CENTERVILLE

A Mid-American Saga

Enfys McMurry

Published by The History Press
Charleston, SC 29403
www.historypress.net

Front cover images courtesy of Appanoose County Historical Society. Back cover images (left to right) courtesy of Dorothy Drake Haines; Mary Ellen Bushemi Cessna; and J.G. Milani.

First published 2012
Second printing 2013

Manufactured in the United States

ISBN 978.1.60949.664.7

Library of Congress CIP data applied for.

Notice: The information in this book is true and complete to the best of our knowledge. It is offered without guarantee on the part of the author or The History Press. The author and The History Press disclaim all liability in connection with the use of this book.

Courtesy of Martha Hoch.

This book is dedicated to Jesse M. Beck (1873–1965), the editor of the *Iowegian* from 1903 until 1945, without whose journalistic skills this book would not have been possible.

Courtesy of Jim Bunnell.

It is also dedicated to Patsy Bunnell (1945–2009), whose ability with a computer was exceeded only by the grace of her personality.

Contents

Contents

Contents

Map of Appanoose County

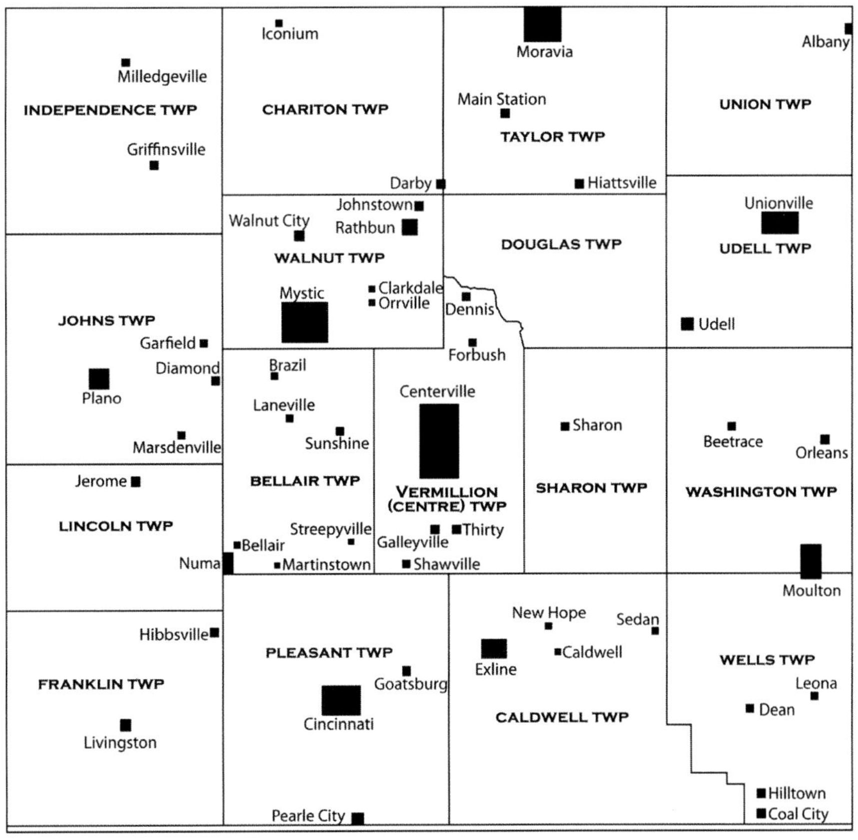

Courtesy of Appanoose County Historical Society.

Chapter 1

The Square

He waited for a killing frost. Then, on a late fall day in 1846, forty-four-year-old surveyor Jonathan Stratton moved through the blue-stemmed prairie grass, the dried seed clusters of asters and goldenrod, the hazel brush and the trees in Iowa's newest county, the twenty-ninth, the one they'd named Appanoose. Behind him, carrying a sixty-six-foot Gunter's chain, pausing in unison and waiting for Stratton's calls, came Ben Spooner and William Smart. Others came to watch: Clancy and Perjue, Crow and Perkins, who three years before had waited for the County to be open, camping on the east bank of the Des Moines River, waiting for the signal. It came with the roar of guns at midnight, a rush through the river, the galloping by flares, the marking of claims.[1]

Stratton lifted the Jacob's staff he'd earlier used to kill a rattlesnake and thrust its iron tip into the ground. He checked the top-mounted compass, located a sight tree, marked it and nearby witness trees with his blaze of three notches on each side, then called for Spooner and Smart. At each extension of the chain, Stratton moved a small horn tally on a leather belt around his waist, checked his total with the two chainmen, recorded his notes in his field book and set temporary wooden stakes on a town he'd named Chaldea.[2]

The site was selected a month earlier. Two commissioners appointed by the State of Iowa came on horseback from Davis and Van Buren Counties to the east. They met at the log cabin of Jackson Perjue with Perjue, Jonathan Stratton and George Perkins, all three experienced surveyors. Perkins was an expert reader of compass coordinates; Perjue had run section lines with the

1832–33 U.S. government survey team; Stratton, on his way west from Erie, Pennsylvania, had platted St. Francisville, Missouri, as well as Jackson and Ann Arbor, Michigan. His "precise rendering" of Ann Arbor's plan, when published in New York City by Nathaniel Currier, had helped lure settlers for the Ann Arbor Land Company. Together at Perjue's cabin that warm September day, the five examined official U.S. township and range surveys. They located the exact geographic center of the new County just south of where the town, forty years later, would place the Jewish cemetery. Then, three-fourths of a mile to its south, one-fourth to its west, the commissioners selected the site for the town. They chose a broad, flat plain circled on the west and north by Cooper Creek and, two miles to the east, by the Chariton River, which flows on a diagonal course from northwest to southeast across the County.[3]

Appanoose was Iowa's newest County, south of Kishkekosh (today Monroe), fourth west from the Mississippi, its southern border touching Missouri. To the west, its jurisdiction until the formation of Wayne County stretched across 150 miles of rolling hills, prairie, oak and hickory forests to the Missouri River. The land was part of the hunting grounds of the Sac and Fox Indians, who sheltered in wickiups and who left a scatter of circular and mysteriously elliptical burial mounds on horizons, as well as the name of a Sac chief for the County title. As they were pushed relentlessly west, news of the new land trickled east. At midnight on May 1, 1843, their land, part of the Second Black Hawk Purchase, was declared open. Settlers rushed in, Clancy, Crow, Perkins and Perjue among them, Stratton, Wells, Jump, Cooksey and Kirby coming up from Missouri.[4]

Long before, fur traders and explorers had penetrated the area. In the 1790s James McKay and John Evans and in 1803 Meriwether Lewis and William Clark ascended the Missouri River at the far western edge of its jurisdiction. Others came north from Missouri looking for honey in trees on the Bee Trace Trail. Daniel Boone, in his last years spent at Femme Osage, made long expeditions north exploring Iowa's rivers, leaving his blaze on a tree at Sand Bank Springs on Shoal Creek, five miles south of where Jonathon Stratton would begin his survey. Daniel's son Nathan Boone in 1832 led a unit of the U.S. Cavalry cutting a path through the area known as the Dragoon Trail from Davenport to Fort Leavenworth, Kansas. It was the same route followed three times by Mormons, popularly renaming it the Mormon Trail. Joseph Smith used it in 1837 when he fled Kirtland, Ohio, making for the Mormon communities of Zion, Far West and Adam-ondi-Ahman near Kansas City. An exodus from those communities followed the trail east to Nauvoo, Illinois, escaping Missouri governor Lilburn Boggs's directive to his state militia that

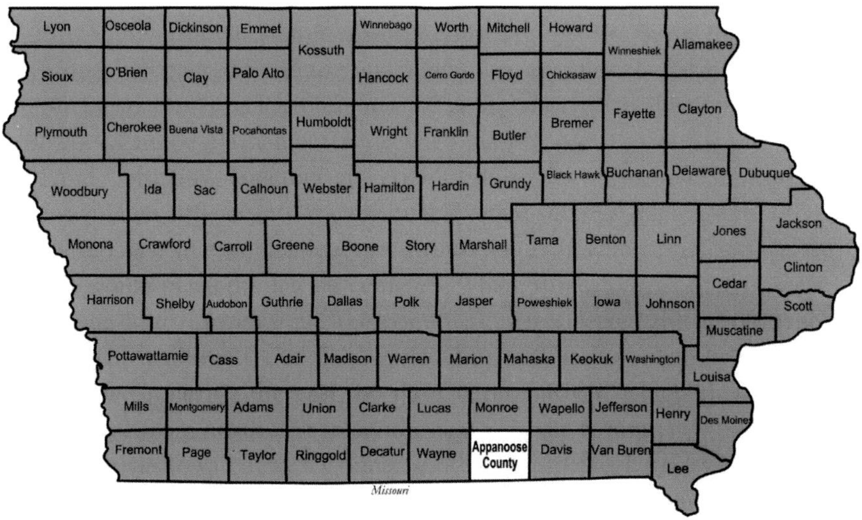

Map of Iowa showing Appanoose County. *Courtesy of Appanoose County Historical Society.*

Mormons "…be exterminated or driven from the state." A third time, after the assassination of Joseph Smith in Carthage, Illinois, an advance party of 143 Mormon men, three women and two children in seventy-two covered wagons pulled by oxen, horses and mule teams traveled west from Nauvoo to their destination in Utah, marking the distances by counting the turns of the wagon wheels. On March 27, 1846, they camped at East Shoal Creek in Appanoose County. There, in the vicinity of the "ring of rocks," Brigham Young was officially declared head of the Mormon Church.[5]

Five miles to the north and seven months later, Stratton began his survey. He began at the south and west lines of U.S. Section 36, Township 69 North, Range 18 West, completing it in less than three months. Then, using a scale of one inch representing three hundred feet, he drew the town plan onto a map. In the lower west quadrant he placed a large (156 feet by 156 feet) open area he named "Public Square." At its center he drew another—this one smaller (132 feet by 132 feet), rotated forty-five degrees and labeled "C. H. Square." Stratton's planning was deliberate, his vision clear. This public square, dominated by the County's courthouse, was to be the heart of the community. It was to be where its people, traveling its twelve converging streets, would meet, do business and exchange news. In time it would do more. The events that took place, the actions of its people on this Courthouse Square, would reflect larger images: those of the nation.[6]

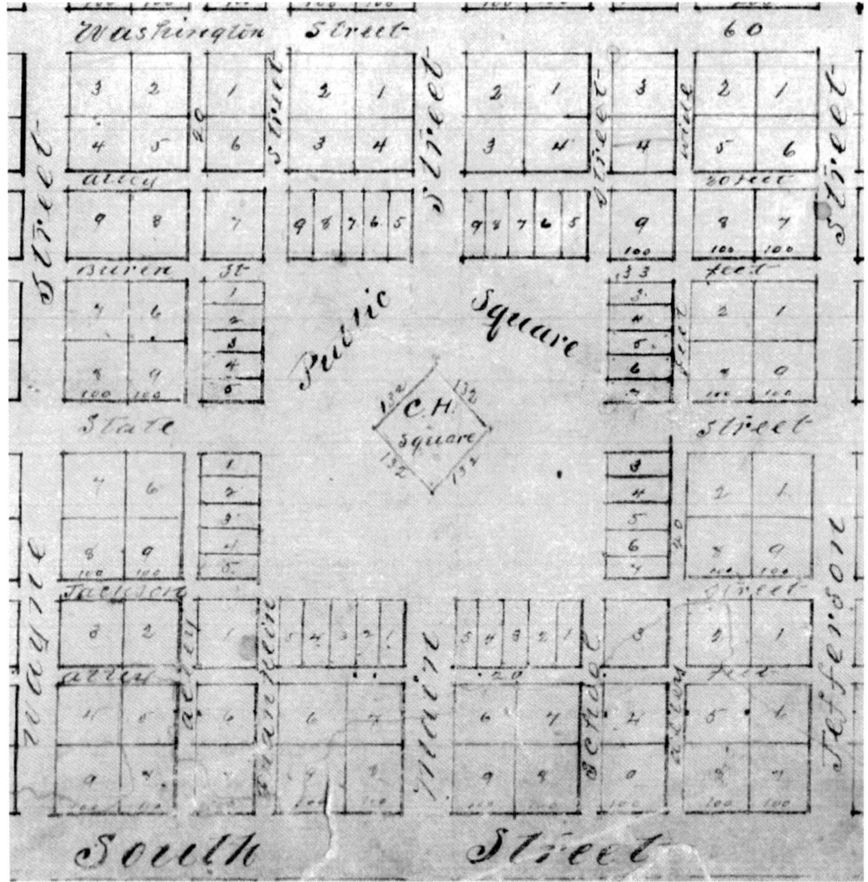

Jonathan Stratton's original plat of Centerville Square. *Courtesy of Appanoose County Recorder.*

On February 1, 1847, Jonathan Stratton rode into his new Square and placed his plan before the Appanoose Board of County Commissioners. By then the name of the town had undergone two changes—from Chaldea to Senterville and from Senterville to Centerville.[7]

Before Jonathan Stratton's plat was completed but the boundaries of Centerville's Square were clear, the sights, the sounds, the shapes of frontier life began to appear.

Thirty-eight-year-old Spencer Wadlington had traveled north and west from Kentucky and built a log cabin northeast of the new Square. He now dismantled it and reerected it on the Northwest block. It became the

Square's first building, the County's general store, an unofficial town hall, a courthouse and the meeting place of the County Board of Commissioners, as well as Wadlington's home, where he slept on deer and bearskins, a bundle of coonskins for a pillow.[8]

People rode in from outlying cabins and tied their horses to Wadlington's hitching rack. They came to buy coffee, muslin, calico and shoes, sometimes bartering with skins—that of a bear worth a dollar, a coon twenty-five cents, a mink ten cents. They stayed to discuss the issues of the day, to listen to the Reverend William Manson give the town's first sermon using a whiskey barrel as a pulpit, to observe court proceedings and to pay their taxes. And it was here on February 1, 1847, the three members of the County Board of Commissioners—Reuben Riggs, George Perkins and J.B. Packard—examined Jonathan Stratton's plat, approved it and ordered the selling of lots: twenty-five dollars for corners, twenty dollars for those inside and for lots off the Square a number of coonskins or pounds of beeswax.[9]

Next door, James Hughes from Indiana opened as the town's first blacksmith. He forged plows and harrows, hammered shoes on horses and replaced Stratton's temporary wooden plat markers with permanent iron ones. For serious crimes, his store substituted as a formal courtroom. Reuben Riggs was the County's prosecuting attorney. Judge Cyrus Olney from Iowa's Third Judicial District sat on the anvil; the Reverend William Manson, clerk to the court, took notes on the blacksmith's bellows. The juries consulted in Wadlington's store or, in good weather, out in the hazel brush.[10]

Across State Street, the Packard family opened a hotel and livery barn and obtained the town's first liquor license. In the evenings they lit the hotel with the town's first kerosene lamp, bought at Wadlington's. A glass bowl held the kerosene, above it thick glass walls, below it a base of brass resting on a four-inch square of marble.

On the Square's Southside, Charles Howell, who had come west from New York for his health, reconstructed a second log cabin store. This mercantile store, formerly on East Maple Street one block to the south, was moved to the corner of Main Street. On Sundays he held the town's first Sunday school classes. Within four years he was confident enough of his prospects, "...far beyond my desert or expectation with business and friends in this state of my adoption," that he began planning the town's first frame building, and he proposed marriage to Lavinia T. Ward back in his hometown of New York City.[11]

Farther east on the Southeast Corner of the Square's Southside, James Jackson, a relative of former president Andrew Jackson, began building the first courthouse. The Board of Commissioners, anticipating a future imposing brick or stone courthouse at the center of the Square, selected this temporary site and gave precise guidelines for the structure. In 1848, despite an accident resulting in an infected knee, Jackson completed the courthouse. It was a one-and-a-half-story log cabin measuring twenty by twenty-four feet, built of sawed and shaved burr and white oak, with space for Jesse Wood to insert a nine-light, eight-by-ten-foot window at each upper gable. Jackson, whose knee was treated by a traveling doctor with the inside of a hornet's nest, would, however, limp the rest of his life.[12]

Across the Square, beyond the brush and trees on the Northside, Ohioan John C. Wright, wielding a cooper's adze, made oak barrels and sold or bartered them for one dollar each. People carried them to Cooper Creek for their water supply, tapping the sides when they wanted a drink "…so the wiggletails would go down to the bottom and the top water was clear." Wright's four sons tanned deer hides and plaited long cattle whips. These they used to drive ten or twelve yoke of oxen to turn the prairie and the hazel brush, which was sometimes five feet in height.[13]

Once a week, nine-year-old Ben Swearingen collected the U.S. Mail from Keosauqua, forty-five miles east in Van Buren County. Returning home, he rode west to the head of the Fox River, across unmarked prairie following his own blazes on trees, swimming the Chariton River when it was in flood and reaching George Perkins's nursery and seed store just off the Square's Eastside. This was now the town's first post office, with Perkins the first postmaster. It was Perkins who oversaw the changing of the town's name from Chaldea to Senterville to Centerville.[14]

The petition to change the name of the town was led by the Reverend Manson. He wanted Chaldea changed to Senterville to honor William T. Senter, Methodist minister, merchant, presidential elector and Whig congressman from Tennessee. The State legislature approved the petition on January 18, 1847, and, assuming Manson didn't know how to spell, changed the first letter. The town now received the official title of Centerville.[15]

From the Square, people left on long journeys: Reuben Riggs to represent the County at Iowa's Second General Assembly in Iowa City or to attend Universalist church meetings and their debates on slavery in Van Buren County; Spencer Wadlington on semiannual visits to St. Louis to buy goods for his store; grocer Thomas Cochran chasing his stolen horses one hundred miles to the west; blacksmith James Hughes and farmer and future postmaster Dan Sparks carrying County school funds to Iowa City, fighting timber wolves in deep snow as they traveled.[16]

But the longest, the most exhaustive journeys were those of Jackson Perjue, now the County's sheriff, with jurisdiction—pending new counties being formed—that extended to the Missouri River 150 miles to the west. He collected taxes, election returns and petitions from this area, then delivered them to the State legislature in Iowa City, another one hundred miles northeast from his home in Centerville.

He explored grievances and apprehended criminals. One such case involved a warrant from Illinois for the arrest of a man named Kane traveling west with the Mormons. Perjue found him near Greenfield and returned him to Keosauqua. The two, Perjue and a handcuffed Kane, took turns on Perjue's horse. Within months, Kane escaped. Traveling in winter, Perjue found him at a camp near Omaha. This time, Perjue returned alone. Kane, charged there with the murder of a Mormon woman, was found guilty by a court of the camp's elders, had his hands tied behind his back and was dropped through a hole cut in the ice of the Missouri River.[17]

When Jackson Perjue returned that cold winter of 1850 to Centerville, he had traveled over 650 miles on that one case. Coincidentally, the County's jurisdiction extending west to the Missouri River was at an end. Six new counties stretching west along the Missouri border were being organized. The boundary of the first, Wayne County, was sixteen miles west of Centerville. The County seat of Corydon was already being platted by Centerville's Jonathan Stratton.[18]

If the western boundary of Appanoose County was now resolved, the one to the south was not. It was an issue applying equally to all ten of Iowa's southern counties that shared their southern borders with Missouri.

Ten miles south of Centerville Square, extending east to west and forming Iowa's entire southern border, including thirty-two miles of Appanoose County, lies the Missouri border. It was determined in 1821 by U.S. surveyor J.C. Sullivan when Missouri became a state. It was marked with tree blazes, wooden markers and mounds of earth and was known as the "Sullivan Line." It ran for 250 miles from "rapids" on the Des Moines River, at the point where it empties into the Mississippi, to just west of present-day Hamburg, Iowa. But over the years, Sullivan's markings eroded, disappeared or became overgrown.[19]

Trouble began in 1837 when the Missouri legislature ordered the border resurveyed. The new surveyor, J.C. Brown, determined the "rapids" on the Des Moines River were not those at its mouth, but "riffles" sixty miles above the mouth near Keosauqua. His line surveyed from there due west gave nine miles of southern Iowa to Missouri. This would have dislocated the geographic center of Appanoose County. With the Missouri border only one mile from

Centerville Square, the town as the County seat would have had to be moved north. This uncertainty slowed the development of the town.[20]

The earliest settlers on the disputed land—Colonel James Wells, Adolphus Stevens, Jack Klinkenbeard, William Cooksey, Austin Jones and Ewen Kirby—were uncertain which state they lived in, and those with ethical objections to living in Missouri, a slave state, refused to stay and left.[21]

To make matters worse, Missouri officials periodically arrived to collect taxes from those who considered themselves Iowa residents. When three honey trees in Iowa's Van Buren County that had long attracted early Missouri explorers were cut down and the perpetrator escaped to safety across the border into Missouri, hostilities accelerated.[22]

Public meetings were held on both sides of the border. When the sheriff of Missouri's Clark County crossed into Iowa's Van Buren County to collect taxes, he was arrested by the Van Buren County sheriff. Violence threatened. Motley armies were assembled, two thousand in Clark, twelve hundred in Van Buren, arming themselves with blunderbusses, ancestral swords, a plough coulter, a log chain, a sausage stuffer and six wagons of supplies—five of these of whiskey.[23]

Before fighting broke out, the dispute, known as "The Honey War," was decided before the U.S. Supreme Court. It ruled the Sullivan Line was the true boundary, with all nine miles part of Iowa. A new survey was ordered. Posts were erected a mile apart; every tenth post of iron marked the official boundary. The words "Iowa" on the north, "Missouri" on the south were imprinted on each pillar.[24]

From the date of the Supreme Court decision in 1851, the growth of Centerville was steady. In 1849 there were 49 inhabitants; five years later, 283, and by 1860, 820.[25]

Chapter 2

The New Settlers

The new settlers came to Centerville traveling in covered wagons pulled by teams of oxen or horses, their hanging cooking utensils rattling above rear feedboxes. Men and boys walked alongside, driving milk cows and steer, pigs and sheep. Women and children rode inside amongst the household possessions and valuables ingeniously secreted in double-bottomed tool chests or in four-by-four-inch, chiseled-out sections of wood camouflaged as parts of furniture. Scouts on horseback circled ahead, testing the best routes, the mudholes, the swamp spots or the best place to ford a river.[1]

The families came from Maine, New York and Pennsylvania; Maryland, Delaware and Virginia; North Carolina, Tennessee and Kentucky. They followed established trails down the Allegheny and Ohio Rivers to St. Louis, then up the Mississippi to Alexandria or Keokuk. Some crossed the Atlantic, arriving at New Orleans or pausing briefly in the East before continuing west. Some came directly north out of Missouri, following the Bee Trace Trail. Or they came from Illinois, Ohio or Indiana, pausing on the Illinois shore to cross the Mississippi, sometimes waiting in long lines for eight days for floodwaters to subside. All of them came pulled by the American dream, part of the spirit that a better life existed and the path led west.[2]

Flatboats, propelled by oars or poles, or double-decker steamboats ferried them across the Mississippi. Wagons were pressed close together. People were jostled. Some pointed to the new land. Others turned to watch the receding shoreline, where the Conger family saw smoke rising from the burning Mormon temple in Nauvoo. Fathers hung quilts so children couldn't see the water. Men held the bits of horses to keep them still. Cows jumped overboard. On the Iowa shore, there were shouts of congratulations, backslapping, hand-shaking, wishes of good luck and farewells.[3]

Across southern Iowa they followed Indian trails worn down by herds of buffaloes. They moved from bluff to bluff, along riverbanks and ridges. They forded the Des Moines at Farmington and were ferried across the Chariton just east of town to reach Centerville Square and form a cluster of small communities around the County.[4]

On arrival, new settlers first located their claims. This was land bought sight unseen for $1.25 an acre from a U.S. government land office in Fairfield, fifty-six miles northeast of Centerville, or Chariton, twenty-five miles northwest. Some paid more—$5 and up from land speculators—and a few received "bounty land" free from the U.S. government in recognition of military service given by ancestors in the war of 1812.[5]

The Appanoose County Claim Society, with branch offices in every precinct, kept records of claims already taken and their boundaries. Its members, all early residents, could intervene in any dispute. When they did so, they wore white caps and carried clubs.[6]

Across the town, across the County, the new settlers forged a community, clearing their land, building their homes, their schools, their churches, stores and a calaboose to hold prisoners north of Centerville Square.

They sawed down trees, selecting the tallest and straightest for their buildings, measuring them with notches cut into the handles of their axes, planing two sides, assembling them into rectangles, mounting one over the other for walls. Gaps were "daubed and chinked," filled with chunks of wood and a mortar of mud mixed with slough grass cut from nearby ponds. Flat limestone rocks were dragged from stream outcroppings to form bases for fireplaces. Slabs of sod were sliced from the land to line chimneys. Small, thin clapboards were split from the ends of straight-grained oak tree stumps, overlapped and held in place with long shaved branches for roofs. Windows were covered with greased paper, greased deer hides or quilts replaced in summer by cheesecloth to discourage flies. Split logs were assembled for benches; slabs of wood balanced on pegs inserted into walls became tables, desks and shelves. Mattresses were filled with feathers, rags or corncobs. They were placed on straw piles or on beds built into corners where slats and ropes radiated from two adjoining walls to a single post fixed into the dirt floor. The buildings were kept warm in winter with logs of wood and occasional lumps of coal that surfaced in the banks of nearby streams. At night, light glowed from candles on tables or on wall hooks or from wicks inserted in lard and anchored inside hollowed-out turnips.[7]

Everywhere, neighbor helped neighbor. Together they raised their houses, turned the ground with wooden plows and planted the corn. In the fall, wheat, rye and oats were harvested, the men swinging their scythes in unison, the cradlers following, the boys raking the ripe grain into bundles, the binders tying them with bands of straw. Then came the flailing of the grain, the wind lifting and separating the chaff.

Together the men took their grain to mills at Bonaparte in Van Buren County and then closer—to mills placed on Cooper Creek, the Chariton River and Shoal Creek. Together they beat out prairie fires and hunted wolves, wildcats, foxes, deer, turkeys, squirrels and an occasional black bear. Women made quilts in groups. For the children they organized singing schools, taffy pulls and spelling bees. They entertained the circuit riders, those ministers of religion who traveled twenty miles a day, each one riding a pony, the saddlebags containing a Bible, a hymnbook, a clean shirt, extra collars and a handkerchief. They attended women in childbirth and sick neighbors unable to wait for one of the four doctors then serving the whole County. They carried whiskey and made home remedies. They gathered herbs: ague root, wild mint, rose hips and pennyroyal, brewing them into teas, broths and syrups. For rattlesnake bites, they boiled and mashed the roots of the cowslip with fresh milk. This they applied as a poultice while the patient drank the residue milk.[8]

Travelers continued to journey through the County. The Mormons now used a more direct route north of Centerville, moving west from Bloomfield through Unionville, Moravia, Iconium and on to Garden Grove in Wayne County. Others still used the old Mormon Trail south of town. There were adventurers on their way to California's Gold Rush, among them Mark Hopkins, who lived in Unionville and who, with Collis Huntington, Leland Stanford and Charles Crocker, would form the Central Pacific Railroad Company. Hopkins died in 1878 worth $350,000,000 and left his name for a San Francisco hotel. The Cody family traveled on their way from LeClaire, Iowa, to Kansas. With them was their ten-year-old son, William, who, forty years later, would return to Appanoose County as Buffalo Bill. There was Erhart Lentz, the drummer boy at the Battle of Waterloo who witnessed the surrender of Napoleon to the British. And there were more gold seekers, the "Pike Peakers" on their way to Colorado. There were roving bands of horse thieves and murderers who, when apprehended, were taken into Centerville for trial and spent time in the town's calaboose. There were Mennonites carrying two gallons of "turkey red" wheat seed from Russia to be planted in Kansas and the Henkle family carrying apple tree saplings from Appanoose County to Oregon. Other travelers took the "Territorial Road" west from

Keosauqua, the route pioneered by nine-year-old Ben Swearingen in 1846 as he delivered Centerville's mail. This brought the travelers directly into Centerville Square, where they shopped at Wadlington's on the Westside, Howell's store on the Southside, and told their stories.[9]

And there were travelers who came, liked what they saw and stayed. One of them was twenty-nine-year-old James Wooden.

On a September evening in 1856, James Wooden rode horseback into Centerville Square to spend the night. He'd left Gosport, Indiana, looking for a suitable town to start a business and raise a family. He'd inspected towns in northern Missouri and looked at Bloomfield in Iowa. His next intended stop was Fort Leavenworth, Kansas. His walk around Centerville Square the next day, Monday, September 8, brought the search to an end. He paid two months' rent in advance for Spencer Wadlington's now-vacated log cabin store and left for Gosport to collect his wife, Amerika, and their seven-year-old son, Albert Edgar.[10]

By 1856, a petition of Centerville citizens requesting town incorporation had been presented to County judge Amos Harris at the log-cabin courthouse on the Square's Southeast Corner. A charter was prepared, ratified by voters and accepted by Iowa's Sixth General Assembly. With it came a pervasive sense of community, energy, focus and optimism that attracted Wooden and other enterprising businessmen.[11]

Under the new City charter, Centerville's first mayor was Spencer Wadlington, the Square's first storekeeper. Now fifty years old, Wadlington had served his community as pioneer storekeeper, probate judge, school inspector, justice of the peace and deputy clerk to the court. His business had expanded into farming and stock raising. He bought 154 acres of upland prairie, another 100 of woodland sixteen miles northwest of Centerville in Independence Township. He left his log cabin, built a brick home just west of the Square on West Van Buren Street and planned a second brick home on his land in Independence Township.[12]

Communities began to connect to each other. Roads—cleared tracks of raw land—radiated from the Square: south to the Missouri state line; north to Albia; east on the State territorial road to Keosauqua, connecting to Burlington, Keokuk and the Mississippi. In response to an order from Postmaster General Aaron V. Brown, John Ferren guided his ox team and sod plough west from George Pratt's Tavern on Centerville Square, creating a furrow twenty-three miles long to Wayne County's Corydon. It took him two days; he was paid five dollars. Following this marked path, galloping on horseback across the prairie with a U.S. Mail bag strapped behind his saddle, went Jimmie Skipper, "a young lad," a star route mailman, to meet pony express riders in St. Joseph, Missouri.[13]

Along the roads, eight-horse stagecoaches owned by the Great Western Stagecoach Company made daily runs between Albia and Centerville. They rolled into the Square, their passengers alighting or embarking at the Oldham House on the Northside, Pratt's Tavern or the Tremont House on the Westside. The horses were rapidly unharnessed by attentive ostlers and led into the livery barns owned by each hotel. Each coach carried six passengers and room for five hundred pounds of luggage in the front and hind boots. When the runs were extended west to Corydon and the Missouri River, the stagecoaches also carried the U.S. Mail, a development that eventually led to the end of the pony express.[14]

Sitting on the outside over the front boot of one of these stagecoaches, holding the reins of the eight horses, was twenty-one-year-old William Strickler. He drove through all weather and never turned back unless a river was too high. In winter he occasionally stopped at night and awoke a sleeping farmer to borrow an axe to dig frozen mud from the wheels of the coach.[15]

In his walk around the Centerville Square that September evening in 1856, James Wooden said he found "...business houses ...perhaps a dozen or so most of them handling general lines." One of these was the Mammoth Store. It stood north of the empty Wadlington store on the Westside. Running it was the remarkable William Bradley.[16]

In the spring of 1856, six months before Wooden's arrival, William Bradley built a store twenty-two by one hundred feet, "...then considered massive," hence the name "Mammoth Store." Bradley was thirty-one years old, born in Pittsburgh to a carpenter so poor he had to fend for himself at an early age. He tried farming, washing dishes, working as an assistant cook and working as an ostler; he carried mail for the government, traveling 240 miles a week; he sold livestock; he tried gold mining in California, fishing, hay hauling, shipping wool, then peddling matches, jewelry, table linen and oilcloths. In Steubenville, Ohio, he ordered a peddler's wagon to his own design and named it "The Star of the West." He traveled the roads, sold goods in southern Iowa and found Centerville en route between Bloomfield and Corydon. He auctioned his goods to Mabry's Menagerie and to Sands and Nathan's Circus, found a wife in Winterset, Iowa, and arrived in Centerville. He established his store with stock valued at thirteen thousand dollars. His business was so successful, he quickly employed several salesmen and two men who drove ox teams hauling his building materials and goods from the Mississippi. When the store was completed, he went to Philadelphia. This time he returned to Centerville with stock valued at thirty thousand dollars.[17]

On the Southside of the Square, Charles Howell, now married to Lavinia T. Ward, was removing the town's first frame store and building its first brick one. Workmen were paid fifty cents a day to dig the cellar and another twelve dollars to move all the dirt across the street with a yoke of oxen. The store—three stories at completion—was the local forerunner of a department store where salt and sugar were wrapped in square-cornered, brown-paper packages and tied with paper string, before paper bags were invented.[18]

James Wooden's business instincts proved accurate. Within months of his move to Centerville, he left the Wadlington log cabin store and built a new frame store across the Square on the Northside, at the west corner lot with Main Street. He expanded into general merchandise and paid the highest price to farmers for thousands of pounds of raw wool, brought in wrapped in old quilts and handwoven blankets. For years, he, his wife, Amerika, their son Albert Edgar, new son Charles Robert and their small dog named Penny lived in rooms at the rear of the building. Wooden made frequent excursions to Chicago to enhance his stock. His wife often accompanied him. They stayed in a hotel there and met a young man they described as a "gallant and courteous man and a great actor." The young man's name was John Wilkes Booth.[19]

Everywhere was movement. Churches were built: the Methodists in a wooden building measuring thirty by forty feet at a cost of eight hundred dollars on the corner of Washington and Jefferson (later renamed Haynes). The Presbyterians met upstairs in the new Howell store and then created a meeting place, the same size as the Methodist church but of brick, south of the Square on the Westside of Main Street. The Baptists chose a frame building west of the Square. Charter member Spencer Wadlington donated the church bell. Dissatisfied with its tone, he had it removed and recast, its metal infused with twenty silver dollar coins.[20]

Stepping stones were placed at strategic points so people could avoid the worst mud when crossing the streets. At night, people carried lanterns, punched full of holes with a candle inside, bought at J.W. Williams's new hardware and tin shop on the Northside. Four coal-oil lamps, one placed on each corner of the Square, issued some light. They were lit by hand in the evenings, extinguished at dawn the next morning. A fence enclosing the Square to stop pigs and cows from running loose was built by Thomas Cochran, pioneer settler and merchant. With the increased demand for water, Cochran dug two wells: one on the Square's Eastside, the second on its North. Both were walled with a fifteen-inch thickness of rock.[21]

Children attended the new two-story frame school off the Northeast Corner of the Square. A bell in the school tower rang out across the town, marking their arrivals and departures. The new school replaced an earlier log building on the same site and stood near the Methodist church, separated by crab apple and plum trees.[22]

Inside the school, children sat on logs and wrote on slabs of wood balanced on pins inserted into the walls. They learned history and geography by singsong: "In fourteen hundred and ninety-two Columbus sailed the ocean blue" and "State of Maine, Augusta, on the Kennebeck River." They learned arithmetic and spelling by rote and repetition. They identified letters by sounds and read from McGuffey Readers and Webster's Blue Back Spellers bought from R.N. Glenn, the druggist on the Square's Northside, or supplied from private homes. For the rules of punctuation, one of the teachers, Mrs. Gill, taught her classes to stop "…at a comma long enough to count to one, at a semi-colon long enough to count two and at a period to go after a bucket of water."[23]

Each new enterprise spawned corollary ones: lumberyards cut and smoothed timber to standard lengths and widths. Blacksmiths supplied nails. Professional carpenters made cabinets, furniture to individual specifications and coffins. A brickyard opened. Mills, now on Cooper Creek close to town, ground wheat, rye and corn, saving long excursions to Bonaparte or—even further—to Alexandria. Stencils imprinted the name of the mill on flour sacks handmade on chain-stitch sewing machines. Wool was cleaned and carded into rolls ready for spinning and weaving. There were tailors and tanners, shoe, boot and saddle makers. Doctors traded their skills from offices on the Square or upstairs rooms over hotels or stores. Pharmacists advertised with window displays of red, blue and yellow liquids in elongated bottles. Lawyers put out shingles: Tannehill and Cumings on the Eastside; Riggs, Harris and Galbraith on the West.[24]

There was increased prosperity. With it came a social shift. The previous egalitarian quality of pioneer life began to erode. The merchants and professional men wore high silk hats and heavy gray shawls. Their new homes were built of brick. They employed servants.[25]

There were public meetings and debates, fairs, picnics, bare-knuckle boxing matches, corn huskings and singing schools. There were dances with a fiddler in an elevated position calling the sets, directing the dances, his voice monotone, his foot keeping time with the music. On Independence Day there were parades, martial music, barbecued beef and local lawyer Judge Amos Harris reading the Declaration of Independence.[26]

As the end of the decade approached, and despite two framework additions, the inadequacy of the log-cabin courthouse became apparent. Court cases were held in other buildings, chiefly the Methodist or Presbyterian churches. In 1858 a change-of-venue murder trial from Davis County brought the issue to the forefront.

Hinton William Smith Hinkle was charged with murdering his wife. The trial, over four days, took place in the Presbyterian church south of the Square on Main Street. People filled the church and overflowed onto the sidewalks. Hinkle was found guilty and was hanged at a public execution by Appanoose County sheriff William Ferren in a natural amphitheater a half mile west of Orleans, near the Davis County border.

It was a hot August afternoon. The crowds that came to watch were variously estimated at five thousand, ten thousand, fifteen thousand. They traveled in wagons. Some walked. Many camped. The rope, made of shoe thread by Ben Deldart, a shoemaker on Centerville Square, broke as it took Hinkle's weight. There was a half-hour delay. Hinkle proclaimed his innocence. Sam Brown from the village of Sharon, who had been on his knees praying, argued the broken rope was a sign from God of Hinkle's innocence. A second rope was brought. The second hanging was successful. To pass the time, the crowd consumed glasses of water sold at five cents a glass.[27]

In a special election in 1860, the voters of Centerville voted 906 to 89 that a splendid brick courthouse should be built, as Jonathan Stratton's plat had indicated, at the center of the Square and at a cost of fifteen thousand dollars. A large courtroom would be part of the design. The architect chosen was thirty-year-old Charles Dunham of Burlington. A national crisis would cause its delay. It was a crisis that for some years had motivated many individuals to move to Appanoose County, specifically close to the Missouri border. And these people were not motivated by business and profit—but by politics and principle.[28]

Chapter 3

Underground Railroad

In 1850, six years before the arrival of William Bradley and James Wooden, twenty-three-year-old John Lankford crossed the Mississippi and reached Keokuk from Indianapolis. He walked across Lee County following the Des Moines River northwest to Ottumwa. Six months later he changed direction and headed southwest into Centerville Square. He became a carpenter and the town's chief undertaker. For the next sixty years, he became a familiar local sight. He was seen walking between his home on Maple Street to his store on the Square's Northeast block or carrying a small table under his arm on his way to the home of a deceased citizen or, perched high on his hearse, driving to County funerals. Year-round he was always dressed in his signature straw hat, no gloves, no overcoat. He might have been impervious to the weather. He wasn't to social injustice, and he wasn't alone. Lankford had selected to live nine miles north of the Missouri border at a pivotal time in American history—and the history of Appanoose County.[1]

The Iowa-Missouri border stretches east to west for 250 miles—32 of those the southern boundary of Appanoose County. Until the end of the Civil War, the line was more than a geographic boundary. It defined a line of demarcation between two societies: one that accepted slavery; one from its inception that outlawed it. Missouri entered the Union in 1821 as a slave state. Iowa, entering in 1846, would become the "...Bright Radical Star ...arguably the most racist free state in the ante-bellum union."[2]

Qualifying it for this description were men committed to increasing civil equality for African Americans and voting their approval of this trend in Iowa's third (1857) constitution. Some went further: they were prepared to assist escaping slaves on their way to freedom in Canada through a system known as the Underground Railroad. In doing so, they broke the law. They risked arrest and violence from slave owners who—supported by the federal Fugitive Slave Law—had the right to cross into free states to recapture their slaves. And there was a further hazard—exposure and attack from neighbors who, in the southern tier of counties, included many Southerners who saw nothing wrong with slavery. The 1850 federal census of Appanoose County shows 38 percent were Southerners.[3]

Despite the dangers, an extensive Underground Railroad system existed in Appanoose County. The movements of its members were necessarily clandestine. They had secret means of communication: a configuration of lights, passwords, handgrips, hand gestures—a clenched fist or open palm to the ear reflecting safety or danger—or the selected pattern of a displayed quilt. The members traveled at night. They altered their routes. They covered their paths and made their records elusive.[4]

Coincidental with the arrival of John Lankford, another abolitionist, John Conger, who had watched the burning of the temple at Nauvoo as he crossed the Mississippi, entered the log-cabin courthouse on the Southeast Corner of Centerville Square. Using the gold he'd hidden in the false bottom of his tool chest, he bought Section 31 of Caldwell Township. The land lay five miles south of Centerville. It was also positioned four miles north of the Missouri border.[5]

Some months later, Conger located the claim of thirty-two-year-old Luther Holbrook, who had arrived with his wife, two sons and a daughter from Lee County, Iowa, seventy miles to the east. It was government land in neighboring Pleasant Township, bought for $1.25 an acre, but so desolate Holbrook's daughter, Eliza, later said, "I think it was very brave of him—not a house, not a tree—just tall prairie grass." Her father's vision was quite different. The new land he'd selected was just three miles north of the Missouri border.[6]

Holbrook arrived in June 1850. That same month he wrote a letter to the *True Wesleyan*, a weekly journal published in New England, edited by Luther Lee and dedicated to the abolition of slavery. It was addressed "To Western Emigrants" and urged those immigrating to Iowa to take a look at Appanoose County, "...the most beautiful, richest, and healthiest place in the Western world."[7]

The letter triggered the arrival of some dozen families. All were abolitionists. At least six came, like Holbrook, directly from Lee County. Two members of the group, Holbrook and J.H.B. Armstrong, were already seasoned members of Lee County's well-established Underground Railroad.[8]

Lee County lies directly east of Appanoose County, separated by Van Buren and Davis. All four counties share their southern borders with Missouri. In 1840 the Congregationalist church members of Denmark in Lee County created the Denmark Anti-Slavery Society.[9]

Twenty miles northwest of Denmark and a year later, the first Quaker community west of the Mississippi followed suit with the Salem Anti-Slavery Society in Henry County. Denmark and Salem were the first of a galaxy of tiny religious communities in southeast Iowa, all dedicated to abolishing slavery and to disobeying the federal Fugitive Slave Law.[10]

Salem's Quakers were the first to aid escaping slaves in 1838. In 1839 Luther Holbrook is recorded as a participant. Another was J.H.B. Armstrong. Holbrook, living eight miles east of Farmington in Lee County, and Armstrong, two miles closer, were helping slaves escape north at the border town of Croton and transporting them to either Denmark or Salem.[11]

Holbrook in 1850 and Armstrong in 1852, accompanied by six other families including the Fulchers, the McDonalds, the Stantons and the Adamsons, all decamped from Lee County, dressed in red shirts and calling themselves the Red Hunting-Shirt Company. Together they forged a new star in the galaxy, a new antislavery community. Its location was seven miles south of Centerville Square, 3.2 miles north of the Missouri state line. They named it Cincinnati for Armstrong's birthplace.[12]

An antislavery Wesleyan-Methodist church was started in Cincinnati. Its minister, the Reverend Henry Jacquis "...never failed in his sermons to denounce the slaveholders and the saloon keeper." A store opened. A post office followed. A doctor arrived. A school was started with a teacher from Lee County's Denmark Academy. Then, one by one, the families entered the log-cabin courthouse on Centerville Square or the U.S. government land office in Chariton, twenty-five miles to the northwest. They bought land, then more land. Within four years Armstrong alone owned two thousand acres.[13]

Records show their purchases and those of abolitionist sympathizers lay mutually contiguous. A broad path stretched from the Missouri border at Pleasant Township north to Centerville, north again to Hiattsville, then east to Unionville and across the Davis County line to Drakesville. From there, escaping slaves were transported to Eddyville and North English or east to Salem, Denmark or Burlington.[14]

On a February morning in 1856, despite winter and poor roads, two of Cincinnati's leading abolitionists left on horseback, traveling 260 miles to Iowa City. There, under the dome of Iowa's capitol, J.H.B. Armstrong and Dr. William Sayres became two of 290 delegates at Iowa's first Republican Party convention.[15]

This new political party, born in Ripon, Wisconsin, to oppose the extension of slavery into two new states, Nebraska and Kansas, was two years old. The party was a natural home for all who opposed slavery, including Iowa's third governor, James W. Grimes, making him the nation's first Republican governor.[16]

In Iowa City that February, the State Republican Party was organized and its platform drawn up; an address was made to the people of Iowa, and eight delegates were selected for the first national Republican convention. One was J.H.B. Armstrong, who now returned to Appanoose County and prepared to leave again for Philadelphia in May, helping to select the country's first Republican nominee for president: that explorer of the Far West, John C. Fremont.[17]

In the November election of 1856, John Fremont carried Iowa. He lost in Appanoose County and in the nation. But the scene was set, the organization in place for Abraham Lincoln in 1860.[18]

Sixteen months later, on the Westside of Centerville Square, Appanoose County Republicans started their own newspaper: the *Appanoose Republican.* The editors were Centerville shopkeeper Joseph I. Place and a farmer and Baptist minister from Franklin Township, west of Cincinnati skirting the Missouri border, Livingston Parker. In support, thirty-nine stockholders signed their names in front of James Hughes, the town's first blacksmith, who had replaced Jonathan Stratton's wooden markers with permanent iron ones and who was now the Appanoose County recorder. First to sign was John H.B. Armstrong. After him were three McDonalds, the Holbrooks, Stantons, Adamsons and John Lankford.[19]

To this core group of Republicans, information gleaned from the 1878, 1886 and 1913 County histories and biographies and individual obituaries in local newspapers yields more. Several describe themselves as "strong anti-slavery." Several freed inherited slaves before coming to Iowa. One described walking for five miles to vote for Fremont. Many qualified their Republican status with the words "staunch," "ardent," "pioneer," "early." Joseph Goss, an Englishman and now boot- and shoemaker on the Southside of the Square, described himself as "a charter member of the Republican Party." Lawyer Joshua Miller said he was "the first organizer" of the party. Dexter Spooner, who ran a freight line from Centerville Square to Keokuk and Alexandria, said he was "a Republican and avowed Abolitionist." In his office over the Oldham House on the Northside of the Square, Dr. Franklin Eells, whose name on the *Appanoose Republican* list of stockholders was number twenty-two, quietly stated just "Republican."[20]

Coincidental with the turmoil of "Poor Bleeding Kansas," several Centerville citizens left for that state. One was Reuben Riggs, one of the town's first pioneers, who left for Marion, Kansas, and died of exposure after being caught in a winter storm. Riggs was a Universalist who had attended antislavery debates in Van Buren County, almost certainly an abolitionist. There was no mistaking Thaddeus Stanton's intention. While still in school, this son of Cincinnati abolitionist Seth Stanton ran away to join John Brown, staying with him and Brown's guerilla chieftain James H. Lane until 1857.[21]

It wasn't the County's only connection with John Brown. Writing in 1950, the Reverend Mott Sawyers recalled John Bridal "…something of a hero in eastern Appanoose County." John Bridal, born in Dorsetshire, England, said he was "personally acquainted" with John Brown and often went to watch him speak in Franklin County, Kansas. Officially, Bridal told an interviewer he knew nothing of the plans for Harper's Ferry. To the young Mott Sawyers, son of Unionville's well-known abolitionists, there was another account: Bridal "…was with John Brown on several raids, was selected by John Brown for the raid on Harper's Ferry and trained under him at West Branch, Iowa for that purpose. . ." But Bridal arrived at Harper's Ferry when "…the attack had already been staged, and Brown and his men were besieged." Too late to help, Bridal left.[22]

Despite growing sentiment in the County against slavery—now aided by a book, Harriet Beecher Stowe's *Uncle Tom's Cabin*, and the issue of the Dred Scott affair—Southern sentiment continued to prevail. At Iowa's Third Constitutional Convention in Iowa City's old stone capitol in 1856, a thirty-eight-year-old Centerville lawyer and the County's representative, Amos Harris, whose voting record opposed equal suffrage, rose to object to property rights for black Iowans. Harris held that the proposed amendment would bring a large number of colored persons to Iowa; he felt himself, he said, instructed by his constituents to use all possible influence "to prevent them from obtaining a settlement in this state."[23]

Slavery was outlawed in Iowa. Racism was another issue. A national crisis with epic consequences in South Carolina in 1861 would begin to propel Appanoose County to reflect the State of Iowa's increasing enlightenment.

Chapter 4

Fall of Fort Sumter

At four thirty in the morning on April 12, 1861, the guns of the Confederate States of America opened fire on Fort Sumter in Charleston Harbor. After thirty-four hours of bombardment, the fort surrendered. Three days later, President Abraham Lincoln appealed for seventy-five thousand volunteers from the North to suppress the revolt and to preserve the Union. Samuel Morse's invention of the telegraph relayed his message around the country. Davenport, on the far side of the Mississippi River's first bridge, was its most westerly receiving station.[1]

U.S. congressman William Vandever of Iowa carried the telegram from there on horseback a further fifty miles west, finding Iowa governor Samuel Kirkwood in overalls and boots tending stock on his farm two miles upriver from Iowa City at Coralville.[2]

"Why the President wants a whole regiment of men!" Kirkwood said on reading the requested contribution from Iowa. "Do you suppose, Mr. Vandever, I can raise that many?"[3]

His concern was soon answered. By the time Kirkwood's own proclamation traveled by stagecoach and horseback to Iowa's county towns and from there to local townships, there were enough volunteers to fill ten regiments.[4]

In the 1860 election, Appanoose County had given a 368-vote majority to Stephen Douglas, Lincoln's opponent. But Centerville's reaction to the national crisis was immediate. Flags displaying all thirty-four states—a middle row of six stars separating two double rows of seven—were placed at the old courthouse, the school, the churches, the private businesses. People talked on street corners.

Spontaneous discussions and "Union" meetings were held throughout the County where political differences were submerged. The *Appanoose Chieftain*—previously a Democrat newspaper—gave up the entire front page, printing arguments by Bishop Hopkins of Vermont against slavery.[5]

In the school off the Northeast Corner of the Square, the school year was almost over. The students were anticipating a long, hot summer. Lincoln's call changed their lives, their intentions. "The big boys all talked war morning noon and night," said Kos Harris, a younger student. As soon as school was over, their teacher, Madison M. Walden—a graduate of the abolitionist Denmark Academy in Iowa's Lee County—enlisted as one of the town's first three volunteers. Joining him were another teacher, William Rhodes from Cincinnati, the abolitionist community six miles south of Centerville, and, from across the Square, shopkeeper John Bashore.[6]

Within days, they were joined by mechanics, farmers, high school graduates, the editor of the *Appanoose Republican*, shopkeepers, the sons of abolitionists, sons of the town's earliest pioneers and those who had voted for Lincoln. There were entire families: four Zimmer sons, aged eighteen through twenty-two, and their gray-haired father, all walking eight miles south into Centerville Square from Walnut Township. "There was no recruiting office," said John W. Fuller, "there was just a parade marching along the streets with flags flying and drums beating and all you had to do to get in the war was walk out and get into the marching column." They called themselves "the Appanoose Volunteers."

They drilled on a vacant lot behind the Bradley Bank on the Northside of the Square. They carried brooms and sticks as makeshift rifles. Wesley Banks and "Uncle Jimmie" Hutchison, two veterans of the 1846 war with Mexico, shouted instructions. The recruits marched in formation. They formed a circle so close that when commanded to sit down, they fell, rolled and tumbled on the ground. Over the hot weeks of May and June, they waited for Governor Kirkwood's call to action.[7]

Recruits for Iowa's First Regiment came from the State's major cities. Without waiting for approval from Washington, Kirkwood prepared second and third infantry regiments. Some Appanoose County volunteers eager for action crossed east into Davis County and joined the Second Regiment, Company G. Kirkwood also recognized local volunteer groups including Centerville's. He had good reason: Iowa faced two other immediate dangers to her security.[8]

In northwest Iowa, a renegade band of Sioux Indians, retaliating for the murder of their leader and nine members of his family, had killed thirty-eight settlers and abducted three more in the Spirit Lake Massacre. Further threats seemed imminent.[9]

In the southern counties of Iowa, not only were slaveholders chasing their escaped slaves across the border in increasingly volatile confrontations with abolitionists—including those in Cincinnati south of Centerville—but Iowans who were Southern sympathizers were organizing into Copperhead groups, joining Knights of the Golden Circle and taking oaths to assist the South. "There are few if any [Copperheads] functioning here," wrote Appanoose's congressman Nathan Udell (a Democrat) in response to an inquiry from Governor Kirkwood. He was wrong.[10]

At least six such camps existed inside Appanoose County. At one, six miles northwest of the Square, some 110 men, each wearing the polished head of a copper penny as a badge, marched and drilled on an eight-acre, grassy ridge surrounded by tall brush and timber.[11]

Their presence and the proximity of the Missouri border created "a constant state of excitement and fear" for the next four years. Rumors of attempted invasions were rife. The first was made days after the fall of Fort Sumter. News came to Centerville that Cincinnati had been sacked, abolitionists murdered, and that the rebels' next stop was Centerville. Farmers south of town placed their families onto wagons, seized their rifles and headed north into the Square. There they were joined by the townspeople, the Appanoose Volunteers and farmers from north of town armed with every available weapon.

The news was a rumor. It served as a warning. The older men of the town formed a home guard. Sentries were placed on roads into the town. Passwords were issued for safe passage at night. Governor Kirkwood promptly organized a military district for the defense of Iowa's borders. Two southern Iowa men—Colonel Morledge of Page County and John Edwards of Lucas—raised regiments and made several expeditions, not only along the Missouri border but crossing into Missouri itself, despite Governor Kirkwood's warning he had no authority to help them there.[12]

On July 4, 1861, the eigthty-fifth anniversary of the country, crowds filled Centerville Square. They had come to witness the departure of their boys, now Company D, Sixth Iowa Infantry. People would later describe their remarkable appearance: "Being nearly all farmers and mechanics accustomed to manly labor, they were of a hardy vigor which enable them, as their history proves, to endure the toils and privations of army life with a spirit amounting to cheerfulness." That day in July, businessman Charles Howell emerged with his wife from their store on the Square's Southside and moved among the recruits. They presented each with a Bible. Teacher Madison M. Walden, now captain of Company D, John Bashore and William Rhodes, the two lieutenants at his side, accepted a silk flag stitched by the ladies of the town. "A power is in motion," said Walden to the audience, "…which unless checked will soon crush into fragments the very foundation stones of that magnificent fabric, the great Temple of American liberty." Seven days later, the company, still without weapons or uniforms, climbed onto covered wagons that formed a long line on the Southside of the Square. People waved and cheered. Many cried. Then, led by the Centerville Brass Band, eighty-four men left for Ottumwa and from there by train to Camp Warren, Burlington.[13]

The men were mustered into federal service on the seventeenth and eighteenth of July and moved to Keokuk, Iowa's most southeastern city, poised on the western bank of the Mississippi and the mouth of the Des Moines River. In less than a month they were at war.[14]

The war began for members of Company D, Iowa's Sixth Infantry, on August 6, 1861, just sixty miles east of Centerville. Rumors in Keokuk were rife that a large Southern force was ready to invade Iowa. Before daylight on a hot August 5, a messenger galloped into the city to report fifteen hundred secessionist troops, led by Colonel Martin Green, were marching north out of Lewis County, Missouri, to attack neighboring Clark County's pro-Union forces, led by Colonel David Moore at Athens.[15]

Directly across the Des Moines River from Athens lay Croton, Iowa. It was a strategic station on the Des Moines River railroad, with direct access to supplies from the U.S. arsenal in St. Louis, the largest arsenal in the slave states, where sixty thousand muskets and other arms were stored. Croton was a tempting target for Colonel Green.[16]

Centerville's Company D awoke to the sound of a long roll beaten on drums. Under the direction of their captain, Madison M. Walden, they joined other companies of Iowa's Sixth and Fifth Infantry Divisions. Still without uniforms but now armed with new Springfield muskets, they were sent, standing room only, on old dirt-and-stock boxcars and flatcars along the railroad from Keokuk to Croton. There they leaped from the train, rolled up their pant legs and waded the river, ready with guns loaded and bayonets fixed to support Colonel David Moore.[17]

The Battle of Athens was already over. One—or several—cannonballs fired by Colonel Martin Green's secessionist troops were lodged in the low hills behind Croton, but Green and his followers were in retreat, returning only under a truce later on the same day to bury their variously numbered dead. Croton became the only place where Confederate cannonballs struck Iowa soil. It was the first engagement for troops from Appanoose County.[18]

Company D returned to Keokuk. Three days later, on August 9, as part of Iowa's eight hundred–strong Sixth Infantry, they marched through the streets of Keokuk and boarded the river palace steamer *War Eagle*. Bands played martial music. Thousands lined the shore. They cheered and shouted farewells. As the boat swung out into the middle of the river, there was a roar of steam whistles, bands playing and bells clanging. As the boat moved downriver, the soldiers listened as a man at the bow took depth soundings of the water with line and lead, shouting with Southern drawls up to the pilot house and mimicked by the soldiers, "f-o-u-r feet!" "e-i-g-h-t feet!" and "m-a-r-k twain!" The boat's destination was St. Louis.[19]

In Centerville, sixty miles west of Croton, a company of volunteer cavalry calling itself the "Mounted Riflemen" was patrolling Appanoose County's southern border. When the news of the Battle of Athens reached town, border responsibility passed to local volunteer home guards led by abolitionist Dexter Spooner. The "Mounted Riflemen" now became Company I of the Third Iowa Cavalry. They moved to Centerville and began drilling. They stayed at local hotels, at Colonel Joe Delay's in the west part of town, at John Potts's, where "Uncle John" complained at the rate the men devoured his pies, and at George Pratt's, who fed the men "like princes." However, recruit Private C.A. Stanton, son of Cincinnati's abolitionist Nathan Stanton and himself an abolitionist, who would rise to colonel and be nominated as governor of Iowa, noted "a twinkle of satisfaction in the eye" of George Pratt when the company received its orders to proceed to Keokuk.[20]

That day was August 29, 1861. The men and their horses left town, stopping at Bloomfield and Keosauqua on their way to Camp Rankin where, on the bluffs overlooking Keokuk, they entered the service of the United States. Their roster is filled with the names of Appanoose County's abolitionists, Republicans and those who had supported Fremont in 1856 and Lincoln in 1860. "Take good care of the girls," Alvah Staley wrote to his wife, the mother of two baby daughters. "I would not be worthy of the name American if I didn't help defend what our forefathers fought and died to achieve."[21]

As the Third Iowa Cavalry was making its way to Camp Rankin, President Lincoln's appointed commander of the Western Department, explorer of the West, the country's first Republican presidential candidate, John C. Fremont freed all Missouri slaves. It was an action that alienated Lincoln, who was well over a year away from a national Emancipation Proclamation.[22]

But there was joy in Company I. First Sergeant Charles Holbrook, son of Appanoose County's pioneering abolitionist Luther Holbrook, guarded a train as it passed through St. Louis, taking the soldiers to Benton Barracks. He wrote home to his parents back in Cincinnati about "…one thing that saddened me all along the route to the camp. There were a great many of Fremont's friends here and as we passed along the children would shout 'Hurrah for Fremont' and I would respond by giving a military salute. But just as my mind would begin to wander from the lover of freedom someone else would shout again so it kept up a melancholy train of thought."[23]

Charles Holbrook and C.A. Stanton were two of fifteen abolitionist men from Pleasant Township, Appanoose County's most active antislavery center. Seven of them would never return home. One would be Charles Holbrook.[24]

Chapter 5

News of Civil War Fighting

By the end of 1861, some 350 Appanoose men had left and were serving the Union cause. These included not just the Sixth Infantry and the Third Cavalry but also those who had crossed early into Davis County and joined Iowa's Second Infantry. There was no news of major military successes, and as 1862 began, the effects of a national economic depression reached Centerville. Trade on the Mississippi River collapsed; food surpluses destined for southern markets caused local farm prices to plunge. Work on the new courthouse in the center of the Square was temporarily halted. Its architect, thirty-year-old Charles Dunham, having overseen the fifty-two-by-seventy-six-foot foundation and marble dedication stone, returned home to Burlington.

In James Wooden's now-established store on the Square's Northside, ticking cost seventy-five cents a yard, calico or print forty to forty-five cents. The bolts remained unsold. People raised flax. They spun and wove it into towels and lengths to save money for summer garments; they did the same with sheep wool for winter ones. Coffee, too expensive for most, was mixed with parched rye or brown meal or came as coffee essence in small tin boxes at ten cents each. Sorghum was substituted for sugar.[1]

Wooden continued to improve his stock with trips to Chicago. Without a bank in Centerville, he carried surplus money in a belt wrapped around his waist and deposited it at J.V. Farwell and Company of Chicago. Back in Centerville, Wooden correctly anticipated a post–Civil War rise in the price of gold. He buried five thousand dollars worth of gold coins in fruit jars in a corner of the basement in his living quarters at the back of the store.[2]

Fear permeated the County. Rumors of bushwhackers coming up from Missouri to steal horses and mules and sell them to the rebel army were rife. The animals collectively contained in barns became prime targets. Farmers hid them in the woods or chased them out into the pastures. The fear was worse south of town near the Missouri border. Benjamin Wells, a farmer and auctioneer, formed the Cincinnati Home Guard. They watched for signs of invading Confederate forces and guerillas.[3]

For the rebels, a point of entry was south of Exline. A cart track followed Shoal Creek north over the State line from Petty Mill Valley in Putnam County, Missouri. A distillery there, a large three-story structure with two-by-two-foot oaken beams put together with wooden pins, alternated as a hideout for bushwhackers and a barracks for Union soldiers. In nearby Bryant's Station, the Bacus's home was repeatedly invaded for food, and well-known Union supporters like Willie Hines were shot and killed when they were called to their doorways.[4]

Just north of the State line at the farm of Elijah and Anna Jane Johnson, twenty or thirty Missouri residents came several times to ask for protection. The women hid in the house, the men in the barn.[5]

In the same Exline area, an attempt was made on the life of physician Dr. J.H. Worthington. He was traveling on horseback between patients, his saddlebags full of bottles and powders, when he heard a rifle shot and a thud in the clay bank at his side. Unable to see any assailant, the doctor coolly dismounted and dug out a bullet. He carried it in his pocket the rest of his life.[6]

But the fear was worse for the children. When Will Delay left Exline with the Third Cavalry, he moved his family into Centerville; his daughter remembered the rumors and how the mothers and children would gather together for safety at night. Four-year-old Elizabeth Stuckey slept with a knife under her pillow. Five-year-old H.B. Williams asked one of the tinsmiths at his father's implement store on the Square's Northside to make him a sword a foot long and slept with it under his pillow.[7]

News of the war arrived in Centerville with the mail at midnight. People waited in the post office between the Howell Building and Joe Goss's boot shop on the Southside of the Square.

Reverend—now, at seventy-one, known as "Granddad"—Manson adjusted his spectacles and opened the mailbags. Inside were letters from soldiers and newspapers from the Mississippi River cities: the *Burlington Hawkeye* and the *Keokuk Gate City* were anxiously scanned for movements of the troops.[8]

In February 1862, news reached the town of victory at Fort Donelson on the Cumberland River in Tennessee. It was the battle that reversed Union despondency and Lincoln's near despair on the course of the war. The pivotal group in the successful capture of the fort was the Second Iowa Infantry; among them were the boys from Appanoose County who had crossed into Davis County and joined Company G.[9]

After a night of freezing temperatures, fierce winds and rain turning to sleet turning to snow, with no tents, no fires, no blankets for protection, General Charles F. Smith, General Ulysses S. Grant's appointed commandant, pointed to Fort Donelson. It stood five hundred yards in the distance on top of a one-hundred-foot hill. "Second Iowa," he shouted, "you must take that fort." Then he added as he led them forward: "You are only damned volunteers. You came to be killed and now you can be. And," he added, "you can die in silence."[10]

In the advance, followed by the Fifty-second and Twenty-fifth Indiana, the Seventh and Fourteenth Iowa, the Second Iowa Infantry pushed uphill in complete silence. They pushed through lines of fire and cannon, across rifle pits and defense walls of horizontally projecting, sharpened points of felled tree trunks. Men died. They fell wounded, but the silence was maintained until the order to shoot was given. The fort surrendered on General U.S. Grant's uncompromising terms, giving his initials the soubriquet "Unconditional Surrender" Grant. The Second Iowa, banners flying, drums beating, bands playing, was the first division to enter Fort Donelson and watch as the Stars and Stripes was hoisted above the fort.[11]

"Chicago reeled mad with joy," said the *Chicago Tribune*.[12]

Major General Halleck—commander in the West, Lincoln's replacement for Fremont—telegraphed from St. Louis the news to Iowa adjutant general Baker: "The Second Iowa Infantry proved themselves the bravest of the brave; they had the honor of leading the column which entered Fort Donelson."[13]

In Des Moines, the Iowa House was in the middle of a roll call. The message of victory at Donelson was handed to the Speaker: "It was the supreme moment of the session. Men wept and shouted for joy. They embraced their enemies and hugged their friends and refused to do any more business that day. The senators soon joined them, vying with the Representatives their glee. And in the evening they 'had it out' at the Demoine House, with Governor Kirkwood as their host."[14]

In Centerville, "Granddad" Manson sent a message to fellow Republicans, two blacksmiths—John Harper and William Henderson—on the Southwest Corner of the Square. They hammered their anvils, bringing out Union supporters who lit candles in each window of the old log-cabin courthouse. Soon much of the County population arrived on horseback, in farm wagons and on foot to join in local rejoicing. They moved along the twelve streets to the Courthouse Square, as Jonathon Stratton's plan envisaged.[15]

If the nation was impacted by the example, the victory, the courage of the Second Iowa, Centerville was doubly impacted. In the days following, more volunteers took up and followed the fife and the drum.

Eighty-six men, Appanoose County's immediate and newest volunteers after Fort Donelson, entered Company F of the Seventeenth Iowa Infantry and Company F of the Eighteenth. The two companies left Centerville without time for training or drilling and were on their way down the Mississippi, the Seventeenth Infantry in April to join U.S. Grant's army, the Eighteenth in July to head west and south from St. Louis for the battles of Springfield, Camden and Poison Springs.[16]

There was good reason for the urgency. Rejoicing at the news of another Union victory at Shiloh fought on April 6 and 7 was quickly followed by the sobering list of casualties: twenty thousand men dead, eight thousand of those Union soldiers, and of those, one in four were Iowans. Iowa's Second Infantry, those who had survived Fort Donelson, lost more than seventy. Iowa's Sixth Infantry, which had moved downriver from Croton, lost fifty-two men killed outright, ninety-eight wounded—many mortally. Thirty-seven were missing and many taken prisoner.[17]

So shocked was the country at the long list, orders were issued by the Union Army to report only the names of those seriously disabled and taken to hospitals. By April 30 that revised number for Iowa's Sixth Infantry was ninety-six—an indication, said Sergeant H.H. Wright of the Sixth Infantry, of "the serious character of their wounds."[18]

Of Centerville's Company D, four were dead, nine in hospital and two were prisoners, including James, one of the four Zimmer boys who had walked into Centerville Square with his gray-haired father in May 1861 to enlist.[19]

The role of Iowa's Sixth Infantry was pivotal to the Union victory at Shiloh. They were part of the Hornets' Nest stand. Outnumbered forty-five hundred to eighteen thousand, these farm boys from Iowa and Illinois, the boys from Appanoose County fighting shoulder to shoulder with those from neighboring Wayne County, fought with tenacity for six hours, giving Grant the critical time to regroup his army and win the battle.[20]

By May, the urgency for new troops increased. Lincoln called for three hundred thousand more volunteers. In response, Appanoose County supplied its largest contingent of 379. And then there were twenty-seven more, men in their forties, fifties, sixties and seventies, saying they were fit enough to fight, an appeal they won in August, forming Iowa's Thirty-seventh Infantry, commonly known as the "Gray-Beard Regiment."[21]

The 379 new recruits were formed into eight companies of Iowa's Thirty-sixth Infantry. The Centerville Brass Band led train after train of horse-drawn wagons filled with volunteers into Centerville Square from the small towns and villages of the County. Companies already created lined up and saluted the new recruits.

On September 2 there was a grand rally. The people of the town prepared a meal, with food served in relays: first the soldiers, then the women, followed by the men. There was music, patriotic speeches, the waving of flags. The soldiers had their photographs taken. They climbed upstairs to David Strickler's Sunbeam Studio over the Bradley Mammoth Store for plain or colored ambrotypes or for melainotype photographs on parchment or leather at Sharp and Bird's Studio on the Southwest Corner.[22]

New testaments were presented again by businessman Charles Howell and his wife, Lavinia. The ladies presented a flag ornamented with a golden eagle, golden stripes and the embroidered words "Presented by the ladies of Appanoose Co. Iowa. May it never be dishonored." Then the men left for Camp Lincoln, Keokuk. Leading them was thirty-one-year-old Lieutenant Colonel Francis Marion Drake of Drakeville, just across the Davis County line. Accompanying him was the company's surgeon, Sylvester H. Sawyers of Unionville. Both men were abolitionists and early Republicans. Sawyers's family had moved to Iowa from Tennessee because of their opposition to slavery and provided a haven for escaping slaves on the County's Underground Railroad. Drake's father, a shopkeeper in Drakeville, advertised his store as selling "Good Union Stock." And in February, Drake's brother William had been killed in Iowa's Second Infantry assault on Fort Donelson.[23]

Chosen by the men to lead Company F was Captain (later Major) William Vermilion from Iconium, twelve miles north and west of Centerville. A trained and practicing doctor, he chose to enlist with the other soldiers for combat. Chosen as captain of Company G was Thomas M. Fee. Only twenty-two years old, he was a new immigrant to Iowa from Ohio, where he trained as an attorney. To lead Company I was Joseph Gedney, a thirty-seven-year-old farmer. All five men would play a prominent role in the town's future.[24]

Chapter 6

Attacks Threaten

In the last months of 1862, the economy of the town began to improve. The Appanoose County Board of Supervisors, complying with an emergency Iowa General Assembly authorization, issued assistance to aid the families of soldiers. This assistance was given by the County Board for seven years, three of those extended beyond the war's end. There was no objection in any year from any board member.[1]

Architect Charles Dunham returned from Burlington, and work on the new courthouse was restarted. Bricks, made by the new team of Thomas Wentworth and Joseph Goss, the boot- and shoemaker, were fired on the Square, just west of the site. Workers piled them on small carts and pushed them to waiting bricklayers and masons.[2]

Builders Callen and Pearson examined Dunham's drawings. They directed his three-story Baroque design, topped with a cupola, the whole structure rising ninety-nine-and-one-half feet from the ground. On the first floor, County offices and fireproof vaults were separated by intersecting halls. On the second floor, long arched windows, each capped on the outside with a central gargoyle, gave light to the jury room and courtroom. Frescoes decorated the walls: the goddess of justice behind the judge, the goddess of liberty behind the accused, an American eagle on the ceiling. Outside, gardeners planted avenues of trees; carpenters encircled the new building with a hitching rack.[3] On the Northside of the Square, James Wooden still made trips to Chicago and expanded his business into groceries, cutlery and clothing. His wife, Amerika, selected and added her selection of hats and shaker bonnets, then popular with the women of the town.[4]

The Great Western Stagecoach Company still ran daily journeys to Eddyville, leaving every evening, except Saturdays, at six p.m. The Western coach left at 7 a.m. Tuesdays, Thursdays and Saturdays to the Missouri River; Mondays, Wednesdays and Fridays just to Corydon. Passengers were now unloaded at a new hotel on the Northside: the three-story framework Keystone, with proprietor L. Whitsell.[5]

On the Northeast block, J.W. Williams expanded his tin shop to a double-front store. Not only were swords made there for small boys fearing a bushwhacker invasion of guerilla Confederates, but Williams sold pots and skillets, tin roofs, gutterings, butter churns, farm implements and cookstoves bearing the Union brand.[6]

In winter he and Howell, on the Southside, sold Peoria wood-heating stoves in two sizes: small for bedrooms, large for living areas. When B.F. Kindig sunk the County's first coal shaft on Manson Creek, one mile south of the Square, Williams and Howell supplied Cannon sheet-iron stoves for the few businesses and public buildings converted to using the new fuel. As coal grew in popularity, Williams sold "…the best coal picks and axes in the world."[7]

On Sundays, Williams started a singing school in the Methodist church close by the school, and Mrs. Williams planted a flower garden. When other women thought her "crazy" in the Civil War to be spending time growing things she couldn't eat, she saved her seeds and gave them away in small packets. The next year, flower gardens bloomed all over town.[8]

William Bradley, with his wife's brother now a business partner, changed the name of the Mammoth Store on the Northwest block to Bradley and Campbell. Goods were placed on counters, and in the fashion of the day, the counters were pushed flat against walls, prohibiting movement behind. A new assistant was hired—John B. Maring, who had visited Centerville before, liked it and now returned to stay.[9]

Thus released, the ever-resourceful William Bradley, confident even in difficult times, began buying farms and land. He offered cash for ten thousand head of hogs, three thousand bushels of potatoes, three thousand bushels of wheat, one thousand bushels of white beans and one thousand green or dried hides. These he drove or carted to the railroads at Ottumwa. With the money, he returned to Centerville and opened the town's first bank.[10]

For some years, he had run a private bank in a wooden frame building on the Northeast block. He accepted deposits from his neighbors and friends, delivered in tobacco sacks. He loaned money at 12 percent interest. In 1863, supported by thirty local businessmen and meeting all requirements of new congressional banking laws, he received charter number 337 and opened as the First National Bank of Centerville—the third oldest in the state of Iowa. People came on horseback, on buckboards and in wagons, buggies and surreys. They tied their horses to the hitching rack around the new courthouse and came to trade in hard metal coin.[11]

New stores opened: fresh beef, mutton and bologna sausage were sold every morning by G. Heygis and at the meat store of German immigrant Martin Hatzenbeeler on the Eastside. On the Southside, Joseph Goss, when not making bricks for the new courthouse, sold boots and shoes. Next door, connected by a small passage, was the Harmonial or Regulator store of Will Wittenmyer. He sold clothing, nails, glass and wallpaper but was better known in the town as the brother-in-law of Annie Wittenmyer, the "angel" nurse their wounded husbands and fathers wrote about from Civil War battlefield hospitals.

At Callen and Pierson's on the Westside, women bought hoop skirts and accompanying underskirts with stiffly starched candlewick inserted along interval casings. The store also sold parasols, umbrellas and fabrics: denim, twill and "cassimeras"—known today as cashmere.

Children, on their way to what Kos Harris called the "ab, bite, cat, fox, rat, mat, sat" school off the Square's Northeast Corner, still bought their McGuffey Readers and Blue Back Spellers at R.N. Glenn's drugstore a store that now offered cures for headaches, jaundice, piles, indigestion and rheumatism. These could be relieved by buying Ayer's Sarsaparilla, Ayer's Cherry Pectoral or Ayer's Cathartic Pills at twenty-five cents a box or five boxes for a dollar.[12]

When out of school, the children stood on the edge of crowds, hearing election speeches of Governor Kirkwood, who was reelected in 1862. A year later, they saw his successor, William Stone, campaigning, circling the Square balancing a large stone on his shoulder.[13]

After rain, the children tossed small objects into the pools that collected in the disused brickyard on the Square. Or they climbed up into the new courthouse cupola to collect pigeon eggs and listen to the wind rattle the windows.[14]

After snow, they coasted on toboggans down West Maple, just off the Square's Southwest Corner, and they stopped in at Guernsey Jordan's Creamery for glasses of buttermilk.[15]

The newspaper *Appanoose Chieftain* was about to close. In an office over the Westside of the Square, a new newspaper was about to start. Dividing his time at the Sunbeam Photographic Studio, David Strickler—always an abolitionist and Republican—bought the newspaper's printing presses and began printing the *Loyal Citizen*. "[W]e shall with our feeble efforts," he wrote in the first editorial, "earnestly labor for the overthrow of the rebellion, and shall devote all our energies to the maintenance of our glorious union."[16]

Local Copperheads nicknamed the newspaper "The Lying Citizen." The term was a reminder of the war not yet over, of the principle of equality still being resisted not just on the battlefield but in Centerville and in Appanoose County and of the fear it generated.[17]

Despite an improved economy for the people of the County, fear became a constant companion. From west to east, all along Iowa's ten-county southern border, invasions—attempted and rumored—assassinations, thefts and activity among Copperheads and Knights of the Golden Circle continued throughout the war. Worry about their soldiers compounded their concern.

In Centerville on August 6, 1862, James Wooden emerged onto the boardwalk in front of his store on the Square's Northside. He listened to the bombardment of Kirksville, Missouri, some sixty miles to the southeast. What he heard was an engagement of Iowa's Third Cavalry, including Appanoose County volunteers, as they chased the rebels of General Price. The war seemed perilously close.[18]

Tom Merritt, who doubled as a mail carrier when not working for Wooden, lifted mailbags onto his saddle at the post office across the Square and took them on to Milan and Winava, both in Missouri. He was twelve years old but was paid a man's pay for the danger from bushwhackers robbing mailbags to get money sent home by Union soldiers.[19]

Bushwhackers did stop another young mail carrier from Centerville. So small he had to be lifted up onto his horse or mule by "Granddad" Manson, Ash Henderson took a route into Ninevah and northern Missouri towns. On his first trip, he was captured by a band of rebels who accused him of being a Northerner and threatened to loot his mail pouch before releasing him.[20]

Another rebel invasion attempt came on July 3, 1862, in the middle of recruitments for the Thirty-sixth Infantry. Cincinnati, its abolitionist ethic well-known, was again the prime target, with Centerville its "accomplice." The town received a warning. It came from John Probasco, "a truly loyal and very reliable man," and other Union supporters in Putnam County, Missouri. Probasco, a New York native who became an ardent abolitionist and Republican in Lee County en route to Missouri, now owned a 640-acre estate just west of Mendota in Putnam County, strategically close—four miles—to the Iowa border, eight miles from Cincinnati.[21]

The people of Cincinnati took proactive action. Walter S. Johnson, the former town postmaster and one of Cincinnati's leading abolitionists, was home, invalided out of Iowa's Sixth Infantry. The townspeople appointed him as their leader. Then, armed with rifles, shotguns and a captain's commission from Governor Kirkwood, Johnson led them south and invaded the state of Missouri.

At Shawneetown and Gault Mill on Shoal Creek, the Cincinnati men linked up with more Putnam County loyalists and the Missouri State Militia. Together they captured thirty rebels, supporters of General Sterling Price and Missouri's secessionist army, in and around the known Copperhead community of Hartford.[22]

In Centerville, there was depressing news from the soldiers. When the Thirty-sixth Infantry reached Keokuk, disease broke out. Some men came home suffering from smallpox, measles, typhoid and dysentery. Those too ill to travel entered Estes House, a five-story, brick structure designed to be Keokuk's leading hotel but rapidly transformed into a hospital. Cots were placed for beds in unpartitioned rooms. Nurses, doctors and orderlies were assigned for duty and Annie Wittenmyer consulted for diets. Up the broad flight of the stairs from the street to the second floor, stretcher bearers carried the sick from the Thirty-sixth Infantry, and wounded veterans in blue were unloaded from steamboat after steamboat from the edge of the Mississippi River.[23]

Not until December 19, three months after they left Centerville, did the War Department consider the Thirty-sixth Infantry fit for active duty. The men were moved downriver to Helena. The decision was a disaster. Malarial swamps, soaking rains, disease-ridden camps and reptile-infested stagnant waters continued to take their toll on the resistance-reduced men. Their numbers dropped from 930 to 630 in five months. Officers fell sick and died on their way home. Their alcoholic colonel, Charles W. Kittredge, was ill equipped to lead and caused constant dissension and rows.[24]

On the first day of January 1863, Appanoose County was enduring the coldest day of the winter. On the same day, Lincoln delivered his Emancipation Proclamation. Appanoose County's Copperheads were incensed. Members of the County's Osborn Camp—its most virulent Copperhead camp—met in a log cabin on Walnut Creek some five miles north of Centerville. They made plans, prepared bullets, contacted Southern rebels in Missouri and planned the murder of the abolitionist Armstrong family, as well as attacks on both Cincinnati and Centerville.[25]

Rumors of the impending attack spread. Long before daylight, couriers started out in every direction, notifying citizens. In the absence of its young men, who were now soldiers fighting and dying on battlefields, boys, women and old men were seen arriving at Centerville Square armed with rifles, shotguns and revolvers.[26]

Mary, the wife of William Vermilion, captain of Company F of the Thirty-sixth Infantry, wrote of her fears to her husband, then in camp in Helena, Arkansas: "I expect I will make a valiant fight, with a woman's legitimate weapons—the broomstick and the shovel."[27]

The rumors also reached west into Wayne County. Within a few hours, forty or fifty armed Wayne County men appeared in Cincinnati, ready to defend Armstrong's family and home. The attack was aborted.[28]

Mary Vermilion blamed much of the trouble on Henry Clay Dean, an Iowa Democrat and superb public speaker who was currently denouncing the Emancipation Proclamation and, according to Mary, "...traveling all over this state and Illinois organizing lodges of the K.G.C. He ought to be suspended." Unknown to the Vermilions, Dean was then inspecting local land as a future home. It lay on the Appanoose County/Missouri border, ten miles south and east of Centerville. He would name it Rebel's Cove.[29]

Reports of new invasion attempts were moving north and east across the County. They reached Unionville, Iowa, on the far eastern end of the County's known Underground Railroad, at the abolitionist home of Dr. Sylvester H. Sawyers. He was then a surgeon in the Thirty-sixth Infantry, serving with his friend Lieutenant Colonel Francis Marion Drake—and Captain William Vermilion—in camp at Helena, Arkansas. Sylvester's wife, Mary, raising five children on her own, watched in terror as an unknown man crouched and crawled through her home.[30]

Across North Fox Creek, to the east of the Sawyers home in Unionville, Hattie Nighswonger remembered "...the day a rumor reached the little community of Drakeville in Davis County where I lived at that time that the guerillas were going to raid the town. I can recall how frightened we were and how the men of the town rallied to its defense."[31]

When Amos Collius came home on furlough to the same area and learned there were Knights of the Golden Circle supporting the rebel cause while he and his comrades were "...standing up to be shot at and braving disease," he took his revolver and raided their meeting alone. "The traitors scattered in haste going out of windows as he entered the door."[32]

People along this border area of Appanoose and Davis County felt that Knights of the Golden Circle and their supporters operated with impunity. In February 1863, two African Americans working peacefully on the southwest border of Davis County were abducted and carried into Missouri. Potential employers of African American men faced threats and harassment. The authorities seemed helpless.[33]

In the same month, at the school off the Northeast Corner of Centerville Square, the bell rang for students to return to class after an afternoon recess. Five boys did not appear, risking "…a severe penalty annexed thereunto," wrote younger student Kos Harris. Half an hour later the boys appeared and marched to the teacher's desk where one, Tice Swearingen, announced they all had enlisted in Iowa's Seventh Cavalry and would start for the front on Saturday. The statement, said Harris, was a bombshell in that classroom. Three girls ran to the front, surrounding the boys, and "…tears, tears, hot salty tears overflowed the school room and school was ended for the day."[34]

It wasn't the only excitement inside the classroom. That summer, sixteen-year-old John Worthington Fuller was sent to Centerville driving a lumber wagon containing the family farm plow to be sharpened at the Williams Store. That day, recruiters were traveling Iowa's southern border, collecting new young soldiers from Pleasant and Caldwell Townships. Fuller tied his horses to the hitching rack on the Square's Northside, encountered a recruiter, lied about his age and joined Iowa's Eighth Cavalry. As this company passed the school on its way to Ottumwa, his best friend saw him and yelled, "Wait for me Johnny!" He climbed out of the open window and joined the march. Fifty-one members of Iowa's Eighth Cavalry, led by Captain Ephraim Cummins, an abolitionist and member of Appanoose County's Underground Railroad at Hiattsville, moved south to Louisville, Kentucky.

At that moment, the eyes of all of Appanoose County's people were turned even further south: to a place named Vicksburg.

Chapter 7

War News Improves

By 1863, more than fifteen hundred Appanoose County men were serving the Union cause. Information on the individual fates of local soldiers was haphazard; sources were scattered and usually reached the town first in private letters, some of which "Granddad" Manson at the post office had permission to open. But regiment locations, telegraphed from official battle-area sources, appeared in the Keokuk, Burlington and, occasionally, Des Moines and other cities' newspapers delivered with the mail.[1]

It was in this way, in the spring of 1863, that the town learned a major offensive involving at least three of the local companies was underway at Vicksburg. No matter how late the evening mail, people waited as "Granddad" Manson adjusted his spectacles and opened up the mailbags.[2]

Vicksburg is a town on the high eastern bluff of the Mississippi River. Henry H. Wright, then a sergeant in Company D, Iowa's Sixth Infantry—also a future sheriff of Appanoose County, later adjutant general of the State and official author of *The History of the 6th Iowa Infantry*—called it "the great Gibraltar of the Mississippi Valley." Lincoln called it "the key" to control of the Mississippi and to the war itself. He assigned U.S. Grant to take it.[3]

Attempts by naval forces, by General Sherman and by frontal attacks all failed. So did long diggings through bayous north of the city, endured by the Thirty-sixth Infantry boys from Appanoose County.[4]

Late in March, Grant ordered his troops to take towns peripheral to Vicksburg: Jackson, Port Gibson, Raymond, Champions Hill, Big Black River.

At the same time, he ordered all lines of communication cut. Now isolated, thirty-one thousand Confederate soldiers were trapped and under siege.[5]

Standing on the west bank of the Mississippi at Helena, upriver from Vicksburg, First Lieutenant Benjamin Pearson from Keosauqua, who had joined Company G of the Thirty-sixth Infantry under Thomas Fee on Centerville Square, watched steamers head downriver "loaded with soldiers." They included boys from Centerville as part of Iowa's Third Cavalry and the Sixth Infantry and battalions of newly freed slaves who had fought "…as brave as the white soldiers" at Milliken's Bend.

Coming north in the opposite direction, Pearson saw Confederate prisoners from Vicksburg, "…the shabbiest looking drove of wolves that ever my eyes beheld." And, more poignantly, he saw a hospital boat "…from Vicksburg with some four hundred wounded soldiers most of them badly wounded and this morning they put off ten that had died."[6]

The wounded were on their way to camp hospitals at St. Helena and upriver at Mound City. Annie Wittenmyer, whose brother-in-law kept the Regulator Store on the Square's Southside, tirelessly visited every one. She was appalled at the unsanitary conditions, the unrelieved suffering of the men, their unsuitable diets.

Surviving bullets that "passed close to [her] eyes" and shells "screaming" over her head at Shiloh, almost drowning and being mired down in mud while traveling on wagons or sidesaddle on horses, arrested by Southerners and attacked by an insane chaplain, Mrs. Wittenmyer, in the style of Florence Nightingale on the battlefields at Scutari, helped revolutionize the care given to wounded soldiers.[7]

At a hospital in Sedalia, she found her own desperately ill sixteen-year-old brother suffering from typhoid; he was served a tin cup of strong, black coffee and a tin platter with fried bacon swimming in grease with a slice of bread.[8]

"Men are dying for the want of vegetables and a greater variety in their food," she wrote back to the Soldiers' Aid Society in Centerville and to others across Iowa. In response she received dried fruit, eggs, butter, cheese, beer, ginger snaps, potatoes, soda crackers and, shipped from Des Moines, five live dairy cattle.[9]

At Helena that hot summer, she found more than two thousand sick and wounded. The conditions in the overcrowded hospitals were deplorable, the Methodist and Baptist churches crowded with the very sick and severely wounded. She found men lying on narrow pews, scant uneven cushions for their heads, their bodies black with swarming flies. Water for the men stood in barrels at the Mississippi River; ice at the landing was melting because there was no authority to issue it. Acres of tents were pitched by the roadsides; mud that had made the roads impassable had turned to dust that at every breeze gusted into the faces of the sick and wounded. Some men were left to die in a wide cypress swamp that was stagnant, green, deadly and heavy with malaria.

Annie Wittenmyer went upriver, "her blood on fire." She ordered, fought for and won four hospital steamers to evacuate wounded Iowa soldiers and take them to Keokuk hospitals, to Estes House and the Medical College Hospital on Seventh Street. Now a heroine to the soldiers and their families, she returned to Vicksburg.[10]

By June 1863 the situation inside Vicksburg was desperate. Grant's siege of the town was so successful that meals were foraged from cattle, horses, mules, dogs, cats, rats and mice. The Vicksburg newspaper on July 2 was written on wallpaper, its tone, two days from surrender, asking for mercy.[11]

Outside, dug into the hillside, waiting for the town to fall, were the thousands of Union troops. Governor Kirkwood arrived from Des Moines and visited every Iowa regiment. He visited the hospitals, visibly moved by the many sick, wounded and dying.[12]

The end for Vicksburg came on July 4, 1863, the nation's eighty-seventh birthday. Annie Wittenmyer watched as the Confederate flag was lowered and replaced by the Stars and Stripes. "What a burst of enthusiasm greeted it," she later wrote. "We waved our handkerchiefs while the men who had faced the cannon's mouth for the flag sobbed in their wild joy and flung their caps into the air." Several days later, 580 miles north, the news arrived in Centerville.[13]

The news of victory at Vicksburg arrived in Centerville late at night. "Granddad" Manson adjusted his spectacles and opened the mailbags. He began sorting letters and extracting the daily newspapers from their packages. His eyes caught the headline "Vicksburg Is Ours." Slowly and hesitatingly, he announced it. Those waiting in the post office rushed out. Blacksmiths were roused from sleep. They hammered their anvils. A cannon was repeatedly fired. Candles were lit in the windows and the cupola of the new courthouse. By eleven o'clock that night, three thousand people were on the Square, "… all crazy with joy …[a]nd all the next day the streets were filled by a moving crowd, too happy to work, careless of the sorrows the war had brought, and indifferent to the future."[14]

The news took longer to reach Mary Vermilion at Iconium, eight miles north of the Square. After midnight on July 13, a messenger galloped on horseback from Moravia post office with the news and a letter from her husband, Captain William Vermilion, reassuring her he was not one of the casualties. "Thank

God!" she wrote to her husband the same night, "The news has come and it is good. Oh, Thank God!"[15]

The next day in Iconium, she saw flags flying and people celebrating and "…not a copperhead to be seen." Then came news of Union victories at Gettysburg, Port Henry, Helena, Charleston. The Stewart family, Mary's neighbors, told her they had "…been up every night but one, since the fall of Vicksburg. Glorifying. They try to have a special jubilee over every victory, but of late the good news comes so fast that it crowds them."[16]

On September 7, 1863, a countywide celebration in Centerville took all day. Soldiers dressed in uniform. Women wore white riding dresses, blue scarves and red caps. Wagons arrived, creating a procession nearly a mile long. Another four hundred wagons came in from the south. Together they circled the Square, five wagons deep with waving flags, streaming banners, men shouting, bands playing, people singing "Rally Round the Flag" and everyone moving through blinding clouds of dust. "We're nothing but black abolitionists anyhow," shouted Henry Maiken to Mary Vermilion above the noise, "and whether we were a few shades lighter or darker was of no consequence."[17]

But the war ground on. The euphoria faded. There were new battles. Casualties continued, and so did the deaths and the news of the wounded, of prisoners taken, of men never found. New recruits left the town as replacements. Men reenlisted and were granted thirty-day furloughs. They came home to their families, members of the Third Cavalry in winter, crossing the Mississippi to Keokuk on their hands and knees in a skirmish line across the ice.[18]

The Iowa they came home to was still experiencing its own turmoil. Governor Kirkwood felt constantly harried by the invasions and activities of Copperheads and Knights of the Golden Circle and thought them "paid agents of the Rebels."[19]

In Keokuk County, sixty miles northeast of Centerville, a young Baptist minister, George Cyphert Tally, "…an uneducated man with more zeal than discretion," made incendiary proslavery speeches and led his armed followers, believed to number one thousand, with threats to "clean out" the Union stronghold of South English. Standing in his wagon, a long bowie knife in one hand, a firing revolver in the other, he was shot dead. His assassination triggered a violent confrontation known as the "Tally War" between pro- and anti-Union forces, only calmed when Governor Kirkwood himself went to nearby Sigourney and threatened the use of force on the "traitors."[20]

There were other disturbances—in Burlington, Iowa City, Fairfield and Ottumwa and in the counties of Muscatine, Washington, Mills and Fremont.[21]

A year later, much closer to home, there were two more.

At the beginning of 1864, for the people of Appanoose County, the geography of the war was changing. Iowa's Seventh Cavalry, including the boys who came late to the schoolroom off the Square's Northeast Corner, were west of Iowa. They were in the Dakotas, Nebraska and Colorado at garrison posts, escorting trains, protecting emigrants, fighting Indians or guarding lines of travel and telegraph.[22]

The Sixth Kansas Cavalry, Appanoose County's overflow of men from Iowa's Third Cavalry, were fighting Confederate guerilla chieftains William Quantrill, "Bloody" Bill Henderson, George Todd and Frank and Jesse James in countless hit-and-run raids and murderous ambushes along the Kansas/Missouri/Arkansas borders.[23]

For all the others, the fighting tilted east. Extra news now came to the town through soldiers' letters, written home and published in the columns of a new local newspaper. David Strickler, who had taken photographs of the soldiers in his gallery on the Square's Westside, printed the *Loyal Citizen* on the unused equipment of *Appanoose Republican*.[24]

The town learned of the men fighting yellow fever, smallpox and heat prostration; they read about battles and casualties at Resaca, Kenesaw Mountain and Missionary Ridge. There was news of the Battle of Atlanta, "Gate City of the South." Samuel Crow, fighting with Company D of the Sixth Iowa Infantry, wrote he had just come from the battlefield and had never seen dead men lying so thick. "I do not think any man in Company D flinched," he added. He concluded his letter with love to all Union people except those "…able to come and fight" but who didn't.[25]

Letters came describing three battle catastrophes involving local men. The Third Iowa Cavalry, misled by General Sturgis on the Guntown Expedition, needlessly lost at least five sons of Appanoose County's Underground Railroad. From Camden, Arkansas, on April 23, 1864, Lieutenant Colonel Francis Marion Drake led a detachment of eighteen hundred men from Ohio, Indiana and the Thirty-sixth Iowa Infantry to a Union supply depot at Pine Bluff. Two days later, at Mark's Mill, they were attacked. Drake was severely wounded and left for dead. Twelve hundred men were killed, wounded or captured, including the men of Iowa's Thirty-sixth Infantry. Those captured were marched to prison at Tyler, Texas, the first fifty-two miles in twenty-four hours without food or rest.[26]

For Iowa's Eighth Cavalry, including the boy who had climbed out of the schoolroom window and the ten boys who had joined from Putnam County, Missouri, the story was worse. At the Battle of Newnan, of 316 officers and men, only twenty returned to Union lines. Any survivors, all under arrest, were

Thirty-sixth Infantry leaders, Francis M. Drake at front, second from left. *Courtesy of State Historical Society of Iowa.*

marched ten miles to Newnan, held for twenty-four hours and then loaded onto boxcars. Their destiny was the notorious Andersonville Prison in southwest Georgia, where thirty-three thousand men were packed into a sixteen-acre camp designed to hold ten thousand. Thirteen thousand men imprisoned there died of disease, exposure or malnutrition. During the summer that the Appanoose and Putnam County men were held there, more than a hundred prisoners died every day.[27]

With the loss of so many men in so many battles, 300,000 more Union troops were needed. Lincoln instigated conscription. In Appanoose County the process was uneventful. It was not the same across the nation. Riots broke out in Manhattan, in Troy, New York, and in Boston.[28]

In Iowa, at Sugar Creek Township in Poweshiek County—seventy miles north of Appanoose County, thirty-five miles northwest of the scene of the Tally War—a "hotbed of rebellion sympathizers" was training its members to assist Missouri's General Sterling Price and his army of secessionists on yet another invasion of the southern Iowa border. The group was doing something more. It was protecting Iowa draft evaders and Union deserters.[29]

On October 1, 1864, two deputy U.S. Marshals rode into Sugar Creek to pursue the evaders and deserters. Both were ambushed and shot by men lying in wait in bushes. One, J.M. Woodruff of Knoxville, died quickly. The other was taken to the nearby farmhouse of James Craver and lived long enough to identify the murderers. He was John L. Bashore, the Centerville shopkeeper who walked across the Square in May 1861 to join two teachers, Madison M. Walden and William Rhodes, as Appanoose County's first volunteers. Bashore's body was returned to Centerville and buried at Oakland Cemetery.[30]

October 12, eleven days after the assassinations at Sugar Creek, was a bright, clear, warm autumn day. Before nightfall there would be news of another Confederate invasion of southern Iowa. This time it would be to Davis County, east of Appanoose.

Before eight that morning, twelve riders wearing stolen Union uniforms, each carrying from two to seven pistols, crossed the Missouri state line into Iowa at Upton, in the southern corner of Van Buren County. They were traveling west into Davis County. For the next nine hours, led by a Bushwhacker lieutenant, Jim Jackson, the twelve swept west along the southern Davis County border. They robbed and terrorized thirty-three homes, and they killed three victims: a farmer, Thomas Hardy, six miles south of Bloomfield; Eleazer Small, a Third Iowa Cavalry veteran; and Captain Phillip H. Bence, on furlough from Iowa's Thirtieth Infantry. Bence was shot in the back of the head, two miles from the Appanoose County border, sixteen miles southeast of Centerville. The four assassinations caused dismay and anger.[31]

On November 9, William Vermilion, still with the members of the Thirty-sixth Iowa Infantry who had survived Mark's Mill, wrote home to Mary: "A little longer must we suffer …and then I hope the war will be no more, and that freedom will reign throughout the land." They had another six months to wait, a further four months before they would be reunited.[32]

Chapter 8

Death of Lincoln

For the next ten months, Captain William Vermilion wrote home to his wife from Little Rock, St. Charles and DeVall's Bluff, Arkansas. He had missed the Mark's Mill disaster, when so many of the Thirty-sixth Infantry were killed, wounded or captured. He was put in command of what was left of Company F, twenty-five men on roll, only thirteen fit for duty. With such depletion, the company remained for the rest of the war in Arkansas and on garrison duty.[1]

Appanoose County's Company D of Iowa's Sixth Infantry, the first group of volunteers to leave town, were now part of General Sherman's Grand Army of the West. It included Ash Henderson, the mail carrier who three years before was so small that "Granddad" Manson lifted him up onto his horse. Now, at fifteen and considerably grown, he lied about his age by three years and joined Company D as a replacement recruit.[2]

From November 1864 to May 1865, Sherman's army marched southeast from Atlanta "to the sea" at Savannah and then turned north. On January 13, the troops entered South Carolina; on March 7, North Carolina.[3]

Between battles and skirmishes, camps were built. News and letters were exchanged with home. For the people of Appanoose County, the soldiers' letters, their diaries and journals stitched kaleidoscoping images. They read of ten thousand Union soldiers approaching Savannah, marching along the Ogeechee Canal towpath in bright moonlight singing "John Brown" and "My Old Kentucky Home," their reflections in the dark green water of the canal.[4]

They read that the men were crossing rivers on pontoons, marching an average of twenty-one miles a day, corduroying roads across swamps with trees, passing through pine forests littered with the bleached bones of dead soldiers.[5]

And there were other images—accounts of cracks in discipline, of drunkenness, pillaging and looting, the destruction of property amounting to a hundred million dollars. In Columbia, South Carolina, cotton loosened from bales was scattered by a high wind, covering buildings, churches, homes and ornamental trees like snow. This was set alight and raged, said Second Lieutenant Henry Wright, like a prairie fire. Then he added, "Not a member of the Sixth Iowa was injured or arrested for disorderly conduct during the stay of command at Columbia."[6]

In March, a letter came to the post office with painful news. It was one of the letters "Granddad" Manson was assigned to open. It was addressed to Jonathan Stratton, the surveyor of Centerville Square. It reported the death of his son Charley, Company D's curly-headed drummer boy, so loved by the soldiers he was looked on as a mascot. "He was killed on the skirmish line," said the letter, "the ball entering his left breast and if it did not pass through the heart, it was very near and caused his death almost instantly. I did not see him until after he was dead but the boys who saw him said he walked a few steps and fell and did not speak after he was struck. He was the life and spirit of the mess and there has been a cloud over us ever since his death …Hoping that you may be able to bear up under this dreadful news."

That night in the post office with "Granddad" Manson was his granddaughter, ten-year-old Mary. Before he took the letter to the Stratton family, Mary remembered, he took her home and knelt in prayer. As the news spread, all of Centerville grieved, too.[7]

In less than a month they would grieve again—this time for their fallen president.

The end of the war came on April 9, when General Lee surrendered to General Grant in the McLean house in Appomattox Court House, Virginia. It was shouted to the Sixth Iowa Infantry as they marched in North Carolina on the Smithfield Road to Raleigh. "It was hailed," said Second Lieutenant Henry Wright, "with shouts of joy and prolonged cheering by the men all along the column. The frantic tumult dying down would soon break out afresh, extending along the line until it died away in the distance like the roar of receding thunder in a storm tempest." William Vermilion heard the news in St. Charles, Arkansas. He wrote home to his wife, Mary, "The news came up this evening that Lee had surrendered himself and [his] army to Grant on terms proposed by Grant. *That ends the war*."[8]

No one was ready for the announcement that came days later.

President Abraham Lincoln was shot on the evening of Friday, April 14, 1865. The president died at 7:22 the next morning. The message was relayed around the country. It arrived first to cities connected by the telegraph. These now included Burlington and Keokuk on the Mississippi. Editors prepared their newspapers.[9]

Members of Company D, Iowa's Sixth Cavalry, had reached Raleigh. They camped on Beaver Dam Creek three miles outside the city, sheltering from a steady rain. With peace now pending, hostile activities were suspended, the men at ease.

General Sherman made the official announcement to his soldiers on April 17 of the murder of Lincoln. Disbelief was followed by grief. Centerville's Ash Henderson and Marion Sharp went from the camp to the Weldon Railroad to get more information. Other soldiers walked into the town of Raleigh. They looked at the giant oak trees surrounding the North Carolina state capitol, at the bronze statue of George Washington at the entrance. Conscious that Lincoln's body was lying in state at the East Room of the White House, they wept as they heard a blind woman sing "The Vacant Chair."[10]

In St. Charles, Arkansas, the news arrived on the sixteenth. Members of the Thirty-sixth Infantry formed a procession, marching with reversed arms and muffled drums. The next day, William Vermilion wrote home to his wife, "We have all got the blues today. We got the news yesterday of the Assassination of Lincoln and Seward. We can't help having the blues my pet. I am afraid of Johnson. Still I hope he is all right."[11]

In Little Rock, First Lieutenant Benjamin Pearson awoke at dawn on the seventeenth to the roar of a cannon. "[W]hen I arose I saw that the flags ware [*sic*] all at half mast and draped in mourning and I hastened to learn the cause and learned with pained heart of the assassination of President Abraham Lincoln and Secretary Seward and his son which had been done on the night of the 14th. Oh how many brave men and soldiers I have saw [*sic*] weep this day & when I met Judge H.C. Caldwell we wept together the Cannon was fired every 30 minutes all this day."[12]

The news reached Centerville on the eighteenth. It arrived on the front pages of the Keokuk *Daily Gate City* and the Burlington *Hawkeye*. Thick black bands bordered each column separating an editorial and twenty-three telegraphed bulletins with accounts of the murder, the scene at the president's deathbed, the swearing in of Andrew Johnson and the pursuit of the murderers.[13]

The whole town went into mourning. Church bells tolled; the courthouse windows were draped in black. People walked softly, they spoke in whispers and they wrapped the hooves of horses to muffle the sound. The *Chicago Weekly Journal* arrived at the Williams tin shop on the Northside of the Square. People read the editorial: "The cup of our calamity is full. The crime of the ages has been committed. The climax of our anguish has been reached." West of town, the J.S. Stamps family shared a copy of the Burlington *Argus* and its description of "the terrible tragedy which has deprived the nation of its Chief Magistrate." James and Amerika Wooden on the Square's Northside read the name of the assassin with disbelief. This was the man they had met in a Chicago hotel and found to be "a gallant and courteous man and a great actor." In response to a proclamation from Iowa's Governor Stone, who had replaced Kirkwood the previous fall, Thursday, the twenty-seventh of April, was declared a day of mourning. People gathered at the town's churches to pray. Travel was brought to a halt, and all secular employment was suspended.[14]

Iowa, with its early and strong antislavery and Republican history, provided a victory for Lincoln in 1860 with a majority of 12,487 and again in 1864 with a more-than-tripled majority of 39,479. Appanoose County, with its Southern influence, voted against Lincoln twice: in 1860 with a majority of 368 going to Douglas and in 1864 for McClellan, but this time the majority was only 46. Appanoose County's soldiers were another story. Men of the Thirty-sixth Infantry voting in Little Rock gave 69 for Lincoln, 3 for McClellan. For the Sixth Iowa Infantry, returns exist only for the whole regiment. Even so, they were overwhelmingly for Lincoln, with only three votes in the entire regiment for McClellan. In Centerville, either by design or by accident, the votes of the soldiers were never added to the count.[15]

In Appanoose County, the murder of the president caused the political ground to change. The loyalty of local Lincoln supporters ran deep. Their early involvement in the Underground Railroad and their connections to the early Republican Party provided a network of people who recognized in Lincoln his humanity, his magnanimous heart, his sense of justice and his vision of the American creed implicit in the words of the Declaration of Independence.

Now his death lifted Lincoln to mythic proportions.

Chapter 9

The War's Effect

As the train carrying Lincoln's body home was reaching Springfield, Illinois, the members of the Sixth Iowa Infantry were marching north from Raleigh to Washington. They crossed the Roanoke River on a pontoon bridge at Robinson's Ferry and entered Virginia. Five days later, they crossed the James River, distributed Union army rations to swarming former slaves and to hungry and demoralized Confederate soldiers, then continued marching north, suffering through an intense heat wave.[1]

Eight hundred miles to the west, the weather was cool as Lieutenant Benjamin Pearson of the Thirty-sixth Iowa Infantry boarded the steam packet *Rodolph* at Little Rock on the first stage of his journey home to Iowa. He traveled down the Arkansas River and then turned north on the Mississippi to St. Louis. He carried with him the flag presented to Company G on Centerville Square three years previously by the ladies of Appanoose County and inscribed "May It Never Be Dishonored." At St. Louis, Benjamin Pearson wrote in his diary, he bought, "beautifull [*sic*] Silk Cords & Tassels of Red, white & blu [*sic*] for it at $12.00 & 8½ yds of beautifull [*sic*] imported gold fringe …for $16.00." He left the flag to be ornamented with a golden eagle and appropriate emblems on one side, the names of the battles the company had fought on the other. On May 19 at Keokuk, he visited his wounded comrades in hospital and arrived home in Keosauqua the next day.[2]

In northern Virginia, the men of the Sixth Iowa Infantry were still marching. From the village of Dumfries they took a six-mile diversion to Mount Vernon. Here they observed "shoulder arms" and saluted at the tomb of George Washington, the country's first president, before marching on to camp at Alexandria.

That night they washed their clothes in the Potomac, looked at large ocean-going steamships and gunboats, bartered with the owners of small boats that sold fish and vegetables and, on the night of May 23, crossed into Washington and formed a camp on the grounds of the Capitol, ready for their part in the Grand Review of the Armies of the Republic.[3]

On May 24 at nine in the morning, a gun signal started proceedings. Major General Sherman, his horse decorated with a wreath of flowers given him by his daughter, led the sixty thousand men he'd led to the sea onto Pennsylvania Avenue at the foot of Capitol Hill. Each brigade was headed by a fife-and-drum corps and followed by six ambulances. Thousands lined the streets. Hundreds more looked on from windows and rooftops. Brass bands played. Artillery was fired. People cheered. They waved flags. Banners stretched across the streets, bearing the names of major battles including Donelson, Shiloh, Corinth, Vicksburg, Missionary Ridge, Atlanta, Savannah, Columbia and Raleigh. The colors of each regiment were unfurled. The soldiers were sunburned. They wore loose shirts and soft hats. They marched in perfect alignment, elbow to elbow, and for the men of the West, including those of Iowa, they walked with a distinguished, looser, longer stride than the soldiers of the Eastern armies.[4]

At the Treasury building, the column turned and passed the reviewing stand on the White House grounds and was greeted by President Andrew Johnson, General Grant and representatives of civil and military authorities.[5]

Within days, the Sixth Iowa was on its way home, traveling by rail to Louisville, hearing endless speeches and long reports before moving on to Chicago, reaching Davenport by the Rock Island Railroad on July 25 and then making their way back home to Appanoose County.[6]

The Thirty-sixth Iowa was still waiting in Little Rock. Nearly a month later, on August 18, William Vermilion wrote home to his wife, "The good news has come at last.... Everybody hollered and threw their hats and chairs and everything else. Captains Gedney and Fee came near tearing my house down. They did break out all the windows."[7]

The Thirty-sixth Iowa Infantry traveled home by steamer to Davenport. There, at the Burtis Hotel, Captains Vermilion, Gedney and Fee and Lieutenant Colonel Drake were reunited with their wives. For Captain Gedney it was bittersweet. He learned for the first time of the death of his son. Sunday, September 3, was the last entry in the diary Captain Gedney had kept through the war: "This is the end of my diary."[8]

Now, for all the men returning home from war, came the time for transition: from soldier to civilian.

When the "boys in blue" returned from the war, they came with their companies or in small groups. A few came alone. There were shouts, cheers, celebrations, a "grand rally" on Centerville Square, processions, torchlight parades and tributes of honor from community leaders and by neighbors.[9]

Fifteen hundred men had served from Appanoose County. Three hundred were killed outright, dying on the battlefields, in the hospitals or as prisoners of war. Most had injuries that would restrict them the rest of their lives. They suffered shattered or amputated limbs, damaged spines, diseased and weakened internal organs and paralysis. They experienced chronic rheumatism, sciatica and lumbago; their most common affliction, chronic diarrhea, was incurable before the advent of penicillin and antibiotics. Many had eye disorders; some were blind, some totally deaf and a few were described as suffering from "nervous disability."[10]

Hank McKeehan was permanently affected by lying on the ground with repeated exposure to snow and rain and by climbing down into wells "thick with men" and boiling the water in an attempt to eradicate blood and oil. John Westerbarger, similarly exposed to harsh conditions, lost his sight in both eyes and lived out his life with his mother near Dean.[11]

R.W. Porter, one of the ten Putnam County, Missouri, State Militia boys who joined the Eighth Iowa Cavalry in Centerville, barely survived Andersonville. Porter's comrades did not. As Sherman's troops drew ever closer to Andersonville, the prisoners, ever weaker, were shuttled in boxcars six times among four prisons before being released in May 1865. Ash Henderson, the fifteen-year-old Centerville mail carrier who had lied about his age and was now a replacement recruit in Company D, the Sixth Iowa Infantry, was a member of the relief detail liberating Andersonville. He carried men from the prison weighing as little as forty-five pounds, men too weak to stand because of scurvy, missing toes and feet.[12]

R.W. Porter was carried out on a stretcher and taken to a hospital in Annapolis, Maryland. He recovered his strength, graduated from crutches to two canes and started home by train to Putnam County via Chicago and from there to Moravia. For days he rested and visited with his wounded captain, Ephraim Cummins, and took a stagecoach that terminated on Centerville Square. A young woman observing his condition asked whether he was from Andersonville. She offered to accompany him on the rest of his journey, then helped him onto her saddle horse. He traveled on alone, crossed the State line into Putnam County and shocked his family, who had assumed him long dead.

"About the hardest task I ever had to do, was to tell what had become of my comrades. Their parents, their brothers and sisters were there to ask where they were," Porter later recalled. Of the ten boys who had enlisted in Iowa's Eighth Cavalry from Putnam County, one was discharged for disability, two died of measles, three were killed in battle, two—Finly Sterret and William Rhoades—died at Andersonville and one, S.W. Allen, survived that prison and lived to get home but "could not rally." The tenth was Porter.[13]

Another survivor of Andersonville whose changed appearance shocked his family was Barney Brayman of Bellair, five miles southwest of Centerville Square, who had enlisted at the age of sixteen in Iowa's Eighth Cavalry. "The strapping youth who had gone off so confidently only two years before now had the shrunken look of an old man," Orr and Mary Kelly wrote in their account of Barney and his brother during the course of the Civil War. A doctor found him "suffering from general debility and irritability of system" and gave him an early discharge on July 12, 1865. Six years later, on November 11, 1871, Centerville's *Weekly Citizen* announced the death of Barney Brayman from tuberculosis: "His disease was contracted while confined in a rebel prison at Andersonville." Brayman was twenty-four years old.[14]

Appanoose County's leading abolitionists shared in the losses, the wounded and the suffering. Livingston Parker was one of the editors of the *Appanoose Republican* before he enlisted in the Sixth Kansas Cavalry, Appanoose County's overflow from Iowa's Third Cavalry. Six years after the end of the war, he wrote, "Of two sons who went out with me in the strength of manhood, one returned maimed for life; the other came not from the battlefield."[15]

John Conger, that first abolitionist who entered the log-cabin courthouse in 1849 and bought Section 31 in Caldwell Township, four miles north of the Missouri border, lost two sons; another two were disabled. Luther Holbrook, whose land Conger helped locate and whose letter to the *True Wesleyan* brought more abolitionists to settle south of Centerville Square, lost his son Charles, who had written to his father describing how he'd saluted "the children of Fremont" as he guarded a train through St. Louis. Luther's brother Solomon, his next-door neighbor in Pleasant Township, lost his son, a prisoner at Andersonville. Henry Adamson had one son killed, the other disabled, and J.H.B. Armstrong, the leader of the Cincinnati abolitionists, had two sons disabled. That did not stop one of them, though blind, from later holding the position of honorary medical director for the State of Kansas.[16]

But whatever their physical condition, these men were changed in more profound ways.

Lincoln's Emancipation Proclamation elevated the war, sealing it forever to the great promise of equality in the Declaration of Independence and the U.S. Constitution. This Centerville's veterans understood. In newspaper interviews and in their obituaries, many described the war as the transformative political event of their lives, causing them to switch allegiance from Democrat to Republican. Many of the people of the town agreed. These included James Wooden, the businessman on the Square's Northside, and Mary Vermilion, who was impatient that emancipation should be "immediate" and not "gradual." And it was understood by Caroline Masters, whose two sons, Hamilton and Harrison, served under Captain Fee in Company G of Iowa's Thirty-sixth Infantry. She wrote to her mother, Margaret Jacobs, on March 31, 1863, three months after emancipation, "I feel proud that I have two sons in such a novle [*sic*] war our country must be saved or we have lost our liberties."[17]

The transformation revealed itself in Appanoose County's voting. In 1863, nine years after the party's birth in Wisconsin, the County trended Republican. From then on, the party increasingly dominated local politics. In the contentious elections of 1866 and 1868, it narrowly missed the moral leadership of the rest of Iowa when Iowa voters led the nation. They granted the right to vote to Iowa's African Americans ahead of Amendment XV of the U.S. Constitution. In 1868, Iowa's courts ruled school segregation unconstitutional; a year later, thanks to Arabella Mansfield of Mount Pleasant, Iowa was the first state of the union to admit women to the bar. By 1880, however, Appanoose County was solidly "on board," voting for James Garfield and eliminating "in a landslide" a line long submerged in Iowa's Constitution that "whites only" could serve in the legislature.[18]

On their return, the votes of the soldiers were embedded in total County returns. Their exact role in nudging forward the transformation process can only be guessed. What *is* known is that the returning veterans took multiple community roles in public service, and almost to a man they were Republicans.

They became mayors, supervisors, sheriffs, justices of the peace, newspaper editors, farmers, businessmen, doctors, lawyers and judges. They served their County in the State House, State Senate and the U.S. House of Representatives. One became attorney general of Iowa, having already served as attorney general of Missouri. One became governor of the State, another lieutenant governor; one was an aide to a governor, another adjutant general and one a member of the Board of Regents of the State University at Iowa City. One became the official biographer of Iowa's Sixth Infantry, and one served as chief doorkeeper of the State Senate for ten years.[19]

And on yet another level, these men were transformed. In what excludes the rest of us, they shared that deep, unspoken bonding of combat veterans in any war in any country. Together they had shared the unspeakable. Together they had survived. And their survival was because of each other.

They met in the mornings for coffee at Joe Holman's six-foot-wide restaurant they called the "Crack in the Wall" on the Square's Southside or on the "goods box" in front of the Wilson Store in Unionville. Over the years, they were joined by veterans from other states who had moved into the County. Joining them, too—admitted to the group and welcomed in the 1920s—was Curly "Bunk" Reed, born into slavery, a veteran of the Sixtieth U.S. Colored Infantry Regiment.[20]

Together they talked of events—of the Battle of Little Bighorn in 1876 and of Ed Ryan from Centerville, who claimed he had survived the massacre, ordered by General George Custer to remain in camp with a dying Seventh Cavalry comrade, and was later afraid to come forward, fearing a charge of AWOL. They listened to each others' stories, held reunions, visited old battlefields and celebrated significant dates—General Grant's birthday, Lee's

Last meeting of G.A.R in 1940; left to right are Bill Shuck, Edward Streepy and Byron Bates. *Courtesy of Appanoose County Historical Society.*

surrender at Appomattox and every year the birthday of Lincoln. On July 4, 1869, they attended the unveiling of a twenty-two-foot monument on Centerville Square, awarded by the people of the town in their honor and their comrades who had fallen.[21]

They had their photographs taken as middle-aged men in dark suits and bowler hats, squatting on grass behind a large, half-furled Union flag; again in their sixties and seventies, their gazes steady, their hair, moustaches and beards thinning and white; and a few in their eighties and nineties, sitting on chairs surrounded and supported by family members, their gazes now vacant and distracted. As the years passed, they attended each others' funerals. They listened to speeches by Captains Vermilion and Fee and Dr. Udell and placed wreaths of flowers and evergreens on their graves every Decoration Day.[22]

Each Memorial Day, whatever the weather, whatever their condition, they marched from the Square to the Levee, one mile south and back. They marched with military bearing and in formation behind Old Glory and the faded, fluttering banners of their companies. And they were watched. They were watched by the people of the town and by small boys unaware that world events would one day precipitate them into their own sacrifices.[23]

Chapter 10

Postwar Expansion

Between 1860 and 1870, the population of Centerville increased by 30 percent. By 1880 it had more than doubled. New stores opened, almost filling the Square. By 1881, a drawing on the back of an envelope—the work of Second Lieutenant Henry H. Wright—showed fifty-seven shops on the Square, twenty-six more in adjacent alleys and side streets, while unlisted were many of the doctors, dentists and lawyers who occupied rooms over the stores.[1]

Eleven of the stores were general merchandising stores selling clothes, dry goods, boots and shoes. One, known for the next thirty years as "Stanton's Corner," was started on the Southwest Corner by Colonel (formerly Major) Cornelius Stanton of Iowa's Third Cavalry. Lieutenant Colonel Francis Marion Drake of Iowa's Thirty-sixth Infantry, not yet forty, was a partner in the ten others.[2]

Six of the businesses were photographic studios. On the Westside was Morret's with its distinctive blue front, Chatterton's with a red front, Thomas Rattan's, a studio shared with Morret, Snedeker's on the Northwest Corner, Goodenoughs on the Eastside and Tom Wales everywhere in between. Wales bought a wagon from A.L. Hanes, oil and paint from Glenn's drugstore and nails, glass and locks from J.R. Wooden; he fitted up a wood-covered wagon as a mobile studio. He sat his clients in front of potted palms, painted curtains and archways and carried with him the chemicals necessary for tintype photographs. He traveled the Square, around the town and west to the Wayne County communities of Seymour, Promise City and Garden Grove, building a large clientele in the process.[3]

The number of grocery stores expanded by ten. Five more advertised themselves as meat markets, including German immigrant Martin Hatzenbeeler, who was still running his store on the Southeast Corner. From his store every morning came the aroma of fresh-roasted coffee. Children on their way to school called out "Guten Morgen, Herr Hatzenbeeler!" when they saw him and ran away when he replied in German. Some went inside to see his prized possession: a twenty-five-by-thirty-inch, red-and-white-figured silk handkerchief carried by his grandmother's brother on Napoleon's disastrous march to Moscow in 1812 and the return to Paris. On Tuesday and Friday mornings, Martin Hatzenbeeler rang a bell over his entrance announcing the arrival of fresh fish from the Mississippi. Packed under ice he'd cut from area ponds the previous winter, he loaded fish onto horse-drawn wagons that traveled to County communities and onto handcarts pushed around the Square, the vendor shouting, "Fresh Mississippi River catfish!"[4]

On the Southside, next to the "Crack in the Wall," where the Civil War soldiers met each morning for coffee, John Pennington and Andersonville survivor Newton Michael opened the Alhambra Bakery and Cracker Factory. They made cakes, pies and confectionery, wrapping their popcorn balls in pink or orange paper. They moved to the Square's "Eyetooth" Southeast Corner and opened a restaurant and ice cream parlor. Whitsell's on the Westside opened an oyster bar in winter, transferring to ice cream in summer. Whitsell's announced the change to the town with a boy circling the Square, ringing a bell and calling, "Ice cream at Whitsell's, ice cream at Whitsell's."[5]

The town's first barbershop opened on the Square's Northside. Its owner was George Barnthouse. Orphaned in Ohio at the age of three and with no known relatives, he'd enlisted in the Civil War at sixteen in Ohio's Fifty-first Infantry. When his name was heard in an army roll call, he was told there were Barnthouses in Appanoose County. After the war, he walked to Moulton, then on to Cincinnati and found a brother, Tom, and, on the Square, a sister, Clara. He stayed.[6]

Traveling businessmen and salespeople were filling the town. The Keystone Hotel on the Northside was improved and changed ownership. Former Mississippi steamboat captain J.K. "Dixie" Boyles added spring mattresses in the twenty-five bedrooms and carpeted all rooms, halls and stairways. In summer, dressed in a white linen suit, he greeted guests and passers-by from under the five-arched porch built out over the sidewalk.[7]

On State Street, just off the Eastside, Susannah and Alexander McKee opened The Jefferson House. They expanded it directly west onto the Square, increased its height to three stories, made several additions and renamed it The Continental, in honor of the completion of the nation's Continental Railroad.[8]

Businesses expanded, more money was exchanged, new services responded and improvements were made.

New water wells were dug—two on the Square's Northside, two on the Eastside, extending the town's total to six. Each was sunk to fourteen feet and lined with fourteen-inch rock walls. The number of coal-oil street lamps was increased, gradually extending north and south of the Square. The hazardous job of lighting them in the evenings and extinguishing them at dawn was given to two young boys for fifty cents a day and the use of ponies for ease in covering the distances.[9]

Sidewalks were built of horizontal wood beams laid crosswise, elevating shoppers to store-entry level, easing loading and unloading for delivery wagons and providing hiding places for small boys. Two large logs from the dismantled old courthouse were laid parallel, their topsides shaved, stones pounded between for dry passage across each intersection.[10]

On the Square's Northside, William Bradley built a new brick bank building. It was half a block west of his earlier bank. It was three stories in height and had leaded-pane windows, and its customers were served across mahogany counters. By 1870, Bradley was expanding his business, opening banks over the next twenty years in nine towns across southern Iowa and northern Missouri.[11]

Bradley's neighbor across Main Street on the west corner, James Wooden, correctly predicted the postwar rise in the price of gold. He dug up five thousand dollars in gold coins and transferred them into greenbacks for thirteen thousand dollars—a profit of 160 percent. He bought one thousand acres of farmland at fifteen dollars an acre, became a private banker, loaned money at interest and became vice president of the First National Bank, working closely with William Bradley, guiding the town's economy.[12]

Across the Square, Bradley's cashier partner and brother-in-law opened his own bank. He named it the Farmers Bank, but gradually people called it by the name of the owner, the Campbell Bank. Campbell celebrated his opening day with the delivery of a bank vault that was pulled—and stalled and pulled again—by two yoke of oxen from Albia Railroad Station, eighteen miles to the north.[13]

The former lieutenant colonel Francis Marion Drake, now a general—as well as a partner in ten of the Square's merchandising stores—still walking with the aid of a crutch after his injury at the Battle of Mark's Mill, crossed the Square to the Southeast Corner. There, on the site of the old log-cabin courthouse, he helped his father create the Appanoose County Bank, later renamed the Centerville National Bank. It was a two-story, brick building with round, arched windows and horseshoe-shaped brick hoodmolds. Upstairs, Drake, now a qualified lawyer, opened an office.[14]

With the increase in the town's population, the school off the Northeast Corner was now too small. A new three-story, brick building, designed by Charles Dunham, the architect of the courthouse, was built two blocks south of the Square. On the day of its completion, the building burned to the ground. Rumors circulated that the principal, S.A. Holt, admired in the town as a successful teacher and Methodist minister, had set the fire. He was now exhibiting symptoms of mental illness of "so peculiar a character" that the Board of Education annulled his contract and ordered him to leave town within an hour. A year later, Holt, now living in Bellevidere, Illinois, was arrested at a Chicago railroad depot for "an outrageous exposure of his person in the ladies' waiting room."[15]

The old wood-frame school building with its bell tower was bought by thirty-seven-year-old James S. Hamilton, who had served as a private with Company I, Iowa's Third Cavalry. He pulled the building to the corner of East State and the Square and opened a store selling the new farm machinery that was revolutionizing American agriculture. Farmers came in wagons and on horseback to inspect, buy and load the "New Manny," "Buckeye" and "World and Ball" reapers and mowers with "iron beams," as well as the "Pitt's" and "Sweepstakes" threshers.[16]

They crossed the Square to the Northside, where James Wooden, now in partnership with his son, secured the John Deere agency. He invited farmers to view the new "John Deere Walking Cultivator" with its steel blade that had won awards at the state fairs of Kansas, Ohio, Nebraska and Minnesota.[17]

Further along the Square's Northside, on the Northwest Corner, Baker and Farley's Agricultural Warehouse advertised the "Princeton Stalk Cutter" and the "Ottawa Clipper Stirring Plows, guaranteed to scour in the most difficult soil." The store also displayed a corn planter, which failed to impress some of the older farmers, who said it would never work because "you couldn't see the corn drop."[18]

But the conversation of the farmers was of the invention of barbed wire and its availability at the general store of James Hibbs of Hibbsville, seven miles southwest of the Square. James Hibbs's store was selling the first barbed wire in the County, and he'd constructed some for viewing across the road from the Antioch Schoolhouse. It was a single-straw wire with soldered barbs, known as the "Glidden wire" for its Illinois inventor. For the first time, prairie farmers could quickly and cheaply define their own land and contain livestock from running free.[19]

Everywhere across the County, a profound change was underway. Farmers were drawn together. Ideas were exchanged. Improved farming methods were debated. The Appanoose Agricultural Society, formed in 1855 but occasionally inactive, was reignited. Joseph Gedney, captain of Company I, Iowa's Thirty-sixth Infantry, who survived being shot at, with bullet holes in his cap, his clothing and his sword belt shot in two, was elected its president for the next ten years. For a further three, he was president of the District Agricultural Society covering Appanoose, Davis and Monroe counties.[20]

Under Gedney's guidance, the County fair was expanded and permanent grounds found on the north edge of town. The society appointed directors—one in charge of each township—and supervisors with specialized knowledge on improving the stock of horses and mules, cattle, sheep and hogs, grains and vegetables. From a central meeting room in the courthouse, they radiated across the County, giving classes, improving farming techniques and talking about new scientific research on soil conservation, which was being advocated by Iowa's Agricultural College and model farm, established in Ames with both male and female students in 1869.[21]

Appanoose farmers joined the Patrons of Husbandry. They formed into fourteen "granges." They and their families met for box suppers and spelling bees; they wrote expository essays and took part in debates. As they shared their grievances, the granges expanded into "cooperatives," buying groceries, lumber, wire and coal wholesale and reselling them to individual farmers for less. When the crops in fifteen northwestern Iowa counties were devoured by an infestation of grasshoppers in 1874, leaving hundreds of farmers destitute, many of them Civil War comrades, the fourteen Appanoose Granges took action. They collected grain, provisions, clothes and money. Under the direction of Iowa's Civil War adjutant general N.B. Baker, they were sent on to distribution points en route to northwest Iowa.[22]

One mile southwest of the Square, on the Manson Branch of Shoal Creek, the County's land was yielding another source of wealth. Ben Kindig was digging a sixteen-foot shaft, extracting two hundred bushels of coal a day and selling it on the Square to town businesses. Half a mile west of town, a "Mr. Talbot" was mining a three-foot bed on Cooper Creek.[23]

Taking note on his return from his service with Iowa's Sixth Infantry, Ash Henderson formed the Union Coal Company, spent ten thousand dollars, dug a shaft on his father's 160-acre farm south of the Square, bought a hoisting engine and horse and confidently followed suit.[24]

The economic transformation of the County was underway, and at its center, at the core of the activity, surrounded by the Public Square, inside the groves of trees, stood the courthouse with its cupola, which, thought five-year-old Ella Williams, was piercing the sky.[25]

Chapter 11

County Celebrations, County Crimes

The courthouse and its park were more than the hub of the County's business activity. They were its social heart, its nexus, its meeting point.

Children still climbed the cupola to collect pigeons' eggs, to listen to the wind rattle the windows and to see on a clear day Corydon, twenty-five miles to the west. A few challenged their own mortality by walking around the roof ledges of the building's second story.[1]

Civil War veterans entered the courthouse and collected their bonuses: money of ascending values—fifty dollars, seventy dollars, one hundred dollars, for years served and wounds suffered—and land "not exceeding 160 acres." They deposited their muskets, "each with a kick like a Missouri mule," in the basement, and they visited their comrades who had offices in the building. Captains Vermilion and Fee and Colonel E.C. Haynes were in offices on the first floor, across the hall from Second Lieutenant H.H. Wright, who was now the County sheriff and, in his spare time, assembling his notes to write the state's official history of Iowa's Sixth Infantry. They looked in on the office of Clerk to the Court Walter S. Johnson, who had led the invasion across the Missouri border for the protection of Cincinnati; as clerk, his desk was covered with boxes as he organized local records. The office of Justice of the Peace Jim Zimmer became a meeting place. Zimmer listened to an occasional veteran expand his war experiences to those present and later muttered, "He didn't get beyond a flat boat at Keokuk."[2]

Outside, a fence divided the courthouse and its avenues of trees from a "commons area." Farmers in town on business unhitched their horses and tied them to strategically placed feedboxes. In summer people stopped to exchange news with their neighbors and enjoy afternoon picnics. Ben Wells, like Walter Johnson one of the organizers of the Cincinnati Home Guard, now the town's auctioneer, rode his horse around the Square and announced community events. In hot weather he sold cold drinks, and people filled pitchers with cold water from a well on the Northeast Corner.[3]

The people celebrated July 4 celebrations and listened to the town bands. They attended the funeral of Jonathan Stratton, conducted appropriately on the Square he'd platted forty years before. They talked of the diminishing numbers of passenger pigeons that had once darkened the sky as they flew west, of the mountain lion caught at Orleans, of the grasshopper infestation in western Iowa.[4]

They wondered if "a great light" that lit up the County for five minutes was a meteor. They looked through Amos Harris's telescope or held up pieces of smoked glass to view an eclipse of the sun when chickens went to roost, cows returned home "bawling" and a few of the County's citizens fell to their knees and "prayed mightily" that the world would not end.[5]

They moved to the Southwest Corner to see T.J. Mobley, "the great rope walker," cross from the top of Stanton's Corner to the top of Merritt's grocery store. They followed the parade of Cole's Colossal Circus, led by Bismark's Prussian Band of sixteen members, to a piece of land two blocks west of the Square on West Washington Street. They stayed to watch performing elephants, bareback riders from the Cirque Napoleon and Herr Paulschoff, who entered the lions' den and fed the animals with raw meat from his naked hand. A month later, Older's Museum, Circus and Menagerie visited town. People now witnessed a horned horse, a "wild uncouth" sea cow and the "only two humped snow white sacred camels in America." They also paid extra money, a half dollar, to see "the petrified body of a man of gigantic size" they called the Cardiff Giant. This exhibit of the Cardiff Giant was attracting thousands of people across the country until an Iowan, Galusha Parsons, a prominent Fort Dodge lawyer, exposed it as a fraud. He told the editor of a Fort Dodge newspaper, the *North West*, "I believe it is made of that great block of gypsum those fellows got at Fort Dodge a year ago."[6]

In the evenings or in the winter, meetings and entertainments were held in the courthouse. Children, including Ella Williams and her brother Haemmerle, carried cookstoves, tables and coffeepots up the winding stairs to the courtroom for church festivals, music conventions, children's concerts and theatrical presentations. At Christmas there was a Christmas tree and presents.[7]

New societies were formed. The Centerville Philomathian Society debated national issues on prohibition, phrenology, female suffrage and capital punishment. Former governor Kirkwood spoke on racial equality. At these events, the rooms were so full "some went away for want of seats."[8]

The Lyceum Club met on Friday evenings. Its members practiced improving themselves in composition, public reading, declamation and debate, and a Musical and Literary Club met there with a single purpose: to raise money to form a town circulating library.[9]

But the talk of the town was about crime. It seemed to the people of the town it was on the rise everywhere.

From the beginning of the County, there had been crimes: fights over land claims, horse and cattle stealing, burglary, barn burning, an occasional murder of passion. Once, a gang of thieves ransacked the Continental Hotel's one hundred rooms and on the same night the Drake and Kirkham hardware store.[10]

Suspects were given a trial and, if found guilty, placed in the City or the County jail. These buildings evolved from wood to stone. When they proved inadequate for the most determined escapees, a nineteen-by-forty-two-foot iron, brick and stone building, with a sheriff's house attached, was built on North Main Street, one block north of the Square.[11]

Occasionally people took the law into their own hands. When Edward Turner, principal clown with the Cole's Circus, attempted to rape a twelve-year-old girl, "considerable indignation was manifested among our citizens, but the law was quietly permitted to take its course." Turner was taken to the Ottumwa jail and released on a writ of habeas corpus.[12]

Returning Civil War veterans had their own accounts of crimes, of violence they had witnessed that far exceeded the demands of eliminating the enemy. Local members of the Kansas Sixth Cavalry had fought against marauding groups of guerillas along the Missouri-Kansas border. They knew of the atrocities of Quantrill, "Bloody Bill" Anderson and their cohorts Cole Younger and Jesse and Frank James. And they knew of the massacre and mutilation of twenty-three unarmed Union soldiers on September 27, 1864, at Centralia, Missouri, 120 miles down the Northern Missouri Railroad then being built toward Moulton.[13]

Seven months after that massacre, nine miles west of town, at sunset on the evening of April 30, 1865, Fred Leach, the driver of the eastbound stagecoach from Corydon making for Centerville Square, was held up at gunpoint at Big Walnut Creek by six men posing as passengers. The mailbags, express packages and the trunks of the other passengers were all broken open and robbed. Robbed, too, were Abraham Sager and his son Polk, who were passing by, returning to Seymour from Centerville. Then the six robbers coolly stood over their prisoners with guns and waited more than an hour for the westbound stagecoach that had left Centerville Square and was driven by Veen Johnson. They robbed it in a similar fashion, stole three horses and headed west and south, robbing houses and travelers on the way. They were never caught.[14]

Speculation about the identity of the robbers at Walnut Creek increased six years later when reports reached Centerville of the robbery of Corydon's Ocobock Bank, twenty-three miles west of Centerville, by Jesse and Frank James, Clell Miller and Cole Younger on June 3, 1871.[15]

There were other sightings of the James boys. J.W. Swinford remembered that, two days before the Corydon robbery, he was gathering wood with his father at the Chariton River east of Centerville. A group of men on horseback stopped to admire one of the Swinford horses and offered to buy it, an offer that was rejected. Swinford noticed the revolvers the men carried when the wind blew back their long "duster" coats.[16]

The night before the Corydon robbery, two men on "fine riding horses" asked for lodging at the Lepper home, an 1870 blue limestone house at Clarkdale, four miles northwest of Centerville. Mrs. Lepper gave them a spare bedroom. She said they kept a light on in the room until late at night, and she heard money "clink" several times. Next morning they paid for their lodging, then left heading west, where they were joined by three more men at the crossroads.[17]

On what must have been the morning of the Corydon robbery, five-year-old Ulysses Grant (U.G.) Bear was looking for cattle and had stopped to drink at a spring near the Galesburg schoolhouse, west of the Lepper home. Six men rode up from the east, all riding bay horses and with cattle whips tied on the horns of their saddles. One dismounted and drew water for the horses. U.G. Bear handed cups of water to the other five, who then asked the way to Corydon before riding off in that direction.[18]

Several days after the robbery, there was a sighting of them at the Continental Hotel on Centerville Square. Again the observer was John Swinford, who was walking a mare and a colt outside the building. A group of traveling salesmen were discussing the Corydon robbery. A man emerged from the hotel and, overhearing the conversation, said it might surprise them if the James boys were then in Centerville. From the hotel came another man who joined the speaker, and the two walked together "down the street."[19]

Either the date or the whole story of the Continental stay could be disputed. After the robbery, a Wayne County posse chased the robbers south and west from Corydon into Missouri, locating them at the house of George Lee, north of Gallatin. In the battle that followed, Frank was injured. Joe Shelby of Lafayette County, Missouri, said Frank's injury was so serious "...he was bleeding from the lungs ...and Dr. O'Rear was attending him ...He was at my house some sixty or eighty days."[20]

But years later, Swinford met Frank James in Nevada City, Missouri, where Frank was running a store. Frank confirmed he and Jesse had stayed at the Continental. Room 28 on the second floor was said to be their room.[21]

Two more homes claim Jesse James stayed there sometime close to the Corydon robbery. One was the Sharp farm, just east of Promise City; the other was the Miles Alcorn farm outside Allerton, where Jesse presented the Alcorn family with a silk handkerchief.[22]

Hours before the robbery at Corydon's Ocobock Bank, W.B. Corbett, a boy of nine, was on his father's farm, four miles west of Corydon. He saw four horsemen ride to his father's place, dismount at a little grove of trees "...to grass their horses and rest ...They lolled around in the shade of the trees and although I did not know it, were waiting for the opportune time when they planned to stage the robbery ...Instinctively I felt afraid of them."[23]

The Corydon robbery took place at noon at the Ocobock Bank on the north side of Corydon Square. One man held the horses and guarded the front door. Another guarded the back door, and two went inside, drew their guns and forced the cashier, Oscar Ocobock, to open the safe. Then all four robbers left with six thousand dollars.[24]

The posse that chased them included W.B. Corbett's father. Corbett himself became Corydon's town marshall for thirty years.[25]

Stories about sightings of Jesse and Frank, barns where they slept and houses where they were fed have been handed down through generations.

Range 16 in Wells Township, at the southeastern part of Appanoose County, was owned by John and Mary Sarah James in 1856. Their great-grandson, Dale Horn, learned the family connection. His great-grandfather, John, was a brother to Robert James, Jesse and Frank's father. John and Robert first moved from Kentucky to Lancaster in northern Missouri. Robert and his wife, Zeralda, moved on west to Clay County, Missouri. John moved north across the Iowa border, settling south of Moulton. The two brothers lost touch, the criminality of Frank and Jesse an embarrassment.[26]

A few miles west of Moulton, in Caldwell Township, the local doctor, Dr. J.H. Worthington, still carried the bullet in his pocket aimed at him in the border disputes of 1861. In August 1876, when five well-dressed men on horseback silently drew water for their horses from Worthington's well, he noticed revolver holsters under their coats. Later that month, the Northfield Raid occurred in Minnesota. Dr. Worthington believed the men were members of the James gang on their way north.[27]

The worry about crime in the area was superseded by another issue. This, the leaders of the community felt, was about Centerville's economic survival.

Chapter 12

Campaign for Railroads

In 1869, an announcement reached Centerville: the Chicago and Southwestern Railroad Company was building a major transcontinental railroad from Chicago to Los Angeles via Cameron and Kansas City. Advertisements appeared in the *Chicago Tribune* soliciting estimates for grading the road and for supplying ties. Profiles of the proposed route were available for viewing at the Chicago office of the company's chief engineer. They revealed Bloomfield and Moulton would be stations on the road; Centerville would not.[1]

For the people of the town, the news was a signal for action. The town's businessmen and City leaders gave speeches. They spoke of the urgent advantages of the railroad: the access to larger markets, the reduced costs of shipping goods, the accompanying increase in the value of property. Others spoke of how Centerville had been bypassed by two previous railroads; the Iowa Central in 1860, before it went bankrupt, prepared a track from Moulton to Albia and missed Centerville by eight miles. And they recalled the recent Northern Missouri Line's track from St. Louis to Cedar Rapids. It was on target to Centerville, but when it reached Moulton, it suddenly deviated east in a sixty-degree curve, reaching Bloomfield after that city paid a hefty gift of money to the company.[2]

The people were agitated. Mass meetings were held on the Square and in the courthouse. A "Kilkenny cat fight" broke out among the three towns of Moulton, Bloomfield and Centerville. The tussle was carefully choreographed by the directors of the Chicago and Southwestern and their major contractor, Snell, Aiken and Company.[3]

On September 22, 1869, at a meeting in the courthouse, J.W. Williams, who owned the tin shop on the Square's Northside, held up a petition. It asked how many men would agree to devote ten days soliciting stock for the company or forfeit fifty dollars. More than twenty leading Centerville businessmen signed it and started out the next morning to canvass the County. Within days, they'd collected $75,000 in stock. They secured the land for the railroad depot from Benjamin Adamson and the rights of way for the track from multiple farmers.[4]

The railroad company's general agent, Judge Aller, requested another $125,000 in cash. The town's business houses closed for three days, and a canvass for more money was made throughout the County. Eight weeks later, on June 15, 1870, the Chicago and Southwestern Railroad changed the course of its track. Its engineers surveyed the best route through Centerville. Rail spikes and joints, supplied by the Pittsburgh Forge and Iron Company, were ordered.[5]

That summer Snell, Aiken and Company opened an office on the Centerville Square. The town filled with supervisors. They brought their families. They included Judge Aller and his wife and daughters. The Keystone and the Continental Hotels were full. Private homes were opened to accommodate the overflow. Colonel E.C. Haynes, in his real estate office in the courthouse, urged people to buy land "before it gets beyond your reach." Land, he said, was still

J.W. Williams and Sons building. *Courtesy of Appanoose County Historical Society.*

available at three dollars to twenty dollars an acre and lots on the Square fifty dollars to one hundred dollars a foot.[6]

On December 3, 1870, Centerville's *Weekly Citizen* described the approach of the track. It had reached Floris "…40 miles east of us; and the entire line from that point to Lineville 42 miles west of us, making in all a distance of about 80 miles, is black with men and teams. The number of hands on this part of the work is estimated at five thousand."[7]

People from the town drove out to watch the work. They watched pilings hammered down into place for the twenty-two-hundred-foot-long trestle bridge, four miles east of town across the Chariton River bottom. Further east, they watched as the track layers were approaching Unionville at the rate of over a mile a day. Farmers in the area, like A.W. and Joseph Hunt, donated hundreds of dollars' worth of railroad ties, hewing them by hand and delivering them for pickup by construction gangs. Alongside the track, separate crews pounded poles into the ground. They climbed ladders. They strung telegraph wire across the distances between the poles. The people who had driven out to Unionville said when they turned they could see the courthouse cupola when they were thirteen miles from town.[8]

By January 14, 1871, the work stopped. The workers under contract to Smith, Van Horn and McKenzie had not been paid. That day people in Centerville reported "a breeze" on the Square. Thirty unarmed men mounted on horses and moving "with military precision" rode to the office of Snell, Aiken and Company Railroad Contractors. They demanded their pay from Snell or not only would all work stop, but much of the work already done would be undone.[9]

The work restarted. By February 10, the track to Centerville was completed. Four days later, the first engine of the Chicago and Southwestern Railroad steamed, roared and whistled its way into the depot, greeted by the town band, the citizens and the children—one shouting, "What's the train whistling for? We all know it's coming."[10]

Its arrival was the first of Centerville's railroads. The second was already being planned—the brainchild of General Francis Marion Drake, who now entered the ninth of his eleven lives.

In 1871, at the age of forty-one, General Francis Marion Drake closed his law office, moved his clients to the office of his Thirty-sixth Infantry comrade Captain William Vermilion, climbed aboard a team and buggy and left town. He inspected land suitable for a track for his Missouri, Iowa and Nebraska (MI&N) Railroad. Its starting point was Alexandria on the Mississippi River, its route across northern Missouri to Glenwood, north to Centerville and west through Wayne and Decatur Counties to Council Bluffs. He consulted his findings with Iowa's state assistant geologist, Dr. H. Foster Bain.[11]

There were more meetings on the Square and in the courthouse. Money was requested; so was stock and donated land. The people of the County were exhausted by such requests. William Bradley spoke in favor of the railroad, pointing out the financial gain; so did Tom Fee and Cornelius Stanton. At least three times, the speaker was Henry Clay Dean, now living at Rebel's Cove on the Chariton River, thirteen miles south of the Square.[12]

During the Civil War, this man's Copperhead sympathies and his hatred for Lincoln were anathema to Centerville's abolitionists. But with the war over, Dean's vision of the area's economic future, with its developing coal industry, coincided with theirs. More to the point, he was a brilliant public speaker, his skills honed as chaplain of the U.S. Senate and as minister of a noted Virginia Methodist church. Editor Madison Walden of the *Weekly Citizen*, who once wrote of a rumor that Dean had broken his arm by putting on a clean shirt, now wrote, "Whatever may be said of him as a politician … we doubt if there could be found in the west a man who would compare with him as a popular speaker."[13]

Dean's speeches lasted two hours. On a hot August day, he kept his corduroy jacket buttoned up to his neck. The MI&N railroad, he told his audiences, was supported by the Pennsylvania Central, "the richest railroad corporation on the face of the earth." One of the backers was Andrew Carnegie. The railroad would be "a grand through route from ocean to ocean." He spoke in towns in the counties west of Centerville.[14]

On June 3, 1871, he spoke to a large crowd outside Corydon's Methodist church. He urged people to back the railroad. It was noon. Thirteen-year-old Adam Ripper was walking along the boardwalk. Nine-year-old Swedish immigrant John Stromsten was sauntering uptown. Everyone else in town was transfixed by Dean's oratory. The two boys watched as four men emerged from the Ocobock Bank. They wore broad-brimmed hats; they carried guns. They fired them into the air as their horses galloped past Henry Clay Dean. They shouted, "We've robbed your bank! Catch us if you can!" The robbers were Jesse and Frank James, Clell Miller and Cole Younger.[15]

On January 11, 1873, the first through train of the MI&N reached Centerville from Alexandria. It was a cold day. People waved along the track. At Centerville, those on board were taken by coach to an evening reception at the Keystone Hotel and a comfortable night's sleep on the host's new spring mattresses.[16]

The two companies opened their own depots. The buildings housed ticket offices, comfortable waiting rooms and cafeterias. The clock placed on the wall at the Chicago and Southwestern was formerly the "train time" clock at the office of the railroad supervisor in Chicago. Next to the clock was a Western Union telegraph office. A Morse code interpreter received news and sent messages. Ten words—not including signature and address—could be sent to Chicago for $1.00 and to Washington, D.C., for $2.20. The same number of words—but including the address and signature—could be sent internationally payable in gold: $10.50 to England, $26.00 to China. The first dispatch sent over the MI&N wires two years later, to Centerville from Alexandria, was addressed to General F.M. Drake: "My compliments. Come in my office and I will talk with you." It was signed "A.L. Griffin," chief superintendent of the railroad.[17]

The transformation of Centerville was underway.

Chapter 13

The Arrival and Effect of the Railroads

The arrivals and departures of the trains became local events. At the first sound of a whistle from the Chariton bottom, boys, sometimes five to a pony, raced to the depot. Circuses disgorged their animals, tents and entertainers. Businessmen and traveling salesmen arrived carrying suitcases, preachers carrying Bibles, deliverymen with supplies, "runners" with messages and documents.[1]

As goods were unloaded, local products were swiftly put on board: grain and cattle for Chicago markets; coal and stone for towns both to the east and west and for the use of the railroads themselves. The business of the town in less than seven years tripled.[2]

The first of the orphan trains arrived. They carried lost and abandoned children collected off the streets and from the gutters and alleys of eastern cities. They were escorted by agents of the Children's Aid Society and the New York Juvenile Asylum and brought west for the possibility of a new life. The children were bathed and dressed in clean shirts and suits for the boys, buttoned-up overcoats and bonnets for the girls. They carried Bibles. Some of them smiled.[3]

A new newspaper in town, the *Centerville Journal*, disapproved. It described the children as the products of "reprobate fathers and mothers, with all of their vicious associations and inherited vices, and impure blood ...spreading the contamination." (It was an early example of the mind-set of the *Journal*'s staff. Thirty-eight years later, the newspaper would change its name to the *Southern Iowa American*, the voice of the Ku Klux Klan.)[4]

Uncon[illegible] people of the town drove to the station. So did County auditor J.B. Maring, who waited with pen and paper to record adoptions. Seven-year-old Joe Fli[illegible] was selected and would become one of the town's most respected and loved citizens. Older boys were chosen for farm work; girls to clean houses or to wait in shops.[5]

On one occasion, the choice of adoption was reversed. A small girl called Lena flung herself at the feet of Maring, clutched his knees, shouted "Poppa! Poppa!" and refused to be moved.[6]

Lena Maring became a fixture in the courthouse office of her new father. She later married Truman L. Allen, who worked in his father's shoe store on the Square's Westside. They became parents of two children, John and Berniece, long respected and contributing residents of the town. They opened Allen's book and news agent store on the Square's Eastside.[7]

Luxurious Pullman dining and sleeping trains occasionally passed through, bound for San Francisco. They carried wealthy citizens from eastern cities at three-hundred-dollar, round-trip tickets. They did not stop.[8]

One luxury train did. It was pulled by two engines: the first gold, the second "doing the actual motive power." It carried railroad executives on their way to Leavenworth and the former Civil War general, now U.S. president, Ulysses S. Grant. He disembarked, saluted and shook the hands of the Civil War veterans lined up on the platform. The *Washington Gazette* reported that the president, "when the train reached Centerville, was in a state of beastly intoxication." The veterans said if he was drunk they'd have known it and he wasn't.[9]

The railroads gave excursion trips to the people of the town. The Chicago and Southwestern's event coincided with the 1871 Fourth of July celebration. Four or five hundred people assembled at the depot. They carried baskets of food. They sat on wooden benches on nine flat cars and carried sunshades. The train traveled to the Chariton River. The people disembarked. They sat under the trees and ate the food from their picnic baskets and listened to the Declaration of Independence read by Judge Tannehill.[10]

The MI&N event lasted two days in June 1873 and cost one dollar. Eight hundred men, women, and children—twice the number expected—thronged the train to Keokuk, where the streets were decorated with flags in welcome. The mayor and leading citizens of Keokuk greeted them on the steps of the Opera House and led them inside. They danced quadrilles to the music of Wittich's String Band. The following day, they were conducted through the Keokuk Library, the Medical Museum and the Hall of the Grand Army of the Republic, and they visited the local public schools. Two paddle steamers, the *Eagle* and the *Cricket*, took them upriver to Nauvoo, affording them a fine view back to the City, the iron bridge and the ship canal. Then they returned to Centerville.[11]

A year later a third railroad, the Chicago, Burlington and Kansas City Railroad, connected those cities. Its stations in southern Iowa were Moulton and Cincinnati. At the same time, it acquired access to the track of the bankrupt Northern Missouri. This gave the company a rail connection to St. Louis. Round-trip excursion tickets from Moulton to St. Louis cost five dollars. They included a "sumptuous dinner at the Southern Hotel and visiting all points of interest."[12]

Colonel E.C. Haynes took a Thanksgiving ride on the Burlington, as the new railroad came to be known. He showed the train's dining-car menu to people at the courthouse. There were Saddle Rock oysters on the shell, followed by a choice of three soups, four choices of fish, seven meats, including pheasant larded aux truffles and pâté de foie gras, selected wines, liquors and cigars, all for seventy-five cents.[13]

But for passengers arriving into Centerville on the Chicago and Southwestern and the MI&N, there was a problem. It had been anticipated.

Both depots were one mile from Centerville's Courthouse Square. Arriving passengers found no sidewalk connecting them to the center of town. In wet weather, they searched along hedgerows for firm footing. Twenty-nine-year-old Scotsman David Dinning stepped off the Chicago and Southwestern into an April blizzard and walked the mile uptown through snowdrifts, a howling gale and blinding snow.[14]

This inconvenience was forecast when the Chicago and Southwestern announced the placement of the first depot. People in the town felt they had met all demands to secure the railroad and maintain harmonious relations with the railroad's executives. An extra outlay of four thousand to five thousand dollars on the part of the company could have placed the depot half a mile from the courthouse. The company refused. The location, said the *Weekly Citizen*, "will offer an inducement to some gentleman of speculative turn to lay off a rival town."[15]

Dexter Spooner, the abolitionist who, in the 1850s, freighted goods between the town and the Mississippi, met each train with his team of horses to haul a "dray load" of merchandise from the depot. Hotel owners on the Square, concerned they'd lose business, began their own services collecting and delivering guests.[16]

But, predictably, around the depots a separate community developed. Tents and shacks clustered close to the tracks for transient workers. Coal mines were dug to fuel train engines; ponds were dug for water. There were machine shops, where forty to seventy-five mechanics made repairs on equipment, a blacksmith and then an iron foundry supplying parts. Engines, amid clouds of steam and blasting whistles, were shunted into a roundhouse for servicing or rotated on circular turntables to reverse the train's direction.[17]

Lumberyards opened; so did Patrick Walsh's grocery store, two barbers, a jewelry and notions store and a post office. Houses were built, as were five hotels: the Depot, the Elmore, the Evans, the Fremont and, with twenty-one rooms, the fashionable Clinton, with thirty-four- and forty-eight-foot porches on the west and north, long shuttered windows, a deck and balcony railings on the roof.[18]

With the railroads came new immigrants, who settled in the area. There were bearded Russian Jews escaping the pogroms of Europe; among the first was Aaron Grinspan, a peddler's sack on his back, selling door to door, then opening a clothing and notions stall near the MI&N depot, and Hyman Chapman, who opened a pop factory on the corner of Elm and Levee. There were Irish Catholics who had laid the Chicago, Rock Island and Southwestern track, who shopped at Patrick Walsh's grocery and post office and celebrated mass on Sundays in Thomas Fleming's Clinton Hotel. And there were Swedish Lutherans, who met in the home of Peter Polson for services in their native language.[19]

Every day the trains brought visitors. Many made their way to the Square. "[A] great many strangers are to be seen on our streets daily," said the *Weekly Citizen*. "Show them around as most of them are looking for locations." Eight months later, the tone had changed: "…tramping beggars are on their rounds, exhibiting their deformities and examining locks preparatory for thieving raids. The county has an infirmary for the destitute and needy and a prison for thieves. The majority of beggars are vagabonds, and consume their gifts in whisky."[20]

The situation was worse near the depots. There were saloons of descending reputation—Thompson's, Fred Kiser's, Tom Froud's. The area was outside the City limits. So when Centerville went "dry," the area around the depots attracted "droves" down from the town. Several of the hotels, including Sammy Stewart's Fremont, transferred their business to liquor supplied by "unsavory toughs" from St. Louis.[21]

There was noise, drunkenness, violence, beatings, knifings, prostitution, shootings and murders. The alias "Beatrice" covered the real identity of a woman living in the area. She wrote to the paper that she witnessed young men "…whose parents are pious and respectable" and town married men involved in "nocturnal debauches and beastly carousels."[22]

Moses Linch, who built a boardinghouse in 1871 close to the Chicago and Southwestern depot, kept a wooden club always near at hand to defend himself. Tom Froud's saloon was pelted with stones; when the owner emerged to defend his property, he was knifed and almost murdered.[23]

George Armour, a tailor who arrived after working in Keokuk, said the place there where men went "to indulge in various vices" was known as "the Levee." The word stuck. Officially named South Centerville, the area became popularly known as "the Levee." Its reputation stuck, too. It would get worse.[24]

Chapter 14

Coal Mining Begins

David Dinning, having survived his April blizzard walk from the Chicago and Southwestern depot, arrived on Centerville Square. Within days the snow melted, and he made his way to the courthouse. Men were laying a new pathway circling the building; others were cleaning the street lamps. Custodian George Bryan was raking dead grass and leaves, his action revealing the fresh, green growth beneath. People were climbing the newly cleaned and carpeted stairway to the cupola. They looked through the new, large telescope Bryan had placed there. They could see improvements in neighboring towns and could identify the color of cattle at Seymour, fourteen miles to the west, and at Moulton, eleven miles east.[1]

Dinning's arrival coincided with Iowa's first inspector's report on coal mining in the State. The inspector was Park Wilson of Mahaska County. Wilson found forty-four coal mines operating in Appanoose County in 1881, employing 387 men. Eight of those mines were within one-and-a-half miles of Centerville Square, two owned by the ever-enterprising William Bradley. All were shaft mines. The coal seam, said the report, averaged almost three feet in thickness and extended "...with more uniformity over the county than the coal of any other county in the state."[2]

Dinning was an ambitious twenty-two-year-old Scotsman from Kilmarnock in Ayrshire when he created a coal mining sensation at Galesburg, Illinois. There, in a mine where the average output was 25 bushels of coal a day, new immigrants Dinning and two Ayrshire friends, David Steele and Robert Livingston—all three of them used to the harsher conditions of British coal mines—pushed their daily output to 125 bushels a day. People in Illinois came from as far as forty miles to see the trio work.[3]

Dinning's ambition now brought him to Centerville. Earlier geologists' reports had said Appanoose County "…lies wholly within the great Iowa and Missouri coalfields." They reported more coal seams existed below the one being mined, and an "inexhaustible mine of wealth" lay beneath the feet of the people of Appanoose County and was within their grasp.[4]

Of the County's forty-four coal mines, David Dinning selected to work at the Relay Mine, one-and-a-half miles west of the Square. Friends David Steele and Robert Livingston joined him from Galesburg. So did three brothers from Scotland.[5]

Three months after his arrival, Dinning joined the Independence Day celebration on Centerville Square. The day started when blacksmith and veterinarian Alvin Pixley hammered his anvil, followed by the firing of thirty-eight guns at sunrise. People crowded into town. A rumor began to circulate. People looked at each other in concern. Others arriving by train hovered at the railroad depot, pausing there for news at the Western Union telegraph office. Three bulletins arrived that day from Washington. Runners carried them the mile to the Square, to the newspaper offices and to Mayor Earlywine.[6]

The first referred to an event at Washington's Baltimore and Ohio Railroad depot two days previously. It read: "President Garfield was shot twice in the B. & O. Depot this morning." It was followed by a second: "President Garfield is dead." Then came another, "…the President is still alive but so much excitement, that the truth cannot be ascertained."[7]

In this state of suspense and uncertainty, the day continued. In charge were two Civil War veterans, Captain J.B. Gedney and J.M. Elgin. There was a morning parade led by Company E, Iowa Second Regiment, of the Iowa National Guard. Then came the town's new fire engine, hook and ladder companies, and the Centerville Brass and Martial Bands. It started on the Westside of the Square, passed through the City's principal streets and returned to the Courthouse Park. There were songs, prayers, an oration and the reading of the Declaration of Independence by the high school principal, Professor Frank E. Stephens.

After a noon picnic, there were toasts given by various speakers. The first of these was to the flag; the second to the press. Toasts followed to Appanoose County, to Iowa, to agriculture, to the law, to the local mining interests, to the common schools and to "our ladies and to our forefathers."[8]

In the late afternoon, the town's first fire engine gave a demonstration of its power. A hose was attached to a well on the corner of the Square. The engine roared into life. Steam issued from its funnel. Water coursed through the hose, burst into view and hurled itself into the air. It was seen as the town's first example of "throwing water."[9]

That evening after dark, people assembled around the courthouse to witness a fireworks display. Five hundred dollars had been spent on fireworks. They were stored in the cupola with the telescope removed. The event was promoted as "the grandest display of the kind ever witnessed in Southern Iowa." Groups of the fireworks were assembled in a formation, each resembling a pigeon. When the fireworks were lit, the "pigeons" were to be pushed from the cupola to travel along a wire stretched to the new Bradley building on the Square's Southside. The fireworks were designed to burst and explode in the air above the crowd.

On the first run, halfway along the wire, the lit "pigeon" suddenly stopped, then started back into the cupola, landing and setting alight the reserve stock of fireworks. The whole cupola with its woodwork burst into shooting rockets and flames. The four men working in the tower found their trap-door exit sealed shut and escaped by jumping through side windows onto the roof eighteen feet below.

People raced to help. The fire department, with the town's new fire engine, went into action. Men climbed onto the roof, dragging up the fire hose, which burst, was repaired and for over an hour supplied a steady stream of water from the Square's four cisterns, finally extinguishing the fire.[10]

Haemmerle Williams from the tin shop on the Northside said the event gave new meaning to the words "the rocket's red glare, the bombs bursting in air."[11]

The next line of the national anthem was given new meaning that night as well—people looked up and pointed, noting that "our flag was still there." Above the fire and the surging crowds below, it waved from the top of the cupola, unscorched and unhurt.[12]

It was the symbol of the country, and not far from everyone's minds was the condition of the country's president.

It took eighty days for President Garfield to die. Throughout that time, bulletins on his health were telegraphed to Centerville, their optimistic tone belying the president's condition. Assassin Charles Gitteau shot him twice—once in the arm, once in the abdomen. Throughout the intense heat, the humidity and swarming mosquitoes of Washington that summer, doctors, using fingers and dirty instruments, extended a "three-inch harmless wound into a twenty-inch-long contaminated gash from ribs to groin." Death came on September 19.[13]

As they had for Lincoln's assassination, local newspapers bordered the news of the death with thick black bands. Mayor Earlywine issued a proclamation. He asked the citizens of the town to attend a memorial service at the Courthouse Park on September 22 and a second one a week later in the new Russell Hall on the Square's Northwest Corner. Committees were appointed to organize events.[14]

Bells tolled. Flags were lowered to half-mast. A letter of condolence was sent to Mrs. Garfield. It was engraved and framed. Arches draped in black and white were built at the Courthouse Park's five entrances. A speaker's stand was prepared. It was decorated with arches, flags and flowers and was surmounted with a life-size portrait of the president, below it the calming words he'd spoken on the assassination of Lincoln, "God reigns and the Government still lives." Black crepe was stretched from street to street. It covered the homes adjacent to the Square and outlined the windows and doors of stores. At J.M. Beall's general variety store, three portraits stood side by side in the window: those of Washington, Lincoln and Garfield. They were wreathed in flowers interwoven with crepe.

On September 22, businesses, public offices and the coal mines closed. Eight hundred to one thousand people formed a procession. They were led by the Light Guard Band and Company E of the local National Guard, all in uniform, followed by the Masons and Odd Fellows, the fire department and school, City and County officials. The procession circled the Square then joined the hundreds of people inside the park.

There were eleven speeches, one of the first by Centerville's Dr. Robert Stephenson, who had served under Garfield in the Forty-second Ohio Voluntary Infantry during the Civil War. A choir sang. At the close of the service, a resolution was adopted. It began by confessing not to understand "the dispensation of God." It ended with a desire "to mingle our tears with those who mourn."[15]

Mrs. Garfield later acknowledged the town's resolution and letter of condolence. It was sent to Dr. Robert Stephenson.[16]

The businesses of the town reopened. Miners returned to work. They included David Dinning, whose reputation for hard work and trustworthiness was rapidly being established. Two years after his arrival, Dinning was secured to sink shafts of new coal mines at Cincinnati, seven miles south of Centerville and poised on the Chicago, Burlington and Kansas City Railroad. Dinning became the operator in charge of five mines, three of which he sank and two he bought. Together with his three brothers, Steele and Livingston, they formed what would become one of the largest operating companies in southern Iowa.

The mines were named for the symbol of Scotland: Thistle One, Two, Three, Four and Five.[17]

Eleven miles east of David Dinning's Thistle Mines, the Chariton River flows through the gentle hills of Wells Township and crosses the State border into Missouri. The river's entire course from northwest to southeast slices the County into two and serves as a sharp geologic divide.

Few coal mines—only early outcroppings, drift, slope and shallow shaft mines—were dug to the river's east. The County's rich coal seam, from thirty-five to three hundred feet below the surface of the land, below the top layer of loam, below the bands of glacial deposits—the limestone, the sandstone, the shale—lay to the river's west.[18]

Three of the County's railroads already existed. Through Cincinnati was the Chicago, Burlington and Kansas City. Two were through Centerville: the Chicago and Southwestern and General Drake's Missouri, Iowa and Nebraska, extended west by 1879 through Brazil, Promise City and Corydon to VanWert. In the 1880s, two new railroads were built: the Centerville, Moravia and Albia Railroad, owned, again, by General Drake, and, in 1887, the Chicago, Milwaukee and St. Paul, seven miles north of Centerville. The tracks of all five straddled the richest vein of coal in the coal-richest part of the State.[19]

By 1886, eight hundred miners were employed in County coal mines, producing 150,000 tons of coal. Two years later their production increased 68 percent to 219,263 tons.[20]

It was just the beginning. Centerville's economy and the County's appearance became dominated by coal. Its social transformation would be even greater.

Chapter 15

The Mines

For forty years, from 1880, Centerville and the surrounding countryside moved in response to whistles. New coal mines were sunk. New spur lines moved the coal to the railroad tracks. The Chicago, Milwaukee and St. Paul cut a diagonal path from Moravia, nine miles north of Centerville, to Seymour in the southeastern corner of Wayne County, spawning new coal mines in Rathbun, Mystic and Jerome.[1]

Around the mines and splayed across the green land, sheds were built, bundled together for mining cages, hoisting engines, pulleys, derricks, air shafts and water towers. There were pyramidal slag piles, stacks of lumber and, at some company towns, rows of twenty-four-foot-square miners' houses, a store, a well, a school and a tavern.[2]

Miners, including boys less than fourteen years of age, were roused at five in the morning with the screech of company whistles. They made their way through the streets to the shafts in their hobnailed boots and leather-kneed canvas work clothes, the orange glow from their carbide helmets wavering and bobbing as they moved through the dark. They carried three-tiered lunch buckets: water at the bottom, sandwiches in the center, dessert in the top. With a signal of three whistles, the men descended in cages, traveling various depths—at one mine in Plano, the deepest in Iowa, to 209 feet.[3]

At the coalface, the men worked alone or in pairs, in thirty- to forty-foot-wide rooms, leaving an eight- to ten-foot pillar of coal to support the roof in the "room and pillar" method of mining. Or—most commonly in Appanoose County, with a coal seam height of only three feet—they worked "the longwall method." Here the miners undercut the coal seam and waited for pressure from the overlying rock strata to break the coal. Large chunks of the coal were then broken with picks and loaded onto pit cars. Each miner fastened a metal washer with his identifying number on the car loaded with his coal. The cars were then pulled by burros or Shetland ponies along tracks to the bottom of the mine, ready for ascent.[4]

The miners used picks, wedges and shovels. They worked the three-foot coal seam on their hands and knees or lay on their sides for nine-, ten-, twelve- or even fifteen-hour days for a six-day work week, from August to April and occasional summer work.[5]

It was hard, dirty and dangerous work. There were falls of slate, rock, coal and "black bat." Men fell down shafts or died of asphyxiation; they were electrocuted, maimed and killed in explosions, crushed by cars or caught in fan belts; and they suffered the rest of their lives from "black lung" disease.[6]

The miners were paid per ton of coal weighed by the coal operator. They were paid in scrip, exchangeable only at company stores near the coal mine in outlying villages or, for mines close to town, at Merritt Brothers and Stanton's Corner on the Southside of Centerville Square, Drake and Lane on the Westside.[7]

For some work, the miners received *no* pay. When they arrived for work, they were required to bail water from the rooms, lower the floor, remove the ceiling, prop the roof and lay track. And because coal owners could not sell small coal lumps, they would not pay for any cut by the miners. To separate the sizes of the coal, operators insisted miners use screens, but the size of the mesh varied from mine to mine, and some operators added spreaders on top of the mesh, which further broke down the coal.[8]

Every year, representatives of the coal miners and coal owners met in the Russell Hall to discuss concerns and the price per ton paid to the miners. The miners asked for more. The coal owners retreated behind stage curtains. The miners waited in knots on the Northwest Corner of the Square. The coal owners reappeared to say they couldn't afford it.[9]

Unmet grievances began to fester. There were strikes at individual coal mines. The miners talked of concerted action. In 1874, three miners in Cincinnati walked to Centerville, entered the courthouse and registered themselves as a union.[10]

Across the country, miners were fighting their conditions. Nationwide, coal mine disasters were reported in local newspapers: 109 coal miners suffocated at Avondale, Pennsylvania. Disaster followed disaster: at Braidwood, Illinois; in Pocahontas, Virginia; at the Frick Coal and Coke Company in Pittsburgh,

Pennsylvania. Closer to home, in 1893, eight miners were killed at Hiteman near Albia; in 1897, at the same mine, nine more were killed when nine cars went out of control. Four years later at the Lost Creek Mine near Oskaloosa, twenty miners were killed and fourteen injured.[11]

Relations between management and labor deteriorated. Strikes in Pennsylvania were broken with murder, arson, threats. A secret organization of miners, the Molly Maguires, fought back using similar tactics. They were infiltrated and exposed. Ten were hung, fourteen sent to jail. Appanoose County's first union, formed in Cincinnati, disbanded.[12]

Despite intimidation, talk of a countrywide union was reported in national meetings. In 1883, an organizer for Knights of Labor, Richard Trevellick, spoke on Centerville Square. He had a heavy cold. He spoke for two hours. The miners, he said, must have an eight-hour workday. Children under fourteen should be in school, not in the mines. The crowd was described as "…very large and appreciative." Local newspapers called Trevellick a "labor agitator."[13]

Seven years after Trevellick, another union organizer spoke to a mass meeting on Centerville Square. L.M. Beatty represented a new nationwide union: the United Mineworkers of America, formed in Columbus, Ohio. This union, Beatty told his audience, divided the nation into twenty-one districts. Iowa was District 13, and four local unions had already been formed in Appanoose County: at Centerville, Jerome, Mystic and Cincinnati. A fifth, Seymour, lay close—just across the County's Southwestern border.

The aim of the union, said Beatty, was the achievement of an eight-hour workday. He also called on all members to support each other and to uphold all wage agreements reached with management.[14]

The eight-hour workday was not achieved until 1899, but in 1895, Appanoose County's miners were ready to exercise their new solidarity.

On April 9, 1895, led by Captain Ramsey of the Salvation Army, who was beating his drum, several hundred coal miners marched south out of Centerville Square. They were from Centerville, Rathbun, Mystic and Forbush, where a fifteen-year-old John L. Lewis, the future United Mineworkers of America president, was then working as a mule driver.[15]

At the Wesley Chapel at Galleyville, the marchers were joined by a hundred more from the mines of Jerome, Numa and Seymour. Their target was Cincinnati, where eighty to one hundred miners, who had gone without work for fifteen months and whose families were "half-starving," were returning to work at twenty to thirty cents per ton of coal below the accepted price agreed to with management.[16]

Cincinnati mayor J.A. Corder was alarmed. He saw the approach of a "mob" now swollen by more miners from Mendota, six miles across the Missouri border. Mayor Corder telegraphed Appanoose County sheriff William Bray. Bray contacted Iowa adjutant general John R. Prime requesting two companies of militia be sent to protect Cincinnati. Extra citizens were deputized. They carried shotguns and Winchesters. The Appanoose Coal Company sent straw mattresses for the soldiers.[17]

Mayor Corder and a group of citizens went out to meet the marchers. Rain began to fall. They could enter the town, Corder told them, but as orderly citizens. The marchers promptly disbanded. Most sought shelter in livery stables and barns. A delegation spoke to the Cincinnati miners. There was no violence or threat to property, but the national press was already alerted.[18]

On April 15, the *New York Times* reported everything in Cincinnati, Iowa, was quiet. Order was maintained by Sheriff Bray. Prime, the adjutant general, withdrew the State militia. Cincinnati miners did not return to work until new agreements were honored. Members of Chatham Square Methodist Episcopal Church in Burlington, Iowa, sent supplies to the needy miners.[19]

As the local coal industry expanded, the struggle between miners and operators became more intense. Miners known to be union sympathizers were targeted by some coal owners as troublemakers. They lost their jobs and were removed from their homes.[20]

Strikebreakers were harassed, intimidated, beaten and strong-armed out of town by union members. Attempts were made to damage their property, even to dynamite an escape shaft where they worked at the Star Coal Company at Rathbun.[21]

In 1886, the Diamond Coal Company, followed by the Relay Mine, installed Harrison and Legg coal-cutting machines. Compressed air from large surface and smaller subsidiary boiler rooms was piped along iron tubes and wire-bound hoses. The air powered the machines that sliced into the coal seam, emitting clouds of fine dust that settled on the miners. Pick miners struck. They feared the new machines would make them redundant. To break the strike, the coal owners at both mines brought in African American miners. Six years before and twenty-one miles to the north, Albia had been the first coal mine in Iowa to attempt this practice. A racial gun battle followed, and twenty-six miles north of Albia in Mahaska County, black strikebreakers found it necessary to form "a mutual protection society." In Centerville, their arrival was relatively stable.[22]

If a few coal owners were insensitive at best, brutal at worst, the same cannot be said for *all* Appanoose County's pioneer coal leaders. Most were honest, considerate and fair. Eleven were exceptional, described as "...all splendid men ...no better men ever pressed beneath their feet the soil of God's footstool."[23]

All but two of the eleven had been coalface miners. For David Steele, James Horridge, the Dinnings, the Orr brothers, the Lodwicks, James Campbell, Joe Turner, the Seddons and the McConvilles, this experience had been in the harsh conditions of English and Scottish mines. For one of these families, the Lodwicks, experience came in the even harsher coal mines of South Wales, where an average of one miner was killed every four hours and miner/owner relations were bitter and prolonged.[24]

The three Seddon brothers—James, John, Tom—worked in the Lancashire coal mines and were "blacklisted" there for their pro-union activities. The McConville brothers, originally Irish Catholic ironstone workers in the granite mountains of County Down, were forced to coalface work in Scottish mines by the Irish Potato Famine.[25]

Harry Ashton, owner of Centerville's North Hill Coal Mine was not a miner. But his unique life had shaped his character. Impressed into the British Army in a London pub in 1854, he was one of 195 of 700 cavalry soldiers who survived the infamous Charge of the Light Brigade in the Crimean War. This military blunder by the Earl of Cardigan and Lord Lucan became the subject of a poem by Alfred Lord Tennyson: "Into the valley of Death rode the six hundred..." Found unconscious on the battlefield, Ashton was transported to the hospital at Scutari and nursed back to health by Florence Nightingale. As he recovered, motivated by his admiration for her and her work, he trained as a nurse and worked alongside her for two-and-a-half years.[26]

A second owner had no coal mine experience. Thomas Jefferson Greene immigrated to Appanoose County from Shelbyville, Indiana, in 1882. He became the owner, operator and salesman of the Watson Mine, south of town. Across the road he built the City Gardens. It covered fifteen acres. It had an irrigation system. Multiple tiny rotating nozzles, inserted along pipes, sprayed fine mist in hot weather. The City Gardens's high yield served three purposes: choice cabbages were shipped across southern Iowa and northern Missouri; fruits and vegetables were sold to visiting circuses; and there was paid employment for the Watson miners in the off-work summer season.[27]

And when T.J. Greene's good friend Harry Ashton suffered financial reversal at the North Hill Coal Mine and was about to lose his home, Greene went to the Ashton home. He said he would take all the coal Ashton could produce at the highest market price, pay cash for it and charge no commission for handling it.[28]

All eleven of these men were unpretentious and egalitarian. They lived in modest homes and committed themselves to the quality of the community. All passed this ethic on to the next generation. One family—the Lodwicks—produced sons who became national figures in aviation, medicine and agriculture.

Coal owners, town officials and miners cooperated to sell County coal in a "booster caravan." A train of General Drake's Iowa Central Railroad picked up coal dealers from across the State, brought them south to Oskaloosa, to Albia and then on to Centerville. The dealers inspected side tracks full of large, bright lump coal; they inspected coal mines, and they viewed mining machinery in operation in local coal mines.

Then, led by grand marshal Colonel C.A. Stanton and the George Landers Band, a parade "three to four blocks long" brought them to the Square for a meal before they returned, walking down West Van Buren Street for their return.[29]

In February 1899, representations of coal operators and miners from across Iowa reached a new wage scale. As part of the scale, operators for the first time accepted the eight-hour workday. It was named the Centerville Agreement, argued and accepted on Centerville Square.[30]

For the miners it was a victory. Men came from outside the City in hacks or on morning trains. They wore badges showing the coal mine they represented. The courthouse park was lined with teams of horses. Fifteen hundred to two thousand people, led by three brass bands, circled the Square. The County attorney, J.M. Wilson, spoke, as did the president of the State Federation of Labor. A glee club sang.[31]

For twenty years, a national pattern for a shorter working day was established in Centerville. In 1895, stores closed at eight each night. By 1900, it was six thirty. With more leisure time, the people of the town could express themselves in sports, in music. Now, coal miners could join too.

Chapter 16

Recreation Expands, Female Leaders Emerge

In the 1880s, Phil Ulrich, the three-forge blacksmith just north of the Continental Hotel on Centerville Square, built the town's first bicycle. It had wooden wheels, iron tires and solid-axle pedals on the front wheel. People came to watch it being built. They said it wouldn't work. They followed him east to the old fairgrounds on Eighteenth Street between Bank and Wall Streets. They stood and watched. Ulrich mounted the bicycle. He circled the track.[1]

Ulrich's bicycle reflected a national trend to outdoor sports. In Centerville, it started a craze. The Centerville Cycling Club was formed. Its members met in a room over Mark Lowther's printing office on the Square. The secretary of the Iowa Division of the League of American Wheelmen and a member of the Oskaloosa Club spoke. This club is for sport and enjoyment, he said, but it has another purpose—to interest the public in improving the nation's roads.[2]

The members met each week. They studied improved designs. They changed their wheels to pneumatic tires. They bought Avery Planter Company's bicycles with central pedal axles, sold in the Centerville Foundry and Machine Company one block east of the Square. Or, for one hundred dollars, they purchased a Columbia bicycle from a catalog available in Duffield and Harlan Drugstore on the Square's Southeast Corner.[3]

New members joined. They held ten-mile handicap races. They made runs down into Missouri, up to Albia and back. Some rode in tandem. The roads were hilly, rough and dirty. Wheels broke. Men fell and were injured. In May 1894, they cycled five miles west to Brazil to see Kelly's Army—five hundred to one thousand farmers, four abreast in a column, marching from San Francisco to Washington to protest their unemployment. When they found it was a false report, they rode back to Centerville, then east to Bonaparte to see the "army" on 134 flatboats sailing southeast on the Des Moines River to join the Mississippi. The cyclists then returned to Centerville, eager to collect "century bars" for one-hundred-mile runs in one day.[4]

Bicycle meets were held at the improved Fairlawn Fairgrounds north of town. Fifteen hundred to two thousand people attended, including riders from Oskaloosa, Ottumwa, Eddyville and Keokuk. Town dignitaries entered the fast competitions, and prices were awarded—a racing bicycle, an upholstered couch, a diamond ring.[5]

On June 29, 1892, the *Citizen* newspaper noted: "The bicycle craze has struck Centerville and the wheel-men can be seen noiselessly gliding in every direction. The ladies are not far behind…"[6]

Across the Square from Phil Ulrich's blacksmith shop, Centerville's first baseball teams—the Blues, the White Stockings, the Merchants—played on land between Washington and Van Buren Streets, or at County fairs, tournaments and Old Settlers' gatherings. They played surrounding towns: Jerome, Cincinnati, Moulton, Shoal Creek, the Mystic Blind Tigers, Hibbsville and, from the Centerville Block Coal Company, the all African American Black Diamonds, noted for their fast-paced baseball and captained by Nat Jeter.[7]

Entrance fees were charged. Money was raised. Hundreds attended games. A new field with a grandstand, surrounded by a fence, was built south of town. Pinch hitter J.C. Harvey, known as "Home Run Johnny," organized the first local baseball leagues. The All-Iowa League represented teams stretching across the southwest tier of the State.[8]

Teams traveled to games by wagons. They rode in passenger trains and on the roofs of freight trains. Flying cinders and smoke affected their eyesight. Competition was heated. A disputed tie score with Seymour resulted in a riot, the umpire escaping through a cornfield.[9]

The greatest crowds, the most intense interest, the time when teams hired professional players to assist them, was any game involving neighboring Wayne County's Shane Hill Baseball Club. This all-farmer team was composed largely from two families, the Whiteleys and the Maytums. They used a catcher's mitt of a horse-collar pad sewn to a work glove and played every game to get home for evening chores. They were disciplined, honest, quiet and courteous. But it was their winning record that made them the team other Midwestern teams wanted to beat.[10]

From 1878 to 1888, they never lost a game. In a match against Seymour, they won 114 to 8. One of the games with a Centerville team was never finished because it was so one-sided. Part of their fame rested on two pitchers. Burt Maytum threw curve balls "impossible to hit." He practiced on two trees—curving around the first and hitting the second. The second pitcher was Hollie Souder, whose star pitching led him to contracts with the New York Giants, with Buffalo and with Montreal.[11]

As their fame spread, teams hired professional players to assist them. As a result, between 1888 and 1898, Shane Hill's winning record was 85 to 88 percent. Only twice were they shut out, each time by teams loaded up with professional players. Their home record, however, remained unbeaten.

There was a Centerville player considered the best. He was "Big Six" Hollingsworth of Nat Jeter's Black Diamonds, who "[n]o white man had any edge on …Had he been white in color the big show would have been his home."[12]

Half a block south of Phil Ulrich's blacksmith shop was the Thompson and Son Livery Barn on East Jackson. The Thompsons loved horses. They owned fourteen rigs, rented them out at three dollars a day and savagely protected the animals from abusive riders. They also owned Sealskin, a horse then rated as one of the seven best pacing animals in the United States.[13]

Sealskin began the County's love affair with horse racing. Then, in the late 1880s, when John Thompson left with horses to sell in Chicago and returned with a $2,100, purebred stallion named Roseberry—a pacing horse with a mile time of 2:27:25, bought in Lexington, Kentucky—the love affair turned into obsession.[14]

The people of the town studied their horses. They raced them on a quarter-mile stretch of Fourteenth Street, past the home of General Drake—the street later renamed in his honor. William Bradley bought horses; so did Leland Sherrard, Dr. Scott, Dr. Sawyers, his brother-in-law John Drake (son of the general) and John Kearville, who kept a harness shop on the Square's Westside.[15]

Lee Jackson came home from western Wyoming. There he'd ridden as a cowboy at the foot of the Snowy Range and along the Green River Valley. He was in demand as a worker with horses, a trainer, a driver and a breeder of trotters and pacers. In 1893, another horse lover arrived in town. He didn't buy horses, but he knew them. He had traveled with fairs and shows, attended races in the daytime and volunteered as a stagehand at nights. Dode Garner was a second-generation natural jockey. Five of his sons would follow suit.[16]

A Centerville Driving Club was formed. Annual races were held. They began on July 4 and lasted three days. Horses were divided into three classes: trotters, pacers and runners. Prizes were awarded—$100 for the best trotter and the best runner; the best pacer, pulling a rider on a light sulky, was awarded $150. The *Centerville Citizen* noted the popularity of the sport was superseding the more traditional July 4 celebrations of firecrackers, peanuts and speeches.[17]

Members of the Driving Club traveled to other race tracks. Roseberry won the Illinois Stakes. His promise as a pacer seemed limitless. In Centerville, Roseberry (number 4765) sired a new generation of horses. It was this legacy that helped the town recover from Roseberry's premature death from a kick in the "stifle"—the thigh area. That legacy included a horse that would bring Centerville international recognition. He was owned by Dr. Scott. His name was Strathberry.[18]

This bay horse, with black points and a small star on his forehead, ran distinctively with "his head high and flesh trembling." He was unknown at the Ottumwa Racetrack in August 1894. In a race described as "the most exciting thing in the history of Ottumwa's racing," he ran in three heats with times of 2:16, 2:16:25 and 2:13:25—an Iowa record.[19]

From 1894 on, his times improved—2:09:75 at Hedrick; 2:08:75 at Malcolm. Then, at the Oskaloosa track on October 9, 1895, Strathberry established a new world record pace of 2:07:75 and then again in 1896 at Lincoln, 2:04:25.[20]

Offers of money for Strathberry immediately reached Dr. Scott. But the horse lived out his life at Dr. Scott's stable on West Franklin Street, siring Doc B.P., champion of Europe, and Strathtelle, a Canadian "wonder horse" that set a time equal to that of his father.[21]

For John Thompson, his love of horses opened a new career. He sold his livery stable on East Jackson, moved to Chicago and joined John Drake.[22]

At twenty-seven, General Drake's son was ready to retire. His wealth, his gambling and his business deals were already legendary. When he was beaten and robbed of twenty thousand dollars in his office in Chicago's Rookery Building, developing his stable of racehorses seemed more attractive. He hired American trainer Enoch Wishard and, from Centerville, John Thompson as his racing and bookmaker's agent. Accompanying Thompson were two of Dode Garner's sons, Charles (Skeets) and Wayne. Together they all sailed for England.[23]

To the people of the town, Phil Ulrich's bicycle was a sign of the times. News traveled faster. People acquired more knowledge. They traveled further. They moved with increasing speed. Events in distant places were known within days of their occurrence: from London, the last days of Charles Darwin, the trial of Oscar Wilde; from St. Petersburg, the death of Emperor Alexander III; from Bombay, descriptions of the funerals of Hindu plague victims, their faces painted, their bodies covered with jasmine and roses; from Mexico, the discovery of ancient civilizations.[24]

The news items arrived by telegraph at the railroad station a mile away. Runners carried them to the town's competing newspapers. "Why can we not have a better telegraph service in this city?" asked the *Centerville Citizen* in 1886. It arrived in 1895. It was placed in the Continental Hotel lobby; messages were received and dispatched daily by Miss Andrews, from 8 a.m. to 8 p.m. The invention was already outdated by the telephone.[25]

Fourteen years previously, attorneys taking breaks from court sessions joined townspeople breaking from work to watch as workmen guyed 150 miles of bright copper wire and six thousand feet of cable up onto the red crossarms of nine hundred black-and-white telephone poles that fringed the edges of the town's streets and alleyways. The poles were continued on to Moulton, to outlying villages at the rate of one-and-a-half miles a day. Four hundred customers were able to exchange instant information on their toll-line Stromberg-Carlson telephones with connections to Burlington and Des Moines.[26]

People wanted to be informed. They wanted cultivated minds. They found it a legitimate ambition. Upstairs, over Miss Oppenheimer's Millinery Store on the Square's Eastside in November 1895, the town's first public library opened. It was known as the "Reading Room." There were comfortable chairs and tables. Books, periodicals and weekly and daily newspapers were available to all. It was the result of twenty years of work, starting with the Philomathian and Literary Societies in the 1870s and the Harper and Brothers publications' circulating libraries in the 1880s. But in the 1890s two women's organizations, the Young Women's Christian Temperance Union and the local chapter of the Philanthropic Educational Organization (P.E.O.), took determined action. Their members circulated subscription lists and collected money. They held benefits and receptions with homemade candies and cakes. They held entertainments, suppers in church parlors and vacant store rooms. They prepared the room over Miss Oppenheimer's Store as the town's first library. For the women of the P.E.O., these actions were a reflection of their principles. Established some eighty miles northeast of Centerville, at the Iowa Wesleyan College in Mount Pleasant, the organization was formed to promote the education and development of women. It was born in 1869, one year after Iowa led the nation in admitting women to the bar—an action triggered when Mount Pleasant's Arabella Mansfield became the first female lawyer in America. It was one year after the State began admitting female students to Iowa's Agricultural College, granting African Americans suffrage and integrating State schools. P.E.O. was a reflection of Iowa's dedication to the encouragement and education of all minorities.

At one of the Reading Room receptions, a parlor orchestra played. Soloists sang. There was a stereopticon entertainment with colored, three-dimensional images of the Chicago World's Fair, a prairie fire, the northern lights and eastern storms. A performance of the play *Arabian Nights* netted fifty-eight dollars. One thousand dollars was awarded by the executors of the will of Barzilla Bowen. Another thousand was presented by General Drake, who inspected the room and declared himself well pleased. More money came from the daily sales—takings at the stores of Major Stanton and Aaron Grinspan, the Russian Jewish peddler, who now had moved up from the Levee and opened a store on the Square's Southside. Alex Dargaval gave a ton of coal. By 1901 the library boasted 2,630 volumes.[27]

The aim of the Reading Room, said Mrs. H.H. Abrams at its opening, was to increase the town's access to vital knowledge and expose its citizens to excellent literature. It had another purpose: to afford "a place of resort for youth of both sexes where they would be free from the contaminating influences of the street."[28]

The fear was not without foundation. Under Iowa law, municipal authorities could determine if liquor was to be sold inside the corporate limits. At each two-year local election, the vote seesawed. The "wets" were granted liquor licenses; two years later the "drys" won. Liquor licenses were then revoked. The saloons and "blind tigers" were ordered closed. Police invaded them and confiscated the liquor.[29]

Small boys in knee breeches were taken to inspect wagonloads of broken bottles in the ditch behind the jail. In the Presbyterian church, during four days of a temperance minister's sermons, eight hundred people signed "the pledge." They wore blue ribbons testifying their intended sobriety. William Bradley organized the Sunday school children of Centerville into a temperance league. They wore small blue ribbons and marched around the Square and back to the Presbyterian church for more talks on the dangers of liquor.[30]

In the meantime, new saloons opened outside City limits and therefore outside municipal control. Many were at the Levee, near the depots, adding to the area's already unsavory reputation. When the "wets" established saloons, the increased number of thefts, burglaries, fights, street brawls, boisterous behaviors, broken windows and incidents of disorderly conduct were extensively reported in the newspapers.[31]

An 1895 New Year's masquerade ball in the Senate Hall, over the Drake and Lane Building on the Square's Westside, deteriorated into a "wild carousal that would have surpassed the debaucheries of a Parisian music hall." The same night, drunks careened across the Square. Sometimes the police were forced to stop arrests, because the calaboose and City jail were full to overflowing.[32]

A man named Mackey, appearing before the Rathbun mayor's court for drunk and disorderly conduct, was "rescued." A gang of his friends burst into the procedures and rushed him from the room.[33]

Men shot up the Square, were robbed for their money and were pushed out of windows. Husbands went home drunk and violent. Thomas Garvin, a repeated offender living in Caldwell Township, was struck on the head and killed with an axe wielded by his eleven-year-old son protecting his mother.[34]

Jesse Jones, living south of the waterworks and emboldened by whiskey, entered the home of his girlfriend, where he shot and killed himself, but only after shooting and killing Lelah Martin and the mother who came to her aid.[35]

The volatile Doc (his nickname) Peak—either drunk or psychotic—was notorious. Time and again, he shut his wife and children out of their home, stole chickens, interrupted evening band concerts on the Square, fought with landlords and police and repeatedly sat in jail.[36]

The even more notorious Sammy Stewart—the Fremont saloon keeper on the Levee—defied every dry law, ran from arrests, kept a running supply of liquor brought up from Missouri and developed such a dangerous reputation that small girls ran past his saloon. Either Sammy or his violent son, Bobby, murdered Dave Milburn for refusing to leave their saloon when requested. In 1892 Bobby met his match—and his end. In jail for liquor law violations, he taunted a new prisoner with such insults and abusive language that the prisoner killed him with an iron poker.[37]

The women of the town were reaching their defining moment.

Across the County, for over forty years, women were moving into positions of community responsibility.

Susannah McKee, the proprietor of the Continental Hotel, was known everywhere for her business acumen. She was declared to be "...without superior in the state of Iowa, and perhaps ...without a rival."[38]

A block north of the Continental, in June 1894, Margaret Needels inherited the *Citizen* newspaper. Her first act was to tell its editor, D.R. Guernsey, that his services were no longer required. He asked who would be his successor. "In a faint voice I replied that I was going to have charge. He looked surprised and then laughed. That was the last straw, and my reply was in no uncertain tone, that after July 1st I would be in charge and walked out. I realized I knew nothing of the business but decided I could use the scissors and the telephone and in some way would make good."

Mrs. Needels made good swiftly. In six months the *Citizen* became the town's first daily edition newspaper. She delegated efficiently. She hired two Northwestern University graduates—Joe Day and Charlie Reimers—as professional news reporters. She spent six weeks at the Morgenthaler Linotype Factory in New York and was the first woman there to take apart, rebuild and operate their linotype machine, one of which she bought and assembled in her Centerville newspaper office.[39]

Appanoose County's women were teachers and school administrators; they ran farms and headed organizations; they were medical doctors, ministers, and telegraph and telephone operators. They played billiards in the Wittenmyer Billiard Hall, declaring they had just as good a right to play billiards—or any game—as their husbands. The town's women's cornet band played at State events, their players—Olive Bradley (William's daughter), Maggie Breazeale and four Kirkham sisters—all described as "outstanding musicians."[40]

Mary ("Mollie") Gibbs Spooner, the granddaughter of the Reverend William Manson, who had preached the town's first sermon over a whiskey barrel, started the Methodist church, named the town and was postmaster during the Civil War, was traveling from New Jersey to Colorado as leading actress with the Spooner Comedy Company.[41]

Margaret Baker, a graduate of Centerville High School, the daughter of A.J. Baker—Civil War general, Centerville attorney, attorney general of both Missouri and Iowa—was winning high academic awards, was writing *Mornings in Florence*, an analysis of John Ruskin's lectures on art, and was about to become head of an English literature department at Oxford University in England.[42]

And it was the women of the town who organized and now were running the Reading Room, presenting opportunities for people to acquire greater knowledge— and to counteract the influence of liquor. At seven thirty in the evening on May 5, 1896, 210 of this last group, opposed to liquor, met in the Methodist church. They marched in a body across the Square, through the double chamber doors of City Hall on West Jackson Street and confronted a meeting of the City Council. They appealed, they said, "in the name of God, pure womanhood and true-hearted manhood." They asked the councilors to preserve "...the purity and happiness of home life" by closing the saloons. They came, they said, "...in the memory of Lelah Martin and her murdered mother and beg you not to sanction the sale of liquor that gave purpose to the hand of the assassin."

The aldermen looked uncomfortable. They glanced at the councilor in the next seat. They endeavored to smile. As soon as the women left the building, the men turned to City matters: extending a two-inch water main into the cemetery, the condition of the City sidewalks and examining a petition protesting changing the name of State Street to State Avenue. The situation with the saloons remained unchanged. The same was not true of the women.[43]

Throughout the winter of 1896, in City Hall and the Reading Room, they tracked City records. They noted, they said, a tenfold increase in crime when alcohol was legally available. They observed thirty carloads of beer and a large amount of stronger liquors shipped into town. They believed "foreign" money was being sent to hire men to secure local signatures and "dictate political policy," keeping the saloons open.[44]

They wrote a letter to the women of Centerville. Volunteers copied the letter and distributed one to every woman in town. "Women of Centerville," it began. "We cannot vote, but it may be we can do something to arouse our voters."

Nine-and-a-half miles west of Centerville, the citizens of Plano had already taken action. When a "blind tiger" was raided twice, they demolished the building, leaving just the door standing that exhibited Sheriff Silknitter's notice forever restraining the owners from selling intoxicating liquors in Appanoose County.[45]

At this time, reports reached Centerville's newspapers of Carrie Nation's attacks on the saloons of Wichita and Topeka, Kansas, and her intention to destroy the bar in Washington, D.C.'s Capitol building. By March, the technique had reached Iowa, when two women using concealed hatchets broke glass and bottles of a saloon in Oxford west of Iowa City.[46]

A month later, eleven Centerville women met at Mrs. William Salters's family home. They discussed tactics. Then, armed with hatchets and hammers, they marched to the Keokuk and Western viaduct and destroyed the Kinder Saloon. They smashed the counter, beer cases and bottles. Now actively supported by John Dailey, who ran a grocery store in the same area, they tackled two more saloons on Eighteenth Street—the Levee. Two days later their numbers had increased by five. Sixteen women attacked the Johnson Saloon, known as "vinegar hill," and three more saloons on the Levee. The situation now was almost a riot, with a lot of fighting and shouting, at least two injuries and several arrests.[47]

The women were urged to stop. But their actions had given them a sense of power. The next step would be to translate it into political inclusion—votes for women. They would have to wait another thirty years.

Chapter 17

Town Fires, Town Improvements

As Centerville's Courthouse Square approached 1900, it assumed the Victorian and Italianate architectural appearance it displays today. Much of it was the result of fires.

In the fifteen years following 1885, there were fourteen major blazes sweeping not only the original sites, but also sixteen adjoining buildings and damaging at least twenty-two more.[1]

At the first sign of any fire, people raced to alert the town. They pulled the rope of Martin Hatzenbeeler's bell—the one that dangled over his store on the Southeast Corner of the Square and announced the arrival of fresh fish—while others sledgehammered the town's official nine-hundred-pound fire bell that rested on the sidewalk outside Firehouse No. 1, just off the Square on West Jackson.[2]

Inside, at the first alarm, Bob and Bob, two strong bay horses, came out of their stalls, in unison like their names. They tripped their own harnesses directly onto their backs. They waited to be attached to the steam fire engine when it was lit by one of the town's forty-two firemen.[3]

The doors of the firehouse opened. The "old tea pot," as the town affectionately named the steam fire engine, pulled by Bob and Bob and driven by Ed Swafford, plunged down the street, bells clanging, smoke rolling from the funnel, sparks flying, live coals peppering the roadway and scattering onlookers.[4]

Behind came the town's other equipment: hooks and ladders, a hose reel with over one thousand feet of hose pulled on wheels over six feet in height.

Horse-drawn fire department. *Courtesy of Appanoose County Historical Society.*

Occasionally "old Mendota" joined the action. This was the previously reliable engine, with two teams of twelve to fourteen men on each side ready to grab its bars and manually pump water in synchronistic rhythm: one side up, one side down.[5]

On each corner of the Square was a large fire well. Water was pumped and dipped out of them, sometimes in great confusion and greater ingenuity when the steam engine refused to perform to capacity.[6]

When Biddle and Riggs grocery store burned on the Northside in November 1891 and the engine refused to raise sufficient steam to "throw" water, firemen climbed onto the post office roof next door and controlled the spread with buckets passed up to them in relays from the nearest well.[7]

When the Keystone Hotel burned on the Northside in September 1894 and again the steam engine's water pressure failed, sides of bacon were added to the machine, which increased the steam and produced a faster supply of water.[8]

The *Centerville Citizen* blamed the owners of wood-frame buildings. "If these frame buildings could be taxed in proportion to the rent received that may …induce their owners to tear them away and build safe brick blocks in their places."[9]

But immunity was not guaranteed brick structures. Between four and five in the morning on February 9, 1893, a furnace overheated in the basement of

Keystone Hotel in the late 1800s. *Courtesy of Appanoose County Historical Society.*

Centerville's brick Continental Hotel. Dense smoke and flames rapidly spread. The panicked hotel clerk, when informed by a cook, and knowing how full the hotel was that night, ran from room to room telling guests to leave, forgetting the fire alarm system installed by Susannah McKee in 1886, which connected his office to every hotel room with a simple switch.[10]

Guests struggled along the landings and balcony but, disoriented on the last stairs, piled dangerously into each other until guided to the exit by shouts from arriving townspeople.[11]

A salesman, slowly being asphyxiated by the smoke and completely lost, fell over a small girl, picked her up and followed her directions to the exit.

William Hale, another salesman, traveling for Jules Fecht wholesale cigar manufacturer of Ottumwa, jumped from a window on the third story and fell through an awning to the ground forty feet below, surviving with "serious injuries" but no broken bones.[12]

Merchant-tailor S.P. Swanson, newly arrived to establish a business in town and sleeping on the third floor, wrapped his coat around his head, bumped into a flower stand, reversed his steps, felt the banisters and followed the shouts to the exit.[13]

A traveler on the third floor dressed himself, adjusted his necktie, donned an overcoat and overshoes, saved three or four lost guests and then lowered himself to the ground with knotted sheets and quilts.[14]

Townspeople, now in force in the snow and ice outside, rushed the survivors—many shoeless—to the warmth of neighboring buildings. And then they watched as the escape routes of two occupants failed.[15]

Samuel Lewis of Greeley was seen and heard at a third-floor window. People motioned for him to go east in the direction of the least fire. He disappeared, returned, threw out his coat and then fell back into the flames. Lewis's body, so badly charred as to defy identification for days, was found in the basement by fireman Lew Davidson.[16]

But the most traumatic failed attempt was that of the proprietress and manager of the hotel and Centerville's first businesswoman, Mrs. Susannah McKee. Trapped on the third floor after repeatedly checking that her guests and workers were safe, she jumped. The forty-foot fall for a "very large" fifty-four-year-old woman was too great. Unconscious, she was rushed to the home of her daughter, Jenny Lloyd Lane, where she died the same day.[17]

By 1895, hydrants and valves were set in several City locations. Next to the fire station, a hose tower was built on its west side where hoses could be dried. The nine-hundred-pound fire bell that sat on the sidewalk was hoisted to the hose tower's belfry. A meeting hall for the firemen was added, along with a sleeping room. A new fire chief, Lew Davidson, spent twenty-four hours a day on duty at the station. It set a pattern for the future.[18]

But despite the fires and the grief over Susannah McKee and the Continental Hotel, the people of Centerville were in a confident mood.

On January 9, 1895, the *Centerville Citizen* noted the town, like the country, was passing through "...the greatest financial depression known in history." Local real estate and business values declined but, noted the newspaper, "Centerville has made a showing that few towns can equal." There were no failures. Banks remained strong. Businesses were in good condition. Everyone looked to the future with buoyancy.[19]

Each day, seventy-four railroad cars carried 350,000 tons of Appanoose County coal out of local depots: thirty from the Rock Island, fifteen from the Keokuk and Western, twenty-nine from the Central. With its level of production, the County was ranked second in the State. Twenty-five trains a day passed through the Rock Island station. They included trainloads of cattle to Chicago. At the depots, freight bills were piled on desks. Finding extra cars to ship grain and hay was difficult. Agents were too busy to talk. Passenger trains were described as "chock full." A Rock Island conductor said it looked as though everyone was going somewhere.[20]

Twenty-two Cherokee Indians, including squaws, papooses and chiefs, peered out on their way to visit northern Wisconsin reservations. The Reverend Alexander C. Jeffries—father of boxing's "great white hope" James Jeffries—intent on evangelizing the world, leaned out scattering religious tracts like snow.[21]

Eager young men bound for Klondike gold were warned by the *Centerville Citizen* to start their sixty-five-hundred-mile journey by April 15. They were further warned that steamers up the west coast to Juneau were fully booked, the cost of a dog and sled to the headwaters of the Yukon was five hundred dollars and the river was free of ice for just three months. The newspaper advised any young man who had never been further northwest than Iconium to spend two hours a day in a zero-degree room of a cold-storage warehouse and bathe in water in which ice is floating.[22]

In Chicago, the World's Fair opened. The railroads vied for business. The Rock Island offered a round-trip ticket from Centerville for $14.75. The Keokuk and Western offered an overnight ticket for $12.50, leaving at 3:05 p.m. and arriving at the White City—as the World's Fair with its white buildings came to be known—early the next morning. Many stayed at Chicago's Dauphin Park Hotel. It advertised in the *Iowegian* as "the Iowa hotel at the World's Fair."[23]

The Woodens, the Fees, the Stantons, the Drakes and the Gosses were the first families in town to attend. So did Haemmerle Williams from the Northside of the Square, to promote the sale of his company's Epworth organs. They witnessed the opening ceremonies, rode on the Ferris wheel and cheered the Iowa State Marching Band that included George Landers and his musicians from Centerville.[24]

They visited the Iowa State Building and inspected the exhibits. They saw native grasses, cornstalks and grains. There were samples of geological strata from Lower Silurian to Cretaceous, sparkling Sioux quartzite, stalactites and stalagmites, twelve-inch cubes of golden sandstone, Allamakee brown hematite, iron ore, lead and gypsum, all assembled in pyramid fashion. They inspected samples of Iowa's best coal. It came from Appanoose County: thirty-five tons carved into a medieval castle with pennanted turrets—a miniature version of the whole Iowa exhibit building. In the main hall, they examined portraits of Iowa's prominent citizens. Among them was one of Susannah McKee of Centerville's Continental Hotel, one of the State's most influential women, now so tragically deceased.[25]

In Centerville the town's optimism was translated into action. Town improvements came under scrutiny. Mass meetings were held. Leaders emerged. Committees were formed and plans made. The Cemetery Association weeded the cemetery and cut and mowed the tangles of grass. Back alleys were cleared of cinders, old boxes, barrels, broken glass, horse manure and dead animals. Health officers Stephenson, Morgan and James, on behalf of the Centerville Board of Health, ordered inspections of property. They recommended disinfectants: "copperas and lime for cellars, premises and outhouse." Cisterns, they said, must first be thoroughly cleansed and then treated with "brom-chlorallum."[26]

Plans for a town waterworks system, long discussed, moved to action when three members of the Israel family, who were shopkeepers on the Northwest Corner of the Square and living in a house on Fifteenth Street, next to the Jewish Synagogue, became desperately ill with typhoid from "water reeking with disease."[27]

On Thursday, October 31, 1895, an early-morning earthquake—a shock felt from the New Madrid Fault some 350 miles to the southeast—awoke the town's citizens. It rattled windows and panicked the superstitious. The same day, a gang of diggers began laying the town's first water mains at the corner of Washington and Main Streets.[28]

Ten weeks later, watched by members of the City council and crowds of citizens, water company officials opened three Eddy-style fire hydrants on the Square. Air first roared through seven miles of mains. Water followed. It spouted into the air. In response to 160 pounds of pressure and amid loud cheers, it rose in cataracts of 100 to 120 feet. The performance was repeated the same day at seventy-two other hydrants around the City.[29]

Most wood-frame and clapboard buildings on the Square were demolished. One—the Breazeale building on the Southside—collapsed, sending the *Iowegian* newspaper crashing into the basement. Some—Russell's Drug Store on the Northwest Corner and Wales Photographic Studio on the Westside—were dragged onto the Courthouse Park, trade continuing there until new brick buildings were completed in their place.[30]

Architects were hired. Sites cleared. Bricks, delivered by horses and carts from kilns west and south of town, were built on top of foundations of local limestone and first-floor, cast-iron facades of posts and sills. Wooden beams, cut to specified lengths, were carried on the shoulders of men from local lumberyards, inserted into brick joist pockets, floorings hammered on top.[31]

The Square's fifteen-year transformation was underway. Building by building, the Courthouse Square began to echo the architecture of its now not-so-new courthouse. Buildings rose with decorated cornices and friezes, classical pillars, overhanging eaves, occasional split pediments and finials. Two, the Hamilton, Bradley, White Building on the Eastside Corner of State Street and the White Building on the Southwest Corner, were designed by returning Burlington architect Charles Dunham. He must have been in a Gothic/Islamic turn of mind.[32]

Both buildings included recessed loggias, oriel windows and terra cotta arches. The Eastside building featured oriel windows with copper balconies

1895 Bradley-Hamilton-White block under construction. *Courtesy of Appanoose County Historical Society.*

and awnings, its roof topped with a copper dome. Dunham's more enthusiastic design on the Southwest Corner included a loggia, stone balustrade and polished granite columns crowned with a decorated ornamental terra cotta arch, its tympanum full of decorations, including an Indian chief's head that people thought could be Chief Appanoose. The building also had gables topped with terra cotta dogs and a steep roof crowned with a wrought iron balustrade.[33]

The people of the town looked at their town with pride. Their timing was appropriate. One of its native citizens was about to become governor of Iowa.

Chapter 18

General Drake Becomes Governor Drake

When General Francis Marion Drake settled permanently in Centerville in 1866 after the Civil War, he had lived six of his eleven lives. He had survived, at sixteen, drowning in the Mississippi; at twenty-two, an attack by Pawnee Indians; and at twenty-four, a fire and shipwreck off the Mexican coast. He had been an abolitionist, a soldier and a businessman. He still had five lives to go. In Centerville, he became a lawyer, a general merchandise businessman and a banker. His Appanoose County Bank stood on the Southwest Corner of the Square. In his absences, Drake's father, John Hamilton Drake, moved from Drake[s]ville and oversaw operations. In this he was assisted by George Barnett and Theodore Perry Shonts, the teenage son of a local doctor, judged by all three men as full of promise.[1]

In the 1870s and 1880s, Drake turned his prodigious energy to railroads. He built five. The first of these was the Missouri, Iowa and Nebraska (MI&N). It started from Keokuk on the Mississippi River and reached Centerville in 1873. The second was the MI&N's extension west from Centerville, with stops, in this order, at the communities of Brazil, Plano, Promise City, Corydon and Humeston, ending at Van Wert in Iowa's Decatur County. He built the Iowa Central between Centerville and Albia, then the Hampton and Belmont, and finally the "3-I": the Indiana, Illinois and Iowa. He saw these railroads as vital economic links for southern Iowa. They also made him a very wealthy man, and in the process he made friends in high places.[2]

On May 16, 1883, one of them, Jay Gould, came to town. He was a New York stockbroker, gambler and a railroad millionaire. He was judged to be the most powerful man on Wall Street. He was included at the top of a list of the nation's "robber barons" and had boasted he'd bought members of Congress. His system of railroads extended from Toledo, Ohio, west to Ogden, Utah; southwest to the frontier of Mexico; and south to Galveston and New Orleans. He owned their connecting telegraphs. He controlled news. Daily he added to his possessions.[3]

In Centerville he leased Drake's Iowa Central. This gave Gould's Wabash a direct route from St. Louis to Des Moines. He negotiated with Drake and the Burlington Railroad to create a faster route between Chicago and Council Bluffs. To do this he used Drake's MI&N extension as far as Van Wert. Drake's wealth grew. It was the Gilded Age. The rich paid no taxes. There were no death duties.[4]

Drake lived with his wife and six children—a seventh, George Hamilton Drake, had died at the age of two—on two City blocks of land between Liberty (renamed Bank) and Wall Streets, south of Centerville Square on Fourteenth Street (renamed Drake Avenue). Their home was a mansion of classical design with bracketed cornices, a roof cupola, long shuttered windows and columned porches.[5]

It was at this home that Drake, in 1880, welcomed a deputation: the Reverend D.R. Lucas, George A. Jewett of Oskaloosa and Professor G.T. Carpenter, who was president of Oskaloosa College as well as Drake's brother-in-law. They requested funds to facilitate moving Oskaloosa College to Des Moines. Drake gave an initial donation of $20,000—more than was asked. It was the beginning of Drake's pattern of "noblesse oblige." For the rest of his life, Drake met every appeal from Drake University, Des Moines, now named in his honor. He gave to a teachers' fund, for a library, to an alumni endowment. He gave $25,000 and $75,000 more for emergency funds, $17,000 for an auditorium and porch, $2,000 for the Drake field, $10,000 for a telescope, $24,000 for a music building and $10,000 each for medical and law buildings. George Barnett, the cashier at Drake's Appanoose County Bank, declared the general had given to Drake University more than a quarter of a million dollars.[6]

It was at their home on Fourteenth Street, too, that Drake and his wife celebrated the marriages of three of their four daughters. The ceremonies were conducted in the parlor. Above each couple hung a large "marriage bell" of fresh white roses. It was suspended from an archway of greenery. In 1881 Eva, the third daughter, married Henry, son of Englishman Joe Goss, the successful boot- and shoemaker on the Square's Southside and, like Drake, an early abolitionist. A year later, Eva's oldest sister, Amelia ("Milla"), married Theodore Perry Shonts, the son of a Centerville doctor, thought full of promise by Drake and all who knew him. "Thede," as he was known, had courted Milla through high school, walking her home, learning to play the violin to impress her. He was now an emerging business figure in his own right and was about to be, at twenty-six, appointed by Drake as managing director of the 3-I Railroad.[7]

The third marriage was Drake's second daughter, Jennie. Jennie was Centerville High School's first graduating student. She married Dr. J.L. Sawyers, grandson of Unionville's abolitionist Elisha Sawyers, the brilliant product of Chicago and Kentucky Schools of Medicine, prizewinner for surgery, gold medalist for proficiency and a student at several European hospitals, including Berlin and Vienna.[8]

The date of Jennie's marriage was June 12, 1883. Twelve days later, Drake, his wife, Mary, and their son John returned home after attending services at the Christian church north of their mansion on Fourteenth Street. Mary complained of "a dizzy spell." Within minutes she was dead.[9]

Drake was fifty-three years old. He never remarried, and personal loss followed personal loss. His home burned. There were more deaths. First his mother, then long-term friends: Elisha Sawyers, Chancellor George T. Carpenter of Drake University; and two comrades from the Thirty-sixth Infantry, Captain William Vermilion and Dr. Sylvester Sawyers, whom he looked on as a brother, the son of Elisha, the father of his daughter Jennie's husband.[10]

On July 17, 1895, a special telegram was delivered to the office of the *Centerville Daily Citizen* on the Northeast Corner of Centerville Square. On the sixth ballot of the Iowa Republican Party, General Francis Marion Drake was the party's nominee for governor.[11]

Thousands met Drake on his arrival at Centerville's Central depot. They followed him in procession through the streets to a Victorian mansion, built by the general on the same land as his previous home, which he now shared with Henry and Eva Goss.

Red, white and blue national flags draped the portico. Among them was the tattered flag of the Thirty-sixth Iowa, the regiment commanded by Drake during the Civil War.[12]

Election Day was November 6, 1895. The general cast the sixty-third ballot at 9:41 a.m. in the Second Ward. He took off his hat. He laughed and asked members of the election board for instructions in casting his ballot.[13]

The results were announced on November 9. It was a victory for General Drake as well as for Centerville. And the town was about to show it.[14]

With the announcement that General Drake was now the sixteenth governor-elect of Iowa, the people of Centerville were ready to celebrate.

Thousands again thronged the streets. Across the town, red, white and blue flags flew from rooftops, windows, pillars and posts. Cannons roared. Bells rang. Whistles, bells, turkey callers and horns blew. Hats were tossed into the air, and handkerchiefs waved. Special trains brought delegations. Telegrams arrived. Bonfires were lit. Fireworks exploded and threw showers of stars across the night sky. Everywhere people cheered.[15]

In Russell Hall on the Square's Northwest Corner and in the Senate Hall over the Drake and Lane Store, there were receptions. The Creston Male Quartet sang. Civil War veterans Colonel Haynes and Captain—now Judge—Tom Fee presided. They introduced speakers, allotting each only a few moments. The speakers praised the new governor-elect. They praised the County—not just the home of the sixteenth governor, but the home, they added amid loud cheers, of Strathberry, their champion trotting horse.

On the Square, the town band, under Major Landers, played popular melodies. At the approach of general, now Governor-elect Drake, the music changed to "Lo, the Conquering Hero Comes." The Square was full. The new electric lights shone on the upturned faces. Small boys sat high in the trees.

"Ladies and Gentlemen, Neighbors and Friends," said Drake to the crowd. "I can only say a few words of thanks to you..." He concluded: "I thank you very much not only for the large vote I have received from this county, but for the uniform kindness that has been shown me by the people of this county. I will try to discharge the great duties toward this state honorably and faithfully."[16]

For the inauguration of Francis Marion Drake as governor of Iowa on January 16, 1896, Centerville was "practically depopulated." Special trains carried people from Centerville to Des Moines. On board was George Landers with the town brass band and a military escort. They accompanied the procession from the Hotel Savery, Drake's new residence, to the east doors of the State capitol. Some stood in the rotunda and heard the chief justice of Iowa's Supreme Court swear Drake into office. He would be the State's last Civil War governor.

The listeners then heard Drake's inaugural address. He praised the history of the State. He called for a State museum, for a soldiers' monument and memorials for Iowa's twelve thousand who died in the Civil War. And he spoke of his vision for the State: comprehensive education for all, from kindergarten through university.[17]

That evening, the new governor held a reception in his official rooms in the State's Capitol. At his side, in the role of first lady, was his only unmarried daughter, Mary Lord Drake. They shook the hands of the members of the

State Senate and the State House and then they greeted the people from their hometown and members of the general public, estimated to be fifteen thousand in number.[18]

Within six months, there was another election, this one for the presidency of the United States. Democrats and Republicans identified themselves by trick celluloid badges: there were bees or elephants or donkeys that sprang open to reveal portraits of their candidates. They held bonfires, exploded Roman candles, listened to speakers and made torchlight parades around the Square.[19]

The 1896 presidential campaign of William McKinley brought ten thousand people to town. The morning parades were led by an Uncle Sam on a golden steed or Captain Ben Wells riding a sleek black horse and dressed in his Civil War uniform adorned with a bright red sash. They were followed by "…a representative of the aborigines of America, who, if they were entitled to the ballot would cast their votes for McKinley."[20]

There were 378 horses, pit mules and ponies. All were mounted and all decorated with flags, plumes and banners and interspersed with floats and wagons, including a sheep on one, "…bleating piteously as it told its story how it had been treated by the Democratic Party." There were torches made by local tinsmiths, with kerosene poured over a central wick and lighted. And there were flambeaus. These were extra-large torches that burned variously colored powders. Both torch and flambeau bearers wore large oilcloth capes and caps as protection from the flares.[21]

The *Centerville Weekly Citizen* took a poll of voters on the Keokuk and Western eastbound train as it headed into Centerville. Of twenty-eight passengers, twenty-two were for McKinley and six for his opponent, William Jennings Bryan. The *Citizen* reporter noted, "The gentlemen who comprised the minority were shackled together and were in charge of the Sheriff of Decatur County who was conveying them to the penitentiary at Fort Madison." Presumably the sheriff was a Bryan supporter.[22]

Election results arrived by telegraph. Extra wires were run to Russell Hall, one in 1896 into the home of Governor Drake, who was in Centerville for the occasion. At Russell Hall, people filled the room "to suffocation." Their numbers spilled across the Northside of the Square. As each state reported its results, each side, Democrat or Republican, cheered so loudly the telegraph operators had difficulty taking messages.

Governor Drake remained awake until one in the morning. "I remained up," he told a *Citizen* reporter, "until I was convinced both Iowa and Ohio had gone safely Republican, and then I went to bed."[23]

Governor Drake's health was another reason he was home. A month earlier, he was hurt when a reviewing stand collapsed at the Burlington semi-centennial celebration. It exacerbated his wartime injury received at Mark's Mill. By March, he was suffering from the "grippe," coughing at times so intensely as to cause dizziness.[24]

Not fully recovered, he traveled by train to Washington for the inauguration of President McKinley. In the mountains of Virginia, the railroad engineer was forced to make an emergency stop to avoid collision with a freight train. The governor was thrown to the floor. Again his back was injured. He was unable to stand for two hours. But despite opposition from his son-in-law, his personal physician Dr. J.L. Sawyers—now his almost constant companion—he was lifted into a saddle by three men and stayed through the inaugural parade from twelve thirty to five o'clock in the afternoon. It would have taken a death blow, he later said, to have kept him away from assisting an old soldier comrade becoming president.[25]

Four months later, Drake fell again—this time on the steps of the State capitol in a severe rainstorm, and this time his left hip—the site of his war injury—was severely fractured. At the same time, diabetes was advancing. He withdrew his name as candidate for a second term as governor.[26]

He came home to Centerville in August. He was carried from the train. His carriage drove slowly to his home, now shared with his daughter Eva and her husband, Henry Goss, and to his room on the southwest corner on the second floor. Dr. Sawyers ordered complete rest, something denied him by the hordes of people in his room in Des Moines's Savery Hotel. Telegraphic reports from Ottumwa stated death was imminent. "I'm not dead yet," Drake replied.[27]

Drake spent two months of treatment in Excelsior Springs in Missouri, returned to Des Moines and then, at the end of his tenure, retired home to Centerville.[28]

It was November 3, 1897. He had another six years to live. They would be the last of his eleven lives. He had lived through drowning, Indian attack, and fire and shipwreck, as well as stints as abolitionist, soldier, businessman, railroad man, banker, lawyer, benefactor of Drake University and governor of the State of Iowa. His final years were to be, for the governor and Centerville, a time of mutual benefit.[29]

Restricted as he was due to one term of office and his ill health, Drake and his administration still made significant contributions to Iowa.

Among them were the purchase of a site and plans for a State historical building; the location and marking of positions held by Iowa regiments at the Battle of Shiloh; and the egalitarian placement of names on the State Soldiers' Monument, where no name "…should be placed …to exalt one soldier over another."

Others included the recodifying of Iowa's laws, controlling loans and savings associations, controlling express delivery services, imposing collateral inheritance taxes and—at least a century in advance of its time—prohibiting the manufacture and sale of cigarettes anywhere in the State.[30]

On March 28, 1896, Governor Drake and a large party of State officials traveled to Philadelphia. He was joined by guests and family from Centerville: Colonel Cornelius Stanton, H.H. Wright—now State adjutant general—the Gosses, the Sawyers and the Shonts. The occasion was the launching of a new battleship at the Cramp Shipyard.[31]

Mary Lord Drake, her father's twenty-three-year-old youngest child, was now first lady of Iowa. She held a large bouquet of roses on one arm. She named the ship the U.S.S. *Iowa.* Then, despite objections from the combined churches of Moulton, the Centerville chapter of the Women's Christian Temperance Union and "two bushels and petitions" received by Governor Drake, the U.S.S. *Iowa* was launched with a bottle of champagne.[32]

Coincidental with Drake's administration, the island of Cuba was flaring into revolt against Spanish rule. Spain's efforts to suppress the insurrection were unsuccessful and violent. Articles appeared frequently in Centerville newspapers. People read the reports of Americans, including two Iowans, Walter Younger of Albia and Paul Gonzales of Keokuk, who were already fighting with the insurgents. They gave graphic word pictures of atrocities by the Spanish.There were pictures of atrocities by the Spanish against the Cubans and against Americans living in Cuba. They described prisoners in Morro Castle fed to sharks or fed poisonous tortillas; they told of Cubans dying of starvation, the mutilation of bodies, of women and girls "outraged" and then shot.[33]

Governor Drake declared himself a warm supporter of the Cuban patriots. He said it was time for the U.S. government to recognize their cause and support them in their struggle for liberty.[34]

In Des Moines, an "Iowa Cuban junta" was formed. It promised a regiment of troops to fight with Cubans against Spain. Hundreds of letters poured in asking for information. Sons of Civil War veterans in southwestern Iowa promised to enlist. So did a company of the Iowa National Guard. Physicians offered their services. Women volunteered as nurses. Cuban flags were made available. In Centerville, young men declared their intention of joining any volunteer brigade.[35]

Then came the headline at the top of the first column on the front page of the *Semi-Weekly Iowegian*: "The Maine Horror." It was February 18, 1898. Governor Drake was out of office, resting in his room on Centerville's Fourteenth Street. Like others, he read the account. Three days earlier, in Havana Harbor, the battleship *Maine* exploded, with a loss of more than 266 American lives. It was the act that precipitated the nation into the Spanish-American War.[36]

Flags flew at half-mast. Feelings ran at fever pitch. They were manipulated and nurtured by headlines in Pulitzer and Hearst newspapers delivered by train, sold on street corners by small boys or read in the Reading Room on the Square's Eastside.[37]

On Monday, April 25, news reached the town that Spain and the United States were at war. President McKinley called for 125,000 volunteers. Orders arrived by telegraph. Members of Centerville's National Guard Company E immediately reported for duty to Captain H.C. Haynes. Among the men enlisting, not as officers but for no higher rank than that of private, were the County attorney, Tom Fee; H.E. Valentine, the town's mayor; Hon. Claude Porter, the State representative; C.H. Elgin, deputy clerk of the district court; and bank cashiers, businessmen and more town lawyers. With them, too, the Third Regimental Band, all loyal members of the National Guard.[38]

The same evening, P.E.O. members organized a public reception in the new armory building at Fourteenth—later Drake—and Maple Streets. Fifteen hundred people attended. More thronged the sidewalk outside. Avenues of the Stars and Stripes lined the hall and flanked the national flag of Cuba. Master of ceremonies and Civil War veteran Colonel Cornelius Stanton introduced patriotic speeches.[39]

The company members were put through a short drill by Captain Haynes. They stood around an artificial fire on the stage. A soloist sang "Tenting Tonight." The Third Regimental Band, led by George Landers, played "The Stars and Stripes Forever." The *Iowegian* reported that "the large audience went wild." Festivities ended at midnight. A line was formed. Each soldier moved along it as members of the P.E.O. sang "God Be with You til We Meet Again."[40]

The next morning they met to have their photograph taken. They sat together in seven rows on the steps of the courthouse. At noon, Company E in blue uniforms and campaign hats, carrying old Springfield 45 rifles, together with George Landers and the Third Regimental Band, marched out of the armory en route to Camp McKinley, Des Moines. Five thousand people lined the streets to the Keokuk and Western depot. As the train departed, there were cheers, tears and high emotions.[41]

Fifty-first Regiment Philippine Expedition Band. *Courtesy of Appanoose County Historical Society.*

It was a pattern repeated along the rail route—at Promise City, all the way to Humeston. At Plano, the commander of the Spanish troops in Cuba, known as "the butcher," was hanging in effigy, men with shotguns firing at it.[42]

Company E, now part of the Fiftieth Iowa Regiment, was moved south to Camp Cuba Libre at Jacksonville, Florida. The Third Regimental Band, part of Iowa's Fifty-first Regiment, was moved via San Francisco to the Philippines.

Company E saw no actual combat, but conditions at the Jacksonville camp caused yellow fever, typhoid and pneumonia. Charles Streepy recalled the rain, the swampy land, the poor food. Private Otto Larson was sent home to Centerville to recover his health. "The sickness in our camp was mainly caused by the unsanitary conditions of the camp and the unhealthy drinking water," he told an *Iowegian* reporter.[43]

While Private Larson recovered, his fellow Company E private William Blakesley did not. His body was returned to Centerville. Sixty comrades home on furlough escorted the remains from the Rock Island depot to a military and civic funeral at Oakland Cemetery. The newspapers reported the deaths from similar causes of three more Centerville men. They served in other units from other Iowa towns. One, Private J.A. Galloway, chose burial at Oakland Cemetery.[44]

During the course of the war, the people of the town celebrated the news of every victory. When Commodore George Dewey's outnumbered U.S. Navy destroyed seven Spanish ships, killing almost four hundred Spanish sailors, a 112½-foot red, white and blue flagpole was raised on the Courthouse Square by workmen from the Light, Heat, and Power Company. At its top, above the Stars and Stripes, they placed a large stuffed American eagle. Blacksmiths fired their anvils. One thousand children from the City schools sang patriotic songs.[45]

Company E of the Fiftieth Iowa and the Fifty-first Iowa Regimental Band under George Landers arrived home separately. The arrivals of both were predictable. Hundreds met the trains, bells rang, anvils were fired, firecrackers roared. The Square was circled at least twice, and each soldier was personally conducted to his home.[46]

For George Landers and the Fifty-first Regimental Band, the Spanish-American War was something of a triumph. Everywhere they played, they received the highest praise: at the Presidio in San Francisco; in Honolulu; from Admiral Dewey; in the pages of the *Army and Navy Journal*; and from Major General Arthur MacArthur, who invited George Landers into his headquarters. He complimented him "...in the highest terms on the excellency of the music, both in point of selection and execution."[47]

The band returned to San Francisco with the Fifty-first Regiment. They sailed under the Golden Gate Bridge. Loud cheers greeted them from the sailors on board the battleship *Iowa* that had been launched by Centerville's Mary Lord Drake three years previously.[48]

The praise heaped on George Landers was no surprise to the people of Centerville. They had recognized his ability from the first day he'd arrived in town. He'd arrived in the 1880s. Twenty-one years old and a transplant from New York, he was hired as an occasional carriage and sign painter, working over Phil Ulrich's blacksmith shop just north of the Continental Hotel. In lulls between assignments, he practiced his E-flat clarinet. The town took notice—George Landers was no musical amateur. He'd trained with New York's Forty-eighth Regimental Band, played with Chicago's Theatre Company Orchestra, and traveled the western United States for three seasons with the John Robinson Circus Band, then a further two years with the U.S. Cavalry Band based in Jefferson City, Missouri. Within weeks of his arrival in Centerville, a deputation of town musicians climbed the stairs over Phil Ulrich's shop, led by local dentist Dr. Blatchley. "You know more about band music than all of us," they said. "We are sent here to employ you as leader of our band."[49]

Landers fused together the best players from the town's existing bands. He named it the Centerville Military Band. Twice a week, the members carried their instruments to a room over a billiard hall on the Square's Eastside. They practiced and rehearsed. They honed their skills. They entered competitions, winning awards and accolades. In 1892, they became the official band of the National Guard's Third Regiment. In their official, full-dress, regulation blue uniforms and tall bearskin hats, this band carried the reputation of Centerville everywhere across the State, enhancing the City's name and reputation. Among the band's repertoire, and in demand wherever it played, were two local pieces: "The Centerville Coal Block Waltz" and "The Appanoose County Blue Grass Quickstep."[50]

Chapter 19

Entertainment and Circuses

Throughout the 1890s and the first decade of a new century, George Landers and his band were not the only entertainment in town. Almost every night, large crowds traveled to Centerville to witness its fairs, carnivals, parades, concerts, musical groups, speeches and events, all loudly promoted by professional "spielers."[1]

Occasionally there was a merry-go-round, and once a "Big Eli" Ferris wheel that carried people to lofty views. There was Lombardo's Venice City Royal Italian Band, a Giggly Alley, an Egyptian dancer, Venetian glass blowers, animals, freak curios, penny picture shows where the image briefly moved and Gorton's "famous New Orleans Minstrels embracing a coterie of high-class artists accompanied by Gorton's Gold Band." Once, there was a snake charmer. He was bitten on the tongue by a rattlesnake, ran panic-stricken to Dr. Reynolds's office on Pill Row and died within an hour.[2]

Tony Sebastian demonstrated his skills as a champion acrobatic roller skater. A magic-lantern projectionist threw images onto a sheet fastened to a wall of the Lankford Furniture Store. Henry Latchford, fresh from London, gave speeches at the high school, the Presbyterian church and on the Square with his personal recollections of William Gladstone, Alfred Lord Tennyson, Robert Browning and Victor Hugo. Dr. Eugene May spoke on "Through Switzerland with a Knapsack and the Ascent of the Matterhorn."[3]

There were political orators promoting socialism and populism. They frequently competed with song-and-dance men selling medicines.[4]

At least two entertainers were run out of town. One was Reverend B.H. Irvin, an evangelist preacher whose "vile and slanderous" preachings so aroused town anger that his tent was torn down and he was pelted with eggs.[5]

And there was Bosco, the snake eater. She was described by her promoter as an Abyssinian freak who was impervious to snake bites and had survived being thrown into a swamp at birth and left to die. She took eight-inch snakes and swallowed them whole. For four-foot snakes, she bit off their heads, peeled the skin down a few inches and then "ravenously" ate the rest. The *Centerville Citizen* declared it "truly disgusting" and "a disgrace to enlightened people that such human depravity should be permitted to be exhibited before curious eyes."[6]

Passenger balloons rose and floated over the Square. They celebrated the beginning of a racehorse meet, the arrival of a circus, the opening of a store. During June 1897, hundreds of sightseers witnessed a series of ascensions by aeronaut John Walters of Allerton. They assembled on the vacant lot off the Southeast Corner of the Square. They watched as the canvas bags were filled with smoke and gas. They heard the bugle blast and the peal of the town's fire bell that signaled take-off.[7]

The balloon lifted rapidly. It floated above them. They cheered as aeronaut Walters waved his handkerchief and then parachuted over the side, landing harmlessly three miles to the east in the Chariton River bottomland.

The next week John Walters returned. This time accompanying him was his small dog, Nero. Both were attached to parachutes. Both climbed aboard. The balloon lifted. It reached thirty feet. A sudden wind blew it dangerously close to the Western Union telegraph lines just east of the lot. Walters attempted to maintain balance. He found his parachute caught by a fastener on the balloon that now suddenly and rapidly ascended. The fastener splintered. Walters, now inverted, fell forty feet, his head and back striking the cone of the roof of the old calaboose just off the Square's Northside.

People ran to help. They carried him to Dr. Reynolds's office on Pill Row. The aeronaut was unconscious. His breath came in deep gasps. He bled profusely from his mouth, nose, ears and a deep wound on his right temple. He lived twenty minutes. Hundreds of the curious lined up outside Dr. Reynolds's office and filed past the body. Walters's body was put on the train. The next day, he was buried in Lineville Cemetery. Pleasure was expressed that the dog, Nero, was safe.[8]

Occasionally the entertainment was unplanned and unexpected.

Between eleven o'clock and midnight on the night of April 13, 1897, an airship passed over Centerville. Bill Peatman saw it on his way home after working late at the brick factory. Civil War veteran Colonel Haynes saw it, and George Bryan observed it through his courthouse telescope. Their descriptions tallied. It approached, they said, from the northwest. It had a steel frame and was lit by numerous lights and a main locomotive headlight that flashed. Bryan observed wings. He heard them "swish" as they passed over the courthouse, and he counted thirteen people "making merry" in the cabin.[9]

Skeptics doubted their story. One said Peatman was beaten so badly at whist the previous night he couldn't possibly be holding his head up long enough to see such a thing.

But sightings of the airship were reported in Kansas and Nebraska, and on two nights it was seen over Milwaukee, the first time in the early hours of the morning. It was viewed by newspaper men, police officers and a guard at the House of Corrections. The next night it returned, this time at nine o'clock, and thousands witnessed it. The object approached from the northeast, hovered over Milwaukee City Hall for fifteen minutes and then disappeared over the lake.[10]

In the late 1890s, there were rose, military and floral carnivals—attempts to rival New Orleans's Mardi Gras, Kansas City's Priests of Phallas or St. Louis's The Veiled Prophet. They were organized by Oakland Cemetery Association, Secret Societies and the P.E.O.

Processions started from the Square. On June 22, 1897, two thousand people lined the sidewalks, sometimes six deep to witness one such event. Small children were lifted onto shoulders or held aloft. A grand marshal on a charger wreathed in bright red roses and poppies led the way. Festoons of fresh roses decorated the floats; on the first, the Centerville Military Band was led by George (now given the respectful title of "Professor") Landers.

The town's organizations and societies followed, each with its own float: the town fire brigade; the members of the P.E.O. on a rose-decorated golden phaeton attended by liveried footmen, a cupid poising his arrow at the crowd; the Welsh Cymrodorion Society pulled by white horses, displaying a June bride attended by eight bridesmaids all in pink and white; the Little Girls' Society in a carriage pulled by Shetland ponies; an African American quartet—their float wrapped in the Stars and Stripes. There were pony carts decorated with clematis and clinging butterflies, carriages garlanded with pinks, lavender, hollyhocks, goldenrods and purple chrysanthemums.

After the parade, children danced around a maypole. They kept time to music from Professor Landers. Each dancer held a long pink, white or green silk ribbon that intertwined with each dance step into a brilliant braid of color on the pole. For the men there was a baseball game: the Fats versus the Leans. The Fats wilted in the heat after the fourth inning and yielded the game to the Leans.[11]

On the Square and on the streets until midnight, crowds of people in masks blew horns, played horse fiddles and acted out myths and legends.[12]

The business community held street fairs. Merchants competed with window displays. Each window was a grotto of color, with incandescent lights and words of welcome in mosaics of coffee and sugar. At a carnival event on September 27, 1899, different-colored wooden arches, painted with stars and flags and mottoes, soared across streets: yellow for East State, white for West State, blue for North Main and red for South Main. Tall pink obelisks, trimmed with blue and white, mounted with stars and a crown of flags at each apex, stood at each corner.[13]

Circling the Square, attached to the tops of the arches and obelisks hung a three-foot banner. Suspended from it were the flags of every nation, interspersed with hundreds of electric lanterns that transformed the scene at night. Below the flags and the lanterns were the booths of every town business, where each artfully displayed its own wares. Moving between the booths, serving refreshments, were waiters from six of the town's restaurants—Murdy's, the Star, Nevins, Beehive, Strickler's and Delmonico's.[14]

But of all the town's entertainment and events, nothing could compare to the arrival of the circus.

Twice a year a circus came to town: the Ringling Brothers, the New Great Pacific, Cook and Whitby, W.W. Cole, John Robinson, Sells, Forepaugh and Barnum and Bailey.

Two weeks before, heralding their arrival, one hundred professional bill posters, seventy-five "paste and bunch" men, four managers and four bill-poster bosses arrived by train in four dormitory advertising cars. They posted posters on the courthouse fence and on every barn, railing and billboard within a fifty-mile radius of the City, keeping careful records of each posting. One day before the show's arrival, a special agent checked each one, renewing any that had been damaged during rainstorms.[15]

The shows arrived on special trains. They were unloaded with speed. People gathered to watch. Tents were erected on grounds at the south end of Seventeenth Street, on the Courthouse Park or in Lane Woods. Fresh fruits and vegetables, cabbages, strawberries and muskmelons were bought at T.J. Greene's City Gardens and carried to cooks in kitchen tents.[16]

Circus day started with a morning parade at ten o'clock. Hundreds lined the sidewalks along Fourteenth Street (later Drake Avenue), down Thirteenth

Street and around the Square. Small boys, uptown before daybreak, sat on curbs. They watched as the parade approached, led by trumpeters, a drum corps and a circus band aboard a carriage pulled by teams of gleaming horses.[17]

Kaleidoscopic images followed: herds of elephants, droves of camels, hundreds of groomed horses, Lilliputian ponies in silver harnesses; tableau cars of purple and gold, scarlet and silver; rickshaws and palanquins; open cages of lions, tigers, hippopotami, seals, kangaroos, ostriches and llamas.[18]

There were beautiful women reclining under silver panoplies, dancers in pink tights and people from hundreds of nations in native costume: Australian boomerang throwers, Turkish harem dancers, tribal warriors, imperial Cossack troopers from the steppes of Russia, turbaned Hindu princes riding howdahs, cavalcades of knights and ladies, masqueraders and harlequins. There were South American gauchos, Bedouin Arabs, detachments of cavalry troopers, and, floating above them all, a collection of international flags and banners.[19]

Music filled the air: military and mounted bands, tom toms, the spirituals of plantation jubilee singers, Scottish and Irish bagpipers and Tyrolean warblers. There were chimes and pipes, bugles, stringed instruments and orchestras, including Centerville's own with George Landers.

Fringing the entire parade—it was sometimes three miles in length—were jesters and clowns running, dancing and rolling, one driving a mule, others interweaving with the crowd. Signaling the end of the parade was the calliope, gloriously colored and sounding its pipe organ with steam and air whistles.[20]

There were two circus performances: one in the afternoon, the second in the evening, when the pathways to the big tents were lined with wick flares. The cost of a ticket was fifty cents; for children, half price. Entries to the sideshows that displayed the bizarre, the deformed and the freaks of nature were free.[21]

John Robinson's Circus was divided into eight separate tents: menagerie, museum, aviary, aquarium, Egyptian caravan, school of trained animals, calisthenic exhibition and the main show. In the last one, people watched a family of high-wire bicycle riders, elephants walking on stilts, Zenobia hurled two hundred feet across the tent from an ancient Roman–style catapult, a three-horn "unicorn" and a Chinese juggler by the name of Ah Fung Jung.[22]

W.W. Cole advertised a three-ring circus, menagerie and theater. He displayed wax reproductions of the famous, including presidents. People saw an undisputed champion bareback rider and twelve sword-carrying "genuine performing Arabs direct from the desert sands of Syria." His greatest star was the famous aerialist Blondin. This Australian star performed on high wires or ropes. He performed blindfolded, running and carrying a man on his back.[23]

But the greatest circus attraction was on September 29, 1899. It was the performance of Buffalo Bill's Wild West Show. People counted it as far more than a circus. It was theater. It was history. It mythologized the Far West, and it educated. The show would give two exhibitions, at two o'clock and at eight o'clock. Admission was fifty cents. Children under ten were admitted at half price, and reserved seats were one dollar.

Appanoose County was familiar territory to William F. Cody. As a boy of eight, he'd traveled the Mormon Trail in a covered wagon. Mrs. Mary Runyon, the mother of one of Seymour's leading physicians, remembered the family. They camped on the Runyon homestead near St. John, Missouri. William's father, Isaac, was antislavery. He took the family in 1852 from Le Claire in Iowa's Scott County to Kansas to be part of making the state free. It was there Isaac was murdered—stabbed while making a free-soil speech.[24]

Now Buffalo Bill, at forty-five, returned at the height of his fame. He'd run the pony express, shot buffalo for railroad camps, written novels—the first Westerns—been an actor and organized a Wild West show noted for its detailed authenticity, then taken it on highly successful tours of eastern states and Europe, giving performances before royalty, including Queen Victoria.[25]

His return to Centerville in 1899 attracted the biggest crowds in memory. People trekked from all of southern Iowa and northern Missouri. Buggies and high-stepping horses overtook them. Sidewalks overflowed. Children got lost.

Circus parade with buffalos riding atop a circus wagon. *Courtesy of Appanoose County Historical Society.*

The parks were full. Wagon after wagon creaked into town. Parents sat on the spring seat, the children on straw spread in wagon beds. The vehicles lined Drake Avenue—since May 1, the new name for Fourteenth Street. Five special trains arrived from distant points. Scalpers worked the crowd.[26]

The Buffalo Bill's Wild West Show parade started from the south of town at eleven in the morning. Two-and-a-half hours later, an estimated crowd of ten thousand to twenty thousand watched its arrival from open-sided, narrow show tents that lined three sides of Centerville's Courthouse Square.

The show began with an explosion of sound. Fast-paced action followed. There was an exhibition of the art of equitation from Cossacks of east Asia, gauchos of Argentina and riders from Europe, the Philippines, Hawaii, Puerto Rico and Cuba. A Mexican expert twirled his lasso in rhythm to music. He roped objects in sight and ended by lassoing himself. There were exhibitions of marksmanship, culminating in the extraordinary talent of Johnny Baker and the even greater one of a small "girl" who "tripped in, bowing, waving, and wafting kisses." Annie Oakley held her rifle backwards over her shoulder and, using a mirror to determine sight, shot the ember off a cigarette. She sliced a playing card held up edgewise, a dime held between a thumb and forefinger.[27]

Chief Flat Iron chased a buffalo and described it as "rare as a white cow, and worth almost its weight in silver." Buffalo Bill rode in with the abandon of a pony-express youth, smashing flying balls as he did so. The old Deadwood stagecoach circled the Square. Sioux Indians attacked. Cowboys chased the Indians, saving the coach and its beautiful female occupants.

Cannons, Gatling guns and volleys from small arms echoed around the buildings in a recreation of the most famous Cuban event from the Spanish-American War—the Battle of San Juan Hill. Rough Riders, the Twenty-fourth Infantry and the Ninth and Tenth Cavalry, all genuine veterans of the battle, marched in from south of the Square. They pitched tents, built campfires and sang army songs. Then came the recreation of the storming of the hill, the rout of the Spanish and the raising of the Stars and Stripes.

Never had Centerville entertained a larger or more noisy crowd. People said they'd never seen a show like it. Twenty years later, it was still the subject of discussion. The date of the Wild West Show was September 29, 1899. Three months remained, not just in the year but in the century.[28]

Chapter 20

The New Century

The new century started cold. Temperatures hovered at four degrees below zero. At the fire station, pails of boiling water simmered, ready to thaw hydrants in case of fires. At Garfield Pond, teams of men sawed ice eight to fourteen inches thick. Their horse-drawn sleds, hauling the slabs to be "bedded-down" in sawdust, slid transversely across the frozen ground.[1]

December 31 was a Sunday. Out of respect for the Sabbath, a New Year's Eve "Holiday Hop" at the armory was held a day early. Private parties, such as the "very recherché affair" at the Vermilion home, were held a day late.[2]

In the afternoon, there were temperance meetings. In the basement of the Pratt Hotel on the Levee, Dr. J.L. Sawyers spoke on the effects of alcohol on the human body. He demonstrated with colored plates and a surgeon's manikin. He passed around the liver of a healthy calf. He followed it with another described as "hob-nailed." It was a liver taken from a young man who had died from liver trouble "…inherited," said Dr. Sawyers, "from his ancestors who were drunkards."[3]

Late in the evening, local Protestants met together in the Methodist church. Messages were read from Queen Victoria, Pope Leo, Emperor William and Czar Nicholas. Across town, Father Nolan exposed the "most holy sacrament" to local Catholics at St. Mary's Church. At one minute to midnight, both congregations joined those across the country in singing the hymn "Old Hundred," and bells rang out to greet the new century.[4]

There were a few millennium predictions of the end of the world, of the Day of Judgement and the imminent Second Coming of Christ. They came from George Salisbury of Reinbeck, Iowa, "the chosen oracle of God," and from the Reverend J.M. Loughridge, addressing the Centerville Men's Meeting, who saw the Spanish-American War as the vanguard and fulfillment of Biblical prophecies. They came, too, from members of the House of David. They walked the streets of Centerville. They spoke on the Square and handed out pamphlets. They gave dire warnings of death from which they alone were exempted. Both the men and women wore their hair long, loose and flowing—the better, they said, for flight through the sky when the last trumpet sounded.[5]

But the tone of the community at the arrival of the new century was generally one of confidence. Appreciation was expressed for the advances in the arts and sciences already achieved and eager anticipation that the new century would produce even greater ones. The editor of the *Centerville Daily Citizen* wrote, "… our great success as a nation is due to the individual efforts of the citizens, and their ability to take advantage of every opportunity." For Mayor Callen it was a time to issue the citizens of the town a challenge and a call for action. "You elect men to office at each election and consider your duties well and truly performed," Mayor Callen told them. "What Centerville needs is concerted action of her citizens for the betterment of the town."[6]

Within five years a new County courthouse, a post office, a free public library, a hospital and three churches were built and dedicated. The town Square and one hundred feet of its converging streets were paved, fifteen miles of sewer laid and four miles of cement sidewalks added. The local water supply was extended, a new telephone company improved services and a newly managed electric company added forty-four street lights, supplied a steam heating system and electricity for businesses, ran a new electric streetcar service from the depots to the Square and planned an interurban service to nearby towns. The town's appearance, said C.W. Vermilion—judge of the Second Judicial Court and son of the Civil War captain and his wife, Mary—was as if the town had undergone one hundred years of growth in just four.[7]

Everywhere there was action. Committees were formed, people in their homes and on the streets consulted, petitions circulated, issues targeted, priorities established. High on the lists was the replacement of the courthouse.

Ever since the 1881 fireworks fire at the courthouse, the building had been deteriorating. The cupola was rebuilt. Iron rods from the County's old bridges were inserted to strengthen walls, corners were reinforced with cement and stone and glass in the windows nearest the corners was replaced with solid masonry. The building continued to deteriorate. New and severe cracks appeared. In 1894 the cupola and second floor were removed; the first floor received a thatched roof of straw.[8]

The situation got worse. The editor of the *Centerville Citizen* called it "squalid" and "wretched" and "…more disgusting than that of a second rate pig incubator." The editor of the *Cincinnati Review* described "…fumigating and irritating odors." Judges suffered "…noxious diseases." Visitors asked: Was it Charlie Wooden's mule barn? Was it a sheep shed? But before the issue of a new courthouse, the chief priority of the people of the town was for general public health.[9]

An "open drain" on East Jackson flowed straight east from the Square, then northeasterly on Sixteenth Street in what was known as "the McKee ditch." Private residential sewers emptied into the same outlet, creating, said residents and health physician C.P. Bowen, "…a very filthy condition with noisome smells issuing there from." The City Council members listened to the complaints. They referred the issue to a committee.[10]

To make matters worse, the Armor Company was slaughtering chickens, then dumping their blood and feathers into a hollow just one block off the Square on South Twelfth Street. Residents had asked for something to be done for more than a year. Their patience was wearing thin.[11]

Two years later and still nothing done, agitation increased. Physician to the Board of Health C.P. Tillmont pointed out other hazards to community health. Each spring, wells were polluted with "…infective material and germ life," which drained from thawing outdoor privies and manure piles, creating disease. And stagnant water, he warned, bred malaria-infested mosquitoes.[12]

Dr. Tillmont was supported by Dr. Charles S. James who, at thirty years of age, was chairman of the practice of medicine of Iowa State Medical Society. Dr. James spoke of the "appalling necessity" for a sewer system, citing the ease of the transmission of typhoid without it.[13]

At the same time, Centerville's medical community had another health worry: there were outbreaks of smallpox across Iowa. From November 1899 to April 1900, the State Board of Health reported 350 cases and 17 deaths in the State. There were currently 12 cases in Des Moines, 21 in Oskaloosa, 8 in Albia. What troubled the State Board of Health even more was that persons "having the disease often make every effort to conceal its real character because of its effect upon their business."[14]

By June 17, 1901, the Appanoose County Board of Health, finally alert to the consequences of contagion, urgently recommended its citizens be vaccinated. When an outbreak occurred in Mystic, the board quarantined the town. When three Centerville men disregarded the order and went to Mystic to visit their girls, they were arrested on their return to Centerville, taken before Mayor Callen and vaccinated. The *Albia Union* considered Centerville's action "silly."

The *Centerville Citizen* fired back. It charged the town of Albia had "carefully suppressed" the smallpox outbreak in their town.[15]

The people of Centerville were in no mood for any suppression of their own. They had waited long enough. In April 1904 a new town council was elected. It would come to be known as "the improvement council." One of its members, representing the town's second ward, was "Professor" George Landers. As the new council assumed office, individuals and groups working together were making other improvements in town. The mood was infectious.[16]

In December 1900, Governor Drake made the offer of a twenty-five-thousand-dollar gift to the Ladies of the Reading Room Association. He would build a new library in Centerville, he said, if local electors would then support it with taxes.[17]

On May 17, 1901, electors of the City voted in favor of a two-mill levy to support a free public library. Two thousand people marched to Drake's home. The Fifty-first Regimental Band, under George Landers, led the way. The Ladies of the Reading Room Association held up a banner. It read, "1,500 majority for the Drake Library. Governor Drake, your $25,000 accepted. Thanks." The former governor, surrounded by his family, emerged and expressed his pleasure. Fireworks exploded. People cheered. The band played "Praise God from Whom All Blessings Flow."[18]

Drake selected a 140-foot-by-140-foot site immediately south of the Armory Opera House on the east side of Drake Avenue. Workers of the J.W. Sanderson Company of Burlington arrived in town, cleared the site and began construction. Stones, St. Louis pressed bricks, corrugated glass for the windows, fluted terra cotta drums and Ionic capitals for the pillars, and a dome of leaded stained glass were delivered and assembled into place.[19]

Before the completion of the library, there was another cause for celebration with more military music, fireworks cascading across the night sky and bonfires on the Square. It was the thirty-five-thousand-dollar post office awarded by the federal government.[20]

Governor Drake presided over mass town meetings. The new post office building, he said, would increase property values 10 percent immediately, 25 percent in three years. People argued about its best location. Store windows around the Square displayed watercolor images of their suggestions. One placed it on the Northeast Corner of the Square. Two placed it directly on the Square itself: on a corner, or on the Southside facing into Main Street. A fourth design extended both Main and State Streets clear across the Courthouse Park,

The new library. *Courtesy of Appanoose County Historical Society.*

creating four Squares. One would hold the post office, one a new courthouse and the other two would be filled with trees and seats, walkways, flowerbeds and fountains.[21]

Frank B. Wheaton, special agent to the federal building committee, arrived at the Rock Island depot from Muscatine. He was met by Centerville's Citizens Site Committee and taken on a tour of inspection. He examined the watercolor images in store windows. He spoke to the site committee members in Governor Drake's office over the Centerville National Bank. He considered all plans but decided on another location: one block south of the Square, on the southwest corner of Maple and Main Streets.

Wheaton's decision reached the town on September 16, 1902. In less than two months, the people voted for a new courthouse and were already raising money to provide the town with a hospital.[22]

Buoyed by their success in achieving the Drake Library, three women of the Library Association formed a Ladies Hospital Auxiliary. They met with local doctors. In response to the doctors' needs, the ladies assembled plans and listed necessities. Across the town, in County villages and in mining camps, people gave what they could afford. Sometimes it was a dime, sometimes a

The new post office. *Courtesy of Appanoose County Historical Society.*

nickel. Two hundred individuals and firms contributed twenty-five dollars, becoming life members.[23]

With ten thousand dollars, the women bought the Aaron Grinspan home on South Main and then the William Peatman home, moving the two close together. Thirty rooms were divided into smaller private ones and wards with two to four cots, with men on the first floor, women upstairs. Gas and electric lights were installed. All corners were rounded. The walls were covered in enamel paint and the floors in linoleum.[24]

An operating room was placed next to a sterilizing room on the northwest corner of the second floor. It was lit by large windows and a skylight. The operating table, described as "…one of the finest made," was of metal and glass.[25]

Women's organizations volunteered for action: the Women's Relief Corps, the P.E.O., ladies of the Methodist church and the MXL Society, the town's oldest social organization, comprising forty married members. They all contributed bedding and linens, a Bible and flowers. John Lankford gave a medicine cabinet.[26]

On Tuesday, November 17, 1903, the hospital was opened to the public. J.M. Beck, the new editor of the *Iowegian*, had just arrived in town, coming by hack from Mystic over muddy roads, and was now ensconced in the newspaper's new office on South Main Street just off the Square. He congratulated the people of the area. To complete this hospital, he wrote, "…shows that the feeling of humanity occupies a high place in the public mind and heart." The hospital had already admitted its first two patients: a boy from Diamond and a man from Brazil.[27]

From his office over the First National Bank, Frank S. Payne—the new president of the Citizens Light and Gas Company—had a perfect view of Centerville Square. Below him, clerks carried boxes of documents from the courthouse, now about to be demolished, to displaced County offices: to the courtroom, clerk's and sheriff's offices on the Westside and to the treasurer's, recorder's, and auditor's offices upstairs over the *Citizen* newspaper building on the Northeast Corner.[28]

In the center of the Square, Jim Dawson, placed in charge of the courthouse demolition, viewed the building and issued orders. Wrecking crews wielded hammers. They swung pickaxes. Boards of cut lumber, doors, windows and bricks were pulled by teams of horses and assembled in organized piles. People pushing wheelbarrows claimed what was usable and bought bricks at $3.50 per thousand.[29]

The 1861 cornerstone at the base of the northeast wall was carefully removed and carried to the window of Kaufman's Drug Store on the Westside of the Square. Masonic members of Centerville's Jackson Lodge extracted and pried open the rusted tin box inserted so carefully in 1861. Dampness had destroyed the contents: a July 18, 1861, copy of the *Appanoose Chieftain*, state and national papers, copies of the Declaration of Independence, Washington's address, a Bible and hymnbook. There were coins: the silver ones blackened, the gold coins retaining their luster, gleaming and reflecting the light from the store window.[30]

Around the Square from the power plant off the Northeast Corner, Frank Payne's own workmen were installing forty-four new electric street lights. They were digging trenches, replacing a deteriorating gas pipeline and positioning hot-water pipes, delivering an effective steam-heating system to buildings, including attachments for the new courthouse.[31]

Payne's workmen were also removing the mule-train track that had brought people from the railroad depots. In its place they hammered seventy-two-pound rails and six-inch-by-eight-inch ties. They raised poles to conduct overhead power wires for a new electric trolley service. At a trial run from the railroad depots to the Square, men and boys climbed into a trolley, an attached freight car and a flatcar. They yelled and cheered as the new system negotiated the new track on a zigzag path, turning alternately north and then west along Eighteenth, Walsh, Sixteenth, Sheridan, Drake, Maple and Main Streets. At the Square the track turned east, then north, passing under Frank Payne's window to the terminus on North Main.[32]

The seven-and-a-half-minute trolley service from the depots to the Square began at nine minutes past ten on the morning of December 18, 1902. One month later, on January 15, 1903, the service transported hundreds of visitors for the dedication of the Drake Library. From Des Moines, two special trains traveled the Wabash and Central tracks. One carried Iowa's governor, Albert Baird Cummins, and three hundred State officials. The other brought five hundred Drake University students, including their band and glee clubs.[33]

Guests were served food at the Armory Opera House, at the Presbyterian church and at another building given by Drake to the town, the Central Church of Christ on Drake Avenue. One thousand bronze medals were sold as souvenirs at twenty-five cents each. On the steps of the library, Governor Cummins gave a speech. Ex-governor Drake lifted a key. He unlocked the door and handed the key to Mayor Callen. People cheered.[34]

The dedication of the Drake Free Public Library would be Governor Drake's last public event. In the afternoons, he still attended to business in his office over the bank on the Square's Southeast Corner. But his health was deteriorating, and in early November 1903, people who saw him commented on his frailty. His war injury, made worse by his fall on the capitol steps before he left office, was increasingly painful. At his home on Drake Avenue, he fell in the tub and broke a rib. He leaned to open a window and injured another. He fought pleurisy, pneumonia, kidney failure and diabetes. His personal physician, Dr. J.L. Sawyers, who was also his son-in-law, was an almost constant companion.[35]

On November 19, urgent messages brought his children and their families to his bedside. Francis Marion Drake died at his home on Friday, November 20, at 10:45 a.m. He was seventy-three years of age.[36]

In Des Moines, the flag on the State capitol was lowered. At Drake University a bell tolled. In Centerville, telegrams and floral tributes were delivered to the home. The Drake Free Public Library was closed and black crêpe placed at the doors. The schools were closed. Work on the new courthouse, now well underway, was temporarily halted. People met in groups: the police, the fire department, members of the bar. Their voices were subdued. They planned events and contributions in his memory.[37]

Drake's body was placed in a copper casket with silver handles and covered with black plush. It lay in state in the new Central Church of Christ he had built on Drake Avenue. Three thousand people walked past the bier. Two hundred schoolchildren placed sprigs of evergreen on the casket.[38]

Special trains arrived for the funeral: from Des Moines, Governor Cummins and members of State government; the president of Drake University, along with faculty, staff and students; from Keokuk and Chicago, railroad magnates, judges and waiters.[39]

There were relatives, friends, town officials and George Landers and the military band, as well as members of the Odd Fellows, the bar, the Masons and the Knight Templars. And there as honorary pallbearers, perhaps those the former governor would have wanted most, were the surviving members of the Thirty-sixth Iowa Regiment—those who had survived Yazoo River, the Battle of Marks Mill and prison in Tyler, Texas. They were now old men, some blind, some deaf, some unable to walk without aid. But on this day, as any other, their military bearing was unbroken.[40]

Chapter 21

The Courthouse, the Clock and Other Public Improvements

By spring of 1903, excavations for the new courthouse were finished, and so were eighteen-inch trenches to support the walls. Workmen followed the plans of Des Moines architects Smith and Gage. A switch from the electric trolley line was built where it turned from Main into East Jackson Streets on the Square's Southside. Workmen built a track into the center of the Square. Now building materials—lime, crushed rock, dressed stone from Quincy, Illinois, and northern Iowa, steelwork from Marshalltown—arrived on freight cars directly into the site from the depots.[1]

By early April, the builder, William Peatman, built a ten-foot fence around the site. This both obstructed views of the building's progress and protected the curious from construction hazards. J.R. Parks, the County auditor, in his office over the *Citizen* newspaper, accepted bids for subcontracting—for heating and plumbing, carpentry and lighting, roofing and painting.[2]

On May 21, a platform was placed over the northeast corner when two courses of stone were built above the foundation. This gave access to members of Centerville's Masonic Jackson Lodge to place the new building's cornerstone. The box, inserted into the stone, measured 8½ by 11½ by 14½ inches. It was made of copper and sealed by Clarence Peatman. It held copies of County newspapers, Masonic-order memberships, pamphlets and photographs of the St. Louis World's Fair, of the old courthouse and of leading citizens such as ex-governor Drake and Jackson Perjue, the town's first sheriff, now eighty-seven years old and still an active citizen.[3]

The ceremony followed Masonic ritual. Members carried assigned objects—a drawn sword, white rods, gold and silver vessels, an architect's plumb, a square, a level, and two large lights. Grain, wine and oil were poured over the cornerstone. Flowers were added along with candles.[4]

Every day throughout that long, hot summer of 1903, freight cars were either pulled or pushed to the site from the depots by the electric trolley. Teams of men working nine-hour days unloaded marble for the flooring and wainscoting, stone veneer, bricks, tiles, art-metal electric light fixtures, brass fittings, grilled ironwork, iron stair-railings and windows. As the building became higher, the teams loaded materials onto hoisting machinery operated by electric motors.[5]

By February 1904, the tower was put in place, then a permanent roof and, in response to public demand, a flagpole at its apex. By August, painters began their interior fresco work. Furniture was delivered: counters, tables, filing cabinets for the courtroom and opera chairs. By early September, County officials—the auditor, treasurer, clerk and recorder—carried their papers from their temporary offices scattered about the Square and moved into their new accommodations on the second floor.[6]

On the morning of Monday, September 12, 1904, the people of Appanoose County inspected their new courthouse. They walked from room to room. They declared everything "beautiful" and "good." Among them were three of the County's early pioneers. There was Judge S.M. Moore, the first County recorder, the first County auditor and County judge from 1863 to 1869. Now unable to see and unable to walk after having been ill for months, he was eager to be there, eager to greet his old friends. Among them, too, was William Crow, who had claimed land that first night in May 1843 when the County was first declared open for settlers, and Jackson Perjue, another first claimer and the County's first sheriff when that office's jurisdiction had stretched to Nebraska. Now eighty-eight years old, he looked the building over and said he'd "…never dreamed of such a structure as this."[7]

The building was officially dedicated that afternoon in the courtroom on the east side of the top floor. There was an invocation, an address of welcome, songs by a male quartet and speeches. Presiding judge Robert Sloan introduced the main speaker. He was Iowa's chief justice, Horace E. Deemer. He traced the history of law and justice from England's confrontation with King John at Runnymede that resulted in the Magna Carta of 1215. Then he formally dedicated the courthouse: "To thee, oh truth! Which needs no flowers of speech, no gifted tongue, which has been said to be the work of God, we dedicate this structure. Here thou shalt all prevailing be."[8]

The new courthouse. *Courtesy of Appanoose County Historical Society.*

Admiration for the new building was universally expressed. One item, a major one, was still needed. For J.R. Wooden, president of the Wooden Bank on the Westside of the Square, it presented a unique opportunity.

James Wooden had good reason to feel gratitude to the people of Appanoose County. He'd arrived in Centerville in September 1856 when he was thirty years of age, looking for a suitable town to start a business. His walk around the Square the next day ended his search. He rented Spencer Wadlington's log-cabin store, collected wife Amerika and son Albert Edgar (A.E.) from Gosport, Indiana, and returned to stay.

Now almost fifty years later, the eighty-year-old Wooden was one of the town's most successful businessmen. He'd migrated from the Wadlington Store to his own Hoosier store on the Square's Northside and built a beautiful classical home with columns, one block to the north. During the Civil War, he speculated in gold and became vice president of William Bradley's First National Bank. He invested in farmlands, real estate and farm mortgages. He was president of the Citizens Savings Bank and opened the Wooden Bank on the Square's Westside. Now, in the spirit of "noblesse oblige," he had an opportunity to thank the people of the community for their fifty years of business. He ordered a town clock from the Seth Thomas Company of Chicago. It would be placed in the tower of the courthouse.[9]

Four plate-glass dials, each almost six feet in diameter and each with electrical attachments for illumination, arrived by train from Chicago. So did the one-thousand-pound bell that would ring out the hours and the half-hours. Walter J. Buckley, representing the Seth Thomas Company, arrived to oversee the clock's installation. Getting the bell to the tower created a problem. Local builders came to assist. Townspeople gathered to watch. From a platform on the building's west side, the bell was lifted by a derrick. It was then swung along a cable that stretched over the roof from the building's chimney to the inside of the tower.[10]

Six days later, on March 13, 1905, Wooden received a subpoena from Judge Eichelberger ordering him to give evidence in court. He arrived in the dark as, for the first time, the clock struck the hour. It was 8 p.m. Immediately Major Landers and the Fifty-first Regimental Band struck up "Hail to the Chief," and a large crowd greeted a surprised Wooden with a reception and expressions of gratitude.[11]

Seven months earlier, across the Square and down Main Street, the new federal post office was dedicated. Music was provided by the ubiquitous Landers and the Fifty-first Regimental Band, and songs were sung by the town's male quartet. There were prayers, an address of welcome and a formal address and dedication by Congressman Peter Hepburn, who had been the prime mover in Washington for the placing of the building in Centerville. A reception followed, and the post office building was open to the public for inspection, the post office officials at their various stations.[12]

The new courthouse and the new post office shared three coincidences. They were constructed at the same time, had the same building contractor—William Peatman—and their dedications were less than a month apart.

There their similarities end. The courthouse design is large, weighty, square, stone and Romanesque; the post office is rectangular, brick with sandstone trim, delicate and Georgian. Above large arched windows, above a balustraded cornice, the post office's steep slate roof is topped by a cupola with a gilded dome.[13]

On June 1, 1904, the Improvement Council—the name given to the town council elected in April 1904 that got so much accomplished—issued a contract for thirteen miles of a sewer system. It was awarded to the Barris-Besley Company of Council Bluffs. Posters advertising for laborers appeared in town and across the State. In the northeast part of town, workmen—paid $1.75 an hour—dug cavities and inserted septic tanks with brick walls and solid bases to receive the sewage.[14]

A thirty-ton, eight-thousand-dollar sewer ditcher, known as Chicago Excavator No. 29 and leased from that city's Municipal Engineering and Contracting Company, rumbled into town. An operator dressed in a suit and bowler hat stood on top of the machine. He manipulated levers. Wheels began to turn. It roared like a locomotive. Steam issued from a central chimney. The machine moved forward. Small scoop-shovels on an endless moving chain dug into the ground, tipping dirt to one side, creating a twenty-seven-inch-wide descending ditch from four to twenty-five feet in depth. The machine at its deepest penetration disappeared from view, except for the top of a bowler hat, a chimney and clouds of steam.[15]

Teams of laborers moved behind the machine. Some placed retaining planks. Some laid sewer pipes, variously measuring eight to fifteen inches in diameter. Some inserted manholes and attached flush tanks. The last team refilled the ditches.[16]

The Iowa Engineering Company of Clinton was also hired. Its purpose was to oversee and coordinate the changes. The firm's excellent reputation was already established in fourteen Iowa communities, six in Illinois, two in Wisconsin, three in Minnesota and one each in Mississippi and Nebraska. The company's president, vice president and chief engineer had studied the best sewer systems of Europe. They had given lectures at state universities. On their arrival in Centerville, the company officials inspected the streets, drew up plans and watched the sewer ditcher at work, and then, for the next year, diligently inspected all work, seeing that contractors performed all requirements precisely.[17]

Centerville's sewer system was completed by December 1905. But the work of town improvements was still not completed.

After the building of the courthouse, the post office and the Drake Free Public Library, as well as the installation of electric lights, sewers and steam and water pipes, the streets around the Square were deteriorating rapidly. Any fall of rain made travel almost impossible. Farmers and doctors abandoned buggies and resorted to horseback. The few hogs came on foot. Grain didn't move at all.

Visitors coming long distances to trade were "disgusted" and described the town as "a muddy mess." Eight-year-old Aaron Cohn, the son of an immigrant peddler, walked uptown from the Levee in 1903 to see the courthouse being built. Fifty years later he still remembered how the rubber boots he wore protected him from "a sea of mud." In the same year, a despairing businessman on the Square's Northeast Corner put out a notice: "Mud—Ten Feet Deep."[18]

Agitation for paving became insistent. There was heated debate on the choice of surface: asphalt, blocks or brick; brick emerged the winner, and a contract was let on September 3, 1904. It was seventeen days after the dedication of the courthouse. Twenty-nine teams, wagons and scrapers of the McCarthy Improvement Company of Davenport arrived in town. They filed in from the north and onto the Square. The date—September 29, 1904—would always be known as "the day Hogan came to town."[19]

When the team, wagons and scrapers arrived on Centerville Square, their thirty-three-year-old foreman, a County Galway, Ireland, native, Edward J. Hogan, was waiting for them. He issued orders and directed activities immediately: "Unload there, get that plow out. Cut a furrow here. Put those scrapers onto the dirt and move lively." Before night that first day, the grading of the Square was well underway. A week later, ten teams graded the yard and leveled the street. They pushed dirt into hollows never less than three, usually four or five, feet in depth.[20]

People came to stare. They couldn't believe the speed of the workers and Hogan's superb rapport with them. "It was," said the *Iowegian*, "the most energetic work ever seen performed by any set of men in Centerville."

The street railway hauled freight cars from the depots. They delivered 250 cars of Purington bricks from Galesburg, 160 of Keokuk stone, 125 of Eddyville sand and 40 of cement from various Missouri locations.[21]

A big concrete mixer was started south of the courthouse, in the street near the car tracks. All day it ground out cement, sand and crushed stone. Carts carried the mixture to the streets, beginning on North Main. Nine hundred yards of six-inch concrete were laid on October 27, one thousand on the twenty-eighth.[22]

On top of the cement was placed two inches of sand. Bricklayers assembled the Purington bricks. The first was laid on the Northside of the Square, on the corner of North Main and West Van Buren. The chief engineer, a Mr. Cox, took a photograph. The bricklayers then moved bricks into position almost as fast as the *Iowegian* reporter could count. Walking behind, engineers from the Iowa Engineering Company of Clinton, those excellent overseers of Centerville's changes, inspected the quality of each brick. A steamroller then pressed them firmly into place, and men wielding big mops worked a liquid mixture of sand, cement and water into the cracks.[23]

They were finished on November 23. It had taken forty days to complete what was judged to be the best paving job ever done in Iowa.

Two nights later, 125 town businessmen held a banquet of appreciation for the McCarthy Improvement Company at the Continental Hotel. D.C. Bradley was the toastmaster. Foreman Edward Hogan was given a gold watch and told that his "...ability to handle men and get things done excited admiration." The owner of the company, P.E. McCarthy, was presented with a gold-mounted, pearl-handled silk umbrella. He was told that when Centerville extended its street paving, the town wanted the McCarthy company to have the winning bid and to have Hogan sent back to be in charge.[24]

By December 9, all restraints on traffic were lifted, and the electric street cars bringing travelers to and from the railroad depots resumed running. The paving was declared in excellent condition. The news traveled to Galesburg. The Purington Brick Company requested a photograph of Centerville Square to use in advertising its bricks. The *Iowegian* concluded, "The job here is recognized as among the very best in the country and this will serve to make Centerville known as a city that wants the best there is and wants it money's worth."[25]

In the same month, the Improvement Council ordered the building of sidewalks, stating that they must be permanent and made of cement or brick, cut stone or granitoid. In response, Ike Manson, son of pioneer "Granddad" Manson, formed the Centerville Sidewalk Manufacturing Company. He mixed, by hand, cement at five dollars a barrel and stone shipped from Ellsberry, south of St. Louis. Cement sidewalks were laid clockwise around the Square, beginning at the Continental Hotel. They were extended along Main and State Streets, the alleyways and the route to the depots. D.C. Bradley ordered the first residential sidewalk in front of his mansion on East Maple Street. The fashion spread. Everyone wanted the "high-toned" cement in front of their homes, paying for it themselves, until fifteen miles of public and private sidewalks laced the City.[26]

In the building of the new courthouse, the grade of the entire park had been razed, destroying the avenues of shade trees. The place looked bleak and bare. Major Landers urged grass-seed planting before the town band resumed its weekly concerts. J.M. Beck, the new editor of the *Iowegian*, wanted trees. A traveling salesman visiting the town said the courthouse yard would be improved with the introduction of squirrels, like the pet fox squirrels he'd observed at Tipton. The Ladies Improvement Association planted four flowerbeds, one at each corner. The P.E.O. Sisterhood presented a five-hundred-dollar, eight-foot drinking fountain from the J.L. Mott Company of New York. It was unveiled south of the courthouse. Water gushed from the mouths of iron lion heads. Crowning the fountain, a statue of Winged Victory held a circle of laurel.[27]

By 1906 the people of the town had good reason to be proud of all the improvements to their City. A second hospital opened—the Graham Hospital, run on the principles of osteopathy. Centerville's children, from primary school through high school, attended brick schools. There were four new brick churches: the First Baptist, the Methodist, the African Methodist and the Swedish Congregationalist. Four more had been extended and improved: the Presbyterian, the Second Baptist, the Jewish Synagogue and the Catholic. Two churches were recycled: the Believers moved out of their summer tents and into the vacated Methodist church on North Main Street; the Reorganized Church of the Latter-Day Saints (the Mormons) moved into the old Church of Christ on Drake Avenue.[28]

The Salvation Army, based on East Van Buren, held "Hallelujah Weddings" under arches of the Stars and Stripes and the Union Jack in Russell Hall and were seen daily on the streets, through summer sunshine or winter storms, with drums beating and cymbals, horns and tambourines sounding. Two religions that had formerly met in private homes now rented halls for regular services:

Inside the Swedish Congregational Church. *Courtesy of Appanoose County Historical Society.*

the Christian Scientists over the Payne building on the Square's Southeast Corner and the Pentecostals over the McCreary Drug Store on the Westside.[29]

And there was another new brick building. The Centerville local United Mineworkers of America (UMWA) now occupied a two-story, twenty-five-by-ninety-foot building on Thirteenth Street. Upstairs it was filled with a large hall and offices for records and business. Downstairs was a storeroom that also substituted as a second hall.[30]

At the same time these town improvements were occurring, other changes were happening. These were national. Their implications were broad. Their effects would be profound. They began with a telephone call from Charles Farrington's new telephone company on North Thirteenth Street.

Chapter 22

The Big Change

It was four fifteen in the afternoon of September 6, 1901, when the telephone rang in the *Daily Citizen* office on the Northeast Corner of Centerville Square. In the basement, copies of the late-afternoon Friday newspaper were just emerging from the printing press. Upstairs, employees were collating, folding and assembling the sheets. A line of newsboys, leather satchels over their shoulders, waited near the door, ready to sell their allotment of copies around town. The telephone call brought all movement to a standstill.[1]

President William McKinley had been shot twice while moving along a reception line in the octagon-shaped Temple of Music at the Pan-American Exposition in Buffalo. The assassin was Leon Czolgosz, a young man concealing a loaded .32-caliber revolver under a handkerchief.[2]

Editor Joe Huston ordered the production of the newspaper halted. He sought verification. Reports conflicted. Western Union sources were uncertain. A contact in Davenport wired the story was false. At five o'clock, confirmation came from the *Ottumwa Courier*. The *Citizen*'s compositor immediately reset the front page. He inserted a two-column spread at the top, right-hand side under a twin, black banner headline in capital letters: "Extra! Extra!" He reprinted a four o'clock bulletin from Buffalo, in his haste misspelling:"McKinley Assasinated." Under the first bulletin, he inserted a second, issued twenty-five minutes later from a Buffalo hospital. This read, "Resting without Pain."[3]

Outside, the news was passing by word of mouth. On Thirteenth Street, five switchboard operators at the Centerville Telephone Company transmitted it to various parts of the City and the County. On the Square, business transactions stopped. People gathered in groups. They seized copies of the newspaper as newsboys emerged from the *Citizen*. Inside the office, editor Joe Huston was besieged with telephone calls.[4]

Over the next eight days, people eagerly read the headline reports of McKinley's condition. On Saturday, the seventh, it was "May Recover"; on Monday, the ninth, "Our President Will Live"; on the tenth, "President Improved"; on the eleventh, "Steadily Improving." But on the thirteenth, there was a change: "The President Has a Relapse." This was followed on September 14, edged with thick, black borders, with "Our President Dead."[5]

On September 19, 1901, three town memorials were held. The fire department, coal miners, businessmen and women, the Fifty-first Regimental Band under George Landers and schoolchildren joined together and walked through the rain to the opera house, to the First Presbyterian Church and to the Christian Church. They sang "America" and "Nearer, My God, To Thee."[6]

Between 2:00 and 2:05 p.m. the same day, at the time of the last McKinley funeral in Canton, Ohio, all trains in the County stopped running. They joined trains across the country. Not a wheel turned anywhere. Trains stopped in cornfields, switch engines in yards; fast mail and fast passenger trains all ground to a halt.[7]

The train drivers were following the proclamation of the country's new president, Theodore "Teddy" Roosevelt, sworn into office on the fourteenth.[8]

At forty-three, he was the country's youngest president. His energy, his buoyancy and his optimism were perfect reflections of the times. Across the country, "The Big Change" was underway. Inventions and forces were radically altering the American way of life. They were also reaching Centerville.[9]

From the courthouse and from the town's offices was the sound of a new business invention. Secretaries tapped out business letters and documents on their Smith Premier or Remington typewriters. In the Continental Hotel, a crowd of traveling men gathered to watch, in astonishment, eleven-year-old Israel Futoransky, the son of Russian immigrant parents Max and Ethel Futoransky, who ran a grocery store on the Levee. Israel could type 135 words a minute. He could keep pace with any dictation. He could maintain the speed without marks on the keys and with his eyes closed. A year later he exhibited his talent at the St. Louis World's Fair.[10]

The town's newspapers reported developments in "wireless telegraphy," of signals sent across space without wires via electromagnetic waves. In 1900, over Vienna, twin floating balloons exchanged signals at a distance of six miles. A year later, at Signal Hill, Newfoundland, twenty-three-year-old Guglielmo

Marconi, flying a kite with trailing antennae, received the letter *s* (three dots) sent across the Atlantic from Cornwall on the southwestern tip of England.[11]

Other inventions were reported: Professor Richard Fessenden's "coherer of greater sensitiveness," and one of the earliest radio-sending apparatuses, invented by William Clifton Cutler, the inventor son of Centerville's early grocer and abolitionist Jacob Rummel. The *Semi-Weekly Iowegian* described how distressed ships at sea sent messages to shore and received help. Other ships were warned of danger and returned to port. The town's earliest radio message was received in December 1908. Dr. J.L. Sawyers, returning to America from Europe, sent a message to his Centerville Baraca Bible Class: "Greetings from Midocean to Baracas. Will be with you 20th: J.L. Sawyers."[12]

On Thirteenth Street, at an empty storefront, a traveling showman invited people inside. They paid five cents, sat on folding chairs in the dark and watched a screen. Grainy, gray photographic images flickered and moved. For two minutes they saw a coastal scene with waves dashing on rocks. For another nickel and for another two minutes they watched a cross-country runner. There were no stories, no sound, no music, but they were the first motion pictures in town, and their popularity was immediate.[13]

Within weeks, three churches—the Christian, the Swedish Lutheran and the Catholic—were advertising "moving pictures." These were of the Oberammergau Passion Play, the scenery "...subjected to Edison's scientific manipulation." Entertainers advertised pictures that moved using a projectoscope. At the Armory Opera House, the Brinton Entertainers from Fairfield used stereopticon double images that "adjusted" to show McKinley's life and assassination, Queen Victoria's funeral, King Edward VII's coronation, the storming of San Juan Hill and the eruption of Mount Pelée in Martinique, the town of St. Pierre destroyed and hundreds killed. People described the images disturbing and said they felt "...like moving from their seats to escape harm."[14]

On Independence Day 1907, thousands of people watched moving pictures in a tent on the Square. Two months later, the town's first movie house, the Lyric, opened on the Square's Westside and a year later, almost next door, the Bijou. It was at the Lyric that people saw Edwin S. Porter's *The Life of an American Fireman* and his groundbreaking *The Great Train Robbery*. In this fourteen-scene, twelve-minute movie, the characters moved, even briefly the camera moved; there were flashbacks and a close-up, uniting to tell what is credited as the first story put into movie form.[15]

But the talk of the town in the early 1900s was of Centerville's John Drake, the son of Governor Francis Marion Drake. At thirty-six, he was a multimillionaire and said to be richer than his father. He invested in stocks and bought a gold mine at Gilt Edge, Montana, and interests in Colorado Fuel and Iron. He gambled large sums of money. He played poker with steel magnate John Gates. He bet on horses, on turns of a card; he bet one thousand dollars for each time a fly landed on a lump of sugar.[16]

In 1902 he returned from England with thirteen racehorses. They'd won at Epsom and at Ascot, ridden by two of Centerville's Garner boys (Charles and Wayne). He maintained stables in England, in Chicago and in Saratoga. The U.S. Treasury Department cross-examined his estimate of the horses' worth at the Manhattan Custom House. In June his horse Wyeth won the American Derby in Chicago. Three months later his horse Savable won the Futurity Stakes at Sheepheads Bay, New York. [17]

The same year, he appeared on the front page of the April 3 edition of William Randolph Hearst's *Chicago American*. Drake had bought an automobile imported from France for William K. Vanderbilt Jr. and was about to drive it from New York to Chicago. What sensationalized this story was its history. Some said it was "voodooed."[18]

The automobile was known as "the White Ghost." Its motor was thirty-three horsepower and was guaranteed to run at fifty miles per hour. On a speed test, it reached fifty-five. William K. Vanderbilt Jr. drove it 138 miles from Newport to Boston and back. On the journey, the auto killed two dogs and one horse and injured a man. Vanderbilt considered it to be jinxed and sold it to Edward Thomas. Thomas agreed the vehicle was bad luck when he drove it on a New York street and killed seven-year-old Harry Theiss.

John Drake bought the auto in 1902 from Edward Thomas. When his Board of Trade and racing associates learned of the purchase, they were appalled and believed Drake's "long-delayed nemesis was at last upon him." A long-term friend believed he brought the biggest kind of voodoo down to perch on his shoulders. "That machine," he said, "...has scared half the coppers in New York, sent all the nurse maids in Central Park into hysterics, populated two or three hospitals, killed all the dogs on Long Island and all the horses in Connecticut." Drake said he wasn't superstitious. His horses at large races were known to wear the number thirteen. At some of those races, the horses won. He drove the White Ghost to Chicago.

The day after the account of John Drake's purchase of the White Ghost appeared in the *Chicago American*, it was headlined on the front page of the *Centerville Citizen*. A month later William Willett of Moulton bought a Haynes-Apperson. He wrote a check for $1,450, an extra $48 for the railroad freight, becoming the first person in Appanoose County to own an automobile.[19]

In Centerville, the first auto was a one-cylinder Cadillac. It was bought in 1903 by Dr. Elbert Ellsworth Heaton. Heaton was a noted physician and surgeon. He studied cancer in England; he studied the stomach, intestines and thyroid in Germany. He loved travel, art and fine craftsmanship. His auto arrived by railroad from Chicago. Fifty people gathered at the Rock Island station to witness its arrival. It stood on the platform, gleaming and polished. It was bright red-orange with black trim. It had a steering wheel projecting from the dashboard at an eighty-degree angle. There was a long, buttoned driving seat and no hood. No one knew how to start it. Carl Ware, the thirty-year-old station agent, turned knobs and twisted levers. The auto leapt forward. Ware grabbed the steering gear and guided the vehicle to the street but was now unable to stop it. People stared in stunned amazement. Others walked alongside shouting suggestions. When Ware got the auto stopped, it was a quarter of the way along Drake Avenue and close to Dr. Heaton's home at 904.[20]

Dr. Heaton and Willett started a fashion. New automobiles arrived. Some operated on steam: the White, the Stanley, the Locomobile, the Rambler, the Pope-Toledo. They had a flash-pan system of boiler that carried up to one thousand pounds of pressure. They sputtered to start, ran two miles at twenty-seven miles per hour, "…breathing flames and smoke," and stopped. They restarted when the steam was back up.[21]

D.C. Bradley, the banker, bought the gasoline-driven, "quiet mile-a-minute" Pope-Hartford. Two doctors, Bowen and Severs, bought the chain-driven Holsman and the high-wheeled Schacht. Another doctor, Hickman, chose a Saxon; Charles Farrington at the Telephone Exchange, a Maxwell; and Frank Payne of the Centerville Light and Traction Company, a Mitchell. More cars came to town. There were brightly colored Lamberts, Overlands and red-and-yellow Willys-Knights.[22]

They were delivered in large boxes, like pianos. They came from Chicago, Minneapolis and Denver. They came without accessories. There were no lamps, no tops, no windshields and no taillights; for some of the roadsters, either there was one door or no doors at all. Some had spoke tires; others waited for the next town visit from traveling salesman Harvey Firestone. Horns were not necessary. Animals were terrified by the noise long before the vehicle arrived, and on Drake Avenue, roadsters driving at the rate of eleven miles an hour were said by the *Iowegian* to endanger the lives of Centerville's peaceful citizens.[23]

By 1907 Centerville's streets were beginning to "swarm" with autos. The drivers, perched high on their seats, wore heavy linen duster coats, driving hats, gloves and goggles and were warned when speeding to keep their mouths shut to avoid strangulation from overloading the lungs, the mouth and the air passages.[24]

The machines were cranked by hand. Sometimes they wouldn't start. Sometimes they stopped without explanation. Rear axles broke, and gasoline was bought in steel barrels at nine cents a gallon from some, but not all, grocery stores. The owners had an urgent need for a town mechanic. He arrived in 1904.[25]

Harry Luther was a native of Clinton, Iowa. He trained as a plumber and worked in a sporting goods store and in the mechanical department of the Tehuantepec Rubber Culture Company in Oaxaca Province, Mexico. On his return to the United States, he worked for the Simmons Hardware Company in St. Louis. He did the ten-thousand-dollar decorating and display exhibit for the company at the St. Louis World's Fair. Then Luther came to Centerville. He was twenty-seven years old.[26]

Luther opened a hardware store on the Northside of Centerville Square. He lit the windows every night with electricity. He placed electric bulbs inside long troughs with mirrors to increase the brightness. His Christmas decorations were the talk of the town. Everything moved. Santa Claus, a sack of toys over a shoulder, walked into woods looking for a Christmas tree. Around him toys moved; trains ran on tracks. High above, a moon and stars shone in the sky.

In 1907 he put a Pope-Hartford touring auto inside his window. People came to stare. It was bought by D.C. Bradley for twenty-four hundred dollars. It was the first car sold in Centerville. Luther replaced it with a flaming-red Brewster. He sold that to Dr. Tillmont, who bought all the extras at the same time: the windshield, the top, lamps, speedometer and bulb horn.[27]

With two successful sales, Luther expanded into auto supplies. He sold motor fuel, motor oils, gasoline and naphtha in barrels and five-gallon cans. A year later, in 1908, he was the first local agent for Henry Ford. The first ten Model T's arrived, then fourteen more, all already sold in town at $850 each. They were black and came with accessories: a hood, windshield, spare tire, rearview mirror, horn, brass headlamps and taillights. By 1913, Ford reduced the cost to $525.[28]

The Ford Company complained that more of their rear axles broke in Appanoose County than any other place in the United States. Luther offered an explanation. The County was the first hilly country for Ford cars at that time. Drivers had to brake down hills, then accelerate up the other side. This put a reverse and forward strain on the axles, Luther told them.

The rear axles were rebuilt. They were made stronger and thicker. Henry Ford wrote to thank Harry Luther.[29]

Luther now opened a garage. Using the skills he'd learned with the Tehuantepec Rubber Company, he operated a vulcanizing outfit with a steam machine to renew tires. He established the town's first curb gas pump and installed a complete auto storage battery service. When local Swedish citizens formed the Centerville Transit Company, he sold them a Ford combined twelve-passenger auto and baggage car. He gave them advice. They opened a taxi service in the Continental Hotel and took passengers to Mystic, Numa and Exline.[30]

Across the town, across the State and across the nation, there was a major consequence to the love affair with the auto. Something had to be done about roads.

Chapter 23

Good Roads Movement

By 1903, the rural mail carriers of Appanoose County had had enough. They faced snow and ice in winter and mud traps in the spring and fall. On foot they became exhausted, leaping between dry "islands" or from side to side of the roads, their feet deep in mud. They joined Iowa's other mail carriers and, at a meeting in Des Moines, called for State action on Iowa's roads. Not only would good roads improve their lives, they said, but, like the telephone and rural deliveries, they would improve the lives of farmers.[1]

Their call was echoed by Iowa's Henry Wallace. Advertisements and articles advocating good roads began appearing in *The Homestead*, Wallace's magazine for farmers. Farm produce, he said, could be moved to towns and railroad depots for more than the present three months a year. Farm income would increase; so would farm property values and the tax base of Iowa's counties. To improve the roads, Henry Wallace championed "the road drag." Its greatest promoter was D. Ward King of Maitland, Nodaway County, northwest Missouri.[2]

On October 31, 1905, a special Burlington train brought King to Centerville. With him was Professor T.H. McDonald of Iowa's new State Highway Commission and representatives of the Burlington and Keokuk and Western Railroads.[3]

At nine o'clock the next morning, D. Ward King addressed a large audience in the courtroom. He showed how to make a drag. He split a log nine or ten inches in diameter into two. The two flat surfaces he faced in the same direction, thirty inches apart and attached each to the other with crosspieces. This simple, inexpensive system will make your roads "from 500 to 1,000 per cent [*sic*] better," he told them. "Sac City," he continued, "has tried it and the race track there is deserted for the roads by horse trainers."[4]

A few hundred spectators followed him outside for a demonstration. They walked to an area including two blocks of West Washington, selected because the road surface there was particularly rough. King attached a team of horses to the first log, climbed on top of the second and drove the horses. Use this process, he said, after a fall of rain. A dozen draggings a year will make the road a smooth surface for travel.

At the close of the event, twenty-five farmers agreed to drag their roads. Prizes were offered by Centerville's Commercial Club, a group of businessmen dedicated to promoting local businesses: fifty dollars for the best mile of dragged road within six miles of Centerville and twenty-five dollars for second prize; ten dollars was offered for the best one-half mile on each mail route, five dollars for second prize.[5]

The County's "Drag Days" became not just an annual road event, but a social one. By 1908 the Retail Merchants Association replaced the Commercial Club. Under the leadership of J.J. Frankel from his store at Stanton's Corner, the association was infused with an energy, a focus, a drive. It awarded more than thirty prizes, provided free hot dinners, free horse feed and merchandise worth five to six dollars from each store on Centerville Square.[6]

The 1913 Drag Day was the biggest one in the State of Iowa. Participants dragged the right-hand sides of their roads from home to Centerville, then the right-hand sides on their return. With 152 drags taking part, the surfaces of 1,791 miles of Appanoose County roads were improved.[7]

On their morning arrival in Centerville, the draggers reported to the front of Harley Link's Photographic Gallery on the Square's Westside and had their individual photographs taken, with a group photograph planned for two o'clock. The draggers then registered at the *Centerville Journal* office, under the *Iowegian* newspaper, on South Main Street. Each registrant received a slip entitling him or her to the thirty prizes and a ticket for dinner served by the Women's Relief Corps in the Grand Army of the Republic room in the courthouse.[8]

The big winner of the day was twenty-year-old Edna Gray. She drove the furthest: thirty-one miles, standing all the way, from the distant reaches of Franklin Township. She left home at three fifteen in the morning and arrived in Centerville Square several hours later, at eleven thirty, so covered with dirt, she said, she felt ashamed. Dirt or not, she was treated like a heroine and picked up prizes all over town, including a rocking chair from Standard Furniture.

The draggers circled the Square, delighting the crowd. There were sixteen drags moving in unison, all flying the Stars and Stripes, and two ten-year-old

Drag Day. *Courtesy of Appanoose County Historical Society.*

girls, Marjorie Faulkner and Juanita Climie, dressed completely in red, white and blue, riding on the drags with their fathers. Mrs. Blanche Talbot, who had driven her drag from Caldwell Township carrying in her arms her seven-month-old baby, was cheered loudly and given a special prize of a velvet rug from Salinger and Goldstein. Fred Pullman attached his drag to his auto, Jockey Thomas to four Shetland ponies, but the biggest applause went to John Mallette from Clarkdale with a specially designed small drag pulled by his pet goat.[9]

If it was the rural mail carriers that helped influence the good roads movement, it was auto drivers who promoted improving long-distance roads.

In America in 1903, Horatio Nelson Jackson, a Burlington, Vermont, doctor recovering from tuberculosis, responded to a fifty-dollar bet. He drove an open twenty-horsepower Winston, with bicycle mechanic Sewell Crocker and a goggle-wearing bulldog named Bud, from San Francisco to New York City in 63½ days. By the time he reached the East Coast, competitors from other auto companies were racing him. Within five years, the fashion reached

Appanoose County. Auto races had cars in competitions to Albia and from Oskaloosa to Centerville.[10]

Across the nation, across the world, long-distance auto races were becoming the fashion: from Paris to Bordeaux, from Peking to Paris and, in 1908, from New York to Paris going west. The races inspired many people to buy autos. They also served as an impetus to governments, civic groups and individuals to build better highways.[11]

In Iowa, groups were developing a River-to-River Road across the State from Davenport to Council Bluffs via Des Moines. In 1912, Oskaloosa's Don McClure, in a green Oakland, raced P.C. Peterson in a Pope-Hartford along the route, arriving in Council Bluffs ten hours and thirty-six minutes later, winning the race by thirty-six minutes.[12]

In Indianapolis in 1912, Carl Graham Fisher suggested a Coast-to-Coast Rock Highway. That was after he'd attached a Stoddard-Dayton to a helium balloon, floated it over the city, built the Indianapolis Motor Speedway, paved it with brick and started the Indianapolis 500. America's Coast-to-Coast Highway was renamed the Lincoln Highway. It would follow a course from New York City to San Francisco, crossing Iowa some sixty miles north of Iowa's River-to-River Road and eighty miles north of Centerville.[13]

In southwestern Iowa, predating both the Lincoln Highway and the River-to-River Road, work was already underway on the Waubonsie Trail, a national highway from Washington, D.C., to San Francisco. On the route, it passed through Indianapolis, Springfield (Illinois), Keokuk, Lincoln and Denver. Between Keokuk and Lincoln, it followed the Mormon Trail across Iowa. This placed Centerville squarely on its route.[14]

The people of the town learned of this road in a meeting of the Wednesday Club on February 9, 1911, in D.C. Bradley's new mansion on Drake Avenue. The speaker was curator E.R. Harlan of the State Historical Society; his subject was the promotion of Iowa's historic trails and associations. The Waubonsie Trail, he told them, named for a chief of the Potawatomi tribe, would be "…a famous transcontinental travel line that will attract tourists across country because of its old associations."[15]

In Centerville, businessmen joined the Waubonsie Trail Association, with its headquarters in Shenandoah, under its president, U.J. Reininger. Farmers residing along the route agreed to keep the road opposite their land in good condition by periodic dragging and filling mudholes. Hills were reduced and grades raised over valleys, culverts and bridges constructed of cement. At each road intersection, three poles were inscribed with a teepee, the insignia of the route.

Underneath, two six-inch black bands were painted, bordering a twelve-inch white one. White signboards, eighteen by forty-eight inches, gave the names of the trails, directions and arrows to towns and their distances.[16]

At crossroad points closer to Centerville, there were extra signs. These measured six by nine feet, exhibited the number of miles to the Courthouse Square and advertised four of the Square's stores: J.J. Frankel's; Ward Howell, shoes; Curtis J. Phillips, clothing; and Standard Furniture.[17]

In 1911, national automobile magazines were directing tourists over the Waubonsie. *Huebingers Map and Guide Book* of 1912 said, "The traveler who once reaches the Waubonsie Trail in Iowa need not ask a single question to keep on the road."[18]

Despite such recommendations, the age of the open road was still remote. For the people of the town, the railroad was the swiftest and most comfortable method for long-distance travel.

By 1904, sixteen daily passenger trains served Centerville. All offered Pullman seats, electric lights, dining cars, improved equipment and comfortable sleeping berths for overnight journeys. They also traveled faster.

The Rock Island tracks from Eldon (thirty-six miles northeast of Centerville) to Kansas City were rebuilt. Eighty-pound steel was laid with miles of rock and gravel ballast. This allowed trains to increase their speed. The California Express cut its journey time from Chicago to Los Angeles by eleven hours.

The opportunities of the railroads attracted the traveling public. The Golden State Limited, en route from Chicago to Los Angeles, Santa Barbara and San Francisco, stopped in Centerville, going west at 5:00 a.m., going east at 1:25 a.m. The El Paso Flyer stopped at 5:15 p.m. going west, 1:00 p.m. going east. At Kansas City, Rock Island passengers could transfer for Jacksonville, Florida, and stations south and east on the Frisco line.[19]

From 1900 on, more travel opportunities became available when the Burlington bought out General Drake's Keokuk and Western. The company's point division offices were moved to Centerville and the roundhouse, where locomotives and cars were repaired, was extended.

On February 5, 1911, the Burlington's new thirty-two-by-ninety-foot depot, with slate roof and brick platforms extending around the building, was opened to local acclaim. Against an interior backdrop of Tiffany brick and dark green "Burlington" woodwork, Mrs. D.C. Bradley served punch. Flower girls handed out 250 carnations. An orchestra played. Members of the Retail Merchants Association greeted members of the public.[20]

With the arrival of the Burlington, the extensive Midwest network system of the Chicago, Burlington and Quincy was now readily accessible. The Burlington offered connecting journeys at Lincoln, Nebraska, for California via the Union Pacific or north to St. Paul to connect to Manitoba, Saskatchewan and the Canadian West via the Canadian Pacific. Also at St. Paul, transfers were available to the crack trains of the Northern Pacific to Wyoming, Montana, Oregon and Washington. The Northern Pacific trains had just broken the world train record, crossing the 3,178 miles from Seattle, Washington, to New York City in 82¼ hours, beating the previous West-to-East-Coast record by five hours and twenty-five minutes.[21]

Both the Rock Island and the Burlington offered from Centerville "low-priced round-trip tickets" for special events and locations: to the Iowa State Fair, to Kansas City baseball games, to the opening of the Mississippi River Dam in Keokuk. Advertisements invited people to visit the Grand Canyon, to see Yellowstone Park: "…it belongs to all the people …have you inspected your property?" And there were "Homeseekers Excursions," offering to show land for sale in Canada, North Dakota, Montana and the American Southwest. Land on the Comanche Indian Reservation was offered for sale by the U.S. government at five dollars an acre; so was the Shoshone Reservation in Wyoming and the Crow Reservation in Montana.[22]

There were private cars and special trains reserved for large parties. They took George Landers and the Fifty-first Regimental Band, personally selected over all other bands by Iowa governor Albert Cummins to accompany him to dedicate memorials to Iowa's Civil War dead on Southern battlefields. They traveled to seven states. They visited Fort Donelson, Shiloh and Vicksburg, retracing the steps of Centerville's Colonels Cornelius Stanton and E.C. Haynes, who six years previously, in 1900, placed markers where the Iowa troops had fought.[23]

More special trains took people to hear President Teddy Roosevelt in Oskaloosa and in Keokuk; they transported Company E, the designated presidential escort, and the much-requested George Landers and the Fifty-first Regimental Band to play at the events.[24]

Some of the trains sped through town without stopping. They carried Mrs. James A. Garfield, widow of the murdered president, and her party on their way to California; the Chicago White Sox, fast asleep at three thirty in the morning on their way to spring training at Mineral Wells, Texas; and six express cars "loaded" with gold bullion labeled as "eggs," going through over the Rock Island line so fast it was "…little more than a blur."[25]

And in 1910, the man who personified gold—John Pierpont Morgan—spent half an hour crossing Appanoose County on the Milwaukee route, ten miles north of Centerville, aboard a replica of the Twentieth Century Limited, so luxurious it was "…one of the finest trains that ever has crossed the state of Iowa." His train, for railroad purposes labeled "the red," was followed by three more "specials," these labeled "the white," "the blue" and "the green." These carried 450 Eastern and Southern bankers, all, with Morgan, on their way to the Thirty-sixth Annual Convention of the American Bankers Association in Los Angeles. For less than one month, the financiers had at their disposal four baggage cars, four buffet or gentleman's club cars, eight for dining, twenty-six compartment, drawing room and sleeping cars—four of which were observation cars, known as ladies' club cars, and each provided with a piano player and a range of records from "Johnnie Get Your Gun" to a Beethoven sonata.[26]

In 1904, people in the town took trains to St. Louis for the World's Fair, officially known as the Louisiana Purchase Exposition. It was opened on April 30 by the click of an electric key under President Roosevelt's hand in Washington, D.C., 730 miles away. Traveling to St. Louis from Centerville was eleven-year-old Israel Futoransky to display his phenomenal typing skills, two local journalists and a crowd of young Centerville men. At the fair, they walked the milelong street called "The Pike." They saw representatives of "every race on earth." They traveled the illusionary Siberian railway and heard recitals on the massive pipe organ in the Iowa Building. They watched the Olympic swimming and diving championships then coinciding with the fair and held in Life Savers' Lake on the western edge of the World's Fair grounds. And they peered through glass to view two twenty-seven-hundred-year-old Egyptian mummies, their bodies wrapped in the original linen, their faces exposed for public viewing.[27]

A year later, people left for the Panama Canal, the vast civil engineering project between the Atlantic and Pacific Oceans, with Centerville's Theodore Perry Shonts as its chief administrator. Neil Stanton, the son of Colonel Cornelius Stanton, went there as operations manager for the Union Oil Company. Lowell Perry, the son of Mr. and Mrs. O.M. Perry, went as a government stenographer, and Eva Shonts, the sister of Theodore Shonts and an aggressive temperance worker, went determined to pressure her brother to outlaw alcohol for men working with steam shovels and bare hands in mud and rain, in temperatures seldom less than 100 degrees, more often 120 to 130 degrees, and fighting malaria and yellow fever at the same time.[28]

Every spring, the J.H. White family came home with trunks and portmanteaus, having spent the winter among the orange blossoms of California. So did the Biddle family and the Williams family of the Square's Northside, who now owned a second home in Pasadena.[29]

Victims came home. There were those who had escaped the San Francisco earthquake, lost everything they owned and slept for weeks in the Golden Gate Park, unable to send letters home to their families, who made frantic daily scans of the *Iowegian* headlines. And there were those not so fortunate: Mrs. Stone and her daughter drowned in the Galveston flood that killed six thousand, their bodies taken for burial to the Felkner Cemetery, four miles west of Centerville.[30]

The trains that served Centerville were powered by steam. They were equipped for and operated over long distances across the country. Between the railroad depots and the Square was the small community street trolley, run originally by mules and then by electricity. An intermediary system was needed, something that, before the advent of good roads, would connect the small towns of the County. It came in the form of the Interurban.

Chapter 24

Modernization: Interurban, Mail-Order Catalogs, Airplanes

By 1900, electric "interurban fever" was sweeping the country and spreading into Iowa. In 1905, Jesse M. Beck, in the editorial office of the *Iowegian*, displayed its symptoms; so did Frank Payne, the head of the Centerville Light and Traction Company.[1]

From his office window over the First National Bank, Payne had watched the workers of his company dismantle the mule track from the railroad depots and replace the three-foot eight-inch gauge with a four-foot eight-inch standard-gauge track of the new trolley service, run by electricity. Now his sight expanded. He visualized a network of linear tracks laid across the green land of Appanoose County. They interlaced the major railroads. They connected people to people, community to community. They could stop at isolated farms, coal mines and villages. And, run by electricity, they were clean, inexpensive and offered frequent service. Above all, Frank Payne could see the unlimited opportunities for Centerville's business community.[2]

In 1905, around Centerville's Courthouse Square, there were seven grocery and meat markets, seven drugstores, five restaurants and hotels, three clothing and millinery establishments, three tailors and an elegant department store, Salinger and Goldstein's. There was a dry goods store, two selling hardware, four banks, a bakery, three jewelers and watchmakers, a bookstore, photographer, cigar-maker and, identified by their red-and-white-striped poles, nine barbershops, where each client was charged twenty-five cents for a haircut, ten cents for a shave, and each had his own shaving mug and had his mustache carefully wrapped in paper before having the rest of his face razored smooth.[3]

Within a block of the Square were plumbers, lumber and brickyards, cement-block companies and iron foundries supplying material for builders and the coal mines. On the corner of East State and Fourteenth Streets for fourteen years was the four-story Bradley and Wells Flour and Grain Mill, turning out one hundred barrels of "the highest patent, straight and clear" flour every twenty-four hours and four hundred bushels of feed and meal, supplying the food industry and County farmers. On Thirteenth Street was a steam laundry and the Centerville Telephone Company, now, under Charles Farrington, extending its toll lines and installing seventeen new telephones a month.[4]

There were also two highly successful businesses that were both started by local entrepreneurs. One was the Pure Ice Company, with ten thousand dollars' worth of equipment making seven tons of the purest ice a day from distilled water drawn from Garfield Pond. It was the brainchild of Steve Martin, who had started as a delivery boy at Stanton's Corner, cut ice for Bill McKee at the Continental Hotel and worked in the coal mines between assignments. His business extended across southern Iowa and into northern Missouri. Local deliveries were by team and wagon to businesses and homes that displayed in their windows the company's red cards requesting delivery.[5]

The second business, started by two local entrepreneurs, was the Hercules Manufacturing Company. Starting in a building on the northeast corner of East Jackson and Fourteenth Streets, forty-nine-year-old Miles Bateman and thirty-six-year-old B.A. "Barney" Fuller developed a tree stump puller so successful in design the company would become the biggest stump-puller manufacturer in the world. In 1905, sales were already extending to every state of the union, to Canada, to the Panama Canal, to South Africa, China, Japan, South America, Australia, Cuba, Puerto Rico, Burma, the Dutch East Indies and to Russia, where it was being used on Czar Nicholas's farm, "Orlovka," at Gatschino, some thirty-six miles from St. Petersburg. A photograph sent to the company of the stump puller in use showed the Russian minister of forestry and—possibly—the Czar himself.[6]

In addition, in the County's fifty-four coal mines operating in 1905, 2,487 miners, lying on their sides, were undercutting and severing 895,000 tons every year from the County's three-foot coal seam, loading them onto mine cars made locally at the Centerville Iron Works or the Joseph Goss Foundry. The cars were pulled by mules or ponies to the bottom of shafts, hoisted above ground, weighed and tipped into railroad cars waiting on sidetracks.[7]

Despite this activity, despite the pride people felt in their new buildings and the manifold town improvements, the business community had reason for concern.

In 1900 an advertisement appeared in a town newspaper. It offered watches, a food chopper, a hanging lamp, a storm collar and a syringe at "Wholesale Prices." At the bottom of the advertisement was a printed box: "Cut this slip out and send it to us with 15 cents in stamps." In return, from Chicago, the customer received a Montgomery Ward mail-order catalog with seventy thousand items at wholesale prices.[8]

Three years later, a cartoon appeared on the front page of the *Iowegian.* It showed a trembling "Home Merchant" watching a wagon labeled "from Sears-Roebuck, Chicago," loaded with boxes and barrels from Montgomery Ward, passing by his store.[9]

The mail-order business was a national phenomenon. Their catalogs were aimed at rural people isolated from the vast range of products sold in good city stores, and they offered them at low prices. A cream separator, for example, important to farmers, had a store price of $100.00. In 1903, Sears brought out three models at $27.00, $35.00, and $39.50. In 1904 the *Iowegian* reported two mail-order houses in Chicago did $62,000,000 worth of business; a year later it was $80,000,000. The catalogs were doing something more: luxuries that were previously the privilege of the wealthy were being turned into "necessities for everyone by the process of mass production and mass marketing."[10]

The 1903 *Iowegian* cartoon was followed by panicky articles, pleas, editorials and even a poem:

Behold a man of Shopless Town;
His name is Obadiah Brown.—
...Instead of buying things for sale
Right here in town, he's sent by mail
For many years and bought his things
From those far off Mail Order things.
No wonder, Obadiah Brown,
This home of yours is Shopless Town![11]

As business continued to languish, Payne's concept to connect the County's small towns to Centerville via the Interurban got the attention of the town. Jesse Beck's editorials led the way: "[Centerville] can become the real commercial center of a splendid contributing territory," he wrote. "Opportunity has knocked. Open." Mass meetings were held, committees formed, money raised and bonds sold; the total was reached after a last-minute, "desperate appeal" with a given deadline of midnight, July 3, 1909.[12]

Work on the new double track began in October. It proceeded north from the Eastside of Centerville Square and Main Street to Madison Street, west to Seventh and alternately north and west for almost seven miles to a terminal opposite the Milwaukee depot in Mystic. On its route it crossed four creeks: Cooper, Hickory, Rock and Walnut, on Cooper and Walnut passing over thirty-foot-span steel bridges. Alongside the track, thirty-five-foot cedar poles were erected with cross arms equipped to carry electricity not just for the train, but at the same time, to light Mystic and to power mines and other industries.[13]

Coincidentally Payne's Light and Traction Company improved its powerhouse on North Thirteenth Street, vastly increasing its horsepower with new tube boilers, power engines, generators, a switchboard, and a combination fire-clay tile and reinforced concrete chimney 140 feet high, six feet in diameter, that now dominated the landscape of the Courthouse Square.[14]

The Interurban service between Centerville and Mystic began with a special dedication run on April 22, 1910. On board were the 165 bond subscribers in Centerville and in Mystic who had made the building of the Interurban possible. Among the group were J.A. and D.C. Bradley, who had contributed together almost twenty-two thousand dollars, and whose father, William Bradley, had come to Centerville in 1856, establishing one successful business after another. Also present were Jesse M. Beck, the editor of the *Iowegian*, and Frank Payne, whose vision of Centerville Square eight years previously, when he had watched the new courthouse being built from his window overlooking the Square, was now realized. The group posed before the camera. The day was cool. They wore hats and overcoats. One supported himself on a cane. They were handed folders with information on the quality of the construction, the powerhouse additions, the improvements planned and the security of their investments. They declared themselves well pleased.[15]

At seven thirty every morning, two green passenger cars of the Interurban departed from the Eastside of Centerville's Courthouse Square. They proceeded up North Main, turned west on Madison to Seventh Street, then north for the twenty-five-minute journey to Mystic. A conductor collected the fares: twenty cents one way; one dollar for three round trips. In a five-minute stop in Mystic, the motorman climbed to the top of the cars and adjusted controls allowing them to change directions, leaving Mystic for Centerville at eight o'clock, a pattern repeated every hour.[16]

Frank Payne, now in partnership with D.C. Bradley, moved his office from the First National Bank to two twenty-foot rooms south of the Owl Drug Store on the Square's Eastside. The north room became the Interurban Waiting

Room, with seats and a spittoon. The south room was President Payne's new office. His company bought land—one hundred by five hundred feet—on the corner of Madison and North Thirteenth Street for repair shops and barns, for switch and freight yards. The ground there was leveled, the "Madison Street hollow" filled up, enabling ease in getting the tracks in from the corner of Main and Madison.[17]

Immediately, the Interurban was a success. "It has proven to be a splendid enterprise for Centerville and is making good returns for its owners," said the *Iowegian*. Farmers in the northwest part of the County were driving their teams to Mystic, leaving them there and taking the Interurban into Centerville. In the first four days of the Interurban's service, businessmen on the Courthouse Square reported an increase in sales, including eleven pairs of shoes and two rolls of carpet—all by travelers on the Mystic track.[18]

In less than two months, "hundreds" were using the train, tempted by a special five-cent ticket. They dismounted at the Interurban Park, a summer resort, northwest of Centerville on Cooper Creek, that came to be known as the Glen Hagan Park.[19]

The park was one-and-a-half miles from the Courthouse Square. On warm May Sundays, people strolled north through the woods and the wildflowers. They crossed Cooper Creek and entered the park. Companies took their employees there for picnics, for dances, for the occasional movie. It became a central attraction for recreation. It was also an anchor for town businesses that supplied its facilities.[20]

On Thursday, June 27, 1912, the Interurban and special trains brought thousands to the park. The event had been publicized for weeks. Posters and bills were placed in store windows around the Square and in small towns across southern Iowa. People paid fifty cents at the entrance, twenty-five cents for those under fifteen. Hundreds more lined the roads to the north, to the west and to the east "without contributing anything themselves," pointed out the *Iowegian*. The attraction was the arrival of Centerville's first aeroplane.[21]

The craft was a white Curtiss box biplane. The pilot sat in an open cockpit. Behind him was the engine. From its crankshaft, chains ran to two propellers mounted behind the wings, which thrust the aircraft forward.[22]

Three times—at four o'clock in the afternoon, five thirty and once again in the evening—people watched the demonstrations. The pilot cranked the engine. He adjusted his goggles and climbed aboard. The plane bumped along the flat land north of Glen Hagan's new country club. It vibrated loudly. It rose into the air. It flew over the heads of the spectators. It circled for five to ten minutes and landed.[23]

Trolley arriving at Glen Hagan Park. *Courtesy of Appanoose County Historical Society.*

When the plane was stationary, people moved forward and examined it. They talked to the pilot. His name was Robert G. Fowler. They had read his name in the newspapers. Nine months earlier he was one of three pilots who flew in a race from coast to coast for a winning purse of fifty thousand dollars offered by William Randolph Hearst. Balloons had been racing each other across America for years. One year before pilot Fowler brought his aircraft to Glen Hagan Park, a balloon racing from Kansas City had passed over downtown Centerville at twelve fifteen one morning, and its occupants called through a megaphone, asking the name of the town. And at Coal City, thirteen miles southeast of Centerville, another balloon in the same race came so low its drag ropes touched the ground, and its pilot, fearing a wood ahead, called out for help; two local men raced to assist, seized the rope and tied it to a stump. But Robert Fowler was not part of a team flying a balloon. He was the hero flying alone in an aeroplane race. He represented the future, and local boys were becoming inspired. Centerville's Pearl Adams, while still a teenager, taught himself to fly and in 1913 invented a hydro-monoplane, his model winning the World's Model Championship at Elmo Field, New York. Pearl gave a lecture the same year in Mystic's United Brethren Church. His subject: "Aviation Past, Present, and Future." In his audience that day—it is tempting to speculate—a nine-year-old Albert Lodwick, the son of a local coal owner, may have been absorbing every word. At the event in Glen Hagan Park and at an Airship Day in Mystic, as he looked at the Curtiss biplane, could he have known that in sixteen years, at the age of twenty-nine, he would be the Curtiss-Wright Corporation's vice president and play a major role in national aviation?[24]

Just west of Centerville's Square, the Interurban track to Mystic crossed the tracks of the Albia and Centerville Steam Railroad, built as an extension of General Drake's MI&N, in partnership with Russell Sage of New York. On the death of General Drake, his interests in the company passed to his son-in-law, Centerville's Dr. J.L. Sawyers; on the death of Russell Sage, to W.A. Boland of New York. Together, Boland and Sawyers renamed the railroad the Southern Iowa Traction Company and made plans for its conversion to an electric Interurban connecting Albia and Centerville with Moravia and Dennis on the line.[25]

Promoting a second Interurban for Centerville, Boland was excited by the possibilities for the town. "I have been an observer of opportunities for investment all over the country…," he told mass meetings in the town. "Centerville should become a great manufacturing city."[26]

By 1912 people watched as a trench was dug on West State Street, up the hill from the railroad terminal built there for General Drake's MI&N in 1871. The depot itself was raised the height of three cement-block layers, the platform moved from the south to the north. In the trench, seventy-pound steel rails were spiked into place and ties laid of first-class oak from Salem, Missouri. The tops of the rails were six inches below the street level; ballast, concrete and brick were inserted, supplying a solid and durable track. Poles were stretched, wire was stretched, but the track remained incomplete, reaching to just the Square's Westside. Frank Payne loaned a car for temporary runs. Teams of horses pulled it across unfinished sections. But Boland and Dr. Sawyers were encountering financial difficulties. In 1914, all their stock was transferred to Frank Payne and D.C. Bradley.[27]

News of the transfer was met with rejoicing. The two men, Payne and Bradley, were described as "two financial wizards." The Mystic Interurban was already the third in the State in net earnings per mile; it was a model of good service and good management. The organizing ability and the operating competence of these two men guaranteed to the town that the Albia line would be "a winner."[28]

Immediately new trolley wires were installed; the track from Madison to Sixth, noted for its curves, was straightened and the West State track discontinued. On Sunday, August 30, 1914, two new green and gleaming passenger cars, delivered from St. Louis, began their run to Albia. People admired them as "handsome" and "metropolitan" in appearance. Each cost seven thousand dollars. Each was forty-six feet in length; each had two compartments—"smokers" and "ladies"; both were made of steel, with side-door entrances, observation ends and a motorman's booth in a corner. An electric freight and a baggage car were added. Both the Mystic and the Albia Interurbans began their journeys from the Square's Eastside.[29]

The long-distance railroads and the Interurbans were changing the County. Big-city newspapers and mail-house catalogs were reaching isolated communities. Ideas were exchanged, meetings attended, speakers heard. Visions expanded. Views enlarged. But the biggest change, and one reflective of the American story, was what was happening to the population.

Chapter 25

Centerville's Jews

For thirty years, beginning in the 1880s, Centerville's newspapers reported the wholesale persecution of Russian and Polish Jews. They reported "…terrible scenes of carnage and bloodshed …bodies of men, women and children being cut down and terribly mutilated …the Russian police and soldiers stood by and offered no resistance." Thousands emigrated to America. Over half a million were crowded into New York's Lower East Side. Many moved on across the country.[1]

Some sixty Jewish families settled in Centerville. In Russia, if not the pogroms, then anti-Semitic prejudice had held them back. But in Centerville as across America, they flourished. They started in menial occupations. They built successful businesses. They became vital contributors to the town's economy and established their own vibrant community.[2]

Aaron Grinspan was the first. He'd left Knyshin in Russia, where he'd learned the weaver's trade so rapidly he'd been made superintendent of the factory. That was before it was known he was a Jew. With his wife, three of six children, no job and "nothing but [his] bare hands," he arrived in Brooklyn and became a master weaver and an expert in wools and cloth. Coming west to Iowa, he was made superintendent of Sherman Brothers Woolen Mill in Des Moines. In 1882 he came on to Centerville, a peddler's pack on his back, and immediately began selling door to door. In less than a year he'd opened a stall on the Levee near the Keokuk and Western depot; in another five he'd expanded it to two South Centerville brick stores; and by 1895 he'd opened a clothing store in the Howell Building on the Southside of the Square. He named it the Bargain Store. It was run by his daughters while he traveled to midwestern city markets seeking bargains, paying cash, building the reputation of his store and importing high fashions, including clothes from Worth of Paris and cashmere underwear. He was about to acquire a partner.[3]

In July 1898, twenty-five-year-old Joe Frankel arrived in Centerville on the early-morning Rock Island train from Peoria, Illinois. Six years previously, in his native Poland, he'd been denied promotion to St. Petersburg because he was a Jew. The same grounds barred him from a university education. Parting from his heartbroken father, he immigrated to America to join three brothers: Charles, Harry and Julius, already running businesses in Peoria. On this July morning, as he climbed aboard the streetcar to the Square, he came as a sales representative for brother Charles's Crockery and Notions Store. In his pocket was a letter of introduction to Aaron Grinspan. It also introduced him to Minnie, Aaron's daughter. By 1905, married for three years to Minnie and the father of a one-year-old daughter, Joe entered a partnership with his father-in-law and stayed in Centerville. The new Grinspan-Frankel store opened to the public in the Stanton Building on the Square's Southwest Corner on March 25; fifteen hundred guests attended. Taylor's town orchestra played music. One hundred dozen carnations were presented to customers who walked the new hardwood floors beneath a sixteen-foot ceiling and examined silks, table linens, hosiery, prints, men's and women's clothing and furniture, all arranged against walls of tinted burlap.[4]

Within five years, Aaron Grinspan, on account of his health, retired. The store, now in just the Frankel name, had a reopening that was another major town attraction. Again the Taylor town orchestra provided music; carnations were given as favors, and frappé was served in the basement. The store was extended onto more floors and a balcony and organized on a city store department plan, with ten women heads of departments, four men and thirty extra clerks for seasonal events and sales. Everything was lit by scores of electric lights—the counters, the displays, the mahogany furnishings and plate-glass mirrors.[5]

For Lewis Salinger, Centerville was his fifth location after emigrating from Poland at the age of seventeen after being denied entrance to university because of his religion. At each place he stopped in the United States, he acquired what would later be valuable mercantile knowledge—bookkeeping in Des Moines, jewelry in St. Paul, clothing in Pocatello and Montpelier, Idaho. He began his business career in Centerville by buying the entire shoe stock of the Surprise Store in 1895 and then offering the shoes at sale prices. He, too, would acquire a partner.

By 1902 he had a partner in Abe Goldstein, who was born in Omaha to Russian immigrant Jews. Salinger and Goldstein took over all three floors of the Lane Building on the Westside of the Square and hired Centerville building contractor B.S. Staley to make sweeping changes. The front stairway was removed, metal ceilings installed, a pair of plate-glass windows inserted and display cabinets and cases, individually lit by electricity, supplied by the Grand Rapids Show Case Company.

Calling themselves "Salinger-and-Goldstein-On-The-Square," their department store would become one of the largest in southern Iowa. Two thousand people came to the opening on August 29, 1903. Music was supplied by Davidson's orchestra. Six hundred favors of roses ran out quickly. The staff, men in blue serge suits, the women in white, were full of apologies. The window displays were pronounced the finest creations Centerville people had ever seen. Richly colored grapevines hanging with fruit intertwined elegant columns studded with shimmering particles and displays of clothing. The store's decorator, Henry Washington, a month later left town, accepting the position of window designer for Marshall Field's of Chicago.

Salinger and Goldstein constantly changed and expanded their merchandise. In 1913, in glass cabinets and cases on the first floor, they displayed 300 hats, 700 suits of clothes, 250 shirts, 700 pairs of men's trousers, 300 overcoats and a boys' suit cabinet holding 300 boys' suits. Like Grinspan and Frankel, they incorporated new ideas observed on business trips to Chicago and New York. After one such visit, they installed an upstairs restroom, covered the floor in green velvet carpet and supplied an easy chair, a davenport, newspapers, magazines, writing materials, a private telephone booth, seven four-by-five-foot beveled plate mirrors and two triple mirrors. It is a place, they said, where a tired mother could rock a restless baby to sleep.[6]

A few of the Jews moved away, seeking larger communities. The Israel brothers, who ran a dry goods store in the Russell block for five years, moved to Des Moines and set up shop across from the Kirkwood House. Moses Rosenbaum, a successful grain dealer in Kuppell, Russia, tried Omaha, then three Iowa cities—What Cheer, Oskaloosa and Centerville—before opening a successful shoe store in Ottumwa. But his three sons remained in Centerville.[7]

In 1893, Moses's son, twenty-three-year-old Sol Rosenbaum, bought a ramshackle wooden building on the Northeast Corner of the Square and sold secondhand furniture. In two years he'd moved across the Square and began shifting his stock to new furniture. In 1908, taking a long-term lease at his business on the Westside occupying three floors, he built a thirty-foot balcony, installed an elevator and advertised a complete stock of up-to-date house furnishings. He called it the People's Furniture Store. Managing it was his son, Lewis, and brother-in-law Louie Ritchell. Sol's older brother, Joseph, opened a scrap-metal yard on South Eighteenth Street—the Levee—in 1895. It grew rapidly into a large plant, called one of the largest in the Midwest. He diversified his lines of brokerage, employed eighty to one hundred workers and in 1911 took on one of his seven children, Sam, as partner and hired another Russian refugee—Jack Levine, who married Joe's daughter. Sol's younger brother, Levi, opened a grocery store in a dilapidated wooden building on South Eighteenth Street. He expanded and improved his services, built a new brick structure and enjoyed a prosperous trade servicing a territory with a thirty-mile radius.[8]

Jewish businesses were now flourishing. On South Eighteenth Street, the Levee, in addition to the Rosenbaum Metal Scrap Yard and the Rosenbaum Grocery there were two enterprises belonging to Hyman Chapman from Russia. One was a grocery store; the other, on the corner of Elm, was a pop factory. Increasing its output ten times in less than twenty years, the plant produced thirty-five different flavors of soft drinks, twelve sold in quart capacities, including ginger ale, birch beer, two phosphates—orange and wild cherry—a cream soda, raspberry and strawberry wines and several ciders, including a "champagne cider." Every day workers packed forty-eight hundred bottles into two hundred wooden cases. They were delivered by cart to the railroad depots for distribution to surrounding towns and cities. On each bottle was affixed the firm's trademark: a picture and the words "Chapman's Twins."[9]

Around the Square, the story was the same. On West VanBuren, James Gavronsky from Riga, Russia, opened the Reliable Culvert Manufacturing Company. On the Northside, Hyman Chapman's brother, Nathan, opened a merchandise store; on the Westside, Gaba and Bromberg Clothing and Furs. Just off the Square, on South Thirteenth, Joe Goldstein (no relation to Abe) from Warsaw, Poland, opened his own business and became known as Joe-the-Tailor. He was just twenty years old and was sent as foreman to a shirt factory in the *Iowegian* building on South Main. It took him, he later said, just eight months to see what a good town Centerville was for his own business. He gave the shirt factory one month's notice.[10]

On the Westside, Max Futoransky, whose eleven-year-old son, Israel, was a typing phenomenon at the St. Louis World's Fair, leased a room from the *Journal* newspaper and opened the Centerville Grocery and Wall Paper Supply House. One door south of the Centerville National Bank, on the corner of State Street, was Friedlanders Clothing Store, which specialized in mohairs, madras shirts "with and without collar attachments," and men's union suits for underwear. In rooms behind the Centerville National Bank, an Austrian Jew, J.O. Schutzbank, opened the Reliable Merchant Tailoring House. Schooled in the best tailoring houses in Lemburg and Vienna and, after arriving in New York City, at the Mitchell School of Garment Cutting, he steadily increased his patronage. Customers arrived at his store. They viewed photographs of new styles sent every month from Mitchells—the only store in town with this service. Clients then ordered their clothes, selecting the style and the finest woolens of the store.[11]

On the corner of Fifteenth Street and Terry in 1894, the Jews of Centerville built their synagogue. They named it "B'nai Israel." Six-pointed Stars of David decorated eleven stained-glass windows, each donated by a Jewish family, their names inscribed beneath. A gallery separated women from the men. A scroll of the Torah was placed in an ark on the east wall, beneath a tabernacle, and candles glowed from chandeliers. Here, Centerville Jews gathered for their Sabbath—from three stars in the sky at Friday sunset to three stars on Saturday. Here they came for their festivals, walking along Fifteenth Street, the men in long black robes, the ultraconservative in brimmed hats and "peyes"—long strands of twisted, curling hair in front of their ears. They came for Yom Kippur, their day of atonement, for Rosh Hashanah, the New Year; for the Fast of Tamuz; for Hanukkah, the Festival of Lights. And here they came for funerals—burying their dead according to their custom in the Hebrew cemetery north of town, the body dressed in plain, white, shroud-like burial clothing and placed in a wooden coffin, the mourners tossing a piece of fresh grass over their shoulders as they left.[12]

Nearby at the synagogue on East Sheridan two more buildings were built; a parsonage for the rabbi and a school where children studied Hebrew every day from four to six o'clock. They came after attending Centerville's public schools, where they excelled academically, winning scholarships to America's colleges and universities, seizing and embracing the opportunity for higher education that had been denied their parents in their countries of origin.[13]

Always they read international news reports and were moved by the continued sufferings of members of their own faith. They collected money for Jews in mob-stricken Russia. They invited to town a Zionist speaker, M. Goodman of Chicago. In response they formed a lodge—the B'Nai Israel Gate, with dues of seventy-five cents a year paid to the national lodge, fifty cents of which was devoted to a four-million-dollar fund based in Austria but largely raised in America, with the aim of buying Palestine and Jerusalem as a permanent Jewish home. An auxiliary lodge was also formed, this for the

Hebrew class with Himie Voxman in back row, second from left. *Courtesy of Bill Voxman.*

young Jewish men and women of the town. They called themselves the Sons and Daughters of Zion.[14]

As a social community they were exemplary. They formed business networks with Des Moines, Omaha, St. Joseph, Kansas City, Peoria and Chicago, at the same time providing social opportunities for their sons and daughters when marrying outside their faith was strongly disapproved. They assisted friends and relatives in immigrating to America and gave support until they were self-sufficient. When they heard Joe Shkolnick, a plumber from Kiev, was in Des Moines with a pregnant wife and two children, couldn't speak English, couldn't find work and was down to his last sixty-five dollars, they brought the family to Centerville. The town plumber was then Carl Polson, a Swedish Lutheran combining plumbing with his South Centerville hardware store, with too much work and no one to help. Polson hired Joe and went further—he had him live with him until he spoke English. Then, with financial backing from banker D.C. Bradley, Polson helped Joe establish his own highly successful plumbing business, first in South Centerville, and then on Twelfth Street, just off the Square.[15]

The Jews of Centerville moved beyond the confines of their own businesses and supported the economy of the wider community. They invested in new non-Jewish businesses—the Pure Ice Company, the Hercules Manufacturing Company, the Centerville Gypsum Company and the Interurban Train Service connecting Centerville to surrounding towns. They were active in achieving paved roads, extending electric lights and giving teeth to the Commercial Club by joining it, becoming leaders and transforming it into the proactive Retail Merchants Association.[16]

For forty years the Jewish community was a vital force in the economy of the town, and its members, with some notable exceptions, were absorbed into the accepted social hierarchy of the town. The story would be different for the town's African Americans.

Chapter 26
Centerville's African Americans

On the afternoon of January 20, 1900, Booker T. Washington, the forty-two-year-old president of the Tuskegee Institute, the country's leading African American, arrived in town. He was invited to speak as part of the Union League Lecture Series run by the superintendent of schools, F.E. King. He stayed in the Continental Hotel on Centerville Square. The town people treated him with deference and courtesy.

That night, he spoke at the Armory Opera House on Drake Avenue. It was the largest audience that had ever gathered there. Every seat was full. Extra seats were moved onto the stage. Scores stood in the aisles and around the doorways. Thirty-six people traveled from Corydon. They included the editors of the *Times Republican* and the *Wayne County Democrat* and the "best people in town." A free seat was given to any African American. They sat together in the balcony.[1]

Washington was introduced by former governor Drake. He complimented the speaker for the leadership of his race. He outlined Booker T. Washington's life: how he was born into slavery; how, on emancipation when he was nine, he supported his mother by working in the West Virginia coal mines; how he walked miles to General Armstrong's School in Hampton, Virginia, and secured an education; and how he'd started the Tuskegee Institute and now, at forty-two, was president, supervising eighty-one teachers and the education of more than one thousand students.

Washington rose to speak. People noted his excellent physique, his keen eyes, his intelligent face. He thanked the ex-governor for his compliments and swiftly addressed the issue of race. He opposed, he said, all suggestions for the return of the Negro to Africa or setting apart some separate territory in the United States to live on, like American Indian reservations. His voice was clear, his oratory unparalleled. Show me a man who hates a Negro, he continued, and I will show you a narrow-minded man. There is only one solution to race relations: that the white man can treat the Negro as a Christian gentleman and that the Negro so lives to deserve such treatment. Thrift, economy, industry, knowledge and power to perform must be linked together in the minds and hearts of the Negro. They don't want charity, he told the audience. They want teachers and leaders. He looked up at the African Americans in the gallery. There was a perceptive increase in their attention. Open a bank account, he said; secure your own home and live in it, and the two races can fight hand in hand for the good of each other.[2]

For Americans of African descent, the County's shared border with slave state Missouri was more than an inconvenience. It was a major obstacle. Until the end of the Civil War, escaping slaves were moved rapidly north out of the County. Those arriving with slave owners were quickly manumitted under Iowa law and left the area—one ex-slave moving as far as Oregon. Those employed as free men were in constant danger of abduction from across the border to be "returned" to slavery. Business people employing them could be harassed, their property damaged. Despite these risks, the 1850 census lists seven Americans of African descent living in the County, thirteen in 1860. Little is known of these earliest citizens. Possibly they were escaping slaves temporarily lodged in protective homes. Miriam Pritchard, going to school in Cincinnati, south of the Square, in the 1850s, remembered "...four Negroes—all grown men—at that school—diligent students trying to learn the alphabet. They stayed at Luther Holbrook's."[3]

The earliest permanent County residents of African descent came to the County at the end of the Civil War. The first was a child. When the son of one of Appanoose County's first residents, Colonel James Wells, found a nine-year-old African American boy following him three times in Texas, where he'd gone to buy ponies, he repeatedly returned him until his mother agreed to her son coming north. Wells brought him to Hilltown, some thirty miles southeast of Centerville, and on his death bequeathed him the land, making Frank Wells one of Iowa's few African American farmers and landowners.[4]

The second permanent resident was also a boy brought north from the South. He was unsure of his age, estimated to be six, but sure of his name—George—and that of his family's owner, Mr. Allen. George Allen became his name. For the slaves of Jackson, Mississippi, emancipation reached them five months late. In the melee following that city's fall in May 1863, in the chaos of slaves fleeing owners and jostling and wounded soldiers making for the river, George became separated and lost from his parents.

Appanoose County's Dr. Nathan Udell, an early Democrat but a convert to Republicanism and then a surgeon with Iowa's Seventeenth Infantry, found him crying and brought him to Centerville. George was passed on to several local families before being raised by John Conger, one of the County's earliest abolitionists. When Conger moved west into neighboring Wayne County, George went with him. Always hardworking and well-liked, George appears in a photograph, presented to the Prairie Trails Museum of Wayne County by Mose Sager of Seymour, with his white friends sitting at the front of a porch in full sunshine. George stands alone behind them, arms folded, in the shadows.[5]

The first family to arrive was the merged family of Isum Trent and his widowed sister, Mary Walden. J.C. Harvey, writing in 1931, remembered them coming to Hibbsville, some six miles south and west of the town, at the end of the Civil War and then moving into Centerville. George Merritt, manager of the *Citizen* newspaper, remembered this family attracting much attention and living in a house on the Southside of the Square. "The white people would gather around the house and lot and watch those little Negro children playing in the yard for hours," wrote Merritt. In the 1870 City election—as soon as the "whites only" clause was eliminated from Iowa's Code—Isum Trent ran for Centerville's City Council. He was not elected but received "many votes." He was regarded as a "worthy man," owned a team of horses, built a brick house in the east part of town and another for Mary Walden's family close by.[6]

From this early nucleus, the African American population expanded. In the 1870 census there were 35 African Americans; by 1880 the number doubled to 74, doubling again in 1885 to 145. The new immigrants were following a national pattern. They were flowing north out of the increasingly dangerous Southern states, where they suffered disenfranchisement, outright discrimination, humiliations, brutality and lynchings: in just one year alone, 1892, there were 155 lynchings in the United States.[7]

Iowa offered the new immigrants safer legal protection, economic opportunity, integrated schools and access to higher education. An African American, Alexander Clark Jr., had graduated from the University of Iowa in 1879 with a law degree. S. Joe Brown from Keosauqua in Van Buren County, a graduate of Ottumwa High School, had been elected to Phi Beta Kappa in 1898, achieved an M.A. from the University of Iowa and in 1902 became one of the State's leading lawyers. In 1902 he had appeared in the district court in Centerville, "showing himself," said the *Centerville Citizen*, "to be a bright and able lawyer."[8]

Of Centerville's African American population, at least five of the men were Civil War veterans who, on emancipation, had immediately volunteered for U.S. Forty-seventh, Fifty-sixth or Sixty-seventh or Iowa's own U.S. Sixtieth Colored Infantry Regiments. Many of both sexes were slaves and had been subjected to degrading and violent events; they included accounts of slave markets. They lived mixed into the community, living on the extreme west end of Washington Street, West Van Buren and near the Felkner farm west of town and the Wilson farm near Unionville. They worked on town property, in the courthouse, on lawns, gardens and farms, in coal mines, as household help and as surrogate mothers. Tom Ridding was a driver to Dr. Charles James, considered one of the town's and the Midwest's most skilled and leading surgeons. Tom frequently aided Dr. James in medical emergencies, earning the local title "Dr. Tom."[9]

When an adventurous young African American teenager by the name of Joe E. Herriford arrived in town, leaving his former-slave parents behind in Chillicothe, Missouri, Susannah McKee, proprietress of the Continental Hotel on the Square's Eastside, recognized his intelligence, his drive and his work ethic. Joe lived and worked at the Continental, running errands, shining shoes at a nickel a shine, attending Centerville High School at Ms. McKee's insistence and treated by Ms. McKee "as though [he] was one of her own children." On his errands across the Square, General (later Governor) Drake often patted him on the shoulder and told him to "[k]eep at it young man." In 1885, Joseph E. Herriford walked across the stage of Russell Hall on the Square's Northwest Corner with seven other graduating students. This made Joe the first graduating African American high school student in the County. He immediately entered Drake University—sponsored and supported by Centerville's Francis Marion Drake, for whom the university is named.[10]

At least four times a year, Centerville's African American community celebrated events, inviting all the townspeople to join them. In late September, on Emancipation Day, they organized a parade, provided a "sumptuous" dinner and gave a program with speeches honoring Abraham Lincoln at the fairgrounds, followed by a dance at Russell Hall on the Square's Northwest Corner. In summer there were ice cream socials, picnics, cake walks and baseball games. At Christmastime, "about 100 of their white friends" were present in a building decorated with flowers, drapery and "Aunt" Betty Cook's lace curtains to enjoy music by the town's mandolin club, sacred songs, solos, recitations, readings and speeches. They opened a church: the Second

Second Baptist Church. *Courtesy of Appanoose County Historical Society.*

Baptist, in a house owned by B.P. Mells. It burned—"the cause of the fire is unknown, and no one had been known to have been in the building for ten days," reported the *Centerville Citizen* on March 25, 1886. They converted the old Lane Hall, west of the Square, as a temporary replacement, then moved to South Nineteenth Street, to the basement of Bradley's First National Bank on the Square's Westside, to East Jackson off the Eastside, until General—now Governor—F.M. Drake gave them land and fifty dollars in cash to build the permanent Second Baptist Church on South Eighteenth Street.[11]

Denied in slavery the right to learn to read, they focused on education, absorbing the alphabet, reading books and ensuring that their children took advantage of Iowa's integrated school system. They took seriously their right to vote, listened to public speakers and informed themselves on issues. J.A. Bandy, a sergeant in the Civil War, gave public lectures on his slave life to the Methodist church, the Grand Army of the Republic and the John Bashore Post. In 1898 they met to form an organization to better their condition. They named it the Afro-American Political Club. In the 1900 election, they met in the Mayfield-Kearney Barber Shop on the Northside of Centerville Square and formed a "Colored Rough Rider Club" in support of the McKinley-Roosevelt ticket. And when they died, they were buried in graves interspersed among the graves of white citizens in Centerville's integrated Oakland Cemetery.[12]

The racial segregation of the audience that night listening to Booker T. Washington at the Armory Opera House was accidental. Free seats were given to African Americans. Either by design or personal choice, they sat together. The image was a pivotal moment in the County's history. The Jim Crow laws of the South, reinforced by the Supreme Court's support of "separate but equal laws" in the 1896 *Plessy v. Ferguson* case, legitimized prejudice and fanned the bigotry of some of Appanoose County's citizens.[13]

Chapter 27

Race Relations in Centerville

A pattern of racial segregation was seeping through the nation. It was in every federal department. In the South, black postmasters were summarily fired. Amendment XV of the U.S. Constitution, adopted in 1870 and guaranteeing that the right to vote "…shall not be denied or abridged …on account of race, color, or previous condition," was openly flouted in twelve Southern states and reinforced by terror. In Iowa, "the bright, radical star" that had given African Americans the right to vote two years before Amendment XV, the laws of equal justice—de jure—remained intact. De facto was another issue.[1]

Robert N. Hyde, a prominent Des Moines African-African, the inventor of a carpet sweeper and H and H Cleaning Soap, entered the J.A. Davis Restaurant in Moulton, some ten miles Southeast of Centerville in 1902. He was refused service. He sued, using two African American attorneys: George Woodson and S. Joe Brown, the Phi Delta Kappa graduate of the University of Iowa. The case was tried in district court in Centerville with a local jury. Hyde lost. The *Centerville Journal*, the most radically prejudiced of Centerville's newspapers and run by the Rinehart family of Moulton, declared the people attending court that day were "amused and entertained." Hyde was described as "influential, has been a delegate to every republican state convention for several years has attended the last three National Republican Conventions …such petting has made him vindictive, arrogant, and bigoted."[2]

When the Fireman's Fall Carnival was celebrated in town, the firemen advertised for a couple to be married as a central event: "Wanted," said the advertisement, "a white couple." When a new amusement hall and roller skating rink opened on North Tenth Street, the manager, F.R. Young, invited all "white" persons of good moral character "for wholesome entertainment." Racial stereotypes were long promoted and preserved by all the newspapers in the reporting of local crime. All over Centerville and Appanoose County, women and men got drunk, spat on the sidewalks, fought and shot and knifed each other; they broke out of jail, attacked the sheriff, beat up their wives, killed their husbands, had abortions, committed bigamy, committed suicide, kept houses of ill fame and suffered from "private diseases." Burglars broke into banks, doctor's offices, hardware, grocery, clothing and drugstores and even the courthouse. They played craps on the sidewalk of South Centerville, threw dice for a dollar on the sidewalk outside the Continental Hotel and caused public disturbances, interrupting public speakers and funerals. But when the perpetrators were African American, they were always identified as "colored."[3]

At this time, a new and, in terms of subsequent world history, sinister force arrived in Centerville. In 1903 Harry Hamilton Laughlin was appointed Centerville High School's principal. He came from Kirksville, Missouri, stayed two years, returned to Kirksville as superintendent of schools, became professor of agriculture at Kirksville Normal School (now Truman State University) and then moved to Long Island, New York.[4]

There, at Cold Spring Harbor from 1910 to 1939, he was superintendent of the Eugenics Record Office, working closely with Charles Davenport, evolving their theories of racial superiority together. Within four years, Laughlin was writing on purifying "…the breeding stock of the race at all costs with a three-pronged program of sterilization, mass-incarceration and sweeping immigration." From 1907 on, twenty-nine states had compulsory sterilization laws, including Iowa, which "…authorized the operation for criminals, idiots, feebleminded, imbeciles, drunkards, drug fiends, epileptics, plus 'moral or sexual perverts' in its custody." Laughlin gave evidence to a U.S. Congressional committee on the "…bad breeding stock that was entering the country and spoiling its inborn national qualities," creating immigration laws in favor of "superior" Nordic immigrants.[5]

By the 1920s, Laughlin's theories had crossed the Atlantic. They were adopted by three of Germany's leading eugenicists, all of whom influenced Adolf Hitler, who fused the theories with his own inner nightmares, unleashing them upon the world. In 1935, after Hitler had come to power, after the Nuremberg Laws, the Nazis recognized Laughlin's influence, giving him an honorary degree from Heidelburg University and describing him as "one of the most important pioneers on the field of racial hygiene."[6]

Harry Laughlin. *Courtesy of Special Collections Department, Pickler Memorial Library, Truman State University.*

At what point Laughlin was in his thinking when he was in Centerville is not possible to decipher. But there are hints. Before he arrived, he described his students in rural Livonia in northern Missouri as "very dull," the school as "20 miles from any civilized animals," and the local people as "75 years behind the times." During his tenure in Centerville, there were unspecified complaints from town business people and accusations of poor discipline at the high school. The president of the school board and two other members wanted to reduce his salary. Serious scuffles occurred between the junior and senior classes. They fought over which class colors would fly over the school. And when the senior class placed a boulder to dedicate to the graduating class of 1905 on the school grounds, the junior class dug a deep hole alongside and rolled it in. The senior class hired a winch and raised it. Some nights later the boulder was blown to pieces by dynamite, breaking eight or ten high school windows and terrorizing the neighborhood.[7]

It is tempting to speculate what role an integrated school system played in the complaints. Laughlin had no such experience in Missouri. But in Iowa, in Centerville, he taught the children of African Americans, Jews, Southern Italians, Sicilians, Croatians, Greeks, Turks and Syrians, as well as those northern Europeans he considered of "superior stock." All the newspapers in town described Laughlin as "brilliant," but his biggest supporter—suspiciously—was the racist *Centerville Journal*.

Laughlin wrote to his mother that his candidates for the school board were beaten, and it was they who had promised to vote for him for superintendent in place of F.E. King, who had moved to Ames. He ended the letter, "I didn't want the place anyhow." Laughlin left Centerville in May 1905.[8]

In September 1905, four months after Laughlin's departure from town, the Drake Free Public Library listed new books added to its collection. Top of the list was "Dixon ...*The Clansman*." It is a novel so imbued with racial hatred, so infused with fears of rape and miscegenation, that the book placed on author Thomas Dixon a serous onus. He was said to be "among the individuals who must share the heaviest responsibility for the radical deepening and broadening of race hatred that occurred in the first decades of the twentieth century in the United States." In another ten years, the book would be made into a movie, *The Birth of a Nation*. Then its influence across the country would be incalculable.[9]

More damage was done in an incendiary speech given in town in 1906 by "Pitchfork" Ben Tillman of South Carolina. He cheerily defied law and justified white domination of African Americans by any means, including murder. "They told our children they were getting ready to kill off the white men, take their women for wives, and make the children serve them as they had once served us. That made us frantic," Tillman said. He talked of voting early and late and often and stuffing ballot boxes so Southern whites remained dominant though outnumbered. "Extermination could be carried out," he said, "but we don't want to do that so domination is the remedy."[10]

Around town, people discussed the speech for days. Its timing must have reinforced those readers of *The Clansman* unwilling to, or incapable of, challenging Dixon's fiction. Civil War veterans were particularly incensed. Tillman had attacked and undermined the justification for their sacrifices and sufferings. To make it worse, he talked of the ease with which Southern soldiers had defeated Northern soldiers when numbers were equal. Out of his selective reasoning, he must have forgotten the Hornets' Nest stand. He must also have been unaware that his audience had not. It was their comrades who, hopelessly outnumbered, had given Ulysses S. Grant the five critical hours to replan, and then win, the Battle of Shiloh for the North.[11]

Jesse M. Beck, the new editor of the *Semi-Weekly Iowegian*, was shocked by the speech. He described it as uncontrolled savagery. "…[S]uch intemperate remarks will never bring peace between the races," he wrote. When Tillman spoke in Des Moines, one newspaper there was more blunt. "…[H]ad he been on as bitter a tirade on the Irish as on the Negro he wouldn't have lasted many minutes, tho' there are twice as many Negroes as Irish in Des Moines." J.M. Beck quoted it in his editorial.[12]

Things for African Americans would only get worse. In 1909, a change-of-venue case came to Appanoose County from Ottumwa. On February 5 of that year, Clara Rosen, soloist and choir singer in the Swedish Lutheran Church in Ottumwa, was attacked, raped and murdered on Gara Street. She was on her way to a lecture at Ottumwa's Methodist church. She was the daughter of a prominent merchant, engaged to be married. She was admired, beautiful, loved and white. Charged with the crime was John Junkin, twenty-six, reform school and penitentiary graduate, opium, cocaine and alcohol addict, inhabitant of Ottumwa's notorious Smoky Row and black. It was a case calculated to fuel and massage the sexual component of white bigotry. Lynch mobs threatened in Ottumwa, Albia, Des Moines, Sigourney and Burlington, each place where Junkin was moved for his safety. Centerville was chosen for the trial, because "it has been the least subject …to the excitement of the mob spirit."[13]

Junkin arrived in Centerville secreted in the baggage van of the 2:33 a.m. westbound Rock Island train. Appanoose County Sheriff John Clark and three deputies transported him to the St. Louis steel cage inside the County jail, north of the Square. Rumors of mobs coming from Ottumwa constantly circulated the town. Two hundred and fifty men were coming on the night train. Local citizens volunteered to be at the station. When the mob failed to arrive, another rumor was heard: the story was a ruse, a trick to distract authorities. The mob members were on horseback. They were coming through woods and across fields and entering Centerville from the northeast. Ex-sheriff William Bray joined Sheriff Clark. He assembled twelve town volunteers to guard Junkin. They worked in sleep rotations at the jail, moving out criminals guilty of lesser crimes. Citizens volunteered as a secret service. They mingled in crowds, joined talks on street corners and visited bars, listening to gossip designed to incite violence. They were joined by Ottumwa detectives. We know every rabble-rouser in our City, they told Sheriff Clark; if they've come to Centerville, we'll know them.[14]

The trial began on May 25, 1909.[15]

Chapter 28

The John Junkin Trial

Before daylight, John Junkin, surrounded by guards, was hurried to the room on the northwest corner of the courthouse's third floor. The trial was conducted by Judge M.A. Roberts of Ottumwa. Junkin was brought into the courtroom along a private passageway and into an entrance on the north side, next to the bench. He wore a dark suit, a light shirt with white turndown collar and a tie, and he carried a derby hat. His demeanor was quiet and controlled. He listened quietly as thirty-nine potential jurors were examined and twelve selected. Records show those who expressed racial prejudice were excluded. Henry Johnson, an African American, was excused. So were four men who opposed the death penalty.[1]

Newspaper reporters sat at a press bench taking notes. Among them was Ruby Rinehart, the daughter of James Rinehart, editor of the *Centerville Journal.* She listened dispassionately, writing the accounts of rape and murder without fear and in a businesslike manner. People called her "the youngest newspaper woman in the world." She was twelve years old. Messengers took the reporters' dispatches quietly from the courtroom, then raced across the Square to the Western Union telegraph office in the Continental Hotel on the Eastside. There, an extra operator was hired to assist in sending wire reports to all Iowa newspapers and to the Associated Press through its Chicago office.[2]

Lawyers for the prosecution and the defense hurried up and down the courthouse stairways bringing witnesses. Jury members were sequestered. They slept on cots that scattered the courthouse top floor, making the place resemble, said the *Semi-Weekly Iowegian*, a city hotel at convention time. The paper went on to report the activity in the courthouse related to the trial, as well as testimony from key witnesses. Food was delivered from the Saratoga Restaurant. A court bailiff accompanied any jurors that had occasion to leave the building. For the prosecution, Clara Rosen's mother identified her daughter's clothing, her jewelry, purse and engagement ring. Mrs. Ray Clutter, who had known Junkin since childhood, told how, three hours after the murder, Junkin called her from bed. He "asked me to write Warden Sanders of the Ft. Madison pen," she said. "Said to write that he was getting along nicely, was being a good boy, working at the chop house, and hadn't been drinking. I wrote it for him. He staid [*sic*] about half hour. He stood up all time. While writing he threw ring down on paper where I was writing and asked if it was any good." She identified Clara Rosen's ring to the court.

Jacob Redman, an Ottumwa Jewish pawnbroker whose accent and descriptions of bartering brought the court to laughter, described a diamond Junkin brought to him, saying he'd found it on the corner of Jefferson and Main. "I told him it was cut glass, would give him 25¢ for it. He wanted $8 and put it back in his mouth. I called boy to look at it. Said to me in Jewish, 'It's a good one.' Boy thot [*sic*] I didn't know it was diamond but I did. (laughter). We stood there and didn't say anything. You know how business is done. (laughter) Finally I offered him a dollar, then $3 and he took out of mouth and finally we made a deal at $5.75." Redman's suspicions were aroused. He was afraid Junkin would return for the diamond. Redman got his family to bed early. Next morning, he contacted Ottumwa chief of police Peter Gallagher, taking the bill of sale, which Junkin had signed using a false name.

The evidence of Ottumwa patrolman Frank Harris was the prosecution's second attempt to introduce vital evidence resulting from Junkin's confession, made in a "sweat" in Albia jail. Before it was ruled out, he described finding Clara Rosen's ring, where Junkin had confessed it would be: at the seven-foot, second sewer trap at Ottumwa's Milwaukee depot.[3]

Junkin's mother was the first witness for the defense. She said she was born into slavery in Missouri, came to Iowa and married an alcoholic, who had been dead for eight years. "John was sent to reform school when 9 yrs. old," she told the court. "I made application because he was a bad little fellow. I couldn't control him …He would play truant, fight, and steal. I would whip him but it did no good. He would go and fight again."

Junkin also gave evidence. He described how he drank whiskey and smoked opium by the age of nine when he entered reform school, emerging seven years later at sixteen. He then listed his moves and jobs before entering the penitentiary at twenty-one for robbery. In those intervening five years, there were seventeen moves and jobs, including one as a bellhop at Centerville's Continental Hotel. "I had some cocaine at pen, also a little gum opium. While there had been about 6 talcum powder boxes that was smuggled in. Just found it in cell."

The defense called on two alienists. One, Dr. H.J. Hoeve, professor of anatomy at Drake University Medical School, told the court he made a special study of the skull with reference to criminology. He had dissected 350, he said, and had 40 or 50 in his possession. He looked at Junkin: "He is a typical criminal by birth, environment, and education," he said. "I never saw a more complete specimen of a degenerate." Professor Hoeve held up the skull of Billy Arholt, a Chicago hold-up man, and pointed to a bulge. Junkin, he said, has the same mark. The arch of Junkin's palate, he said, is very high. He "has a bully like, don't care walk." Junkin was told to stand. "His arms are too long," the professor continued, "his lower jaw too large, the back of his neck too thick." Dr. Hoeve pointed for the jury to Junkin's "big feet, long arms, great distance between the ears, large jaw, thick neck, heavy lips, large nostrils."

In charge of John Junkin's defense was Judge J.C. Mitchell. In his summation, he told the court he opposed capital punishment on principle. His attitude to race, however, was quite different. "I am of Virginia and Kentucky blood," he said. "I have their view of the Negro. I believe our greatest mistake was when we adopted the 15th Amendment and put him on an equal with the white man."[4]

At 7:55 p.m. on Tuesday, June 1, the jury returned its verdict. Junkin was declared guilty and sentenced to death by hanging. The prisoner appeared stoical, calm and controlled. When asked by Judge Roberts if he had anything to say, he shook his head. He was led from the court. Clara Rosen's brother, with a gun, rushed officers on the circular back stairs before being disarmed. Her parents thanked the jury. Cheering broke out among a crowd at the courtroom door. Judge Roberts ordered "this nonsense" to stop.

Outside people came running, assembling on the north courthouse lawn. For the first time, they appeared threatening. Ex-sheriff Bray, handcuffed to Junkin and surrounded by twenty-five armed guards, pushed through the crowd, beating off potential attackers with clubs. Junkin was rushed to the Interurban streetcar that raced at top speed to a waiting Rock Island train for the journey to Fort Madison and its prison.[5]

Judge Mitchell now appealed to the Iowa Supreme Court for a new trial for Junkin. Harry Laughlin's influence permeated his words. Mitchell described Junkin as a moral pervert. He went further: "When he stands," said Judge Mitchell, "he looks like a baboon standing on its hind legs. His massive arms hang almost to his knees. If he were stripped and put in a cage he could easily be passed off upon the unwary as a beast the nearest to a man in the transition from beast to man." The appeal was denied.[6]

Junkin was executed at 12:20 p.m. on July 29, 1910, in Fort Madison Prison by Appanoose County sheriff John Clark. He used a fifty-foot, three-quarter-inch hemp rope ordered through Davison Brothers Hardware on the Northside of Centerville Square. It was a slow death. The neck was not broken. Before he died, Junkin apologized to his mother for all the trouble he had caused her and asked forgiveness of the family of Clara Rosen. He donated his body to Professor Hoeve.[7]

For some years afterward, the professor gave public lectures on his examination of Junkin's body. He used slides to illustrate his talk. He pointed out to his audiences how the brain of Junkin was more like that of an animal than a human being. The brain was almost smooth, like the "brain of a beast," he said, instead of full of convolutions like a normal human being. The cells of the brain were far apart—another animal likeness—not close together, and the cells were not deep. He held up a portion of Junkin's breast, stating it was covered with a layer of muscle ordinarily discovered only in the development of the lower animal. Sometime later, Drake University fired Professor Hoeve. Two reasons were given for the request for his resignation. It was charged he had not attended church in two years and he stayed out nights with the boys and had a bad influence over them.[8]

It would take more to reestablish equilibrium in Centerville. Jesse M. Beck, editor of the *Semi-Weekly Iowegian*, led the charge. On the day of the verdict, he wrote in his editorial: "…it was an individual not a race that killed Clara Rosen." Junkin, he continued, was no lower than members of the white race who have committed crimes just as shocking. "The Negro race should not as a whole be condemned. The white man has taught the Negro many of his vices. In Smoky Row district in which Junkin has spent much time are white men living just as degraded as he has lived. Evils that infest such districts have been permitted by the white man,—liquor selling, opium dens and prostitution."[9]

Four months later, a lynching inside Appanoose County jail seemed a real possibility. Fifteen inmates there, seven charged with penitentiary offenses, found the crime of a new inmate so revolting they were on the point of violence. The inmate was John Hicks. His charge: the rape of his three-year-old niece. The little girl was said to be seriously injured, needing the attention of three physicians, and was still in critical condition. The medical testimony of one of the doctors, Dr. C.P. Bowen, so upset the defense it brought the trial to an abrupt halt. John Hicks withdrew his plea of innocent and pled guilty.

The judge sentenced him to ten years at Fort Madison. In writing of the arrest, of the dispute at the jail and of the trial, Jesse M. Beck inserted one word, an unusual description of Mr. Hicks. The word was "white."[10]

The following year, Beck headlined a story from the *Creston Advertiser Gazette* titled "Civil Rights for the Negro." In it, the Creston paper reported on a case in Corning where the Fair Association banned a Mr. Bagby, an African American trainer of horses and driver, from the use of the track. Judge Towner's ruling was clear: "The Association being a public institution, had no right . . . to exclude Mr. Bagby because he was a colored man." Beck's postscript recorded, "This case will be of local interest especially to the colored men," and then came his revealing comment: "It shows Judge Towner's heart and mind are both right."[11]

Judge Towner was also on the side of Iowa law. Across the country, in July 1910, the same month Junkin was hanged, there were outbreaks of violence, including eleven deaths. When Jack Johnson, the African American boxer defeated James Jeffries, who was labeled "the great white hope" and whose father had thrown religious pamphlets from the Rock Island train as it passed through town, violence broke out across the country, and measures were taken to stop showing pictures of the victory to prevent further violence.[12]

Beck wrote another editorial: "While prize fighting should not be the measure of the two races, it is to the credit of the black man that he has been able to achieve this distinction." He listed the qualities of good boxing: the quick eye, the subjection of the body to the training of the mind, long and determined practice, and self sacrifice to reach the acme of perfection."

He concluded, "The white man should have enough self control to meet defeat squarely and not seek to wreak his disappointed feeling upon the colored man who happens to be exuberant over the outcome."[13]

Beck's own self-control, his own fairness, provided a moral compass for the town. In another twenty years' time, Beck's test would be even greater.[14]

Chapter 29

Immigrants: Diversity and Integration

Between 1900 and 1918, the rich racial and national diversity of Centerville was approaching its peak. In this, the town was no different than any town or city in America. What made it different was its size: 6,951, and the ratio of natural-born citizens to immigrants—less than five to one.[1]

What drew the new immigrants were the coal mines. For more than fifty years, they attracted workers. African Americans from the South were joined by immigrants, not just from traditional northern European countries, but from Italy, Greece, Syria, Bohemia, Turkey, Croatia, Austria, Finland, Hungary, Portugal, Serbia, Czechoslovakia, Madeira, Russia, Poland, Canada, Mexico and China.[2]

Except for the last three countries and the 486 African Americans, the new immigrants entered the country through Ellis Island. They came from the Italian villages of Arsie, Riolo and Fonzaso; from the Croatian villages of Lokve, Fuzina and Slavica. As their ships sailed into New York Harbor, they looked at the Statue of Liberty, and at night, through the windows of Ellis Island, they saw the lights of New York City. The immigrants wore luggage labels tied to their lapels, each bearing two printed words they'd been trained to repeat to U.S. immigration officers: "Centerville, Iowa," the first word occasionally altering to "Seymour," "Cincinnati" or "Mystic." Officials examined their passports. Doctors gave medical examinations. Some immigrants had their heads shaved. Some were refused entry.[3]

For the successful immigrants, coal mine representatives and sponsors guided them to trains for the journey west. Railroad conductors were alerted to the town where the immigrants would disembark and pointed directions from the station to the homes of welcoming committee members. Some rode uptown from the Centerville depots. They looked at the palatial residences on Drake Avenue known as "The Gold Coast," the new churches, the post office, Drake Free Public Library, the new courthouse; and they looked at the free public schools their children would attend, stitching their families into the fabric of America.[4]

The immigrants settled into isolated coal mine villages scattering the County: Mystic and Rathbun; Clarkdale, Plano, Brazil, Sunshine, Jerome and Numa; Cincinnati, Exline, Thirty, Streepyville and Goatsburg. They began work in the coal mines, starting as assistants to sponsors; then, as independent coal miners, they collected fifty dollars a month and saved to pay the ship passages of family members.[5]

When the families arrived, they lived in the coal camps, row after row of uniform, small wooden homes. Saving money remained an ethic. The wife earned money by taking in boarders, by sewing and selling garden produce. The children picked coal from the slag piles and sold it door to door. The family's aim was to buy five acres, build a four-room home, keep a couple of cows and hogs, chickens and rabbits, and raise a large garden. Slowly, across the County, accordions were heard along with the mellow mandolin sound of tamburitza orchestras. And on a shale-surfaced court at the back of Bona Polich's tavern in Rathbun, men played bocci ball.[6]

On Saturdays the men dressed in suits and hats, their wives in long skirts and babushkas. They paid the nickel fare on the Interurban and joined the people of the town on Centerville's Courthouse Square, where the stores stayed open until late at night.[7]

The sidewalks teemed with life. Men greeted each other and stopped to talk. Women pushing baby carriages visited with friends. People collided. Others stepped into street traffic. Centerville police urged pedestrians to follow patterns established in large cities and keep to the right-hand side.[8]

Shop assistants stood at doorways, inviting people inside. Free gifts and souvenirs were distributed. Music played from a loudspeaker at Harry Luther's. Up-to-date baseball bulletins were posted at the Keck-Davis cigar store. A large thermometer on the north side of Lankford's Funeral Parlor gave temperature readings.[9]

People bought popcorn and roasted peanuts from "Blind Jim," the Bandfield Store wagon on the Square's Southside. They sampled different flavored ice creams and Underwood's hand-rolled chocolates, sitting at the marble counters of Gus and Santi Milani's Northside ice cream parlor. They drank sarsaparilla

Inside Milani's ice cream parlor. *Courtesy of J.G. Milani.*

at Delmonico's, Coca-Cola and chocolate ice cream sundaes at the Square's eight drugstore soda fountains. These included the Elite, now renamed the Owl, and the Red Cross drugstore, whose owner, Carl Weeks, was building a fortune from his Armand cosmetics and was about to travel the world and build an antique-filled mansion—Salisbury House—in Des Moines.[10]

They bought Kansas City, Des Moines and Chicago newspapers and local newspapers from the *Iowegian*—now merged with the *Daily Citizen*—in its office just off the Square on North Main Street or from newsboys shouting headlines on street corners. Some of the news was of events back in "the old country." There were bloody revolutions back home in Russia and in Portugal; torture of Bulgarians in Turkey; earthquakes in Mexico and two in southern Italy—the first killing 200,000, the second 76,000. In April 1912, the news of the sinking of the *Titanic* on its maiden voyage was accompanied by another headline: "Mystic Man Loses Wife and Children."[11]

The Mystic man was Franck Lefebvre. He was an immigrant from Lievin in the northernmost part of France, known as the Nord-Pas-de-Calais. He worked in Mystic's Lodwick mine with his thirteen-year-old son, Anselme. Franck saved money and sent tickets to his wife, Marie, and four children: fifteen-year-old Mathilde, eleven-year-old Jeanne, eight-year-old Henri and six-year-old Ida. The five boarded the *Titanic* in Southampton April 10, 1912. They traveled steerage. In the catastrophe that followed on April 14, 75 percent of these passengers died. The bodies of Marie and her four children were never recovered, or if they were, they were never identified.[12]

Within days, there was news of unclaimed children. They were thrown into lifeboats by parents on the doomed ship. Thirteen of the children were said to be French; two of the youngest were being cared for by a Miss Margaret Hays at West Eighty-third Street in New York. In Mystic, local people collected money for Lefebvre to travel to Chicago. There, at the French consulate's office, photographs of the children were examined—those of Lefebvre's, those from Miss Hays. The children were not his, and Lefebvre returned to Mystic.[13]

In less than a month, his life changed again. An examination of his papers showed he'd entered the United States illegally. He had eloped from France with another woman he claimed was his wife. Lefebvre and his son and the woman and her daughter were arrested by an immigration inspector named Whitfield. They were brought to Centerville on the Interurban, placed in the County jail and then deported back to Lievin.[14]

After dark, Appanoose County's immigrants joined with others and watched as the town lights were turned on: twenty-four electroliers, six to each side of the Square, with an ornamental iron post supporting five globes. Sometimes, in celebration of special events, brilliantly colored lights ran in streamers from the topmost pinnacle of the courthouse tower to the electroliers and then leaped from electrolier to electrolier, circling the Square.[15]

The most popular entertainment was now the movies. People attended movies at the new Orpheum cinema. They watched *With the German Army* and *Within the Crimson Lines* and, despite objections by the Des Moines chapter of the NAACP, D.W. Griffith's three-hour *Birth of a Nation.* This movie version of Thomas Dixon's novel *The Clansman* was, from a cinematic perspective, considered brilliant and revolutionary. But its blatant racism, with its celebration of the Ku Klux Klan, distorted many viewers who were unable or unwilling to challenge its lack of authenticity.[16]

One of those was the president of the United States: Woodrow Wilson. The movie was shown in the White House to the president, along with members of his staff and cabinet. At the end of the showing, Wilson was reported to have said, "It is like writing history with Lightning. And my only regret is that it is all so terribly true."[17]

Birth of a Nation was shown in Centerville at least twice. Its immediate impact is unknown. But it prepared the groundwork for an event seven years later. The Ku Klux Klan arrived in Centerville in 1922. When it came, the town had too many ready and eager converts. When the KKK left, a residue of divisiveness and bigotry remained. It would permeate the town for more than fifty years.

Before 1922 there was another pressing concern. The County's new immigrants had to be integrated. They had to be Americanized.

In August 1911, Mayor Silas "Bolar" Bryant of Centerville received a report from the State Board of Health. Immigrants from cholera–infected areas of Europe were moving into Appanoose County. The news reinforced the public health concerns of local doctors. They were dealing with outbreaks of contagious diseases caused by lack of hygiene and the casual disposal of waste and excrement. In one year, 1904, 32 percent of County deaths were due to tuberculosis transmitted by infected sputum and between families refusing to open their windows, embrace fresh air and eat healthy diets. There were repeated outbreaks of typhoid and smallpox, and there was at least one case of polio.[18]

Three cases aroused local emotions. All three were cases of people with highly infectious diseases put off trains for Centerville's doctors to administer. One patient suffered from smallpox, another from leprosy, and in 1907 there was a story so full of danger and pathos that the people of the town felt both anger and sympathy.

It involved Mary Rebecca VanNess, now Mrs. Alonzo Snyder, born and raised in Centerville, who had moved to Ottumwa and was now penniless and dying of tuberculosis. Seeking treatment, she moved from Ottumwa to Davenport, back to Ottumwa, to Colorado, back again to Ottumwa. She was brought to Centerville on a cot, too sick to sit up, too weak to speak, escorted by a Wapello County overseer of the poor and deposited at Centerville City Hall. It was an act, said the *Daily Iowegian*, that would have made Scrooge of Charles Dickens fame a full-blown philanthropist. She was moved to Centerville Hospital and died two days later.[19]

Many of the cases, like Mrs. Snyder, involved natural-born citizens. But the new immigrants were posing new health challenges. Mayor Bryant ordered a close watch be kept on them. Doctors fanned out across the County. They gave talks at schools, at churches, at the Miners Hall and under the auspices of the Trades and Labor Assembly. The talks were free. They included stereopticon illustrations. Schoolchildren were vaccinated against smallpox. School District No. Two in Franklin Township, the site of the polio case, was ordered to close for three weeks. Eighteen-inch yellow cards labeled "Quarantine" were placed on the homes of anyone suffering a contagious disease. The worst cases were transferred to the County Pest House, four miles east of town.[20]

War was declared on flies and those places where they bred: outhouses and manure piles. Dr. J.L. Sawyers warned his audiences that one person infected with tuberculosis could infect a whole community. Five thousand tubercle bacilli, or TB, can exist in one fly speck, he told them, sixteen million on a postage stamp. People were advised to use netting over open windows. Garbage was ordered burned or stored in dustbins with tight-fitting lids. Spitting was outlawed. Public drinking cups were replaced with individual ones. Refrigerators were promoted as "germ free," and the town's drugstores advertised jointly: "Hope, rest, fresh air, and—Scott's Emulsion."[21]

Another serious concern involving the immigrants was the local increase in crime. Italian beer picnics at Rathbun were turning into annual free-for-all riots with clubs, hatchets and pistols. Sheriff Climie, trying to keep order, was almost killed; so were bystanders trying to help. An article reprinted from the *Cedar Rapids Gazette* years before warned that Italians were immoral, resistant to education and not self-governing. Where they existed in Iowa, the newspaper said, riots were frequent, murders a matter of everyday life, with the pistol and stiletto their arguments. In Centerville it seemed a life-fulfilling prophecy.[22]

Fights broke out between Italians and native-born citizens in the Miners Hall on Thirteenth Street. When they spilled into the street, arresting officers were attacked. South of town, men with Italian names murdered each other: Sisto Varetti and Bartello Galvan, Tony Bartello and Frank Rucci.[23]

Irishmen celebrating St. Patrick's Day, expounding upon the virtues and achievements of St. Patrick, got drunk and started fighting with rocks, bricks, curses and "vile execrations." Those who were sober declared they were Fenians ready to fight any Englishman, and if the English enlisted Canadians to fight in Ireland, they were armed and ready to raid, to go north across the border and take on "the Canucks."[24]

Syrian peddlers were harassed. Jewish businesses were robbed. A Mexican was shot to death; so was a German—the head of North Hill coal mine. An Austrian was found beheaded near the town reservoir; Italians and Austrians were the targets of pickpockets. Men attacked and murdered men with knives and guns. They killed their wives and murdered women in broad daylight on the main street of Unionville and with a hatchet in Mystic. On an Interurban run from Mystic, men with guns pulled the trolley from the wire, put the car in darkness and, with its air exhausting, ran it down a hill. As conductor Johnson and motorman Swanson fought for control, a gun was shot at Johnson's face, but it failed to fire.[25]

Burglaries were increasing; so were accounts of betting, gambling and drunkenness. A lot of the reports came from South Centerville, Galleyville, Goatsburg and Thirty—an Italian community around Mine Thirty, a mine south of the Square.[26]

People were concerned. The churches held meetings. The ladies of the Baptist Mission Circle discussed "Aliens or Americans?" At the Wednesday Club, the issues included discussions on "Immigration" and another on "Peace and Arbitration." A night school for foreigners, preparing them for citizenship, was begun in Garfield School. The Women's Relief Corps (WRC) presented seven American flags to the courthouse—one to be waved from each of seven windows. Both the WRC and the P.E.O. presented flags to every classroom in the town's schools. They also requested more patriotic songs be sung there and readings be given of moral principles in the Bible.[27]

At this time in its history, the calendar of the town was crowded with events and opportunities. They were now seen as occasions for immigrants to attend and absorb the American way. There were concerts at the Drake Avenue Armory Opera House given by the Minneapolis Symphony Orchestra and the Mountain Ash Male Voice Choir and repeat performances of *Uncle Tom's Cabin* using real hounds. Tango lessons were taught at the new Elks Club, just off the Square on East State Street.[28]

On October 29, 1915, all businesses and all industries closed for the day. Thirty thousand people converged on Centerville Square for a free performance by the U.S. Marine Band under the direction of Lieutenant William Santelmann. Attired in their dress uniforms of scarlet jackets, blue trousers with white stripes and scarlet caps with gold braids, the band delighted immigrants and native-borns alike with a variety of music from Beethoven and Wagner overtures to the ragtime music of Irving Berlin and George M. Cohan, followed by a Strauss waltz.[29]

Periodically through the years on Centerville Square, there were public speakers: Billy Sunday, Helen Keller, William Jennings Bryan, Carrie Nation, Eugene Debs and "Big Bill" Haywood. Beginning in 1904, there were ten-day Chatauqua Assemblies. They were held at Glen Hagan Park, with more speakers, bands, choirs, entertainers, troubadours and performing cats and dogs. On September 1, 1908, the biggest Chautauqua attraction was for the speaker Theodore Perry Shonts.[30]

To the immigrants, to the people of the town, "Thede" Shonts was the embodiment of the American dream. He was a local boy, the product of Centerville's free public schools. He married Amelia, whose father was the former governor and general Francis Marion Drake. One of his two daughters

Quarantine notice. *Courtesy of Appanoose County Historical Society.*

had married into the prominent East Coast Bingham family. The other was about to marry a French duke. Shonts headed railroads. He was selected by President Teddy Roosevelt to be chairman of the Panama Commission. Now, two years later, he was president of the Interborough Metropolitan Street Railway Company of New York.

He arrived in Centerville in his own private railroad car. He wore a pince-nez and a mustache and had a bulldog expression. He tackled problems appalling in their magnitude. In Panama he'd taken on the fight to end yellow fever. He undertook them with characteristic American enthusiasm and determination. He worked unremittingly at construction, at operations, at finance. In New York, subways were laid, elevated railroads built, politicians subdued and labor difficulties solved. The subject of his speech that day in Centerville was transportation. It was, he told his audience, the secret of American's greatness.[31]

But a new form of entertainment—the movies—was emerging as the most popular. They were still silent, so there was no language barrier for the immigrants. New picture houses opened in addition to the Lyric, the Bijou and the Orpheum. The Star opened on Thirteenth Street, the Comet on the Levee, and the repertoire of the Drake Avenue Theatre expanded to include movies. In October 1913, Robert and William McKee—two sons of Susannah, who had died in the Continental fire—built the Majestic on the corner of Thirteenth Street and Maple. It was elegant and comfortable. There were soft opera chairs and thick carpets; a pipe organ; an orchestra of pianist, violinist, drummer and trumpeter; and twenty-one switches to control stage lights. The breakthrough movie, however, was shown at the Drake Avenue Theatre on February 4, 1915; its title was *Tillie's Punctured Romance*. It was advertised as "A Six-Reel Keystone Riot." The director was Mack Sennett, his leading actor identifiable in the advertisement despite his misspelled name: "C. Chapman."[32]

Left: Theodore Perry Shonts, chairman of the Panama Canal Commission. *Public domain photo.*

Below: Majestic Theatre. *Courtesy of Appanoose County Historical Society.*

Not only had Chaplin arrived in Centerville, so had silent comedy in the form of the wild, physical actions of the Keystone Cops. Laughter would soon be needed. Thousands of miles across the world, events were shaping that were beyond the control of the people of the town. Their impact would test everyone, most particularly the County's new immigrants.

Chapter 30

World War I: Outbreak in Europe, Effects in Centerville

On the thirtieth of June, 1914, the people of Centerville read a thirty-two-line paragraph that appeared halfway down the center front page of the *Semi-Weekly Iowegian*. It was headlined, "Austrian Heir Is Assassinated." Two days previously, on a crowded street in Sarajevo, a Serbian nationalist, Gavrilo Princep, had fired two shots at an open automobile. The first pierced the neck of Archduke Franz Ferdinand of Austria; the second, the abdomen of his wife, Sophie. Within minutes both were dead. Within a month, Europe was at war. Austria invaded Serbia, Austria's ally Germany declared war on Russia and invaded both Belgium and France and England entered in defense of Belgium and France.[1]

Appanoose County had immigrants from all the belligerent parties. There were 68 Germans, 80 French, 808 British, 71 Russians and 116 Belgians. Within the County, 593 had declared themselves as Austrians, submerging their identities as Czechs, Croatians, Bosnians or Montenegrans; and there were Serbians, including Theodore Maximilian Streu, the Rock Island agent in Numa, with a claim to the throne of Serbia, his grandmother a descendant of Obilitch, hero king of Serbia.[2]

All the immigrants had friends and relatives back home. War now interrupted and silenced communication. Local alarm was also expressed for Centerville citizens vacationing in Europe. They were now stranded, unable to cash their checks, unable to get transportation to European ports, as trains had been commandeered for military uses.[3]

The headlines of Centerville's newspapers escalated in prominence and size as the intensity of fighting increased. In addition to local papers, people anxious for more details subscribed to the *Des Moines Capital*, the *Des Moines Register and Leader*, the *Chicago Tribune*, the *Chicago Herald* and the *Kansas City Star*, all delivered in bundles from early morning trains.

Everywhere people read the news. The reports were discussed on the streets, in coal mines, in barber shops and at drugstore soda fountains. Men with names like Bubniak, Kauzlaric, Kunda, Zima, Poli, Milani, Padovan and DeZorxi entered the courthouse in the center of the Square. When they emerged they were Americans. They waved small American flags. People cheered.

Feelings across the town were tense. There were occasional brawls. A fight near Mine Thirty between an Austrian and a Belgian landed the two in court for a severe warning from Judge Lane. "Timely words of counsel," wrote Jesse M. Beck, editor of the *Semi-Weekly Iowegian* and now the *Centerville Daily Iowegian*, and he reprinted an article from the *Chicago Herald*: "We must have no fighting here ...many thousands of Americans of European birth or extraction are deeply stirred by the wars ...their emotions are natural ...But we are Americans, and this is not our war." Thomas Phillips, in a letter to the *Iowegian* editor, argued against all war, finding it incompatible with Christianity. He ended, "I pray the United States ...will not be in this scrap."[4]

In the *Iowegian* office on South Main Street, the Associated Press telephone service delivered daily dispatches—seventeen on just August 6. They came direct from London, Paris, The Hague, St. Petersburg and Brussels. Occasional uncensored reports were from Berlin. They came via the Gold Schmidt Wireless Company's station in Tuckerton, New Jersey. The information was relayed to the newspaper's new Goss "Comet" flatbed web-perfecting press that roared into life, printing on a continuous roll of paper, folding and cutting the newspapers at a rate of thirty-five hundred eight-page papers per hour.[5]

Within days, the telegraph wire service gave accounts of the war's first engagements. On August 4 the Germans violated the neutrality of Belgium. They crossed the River Meuse at Visé, north of Liège. Their cavalry was first, then came rows of infantry, monocled officers—pistols drawn—in automobiles, motorcyclists circling and accelerating, laying telegraph wires, horse-drawn artillery and field-kitchens on wheels.[6]

In Centerville, members of the Belgian community were in a state of high anxiety. The John Kennis family had left their fourteen-year-old daughter there with her grandmother. Not waiting for the printed newspaper, they collected in clusters around the *Iowegian* office, hearing the dispatches direct from the telephone operator. On August 13 they heard Belgian refugees by the thousands were crossing into Holland. From Amsterdam came messages describing the atrocities they'd witnessed. They told of priests and civilians shot, villages razed, churches set alight, the dead lying in ditches—a seventeen-year-old boy, an old man—of soldiers, horses, wagons, carts, automobiles and bicycles lying in confusion in the roadway, the body of a gray-haired man still clutching his umbrella.[7]

The news was no better for Centerville's French population. Fighting was underway on the 250-mile frontier from Switzerland to Belgium. Key cities in Alsace and Lorraine had fallen. Paris prepared for a siege. Stocks of food were placed in state warehouses. The *Iowegian* reported that the Bois de Boulogne and grounds of the the Chateau of Bagatello were transformed into vast pastures, with cattle guarded by French Army Reserves wearing the large shirts of drovers.[8]

And a new weapon of war was at work. Bombs were dropped from zeppelins flying over the cities of Liège, Antwerp, Paris, London, Scarborough, Yarmouth, Kings Lynn and Sheringham. They destroyed houses, killing their inhabitants, tearing great holes in sea walls and roadways. Unexploded bombs were described as giant lead plumbs. One lay broken open, lumps of yellowish substance oozing onto the ground. British aviators in open cockpit biplanes flew through the high mountains of southern Germany and bombed the zeppelin factory in Friedrichshafen on Lake Constance.[9]

Americans, including those from Centerville, cut short their vacations and hurried home. The daughter and son-in-law of Dr. Blatchley, Centerville dentist, departing Cherbourg harbor on the American liner *New York*, heard five guns fired, indicating France was at war. Passengers on board the New York–bound *Minnehaha* anchored at Sheerness in the Thames Estuary witnessed an air battle fought out directly overhead. Two German aircraft bound for London were intercepted by three British aviators. Amid shells bursting around them like fireworks, the planes alternately dodged, circled, twisted, climbed and dove in and out of cloud banks. The British finally chased the German planes back out to sea.[10]

The pastor of Centerville's Presbyterian church, the Reverend Wm. McCoy, as well as E.G. Campbell, C.A. Carlson and H.G. Hanson, all traveling home on boats from their native countries of Ireland, England, Sweden and Norway, traveled on boats that deviated from standard routes. Fearful of bombs and U-boat attacks, the captains followed paths north of Scotland and ordered all lights extinguished, all portholes blanketed. John Swab was caught in his native Croatia. He witnessed his friends departing for war. He planned his route home, he and his wife going through the mountains of Slovenia into then-neutral Italy and having their American passports minutely examined at every frontier over and over again.[11]

By the end of August, President Woodrow Wilson restated his intention of keeping America neutral. Sixty thousand Americans did not agree. They crossed the country's northern border as volunteers for the Canadian army, already at war in support of England. Two were from Centerville. One was Harry Luther's red-headed mechanic, Earl Gaughenbaugh, who entered the Foreign Legion of the Canadian forces. The other was fifteen-year-old Harley Miner. He entered the British recruiting office in Des Moines. "Are you a British citizen?" asked the recruiter. He said he was not. "Well you take a walk around the block and tell us you are a British citizen," the recruiter replied. Miner served twenty-eight months in the British army, eleven of those in Europe. When it was realized he was underage and an American citizen, he was discharged. He immediately joined the American army and served more than seven years.[12]

Wire service messages from Europe continued to arrive at the *Iowegian* offices. In the first eight months of the war, six million men were reported dead, wounded or captured; seven billion dollars were already lost in expenditures. Reports came from the battlefields, from Flanders, Verdun, Gallipoli, Ypres. It was at Ypres, in the second battle, that a yellow-green cloud of chlorine gas moved through bright sunshine toward French and Canadian trenches. It engulfed the unsuspecting and unprepared men in slow death, excruciating pain and panic. One was Earl Gaughenbaugh, gassed and invalided for months in hospitals in France and in England. His parents, southwest of Centerville Square, waiting for news and letters.[13]

More nations entered the conflict: Turkey, Greece, Bulgaria, Romania, North Africa, Italy. Joe Milani on Centerville's Square's Northside received a letter from the Italian Consulate in Chicago. It ordered all Appanoose County's Italian men aged twenty to forty, even those now American citizens, home to Italy to fight. British recruiting officer Ernest Hugh Fitzpatrick arrived from Chicago to collect all eighteen- to forty-five-year-old British men.[14]

Travelers passing through town, visitors and Chautauqua speakers all gave graphic accounts of the war. Marie Van Gastel, a Belgian nurse, told of the horrors of the invasion of her country and the fall of Antwerp. She described hundreds of citizens lined up and shot by machine guns, of children crying as they searched the bodies for their parents. She related how German soldiers burst into hospitals and tore bandages from patients before mutilating and shooting them. On Centerville Square, a quartet of wounded soldiers sang patriotic songs. They were British and Canadian army veterans, one with an amputated leg, one suffering from shell-shock, another wounded in the back, a fourth shot through the lungs. Verne Marshall, editor of the *Cedar Rapids Gazette*, who had served in a volunteer American ambulance corps at Verdun, spoke to Centerville's high school history class. He described how, in a strip of land twelve to fifteen miles in length, between two hundred yards and three miles wide, one million men had died. Clermont Mestraud, known to the town as a traveling salesman for the Edison Company before he returned to France, met at the Owl Drug Store with an *Iowegian* reporter. He had been the driver for the American ambassador to France. They had driven from Paris to Rheims. The ancient cathedral there lay in ruins, he told the reporter, its vaulted roof half shot away, the gargoyles and intricate stone lacework jumbled and shattered, its rose window pulverized. On route, he and the ambassador witnessed in the scorching sun heaps of bodies overrun with rats. Men with medicated cloths across their noses lifted them onto forty freight cars and shunted them down cliffs and into the sea.[15]

From the North Atlantic came reports of submarine attacks on neutral ships, including those clearly marked as U.S. ships carrying food and clothing for the starving of Belgium. Then came the news of the Cunard liner, the *Lusitania.* This pride of the British navy, the largest, fastest, most luxurious passenger liner of her time, sailed from New York for Liverpool on May 1, 1915, carrying two thousand passengers and crew. Six days later, at 2:10 in the afternoon on May 7, when she was twelve miles south of Kinsale Head on the coast of southern Ireland, the *Lusitania* was torpedoed by German U-boat number twenty. She sank in twenty minutes. As a result, 1,201 died, 128 of them American citizens, most of them women and children.

The world was shocked. This was a passenger liner, its cargo innocent travelers. In Centerville the event had special impact. Three Centerville families—the Shellcrosses, the Monks and the Eatocks—were believed to be on board, traveling to visit relatives in England.[16]

Jesse M. Beck, the *Iowegian*'s editor, was in Chicago as the news broke. It was the hometown of many of the victims. Before returning to Centerville, he watched as extra editions of newspapers appeared on Chicago streets and crowds assembled on sidewalks outside the Cunard office. The feelings were intense, the expressions on the faces of the people self-controlled. He heard one or two inflammatory remarks, but the general feeling was that any response should come from Washington. And it should be firm.[17]

The Germans, responding to the shock, argued the *Lusitania* was carrying munitions. Their embassy in Washington, they said, had warned that any British ship could be attacked. This warning had appeared in the *Des Moines Register* on

April 23, a week before the *Lusitania* sailed from New York. It was repeated in the *New York Tribune* and other East Coast newspapers the day of departure.[18]

In Centerville, people anxiously scanned the lists of victims and the interviews with survivors, looking for the names of the three Centerville families. The tone of the town, like that of the country, had altered. The *Semi-Weekly Iowegian*'s headlines confirmed the change: "War May Possibly Come," "U.S. Demands That Germany Stop It," and "Unless Germany Backs Down on Submarine Policy U.S. Will Sever Relations or Go to War." At the end of the Saturday afternoon moving picture show at the Armory Theatre, the orchestra played "The Star-Spangled Banner." The audience rose to its feet.[19]

Confirmation of the certain safety of the Shellcrosses, the Monks and the Eatocks did not reach the town until the eighteenth, eleven days after the event. The three families had heeded the warnings. They transferred their tickets to another Cunard liner: the *Transylvania*. Even so, their journey across the Atlantic to Glasgow was fraught with danger. Passengers reported seeing a periscope and a conning tower in the water off the north coast of Ireland. The captain followed a zigzag path and so avoided the white wake of a discharged torpedo. All the *Transylvania*'s lifeboats were prepared. The passengers spent the nights on deck. It was later learned that the *Transylvania*, like the *Lusitania*, was carrying a secret cargo: munitions.[20]

As the people of the town waited for action from Washington, they responded to national appeals. They shipped carloads of horses and one thousand mules to the British army. In an appeal from the *Chicago Herald* to fill a ship with Christmas gifts for war-orphaned children in Europe, they carried blankets, comforters, clothing, dolls, crayons and toys to the local collection point. This was D.A. Lee's coal mine office in the Continental Hotel's extension on East State Street. A month later, the appeal was far more urgent. It came from the chairman of the American Commission for Relief in Belgium. His name was Herbert Hoover, a native of West Branch, Iowa. "This is not a quest of charity or relief to the chronically poor," he told the Associated Press, "it is a question of feeding an entire population …America must feed Belgium this winter." Three million Belgians were already starving, another seven million would as well, unless help was immediate. Centerville's businessmen and farmers responded the next day. A noon luncheon was held at the Sargent Café. County grain elevator owners were appointed as agents to receive corn. J. Rosenbaum and Son in South Centerville agreed to accept contributions of grain. People across the County dropped coins into donation boxes on store counters. Banks—the First National, Centerville National, the Wooden—accepted larger amounts. All consignments were loaded onto trains and shipped to national collection points free of cost by the Chicago, Burlington and the Rock Island lines. Promise City sent a car of corn weighing 52,224 pounds, Ottumwa 30,000 pounds of pork and 45,000 pounds of lard. It was a pattern for the war for appeals for the suffering French, the Serbians, the Jews of Russia and Poland and for the Armenians dying in Turkey.[21]

On February 3, 1917, news reached the town that President Woodrow Wilson had broken diplomatic relations with Germany. Flags were hung on businesses and residences. The largest were seen flying in South Centerville at the Anderson Produce House, over the Burlington Railroad roundhouse and office and on a new flagpole at Jim Shanks's drugstore. Around town, at places of work, in the noon hours and in the minutes before working time, clusters of men and women discussed the chances of war, the possible call for a volunteer army. Naturalized citizens joined the American-born, unified to voice their support: "The hyphen," said Jesse Beck at the *Semi-Weekly Iowegian*, referring to the mark between country of origin and America, such as Italian-Americans, "has disappeared in Centerville."[22]

Chapter 31

War Declared

When President Woodrow Wilson broke diplomatic relations with Germany, Iowa's volunteer army—the National Guard, including Centerville's Company D—was already at war, not in Europe but on the Mexican border. There they were fighting Pancho Villa and his followers, Mexican bandits who had murdered seventeen American mining engineers in Chihuahua and then crossed the U.S. border, killing another seventeen—these in the town of Columbus, New Mexico.[1]

As tensions with Germany increased, Iowa's National Guard was ordered home on February 22. Company D arrived back in Centerville, bronzed and battle-hardened after intensive routines directed by an officer from the Midwest, a native of LaClede, Missouri, seventy miles south of Centerville, a graduate of Kirksville Normal School: Brigadier General John J. "Black Jack" Pershing.[2]

On April 2, 1917, President Woodrow Wilson declared war on Germany. Members of Company D were ordered to the armory. They were inspected by a federal appointee: Colonel Carl Reichman. Captain Glenn Haynes, who had been the company's first sergeant in the Spanish-American War nineteen years previously, resigned as postmaster inspector at Mount Vernon, Iowa, and returned to command Company D. New volunteers were sought by order from Guy E. Logan, Iowa's adjutant general.[3]

The recruiting office was placed in the front window of the Goldstein Store on the Square's Westside. It was decorated in national colors, large flags, recruiting posters sent by the State, a copy of an 1865 newspaper carrying the news of President Lincoln's assassination and a table for the recruiter, Lieutenant Harry Peavey. Crowds watched on the sidewalk. New recruits sat on chairs, then stood one by one, right arm raised, and took the federal oath. There were sudden explosions of light as photographer Ray Link took flashbulb pictures.[4]

Outside, the Centerville town band played patriotic music. Everywhere were the colors red, white and blue. Festoons of bunting decorated the courthouse; people carried individual flags, handed them by members of the Association of Commerce; they wore smaller ones or red, white and blue ribbons in their coat lapels. Fleets of automobiles carried the new soldiers, recruiter Peavey, citizens led by Mayor Fox and the town band to outlying County towns, where they were greeted with more patriotic music, the waving of flags and cheering as new volunteers stepped forward. The U.S. Navy, represented by a gunner's mate and a boilermaker, accepted new inductees in the courthouse. The new sailors were sent to naval stations near Chicago and then to training ships on the East Coast. In Centerville High School, military training was started. Eighty-eight boys were formed into two companies. Twice a week after school, they marched and drilled following instructions from Company D.[5]

The Centerville division of the Burlington Railroad gave a large portion of its rights of way to the City and to the County towns it served for community gardens. Coal mine owner David Dinning followed with fifteen acres of his own. People gave scattered empty lots. They also volunteered to provide seed and regular garden maintenance. The proceeds of the produce were to go for war purposes or to feed the poor. A local chapter of the Red Cross was formed. It met in the Association of Commerce room over the Stephenson Drug Store on the Northside of the Square. D.C. Bradley took the chair. Plans were made to train nurses to battle-line readiness, to prepare hospital garments and surgical supplies and to assemble the names of nurses, doctors and volunteers to serve in ambulance corps in France. The Red Cross members divided the City into seventeen districts. They made a house-to-house canvass requesting new members and donations. There was a captain in charge of each group. He was accompanied by a girl dressed in a white nurse's uniform marked with red crosses.[6]

By early July, Company D established a camp in South Centerville just north of the Hercules plant on land donated by D.C. Bradley. Rows of tents were erected facing east. Officers' tents faced north at the south end of the company rows. The Burlington Railroad gave permission for the men to use their pond for bathing purposes. Each morning the soldiers were awakened with a five thirty morning call. They retired with taps at ten thirty each night. During the day, they trained, marched and drilled. They ran distances. Paul Davis from Unionville, who had run a ten-second hundred yards in high school, set the pace. They practiced at a rifle range brought into camp from three to four miles east of the City. They adopted three mascots: a kitten, a fox and an eight-year-old boy named Sam Beardsley, who joined their trainings and drillings, walking their eight- and ten-mile hikes without exhaustion. In the afternoons, there were lectures. Captain Haynes recited the articles of war, the rules for conduct and punishments for infractions. Dr. Frank Sturdivant spoke on cleanliness, on sanitation and on avoiding moral laxity. Medical examinations were conducted by Major Russell and Lieutenant Van Meter of the U.S. Army Medical Corps. They discharged three men as unfit. One cried. To the others they administered the first antityphoid prophylaxis. The second was administered ten days later. In spare moments, the soldiers played baseball or they wrestled, pitting themselves against two of their members who were professional wrestlers. They changed the names of wrestling holds: the full nelson became the "German hug."[7]

The date for Company D's departure was undetermined. Concerned with the soldiers' uncertainty, the people of the town organized entertainments and acts of appreciation. There were marches around the Square led by Mayor Fox carrying a flag, musical evenings at Drake Avenue Theatre, a County picnic, free tickets to the Hagenbeck-Wallace Circus, an auto tour with seventy-five private automobiles taking the men to Moravia, Unionville and Udell for desserts, music and cigars at all stops. The Association of Commerce sent a crate of fresh oranges and ice water on the hottest days. The ladies of the town supplied fresh lettuce for Sunday salads. The ladies of Plano brought ice cream and cake. The local chapter of the Eastern Star stitched each soldier a "comfort bag." These contained a series of pockets containing useful articles—a toothbrush, needles and thread, a few buttons.[8]

Half a world away, the first American soldiers were arriving in Europe. Telegraphed messages at the *Iowegian* office described the scenes. Millions of Londoners waving American flags gathered and cheered the soldiers. At the gate of Buckingham Palace, King George V, Queen Mary and other members of the royal household raised their hands repeatedly, saluting the flag of the United States. From the window of the war office overlooking Horse Guards Parade, there were greetings from Prime Minister David Lloyd-George. In Paris the scenes were similar. "Lafayette, we are here," said U.S. Colonel Charles E. Stanton at the tomb of the French aristocrat who had crossed the Atlantic in 1775 and was a hero at Valley Forge and at Yorktown. General

Pershing followed; he hoped, he said, his American forces would "vanquish for the liberty of the world." Liberty was on the American mind that day. It was July 4, 1917.[9]

Thirty-eight days later, in Centerville, Iowa, it was just after noon on August 11. A United Press wire service message was received at Centerville's *Iowegian* office on South Main Street. A reporter rushed it down to Company D's camp near the Hercules plant and delivered it to Captain Haynes, who called the men together to hear the bulletin. Company's D's members had all anticipated they would be sent first to Deming, New Mexico, with the rest of Iowa's National Guard. When the news was read, it brought loud cheering. Company D was selected to be part of the 168th Infantry of the army's Forty-second Division. Comprising National Guard units from twenty-six states, arcing across the country from California to Georgia, Oregon to Alabama and the District of Columbia, the division was led by its chief of staff, Colonel Douglas MacArthur, who named it "the Rainbow Division." They were to depart for France immediately.[10]

Centerville's contribution to the Rainbow Division left town aboard cars of the Interurban at six thirty Friday morning, August 17, 1917. The night before,

World War I men departing. *Courtesy of Appanoose County Historical Society.*

thousands greeted them on the Square with speeches, the presentation by the WRC of a silk flag and $236.68, a spontaneous offering in change, tossed onto a piece of canvas by the crowd. The Friday morning departure was personal and emotional. There were private embraces, tears, farewells and handshakes, the soldiers leaning from the car windows. As the train slowly exited the Square onto North Main Street, bands played, and there were the sounds of cheering. Hands, hats and handkerchiefs were waved until cars were lost to view.[11]

At that moment, they were not the only Centerville soldiers and families preparing for departure to war. On June 5, President Wilson had set into motion the draft. All unenlisted men aged eighteen to thirty-one were ordered to register and await their selection in a national lottery system. As Company D departed from Centerville Square, another 412 of Appanoose County's men had been called to service.[12]

The men had registered on June 5, 1917. They registered in the County Auditor's Office in the courthouse on the Square and in registration booths in area voting precincts that opened at seven in the morning. Before nine o'clock that night, 2,428 men emerged with official registration cards giving their name and a number. Joining them were twenty-five carnival men working for the Hallenbeck-Wallace Circus and two Mexican miners giving their address as a boxcar in South Centerville.[13]

Forty-four men refused to register at all. They were immigrant miners working at Thirty, Streepy, Shawville and Numa. They were arrested and placed in the County jail. They said, via an interpreter, that their Italian newspaper told them if they weren't citizens they were exempt from a U.S. draft. Town rumors gave an alternative political reason. They were all, it was said, from the northern provinces of Italy and all part of "a rabid socialist and anarchist" cell circulating seditious literature opposed to all government and all its officials. They appeared at the courthouse and were sent to Ottumwa to appear before a federal grand jury. A special car of the Interurban took them to Mystic, then on to Ottumwa in the rear car of the Milwaukee Railroad number eight. Together with their interpreter, John Azzolin, and Centerville's Joe Milani—the agent for the Italian consul in Milwaukee—watched by hundreds and followed by fifteen of their emotional mothers and wives, they marched from the station, two or three abreast, up Market Street to Fourth and west to Court Street and jail. Within days they were transferred to jail in Des Moines. They returned to Centerville, deposited fifty dollars each at the post office to buy a Liberty Bond—and then registered for the draft in the County Auditor's Office in the courthouse. Two still refused. Peter Azoo, an Armenian, and Louis Markeni, an

Italian, chose prison terms. They served a year in Appanoose County Jail and were then escorted by federal agents to St. Louis and deported.[14]

All of Centerville's registered men now awaited their selection in a national lottery system. It was held in Washington in U.S. Senate room 226 at nine thirty in the morning on July 19. Two blindfolded men drew, from glass bowls, gelatin capsules, each containing the number of a registered American. Four hundred and twelve of Appanoose County's men were called to service. The list included three local men who had at first refused to register. Medical examinations followed. Those considered unfit or in occupations vital to the national interest were issued red, white and blue metal buttons, the words "Exempted U.S." inscribed in a concentric circle in the center.[15]

For the next year, the drafted men left the town in groups of varying sizes and on alternating dates. For all departing soldiers, there were prior dinners and farewell speeches, waving crowds and the town band playing at the Interurban or Rock Island depots. This pattern was also followed for six of Centerville's African Americans. They left together on the Interurban on October 15 for Camp Dodge to join all African American companies from Illinois, Minnesota and North Dakota. Camp Dodge was the only camp in the country for training African American officers. From Camp Dodge, 639 of them qualified and graduated. When they were assigned to the Ninety-second Army Division, however, their qualifications were ignored. They served under only white officers.[16]

The drafted men were scattered among various sections of the army and the navy. Company D—now the 168th Infantry—remained as one unit throughout the war. It trained at Camp Mills, Long Island, as part of the American Expeditionary Forces led by the same Missouri man they'd known on the Mexican border: John J. "Black Jack" Pershing, now commander General Pershing. The 168th Infantry arrived at LeHavre, France, in the bitterly cold December of 1917. Unheated railroad cars labeled "Hommes 40—Chevaux 8" transported them east into Lorraine. By February 24 the men yielded the cold and the ice of barns, attics and outbuildings for the cold, ice, mud, lice and constant shelling of the trenches. When the Germans realized Americans were nearby, they increased their shelling from 150 shells a day to more than a thousand, and their airplanes flew almost continuously overhead, dropping bombs. News from the battlefront was limited. Letters home were censored. Where the men were fighting, the circumstances of their war, were unknown to their families and the community. When news did come, it was sudden and brutal: the news and the names of those killed in action. On March 5 the people of the town read of the first three Americans dead. The list included an Iowan—Private Merle D. Hay of Glidden. At the moment of the reading, their own Centerville men were in a desperate battle. An hour before dawn, it began with a sudden and intense barrage of shelling. As it lifted, members of the Fifteenth Bavarian Sturm Battalion, tossing hand grenades in front of them and armed with knives and pistols, rushed their trench. The 168th fought off their attackers, but there was a cost.[17]

News of Appanoose County's first casualties reached the town early on the morning of March 11—three men killed in action, two wounded. The list was an error. After two weeks of memorial services and an outpouring of sympathy to their families, it was learned that two listed dead, John Ellis and Russell Selix, were alive. Four men were dead— Guy Worley, Merrill Morrison, Ira Rogers and the first to die from the County, Ray Walden. A letter from the Company D chaplain to Hattie Elwood, Ray Walden's sister, described the funeral in the French village of Badonville given to all four boys: "We buried them …in the little cemetery on the hill overlooking the little French village and the trenches …I wish you could have seen the tribute of love and respect paid Ray and his comrades by the French people. Thousands of them lined the streets as we passed by and saluted the dead heroes."[18]

The 168th Infantry, as part of the Rainbow Division, left Lorraine in July. Their next battles lay in a narrow ellipse west to Champagne, between Suippes and Chalon, further west to the valley of the Ourcq and Chateau Thierry, then back east, chasing the Germans to St. Mihiel and the Argonne. Occasionally an unidentified man fought alongside them in the trenches. He wasn't in uniform but a turtleneck sweater, riding breeches, cavalry boots and smashed-down cap, sometimes with a sweater marked with the letter *A*, sometimes a four-foot knitted muffler. He wore no helmet, rejected a gas mask and answered to "Buddy" or "Say You." Only later did they learn it was Colonel Douglas MacArthur.[19]

The men marched the distances between battles in full kits and in shoes so inadequate they left blood stains on the snow. They survived bombardments described as "paralyzing" and "crushing," repeated gas attacks and peppering by machine-gun fire delivered from Von Richthofen's scarlet-nosed Fokker aircraft that circled, plunged and looped above them, yellow scarves flowing out behind the pilots. Occasionally above them was another phenomenon. They noticed it first in Lorraine. The soldiers were waiting for an attack. A rainbow appeared. The attack failed. "A coincidence," they thought at first. But the rainbow appeared again in Champagne, at the Ourcq, a brilliant one at Chateau Thierry, at St. Mihiel, in the Argonne, over the Meuse and over the Rhine as the division crossed into Germany. "The rainbow has been to us a vision and an omen," wrote John Johnson to his wife. "The men don't talk about it much but when the rainbow appears you can hear a murmur go down the line. As we came over the last big hill and started down into the Rhine valley we saw the rainbow and instantly you could hear the shout …'There she is…'"[20]

Chapter 32

The Home Front

News of war dead, injuries and suffering fueled anti-German feelings in the United States. In Iowa, fights broke out in Waterloo and Fort Dodge. In Audubon, there were two attempted lynchings, in Sigourney a fatal knifing. U.S. attorney general T.W. Gregory issued a blunt directive to German immigrants sympathetic to their homeland and sent it to U.S. Marshal Nick Reed for the southern district of Iowa: "Obey the law; keep your mouth shut." Iowa's governor, W.L. Harding, fearing public disorder, canceled a concert at the Des Moines Coliseum by German operatic star Frieda Hempel. A month later he issued a public proclamation: "Talk English or not at all. Henceforth, all foreign languages are barred in schools, churches, theaters, in all public gathering places and over the phone."[1]

Centerville did not escape the tension. The local school board requested the resignation of a high school economics instructor on the grounds she'd spoken pro-German views, and rumors circulated—completely groundless—of a group of teachers at St. Mary's parochial school with similar opinions. When a woman who rented a room at a home on East Van Buren was heard speaking German and then disappeared, she was considered a spy. And when two people were selling "court plaster" door to door, it was believed the plasters—applied for cosmetic or medical reasons—were filled with lockjaw germs and were part of a German plot aimed at killing those who applied them. There were arrests of three Centerville people: a man insulting a new recruit to the National Guard, and two women who thought anyone trying to raise money to help soldiers were "cut throats." Those who refused to contribute money to buy Liberty War Bonds were given hearings in front of the Appanoose County War Council. If they still refused, their names and townships were exposed in the *Iowegian* under the headline "Slacker List Is Published."[2]

Wearing a legitimate exemption button did not guarantee immunity from being called a "slacker." The worst incident was in Plano, when effigies of two exempted men, their names applied in bright yellow paint, were hung on the telephone wires in front of the Plano bank on the main street. Yellow paint was also applied to two barber shops on Centerville Square. One on the Westside had its doors, windows, panels of the building and the barber pole liberally daubed. A trail of paint across the Square led to a second barber shop similarly treated. The motives were obscure. One barber had a son in service; both had contributed to community efforts at supporting the troops and the war effort.[3]

But for most of the citizens, it was a time for positive action. Frank Payne of Iowa Southern Utilities became chairman of five Appanoose County Liberty Loan Campaigns. Every day, he left his office on the Square's Eastside and met with a team of volunteers in the Association of Commerce room. The team included members of the War Service Council and seventeen members of the Women's Committee, led by Mrs. John B. Taylor with extra aid from high school girls. Together they mailed hundreds of circulars and thousands of letters, checked records of thirty County precincts, kept careful records of sales, deposited money to banks and duplicated all copies by hand.[4]

Posters by national artists—Strothman, Norton, Everett, Pennell, Raleigh, St. John, Young, Williams, Christy, Whitehead—part of ten million posters sent out by the U.S. Treasury Department, were placed in doors and in display windows of every store and public building in town. Some stores displayed more than one. The Continental Hotel and Appanoose Cafe showed two; there were three at Goldsteins, four at Standard Furniture and the Centerville National Bank and five at Lankford's and Riggs Grocery.

The posters showed different graphic images: the bloody handprint of a German soldier or his boots marked with blood; a bloody bayonet in the smoking ruins of a cathedral; a German invading the home of a frightened girl and baby; one dragging a young Belgian woman. At Peatman's Hardware, Phillips, Lowrey's and Rosenbaum's, a poster displayed a mother pleading with one arm outstretched, the other arm holding a baby to her breast, a small child clinging to her skirt. At Milani's, the Red Cross Drug Store, Frankel's and Parker's Clothing, there was the image of a crumbling Statue of Liberty and a smoking New York City; at Riggs, Purity Bakery and Climie's, an image of "Victory" bearing a sword in one hand, an American shield in the other, flanked by an American eagle and a flag; and there was a second poster of

"Victory" pointing out to sea over the gun crew of an American battleship. But the window receiving the most attention was Frankel's. There, a poster of an American soldier was displayed with a bayonet over the body of a dead German, in front of it a store dummy in German helmet and mask lying flat on its back, a bayonet thrust deeply into its chest. With the posters were statements: for the handprint and boots, "Keep these off the United States." Others said, "Huns or Home?" or "The Hun—his mark," "Remember Belgium," "For Victory" and "That Liberty shall not Perish from the Earth."[5]

Throughout the war, the stores on the Square decorated their windows with patriotic themes. The Kraft-Triebswetter Clothing Store on the Southside displayed the old Civil War Thirty-sixth Iowa Regimental battle flag. In front were photographs of those in service. On a pedestal in the center, an enlarged picture of Captain Glenn Haynes of Company D was draped in national colors. At the Centerville National Bank, passersby inspected a large framed document in French. It was the official transfer of Centerville's Lazelle Sawyers from the French to the American army. It expressed gratitude for his early volunteer service to France in their ambulance and munitions corps. On the Northside of the Square, Santi Milani's fruit store was the central collection station for plum pits, nut shells and date seeds. They were washed, dried and shipped to Des Moines at Santi's own expense for their conversion into suitable charcoal for gas masks necessary for the soldiers on the battlefields. In one week, Moravia sent 225 pounds, Mystic 78 and Lowrey's grocery on the Westside of the Square sent 56 pounds.[6]

At the Courthouse Park, the Red Cross held regular auctions to raise money. Auctioneer "Phip" Wells, whose father, Ben, was the town's earliest announcer and auctioneer, long remembered selling a goose that was given back and auctioned again and again until the sales netted twenty-five hundred dollars. The biggest single Red Cross fundraiser occurred on Labor Day, September 2, 1918. Two exhibition baseball games were held. Members of two teams, hot rivals in the 1880s, now twenty-five years older, came out of retirement. On one side were the "Old Timers" drawn largely from Appanoose County, led by Professor J.C. Stamps. On the other side was Wayne County's Shane Hill team. In its day, Shane Hill's winning record was almost unbroken and was famous across the country. The games—one in Seymour, one in Allerton—were advertised in the *Des Moines Register*. People traveled from across the State. Centerville practically emptied. People thought it the biggest baseball game ever in southern Iowa. Burt Maytum, Shane Hill's 1880s star pitcher, whose curveballs no one could hit, threw out the first balls. His team, Shane Hill, won both games. All proceeds went to the Red Cross.[7]

In the Red Cross Society's rooms over the Stephenson's store on the Northside, activity was constant. Sewing machines vibrated as mothers of the soldiers and other volunteers made "cootie-proof" underclothing for the boys in the trenches. They cut the cloth from donated cross-barred dimity and unbleached muslin, then sent the completed garments on to the University of Iowa, where they were chemically treated and returned without charge. Every Wednesday they were joined by twenty-seven of the town's African American women, collecting and making clothes for the Belgian Relief Fund. Red Cross volunteers prepared sandwiches, coffee, pies and fruit. They took them to the Rock Island depot. They met trains on their brief stops in Centerville and passed the food through the windows to in-transit sailors and soldiers between assignments. Junior Red Cross auxiliaries were started in County schools. Students volunteered at the Red Cross rooms, rolling bandages, packing boxes of clothing for European refugees in northern France, Belgium, Italy, Romania, Serbia, Greece, Montenegro, Albania, Czechoslovakia, Poland and Palestine. Each school adopted a French war orphan. The children exchanged letters and photographs. They sent money and supplies. Children and adults in Sunday schools gave money in response to an appeal from President Wilson, from Sir Robert Borden, the premier of Canada, from Teddy Roosevelt and from William Taft. The appeal was on behalf of the Armenian people driven by the Turks into mountains and deserts, massacred, deported and dying of exposure and disease, the women sold into slavery.[8]

At Drake Free Public Library, people carried in donated books for the troops, bringing four hundred on one occasion. They selected those by popular authors: Zane Gray, Rex Beach, Jack London, Ralph Connor, Owen Wister and the short stories of O. Henry. The books were forwarded to the American Library Association offices in Washington, D.C., and shipped to YMCA, Red Cross and Salvation Army huts, hospitals and canteens in France. In the corps room of the Women's Relef Corps, women worked over a County service flag spread across tables. They collected and assembled the names of all in service—members of Company D, all draftees and all volunteers, including nurses serving in Europe's Red Cross hospitals. They stitched each name onto a star, then sewed the stars onto the flag.[9]

But for the people of the town, throughout all their activities, their daily focus was the news from the battlefields of Europe.

News of German reversals and retreats first reached the town in July 1918. On the second, the people of the town learned from a United Press report in their morning newspaper that American forces were advancing west of

Chateau Thierry. They had taken the village of Veaux, the military target Hill 192 and Roche Wood, and were penetrating the Ceranbaut Wood. They had inflicted heavy losses on the enemy and taken 450 prisoners. Two weeks later, on July 19, the *Iowegian* headline measured two-and-a-half inches: "30,000 Huns Captured"; underneath, a second headline, one-inch high, read "Soissons Falls before the Victorious Allies."[10]

Spontaneously in response on that morning, the town band walked the streets of Centerville playing martial music. At its head, a large flag was carried by a boy or girl at each corner. The next morning it happened again. The town's former residents of England, France and Italy, representing the Allied forces, joined in, carrying their national flags. They marched to the residence of Colonel E.C. Haynes, a veteran of the Civil War and the father of Glenn Haynes, the captain of Company D, now on the battle line in France. There were brief speeches by Iowa state senator James Wilson, Mayor William Fox and a new candidate for Congress, D. Fulton Rice.[11]

From that date on for four months, until the end of the war on November 11, the parades became a daily Centerville phenomenon. At ten thirty every morning, shopkeepers on Centerville Square shut up their shops and followed Mayor Fox carrying a flag. They walked around the Square twice, frequently joined by onlookers. One parade was held in Mystic, but on Centerville Square they were held every morning at the same time, including Sundays. The parades began at the City Hall when the metropolitan papers arrived. Mayor Fox stood on the front step. He announced the headlines: "British Smash Thru," "French Pinch Another Salient," "Yanks Bite in Again."[12]

On Saturday nights, there were expanded versions. The parades began with the firing of anvils at eight o'clock. The marchers entered the Square from the Southwest Corner. An Uncle Sam and a Miss Columbia were at the front. The Centerville band followed, the flags of Allied nations represented by 150 women divided into groups and all wearing white, the colors of each nation on their arms. Next came a float of children dressed as Red Cross nurses, four bearing a stretcher with an improvised wounded soldier. There was a martial band, old soldiers, veterans of the Civil War and the Spanish-American War, some on crutches, citizens and more children. They were followed by the fire wagon decorated with flags and bunting, then automobiles. Watching were crowds on the sidewalks, standing at attention, hats removed, right hands placed over the left breast.[13]

As the European War limped toward armistice, two premature peace reports reached the town. For one, on October 7, J.M. Beck was awakened from his sleep at four in the morning by a telephone call. Ever the careful editor, he left

World War I daily parade around the Square with Santi Milani. *Courtesy of J.G. Milani.*

his bed for the *Iowegian* office to read overnight telegraphic press bulletins that could confirm the rumor. There were none. He phoned newspaper offices in Des Moines. They had no confirmation either but did report the Germans were "putting out peace feelers." That was enough for people to celebrate in the streets and circle the Square.[14]

But when they learned the terms of the peace feelers—that negotiations would be with the traditional ruling class of Germany, the Hohenzollerns and the Hapsburgs—the tone of the daily marchers changed. This time the people of the town waited for a signal: the sound of a fire whistle that sounded at noon. They stepped outside. The merchants and their clerks stood in the streets, housewives in groups on lawns. Workmen assembled at their places of employment. At the sound of a second whistle, they all faced east and shouted in chorus, "No!"[15]

The news of Centerville's daily parades and the town's method of expressing disapproval at the early peace terms spread. Visiting citizens took the ideas back to their own towns. News reached metropolitan newspapers and across the country. Writing about it all, editor Jesse Beck noted the spirit of the town: "When peace really comes there will be one of the biggest jubilees on record." A month later on November 7, there was a second false peace report. This time it was declared authentic by official wire reports from Paris and Washington.

Two-and-three-quarter-inch headlines stretched across the *Semi-Weekly Iowegian*: "Germans Quit." Within five minutes the anvils boomed, the fife and drum crops were in action, the fire and coal mine whistles blew, church bells rang and marchers circled the Square. Despite the prematurity, the town knew final victory was just days away.[16]

That news of final victory reached the town November 11, 1918—the eleventh hour of the eleventh day of the eleventh month, Paris time. In Centerville it was four in the morning. The United Press bulletin began: "Germany Licked! Kaiser Canned! War Over!" "End World War," said the *Iowegian* headline. By six that morning, the news filtered from the *Iowegian* office to the first employees arriving on the Square. Mayor Fox was telephoned. He issued a proclamation declaring the day a public holiday. Schools that had just opened closed for the day. The coal mines emptied, County offices were shut. By eight o'clock again the anvils boomed, fire whistles blew and the church bells rang. Deputy Clerk to the Court Howard H. Henderson, who had an apartment on the third floor of the courthouse, threw up a window and shouted down to the Courtyard as to what was going on. "Didn't you know?" came back the answer. "Germany has just surrendered in six different places." A parade started around the Square. Every few minutes it doubled in size. It turned east onto State Street, then right, marching over the south part of the City, back again and then was temporarily disbanded. The news traveled to County towns. People began arriving on trains and wagons for an evening of music, bands, speeches and cheering.[17]

The official town parade occurred three days later, on November 14. The *Iowegian* called it "a monster." It began at the post office corner and started with the sounds of the anvils and fire whistles. The police led the way, followed by flags representing each Allied nation, bands from five County towns as well as Centerville. There was a decorated auto containing Kenneth O'Daughrity, a member of Company D, home early recovering after having a leg amputated. Sitting beside him was Colonel E.C. Haynes, the father of Company D's captain, now Major Glenn Haynes. Lodges and secret societies followed, the Women's Relief Corps, the Grand Army of the Republic and railroad employees. Everywhere there were imposing banners. Red torches flamed in the dark. Flags waved. A bonfire was lit on the Square's Southside, an effigy of the Kaiser was doused in kerosene and burned.[18]

On the morning of December 1, 1918, nineteen days after the armistice, Company D was in the Rhineland on a march to Koblenz. Its commander, Major Glenn Haynes, had received a letter from D.C. Bradley in Centerville. It contained a draft for six hundred dollars, collected by members of Centerville's

P.E.O. from the people of Appanoose County. It was a gift to the soldiers to be spent for their enjoyment. Haynes later recalled he borrowed a horse and found his men waiting in line in the rain for their rations and told them of the gift. Out of ninety men from Centerville, twenty remained. Seventy had been killed, wounded or were ill in hospitals. "I don't remember now if it was the following day or several days later that a committee of three members of the company came to my billet," Haynes recalled. "They had brushed their worn-out clothes and shoes. They were cleanly shaved and standing at attention. They gave me a piece of paper signed by all twenty remaining men." The letter expressed gratitude but requested the money be returned and "made a nucleus of a fund to be raised for the erection of a memorial for the men from Appanoose County who have given their lives in the war."[19]

As 1918 turned to 1919, the people of the town began collecting money to meet the wishes of Company D. At the same time, they planned celebrations for the return home of their men. While they waited, another crisis was about to unfold. This would not be on a distant and foreign battlefield. This one would be at home.

Chapter 33

The Great Flu Epidemic

For its victims it began with a headache. Following that came aching muscles, uncontrollable shivering, burning eyes, ascending fever and delirium. Blood invaded urine, sputum and saliva. The face and feet darkened, the patient gasped for air; death followed—by drowning.

The source of the 1918 flu epidemic remains a mystery. It was recorded first in February 1918 in a mild but highly infectious form in San Sebastian, Spain. By March it was sweeping Europe, affecting French, English, American and German troops, hindering their ability to fight.

There was a summer lull. Then the disease returned, and this time it was lethal. Half a million Americans died. Worldwide the number was twenty million to one hundred million people. And there was a pattern to its victims: babies and children under five, the elderly seventy to seventy-four and young, apparently healthy, adults aged twenty to forty.[1]

In Centerville the mild form arrived with spring. On April 8 the *Iowegian* noted: "An epidemic of an ailment resembling la grippe, which has been afflicting many of the residents of Centerville the past week, seems to have entered the school Friday, and the afternoon session in some rooms was attended by only a very few pupils ...It seldom develops into anything serious ...lasting only two or three days and in some cases only one day." Within a month, Centerville's "mild" disease caused five deaths. The ages of the victims were an ominous portent: thirteen-month-old Francis Underwood; eighteen-year-old Charles Bailey; Kirk McDonald, a soldier of twenty-three, who died at Camp Dodge; Fanny Dwyer-Brownfield, twenty-seven, a teacher at Lincoln School; and Oliver Hiatt, seventy-seven, a Civil War veteran.[2]

The outbreak prompted a campaign by local physicians against lapsing sanitary conditions. "Filth breeds disease," they argued and pointed to continued spitting on sidewalks, especially around the Interurban depot and the taxi rank on the Eastside of the Square, to undrained basements, leaking drainpipes, swarms of flies, barrels of chicken feathers and blood and decayed and decaying food in the alleys. And, they continued, within fifty yards of a restaurant and meat market, an old water closet, once removed, had been moved back by the owner, its "candy buckets" fully exposed and the stench intolerable. The town responded. The street flusher—owned jointly by the City and businesses since 1914—fanned clean water, spraying down the alleys, around the Square and the sidewalks.[3]

Then, in September, the lethal form of influenza arrived. On the twelfth, stores on Centerville Square reported two or three of their clerks had the disease. There were six at Iowa Southern Utilities, and at the Car Barn the foreman, the roadmaster and four workers were all ill, one so seriously he was admitted to the Graham Hospital on East State Street. It was the same across the country. The death toll began to rise, with U.S. Army and Naval bases affected the most. The *Semi-Weekly Iowegian* reported 41 dead in Boston, more at naval and army camps and in cities and towns within a twenty-five-mile radius of the city. In the Naval Yard at Philadelphia, 800 were ill. At Camp Dix, New Jersey, 1,800, with 34 deaths in a twenty-four-hour period. At Camp Devens, Massachusetts, "a scene out of hell" was said to exist, with 10,789 suffering the disease. At the Great Lakes Naval Station in Chicago, 8,218. By September 25, the army reported 22,992 cases, with 3,000 for just that morning. The article ended with the careful words: "The total number of deaths was not announced."[4]

In the absence of an open dialog on the number dead, bizarre rumors substituted. They were repeated in Centerville. The number of dead at Camp Dodge was said to be 150 a day; the number suffering the disease many thousands. The rumors became grotesque: twelve doctors and one nurse, it was said, had been shot at the camp for administering a substance that would hasten the deaths and spread of the disease; the number of doctors supposedly shot increased with each repeating. The Germans were blamed. Their submarines operating along the Eastern Seaboard were thought to have sent agents ashore to release germs in theaters and other places where large numbers of people assembled. "Sure the Germans started it," said a man interviewed on Centerville Square, "but it got beyond them and has now gotten into their own ranks."[5]

In late September the first bodies came home to Centerville's Rock Island station from distant military places: Floyd Mincks, twenty-one, from the army's Camp Dodge; Everett Traxler, twenty-one, from Puget Sound Naval Station; Byron Bradley, twenty-one, serving in the army's Medical Corps at the Rock Island arsenal; Roscoe Guernsey, thirty-five, from Denver, where he was entering the army's Judge Advocate General's office; Fred Houser, twenty-seven, working for the railroad at Eagle Grove. In early October the first deaths occurred inside Centerville—on October 7, B.F. Thomasson of North Seventh Street, seventy-nine years old; on October 14, Paul Lamentia, a young businessman on South Twentieth Street, who had contracted it in Chicago.[6]

Local physicians saw no reason for panic. The disease had been caught away from home by all the victims; Thomasson was old and infirm. Then on Thursday evening, October 10, the town's complacency about the disease ended. A rumor spread by word throughout the town. People, shocked and incredulous, asked for confirmation. Fifty-four-year-old Robert A. McKee was dead. He was one of the town's leading and most successful citizens. He was the owner of the Sunshine coal mine, stockholder at the Commercial State Savings Bank, a member of Knights of Pythias, the Benevolent and Protective Order of Elks and the Methodist church and one of the builders of the new Majestic Theatre on North Thirteenth Street. He was the son of Susannah McKee, the owner of the Continental Hotel who had died in the fire in 1893. He lived at an elegant address, 606 South Main, and was known for his energy, business acumen, his spirit of optimism, his dry Irish wit.[7]

As the national death toll rose, controlling panic was now an issue. Bulletins appeared in local newspapers. The *Iowegian* sent them on to Mystic. There they were posted, bright yellow notices, on the windows of Forsythe's Drug Store and the doors of the Interurban and Milwaukee stations. The entire state of Utah was shut down; so was Chicago and all of Illinois. The Health Board of Des Moines ordered a quarantine. Every theater, store, movie house, pool room, church and all public gathering places in the city were ordered to close and streetcars to carry only seated passengers. Ottumwa, Cedar Rapids, Ames, Iowa City and Cedar Falls followed. Two days later so did Clinton, Boone and Fort Madison. By October 12, eighty-four Iowa towns reported cases of the flu, six thousand across the State. Des Moines had one thousand cases, including Governor Warren L. Harding. Missouri Valley in Harrison County had eight hundred cases. Villisca in Montgomery County reported sixty-seven cases diagnosed on one day. To add to the difficulties there was a scarcity of physicians. Many had entered military service; others were ill. Spirit Lake reported its only doctor was one of the town's fifty victims. At Millersburg no doctor could be found for four hundred flu patients. In Seymour, west of Centerville, the disease claimed Wayne County's reliable and loved forty-one-year-old Dr. R.K. Ingersoll. But on the issue of a town quarantine, Centerville held out.[8]

At a town council meeting on October 11, the day after Robert McKee's death, members consulted Dr. Frank Sturdivant, the local doctor who had spoken to Company D about cleanliness and moral laxity. At thirty-five, Dr. Sturdivant was achieving a national reputation as a bacteriologist and pathologist. The following week he had joined the Mayo Clinic in Rochester, Minnesota, as assistant to Dr. Edward C. Rosenow, working on an anti-influenza vaccine. Dr. Sturdivant thought Centerville's conditions, "no worse than they are," made quarantine unjustified. It would be necessary to close the mines, he pointed out, all industries employing twenty-five or more people, stores where there is heavy trade, schools, churches and theaters. None of this would halt the spread of the disease, he said, so long as people were allowed to congregate at other places. In a unanimous vote, a local quarantine was rejected. Seven days later, on October 17, they had no choice but to reverse themselves. Guilford H. Sumner, M.D., secretary and executive officer of the Iowa State Board of Health, issued a Statewide quarantine. Centerville's Mayor Fox ordered the closing of the town's theaters, moving picture shows, public schools, churches, lodges, social and political club meetings, public funerals and pool halls. The Red Cross alone was allowed to continue. With his order, Mayor Fox combined one of his own: a reinforced order prohibiting spitting on Centerville's sidewalks.[9]

The quarantine lasted one week. It was, by accepted standards, unusual. Stores remained open; so did the mines, and the daily patriotic parades continued. The drugstores were open, as were the cigarette counters, the hotels and the eating houses. The Midway News and Lunch Room on Thirteenth Street was busier than usual selling the latest newspapers and magazines, and the Majestic Theatre was closed for movies but open for the sale of its ButterKist popcorn. On the Sunday of that week, church bells were silenced, the streets strangely deserted. By late morning, small knots of people began to gather in groups, a few strolled aimlessly or sat or lay on the courthouse lawn enjoying the bright fall sunshine. Some people took joyrides in their automobiles. Fragments of conversation were overheard: "Gee whiz, a man will have to get a permit from the board to kiss his own wife, pretty soon"; "It'll take three or four of the very best games right out of the football season"; "I think it's the right thing to do and we ought to be willing to take care of ourselves."[10]

On October 24, the State Health Office lifted its order and allowed each community to observe its own quarantine in response to its own situation. For Centerville, the quarantine ended. The church bells rang out on Sunday, bringing the faithful to worship. Braving blustery rain showers, people congregated in groups and around soft-drink stands and ice cream parlors. A week later the disease increased, and the death rate rose. October's death rate in Appanoose County numbered eight. In November it was fifty-one, in December sixty-one. Articles offering advice and countering panic appeared in newspapers. People hung asafetida on string around the necks of their children. They entered the town's drugstores. They took liquid or tablet-form laxative Bromo Quinine, aspirin or Dover's powders at the first signs. They consumed large quantities of garlic. They brewed Bulgarian Blood Tea, inhaled Booth's Hyomei or Men-Tho-Eze and drank Chamberlain's Cough Remedy and Foley's Honey Tar. On throats and chests they spread goose grease and turpentine, Vick's VapoRub or Begy's Mustarine that came in yellow boxes and was said to be "...the first, and best improvement on Grandma's old-fashioned Mustard Plaster." The careful followed the advice of U.S. Surgeon General Rupert Blue. They avoided crowds, wore face masks covering the nose and mouth, shunned common drinking cups and roller towels and slept with open windows.[11]

In December, Mayor Fox, together with Mayor Oughton of Mystic and Dr. G.F. Severs of the Iowa State Board of Health, attended a meeting in Chicago on the disease. Doctors and health authorities from across the country offered their observations. Quarantine, they said, is not an effective means of controlling the disease. What works is the observance of sanitation and the isolation of those afflicted. On his return, Mayor Fox ordered the printing of the same yellow cards that had been issued in response to earlier contagious diseases. They were distributed to the town's doctors to place them on houses of the patients who were sick. This, Mayor Fox argued, was not a quarantine but a warning to the public.[12]

The disease now preoccupied the town. The County's twelve doctors were exhausted. They barely slept. They visited the sick, finding three, even four, victims in one home. On the Square, almost every business was affected: Shkolnick's Plumbing and Heating service, clothing stores, the Appanoose Telephone Company, the *Iowegian* newspaper. The superintendent of the Graham Hospital was ill, as were the husband of a high school teacher, a popular drugstore salesman, brakemen and engineers at the railroad stations, one of the town's undertakers, the town's Civil War veterans and the area's coal miners. It raged in the County's smaller towns, in Brazil, in Dean. Moulton was relatively free of sickness after its physicians inoculated hundreds of its citizens with anti-influenza serum.[13]

The disease cut across social and ethnic classes. It took the life of a young Mexican Rock Island worker living in a boxcar in South Centerville and twenty-nine-year-old Bettina Bradley, now married to Theodore Stuart, assistant attorney general for Colorado, a lawyer for the Colorado Southern and the Denver and Rio Grande Railroads. She became ill visiting her parents, the D.C. Bradleys, and died at their mansion on Drake Avenue. Whole families were dislocated. Fathers died. Mothers died leaving three, four, five children. In Mystic, Polish immigrant Mrs. Alfred Dudegne left nine children aged one to sixteen. Parents were too ill to attend the funerals of their children. Families recovering from the loss of a son in battle now bore the loss of another to flu. Both mothers and fathers died within days of each other: Lottie and Fred Houser left two children aged five and two; the Will Eddys left six children, the oldest seventeen. Parents and children died within hours of each other, their funerals held jointly, such as Reuben Barton and his eight-year-old daughter, Minette. Mrs. Clyde Weeks and the youngest of her four children, eighteen months old, died on the same day; seven-year-old Edna died two days later. All three were buried together in the same ceremony in Mystic's Philadelphia Cemetery. On November 25 there were four deaths in Centerville and vicinity within twenty-four hours. On the twenty-ninth, five deaths occurred in eighteen hours. Unionville, Missouri, twenty-two miles south of Centerville, held nine funerals on one day, November 16—all victims of the disease.[14]

In January 1919, the number of deaths in the County declined to fifteen; by March it rose to twenty-two and then dropped steadily, virtually disappearing by June. In 1920 there was a secondary attack. Both town hospitals were full, turning away patients who were less afflicted. But this flu was far less severe. The five hundred estimated cases reported, said the *Semi-Weekly Iowegian*, "…do not cause alarm at all, altho [*sic*] people are prone to remember the awfulness of the influenza stricken city last year." Beginning in March 1919, another frightening epidemic touched Appanoose County. It was believed to be linked to influenza. It was a brain disease that worldwide killed an estimated five million people. Its name was "lethargic encephalitis," commonly called "sleeping sickness," its etiology still not understood. Patients slept continuously but could be roused to answer questions. In the case of Mrs. Harry Tissue of Moravia, she started cooking potatoes as though sleepwalking and fell asleep before the water boiled. Mrs. Tissue recovered completely, living an active and normal life, including more pregnancies. Seventeen-year-old Lucile Hendersheldt of Exline also recovered; John Bradley of Twentieth and Cottage Streets in South Centerville did not.[15]

Now, exhausted by disease and death, the people of the town turned to welcoming home their own men, those who had survived battle, trench warfare, gas attacks—and the deadly influenza pandemic of 1918.

Chapter 34

The Boys Return Home

On April 17, 1919, Centerville's Company D, as part of the 168th Infantry, boarded the U.S. troopship *Leviathan* and departed Brest Harbour on the Atlantic Coast of France for home. Eight days later they sailed through the Narrows into New York Bay and docked at Hoboken. There were forty boats, whistles, tugs decorated with flags and banners and crowds of cheering people. Some of the boats represented the home states of the soldiers. On one was a banner: "Iowa Welcomes Her Boys of the 168th." Among those on board was Mayor Fox of Centerville. The following morning, he managed a short conversation with now-Major Glenn Haynes. He then hurried back to Centerville.[1]

The boys had been absent for twenty months. Since the November armistice of 1918 and despite the raging flu epidemic, the people of the town were planning their welcome home. Meetings were held at the Association of Commerce room on the Northside of the Square. Committees were formed. A soliciting committee canvassed businesses for money. An appreciation committee was made of mothers, veteran soldiers and the War Emergency Bureau members. They rented the old *Daily Citizen* editorial room on the Square's Northeast Corner as a Soldiers and Sailors Club Room where the returning men "could drop in and occasionally regale themselves with reminiscences of the experiences through which they have just passed." Donations arrived for the club room: a leather davenport, a bookcase, books, a phonograph, records, tables, rugs, ferns, magazines and framed, mounted pictures of General Grant, General Sherman and President Wilson. Stationery was provided, imprinted with "Soldiers and Sailors Club Room, Centerville, Iowa. Maintained by the Folks Who Appreciate." Iowa Southern Utilities gave half-rate on the electric bill; cigars were provided, along with half a bushel of sugared popcorn and a basket of fresh fruit, the last three to be delivered on the return of the soldiers.

A decorative committee considered the town's appearance. The plans took form. National and Rainbow Division colors decorated the town. Large "reception buttons," six feet in diameter, were supplied for every storefront. Smaller "Rainbow Division Welcome Home" buttons for individual wear were sold for twenty-five cents apiece by enthusiastic boys and girls who were stopping people "every ten steps." On the Southside of the courthouse, a reviewing stand was built for the relatives of the soldiers. A special section, decorated with gold stars, was reserved for those who had lost a son. Spanning the courthouse's south walkway, close to the street, a Victory Arch was added. Made of a wooden framework and weighted by sand, it carried the names of all Appanoose County boys who had lost their lives in service.[2]

A parade committee planned a demonstration organized into three divisions. In the first was Major George Ogle; the police; Boy Scouts surrounding Mrs. May Fisher dressed as Columbia and Miss Madge Dale as Peace; the Centerville Band; and the Red Cross ladies, forming a large rectangle left empty to accommodate Company D and the soldiers and sailors invalided or discharged early. In the second division, behind Captain Ellis Pixley, were the local drum corps dressed in colonial costume; veterans of the Civil War and the Spanish-American War; the Women's Relief Corps dressed in colors of the Rainbow Division; professional and businessmen and the carpenters. In the third division, led by Colonel Phillip Wells, was the Unionville Band carrying its instruments, the "Colored Band" furnishing the music, and church organizations.[3]

A thousand miles away across the country, the 168th Infantry was still under military control. From Hoboken, New Jersey, the members were taken to Camp Upton, Long Island, "deloused" and assigned to quarters in barracks, where they waited for their turn to travel home, a process that took two weeks. The 168th, now thirteen hundred men and sixteen officers, traveled west on three trains, crossing the Mississippi and entering their home State at Dubuque, Davenport and Keokuk en route to Camp Dodge and Des Moines for their official discharge. It was the eleventh of May. Across Iowa, at every city, every village, every hamlet along the parallel routes, there were cheering people, parades, flowers and food. At countryside crossroads, small groups of rural people gathered to wave and shout greetings as the trains passed by. The three trains converged on Des

Moines during the night of May 13. Despite the hour, thousands greeted them, and with dawn on the fourteenth, thousands more joined.[4]

Des Moines declared a public holiday. The sky was blue, the weather sunny and warm. Special trains arrived from across the State. One carried 130 people from Centerville. The number included Appanoose County's invalided soldiers already home. People jostled on the sidewalks. They carried flags, banners and armloads of flowers to throw at the feet of the soldiers. Bunting stretched across the streets and the hill leading up to the State House, ending at an Arch of Triumph, a court of honor and reviewing stand for the governor and State leaders. For the soldiers, there was lunch at the coliseum, then came the parade. Colonel Tinely was its leader, followed by his majors—including Glenn Haynes—the Regimental Band and the uniformed soldiers in their helmets, carrying gas masks and rifles. Behind them came more than three hundred discharged or convalescent soldiers and, at the end, in automobiles, the disabled members of the regiment from the hospitals at Camp Dodge and Fort Des Moines. Through the applause they marched, across the flowers, under the Victory Arch, through the court of honor and past the reviewing stand. Their service was now ended, but they marched with the characteristic discipline of the Rainbow Division.[5]

On Saturday, May 17, 1919, Company D arrived back in Centerville on the Interurban from Albia. It had been decided there would be two celebrations. This, the first, was to be short, honoring the needs of the men and their families to be together and in private. Thousands lined the sidewalks. On the Courthouse Square, the windows of the buildings were full; so were the tops of the roofs. The fire whistle blew as the train carrying the soldiers reached the junction on Park Avenue. The men dismounted, were rushed to West State Street in autos and took their place in the parade, inside the rectangle surrounded by Red Cross ladies. People noted their uniforms, their stripes, chevrons, red and green silk citation cords, medals and insignia. Below the left shoulder they saw the red, yellow and purple rainbow of their division, the blue letter *A* of the First Army Corps and the red circumflex declaring their official discharge. The parade circled the Square, marched under the Victory Arch and past the reviewing stand. On a command from Major Haynes, the men marched backwards to form a platoon. Now they could watch the remainder of the parade pass before them. At the end of the parade, the men were dismissed. Then the gaze of onlookers turned upward. Two rainbows appeared, one close to the sun, the other closer to the horizon. They were seen across the State. Professor W.D. Morehouse of Drake University offered a scientific explanation. The boys of Company D chose another.[6]

Return of the boys from World War I at the arch on the Square, with Red Cross ladies surrounding the boys. *Courtesy of Appanoose County Historical Society.*

The second celebration, an appreciation day for all soldiers and sailors, was held on September 11. There was no parade. This was to be a day for neighbor to meet neighbor, to speak with the soldiers, to relax and enjoy. Again the town was decorated, this time with professional help from the Henry Field Company of Shenandoah. The courthouse was draped from roof to foundation. So was the Victory Arch, the electrolier lights and the streets approaching the Square. In the morning the soldiers and sailors registered and received a registration tag and free tickets for meals at the four uptown churches, the Catholic church and the Women's Relief Corps, as well as tickets for a performance of *Fair and Warmer* at the Drake Avenue Theatre, all movie shows and Coca-Cola drinks at the drugstores. At the Red Cross canteen for the soldiers, there were free cigarettes, gum, popcorn and ice cream.[7]

At two thirty in the afternoon at the bandstand, there was a presentation of the Croix de Guerre to Sergeant Bernard Nelson, the son of the Axel Nelsons of South Twentieth Street. It was awarded by the French government as a token of valor for the sergeant leading two squads of men, who at the height of battle cut a path through barbed wire and silenced enemy machine guns. Soldiers who had received their awards earlier were also recognized and "victory pins" made by Centerville people were given to every discharged soldier and sailor. There were two speeches, one from Senator James Wilson of Centerville, currently running for lieutenant governor of the State, and the Honorable Nate Kendall of Albia, candidate for nomination for governor. Kendall was known as "the silver tongued orator," and he had a special affinity with Centerville. He was married to Belle Wooden, daughter of Southside Clothing Store owner A.E. Wooden and the granddaughter of J.R. Wooden, one of the town's pioneers. The Herring Motor Company of Des Moines sent an eight-cylinder airplane. People flew above the town at ninety miles per hour for fifteen dollars, or one dollar a minute. There was a wrestling match between Company D's Cela Seals and two challengers. A magician entertained with tricks no one could explain, and there was a baseball game between Centerville and Unionville that descended into a near riot. It was broken up by the police, and it was followed by the umpire retiring, a new one taking his place. In the evening a military dance was held in the armory, the Majestic orchestra furnishing the music. It was described as one of the largest dances ever held in town. As the day ended, said the *Iowegian*, "everyone had the time of his life throughout the entire day of celebration."[8]

Of the soldiers who had departed from Centerville Square in 1917 and served the nation, fifty-five had died. For those who returned, their lives were forever altered. Deteriorating wounds led to surgeries; some caused early deaths; some, like John Stevens of Hilltown, shot in the head at St. Mihiel, suffered the rest of a long life with severe headaches, partial blindness and a lame gait. More than 160 men, including every member of Company D, suffered the effects of chlorine and mustard gas—some severely. Cleo Pickering was so affected he was brought home "in a basket." For Carroll Horn of Moulton, the gas affected his larynx to such an extent he was unable to speak for months until, exasperated, it suddenly returned when he shouted at a team of horses negotiating a creek. Major Glenn Haynes, for the rest of his life, jumped at the sound of a Klaxon auto horn—the same sound that warned soldiers of an impending gas attack. Many were treated in government hospitals in Colorado and California and as old men were distinguishable to small boys by their spectacles with green lenses.[9]

Perhaps the most serious effects, the most locally underreported, were from the condition then called "shell shock," today known as post-traumatic stress disorder. Base Hospital 117 in France recognized the symptoms, calling them "war neuroses," and attempted to treat the victims with what was then "the highest standards of neurological science." In Centerville, several soldiers on their return were described as "restless," one or two as "changed," one as "violent." One suffered from narcolepsy and was found unconscious on

Cemetery Hill, another time in South Centerville. One went missing. At least one committed suicide. Some were placed in veterans' hospitals; one wandered away. Several became addicted to narcotics and alcohol and were committed to the top floor of Independence Asylum in Missouri, where one was murdered.[10]

Most of the men, despite injuries, reentered civilian life, their experiences broadening them and in the process enriching the community. Earl Gaughenbaugh, who had left town in 1914 to fight with the Canadian army, became sheriff of Appanoose County for eight years, from 1923 to 1930. Lazelle Sawyers, who, fresh out of Princeton, volunteered for the French Mallet Ambulance division, joined the Bankers Trust Company of New York City, then came home, becoming president of the Centerville National Bank. Russell Selix, whose death in France was a reporting error, became a Baptist minister. Bernard Nelson, who was awarded the French Croix de Guerre on the Square in the September 11 celebration, returned to France and studied medicine at the Sorbonne. Howard Anderson and J.C. Clymo supervised the building of railroads in Siberia. Mike Sklavos, who had been Major Haynes's orderly during the war, and George Kostas set up a shop on Thirteenth Street, the Midway. They called it the Rainbow Ice Cream Parlor to honor the army division in which they served. In less than a year, they could afford larger quarters, moving onto the Square three doors south of the Continental Hotel. Charles Orey of North Fourth Street brought home an English bride, and J. Dilts planted poppies in his Centerville garden with seeds from Flanders Field, brought home by a grandson who had served in the A.E.F.[11]

Over the years, the men gave speeches to high school classes, to local churches and to organizations. They formed American Legion chapter number 214. They named it for Ray Walden, the first man from the town to die in battle, and they won Iowa's "Murphy's Mug" for the biggest increase in membership for the year 1926. They attended the funerals of fourteen soldiers whose families requested their bodies be brought home. Every year, Company D held its annual banquet on March 5—the anniversary of the first day the Germans attacked them and were repulsed. They helped each other find employment, assisted their comrades in need and canvassed the County for money for a memorial to French dead at the Battle of the Marne and for a campaign to rebuild the French town of Belleau as a memorial to American dead at Belleau Woods and Chateau Thierry. They traveled together to reunions and to special events. Over Christmas 1919, they were in Laclede, Missouri, for the homecoming of General Pershing. In 1920 and in 1924, they were in Des Moines when Pershing visited camps and hospitals and was welcomed at a reception at Hotel Fort Des Moines by now-Governor Nate Kendall and the first lady, Belle Wooden of Centerville. People recalled their personal contacts with John J. Pershing. Mrs. Frank Mohler's brother and sister attended grade school with him in Laclede. Elizabeth Bidwell on South Twentieth Street stayed in the Pershing home when her own home was destroyed in a tornado. She remembered the young Pershing sliding down banisters, leaping backwards over the newel post and letting out a "whoop" that awoke her baby. L.W. Orr of East Franklin was a student with Pershing at Kirksville Normal School, now Truman State University. Orr remembered Pershing was not good at math, but he could "pitch the hardest straightest ball you ever saw." There was a soldier with a more recent memory. John Tunnell, who enlisted in Centerville in 1917, was stationed in eastern France. In a lull in fighting, he took some cartoons cut from recent *Semi-Weekly Iowegians* to the general. "To heck with the cartoons," said Pershing, "who's here from Centerville?"[12]

The most important day for the soldiers was each anniversary of the armistice. Those who had been in battle remembered back to the sound of a German bugle, the silence that followed and the singing of German troops in their trenches. It was too late for Wayne Minor, fighting in the Ninety-second African American Division. He had acquired a sterling reputation as a soldier. Minor was killed three hours before the 11 a.m. armistice. Earl Gaughenbaugh remembered being almost killed. After recovering from the gas attack at Ypres, he was at Cambrai with Canadian forces. One of the last German shells exploded near him. He was dragged unconscious into a Belgian peasant's hut and revived with a bottle of wine. Some remembered Paris. Spontaneously with the armistice, people poured onto the Champs-Élysées and the Place de la Concorde. Sounds of American jazz spilled from the cafés. People embraced. They kissed, and they asked American soldiers to teach them to fox-trot. They danced on the sidewalks.[13]

All the men were deeply proud of having served in the Rainbow Division. They knew they had spent more days in the face of the enemy, been opposed by the best German divisions, gained more ground against them and marched further in its operations than any other division in the A.E.F. They knew of General Pershing's praise: "The share which the forty-second division has had in the success of our armies, should arouse pride in its achievements in all ranks." As they prepared to board the *Leviathan* on their way home, Vice Admiral Moreau, the governor of Brest, read them a letter of eulogy from Premier Clemenceau of France. But for the Iowa men, the 168th Infantry, their most treasured memory was the praise from Douglas MacArthur. When a French staff major congratulated MacArthur on the military bearing of the men, he replied, "Is it any wonder my father was proud of this regiment?"

The 168th was the Fifty-first Iowa Infantry, led by Douglas's father Arthur MacArthur in the Philippines in the Spanish-American War.[14]

In contrast to the ecstatic cheering of armistice in 1918, the yearly anniversaries in Centerville became increasingly somber and reflective. Fifteen minutes before noon, the bells of the City tolled. The stores closed. The courthouse clock struck twelve, and for two minutes the citizens of Centerville stopped and stood in silence. There was a roll call of the dead, and there were speeches. The speakers declared their gratitude for the "end of the war that would end all wars." Others were already skeptical of the phrase. Fritz Haynes, the brother of Glenn, the son of Civil War veteran Colonel E.C. Haynes, had chosen to fight not as an officer but as a private soldier in the trenches. In the months after armistice, he heard America's respected journalist William Allen White speak at the University of Paris. Fritz quoted him in a letter home to Centerville. White foreshadowed World War II: Beware, he cautioned, of a Germany that may become "...a new and strong nation [and] leap up in arms to strike, but still breathing the spirit of revenge and imperialism." In South Centerville, Nels Nelson, an inspector for the Quincy Railroad, remembered a book his grandfather kept next to his Bible in South Vissing, Denmark. It was called *How to Get America.* The book, written by Prussian officers and approved by Chancellor Bismarck, laid out a German plan to conquer Europe first, then England, then America. Nelson's mind as a child was imprinted with one phrase from the book: "With the United States in our hands, the rest of the world must follow, for we are God's chosen people who will rule the world for Him."[15]

Already the next "rough beast," its hour come round at last, was "slouching" into history. Adolf Hitler started his Nazi Party in 1919 with seven members. By 1923 they numbered seventy thousand brown-shirted men, goose-step marching and armed. On November 7 of that year in Munich, after a mass rally in the Burgerbrau Beer Hall, they smashed trade union offices and republican newspapers, raided Jewish homes, tried to take over the railroad and the post office and planted swastika flags on the main square. The world, tired and exhausted, looked away.[16]

Chapter 35

Prohibition

On January 1, 1920, the Eighteenth Amendment to the U.S. Constitution became law. "Prohibition" outlawed the manufacture, sale or transportation of intoxicating liquors. The State of Iowa was already "dry." Its own Prohibition law, and before that arbitrary local "mulct" laws, had allowed law enforcement officers to invade Appanoose County homes, confiscate liquor and fine or imprison those involved.[1]

For Appanoose County's immigrants, for those from southern and eastern Europe, it's doubtful whether any single law could have been more alien to their way of life. For the Italians, the Sicilians, the Croatians and the Greeks, wine was integral to their culture, part of their enjoyment of life. Prohibition laws propelled hundreds of these County immigrants to become lawbreakers. Some went further: their bootlegging activities absorbed them into a criminal class. Violence became common, and Centerville was a haunt of gang members from St. Louis, Kansas City and Chicago.

For the women who had smashed the saloons of South Centerville, Plano and Mystic, for the ministers, for the members of the Women's Christian Temperance Union and the Anti-Saloon League, their immediate objective was realized. Eliminating alcohol, they believed, would end poverty, disease, crime, insanity, degeneracy and the disintegration of the family. It would empty asylums, poor houses and jails.[2]

On Sunday, April 26, it was the subject of this last group that packed the Presbyterian church to hear the new pastor, thirty-eight-year-old Dr. Mott Sawyers, the distinguished son of the respected Sawyers family, deliver a sermon on "Why Is the Appanoose Jail Empty?" "Prohibition," he said, "has taken the place in a nation where drink was responsible for most of its crime." He pointed north to the County jail. "In February a year ago," he continued, "there were 50 prisoners in the Appanoose County jail ...This year there were 29. In March a year ago there were 39 prisoners ...This year there were only 11. During the month of April a year ago there were 27 ... This year there have been only 8 ...The county jail has been empty twenty days during the month of April and at the present time there is only one inmate." It was the same across the nation, he said. "If the nation's moral progress increases during the next year at the rate it has this year, there will be no prisoners."[3]

It was a wishful hope. Six days into the new national law, Deputy Sheriff Harry Trigg and Constable Thomas made their first raid. It was in Clarkdale, four miles north and west of Centerville, halfway down a well at the home of Sam Kansara. They found eight gallons of white whiskey, twelve large boxes of raisins and a half-barrel of raisins in process of souring.[4]

In May it was Clarkdale again, where they found six gallons of white liquor and five barrels of souring raisins. Then in June, accompanied by Sheriff Elgin and State agent Webb, they searched a coal mine one mile north of Mystic, leased to a John Frost. Blocked by hip-high water, smoke from the mine furnace, a rock wall, a door they broke with a battering ram, sixteen feet of "gob" dirt and black damp that almost killed agent Webb, they found a room with a three-burner still and fourteen barrels of soured raisins.[5]

The next raids were south of the Square and south of the town. This was the area that had already dominated the earlier raids under Iowa's Prohibition laws and local mulct laws. It was the area that would now dominate the raids, the murders and the violence of the next decade.

On September 29, nine months into national Prohibition, a man was arrested at the Rock Island station as he boarded a westbound train. In his suitcase were two gallon jugs and a quart bottle of "grappi." He told police he'd been coming to Centerville three times a week, where he bought liquor in town and then delivered it to a poker joint and a "blind tiger" at Trenton, Missouri.[6]

At the Blue Front, a small store near the Rock Island crossing on South Eighteenth run by Mrs. Nicolo Vinceri since the Black Hand murder of her husband, police found five pint bottles hidden in the false bottom of a table. In the cellar they found a gallon jug, a second one in a sand pile. At Number Thirty Mining Camp on October 4, in a surprise raid of the home of Louis Succo, they found a bushel basket heaped with bottles of "perfectly good well-tempered grappi" being consumed by ten patrons.[7]

These were mostly small operations, producing a few gallons of wine. They were well-known as "white mule," "dado" or "dago red," a corn whiskey called "hooch" and "chautau" or beer. The products of the small operations were shared among friends or were sold in "blind tigers" or in "speakeasies." They were usually served from fruit jars, giving a habitual imbiber a characteristic horizontal line below the bridge of the nose. Some men were known as "liquor leggers." They carried liquor and served it from specially made pockets with tiny cups.[8]

Five days after the raid at Mine Thirty, Sheriff Elgin and Deputy Harry Trigg found an operation that was quite another story and catering to different clientele. They found "a first class still …a credit to a small brewery." It was in a farm just west of Streepyville. In the basement, the two officers discovered a heavy copper kettle of forty-gallon capacity, a copper lid and wing screws for clamping the two together, making a steam-tight enclosure. In the center of the lid was a large retort and a long copper coil for condensing wine. Next to the kettle they found an elaborate set of burners, operated by kerosene and ready to cook five barrels of mash that stood close by. The officers commented on the cleanliness of the operation. It appeared to them to be sophisticated. Only much later did it occur to them the operation was something more significant.[9]

At the end of 1920, the first year of Prohibition, seven raids had been conducted in Appanoose County. In 1921 there were sixty-three, when the average for any other Iowa county was twenty to twenty-five. More and larger stills were discovered. There were larger hauls. Stills were producing 25 gallons of grappi, 300, 500, 620, even 2,192 gallons. Officers found 162 bottles of beer, then another 176 and later enough to fill two Ford police cars. The amount of liquor being found, the still at Streepyville, the selling of grappi to Trenton and a report that Centerville grappi was being transported to Des Moines hinted at something else: professional organized activity on a large scale.[10]

This was confirmed in February 1921 with the first arrival in town of two federal agents who were sent "to make a clean up by someone who knew that there was a need for it." Together with Deputy Trigg, the two agents searched South Centerville, Shawville and Mine Number Thirty. They smashed large quantities of wine and mash and took away samples for an analysis of the content of alcohol.[11]

Their report listed everything well in excess of the half of 1 percent allowed by law. Local beers were 3 to 7 percent, wines 7 to 10 percent and Appanoose County whiskey above 44 percent. The reputation of local liquor was spreading. Not even visits by federal agents contained it. Three travelers arrested for drunkenness told Mayor Fox they had heard of Centerville grappi and had come to sample it. They said it was "stronger" and "more deadly" than the rumors and "…after a few swallows they were able to testify to its staggering powers." The liquor sold by Mrs. Vinceri at her store on South Eighteenth Street was described as "good grappi"; that of Louis Succo at Mine Number Thirty "perfectly good" and "well-tempered"; five gallons taken from the Louis Varese home in June 1921 "…of the best grade and contained …four and one-half gallons of alcohol"—it could have "rendered 40 men practically unconscious." Matt Supertina made such superior grappi at Goatsburg, eight miles south of Centerville Square, it was in demand in New York City. When his operation was discovered and closed down, he told Justice Zimmer, "I can get $40.00 a gallon for grappi in New York City."[12]

The raids, the arrests did not slow local production. Ten carloads of California grapes were said to have arrived in the summer of 1923. They were consigned to Streepy, to Number Thirty and to other camps. One carload of grapes was estimated by the *Iowegian* to weigh twelve tons, or twenty-four thousand pounds. Twenty pounds of grapes made three gallons of wine. One carload of grapes could yield thirty-six hundred gallons of wine; multiplied by ten for the ten carloads, there had to be thirty-six thousand gallons of grappi in Appanoose County. With a return of ten dollars a gallon fifty miles west in Leon, and forty dollars a gallon in New York City, the economic incentive was obvious.[13]

The odor of alcohol gently permeated the town. It settled around the courthouse cellars where the grappi and grappi-making equipment were taken. Thieves broke in through basement windows. They tipped and sampled the wine; they stole the equipment. The next confiscations were locked into Justice Zimmer's office and Justice Bryant's on an upper floor. The liquor leaked. It soaked through the floor and trickled through to offices and rooms below.[14]

First-class-quality whiskey bottles, labeled products of the Consolidated Distilleries of Canada, such as Old Kentucky and Old Crow, were donated to local hospitals. Other bottles were smashed at the rear of the police station on West Jackson and the County jail on North Main, shards flying into the faces of police officers. Gallons were emptied into Cooper Creek and the ground nearby, causing, on one occasion, an Interurban freight train to "buck." When crew members descended to find the cause, they saw two hoboes, red bandannas tied around their possessions, running to find the source of the smell. As the two watched one thousand gallons mix with the water and the dust, they looked at each other and shook their heads, and tears descended their cheeks.[15]

Sheriff Gaughenbaugh (kneeling) with confiscated equipment during Prohibition. *Courtesy of Appanoose County Historical Society.*

In the middle of their raids searching for illegal liquor, Centerville police were notified of a new concern. A federal agent and a State narcotics agent from Des Moines warned that Centerville was the opium-district center of southern Iowa and that an organized band of dope peddlers was using the City as its headquarters.[16]

For years, local police had known about Fred Taylor. Since the death of his father, he was running the family music store over the City Book Store on the Southside of the Square. Several times he'd been arrested and sent for treatments but had relapsed. Now he was watched and arrested again. He was found to be carrying on his person fifty grains of morphine, a syringe, a needle and small envelopes of powdered morphine, ready for sale at two dollars a package. He was lodged in the City jail, denied visitors and ordered isolated. There was a two-year lull in dope trafficking. Then it started again.[17]

Doctors' offices were raided for opiates: Dr. Sawyers's office over the Frankel store; Dr. W.B. Miller's over the Fritch Pool Hall on the Southwest Corner. Addicts circled the Square. They searched doctors' cars. They stole surgeons' cases, ransacking them for morphine. Many appeared in a "pitiable" condition. Some sought help. One young man asked the County attorney, C.W. Howell, to be sent to the asylum at Independence, saying, "I would rather die than go on as I am going now."[18]

The adopted treatment policy of addicts was to give them "a shot" and order them out of town. In 1923 this changed. There was a new sheriff in town. It was Earl Gaughenbaugh, who had survived World War I trenches, gas attacks, wounds and unconsciousness. He ordered the established policy reversed. Addicts were no longer given "a shot." They were placed in the County jail. Mayor Keller kept records on cards. Each listed a known addict. They included high school students and several from the town's wealthy families. The *Centerville Journal* was alarmed. It quoted a local druggist, who saw a new "society" class of addicts who, unlike those desperate on the Square, could practice their vice secretly, undetected by anyone except their physicians.[19]

Throughout it all, there was still plenty of drunkenness from alcohol in the town. Intoxicated people drove cars too fast, were rowdy, were arrested for disturbing the peace, ran down children, got in fights and seduced young girls. Drunks were found unconscious behind Swearingen's Pool Hall or sitting in the middle of Drake Avenue, unable to navigate or even stand. One broke a collar bone, tore a shoulder and fractured a skull after mistaking an upstairs window for the front door. Paul, the son of druggist Mose Beer, dressed in a pair of summer trousers known as "ice-cream pants" and a black-and-white hat, directed traffic on the Square's Southeast Corner. At the same time, across the Square on the Northwest Corner, his friend Charles Pyfer also directed traffic while holding aloft a large black umbrella. Four men, all "two sheets to the wind," sat in a car on the Square on a warm summer evening. Sheriff Gaughenbaugh leaned down to the open window, asking, "Gentlemen, can I be of any assistance?" A long pause followed and then a voice answered: "Not unless you can sing tenor."[20]

Some, including high school students who either couldn't find the liquor or weren't able to afford it, resorted to Bay Rum Hair Tonic, available at Woolworth's or the McLellan's stores, or rubbing alcohol, ignoring clear warnings on the label that if taken internally "…it will cause violent gastric disturbances."[21]

The drunks were all arrested and put into jail, appearing before the mayor the next morning to pay fines. These were twenty dollars for the first offense, increasing amounts for subsequent arrests. A sixty-three-year-old Irishman—a lumberjack who, according to the newspaper, had mixed his Irish with too much Scotch—told the mayor he had no money. He paid his fine by sharpening the City's saws and axes and then performed an impromptu clog dance of gratitude to the mayor and bystanders. Some drunks, judged to be habitual offenders, were sent to the Independence asylum for treatment until that institution became too full and refused new patients.[22]

In due course, the names of the drunks appeared in the local newspapers. An exception was made in the case of those judged to be from prominent and wealthy town families. They were given sobriquets: John Doe One or John Doe Two. John Doe One, a habitual offender, when arrested was described as "pickled, kippered, stewed and wall-eyed."[23]

But for Centerville in the early 1920s, alcohol and dope were not its only problems. One was superseding them. It was murder.

Chapter 36

Violence and Murder

On the evening of June 16, 1920, thirty-six-year-old Sicilian immigrant Tony Matto had just finished his shift work at Mine Number Thirty. He washed, changed his clothes in a room he rented at fellow Sicilian Luciano Tobia's boarding house, put fifteen cents in his pocket for a movie ticket and walked north along the east sidewalk of South Eighteenth Street. At house number 1607, he stopped and walked up the path of the house of George Russo. On the porch was George's eighteen-year-old daughter, Carmela. Matto, witnesses later said, leaned toward her, whispered and took her arm. Within minutes Tony Matto was dead. Carmela shot him once in the yard of her home, then six or seven times more as she chased him down the back alley. She then returned home, telephoned Officer John Maring at the police station and said, "I have just shot a man, come and get me."[1]

Carmela Russo was single. Tony Matto was married. Both were immigrants, and both were part of Centerville's tightly knit, densely compacted Italian-Sicilian community living around the Rock Island crossing on South Eighteenth Street. The 1920 U.S. census of Appanoose County shows immigrants from forty different countries of national origin. In comparison, Peoria, Illinois—considered a benchmark of immigrant diversity—lists forty-four on its 1930 census. But Peoria's population at 111,827 was more than thirteen times the size of Centerville's 8,486; Peoria County at 141,367 more than four times the population of Appanoose County's 30,535. The largest contingent of Appanoose County's immigrants—746 on the 1920 census—were Italians. They left their hillside villages in northern Italy and came to mining camps around the County, but chiefly south of Centerville Square to Thirty, Streepyville, Numa, Shawville, Seymour or, like Carmela Russo and Tony Matto, to South Centerville around the Rock Island Railroad. On arrival, each immigrant moved into a boardinghouse run by an immigrant or lodged in a private immigrant home until he could afford his own house and send money to Italy or Sicily for other members of his family to join him. The Italian immigrants could maintain their own way of life almost without interruption. They mixed with each other, enjoyed Saturday night dances in the kitchens of friends and attended familiar services and rituals at Centerville's St. Mary's or Numa's St. William's Catholic churches. They shopped in their native language at Italian grocery stores: Vinceri's, Grazian's or Arduino's in South Centerville; Milani's on the Square; Poli's at Streepyville and in Seymour; and Joe Brazzalle's at Thirty, which specialized in imported cheeses and ingredients for Italian dishes.[2]

They celebrated Italy Day in May with town parades that started at the post office and circled the Square. Public speeches were given at the bandstand by the postmaster representing the federal government, the mayor, the senator, a reverend, Philip Buscemi representing local Italians and the Honorable Paul Parisi of Chicago, who spoke in Italian. The mayor presented the key to the City of Centerville for the evening. The parade was led by Santi Milani, Italians of the Centerville Society of Generale Caneva, the Italian band from Seymour, the Italian/Croatian band from Rathbun, the Italian Foresters of Numa and members of the Columbia Society of Seymour. Following the marchers came flag-decorated floats full of children dressed in Italian national costumes, and people shouted, "Viva l'Italia. Viva l'America" and waved the national flags of both countries.[3]

Most of Centerville's Italians and Sicilians took advantage of the opportunities in their new country. Their children attended free public schools. One of them, Philip Buscemi, in 1915 had taught private evening classes to sixteen Italian men, aged sixteen to thirty-five, to help them speak and write English. They came from work in the mines and met five nights a week, from seven to ten o'clock, in a room donated by the Centerville School Board. All the Italians imported traditional village and family patterns with their prescribed male and female roles. Some of the southern Italians and Sicilians, those from an area of grinding poverty and corrupted authority, went much further. They imported strict rules for conduct and violent revenge for its infringements. The murder of Tony Matto by Carmela Russo was part of that pattern.[4]

For nine years before the Russo/Matto murder, a pattern of accelerating violence was occurring in the area: a hatchet murder in Mystic; Robert Kelly's killing of his entire family at the Drum and Monkey Mine; a shooting on the Interurban; Joe Gonzales found dead in his boxcar at the Keokuk and Western depot, a bullet hole over his heart. Sarah Williams, who ran a "disorderly house" on Houser Row in South Centerville, shot and killed Effie Mills, whom she saw as a competitor for the attentions of Logan McDonald. And in Unionville, northeast of Centerville, in the middle of the day in the middle of Main Street, Alice Gerlach was shot and killed by her cousin Frank Smith, who said he was forced to kill her "against his will," because a woodpecker pecking at his roof awoke him that morning, a sure sign that violence must follow.[5]

Then events took a disturbing and ethnic trend. Pearl Traxler, a thirty-one-year-old Appanoose County man from Cincinnati, emerging from the Frank Danna Dance Hall near the Interurban Park northwest of the town, was shot and instantly killed by Italian immigrant Frank Dangelo, jealous because Traxler had danced with Linnie Hinkle. At the same time, the lives of local citizens were threatened with Black Hand letters. This organization—La Mano Nera—was born in Sicily in the 1750s and imported to the United States in the 1880s. It started as a protection society offering modest insurance and burial benefits for immigrants from southern Italy and Sicily. It degenerated, demanding extortion money, particularly from successful immigrants, and it settled personal feuds with brutality. Bionchi Luizi told friends he had refused to dynamite the home of the Seymour town marshal and now feared for his own life. He chose suicide, throwing himself down a Seymour mine shaft. That was 1911, the first reported local Black Hand activity. Six years later, Sam Massey reported he feared for his life from "the gang." He kept hiding and clutching his pocket as if it contained a gun. Local authorities committed him to Mount Pleasant Asylum. Two months later, a badly frightened unnamed foreigner, a section hand on the Rock Island, asked for police protection and got it. He was secreted at the police station until he could safely leave town.[6]

These incidents remained unconnected until the night of October 31, 1918. At one twenty in the morning, the home of Italian immigrant Tony DeZorzi at the corner of North Tenth Street and West Van Buren, just off the Square, was blown apart by dynamite. The family escaped serious injury. DeZorzi showed the police three letters he'd received in the last weeks, all signed with a hand imprinted in black ink. The first was postmarked from a town in Pennsylvania, the last two from Chicago. All three demanded money in increasing amounts, the last for sixteen thousand dollars. All included death threats. The last letter gave the threat in graphic form. It included a precise artist's drawing of Tony DeZorzi lying in a coffin with a stiletto knife sticking out of his heart. Bloodhounds brought from Agency, near Ottumwa, followed a trail down alleyways and across streets from the DeZorzi house to the home of Frank Danna, the dance hall owner, already under suspicion for his involvement in the murder of Pearl Traxler. Sam Falzone was charged along with Danna. More Black Hand letters appeared—at Rathbun; to Centerville businessman Noah Ressler to put five hundred dollars at the back of Fisher Lumber Yard or be shot. They also went to Mayor Fox, who had sworn to clean up the town, and to Sheriff Gaughenbaugh, who was carrying out Fox's directive.[7]

The town's court dockets were dominated by Italian names—Salamone, Bellegante, Mioto, Pampio, Cora, Beraha, Sacco, Torreseni. The chief area of crime was South Centerville. In 1913, Tony Bartello—who had already killed Joe Long—met Frank Russi in a duel just east of the Eighteenth Street Rock Island crossing. Both died. Russi was a lodger in the Russo home. Carmela was then eleven years old. In Galleyville, further south, Sisto Varetti knocked at the door of Bartello Galvan, shot Galvan through the door and then committed suicide. On February 2, 1915, Jocomo (or Giachimo) Trapina—a boarder in the home of Sam Falzone—was found, his throat cut from ear to ear, on the railroad track on South Eighteenth and Stewart. A wide swath of blood and two sets of footprints in the snow revealed the victim was dragged from the east. No one was charged, but suspicion fell on Ben Zucarelle, who had changed his name from Campanelli when he'd escaped from Orrville, Illinois, where he was serving a murder sentence. He was a witness at Trapina's inquest held in the Lankford Funeral Home on the Square. He was urged by his wife not only to view Trapina's body—against his will—but to kiss it. This was a southern Italian belief that a person so kissed would not haunt dreams. On February 10, 1920, miner and storekeeper Nicolo Vinceri rose at five in the morning, dressed, lit his lantern, took a bucket of oats and left his house on South Seventeenth for the barn. He was ambushed, shot and killed. Again no one was charged. There were rumors of an Italian stranger in town who left on an early morning train. Mrs. Vinceri told police they had received Black Hand letters and feared for their lives. Four months later, almost directly across the road, Carmela Russo killed Tony Matto.[8]

The *State of Iowa v. Carmela Russo* trial began September 20, 1920, at the courthouse on Centerville Square. Every seat was taken, with women outnumbering men three to one. People stood in the aisles. John Luse, the bailiff, and Ash Henderson, the doorkeeper, struggled to maintain a narrow pathway through the dozens blocking the entrance. The trial lasted ten days. In that time the court heard how, when Tony Matto arrived from Sicily, he became one of the lodgers at the Russo home. The defense described

Matto's three-year repeated sexual advances to Carmela and an incendiary letter Matto had written to Cosimo Malone, Carmela's fiancé. The letter told of Carmela's intimacies with her cousin and with Tony Matto. It also claimed Carmela had obtained an illegal surgery in Des Moines. After reading the letter, Cosimo Malone ended the engagement. When Carmela spoke in her own defense, her voice was calm, clear and controlled. "Are you sorry you killed Tony Matto?" asked one of her lawyers. "As God is my judge, Mr. Wilson, I cannot say that I am."[9]

There was considerable sympathy in the town for Carmela. She was well liked. She came to Centerville at the age of six, attended McKinley School and spoke her own native Italian, English and Spanish well. She worked in the courthouse for the Appanoose Title and Abstract Company. She assisted immigrants in their applications for citizenship or those who registered for the draft in World War I. Character witnesses described her as "peaceful," "quiet," her reputation as "good." An open letter to the women of the County on behalf of Carmela appeared in the newspaper. People signed petitions for clemency on the counters of seven stores on the Square—all four drugstores, at Frankel's, the millinery parlor of Mrs. E. Kimber, and the confectionery store of Santi Milani. More petitions appeared around the County, and as the news spread , they appeared around the State.[10]

Carmela was convicted of manslaughter. She was sentenced to eight years in Rockwell City Reformatory. Before she left on the train, she was married to Cosimo Malone. It was the end of the first installment in the lives of Carmela, Cosimo Malone and the Russo family. The same can be said for Centerville's connection to murder and violence.[11]

More bodies were found alongside railroad tracks and on crossings: Dan Gill at Streepyville; John Swab at Galleyville; Joseph Farris on the South Eighteenth crossing; Elvin Kirkman, fourteen years old, at Coal City, south of Moulton; Celestino Colombo, east of Numa; David Weston in the river below the Dennis Interurban Bridge. The remains of the victims were badly mutilated to obscure criminal activity. Drivers of trains reported seeing men running from the vicinity of the bodies; autopsy reports showed David Weston had not died by drowning, as it appeared, but by violence to the transverse colon and solar plexus.[12]

Tony Montegna, an Italian ice cream vendor pushing his cart a block west of the Rosenbaum Junk Yard, near the Rock Island crossing on South Eighteenth Street, shot and killed Mexican Ben Cardanas in an argument over an ice cream cone. Ten-year-old Wiladine Jeters was killed by a bullet intended for her father,

Harry. It was fired by Roy Johnson in a house gambling party south of the Eighteenth Street crossing.[13]

William "Crip" Hamilton, a sixty-year-old, well-known Centerville taxi driver, picked up passengers at the taxi rank at the Continental Hotel on the night of August 20, 1921. Hours later he was found murdered, seven miles east of town on the Moulton Road. He had a bullet hole in the back of his neck, another through his chest. Suspicion fell on a gambling den in a Moulton boxcar infamous for bootlegging and "wild women." It also fell on two young men from South Centerville: Bruce Henry and Harvey Hicks.[14]

At one of David Dinning's Cincinnati mines, Thistle Number Four, watchman Axel Johnson Deer, sixty-two years old and an immigrant from Norrkoping, Sweden, was murdered. He was found in a tent where he lived on the company grounds, three axe wounds to his head.[15]

Some deaths were suspicious: for example, Battista Battistello and Pete Govanni, who fell from moving cars or from cars overturned by multiple burst tires. Some simply disappeared and were declared missing: Guiseppe Travona and Tony Sebben, both from Thirty, George Grando from Rathbun, Gus Petrani from Galleyville. Some died violently in Chicago: Antonio Guiseppe; Filadelphia Todora; Pagliachi Kaskyski; and Sam Falzone, who in Centerville in 1918 had been charged with conspiracy in the dynamiting of Tony DeZorzi's home on North Tenth Street and West Van Buren. Santo Cellebron, who was driving trucks into Cicero, possibly carrying grappi from Appanoose County, was shot for "talking too much." Louis Cora was shot in Chicago but somehow returned to Centerville and was attended by Dr. W.B. Miller, who removed three bullets from his head.[16]

In December 1921, the *Iowegian* noted Centerville's Southside was being invaded by "some who are tough and growing tougher."[17]

Shots and cries were heard in the night. Fights swiftly became violent. John Buhr, failing to kill John Scavuzzo by a bullet through the door, killed Scavuzzo's two horses instead. Outside the Rainbow Candy Store on the Square's Eastside, Charles Raney pulled a gun on Pete Titone and then a razor on Tony Swob. There were fights at Huff Swearingen's Pool Hall, and outside the Wooden Bank on the Square's Westside four women bearing grudges were pried apart after fighting; two women in town from Promise City were attacked by another two women, hitting one on the head with a hoe, the other with a hammer.[18]

There were family fights and family feuds. Elizabeth Cambruzzi was shot by her stepfather, Barney Datto, for resisting his advances. She pressed charges then dropped them, and the two left court arm in arm. Mrs. Datto promptly filed for divorce—for the fifth time. On the main street of Brazil, five miles west of Centerville, Basilio Brodi shot John Logsdon, his father-in-law, in what was called the rear of his hip. Brodi also charged Logsdon with a statutory offense against Logsdon's daughter, who was Mrs. Brodi. Logsdon countercharged that he was removing his daughter from Brodi's violence. When Brodi was found guilty and sentenced to thirty years for attempted murder, he sobbed, fell to the courtroom floor, was carried back to jail, threatened to kill all those who had a part in sending him to prison, butted his head on the jail's iron walls, bobbed it on the floor, said, "Me, I will go to the cemetair and not to the penitent" and set his cot on fire and then laid on it.[19]

There were holdups on roadways, at Mine Thirty, at the Judy Plant and at Brazil's railroad ticket office. Passing bad and forged checks caused alarm at the stores and the banks. In the first three years of the 1920s, the *Daily Iowegian* and *Citizen* reported sixty-three major cases of robberies and urged the retail merchants to install burglar alarms, called electronic policemen. The retail merchants urged the Association of Commerce to push for better police protection.[20]

Bullets flew through windshields, through the tires of cars, through windows at the Kauzlarich home and through a window at Rathbun School, just missing the teacher and the children, the bullet embedding itself in the blackboard. At the Mike Buban home, south of the City, a brick shattered the glass of the window and hopped across the floor, injuring one of his children.[21]

Evidence began to appear that national organized gangs were involved in local crime. At the Rock Island depot on the night of March 19, 1921, thieves stole the eastbound registered mail pouch containing nearly one hundred thousand dollars. The theft was part of a network of thefts masterminded by John W. Worthington and Owen T. Edwards, the president and vice president of the Central Securities Company of Chicago.[22]

The next evidence came on October 11, 1921. On his way home from work at one in the morning, Centerville policeman H.A. "Slim" Edwards offered assistance to three men working on a Ford touring car on South Twelfth Street, two blocks south of Maple Street. In response, a bullet shattered the bone in his left leg, a second deeply creased his left wrist and a third hit him just above the heart. Edwards, on the ground and believing himself to be fatally wounded, pulled his gun from a shoulder holster and fired at the men, who were trying to start the car by pushing it down Twelfth Street, one of them trying at the same time to remove the car's license plate. The three men abandoned the car and scattered on foot.[23]

Edwards survived. The critical bullet, aimed at his heart, was deflected by his officer's metal badge. Clues from the abandoned car, from its engine number

Sheriff's badge that protected against gunshot. *Courtesy of Gary Craver.*

number—3252844—identified the car owner as Luke Kennedy, a member of the notorious St. Louis Hogan Gang. Appanoose County sheriff Elgin traveled to Jefferson City with extradition papers. Before Elgin returned to Centerville, Luke Kennedy, handcuffed to a St. Louis police officer, appeared at the hospital bedside of the recovering "Slim" Edwards. The officer presented Edwards with an affidavit to sign that the prisoner before him was the man who had shot him.[24]

Edwards hesitated. The attack had happened in the dark. His assailant had worn a hat and had several days' growth of beard. And, Edwards thought, the man who shot him was taller. But he prepared to sign the document. It was at this moment that the County attorney, Tom Fee, entered the hospital room, intercepted the affidavit and tore it up. The two visitors from St. Louis were imposters. The "police officer" was Jacob Mackler, the gang's attorney.

Charges against the real Luke Kennedy were dropped, a grand jury citing insufficient evidence. Kennedy returned to St. Louis. On April 17, 1922, less than six months after his alleged attack on "Slim" Edwards, he was shot to death as he sat in his car on Hamburger Avenue. Ten months later, attorney Jacob Mackler, the phony police officer, met the same fate as he sat in his car at Twelfth and Howard Streets. The assassins were members of a rival St. Louis gang: Egan's Rats. Its leader, its prime marksman, was a man calling himself William P. Colbeck, a man already familiar with Centerville. The assassination of Jacob Mackler was on February 14, 1923—St. Valentine's Day. Six years later, to the day, at the SMC Cartage Co. at 2122 North Clark Street in Chicago, a man calling himself Fred Burke adopted Mackler's ruse of dressing as a police officer in the infamous shooting that would come to be known as the St. Valentine's Day Massacre.

The people of the town collected a gift of money for "Slim" Edwards. He left St. Joseph Hospital on December 22, 1921. He had spent eleven weeks in recovery. He would limp the rest of his life.[25]

Chapter 37

Morality and a Movie

For the town, as for the country, in the first years of the 1920s, the problems went far beyond alcohol, murder, theft and infiltration by gang members. General morality and discipline seemed to be in free fall.

Children entered houses when owners were away and threw armloads of dry grass over rugs and furniture. They destroyed magnolia and shrubbery bushes along Maple Street. They plugged the courthouse water fountain with matchsticks, giving an unanticipated shower to the next user, and they chalked algebra and geometry problems on the outside walls of the Wooden Bank and the Strickler Store.[1]

Some of the acts were more sinister. They shot out the porcelain gravestone portraits of Italians in the cemetery. On South Sixteenth Street, they dragged a store dummy onto the road and liberally doused it with red paint, causing motorists to swerve in horror and report another Mafia-style murder.[2]

Children begged outside movie houses and on street corners. One evening, a reporter for the *Centerville Daily Journal* counted them. He started in South Centerville, walked uptown, circled the Square a few times and counted seventeen. The Reverend J.R. Hanley of the Methodist church counted many more. The children requested money for cigarettes, for movies and for food—the last option running a poor third. Many of the children were from good families not in need of alms.[3]

Children ran away from home; some were abandoned, some neglected. Some, like a fourteen-year-old Cincinnati boy overwhelmed by responsibilities since the death of his mother—cooking meals, washing clothes, running the household—burned his cherished school books and papers and shot himself. One spent the night, undetected, on a cot in the armory; another, a girl of fourteen, wandered the courthouse at closing time and spent the night as a guest of the sheriff. Boys and young men loafed on Thirteenth Street across from the Majestic Theatre, in stairways and outside buildings on the Square, exposing pedestrians to obscene language and causing them to deflect their paths into roadways.[4]

Young men cruised in cars. Girls were harassed, some abducted, some raped; four of those were under age—fifteen, twelve, eleven and eight, the eleven-year-old by her own father. Reports of window-peeking were almost nightly. City police estimated three to six such voyeurs were operating independently across the City. Only two were caught, and they were young boys watching the showgirls as they changed between acts in the Drake Avenue Theatre basement.[5]

The reputation of the town was spreading across the State, and it was not good. In July 1921, the *Des Moines News* placed a story about Centerville's violence on its front page. The article cited twenty-one deaths in the area of South Eighteenth Street in the previous fifteen years, "...not by accidents or mad rushing waters, but by the modern revolver, knives, bottles, picks or anything that the murderer might lay his hands on while in the mood for killing." A business visitor at the Continental asked, "Why is it that the only time you see Centerville mentioned in the city papers, is in connection with some murder or sensational case?"[6]

The people of the town had had enough. They demanded action. Children were ordered off the streets by nine at night or action would be taken against their parents. Loafing in hallways and across from the Majestic was prohibited. Men making "wise cracks or obscene remarks" to women were ordered arrested. Better police protection of property interests in the business district was urged at a meeting of the retail bureau of the Association of Commerce. People expressed the opinion that, with so many men unemployed and with the general tendency to crime, depredations of the most serious sort may be expected in the future unless some action was taken.[7]

Extra officers were hired. Three patrolled the Square and back alleys every one-and-a-half hours from midnight until dawn. To assist them, businessmen kept both their stores' interior and rear electric lights shining throughout the nights. The Kraft-Triebswetter Store installed the town's first burglar alarm: any interference with a window or door resulted in a loud siren and flashing lights.[8]

The sheriff acquired a "Bertillon System." People were invited to view it at the courthouse. They thought it looked like a victrola or an icebox or a safe for contraband whiskey. Then the sheriff opened its doors, revealing photographs and details of known criminals and equipment for taking fingerprints. It was thought this "scientific" police work would deter criminal activity. Looking at the photographs, Centerville mayor Dave Rees commented on the youth of the criminals. Justice James C. Cropsey of the New York Supreme Court was quoted in the *Iowegian*: "Over 80 per cent of criminals are less than 25 years of age." In Centerville, as well as over the United States, agreed the *Iowegian*'s editor, it is the youth of the nation that are doing the unlawful.[9]

Across the County, people took action. When they judged children to be neglected, they contacted the County attorney, Tom Fee, who sent the children on to State orphanages. When a fifteen-year-old boy without a home or parents stole clothes in Moulton but was judged to be a fine person, attorney Fee paroled him to a good home. When the discipline of a child in Centerville was judged to be brutal, neighbors demanded the arrest of the mother. Residents in Exline wrote to Fee asking for an investigation of a family there that was treating a young orphan girl living in the home as "little better than a slave." And miners at Galleyville went on strike, refusing to work with a man who had placed his three-year-old sick child, who was also said to be "defective," to live in a coal shed.[10]

"Peeping Toms" were chased with shotguns. When they ran away, bloodhounds were brought from the town of Agency. An attempted bank robbery at Moravia incensed both local residents and farmers. They formed themselves into a group. They kept shotguns behind their doors. They called each other to action at perceived dangers. They called themselves vigilantes and formed a chapter of the Law Enforcement League. Other communities in the County followed suit. Some called themselves special "Roadside Vigilantes." They patrolled County roads late in the evenings and put a stop to "indecent petting parties." Other members formed themselves into posses and joined the sheriff on local grappi raids. And everywhere people tried to explain why crime was increasing and morality declining.[11]

To Jesse Beck at the *Iowegian*, the cause of the crime wave sweeping the country was the upheaval that followed the World War. Men came home traumatized by battle, dislocated from former values and, too often, unable to find employment.[12]

To Dr. Osborn at the Methodist church, it was poor church attendance. For the Reverend Staples at the Baptist church, it was because people were following false gods: those of pleasure, success, the flesh and selfishness. For the Holy Rollers in their tent behind Max Chapman's Store on the Levee, it was all the work of the devil. He was everywhere, they said. They preached in a tent round in shape "to keep him out of the corners."[13]

Others pointed to the movies. They thought it was "the seductive movie kiss" combined with the privacy afforded by automobiles. Stars dressed provocatively. Some of their personal behavior broke into scandals that filled local newspapers—stories of rape and murder, sexual orgies, rampant alcoholism, drug addictions and rotating marriages and divorces. They involved the stars that the people of the town loved and watched night after night in packed audiences at the Majestic and the Ritz movie houses. They involved Roscoe "Fatty" Arbuckle, Olive Thomas, Wallace Reid, Barbara La Marr, Desmond Taylor, Mary Miles Mintner, Edna Purviance, Pola Negri, Mary Pickford and Charlie Chaplin.[14]

In May 1921, just ahead of the film world's scandals, Leo Moore, the manager of the Majestic Theatre on Thirteenth Street, hurried to the *Iowegian* office on Main Street, just south of the Square. He had just received notice that the First National Film Company of New York was on its way to film scenes of its comedy-drama *The Wonderful Thing* in Centerville and at the D.C. Bradley/Link Harbold Hog Farm at Walnut Creek near Plano, nine miles to the west. Director Herbert Brenon had visited Centerville years before. He never forgot "its beautiful public Square and splendid business houses," and he never forgot the rolling hills and fertile valleys of Appanoose County. He was known as "Brenon the Great." His salary was said to be two thousand dollars a week.[15]

Norma Talmadge. *Library of Congress.*

The stars of the movie were Norma Talmadge and Harrison Ford, two of the foremost silent-movie picture stars of their day. Both were well-known to Centerville movie audiences: Norma Talmadge in *A Daughter of Two Worlds*, *She Loves and Lies* and *The Branded Woman*; Harrison Ford in *A Lady In Love.*[16]

The Bradley/Harbold Hog Farm north of Plano was selected because of its reputation and appearance. It was the largest hog feeder in the country. It shipped thousands of top-quality Duroc Jersey hogs. Its reputation for hygiene was unparalleled. Its white-trimmed, red buildings sat in a depression that crossed Walnut Creek, nestled in hills, green trees and a bridge. On the news of the farm's selection, the fenceposts were given a fresh coat of white paint and a large sign—"Boggs' Hogs," reflecting one of the characters of the movie—was painted in Centerville and placed prominently at the farm.[17]

Members of the film company arrived—the personnel on May 21, the stars on May 23. They were entertained at D.C. Bradley's mansion on Drake Avenue. In the evenings they drank Coca-Cola and danced to the music of a phonograph in the Red Cross Drug Store on the Square's Southeast corner. People watched them through the windows.[18]

The crew and the stars stayed at the Continental Hotel. They had breakfast in their rooms. Miss Talmadge was said to be slightly indisposed with "rose fever." She sneezed, and her eyes itched. Miss Talmadge described it as a mild cold, a type of hay fever. Some of the local boys suspected it was a mild hangover. Today it is considered an allergy.[19]

People waited and watched in the Continental lobby. Norma Talmadge came downstairs with director Brenon. People described her as "radiant" and "indescribably attractive," with a "beautiful chisled [*sic*] placid" face and in manner "just a nice whole-hearted girl whose head is not in the least turned by thousands upon thousands of worshipping fans." Outside the hotel, William S. Bradley (grandson of William Sr.) waited at the wheel of the Bradley auto. He drove Miss Talmadge, Harrison Ford and director Brenon west to the hog farm, where filming began. It was a signal for citizens' cars. They followed in a procession. They came from eight or nine states. They blocked the public road for one-and-a-half hours. Fifteen hundred people on foot watched events. They included two high school students, Carl Brunow and Leo Schutzbank, the son of the town tailor. Both were loaded with cameras and full of enterprise. The *Des Moines Register* flew in its best reporters and photographers. So did the *Des Moines News*, the *Des Moines Capital* and the *Omaha World-Herald*. The manager of the film company said he was grateful for all the interest, but they had never "been up against" so many spectators. A detachment of Company G arrived to keep people back from in front of the camera.[20]

Other scenes were filmed on the Square, with the courthouse at its center, and at the Burlington/Quincy depot in South Centerville. At the station, a special Chicago, Burlington and Quincy train was backed up to the depot. Cameraman Roy Hunt focused his motion picture camera. Norma Talmadge

Harbold Farm, which was used in the production of *The Wonderful Thing*. *Courtesy of Richard Gorden, Plano Museum.*

descended from the train. She wore a dress of light tan grain silk, a sand fox fur, long white kid gloves and a green straw sailor hat. Assisting her was William Harvey, the local Quincy conductor, who described the experience as one of the highlights of his career. Watching was W.S. Alexander, the station's manager.[21]

The First National Film Company left Centerville on its way to New York via Chicago on May 24, traveling on the 11:59 p.m. Golden State Limited from the Rock Island station. Director Herbert Brenon hoped that the picture would be released within a month and that manager Leo Moore of the Majestic Theatre would be the first exhibitor.[22]

The film was released in September 1921. Its advertisement covered one page of the *Iowegian*. It was first shown at the Majestic Theatre on October 11 and for the following three days. Crowds filled the building to the door. More crowds assembled, waiting for the second showing. Centerville was in films. The courthouse, the Burlington depot and the Bradley/Harbold Hog Farm were all flashed onto the silver screen. Then appeared the caption: Centerville, Iowa, U.S.A. People began to talk in excited whispers. They commented on Norma, on the hog farm, on thirteen-year-old, freckled Clarence Brand of Plano, whom director Brenon pulled out of the crowd to deliver a telegram. And they commented on the courthouse.[23]

Three years later, in Ching Chow, Honan Province, China, a Centerville girl, Trissa Darnall Smith, and her husband went to the YMCA to watch an American movie in celebration of George Washington's birthday. She wrote home, "I was so surprised when the film showed a telegram from Centerville, then next came the courthouse and I was about wild. I stood up and squealed 'That's Home, where I was born and raised.' Then I sat down and began to cry …those on both sides of me started crying and I saw the rest of the picture in tears. It showed the square and courthouse, the Burlington station and some farm homes. Here in the heart of China…"[24]

Chapter 38

Jazz, the Charleston, the Changing Role of Women

Much of the blame for deteriorating morals was leveled at jazz. It was first heard in Centerville in November 1918 when Harry Payton's Five-Piece Jazz Band, with William S. Bradley—the son of D.C. Bradley, grandson of William the banker—at the drums, played at dances, Halloween masques and at City Hall. It swiftly became "a craze." Orchestras used to playing waltzes, polkas, tangos and foxtrots added the word "jazz" to their advertised repertoires, and across the town young piano players began syncopating their rhythms, calling it "ragtime." The *Centerville Journal* described ragtime as "ragged incoherence" and jazz as a step further into incoherence. Harold Hoyer, the pianist for the silent movies at the Majestic, said the music wouldn't last. He then promptly formed a jazz group of his own.[1]

There were warnings of consequences. A teacher at Centerville High School said jazz was ruining the moral and intellectual minds of students. Walter Merritt, the principal of North Des Moines High School, said a jazzy tune will turn "a roomful of well behaved students almost instantly into a rough rowdy crew, who cannot be trusted without a chaperone."[2]

Despite the warnings, the town jazz "craze" grew. Dance halls on the Square's Northwest and Southwest Corners and the Majestic Theatre imported jazz bands from across the State and beyond: Wetzel's Jazz Hounds from Des Moines, the Schubert Shimmy Band from Washington, Eddy's Famous Lightning Jazzadores of Chicago. At the Drake Avenue Theatre, the Bronze Bostonians, with the "famous Creole Beauty Chorus" appearing in person, took the town by storm. Movies at the Majestic—*The Sins of St. Anthony* and

On with the Dance—promoted the music, showing professional dance bands and demonstrating "shimmy dances."[3]

New warnings against the new music were heard. These suggested dire moral consequences. Jazz was described as "intoxicating," as "musical bolshevism," as "the cause of insanity" and as "erotic." Underlying these were hints of a social and sexual revolution. The Illinois Vigilance Association reported that "moral disaster is coming to hundreds of young American girls through the pathological, nerve-irritating, sex-exciting music of jazz." In Omaha, saxophonists were ordered to sit down when playing, because when they stood they encouraged dancers "to engage in wiggly-wobbly body movements." And Carrie Nichols of the Women's Ward of the Des Moines City Jail said, while blushing, "The sensual motions, the body rubbing of jazz dancing, have started many a girl towards [this] ward."[4]

People began watching the town dances. Complaints arrived on the desks of the mayor and the chief of police. The authorities issued warnings. "There are several different ways of dancing…," they said. "There is the right and the wrong way." Because most of the dancing was "the wrong way," dances were halted at Relay and at Streepy. Saturday-night dances at the hall on the Square's Northwest Corner were canceled, the hall ordered closed after complaints that couples were dancing in too-close physical proximity and that, between dances, "indecencies" were taking place in the alley behind the hall.[5]

Lurking in the criticism was the issue of race. Centerville police received complaints that "…some of the colored folks in the southwest part of the city were disturbing the peace late Saturday night." Constable Phares and other officers went to investigate. "Jazz" melodies on a piano, singing and a general good time were in progress, "…but the colored folk were doing nothing out of the way and no arrests were made or charges filed." A year later, editorials in the racist *Centerville Journal* said the word "jazz" had been traced "to its jungle lair." And in the "general noise and confusion" of jazz music, "African savages beating on their tom toms should think jazz is fine."[6]

By 1925, a fresh wave of enthusiasm, accompanied by an equal one of disapproval, greeted a new dance: the Charleston. The *Iowegian* described it as a "contortion." Some dance halls in Iowa's capital city banned it. It was first heard in Centerville at the Drake Avenue Theatre with Schaffner's Syncopating Savages. The company, with both black and white performers, offered a revue that included demonstrations by three African American professional Charleston dancers and prizes for the best amateur local dancers in a Charleston contest. The first prize went to Rollie Jeter, the second to William Penn, the third to William's sister Irene. All three were African Americans. The company promptly announced two competitions: one for white dancers and a separate one for black dancers.[7]

Implicit also in much of the criticism was the changing role of women. Their appearance altered: they bobbed their hair, shortened their skirts, eliminated sleeves and discarded stockings. They entered Goldsteins-on-the-Square and replaced their whale-bone corsets with Madame X's "new scientifically treated rubber girdles." They consulted visiting dermatologists at Mose Beer's drugstore. They bought Elizabeth Arden's beauty products and Carl Weeks's Armand cosmetics at the Red Cross Drug Store and Helena Rubinstein's at the Owl. Household work was reduced with the Hoover Beating-Sweeping Suction Cleaners, washing machines, irons, toasters and sewing machines, all run by electricity, conveniently supplied by Iowa Southern Utilities from its power station off the Square's Northeast Corner.[8]

With their increased leisure time, the women turned to public affairs. When Iowa granted partial female suffrage, Frances Goss—her husband, Thomas, was the son of abolitionist Joe Goss—ran for the Centerville School Board in 1913. She was elected, topping the poll over three well-known men. Her initiative, leadership and independent ideas swiftly propelled her to becoming chairman of the board. In 1916, a statewide amendment granting Iowa women the vote lost. But in Appanoose County it passed. The County's all-male voters supported the amendment, and they did so by a sizeable majority. In another four years the Nineteenth Amendment to the U.S. Constitution—that the right to vote would not be denied on account of sex—became the law of the land. Appanoose County women swiftly registered. For the first time in a presidential election, on November 2, 1920, they entered Appanoose County's forty-four polling stations from early in the morning until they closed and in "large numbers." They emerged, it was said, with "sphinx-like expression." Within a month, five women were listed among fifty potential jurors. Mary Dershem of Numa on January 11 and Mary Kerby of Centerville and Jenny Garrett of Washington Township on the twelfth took their places on an Appanoose County jury. Some people anticipated nervousness, crying and fainting. The *Iowegian* reported, "…no men ever carried themselves with more ease, clear thinking, and calmness."[9]

Across the country, women were becoming aviators, lawyers, doctors, architects, engineers and justices. They were swimming the English Channel and setting altitude records and new records at track and athletic events. They were exploring the upper regions of the Nile, entering national politics, becoming governors and directing opera companies and all-male orchestras. In Appanoose County, Moulton's Nellie Walker was one of the nation's most accomplished sculptors; Mystic's Louise "Luby" Quist, told watchmaking was not a suitable career for a woman, was inspector of watches for the Kansas City division of the Milwaukee Railroad. Centerville's Mabel Lee, a national expert advising the U.S. Army on the fundamentals of body mechanics and conditioning, was head of the physical education department at the University of Nebraska. Estella Gordon, from the Appanoose Abstract Company, caught the Rock Island train to Chicago to become the field manager of the Compton Publishing Company. Two women doctors—Ida Nulton of Lancaster, Missouri, and Mary J. Bawden at her office on West Washington—served town patients. Mrs. Harry Longanecker, Frank Payne's secretary at Iowa Southern Utilities, developed such skill and competence she could have run the organization herself; and Alma Farnsworth Monteith, widowed with four small children to support, the youngest six months old, moved home to her family at Exline, became office manager for a coal company, and then was Appanoose assistant County treasurer. Assistant auditor Lizzie Malaney for fifty years set type by hand at the *Iowegian* office, and she operated the newspaper's first linotype machine. And Nate Kendall, a long supporter of female suffrage, married to Belle Wooden of Centerville and in 1920 elected the governor of Iowa, announced he would appoint women to key positions in his cabinet.[10]

For some people, the changing role of women was leading to the breakdown of the family. The "Divorce Rate Is Appalling," said one headline. It cited an Iowa State Department of Health statistic that in Appanoose County, one in every four marriages was ending in divorce. Father Alexander at St. Mary's Catholic Church described it as America's greatest evil: "…that abominable thing," he said, "…which is sanctioned by the courts we call divorce." Father Alexander went further, decrying the use of birth control methods, then administered at the discretion of local doctors and advocated in a speech in Des Moines by Margaret Sanger. He described the methods used as blocking "the laws of nature in the name of hygiene." Judge F.M. Hunter of the district court looked at the list of sixty-one divorces before him. "Time was when a woman married," he said, "she became practically dependent upon the man." Education and training have changed her condition. "They now have a feeling of independence, and they no longer tolerate from the husband what they formerly feared."[11]

Judge Hunter and Father Alexander might have considered that divorce was preferable to women committing suicide. Between 1900 and 1913, there were a number in the County. Ten were reported, others hinted at. The victims had taken carbolic acid, strychnine, laudanum, lye or an overdose of sleeping tablets. All were married women, and many were mothers with young children. Most left notes citing "family troubles." One, a woman, living east of Darbyville, some five miles north of Centerville, was accused of being a member of a suicide club, teaching the unhappy and the trapped how to die out of their unhappiness.

Meanwhile, something approaching a community suicide was about to occur.[12]

Chapter 39

The KKK Arrives

In early January 1923, George N. McDonald drove into Centerville in a black Lexington Minute Man Six. He was a Texan, tall and fashionably dressed. He ostentatiously exposed rolls of hundred-dollar bills, peeled them off, rerolled them and returned them to his coat pocket. George N. McDonald was a Ku Klux Klan organizer, and Centerville was his target.

He quickly began his work. He identified and approached those he considered the leaders of the community: the ministers of religion—so long as they were Protestant and white—prominent businessmen, editors of the *Daily Iowegian* and *Centerville Journal* newspapers and members of the vigilante Law Enforcement League.[1]

On January 16, a *Daily Iowegian* reporter circled the Square, eliciting reactions from the town's bankers and leading businessmen. "KKK seems to stand for Kill, Krucify, and Koverup," said one. "Anything that needs a mask," said another, "is un-American and anything that is un-American should not be encouraged…" On January 24, Jesse M. Beck, the editor of the *Daily Iowegian*, placed a large ten-by-eight-inch cartoon on the upper half of the front page of the newspaper. It showed three figures; two of these were a grinning alcoholic, his pockets bursting with liquor, and an evil-looking speedster, horns emerging from his head, hands gripping a steering wheel. The two flanked a masked, hooded KKK figure towering behind them. The cartoon was titled "The Three (Dis)Graces."[2]

At the same time, the Reverend Mott Sawyers, pastor of Centerville's Presbyterian church, wrote two articles for the *Daily Iowegian*. Both opposed the KKK. Mott Sawyers had supported Prohibition and was a member of the County's Law Enforcement League. But when it came to racial prejudice and religious intolerance, he was coded with abolitionist credentials. His two grandfathers, Elisha Sawyers and John Miller, left Tennessee for Appanoose County in the 1850s because of their objection to slavery. Both provided safe havens in Unionville on Appanoose County's Underground Railroad. And as a small boy, Mott Sawyers had listened to the stories of John Brown and his raid on Harpers Ferry from a follower of John Brown: John Bridal, then bearded and ancient, when he rode into town on horseback.[3]

"An organization like the Ku Klux Klan is a menace," wrote Sawyers on February 3. "The American government is the outcome of a long period of self-control, anxious thinking, free exchange of ideas and conscientious effort to establish justice and liberty among men. Its principles are few but clear, —the inalienable right to life and liberty, no discrimination on account of race, religion or previous condition of servitude, —the settlement of all differences by the orderly process of law . . . the Ku Klux Klan is against every one of these principles. It proposes to say what a man shall do with his liberty, and even his life. It seeks to discriminate against men on account of race and religion. Instead of following the due process of law it proposes to regulate morals by midnight courts of masked men and medieval punishments."[4]

The following day, a Sunday, at the Central Church of Christ on Drake Avenue, the church pastor, the Reverend J. Roy Wright, addressed his evening congregation. His subject was "Why I Do Not Oppose the Ku Klux Klan." J. Roy Wright was a powerful speaker. He was expanding the size of his congregation. Those present listened attentively. The Reverend Wright told his audience he supported the Klan's secrecy and its right to act outside the due process of law, and he justified their masks. He supported segregation and Jim Crow laws. At the same time, he denied he had ever been a member of the KKK, was not a current member and said, "I never expect to be a Klansman."[5]

It was, if not a dishonest claim, a premature one. By July 1923 the "Kluxers," as they were called, were busy everywhere in the County, silently infiltrating organizations. By October, the Reverend J. Roy Wright was not only a member of the KKK, he was appointed "Exalted Cyclops"—the president of the Appanoose County Klan. By the third week in October, the organization's wall of obscurity began to erode.[6]

Many of the businessmen of Centerville awoke to find copies of the October 15 *Arkansas Traveller*, a Ku Klux Klan newspaper published in Little Rock and El Dorado, Arkansas, on their doorsteps. A banner headline stretched across the top of the front page. It read: "Centerville, Iowa, Needs Klan." The anonymous writer repeated sensational points made earlier by the *Des Moines News*. Centerville was the "City of Crime," the Rock Island crossing on South Eighteenth Street "The Death Crossing …the scene of more murders and crimes than any other one point within the bounds of our state."[7]

In the same article, Joe Montegna was called a "wop," illegal liquor stills "dago booze joints." The article then turned to Centerville's Jews: "Seventy-five per cent of the business carried on in the city is controlled by the Jewish population. Consequently they domineer the municipal government. Many of these so-called leading citizens have accumulated their fortunes either directly or indirectly from the manufacture or sale of liquor."[8]

There could have been no doubt about the Klan's philosophy. The *Iowegian* in October 1923 reported on a speech given by Dr. H.W. Evans, "Imperial Wizard" of the Klan, in Dallas, Texas. He supported restricting immigration; he said that the Negro, "both by biology and anthropology," could not attain the Anglo-Saxon level, that the Jew was an "absolutely unblendable element" and that Catholics subordinated the presidency at Washington "to the priesthood at Rome." They believed in "100% Americanism." This they interpreted as Christian, gentile, white, native-born and Protestant. They denounced Catholics, Jews, African Americans, Orientals, bootleggers, pacifists, Bolshevists, socialists and the theory of evolution and immigrants from "non-Nordic nations."[9]

Fifty thousand of these new immigrants were pouring in monthly through Ellis Island. By February 1921, "the jam …had become so great that immigration authorities were hastily diverting New York–bound ships to Boston." These immigrants were fumigated and then released into a country where unemployment was high and where many of the 4.5 million returning members of the armed forces could not find work. Many of the immigrants imported political opinions judged revolutionary and dangerous. They were blamed for disease "from vermin-infested clothing," for political agitation, for violence and for bombs, including one on September 16, 1920, when a wagon loaded with dynamite exploded outside the Wall Street, New York, office of J.P. Morgan, killing thirty-eight and wounding hundreds.[10]

The stories were carried in Centerville newspapers. So were accounts of revolutionary activities closer to home. Workers in St. Paul, Minnesota, in 1921 were calling for a May Day uprising. In November of the same year, to control strikers at the Morrell Packing Plant in Ottumwa, forty miles northeast of Centerville, four units of the Iowa National Guard were patrolling the streets carrying machine guns. And of three thousand "Radicals" across the country arrested for "planning a Soviet Government in the United States," thirteen were "Reds" from Des Moines, where several tons of radical literature were seized.[11]

There was alarm in Centerville. Many of the officials in the town were receiving "Red" International Workers of the World (I.W.W.) literature. The camp at the Streepyville mine was said to be "inundated" with I.W.W. and socialistic material. Talk had long persisted of anarchists, Bolshevists and socialists at Streepyville and at Mine Thirty. People recalled the forty men who refused to register for the draft and the well-known anarchists who were deported, one of them Luis Marchini.[12]

At the post office on the corner of Main and Maple Streets, local postmaster H.C. Haynes reported that "Red" literature was flooding the mails. "Much is in sealed envelopes," he said, "and sent to people on regular mailing lists."[13]

Father M.J. Kaufmann of St. Mary's Catholic Church told a group at a Kiwanis Club luncheon he'd been in the homes of immigrants and had seen the literature. It came from radical foreign papers, from the I.W.W., from the Communist Party, the Non-Partisan League and from the Committee of 48. "What they say is a menace to social order and Christian ideals," he said and appealed to the community to get immigrants Americanized.[14]

In the nation's capital, efforts were underway to restrict the immigration of the world's "huddled masses." Quota bills were passed. Chairing the Immigration and Naturalization Committee for ten years throughout all three bills was racist Albert Johnson. Testifying before a full House committee, giving evidence in support of restricting the immigration of Slavs, Asians, Africans and southern Europeans but expanding the quota from "Nordic nations," was Albert Johnson's good friend, whom he introduced to the committee as "Expert Eugenics Agent." It was Harry Laughlin, principal of Centerville High School for two years, from 1903 to 1905, who left the town telling his mother he had no wish to remain.[15]

It was perfect timing for Appanoose County's Ku Klux Klan. Its members launched a campaign against Centerville's postmaster's son, Glenn C. Haynes. Then running for Iowa governor, Haynes, who had led Centerville's National Guard through World War I, was loved by his men and the community. The Klan objected to Haynes's opposition to Albert Johnson's selective immigration bills. On February 3, 1924, Haynes spoke at the Italian Southside Community Center in Des Moines. He said, "I believe in admitting to this country any foreigner who can come up to the physical, mental and moral standard of the average American. I will do all I can to work against the measure."[16]

It was also the moment for Appanoose County's Klan to announce its presence to the people of Centerville.

Chapter 40

The KKK Emerges into Public View

On the evening of March 19, 1924, four blocks southwest of the Courthouse Square, a dull red light glowed at the back of Centerville High School. Suddenly it intensified. A cross, eight feet high and five feet wide, burst into flames, flaring into the dark night for two hours. Moments later, a second cross burned, this in full view on top of Cemetery Hill, just east of town.[1]

Five nights later, seven miles to the south, Cincinnati—the birthplace of Appanoose County's Underground Railroad—was the target. Three robed, hooded, masked men emerged from a car on the west side of Cincinnati's square. They carried a cross to the square's center, set it upright into a previously prepared hole, set the cross alight and drove away. Within minutes, on an abandoned coal mine three blocks to the east of Cincinnati's square, another cross burned.[2]

By early April, members of the Klan were meeting in a room on Centerville Square's Northside. They were distributing onto town doorsteps copies of the *Iowa Fiery Cross*, a Klan newspaper published in Des Moines. More copies were dropped over Numa and Centerville from low-flying aircraft, the undersides emblazoned with the words "Appanoose County Klan." More burning crosses were appearing. In swift progression, they exploded into life on the slag pile at Thirty, at Galleyville, near the Rock Island track crossing on South Eighteenth Street and at Numa.[3]

The same month, the Klan's tentacles were deeply embedded in the local Democratic Party and the Law Enforcement League. Alert to the eroding boundary of the league, town lawyers Tom Fee and William Hays began asking potential jury members if they were members of the Law Enforcement League. The Klan objected. Using its two members on the Board of Supervisors, the Klan submitted its own list of choices for election judges who, in the 1920s, selected jury members. With their own Klan members on juries, the Klan could control trial outcomes. This was later described as "…the most colossal attempt at jury stealing ever perpetrated in the United States."[4]

In July the Klan made a bolder move when 157 of its members arrived at the County Republican Party Convention at the Drake Avenue Theatre. They outvoted the fifty-one traditional party members they termed "the old guard." C. Elgin was ousted as chairman; traditional committee members and delegates were overturned. The Klan voted in their own delegates to the State Republican and the State Judicial Conventions. Both political parties were now under Klan control. Effective organized Democratic opposition to it was now emasculated.[5]

With the crosses, with the activity, Appanoose County's Klan not only announced its presence, but it had a thorough organization and extensive membership. On one level, the converts were the unsuspecting, the poorly educated, the fearful and those who, beneath a veneer, were always racial and religious bigots. On another level, the story was quite different.

Among the County's earliest converts were ministers of the leading Protestant churches. In addition to J. Roy Wright at Drake Avenue Christian Church—now "Exalted Cyclops" of the County Klan—there were others: E.J. Shook, Methodist; S.E. Waters, Pentecostal-Ecclesiastical; Russell Archibald of the Latter-Day Saints. One minister, Frank E. Peterson of the Lutheran church, wobbled, was used by the Klan, regretted the event, turned against the Klan and worked to keep his church out of the fray. J.O. Staples at the Baptist church refused to be involved. He retired and was replaced by the Reverend P.H. Peterson. In town for less than a month, P.H. Peterson became a Klan supporter.[6]

Around the County, the story was the same. In Mystic, Cincinnati, Moravia, Plano, Jerome, Moulton and Fairview, Protestant ministers were supporters of the Klan or remained silent, refusing to speak out. One Protestant minister stood alone: the Reverend Dr. Mott Sawyers of the Presbyterian church, who a year earlier called the Klan "a menace" and its members violators of the principles that formed America.[7]

Throughout 1924, Appanoose County's Klan built its powerbase. Two County newspapers, the *Cincinnati Review* and the *Mystic Telegram*, became the organization's mouthpieces. By August there was a powerful third. Seventy-one Klan members bought out the always marginally racist *Centerville Journal.* They renamed it the *Southern Iowa American* and moved Glenn Reed up from the *Cincinnati Review* to be its editor. From its office just off the Square at 120 North Twelfth Street, this daily newspaper issued its first edition on September 17, 1924. Editor Glenn Reed, together with G.N. McDonald and the Reverend J. Roy Wright, now became Appanoose County's KKK trinity.[8]

If anyone still nursed doubts about the Klan's intentions, Glenn Reed's polemic writing could swiftly dispel them. When Clifford Perry, an African American, was killed on a building site in Des Moines, Glenn Reed's headline read, "Brick Was Harder Than This Negro's Head." He quoted Dr. Caleb A. Riddle, pastor of the Central Baptist Church in Dallas, Texas, who said, "I haven't time for a lengthy discussion of white supremacy. Suffice it to say we believe in that, we stand for that. . ." In writing of New York's Tong Wars, Orientals were described as "excrement"; the death of one was reported as "Another Chink Killed…" In giving a "Good Program for Americans," "wiping out the alien vote" was an item; so was expelling Romanism, which was "undermining Americanism." The country's "moral disintegration" was blamed on "anti-Christian Jews, in our theatres, our motion pictures, and in American business circles." To Reed, "Native born, white Gentile Americans have simply awakened to the imperative need of supporting their own blood and kind."[9]

Throughout the summer and fall of 1924, the KKK was now confident enough to emerge into public view. Dressed in full regalia and masked, they held exhibitions and parades. Funerals for Jacob Kelse in Numa, for John Meade at Mystic and for William Henry Brown at Centerville's Methodist church were theatrical displays. Brown's stopped all legal proceedings in the courthouse, and faces crowded its windows. The streets were full. Eighty Klan members attended, including delegations from Albia and Burlington. Outside the Methodist church, the Klansmen formed an avenue through which Brown's body was conducted to the car. G.N. McDonald and the Reverend J. Roy Wright, visors up, led the cortege, together with Burlington Klansmen, around the Square, exiting on East State Street at the Continental Hotel.[10]

Meetings were held at the Harry Gault farm north of Cincinnati; twenty-four hundred to three thousand people attended. There were more meetings at the Clyde Hiatt farm three miles west of town, at the John Morrison farm north of Centerville, at the Tyner place, near the Iconium Christian Church, at Bert Long's place three miles east of Seymour and on the Square at Moravia, with a crowd of six thousand all warmly welcomed by Mayor Winsler. At the three-day Moulton Jamboree, the local entertainment committee there asked the County Klan to hold an open public lecture. Several thousand attended; five hundred signed membership cards and were initiated at a meeting a week later two miles north of Moulton.[11]

The meetings were held after dark. Red lanterns guided cars and those walking on foot. Crosses were burned or electrically lit. Robed Klansmen clasped hands and circled the cross. They sang hymns and said prayers and listened to speakers—often Reverend Paul Henry Packard of Des Moines.[12]

More crosses were burned—at Rathbun on top of the coal mine; and at Numa, where the KKK formed a line at the Methodist church, marched around the Square and sang "The Old Rugged Cross, "Onward Christian Soldiers" and "America" while a fourteen-foot cross burned.[13]

There were what appeared to be acts of generosity. At midnight on May 15, five robed men walked the road between Unionville and Udell, nine miles northeast of Centerville Square. People watched from behind curtains. They later described their fear. The robed figures knocked on the door of the Calvin Doll family. They presented five ten-dollar bills as a contribution after a fire had destroyed the upper story of the Doll home.[14]

KKK funeral in Cincinnati. *Courtesy of Becky Morgan.*

On October 1, forty Klan members delivered one hundred dollars to Joe Sacco—an Italian Catholic immigrant—who lived two miles west of Centerville. Joe's son had been accidentally shot while hunting and was in the hospital. On November 24, a gift was made to Mrs. William Binns, who lived southeast of Cincinnati and whose husband had deserted her and six children, ranging in age from nine months to thirteen years. Klan members brought several sacks of flour, blankets, meat, groceries, enamelware and shoes. They returned on Thanksgiving Day with clothing, fresh fruit and two tons of coal.[15]

At Christmas time they contributed seven hundred to one thousand dolls and toys to the Women's Relief Corps for distribution among the poor. They gave twenty dollars to the Ingram family in need in Seymour and helped a family walking to New Mexico from Ohio with a tubercular daughter—the Klan paid for a night's stay at the Dodge Hotel in Cincinnati.[16]

Churches also benefitted: the Methodist church in Numa received fifty dollars, the nearby Christian church in Numa twenty-five. Robed figures appeared during services, presenting fifty dollars to area ministers: Reverend Roll at Confidence; Reverend F.J. Robins at Brazil's Methodist church; Reverend Frank E. Peterson at Centerville's Lutheran church; and Reverends W.O. Jones and R.C. Rowe, conducting revival meetings at Fairview. At a revival meeting in a tent at Moravia, the Reverends Rowe Sr. and Rowe Jr. received another fifty dollars, as did the evangelist Reverend George Bennard, composer of the hymn "The Old Rugged Cross," living at the time at Lucas, some thirty-four miles northwest of Centerville. But when they presented thirty dollars in coins at Plano's Methodist church, they hadn't reckoned with the church's treasurer, James (J.T.) Sherrard. He handed the money back, saying, "Christ was sold for 30 silver coins, I return your money."[17]

Not only did the Klan fail to reckon with Sherrard, it also hadn't reckoned with those in the County who would now fight back.

Chapter 41

Opposition to the KKK

In combating the KKK, church treasurer Sherrard was not alone. Neither were the Reverend Mott Sawyers at the Presbyterian church or Jesse Beck at the *Iowegian*. They were three of the many who resisted the Klan from the start. There were more.

Pete Agnessen was an immigrant Belgian coal miner, a union leader who lived on North First Street. He spoke on Centerville Square on August 7 following a weekly band concert. The Square was packed with people to hear him, "the downtown section almost at a standstill." Agnessen was joined by John Wilkinson, a former Secret Service agent, a skilled debater and an experienced opponent of the KKK in Oklahoma. When Wilkinson learned Reed, Wright and McDonald had tried to prevent the meeting, he offered to publicly debate them. He repeated this offer at all his next speeches, given at nightly meetings with Agnessen at Numa, Moulton, Moravia, Mystic, Cincinnati, Plano, Jerome, on the L.L. Evans farm north of Seymour, at Udell, Barger's Corner and Moulton.[1]

The Klan leaders refused all offers. Using their three newspapers, they chose instead to attack the character of anyone who opposed them, to smear their names, to denounce their reputations. To that end, truth was obscured, distorted and manipulated. In cavalier fashion, they added names to their petitions and endorsements, forcing those so used—like Dr. W.B. Miller—to advertise their strenuous opposition. John Wilkinson was described as "a wife deserting crook," "a paid community agitator," "anti American," "pro-bootlegger" and "a repulsive foul-mouthed tool of the Underworld." When he refused to be silenced, a headline read, "Slimy Serpent Still Spreads Vile Slush." Pete Agnessen was a "flannel-mouth," "a poker playing cock-fight promoter," "an infidel" and "a Bolshevist"; the Klan circulated a petition to deport him. It failed. Agnessen was a U.S. citizen.

The crowds at the anti-Klan meetings were, the Klan said, "bootleggers, murderers, gamblers ...Catholics, Jews, crooked politicians, foreigners and some disgruntled weak-kneed, jelly fish, back-boneless Protestants." The crowd resembled "an Italian bull-fight or cock fight crowd," and gas masks ought to be issued at the anti-Klan lectures "to guard against casualties from asphyxiation by the garlic route."[2]

George Russo—Carmela's father—who supported Agnessen and Wilkinson, was "an Italian leader." Carmela, home from Rockford reformatory, was "that convicted murderess"; a second daughter, Constanza, was called "a thief" accused of stealing a dress from J.J. Frankel's store on the Square's Southwest Corner. J.J. Frankel himself was "that Jew merchant" and was accused of making "advances upon pure American Protestant womanhood by talking "vile insinuations" to his sixteen-year-old employee, Rosetta Kirk. When Frankel advertised a "closing out sale," Glenn Reed said, "[H]e is simply using his natural race instinct to make money." When rumor spread that other Jews were leaving Centerville on account of Klan activities, the *Mystic Telegram* said, "... Centerville will be a good town without them. If it wasn't, the Jews wouldn't be there—to get the 'cream.'"[3]

But the most sustained attack from the Klan and all three newspapers was directed at Jesse M. Beck, editor of the *Centerville Daily Iowegian*, their single competitor. He was accused of undermining the financial success of the *Southern Iowa American* by failing to announce the *Southern Iowa American*'s presence in town, of buying up all the daily press-news services, of "whitewashing" the "old ring" who led Centerville and of lying about the *Iowegian*'s circulation. Taylor McCoy wrote to Jesse Beck, withdrawing his subscription, because the *Iowegian* published an anti-Klan advertisement; so did Amos Carr, a farmer living southwest of Cincinnati.[4]

The town was becoming increasingly divided. Business advertisements began openly revealing their political persuasion. "Koontz Klean Koal" was offered for sale. "Eat at the American cafe: Kool Klean Komfortable," said another. On the Square's Westside, Shaw's Hardware offered "K.K. Kutlery," and E.K. Elledge sold "Triple Knee" socks. Clark's Grocery on the Northside advertised its promotions split into four sections, the division lines forming a Klan cross, and said its service was "100% Effecient [*sic*]."[5]

The "100%" KKK chant was also used in South Centerville, where the Collins Company displayed itself as giving "a 100% Filling Station Service." And in Cincinnati, H.L. Adams's Bakery said it did business in "the 100% way."[6]

The town's divisions were becoming dangerous. Guns bulged in pockets. The congregations of both the Methodist and the Christian churches divided, members opposing the Klan leaving to meet elsewhere. Klan supporters shopped at Klan stores and boycotted those suspected as anti-Klan, and one funeral home was said to refuse to take Catholic bodies. In the November election, with both political parties compromised, it was inevitable that Klan candidates were elected. "Kluckers Klean Kounty," said the headline in the *Mystic Telegram*. In such an atmosphere, it was inevitable there would be fights.[7]

The first occurred in the primary election in June 1924. Klan members supported the candidacy of Burbank for governor and not local World War I hero Glenn Haynes. In the early hours of election-day morning, Klan supporters led by G.N. McDonald pasted "Burbank" signs on windows, doors and sidewalks. An especially large "Burbank" sign was painted on the sidewalk outside the Rainbow Cafe, owned and run by a World War I veteran, Mike Sklavos, who had named the cafe in honor of the Rainbow Division. Haynes supporters retaliated. They painted "Haynes" over "Burbank," and a free-for-all fight was the result. Other fights occurred the same day: outside the Stephenson Drug Store with the KKK office upstairs; another a short distance off the Square; another fight in Mystic.[8]

By August, fights were reported in Numa, another in Moulton and one at a Klan meeting on the Andy Lookabill farm between Unionville and Udell. In October, Pure Ice Company's Steve Martin, who was strongly anti-Klan, dressed in a found Klan robe and talked his way into the Klan office over the Stephenson Drug Store. The Klan discovered him, placing his photograph prominently in the Klan newspapers.[9]

The worst and potentially the most violent fight occurred in early December. The Rusty Wood and Pete DeMarchi homes at Sunshine, three miles west of Centerville, were raided by Constable Tait of Mystic and a posse of fifteen men. The conditions there, said the *Southern Iowa American*, were deplorable. Everywhere was the smell of booze, and there were "spaghetti eaters with violins reeling off the strains of popular passion-exciting ragtime." Several couples were dancing, continued the newspaper, "doing movements that make modern dance the degrader of manhood and womanhood." Cars were coming and going from Des Moines and Seymour. The *Southern Iowa American* listed the names of those involved. The list included the name of a well-known local boxer, Johnny Delmar.[10]

Next evening at six forty-five, Glenn Reed, his father, his son and his friend left the *Southern Iowa American* office on North Twelfth Street and started for home. Reed was accosted by Johnny Delmar, who insisted he was not at Sunshine during the raid. Reed contradicted, and a fight occurred.[11]

At two thirty the next afternoon the fight started again, spilling raucously from North Twelfth Street onto the Southwest Corner of the Square. This time it was an open battle—some called it a riot. Large numbers of supporters of both sides fought using knives, blackjacks and guns. The trigger of one gun, a .25-caliber automatic, was heard to snap. The gun failed to fire.[12]

The warning to authorities was now clear. Over the town, stories emerged about the Klan's increasing intimidation techniques to get people to join and about the increasing amount of dollars demanded for membership dues. The dues had been twelve dollars; from some, fifty dollars was now being demanded. Burr Van Ness went to a KKK meeting upstairs over the National Bank on the Square's Southside out of curiosity. When he stood up to leave, Klansmen blocked his exit, and he had to fight to get down the stairs. In Moulton, local physician Dr. Downing was telephoned by the Klan and told to come to their meeting north of town. He drove there thinking someone was ill. Instead, he was confronted by Klansmen with guns and ordered to join their organization. When he refused, the Klansmen locked the gate, and he was told he couldn't leave until he did join. "I'll drive every one of you down and drive straight through that gate," he replied. "I won't join your organization." He left.[13]

In Centerville, fires broke out in town. One was on the Northeast corner of the Square at the Purity Bakery, owned by local builder B.S. Staley, who was anti-Klan. The pro-Klan Lacey-Morrison Garage and the Clark Grocery were set alight; cans of gasoline close by were ready to explode. Newspapers, both the *Iowegian* and the *Southern Iowa American*, reported violence between Klan and anti-Klan forces across the country. In Herrin, Illinois, the violence resulted in murders.[14]

The day after the riot on North Twelfth Street, the County attorney, C.W. Howell, noting the deteriorating situation, ordered all citizen gun permits revoked. Bricks were thrown through the *Southern Iowa American* office window on North Twelfth Street. Many were errant throws, crashing through the Sunshine Coal Company window next door. Sam Carpenter lost count of how many times he replaced his coal company's window. Sheriff Gaughenbaugh and specially appointed officers searched every pool hall on the Square and across the City. They confiscated weapons and anything that could be used as one.[15]

Tensions approached the boiling point. A showdown between the town's Klan and anti-Klan forces was becoming inevitable. The event would be the Centerville City Council election. The date: Monday, March 30, 1925.

Chapter 42

The Showdown

The Klan moved first. On February 25, two of its members entered the City clerk's office in City Hall, just off the Square on West Jackson Street, and filed seven names for the City Council. They called themselves the "Citizens Ticket." Ten minutes later a Republican ticket was filed. There had been no mass meeting and no caucus. Since the Republican Party's takeover by the Klan, this was a second Klan ticket.[1]

Two blocks away, a group of men who opposed the Klan met in secrecy in Dr. Bamford's clinic on South Main Street. They discussed their opposition to the Klan. They talked of the changes in the town, the distrust, the discord, the loss of confidence in the town's future, the stagnant economy and the dragging employment. What started as private conversations now evolved into political action.[2]

In the North Twelfth Street office of the *Southern Iowa American*, editor Glenn Reed was puzzled. It was March 9. The closing date for nominations was the fourteenth, five days away. Klan supporters were asking him who the opposition would be. "Well," he wrote, "they will soon have to throw down the curry comb and rush them into the open. They hate to do it, but 'business is business; and law is law.'" On Friday, March 13, he worried again: "The 'dark horses' in the city campaign must be filed as candidates before tomorrow night if their names are to appear on the ticket in print."[3]

That very evening, in the Association of Commerce room above the Miners Hall on Thirteenth Street, just off the Square, almost one hundred people were attending a meeting. All were anti-Klan, and all knew of the meeting by word of mouth. Any attempt to advertise their meeting, any loud pronouncements of it, they knew, would invite invasion and domination by Klan members intent on crushing their opposition. That night they unanimously voted for an anti-Klan, non-partisan ticket. They called themselves the "Lincoln League." The next day, moments before nominations closed, the ticket was filed in the City clerk's office.[4]

Glenn Reed was furious: "The editor of this column is puzzled, amazed, insulted, tickled, flabbergasted and also bloomin' sore at the thing that has been pulled without his knowledge, advice or consent." Three days later, the "straw" Republican ticket was withdrawn. Centerville now faced a direct confrontation: On one side, the pro-Klan Citizens Ticket; on the other, the anti-Klan Lincoln League. For the next twelve days, what followed was a campaign so vitriolic and so personal the community became traumatized.[5]

At least some of it must have caused hilarity. The Klan's "Exalted Cyclops"—the Reverend J. Roy Wright—wrote three articles in the *Southern Iowa American*. The articles were flattering, even obsequious, to those the Klan had rejected but whose votes it now courted.

In "The Ku Klux Klan and the Jew" and "The Ku Klux Klan and the Roman Catholics," he said Klansmen had no prejudice toward either group and would uphold their rights if they were ever under attack. In "The Klan and the Colored Race," he wrote, "The Negro is regarded as a brother race by the Klansmen." All the Klan objected to, he continued, was interracial marriage, because the Klan wanted to protect "the purity of the Negro race as he would his own."[6]

The tone of those articles was the exception. The *Southern Iowa American* launched daily slanderous attacks aimed at Mayor Keller, Frank Payne and Ed Bulmahn at Iowa Southern Utilities, B.S. Staley, editor Jesse Beck and William and D.C. Bradley. They called the Lincoln League "the Liquor League" and ordered the arrest of John McConville for voting when not a citizen. McConville was born in England to American citizens. This made him an American. His case was dismissed. He voted on March 30 for the anti-Klan ticket. The Klan left the Agnessens, the Russos, the miners, the farmers and the town's workers alone. Their intention was deliberate. It was targeted at those with education and those in the town who wielded power. Having already assisted in poisoning the town's racial and religious divisions, the Klan now created a new one: class. Its effects would last decades.[7]

Both newspapers introduced their candidates and published their advertisements. The Lincoln League daily, via the *Iowegian*, published articles giving its position on issues facing the town and how to mark the ballot. They held public meetings, and they held a private one, this one behind the closed doors of the Second Baptist Church with a large congregation of African Americans. Registration was reported to be heavy.[8]

On Thursday, March 26, four days before polling, the *Iowegian* published a list of endorsements for the Lincoln League. There were 235 signatures. Two days later, on Saturday March 28, the list was republished, this time with 245 more signatures added overnight, then another 34 handed in the same day but too late for publication.[9]

Perhaps by design or by accident, the Majestic Theatre that week was showing the movie *Abraham Lincoln—The Man of the Ages.* Its advertisement in the *Iowegian* stretched across two full pages. There were six images of Lincoln in different poses, each accompanied by a quotation from his most famous speeches. All seemed apropos to Centerville's struggle. Perhaps the best was the first: "You can fool some of the people all of the time, all of the people some of the time, but you cannot fool all the people, all the time."[10]

The polls opened on March 30 at 7 a.m. Lines quickly formed at three rooms in the courthouse: the Farm Bureau for the First Ward, First Precinct; the Grand Army of the Republic room for the First Ward, Second Precinct; the engineer's room for the Second Ward, First Precinct. Across the Square, voters in the Second Ward, Second Precinct, voted in City Hall. Voters in the Third Ward, First Precinct, voted in Bever's Barber Shop on South Eighteenth; those in the Third Ward, Second Precinct, at the Roth Store on South Main. By three o'clock, with four hours of polling still to go, lines were still forming at the polling stations. It was the heaviest vote in Centerville's history.[11]

Everywhere was quiet. There was no evidence of betting on the election result. No voter wanted to jeopardize his vote or pay a heavy fine. Sheriff Gaughenbaugh warned any disturbance, any infraction of the law, would meet with speedy arrest and punishment. Five State agents and a company of the National Guard were held ready in case of unrest. When Gaughenbaugh learned many men from neighboring towns were coming to Centerville "to see the fun," he said, "There ainta gonna be no fun."[12]

The polls closed at 7 p.m. The counting began. The Lincoln League swept the polls, with majorities at each precinct from five hundred to nine hundred votes. As the result became known, the celebration on Centerville's Courthouse Square was instant. Bands, drum corps and sirens sounded. Impromptu parades went in every direction. Cars in long processions circled and recircled the Square and residential districts with their horns blaring. At the theaters, the movies and the entertainment were halted and the result announced. People stood, clapped and shouted. People sang, marched and danced. Fireworks, including cannon crackers, skyrockets and Roman candles exploded over the town—a scene that continued into the early hours of the morning.[13]

Chapter 43

The KKK Defeated

Lincoln League Win Election" was the KKK's *Southern Iowa American*'s succinct headline the next morning. Jesse M. Beck's *Iowegian* headline read, "Lincoln League Wins in Monster Vote." The Hearst International News and the Associated Press carried the result across the State. If the headlines of the two newspapers were not widely divergent, their coverage of the town's election-night celebration was. To the *Iowegian*, it was "a hilarious display of joy" in which whole, huge gatherings of citizens were law-abiding, the people in the parades "...as genteel and reputable and orderly as can be found in the entire city," and, with the exception of a few, there was "little evidence of liquor." To Glenn Reed, the celebration resembled "...a charivari with cowbells and fireworks." He saw instances of drinking "everywhere," much of it sustained with shouts of "Liquor League, I'll say Liquor League." He said that vulgar and obscene language was used promiscuously and women were insulted. Many demonstrations occurred outside the Klan office on North Twelfth Street with shouts of "Come out all you Kluckers"; "Get off the streets you sons of b——s"; "We've got em over a barrel now"; and "There'll be a hot time in the old town tonight!" And at one place on the Square, Reed found it particularly objectionable that "Negroes and whites were seen to be passing their bottle from mouth to mouth."[1]

"Charity for All" was the title of Jesse Beck's editorial on November 4. It quoted Ulysses S. Grant, who, at the end of the Civil War, advised the opposition to return to their farms and their stores and their offices and resume their work as citizens of a common country. "And that," concluded Jesse Beck, "is what we must do in Appanoose County." Glenn Reed felt differently. He said he'd been approached by "many people" with an apology for having voted for the "Liquor League." "Too late," he wrote. "The so-called emancipators who set the bootleggers free should have been near Thirty and Streepy last night. That portion of their party are [*sic*] still emancipating." Reed was about to be distracted. He faced a more pressing concern.[2]

The day after the election, a small notice appeared in Reed's newspaper. It said, "Your pledge of ten dollars is due." It was signed by G.N. McDonald and underneath his name there was another name—that of a fictitious company, "Southern Oil, Land and Development." The initials, it was noted, created a code: SOLD. Glenn Reed left Centerville, returning to edit the *Cincinnati Review* south of town and renaming it the *Hawkeye X-Ray*. His spleen was still not vented. Again he launched attacks on Jesse Beck, describing his policy as "contemptible cussedness …If there was ever a newspaper that seemed more plainly sold out to 'interests,' bootleggers, thugs and crooks it has not came to our attention." The *Hawkeye X-Ray* lasted seven months. Reed and his family moved to Louisville, Kentucky. His printing press was sold and moved to Brashear, Missouri.[3]

G.N. McDonald left town soon after the election. He was reported to be in a Klan parade in Sioux City in September, and then it was rumored he'd returned to Texas. His exact whereabouts were unknown. The Reverend J. Roy Wright continued to receive support from the Central Church of Christ and remained as the church's pastor for the next three years. He died at his home on West Washington Street in Centerville on August 4, 1928. He was just forty years old and suffered from asthma.[4]

The Reverend E.J. Shook of the Methodist church remained steadfast to the Ku Klux Klan. Even after the City election, he spoke to a KKK rally in Moravia: "I am a Klansman," he said, "because of the character of its opposition. The selfish politicians, the covetous businessman, the bootleggers, libertines, gamblers and other grafters …I must classify myself as standing as a member of this great constructive order [the KKK]." For the people of his church, it was too much. In September they circulated a petition requesting the removal of Shook as the church's pastor. Dr. Shook was transferred to a smaller pastorate in Sigourney, Iowa.[5]

The *Southern Iowa American* was bought by Louie R. Scott, the publisher and editor of the *Mystic Telegram*, with $5,625 given by twelve stockholders. Scott's tenure at the *Southern Iowa American* was as financially precarious as Glenn Reed's. There were sparsely worded advertisements stretching across multiple pages and repeated requests for new readers, for new local stories and for subscriptions to be paid by existing readers. In less than a year, its daily edition was replaced with a semi-weekly one. Three months later it advertised, in three-inch letters, a "Cooperative Profit Sharing Salesmanship Club." Prizes were offered worth almost four thousand dollars to members who could enroll the most new readers. There was a qualification for participants. Only "… reputable white men and women" could enter.[6]

In less than a month, the stockholders foreclosed the *Southern Iowa American*. They also sued Louie Scott for their investment. He countersued for twenty-five thousand dollars for their libelous accusations of "the lackadaisical manner" in which the paper was run. Scott lost his case.[7]

For many years, meetings of the Klan still continued in the County—their advertisements ever smaller, the number of their members dwindling. There were disputes and occasional fights. Dr. E.E. Bamford, who opposed the Klan from the beginning and in whose clinic on South Main the concept of the Lincoln League was born, was the subject of one. Threatening notices from a supposed adjustment company in Chicago were mailed to his patients, ordering the immediate payment of medical bills. It was, said the *Iowegian*, "a diabolically conceived plot" to injure a man and his business. The patients owed no money. Glenn Reed, misquoting a rodeo rider, was involved in a fight at the Merchants Hotel on West State Street. Reed received two black eyes and a broken nose. Worse scandals were breaking out across the country. In April 1925 in Vinton, Iowa, Mrs. C.B. Cook, active prohibitionist and Klan leader, was assassinated, her assailant never caught. The same month in Indiana, D.C. Stephenson, the "Grand Dragon" of Indiana's KKK, was charged with the kidnapping, rape and murder of Madge Oberholtzer. For months, newspaper headlines ran lurid accounts of the Klan's activities in Indiana, exposing graft, corruption and political secrets.[8]

In 1925, the Pulitzer gold medal for "the most disinterested and meritorious public service rendered by an American newspaper in 1925" was awarded to the *Columbus Enquirer Sun*, a Georgia newspaper in the heart of a region of KKK activity. It was awarded, said the judges, for the newspaper's "brave and energetic fight against the Ku Klux Klan, against the enactment of a law barring the teaching of evolution, against dishonest and incompetent public officials, against lynching, and for justice to the Negro."[9]

By the 1930s, Appanoose County's battle with the Klan appeared to be over. The *Mystic Telegram* closed; the *Southern Iowa American* and all its equipment were sold. The purchaser, ironically, was Jesse M. Beck, the editor of the *Iowegian*. A generation of children were raised never hearing of their town's struggle with the KKK. Robert Beck, Jesse's son, became a good friend of the son of Joe

Allison, who had run for mayor on the Citizens Ticket. A few children recalled being hidden from views of cross burnings or protected by parents from Klan gatherings. A few others, exploring their grandparents' attics, discovered discarded KKK robes and were hushed into silence. By the 1940s and '50s, those same children were unconsciously helping to undermine the Klan. Anti-Klan journalist Stetson Kennedy had infiltrated the higher workings of the Klan in Georgia and given the Klan's secret rituals and code words to the writers of the popular radio adventure series *Superman*.[10]

But beneath the protection, beneath the silence, there was a legacy. Families had been riven, suspicion between neighbors intensified, and businesses supported or boycotted for decades. And on a deeper level, racial, religious and class divisions became calcified. Their influence would permeate the community. They were there, ready to be confronted again and again as the town—as the country—attempted to live out their national heritage: that all men are created equal.

Chapter 44

Radio

In his new shop just off the Square, next door to the *Iowegian* on North Main, Harry Luther was tinkering. Using two vacuum tubes, a condenser, receiver, loop aerials, batteries and headphones, he displayed to a fascinated town its first radio receiving set. The date was October 1, 1920. Luther's radio launched the town into a new era. The train and the automobile gave travel from the town to distant locations. The radio offered the world without leaving home.[1]

Across the nation, radio was the "craze." Stores were being mobbed by people eager to sign up for a three-month delivery. Local people reported that counters in Kansas City and Chicago were bare. But, said William S. Bradley, Harry Luther's store in Centerville had "more stuff in his show-cases than all the Chicago stores combined." Some of his supplies Luther now moved diagonally across the Square to his garage on East Van Buren. There the town's boys and young men built more radios. They listened through headsets to sounds coming across airwaves. At first, they heard codes from Washington, D.C., and Arlington, Virginia, and those from a radio station in Norway contacting New York City. There was a telephone conversation between Santa Catalina Island and Los Angeles said to be a freak of static electricity. And then voices were heard clearly: opera singer Lucien Muratore from the Chicago Grand Opera on wavelength 360 meters and, on wavelength 330 from KDKA in Pittsburgh, Pennsylvania, agricultural and market reports sanctioned by the U.S. Department of Agriculture.[2]

Jack Porter, the pressman at the *Centerville Journal*—nineteen months before it was sold to the KKK—set up a radio at his office and wrote a weekly column for radio enthusiasts. He listed wavelengths of stations and gave advice on building rooftop aerials to improve reception. Farmers bought sets and received daily market reports and weather forecasts. Music lovers listened through headphones to such options as a concert in Omaha or a band recital in Milwaukee. Opera aficionados heard *Pagliacci*, *Samson and Delilah*, *Cavaleri Rusticana* and *Il Travatore* from Chicago's Metropolitan Opera. Jack Porter, on Sundays at his residence on South Fifteenth Street, sat back in his easy chair, smoked his pipe and listened to radio chapel services from Swissvale, Pennsylvania, and Detroit, Michigan. The Elks Club put a radio in its club room. Manager Leo Moore installed one at the Majestic. By April 6, 1922, fifty radios were known to be operating in Appanoose County.[3]

On April 13, William Bradley installed the town's first radio station. He placed it at the First National Bank on the Square's Northside. Workmen erected an aerial on the roof. The station was one of eight in Iowa, one of four regularly broadcasting evening programs. It had its own power plant. It delivered five hundred watts of electrical energy at one thousand volts direct current, tapping some from the Interurban trolley wire. The station radiated three-and-a-half amperes in the antenna, drawing 220 milliamperes plate current. Its call letters were WDAX.[4]

On April 22, a Saturday evening, seven days from its installation, WDAX joined the *Centerville Journal* for a broadcast concert featuring all-local artists. More than a thousand people packed Twelfth Street from Maple to the Square. They waited outside the *Journal* office. They watched Jack Porter operating his receiver set in the front window. The program began at 7:30 p.m. from the First National Bank broadcasting station. The signal was sent to the *Journal* office, and Jack Porter transmitted it to a Magnavox loudspeaker located in the transom over the door. The listeners heard the jazz of local boy Paul Beer and his Synchopatin' Five; Mrs. Gladys Cooper, the popular Centerville soprano, in a selection including "Myfanwy," a love song from her native Wales; a three-minute address on Clean-Up Week from the Reverend Mott Sawyers; John and Patrick McConville playing a duet on dulcimer and accordion and causing "a sensation"; the Harmony Four Male Quartet in a selection including "My Wild Irish Rose," "Peggy O'Neil" and "Until the Dawn"; and Miss Marjorie Piper in a violin solo titled "Souvenir." The reception was described "in fine shape." As an overflow crowd at the Majestic four blocks away listened to the Harmony Four begin "Peggy O'Neil," the Majestic orchestra, spontaneously, began playing the accompaniment very softly and to the delight of the audience.[5]

WDAX's signal reached great distances. Reports arrived that it was heard 350 miles away in Mount Hope, Wisconsin; 380 miles in Pittsburgh, Kansas; 425

in Goodland, Indiana; 440 in Bellingham, Minnesota. A band concert given in the Courthouse Park Pavilion in September 1922, relayed to the bank by a wire connected to a microphone and then transmitted through the airwaves, was heard over a radius of one thousand miles and penetrated sixteen different states. Elmer Sharp of Sharp's Hardware Store on the Square, vacationing in an Excelsior Springs hotel in Missouri, heard WDAX by connecting his wiring to the bed springs and to the hotel water pipe, thus establishing a ground. Almost immediately he heard William Bradley broadcasting market reports and saying, "This is station WDAX at the First National Bank broadcasting station, Centerville, Iowa, signing off." Elmer said it made him homesick. Within a week, the guests at the Excelsior Springs hotel had plenty of radio entertainment, and they considered Elmer about the smartest radio amateur they ever met.[6]

WDAX ceased operations suddenly and unexpectedly. "Death," said the *Iowegian* on December 21 1923, "was sudden, unsuspected. Painless and wholly unpreceded by any infirmity. Yesterday WDAX was doing nicely and today it ceased to exist." The cause was a letter received from the government department canceling the station's license because it was not run by a licensed operator.[7]

The loss of WDAX was a disappointment to the people of the town. But nothing could halt their enthusiasm for radio. They heard the primary election returns in 1922; President Calvin Coolidge's speech in New York City; and his reelection on November 1, 1924, when Centerville's Universal Car Company invited everyone to the Appanoose County Courtroom or P.A. Hollenbeck's Exline store to hear the results live over a Kennedy radio set and loudspeaker. Four months later, on March 4, 1925, half a million Iowans gathered on farms, in towns, in villages and hamlets, in factories, in halls and in schools to hear, for the first time, the first presidential inauguration ever broadcast. They heard it relayed from Washington, D.C., by the American Telephone and Telegraph Company to WHO broadcasting station of Bankers Life Company in Des Moines. In Centerville, the new "radioman" in town—Ira Durham—installed Atwater Kent radio receivers and loudspeakers in the high school, the grammar school and the County Farm Bureau office. Others were placed in Davison Brothers Hardware and other businesses. Many more people listened at home.[8]

By September 1924, the *Centerville Daily Iowegian* was publishing the "Daily Radio Program," a newspaper feature citing fifty radio stations across the United States, their wavelengths, their programs and their times of broadcasting. Burdell Kirkhart on East Maple, using a Radiola IIIA with a Radiola loudspeaker, in one evening tuned in to forty-three stations and had witnesses to prove it. The stations included some in Canada, some on the Atlantic coast and some on the Pacific coast.[9]

Late at night, American stations tagged "stand-by" silent hours to allow reception from England, from Europe. The record for the earliest and furthest station heard in town went to B.S. Robley, a car salesman with the Universal Car Company, who lived on West Maple. On a set he'd built himself and said to be one of the best in Centerville, he heard London, England. It was Sunday, November 25, 1923. The station letters, he said, were "H2 something"—probably H2O, quipped the *Centerville Daily Iowegian*, seeing as how the signal came across the water. A few days later, Mrs. Harry Payne on North Eighteenth heard Edinburgh, Scotland. H.E. Jennings at the Alexandria Apartments on Haynes Avenue was listening to SBR, the call letters for Brussels, Belgium, on wavelength 266 meters and 5NO, the call letters for Newcastle, England.[10]

The radio sounds came through flashing lightning, thunder, rain and storms that broke power lines. They came through more than five hundred feet down below the surface of the earth and three hundred feet back into the cavernous workings of Centerville's gypsum mine. A week-long, severe ice storm in February 1924 changed how the town received its news. Telephone and telegraph wires across the Midwest were down. Long-distance communication was impossible. The major news associations—AP, United Press and Reuters—sent national and international bulletins by radio. Jesse M. Beck was listening at the *Iowegian.* "Had it not been for the radio," Jesse Beck wrote, "…this community would have had to wait longer for much of its news."[11]

The radio delivered health talks, food information and lectures from Iowa's universities at Ames and Iowa City. There was entertainment, from classical music to jazz. From New York City via NBC came the Ziegfeld Follies, with Eddie Cantor interviewing channel swimmers and nonstop air fliers. From Hollywood, listeners heard John Barrymore rendering Hamlet's soliloquy and, to the delight of everyone in Centerville, Esther Campbell, Centerville's "Whistling Girl," now twelve years old and studying whistling in Los Angeles, where she was about to whistle her way into Disney's movie *Snow White and the Seven Dwarfs*. They heard of Corydon's George Saling winning the gold medal for hurdles at the 1932 Olympic Games; they remembered him representing Corydon High School and winning at Centerville High School track meets and at the Drake Relays in Des Moines. They also heard an interview with Centerville's Harold "Swannie" Swanson talking about Hollywood and his emerging career there as a top-notch literary agent.

When radio carried the World Series, Harry Luther on South Main Street placed a loudspeaker on the outside of his store, operated for the first time in town by light current without batteries. For the 1927 Dempsey-Tunney boxing match, Ira Durham placed a loudspeaker on his shop on the Square's Eastside and provided food and beverages inside. For the same event, Garrett and Phillips, the local agents of Freed-Eisemann sets, placed a radio in the south window of the recorder's office in the courthouse.[12]

When radio programs covered the discovery of King Tutankhamun's tomb in Egypt, a national fashion rage was engendered. Women's clothing stores in Centerville, from Goldstein's to Frankel's, were selling, said the *Iowegian*, "Tut hats, Tut gowns, Tut waists, Tut sweaters, Tut gloves, and even Tut headdresses and hairdresses." In June, a King Tut bathing suit was seen at Centerville's swimming pool.[13]

In 1925, when WGN Chicago carried live the trial of Thomas Scopes, a high school science teacher in Tennessee, for teaching Charles Darwin's theory of evolution, fourteen-year-old Dale Jones said he was glued to the radio and so was everyone he knew. When science lectures on the subject were given by the Reverend Mott Sawyers of the Presbyterian church, the rooms were filled to capacity. Reverend Dr. Sawyers held Ph.Ds in philosophy and science from Princeton University. He saw no clash between religion and science.[14]

In 1926, William S. Bradley's old radio station WDAX came back briefly to life. It was reconditioned and renamed PAVE. It operated for thirteen days, from April 1 to April 13. Programs consisted of educational and musical numbers interspersed with talks urging people to vote "yes" on April 14 for paving the County's roads. The station offered rewards for the best slogans of the campaign.[15]

Four mud-covered vehicles came into town. One was an automobile, laden with chairs, high boots, ropes and shovels, labeled, "We Just Came in from Moravia." Another was a Ford car, wobbling precariously from side to side. Slogans were everywhere: "Pave or Perish," "Pave Don't Rave," "Come Dave Let's Pave," "Pave or Push." The winners were two tiny children, Muriel Fannon and Jack Calhoun, each carrying a banner that read, "I Am Too Small to Vote, Are You?" The winner from the high school was Rissie Cridlebaugh's "Put Aunt Lizzie and Uncle Henry on the Great White Way." The winner of the general category was Gilbert Pullen of North First Street. He drove a dilapidated Ford truck, laden with coal and covered in mud, with a slogan: "Help Me out of the Mud."[16]

The bond issue passed with a majority of three thousand. By August, three hundred feet of concrete were laid on what was then Highway 3 west of town. By July 30, 1929, after a "yes" vote for a $100,000 State bond issue, pavement was laid connecting Centerville to Corydon, twenty-three miles west. Four months earlier, a Studebaker Commander roadster roared over five miles of the completed road west of Centerville. Its speed was registered at ninety-three miles per hour.[17]

Chapter 45

Speed and Flight

The fast-moving Studebaker west of town was a sign of the times. Speed and breaking records for covering new and vast distances rapidly were becoming a national obsession.

Specially designed sports cars were roaring across Utah's Bonneville Flats. Steamships on the Atlantic were fighting for the Blue Riband Trophy, awarded for the fastest crossing of the ocean. Witnessing one, aboard the Cunard liner *Mauretania* then challenging the North German Lloyd liner, the *Bremen*, was Centerville's jockey family, the Garners, on their way to see their son Guy winning on French race tracks. Train speeds accelerated. Vegetable trains roared through Appanoose County carrying fresh produce to eastern cities from the Imperial Valley of California and from Yuma, Arizona. The crack Golden State Limited, cutting its time from Los Angeles to Chicago by 105 minutes, rushed through town carrying passengers, sometimes favorite film stars, to California. People from the town lined the Rock Island tracks to catch glimpses of them: Tom Mix in 1922; Pola Negri in 1926, accompanying her the flower-covered, silver-bronze casket bearing the body of Rudolph Valentino, the sheik of their movies, dead at thirty-two of appendicitis and a perforated gastric ulcer. But nothing excited the human imagination like the speed, the covering of impossible distances, then being achieved by human flight.[1]

Dirigibles were flying around Europe as early as 1909. The first to cross the Atlantic was the British R-34, gliding into Mineola, Long Island, in July 1919, her crew emerging haggard, their eyes bloodshot after 108 hours and twelve minutes without sleep. Repeated failed efforts were made to cross the ocean in propeller-driven, fixed-wing aircraft. On June 16, 1919, two British fliers—Captain John Alcock and Lieutenant Brown—flew across the Atlantic successfully in a Vickers Vimy biplane. They flew the 1,930 miles from Newfoundland, landing in a bog in County Galway. Their time: sixteen hours and twelve minutes.[2]

The first into Appanoose County were the barnstormers. These aviators, usually former World War I pilots flying in Army surplus or Curtiss Orioles at one hundred miles per hour, became regular attractions at July 4 celebrations, fairs and school homecomings. They landed in fields at Moulton, Moravia, Seymour and Corydon. In Centerville, they touched down on the field north of Mine Thirty or on the John Curl farm to its south. They flew low over the Courthouse Square. They waved to the upturned faces. They dropped packets of Wrigley's Chewing Gum attached to small parachutes for free-flight tickets. One such parachute landed on the Continental Hotel Annex roof and was won in a mad scramble of boys up the fire escape by fourteen-year-old Paul Beck, the son of the *Iowegian*'s editor. Without a free ticket, the pilots charged a dollar a minute for a flight, ten dollars for a ride and a loop, fifteen dollars to circle the town.[3]

Some of the pilots were stunt fliers. They performed dives, flip-flops and repeated loops. One, flying midpoint between Centerville and Mystic, ascended to an altitude of nine thousand feet, then descended in two tailspins of three thousand feet each. Sometimes two pilots flew two planes and worked in tandem. They swung on trapezes under a swift-moving aircraft. They walked on wings. They jumped in midair from one plane to another.[4]

Over the years, unidentified planes flew over the town. They occasionally roared over the Square, awakening people from sleep. One flew from Chicago to Kansas City, above and following the Rock Island track. Engineers leaned from cab windows. Telegraph operators at different stations kept records of its location and the times it was making. Another, issuing great clouds of smoke, made an emergency landing near the Sunshine coal mine west of town. Spectators raced to the scene. They watched the pilot remove the gas, strain it through a chamois, refill the tank and fly on.[5]

Charles Eddy, a farmer living south of Exline, could set his watch and exchange waves with the pilots of the Chicago-to-Dallas U.S. Mail flights. "Four," he said, "go over every day: 3 a.m. and 11 a.m. for the Westbound, 5 a.m. and 4 p.m. for the Eastbound." He could also judge the weather by the height the aircraft was flying: high on clear days, low in bad weather. Paul E. Johnson, U.S. Air Mail pilot flying the Chicago-to–Kansas City leg of the Dallas flight, confirmed Charles Eddy's observation. Interviewed by the

Kansas City Star, Johnson described how in bad weather conditions and low visibility he was compelled to fly dangerously low over Appanoose County, skimming treetops, avoiding barns, bridges and houses that could suddenly loom out of fog.[6]

Speeds continued to increase, records continued to fall and technology continued to improve. Nonstop flights were recorded in the *Iowegian*: Jimmy Doolittle from San Antonio, Texas, to Jacksonville, Florida, in 1922; Lieutenants Macready and Kelly across the United States from New York to San Diego in 1923; French aviators L'Martre and Arrichards from Paris to Senegal in 1925. One year earlier, three U.S. Army Air Service pilots—Lieutenants Ogden, Nelson and Smith—were the first to span the globe, flying west from Seattle. They flew in four custom-built biplanes known as Douglas World Cruisers, making multiple stops en route for fuel, food and supplies. Journeys across the Atlantic Ocean that did not stop were being made by the dirigibles, but the goal of aviators was to cross it in fixed-wing aircrafts in the style of Alcock and Brown. The goal was enhanced when a French-born American, Raymond Orteig, who owned two Manhattan hotels, the Lafayette and the Brevoort, offered a prize of twenty-five thousand dollars for the first nonstop New York-to-Paris flight.[7]

In September 1926, French aviator René Fonck's flight plan to claim the Orteig Prize appeared in the *Iowegian*. Taking off from a Long Island runway, his aircraft exploded in a gully. Fonck and one other of his four-member crew escaped. The other two did not. The next bid for the Orteig Prize came from two French war aces: Charles Nungesser and Francois Coli. They left Paris's LeBourget Airport on Sunday, May 8, 1927. They were to arrive in New York on Monday. It was expected they would win the prize. The two men never arrived. Somewhere over the Atlantic, they were lost. Eight more aviators now prepared to make the flight. One was Admiral Byrd, the first to fly to the North Pole. Another was Clarence Chamberlain of Denison, Iowa. One of the eight planned to fly solo. He was twenty-five-year-old Captain Charles Lindbergh, who had barnstormed in Iowa—possibly in Centerville—and carried the U.S. Mail between St. Louis and Chicago. Lindbergh took off from Roosevelt Field, New York, at 7:51 a.m. on Friday, May 20, 1927. He was flying a silver-colored Ryan plane he'd named *The Spirit of St. Louis*. Interest was intense. Jesse Beck checked United Press news service plans.[8]

The United Press had dispatched one hundred special correspondents to remote points in Newfoundland, Nova Scotia, Ireland, England and France. Nineteen were on the Irish coast, another nineteen in France's River Seine Valley, practically as many in England. Each was notified of Lindbergh's departure and each given a description of the plane. The Commercial Cable Company, R.C.A., the Western Union telegraph company and the Independent Wireless Service stood ready to gather the reports and transmit them to the UP office in New York. Operators there transmitted the accounts to all those receiving UP services, including Centerville's *Daily Iowegian*. Ships at sea, the Coast Guard, the International Ice Patrol and radio and cable companies joined the watch. No one slept in the newspaper office. Many more were awake across the County.[9]

In Centerville, editor Jesse Beck hovered near the *Iowegian*'s telegraph printer. The telephone rang constantly with inquiries. People stepped into the office on North Main Street asking to hear the news of Lindbergh and to read the immediate bulletins direct from the machine. By eight fifty-one on Saturday morning, Centerville time, Lindbergh had been in the air for twenty-seven hours. A half-hour later, at nine twenty, Jesse Beck recalled, the reports telegraphed to his printer began to show a consistent pattern. A message was received from Queenstown, Ireland. The commander of the County Kerry Civic Guard reported sighting a plane believed to be that of Charles Lindbergh over Smerwich Harbor, north of Dingle, on the country's southwest corner. Half an hour later, a sighting was made over County Cork, then over England at Plymouth. All reports said the plane was flying at a great height and following a consistent southeasterly flight path. At one thirty in the afternoon in Centerville—eight thirty that night in France—the telegraph machine printed a sighting of a plane several thousand feet high over Cherbourg, and then Bayeaux, flying in the direction of Paris. Lindbergh landed *The Spirit of St. Louis* at LeBourget Airport Saturday, May 21. It was 10:21 p.m. Paris time, 3:21 p.m. in Centerville. One hundred and fifty thousand people stood waiting to greet him. As Lindbergh taxied to a stop, they moved toward him in a human tide. Three minutes later, the news reached the UP office in New York. In another minute, it was in San Francisco and in another two in Centerville. Jesse Beck immediately prepared an extra edition of the *Iowegian*; the word "Extra" measured three-and-a-half inches, above it the headline "Lindbergh Lands in Paris 3:21."[10]

Everywhere, the report was telephoned to radio stations and announced on the air while bands played. In Centerville and in towns across the country, whistles shrieked and bells rang. In theaters and movie houses, the bulletin was read to audiences amid wild cheering, and people shouted the news to each other. In Centerville, those with the deepest sense of pride were the Swedish immigrants. In Mystic, one of them, Gustav Swanson, collected the Swedish-language newspapers delivered by Milwaukee train from Chicago, full of the news and photographs of Lindbergh's triumph. These he showed in Mystic and in Centerville, so brimming with pride people believed Gustav and Lindbergh must be cousins. They were not. But Gustav had immigrated into America from Vastervik on Sweden's east coast; Lindbergh's grandfather had come from Smedstrop, across the peninsula, and that was enough.[11]

Lindbergh was now a hero, mobbed across Europe and, on his return, in America. Centerville's mayor Jim Keller, Mr. and Mrs. E.A. Markley and J.H. Adamson left town to represent the County at the official welcome in Washington and to witness the presentation of a new U.S. medal, the Distinguished Flying Cross, to Lindbergh by President Calvin Coolidge.[12]

In Centerville, people listened to the proceedings on their radios. Within weeks they were buying "Lindy ties" at Rosenbaum's Clothing Store, the ties covered with airplane designs and imprinted with the words "New York to Paris." They danced a variation of the Charleston known as the Lindy Hop at local dances, and they listened and sang the songs, the marches, the hymns, waltzes and fox-trots all composed in Lindbergh's honor. On August 29, 1927, Lindbergh flew into Des Moines. Seven cars traveled in convoy to witness the event: five from Centerville Square, joined en route by one from Moravia, another from Corydon. The trip was completely free—courtesy of the Appanoose Chevrolet dealers, a reward to those who'd bought Chevrolet cars between the date Lindbergh arrived in Paris and the date he arrived in Des Moines. Just before two in the afternoon, the forty-three guests from Appanoose County watched as Lindbergh and *The Spirit of St. Louis* roared over Des Moines Airport, circled several times and landed. Lindbergh made a short speech. He was welcomed by Mayor Hunter of Des Moines, then taken on a tour of the city by the mayor and the governor of Iowa, John Hammill. It was a day, the returning local residents said, they would long remember.[13]

Lindbergh's flight unleashed an even greater interest in aviation. In Centerville, excitement was further fanned when it was learned that a new nonstop distance record was set from New York to eighty miles southeast of Berlin and that one of the two pilots was an Iowan: Clarence Chamberlain of Denison. Days later, Danley Benjamin, who worked at Looten's Bakery on the Square, bought the town's first aircraft. It was a standard model but powered with a new eight-cylinder OX5 Curtiss engine. The wings of the aircraft were silver, the underbelly yellow, the fuselage dark blue. People watched him play hide-and-seek in the clouds above the Courthouse Square or chase another pilot, Leroy Bartholomew, the two cavorting over each one of the County's towns.[14]

The talk in town was now for a Centerville airport. Speakers promoted the idea, the Association of Commerce was enthusiastic, the U.S. Department of Commerce sent an observer and Vern Price was placed at the head of the town's Aviation Committee. Money was raised and 160 acres leased on the Herbert Streepy Farm, three-and-a-half miles southwest of the town. Volunteers removed cross fences and haystacks; formerly plowed land was disked and harrowed down; uneven areas were smoothed. An area was fenced off for auto parking, for concessions and refreshments. A telephone was installed. Markings for the landing strip and for stalls for planes after arrival were whitewashed.[15]

The opening of Centerville Airport was held on Monday, June 18, 1928. It was called "Aviation Day." It was raining and foggy, but up to fifteen thousand spectators arrived to witness the events. Increasing the excitement was that morning's news. It was given on radio bulletins. It was the headline in the *Iowegian*: "Girl Flyer Reaches England." Amelia Earhart, the first woman to fly and copilot across the Atlantic Ocean, had in fact reached Wales. Her trans-Atlantic airplane, *Friendship*, had landed in an estuary at Burry Port on the Carmarthen coast. She and her two crewmen—Wilmer Stulz, the pilot, and Lou Gordon, the mechanic—were taken ashore by motorboat.[16]

At Centerville Airport, the day began with the arrival of the *Des Moines Register*'s five-seater Fairchild monoplane, named *Good News*. At a window, George Yates, the newspaper's chief photographer, was busy taking aerial shots over Centerville Square and the new airport field. Next came twenty-two planes as part of the Iowa Good Will Tour. These planes raced each other between ten different Iowa cities for four days and a winner's prize of one thousand dollars. The first city, in honor of Aviation Day, was Centerville. The planes left Des Moines at two-minute intervals. Timekeepers recorded their arrival times and relayed the results to a head checker. The winner of the first lap was Carl Christenson of Des Moines, flying a Waco with a time of forty minutes.[17]

Throughout the day, the National Air Transport Company ordered U.S. Air Mail planes to deviate from their routes and fly directly over Centerville Airport. Courtesy of the assistant secretary of war, airships of the U.S. Army's Seventh Air Corps flew in from Omaha, giving demonstrations of their skills before landing. The governor of the State, John Hammill, arrived also by air. The flag was raised. The governor officially opened the airport and gave a speech on the marvels of aviation and on good citizenship, using Charles Lindbergh as an example. Private planes arrived. Among them were a large bomber from Chanute Field in Illinois, piloted by Captain J.J. Devery; a little, bird-like Velie from Moline; and a black-and-orange, giant Stinson Detroiter with Eddie Stinson at one of the two controls. From Ames came a bright yellow-and-black plane with the number thirteen on its side and flown by African American Herman Banning, carrying a surprise passenger. Centerville plumber Joe Shkolnick, whose car was marooned in Des Moines because of the rain and who wanted to be home for Aviation Day, had hitched a ride. There were other aircraft: Pheasants, Eaglerocks, Whitey Sports, Arrow Sports, Humming Birds and, from Monmouth, Illinois, a Ryan—a duplicate of *The Spirit of St. Louis.*

The planes held races. There was a race for "a dead stick landing," another for dropping from an altitude of two thousand feet "with motor dead," some for stunts and some for circling Streepy and Number Thirty mine dumps three times for a distance of twenty miles. For boys fifteen and under, there was a model aircraft competition. These were demonstrated in the evening when the celebrations moved to the Square. Dwight Monteith flew his miniature tri-motored Fokker, George Phillips his miniature copy of *The Spirit of St. Louis.* The town band played. There was a clown contest and, under the stars on the Courthouse Park, a free dance.[18]

On February 29, 1929, Charles Lindbergh, piloting a Sikorsky Amphibian, left Miami Airport for the Panama Canal Zone. He was carrying the first air mail between North and South America. At Cristobal, he unloaded six bags of mail, picked up a similar amount and returned to Miami. Those mailbags contained two letters for Centerville. One was to Mrs. Melissa Triebswetter from Mrs. Blanche Dingeman. Mrs. Dingeman was living in the Canal Zone with her husband, Ray, who was working there. The second letter was to Mrs. Joe Goldstein on South Fifteenth Street. It was from her brother, Captain Charles Ritchell, stationed in the Canal Zone with the U.S. Army. The two letters became known as "the Lindy letters." They were put on display at the *Iowegian* office and Joe Goldstein's store on Midway, also known as North Thirteenth Street.[19]

Six months after Lindbergh's flight to the Canal Zone, at eleven forty on the night of August 7, 1929, Dr. Hugo Eckener, director of the German Zeppelin Company, piloted his airship, the Graf Zeppelin, out of Lakenhurst, New Jersey, heading east. This would be, he announced, a new flight. His Graf Zappelin would circle the world in three hundred hours. He reached Friedrichshafen August 10, Tokyo on August 14 and Los Angeles on August 26, then he set a course for Chicago. On August 28, 1929, the people of Kansas City were up at dawn. The temperature was warm; the sky cloudless. Parked cars congested traffic; housetops and office buildings were thronged with sky gazers. The Liberty Memorial in Kansas City was jammed. At nine thirty-eight that morning, traveling at seventy-five miles per hour, the Graf Zeppelin approached from the southwest, passing directly over the city. On the road to Excelsior Springs, on a hill a few miles northeast of Kansas City, *Centerville Daily Iowegian* reporter Charles DePuy stood transfixed. He heard the airship's engine first and then saw its pointed nose sliding through the blue and disappearing, "an indistinct smudge of mist against the early morning light." A few miles away, veterans of World War I, still nursing wounds suffered at the hands of Germans, watched from the Excelsior Springs Hospital. They were cheering.[20]

In Centerville, excitement was mounting. Radio reports and wire news services were estimating the continued course of the Graf Zeppelin over the Midwest. They predicted its path across Appanoose County. People drove their cars. Some headed for the new airport, others to Mystic, still more to Exline and Moulton. Jesse Beck described them as all "hot and bothered." He placed long-distance telephone calls to Princeton, to Trenton and to Milan, where the airship at that moment was passing just to its east. The Graf Zeppelin was now approaching the Iowa line. Brakeman Steve Crawford and fireman Dick Thompson were on board their freight train, laboring up a hill between Arbela and Memphis, Missouri, eight miles south of the border. They were, at that moment, discussing their misfortune at not having the day off to see the zeppelin. They saw Red May on the caboose moving his arms at them agitatedly, pointing upwards, going through wild contortions. They ignored him, only later to learn the Graf was directly overhead and they had missed it. The airship crossed the Iowa line some twenty miles southeast of Moulton. People climbed to the top of the town's water tower. Others drove onto the Coatsville Road. The airship was just visible as it moved across the corner of Davis County and directly above Milton and Keosauqua in Van Buren County. In Ottumwa, people watched through telescopes as the ship passed thirty miles to the south. It moved over Morning Sun at one forty-five in the afternoon and Davenport at three minutes after two, reaching Lakenhurst on August 29 at seven twelve in the morning. The trip had taken twenty-one days, seven hours and thirty-two minutes. It was a record world flight.[21]

Across the country, Dr. Hugo Eckener was congratulated, but there was more on people's minds—including those in Appanoose County. It was 1929. The stock market was wobbling; banks were insecure, and the economy was in trouble.

Chapter 46

Decline in the Coal Industry

At the end of World War I, wartime markets in Europe disappeared. Government contracts were canceled. European farmland returned to normal production. Farm prices, high during the war, dropped. Corn prices plummeted. Wheat dropped from $2.26 a bushel to less than $1.00. Farmers were unable to pay their debts. Some began losing their farms. The 1930 U.S. Census showed the population of Appanoose County had dropped 5,751 since 1920: 2,476 of that in the towns, 3,275 for the rural population. And for the farmers still at work, there was a severe shortage of farm help, but, said Jesse Beck's headline, "Jazz, Shows, and City Lights Hold Hands Away."[1]

For the County's coal industry it was worse. Throughout the 1920s it was in decline. This, the vital foundation of the local economy, the production of coal, had reached its peak in 1917. In that year, the output of its coal mines was 1,672,000 tons. From then on, it was all downhill, reaching 590,848 in 1930. People were heating their homes with electricity and oil; the railroads—once the greatest consumers of local coal—were buying cheaper coal, much of it non-union, from Illinois, Indiana and Ohio.[2]

The miner was already disaffected. His life was always a miserable one. His work was backbreaking, dirty and dangerous. Coal mine accidents were reported almost weekly in the *Iowegian*: 47 dead in California, 164 in Alabama, 80—then another 38 and another 162—in Pennsylvania, 41 in New Mexico, 33 in British Columbia, 439 in a single explosion in South Wales. Nothing approaching these numbers occurred in Appanoose

Inside a coal mine. *Courtesy of Appanoose County Historical Society.*

County. But there were cave-ins, "kettle-bottom" roof falls and multiple serious injuries—ninety-six in just one year, many incapacitating the miner from ever working again.[3]

Even above ground, there were accidents caused by the coal industry's dangerous residue. Shale dumps exploded. One, dynamited at Galleyville, showered burning dust and red-hot cinders over eleven men, blinding them, incinerating their clothing, blackening them beyond recognition and causing excruciating pain, for three of them eventually relieved by death. Small boys, though warned, used the shale dumps as playgrounds. They climbed to the tops of the "pyramids," grabbed inactive cable ropes and swung on them, exposing their hands to mangling when the cables began moving and to certain death when flung with the contents of an ascending car. Other boys explored abandoned mines and mine shafts, becoming victims of leaking gas. One such accident, on July 4, 1918, was throughout the 1920s and '30s still seared into the local psyche. Fourteen-year-old Vincel Kovacevick collapsed almost as soon as he entered a disused airshaft of Thistle Number Two coal mine, two miles northeast of Cincinnati. Forty-two-year-old August Kauzlarich raced to save him, lifted the boy onto his shoulders and collapsed himself. Both died. The act earned for Kauzlarich a bronze Carnegie Medal for heroism, inscribed with his

Carnegie Medal awarded to August Kauzlarich. *Courtesy of Linda and Fred Polich.*

name, and five dollars a month was given to his widow, Antonija, to raise their nine children.[4]

It was at this time, in the late 1920s, that Appanoose County's coal owners, forced to compete in a shrinking market, cut costs. The costs included cutting the wages they paid their miners.[5]

By the early twenties, the country's coal miners' union, the United Mine Workers of America (UMWA), was led by a man well-known in Appanoose County. Born just outside Lucas, some thirty-eight miles northwest of Centerville, John Llewellyn (John L.) Lewis as a young man had worked in the Forbush and Rathbun mines and collected his wages from the Whitebreast Mining Company's office on the Northside of Centerville's Courthouse Square. In 1924 President John L. Lewis negotiated a national wage agreement with coal owners called the Jacksonville Agreement. It placed a coal miner's pay at $7.50 a day. For many coal owners, this was too much. Appanoose County's coal owners were prepared to pay $5.00 a day. John L. Lewis ordered UMWA miners to strike until operators agreed to the negotiated Jacksonville Agreement of $7.50 a day.[6]

Complicating the situation in Appanoose County was another coal miners' union. Originally started in Macon, Missouri, it was called the United Brotherhood of Miners. Centerville's J. "Pete" Agnessen, the same Belgian coal miner who'd courageously fought against the KKK, left the UMWA, joined the Brotherhood and became its president. Members of the new union, facing the realities of a shrinking coal industry, were prepared to work for five dollars a day.[7]

The United Mine Workers of America went on strike March 31, 1927. The County's coal mines shut down. There was an exception: the Empire coal mine, near the country club, less than two miles northwest of Centerville Square. Striking miners, the members of UMWA Local no. 553, met at the Miners' Hall on Thirteenth Street. Rumors of a riot percolated the town. One hundred of them marched from the Union Hall down Midway and along the Southside of the Square. Waiting for them was Sheriff Earl Gaughenbaugh. He asked

Joe Allison, the marchers' leader, where they were going. The miners were on a peaceful mission, Allison replied, were unarmed and wanted to speak to the workers at the Empire mine about what he termed "an inharmonious situation." The sheriff accompanied the marchers to the mine and remained with them during their stay, then accompanied them back into town. The Empire mine remained open, the miners, now members of the Brotherhood, were working for five dollars a day.[8]

Feelings intensified. The UMWA held mass meetings. A crowd of one thousand assembled and listened to speakers for five hours and again, after a break, for several more hours in the evening on the Southside of the courthouse. The language of the speakers stirred the crowd. The coal owners were called "cowards"; the Brotherhood was seeking to "betray" the miners with "subtle and poisonous influences," and, worse, it was in league with the owners to break the UMWA. The next two mass meetings, a week apart, were held in Mystic. Over the years Mystic had long been a center of union activity. Nationwide speakers had addressed crowds there: "Big Bill" Haywood, Eugene Debs, John L. Lewis on multiple occasions and Mother Jones, beloved by miners across the country and whose rallying cry was "Pray for the dead and fight like hell for the living." When three more coal mines opened under the Brotherhood's pay scale and all three—the Barrett, the Winifred and the Garfield—were in the Mystic-Brazil axis, Mystic now became the focus of heated exchanges. Mass meetings were held on the vacant lot next to the Miners' Hall on Main Street. There was more incendiary language.[9]

Striking UMWA men began picketing the Barrett mine. Miners working there were escorted to and from work by Mystic's town marshal and night watchman, William McFall. They walked the road between a gauntlet of men, women and children. There were threats of violence, dog barks and cat calls. Centerville attorney Tom Fee acquired a court injunction to prevent picketing at the mine. Crowds then gathered at the homes of three of the Barrett miners. Taunts were shouted and more threats, including tarring and feathering the men. One Barrett miner procured a gun. He threatened anyone who entered his yard or approached his house. People feared the trouble would lead to bloodshed. Sheriff Gaughenbaugh was called; he ordered the crowd to disperse.[10]

Parades, picketing and marching became daily occurrences on Mystic's east side. Despite a second court injunction preventing such action, one hundred men and more than one hundred women and children gathered on the road to the Winifred mine. UMWA letters were painted on cars. A boy played an accordion. An old man danced. At Cooper Creek Bridge, on the paved highway just west of Centerville, cars driven by UMWA officials repeatedly swerved in front of two carloads of Winifred miners on their way to work. One of the officials shouted, “Stop that car. That damned car is not going to Mystic today.” It didn’t that day or any day thereafter. The miners returned to Centerville and refused to work at the Winifred again, saying the tactics of the pickets were life threatening. Back in Mystic, the marchers carried banners, sang songs and shouted hurrahs for the UMWA. At five o’clock one afternoon, thirty of the pickets walked to the Winifred gate to speak to the miners as they left work. The women and children shouted “Scabs, Sons-of-bitches—low lived trash, yellow dogs and rotten trash.”[11]

By August 12 the same pattern began at the Garfield mine west of Brazil. Two hundred and fifty pickets asked to speak to the miners. Sheriff Gaughenbaugh was called, and so was William S. Bradley, the Garfield’s owner. Bradley walked to the shaft between the lines of pickets and granted them ten minutes to speak to his miners. The Garfield miners listened. They were asked to quit work. They refused “in strong terms” and returned to work. Gaughenbaugh asked the crowd of men to disperse. They refused. Gaughenbaugh called for Deputy Charles Ware to bring police and a force of local deputies. Then he wired the State’s attorney general for reinforcements to quell a situation he saw as more and more ominous.[12]

Thirty days later, William McFall, Mystic’s town marshal who had been escorting the miners working at the Barrett, the Winifred and the Garfield, drove a short distance north of Mystic, crossed the Little Walnut Bridge and stopped his car. He lay on the road, used his coat as a pillow and shot himself.[13]

If the shock of McFalls’s suicide cooled the situation, the effect soon wore off. Within five days, on the Walnut Creek Bridge west of Brazil, was another act of violence.

At five o’clock in the afternoon of August 18, four men employed at the Garfield mine left work for the day and together began the drive home. As their car approached Walnut Creek Bridge, its path was blocked by a Ford roadster apparently stalled on the bridge with no space to pass. The man with the Ford requested help from the four Garfield men to move his car. Three of the men—William Taylor, Ira Mullen (Garfield’s engineer) and Carey Raney went to his assistance. As they did so, fifteen or more men who had been hiding under the bridge rushed up in ambush. The three were beaten and kicked, Taylor and Mullen into unconsciousness; Raney was badly hurt and Lester Hazeltine, who’d remained with the car, was badly bruised. The assault was interrupted by the arrival of Garfield’s owner, William S. Bradley. The attackers ran in all directions. Bradley drove the injured men into Centerville to St. Joseph Hospital. On regaining consciousness, Mullen said he'd been threatened on several previous occasions, including with death. His incapacity now, as the mine's engineer, closed the Garfield mine for several days.[14]

Sheriff Gaughenbaugh hired extra deputies. They were law enforcement officers from outside the County. They provided an armed guard for miners at the Barrett, the Garfield (as soon as it reopened) and the Winifred mines, those without cars who walked to and from work along the railroad track lined with camps of UMWA strikers.

Local citizens urged Iowa's Governor John Hammill to send troops. So did the coal owners. On August 26, eight local coal operators, Sheriff Gaughenbaugh, local peace officers and officials from district thirteen of the UMWA were closeted in a meeting with Governor Hammill in his Des Moines office, from ten in the morning to two thirty that afternoon. The UMWA members agreed to the governor's terms: a picket of not more than thirty would be allowed at a coal mine; parades and pickets must be orderly, lacking violence and obscene language.[15]

By mid-September, the County attorney, W.B. Hays and Sheriff Gaughenbaugh observed violations of the governor's terms. They counted between two hundred and three hundred pickets—well in excess of the maximum of thirty—many of them subjecting the miners at work to profane language and attacks from rocks, clods and eggs. When, on Wednesday, September 21, Gaughenbaugh and his deputies ordered a large crowd of pickets at the Garfield mine to disperse, they were greeted with jeers and outright refusals to move. The next day, more deputies, eleven police officers from Des Moines, arrived in Centerville, responding immediately to a request from Gaughenbaugh that was reinforced by the Appanoose County Board of Supervisors. In addition, the sheriff obtained a supply of tear gas.[16]

Sometime before the miners working the Garfield emerged on their way home on Friday, September 23, a crowd of pickets gathered near the mine. They numbered two hundred. There were UMWA officials, some from other districts, union members on strike, and their wives and children. They lined the road both to the east and to the west. Some sat in cars parked along the road for several hundred feet. They were quiet and orderly. There were no shouts and very little singing. Sheriff Gaughenbaugh, with five or six local deputies and the eleven Des Moines police officers, arrived. They parked their cars on the east side of the railroad tracks leading to the Garfield. They briefly conferred. Then, with Gaughenbaugh in the lead, they marched toward the pickets in a phalanx. The pickets noticed the officers were heavily armed. There was "a considerable stir" and "much murmuring." The sheriff asked the union officials to disperse the crowd. The officials replied they could not make the people leave. Gaughenbaugh approached the pickets several times and clearly he warned them he would use tear gas. Some pickets left immediately, driving away in their cars. Others moved away some distance and out of range of any action. Gaughenbaugh, himself a survivor of World War I's chlorine and gas attacks, waited, giving plenty of time for all who wished to leave to do so. He then walked to the west end of the pickets, lit a tear-gas bomb and carried it slowly along the north side of the road, allowing a wind from that direction to carry the fumes across the highway to the pickets who had remained, most of whom now scattered. The sheriff and the deputies moved to the mine. As the Garfield workers emerged, they were searched for weapons and then escorted home.[17]

"There is but one step left," said Governor Hammill when he heard the news. "Unless law and order is maintained in Appanoose County, troops will be sent there." Sheriff Gaughenbaugh thought this unnecessary. He hired more police officers from Des Moines. He placed them at strategic locations where trouble could erupt. The mayor of Mystic ordered a ban on all UMWA marches. At the same time, Gaughenbaugh dismissed local deputies who, by their residence, he said, had not acted impartially and before the arrival of out-of-County officers had placed the entire burden of crowd control onto his shoulders. Furthermore, he'd placed confidence in UMWA officials to help control the pickets. Instead, they'd brought in UMWA officials and pickets from out of the County who were inciting more trouble, which left him feeling double-crossed. A few strikers were furious at the use of tear gas. The mother of a small girl who suffered in the gas attack called at the office of attorney C.W. Howell on Centerville Square to demand retaliation. Among others there was an undercurrent of bitterness.[18]

Chapter 47

More Coal Mine Violence

On the night of September 27, four days after the use of tear gas at the Garfield, fifty to sixty sticks of dynamite were stolen from the Young mine at Clarkdale. The next night, an explosion rocked Mystic. An electric light pole, fuse boxes and the main twenty-two-hundred-volt leading wire to the mine machinery at the Winifred were destroyed.[1]

The County had reached a turning point. Jesse Beck's editorials called for restraint. The parties involved in the mine controversy, he wrote, need to do the most sober and thoughtful thinking of their lives. We are a nation of laws, he continued. The alternative is chaos.[2]

There were letters to the *Iowegian* and a circulated petition about the cost to local taxpayers for the out-of-County police officers. The local deputies, said the petition, before they were dismissed were paid $3.50 a day, with nothing extra for living expenses. But those from out of the County were being paid $7.00 a day, with extra for room and board and gasoline. The issue agitated local farmers, some of whom had been deputies. They already had financial issues of their own. Fifty of them met in Plano to express their concern. They called for more meetings.[3]

There were still sporadic acts of violence and still some picketing. Two Mystic women who had thrown rocks and chunks of coal at mine workers were charged with committing assault with intent to do great bodily harm. Their case was taken directly to a grand jury. They were found guilty and placed in the Appanoose County Jail. One of them claimed she was pregnant. She was immediately released. Violators of the governor's thirty-person limit for pickets at mines were also arrested. They were charged with contempt of court. By November they included four UMWA officials. Judge W.M. Walker ordered them to spend November 14 in jail and pay fifty dollars each in fines and, in addition, the costs of the court proceedings, including witness fees and the court reporters' expenses. Twenty-four hours later, their stay was extended when they refused to pay their fines. They called for tubs of boiling water and scrubbing brushes. "I would like to see Appanoose County's jail something less like a pest house," Joe Morris, the State president of the UMWA told an *Iowegian* reporter, "and more of a place in which men might become penitent rather than broken in body and soul."[4]

Winter was approaching. UMWA pay-strike benefits were five dollars a week to each union member and fifty cents a week extra for each child in the family. Some members, such as French immigrant Emil Gerard as well as Frank Powell, were denied any benefit, because at their homes on Walnut Hill they kept a couple of cows and some chickens. Russian immigrant Lige Burcaski of Mystic wrote, "I can't live on $5.00 a week when there are seven in the family …not only me but a lot of other men were going to start to work." In another letter, S. Boslem of Centerville, who had a family of ten, agreed. He said the UMWA is the best friend the miners and operators ever had but noted, "I fully realize what another winter will mean if I do not secure work." William Allan, the superintendent of the Numa Coal Company, who had worked in Iowa mines for forty-three years, said he'd never seen conditions so bad. One man had told him if he had to live on charity through the winter, he'd prefer to go to the County Farm with his wife.[5]

On November 9, John C. ("Shady") Lewis, head of the Iowa State Federation of Labor, toured Appanoose County mine camps to determine the condition of the miners who were not working. Responding to his reports, relief committees were established in Des Moines. The Salvation Army collected large amounts of money, clothing, food and shoes. So did the entire Des Moines Order of Moose, the UMWA and the State Federation of Labor. Donations were collected at a central location, a room at Drake University Observatory. The Red Cross refused to take part. They refused to assist striking miners, apparently forgetting it was those same miners who, in 1918, had donated their entire one-day wages to the organization.[6]

Carloads of food and clothing arrived in Centerville and Mystic by train. There were thousands of pounds of sugar, beans, rice, cornmeal and canned milk. Seven Des Moines women distributed the clothing at the Mystic Miners' Hall. Some of the Mystic women reported they had found coats of a better quality than they had ever known.[7]

Throughout the winter of 1927–28, more of the County's mines opened paying the Brotherhood's five dollars a day. By January of 1928, six hundred of the County's miners, all Brotherhood men, were working. But UMWA miners were still on strike. The troubles in Appanoose County were not over.[8]

Appanoose County's clash between its two coal mine unions was getting the country's attention. Reporters arrived in town. They asked questions. They wrote articles in the *Black Diamond*, in other national coal-trade journals and in the *Chicago Tribune*. Their editors considered the story "tremendously important."[9]

Much of the clash revolved around the realities of Appanoose County's geology. The coal seams were narrow, and they were deep. Extracting the coal was slower and more expensive than coal extracted from coalfields where the seams were wide or near or on the surface. In the mines of Pennsylvania, the average output of coal with the latter conditions was five or more tons per day per miner. Working in the limitations of Appanoose County mines, it was two tons per day per miner. These circumstances made the local area what was labeled a "high cost coalfield." The position of the Brotherhood of Miners was that the miners should negotiate their wages dependent on local mining conditions. Local owners and operators were specific: "…we can only pay so much for mining coal in this field and keep out of bankruptcy." In wage negotiations, the Brotherhood and operators determined $5.00 a day a fair wage. By insisting on the Jacksonville $7.50-a-day scale, the UMWA's president John L. Lewis was doing more than putting his members on strike. His aim was seen by the Brotherhood as something more sinister. It was to close all "high cost mines," something he'd spoken and written about. To the Brotherhood, the end result of the insistence on the Jacksonville wage spelled the eventual end of all coal mining in Appanoose County.[10]

More and more miners were swayed by the Brotherhood's arguments and joined the new union. But not all. For another three years, the local struggle continued and spread across the County, much of it confrontational and violent.

Men were beaten and threatened with guns in Brazil and at the Sunshine mine west of Centerville. Bullets were fired at H.C. Shadden as he walked through Centerville Brickyard on his way to work at the Diamond Lump Coal Company. The two bullets were deflected by his sheepskin jacket, a spent one then falling onto the lid of his dinner bucket. Pickets, well in excess of the stipulated 30, sometimes as many as 200 to 250, confronted miners at the Numa Coal Company and the Iowa Block Coal Company in Exline. Pickets surged at the Center coal mine. John Sieren, the Center's pit boss, was beaten. Two pickets arrested and placed in a deputy's car were hauled to freedom by a cheering crowd, and Maurice Bernard, one of the operators of the Empire coal mine near the country club, was beaten into unconsciousness over a mine car full of dirt. Patches of shingle and roofing nails hammered upright through boards were laid in wheel tracks to pierce the wheels of officers and deputies called to "emergencies" by fake telephone calls.[11]

The theft of two thousand gallons of gasoline from the Sinclair Oil Company storage tanks at the Rock Island depot yards heralded attacks on coal mine property. Tipples and shafts mysteriously caved in at Streepy and the Empire. Fires of incendiary origin occurred at Center, Streepy, the reopened Empire, the McConville mine at Dennis, a home formerly belonging to a coal operator on North Main Street in Centerville, the offices of the Electric Coal Company in Mystic and a seven-room Mystic boardinghouse owned by the same company. Called to the Winifred, Sheriff Gaughenbaugh found a piece of black blasting fuse, the cotton at one end soaked in gasoline, a gasoline bottle close by. At Brazil, the tipple at the Hawkeye mine burst into flames, and the fire reached the storage batteries used for power. A loud explosion destroyed mine cars and two electric mine locomotives. A length of pipe filled with black powder, driven into a dirt dump, set off another explosion, destroying the fan house and all remaining Hawkeye surface buildings. Tampered telephone lines delayed the arrival of help. Damage at the Hawkeye was estimated at fifteen thousand dollars. The mine never reopened.[12]

By mid-January of 1929, two thousand miners belonging to the Brotherhood—now with a changed name: the Southwest Miners of America—were all employed full-time in mines, being paid five dollars a day, working to full capacity, their coal leaving Appanoose County at the rate of thirty-five hundred tons per day. Relations between miners and operators were described as "amicable," their view of the future "optimistic." In contrast, the UMWA members were still on strike. Between 93 and 165 families from Centerville to Seymour, Mystic to Rathbun, Numa to Jerome and Exline and Cincinnati were still receiving relief. Each week flour, sugar, coffee, milk, meat, beans and clothing arrived at the Miners' Hall on Thirteenth Street in Centerville and was then distributed. The items were sent courtesy of the UMWA's Bandanna Committee in Des Moines. It was a situation conducive to discord.[13]

Two men, both members of UMWA's District Thirteen executive board—the two men who'd stayed at the Continental through all the troubles, who'd attended every UMWA meeting together, who'd been on every picket line, who'd served their sentences together in the Appanoose County Jail and even scrubbed it together—began to feud. District Thirteen's UMWA president Joe Morris accused Tom White of submitting excessive expense accounts and of insubordination. He had him suspended.[14]

On the national level, it was worse. At the 1927 UMWA Convention in Indianapolis, police were called to quell disturbances. John L. Lewis's leadership was challenged. Delegates questioned his four-thousand-dollar pay raise. He was described as dictatorial, of quelling and bullying those who disagreed with him. Some referred to him as "the Editor-in-Chief," as "The Whole Show," as "The King" and "The Czar." Lewis countered. He accused his critics, including Appanoose's Pete Agnessen, of undermining the solidarity action of miners. Many of his critics, he said, were Communists. He had them expelled.[15]

By 1930, there were two UMWA conventions: John Lewis's at Indianapolis, and a breakaway, reorganized or "rump" UMWA convention at Springfield, Illinois, that demanded John L. Lewis's resignation. Two of the "rump" union leaders spoke in Centerville's armory—or tried to. The meetings were near riots, with, said the *Centerville Daily Iowegian*, so much shouting, cheering and jeering and so many epithets—"of a very colorful variety flickering back and forth so rapidly"—it made accurate reporting impossible. "None of the speakers ever got a chance to have their say," continued the *Centerville Daily Iowegian*. "Not even soothing music supplied by the Centerville Band could keep the audience calmed."[16]

Dissension was also breaking out inside the Brotherhood. When Pete Agnessen wanted a coalition between the Brotherhood and this "rump" breakaway UMWA union, things came to a head. Members of the Brotherhood rebelled. They declared themselves independent of Agnessen's leadership and closed the organization down. Between 145 and 150 of them then walked to Thirteenth Street, into the Miners' Hall, and rejoined the UMWA. Pete Agnessen was not one of them. He was no longer a coal miner. He was now a businessman, selling coal for the Old King Coal Company.[17]

A year later, UMWA president John L. Lewis came to Centerville. He spoke at a mass meeting in the Courthouse Park. Thousands attended. "If miners in the county will return to the UMWA," Lewis said, "a scale will be made which recognizes differences in working conditions …that exist for southern Iowa." Eleven days later, Appanoose coal miners, now 100 percent members of the UMWA, and Appanoose's coal operators struck a temporary agreement. The mines reopened. The coal miners returned to work. Their salary: $4.00 a day, $3.50 less than the Jacksonville Agreement they'd demanded for so long, $1.00 less than had been paid to the members of the Brotherhood. It was hardly a good time to bargain. 1931 was an ominous year. Starving and threadbare miners were being shot in New Orleans, Harlan, Kentucky and in the coalfields of Illinois, Ohio and Oklahoma. And there was more.[18]

Three years previously, in 1928, Herbert Hoover passed through Centerville on a special train. He was an Iowan on his way back to the village of West Branch. He was going there to visit his old home, to sit at the table with relatives, to meet acquaintances of his boyhood. On November 6, he was elected the nation's president. But it was now 1931. The entire economy was snowballing downhill. The prize for national understatement went to ex-President Calvin Coolidge: In a syndicated press column on January 20, he said, "The country is not in good condition."[19]

Chapter 48

Stock Market Collapse

There were warnings, and there were premonitions. They came early, and they came clearly. They came from editor Jesse M. Beck and from J.A. Bradley, Centerville's conservative and steady banker. Bradley, ten years before the stock market crash, warned of "agents" flooding Appanoose County, selling dubious stock with questionable authenticity. Sheriff Gaughenbaugh, armed with a federal indictment, walked into the Continental Hotel to arrest resident Ben P. Bagby and return him to St. Louis to answer charges. There were forty counts in the indictment. Bagby was charged with defrauding the public and, together with twelve conspirators, with using the U.S. Mail in the process. Bagby had lost his investors more than two million dollars. This included three hundred thousand dollars in the International Aerial Navigation Company and twenty thousand in the Western Bond and Mortgage Company. In Centerville, he'd been selling land in Florida and stock for a poultry company in Moravia and a creamery in Albia.[1]

At the same time, throughout the 1920s, from across the State, news of bank closures were reaching the town: three at Perry, two at Grinnell, more in counties to the west and the north—then to the east, the Manning Bank, the fifth to close in Keosauqua. Rumors swirled Centerville. What was called a local "joker" entered a pool hall and wanted to bet that a certain bank in town would not open on the next Saturday morning. Saturday's date was January 1, 1927, New Year's Day, a public holiday. "Irresponsible talk!" said an indignant Jesse Beck at the *Centerville Daily Iowegian*. "[It] may often bring great consequences. A Chicago cow kicked over the lantern and Chicago burned. An ancient goose is said to have squawked and Rome was saved ...Centerville banks are all solid. They have been run by careful bankers ...Centerville bankers have been the envy of bankers in other parts of Iowa because of the large cash balances and surpluses they have in their banks."

The County's banks began publishing official reports of their resources and liabilities. They were printed in the *Centerville Daily Iowegian* for all to read. They were copies of the reports made to the State Superintendent of Banking. They were required by law. By April 1927, the people of the County were paying their taxes so promptly, the Board of Appanoose County, forced to seek new places to store money, raised the deposit limit of town banks.[2]

A layer of confidence returned to the town. Business people were taking stock. So did the town council. There was a waiting list for business locations. Hamburger and sandwich shops opened. So did a delicatessen, a tea room, a new café, two new restaurants offering four-course meals for fifty cents and a roadside inn west of the City limits with a dance floor and a soft drink and soda dispensary, its building decorated with outside lights, electric Japanese lanterns and flower boxes. On the Northside of the Square, Santi Milani, who for seven-and-a-half years was superintendent of Detroit's Bailey Art Company, decorated his confectionery shop with mural paintings and intricate plaster designs. He extended the business with a luncheon service and invited the public to examine the new kitchen. On the Westside, Sam and Charles Katter, both immigrants from Beirut, Syria, imported Oriental rugs, linens and mosaic filet cutwork. The McKee Shoe Store decorated its name in octagonal ceramic tiles on the sidewalk. Allen's News Shop opened on the Square's Eastside; a block to the north, George Swearingen, next to his pool hall, opened a newsstand and candy and cigar stall. At the drugstores, new soda fountains were added. The one at the Red Cross offered toasted sandwiches. The one at the Owl extended for fourteen feet, was of shining nickel and snowy-white vitreolite and had space for six different kinds of ice cream, some already packed for home delivery.[3]

Buildings were remodeled and redecorated. The Wooden Bank expanded into a newly acquired store to its west and increased the size of its lobby. On the Northside, J.A. Bradley's First National Bank was undergoing a thirty-five-thousand-dollar renovation. Carved Bedford-stone facades with plasters, rosettes, festoons and a split pediment were applied to the brick exterior; beveled windows were inserted. The interior floor was lowered and covered with ceramic mosaic tile bought from the Katter's on the Square's Westside. A mezzanine was added. Fitments were of marble and black walnut; Bradley's private office featured an addition of mahogany wainscoting. The building's new appearance earned it an article in the September 1928 issue of the *Northwestern Banker*—the oldest financial journal west of the Mississippi. It described the building as "a study in gray and marble and walnut."[4]

Around the Square, grocery and department stores offered new services and new stock. The owner of one, J.C. Penney, stopped in Centerville as part of a tour of his Iowa stores. The *Iowegian* called him "the Napoleon of commerce." He arrived in a fleet of large and expensive cars. He inspected his store in the Dinning Building on the Square's Southeast corner. He met the twenty employees and manager John Heimes and Mrs. Heimes. Local businessmen assembled at the Association of Commerce room on Thirteenth Street. They waited to honor him with speeches and a banquet. Penney was uncharacteristically late. He'd learned of a personal story and taken a detour. His fleet of cars bounced and swerved over one of the worst roads in Centerville to a small house surrounded by a picket fence near the brickyard. He went to meet Mrs. Henry White, an African American who'd worked in the household of a member of the Penney family. Penney then returned to the Association of Commerce room to give a speech, to shake the hands of all present. A reporter for the *Des Moines Tribune* who was present noted that the food had cooled.[5]

On Saturday evenings, people again crowded the Square. Cars lined the streets. Stores were busy. Bradley's First National Bank stayed open until eight o'clock. Traffic officers directed at intersections. They blew whistles. The sounds fused with the throb of auto engines, the movements of hundreds of walking feet, the proselytizing of evangelists on the Northwest Corner, a jazz orchestra across the street and, a block to the south, a blind musician on a battered violin. And occasionally, practicing on a Saturday night in a room over Swearingen's Eastside pool hall, the town band played under the direction of William Gower. At the sound of a certain note played by the E-flat clarinet player, a young Himie Voxman, a dog in the building would let out a howl.[6]

People paused to examine displays in store windows, such as, at the Western Union office on South Main, a section of the ocean cable laid from Newfoundland to Penzance in England that carried twenty-five thousand letters per minute. Harry Luther's was now identified by a suspended, electrified, twenty-foot sign. In the window, a miniature Rock Island fast-passenger locomotive circled a track emerging from tunnels and forests, pausing at crossings, whistling into towns. Built by Centerville's Ed Boggs, it was four feet long, twelve inches in height. It was complete with injectors, sand dome and pipes, running lights, running flags and water pumps. Lights of the red fire glowed from the swinging door of the firebox and the ash pan. A brilliant, tiny headlight illuminated the track ahead. Luther's competition,

Ira Durham, was now the appointed distributor for the Majestic Radio, "the Mighty Monarch" of the air. All the radios in his window and in the store were operated direct from lighting currents. There was not a battery in sight, and rumors were spoken of television.[7]

The two movie houses did a brisk business. A metal canopy, built nine feet out over the sidewalk, protected waiting customers at the Ritz. This was granted by a special amendment to City Council proceedings. On the outside of both the Ritz and Majestic were Vitaphone signs indicating their movies were "talkies."

Lights surrounded "blazers": framed advertising posters announcing the next movies. Both houses defied the ban on Sunday showings, paying the five-dollar fine and four-dollar costs, arguing through attorney Tom Fee their theaters were not public disturbances and attendance was entirely optional.[8]

Around the Square, the electric trolley service to the railroad stations was discontinued. Three motor coaches took passengers from the Interurban station at the Bradley building north of East State, around the Square to Main Street. They then followed the same route south to meet arriving and departing trains. The buses were green and cream. They had nickel fittings. People entered through a hinged door; they sat on leather-covered seats; they walked on regulation streetcar rubber matting. There were electric lights with frosted window shades and ivory push buttons to open and close windows. The cash fare was ten cents per person or twenty-five cents for four tickets bought in the waiting room.[9]

On the outer rim of the Square, auto dealers replaced the blacksmiths. Packards were on display at Glen Norris's on Jackson at Haynes; Dodges with the first car radios in town at the Carmer Motor Company; Chevrolets at the Universal Car Company on North Main; and Fords at the Fisher garage on West Van Buren.[10]

As the critical year of 1929 began, Iowa's governor, John Hammill, speaking to the State legislature, saw a bright future. Centerville's key businessmen and factory owners agreed. They wrote articles in the *Iowegian* outlining their optimism, agreeing with C.R. Wooden that they could anticipate "sustained prosperity." The Rosenbaum plant on the corner of Cottage and Eighteenth was sending out two thousand or more carloads of iron a year, shipped to steel mills in Chicago, Pittsburgh, Philadelphia, St. Louis and Buffalo. Centrox Dairy was anticipating a steady increase in its output of three million pounds of butter and sixty thousand gallons of ice cream. Centerville Clay Products confidently tore down its brick and tile plant in South Centerville and built a new plant at the foot of Van Buren Street, near the old Iowa Central depot. Six of a proposed ten kilns were immediately constructed. They were beehive in shape and in row formation. Each kiln could process 2,862 bricks. Every two weeks, the plant could process and ship half a million bricks. S.A. Martin at the Pure Ice Plant was expanding its number of substations in a hundred-mile radius. In Centerville, he installed an ice server. Patrons drove to the plant's delivery platform, held up one finger and collected an immediate twenty-five-pound cake of ice, automatically served from a rod on the outside of the building. Two fingers yielded a fifty-pound cake, three a seventy-five-pound and four one hundred pounds. The Hercules factory served a large order for stump pullers for the Amtorg Company in Russia and anticipated an order for a larger amount. Russia was now a long-term satisfied customer. Town banker Jim Bradley remembered that, years earlier, on a visit to Russia, he saw some brightly colored objects in St. Petersburg that bore an inscription: "Hercules Manufacturing Co., Centerville, Iowa U.S.A." A special spur track of the Interurban arrived daily on the Square's Northeast block. Cars of groceries were delivered to the Jennings-Christopher Wholesale Company.

Other cars, full of coal, were pulled by cable, opened beneath and dropped their deliveries into the basement of what was emerging as the town's most significant business: Iowa Southern Utilities. By 1927, the company's peak production was eight thousand kilowatts. This was enhanced with a new eight-hundred-horsepower boiler, three six-hundred-horsepower boilers, super heaters, stokers and economizers to produce seventy-five hundred horsepower. It served electricity to twenty-two southern Iowa towns inside a triangle from Newton and Grinnell in the north, Burlington and Washington in the southeast, to Mount Ayr and Creston in the west. In 1929, it was about to expand internationally to Moose Jaw, Saskatchewan.[11]

Such was Centerville on the cusp of the Great Depression. The *Centerville Daily Iowegian*'s headlines recorded the stock market's ascent in 1928: "Stocks Gone Mad," "Stocks Continue Dizzy Climb" and "Went Wild on Stock Markets." At the beginning of 1929, the upbeat pattern continued: "Wall Street …in Optimistic Mood"; "Business in Upward Trend." By March there was a hesitation: "Bad Day for Stocks." Then, on October 28, under a front-page banner, came the "Extra": "Stocks Crash in Today's Trading." The next day, the twenty-ninth, "Stocks Continue Downward Trend on Today's Trade." By November the headlines were bleak: "Socks [*sic*] Crash at the Close of Today's Trading" and "Stock Market in Another Slide Downward Today." On November 13, Jesse Beck had reason to warn again. "This paper called for caution at various times. Now the caution needs to be along the line that the people should not lose confidence in the future…"[12]

Chapter 49

Bank Closures, Drought and Grasshopper Infestation

For the rest of her long life, Gail Sherrard Tuttle never forgot the emotional effect of the stock market crash. She was then nineteen years old, a student at Simpson College, living in Plano. She remembered her own "sinking feeling," the devastation of relatives, friends and neighbors, the fear when photographs of bread lines began appearing in newspapers.[1]

For a time, life for the people of the town seemed to proceed as usual. Children still ran across the Courthouse Square on their way to school, checking the time on the courthouse clock, now with its newly washed face and repainted numerals. On Monday mornings they climbed up into the clock tower with the janitor. They watched him wind the clock. They listened to the murmuring of pigeons, the whistling of November winds. People gathered as usual on Armistice Day. At quarter to noon, the bells of the town tolled. All businesses closed. At noon people paused for two minutes of silence. They placed wreaths at the Civil War Monument. They lingered to talk, to look at the three hundred names of those who never returned from that war, now inscribed on bronze tablets placed over those on marble obliterated by time and the elements.[2]

In the early days of December 1929, the people of the town decided on an early Christmas. Workmen installed colored lights and signs around the Square, on the trees, on the courthouse and along Eighteenth Street in South Centerville. Soon after dawn on Saturday, December 14, and despite thick fog, cold and rain, fifteen hundred children were waiting. Between them, dogs leaped, cavorted and barked. Santa Claus, riding in Danley Benjamin's plane, swept over the City. He circled above the Courthouse Square. He landed at the grammar school field. Hundreds ran to greet him, to march alongside the plane, forming a cheering cordon as the plane was hauled uptown to the Square, halting with its nose touching the chains of the horse-hitching rack. To cheers and shouts, Santa emerged, tossing candy—more than two thousands sacks of it—to the waiting children. Jesse M. Beck noted their diversity: girls and boys, black and white, American, Italian, Jew and Gentile, Protestant and Catholic, rich and poor— "…they were all alike to Santa…"[3]

That year the stores remained open late in the evenings on Mondays, Tuesdays, Fridays and Saturdays. They were stocked with Christmas goods. Shoppers traveled on better roads from longer distances. They filled their cars with gasoline sold at thirty of the town's filling stations. The shoppers paid particular attention to two of the newest stores on the Square. They were Gambles, which had opened in February, and Spurgeons, which had just bought the Katter store on the Westside. But there was a mystery.[4]

For over a year, rumors had floated and were confirmed that the Montgomery Ward company was coming to Centerville. Their representative arrived from Kansas City. He inspected sites and possible locations. He was looking for, he said, a large building with two stories and a basement. He found it in October when Bernstein's Standard Furniture Store on the Square's Northeast Corner became vacant. Lawyers arrived from the company's head office in Chicago. They examined plans of the building. They took measurements. They discussed possible structural alterations. They read the terms of the lease and the date of possession. They announced plans to open the store on January 1. Suddenly on December 15, all papers, all unsigned, were returned. All plans were canceled. The people of the town wondered. It was two months after the stock market crash. Was this the response to a troubled economy? Was it a sign of coming events?[5]

Their thoughts were swiftly rebuffed by news reaching them by radio and by the *Centerville Daily Iowegian*'s new United Press high-speed, automatic-printer telegraph, just installed by the American Telephone and Telegraph Company. President Hoover was giving optimistic speeches to Congress. He recommended a reduction in taxes. He gathered the nation's captains of industry to conferences aimed at promoting business confidence.

They included John D. Rockefeller Jr., J.P. Morgan and Henry Ford. They represented millions of men and billions of dollars. Henry Ford said he'd raise wages and expand his operations. James A. Farrell, president of the United States Steel Corporation, A.W. Robertson, chairman of Westinghouse, and Samuel P. Arnot, president of the Chicago Board of Trade all gave optimistic previews of the nation's economy, as did George B. Everitt, president of Montgomery Ward, fifteen days after his company had pulled out of Centerville. Jesse Beck, reading the reports, thought "the panic" was over. The State superintendent of banking, L.A. Andrews, thought 1930 would be "a very good year" for Iowa's banks. Clifford DePuy was even more upbeat. He was the publisher of the *Northwestern Banker*, the oldest financial journal west of the Mississippi and the same journal that had described J.A. Bradley's renovated First National Bank as "a study in gray and marble and walnut." Speaking to investment bankers in Des Moines at the beginning of the new year on January 7, he said a new period of prosperity had entered Iowa and it would continue throughout 1930.[6]

Fifteen days later, on January 22, Centerville's Southside Savings Bank, the Bradley Bank in Mystic and the Security Savings Bank of Promise City failed to open. The principal stockholder of all three was William S. Bradley, nephew to the conservative, steady and safe J.A. Bradley, the banker at the First National on the Square's Northside. This Bradley, William S., was described by one writer as "a reckless plunger and speculator in business." But there was another side to the story. William's father was D.C. Bradley, brother to J.A. Bradley. D.C. was popular and, unlike his brother, noted for his support of community projects, for an aggressive loaning and business style. By 1927, he was in deep financial trouble and called in his son William S., hoping for his rescue. Another writer said, "Bill didn't have a chance and his father knew it." The father died in 1928 at his mansion on Drake Avenue with, according to Roy Oughton, D.C.'s long-term manager, "a broken heart." His son, twenty-nine-year-old William S., a World War I captain and a graduate of the University of Pennsylvania, now with union disturbances and a faltering national economy, faced the consequences.[7]

The extent of his father's enterprises was now revealed: ten farms in Appanoose County totaling more than four thousand acres, filled with top-quality livestock, farm machinery, tools, equipment, grain, hay, feed and supplies. There were eighteen Centerville town lots, two more in Mystic and a residence in Cincinnati. He held controlling shares in his failed banks, thirty more in the Appanoose Abstract and Title Company, one share of capital stock at Centerville's country club, and he owned three coal mines. These were the Iowa Block at Exline and two at Mystic—the Barrett and the Garfield, the site of so much agitation two years earlier.

On February 17, 1930, William S. Bradley filed a voluntary petition for bankruptcy. His assets were placed on sale—a process not finalized for five years. In that time, the men working in the mines were paid once, on January 25, three days after the banks' closures. That was the last paycheck at the Garfield until eight months later in September, when the mine was bought by J. Rosenbaum and Son of Centerville for twenty-five thousand dollars and the mine reopened. In that intervening eight months, there was considerable social unrest. It was the middle of winter. The miners needed the money. So did those with deposits in the banks. At the Mystic bank, these included miners and their families, widows and the guardians of children, Mystic Independent School District, the Mystic Telephone Exchange, three lodges, a new coal company and two union locals. On the day his bank closed, Bradley apologized and said he hoped to pay each depositor in full. When a final settlement was reached in 1935, the depositors at the Bradley Bank in Mystic received 8 percent of their money; those at the Southside Savings Bank 26.5 percent. Bradley left Appanoose County and made his home in Texas. In 1932 he joined the Roosevelt administration. In 1950, during the Truman administration, he moved to Washington, D.C., and became assistant secretary of commerce.[8]

Even before the failure of the three banks on January 22, 1930, the County's charity organizations were witnessing social conditions deteriorating, the finances for their amelioration dwindling. They combined their efforts into a new organization called the Social Service League. Nine days after William Bradley filed his petition for bankruptcy, the new Social Service League appealed for public help. The members pleaded for donations of used clothing, for shoes and stockings for barefoot children they had witnessed in the coldest weather, for baby clothes for the newborn. The situation was about to get worse.[9]

In retrospect, the people of Appanoose County thought 1930 started inauspiciously. First was the failure of three banks. Then, between midnight and two in the morning on February 3, 1930, the Iowa Southern Utilities basketball team, arriving back on the Square from a game in Albia, smelled burning wood. They found the Rosenbaum Clothing Store on the Southside on fire. Minutes later, the *Iowegian* job-printing man on his way home from work found a blaze at the Drake Avenue Theatre. He tried to douse it with snow. The two fires were too advanced. Both buildings were destroyed. The Drake Free Public Library, next door to the Drake Avenue Theatre, was damaged. So was the big LaFrance fire engine that had arrived to help but stalled with a broken chain drive when too close to the theater fire.[10]

By April, default cases were dominating County court proceedings. Delinquent tax lists, printed in the *Iowegian*, were getting longer. Advertisements from stores appeared requesting immediate payment of bills. The County's allotted Pauper Fund was overdrawn by $16,000; so was the General Fund by $25,000 and the Juvenile Fund by $12,500. Covering the overdrafts with transfer money from the Emergency Fund and the Insane Fund drew objections from the town's Tax-Payers League. There was worry about County bonds of $322,000 that would be due in a few years.[11]

In May there was more bad news. The 1930 U.S. Census report for the County showed a drop in population of five thousand. The town's leaders were shocked. They asked for an extension of time, convinced the heavily immigrant population in the Third Ward in South Centerville had not been counted. They counted again. The census number remained the same. Jesse Beck blamed the population drop on already existing depressions in two of the County's leading industries: coal mining and farming.[12]

Local coal mines had fought back after the troubles of 1927 and 1928. In addition to Iowa Southern Utilities' steady yearly purchase of eighty thousand tons, the mines found new markets, citing that Appanoose coal scored high in BTUs. They were awarded contracts for State institutions. Every week, tons of County coal was shipped to the State university; to the hospitals at Clarinda, Glenwood and Mount Pleasant; to the reformatories at Rockwell City and Anamosa. By March 1931, Appanoose County was Iowa's leading coal-producing County. The miners at two local coal mines—Sunshine and McConville North—were breaking records for daily outputs. Those at the Empire Coal Company were treating their furnace coal with a solution of calcium chloride. They called it "dustless." To ship the coal around the Midwest, they bought twelve railroad cars. On the outsides they painted scenes of the Empire coal mine, even a slag pile surrounded by trees, a map of Iowa showing the location of Centerville and the words "The Home of 8,000 Friendly People and Empire Dustless Fuel."[13]

But now two new issues threatened the local coal industry. Miners in northern Missouri were working for $3.75 a day. In Illinois, the miners' daily wage of $6.10 was being dropped to $5.00. In Illinois, there were protest marches and confrontations. A picket was murdered at Zeigler, and students in Kincaid, showing solidarity with their fathers, walked out of their high school when they learned the school was buying coal from mines paying a lower wage scale. Appanoose miners were wondering about the effect on their $4.00 a day.[14]

The other threatening issue was what was happening to the railroads. They were critical to the County's new and distant coal markets, and they were in trouble. Business on the nation's railroads was being undercut by cars, motor buses and improved highways, as well as from aircraft and from pipelines carrying oil and natural gas. The *Iowegian* was reporting that passenger services across the country had dropped by one-third and 370,000 employees had lost their jobs. Centerville businessmen attended a large mass meeting called by employees of the Burlington Railroad. The Burlington had division offices in Centerville. It had terminals running in four directions. It had a roundhouse where engines and carriages were repaired and rebuilt. It employed a large number of crews that made their homes in Centerville. It paid forty-five thousand dollars in Appanoose County taxes. Its payroll was more than a third of a million dollars, with another half a million paid in wages and for supplies. At the mass meeting that night, Centerville's businessmen were united. They pledged all their shipping to the railroad and said they would refuse to patronize road-truck deliveries from other towns.[15]

Depression in the local farming industry was even deeper. Like farming across the country, it had never recovered from the loss of markets following the end of World War I. Farm products kept dropping in price. Appanoose County farmers constantly sought to improve their yields. They traveled to watch farming demonstrations—plowing on the Douglas Vinzant farm, the McCormick-Deering Corn Picker at the P.M. Phillips farm and the first combine cutting and threshing machine in southeast Iowa at the Bradley farm at Sedan.[16]

They studied soil building. Eleven railroad carloads of acid phosphorous were shipped to use as crop aid and fertilizer. Ten experimental plots were selected. One hundred and fifty to three hundred pounds of the phosphate were added per acre of soil that was then seeded with oats, barley and alfalfa. Farmers traveled again, this time to witness the resulting greater crop yields. This was particularly noticeable with alfalfa. It was, they learned, a soil-enriching legume crop. It was high in food value and well adapted to the needs of Appanoose County. To encourage its adoption as a crop, the local Farm Bureau, together with the Association of Commerce, held a competition for the best field of alfalfa. On November 15, 1927, the first "Alfalfa Banquet" was held. Each farmer brought a businessman as a guest. The two groups amounted to 170. The Cincinnati Christian Church ladies served a meal at fifty cents per plate. C.D. Kirkpatrick, a master farmer of Keota, Iowa, was the principal speaker. Prizes were awarded. The winner of first place was William Miller of Union Township, known from that moment on wherever he went as "Alfalfa Bill."[17]

The Alfalfa Banquet became an annual event. It was copied in other Iowa counties and in other states. In its second year in Centerville, the main speaker was Henry A. Wallace, Iowa's experimental scientist, a social scientist, the world's greatest authority on hybrid corn and the second-generation editor of the farm journal called the *Wallace Farmer*. He was just four years away from becoming the nation's secretary of agriculture.[18]

The improved yields of the farmers resulted in more and better crops. This drove the prices ever lower. And then there was the weather. In June, July and August of 1931, temperatures hovered in the high nineties and low one hundreds. People watched the red alcohol climb in the fine glass tubes in thermometers on the Square and at the government recording station at the Pure Ice plant. People broke eggs on cement sidewalks and watched them fry. By July 8, United Press bulletins in the *Iowegian* said 368 people were dead of heat prostration in Chicago, 164 in Wisconsin, 65 in Indiana, 114 in Missouri and 173 in Iowa. On July 30, the heat took the life of a farmhand on the William Eddy farm. Three City businesses—Swift and Company, the Hutchison Ice Cream factory and the Pure Ice plant—opened their refrigerated rooms for anyone in distress. Animals were dying—more than a hundred head of horses and stock in one week. A farmer in Lincoln Township lost a team of horses worth four hundred dollars. Over 50 percent of the County's farmers plowed at night, by moonlight or flashlight, from three o'clock to shortly after sunrise. And then came the grasshoppers.[19]

In late July came the reports that they were laying bare whole counties in South Dakota and Nebraska, the borders of Minnesota and Iowa. They were devouring everything containing vegetable fiber. They ate wagon tongues, fenceposts and clothing. Farmers raked dead hoppers into piles and burned them. Bonfires dotted the plains. Crops almost destroyed by the heat and the drought were finished off when the grasshoppers swarmed in. In South Dakota, whole families moved northward in covered wagons, driving half-starved herds before them. More than three thousand head of cattle were shipped in one week from South Dakota to northern Nebraska.[20]

By July 28, hordes had invaded Iowa's western counties. By the thirty-first they were in Appanoose. Farmers reported they were in their fields. They were damaging lawns and flowers. On the roads, driving into a swarm of the insects was like driving into a snowstorm. Car radiators were jammed full of their dead bodies. Every morning they were swept off the Square and all downtown sidewalks. Iowa's State agricultural director Mark Thornberg announced a fund of fifty thousand dollars to battle the grasshoppers. Aircraft flew overhead spraying bran mash laced with arsenic.[21]

It seemed man and nature had conspired together to ruin the farmer. Across Iowa, it would take just a spark to light the tinderbox of grievances. But first, Appanoose County had to address its increasing numbers of the unemployed, the poor, the destitute and the hungry.

Chapter 50

The Great Depression

The farm sales in Appanoose County began on October 6, 1930. Advertisements for them appeared in the *Centerville Daily Iowegian*. They included instructions to locate the farm and named a local church whose ladies would serve luncheons. At first the advertisements listed the sales of animals: thirty head of cattle, a gray suckling mule colt and forty-five white Pekin ducks at the Roy Vandike farm southeast of Exline. Two days later, on the eighth, thirty-four purebred Guernsey cattle at Centerville's Prospect Farm were advertised; the following day, an ad listed forty-seven cattle, hogs and buck lambs at the farm of S.H. Porter northwest of Udell. Within a week, advertisements included the sales of saddles, tractors, plows, farm machinery and household furniture.[1]

There were community auctions held at Centerville's High Gate Yard. Multiple farmers called at the *Iowegian* office to list their livestock, their grain, automobiles, furniture, rugs and "good oak posts." On the southside steps of the Appanoose County Courthouse, auctioneers called out bids on land—107 acres east of Centerville, 120 acres northeast of Plano. Seven farms and fifteen homes were listed for sale at Speers Real Estate Office over the Brody Store on one day. In one year, 1931, eighty-seven farms and town properties were sold by the Appanoose County Sheriff—all foreclosed by court order.[2]

The value of County land was in free fall. An acre, previously worth $75 to $125, now sold for $10 to $15. On the market, oats commanded eight cents a bushel, corn twelve cents, pork three cents a pound and beef five cents. Farmers were unable to pay bank mortgages. This placed the still-open banks in crisis. Ten Appanoose County banks reduced the rate of interest they paid on savings and time deposits. Two banks, Centerville National and the Commercial State, merged. The four banks on Centerville Square placed a two-cent tax on each written check. More banks closed: Mystic Industrial Savings, the National in Seymour and three State Savings Banks—one in Moulton, one in Dean and one in Moravia. On July 16, 1932, came the biggest shock. A notice appeared on the door of the Wooden State Savings Bank on the Square's Westside: its business was "…temporarily suspended for the purpose of possible readjustment."[3]

Dr Bamford of the Bamford Clinic on South Main Street spoke out. What is happening to farmers, he said, is universal, ruthless and pitiless. "The history of the world teaches that any nation in which Agriculture has been allowed to perish, that nation has perished also. History does not record one exception."[4]

For the farmers there was a new grievance. State veterinarians, hypodermic needles in hand, were moving onto the farms of Appanoose County and those of every county in Iowa. They were enacting an Iowa law making the tuberculin testing of cows compulsory. They injected a single drop of tuberculin—a clear, sterile serum derived from the tuberculosis bacillus—into the thin skin on the underside of a cow's tail. A red lump at the injection site forty-eight to seventy-two hours later indicated a tubercular cow—one that must be destroyed. J.M. Tucker, a farmer at Moravia, wrote to the *Iowegian*: This policy, he said, "… is robbing farmers of our best cows." He urged Appanoose County farmers and stock breeders to copy the revolt that was happening in Cedar County. There, at the William Butterbrodt Farm near Tipton, State agents had been forced to withdraw when one thousand farmers standing shoulder to shoulder in the barnyard blocked their path. A meeting by all Iowa's protesting farmers occurred in Des Moines. Twelve hundred farmers from Cedar County and adjoining counties, some from western Iowa and a few from Appanoose County, marched through the streets to the State capitol. They wore small blue cards on their lapels demanding the TB tests be made optional. They interrupted regular State legislature business. They shouted "boo's" and "no's." They stamped their feet. They packed the aisles.[5]

The experience had a sobering effect on those who'd attended from Appanoose County. They distanced themselves from the objectors. Testing on the County's 31,082 cattle began and by September was completed without incident. The same could not be said for Cedar County or Muscatine, Henry, Des Moines and Chickasaw Counties. State veterinarians were kicked and showered with water, handfuls of mud and barrages of eggs; they were threatened with guns and clubs and had their automobile tires punctured and their car windows smashed. Two hundred farmers wielding pitchforks at one farm defied sixty-five sheriffs' deputies attempting to protect the vets.[6]

Iowa's usually mild-mannered governor Dan Turner had had enough. He called out the National Guard. It included Centerville's Company G of Iowa's 168th Infantry. The local men served twice: once in Cedar County, once near Burlington. Armed with rifles and machine guns and divided into detachments, they protected State vets as the tests were successfully administered. Among the vets, ordered to the scene by the State's secretary of agriculture, M.G. Thornberg, was Centerville's Dr. C.R. Fry. When Company G returned home, it was almost time for Thanksgiving. They had served for sixty-four days.[7]

The fight over compulsory bovine tubercular testing was over. The distress of farmers was not. The market price of farm products continued to fall. The number of foreclosures continued to rise. Enter Milo Reno. He was president of the Iowa Farmers Union, guest writer and occasional editor in chief of the *Iowa Union Farmer.* He called on farmers to strike, to withhold their produce from the market until prices rose. He named the campaign the National Farmers Holiday Movement.[8]

His call had the greatest effect in northwestern Iowa. It spread to farmers in the Dakotas, Nebraska, Minnesota and Wisconsin, the area that had suffered the most with heat, subsequent drought and grasshopper invasions. Milk, selling for two cents a quart, was spilled across highways. Trucks carrying livestock and produce to market were stopped. Trains were halted, seals on freight cars broken open, cattle and hogs released into fields. Farmers assembled poles, railroad ties and spiked logs to throw into the paths of produce-laden vehicles heading to market. People in cities drove out to see them as they huddled by night fires dressed in blue denim overalls and jackets. Occasionally there was violence. Men died. Fourteen pickets at Cherokee were shot but survived.[9]

In October 1932, the Holiday Movement acquired a new objective: a moratorium on taxes and a halt to foreclosures. Farmers disarmed sheriffs at foreclosure sales. They marched to state capitals. In the Iowa town of Primghar in O'Brien County, six hundred angry farmers showered sticks and stones on the sheriff and twenty-two assistants and forced them to kiss the American flag after a half-hour battle. At Denison in nearby Crawford County, two hundred farmers attacked fifty special deputies with clubs that sent six for medical treatment.[10]

But the most serious event happened in Le Mars in Plymouth County. There, a group of men, blue bandannas covering their faces, dragged Judge Charles C. Bradley from his courtroom, beat him, mauled him, smeared him and filled his trousers with grease and grime, took him into the country, put a noose around his neck, jerked the judge from the ground until he fainted, ordered him to pray and then, with some apparent remorse, released him.[11]

The news of the attempted lynching of Judge Bradley incensed Iowa's new governor, Clyde L. Herring. He declared immediate martial law in Plymouth County and dispatched Centerville's Colonel Glenn C. Haynes of his staff by air to Sioux City. Haynes was placed in charge of martial law in Le Mars. He arrived there with a machine gun company of one hundred National Guardsmen. Moving cameras recorded the scene. Machine guns were mounted on the roof of the Plymouth County Courthouse. Machine guns controlled the scene at two foreclosure sales. Colonel Haynes ordered militiamen with fixed bayonets to patrol the streets both day and night. The soldiers wore helmets in case of emergency. Haynes placed a fourteen-man hospital corps to be in attendance. Farmers at Primghar and at Granville—twenty miles south—held meetings. Nine men thought to be ringleaders were immediately arrested. Assistant attorney general Leon Power arrived from Des Moines to determine if they should be court-martialed or tried by a criminal court. Rumors said the revolt was spreading from the Minnesota line to Clarinda, 120 miles west of Centerville.[12]

By May 5, seven days after the declaration of martial law, a total of 146 men were under arrest—84 in Le Mars and Sioux City, 62 at Denison. Five days later martial law was lifted.[13]

Governor Clyde Herring received praise for his swift action. It came from bar associations, from chambers of commerce, from prominent citizens and from newspaper editors. One of the editors was Jesse M. Beck at the *Centerville Daily Iowegian*, who said he could not have dreamed the action against Judge Bradley could be possible in Iowa.

Appanoose County farmers were not involved in this fray. But in one person they felt great pride. Restoring order to Plymouth County was Colonel Glenn C. Haynes. He was a Centerville boy, a product of Centerville schools. He was the son of a local Civil War hero. He had led Company E through World War I. He had been attacked by the KKK for opposing Albert Johnson's and Harry Laughlin's racist Immigration Quota Bill that limited the immigration into America of Slavs, Asians, Africans and southern Europeans. Glenn Haynes was already a local hero. For two nights in May 1933 the people of the town sat in the Ritz Theatre on Centerville Square's Northeast Corner. They went for a "special showing" listed as a movie. Its title: *Col. Glenn C. Haynes in Charge of the Le Mars Disorder.*[14]

In the early 1930s, Pollyanna statements about the national economy were reported in the *Centerville Daily Iowegian* and broadcast over local NBC radio stations. They were made by President Hoover and national leaders: "Brighter days lie ahead," said President Hoover to bankers at Cleveland, Ohio. "The worst of the depression is over," echoed Rome E. Stephenson, president of the American Bankers' Association on an NBC broadcast. "Today the depression has run its course," newspaper publisher Paul Block said in an article. The statements belied events. Juxtaposing them, the people of the town read and heard of new crises. Stocks slumped to new lows. Bank failures soared. So did unemployment. Millions of the jobless were walking the streets. Bread lines were forming in cities. Demonstrations of the unemployed were turning violent in New York; Chicago; Okalahoma City; Terre Haute, Indiana; Bisbee, Arizona; and Salt Lake City. Hundreds were marching to state capitals. Thousands were converging on Washington, D.C.: twelve thousand from Pittsburgh, traveling in an eight-mile-long serpentine caravan of trucks and automobiles; 300 World War I veterans—the advance group of the "Bonus Army"—from Portland, Oregon, rocking and swaying across the Rockies in Union Pacific freight cars, their numbers swelling to twenty thousand by the time they reached the nation's capital to request advance payment of their soldiers' bonuses.[15]

In Iowa, State funds were "near exhaustion." Thousands of tax assessments were unpaid. There were 1.5 million dollars in State funds frozen in closed banks. State salaries were slashed. Grants to State universities, institutions and hospitals were cut. Appanoose County reflected the whole. The Pauper Fund was consistently overdrawn. By late 1931 so was the General Fund. The district court processed more default cases. There were more foreclosures. There were more auctions: people's personal shares of stocks and bonds sold from the south door of the courthouse; their jewelry, silverware and personal possessions from the sidewalk outside Humphrey Jewelry on the Square's Northside.[16]

Stores closed: Max Rosenbaum's, Katter's, Morris's, the Nelson Shoe Store, Strickler's Dry Goods, Graham's Department, Davison's Hardware, Chapman, Lowrey Grocery and the Hibbs store on the Square's Westside. Cars were not selling. Some owners stored the ones they had to avoid the payment of licenses. The Glen Norris Garage that sold Packards and Hudsons, Chryslers and DeSotos was declared bankrupt. Wages for coal miners were dropping by 21.8 percent. The salaries of Centerville's mayor and all City employees were cut by 20 percent. The Centerville School Board reduced the salaries of its teachers by 5 percent. Clarence McCracken, the Appanoose County superintendent, dropped one hundred dollars from his own salary. The manager of the Western Union office on South Main received instructions from headquarters that all money orders were not to exceed fifty dollars. Justice of the Peace D.W. Bryan resigned, saying his office was not generating enough income to justify continuing. For two years—1929 and 1930—no advertisements appeared in the Centerville High School yearbook. In 1933 there was no yearbook at all. Local photographer R.C. Link offered a substitution. He took every senior's picture free of charge.[17]

For abstractor and realtor W.E. Law, the financial reverses were too much. He attempted suicide with a revolver but recovered. A year later he was successful by hanging himself in the cloakroom of his office just off the Square on West Jackson Street. People were shocked. Law was well-known and well liked. He had appeared in good spirits. He had talked with friends and displayed no despondency.[18]

But most of the members of the business community fought back. They fought against counterfeiters, peddlers of bogus coins, false rumors, street vendors flooding the town and mail-order houses whose catalogs they saw lying "in heaps, stacks and rows" in Centerville Post Office, offering prices and conveniences that undercut the local economy. Merchants wore small red buttons with, in white letters, the words "Business is Good." They held competitions, "special stimulator" sales, "clear the deck" sales and "All Centerville Days" sales. Above all, they threw their energies to those less fortunate than themselves.[19]

For some time, the town's charity workers were being overwhelmed. People were knocking on their doors day and night; at the same time, others were telephoning, and there were those, uncounted, too proud to ask for help. Fifty local charities had already fused into the Social Welfare League. Its members met regularly identifying those in need, coordinating with the County's new social worker, Pauline Boyd, planning activities and avoiding duplication of effort.[20]

Appeals were made for clothes and bedding. These were delivered to Mrs. Boyd's office on the third floor of the courthouse, to Mrs. Roxie Miller at the Miller Funeral Home, to the Payne Building on the Square's Southeast Corner or to a room just east of the Ford Garage on West Van Buren. Appeals were made for vacant lots or plots of land, and they were distributed to those without gardens. Seeds for vegetables were assembled and distributed free of cost. Elderly women from southern Iowa and northern Missouri came to Centerville. They taught women how to card and spin raw wool and to weave it into comforters.[21]

At the school, the pupils formed a "Student Relief Committee." They organized donations around a day of the week: Monday, potatoes; Tuesday, clothes; Wednesday, vegetables; Thursday and Friday, a nickel or a dime dropped into the barrel-shaped boxes on each teacher's desk. The school nurse, assisted by the teachers, identified those students in need of winter clothing, those undernourished and those needing medical attention. The Elks Club delivered forty-eight pints of milk a day to those judged undernourished. The Kiwanis Club sponsored a room at St. Joseph Hospital free for the treatment of underprivileged children, and local doctors pledged free service. When a citywide survey revealed 73 malnourished babies and young children all under school age and therefore not receiving free milk, the Business and Professional Women took action. They placed empty milk bottles on doorsteps, businesses and on counters in stores. Attached to each was a card requesting donations and the purpose of the contribution. As the Depression deepened and the number of malnourished babies jumped from 73 to 196, they knocked on doors for donations, held a carnival on Haynes Avenue and sold tickets for a benefit show at the Ritz Theatre.[22]

Benefit shows at the Ritz and the Majestic were frequent. An old overcoat served as a ticket admission to one; two or more eggs, a sack of potatoes or apples, canned vegetables or canned fruit to another. As Christmas neared, there were shows for children—the admission: a toy. Children from all over town arrived. They carried big dolls, small dolls, teddy bears, mechanical toys and airplanes. They came pushing buggies and pulling wagons. The toys were transferred via Steve Martin's ice wagon to the Milani Ice Cream Factory on West Van Buren, temporarily converted into a "doll hospital." The building was heated by coal donated by the Old King Coal Company. The local troop of the Boy Scouts cleaned and made necessary repairs, referring complicated ones to the Kiwanis Club members. The Boy Scouts then painted and polished each toy. Students at Centerville High School's economics classes dressed the dolls.[23]

Christmas food baskets were assembled for needy families, their numbers increasing every year. And there was a Christmas party held at the armory on each Christmas Eve for underprivileged children—five hundred of them forming a line to the Square, waiting for the doors to open. A huge Christmas tree, a gift from the Horne Fruit Company, occupied the stage. It was surrounded by toys, clothing, candy, nuts and one thousand popcorn balls. It was brilliantly lit and spray-painted in variegated colors by employees of Iowa Southern Utilities. The highlight was the arrival of Santa Claus. The children cheered and clapped. Then, one by one, the names of the children were called, and each child received a personalized gift.[24]

Throughout the Depression, whatever the financial despair, somehow the people of the town found ways to keep giving. A refrigerator was auctioned at the bandstand. A benefit dance in South Centerville, with all proceeds going to the Christmas fund, was well attended despite a snowstorm. At the post office all workers, from postmaster H.C. Haynes down to the messengers, pledged a day's salary. The City Barbers of Local 369 forwent their annual banquet, sending the money for its cost to the Christmas fund instead. At Exline, local postmaster G.W. McClaskey asked for donations "each time you collect your mail." Similar appeals went out in Numa, Mystic, Rathbun, Moravia, Unionville, Moulton and Cincinnati.[25]

The situation continued to decline. Unemployment continued to rise, in Appanoose County often reaching over 25 percent—the highest in Iowa. For the coal industry, the position was dire—1,074 County miners were without work. Many men in Mystic had not found work since 1927. Those who did were making six to ten dollars a week, sometimes for two weeks; larger numbers were making nothing at all. Local people, unable to afford coal, were burning wood and corn. Markets continued to prefer oil and natural gas, and mild winter weather further reduced demand. Operators asked miners to take a 25 percent drop in wages. Some used subterfuge, paying their workers less than UMWA-agreed prices, a situation that lead to sporadic strikes.[26]

And if all this wasn't enough, there was the problem of the hoboes.

Chapter 51

Transients, Hoboes and Violence in Appanoose County

There had always been transients: those on foot traveling the old Mormon Trail, those in covered wagons heading west and those riding the rails—the adventurous, the restless and the drifters. Some stayed a night or two, up to forty sleeping in boxcars or in haymows or undiscovered on the Courthouse Park. Amnesia victims and shell-shocked veterans, half-frozen, their hands swollen with pus, could be found foraging for food in back alleys. And some, having fallen from perches between freight cars, were found dead alongside Rock Island tracks with head injuries rendering identification possible only from fingerprint records at the Bureau of Identification in Washington, D.C.[1]

Some of the transients offered spontaneous entertainment. A traveling amateur escape artist performed on the Courthouse Square, strapped in a straightjacket, padlocked with chains and tied with ropes, freeing himself in just over a minute. Roving bands of gypsies, some in Cadillacs loaded with children, were hurried out of town by the sheriff. Other gypsies, genuine Romany, traveled as fortune-tellers; one taken before the mayor on a charge of disorderly conduct protested in broken English that she was not a transient but a phrenologist who "read de head, de coco, de bean."[2]

Some of the transients were "regulars." Jimmy Clark did odd jobs around town. "Old Sport" Tom Henry played a battered violin, tapping the beat with his foot at the same time. One transient was known only as "the Old Scissors Grinder." There was "Hairbreadth Harry," who called himself "the King of the Bums" and told a *Centerville Daily Iowegian* reporter he was "the biggest shot that ever set foot in Centerville." And there was Ezra Temple, a self-styled preacher, a Baptist with long, flowing, snow-white hair and beard. He preached on every street corner and carried his belongings suspended from a cane balanced over his shoulder.[3]

With the Depression, the number of transients increased. They also changed. Jim Spooner, the night patrolman, noted it; so did Charles Magee, the Rock Island agent, and Jesse Beck at the *Centerville Daily Iowegian*. There were still what Beck called "just plain 'bums,'" allergic to work "even with a golden pick or silver shovel," panhandling all over town for handouts at homes and restaurants, bake shops and stores, leaving signs—marks that identified for fellow transients the degree of generosity received. But there was a change. In ever-increasing numbers, there were "hoboes" as distinct from the "bums," and this group was becoming dominant. These were men out of work and seeking employment. Many appeared respectable, clean and timid about asking for aid. They offered services in exchange for food. They mowed lawns, chopped wood or sharpened knives and scissors. In many cases their services more than

Hobo in front of Luther's store. *Courtesy of Appanoose County Historical Society.*

paid their way. By 1932, women were riding the rails into Centerville; so were children, newly married couples and families.[4]

Night patrolman Jim Spooner had the most contact with the transients. He acquired the title as the town's most "depression conscious" person. Throughout the winters, he ran Centerville's "hobo hotel"—the heated City Council chamber. The room had two nicknames—"Spooner Hotel" and "The Walled off Astoria." Arriving transients collected newspapers from the mayor's office, spread them as mattresses on the pine-board floor and rolled their coats for pillows. There was a separate room with a toilet, mirror, hot and cold water, soap and towels. Jim Spooner observed the clients: there was every nationality except Chinese or Japanese. He noted fourteen members of the Yaka Indian tribe, eighteen African Americans stranded by a bankrupt carnival company and four sailors from New York City heading to San Francisco to try for work on ships out of West Coast ports. The hoboes observed a strict code of ethics. Anyone who stole or was drunk or quarrelsome was "strong-armed" out, not by Jim Spooner or the City police, but by the hoboes themselves.[5]

City Council members complained of itching. There were rumors of "cooties." The "Walled off Astoria" was temporarily closed, the hoboes transferred to the County jail, sleeping on the concrete floor between the cages, enjoying a good breakfast until their surging numbers became too large to accommodate. The council chamber reopened, and new locations opened in town—one by the Burlington roundhouse, one in a steam-heated, twelve-by-fifteen-foot room in the northeast corner of the Kearville Garage on South Twelfth Street, and one in "the Jungle House." This was the blacksmith shed at the Center coal mine, where bunks of freight-car doors were arranged in double decks and an iron stove was fed by old fruit boxes, barrels and meat racks used in refrigerator cars, tossed out from passing Rock Island trains.[6]

Throughout 1932 and 1933, whole families were passing through Centerville on foot, their situations desperate. An arriving woman deposited her five children, aged between six and fifteen, at the Appanoose County Social Welfare League office, saying she could not care for them anymore and walked away. A nine-year-old girl, her feet swollen, bruised and infected from long miles of walking with her father, was taken in by the Virgil Law family, seven miles southwest of Cincinnati, while her father walked on, seeking work. A husband, wife and seven children aged four months to twelve years were stranded at the Sharon Schoolhouse, three miles east of town, when one of the horses pulling their covered wagon, exhausted after five hundred miles, died. Families of transients were seen trudging wearily, one along West Maple Street; two more families came through Numa, all pushing small handcarts made of cultivator wheels containing children and possessions; a fourth family offered its few bedclothes to pay local bills; yet another offered its camp stove for something to eat. A sixty-seven-year-old husband, his wife in her late fifties, inadequately clothed and without blankets, slept on newspapers under Cooper Creek Bridge, just west of Centerville. The temperature was at freezing point, and they refused offers of a warm place for the night. Six miles to the east, a father, mother and two children camped at the Rock Island bridge over the Chariton River, the temperature that night at six degrees.[7]

Acts of charity were boundless. As soon as a predicament was seen, the people of the town, of the County, responded. Doctors treated the worst medical cases free of charge. Sweaters, shoes, galoshes, blankets, money and food were given to families—even a horse for the family stranded at Sharon Schoolhouse.[8]

One of the dozens of men looking for work anywhere was immigrant Ben Dorovich, living in Cedar Rapids. He lost his business, his home, his car, his savings and two children—one to infantile paralysis, the other to pneumonia. He told an *Iowegian* reporter the wolf wasn't at his door, "he's come inside my house and we sleep together."[9]

The wolf could now be said to be sleeping with Appanoose County's 450 unemployed. For them, starvation was imminent. In response, the national Red Cross shipped thirty thousand pounds of flour to the County. In her office on the third floor of the courthouse, the Overseer of the Poor—Elizabeth Goodson, since the departure of Pauline Boyd to Iowa's troubled Plymouth County—filled out applications for those who qualified. The flour arrived by rail in carloads: ten thousand pounds, followed by fifteen thousand for Centerville, five thousand for Mystic, with allotments for Numa, Unionville, Plano, Cincinnati and Dean. People lined up at distribution points—the welfare office on West Van Buren in Centerville, the Paul Dixon Legion Post in Mystic.[10]

The recipients were but a fraction of the millions now unemployed throughout the country. The states, the cities, the churches and private charities were exhausted. Federal relief appeared the only answer. On July 19, 1932, the *Iowegian* reported that, by one stroke of the pen, President Hoover signed into law the Reconstruction Finance Corporation. By so doing, he committed the federal government to "the most far-reaching relief plan in history."[11]

For Hoover it was too late, even in his home state of Iowa. The country held a presidential election on November 8. Two Centerville High School senior students wrote articles in the School Section of the *Iowegian*. "Vote for

Hoover," said Bob Beck; "...he was a poor boy born in an Iowa home and grew up an orphan, getting an education largely by his own efforts. Roosevelt grew up in the home of rich parents, and did not mingle with common American boys and girls." James Bradley looked squarely at Hoover's record. "Vote for Roosevelt," he said; "...the story of the last three years is a recital of economic collapse."[12]

Voting in Appanoose County's thirty precincts was heavy. That night, people followed the election returns over their radios. Both CBS and NBC rebuilt their studios. Results were transmitted by telephone and telegraph, assembled on large tally boards, then relayed to the public by radio special announcements. The country elected a new president: Franklin Delano Roosevelt. And Appanoose County, for the first time in its long post–Civil War Republican record, had gone Democratic.[13]

Roosevelt would not be inaugurated until March 4, 1933. By then the Depression got worse, and in Appanoose County the situation veered toward violence.

By January 1933, three months before the presidential inauguration, the situation was urgent. Unemployment continued to escalate. Everywhere men sought work. When two new homes were being built on West Van Buren, forty men applied for jobs, another forty the next day. When there was a suggestion that the offices of County auditor, recorder, sheriff and clerk to the court needed deputies, the courthouse was deluged with scores of applicants. Restaurants served free meals to the unemployed—105 in two days at the Peacock Inn "... to women and children," said manager M.S. Kassem, adding, "...few men take advantage of the services offered."[14]

Committees were formed to discuss the situation. Meeting rooms were filled to capacity. Solutions were offered: create public works; make payment in "scrip." This was the proposal of Steve Martin of the Pure Ice Company. Beginning on February 20, 1933, twenty-three men, a different twenty-three each day thereafter, all judged with families in the greatest need, worked for Appanoose County and the City of Centerville. They built windows for the Centerville Fire Department, sawed wood at the City maintenance shed. They repaired Centerville's shale streets. They cleansed brush on County roads in Sharon and Pleasant Townships. The men were paid $1.50 a day on three pieces of paper "scrip," each worth fifty cents, each printed and signed by the County auditor, and each roughly the size of a dollar bill. The men used scrip to purchase necessity items from stores displaying a red or green card. In exchange for the item, the merchant affixed a stamp on the back. When the scrip was filled, the merchant attached a two-cent tax stamp. It was then redeemable and part of the merchant's payroll.[15]

"Scrip" provided for immediate business transactions. But it was temporary, it was limited, it was short-term and it was not enough. The County applied for federal help. On February 28, $13,400 of President Hoover's Reconstruction Finance Corporation (RFC) was granted to the County. Local scrip was now stopped. Centerville's number-one scrip bill for fifty cents was purchased by the Chase National Bank of New York City and placed in its internationally known museum.[16]

The committee in charge of the RFC fund was headed by social worker Elizabeth Goodson. An office was opened over the Centerville National Bank. RFC work cards were issued to the qualified unemployed. Twenty more acres of land and a series of vacant lots were plowed and divided for municipal relief gardens. RFC cardholders drew lots for their gardens at the Payne Building on Thirteenth Street. Seeds were given free. For extra help, the Red Cross sent 330 barrels of flour to distribute to the needy.[17]

Applicants wildly exceeded predictions. The rush for aid was so rapid that Elizabeth Goodson at the RFC office was unable to investigate the legitimacy of every applicant. Rumors began to circulate. There was open criticism of the means of distribution used by the RFC office. And suggestions were rife that some had received work cards and flour who didn't deserve them. By April 24, the funds were dangerously low. Additional relief-work cards were not issued. By May 20, the town's two relief sources, the RFC and the Red Cross flour, ran dry at the same time. Exacerbating the situation was exceptionally dry summer weather. The relief gardens badly needed rain, and the lack of it was shortening the farm harvest, limiting available seasonal farm labor.[18]

For weeks the town hovered on the brink of violence. Daily, hundreds thronged the Courthouse Square. There were marches, mass meetings, huddled conferences and dire threats. Charles DePuy at the *Iowegian* saw men fondling the trigger of the English field gun on the south Courthouse Park and was grateful it had been brazed shut at the breech. At one meeting, someone shouted, "Let's go and get her," meaning Elizabeth Goodson, whose office was a few steps away on the Square's Southside. The path of the men was blocked by Chief of Police John White and several deputies standing at the foot of the stairs heading to Miss Goodson's office. Miss Goodson must have been alarmed for some time. Eight months previously, her equivalent in Charles City, some 160 miles to the north, had been dragged from her office by seventy-five men and beaten unconscious. And everyone must have recalled the fate of Judge Bradley in Plymouth County.[19]

Shortly after nine in the morning on June 1, three to four hundred of the unemployed marched to the south door of the courthouse. They wanted to speak to members of the County Board of Supervisors. They were stopped by Sheriff Roscoe Wales, supported by other City and County officers. The County Board was not in, they were told. We'll wait for them on the Square, was the reply. It was the first of several such marches and meetings with the supervisors, the numbers of marches ever increasing and swollen by more unemployed from Mystic, all of them congregating on the Square. It was an atmosphere ripe for rumors.

One of the first was that eighteen sacks of Red Cross flour were being stored in Exline. The news triggered another march. Sheriff Wales phoned to Exline ahead of the marchers and ordered the flour be locked away. He then drove himself to confront them. The eighteen sacks were for the older people dependent on the County, he told the men, and any attempt to break in and forcibly remove the flour would lead to trouble. The men returned to Centerville.[20]

Another rumor led to another march. It was that workmen on the Number Thirty road-shaling contract were not Appanoose County men. A large group of the unemployed met at the Galleyville dump, interrupting work, demanding work stop altogether and causing the arrest of four leaders by Sheriff Wales. Their imprisonment led to yet another march. This time, 150 circled the Square, then turned north to the County jail. They were again met by the ubiquitous Sheriff Wales, his deputy, constables and officers. Demand for the freedom of the four imprisoned men was voiced and refused. A voice shouted, "Let's go." The crowd surged to the back of the building, ready to storm the County jail. They were halted again by the sheriff and officers, who had fallen back to the second position and steadfastly held their ground, their quiet firmness winning the day. The four men imprisoned were released legally the next day on bond furnished by a local contractor.[21]

Across the town, there was despair. People talked of their nation in crisis, banks tottering, the whole country paralyzed. All they could do was wait for the new administration they'd helped elect.[22]

Chapter 52

Roosevelt Inaugurated

On March 4, President Roosevelt was inaugurated. He acted boldly and quickly. Even the *Centerville Daily Iowegian*, which had strongly opposed President Roosevelt's election, now considered "…his wise and conscientious action …can make him into a national idol." The president's first act was to close all banks. When they reopened, twelve Federal Reserve banks were pouring a stream of new currency into the nation's banking system. All three Centerville banks had remained "rock solid" throughout the Depression. Such was their record, they were swiftly certified. The two national banks—the First National and the Centerville National—reopened on Tuesday, March 14; the town's private bank—Iowa Trust and Savings—on the fifteenth.[1]

Across the nation, confidence surged. It was reinforced by the president's first radio "fireside chat," reassuring the public that the reopened banks were sound. Three days later, the stock market had its largest one-day increase in history. In Appanoose County, people responded in kind. From lockboxes and sugar bowls, from fruit jars and mattresses, they carried their hoarded, often musty-smelling money to the banks so rapidly local bankers were rushed to process it. In the same way, they carried in their gold and gold certificates—a roll in Oskaloosa was said to be wrapped around a bedbug. Within three days, Centerville's three banks had submitted gold to the Chicago Federal Reserve Bank worth $145,351.50.[2]

Now the administration turned to measures to provide relief and work for the unemployed, to stimulate agriculture and to help farmers. Programs targeting unemployment and farming were of immediate concern to the people of the County. In both they had good reason to feel extra confidence. At the helm of these programs were Harry Hopkins and Henry Wallace. Both were men from Iowa.[3]

Six weeks into the new administration, First Lady Eleanor Roosevelt took a night flight over Washington, D.C. She looked down on the lights of the city, the illuminated dome of the Capitol, the shaft of the Washington Monument, the portico of the White House. At the controls of the aircraft, slim and elegant in the white evening dress and white kid gloves she'd worn to dinner in the White House that evening, was the first lady of the air: Amelia Earhart.[4]

The event was reported in the *Centerville Daily Iowegian.* For the people of the town, it was an example of how the Roosevelts were breaking precedents. Eight miles to the west in Jerome, the article was absorbed by Dorothy Owen, who would later be town librarian of Centerville for thirty-three years. It was news of her heroine, Amelia Earhart, and an indicator of how both first ladies were challenging barriers and changing society in the process. People read another *Centerville Daily Iowegian* article. It was written by UP reporter Raymond Clapper. He listed twenty tradition-breaking actions by the president in his first twenty-five days as chief executive, five more by the first lady. The list included changes in daily routines; the first woman—Frances Perkins—appointed to the Cabinet; the nationwide bank holiday and gold embargo; the recognition of White House messenger Eddie Savoy, an African American, on his retirement; and the president's immediate focus: a proposal for a direct attack on the unemployment and hunger of fourteen million Americans.[5]

The proposal was issued by the president on March 21, seventeen days after his inauguration. It fell into three parts: public employment for the unemployed, grants of money to states for relief and the creation of a public works program. For the first of the three, Roosevelt created the Civilian Conservation Corps—the CCC. Under it, 250,000 men, aged eighteen to twenty-five with dependents, were to be recruited from the jobless and put to work on reforestation, soil erosion and flood control projects. Within three days, forest service officials selected thirty-eight camp sites in nine states. Excepting Arkansas, all were east of the Mississippi, from Pennsylvania south to Florida. Labor Department representatives in sixteen large Eastern cities selected men for the vanguard army. Included were members of the dissolving Bonus Army.[6]

The men were examined, instructed in forestry work, given work overalls and shoes and paid a dollar a day and their keep, all under the control and supervision of the U.S. Army. William Green, president of the American

Federation of Labor, denounced what he called the "regimentation of labor in its hour of depest [*sic*] distress …it smacks of fascism, Hitlerism and a form of sovietism." Despite such objections, by June 1, the *Centerville Daily Iowegian* reported, there were 1,556 CCC camps across the country, employing three hundred thousand men.[7]

On April 12, CCC representatives arrived in Iowa. They traveled the State. They selected five work sites for immediate work: Albia, Chariton, Glenwood and two State parks, Backbone in Delaware County and Lacey-Keosauqua in Van Buren County. Within days, they had selected more sites, with twenty-six as the total number. At the same time, five thousand young Iowans from the State's major cities, some of whom, said the *Iowegian*, "have not eaten three square meals in one day for months," began entering the white-capped tents at Fort Des Moines to be examined, conditioned and trained. Ten days later, 212 left Des Moines for the camp at Albia, known as "Camp Number One." Two hundred and fifty more went through Centerville on Rock Island number thirty, dismounting at Paris some twenty miles northeast of Centerville, ready to pitch camp at Bunch Lake, known as "Camp Number Two." Another five hundred piled into train cars and were sent from Des Moines to Shenandoah, Oskaloosa and Winterset.[8]

Over the bank on the Southside of Centerville Square, Elizabeth Goodson's welfare office was swamped with inquiries and more than a hundred applicants for the County's quota of forty-five. By mid-May, the first ten had been selected and sent for training. One, an African American, was said to have been sent to "a colored camp." Another eight men, all over twenty-five years of age and all experienced in supervision, were hired by the CCC as "straw bosses."[9]

The recruits wrote home from distant locations in Wisconsin, Minnesota and other parts of Iowa. They described their daily routine: reveille at 6 a.m., daily medical inspections, three square meals a day, eight hours of work except on Saturdays and Sundays, lights out at 10:30 p.m. All enjoyed the experience and were anxious to sign up for another six months of their year allotment. From their payment of thirty dollars a month, they retained five dollars and sent twenty-five dollars home. By September 1933, thirty-nine men had left Appanoose County. Their wages in the process removed thirty-nine families from the County Poor Fund.[10]

The following year, in April 1934, Captain Vernon C. Koons and Second Lieutenant John McCrory of the U.S. Army arrived in town. They contacted lumber dealers, plumbers and trade people. A CCC camp was to be placed in Centerville. It was a relocated camp—Unit 774th Company, from Winterset. On May 12, 198 arriving recruits began setting up wall tents at the north end of

Seventh Street, once the Wooden pasture, now the property of ex-Governor Nate Kendall, giving the camp the occasional title "Camp Kendall."[11]

The primary assignment of the Centerville camp workers was to correct the worst incidents of soil erosion identified by County farmers, the Farm Bureau and CCC field engineers. By May 18, the men at the camp were divided into four platoons and were working at correcting gullies at the E.G. Irelan farm, two miles southeast of Cincinnati, the G. Felkner and Ed Simmons farms west of town and the Harvey Main farm in the north part of the County. They built dams a short way downflow from the head of the ditches or gullies. They used two methods: the "woven-wire dam" for most gullies, "the baffle dam" for deep gullies. At the E.A. Caylor farm, where erosion was causing water to spill across a highway, they used a third method—a concrete dam and dike. With the first two methods, they piled straw or brush with dirt, pounding them into place against the dam on the upstream side. The gully was now filled in, making the field smooth and the area previously marred by the gully ready for cultivation.[12]

At the E.G. Irelan farm, new techniques were used: willow twigs were thrust down through the impacted straw and mud. They were designed to root. When they did, natural dams were created in the process, creating prime nesting locations for quails. And to prevent unnecessary wash, black walnuts were planted—on the Irelan farm, five thousand were planted in two days.[13]

In July 1934 the Centerville recruits began work at the park four miles east of town, on the banks of the Chariton River. In December of 1930, it had been named The Bluffs State Park. The name Sharon Bluffs State Park would appear later. For over ten years, this park had been promoted by Professor L.H. Pammell, head of Iowa State University's botany department, chairman of the Iowa Conservation Board, whose son was married to Mona Thompson, the daughter of Centerville physician Dr. J.I. Thompson. Pammell was a passionate conservationist, a supporter and visitor to national parks, and had helped create thirty-eight State parks in Iowa. At The Bluffs, he marveled at the variety of wildflowers, the ferns and the big hickory trees with their mammoth hickory nuts found, he said, only in Appanoose County. This park, he continued, contained more native Iowa plant life than any other park in Iowa.[14]

The CCC workers built at the Bluffs a shelter house, twenty miles of trails through the woods, a suspension bridge across the river and a fence around the park. Their work was a fitting memorial to Dr. Pammell. On March 24, 1931, his death had been reported in the *Iowegian*. He had died on board a train at Provo, Utah. He was on his way home to Iowa from California.[15]

On August 14, 1934, Rex Parsons, the superintendent of Centerville's CCC camp, addressed the town's Association of Commerce. He listed details of the business asset that his camp was to the town. It was part of a whole story. President Roosevelt's other programs were also taking effect. Conditions in the town were improving.[16]

Chapter 53

More New Deal Programs

More "New Deal" programs followed. On June 1, it was FERA—the Federal Emergency Relief Administration. At its head, Roosevelt appointed an Iowan. Harry Hopkins was born in Sioux City, graduated from Grinnell College seventy miles north of Centerville and was known to one of the assistants at the welfare office in Centerville. Hopkins directed five hundred million federal dollars to states for direct relief to the needy. Elizabeth Goodson, in the welfare office over the Centerville National Bank on the Southside of the Square, distributed $1.00 to $5.50 a week, with extra for clothing and rent, to the County's 755 destitute families. With the approach of winter and the termination of fresh produce from City gardens, foodstuffs arrived for distribution: thousands of pounds of flour, butter and pork, as well as eggs, cheeses, cereals and canned vegetables.[1]

By November 15, thinking—accurately—that the needy preferred work over the dole, Hopkins created his second brainchild: the CWA, the Civil Works Administration. It was a temporary work program for the winter of 1933–34. In Centerville, men waited in lines outside the welfare office, the City Hall and the new federal reemployment office upstairs in the Farrington Building on Thirteenth Street. By December 4, 1,514 men had registered for the County's initial allotment of 614. Five days later, ten women joined the lines, then thirty-nine more, one aged seventy-six with an unemployed husband, now injured after cutting wood to keep them warm.[2]

By mid-December, 923 of the unemployed were working at different projects scattered across the County. They resurfaced streets and rural roads with shale and crushed rock. They dug a half-mile ditch, fourteen feet deep, thirty feet wide, to divert the flow of the Chariton River in an attempt to decrease flooding. In Moulton, Rathbun, Moravia and Unionville, they made all-weather streets. At area schools they built additions, dug wells, repaired foundations and spoutings, laid brick sidewalks and leveled grounds for athletic fields. In Centerville, 820 feet of sewer was laid in the northwest part of the City, where raw sewage was entering Cooper Creek and being drunk by cows supplying the town with milk. Trees were planted at the City park and ground leveled for tennis courts. At the airport, two runways were measured out and shaled. Books were repaired and the walls decorated at Drake Free Public Library, and at the courthouse there was more decorating. The walls were washed and painted, the woodwork varnished, floors and sub-sills replaced and the main doors cleaned and decorated, revealing to the town their long-forgotten, gleaming copper beauty.[3]

For the nation's beleaguered farmers, federal relief came from Washington on May 12 with the AAA—the Agricultural Adjustment Administration. For the farmers of Iowa, the relief was interlaced with pleasure in the president's choice for secretary of agriculture. The credentials of forty-four-year-old Henry Agard Wallace lay deep in the good earth of Iowa. Born on an Iowa farm near Orient, a hundred miles north and west of Centerville, he was educated at Iowa State University, was a brilliant scientist, absorbed Gregor Mendel's theories of genetics and developed hybrid corn. He was the publisher and editor of *Wallace's Farmer* that was started by his grandfather and continued by his father, Henry Cantwell Wallace, who was secretary of agriculture under two presidents, Harding and Coolidge. Henry Agard had spoken on farms and in Centerville at Alfalfa Banquets. He listened to the hardships of small farmers, read their letters to his newspaper and was committed to improving their plight. And there was an extra bonus for the people of the town. Centerville's William S. Bradley was appointed a member of Wallace's AAA.[4]

Under Wallace's AAA, farm loans were available. For Appanoose County farmers, they were issued from the Federal Land Bank in Omaha. The loans were part of a contract between each farmer and the government—one, it was hoped, that would create an economic domino effect. The farmer must decrease his production to raise farm prices, in order to increase a flow of money that would create a demand for goods, that would in turn boost national employment. The Appanoose County Farm Bureau Office in the courthouse was the busiest place in town. Large piles of forms and data sheets were piled everywhere. Two stenographers were hired to assist bureau chief Edna Withrow. Stepping around the CWA workers who were redecorating the courthouse, farmers filled in their applications for the corn-hog program, for corn loans and for soybean and wheat seeds for planting.

Five local farmers were now federally appointed directors of the loan program. They discussed with each farmer his production figures. They made inspections. Farmers then signed to reduce their acreages, plow undesirable land, seal excess corn in cribs and cut hog, beef, sheep and chicken production by slaughter. Four tons of roosters were taken for slaughter on June 28, 1934, to the Swift plant off the Levee. On August 21, sixteen carloads of cattle were shipped to east St. Louis. Hundreds of others—cows and young calves—were shot and buried in specially dug trenches along the Burlington right-of-way.[5]

Interweaving FERA, the CWA and the AAA was the NRA—National Recovery Administration. It set codes for every business, outlawing child labor and controlling working hours and conditions, prices and wages. The NRA had a symbol: a blue eagle clutching a wheel in one claw, three lightning discharges in the other. And there was a slogan: "We Do Our Part." It began enthusiastically: 250,000 supporters marched down New York City's Fifth Avenue. There were pledges and patriotism and songs. Two hundred thousand employers across the country signed the codes. It made them eligible to hoist the blue eagle banner above their establishment. The *Centerville Daily Iowegian* reported that more than a million jobs had, as a result, opened in retail stores across the country.[6]

In Centerville there was a mass meeting of business owners at the Association of Commerce on Thirteenth Street. They agreed on general opening and closing hours. Stores were to open at eight in the morning, close at five in the afternoon, nine on Saturday evenings. More flexible hours were agreed for restaurants, drugstores, barbers and grocers. On August 3, forty-eight Centerville businesses took out a full-page advertisement in the *Iowegian*, pledging their full support of the NRA codes. Other businesses followed. Town businesses flew the blue eagle banner. Stores placed the symbol in their windows. People checked for the blue eagle label on bicycles unpacked at Davison's Hardware Store. Coal miners refused to work in mines not displaying the blue eagle.[7]

And as was inevitable in Centerville, a big parade was planned. Former Centerville businessman Carl Weeks was to be the speaker. He had opened the Red Cross Drug Store on the Square's Southeast Corner. He had manufactured Armand cosmetics and was the owner of Salisbury House, filled with art and European antiques in Des Moines. The parade occurred on September 7. It took half an hour to pass a fixed point on South Main Street. It was headed by a combination of Centerville High School and municipal bands all dressed in white and led by a drum major. Following came the police, Company G of the National Guard, decorated cars from every County town, more than 185 United Mine Workers of America marching four abreast and decorated floats representing every town business. Thousands lined the sidewalks and jammed the downtown. There was entertainment and music and speeches, with Judge Utterback a last-minute substitute for an indisposed Carl Weeks. And everywhere banners and flags flew signs of the blue eagles.[8]

Despite the programs, unemployment remained high. The CWA, always intended as a temporary program, closed in February 1934, and both the NRA and AAA programs closed when the United States Supreme Court ruled them unconstitutional. Centerville's unemployed numbers approached twenty-five hundred—some with college degrees. For a few, employment was possible with Harold Ickes's Public Works Administration (PWA), with projects far from Centerville: building the hundred-mile causeway from Key West to the Florida mainland; and the dams—the Grand Coulee in Washington, the Bonneville in Oregon and the Boulder in Nevada (later known as the Hoover), visited and described in the *Centerville Daily Iowegian* by Jesse Beck's son Paul. For the rest, they were back to dependency on FERA and Elizabeth Goodson's welfare office over the Centerville National Bank.[9]

In spring 1935, President Roosevelt by executive order started the Works Progress Administration (WPA). Administrating it again was Harry Hopkins. He spent billions employing workers for reforestation, flood control, rural electrification and slum clearance, and he hired writers and artists who painted murals in post offices. In Centerville, the WPA office opened over the City Drug Store on the Square's Westside. Seven hundred of the local unemployed lined up to register and began work immediately. They built six farm-to-market roads and placed signs south of town marking the route of the Mormon Trail. With the blessing of the State Public Health Department, they rebuilt outside toilets for those beyond the limits of a sewer system. They rebuilt them with concrete floors and risers, ventilated pits and self-closing seats. They made them fly-tight, almost odorless and free from surface drainage. The WPA workers also built a new eighty-five-by-eighty-five-foot County Home, a model of cleanliness, sanitation and comfort. They rebuilt the Central School and a fifty-five-thousand-dollar, state-of-the-art City swimming pool.[10]

Under Roosevelt's multiple programs, hundreds of thousands of federal dollars poured into Appanoose County, and work was given to thousands without jobs and almost without hope. The list included sixty-eight old-age pensioners climbing to the third floor of the courthouse to collect a monthly allowance. To them all, Roosevelt was a national hero. He had lifted their spirits and their self-esteem. Orace McCutcheon, saying he could not take care of his own family, collected his eighteen-month-old child from his father, who had kept the baby while Orace was out of work. Another Centerville man, without steady employment for twenty years, showed his paycheck to neighbors with pride. And on Centerville Square, there was a near fight when a criticism of Roosevelt was overheard. The listener said he took any criticisms of Roosevelt as quickly as if the remarks were about his own wife. Roosevelt's supporters listened to the president's "fireside chats," placed their signatures at the Western Union office on a giant birthday card to him, submitting at the same time twenty-five cents each for infantile paralysis research, and they rallied for him when renominated by his party in 1936 and 1940.[11]

There were plenty of criticisms. In September 1934, U.S. Representative Lloyd Thurston of Iowa stopped into the *Centerville Daily Iowegian* office. He supported the president's original relief program, he said, when there was an urgent humanitarian need because men, women and children were actually hungry for food they did not have the money to buy. But he did not support what he called "the orgy of indirect relief" that followed. A year later, speaking to Centerville's Republican Women's Club, U.S. Senator J.L. Dickinson of Iowa decried the lost American prized possessions of liberty and individualism and accused FDR of being "red." So did Floyd M. Edwards of Promise City, who, in a letter to the *Iowegian*, said the president was trying to "Russianize" the country. Replying in another letter, T.W. Killion wrote that if Hoover had been elected in 1932, it "...would not have been six months until a bloody revolution would have broken out..."[12]

Beyond the adulation, beyond the criticisms, President Roosevelt's programs—in particular the CCC, the CWA, the PWA and the WPA—had an unanticipated result. The millions of men across the nation who had worked in them would soon have to fight in a war that already was looming. These men would be ready to serve their country, and they were immediately ready, in superb physical condition.[13]

In September 1936 two special trains passed through Appanoose County. On the afternoon of the twenty-eighth, one carried the Republican candidate for president, Kansas governor Alf Landon, traveling on the Milwaukee route. The train slowed at Moravia, Rathbun and Mystic. It stopped in Seymour. At each station, the crowds were showered with sunflower presidential badges. At Seymour, Governor Landon waved and spoke to the crowd of fifteen hundred from the train's rear platform. He urged the voters to "...plow the New Deal under."[14]

Earlier that month, during the night of the fourth, a train carrying President Roosevelt passed through Moulton on the Wabash route. It was preceded by a one-car "feeler" train, testing the safety of the track. The president's train, flying white flags and interspersed with Secret Service agents shining flashlights, came next. It eased its speed to take on coal and water. It was three in the morning. The president, in the ninth car, a Pullman observer, was asleep. Fifty supporters were at the depot, and WPA workers provided extra guards for the track and tested the bridges. They did not see their president. But they were close, and that was enough.[15]

Two months later, on November 4, 1936, President Roosevelt won forty-six states, including Iowa, out of the then-total of forty-eight. He carried Appanoose County with 6,609 votes to Governor Landon's 5,511—a majority of 1,098. He would carry the County again in 1940. But his majority would be only thirty-five, and he lost Iowa.[16]

Chapter 54

Organized Crime in Centerville

There were always rumors—rumors that throughout Prohibition some of the County's illegal stills were too sophisticated to be local operations. One raided on a farm west of Streepyville was described as very clean, "a first class still ...a credit to a small brewery." So were a still at "House No. 49" in Bellair Township and one at Victor Christina's cellar. The quality of the local alcohol was known. It was in demand in New York City, Chicago and Des Moines. It was shipped out of the County by car. Mysterious aircraft landed and departed quietly.[1]

On Sunday afternoons, men dressed in silk suits and fedoras arrived. They came in expensive cars. Curtains occasionally covered the windows. They came into town from the east and turned south. They stopped in at the back room of a bar at Thirty. Or they went to the homes of well-known Italian families. They gambled. They played poker for high stakes. They sang songs, drank wine and were watched by small children, warned not to name one of the visitors—the man from Chicago with a scar running the length of his cheek. Reports do not reveal local police raiding these events. But the town was warned: "Thirty and the south end of Centerville," said the *Centerville Daily Iowegian*, are "being invaded by some who are tough and growing tougher." Southside merchant Tony DeZorzi went further: "These are members of the Mafia in Centerville. They are morose and quick tempered and no one knows how to take them."[2]

The town's link to an organized gangster underworld was becoming clear. Men left on temporary visits to Chicago and were never heard from again. Louis Cora was shot there three times in the head by John

Nickelle. Somehow he lived and returned home to Centerville to have one bullet in the roof of his mouth and another in the lower left side of his neck successfully removed by Dr. W.B. Miller. Others were not so lucky. Filadelphia Todora was beheaded. More bodies of Centerville people were found, mostly in Cicero, the area of Chicago by 1924 dominated by Al Capone. Angelo Normali was murdered there by Raymond "Mondo" Terrazoni, who'd followed him from Streepyville; so was Mary Todao at the hands of Giovanni Lescari. John Castenaro, well-known in Centerville mining circles, was buried alive at the rear of a garage on Cicero's West Thirtieth Street, his hands and feet bound, a rope wound tightly around his neck, his head covered with a sawdust sack. Santo Cellebron, a chauffeur from South Centerville, was caught in Chicago with six thousand gallons of wine, valued at forty-two thousand dollars, and indicted as one of seventy-nine Cicero gangsters. He was now ready to be a government witness, investigating conditions in Cicero. For this decision he was summarily shot "for talking too much." And Sam Falzone, living in Chicago after being pardoned for dynamiting the Centerville home of Tony DeZorzi, died when his own home exploded.[3]

"Innocent" explanations for the deaths were spread around Centerville. They were about misunderstandings, it was said, or the result of triangular love affairs. In Louis Cora's case, he was simply trying to get a gun from John Nickelle and return it to its rightful owner in Streepyville. Santo Cellebron, now spelled Calabroni, was completely innocent of any gang or liquor feuds. This last account was sent into Centerville by a Mr. and Mrs. Smaniotto living in Cicero.[4]

The Smaniotto version of the Cellebron murder did nothing to quell local gossip. Both Smaniottos were well-known in Centerville. Lena was a local girl from Numa. Bob had worked as a coal miner at the Prairie Block Coal Company and had boarded in Numa at the home of Natutale Belerino. Now married, the two lived in Cicero, where Bob joined the ranks of Al Capone. It was with this contact that Bob set up a whiskey still on the Streepyville farm of Lena's brother, Ray Owens, periodically returning to check on the operation and run off a supply. In 1924, the still was raided by Sheriff Gaughenbaugh. Lena's brother, Ray, was arrested. Ray consistently refused to identify the still's real owner.[5]

In Chicago, Al Capone held a raffle for a new car, manipulating the result so Lena won the prize. Lena couldn't drive. Her sister Anna Owens (Rhodes) could. The car was used repeatedly to deliver whiskey into Centerville, where sales immediately spiked. To recognize Anna's contribution, Capone held a

Al Capone raffle car. *Courtesy of Goldie Dwight.*

baby contest and again manipulated the result so Anna's son, Dennis, won the ten-dollar gold piece first prize.[6]

The size of fines issued for liquor offenses reflected the opinions of law officers. The greater the fine, the more extensive and dangerous the bootlegger's crime. Most bootleggers were fined $100 to $400. Ray Owens paid $61.65, and for a six-months sentence, he spent only the nights in jail, driving Sheriff Gaughenbaugh to his various appointments during the days. Dominic Cora, Louis's brother, was fined $900. But $1,000, "one of the heaviest liquor nuisance fines ever handed down," was given to Bob Smaniotto's brother Frank, whom the *Centerville Daily Iowegian* named "one of the kings of the Appanoose County bootleggers." Frank did not appear to answer the charge. He said if he did, he'd blow the roof off the County courthouse. Instead, he swiftly left town, abandoning his clothes, his furniture and his house on Drake Avenue—all placed on auction at the sheriff's sale. Not a single person bid so much as one cent on any of Frank Smaniotto's possessions.[7]

Frank presumably had joined his brother Bob in Cicero. In less than a year, Chicago's gangland was again openly operating in Centerville. This time the target was a well-known Italian family on South Eighteenth Street, the Russos. In June 1920, Carmela Russo shot and killed Tony Matto. He was, she said, endangering her engagement to Cosimo Malone by sending him a letter impugning her "honor." By 1923, she had served three years of an eight-year manslaughter sentence, been pardoned by Iowa's governor, married Cosimo Malone, given birth to two daughters and was back in Centerville. "Finished," said the *Centerville Daily Iowegian*, when Carmela arrived home; "...the last word has been written and the book containing [this story] is closed." The *Centerville Daily Iowegian* was wrong. In February 1925, Carmela filed a petition for divorce at the Appanoose County Clerk's office. Malone, she said, beat her unmercifully and repeatedly had threatened her life and the lives of her two children. The divorce was granted on March 31.[8]

Cosimo Malone was enraged. He was now living in Chicago. He appeared at the Russo home, sometimes alone, sometimes in the company of associates. There were confrontations and demands. There were dire threats to kill, to cut, to tear. Police officers were called to be present. On a late night in September, Constanza, Carmela's fifteen-year-old sister, disappeared. People gossiped: "Certain customs brought to America from the old country" were being observed. The *Centerville Daily Iowegian* asked if it was a practice of the organization "of which Malone is a member." Or had Carmela secretly aided in the abduction of her sister to appease the wrath of Cosimo and so end the danger to herself and the Russo family? George Russo, the father of the two girls, was unaware of such explanations. When Constanza surfaced in Chicago, saying she was in a trial marriage to Cosimo Malone, George, believing his daughter was disgraced, cut her off from her family and her inheritance.[9]

Constanza's "marriage" lasted a week. She escaped to the home of Dominick Gragliano in Rock Island. Malone chased her. He shot her twice, the bullets entering her jaw and her shoulder. While recovering in a hospital in Rock Island, she received a telegram from her father: "Glad you were shot. Too bad you're not dead." When Constanza recovered, she returned to Centerville. There was a visible scar on her neck. She appealed to Sheriff Gaughenbaugh. She asked for protection, fearing retribution from two gangs: Malone's in Chicago, and Gragliano's in Rock Island. Constanza was cared for in the County jail and given protection in the Girls Reformatory at Mitchellville. Malone was eventually arrested in Illinois and served a sentence for the attempted murder of Constanza.[10]

But even in a town as accustomed to murder as Centerville, two reports in February 1929 left people shocked and even numbed.

At ten thirty in the morning on Thursday, the twenty-eighth of February, 1929, Centerville attorney David Fulton Rice left the Appanoose County Courthouse to return to his office. Waiting for him, hovering at the foot of the stairs leading to Rice's office over the City Book Store on the Square's Southside, dressed in a brown coat and a black hat, was forty-four-year-old coal miner George Domyancich.[11]

A year earlier, Domyancich had retained Rice as his lawyer to file a case of slander against fellow Empire coal miner Tony Karlotto. Domyancich wanted twenty-five thousand dollars in damages. Karlotto was calling him names, he told Rice. He was calling him "dirty" and "filthy." Bank officials in town were laughing at him. Other Croatians were holding meetings to plot against him. People were threatening to kill him. Cars were driving past his house at Thirty late at night. He couldn't sleep. He sat at his window with guns laid out on a table. He kept another under his pillow when he tried to rest. He didn't understand the legal procedures and delays of his case. He confronted district court judges Smith and Dalshiel in the courthouse. He visited D. Fulton Rice every day, sometimes twice.

Rice was on the verge of a brilliant career. He had worked as a teacher in Jerome and saved his earnings to study law at Drake University and the University of Michigan. He served his country in the World War as an aide in the U.S. Army Judge Advocate's office. He was elected to the State legislature for two terms and two extra sessions. His name was proposed as candidate for governor of Iowa. He was married, the father of two children, a third expected in another month. He was considered handsome, charming and even lovable.[12]

When, on that morning, Domyancich saw D. Fulton Rice emerge from the courthouse, he hurried to meet him on the south walkway. Witnesses said there was an exchange of words. Fulton Rice continued to walk south. Domyancich pulled a .38-caliber revolver from his pocket and shot Rice twice in the back, killing him instantly. He then walked on to the courthouse, handed his gun to Sheriff Gaughenbaugh and said, "He no handle my case right."[13]

Domyancich's act was a study in futility. Had he waited twenty-four hours, his name would have been cleared. Tony Karlotto had already defaulted the case against him, and in a month he was dead—of blood poisoning—in Chicago. At seven on the morning of April 4, Mrs. Rice gave birth to a son. The baby appeared healthy but began to grow weaker and died at nine that morning. Domyancich "will be called upon to answer another murder," said the *Moulton*

Gaughenbaugh with Domyancich at spot where D. Fulton Rice murder occurred. *Courtesy of Appanoose County Historical Society.*

Tribune. Domyancich's trial for the murder of D. Fulton Rice began on April 22. He was tried in Ottumwa, taken there "for safe keeping" quickly and quietly by Sheriff Gaughenbaugh. Three days later, Domyancich changed his initial "not guilty" plea to "guilty." He was taken the same day to Fort Madison prison to begin a life sentence. In September, less than seven months after his crime, Domyancich committed suicide.[14]

Interweaving the murder of D. Fulton Rice, the people of the town were reading of another. It happened two weeks earlier and three hundred miles to the east. Slowly its tentacles reached Centerville.

On the morning of February 14, 1929, also at ten thirty in the morning, four men entered the garage of the SMC Cartage Company at 2122 North Clark Street in Chicago. Two were dressed as policemen. They carried machine guns. They ordered seven men in the garage, members of the Bugs Moran gang, to line up against a brick wall. They then opened fire.[15]

The "St. Valentine's Day Massacre," as it came to be known, shocked the nation and much of the world. Centerville was no exception, although its links to the crime were not yet established. For days after the massacre, AP reports appeared on the front page of the *Iowegian*. Public opinion in Chicago was said to be "at its highest pitch of indignation," and it "clamored ...for a purging of

Chicago—[a] general housecleaning of the gangster element responsible…" Pastors from one thousand churches met on the Chicago "Loop." Evangelist Dr. W.E. Biederwolf declared, "Men are going from bad to worse to Chicago …Sodom and Gomorrah were righteous [in comparison]."[16]

At Centerville's First Methodist Church, the Reverend H.B. Scoles issued a warning to his Sunday morning congregation. Chicago, he said, was reaping what it had sown. The City of Centerville must awaken to the corrupting moral and degrading conditions in its own town before it was too late. Reverend Scoles did not name the corrupting situations. His congregation was aware of them, and eight years previously, gang warfare had struck the heart of the community when policeman "Slim" Edwards was shot and almost killed on Twelfth Street by Luke Kennedy of the St. Louis Hogans Gang. Kennedy was himself killed in St. Louis by a rival gang, Egan's Rats. Its leader and chief assassin was William P. Colbeck. By 1928, the man was in Centerville, giving the name "Jack Burke." He was presenting himself as a roofing contractor. He "flashed diamonds and a bloated bank-roll in a blasé manner," said the *Centerville Daily Iowegian.* Accompanying him was a Centerville girl who had worked in a local hotel. Following him were St. Louis detectives. They reported he was also wanted in New York City.[17]

By March 5, Chicago police were naming suspects. On the list was Frederick R. Burke, an import from St. Louis, who, they believed, had dressed as a policeman and had wielded the Tommy gun in the massacre. If the people of Centerville did not yet connect Fred Burke to Jack Burke, they had good reason. They were processing the shock of the Fulton Rice murder.[18]

In fact, Chicago police were deadlocked in solving the St. Valentine's Day Massacre. Science provided the first breakthrough—the science of forensic ballistic technology. U.S. Army Major Calvin Goddard had made a study of the lands and grooves of gun-barrel rifling. They left distinctive marks on bullets, he said. It was possible to measure the "helixometer," the left- or righthand twists and degrees of spiraling that could identify the gun's make and the model. He could chemically restore ground-off serial numbers on firearms. A year before, Major Goddard examined the bullets fired into gangster Frankie Yale on a Brooklyn sidewalk. It was the first murder by the Thompson submachine gun—the Tommy gun. He now examined seventy spent .45-caliber shell casings and thirty-eight bullets taken from the bodies of the St. Valentine's Day Massacre victims. The killers, he said, had used two Tommy guns and a shotgun. Furthermore, he said, the bullets fired into Frankie Yale had been fired by the same Tommy gun.[19]

Oscar V. Payne, hired by General John Thompson to design the Tommy gun. *Courtesy of the Helmer Collection.*

When this information reached Centerville, there had to have been some sense of irony. The inventor of the Tommy gun was from Centerville. Oscar V. Payne was one of the popular boys of the community. He had attended Centerville schools, fished with "the gang" in Cooper Creek and the Chariton River and played baseball under the sputtering arch lights on West State Street. Payne was gifted with the ability to take an abstract idea and work out a suitable design. He taught himself drafting and engineering. At sixteen he'd invented an "Oscar," a propeller pitch indicator used in propeller aircraft. At twenty he studied patent drawings and disassembled the only antique Roberts firearm in the U.S. Army Ordnance Department. His ability was duly noted by General John Thompson. The United States was about to enter World War I. Thompson hired Payne to work on war machinery.[20]

If it was understood what guns killed the Bugs Moran gang, who committed the crime was still unsolved. There were conjectures, theories and suspects, but nothing definitive. The second breakthrough came in December, ten months after the crime. Fred Burke, alias Jack Burke, and now alias Fred Dane, was drunk. While posing as a retired businessman in St. Joseph, Michigan, under the name Fred Dane, he was involved in a minor traffic accident. When twenty-four-year-old policeman Charles Skelly insisted Burke report to the police station, Burke shot him. Skelly died three hours later. Michigan police set up roadblocks and found Burke's wrecked car, with papers identifying its owner as Fred Dane, with an address in Stevensville. A search of the address yielded firearms, ammunition, bulletproof vests, almost three hundred thousand dollars in bonds stolen in bank robberies and machine guns that were perfect matches with the bullets from the St. Valentine's Day Massacre victims, as well as those taken from the body of Frankie Yale. One other item found in Fred Dane's house—shirts embroidered with three letters *FRB*— helped identify Frederick R. Burke.[21]

Evading both the police and the FBI, Fred Burke drove out of Chicago on the last day of 1929. He was now America's most wanted criminal and called "the most dangerous man alive." Posters with his photograph were being placed across the County; a reward for his capture was set at $101,000. He adopted another alias: Richard F. White. He drove through the worst snowstorm of the season to an isolated farmhouse in Sullivan County, Missouri. He was now just twenty miles south of Centerville.[22]

Chapter 55

Fred Burke and National Gangs

Fred Burke, now Richard F. White, had found refuge in the farmhouse of Mrs. Amanda Bailey. She was the seventy-seven-year-old mother of Harvey Bailey, who had spent a dozen years sweeping across the Midwest, from Texas to Wisconsin, Ohio to the Dakotas, robbing scores of banks. Burke and Bailey were firm friends. They had met at Paddy Ryan's Saloon and Restaurant in Cicero. They occasionally assisted each other laundering stolen money and negotiable securities. But there was a difference. Burke was a close associate of Capone and a killer. Bailey knew Capone, he even liked him, but he remained free of syndicate associations, independently planning his own smooth professional crimes and never killing.[1]

In Sullivan County, Burke told people he was an oil and real estate broker. He needed to be gone on business for a week or ten days at a time. He was partially retired and looking for tranquility and peace. Burke was well liked. He was expensively dressed, well-spoken, educated, quiet and concerned about others. He carried fifty-dollar bills in his pocket and used them to pay for items in nearby Green City stores, always ending with, "Keep the change." Occasionally he changed into overalls, worked as a farmhand for Mrs. Bailey and helped farmers get their grain to the Rodgers Grist Mill in Pollock. In the evenings he'd join neighbors and play cards at the nearby farm of Barney and Lee Anna Porter.[2]

Bonnie was the attractive, blonde, twenty-one-year-old daughter of the Porters. She was a student nurse in Kansas City and made frequent visits home. On June 17, 1930, six months after Burke's arrival, Bonnie and "Richard F.

White" were married. The two drove north across the Iowa border to Centerville, collected Bonnie's aunt, Eliza Stuckey of 900 South Main Street, and neighbor Ethel Swanson and entered the Appanoose County Courthouse. On the walls of the sheriff's office in the same building were four photographs of Burke. They were assembled on a poster sent by the sheriff of Berrien County, Michigan. It offered a reward "for the capture of Frederick R. Burke, alias Thomas A. Camp, Fred Dane, Theo Cameron, F.A. Campbell, Jas F. Lewis, etc."[3]

Fred Burke mug shot. *Berrien County, Michigan, Sheriff's Department photo, public domain.*

Using yet another alias, Burke signed a marriage license with Bonnie Porter. He declared he was Richard F. White, his age thirty-four, his birthplace Kansas City, his place of residence De Kalb, Illinois. The two were married the same day by Centerville's new Lutheran minister, the Reverend Wenzel Bloom, at the church parsonage on East Walsh Street. Reverend Bloom later said he had had reservations. The bridegroom seemed too old for the bride, and he had "the appearance of a man who leads a somewhat loose sort of life …," but "he seemed a perfect gentleman."[4]

The couple left on an extensive honeymoon out West. On their return, they moved into rooms on Kansas City's Park Avenue and began negotiations to buy a home. Burke continued on his business trips and made occasional stays at the Porter home. Some people began to wonder about him. Ramah Peek noticed how he always lifted a child on his lap whenever he was in company. Saline Vance didn't like how he was always looking around over a crowd. "I think he's a hoodlum," she told her Aunt Etta and her daughter, Evelyn. "Hoodlum," "gangster" and "bootlegger" were all possible explanations for Burke and his money; the descriptions "killer" and "multiple killer" they never even dreamed. But then they, and Burke, hadn't reckoned with an alert twenty-nine-year-old attendant in Green City's Shell Gas Station.[5]

Joe Hunsaker was an insatiable reader of detective magazines. In 1929 and 1930, these magazines carried accounts of the St. Valentine's Day Massacre, the murder of policeman Charles Skelly and descriptions of the main suspect, Fred Burke. Hunsaker was suspicious, and when one of the magazines carried a photograph, he was sure. "The shape of his nose had been changed by an operation," said Hunsaker. "He had even changed his teeth …I could still see that he was Fred Burke."[6]

For a year and a half, Hunsaker watched Burke and tightened his evidence. He wrote to the Department of Justice in Washington, D.C., to J. Edgar Hoover, to the chief of police in St. Joseph, Missouri. He collaborated in secret with Green City businessman Allen Morrison. They maintained secrecy by sending letters by departing trains, avoiding the local post office where the addresses on their envelopes might start gossip. And when Hunsaker observed Burke was staying at the Porter home, he alerted authorities, and they took immediate action.

At first light, a few minutes before six o'clock on Thursday, March 26, 1931, the Porter home was surrounded. Four policemen from St. Joseph, Missouri, and three from Milan, the Sullivan County seat, were all armed with Tommy guns and shotguns. Burke was asleep when arrested and offered no resistance. He was processed in St. Joseph Police Station, Missouri, and extradited to St. Joseph, Michigan. He served a life sentence for the murder of Charles Skelly at Marquette State Penitentiary, dying there of natural causes on July 10, 1940. His wife, her parents, their relatives, friends and neighbors were shocked. They claimed no knowledge of his real identity or of his record. Bonnie moved to Chicago, visited him several times, divorced him and remarried.[7]

The discovery of Burke in a place as remote as rural Sullivan County, Missouri, was seen as part of a trend. The crime center of the nation is shifting, said the *Centerville Daily Iowegian.* Kansas City, "the Heart of America," has become its capital, attracting gunmen from Chicago, Detroit, St. Louis and Cleveland. The Union Station Massacre there and the kidnapping of leading citizens across the Midwest were all examples. Appanoose County, the *Centerville Daily Iowegian* continued, "because of its situation on the Iowa-Missouri line, and because of the cover offered in the hills to the south, has become a hide-out or vacation spot for major criminals when other places got too hot for them."[8]

It wasn't just the geography of crime that was shifting; so was its target. Bootlegging was being superseded by bank robbing, and the banks of Appanoose County were temptingly close to the Missouri border. As early as 1923, professional robbers were penetrating the area. A hole was bored into a bank at Bunch. Two business safes were blown in Moulton. The State Savings Bank in Moravia was robbed three times in eight years, losing a total of $10,300. The Dean Savings Bank, less than three miles from the border, was robbed for $1,000 on December 6, 1929. The Citizen's State Bank in nearby Cincinnati was held up twice: for $4,200 on May 26, 1932, for $1,000 on November 24, 1937.

On October 3, 1932, it was a bank on the Centerville Square—the Iowa Trust and Savings on the Eastside. A single gunman forced the assistant cashier, the bookkeeper and a customer to lie on the floor. He scooped $2,662 out of two counter drawers and fled. To authorities, the crime—in comparison to the others—seemed an amateur affair. The gunman was quickly identified and arrested. He was Jack Budiselich, born in Rathbun, who had lived in Chicago and by the age of nineteen had already compiled a long police record in both Chicago and Appanoose County.[9]

J. Edgar Hoover was noting that the nation's leading gangs were dashing about the Midwest, leaving a trail of bloodshed, and Iowa was part of their "crime corridor." Throughout the 1930s, local law enforcement officers were receiving alerts. In the vicinity were four robbers of a Kansas City bank who had kidnapped two Knoxville night watchmen; five Indiana escaped convicts; and two "Honeymoon bandits" who had robbed businesses in Osceola and married in Lancaster, Missouri. So were the associates of bank robbers: Harvey Bailey, who had introduced Fred Burke to Sullivan County; Machine Gun Kelly and his wife; Fred Barker; Alvin Karpis; Verne Miller; and Wilbur Underhill. In early March of 1934, when John Dillinger escaped from the Lake County Jail in Crown Point, Indiana, there were sightings of him and his gang members in Dubuque, Waterloo and Cedar Rapids. Federal officers scoured Iowa highways and tourist camps. Centerville police checked suspicious arrivals at the Continental Hotel. Captain Sandstrom of Company G, Iowa National Guard, received orders to have the hammers removed from the automatic pistols and the firing pins from the rifles stored in the local armory, rendering them useless should Dillinger attempt a robbery in Centerville.[10]

In the same months, Charles "Pretty Boy" Floyd was said to be using southern Iowa and northern Missouri as a "hang-out." He had relatives in Cincinnati and was known to visit them. He was seen walking in the street by a local minister. He and a female companion ate in the Blue Bird Cafe on the Square's Southside. On October 15, 1934, a car believed to be Floyd's, a burning wreckage of a Ford DeLuxe V8 sedan, was found three miles west of Numa. Bullet holes were seen in its body. State agent A.C. Height arrived to examine it. The car burned here, he said, perfectly answers descriptions of the one used by Floyd in a shoot-out four days previously in McIntire, Iowa. There were sightings of "Baby Face" Nelson. FBI agents searched for him at 625 West Maple—a home that rented rooms to travelers.[11]

But it was the two alerts involving the Barrows gang that aroused the greatest excitement. On July 29, 1933, the Wayne County sheriff's office telephoned Appanoose County deputy sheriff Ray Brunson requesting help.

Centerville's officers were asked to be armed and drive west on Highway 3 (today's Highway 2). A large green coupe with yellow wheels and a rumble seat, said to be carrying three members of the Barrows gang, had just turned east on the road out of Corydon. Wayne County officers were following. The joint pursuit was fruitless. Later came reports that the car had turned north. It was seen with three occupants—one lying down in the car as though injured. They were seen on the Clarkdale road, and on the same night a farmer's store in Plano was broken into and twenty dollars taken. It was five days after the gang's shoot-out at Dexter, Iowa. Clyde Barrow's brother Marvin was dying in a Perry hospital. Blanche, his wife, was under arrest in Des Moines. The remnants of the gang—Bonnie and Clyde and one other—the police thought were taking back roads, dodging and twisting to avoid capture. They were being pursued in eight states, stealing cars, abandoning them and burning them. By April 9, 1934, they were rumored to be back in the vicinity, stealing an Oldsmobile coupe in Indianola, burning it north of Mystic and again disappearing. The pattern ended with the death of Bonnie and Clyde, shot by a squad of Texas officers at Black Lake, about ninety miles south of Shreveport, Louisiana, on May 23, 1934. But new images were superimposing themselves—images more sinister than gangsters, more threatening than depressions.[12]

Chapter 56

World Aggressions Disturb Centerville

The images were coming to the town on radio reports, in newspapers and via Fox and Movietone newsreels at the Majestic and Ritz Theatres. Japanese soldiers using machine guns and bayonets were massacring twenty-seven hundred Chinese peasants, women and children in Manchuria.[1]

In Germany, Adolf Hitler came to power. Twenty thousand of his six hundred thousand brown-shirted stormtroopers massed and drilled in Berlin. They were goose-stepping, saluting swastika flags, wearing swastika armbands, raising their arms and shouting "Heil Hitler!" More than four thousand German Jews were fleeing into Czechoslovakia, another five hundred thousand into Spain. Clutching an ancient umbrella and a battered violin case, the world's best-known genius, Albert Einstein, boarded a ship at Bremen bound for America. Jews remaining in Germany were subjected to indignities. Their businesses were boycotted. Their doctors were restricted to autopsies and only on known Jewish bodies. They were ordered to surrender their passports. They were stripped of their civil rights. The names of their twelve thousand war dead—those who had died for Germany—were erased from memorial monuments.[2]

In Italy, Mussolini's black-shirted Fascists were in power. They were bombing and poison-gassing their way into Ethiopia. Mussolini and Hitler were forming an alliance. In Spain the two helped overturn a democratically elected government. They were testing their military equipment on the defenseless Spanish.[3]

Hitler was talking of "Lebensraum": more land for his people. The Saar, rich with its coal mines, iron and steel works, was returned to Germany by popular vote. Those who opposed became refugees. Newspaper photographs showed them carrying their children, their suitcases and their possessions and walking to new homes in France. Contravening international agreements, Germany was rearming. Conscription was introduced. An air force was created. German army officers were seen wearing gas masks.[4]

In England, the member of Parliament for Woodford, Winston Churchill, alert to the situation in Germany, was warning the British were in "mortal danger." The Royal Air Force opened eleven recruiting stations. The British voted for rearmament. So did the French, increasing their defense budget by 640 million francs (108 million U.S. dollars) and reinforcing the Maginot line, their 250-mile hidden fortifications in eastern France, from Flanders to Switzerland.[5]

In Centerville, Mrs. Dave Rosenbaum on South Main Street shared with her neighbors letters from her nephew, Lester Ziffren, UP's chief correspondent in Spain. Along with sharing fried shrimp, fresh bola cheese and beer with fellow war correspondent Ernest Hemingway in Madrid's cafes, he described to her the Nazi and Fascist bombings and the despair of the Spanish people. Similarly, letters came to Centerville families from sailors who had witnessed the bombardment of Bilbao; another came from Fred Evans, a representative of the Flexible Shaft Company of Chicago, to his father in Seymour, describing his escape from Pamplona, crossing the Pyrenees into France.[6]

People returning home from vacations in their countries of national origin—Santi Milani from Italy, Joe Shkolnick from Russia—had long reported ominous reactions to what was happening in Europe. Incoming immigrants from northern Italy had their own accounts. The Lira family of Numa hated Mussolini and everything fascism represented. Italian-American Mary Buttel was long traumatized by being slapped in a fourth-grade class in Giorgio di Perlena, Italy, for criticizing Mussolini. Missionary friends of the Presbyterian church, running hospitals, orphanages and churches in China, were writing to the Reverend Mott Sawyers for years of a rapidly deteriorating and threatening situation. Jesse Beck at the *Centerville Daily Iowegian* worried about his cousin, Roy Ghoulson, working at the Asia Life Insurance office in Shanghai, who wrote, "The Japanese have gone 'hog mad.'" And members of the B'nai Israel Synagogue on Fifteenth Street and Terry tried to work out strategies for getting aid to Jewish refugees.[7]

The reaction of most of the County's immigrants was in sharp contrast with their reaction to news of aggression before World War I. Then the immigrants were new arrivals, their separation from relatives, friends and the "old country" more immediate. At that time, they had besieged the *Centerville Daily Iowegian* office, seizing information from AP dispatches before they could be printed in the newspaper. But it was now twenty years later. The process of assimilation was underway. Many were well-established in the new country. They owned successful businesses and—what would have been an impossibility in their country of origin—they owned their own land. Their children were attending America's free public schools. Education offered them a direct route to opportunity and advancement. This the immigrants fully understood. They backed their schools. Even with the backdrop of Depression, they supported the creation of Centerville Junior College. And they backed their children. When the Rathbun boys' basketball team, too poor to have uniforms, qualified for State tournaments, a shaft bucket was lowered into coal mines and money raised for team jackets. In impoverished Numa, when the girls' team needed new basketball shoes, their fathers, working part-time in the coal mines, the rest of the time for the WPA, asked to buy them "on time." And when a new high school in Centerville was built replacing the one destroyed by fire, they were among the hundreds inspecting the new facilities.[8]

The reports of war and aggression in Europe and Japan seemed at first remote. Many hoped they'd stay that way. Some had bitter memories of America's intervention in World War I. Robert Fell, writing in the *Centerville Daily Iowegian* said, "…I want it distinctly understood I'll be hiding in Tahiti when the time comes for us to save poor, dear Europe's skin." Those in the town who were strongly isolationist agreed.[9]

It wasn't just the war that the people of the town were negotiating. There was the Depression, and then there was another issue—one that must have made the southern European immigrants wonder if their move to Iowa had been the right one. It was, again, the weather.

Chapter 57

Extreme Weather

By the mid 1930s, loose dirt propelled by high gales was blowing through the town. Rain fell, each drop forming a globule of mud. Housewives found clouds of dust settling in clean homes. It deposited on bedclothes, furniture, drapes, floors, walls and ceilings. It flew through cars with sealed windows. It was sucked into carburetors, damaging cylinder walls and pistons. Storm followed storm. They roared in from the west. High gales and blinding, choking clouds of dust arrived like dense fogs, obscuring lights, blotting out the sun. They came in different colors: reddish-brown, dun, violet, saffron. On Centerville Square, boys with brooms swept the dirt into the street, the wind promptly depositing it back on the sidewalks. Tons of shale were lifted off County roads. Farmers found spring seedlings uprooted, winter wheat damaged, ears of corn stripped from stalks. Rich farm soil was swept away. Out West it was far worse. In a May 1934 editorial, Jesse Beck stated that an estimated five million dollars of Texas soil had landed in Nebraska. Nebraska and South Dakota soil was landing in Iowa. Frank Swab, motoring to Centerville from his naval base in San Diego, drove through two hundred miles of it between Deming, New Mexico, and El Paso, Texas, barely able to see the radiator cap on his car. Graphic photographs appeared in the *Iowegian*: people in Boise City, Oklahoma, covering their faces with dust masks; handkerchiefs covered faces on the streets of Kansas City, where clouds of the dust were paralyzing traffic. In Hays, Kansas, drifts were reaching the roofs of houses; in Cimarron Valley, Oklahoma, to the tops of trees; at Gregory, South Dakota, to the eaves of barns. Letters arrived in Centerville describing conditions. One, on March 17,

1935, to Mrs. Raul Lockman in Moravia from her sister in Burdett, Kansas, said she didn't advise anybody to move west to live, "…to be thankful for the rain and mud of Iowa."[1]

And then came the winter and summer of 1936—the year of bad weather no one ever forgot.

It began on December 20, 1935, when the temperature was three degrees below zero. For the next eleven days of 1935 and fifty days of 1936, the mercury remained at zero or sub-zero. Thirty-six times it occasionally reached single positive digits, but between January 22 and February 20, it never came above zero, with a reading on the night of February 5 of twenty-four degrees below. It wasn't just the temperatures. Snow piled on snow, blizzard followed blizzard, with repeated lashing winds that lifted snow into deep drifts and froze them so solidly vehicles could drive across the tops. Trains stalled. Car brakes failed. Furnaces broke down. Water mains froze. Schools closed. Mail piled up at the post office. Petit jurors were unable to reach the courthouse. Grocers' supplies were short. Heating materials unavailable. Twenty-five truckloads of coal were snowbound at Jerome, more near Numa. Entrances to coal mines were blocked. Miners dug their way to work, then became marooned inside coal shafts. People chopped up their garages and their porch columns. They burned corncobs and cornstalks. People sought refuge. City Hall opened at night; so did the steam-heated buildings and the Dinning building on the Square's Southeast Corner. The National Guard cleared Rock Island tracks and yards. Highway employees worked days and nights to keep roads open. They dynamited drifts. One south of Streepyville was higher than an automobile and longer than several hundred feet.[2]

Animals froze and died, a dead dog like a statue against a fence between Centerville and Mystic, birds in full flight, others dropping off barber poles and porches. People died. They suffered from pneumonia, from bronchitis and from being too cold. Funerals were delayed. Friends of the deceased dug pathways through cemeteries. Doctors traveled to the sick on sleighs, skis and snowshoes. Dr. Leffert gave telephone instructions to a Unionville neighbor who was attending the birth of Mrs. Rolly Morrison's baby. He left at midnight to reach her, arriving at six o'clock the next evening. He drove two miles on the Rock Island track. He repeated this on his return journey, to be almost hit by the westbound Apache Limited.[3]

The severe cold weather ended on February 22. The spring that followed was brief. On June 19 the temperature reached 100 degrees both day and night. On July 15, with the mercury reaching 110 degrees, an egg was successfully fried on a heavy iron manhole cover at the intersection of

Main and Maple Streets. Discarded turkey eggs at the Merritt Farm south of Seymour spontaneously hatched. Vegetation dried. Crops were ruined. Fire swept fields of tinder-dry grass. People died of heat stroke. The healthy suffered prostration and exhaustion. The feet of Centerville's prize-winning band, marching in the streets of Kansas City, stuck to melting hardtop. The brass players stopped playing, unable to bear the brass pieces in their mouths, and the reed players, including E-flat clarinetist Himie Voxman, spat into their instruments to keep them from drying out. In a fifteen-minute hailstorm on July 20, temperatures dropped twenty degrees. By August 13 the heat returned, remaining at or above 100 degrees for a further sixteen days.[4]

But despite the vagaries of Iowa weather, despite deteriorating international news, despite the Depression, life for the people of the town proceeded with some normalcy. They paid $6.35 for special coach, round-trip excursions on the Rock Island trains to the Chicago World's Fair. They danced to Jimmy Toussaint or "King of the Accordion" Louis—or Lawrence—Welk at the Dreamland Ballroom in Mystic and to Dale Larson's nine-piece orchestra at the armory. They heard the Augustana Cappella Singers from Rock Island at the high school auditorium and Centerville's own singers taking part at Easter performances of Handel's *Messiah*. At the Majestic and the Ritz, they watched their favorite movie stars: Shirley Temple and Charlie Chaplin, Fred Astaire and Ginger Rogers in *Top Hat*, Clark Gable and Claudette Colbert in *It Happened One Night*. Everyone in town tuned their radios on May 5, 1934, when Mack Garner, a member of Centerville's famous jockey family, won the Kentucky Derby, riding Cavalcade, and then rushed to see the event on Fox newsreel at the Majestic Theatre.[5]

Circuses, carnivals, stunt-flying shows and one-day exhibitions still arrived in town. They came with their processions of animals, acrobats, freaks and oddities, their musical bands, fluttering flags and their distinctive odors of sawdust, tan bark, popcorn and candy floss. In September 1935, from Long Beach, California, there were two penguins, Ike and Mike, a giant octopus and Madame Sirwell's troupe of trained fleas that kicked footballs, juggled, pushed little carts, danced and ran a merry-go-round. They were exhibited with a sixty-eight-ton whale in a one-hundred-foot, specially constructed steel railroad car secured on the I.S.U. depot siding just off the Northeast Corner of the Square. D.D. Roland, "the human fly," scaled the outside wall of the National Bank on the Square's Northside, shifting to the corner twenty feet from the top, unaided except for his own hands and feet. He then walked the roof ledge blindfolded, with his wife astride his neck.[6]

Mack Garner astride Cavalcade. *Courtesy of Appanoose County Historical Society.*

But much of the activity revolved around education. The 1930s and the 1940s were considered a "golden age" for local schools. Students were winning academic awards; their debate teams winning contests, the Centerville High School band regional and national prizes, its individual members number-one ratings year after year. For many, these were the first steps in prominent careers. Centerville superintendent Everett Fannon coaxed boys who'd left school early and were working in coal mines to return and join the football team. For twenty-eight games, the team never lost. In the 1935 season, it was undefeated and untied. Centerville's girls' basketball team, the Redettes, went to State championships five times. They won the championship in 1935 and again in 1936 and were finalists in 1937 and 1938.[7]

In the County's small communities, the first-generation daughters of the immigrant coal miners took to basketball with a vengeance. The girls' team at

Mystic went to the State championships three times; the girls at Numa, despite a school enrollment of less than fifty, went to the State championship games four times in seven years; the girls at Numa's arch rival, neighboring Seymour, qualified for State championship play a record of fifteen times. In the 1941 State tournament, Numa beat Seymour in the semifinals and won the State championship. Revenge for Seymour would come six years later when they beat Numa in the 1947 State championship final. Numa's 1941 team was described by authority P.H. Jarman as "the greatest ever to win a state title." The team called itself the "Minerettes." Three of them had Croatian names: Zunich, Kauzlarich and Tometich. A fourth, cocaptain Eleanor Lira, had parents from northern Italy who were the fierce opponents of Mussolini and the Fascists.[8]

These academic and sports successes were silver linings for the community in a dark time. The international news reports were making it ever darker.

Chapter 58

New World Aggressions: Hitler Invades

New aggressions, new crises were dominating newspaper headlines. Japanese forces were attacking along the length of the Chinese coast, ringing Shanghai, penetrating inland, bombarding NanKing, exploding railroad cars packed with Chinese refugees off railroad tracks and killing another two thousand in Canton. A *Centerville Daily Iowegian* reporter watched a film at the Majestic Theatre. It was a documentary with unedited pictures of the bombing and atrocities in Peiping. He was shaken. "No parades, no lilting bands, no gold braid and flashing sabers," he wrote, "…just blood, misery, pain, horror, detached arms and legs, crushed heads and dead bodies." Children in one Centerville home looked over their 1937 Christmas presents and placed those marked "Made in Japan" in the ashcan.[1]

In Europe, Hitler had sent Nazi troops goose-stepping across bridges into the demilitarized Rhineland. The French, watching from their Maginot line, reported 56,000 regular German troops and 250,000 of other military groups were on their border. Some were erecting the German version of a fortified trench: the Siegfried Line.[2]

In March 1938, Hitler's troops were marching over borders again—this time into Austria. Tens of thousands of cheering Austrians lined the streets of Vienna. Swastikas flew over the chancellery and the Schoenbrunn Palace. They flew in villages. Flowers decorated stores. Inscriptions were seen: "Welcome to our Fuehrer." One-hundred-and-twenty-foot pylons supporting golden eagles and oak-wreathed German flags were built at intervals along Vienna's main street, and a sign was placed at the front of a fashionable city restaurant: "No Jews wanted."[3]

Jewish lawyers were ejected from the Vienna Bar Association; Jewish physicians from Vienna's emergency hospital. Vienna's orchestra conductor and opera director, Bruno Walter, was dismissed. Eighty-two-year-old psychoanalyst Sigmund Freud, seriously ill after being visited by Nazi police, was moved to London after friends paid a large sum of money to the Nazis. The Jews in Vienna were forced to tear down their own synagogues. A photograph, smuggled out to the Central Press, appeared in the *Centerville Daily Iowegian.* It showed elderly Jews force-scrubbing the streets of Vienna, supervised by smiling Nazi officers. The death rate of Jews jumped from 4 to 140 per day. Those attempting to leave the country found all borders closed. A secret underground helped one thousand into Switzerland. Some jumped from trains. Seven thousand committed suicide.[4]

In Germany their plight was even worse. Polish Jews living in Germany were rousted from their beds at night and ordered to leave the country. Thousands were herded into what were termed "concentration points." Jews were forbidden to leave their homes except with police permission. They were ordered not to appear on Berlin's principal streets, in public buildings, national memorials, theaters and other public places. Using the excuse of the assassination of a German diplomat in Paris by a young Jew, mobs roamed the streets of Berlin, Cologne, Hamburg, Dresden and Vienna. Dozens of synagogues were raided, desecrated or burned. At night, every Jewish storefront was smashed. Shards of broken glass littered sidewalks and streets, giving the November 1938 event the name Kristallnacht. Jews were levied a 20 percent tax to pay the four-hundred-million-dollar fine imposed by the Nazis, who held all Jews responsible for the assassination. The tax was to be collected in four installments. No mercy would be accorded, the government continued, in this, "...the last chapter of the Jewish question in Germany." Hundreds of Jews were being arrested and taken to undisclosed locations.[5]

Boatloads of Jews were attempting to reach Peru, Chile, Bolivia and Colombia. There was talk of them finding land in lower California, British Guiana, Tanganyika. They were turned away from Romania and Turkey. Nine hundred and twenty aboard the Hamburg-America liner *St. Luis* were refused permission to enter Cuba. They were refused entry to the United States. The *St. Luis* was forced to return to Germany. Antisuicide committees patrolled the decks.[6]

In the *Centerville Daily Iowegian* office, the news items sent by Associated Press reporters were disgorged at a sixty-words-a-minute clip from two AP teletype machines, photographs from a Wirephoto machine. Their constant automatic chattering attracted much attention. People came to watch. It was in this way many read of Howard Hughes's record-breaking flight around the world. They watched as a photograph of Hughes's ticker-tape welcome in New York City appeared and identified Al Lodwick from Mystic, Hughes's indispensable manager, sitting to his left, dressed in a white suit. But in the arrival of news, there was competition.[7]

On May 12, 1937, Charles DePuy and his two daughters were awake at four in the morning to hear the coronation of King George VI broadcast live from London, England, and carried over all radio networks. DePuy noticed lights in houses across the town. Others were listening, too.[8]

Until this date, radio emphasized entertainment: Bing Crosby, Edgar Bergen, Amos 'n' Andy, the ill-timed broadcast production by Orson Welles of H.G. Wells's *War of the Worlds* and, from the powerful fifty-thousand-watt WHO station in Des Moines, sports reporter Ronald "Dutch" Reagan. There were exceptions. News took priority over entertainment for election results, the inauguration of a president, the Scopes Monkey Trial and Herbert Morrison's emotional description of the Hindenburg disaster.[9]

One year later to the day of King George's coronation, on May 12, 1938, people in Centerville and across the nation tuned in to the Columbia

Albert Lodwick (in the white suit) with Howard Hughes. *With permission from Bettmann/Corbis.*

Broadcasting System. They heard a live news report from London. In England, it was eleven thirty at night; it was six thirty in the evening in New York, five thirty in Centerville. What people heard that night was transformative. It was the first live, uncensored eyewitness account of the Anschluss, Hitler's takeover of Austria. The reporter was William L. Shirer, a native of Cedar Rapids, who had witnessed the Nazis marching into Vienna and, to avoid Nazi censorship, had flown to London to deliver his report from the headquarters of the British Broadcasting Corporation. Radio's unprecedented speed and immediacy catapulted radio journalism to the forefront of news dissemination. It was the brainchild of Edward R. Murrow, twenty-nine years old, living in London, who could see the evil of Nazism and the urgent need to inform Americans.[10]

Murrow had already hired Shirer. He now assembled a team of talented, courageous, young American reporters and distributed them to key European cities. CBS began broadcasting evening news "roundups," with the reporters telling their news stories live from Europe to America, hours before the stories appeared in print. Other networks followed. Across Centerville, people tuned in at seven each night. For the Smallwoods in Mystic, the Morrows in Moulton, the Harringtons in Unionville, work and conversations stopped. Families listened together. As the situation in Europe deteriorated further, entertainment programs were interrupted with increasingly ominous bulletins. And when reports were undermined by poor transmission, the strong WHO/NBC station in Des Moines with a young news director, Jack Shelley, moved to the forefront.[11]

By October 1938, Hitler's Nazis marched into the dismembered Sudetenland. Six months later, he bullied his way across a frontier he had guaranteed to respect and invaded Czechoslovakia. Trapped inside the country was the Adam Slaka family of Centerville. Almost immediately Hitler was looking east again, this time to Poland. England and France, both participants in the dismemberment and sellout of Czechoslovakia, now promised to defend Poland.[12]

No one now was in any doubt of Hitler's intentions. Borders were closing. The frontier of Hungary at Czechoslovakia appeared a solid wall of barbed wire, steel and concrete. The troops of Belgium were mobilized. So were those of the Netherlands. Sweden called up a reserve class for "preparedness service." The U.S. Department of State constructed bombproof shelters in U.S. embassies and consulates in Europe. In France, leave was canceled for members of the army, navy and air force. French women replaced men in civil positions. Trainloads of three hundred thousand reservists were sent to reinforce the Maginot line, many moving silently to the trains at Gare de l'Est as if they'd been practicing for it since the last war. A partial blackout of

French coastal cities was undertaken. The French Ministry of Public Works ordered the evacuation of Paris. Nurses in the American Hospital in the city were issued gas masks and flashlights.[13]

In Britain, a case of emergency was said to exist. Talk was openly of "the next war." Income tax was increased from 25 percent to 27.5 percent. All leave for the country's armed forces was canceled. Officers and men were called to operate antiaircraft guns, searchlights and air defenses. Munitions factories were operating on twenty-four-hour schedules. The royal throne was removed from Westminster Abbey to an undisclosed location. Air-raid shelters were built in back gardens; one was created in a dungeon at Windsor Castle for the king, queen and two princesses; one in the grounds of Guy's Hospital in London was dug by the nurses for the patients. Roadside signs were removed. In London, through nights of drizzling rain, elderly men dug trenches in parks and vacant lots. Neighbors brought out bread and butter and steaming pots of tea. Tape was placed in criss-cross pattern across windows. Volunteers went door to door with instructions of how to prevent any display of light at night. At London Zoo, plans were made to kill poisonous snakes and spiders should bombing cause a danger of their escape. People were fitted with gas masks. Children evacuated from London's Docklands on trains to country areas to escape the bombing, carrying their gas masks over their shoulders. Very small children were issued bright red masks with floppy Mickey Mouse noses. For babies, larger masks with padded interiors were supplied.[14]

Americans living in Europe were urged to return to the United States. Warships, cruisers and destroyers sped across the Atlantic to help collect them. The U.S. minister to Prague, the U.S. ambassador and the commercial attaché in Berlin were recalled to Washington. Before he left, the ambassador to Germany urged all Americans to return home. So did Joseph P. Kennedy, the ambassador in London, the ambassador in Poland and the ambassador in Paris. In London, steamship offices were jammed with Americans booking passages. Three ships left Britain with record manifests. Americans at Le Havre fought for cots set up in salons and recreation rooms aboard the *Ile de France*. Charles H. Schwab, the seventy-seven-year-old chairman of Bethlehem Steel, recovering from a heart attack, was carried aboard the liner *Washington* at Southampton, passing hundreds of cots lining lounges and passageways. The *Manhattan* added five hundred extra cots to transport seventeen hundred home.[15]

By June 1939, Winston Churchill said war was likely by July, August or September. On August 24, *Centerville Daily Iowegian* reporter Charles DePuy walked to the courthouse and around the Square, interviewing people on the street. All condemned Hitler. One called him a madman. Most, like Tom Olds at O.K. Furniture, believed a war was going to happen "…but I hope they keep it on the other side of the water." Next day, August 25, editor Jesse Beck wrote, "As this Editorial is written on the afternoon before its publication, there is no assurance that a general European war will not be waging by the time this is printed …Only undreamed of diplomacy or an act of Providence can prevent it." There were six days to go.[16]

In the *Centerville Daily Iowegian* office on South Main Street on August 30, Charles DePuy complained that the continuous "They will," "They won't," "They will," "They won't," "They are," "They aren't," "They are," "They aren't" created a jittery clattering of the teletype machines that was irksome. He was ready "…to quit worrying and go fishing." He didn't. German troops, German tanks, German aircraft and German armored cars were already moving into position on the Polish border. On September 1, Poland was invaded. British prime minister Neville Chamberlain declared, "…unless Germany would suspend aggressive action and withdraw her forces from Poland, Britain would unhesitatingly fulfill her obligations to Poland." The French agreed. There was no reply. On September 3, England and France declared war on Germany. War in Europe was underway.[17]

Charles DePuy again walked Centerville Square seeking local reactions. All held Hitler responsible. Many thought the world would be a better place without him. Some suggested his annihilation. Mayor W.R. Blakeslee hoped the war would stay in Europe. Insurance and realtor Bill Cree thought Americans were still trying to figure out why they'd got into the last war: "If we jump into another scrap it will be the same thing again." For Drake University student Jack Trimble, there was another reaction: "We'll be marching before long."[18]

Chapter 59

Military Preparations at Home

Jack Trimble's prediction was shared by Jesse Beck, the *Centerville Daily Iowegian*'s editor, who had wondered for months if the United States was actively preparing for war. Associated Press news items seemed confirmation. The War Department was planning to train 100,000 civilian pilots and 125,000 mechanics. President Roosevelt was asking for a national defense budget of $552,000,000 to build Atlantic and Pacific bases, for airplane construction, to improve seacoast defenses, to strengthen the Panama Canal Zone and to assemble ammunition, guns, rifles, tanks and gas masks.[1]

By spring 1939, people watched equipment never before issued to the local National Guard unit—Company G, 168th Infantry—arriving at Centerville's armory, just off the Square on East Jackson Street. There were bright green trench mortars, automatic rifles five times more effective than previous models and complete new uniforms of cotton and elastique cloth, straight legs replacing traditional breeches. Recruiting officers arrived from Ottumwa with more frequency. They interviewed possible recruits in a room at the post office.[2]

By August, when the British were digging air-raid shelters and Americans in Europe were booking passages to get home, Company G was ordered into an "Emergency Mock War Drill." The company was to imagine an "enemy" had driven through Numa. Troops were landing from planes. They were taking over Centerville Airport. Captain Dewey Bear mobilized his men. Under full equipment at seven in the evening on Saturday, August 5, they emerged from the armory and marched south out of town. The enemy engaged them in mock maneuvers: combat at the lower reservoir, strafing from an armored car on the upper reservoir dam and a machine-gun attack at the airport before Company G successfully retook it, established order and then pitched camp in the dark.[3]

Thousands of miles and one month away, on September 1, Poland was invaded in "blitzkrieg"—lightning war. Shrieking Stuka aircraft, equipped with sirens to increase their scream, dive-bombed, terrorizing both soldiers and civilians. The attacks were precisely coordinated with seventeen hundred tanks and 1,516,000 marching panzer troops. They were blowing up trains, rail lines, supply depots and stations full of mobilizing soldiers. They were strafing streams of fleeing refugees. They destroyed the Polish air force on the ground. Within twenty-four hours, the Luftwaffe controlled the Polish skies. On September 3, England and France declared war on Germany. World War II was on. It cast a pall over the town of Centerville.[4]

Of all the people of Appanoose County, those in the highest state of anxiety were Centerville's Jews. They were emigrants from Poland and Russia. They had family members still there, part of Poland's 3.5 million Jewish population, the largest in Europe. They knew the plight of Jews in every country occupied by the Nazis. They now feared for their relatives. From his new home on the corner of Drake Avenue and Terry Street, Joe Goldstein, the owner of Centerville's Economy Cleaners, was using all means to contact his family in Warsaw without success. An AP report on the front page of the *Centerville Daily Iowegian* on September 12 gave some comfort. Every thirty seconds—each night, every night—from Warsaw's radio station, the eleven opening notes of Chopin's Polonaise in A Flat were played on a xylophone. Polish composer Frederic Chopin died in Paris in 1849, but his heart for ninety years lay buried in Warsaw's Church of the Holy Cross. The notes were a signal to the world that Poland still lived.[5]

Centerville's Jews were ardent Zionists, supporters of a homeland for Jews in Palestine and long-term contributors to the national United Palestine Appeal. In this they were supported by Centerville's BPW, the Wednesday Club, the Association of Commerce, the Methodist church and ordinary citizens of Centerville and Ottumwa, who contributed four thousand dollars in 1939. Joe Frankel, owner of the department store on the Southwest Corner of Centerville Square, was a member of the National Council for Palestine and Iowa's 1939 sole delegate to the National Jewish Conference in Washington, D.C. Together at their synagogue on the corner of Seventeenth and Terry Streets, Centerville's Jews met to pray, to support each other and to repeat together the words of Psalm 137, rededicating themselves to Jerusalem.[6]

On September 17, the Russians, in a startling—and temporary—pact with the Nazis, invaded Poland from the east. The Poles were caught in a vise, their country divided between Germans and Russians. On September 27, an announcer on Warsaw radio said, "We will never give in while one of us is alive." The announcement was followed by silence. That night, the sound of the xylophone was no more. The following day, a Polish flier escaped his country through a barrage of German shells. "In a husky voice," said the *Centerville Daily Iowegian*'s AP report, he told of the starvation, the incessant rumblings of siege guns and the civilians creeping from cellars during lulls of artillery fire and air raids to bury their dead in parks and public places. A pall of black smoke hung over Warsaw. "From the air the city is a horrible sight," he said. "Hardly a building is intact."[7]

In his home on Drake Avenue, Joe Goldstein again tried to contact his family in Warsaw. Failure was the result. It was all too much. Joe died of a heart attack on Monday, October 23. It was six weeks after the Nazi invasion of Poland. Joe was fifty-three years old.[8]

As Poland succumbed, the people of the town were reading that Canada, Australia, New Zealand and South Africa all were entering the war in support of Great Britain. They saw photographs in the *Centerville Daily Iowegian* showing Canadian militiamen in Halifax, Nova Scotia, bidding good-bye to their families, and tarpaulined aircraft minus their wings being loaded by cranes onto vessels in New York, bound for England.[9]

For some months, Hitler was holding his fire against the French and the British. It was called "the phony war." It wasn't without incident. German submarines and mines were sinking British ships. On the second day of the war, it included the British liner *Athenia* off the Hebrides, on its way to America. It sank with a loss of 117 passengers, 28 of them Americans. One of the survivors was nineteen-year-old Martha Bonnett of Chariton. On her return home, she spoke in Centerville to a full Methodist church, describing the night of terror.[10]

Then suddenly, dramatically, the seven-month "phony war" in western Europe was over. Without warning, on April 9, 1940, the Germans invaded Denmark and Norway. One month later, on May 10, using the terrorizing blitzkrieg tactics they'd perfected on the Spanish and the Poles, they invaded Holland, Belgium and Luxembourg. They bypassed the Maginot line, smashed through the Ardennes, invaded northern France and cut off thousands of British Expeditionary Forces trapped on the beaches of Dunkirk and subjected them to continuous Stuka attacks. The people of England's southeast coast took action. They crossed the English Channel in sailing boats, fishing boats, rowing boats, anything that would move on water and save lives. Winston Churchill, about to become prime minister of England, hoped in this way 30,000 men could be saved. The actual number was 338,220. It included 123,095 Frenchmen, rescued to fight again. The Germans now swung south. In two weeks they cut the French army to pieces, and by June 14, two months after their invasion of Denmark and Norway, they were marching into Paris.[11]

For those two months, the people of Centerville, like those of the nation, heard and read the news and reeled. Businessmen John Jensen and Pete Hansen, both immigrants from Denmark—Hansen with four hundred family members in one Danish city—failed to get responses from relatives. Neither could others from western Europe, including Norwegian immigrant Ann Henshaw, whose cousins Gudrun, Finn and Sigrid lived in Oslo, which was then being bombed. It was early May. It was tulip time in Pella, the Iowa city sixty miles north of Centerville that each year celebrated its Dutch heritage. The news of the invasion of Holland, said Jesse M. Beck, who was visiting the festival with his wife and friends—the Barney Fullers and the Jack Warrens—cast gloom over the event. The people of Pella and the thousands of visitors that day paused to pray and send a cablegram of concern and sympathy to the citizens of Holland.[12]

One hundred and ninety miles southwest of Centerville, 133 of the town's high school musicians were in Kansas City. They had participated there in the National-Regional High School Music Contest. They were waiting for the Rock Island gates to open at Union Station for their return train to Centerville. Thousands of people thronged around them. Newspaper boys were hawking war headlines. Groups of people stood reading the headlines. War was the topic from radio loudspeakers; war was the talk on every tongue. Just then, through some spontaneous mutual action, the Centerville boys and girls began to sing "The Star-Spangled Banner." Everyone in the station came to attention, loudspeakers were silenced, hats were removed and hush replaced the earlier hubbub. The event brought tears to the eyes of hundreds, and those who heard it, those who were there, said they would never forget it.[13]

Chapter 60

The Nation Recruits, Murrow Broadcasts, the Red Cross Appeals, Company G Leaves

As it was in Kansas City's Union Station, as it was across the nation, war was now the talk of Centerville. Faces were long, conversation animated. Newspaper carrier boys shouted AP headlines from street corners. NBC, CBS and Mutual reporters described scenes daily from Europe on radio. A loudspeaker on the outside of Harry Luther's store carried late bulletins.[1]

President Roosevelt, addressing a joint session of the House and Senate said, "These are ominous days ...days of swift and shocking developments." He asked for a defense budget increase of $890,000,000 for the U.S. Army, the U.S. Navy and the Marine Corps and stressed the need to immediately and urgently develop U.S. air supremacy. Jesse Beck, on Monday, May 13, in his first editorial since the blitzkrieg of Holland, Belgium and Luxembourg, wrote, "We are coming to a terrible dilemma ...Will we stay out?" Robert Fell, the same *Centerville Daily Iowegian* writer who'd said six years earlier he'd be hiding in Tahiti if asked to defend "poor, dear, Europe's skin," now asked, "Must we wait for Hitler and Company to stub their toes and break their necks?"[2]

Britain stood alone. "We have just one more battle to win," Hitler's propaganda minister Joseph Goebbels, talking of Britain, told cheering thousands. In response, Winston Churchill, now Britain's prime minister, told his people he had nothing to offer "...but blood, toil, tears and sweat." With the invasion of the island imminent, he said, "We shall fight on the beaches, we shall fight on the landing grounds, we shall fight in the hills; we shall never surrender..." The speech went around the world. It was reported on the front page of the *Centerville Daily Iowegian*. *Time* magazine, sold in Allen's bookstore on the Square's Eastside, carried it in full.[3]

Within weeks, extra military recruiting officers were in town, bolstering local efforts. Enlistments were sought for cavalry, for infantry, for engineers, for medical detachments. Representatives of the Civil Aeronautics Authority arrived and made arrangements with Centerville Junior College to open an aviation school at the airport. Student pilots, required to be enrolled in a college or graduated from one, signed up in Junior College rooms on the top floor of the high school.[4]

At the armory, Captain Dewey Bear received orders to—again—increase the size of Company G. By August the company was in training with fifty thousand other Midwestern guardsmen at Camp Riley, Minnesota. They were issued M-1 rapid-fire rifles, four new light machine guns and were called to serve for twelve months active duty.[5]

On September 16, 1940, President Roosevelt signed the nation's first peacetime conscription bill. A month later, on Sunday, October 16, American men aged twenty-one to thirty-six were signing up for the draft at the rate of 1,250,000 an hour. In Centerville, the Square was ringed with flags. Loudspeakers broadcast repeated renditions of "God Bless America" and the national anthem. The sun was shining. Local men signed up at six uptown precincts and at twenty-four more precincts in the County's townships. Lines formed. They included traveling men and transients. There were medical examinations. Each man took the oath of allegiance. There was much bantering. The men made mock farewells, calling each other "Sarge" or "Corp" and saluting.[6]

Serial numbers were assigned to the recruits. They were posted at the foot of the stairs leading up to the local Selective Service office on the second floor of the Centerville National Bank, on the Square's Southside. On October 29, the men gathered in groups around radios as the numbers of the first draft were announced from Washington, D.C. One by one, each number, encased in a cobalt blue capsule, was drawn from a large glass bowl by blindfolded government officials. Secretary of War Henry Stimson drew the first at 12:16 p.m. EST. It was number 158. Six thousand, one hundred and seventy-five men in the nation's 6,175 draft areas held the 158 number. They were the first men drafted for military service. In Appanoose County, number 158 was Marvin Luse of Mystic. "I'm rarin' to go," he said.[7]

As America was arming itself that summer and fall of 1940, Britain was in mortal peril. Prior to invading across twenty-six miles of the English Channel, the Nazi Luftwaffe was bombing the British, attempting to eliminate the Royal Air Force (RAF), paralyze the country and demoralize its people. This "Battle of

Britain" began in earnest on July 10, 1940. It continued across August, reaching its violent crescendo in September with daylight bombings of London, then in October and November bombings at night.[8]

Across Centerville, across Appanoose County, across the nation, people in comfortable living rooms were tuning their radios to hear Winston Churchill's speeches to the British people carried over U.S. networks. They heard American correspondents' reports from London. Night after night, CBS's Ed Murrow began with three words, a characteristic pause over the first: "This …is London." He took his microphone onto rooftops and onto streets. American listeners heard the warning sirens, the sounds of British feet walking without panic to air-raid shelters. They heard the sounds of bombs falling, the antiaircraft guns, the whistles of police officers and air-raid wardens, the bells of ambulances. *March of Time* newsreels, shown at the Majestic Theatre, showed the devastation of London, graphic pictures of its victims, young RAF pilots racing to their Spitfires and Hurricanes and rising to intercept the incoming Dornier bombers with their escorts of Messerschmitts. American reporters, sharing their experiences and their dangers, were identifying with the British people. So were most Americans.[9]

Thousands of Americans were already embedded in Allied infantry divisions. Rumors existed of a secret American Expeditionary Force fighting in Europe in Canadian uniforms. A Roosevelt—Kermit, President Teddy Roosevelt's son—declaring the fight against Nazism "a clear cut moral issue," was a second lieutenant in the British Army. A group had joined the RAF calling themselves "the Eagle Squadron." Hundreds were flying instructors in Canada. Dozens were ferrying England-bound planes. Some of these planes were seen over Centerville. They were all metal, devoid of insignia, twin-motored and with mid wings.[10]

The people of Appanoose County were no exception in their sympathy with the British. On Flag Day, speaker Reverend Dr. H.E. Trimble said, "Our sympathies are all with the Allies." A song, written by Centerville's Mrs. E.J. Riepe began,

Help Britain all we can
Pray with all our might for valiant Englishmen…

Centerville people volunteered to adopt British refugee children. They started a Bundles for Britain organization. Donated shoes were collected in a barrel placed on the Square's Westside, outside Dunham's Central Shoe Store. It was painted red, white and blue. Centerville mayor T.J. McIntire was the first to make a contribution. Knitting clubs were started. Knitting needles flashed furiously at parties and social gatherings. The country club was as thick with knitters as it was with golfers. Children in Mystic's seventh-grade class learned to knit and purl, making sweaters for Norwegian refugees in England.[11]

Money was collected for the people of Finland, for the people of Greece, for the American Red Cross that was desperately coping with millions of exhausted, frightened, hungry, homeless refugees streaming out of Dutch, Belgian and French cities. In Centerville there was a "Blitzkrieg of Mercy." Pilot Douglas Alexander, his aircraft mimicking a Stuka, complete with a siren, "dive-bombed" every town in the County, dropping not bombs but five thousand pamphlets requesting money and assistance for the Red Cross. Carter English, the manager of the Majestic Theatre, donated an upstairs room for the organization. It became a center to assemble and ship surgical equipment, money for British ambulances, baby layettes, garments, scarves, gloves and socks for children, for adults and for refugees.[12]

Stories of local Nazi sympathizers circulated. One in Moravia and one in Moulton were said to have contributed money to pro-Hitler organizations. There was a sudden rush of applications for U.S. citizenship. At Garfield School, preparation classes were held two nights a week. Successful applicants entered the courthouse and emerged waving small American flags. Remaining aliens, three hundred of them, were registered and fingerprinted at the post office.[13]

Just after Thanksgiving, on November 27, 1940, the first two County men in the first peacetime draft were called to service. They were Clarence Bandy, an African American, and James Harry Morrow. Both were volunteers, preempting Marvin Luse, who had already enlisted in the County's National Guard, Company G. A special T-bone steak dinner was served to them at the Blue Bird Cafe before they left on a Rock Island train to Des Moines en route to Fort Snelling, Minnesota. Within weeks, three more were called to service: Sanford Rosenbaum, whose brother Theodore had already enlisted, Theodore Roosevelt Bishop of Moulton and, on January 10, 1941, the first to be drafted from Seymour: Max Morrow. Jesse Beck wrote, "...one by one, youths have sort of quietly slipped away from this community to take their places in various divisions of our army and navy."[14]

The Commander in Chief of that army and navy, President Roosevelt, had been reelected in November 1940 for a third term. He was sworn into office on January 20, 1941. The next morning, Company G received mobilization orders. On March 1, led by Captain Dewey Bear, eighty men marched out of the armory and down Drake Avenue singing the "Iowa Corn Song." Thousands lined the streets. They were completely silent. Some were crying. Precisely at 10 a.m., the company departed on a Rock Island train en route to Camp Claiborne, eighteen miles south of Alexandria, Louisiana. Their intended stay was for one year.[15]

By early April 1941, war materials were being transported on Rock Island and Milwaukee freight trains at high rates of speed across the County. Army planes and bombers were seen flying daily over Centerville Airport. Convoys of canvas-covered army trucks, Red Cross ambulances and motorcycle couriers were escorted through town by highway patrol officers, their destinations unstated. Children watched from the windows of the Central School on Drake Avenue. A bug-like U-boat fighter was displayed on the Square. Army jeeps were demonstrated out at the County fairground, car enthusiasts in awe of their four-wheel drive. People donated blood at the district health office in the courthouse. At the post office, under a sign that read, "Faith in America My Country," they bought ten thousand dollars in U.S. defense bonds. Government classes were held to teach industrial skills to meet the growing demand for trained workers in defense shops and factories. Four aircraft companies conducted interviews at the Continental Hotel and the junior high school for aviation workers. The Hercules plant in South Centerville received War Department contracts for thirty-foot-long, steel shell-loading tables, for work benches, for two-wheeled steel carts and for flask lugs for Rolls Royce aircraft engines.[16]

It seemed to the people of the town that the country was moving inexorably toward war. Jesse Beck felt the country was committing itself against Germany "almost as definitely as if we'd made a declaration of war." President Roosevelt's fireside chat on May 27 provided them all with confirmation.[17]

Chapter 61

Roosevelt Speaks to the World, Germany Attacks Russia, First Aluminum Drive

On the evening of Tuesday, May 27, across the County, across the nation, people sat by their radios. The president delivered his fireside chat into a cluster of microphones at a desk in the East Room of the White House. Facing him, seated in a semicircle, were key diplomats; behind him, massed closely together, twenty-one American flags. He told the nation that "an unlimited national emergency" existed. Hitlerism, he said, must be "forcibly checked now." He asserted the doctrine of "freedom of the seas" and said the delivery of goods to Britain was imperative: "I say this can be done; it must be done; it will be done." The speech was carried by direct radio transmission to every corner of the world. It was translated into fourteen different languages. In Berlin it was branded "an open act of war." Crowds, gathered in London hotels before dawn to hear the speech, cheered throughout the broadcast. In Canberra, in Ottawa, throughout Britain's empire, the president's words were heard with jubilation.[1]

Events moved swiftly. A second draft registration was announced for all men who reached the age of twenty-one since the first registration on October 16, 1940. Appanoose County's 126 eligible men reported to the County draft board office over the Centerville National Bank on the Square's Southside. At the same time, new recruiters for the navy and the Marines arrived in town and interviewed applicants in the post office.[2]

Within forty-eight hours of the president's speech, the length of military duty for the country's National Guard units shifted from one year to "indefinite." Two days later, in the high school auditorium, an Appanoose

County branch of the USO—United Service Organization—was formed. It swung rapidly into line with the nationwide movement, collecting money for recreational centers near military camps where off-duty men could read, relax, meet friends, play, eat and engage in what the *Centerville Daily Iowegian* described as good "wholesome" activities. The primary focus of the meetings at the high school was of the Appanoose men in Company G. Robert Stevens, a veteran of World War I, described to the audience the loneliness of the soldier, the private moments of boredom.[3]

Reports from the men of Company G indicated they were in rigorous training and in temperatures of 90 to 110 degrees. They practiced marching and hiking across fields, over creeks and through swamps. They took part in mock battles. They "entrucked" and "detrucked" under constricting time limits. They were part of a "big show" of maneuvers in Louisiana involving five hundred thousand soldiers with battles, planes and artillery—all complete warfare, minus the bullets.[4]

As their reports reached Centerville, ham radio operator Lloyd Stansberry, whose amateur station was WYGWW, contacted two Louisiana stations—CEW and W5BMM—and arranged for messages to be exchanged between the Company G men and their families and friends, free of all costs. Red Cross members volunteered as liaison contacts between the men and their families with worries back home: mothers ill in the hospital, wives alone coping with money transactions. The Centerville Women's Club placed baskets on each side of the Square, where local and County residents could place their old magazines for shipment to Camp Claiborne.[5]

The Red Cross also began nursing classes. Its members anticipated a shortage of nurses as more and more of that profession moved to army and navy hospitals. The classes were held in an equipped room adjoining the County draft board office. So large was the local response, superintendent of schools E.W. Fannon provided a classroom for additional instruction at the high school. And to accommodate the schoolchildren who wanted to participate, a Junior Red Cross was formed.[6]

With more and more sympathy to the plight of the British fighting alone against the Nazis, the ties between America and Britain were solidifying. Breaking her best-kept secret of the war, the invention of radar by scientist Robert Watson-Watt, Britain asked for a volunteer army of thirteen thousand American technicians. They were to assist in making radar devices and operating the dozens of high-level and low-level radar stations then ringing the British coastline. As the technicians crossed east over the Atlantic, seven thousand young Englishmen were arriving in the United States to train as pilots. Mystic's

Al Lodwick, running his own School of Aeronautics in Lakeland, Florida, told the *Centerville Daily Iowegian*'s Jesse Beck that three hundred of them were assigned to his school. They were described as the finest of their youth; "[t]hey come from good homes, [they] are intelligent, and they have courage."[7]

Then suddenly, on June 23 and for the next twelve days, in the headlines of the *Centerville Daily Iowegian*, in news flashes on the radio programs and shouted by Harry Luther's loudspeaker on the Square, was bombshell news from eastern Europe. On June 22, 1941, in one of Hitler's characteristic acts of reversal, he attacked Russia, turning the parties he'd guaranteed a ten-year, non-aggression treaty into his enemy. Three million German soldiers, three thousand tanks and twenty-seven hundred aircraft, in an operation code-named Barbarossa, plunged across the Soviet border. They thrust toward Minsk, the key rail junction to Moscow, and swept in droves into the rich breadbasket of southwestern Russia. Hitler used blitzkrieg and panzers, infantry, screaming Stukas, death squads of the S.S., summary executions, wholesale rape, burning and plundering. The operation, he thought, would take one month. He hadn't reckoned with the Russian people. Urged by their premier, Joseph Stalin, they fought with guerilla warfare and a vast "scorched earth" policy—destroying all supplies, food and equipment ahead of advancing German troops. Within weeks, there were AP reports of one million German casualties in Russia; in two months, there were three million. President Roosevelt described the Russian resistance against the Nazis as "magnificent." To Winston Churchill, "…any man or state who fights against Nazidom will have our aid." Soviet Russia was now joined with Britain and America in a unified fight against a common enemy. Stalin called the British and Americans "joint allies."[8]

Predictably, tensions with Germany intensified. A *March of Time* newsreel at the Majestic Theatre chronicled Hitler's track record of broken promises, including those made to Russia. "It is small wonder," said Jesse Beck at the *Centerville Daily Iowegian*, "that many sound thinking Americans frown with apprehension when Hitler states that he has as much chance to conquer America as he does the moon." The president was one of the skeptics. He ordered German consulate offices in the Canal Zone, Hawaii, the Philippines and the West Indies to close. Hitler responded, ordering all U.S. consular employees to leave Germany, Norway, Holland, Belgium, Luxembourg, occupied France, Serbia and Greece. The president sent U.S. forces to Trinidad and British Guiana in the Caribbean, to Greenland and to Iceland. Nine hundred and fifty American technicians were sent to Northern Ireland to work on a construction project of an undisclosed nature. Northern Irish bands scrambled to buy copies of "The Star-Spangled Banner." The area's leading newspapers, the *Northern*

Whig and *Belfast Post*, said the establishment of U.S. bases in this part of Britain "may be nearer than is realized." Strategic points of defense were thus formed in the south and north Atlantic. What was also formed was a vital land bridge to Great Britain. Further reinforcing this connection, from August 10 through August 14, was a secret meeting between President Roosevelt and Winston Churchill on board U.S. cruiser *Augusta* off the coast of Newfoundland. On board the ship, witnessing the arrival of the dignitaries, was a navy ensignee, Centerville's Bob Middleton, son of patrolman Ike Middleton. In a letter home to his parents, Bob said he had never seen ". . . so many important people together in all my life. The ship was full of them." Bob knew he was part of history. It was the thrill of his lifetime.[9]

The news of the Nazi invasion of Russia and the defensive measures of the president were, if anything, a stimulus to the people of the County. The government called for a drive to collect scrap aluminum to build new aircraft. Centerville mayor Albert Fleming placed two concentric, circular storm fences on the lawn of the courthouse. The inner circle was a corral for deposited aluminum. The outer circle provided a barrier for the first. Volunteer workers, appointed to each City and County precinct, moved door to door, estimating donations. Boy Scouts and Girl Scouts followed, collecting the items and placing them on accompanying City trucks. In the country, contributions were left by rural mailboxes, collected by mail carriers and delivered into bins at the County sheds at the western edge of Centerville. One farmer at Unionville asked for a City truck. He had more scrap, he said, than any mail carrier could haul. At Mystic, housewives yielded their newly acquired, prized aluminum kitchen utensils—the wife of funeral director Ray Swanson with tears in her eyes.[10]

At the end of the first day, the inner corral on the courthouse lawn was "well-filled." Six days later it was heaped high, overflowing into the protecting outer circle, and included a forty-five-pound aluminum washing machine from local fire custodian Joe Milani. A U.S. Marines officer in town to enlist new recruits circled the collection, taking photographs. Wooden and wire handles were removed, everything weighed, and 3,630 pounds of the County's aluminum was loaded onto trucks and headed for Des Moines. The arrival of the Appanoose trucks at the big State aluminum bins made the front pages of Des Moines's evening paper, with large photographs in the *Des Moines Tribune*. The trucks, loaded to the hilt with aluminum, their high sideboards decorated with hanging teakettles and clattering utensils, eliminated a previous mood of apathy and caused a considerable crowd to gather. The waiting bins allocated to Appanoose County metal were rapidly filled. Leftover Appanoose scrap was placed in bins of other cities. It was the largest delivery to Des Moines up to that time, August 1.[11]

For Jesse Beck, the response of the people of the County to the aluminum drive was heartening. "It means," he wrote, "we are still patriotic, willing to help our country, and foresee a fight to the finish against forces that threaten democracy."[12]

But where to draw the limit of that fight was becoming fraught with emotion. There was anxiety in the town; there was despair and anger and resignation.

Chapter 62

Public Opinion Veers

Letters from friends and relatives arrived in the County with disturbing accounts of wartime struggle and survival, the anticipation of worse to come, their hope for American help. They came from Daisy Geynet in Chateauroux, France, to her sisters Leona Caster and Huse Cochran in Exline; from Mrs. J. McWilliams in Luphinnas, Scotland, to her sister Margaret Dooley on Centerville's North Seventeenth Street; from Dominic Maddollozo in Mussolini's Italy to his good friend John Padovan in Numa. Mothers, like Johanne Mont Thurston out on Soap Creek, empathized with the suffering of European families but felt their own fear "for the 19 year old who glances with young eyes at the 'Enlist Now' posters—who lights up with admiration at the sight of soldiers' uniforms."[1]

In May, Charles DePuy at the *Centerville Daily Iowegian* veered between pacifism and resignation. He described the Utopia that there could be if the money currently being spent on war was converted to peaceful, humanitarian needs. Then, in words reminiscent of Mark Twain, he wrote, "So let's forget about Utopia and well-fed and happy children …Let's get ready to fight. Let's kill a lot of young men who want to live. Let's fix things up so that future thousands of children can have broken hearts and undernourished bodies. Let's whoop and hurrah and go to war because we've got to save the world and democracy…"[2]

In mid-August, two days after he'd reported the Churchill/Roosevelt meeting, Jesse Beck made his position in the debate clear: "America must not go to war. That would be a tragedy of the worst sort. That must be avoided. It can be avoided." His solution was that America "must supply Britain, Russia, and the fighting allies of Europe, give them the weapons that they need to achieve victory, for if they fall in battle, if the Nazis conquer them, who is there among us who can say that we are safe."[3]

The strongest opposition to American intervention was the America First organization. Its leader was Charles Lindbergh. He spoke at Madison Square Garden to twenty thousand people; in the Arena at St. Louis to fifteen thousand; and in Philadelphia, at the Hollywood Bowl, at the San Francisco Civic Auditorium. People tuned in to hear the speeches carried over NBC Blue, NBC Red and CBS networks. His views were well-known. By aiding Great Britain and other countries, he said, the United States was "encouraging war, prolonging it and increasing bloodshed in Europe." In Centerville, Lindbergh's popularity began to fade. On September 11, 1941, he spoke in Des Moines at the coliseum. Thirteen invited Centerville businessmen refused to attend. Bob Chenoweth at the City Drug Store said he wouldn't drive anywhere to hear Lindbergh. Frances Gerdon at the Red Cross Drug Store said he wouldn't even listen to him on the radio. Attorney Purley Rinker thought Lindbergh an extremist, and Mike Buscemi thought him definitely "tootsy totsy."[4]

Even beyond Centerville, in the fourteen years since his "Lone Eagle" flight to Paris, Lindbergh's reputation as a national hero was eroding. In his many travels, he'd examined aviation systems, including those of Germany. He toured Luftwaffe factories and examined Nazi aircraft. He was escorted by Nazi leaders and was considering moving his family to Berlin. On one visit, Hitler's air minister, Hermann Goering, with the words "By order of the Fuhrer," presented him with the Service Cross of the German Eagle. It was a golden cross with four small swastikas finished in white enamel, strung on a red ribbon with black borders. The timing of the award was imperfect. Twenty-two days later was Kristallnacht. In one night in November 1938, with Nazi brutal attacks on German Jews, the whole world was exposed to the barbarism of the Third Reich. In America, the award to Lindbergh compromised him. It linked him to the Nazis. He received requests to return it. He never did.[5]

Two Centerville men did attend the meeting in Des Moines: the town's two principal newsmen, Jesse Beck and Charles DePuy. In a capacity crowd of eighty-five hundred, their seats were close enough to Lindbergh to touch him. The talk was carried over a Mutual radio hookup. Lindbergh was introduced by the Reverend L.K. Bishop of Des Moines. When the reverend held up an arm to give the invocation, he was greeted with shouts of "Heil Hitler." The shouts set the tone. The meeting was boisterous and noisy. There were boos, cheers, catcalls and roars. Lindbergh told the audience it was the British, the

Jews and the Roosevelt administration that were plotting to drive the United States into war. At least once, the heckling was so loud that Lindbergh was forced to stop. Twice he attempted to continue. His ability as a public speaker didn't help. Charles DePuy thought that as an orator, Lindbergh was a good aviator. Lindbergh concluded his speech by saying that the United States was "on the verge of war for which we are still unprepared ...a war which cannot be won without sending our soldiers across the ocean to force a landing on a hostile coat [*sic*] against armies stronger than our own."[6]

As the summer of 1941 yielded to autumn, an isolationist stand was harder to support. American boats were being torpedoed and blown up. American lives were being lost. By September 12, the president ordered the navy to "shoot on sight" any enemy submarine. Following his order, four more U.S. boats were torpedoed. "We are steadily going in the direction of war," said Jesse Beck. American opinion was hardening. In its convention in Milwaukee, the American Legion called for the defeat of Adolf Hitler "and all he stands for." Gillespie, Illinois, the hometown of a victim of one of the torpedoed boats—the *Kearney*—sent a telegram to Washington: "The Nazi attack against America must be answered and smashed." In a fiery address on November 19 to Centerville's Federated Women's Club, Iowa's Lieutenant Governor B.B. Hickenlooper said, "It would be a sad commentary on this generation if future Americans, as yet unborn, should point their fingers at us and say that we lost for them their rightful heritage of freedom..." And interlacing all the stories from Europe were reports of rising tensions with Japan.[7]

As early as February 1941, nine months before Pearl Harbor, *Centerville Daily Iowegian* editor Jesse Beck thought war with Japan more than a possibility. Japanese aggression was moving south from China. Hitler's defeat of the French and the Dutch and his threats against the British had weakened the hold of these countries over their colonies in Indo-China, the Dutch East Indies, Burma and Malaya. The Japanese were eyeing them, hoping for good pickings of tin, bauxite, rubber, oil—the raw materials they wanted, that they needed, to expand their economy. But they had a stumbling block: the menace, to them, of American power. In the same February edition of the *Centerville Daily Iowegian*, there were photographs of American Curtiss-Hawk fighting aircraft being shipped to the Dutch East Indies and to British forces in the Far East. Two days later, the people of the town read that the Japanese were warning that U.S. and British action in the Pacific could cause a "dangerous situation." The Japanese felt there was a plot to "encircle them."[8]

The *Centerville Daily Iowegian* reported more incidents. Between February 28 and March 3 in Hawaiian waters, U.S. customs agents seized nineteen Japanese fishing boats. They were believed to be involved in espionage. There were reports the boats carried expensive radio and photographic equipment and navigation charts unconnected with fishermen's work. The reports tallied with rumors of Japanese naval officers posing as fishermen along the U.S. Pacific coast. Perhaps by coincidence, on March 8 the first U.S. city to try the wartime practice of "blackout" was a West Coast city: Seattle. All the lights of that city were switched off for fifteen minutes, from 10:40 to 10:55 p.m. Only navigation lights in the harbor, running lights on a moving train, isolated lights from an aircraft company and a shipyard working on defense orders broke "the island of blackness."[9]

By June, the *Centerville Daily Iowegian* reported that Japan was reaffirming its union with Germany and Italy—the Axis. The union had clauses of mutual defense. In July, the people of Centerville read the Japanese were mobilizing one million troops. The next day, President Roosevelt ordered the freezing of Japanese financial assets in the United States; Great Britain and the Netherlands followed suit. And they cut off not just Japan's sources of credit, but Japan's critical imports of rubber, scrap iron and, most significantly, oil.[10]

By October, Tojo, Japan's new premier, asked his nation for "iron unity among all the fighting arms and people to cope with the encirclement of Japan by foreign powers." Japan, he said, was facing "the critical hour." The possibility of war with Japan was now the topic of conversations in the Appanoose County Courthouse, in work places, at dinner tables across the County—with the Seddon family in Mystic, with Henry Adams at the Red Cross Drug Store. Throughout the last months of 1941, they read an escalating pattern almost daily. The U.S. Navy was ordering passenger boats of two American shipping lines to avoid Japanese-controlled Shanghai. By November 26, Americans living in Japan were advised to leave "promptly." By the twenty-ninth, the *Centerville Daily Iowegian* headline read, "Far Eastern Situation Very Critical." By December 1, Americans in Shanghai were ordered to leave "as soon as possible." So were Americans living in Thailand. There were reports of "unabated Japanese military activity" on the border of Thailand. Bangkok radio warned Thai people to be ready for any emergency. The British were rushing military reinforcements to Singapore, the Australians tank troops to defend the Dutch East Indies. The headlines of Jesse Beck's articles appeared ominous: on December 5, "Japan Sizzling over Alleged Encirclement;" on December 6, [British] "Prepare for Showdown in the Far East…"[11]

In Centerville, preparations for Christmas were well underway. People were dragging home Christmas trees from Perry Produce across from the post office. City merchants, wanting this to be "the greatest Christmas," had got in their orders early. Around the Square, window displays were bursting with greens and reds, silvers, golds and patriotic red, whites and blues. The courthouse at night was a fairyland of light, and huge candles stood on each side of the building. There were rapid sales of two-dollar Arrow and Enro shirts at Bob Elgin's, Lentheric cosmetics and toiletries at Steven's Walgreens Drug Store; a special one-dollar sale at the City Book Store of Lloyd C. Douglas's best-selling *Magnificent Obsession*; and house slippers priced between $0.39 and $2.49 at Brody's on the Northwest Corner. Gambles on the Southside, Spurgeon's on the West opened special toyland sections, open nights beginning at seven thirty with free packages of Cracker Jacks for children accompanied by adults.[12]

On Saturday morning, the sixth of December, at exactly nine thirty, Santa Claus drove into the Courthouse Square, brilliantly dressed in a fiery red suit and riding on an Eskimo sled pulled by a team of barking Northland huskies. Three to four thousand children and their parents cheered loudly. There were free rides on the Eskimo sled, free movie shows at the Ritz and the Majestic and thirty-eight hundred sacks of free candy.[13]

Across town at the high school, members of Centerville's Federated Women's Club were preparing the auditorium for a Tolerance Rally to be held at three o'clock the following day. A team from the Des Moines Round Table, consisting of a Jewish rabbi, a Catholic priest and a Protestant minister, were to discuss national unity, moderated by Alfred Severson, professor of sociology at Drake University.[14]

At that moment, thousands of miles to the west, unknown and unseen, maintaining radio silence and taking a northerly course to avoid detection, the Japanese fleet of two battleships, two heavy cruisers, eleven destroyers and six big aircraft carriers carrying 423 air planes were on route from the Kuril Islands for their rendezvous with infamy.[15]

Chapter 63

December 7, 1941: Pearl Harbor

It was Sunday, December 7, 1941. The attack on Pearl Harbor came in two waves: the first at 7:49 a.m. lasting thirty minutes, the second at 8:50 a.m. for sixty-five minutes. At the end, 2,403 American sailors, soldiers, marines and civilians were dead, and 1,178 more wounded. Out of 394 airplanes on the island, 188 were destroyed, another 159 damaged. Of 94 warships in the harbor, 18 were sunk or suffered major damage. Eight of these were battleships: the U.S.S. *Arizona* damaged beyond repair, the U.S.S. *Oklahoma* shattered and capsized.[1]

In Centerville, five time zones to the east, it was midday. Morning services were over. At the Majestic on Thirteenth Street, posters advertised that evening's movie. Its title was *International Squadron*. It featured a former WHO Des Moines broadcaster, now a Hollywood star—Ronald Reagan—as "the lovable, laughing, reckless" American Eagle pilot flying with the British Royal Air Force. In the Hotel Continental Coffee Shop, it was the first day of the Christmas menu: chicken noodle soup, roast turkey, prime rib of beef, loin of pork, young guinea, golden fried chicken, vegetables and dessert—all for fifty-five cents.[2]

By mid-afternoon, twenty-one-year-old Helen Carlson was visiting her friend Mary Montgomery in an apartment behind the high school. Inside the school's auditorium, twelve-year-old Betty Morris (later Bear), her mother and grandmother were attending the ecumenical meeting to promote national unity and tolerance. On West Maple Street, twenty-six-year-old Robert Beck and Bill Sharpe were hanging a light fixture. Further east, newlyweds John and Virginia Koestner were filling their car at the Skelly station and chatting with the owner, Thayn Bryant. In Mystic, the Seddon family had finished its Sunday dinner. Seventeen-year-old Bob remained at the table, arguing with his father about United States–Japanese relations and their warlike tone. Bob thought war was likely; his father responded, "No we won't go to war with Japan. This tension has existed for years." Bob's father then left the house for his afternoon coffee and talk with friends at the local gas station, and Bob turned on the radio. Half a mile to the west, twenty-two-year-old Maurice "Reese" Hudson and his wife, Norma, were walking from Mystic to his parents' house in Brazil. Out at Soap Creek, in a 1928 Model A roadster, eighteen-year-old Joe Wilson was delivering Sunday newspapers. And diagonally across the County, just east of Seymour on Shoal Creek, Maurice Stamps and his brother Boyd were listening to a radio broadcast of a football game between the Green Bay Packers and the Chicago Bears.

Their lives, and those of everyone they knew, were about to change.

The first news of the attack on Pearl Harbor reached the town via radio. Maurice Stamps's football game was interrupted. Betty Morris, her mother and grandmother had left the high school ecumenical meeting and were arriving home at Rathbun, her grandfather Matt Blazina waiting for them in the driveway with the news. In Mystic, Bob Seddon heard it on his radio and was chasing after his father to tell him. And halfway on his walk between Mystic and Brazil, Reese Hudson heard it when Jesse Low came running out of his house shouting that Reese, who'd been drafted and inducted three months earlier, had better get in contact with his army unit.[3]

Most people that Sunday afternoon were bonded to their radios. The news was also moving by word of mouth. Within minutes of it reaching Moulton's Main Street, all activity on a traveling roller-skating rink stopped. One of the skaters, eleven-year-old Phyllis Morrow (later Cosby), ran home to tell her parents, whose initial disbelief evaporated when they turned on their family radio. The Morrows, like everyone, were learning the full horror. It wasn't just Pearl Harbor that had been attacked. The Philippines were under attack. So were Thailand, Malaya, Sarawak, British North Borneo, Hong Kong and three islands in the Pacific: Naura, Guam and Midway.[4]

If shock was the initial reaction, for more than thirty County families it was accompanied by high-level anxiety. They had family members known to be serving at Hickam Field and Pearl Harbor—on the ill-fated *Arizona*, the capsized *Oklahoma*, the injured *California*, the damaged *West Virginia* and six other battleships. And Appanoose County men were serving in the Philippines and on Wake Island. The enormity of it all was causing a fear that bordered paranoia. Where would the Japanese attack next? Was anywhere safe? Several weeks previously, Charles DePuy, in his *Centerville Daily Iowegian* column, had noticed a considerable number of Japanese using bus lines in and out of Centerville. People now asked: Were they collecting data pertinent to military action? Were they planning sabotage here in Appanoose County?[5]

At midnight there was a special phone call from the FBI to W.O. Frame, superintendent of the Burlington Railroad in Centerville. The call also went out to all transportation lines of all descriptions throughout the County. No transportation, it said, was to be given to any Japanese person in the United States. The call was followed by a wire from the Secretary of Air Commerce in Washington, D.C., to Sheriff Jack Bailey and Chief of Police Ray Brunson. All locally owned aircraft and planes were to be grounded, and authorized police officers were to guard Centerville's landing fields and keep them under twenty-four-hour surveillance. The action was to prevent Japanese nationals from breaking into hangars or taking a plane by force to make a getaway to the coast or to Mexico. Patrolman Richard Davis was immediately assigned to night duty at the airport. Officer Carl Ware replaced him for day duty. Both men were to be in constant contact with officials at City Hall. If any period more than an hour passed without such contact, an investigation patrol was to be sent out.[6]

That same night, the Hercules Manufacturing plant announced it was closed to all visitors, and strict rules would be instigated to prevent sabotage. The plant was manufacturing requirements for twelve U.S. Defense Department contracts. They included flask lugs for Rolls Royce airplane engines, unspecified materials for trench mortar bombs and equipment for shipbuilding yards in Wisconsin and Nebraska. A similar announcement came from the Iowa Southern Utilities plant off the Northeast Corner of the Square. It supplied light and power to more than one hundred Iowa towns and communities. This, the announcement said, was vital to moral and defense preparations. For this reason, the big plant would be closely guarded and admission to any facility closed to any visitor except by a special pass issued from the main office. The doors to this plant, previously open to anyone who might enter at any time to observe the activity and machinery, were now closed, sealed by steel-wire gates, open only to plant officials.[7]

There were no ominous rumblings of gunshots or bombs to be heard in Centerville that night and no questionable aircraft drones overhead. But as the night deepened, some of the people in the County covered their windows. Others watched the sky and waited for the light of dawn.[8]

Chapter 64

The Day after Pearl Harbor

The next day was Monday, December 8. The weather had changed. A high wind tore furiously at a flag on top of the courthouse yard flagpole. Dark, sullen clouds hung low in the sky. *Centerville Daily Iowegian* columnist Charles DePuy, his head low to keep the wind from his eyes, walked the Square, seeking reactions. He met Carl Stevens, a sailor just arrived home from San Diego Naval Station for a fifteen-day furlough. He had heard the news. He shook his head and said he was already leaving to return to his California naval base.[1]

In the Red Cross Drug Store on the Square's Southside, DePuy found people listening to a radio. The radio commentator's voice was slow, steady and nasal. Between items, customers talked of the last war. There was an air of resignation. Henry Adams said the attack was no surprise to him. Don Ellis thought we'd listened to Japan too long. Bob Chenoweth agreed, and so did V.W. Munn, the jeweler. Standing on one side was W.M. Evans, chairman of the local draft board. "We had orders to speed up our draft calls before this happened," he said. He thought those newly released from the army would be the first to go, and he expected the navy to begin conscripting men.

Charles DePuy's next stop was the Continental Hotel. There he found silence, except for the sound of the radio. Traveling salesmen were standing in groups, listening to the announcer. They looked worried. There was confusion. They wondered what to do next. Some were told by their companies to sit and wait, others to return home. The time was almost eleven thirty in the morning. The radio announcer was starting to describe the scene in the U.S. Congress. The president was about to speak. Charles DePuy moved on.

Across the County, as the speech began, people became quiet. They adjusted their radios and increased the volume. Six miles northwest of Centerville, students in Mystic High School were gathered in the assembly room in lines according to their ages: juniors and seniors at the rear, seventh and eighth graders in front. They were silent and watched as, four feet above them on the stage, superintendent H.G. Golden placed a console radio. Sixteen miles to the east, all of Moulton High School's students were assembled in the study hall. Superintendent Werner Wegner tuned the radio and checked that all could hear. In Centerville, Charles DePuy had reached the City's high school. The students were listening to radios in their classrooms.[2]

The president began: "Yesterday, December 7, 1941—a date that will live in infamy…" At the end he finished: "I ask that the congress declare that since the unprovoked and dastardly attack by Japan on Sunday, December seventh, a state of war has existed between the United States and the Japanese empire." The national anthem was played. The Centerville students, without prompting, stood to attention and pledged allegiance to the flag.[3]

Also listening to the speech and assembling the full text for page two of that evening's edition of the *Centerville Daily Iowegian* was Jesse Beck. Since early morning, the newspaper office was the most hectic place in town. Jesse Beck, the paper's news desk editor, was processing twenty-eight thousand words of news copy streaming in over two Associated Press teletype machines, clattering out multiple stories nonstop at the rate of sixty to sixty-five words a minute. Developments piled on top of developments. News items occurred that were outdated within minutes. Events of momentous importance were being transmitted. The pressure was so heavy, so intense, Jesse Beck couldn't leave the machines, and at noon he ordered a sandwich to be delivered to his desk.[4]

From Centerville High School, Charles DePuy was walking the four blocks back downtown to the *Centerville Daily Iowegian* office. He noticed there was now a little sunshine and more blue in the sky. The wind was still strong. The flag on top of the courthouse yard flagpole was still being hurled about. Its edges were raw. But, he noted, it was still there.[5]

Inside the office, it was one thirty. Jesse Beck was desperately trying to assemble the front page of the newspaper. AP had fired out seven news leads, one displacing the other, causing Beck to wonder if he'd ever be able to pull together a comprehensible, understandable story. By two o'clock, he began the front page dummy and determined the two-word banner headline: "War Declared," the all-capital letters two-and-a-half inches in height and colored bright red. By four thirty, the eight-page *Centerville Daily Iowegian* had rolled off the presses and been assembled and delivered by circulation manager Clyde Triebswetter to waiting newspaper delivery boys in Centerville, Mystic and all County towns. By early evening, the people of Appanoose County were reading accounts of Pearl Harbor and the president's speech in their newspapers and listening to developments on their radios.[6]

Within twenty minutes of the president's speech, Congress voted a formal declaration of war against Japan. Britain had already done so in a note given to the Japanese chargé d'affaires in London at one in the afternoon (six in the morning, Central Standard Time). "It only remains now," said Prime Minister Winston Churchill, "for the two great democracies to face their task with whatever strength God may give them."[7]

Air raids were sounded in New York City. There were unconfirmed reports of an imminent attack by hostile planes. From Long Island to Montauk Point, people braced themselves for a possible attack. Civilian defenders for Suffolk County at the eastern tip of Long Island were called for immediate action. Civilian defense officers for New York, New Jersey and Delaware met in emergency sessions. All firefighting equipment was placed at vantage points at La Guardia airfield. All planes were cleared from runways. A million children in New York and thousands on Long Island were sent home. Blackout practices were ordered for all New York cities. A report from Boston at two in the afternoon, Eastern Standard Time, said hostile forces were outside the city.[8]

On the West Coast, at least two squadrons of Japanese planes were seen from San Jose to the huge naval yard at Mare Island. They conducted reconnaissance flights over industrial plants ringing San Francisco but dropped no bombs. U.S. Army interceptor planes chased them but were unable to determine where they went. The army and navy began searching for the possible base: an enemy aircraft carrier some five hundred to six hundred miles off the coast. Three blackouts in one night were ordered in San Francisco. In Los Angeles and Oceanside, radio programs were interrupted for blackouts "by order of the Fourth Interceptor Command" when planes of unknown origin were seen. Public announcement vehicles toured the streets to ensure blackout compliance.[9]

In Washington, Secretary of the Treasury Henry Morgenthau ordered the nation's borders closed to Japanese nationals. All financial transactions with them were banned. Within hours of the bombing of Pearl Harbor, 736 Japanese were arrested in the United States and Hawaii. Daily, more were taken into custody. Thousands of Americans of Japanese birth or parentage were forced from their homes and businesses. Exline's Bill Hutchison, serving with the Coast Guard at Treasure Island in San Francisco Bay, was awakened from his sleep on the night of December 7. He dressed and was armed and assigned to duty throughout the night outside a Japanese dry goods store on Mission Street in San Francisco. He was to prevent anyone from entering. He described, in a letter home to his parents in Appanoose County, the look on the faces of the elderly Japanese owners when he told them they could not enter their own store.[10]

Across the nation, troops were assuming guard posts at defense industries, key buildings, strategic bridges and public utilities. In Centerville, in the middle of America, so far removed from either coast, the fear was not as acute. People listened to the president's fireside chat on the night of the ninth. They listened to it broadcast from the stages of the Majestic and Ritz Theatres. And 360 County farmers and businessmen attending their annual Alfalfa Banquet listened to it on special radios installed for the purpose inside the dining room of the Central Church of Christ on Drake Avenue. "The country is at war," the president told his audience, but "we are going to win [it] and we are going to win the peace that follows."[11]

The war was about to expand. On December 11, two days after the president's fireside chat, Germany and Italy declared war on the United States. Premier Mussolini had shouted it from the balcony of the Palazzo Venezia in Rome. Adolf Hitler announced it to the Reichstag in Berlin's historic Kroll Opera House. When the news reached Washington, President Roosevelt requested from Congress declarations of war against both countries. His request was passed immediately and unanimously. "Never before," said the president, "has there been a greater challenge to life, liberty, and civilization."[12]

Chapter 65

Mobilization and Rationing

Across the nation, action was replacing shock. In urban and rural communities, military recruiting offices were jammed. The day after Pearl Harbor, all across the Midwest, lines of young men waited in front of courthouses and recruiting offices—some of the offices announcing they would remain open twenty-four hours a day, seven days a week, to process the rush. At the gates of Jefferson Barracks in St. Louis, Missouri, ninety men, all army deserters, surrendered, saying they now wanted to do their duty. In Iowa, enlistments for all branches of military service increased dramatically. Selective Service officials were deluged with enquiries from registered men wanting to enlist rather than wait for the next draft. Men in their fifties, sixties and seventies were volunteering, one in Des Moines "fighting mad" at being unable to pass the required visual tests.[1]

Everywhere, veterans of World War I were volunteering. Harley Miner, who ran away from Centerville and joined the British Army in 1914 when he was fifteen and was now forty-two years old, enlisted with his nineteen-year-old son, Bobbie. Mystic's Howard Fuller—age forty-four—who'd served in the First World War's 803rd Aerial Repair Squadron, joined with his eighteen-year-old son, Ted, his twenty-year-old son, Jack, already serving with the Canadian Air Force. Centerville patrolman Ike Middleton, a sailor in World War I and the father of son Bob, a sailor on the U.S.S. *Augusta*, signed up, and so did Fay Seals, whose two sons, Aubrey and Ray, were members of Company G, the local National Guard unit currently in training at Camp Claiborne. And all the veterans at Appanoose County Post 526 formally offered their service to "the Community, State, and Nation."[2]

Whole families of brothers were joining. More than seventy-five Appanoose County families provided two or three sons each. The Howe family, the Phillips/McCoys, the Johnsons and the Allens all provided four. The Adams family of Exline and the Robbinses of Cincinnati each sent five sons. The King family of Udell sent all six of their sons. And from Waterloo, 120 miles northeast of Centerville, it was duly noted, the five sons of Mr. and Mrs. Thomas Sullivan enlisted in the navy together. They trained together. They were assigned together on the U.S.S. *Juneau.*[3]

By December 11, American flags were flying from the homes and businesses of the County. A particularly large, beautiful one hung at the front of the Ray C. Walden American Legion Post on Drake Avenue. The Legionnaires watched a small boy, unaware he was being seen, walk up to it, feel the silken folds and the golden cord, turn and walk away. Then he stopped, did a sharp about face, smartly saluted the colors, turned and walked away. At the high school, students made a large, white flexiglass *V* for victory sign and placed it over the school's east front entrance. They equipped it with seven one-hundred-watt electric lights, one homeroom class in turn each week bearing the one-dollar expense of their maintenance. At the retail stores, in school classrooms and from their newspaper carriers, people bought ten-cent defense stamps. In banks they bought Series E defense bonds at a minimum price of $18.75. By December 16, eight working days after Pearl Harbor, Centerville National Bank had exhausted its stock. So had its supplier, the Federal Reserve Bank of Chicago.[4]

At the armory, men volunteered for a new National Guard unit to replace Company G. At City Hall a Civil Defense Committee was formed. Extra guards were sent to patrol local rail and communications lines, the Centerville Water Company, the pumping station, the two large reservoirs and their surrounding acreages; high overhead, a volunteer Air Patrol, based in Ottumwa, flew sorties. An Emergency Ambulance Corps was formed. Classes were started in first aid and lifesaving techniques. Local Boy Scouts served as fire watchers, message carriers and auxiliary first-aid assistants. Police matron Nettie Bever organized a women's rifle unit. The women practiced marksmanship and outdoor marching.[5]

At the *Centerville Daily Iowegian* office and at the Rock Island station, editor Jesse M. Beck and station agent G.N. Garrett received government orders not to report the movements of trains carrying troops or military equipment and the convoys of army trucks passing through the area. A similar order reached Tom Wood Jr. at the Centerville Pure Ice plant. He was ordered not to release weather information, and the public at large was told to avoid loose talk about weapons, military equipment and the defense contracts at the Hercules Manufacturing plant.[6]

Upstairs over the Majestic Theatre on Thirteenth Street, five hundred women volunteers for the Red Cross began meeting in relays, their activities expanding from one room to the entire upper floor of the theater. Over the Samson Electric Store on the Square's Westside, more volunteers established a "Bundles for America" workroom. There they recycled clothes and furnishings, shipping them to the U.S. Army and Navy Relief Society for distribution to needy military families.[7]

All resident aliens—there were forty-nine Italians and one German—were ordered to surrender to Sheriff Jack Bailey their guns, any radio-sending and receiving sets and their cameras. They were told to apply at the post office with three photographs per person for certificates of identification. Those who had not acquired U.S. citizenship were told to do so.[8]

Rumors "thick and fast" spread across the town. Suspicious activities were reported of five local individuals. They were a labor leader, a tailor, an Italian, a teacher and a medical doctor. FBI agents arrived. They ran surveillances of suspects and conducted interviews. Convinced all Italians were about to be arrested and killed, one Italian miner—Andrew Giocolletto—chose suicide, throwing himself down the shaft of the Enterprise mine north of Promise City.[9]

Recruiters for the U.S. Coast Guard and Marines arrived in town more frequently. Quietly, silently, day after day, men bound for war boarded buses outside Allen's bookstore on the Square's Eastside. Charles DePuy watched them and yearned for "the parades, the flags and lusty booming farewells" of World War I.[10]

Two days before Christmas 1941, two weeks after Pearl Harbor, Japan's swift seizures of the world's crude rubber plantations caught up with the nation. The country faced an almost complete tire famine. Stocks of tires, inner tubes and rubber shoes were frozen. Tire rationing was announced. Appanoose County's allotment of new tires was assigned on January 1, 1942: fourteen passenger-car tires, twenty-four for trucks. Medical and veterinary professionals received priority, so too ambulances and public service vehicles. Applications were taken by a local tire-rationing board above the Davison Hardware Store on the Square's Northside. Burlington Trailways curtailed its bus services. Stores restricted home deliveries. Servicemen at Iowa Southern Utilities pedaled to emergency calls on shiny new bicycles. The drivers of cars without priority began inventing their own methods of extending the life of their tires. They patched their tire holes with pieces of leather cut from old boots. The cars were driven with a distinctive "ker-thump" sound. The Goodyear Tire and Rubber company made the Centerville Goodyear Service Store on Haynes Avenue, the town's official Tire-Life Extension Station.[11]

Across the town, across the County, radio news reports were heard. News flashes on newsreels were watched at the Majestic Theatre. Newspapers were read—those from Kansas City and Des Moines, along with the *Chicago Tribune*, the *Chicago Sunday Times Herald* and the *Iowegian*. They were spread across coffee shop tables and over store counters. Bulletins were shared between owners and customers. Drake Free Public Library reported a surge in the reading of books on world affairs. At the schools, students were reading textbooks on world history. They studied maps and held discussions with expanded current issues of *Readers Digest* and *Scholastic Magazine*.[12]

The people of the town saw crack passenger trains put on sidings while freight trains, loaded with munitions, roared through with right of way. They saw freight cars sandwiched between elite passenger coaches. They saw army planes flying in formations across the sky. They heard them at night. Silence had now descended across the movements of troops. The locations, the destinations, the fates of their own men was their highest source of anxiety. Mrs. Josie Stuckey of Udell heard from her son Dale. He'd survived Pearl Harbor and mailed home a piece of a Japanese plane. The R.E. Erskine family of Plano received a delayed letter from their grandson, who had been killed at Pearl Harbor aboard the U.S.S. *Arizona*. Henry Kijak of Jerome was a prisoner of the Japanese capture of Wake Island. But there was no news of Company G. Then, seven weeks after Pearl Harbor on January 26, they learned the first American army forces had arrived in Northern Ireland. There was no mention of which units, their sizes, their points of departure, their dates of sailing. "Are Our Boys There?" asked Jesse Beck. They were not. Not yet.[13]

Chapter 66

Northern Ireland, the Doolittle Flight and the Battle of Midway

The men who'd arrived in Northern Ireland that January day were the first U.S. soldiers to reach the British Isles. They numbered several thousand of an unnamed infantry division, almost all the soldiers from the Midwest. They arrived in Belfast in a convoy of gray transport ships crossing the twenty-four-hundred-mile, submarine-infested Atlantic without incident. So great was the secrecy of their arrival, only a small group of curious onlookers observed it. But, when a military band suddenly struck up "The Star-Spangled Banner," there was a cheer, followed by an electrifying cry that ran like wildfire through the city. "The Yanks are here!"[1]

The first American ashore was twenty-two-year-old Private First Class Milton Henke of Hutchinson, Minnesota. He was the son of a German immigrant to the United States. He held up a postcard from his father that read, "Give 'em Hell." Thousands of spectators crowded onto the Belfast streets. The troops marched out of the dockland, full packs on their backs, steel helmets on their heads. They swung along to their state songs, to the "Iowa Corn Song" and to "Marching through Georgia," the Stars and Stripes fluttering at their head, to the camps built by American technicians seven months previously that then had been described as "of an undisclosed nature."[2]

Within hours, photographs appeared in the *Iowegian*: of Private Milton Henke stepping ashore, the troops marching through the streets, the twenty-four nurses from Kentucky who accompanied them. The photographs were sent by AP's new Telemat Service, wirephotoed to Chicago, converted into engravings, changed into mats and sent on by Rock Island train into

Centerville, where editor Jesse Beck had already been warned of their arrival times and their sizes.[3]

Company G, the town learned, was still at Fort Dix, but John Koziol of Mystic, a transfer to another unit, was identified among the marching men by his wife, Marie. It made John Koziol the first from Appanoose County to arrive in Northern Ireland. Three days later, the first from Centerville was another transfer: Charles Pancrazio. The two were part of tens of thousands of U.S. soldiers arriving on ships in Belfast by day and by night. The ships, screened by antiaircraft guns, were unloaded of men by army and navy specialists working in teams with peak military efficiency. The empty transport then immediately returned back across the Atlantic for more men and equipment.[4]

On May 21 came confirmation of the arrival in Northern Ireland of Company G. "Arrived safely," Major Dewey Bear wrote to his wife and small son in Centerville: "good accommodations, excellent health, happy birthday Jimmy." And from Captain Charles Apgar to his wife: "Arrived safely, beautiful country. Love to all."[5]

As U.S. troops were reaching Northern Ireland, the news from the Pacific was bleak. The Philippines had fallen. Twelve thousand five hundred U.S. troops and sixty-eight thousand Philippine soldiers and civilians, despairing of a U.S. rescue, surrendered on the Bataan Peninsula. Already starving from one-third rations, they were now force-marched by their Japanese captors for sixty-five miles to prison camp in a death march famous for its barbarity, twenty-five thousand dying en route. A week later, another ten thousand men surrendered on Corregidor and were subjected to the same fate. In Southeast Asia, the Japanese were achieving their every objective. They seized Sumatra, Java, Bali, Timor, a ribbon of islands that now opened up their path to India and Australia. By February 27, 1942, the Japanese were bombing India, Colombo and Trincomalee in Ceylon, and on March 16 the city of Darwin in northern Australia. On February 24, off the coast of California, fifteen Japanese shells were fired from a submarine at an oil field and refinery near Goleta, seven miles north of Santa Barbara. The next day, an unidentified object was seen moving slowly down the coast from Santa Monica, and so were two aircraft over Long Beach. Air-raid sirens wailed at 2:25 a.m. in Los Angeles. Tracer bullets, exploding shells and searchlights criss-crossed the sky along a ten-mile front to the south.[6]

In those early months of 1942, before America's war production was in full effect, fighting a superior Japanese fleet was limited to "hit and run raids." Of these, the most dramatic, the most morale-boosting for Americans, was the raid on April 18. On that date, four months and ten days after Pearl Harbor, eighty crewmen in sixteen B-25s, led by Lieutenant Colonel Jimmy Doolittle, took off from an aircraft carrier, the U.S.S. *Hornet*, 650 miles from the Japanese coast, on a potential suicide mission to bomb Tokyo. With the B-25s' limited range, the planes could not hope to return. The bombs were dropped on Tokyo and four other Japanese cities. The planes then flew on, some to safety of China, some crash landing, some crewmen bailing out, some captured.[7]

As they left the *Hornet*, escort planes flew part way. The pilot of one, flying his F4F Grumman Wildcat fighter aircraft, was Centerville's ace pilot, Johnny Talbot. Within three weeks he'd be in the air again—this time one of the U.S. pilots so outstanding in their skill and courage that they made the Battle of Midway the turning point of the Pacific war. Those pilots sank four Japanese aircraft carriers and two heavy cruisers, put four destroyers out of action as well as 437 Japanese aircraft. One hundred and forty-five U.S. aircraft were lost: the slow torpedo bombers shot down, the F4F Grumman fighters running out of fuel and ditching in the ocean. Johnny Talbot was one.[8]

John Talbot had thirty seconds to exit his cramped cockpit and retrieve a life raft from the rear compartment. In thirty seconds, the plane sank, dragging John underwater, his foot caught on an aerial. He fought free. Then came his struggle for survival. The raft would not automatically inflate. His air pump wouldn't work. Using his breath to inflate the raft, only one side would fill with air, a valve left open on the other side. His supply of food had been pilfered. He had half a canteen of water and a bottle of malt tablets. Somehow John Talbot survived. He survived through four bitter cold nights and five days of scorching sun. Sharks circled. Aircraft searching twenty-five million square miles of moving ocean flew high overhead, missing him until the fifth day. John was rescued by a PBY Catalina patrol plane. Severely burned, dehydrated and exhausted, he was taken on a stretcher to a hospital in Pearl Harbor. His arrival there was filmed by Hollywood director—now naval commander—John Ford in the U.S. government production *The Battle of Midway*. It was shown at the Majestic Theatre, people jumping to their feet and pointing, "That's Johnny Talbot!"[9]

Johnny Talbot. *Printed with permission from J.M. Talbot.*

By the time of John Talbot's rescue, men were leaving Centerville for war in ever greater numbers: twenty-two, thirty-seven, forty-three, ninety. Since the nation's third draft, U.S. Army recruits now dominated. At each departure, throngs of relatives and friends gathered outside Allen's News Shop and the Burlington Trailways Bus Station on the Square's Eastside. Free donuts and coffee were supplied by Buscemi's Blue Bird Cafe; a canteen bundle of cigarettes, apples, candy and cookies was given to each recruit.[10]

Women began leaving to join the WAACs at the national training base at Fort Des Moines. They were greeted there by Colonel Thomas N. Gimperling, who told them, the corps "...will tolerate no petulance or capricious feminine temperament." Other Centerville women left for the navy's WAVES, for the Coast Guard's SPARS and for the WOWs, volunteering as Women Ordnance Workers. African Americans were leaving, their departures separate, their destination camps segregated. When the U.S. Navy lifted its racial exclusion policy, Centerville's twenty-year-old Casey Bolden was the first African American in Iowa to enlist. "I'm proud of that boy," said his father, an employee of the *Centerville Daily Iowegian*, to editor Jesse M. Beck.[11]

As more and more men left their places of employment for military service, national labor-supply experts urged employers to "...forego prejudices against the weaker sex, as well as color, racial and religious prejudices." In Centerville's theaters—the Majestic and the Ritz—an all-female staff replaced men. Seventeen women in town trained as air-raid wardens. They studied war gases, identifying them with "sniff kits," learning the first-aid treatment for each type, how to protect themselves and how to evacuate the community should it be attacked. Thirty-five-year-old Ruth M. Fuller, the first woman pilot in Appanoose County, served as a sergeant in the Civil Air Patrol. Twenty-two-year-old Helen Carlson was one of some thirty young women who volunteered for the U.S. Air Force Ground Observer Corps, learning to identify both friendly and hostile aircraft by their distinctive shapes. At the National Youth Administration (NYA) workshop at the fairgrounds in northwest Centerville, girls were welding. In Iowa, of 3,390 youths preparing themselves for war industries, 1,588 were young men, 1,801 young women. NYA Centerville girls were being accepted as sheet metal workers and spot-welder operators at aircraft companies in Des Moines, Rock Island, Minneapolis, Seattle, Wichita and Kansas City.[12]

As war production shifted into full gear, dress codes for women were issued: women were to wear pants, low-heeled oxfords, no peek-a-boo blouses. There was to be no jewelry and no fingernail polish; all hair had to be firmly wrapped in head turbans. Centerville's four dress shops immediately responded. "Slacks ...in step with the times ...to do a man-sized job," said the Spurgeon's

Pauline VanNoy in welding gear, with her daughter Charlene Lamb. *Courtesy of Charlene VanNoy Lamb.*

advertisement offering slacks from $1.00 to $3.98 and slack suits from $1.98 to $8.75. Milady's Shoppe and Brody's on the Square's Northside followed, and so did Jensen's on the Southeast Corner.[13]

More and more young women left for the new opportunities that also gave them the pride that they were serving their country. Barbara Clarke left Centerville to work on bombers under production in Wichita. Jean Harrison was assembling the first layer of gas tanks in P-47 Thunderbolt aircraft. Because of her small size, twenty-year-old Doris Kennedy, working on aircraft in Kansas City, was assigned the job of crawling into tail sections to put in place delicate and precise electric wiring. Pauline VanNoy joined her husband in Vancouver, Washington, and became a welder working on submarines at the Kaiser Shipyard, where women workers were valued for welding finer seams than men. Twenty-five-year-old rural school teacher Leila Riggs spent a summer in Chicago working night shifts as an inspector of valves for forty-pound bombs. The women worked forty-hour weeks in swing shifts at sixty cents an hour—more for overtime. From a Seattle shipyard, Mary A. Large wrote home to Centerville; she'd been transformed from a three-dollars-a-week housemaid to a sixty-dollars-a-week welder.[14]

The war was changing women. It was changing men. It was also changing the home front, where all Centerville eyes were fixed on victory.

Chapter 67

The Home Front: Salvage, Metal and Rubber Collections

For the people of Appanoose County—as for everyone across America—there were three wars: the one in the Pacific, the one in Europe and the one on the home front. As the country geared itself into wartime production, vital raw materials were critically short. The War Production Board, created by executive order in January 1942, called on the nation to supplement the supply by recycling waste materials. The premium need was for metals and rubber. Also needed were dark and light greases to create explosives; nylon and silks to make into gunpowder bags; paper and rags to form corrugated boxes to carry food and ammunition to the troops and to carry blood plasma and surgical dressings; and in 1944, milkweed pods to supplement kapok, used to line life preservers and life vests. Throughout the war, there was a national Victory Book Campaign, aiming to collect a million books to stock USO houses, army day rooms, ships and U.S. Navy bases. This expanded into a drive for phonograph records for troop entertainment.[1]

In Centerville, salvage collections began in January 1942. By August the collections became part of organized national drives. Kickoff meetings were held at the Association of Commerce rooms on North Thirteenth Street. They were full to capacity. County chairman Steve Martin divided the County into townships and precincts. Captains and chairmen were appointed. Assignments were issued for each area. When the one for Moulton was announced, S.A. Southern, the chairman of Moulton's drive, told the meeting, "We'll get it. We'll get it all. It's our chance to do our part." Those at the meeting warmly concurred.[2]

By June 6, two circular storm fences, painted bright red, formed corrals on the Southside of the courthouse yard. One was for rubber, the other for metal. Extra collection points were given across the County: gas stations for rubber; junkyards for metals; grocery stores for grease; hosiery stores and the courthouse Grand Army of the Republic room for nylons and silks; the ends of sidewalks for tied bundles of paper; phonograph records to American Legion posts; and books to a box in the lobby of the Drake Free Public Library. Jesse Beck printed a skunk and a verse at the masthead of his newspaper:

We'll beat Hitler,
The dirty skunk,
If you'll turn in,
All your junk.[3]

For the next four years, citizens scoured the streets, the roads and the fields of Appanoose County: small children pulling loaded toy wagons; Boy Scouts; Girl Scouts wearing identifying kerchiefs; Legionnaires; neighborhood groups; women of the North Bend Church Ladies Aid, tearing sheets into bandages; the Women's Salvage Army; paper troopers from Centerville schools—the letters P.T. in blue stitched onto their yellow arm bands; rural children out on Soap Creek, filling onion sacks with milkweed pods. Following them were trucks with loudspeakers borrowed from the City, the State Highway Commission, the Pure Ice Company and Gavronsky's Junk Yard.[4]

By June 9, 1942, 105 tons of metal were collected from the County's farms. They rattled into Centerville in extra trucks supplied by Triple A and the Farmer's Exchange. The metal was weighed on the City weighing scales next to City Hall, just off the Square on West Jackson Street. By August 11, it was reported, three Centerville streets alone were yielding 5,180 pounds of waste materials. Some of the scrap brought scrip money for the donor in a campaign titled "Scrip for Scrap to Whip the Jap." Others received sixty cents for one hundred pieces of scrap metal, ninety cents a pound for rags, one cent a pound for rubber, four cents a pound for light grease (three cents for the dark variety) and seventy-five cents for batteries. Scrap metal and rubber collections could give free admittance to movie shows. Two hundred pounds of metal earned one hundred free baby chicks from the Swift and Company Uptown Hatchery on East Jackson Street, across from the armory. It earned the children at Lincoln School a new gas stove from Grant Venell of Venell and Company and a Christmas party for those at Garfield School.[5]

Most of the scrap was given in unpaid straight donations. Rubber seat cushions were tossed into the rubber corral on the Courthouse Square. Two-year-old Donnie McCoy threw in his two beloved rubber dolls, hoping they would hurry home his father, then serving with the A.E.F. (American Expeditionary Forces).The rubber mats disappeared from the foyer of the Blue Bird Cafe, from the Ritz Café and the entrance to Beers Drug Store. When a boy on a bicycle witnessed two smaller boys deliver a coaster wagon full of rubber dolls and boots to the DX station across the street from the Majestic Theatre, he pulled the two rubber handgrips from his handlebars and added them to the pile. By June 29, 172,000 pounds of rubber had been collected from the County, 62,000 pounds from the City and 3,000 pounds from the courthouse corral.[6]

For the County's metal collection, objects were given that were museum pieces and vital objects of County history. There were Civil War muskets; an old saber; an ancient musket made in Liege, Belgium; a relic bayonet; shell clips; a frontier revolver; an antique Philippine machete with a teakwood handle; and braces from a 1913 pusher airplane flown by local aviator Pearl Adams. Two ornamental iron hitching posts—known as Adam and Eve—that originally graced the entrance to Governor Drake's mansion on Drake Avenue were added to the pile. So was the World War I British howitzer cannon that had stood for more than twenty years on the Eastside of the courthouse yard and was now rendered into pieces by W.O. Wright, wielding an oxyacetylene torch. From the middle of the street, between the Continental Hotel and the First National Bank, 27,960 pounds of old streetcar rails were dug up, their demise watched over by Alex Orr and Casey Swanson, two of the town's earliest Interurban conductors and motormen. And over at the City Drug Store on the Square's Westside, Bruce Johnson squeezed Unguentine ointment out of one hundred sample metal tubes into a glass jar and collected more empty metal tubes brought in from customers.[7]

In all the collections, the County's children were everywhere. When seventh- and eighth-grade students at Washington Junior High learned the national need for leaded nickel silver was "distressingly urgent," they made house-to-house calls across the County, collecting old keys, particularly the richest source of nickel silver: those from Yale locks. They put collection boxes in the schools. They hung keys on a string across a classroom. They chanted the national motto: "Key Tokens for To-KEY-o!" Children pulled junk into piles in school yards. Their coaster wagons strained under thousands of pounds of scrap. They groaned and squeaked to the school grounds. Front axles broke. Teakettles were collected, as were gas pipes, bedsteads and stovepipes. On two special tin-can day drives in January 1943 and on August 31, 1944, it was an unusual home, wrote Jesse Beck, that did not receive from one to ten calls every day from schoolchildren on the "tin hunt." They piled them up at the back doors in alleys, on vacant lots and on back porches. There wasn't a dog in town, continued Beck, that had any worries about having a can tied to his tail, because "there weren't any cans left to tie, if anyone had been mean enough to do it." The children dug up rails from abandoned tracks. Panicked railroad officials, convinced the children had mistakenly dug up currently used tracks, insisted on seeing the location. The children's judgment had not been wrong. Beck at the *Iowegian* expressed his pleasure at the efforts of the County's youth. They were, he said, "an inspiration to the older people who have been working hard at scrap collection."[8]

By September 14, three months since the beginning of the County's scrap drives, the County was receiving congratulations from Herbert Plagman, executive secretary of Iowa's State drive, for having exceeded its quota. County chairman Steve Martin reported total collections had taken the County "well beyond" its target goal of two hundred pounds per person. It had placed Appanoose County in the top fourth of all Iowa counties.[9]

But it wasn't enough. The War Production Board in Washington, D.C., appealed nationally for more scrap—millions more—and the situation was urgent. The board sent representatives to communities. They were to organize new local collections using government trucks and WPA labor and to pay prices that would, Jesse Beck pointed out, undercut local businesses and money. One of the War Production Board's representatives waited at the Continental Hotel. A quickly assembled meeting of County officials preempted what they considered the stigma of government help. Centerville mayor Albert Fleming issued a proclamation: Thursday, October 22, was to be a Centerville Scrap Holiday. All stores and offices were to close and reopen in the evening from six to nine thirty. This, he said, would release "all able bodied citizens [to] join in the drive to collect the scrap so badly needed by our Government in the war effort." Publicity was given by County newspapers and by State radio stations. The holiday was extended from Centerville to being an Appanoose County Scrap Holiday.[10]

Appanoose County's action was not isolated. Across Iowa, it was happening in her cities: Waterloo, Clarinda and Fort Madison. It was happening in her counties: Franklin, Ida, Audubon, Adams, Clay, Montgomery and Cass. It was happening across the nation. The *Centerville Daily Iowegian* reported scrap holidays in Pennsylvania and in Texas. In Jefferson County, Alabama, church bells rang, calling residents to join the one-day scrap drive.[11]

In Centerville on October 22, it started with a 7:30 a.m. whistle. Sixty-four trucks began rumbling onto the Square. Crowds of released workers waited: managers, laborers, shop assistants, dentists, druggists, businessmen, lawyers and coal miners. Sitting at a table on the Southside of the courthouse walk was Dwight Selix, spread in front of him sheets of paper. They listed each truck, its designated complement of men, its predetermined township, its predetermined route marked on maps. A raw October wind blew the papers. Heavy gray mists in the east blocked the sun. A light rain began to fall. But, observed the *Centerville Daily Iowegian*'s Charles DePuy, the whole operation was organized as smoothly as any military maneuver.[12]

The first truck to be weighed pulled up at the Centerville City scales shortly after nine that morning. It was from Exline. An American flag waved over the driver's cab. Its scrap metal weighed six-and-a-half tons. By ten o'clock, the line of trucks was several deep. The City scale had more than it could handle. A long waiting line continued well into the afternoon.[13]

A total of 918 tons was collected. It came from homes, shops, farms, hills, valleys, ditches, vacant lots and barns. As the scrap moved along the roads of the County, Charles DePuy observed the metal was broken and unused, and much was covered with rust. But, he wrote, it was the stuff for smelting plants, ready to be converted into shining guns, tanks, planes and ships.[14]

If the country urgently needed scrap, there was a higher need: money. After Pearl Harbor—with war declared on two fronts—the need was acute. People were asked to buy U.S. Defense Saving Bonds. And again, the people responded.

Chapter 68

The Home Front: Savings Bonds, Defense Stamps and Rationing

People of the town were already buying U.S. Defense Bonds, the most popular the Series E savings bonds at $18.75, maturing in ten years to $25.00, and Defense Stamps in ten-cent or twenty-five-cent denominations. Between 1942 and 1945, the national urgency for the public to buy bonds was organized into eight defense war-bond drives. Each city, each town, each county was given, for each drive, a set target amount and a set target date. All four radio networks—NBC Red and Blue, Columbia and Mutual—combined to broadcast kickoff appeals. People in Appanoose County tuned in to hear appeals from the president; from Henry Morgenthau, secretary of the treasury; from Hollywood stars—Bob Hope, Bing Crosby, Frank Sinatra and Judy Garland, as well as Iowa native Captain Glenn Miller and his Army Air Force Band, and Ronald "Dutch" Reagan, the sports reporter they knew from WHO Des Moines, acting the part of a soldier in a foxhole, wondering what Americans were doing to help him.[1]

As the drives began in Appanoose County, Clarence Hood, in charge of all eight drives, explained their purpose. "Taxes," he said, "will never produce all the money needed to finance the war. The balance must be secured thru the American people." In Centerville, the drives began with parades, marches, "Paul Revere rides" with people on horseback, concerts, dances, speeches from wounded World War II soldiers and sailors, and visits by Hollywood stars Paul Kelly and Marjorie Woodworth. Jesse Beck placed a red savings bond, topped by an eagle and cut with a large *V* for victory sign, on the masthead of the *Iowegian*. A large thermometer was built onto the side of the courthouse.

At its top was written the set target amount for the current drive. At each one-hundred-dollar sale of a Defense Bond, Centerville fire custodian Joe Milani blew the town's fire siren and pushed up the level of the thermometer's graduated meter. When a single bond purchase for seven thousand dollars was made in July 1942, he blew the siren seventy times. On the third anniversary of Pearl Harbor, Oscar Jones, a popular graduate of Centerville High School, an African American, now a coxswain in the U.S. Navy and home on leave, fired a salute bomb from a mortar on the Square for every one thousand dollars of E bonds sold. He did that until one in the afternoon, when the bomb supply was exhausted, and Joe Milani's fire siren took over.[2]

At each drive, store windows were decorated with photographs of the County's young men fighting for their country. The photographs were flanked by flags, military insignia and patriotic symbols. Girl Scouts, women's club members, 4-H Club girls and precinct workers made house-to-house appeals. They circled the Square wearing red, white and blue streamers. They carried decorated trays of Defense Stamps. They sat at booths inside shop entrances, selling one-dollar cellophane-wrapped corsages made with ninety-eight cents worth of Defense Stamps, arranged on a background of red, white and blue imitation petals, leaves and stems. They sold smaller versions as boutonnieres for lapels. There were special incentives. A local beauty dressed in red, white and blue, sitting in a decorated wheelbarrow, was pushed around the Square in turn by businessmen who'd bought bonds. Out at the Appanoose County Fair, fifteen-year-old Dorothy Drake, Miss 4-H, wore a dress sent from Younkers Department Store in Des Moines. It was of white net overlaid with red and blue defense stamps. She carried a bouquet of more war stamps. At the fairground, an army jeep gave free rides to adults who'd bought twenty-five dollars of war bonds that day—or five dollars in Defense Stamps to anyone under twenty-one. On the twenty-eighth of August, 1942, the E.A. Hull Insurance Agency placed a car on the Southeast Corner of the Square. It had been parked near Hickam Field, Honolulu, on December 7, 1941. It was riddled with Japanese bullet and shrapnel holes. Look at the car, urged E.A. Hull, "Then—Act—Buy Bonds and More Bonds …'The Car from Pearl Harbor' Must Not Happen Here."[3]

Stores and businesses made special offers. The Ritz and the Majestic Theatres gave free movie tickets with proof of a bond purchase. Waggoner's Poultry Equipment and Feed Store on North Haynes gave free Defense Stamps in exchange for returned feed sacks. Beers Drug Store gave a free packet of cigarettes with the proof of purchase of a fifty-dollar E bond; at the Supply Store, that fifty-dollar E bond earned a pound of bacon. At the City swimming

Dorothy Drake wearing a dress made of war stamps. *Courtesy of Dorothy Drake Haines.*

pool, stamps were given to patrons when a specially rigged alarm clock rang at intervals. The country club issued stamps in return for entry fees and awarded bonds as prizes. And bartenders at the town's nightspots served "Slap the Jap" cocktails: in return for twenty-five cents, a customer received a twenty-five-cent Defense Stamp and a glass of water.[4]

Every age group was buying bonds and stamps. Ninety-eight-year-old Civil War veteran Edward Streepy made a trip into town to buy fifteen hundred dollars worth of bonds in one day. In Mystic, tiny Sandra Sue McNamar emptied six dollars in pennies, nickels and dimes out of her penny bank and marched downtown to give it all to Uncle Sam. Nine-year-old Harry Frink worked as an odd-job man, earned $1.45, borrowed a nickel from his father and spent it all on Defense Stamps. Fourteen-year-old Junior Roush became the County's star war-bond salesman by selling more bonds than anyone his age in the state of Iowa. A "Minute Man Flag"—a pennant—flew over the Swift and Company plant in South Centerville, indicating 100 percent of the workers there had subscribed 10 percent of their income to war bonds. Parents and grandparents bought bonds decorated with borders of Walt Disney characters for babies—two-day-old Robert Leroy Hobart and three-day-old Tommy Warren Wallace. Stamps were sold by students each morning before classes at a booth in Centerville High School's main hall and at Lincoln School, where ten-year-old Carolyn Snodgrass (later Bauman) assembled them in small books. At a night football game against Fairfield, the Centerville High School band—led by Mark Kelly and Frank Minckler—made complicated maneuvers with flashlights illuminating the letters that spelled "Buy a Bond" as they played Irving Berlin's "Any Bonds Today." They then rapidly regrouped into a heart to the music of Victor Herbert's "Sweethearts."[5]

Then there was rationing. The rationing of tires had begun two weeks after Pearl Harbor when the County had been assigned fourteen tires for passenger cars and twenty-four for trucks. In less than a month, in January, as national auto plants converted to the production of military vehicles, the manufacture of new automobiles for the public was frozen. The County was told its new car allotment for all of 1942 was to be twenty-four vehicles. The sales of cars dropped like stones. Centerville's four car dealers thought their outlook dismal. People joked about reinstalling the Square's hitching racks. There was a "bike rush" at Purley Munden's Bicycle Shop on Short Street off Haynes Avenue. The entire stock of bicycles at Harry Luther's store on the Square's Northside sold out. Iowa Southern Utilities' workers were seen traveling to service calls on bicycles. Rural children, determined to complete their education, rode bicycles to schools distances away. Travelers and businessmen began transferring to public transportation. The Burlington bus lines, the Centerville division of the Burlington Railroad and the Rock Island depot all reported increases in passenger service. A local office for the Statewide Share-A-Ride Club was established at the Victory Hotel on West State Street. People collected in groups on Highway 2, hitchhiking for rides to Mystic.[6]

At the same time, there was a severe shortage of sugar. The supply from the Philippines was completely cut off, the one from Hawaii limited and purchases from Cuba not immediately available. Centerville grocery stores limited purchases. Jesse Beck reported "the faint essence of [a] sugar panic" in town. The Office of Price Administration in Washington, D.C., issued ration books. Appanoose County clerk Mage Luse received instruction to store them in the courthouse. People lined up at County schools to fill in application forms citing their needs, the size of their families and their intention to can fruits. Teachers assisted and acted as registrars. Superintendent E.W. Fannon supervised. There were discussions about sugar substitutes. Housewives reported honey was an excellent alternative for making bread and baked goods. The Pure Ice Company offered a recipe for homemade ice cream: corn syrup, milk, salt, vanilla and heavy cream. The first ration book—it was specifically made for sugar—was available in May 1942. It contained twenty-eight war ration stamps. Each stamp was valid for one week's sugar supply. As other shortages occurred across the war years, there was a second ration book, a third and a fourth. The new books were more "comprehensive," covering not just sugar but coffee, shoes, meats and fats, canned vegetables, fruits, juices and soups, fuel oil and gasoline. The books contained eight pages of twenty-four coupons each. The stamps came in colors: red, blue, green and brown. They had a letter, a number and a design.[7]

On October 1, 1942, in order to conserve the nation's rubber stockpile, a wartime speed limit of thirty-five miles an hour went into effect. Tires were inscribed with numbers. They were inspected every four months; the wear on the tires was expected to tally with the mileage recorded on the odometer. After December 1, 1942, there was a more effective deterrent to breaking the speed limit: gasoline was rationed. Violators could lose their gasoline coupons. For the distribution of the rationed gasoline, vehicles were placed in categories according to their use. Identifying colored stickers were placed on the lower righthand corner of windshields. The letter *A* in white on a black background indicated a car used for private transportation and qualifying the owner for only three gallons of gasoline each week. Category *B*—white on a green background—was for those workers judged essential to the war effort and entitling them to eight gallons. Red *C* letter stickers were for physicians, ministers, mail carriers and railroad workers, allowing them whatever number of gallons necessary. The letter *T* was for truckers, who were permitted five gallons a week, and five gallons were issued for the letter *R*—the owners of non-highway vehicles such as farm tractors. Farmers felt increasingly isolated—the result of the last category.[8]

If these measures were inconveniences, there was a constant and sobering reminder. It was the sight of the endless processions of young men climbing the stairs to the recruiting office over the National Bank on the Southside of the Square.

Chapter 69

Letters from Soldiers

Men were leaving the town for war in increasing numbers. They left for the navy, the army, the army air force. Career army soldiers, their terms completed, were ordered to return to active duty. Men ages twenty to forty-four, men eighteen and nineteen years old, left in large groups of forty-two, seventy-three, eighty-three, the County's African Americans in separate departures. They all left in the dead of night to board special cars on Rock Island and Burlington trains. They left led by a color guard and the town band. They left surrounded by families and jovial well-wishers.[1]

But by August 1942, the tone of the departures changed. Five of the County's young men were already dead, killed stateside in accidents while serving in the military: Jack Packard and Robert Gilliland, when the truck they were driving ran off a gravel road on the edge of Des Moines; Centerville's Chase Fannon, the son of the superintendent of schools, a champion golfer, killed when the aircraft he was flying suddenly dipped and veered and crashed into the Missouri River two miles northwest of Fairfax Air Base, Kansas City; Brazil's Anthony Javonovich, lost in an aircraft somewhere between Florida and Bermuda; navy gunner Danny Lutrell of Mystic, killed by a subway train in New York City. At the same time, people of the town were reading of their men fighting at the Battle of Midway and the Coral Sea, of attacks on Allied shipping at Port Moresby, New Guinea; of fighting in the Solomon Islands, and of U.S. Marines in hand-to-hand combat at Guadalcanal. Now the departures were more somber.[2]

It was at this point that a pattern was established that continued throughout the war. Families wrote letters and sent parcels from the post office to their men at military addresses around the world. The *Centerville Daily Iowegian* staff sent copies of the newspaper. When they were able, the men wrote home, their letters censored, the names of places deleted. Appanoose County listened to the course of battles and events within moments of their occurrence. Within hours they could hear reports on the radio. They could read detailed accounts and news analyses sent by 179 AP war correspondents to the *Centerville Daily Iowegian*'s two teletype machines and translated immediately into the newspaper's headlines. But where the local men were fighting and what was happening to them was little more than guesswork. This news arrived weeks, sometimes months later, and the silences were almost unendurable.[3]

At the *Centerville Daily Iowegian*, Charles DePuy began a new column. It was called "Columns Write." "It will be dedicated," he wrote on the first day, "to the men at the front...a sort of central exchange for news from the home folks to the boys and vice versa." For the next four years, "Columns Write" featured excerpts from the men's letters. The *Moulton Tribune* and the *Mystic Sentinel* did the same. At Mystic, there was something extra. The Methodist church bell rang every day at noon, reminding everyone to pause in silent prayer for the men in service. And at Mystic's funeral parlor, residents of the town were seen standing at the window reading hundreds of letters sent by GIs who'd written to mortician Ray Swanson from all over the world. The letters, frequently with a photograph attached, were cellophane-taped to the inside of the window. Every day, Ray was seen replacing the older letters with the newer ones. When the GIs learned what he was doing, they wrote on only one side of a sheet of paper. As the number of letters expanded, Johnny Milburn at Mystic's Pool Hall followed the same pattern.[4]

The first letters from the men overseas came from Company G in Northern Ireland. They described the beauty of the Irish countryside, with its trim hedges and thatched roofs, and the narrow streets—"narrower than pill row," wrote one, making the comparison with Centerville's Thirteenth Street. The letters came from New Guinea, describing the fish, the coconuts and the bananas. They came from Australia, and there was a transoceanic radio interview from Australia. Mrs. Opal Buscemi at the Blue Bird Cafe on the Southside of the Centerville Square heard her nephew, ace army photographer John Buscemi, talk. His work was appearing in *Yank* magazine and in the *Saturday Evening Post* people were buying at Allen's bookstore on the Square's Eastside.[5]

As well as writing letters home, members of Company G were in training. As part of the 168th Regiment of the Thirty-fourth Infantry, the red bull insignia on their sleeves, they were battling in maneuvers, fighting through smokescreens and climbing over barb-topped stone fences. There was more training in Scotland at Inverary, where volunteers in commando units joined British units to train for amphibious raids and mountain warfare.[6]

In Centerville, in the fall and early winter of 1942, the headlines of the *Centerville Daily Iowegian* came from North Africa. They told of the British Eighth Army, led by General Bernard Law Montgomery, routing a battered German panzer army from Egypt in a two-thousand-mile retreat west across the coast of Libya; at the head of the Germans was General Erwin Rommel. And there were new headlines. They told of RAF bombings in northern France; of B-17s—the Flying Fortresses of the U.S. Army Air Force—flying out of English bases in precision raids over Rotterdam and Utrecht; of U.S. troops fighting to regain Kiska in the Aleutian Islands; of the destroyer *Jarvis* with 250 Americans aboard, missing somewhere off the Solomon Islands. They told of the titanic struggle for Stalingrad, the Russians heroically fighting the Germans hand to hand, building to building, with the invaders "walking knee deep in blood" and the bodies of hundreds of Hitler's grayish-green-clad soldiers piled high on Stalingrad streets. And the headlines told of President Roosevelt's blunt warning to Hitler to expect a second front to relieve the Russians, with attacks coming from a dozen possible different points in Europe.[7]

On the morning of November 9, people in the town read the headline "U.S. to Hit Axis through Tunisia." The second front, code-named Operation Torch, started in secret and at midnight on November 8, 1942, at three North African locations: at Oran and Algiers on the Mediterranean coast and at Casablanca on the Atlantic. The objective was to move troops rapidly east across North Africa to Libya, meet up with the British, trapping the retreating Germans in the process. At Casablanca, the American fleet of 174 vessels, straight from Hampton Roads, carrying thirty-five thousand troops commanded by General George Patton, faced fire from the French fleet and promptly responded. At the guns of an Armed Guard Liberty Ship, the *Samuel Griffin*, one of the fleet's escort ships, was Tracey Corder of Moulton. His fire was aimed at the brand-new French battleship *Jean Bart*, the ship eventually silenced by U.S. Navy torpedo planes. Fifteen miles to the northeast at nearby Fedala, Leonard Knecht, son of the Reverend L.P. Knecht, former minister of Centerville's Seventh-day Adventist Church, disembarked from the *Joseph Hewes*, dodged artillery fire from the shore, cleared a path at the docks to unload equipment and saw his ship sunk by two torpedoes launched from a submarine.[8]

At Algiers, the 168th Infantry, including Centerville's Company G and led by Dewey Bear—now Colonel Dewey Bear—landed in the first wave amid probing flashes from French searchlights and the sounds of gunfire inflicting severe damage on two small ships attempting to smash a boom at the entrance to the harbor. In a little more than twenty-four hours, an American flag was planted on the beach, the harbor and the heights above it were secured and a cease-fire agreed to at the city's main fort.[9]

At Oran on the Mediterranean coast, eighteen thousand arriving American and British troops, coming direct from Great Britain and commanded by British officers, faced gunfire at two of three selected beaches. At the third, at Arzew some twenty miles to the east, the Nineteenth Combat Engineers left a British ship, the *Letitia*, and arrived on shore without incident. Among them was Reese Hudson, who, with his wife, Norma, had heard the news of Pearl Harbor as they walked from Mystic to Brazil.[10]

On November 12, four days after the AP reports of the landings in North Africa appeared in the *Centerville Daily Iowegian*, Jesse Beck asked, "Are Our Boys There?" Solid news of Company G's involvement did not arrive in Centerville for thirty-three days. And the news then was of the death of twenty-two-year-old Noah Davis of Centerville, killed on the first day of the invasion by a sniper at El Biar, a suburb of Algiers. Noah Davis became Appanoose County's first confirmed battle death of World War II. On learning of the death of Noah Davis, the mood of the town was described by Charles DePuy as "frantic." The mood defused a little when the first letters, forty-three of them, arrived together at the Centerville Post Office five days after the *Centerville Daily Iowegian* report of the death of Noah Davis, thirty-eight days after the landings in North Africa. Those forty-three letters arrived on December 16. What followed was silence again.[11]

Long silences were also distressing hundreds of Centerville and Appanoose County residents who had close relatives in enemy-occupied countries. John Jensen, the owner of the Jensen's store on the Square's Southeast Corner, had letters returned unopened that he'd sent to his eighty-year-old father, living alone in Denmark. H.O. Kelley, the head of Appanoose County's Red Cross, said messages could be sent via his organization, but they could say little more than "We are well, how are you?" and some messages could be attempted via Switzerland. It was a slow and sometimes futile process, but this method worked for Bona Polich of Rathbun, who made contact with her family in Fuzine, Croatia—the hometown of so many of the County's Croatians. It didn't work for the large local population of those from Italy, a belligerent country.[12]

In each home of a serviceman across the County, the Veterans of Foreign Wars placed a window card bearing a star emblem: a blue star for a serviceman in domestic service, silver for someone serving beyond U.S. borders and a gold star for those who'd made "the supreme sacrifice"— the first placed on the window of Noah Davis's family on South Ninth Street. In Mystic, in Plano, in Numa, in Exline, in Moulton, in every County town and in Unionville, Missouri, large community billboards with the names of each local serviceman prominently displayed were placed in public locations on squares or painted on the sides of red brick buildings. On Centerville's Fifteenth Street, local artist Ban McCormick was carving four large honor-roll plaques from mahogany and white pine, honoring all Appanoose County servicemen. Each plaque was topped by an eagle, each name recorded in gold on a black background, the completed plaques placed permanently on the entry corridor of the County courthouse.[13]

Radio news reports were heard across the County. The voices were those of H.V. Kaltenborn, Andy Rooney and Winston Burdett. They reported from battlefields; their voices entered homes and offices. So did the voice of twenty-four-year-old Charles Collingwood, whose reporting for CBS from North Africa won him a coveted George Foster Peabody Award. Some listened through the night to shortwave radio broadcasts. On December 7, 1942, Will Seath, listening in Numa, heard a British broadcaster announce from an undisclosed location that he was interviewing some American men overseas to say words on the anniversary of Pearl Harbor. "There are a bunch of boys here," the announcer said, "from Centerville, Iowa." Everywhere in town, in small County towns, in farmhouses, in offices and in schools, newspapers were read assiduously: AP reports, AP maps, dispatches and photographs sent via AP telemat from the U.S. Army Signal Corps. They showed troops landing in North Africa and in the Aleutian Islands; they also showed men, heads bowed, at a graveside ceremony for their fallen American comrades on Guadalcanal.[14]

In the town, there was a sense now that the war would be prolonged, the suffering just beginning. They looked for signs: flocks of ducks flying across the sky, great *V*'s against the autumn sky; potatoes cut open revealing *V*'s; and three stars in the northwest evening sky forming a perfect *V*, a brilliant one at the point. "In terms of victory," wrote Jesse Beck, "with *V*'s of all sizes in evidence on every side …so far as morale is concerned victory is no idle fad."[15]

Chapter 70

News from Africa, Guadalcanal, Kiska and Stalingrad

Iowa's winter of 1942–43 was long and hard. Snow fell in September and didn't melt until spring. Day and night temperatures hovered around two degrees, one night falling to nineteen degrees below zero. On New Year's Eve, Charles DePuy found everything wrong on Centerville Square. He found it empty, hollow, devoid of celebration. "You can't take 1,000 of the county's youth away," he wrote in his column, "without noticing a change."[1]

The news wasn't much better. All five Sullivan brothers from Waterloo, who'd enlisted together, who'd served together, died together when their boat, the U.S.S. *Juneau*, was destroyed in the Battle of Santa Cruz in the Southwest Pacific. In that same part of the Pacific came the delayed news of the sinking of U.S.S. *Hornet*—a survivor, Centerville's Harvey "Bud" Pearl Van Doren, swimming three miles for an hour and a half before being rescued. And Delmar Rak from Exline, a staff sergeant with the Thirty-seventh Bomb Squadron, was missing somewhere over the Mediterranean, in a secret mission—his death confirmed four months later.[2]

In North Africa, the British Eighth Army was pushing Nazi general Erwin Rommel and his Afrika Korps in a one-thousand-mile retreat west from Egypt across the coast road of Libya into Tunisia. American troops, including the Thirty-fourth Infantry and Centerville's Company G, were moving rapidly east to meet the British and trap Rommel's forces in a pincer movement. Ahead of the American troops, building roads and reinforcing bridges, were the combat engineers in weather conditions General Patton described as "truly appalling." For Mystic's Reese Hudson in the Nineteenth Combat Engineers, what began now was a battle of mud, mines, booby-traps, bombed-out roads and blasted bridges. The engineers worked through rain and cold, with heavy machinery and with picks and shovels. They forfeited sleep and food, and they, like the soldiers who followed them, faced constant bombardment from German Focke-Wulfs, Messerschmitts and screaming Stukas.[3]

By late January, the news appeared a little more cheerful. Russia had won its epic struggle for Stalingrad. Germans were surrendering there by the hundreds of thousands, their losses estimated at 1.5 million killed, wounded, missing or taken prisoner. Nine days later, on February 9, the headline of the *Iowegian* read, "Japanese Withdraw from Guadalcanal." It was there, on that Pacific island, that Appanoose County boys were fighting, and there Centerville's Dr. E.F. Ritter, serving with the U.S. Sixth Engineers, was head of the field hospital. He was performing surgery under the trees; his assistant was Hollywood film star and conscientious objector Lew Ayres. Three of the County's servicemen who'd fought on Guadalcanal came home to Centerville and told their stories. The fourth, John Wynn Ross of Cincinnati, had died on Guadalcanal of strep throat, malaria and pneumonia. The surviving three described the conditions they'd endured: the malaria-infested jungle, the constant rain, the filth, the vermin, the incessant falling of Japanese bombs, the snipers, the attempt at sleeping in tents where mosquitoes sounded like swarms of bees, the swimming in the shark-infested ocean. The experiences had given them a professional respect for but an ethnic hatred of the Japanese. One carried Japanese teeth in his pocket and on his wrist a bracelet made of metal from a Japanese aircraft. Another, African American Charles Davis, had a more lasting memento: a permanent limp from a Japanese bayonet thrust into his left thigh.[4]

By February 14, the news from North Africa turned ominous. Two German panzer divisions led by General Rommel overran American defenders from Faid Pass to Gafsa in central Tunisia; survivors were reeling back fifty miles to Kasserine Pass. The Germans followed, got there on February 18, captured it, surrounded the 168th Regiment, including Centerville's Company G, and cut it to pieces. An unconfirmed International News Service radio report was heard in Centerville. It named Captains Charles Apgar and Floyd Sparks—two Company G officers—saying they were in the "thick of the present sharp battle with Rommel's troops." Jesse Beck immediately sought confirmation. By Monday, February 22, he'd sifted and assembled information gleaned from the *Chicago Times* and from a delayed AP report that arrived on the *Centerville Daily Iowegian*'s teletype machines that morning. Company G was indeed involved. The names of men, casualties, were listed from Centerville, Cincinnati, Albia and from one group led at night by Major Robert Moore of Villisca in Iowa's Montgomery County, escaping so close to the German eighty-eight-millimeter gun position, said Major Moore, "we could've reached out and touched the guns." But not all men had escaped, and the people of Appanoose County knew it. With their anxiety level high, they waited. They waited for twenty-two days.[5]

Throughout that time, at the *Centerville Daily Iowegian* office on Main Street, editor Jesse Beck was juxtaposing any news from North Africa with the fighting of the County's men on the islands and atolls of the Southwest Pacific. In early March, in what Associated Press labeled "an amazing victory," U.S. and Australian pilots flew their bombers low over the Bismarck Sea, successfully eliminating a Japanese convoy of twenty-two ships carrying fifteen thousand Japanese troops. Among the crews of the U.S. planes were Robert Gibson of Unionville, Missouri, who'd trained at Centerville Airport, and Centerville's Sandy Cortesio, injured on his forty-sixth mission.[6]

On the Solomon Archipelago, U.S. soldiers were advancing west from Guadalcanal to the Russell Islands to the New Georgias and the Trobriands. On the other side of the Solomon Sea, a complementary action was evolving. The two actions were named Operation Cartwheel. On the north shore of Papua, New Guinea, Americans and Australians were landing in a series of shore-to-shore amphibious landings, fighting in conditions worse than those experienced at Guadalcanal. And in the considerably colder climate of the North Pacific, the two Aleutian islands of Attu and Kiska were recaptured, bringing the news to Mystic of the town's first battle death: that of Robert Marshall, whose letter home to his parents would arrive in Mystic after the announcement of his death. And after the fight for Kiska, Centerville's Bill Darnell was hospitalized with two frozen feet and a frozen hand.[7]

By this time, telegrams were arriving to more homes across the County. These came from Africa, and these for the next two-and-a-half years would become all too familiar. They were labeled "Killed in Action," "Wounded in Action" and "Missing in Action." Keith Stegner's family on North Main received a "Killed in Action" telegram. So did the family of Ray Seals on South Eighteenth. "Wounded in Action" telegrams came to the John Benac family on South Sixteenth, the family of Floyd W. Ross in Cincinnati and to the West Washington Street home of Jack McCoy, whose son, Donnie, had thrown his two rubber dolls into the first scrap-drive corral on Centerville Square "to help his Daddy come home." "Missing in Action" telegrams were delivered to eleven County families. Forty days after the men's disappearance, the War Department thought the missing men were prisoners of war. By April 1, forty-five days after the Battle of Kasserine Pass, Charles Burkhiser's family received confirmation. Charles was heard on a shortwave radio message from Germany picked up in Charlottesville, Virginia, the news sent by letter to the Burkhisers in Numa from the family who'd heard the message in Virginia. By this same method, Paul Slavin's family heard he was alive. So did the families of Rocco Pravdica and Gail Bailey. By the end of April, the missing men were writing home, prisoners of war of the Italians or the Germans. Their letters appeared in "Columns Write." They gave their addresses, with the word "stalag" followed by an identification number.[8]

After Kasserine Pass, a new Allied offensive was underway in North Africa. The Germans and Italians were pushed north to the sea and encircled at Tunis. Hill 609 was the target given the Thirty-fourth Infantry, the "Red Bull" Division, including the surviving members of Company G. Richard Wilson of the *Des Moines Register* witnessed the action. He saw the men from Iowa shatter the German and Italian line, collapsing their resistance, taking the flat-topped natural fortress and providing, by its conquest, the pathway for U.S. and British troops to enter Bizerte. It was where Company G's Sergeant Verl Farnsworth from Exline was shot in the head and lost a month of his life, saved by doctors riding to the front lines. By noon on May 1, Axis prisoners by the tens of thousands were surrendering. The battle for North Africa was over. On July 10, the *Centerville Daily Iowegian*'s two-and-a-half-inch banner headline read, "Sicily Invaded."[9]

Chapter 71

Sicily Invaded, Company G Goes to Italy

In darkness early on June 9–10, 1943, the U.S. Seventh Army under Patton, the British Eighth and Canadian First Infantry Division under Montgomery disembarked from LST (Landing Ship, Tank) beaching crafts west and east of Cape Passero, Sicily. Within hours, 150 miles of shoreline were secured, and the men were moving inland.[1]

Centerville's Company G, as part of the 168th Infantry, the Thirty-fourth "Red Bull" Division, was still in North Africa. They were at Bizerte, fueling the B-17s and B-24s on their way to bomb Sicily, Naples and Rome. They were unloading ships arriving from the United States. Moulton's Tracey Corder and Unionville's Richard Harrington each made four such trips, bringing supplies and military equipment, including tanks for Patton with the ace of spades decorating their sides. And the men of Company G were setting up staging camps for the thousands of surrendering POWs in North Africa, furnishing the cooks and digging the latrines. Watching the scene, a German major complained to a U.S. lieutenant colonel: "This situation is terrible," he said, "there is no organization. It is inexcusable. Such confusion would not be permitted in the German Army." "Yes," responded the lieutenant colonel, "but we received poor information. We heard from your radio that Germans would fight to the last bomb and the last man. I came here to bury your fellows, not to watch you surrender." He turned his collar to reveal a cross. The lieutenant colonel was frontline chaplain Deloss Marken of Des Moines's Cottage Grove Avenue Church of Christ.[2]

In late July, the Thirty-fourth Division was moved east from Bizerte to Oran and assigned in reserve to Mark Clark's U.S. Fifth Army that was preparing for an invasion of Italy. The Thirty-fourth trained and integrated with the 100th Infantry Battalion, composed of Hawaiian Americans who'd volunteered as soon as Americans of Japanese ancestry were declared eligible for service, among them Daniel Inouye, who would one day serve six terms as Hawaii's U.S. senator. Their papers had been assembled and delivered to their departing ship in Honolulu Harbor by Maurice Stamps of Seymour, who was serving in the adjutant general's office at Fort Shafter.[3]

In Sicily, the Seventh Army was already reaching the north coast. Reese Hudson with the Nineteenth Combat Engineers was spending his days unscrewing detonators on hundreds of mines, bulldozing holes and finding bypasses around blown bridges. In a letter home to his parents in Brazil, he described Sicily as "the hilliest place I ever saw. A person is always going up or down." Corporal Floyd Purvis of Mystic thought Sicily "an awful place to call home," but he appreciated the cheering, the crying, the clapping and the singing when the first U.S. motorized units drove through the village of St. Antaino. Richard Stockwell wrote home to his parents in Moulton that he was sleeping in foxholes, was sometimes asleep before he hit the ground and hadn't taken off his shoes for seven days and seven nights. "The other day," he wrote, "I went into an old cathedral, hundreds of years old and knelt to pray with a nun, made me feel better, but it seemed pretty strange to be there covered with dust and not able to talk their language." And at the end of the letter, he asked, "When did the Jerries ever get that cock-eyed idea that they were some sort of master race? I don't think they care much for us since we've put a dent in the idea."[4]

Richard Stockwell's "dent" was well-timed. Within four weeks of the Allies landing in Sicily, Mussolini had been removed from power, the Italians were withdrawing their troops and exploring an armistice with the Allies and Patton's Seventh Army had reached Messina and met up with the British and Canadians as the Germans were in full retreat across the straits of Messina to Italy. Victory at Sicily was complete. The next Allied target was Italy.[5]

On the third of September, 1943, Montgomery's Eighth Army of British and Canadians crossed the Straits of Messina, landed on the toe of Italy and took control of Reggio and Calabria. Six days later, on the ninth, Mark Clark's Fifth Army landed south of Naples on the Bay of Salerno. The day previously, Italy had unconditionally surrendered to the Allies. But any comfort this news gave to the landing forces was swiftly erased. Nazi tracers and flares blazed onto the Salerno beaches. There were repeated attacks by aircraft, infantry, tanks and gunfire strategically delivered from German positions on inland hills.[6]

In Appanoose County, day after day, people were listening to radio reports and reading newspaper accounts. The fighting remained fierce, at times so critical Allied troops were forced to yield ground and the failure of the whole operation was threatened. Four days into the attacks, a British hospital ship, the *Newfoundland*, arrived offshore to tend to the wounded. Nazi pilots targeted, bombed and sank the ship despite its clear markings: bands of green lights and brilliantly illuminated red crosses. Six British nurses and seventeen crew members were killed. Escaping were fifty-two nurses assigned to the U.S. Fifth Army. Escorting them efficiently and calmly was their chief nurse, Helen Wharton of Mystic. Her demeanor was no surprise to her hometown. She had displayed it on the Mystic girls' basketball team that had competed in the State tournament in 1927, earning her placement as All-State center.[7]

To hold the Salerno beachhead, reinforcements were arriving: U.S. airborne divisions, British armored divisions and extra infantry divisions, including the Thirty-fourth, the "Red Bull." Further critical support was also arriving with the British Eighth Army that had advanced north from Calabria. The *Centerville Daily Iowegian*'s headlines that late September began to assuage local anxiety: on the sixteenth, "Allies Throw Back Nazi Forces"; on the eighteenth, "Allies Move Forward 11 Miles"; on the twenty-second, "Fifth Army Approaching Naples"; and on the thirtieth, "Naples Evacuated by German Troops." By early October, the next Allied aim was north to Rome. The distance was one hundred miles. The journey would take them eight months. Significant amid their obstacles: the terrain.[8]

Dominating the geography of Italy is a central, ten-thousand-foot, mountainous spine. From it, rapid rivers in deep valleys flow west and east to the Mediterranean and the Adriatic. The Germans, defeated in southern Italy, built a new line of defense laterally across this spine. They blasted bunkers into the solid-rock mountainsides, camouflaged machine-gun nests and mortar locations on surrounding hills and laced approaching riverbanks, vineyards and olive groves with mines. Straight into this line of defense, the Thirty-fourth, the "Red Bull" Division, headed. As part of a task force, it was instructed to move sixty miles north, to cross the Calore and Volturno Rivers along a serpentine highway with dangerous U-curves, precipitous ledges, blown bridges and roadblocks, all the while providing German snipers with open targets. The Company G tank driver, Centerville's John Sisul, having witnessed several tanks falling over edges, negotiated the most dangerous positions alone, insisting his crew disembark.[9]

By mid-October, autumn rains fell. They fell for days, pouring constantly and accompanied by cold, gale-force winds. Rivers changed to raging torrents. Roads changed into seas of mud. The men were without specialized winter equipment. They lived in sodden clothing with no waterproof boots, their feet so cold and wet, trench foot was inevitable. By late October, the rain changed to snow, increasing the cold and the misery. At night in the mountains, with temperatures below freezing, the men lay, the thin snow sifting over them. They had been seventy-six successive days fighting the enemy. Ahead of them was the hill and the great sixth-century fortress abbey of Monte Cassino.[10]

For the men flying the air attacks from the U.S. air bases in southern Italy, targeting enemies in the north, the bad weather had provided a respite. It also afforded breaks for the men in the Fifty-seventh Service Squadron. One of them, Staff Sergeant George Cortesio from Centerville, drove south along the coastal highway from Paestum to the Calabrian village of Motta Saint Lucia. It was from this village that his grandfather, Giacinto Cortesio, with his wife, Rusaria, had emigrated to America, settling in Clarkdale, north of Centerville, in 1906. George wrote home to his father, Frank, in Mystic. He described the village and its fountain and finding the home of his grandparents. When he gave his name at the door, "Aunt Carmela, Teresina and Francesca were so glad that they were crying. Soon all my cousins were there and I really got a lot of kissing. I was the happiest guy in the world when I saw them and I bet mom will be twice as happy to know that I saw her sisters and relations ...I always did tell her that I wanted to see our people over here but little did I realize that a war would have to bring us together."[11]

George Cortesio's letter appeared in Charles DePuy's "Columns Write" on November 26, 1943. Two days later, in a Sunday telegram to Mystic, there was quite different news. It was delivered to Mr. and Mrs. Sam Beers and gave the news of the death of their son and only child, Sergeant William Booth Beers. Serving with the 168th Infantry in the mountains of Italy, Bill had stepped on a mine and died from his injuries. Similar news from Italy arrived to the parents of Ersal Wakefield, who lived on the Exline-Sedan highway, killed by an artillery shell. And there were the wounded, four from Centerville: Private First Class Paul Atkinson, Charles Tovrea, Sergeant Roy Long and one of the officers of Company G, Major Floyd Sparks.[12]

The town braced for more bad news. In the Pacific, its men were continuing to fight on west across the Solomon Islands to Vella Lavella, the Treasury Islands and to Bougainville, where Centerville's Royal Simmons—a Seventh-day Adventist, therefore unarmed—was a medic on the front lines, bandaging, administering sulfa drugs and giving morphine to the wounded. In the dual drive across the Solomon Sea, local men were fighting inland alongside Australians at Lae, Salamana, Finchafen, Arawe and Saidor. They were delivering the vast military equipment needed for the battles. They were fighting on submarines. County men were in army air force crews, flying dangerous missions over Europe. And Company G, the Thirty-fourth Infantry embedded in the Fifth Army, was still fighting in Italy.[13]

In the last days of December 1943, two top generals—Eisenhower and Montgomery—left Italy for London to plan the promised invasion of western Europe. On his departure, Eisenhower declared without qualification, "We will win the European war in 1944."[14]

Chapter 72

Military Aircraft and Employment Come to Centerville, Fighting in the Gilbert Islands, GIs Arrive in England

As the war entered its third year, men and women in uniform, home on leave or on furlough, were familiar sights on the streets of Centerville. Troop trains were racing across the County, children from Sara Ritchell's McKinley School class waving small flags at the sides of the tracks. At the depot on the Square's Southeast Corner, men called by the draft climbed aboard Des Moines–bound buses. They were those reaching their eighteenth birthdays and young family men with children. Convoys of army trucks stretching for miles entered the town from the east and then turned north. Military aircraft every day flew overhead in close formations, and aviator cadets from the Naval Air Station at Ottumwa practiced loops, circles and dives. Douglas C-47s made regular landings at Centerville Airport; so did BT-13s. Some came out of the night, their red-and-green wing-tip lights visible on the horizon, and roared overhead, said Jesse Beck, "like thunder on wings." Once a Martin Marauder with a faulty oil gauge made an emergency landing en route to Chicago. It came hurtling down out of the sky, landing on Centerville's half-mile shale runway with a landing speed of 165 miles per hour, the brakes screaming, the plane skidding to a stop eight feet short of the airport's north fence. On another occasion, a P-38 flew over the Square so low people ducked into business places, convinced it was about to crash land. Deputy Sheriff Gib Swanson swore the pilot ticked the courthouse. Unofficially people believed they knew the pilot. He was a local boy who'd promised his friends the next time he flew over the town he'd let them know. He also let them know at Mystic High School, where he'd graduated in 1943. He flew past the second-floor windows, then buzzed the school windows a second time.[1]

The bus depot on the Square's Southeast Corner was also busy transporting men and women leaving town for "vital war work" advertised in the newspaper by the local U.S. Employment Service on North Thirteenth Street. More than fifty were youths trained in welding and metal work at the NYA workshop at the fairground on the north end of Seventh and Eighth Streets. They were on their way to join colleagues working in the shipyards of Seattle, at Portland, Oregon, and to work on the "new super bombers," the B-29s, on the west coast. In the space of two months, 825 County people left to work as clerks, typists and stenographers for the FBI and the navy department in Washington, D.C.; to take multiple positions at the port of Hampton Roads, Virginia; or to work as electricians and carpenters building airports on a Canadian-Alaska project. Guy Evans, head of the employment office, worked on what he was told was a "vitally important" government project of which he knew nothing. He and other workers at the office worked night and day, Sundays and holidays, to convince people to leave their current work and homes for an unknown location, for an unstated "great military secret" that offered "large wages and patriotism." The office recruited 220 people, 125 from Appanoose County, most of those from Centerville. One year later, the place was revealed: Pasco, Washington State; the military secret—the atom bomb.[2]

All these citizens leaving the County created a local employment crisis. Businesses made competitive offers. Gambles on the Square's Westside advertised for women to sell insulation, siding and roofing, with salary and commission and a guaranteed permanent postwar position. The Hercules Manufacturing plant in South Centerville paid fifty to eighty-five cents an hour in "patriotic" essential war work, making parts for ships, invasion barges and troop transports. In Ottumwa, the John Morrell meat-packing plant offered seventy cents for overtime work, vacations with pay, free life insurance and a retirement-income plan. On farms where the need was acute, the State of Iowa imported three hundred to four hundred Mexican laborers from Texas. The State's prosperous farms advertised salaries of sixty-five to eighty-five dollars a month, with liberal allowances for married workers; they offered room, board and laundry for workers who were single. In agriculturally less-prosperous Appanoose County, Centerville businessmen formed a Business Men's Farm Aid group. They worked in harvest season or for any critical need. They worked the evenings after five o'clock, forming themselves into teams with captains and equipment. At the Arthur E. Sager farm northwest of Plano, the first emergency crew rolled in and stored nine loads of hay between six and darkness, complaining that had the moon been bright enough they would have shocked oats after supper. The *Centerville Daily Iowegian* struggled with a reduced staff. Drawing on a frontier days' notice, the paper placed its own apology: "Don't Shoot the Piano Player ...He Does the Best He Can!"[3]

The *Centerville Daily Iowegian*'s "piano player," editor Jesse Beck, was working overtime at the newspaper's two AP teletype machines. His November and December 1943 headlines—the Allied bombing of Berlin, the Russian advances in Kiev and the Crimea—were being nudged out by AP wire photos and reports of a giant leap by U.S. forces onto the Gilbert and Marshall atolls in the central Pacific. Making the leap possible were six cutting-edge, new aircraft carriers—newer, faster, stronger destroyers, cruisers and battleships, escorting the fast "attack transports" full of marines and infantry men. Those rubber collections, the many metal drives, the waste paper, fats and silk campaigns all fed into a national wartime production of 296,000 military aircraft, 102,000 tanks and 88,000 ships and landing crafts. This was accomplished at accelerated speeds, and it was done despite the diversion of some twenty million Americans into the armed forces. At the shipyards of Seattle and Portland, the time to build one Kaiser Liberty Ship was cut in 1943 from twenty-seven days to 10.3 hours. Contributing to the new efficiency were the many NYA Centerville graduates, among them welders Pauline VanNoy and Mary Large from near Exline, who was the first woman on the West Coast to become a member of the union and a journeyman welder with all rights and privileges.[4]

The invasion of Makin—the first of the Gilbert atolls—was reported in the *Centerville Daily Iowegian* on November 23. Resistance was light, the island taken in two days but not without challenges. *Yank* magazine ace photographer John Buscemi, born in Centerville and with many relatives and friends in the town, waded ashore with *Christian Science Monitor* correspondent John Beaufort, the two under enemy fire. He wrote to his aunt Opal Buscemi at the Blue Bird Cafe on the Square's Southside: "I saw our own planes burst and disappear into the black smoke. I got scared many times. The first night on Makin was the most horrible and miserable night of my life. We were in a foxhole and you could reach out and grab a handful of mosquitoes. The constant sniper and machine fire was worse ...Miller [writer Merle Miller, an Iowan from Tama County] and I are leaving on another mission in the near future."[5]

The next mission was the second atoll of the Gilberts: Tarawa. There the Marines were waging a desperate battle that would kill one thousand of them and wound two thousand others. The best available maps failed to show how close to the surface was an offshore reef. It caught and immobilized incoming landing crafts, forcing the Second Marine Division

John A. "One Shot" Buscemi with his camera. *Courtesy of Mary Ellen Bushemi Cessna.*

to wade ashore under withering and intense enemy fire. The first assault wave was described by Private First Class Charles "Curly" Kauzlarich of Rathbun in a letter to his brother Bill. "When I hit the beach," he wrote, "I thought I was in hell. All around me Marines were falling, some in instant death, others with gaping wounds. In the sky above us our Navy planes were swooping low strafing enemy positions. I could hear the chatter of Japanese machine guns and the sharp reports of rifles and the tremendous burst of mortar shells." Injured when a grenade exploded near him, he crawled from a shell hole when he spotted a corpsman. "Then everything got dark in front of my eyes," he wrote, "and then I passed out."[6]

When news of the fighting reached Buscemi, he prepared his Rolleiflex and Speed Graphic cameras and flew onto Tarawa. From the approaching seaplane, his first sight was hundreds of dead marines floating in the water. The surviving marines had fought on, battling the Japanese, who were defended in five-foot-thick concrete blockhouses and pillboxes made out of sand-filled oil drums. The island was secured in seventy-six hours.[7]

As each island was made safe, U.S. Navy Seabees built runways for the U.S. Seventh Army Air Force to target the next military objective. They built piers on coral reefs where ships could deliver supplies. The Forty-seventh Bomb Squadron Ordnance team arrived to set up camp, to service and prepare B-26 aircraft and to load them with three-hundred-pound bombs. One of the team was Motor Sergeant Bob Traxler of Exline. He drove Chevrolet ton-and-a-half trucks, pulling trailers carrying bombs to the aircraft.[8]

Across the world, thousands of young American men were arriving in Great Britain. Captain Jack Brody wrote to his wife on Centerville's East State Street that his arrival had dispelled his doubts about going. When he traveled from the port, he told her, "...the English people went out of their way to run to the siding to wave at us, and shout 'Welcome Yanks,' or 'Good Luck Americans' ...Old, middle-aged and young waved at us. I saw small babies just learning to walk practically crawling up a steep slope just to greet us. And in the not too far distance was mute evidence of what they had been going through." Former Centerville police patrolman Roy McFarland, now in the navy, wrote a letter to his former colleagues at City Hall. He, too, noticed the same evidence as he arrived in England: "We can really appreciate what the British went through ...for we have seen some of the ruins down along the Channel. They took an awful beating." Captain Brody and Roy McFarland were on their way to U.S. bases. Thousands of Americans were billeted in British homes. At one of them, Mr. and Mrs. H.W. Powell of Senghenydd, South Wales, wrote to Frank Sadaro's parents in Centerville: "You can surely be proud of your son who with other American boys here are a fine type of American youth ...we are happy to have the privilege of doing something for him in return for the great kindness your people over there have shown our boys for which we as parents are deeply grateful."[9]

Soon, that American kindness would translate into military action.

Chapter 73

News from Monte Cassino, Anzio, the Marshall Islands and New Guinea

Some nine hundred miles to the southeast from Great Britain, the U.S. Fifth Army's Thirty-fourth Division, which included the 168th Infantry and Centerville's Company G, was still fighting in the mountains of central Italy. It was January 1944, the weather appalling, the coldest in fifty years. Temperatures were below freezing, the men digging into stones, sleeping behind rocks and in half-caves with no blankets. Scripps Howard war correspondent Ernie Pyle observed the Thirty-fourth Infantry. People in Appanoose County were reading his syndicated articles appearing regularly in the *Des Moines Register*, occasionally reprinted in the *Centerville Daily Iowegian*. Night after night, Pyle watched as the Thirty-fourth's mules, carrying packboards of provisions—K and D rations, water, miles of telephone wire, ammunition, first-aid packets, sulfa drugs and mail—started up the treacherous, exposed mountain trails. The mules traveled one third of the way. The packboards were then transferred to supply and kitchen men, Corporal William Archer of Mystic and Sergeant Jack Calhoun of Centerville. They walked the last, bitter two-thirds distance to reach their buddies at the top.[1]

By January 10, the Thirty-fourth's assignment changed. For days and nights, they were in street-to-street, house-to-house, hand-to-hand, grenade-and-bayonet combat with Germans hiding in the villages of the Liri Valley. Fifteen days later, their assignment changed again. The Thirty-fourth was ordered to undertake what would be the first of three futile attempts to storm Monte Cassino itself. They were to cross the flooded Rapido River, take all the hills north of the monastery and circle to seize Highway 6 in the valley below, in the process isolating both the monastery and the town of Cassino. The men were rowed across the Rapido silently and at night by the Nineteenth Combat Engineers, among those at the oars Reese Hudson of Mystic. They now faced thick minefields, reinforced bunkers, steel pillboxes and massed artillery, some of it on portable bases that moved, appearing and disappearing into mountainsides. And they faced conditions in the mountains so extreme that the exhausted, the frozen and the injured had to be bodily lifted out of foxholes and carried down to medical aid stations. The *Des Moines Register and Tribune*'s Gordon Gammack traveled with the Thirty-fourth. His articles appeared in the *Centerville Daily Iowegian*. He described the Thirty-fourth's undertaking as "a mad, weird, horrible struggle in cold rain and snow of men sworn to kill or be killed." The depleted regiment, its members having exceeded human endurance, were sent for rest and relief as hundreds of B-17s bombed the sixth-century monastery. Within days, the "Red Bulls" were issued a new, emergency assignment: to support the besieged Allied forces on Anzio beachhead, seventy miles to the northwest.[2]

At Anzio, four British and U.S. divisions had landed on January 22. The beachhead, completely flat, relatively small (eight by ten miles), heavily criss-

Maurice Hudson. *Courtesy of Maurice Hudson.*

crossed with canals and drainage ditches and just thirty miles south of Rome, seemed the perfect location for a surprise, rapid capture of that city. Eight days later and solidly congested, the troops were trapped, pinned on the beach, their advance stalled, with no rocks or caves for shelter. The men dug their way underground into foxholes, into the sides of ditches and canals and remained that way for four long months, besieged in squalor and constant danger from bombing and shelling. The enemy, ensconced in the hills overlooking the beach, could see everything, sinking ships that were carrying supplies with guided bombs.

Into this, arriving at night on LST boats from Naples, came the Thirty-fourth Division. Somewhere always close alongside the fighting men, Ernie Pyle witnessed the action, and his accounts continued to appear in the *Des Moines Register*. He described getting off a boat at Anzio "...feeling pretty much like a clay pigeon in a shooting gallery." When he saw the daily conditions, he wrote, "On this beachhead every inch of our territory is under German artillery fire ...our army had moved underground ...this is the first time our entire ground force has had to burrow beneath the surface." German shells fell. They fell everywhere. They fell on clearly marked U.S. field hospitals, killing twenty-seven at one and wounding more than sixty, killing another six Red Cross nurses at a Red Cross hospital where the patients, all soldiers, urged the surviving nurses to go to the foxholes "and forget about us." The bombs fell on LSTs, on one carrying diesel oil, igniting the ship and killing 24 of the 108 on board. Coxswain Robert Hanrahan from Unionville escaped but was lying injured on the beach for sixteen days.[3]

There were extraordinary acts of courage: signal corps men, like Private First Class J.C. Kilbourn of Allerton, climbing up poles, placing wires in the darkness, feeling with their hands, setting up crucial lines of communication; the ever-present engineers, stringing barbed wire entanglements at night on the beachhead; medics making dashes for the badly wounded, some of the injured lying there and suffering until dark. There was Lieutenant Helen Talboy of Des Moines, leading nurses who seemed at breaking point, some crying soundlessly for the dead and the dying, the tears on their cheeks in the cold moonlight the only sign. There was Ann Goplerud of Osage, Iowa, the first Red Cross volunteer on the beach, who sang to the troops on the front line, in hospitals, anywhere, earning her the sobriquet "Anzio Ann," the symbol of the girl back home. And when Centerville's Second Lieutenant Wallace "Dutch" Koestner learned ammunition was urgently needed for men on the front line, he and a comrade found a cart and a brace of oxen, removed their helmets and weapons, lowered their trousers over their boots, donned peasants' coats and walked under fire, over two miles of a road unswept for mines and in full view of the enemy, to the ammunition dump, collected a load and returned over the same route.[4]

To the villages and the towns of Appanoose County, telegrams were arriving—those that engendered fear. Three went to Unionville. They reported the deaths of Private First Class Wilbur Lewis, captured by the Nazis in a tank battle at Cassino and dying there under their care three days later; and the death of Private Ralph Elder, killed on the road to Rome. Both men were twenty-eight years old, both were married and both were the fathers of small children. The third telegram was a "Wounded in Action" telegram, reporting the injury of Robert Hanrahan, the coxswain serving in the amphibious landings on Anzio—the one whose LST carrying diesel oil had ignited, killing 24 of the 108 on board.[5]

To Numa two telegrams arrived. One gave the death of Corporal Harold Willits at Cassino. He was head of the music department and an instructor at Numa High School. So gentle, so kind a man, no one who knew him could equate him with any kind of warfare. He was killed, it was reported, carrying the stretcher of a fallen comrade. The second telegram was of an injury. A severe shrapnel leg wound had hospitalized Alfred Ostino, a member of Numa's closely knit Italian community.[6]

Another two telegrams went to Moulton. A "Killed in Action" message was delivered to the home of the town's former mayor L.B. Swartz. William "Bill" Swartz, just twenty years old, was a "crack shot" serving with the U.S. Rangers. He was killed on dangerous secret missions, his father was told, "back of German lines" somewhere over Italy. Moulton's second telegram was a "Wounded in Action" report. Sergeant Earl Brinegar, an Appanoose County farmer, husband and father, had been wounded for the second time at Cassino.[7]

To Exline went the report of the death of Eugene Sales, a naval motor machinist, killed in the landing operations at Anzio beachhead. He left a wife and a seventeen-month-old daughter. Mrs. Lottie Ross of nearby Cincinnati received a "Missing in Action" telegram. She had four sons, all serving in reconnaissance in the navy. This reported the youngest, Loren, twenty years old, a private with the Cavalry Reconnaissance Troops, missing on the Anzio beachhead.[8]

Five telegrams arrived in Centerville. Three reported deaths. Two twenty-six-year-olds, both privates, both serving with Company G, were dead. Jack Brown was killed at Cassino, and Lester "Jug" Brinegar, one of seven children living on South Nineteenth and known all over Centerville, was killed at Anzio. Two streets to the east, on South Seventeenth, Mrs. Ella Johnson learned of the death of one of her ten children, Private James Johnson, twenty years old, dead at Anzio. A "Wounded in Action" telegram told of Private First Class Delmar Kennedy, wounded at Anzio. The fifth telegram reported Private Amos B. McGhghy missing in action at Anzio.[9]

To these reports came more: news of death and injuries in the Pacific theater.

After Tarawa in the Gilbert Islands, the next military target was the atolls comprising the Marshall Islands. This was thc next *Yank* magazine assignment for Centerville's John Buscemi. He cleaned and oiled his cameras, wiped the lenses free of the fungus that the high humidity caused to accumulate daily and landed on Kwajalein with the Seventh Infantry Division. Kwajalein was secured in four days. John Buscemi's photographs appeared in *Yank* magazine in early March. Buscemi then moved 350 miles northwest with the Twenty-seventh Division to Eniwetok, landing there on February 19 together with *Yank* writer Merle Miller and correspondents and photographers from other services. Here resistance was heavier. The men moved forward through a rain of sixty-millimeter knee mortar shells. Buscemi was hit. He suffered shrapnel wounds to his left leg, cheek and neck. There was a considerable loss of blood. Litter bearers carried him to an aid station. He asked Miller about the condition of his cameras. "To reassure him," Miller said, "we put the cameras on the litter where he could keep his eyes on them." Placed on a landing boat, the wounded Buscemi was taken for immediate surgery to the medical unit on board U.S.S. *Neville*. His last words as the anesthetic was administered were, "Be sure to get those pictures back to the office." John Buscemi died in surgery.[10]

The news reached Centerville by telegram ten days later. It was delivered to his uncle, Jesse, at the Blue Bird Cafe on Centerville Square's Southside. The news swiftly spread across the town. John Buscemi was born in Centerville and had attended the local schools before his father, Pietro, moved the family to Gary, Indiana. John returned to Centerville often and was popular, with his good looks, his energy, his spontaneous friendliness. People recalled the last time he visited the town. Before leaving for overseas he'd flown into the airport with a pilot friend.[11]

As the Marshall Islands of Kwajalein and Eniwetok were secured, General Douglas MacArthur's troops were advancing west along New Guinea's north coast. MacArthur received detailed and precise reconnaissance intelligence in advance of his landings from 138 men selected to be "Alamo Scouts." These men, exposing themselves to incredible danger, worked in teams of six or seven. They operated behind enemy lines. They moved silently in camouflage with painted faces and hands. They collected data on enemy troops, their numbers, their locations, the physical circumstances that U.S. invading troops would face. One of the scouts was Staff Sergeant Verne M. Miller, whose home was Jerome, some eight miles west of Centerville.[12]

Working confidently with this received intelligence, MacArthur's infantry began leaping ahead hundreds of miles, bypassing thousands of Japanese troops. They leaped to Aitape, to Hollandia, to Biak Island. At Hollandia, Centerville's Trenton Mericle, a member of his infantry unit, collapsing under the combined weight of a machine gun, tripod and packs, recovered to make the amphibious landing and fight to take Japanese airstrips at both Hollandia and Biak Island. In both places Trenton survived four direct sniper attacks. Even luckier was Moulton's Fred Swartz, whose younger brother died in Italy. Fred was heard on the radio. In a heated clash with the Japanese on New Guinea, a bullet had pierced his helmet and plowed a furrow in his hair "as close and clean as though it had been done by clippers."[13]

Not all Appanoose County men in that area of the Pacific were as fortunate.

A telegram announcing the drowning death of Cecil Gerdon, a chief commissary steward in the navy, was received by his brother, an official at the Red Cross Drug Store on the Square's Southside. Another went to Rathbun: Private First Class Joseph Francis Morris was killed serving with the marines in the Pacific. And there were the wounded—on New Guinea, Private First Class Paul Kauzlik, who was employed by the Economy Cleaners on Thirteenth Street, and Byron Inman, whose parents lived west of Centerville. Byron's injury happened at Aitape. He was wading in a stream, circling to eliminate a Japanese ambush. A Japanese sniper shot him in the left eye; the bullet simultaneously severed the optic nerve to the right eye. Byron survived, but he was permanently blinded.[14]

With repeated successful offensives across the Pacific, the United States was now poised to attack the Mariana Islands—Saipan, Tinian and Guam. With a U.S. victory, these islands would provide bases for bombing operations, taking the war directly to Japan itself.[15]

But much of the town, following the radio reports and the headlines in the *Centerville Daily Iowegian* and other newspapers, was now focusing on western Europe.

Chapter 74

Preparations for Western European Invasion

As General Eisenhower arrived in London to command the planned invasion of western Europe, his prediction "the European War will be over in 1944" was being discussed in Centerville. "There are people who think this year may 'wind up' the war," said Charles DePuy to the troops in his "Columns Write" early in the year. "We hope they're right one hundred per cent ...We want you back here in 1945 without fail, but before that if possible." At the Legion Hall on Drake Avenue, the County's veterans of three wars were giving their own predictions, writing them down on slips of paper. Their consensus: the war with Germany would end in August or September 1944, the war with Japan in 1945 or 1946. Both wars, these men insisted, must end with unconditional surrender, but unlike Charles DePuy, they didn't see the boys returning home until "1950 to never."[1]

At the same time, Eisenhower and the chiefs of staff from Britain and the United States were refining their plans. Americans in their smooth, tailored uniforms of olive jackets and beige trousers were flooding into Britain in a tidal wave. Hundreds of thousands were arriving every week, 1.5 million by May 1944, pouring into a country smaller than Iowa. There had been portents: at first a scattering of officers; 950 civilian technicians in Northern Ireland; 13,000 more making radar equipment and operating radar stations ringing the British coastline; 10,000 Americans committed to the Allied cause who'd enlisted in the Canadian Army and the Royal Canadian Air Force; and those famous fliers of the Eagle Squadron who'd joined the British Royal Air Force, flying bombing missions across occupied France. And at more than eighty airfields in southeast England, where they lived in barracks and huts and squad tents with wooden floors, were thousands of the U.S. Army's Eighth Air Force. Every airman flew twenty-five missions in a crew of ten aboard "Flying Fortresses"—the B-17s—each aircraft given a nickname. Each mission's target was to destroy the Luftwaffe and the German industrial might by precision strategic bombing in daylight, complementing the RAF's bombing at night. The Eighth's first mission was a daylight attack on the marshalling yards at Rouen in which the lead plane was flown by Paul Tibbets of Des Moines.[2]

One of the early airmen serving with the 413th Squadron of the U.S. Army's Eighth Air Force was Eugenc "Gene" Wilcox of Moravia. Within three months, he'd participated in enough combat missions to qualify for the Air Medal, two oak leaf clusters, and promotion to first lieutenant and to pilot duty. In August 1943 Gene flew a B-17 named "Alcohol Annie" on a mission to the Ruhr. "There's no milk run to the Ruhr cities," he wrote, "no place in the world where the flak is so thick or the fighters so bothersome. The British nick-named the Ruhr 'Happy Valley,' which is like calling Dante's Inferno 'Playland.'" On that flight, Dante's Inferno became Lieutenant Gene Wilcox's reality. As "Alcohol Annie" approached the German coast, the plane's third engine was hit, then the fourth, followed by the first. Two shells struck the nose; one went through the navigator's compartment and yet another, fired from below, went through the cockpit between—but just missing—Gene Wilcox and his copilot, Phil Stratton from Kansas City. With five of the crew killed, one wing on fire and billowing smoke and chunks of metal dropping from the under carriage, Gene Wilcox turned back and ditched the plane in the ocean. He and the four other survivors spent two days and nights on a raft on the surface of the North Sea until rescued by the RAF. Gene wrote of the account. It was published in the national magazine *True* and featured in the movie *Five Came Back*. At the end of the article, he wrote, "I want to go again, as I did when I was a kid in high school, over to the county seat towns—Albia and Centerville—go to the movies and have dates, see my folks again, and see a girl I haven't put eyes on for two years." Gene's wish never transpired. Given the choice of a ground job or flying again, he chose the second. In late September 1943, Gene Wilcox failed to return from a mission over Europe. His remains were never found.[3]

The loss of Lieutenant Gene Wilcox, his crew and the B-17 he was flying was an instance of the huge damage being inflicted on the U.S. Army's Eighth Air Force. One month after Gene's disappearance, in a six-day raid on the ball bearing plants at Schweinfurt, the Eighth Air Force lost 148 bombers and their crews, totaling 1,480 men.[4]

When the bombers left their English bases on bombing missions, they flew in perfect *V* formations. Watching them, photographing them with his Leica camera, sketching and taking notes in his sketchbook was artist and Centerville native Manuel Bromberg, a member of the U.S. War Artists Unit. He also watched their return, noting the holes in their formations, indicating the planes lost.[5]

By early 1944, the world's newest and fastest fighter planes—the P-38 Lightning, the P-47 Thunderbolt and the P-51 Mustang—were offering bombers some protection. They escorted aircraft to bomb Germany. They escorted them across the North Sea from England and north up the Italian peninsula. These aircraft, too, were targets for the German Messerschmitts and Focke-Wulfs. Flying in the first P-38 Lightning group to operate from British bases and penetrate deeply into Germany was Lieutenant Raymond Lee Sumpter of Cincinnati. After Sumpter completed ten missions, qualifying him for his first oak leaf cluster, his father in Cincinnati learned he was missing in action. Three months later he was pronounced killed in action.[6]

Escorting the B-24s of the U.S. Army Fifteenth Air Force north out of Italy were P-47s and the P-51 Mustangs—the latter named the "Red Tails" for their bright red-painted tails. Centerville's Phil Brunow, a waist gunner on one of the B-24s flying north from Cerignola Air Base in Italy, remembered the "Red Tails." They were operated by the Tuskegee Airmen, the all-African American crewmen who knew they were fighting two enemies: fascism abroad and racism at home, four years before President Harry S. Truman desegregated the U.S. Armed Forces.[7]

New reports of aircraft deaths, wounds and escapes were arriving in the County. Killed were Staff Sergeant Carl Hampton of Mystic and Flying Fortress bombardier Brice Cain of Moravia. Missing were two from Udell—Lieutenant Clifford "Wendell" Swank, raised there after the deaths of both his parents, and Staff Sergeant Jack H. King, one of the six sons of Walter King serving in the war; another missing, from near Udell, was Lieutenant Dale Stuckey, who'd survived Pearl Harbor, was reported missing and then was changed to prisoner-of-war status after an air crash. And another prisoner of war, Centerville Staff Sergeant Chester C. Strickler, was also shot down, his left leg broken. All six men were reported lost somewhere over Europe. Two Centerville men, paratrooper Richard Kelly and Private First Class Paul Atkinson, were injured and patients in an English hospital. And Staff Sergeant Jack Trimble, the son of the pastor of the Central Church of Christ, who was serving as a nose gunner and engineer, was one of only two men out of a crew of eleven who survived being shot down over Germany. "The worst part of it all," wrote Jack to his parents, "was when we returned to the hut where we had all lived together, and the other men were not there."[8]

The people of the town knew the bombing was preparatory for the big invasion. And they knew it was vital for the invasion's success. Radio news reports were heard across the County. From WHO, the NBC station in Des Moines, there were fifteen every weekday, five on Sundays. And on Mondays, Wednesdays and Fridays, there were accounts and analyses by H.V. Kaltenborn, who won ten awards for his wartime work, including the Dupont Radio Award. At the *Centerville Daily Iowegian* office on Main Street, dispatches were printed from AP reporters around the world; so were opinion pieces and reprinted articles. Morgan Beatty, who also worked for NBC News, warned readers that "the hour of maximum sacrifice to win the war is just around the corner." Winston Churchill compared the coming Allied offensive to Gettysburg and Waterloo, because "it would be accompanied by bitter sorrow because of the losses." An article reprinted from *Colliers Weekly* was frighteningly specific. The author was Quentin Reynolds, veteran war correspondent, who'd been an eyewitness to battles in four countries, including the one at the Salerno beachhead. The landing troops, he wrote, will be "compelled literally to blast their way through concrete for fifty miles while battling crack and superbly equipped German troops." He wrote of the countless mines fortifying the coastline from Normandy to Spain. He described the shore batteries, the machine guns, mortars, high-explosive grenades, the constant avalanche of destruction from the Luftwaffe, the concrete- and steel-reinforced pillboxes, the blockhouses and the long-range guns, expertly camouflaged.[9]

Everyone in Centerville, in Appanoose County and across the nation was under intense strain. Everyone was waiting for D-Day, waiting for word their boys had battled their way up from the beaches of western Europe and established secure locations. There was one source of comfort. The Allied Command had selected where the invasion landings would occur: a forty-mile strip of the Normandy coast between the Orne River and the Cotentin Peninsula, the eastern sector assigned to the British, the western to the Americans. They also had selected a date: June 5, 1944. But the decisions were top-level secrets known only to a few high-ranking Allied officers. The Nazis were unclear, and the Allies further confused them with deception. Maps were published in the world newspapers. People in Appanoose County studied them in the *Centerville Daily Iowegian*. They showed possible invasion routes into western Europe from the east, from the south, from England via Norway, Holland, the Bay of Biscay, Normandy and at the narrowest point of the English Channel to Calais. False radio messages were sent; dummy parachutists, decoy aircraft and papier-mâché tanks were assembled in the roads and fields of Kent and Sussex opposite Calais.[10]

Supplies, warships and transports were filling the harbors along England's south coast; so were thousands more troops, sent to camps according to the beaches in France that would be their destinations: the British to Kent, to East and West Sussex; Americans to Dorset, Somerset and Devon. Lowell Marshall wrote home to his parents in Centerville, "The countryside is more beautiful than you could ever imagine."[11]

There were occasions of public goodwill. Private First Class Cecil R. Cline of Exline represented Iowa at a civic reception and dance held to honor good relations between England and America at the invitation of the lord mayor of Leicester, and thousands of Londoners applauded as three thousand Americans marched through central London. There were private moments of happiness and goodwill. Centerville's Private First Class Ray Simmons married an English bride, Lola Steight, in Dursley, Gloucestershire, his best man another Iowan, Private First Class Charles Biery from Ida Grove. Corporal William Callen of Moravia located his one and only brother, one he hadn't seen in two years. "It was the happiest day of my life," he wrote home to his mother, "'Arch' got the day off and we talked about everything back home..." And there were events that rendered emotion. Lowell Marshall and his fellow soldiers were invited to a Mother's Day service at a local church. The minister urged each to be "...the boy your Mother thinks you are ...Many handkerchiefs were waving," continued Lowell, "and the guys didn't all have colds, either."[12]

Everyone knew their men in England were undergoing rigorous training. AP wire photos appearing in the *Centerville Daily Iowegian* showed lines of troops marching in strict formation. Another showed soldiers under full backpacks heading to camp fifteen miles away over rough, open English countryside. For training specific to the invasion landings, the beaches on the southern coast of Devon were considered good replicas for those in Normandy, which for the Americans were now coded Omaha and Utah. In late April, long convoys of tanks, jeeps, trucks and troops clogged the narrow streets of the villages and towns that bordered the coast. On the beaches, troops exercised practice runs, rehearsing for D-Day over and over and over again, every detail, every maneuver carefully timed. Ships, transports and LSTs were loaded with jeeps, tanks and trucks, a special waterproof fitment placed over exhausts. Also on board were combat engineers of the First Engineer Special Brigade. Infantry loaded aboard LCIs (Landing Craft Infantry) practiced climbing across the sides and descending toward the ocean on rope ladders. Centerville native and artist Manuel Bromberg, wearing his correspondent's patch, carrying his Leica and a sketchbook, was embedded with Headquarters Company 116, scheduled to land on D-Day plus thirty minutes. He was issued waterproof covering. It smelled and was stiff and clammy. Chaplains and priests offered prayers. Men of all faiths attended. When the LCIs opened up, they disgorged the infantry, the men hitting the ground, Manuel Bromberg among them, crawling toward a bluff; Bromberg turned to capture the images.[13]

On one of the larger exercises on April 27–28, labeled Operation Tiger at Slapton Sands, nine German E-boats—high-speed boats that could lay mines and fire torpedoes—spotted a convoy of eight U.S. LSTs and attacked. As a result, 638 U.S. servicemen were killed; another 308 died from friendly fire. Centerville Private First Class Joe Coates, a member of the 147th Amphibious Combat Engineers, stationed at Paignton and a participant in the training operation, remembered hearing about boats sinking. So did Manuel Bromberg. But the disaster was a closely guarded secret. According to the Combined Operations website, "No official communiqué was issued and the staff of the 228th Sherbourne Hospital in Dorset, who received hundreds of immersion and burn cases, were simply told to ask no questions and warned that they would be subject to court martial if they discussed the tragedy."[14]

By May, the USAAF and the RAF were bombing Nazi installations along the French coast relentlessly and incessantly. Articles from AP cited inland rail lines and rail centers, airfields, known naval and submarine bases, war factories, chemical plants and Messerschmitt assembly plants that were being targeted and reduced to rubble. In Centerville, people attended the Majestic Theatre for a three-day showing of the four-reel documentary *The Memphis Belle*. It was named for the first Flying Fortress, the B-17 of the U.S. Army Air Force, to return home after completing twenty-five missions. Every scene of the documentary, written and directed by Hollywood director William Wyler, then a lieutenant colonel, was made under actual combat conditions by photographers and crew members of the U.S. Eighth Air Force. Those who attended the showings at the Majestic were made graphically aware of the dangers the crews faced. They saw crews shot down. They saw the deadly flak and the attacks from the constantly present Luftwaffe. The *Centerville Daily Iowegian* declared it beggared description through words.[15]

Reports from Great Britain were appearing daily in the *Centerville Daily Iowegian*. Preparations for D-Day were clearly accelerating. British main-line passenger train schedules were being slashed without warning. Troops were given priority on those still running. Soldiers and sailors of the American Expeditionary Forces were leaving camps and homes where they'd been billeted. More came by sea in transports. More LSTs arrived. Communication was silenced. All travel to Ireland—where German diplomats and spies were harbored—was heavily restricted. At night, ships moved south from the Firth of Clyde and Belfast, past Liverpool, Swansea, Bristol. They got into formation, turned left at Lands End and made for their designated ports. At night, British people watched the skies above their gardens, where the drone of waves of aircraft moving south could be heard. Guarding the eastern Atlantic and the English Channel, brilliantly, from submarine attacks was the navy patrol. Lieutenant Richard Owen of Jerome, the pilot of a twin-engine aircraft with Patrol Bombing Squad 212, scanned the ocean, dropping bombs on target. So did Seaman First Class Danny Chriss of West Maple Street and Lieutenant Commander Cleo Kerschner of South Eighteenth, in charge of air patrols that had sunk ninety U-boats, and so did Corydon's Calvin Sharp, well-known in Centerville, his mother's hometown, who lost his life when the aircraft he was aboard developed engine trouble and lost altitude, and his parachute failed to open in time.[16]

By June 3, USAAF pathfinder John Koestner of Centerville was waiting at an air base in southern England. He was waiting for instructions to load his C-47 cargo aircraft with paratroopers of the 82nd and 101st U.S. Airborne Divisions. At English harbors, hundreds of LCTs and LCIs were filled with infantrymen; British people lined the shores, waving good-bye and shouting good luck. In one of the LCIs, scheduled for the first-wave landing on Omaha Beach, Centerville's Private First Class Ray Simmons, married just thirty-four days, prepared himself. A Seventh-day Adventist like his brother Royal on Bougainville in the Pacific, he was a noncombatant. He was unarmed and ready to operate a medical unit. Radio silence prevailed. No lights were permitted.[17]

By early June 4, there was a thick, low cloud cover. It began to rain. A wind churned the English Channel into high waves. For the men already loaded aboard ships and transports, it was cold, wet misery. Many vomited. The weather report for June 5—the planned date of the invasion—was worse. Eisenhower decided to postpone the invasion by one day, moving it to June 6.[18]

But for the people at home, the headlines for almost a week were not about Normandy. They were about Italy, some nine hundred miles to the southeast. And they focused on the city of Rome.

Chapter 75

The Liberation of Rome, the Invasion of Normandy Gets Underway

In May 1944, as preparations for the invasion of Normandy were poised on England's south coast, in Italy German forces were in a northerly retreat. The British Eighth Army, reinforced with Americans, Canadians, French, Poles, Indians, South Africans and Moroccans, aimed yet again at Monte Cassino. After three months of bloody fighting, the Second Polish Division captured the ruins of the monastery, enduring appalling losses but driven to avenge what the Germans had done to their homeland. The date was May 19, and the Liri Valley now gave access to Rome, one hundred miles to the northwest.[1]

Four days later, the troops pinned for five months in their foxholes on Anzio beach broke out. Preceded by a fifteen-minute artillery preparation, the great exit from the beachhead smashed into action. Iowa's "Red Bull" Division—the Thirty-fourth Infantry—was assigned to hold the perimeters, allowing the First Special Forces on the right, the Third Infantry in the center and the First Armored Division (including the 168th Infantry, full of Appanoose County boys) on the left to pierce through the German iron ring of defense.[2]

Progress was rapid. The Germans defending that ring reeled back in confusion. Hundreds were captured and placed in prisoner cages. Flying overhead, B-24 Liberator Bombers and B-17 Flying Fortresses of the U.S. Army's Fifteenth Air Force, based in Italy, hammered at Nazi lines in a fifty-mile radius of Rome. They flew across the Adriatic, pounding airfields and aircraft plants in Vienna and Graz, the railroads at Zagreb and the chief source of Nazi oil—the Ploesti oil fields in Romania. At least nine Appanoose County families, among them the Brunows and the Hobarts, whose sons flew with the Fifteenth in Italy, anxiously listened to radio news reports, in particular those of H.V. Kaltenborn and Robert St. John.[3]

The U.S. Fifth and the British Eighth Armies fought on north. The advance was day and night at top speed. They traveled through fields of red poppies and flat stretches of golden grain. Private First Class Floyd Purvis noted with his Appanoose County farm-boy eyes and wrote home to his parents, "They do raise some corn, alfalfa, and other grains ...but their main crops are wheat, oats, tomatoes, and beans."[4]

The men pushed on, fighting through towns and villages: Cisterna, Lanuvio, Velletri. They passed ditches full of crosses carrying British, American and German names. They found "carpets" of dead Germans, mounds of their discarded equipment and columns of two thousand German prisoners, worn and bewildered, streaming to the back to join twelve thousand already surrendered.[5]

Ahead, as ever, were the engineers—the Nineteenth Combat, Reese Hudson among them—clearing mines, repairing destroyed bridges. At each advance, members of the Signal Division, including J.C. Kilbourn of Allerton, were tirelessly linking units by telephone, maintaining constant contact between division headquarters and the corps along the line and to the rear.[6]

AP reports in the *Centerville Daily Iowegian* told of their advance. On May 29 they were "nearing Rome." On the thirty-first, they were "within 18 miles." They had captured high ground in the Alban hills and could see Michelangelo's dome of St. Peter's Cathedral. By June they were "within 14 miles." On June 4, the Fifth Army rode triumphantly into Rome. It was a Sunday. The news reached Centerville via radio. The next day, the fifth, people in the town eagerly read the *Centerville Daily Iowegian* headline. It read, "Fifth Army Drives across River." They learned the Fifth Army—containing men from Appanoose County—had moved beyond Rome. It was moving north across the River Tiber, pursuing the Germans with hardly a look at the ancient monuments of western civilization, all preserved in a no-bombing agreement between the Germans and the Allies. But what the troops did see were the thousands of Italians lining the streets who, wrote AP reporter Noland Norgaard, cheered and rushed to kiss "the bearded and grimy liberators."[7]

At that moment, nine hundred miles to the northeast, it was still raining in England, the channel still stormy. Hours before, Eisenhower had received the latest meteorological prediction. There would be a twenty-four-hour clear spell beginning late on the fifth. There was a five-minute silence. Eisenhower's response: "O.K. We'll go." The order went out at 4:15 a.m. on the fifth.[8]

On June 6, the initial assault fleet of nearly six thousand ships put out from a dozen different English ports. Among them were men from Appanoose County, including Joe Coates, Robert McGuire, Richard Southern and Private First Class Ray Simmons—the Seventh-day Adventist—unarmed and with the Medical Corps. Waiting at an airfield in a Pathfinder C-47 Paratroop Transport Aircraft was Staff Sergeant John Koestner of Centerville, a radio operator. He noted the aircrafts were painted khaki, three white stripes on each wing, steel plates under seats, fresh water in the tanks to clean windshields of sea-water spray as they flew low under German radar. Near midnight, thirteen thousand paratroopers, each face blackened, the equipment of each weighing eighty-five to one hundred pounds, were driven to the airfields to board the waiting Pathfinders. Among them, one of the 82nd "All American" Airborne Division, was Private First Class Harold L. Parris of Mystic. The engines whined. They roared into action. They taxied down the runway and lifted from the concrete surfaces. The planes flew in *V* formations of nine planes. The center plane of the first three served as an immediate point, with visible, winking, red-and-green navigation lights.[9]

John Koestner's Pathfinder C-47, at the lead of the third flight, arrived over the French coast, greeted, he said, by what looked like a "Fourth of July celebration" of tracer shells and searchlights. In the forty-five-minute journey, he'd been tensely listening to his radio, fearful of being signaled that the invasion had been called off a second time. The Germans were jamming the radio signals, and he was terrified at the thought of his three planes dropping the 82nd and 101st U.S. paratroopers when there was no back-up. Nearing the target, anxious at leaving his steel plate–reinforced seat, he moved to a window to signal the other two C-47s with a green flashing light that they were over the drop zone.

John Koestner. *Courtesy of Virginia Koestner.*

It was the return trip to England that John Koestner would never forget. The clouds had cleared, and eighty-five hundred feet beneath him lay the Allied invasion fleet. "They were so thick, it looked like you could step ship-to-ship back to England," and there were the thousands of planes and troop gliders all flying toward France, looking "like a huge flock of geese."

The invasion was underway. From the moment the first barges started across the

English Channel, President Roosevelt, working behind blackout curtains in his White House bedroom, was informed of the invasion by telephone calls from the army's nerve center in the Pentagon. Soon the news was flashing around the country. In Appanoose County it arrived just after midnight.[10]

Chapter 76

June 6, 1944: Normandy

That morning of June 6, 1944, the thousands of ships, the thousands of aircraft that had turned the English Channel into the congested, broad highway that John Koestner witnessed from his C-47 as he flew back to England, were delivering Allied forces onto five Normandy beaches. They were landing between six and seven-thirty in the morning, French time, coinciding with predictable tides. To the east, the Canadians and the British at Juno and Sword met little initial resistance, but the British at Gold suffered heavy losses to two battalions.[1]

For the Americans at Utah—the furthest beach to the west, at the base of the Cotentin Peninsula—landings began at six thirty. The beach was protected from the wind. The seas were smooth, but craft floundered on mines. Some were swamped. Men landed shoulder deep in water, some a mile off target, their heavy equipment pulling them under. Within hours, reinforcements arrived, among them the 634th Tank Division. On board, the emblem of a black cat with a tank in its mouth on his shoulder, was personnel officer Tom King. Tom was one of the six sons of Walt King of Udell, all six serving their country. Tom's assignment on landing: to count the dead and wounded.[2]

But of all the landings, nothing compared to the catastrophe that was occurring on Omaha Beach where the First, "the Big Red," and Twenty-ninth U.S. Infantry Divisions were arriving, among them Mystic's Joe Coates, Moulton's Richard Southern, Cincinnati's James Lee Harrington and, in the first wave, Ray Simmons. Waiting for them were Germans of one of the best German divisions. The Germans were tunneled into foxholes and sand dunes.

Joe Coates. *Courtesy of Joe Coates.*

They were in deep trenches, providing them with underground protection and magazines of extra ammunition. They were armed with machine guns and mortars capable of firing shells in high trajectories. They were in concrete pillboxes and reinforced bunkers that housed heavy artillery. They were waiting with more artillery on the cliffs, their 88-millimeter projectiles designed to match those on the cliffs opposite, delivering shells at cross angles to rake diagonally across the beach. And on top of Pointe du Hoc, the clifftop to the west, were five 155-millimeter guns. Every inch of the Omaha Beach had been presighted for fire. And there was more. Lacing the underwater area, the beach, the shingles and the bluff fifty yards away were mines, wires, barbed-wire entanglements and "Rommel's asparagus"—steel beams tipped with more mines.[3]

As the men of the First and the Twenty-ninth approached the shore, a northwest wind pushed the landing crafts off course. So did a rapidly rising tidal current. Appanoose County's five men witnessed landing boats being mined and swamped, men drowning, tanks floundering, artillery shells exploding into action, firing down and across, pinning all the men on the beach. Men on the LCIs and LCAs (Landing Craft Assault) were shot, their officers, captains and sergeants killed. The lieutenant on Moulton's Richard Southern's craft said he'd be the first off onto the beach. He wasn't. Richard was the first off, climbing down a rope carrying too much weight, including a twenty-nine-pound radio, crucial for communication. He landed waist-deep in water, chest-deep after a sandbar. Bodies were everywhere. They touched each other, floating in the sea. Men pulled the wounded away from the water, attempting to drag them to the bluff, to the base of the cliffs. Richard Southern fought across the beach; so did Joe Coates, who'd landed neck-deep in water, Bob Nevins and Robert McGuire. And so did the unarmed Ray Simmons, who reached

Richard Southern. *Courtesy of Richard Southern.*

the one-hundred-foot bluff fifty yards away with no recollection of how. He set up his medical unit and began administering sulfa drugs and plasma to the rapidly arriving wounded—the first so badly hurt, medical attention seemed immaterial.[4]

From the moment the first invasion barges departed from England, President Roosevelt, working behind blackout curtains in his White House bedroom, was informed by telephone calls from the army's nerve center at the Pentagon. They continued as the news flashed around the country. In Appanoose County it arrived just after midnight. From then on, few slept. They sat by their radios until two, three, four and later in the morning. Reports were relayed from the BBC in a reciprocal arrangement with American broadcasters. At the *Centerville Daily Iowegian* office on South Main Street, editor Jesse Beck worked without sleep throughout the night. He drew his information from radio reports and those from Europe sent by Wes Gallagher on the newspaper's two AP teletype machines. Before light, a notice was posted on The Smoke Shop on Centerville Square's Eastside. It read, "The Smoke Shop ...Will Remain Closed Until the Beachhead in France Is Firmly Established."[5]

Reports arrived intermittently. From Juno and Sword, the British and Canadians were advancing toward Caen. The British who had survived Gold were moving inland in the direction of Bayeaux. On Utah, arriving American troops were connecting with the 82nd and 101st U.S. Airborne Divisions and moving west to take control of the Cotentin Peninsula and target Cherbourg, the vital seaport on its northern tip. On bloody Omaha, reinforcements, pretimed to arrive within minutes of each other, were further clogging the congestion unable to move off the beach. General Omar Bradley, in charge of the landings, was considering evacuation and ordering arriving reinforcements to land at Utah or the British beaches. Then came the message: "[We are] advancing up heights." It was noon in Normandy, six in the morning in Centerville. Jesse Beck began tentatively assembling the reports to form that day's extra-edition newspaper headline. It read, "Invasion Holds." The all-capital letters measured almost two-and-a-half inches in height.[6]

Across Appanoose County, as across the nation, churches opened. People gathered to pray. In Philadelphia the Liberty Bell rang out. In a Brooklyn shipyard, hundreds of men and women on night shift knelt by the glare of arc lamps on the decks of unfinished Liberty ships and recited the Lord's Prayer. They gathered to pray in Virginia at the home base of the Twenty-ninth Infantry, their men then fighting and dying on bloody Omaha. They prayed in Moberly, Missouri, the hometown of General Omar Bradley. They did in Albuquerque, New Mexico, summoned by sirens and whistles that announced the news. They did in New York City at the Stock Exchange, at the World War I Eternal Light memorial, at Lord and Taylor's department store, at the U.S. Veterans Hospital, where patients, still hospitalized from World War I, in pajamas, in bathrobes, walking on crutches and on canes, left their beds, gathered on the hospital lawns and bowed their heads in silent prayer. They did at Iowa's Fort Des Moines, where members of the Women's Army Auxiliary Corps met at the post's chapel or prayed alone on their bunks. All day, the women seemed distracted. One poured syrup for her hot cakes into her coffee. Another, Private Victoria Chase, whose home was near Nevers in France, said, "Thank God. I know how happy my people will be." It was a joy shared by a group of French sailors in New York City. They linked arms and danced down Broadway.[7]

Throughout the day, radios were heard across the nation, the voices of the king of England, General Eisenhower, President Roosevelt and Ed Murrow. Everywhere, the invasion was the subject of conversations. Everywhere, newspapers were studied. In Appanoose County, it was an unusually cold and rainy day for early June. In Mystic, Ned Clark's once-a-week cream route to collect eggs and cream for Meadow Gold Creamery was canceled because of the rain and mud. Thirteen-year-old Bill Smallwood joined the town's men. They sat huddled by a roaring fire in the stove of the East End Market and listened to the radio reports. Their thoughts, like those of the nation, focused some four thousand miles away on the other side of the Atlantic Ocean.[8]

Chapter 77

Fighting in France, in Italy and in the Marianas, Japan Bombed

By late afternoon Centerville time on June 6, darkness was falling in Normandy. On Omaha Beach, men dug in for the night. Mystic's Joe Coates, on the sand, slept fitfully. "Bed Check Charlie," a German pilot flying at night, trying to blow up a nearby barge loaded with ammunition, kept him awake until the plane was shot down and fell into the sea. Moulton's Richard Southern and Centerville's Bob McGuire were inland, up on top of the bluffs. Both dug holes into the ground with their trenching shovels and slept, despite the shellfire and the sounds of aircraft.[1]

By dawn, reinforcements of men, tanks, guns and supplies, waiting all night off the Normandy shore, were unloaded. Arriving on Omaha Beach with the Second U.S. Infantry was Moulton's Elvin Jay. Everywhere, he saw bodies: "We just had to go through them, and do what we came for." Embedded with the GIs that day, arriving on Omaha, having rejected General Omar Bradley's offer to accompany him, was reporter Ernie Pyle. In his syndicated column, Pyle described the submerged tanks, the burned-out trucks, the shell-shattered jeeps, the sea infested with ships, the bodies of soldiers sprawling grotesquely in the sand, others lying in rows covered with blankets, "the toes of their shoes sticking up in a line as though on drill." In Centerville, Pyle's accounts, and those of AP's Hal Boyle, also arriving with the troops, were read in the *Iowegian* and in newspapers from Des Moines, Chicago and Kansas City, delivered in bundles into Appanoose County from early-morning trains. With the newspapers came AP photographs: at first, images of troops departing from England. Days later there were the disturbing images of wounded Americans en route to English hospitals, of rows of the dead covered with sheets, awaiting burial. For the people at home, there had been no news from their men since their departure from England. They had no knowledge of who was injured, who was dead. In the absence of personal news, it was the immediacy of radio reports that people craved. For days following the invasion, everybody in Appanoose County, wrote the *Centerville Daily Iowegian*'s Charles DePuy, was spending most of their time listening to the radio. Broadcast networks followed planned invasion schedules. Regularly listed programs were interrupted and canceled. Radio reporters had landed with the troops, but there were no transmitters until the eighth day. The first radio "scoop" was from ABC's George Hicks, offshore on June 6 aboard the *Ancon*. His report was sent by a returning ship to Edward R. Murrow in London, who promptly sent it on to American audiences. When it was broadcast, it was two in the morning on June 7 in Appanoose County, but most people were awake. They were listening through the static, the sounds of battle, the exchanges between Germans and Americans.[2]

On day two of the invasion, radio programs and the *Iowegian*'s headline reported all Germans were cleared from the landing beaches and the Allies were pushing inland. To the east, the British and the Canadians were advancing on Caen. From Omaha, the U.S. First Infantry, including Richard Southern and Bob McGuire, was moving south and west toward St. Lo. From Utah, the Fourth Infantry, including Udell's Tom King and Mystic's Roy Davis, as well as the 82nd and the 101st U.S. Airborne Divisions, including Mystic's Harold Parris, were moving west onto the Cotentin Peninsula, aiming at the vital seaport of Cherbourg. And arriving on all the beaches from southern England were endless streams of Allied ships, carrying more reinforcements, more men, more vehicles, more equipment, more supplies. The U.S.S. *Thompson*, with engineer Richard Harrington of Unionville, brought in the chief of staff of the U.S. Army, George C. Marshall, General Eisenhower, General Henry "Hap" Arnold and Admirals King and Kirk.[3]

Aboard an arriving LST on Omaha was Centerville-born artist Manuel Bromberg, a member of the War Artists Unit, embedded with HQ 116 Regiment, assigned to record scenes on the beaches in paint on canvas. He carried a small, hip-pocket sketchbook, a Leica camera, a carbine and a letter signed by General Eisenhower in English, French and German, requesting the artist be given every assistance. At Utah Beach, the reinforcements included the 561st Field Artillery, the commanding officer Captain Karl O. "Hap" Holliday of Promise City, known everywhere in Centerville. Another arrival was the S.S. *William Pepper*, carrying seventy-five hundred tons of ammunition, its crew, including two brothers from Unionville—Donald and Bob Cross—grateful at surviving a perilous journey that included being lost in fog and emerging into the middle of a five-mile minefield.[4]

Ernie Pyle, moving with the troops through the Cotentin Peninsula, thought the Normandy countryside "a dreamland of beauty ...too wonderfully beautiful to be the scene of war." For the men fighting there, it was a struggle not just fighting the Germans, but coping with relentless wet, stormy weather and the "bocage," the field boundary hedgerows formed by two thousand years of collected earth and tangled roots. Inch by inch, the men fought, pushing the Germans north to Cherbourg. Private First Class Roy Davis wrote home to his parents in Mystic, he "could see the Germans coming out of their foxholes all over the place with their hands up."[5]

In Italy, seven hundred miles to the southeast, members of the U.S. Fifth Army, which included the Thirty-fourth "Red Bull" Division with Centerville's Company G, were also seeing Germans leaving their foxholes with their arms up. Coordinating their aim north with the British Eighth Army on Italy's east coast, the American Fifth was securing the west coast. The troops were moving so rapidly through Civitavecchia and Tarquinia, they were overtaking German rear guards, taking prisoners, finding the highways en route to Leghorn littered with enemy dead and abandoned equipment. Reese Hudson with the Nineteenth Combat Engineers was dismantling mines, building pontoon bridges, clearing roadways. He wrote home to his parents in Mystic, describing every village, every town, reduced to rubble and the children begging for candy. Describing the retreating Germans, Reese wrote, "They left us one thing, though—the fleas."[6]

For the people in Appanoose County, for eight days the fighting in Normandy was dominating the news. There was a change on June 15 when people read a two-and-half-inch banner headline: "Bombs Hit Japan"—the first bombing of that country since Jimmy Doolittle's "suicide" mission two years previously in April 1942. Flying from Chengdu, China, over Japan, pilots of the U.S. Twentieth Air Force bombed key Japanese industrial centers. A month later, the people of Centerville learned the organizing and the planning of the raid was the work of a thirty-one-year-old colonel: Dwight Monteith of Centerville, the assistant operations officer of the Twentieth Bomber Command. Everyone in town remembered Dwight. He was a 1930 graduate of Centerville High School whose mother, Alma Monteith, had worked at the County auditor's office. Homer McClellan recalled Dwight's early work ethic. S.A. Martin of the Pure Ice Company was similarly impressed and supported Dwight's passage through the U.S. Academy at West Point.[7]

On the same day, June 15, on the *Centerville Daily Iowegian*'s front page, was a smaller headline: "Reports Landing Attempts on Two Jap-Held Islands." The islands were the Marianas: Saipan, Tinian and Guam, obvious strategic locations for airfields for the B-29s targeting Japan. Mapping the landing sites in the War Plans Section of Admiral Nimitz's office in Hawaii was Lloyd "Pat" Patterson of Seymour. Backing the invasion forces moving into the Philippine Sea was the greatest armada the world had ever known. On board one of the aircraft carriers, the *South Dakota*, the division commander of the ship's five-inch guns was Robert "Bob" Beck, the son of the *Centerville Daily Iowegian*'s editor. Among the accompanying destroyers was Mystic's John Golden, on duty at the radar screen of the U.S.S. *Patterson.* And landing on Saipan amid torrents of Japanese artillery and mortar fire was a seventeen-year-old marine in the front line of the Second Infantry, Centerville's J.B. Kelley. J.B. moved through the continuous gunfire and bomb explosions to string phone wires from reels leading from the big guns to the front lines, giving coordinates so the artillery knew where to aim their fire. Amid the shelling, he was constantly retracing his steps, splicing and resplicing the wires severed as the landing tanks and amphibious tractors rolled inland. The fighting on Saipan lasted twenty-three days. The battle-hardened American troops, J.B. Kelley among them, were sickened by the sight of banzai assaults on hundreds of Japanese civilians: men, women and children being killed by their own soldiers or committing suicide rather than surrender.[8]

Four days into the fighting on Saipan, the U.S. fleet, including the *South Dakota* and the U.S.S. *Patterson*—part of Task Force 58—turned to counter an approaching Japanese attack. In the two-day confrontation known as the Battle of the Philippine Sea, seven Japanese ships were torpedoed or bombed and 243 out of 373 Japanese aircraft shot down, with the loss of 29 American. Commanding the five-inch guns of the *South Dakota*, with seven enemy planes to their credit, was Bob Beck. One of the gunners, amazed at Bob's "cold as ice ...steady as a clock" demeanor directing the gunfire, wrote home to Bob's parents. "I was scared to death," he wrote, "but if Bob was, you couldn't tell it."[9]

As the men were fighting in that deadly combat, the people at home were learning the port of Cherbourg, at the tip of the Cotentin Peninsula, was in Allied hands. One of the first American soldiers to set foot there, reported the *Centerville Daily Iowegian*, was Staff Sergeant Robert Thistlewaite of Udell, a member of the Seventy-ninth Division. And what the soldiers saw were the port facilities, so vital for the arrival of Allied reinforcements, that had been totally leveled by the surrendering Germans. The port was rebuilt in record time by the 333rd U.S. Engineers, Adjutant Larry Mahoney of Unionville, twenty miles south of Centerville, overseeing barges full of supplies being towed across the English Channel from South Wales. "There were many good Germans," he reported; "more than one would point to the ground where I was about to step and say, 'Mine!'"[10]

Throughout that high summer of 1944, the people of Appanoose County followed the war on their radios and in their newspapers. At the Majestic and the Ritz, they watched Fox newsreels and War Department delayed-footage motion pictures that showed the liberation of Rome and, from the Pacific, the battle for New Britain. They watched two full reels of preparation for D-Day on Normandy and fifteen minutes of the actual invasion, the audience anxiously scanning the images for familiar faces. There were occasional letters in Charles DePuy's "Columns Write." One told of soldiers quietly celebrating July 4 in their trenches; another told of Private First Class Carl Trent of Numa on that same day standing guard over "Old Glory" as it was flown in the Piazza Venezia in Rome. And on July 4, in a Paris thick with rumors of the approach of Allied troops, AP reporter William Smith White told of one hundred French people toasting American independence at Maxim's, the world-famous restaurant. No Germans were present but the news reached them. They closed the restaurant.[11]

By early July, U.S. troops were moving south, breaking out of the Cotentin Peninsula in what AP reporter E.D. Ball described as "a typical Patton rampage." He sent his tanks forward and, when they encountered opposition, he sent them around, surprising and cracking the Germans from the rear. The First Infantry under Omar Bradley, Richard Southern and Bob McGuire among them, Patton's Third, including Centerville's Bob Nevins, and the Second Infantry with Elvin Jay were all pushing into Brittany in record time. People at home read of the towns liberated: Coutances, Avranches, Brest, Rennes. Now the troops turned east, breaking out of Normandy and Brittany into open France, outflanking the Allies and Germans to their north, racing under Patton toward Le Mans. Moulton's Richard Southern remembered the cheering that greeted the soldiers in every village. Corporal Clair Callen of Moravia wrote home to his mother, "Every house that you pass over here, you are met at the roadside by the people with a bottle of wine or pitcher of cider." Second Lieutenant Veryl Myers wrote home to his wife in Centerville, "...it will always remain a mystery to me how a great, thrifty, and energetic nation such as this could be so happy when all their earthly possessions are in shambles and rubble. They line the roads and streets from early morning until late at night holding up their hands in the sign of *V* for Victory." Le Mans fell on August 8. Patton now took the men north to meet the Canadians at Falaise, in the process trapping and killing ten thousand Germans, taking another fifty thousand prisoners in the Falaise Pocket. Photographs appeared in the *Iowegian*. From Le Mans, Paris was just 110 miles away.[12]

In a fresh invasion, the American Seventh Army, under General Patch, and the French First were entering southern France and proceeding north. It was August 15, seventy-two days since the invasion of Normandy. Still no news had reached Appanoose County of their men who might be dead. That was about to change.

Chapter 78

Reports of Deaths to Appanoose County, a Fresh Invasion of France, Paris Liberated

The first Appanoose County man killed in Normandy was twenty-one-year-old James Lee Harrington of Cincinnati. He died on Omaha Beach on D-Day, pulled under water by the boat's propeller as he tried to disembark. Not until one month later, on July 6, was he reported "missing in action." His death was not confirmed to his parents until six months later, on January 6, 1945.[1]

That summer of 1944, as the men fought on the Cotentin Peninsula and deeper into Normandy, news of deaths came steadily to the community, and, in the pattern of war, they came late, arriving weeks and months after the event. Staff Sergeant Richard L. Patterson of Exline was last heard of on June 19 when he was aboard an LST sunk by enemy mines off the coast of France, and Marvin Burton, whose sister lived in Moravia, missing since June 18, was not confirmed dead until April 26, 1946—two years later. Nineteen-year-old Pearl Dee Glasgow was killed on July 27; the news of his death reached his parents in Udell on August 31. Another Harrington—Private First Class Earl Harrington, born and raised in Exline—was killed on August 10, the news reaching Centerville on September 14. Earl was serving with the medical corps of the Twenty-eighth Infantry. Despite being hit by machine-gun fire, he crawled to tend to a wounded soldier, successfully completed the dressing, then threw himself across a second soldier to protect him from gunfire flak that ended his own life. It was an act of heroism that earned him a Distinguished Service Cross, delivered posthumously to his family.[2]

In the same month of August, Private First Class Charles Ward of Moulton was killed, as were five men from Centerville, including Private Gerald Kennedy of West State Street, Chief Warrant Officer Howard Chriss of West Maple, and Sergeant Arthur Sobieski of South Twelfth Street, a member of the 581st Ambulance Company—his wife, Christine, was the dearly loved music teacher at Mystic. On Saturday, August 12, a rumor spread across the town—Lieutenant Theodore (Teddy) Rosenbaum, the son of one of the town's leading families, the winner of local awards for leadership and character, loved by everybody, had been killed. The rumor was confirmed the next day when thirteen-year-old Nan Krapfel collected a telegram from the telegraph office on East State Street and delivered it to Teddy's parents, who were playing bridge with Nan's parents at their home on East Washington. Teddy, serving with the Ninetieth Infantry, was killed on July 12 in the breakout from the Cotentin Peninsula to St. Lo. So was Private First Class Roy Davis, who'd written home to his parents in Mystic describing the German soldiers coming up out of foxholes with their arms raised. Roy Davis's death was not confirmed to his parents until November 23, five months later.[3]

There were deaths reported in Italy and in the Pacific. Staff Sergeant Carl Hobart, an engineer and nose-turret gunner on a Fifteenth U.S. Air Force Liberator bomber, whose father was the typesetter at the *Iowegian* office, was killed instantly on June 22 while flying a mission over Bologna in northern Italy. Another man, copilot Lieutenant Charles Bland, also of Centerville, was killed on July 16, flying over the oil refineries of Ploesti, Romania. And to the McDonald family of Iconium, notification arrived of two sons killed: Private First Class William McDonald in Italy on July 26 and, two weeks later, Corporal Joe McDonald in the Pacific.[4]

The news of the deaths in Italy was a stark reminder to everyone so focused on the war in Normandy of what war correspondents in Italy were calling "The Forgotten Front." By early August, many of the men and units fighting there, including some embedded in the Thirty-fourth Division, were being withdrawn to fight in the invasion of southern France. Watching their departure from Italy was Frank Miles, Iowa newspaperman, lecturer and editor of the *Iowa Legionnaire*. Miles visited the *Centerville Daily Iowegian* office on North Main Street. He told Jesse Beck he was leaving Des Moines for Italy to interview the Iowa men fighting there. As he prepared to leave his home, he was presented with a second purpose: to visit the grave of his son, thirty-one-year-old Lieutenant Bill Miles, a pilot of a Liberator, killed by flak over the island of Elba, off the western Italian coast.

On the morning of August 15, people across the country learned what Frank Miles in Italy was observing. U.S., French and Canadian forces were landing between Nice and Marseilles. Centerville's Staff Sergeant John Koestner, who'd dropped the first paratroopers on the Cotentin Peninsula in June, was repeating the mission onto southern French beaches. Moulton's Tracey Corder, a gunner aboard the *Samuel Griffin*, remembered how hot it was that day as he watched the Fifty-seventh Service Squadron, with Mystic's George Cortesio, unload their LCT (Landing Craft, Tank) after moving from Italy. Moulton's Leroy Brinegar, sitting in a gun turret, also remembered the heat, regretting he had to keep his shirt sleeves rolled down to prevent powder burns. The objective of the invasion into southern France, read the people of the town in that morning's *Centerville Daily Iowegian*, was to move up the Rhone Valley and connect with the Allied armies advancing out of Normandy.[5]

Overnight, the Germans were being attacked from a new direction. Montgomery's British and Canadians were pushing northwest along the coast into Belgium. At the same time, the U.S. First Army was racing north and crossing the River Seine. Patton's Third Army was erupting north and east, crossing the River Loire, liberating Orleans, reaching Versailles, being twelve miles from Paris and within sight of the Eiffel Tower. Five days later, on August 23, NBC radio news announced Paris was being liberated. On the morning of the twenty-fifth in Paris, crowds were thronging the long southern avenues reaching into the city. There was an early morning mist and the promise of a hot day. The crowds saw the approaching tanks. The star visible on their fronts indicated they were American. But, under Eisenhower's instructions, at the turrets of the tanks were soldiers of the Second French armored division. Excitement reached the level of frenzy.[6]

Entering Paris behind the tanks carrying the French Second Armored Division was correspondent Ernie Pyle. He was in a jeep with other Americans following the tanks. The jeep was constantly swamped by swarms of French women and beautiful young girls kissing and hugging them, one very short woman using a ladder to reach them. There were still German snipers, and machine-gun fire could be heard. But, wrote Pyle, "...they were doomed. There was a full French armored division in the city, plus American troops entering constantly."[7]

Across Paris, church bells rang; Nazi flags were replaced with French tricolors. "La Marseillaise" was sung everywhere. Later that day, there was a formal Nazi surrender, led by General Dietrich von Choltitz. Ordered by Hitler to demolish and level Paris, von Choltitz apparently disobeyed. Instead, he identified to the liberators the locations of dynamite placed in the buildings prepared for demolition. Notre Dame, the Eiffel Tower, the Arc de Triomphe, the architectural beauties of the Place de la Concorde and the Champs-Élysées were all intact. Photographs of the buildings appeared in the U.S. newspapers, reassuring travelers the Paris they'd known and loved was still in place.[8]

Other photographs also appeared in American newspapers—of U.S. soldiers being enthusiastically kissed by Parisian girls. In Des Moines, a *Life* magazine reporter and cameraman sought interviews, asking Iowa girls what they thought of "this victory kissing business." Sally Akes, a twenty-one-year-old waitress from Centerville, sided with the French girls saying, "...the Des Moines girls would do the very same thing." Her neighbor, a woman with a husband serving in France said, "What he does over there is his own business but what he does when he gets back to the U.S.A. is mine."[9]

The city of Paris was bypassed by the men of the U.S. First Army. They passed north and east toward the German border. They reached Soissons and Chateau Thierry. Richard Southern of Moulton was conscious he was stepping on ground where his father had fought twenty years previously in World War I and where hundreds of Americans lay beneath the white crosses at Soissons cemetery.[10]

The U.S. First, the Second and Patton's Third Armies—Appanoose men among them—were approaching the German border, German soldiers en masse retreating in front of them. As people at home followed radio bulletins and newspaper headlines, it seemed the progress of the troops in Europe was taking the form of a rout. In less than two weeks, the British had captured Brussels and Antwerp; Americans had crossed the Rhine into Germany and conquered Aachen, the first German city to fall. The U.S. Seventh Army ascended the Rhone Valley rapidly. Centerville's Private First Class Lee Rice was one of the six engineers replacing blown bridges from Aix-en-Provence to Lyon. The Seventh joined up with Patton's Third Army at Dijon. By the fourteenth of September, all of Belgium and Luxembourg were in Allied hands. At the same time, the Russians were pressing Germany from the east, sweeping ever closer to German soil. In Italy, the story was the same. The British Eighth and the U.S. Fifth were continuing their tandem progress north. There were still stories of deaths and woundings and a brilliant escape by Russ Daniels of Moulton, who was captured but then brought his left arm down and back and tossed the Nazi headlong into a rushing stream. Within five weeks, beginning on August 3, South Africans fighting with British had entered Florence, the U.S. Fifth was in Pisa and both British and American forces high in the Apennines were attacking the formidable transpeninsula Gothic Line.[11]

To the people of Centerville, victory in Europe seemed imminent. "Germany Licked" was the title of Jesse Beck's editorial on September 7. The town's businessmen met in the Association of Commerce rooms on North Thirteenth Street to plan a celebration as soon as the news of Germany's surrender reached the town. But they waited. And they waited. "We're waiting," wrote Charles DePuy to the troops in his "Columns Write," "...with our fingers crossed."[12]

While they waited, they watched Pathe and Fox newsreels at the Majestic and Ritz Theatres. They collected clothes for the Russians, the French, Belgians, Dutch and Yugoslavs. More young men were inducted into the armed forces, some drafted before graduating out of high school. Orientation flights were given at the airport for prospective air force cadets and air force enlisters. In the Red Cross room over the Majestic, blood-donor clinics were held; so were box suppers and dances to raise money and to assemble gifts for every wounded, sick and disabled serviceman brought home from the war's battlefields to government hospitals.

The war along the German border had settled into what General Eisenhower called "the dirtiest kind of infantry slugging." Soon the bleak news would arrive in Appanoose County: fifteen more of its young men dead.[13]

Chapter 79

Deaths in Germany, Italy, Palau and the Philippines

Of the fifteen Appanoose County men killed in the fighting along the German borders, seven were from Centerville: Private Guy Keaton of East State, who through high school worked at Dawkins Hamburger Shop on North Main; Private First Class Sammy Frank of South Nineteenth, who would be on the front line in France for just twenty days; Private Raymond "Jim" Sleeth of East Wilson, the father of a two-and-a-half-year-old son; Private James Orris Buck, twenty years old, of Drake Avenue; Corporal "Jack" Warren, who operated the Phillips 66 station; twenty-nine-year-old Sergeant John Sebben, who worked at the Centrox Dairy; and Santos Reyes, who lived in a boxcar near the Eighteenth Street crossing, who supported his mother after the death of his father and who had a statewide reputation as a fine amateur boxer.[1]

Telegrams carrying the news of eight more deaths went to outlying communities: to Brazil, twenty-year-old Eugene Clark, the only child of the former postmaster and depot agent; to Udell, Lieutenant Lawrence Swank, born to a family of attorneys on a farm one mile east of town; to Exline, Sergeant Chester Caster, killed as he drove a tank near Mons, Belgium; to Cincinnati, Private William Robbins, killed when "engaged in a hazardous undertaking," leaving a wife and four children under four years of age. Two telegrams went to Numa, one reporting the death of Private Howard P. Wyldes, leaving a wife and two sons, another reporting of death of Sergeant Clarence Oral Purvis. Within days, Clarence's wife and parents received photographs of his grave at Andilly, decorated with flowers by local French civilians and visited by two

Appanoose comrades, Sergeants Clyde Holbrook and Ralph Craver. To Mystic, a telegram went to the home of Private Grover Bills, who left a wife and a baby daughter. And one went to Clarkdale to a widowed father, Frank Caraccio Sr., reporting the death of his twenty-three-year-old son, Staff Sergeant Frank Caraccio Jr. The manner of Frank Caraccio Jr.'s death came later. With some of his comrades pinned down by enemy fire, totally disregarding his own safety, he set up a machine gun, blasted enemy positions and saved his comrades but was killed by a hidden enemy gun. It was an action that earned him a Silver Star. It was presented to his father and his sister Helen at Centerville's St. Mary's Catholic Church.[2]

At the same time, there were more notifications of deaths arriving from Italy. A notice to Unionville reported the death of Sergeant Edwin Mathes from wounds he sustained a day earlier; another was to Mystic regarding Robert Baker, wounded three times, killed on reentering the infantry a fourth time; to Moulton, twenty-three-year-old Private First Class Charles Vanlandingham, a member of Centerville's National Guard Company G; and to Exline, the death of Private Amos McGhghy, like Charles Vanlandingham a member of the Thirty-fourth "Red Bull" Division.[3]

What was now apparent to the town was that the plans for V-E celebrations were premature. At the same time, their attention was being pulled back across the Pacific. There, the U.S. victory on the Mariana Islands of Saipan, Tinian and Guam opened up the far western Pacific to the U.S. advance. Even before their capture was complete, airfields were built, and Mariana-based B-29 Superfortress aircraft were bombing Japan. The first target was the Musashi aero-engine plant on the edge of Tokyo. One of the B-29 pilots was Plano's twenty-six-year-old Gerald DeVore, his crew witnessing that both bombs and rockets had hit the factory. "It was burning and smoking," he reported.[4]

Drawing ever closer to the Philippines, hundreds of U.S. naval vessels made for Peleliu in the Palau Islands, among them the U.S.S. *Patterson* with Mystic's John Golden aboard. They began pre-invasion bombardment. Waiting on an LST, Technical Sergeant Merle Reisner of Centerville's South Nineteenth Street described in a letter home to his mother the pounding of the beach, the clouds of smoke, the slicing of huge coconut palms, the fires, the deep craters. His letter, after he'd survived the invasion, began, "Praise the Lord the ammunition passed me." Marine Bill Kauzlarich wrote home to his parents, the Julio Kauzlarichs of Rathbun. He, too, survived the invasion. And so did Centerville's eighteen-year-old Wendell Thomas. Wendell was commander with the 710th Tank Battalion fighting for days on Palau on a four-by-eight-mile stretch of coral and thick vegetation in sweltering heat and daily rain.[5]

Plano wall of names of those who served in World War II, with Cecil Wakefield. *Courtesy of Richard Gorden, Plano Museum.*

Bill Kauzlarich's and Merle Reisner's letters arrived in Centerville coincidental with new headlines from the Pacific. On October 19, the *Centerville Daily Iowegian* headline read, "Philippine Islands Invaded on the 20th: 'I Have Returned'—MacArthur," and some days later, people saw a photograph of MacArthur wading ashore on a twenty-mile beachhead on Leyte. Seventy-three U.S. transports and fifty LSTs had entered Leyte Gulf.[6]

Four days later, a Japanese naval force moved in to attack. The Battle of Leyte Gulf would be the largest naval battle in history. The U.S.S. *Patterson*, with Mystic's John Golden, was also there, a part of Task Force Thirty-eight. Confronting four Japanese carriers off Cape Engano, the *Patterson* crew witnessed kamikaze attacks exploding the U.S.S. *Belleau Wood* and the U.S.S. *Franklin*. They pulled survivors from the sea, the ship's medical team working heroically around the clock to save lives. One life that was lost was Mystic's John Robert Thompson, an honor student graduate, a specialist radio technician first class, trained at Texas A&M. Centerville's Kenneth C. Henke somehow did survive. He was aboard the *Abner Read*, a soundman on the bridge, his job to detect enemy submarines. A kamikaze plane disabled by antiaircraft guns crashed onto the deck, burst into flames and broke the ship's water mains, the flaming gasoline igniting two of the *Read*'s powder magazines. Ordered by the captain, the crew abandoned ship and jumped into the sea, trusting in their life jackets. Japanese planes made strafing runs on the men in the water—the nearest bullets fifty yards from Kenneth.[7]

Further south at the San Bernadino Straits, one of Centerville's African American community, Robert "Bob" Bandy, steward first class, was aboard the hit destroyer U.S.S. *Johnson* and thrown into the sea. Bob couldn't swim, had no life preserver and was suffering from internal injuries due to the blast concussion, but he made his way to a raft. He survived there for two days and three nights before being rescued. On the first day he was one of ninety men on the raft, but when rescued, the number was thirty-three. "Some of the men died," he told his mother and friends on East Bank Street when he was home recovering. "Some of the wounded went crazy and so did some of the men who drank salt water. At night the sharks got a few..."[8]

The Centerville in which Bob Bandy was recovering had politics on his mind. 1944 was an election year. President Roosevelt, the Democrat, was running for a fourth term. His opponent was Governor Thomas E. Dewey, the Republican candidate. In late September, Dr. George Gallup, the originator of the world-famed Gallup Poll, arrived in Appanoose County with two assistants. They carried briefcases. They stayed at the Continental Hotel on the Centerville Square. The purpose of their visit, Dr. Gallup told a *Centerville Daily Iowegian* reporter, was to conduct an in-depth poll of the people of Washington Township. For forty-four years, Dr. Gallup explained, as went Washington Township, Appanoose County, Iowa, U.S.A., in its political choice, so went the nation.[9]

The *Iowegian* reporter noted the condition of Dr. Gallup's shoes. They were scuffed. The color was worn off the toes by wet grass, mud and country highway travel. "I have no patience," Dr. Gallup continued, "with the armchair boys back in New York, who try to figure things by remote control and that's why I'm out here." He and his team cross-sectioned Washington Township, by blocks in Moulton and by school districts in the outlying area. At the Morrow home in Moulton's Seventh Street, the door was answered by thirteen-year-old Phyllis Morrow, "My parents will vote Democrat," she told the team. "They will not vote Republican."[10]

In the presidential election returns on the night of November 8, President Roosevelt was reelected with a popular majority of 3.5 million over Governor Thomas Dewey. American servicemen around the world had voted at their camps. Many of them in London watched the results posted at the Red Cross Rainbow Corner at Piccadilly Circus. The president lost the State of Iowa but he carried Appanoose County by eighty votes. And Washington Township, Dr. Gallup's political guinea pig? It upheld its forty-four—now forty-five—year tradition, casting 330 votes for President Roosevelt, 315 for Governor Dewey. Election night in Appanoose County, said the *Centerville Daily Iowegian*, was almost peaceful. In the past, election night was a time for extra police and a busy "Black Mariah" police wagon, with arrests for intoxication and fistfights. This year, the police reported, there were only two cases of drunkenness and one fistfight. Perhaps the sobering influence was the news.

Chapter 80

Battle of the Bulge

In Europe, the weather had now turned cold. Through November and into December, U.S., British, Canadian and French forces were fighting all along the border from Holland to Switzerland and were poised to plunge into Germany. The First and the Ninth U.S. Armies were penetrating toward Cologne and the dense cold thickets of the Hurtgen Forest. It was here Moulton's Richard Southern suffered a severe traumatic back injury. He was transported by medical units to Liège and flown to a hospital in England. The Second Infantry, with another Moulton man, Elvin Jay, was taking a twenty-seven-mile holding position at the Siegfried Line. Elvin's job, and that of his unit, was to carry ammunition to the gunners at the front line. They moved at night. They tied wires to trees to find their way in the dark. They used passwords to identify each other: "George," one would say; "Washington," the acceptable reply. Patton's Third Army was battling through snow and sleet, their tanks, one driven by Centerville's John Sisul, painted white. They battled through snow and sleet in Lorraine, targeting the city of Metz. Centerville's Louis "Sol" Kauzlarich with the Third Army was moving every night, unwinding telephone wire from reels on his back and attaching vital links of communication. Patch's Seventh Army and the French First had driven the Germans out of Alsace and were moving through deep snowdrifts toward Strasbourg. It was here that Centerville's Sam Montegna in the Seventh Army tried a cheerful letter home to his parents on South Sixteenth Street: "...I am getting along pretty good. So please don't worry about me." In fact, Sam's right leg had been smashed. He'd spend two years in the hospital, endure multiple surgeries before he could walk and suffer lifelong nightmares.[1]

It was along this border, along an eight-mile front in the Ardennes early on the morning of December 16, that the Germans violently counterattacked in the Battle of the Bulge. Radio bulletins alerted the nation. Reports came to the Midwest from a new young reporter placed with the U.S. First and Ninth Armies. He was Jack Shelley of WHO, Des Moines. By Monday December 18, people heard his reports and read AP reports in the *Centerville Daily Iowegian.* American lines had been penetrated and overrun. The Germans, in what one reporter called a colossal gamble, had thrown in hundreds of tanks, parachutists and panzer divisions, many dressed in U.S. uniforms to create confusion in the area. The Germans were massacring unarmed U.S. soldiers, officers, medics wearing identifying armbands and Belgian citizens who couldn't believe the change of events. Neither could the people of Appanoose County.[2]

The U.S. First and Second Armies fought back. They fought through snow and cold and freezing rain. They burrowed into foxholes in the snow that filled with dirt and water, soaking their clothes and their leather boots, which would freeze, causing blisters and trench foot. Lieutenant Dick Stockwell of Moulton was experiencing the sheer terror of leading an attack in the moonlight on twenty-one German trucks, an attack in which sixty-five Germans were left dead. Exline's Sergeant Kenneth Hatfield, a teacher in real life, noting that he was "never much of a fellow to fight," left a covered position and, though exposed to arms and tank fire, manned a machine gun and halted the enemy crossing a key river. Lieutenant James Ruby of Seymour, using the German language he'd learned at home, successfully got a group of Germans to surrender, only to have to cut them down when, one hundred yards away, the Germans pulled out hidden weapons and began to shoot. Centerville's Sergeant Andrew Golick won a Bronze Star for repulsing several attacks against his company. Another went posthumously to Corporal Ersal Wakefield of Exline for holding off an attack singlehandedly with a machine gun. Sergeant Harry Horrocks of Mystic, who had already won a Silver Star near Metz, had fought sixty-one days at the front line without relief, had four times been wounded in action and found himself again at the front line. First Lieutenant Robert Dudley of Centerville won a Silver Star for destroying twenty-seven Nazi tanks, and another Silver Star went to Private First Class Lloyd Parcel of Livonia, Missouri, who'd entered the service from Centerville. When Lloyd's rocket launcher refused to work, he waited alone with five German tanks approaching while comrades sought reinforcements. Then, surrounded by enemy infantry with machine guns, he threw hand grenades, destroying tanks, guns and crew.[3]

The focal point of the Battle of the Bulge was Bastogne, where a network of roads met, all essential to the German advance. Socked in by bad weather that prevented U.S. aerial reinforcements, American troops holding the town were surrounded, outnumbered and cut off. When ordered to surrender by the Germans, U.S. General "Tony" McAuliffe gave the one-word reply: "Nuts!" Next day the sky had cleared and aerial reinforcements began arriving with supplies. Patton swung the Third Army around, reversing its direction from east to north. Now including Moravia's Marvin Gardner, Patton's men broke through the German encirclement and saved Bastogne. Field medics began collecting and stabilizing the wounded, moving them to hospitals. The medics, like Ray Simmons on Omaha Beach and Promise City's Leck Tuttle at the Battle of the Bulge, gave aid on the edges of battlefields. Surgical teams amputated on kitchen tables and on hilltops. Centerville's Major Bruce Howar, a doctor with the U.S. Medical Corps, worked under tents and, in Belgium, in an insane asylum converted to a hospital. Nurses in the air evacuation program—Centerville's Carol Willier was one—flew the injured by Air Transport Command to Britain. One hospital there was the 106th General in Wimborne, Dorset. Centerville's Private First Class Charles Lampkin worked there as a quartermaster supply clerk. He recalled the busiest time at the hospital was during the Battle of the Bulge.[4]

Reports of deaths from the Battle of the Bulge arrived in Appanoose County from late December 1944 to April 1945. There were fourteen. The first was that of twenty-eight-year-old Private Jesse Wyldes of Numa, and it came as a double shock. Four days earlier, Jesse's brother, thirty-four-year-old Howard, was reported killed. Their family in Numa included Jesse's wife and two small children and Howard's wife and two small sons. The parents of both men were coping with the double tragedy less than a week apart.

To a neighbor of the Wyldes, a stepmother, news arrived of the death of Staff Sergeant James Lowell Allan. James, whose mother had died when he was six, his father when he was ten, was known in both Numa and Centerville as a talented softball pitcher. At twenty-five he'd moved to Independence, Kansas, where he worked as an accountant at the home office of the Sinclair Oil Company. He was the father of a nine-month-old daughter and the brother of Vern Allan, managing editor of the *Wright County Monitor* in North Central Iowa.[5]

Six notifications of deaths arrived at Centerville homes. The first, on January 2, was that of eighteen-year-old Sergeant James "Jim" Samson, the only child of the Samson family of South Main Street, a twin sibling having died at birth. Jim was trained in the air corps but was transferred into the infantry weeks before his death. Six days later, the news of the death of Private William Seath arrived at the North Main Street home of his parents as a dinner with seven family guests was in progress. A 1931 graduate of Centerville High School and a student at Centerville Junior College, thirty-two-year-old William, before enlisting, was an employee of Swift and Company in Fulton, Kentucky, where he left a wife. Neighbors on the next block of North Main Street, the John Bennett family, twenty-two days later were told of the death of their twenty-eight-year-old son, Private First Class Robert Bennett. In one of his letters home, he told his parents how he and his fellow soldiers were tracking Germans in the snow much like men back home used to track rabbits. Then, with a feeling of premonition, he added: "My luck has held out about as long as it probably will." He was killed January 11.[6]

At 820 South Nineteenth Street on February 27, Mrs. Minnie Bever arrived home from her nursing duties at St. Joseph Hospital to learn of the death of her thirty-year-old son and only child, Technical Sergeant Forrest Bever. Forrest was serving with Patton's "Blue Ridge" Division. He'd written home on January 31. He told his mother he had recovered from wounds to both arms, both legs and to his back. He was back fighting, and it was "very cold." Not only was Forrest Mrs. Bever's only child, she was a widow. Her husband, well-known in South Centerville as a barber, had died three years previously.[7]

The next day the news of the deaths of another only son and only child reached the Brundage home on South Drake Avenue. Private George Brundage was nineteen years old and, like Forrest Bever, serving with Patton's Third Army. He died at Bastogne on February 6. And to South Sixteenth Street, the news came that Second Lieutenant Clifford Collins, thirty years old, who was born in Centerville, who graduated from Centerville High School, who ran a local oil station, had died from wounds while serving with a battery armored artillery division.[8]

Two telegrams went to Mystic, one to the house of Private Carl Bozwick, serving with the Ninth Armored Infantry, killed on January 4. The second went to the home of Lieutenant Bruce McKern, a C-47 pilot flying supplies into the front and flying wounded soldiers back to England. The telegram announcing Bruce's death arrived at the home of the Eugene McKernses as Bruce's wife, Pauline, was returning home with Bruce's baby daughter, Lana, born on March 11.[9]

One telegram went to Unionville, to the home of the Paul Harringtons, to report the death of their twenty-four-year-old son, Technical Sergeant Neil Forrest Harrington. Neil, known as an avid reader, interested in politics, a basketball and baseball star, popular, charming and intelligent, had died on

New Year's Day, January 1, 1945, serving with the Seventh Army. One telegram went to Sedan giving news of the death of twenty-seven-year-old Private George Ivan Kerby, serving with the Seventh Army, killed on February 23. To Cincinnati another telegram was to the home of the Benjamin Haineses, reporting the death of their son, Private First Class Orris Haines. Serving with the Second Infantry, Orris, armed with a Browning automatic rifle, crawled forward in a wooded area, fighting back Germans for three hours before being killed himself on February 20. And yet another telegram reporting a death in the Battle of the Bulge, but not reported until April 28, was of Bernard Forsythe of Moulton, a graduate of the high school there, killed three months previously on January 12 while serving in the Seventh Army.[10]

Chapter 81

Fighting in the Pacific, the Philippines, Iwo Jima

On the morning of January 10, the *Iowegian* headline read, "Yanks Drive toward Manila." The day before, January 9, the fighting in the Philippines moved from Leyte to Luzon. Men of the U.S. Sixth Army had landed along fifteen miles of beaches at Lingayen Gulf on Luzon's west coast. Preceding the invasion was an air bombardment of shells, bombs and rockets from escorting ships. One of these, again, was the U.S.S. *Patterson*, its crew, including Mystic's John Golden, rescuing survivors of the *Ommaney Bay* that had been subjected to a kamikaze attack.[1]

Aboard an Australian ship waiting to land was Technical Sergeant Merle Reisner. He'd written home to his mother on Centerville's South Nineteenth Street describing the bombardment of Peleliu. He now wrote to her again, describing the scene at Lingayen Gulf. "Arriving at daybreak when the shadows of night began to fade on this eventful morning, I began to think the entire fighting power of the USA was at hand ...This shelling was for three hours, after which I hit the beach with the tenth wave in water over knee-deep. My pack and rifle were partially submerged, but that did not last long." Twenty-four hours later, AP was reporting sixty-eight thousand U.S. troops had poured ashore, and tank-led units were driving south across flatlands toward Manila, less than 120 miles away.

All along the beaches when the smoke lifted, Filipino civilians were welcoming the American arrivals, some refusing to take cover during the shelling so they could be the first to greet them. Merle Reisner described how they waved and how they shouted, "God Bless America, may you live forever," and the children sang "God Bless America." Throughout their stay, the Filipinos served the troops chicken dinners and wine made from coconuts. They did their washing, returning clothes and towels immaculately clean, everything pressed, even their socks. "During those dark days of Bataan and Corregidor," wrote Merle Reisner to his mother in Centerville, "General MacArthur ...made the following statement, 'I will go, but I'll return.' This, we have now successfully completed, and, at present [we're] forging ahead toward final victory in the Philippines."[2]

The final victory was still months away. Within a week after landing, there was a full-scale battle on Luzon, with fighting in the jungles and deadly, atrocity-filled, house-to-house fighting by the Japanese in the streets of Manila and reports of more atrocities, more massacres of towns, villages and whole communities. The murders included the daughter of Ezra Temple, the well-known evangelist who'd traveled with the hoboes in Iowa, as well as her daughter's husband and their three sons.[3]

In a daring raid twenty-five miles behind Japanese lines, the all-volunteer Alamo Scouts, working in teams, rescued five hundred Allied prisoners slated for certain death from a stockade near Cabantuan. The Scouts, which had originally included Verne Miller of Jerome, had collected intelligence behind enemy lines for General MacArthur all across the Pacific. The prisoners rescued from Cabantuan were some of the men who endured the Bataan Death March. They survived torture, disease and starvation. One of them was Sergeant Harold Malcolm Amos. His sister received the news of his rescue. She was Roberta McDonald of Centerville Beauty Shoppe. Another, liberated from the Santo Tomas internment camp in Manila, was Maurice Furstenberg, the brother of Bertha Gavronsky who, with her husband, James, lived on Haynes Avenue.[4]

Survivors all had their own descriptions of the horrors experienced at the prison camps. A Filipino colonel who'd survived Camp O'Donnell estimated that forty thousand American and Filipino soldiers, half of all prisoners, had died of disease, malnutrition and mistreatment. In the early days of the infamous Death March of Bataan, he said, several hundred died daily. Russell Brines, a writer for the *Centerville Daily Iowegian*, found a cemetery about seven hundred yards northeast of the main building. Tall grass covered the graves. Brines found small crosses made of unpainted laths, dog tags of the dead fixed on the backs, occasionally with names and words like "Rest in Peace" hacked out by surviving comrades, some painted in ink, some burned, one hammered in tin. Fellow prisoners kept records of the fate of their comrades. They wrote them on the backs of Japanese-printed forms, on milk-can wrappers or cigarette papers, carefully burying them, providing rescuers with the most important source of information in identifying the victims.[5]

Some survivors just walked out of the jungle. One was Captain Robert "Bob" Lapham of Davenport, Iowa. He emerged wearing rope-soled shoes with the toes cut out. He was in native clothes, followed by thousands of Filipino guerillas he'd led in nearly three years of hit-and-run fighting against the Japanese. People back in Davenport had trouble fitting the character of Bob, the hero guerilla, with the Bob they knew—quiet, well-dressed, well-mannered, unassuming and so handsome, reported his high school principal L.E. Keller, "he made girls' hearts pop."[6]

Throughout the fighting in the Philippines and the whole Pacific war, the sheer logistics of moving men and material was, to an untrained eye, impossible. Lieutenant John Valentine, speaking to Centerville's Association of Commerce, described the task as Herculean. Reporter Ernie Pyle, who'd moved from reporting the war in Europe to reporting in the Pacific, wrote on February 16, "Covering this Pacific war ...I can't get my mind around it, or get my fingers on it ...Distance is the main thing ...distances in Europe are hundreds of miles at most, out here they are thousands. And there's nothing in between but water."[7]

Centerville's Jerry Kirkpatrick, aboard the U.S.S. *Levy*, kept a diary. His ship ran supplies, oil, ammunition and troops, traveling huge distances from New York and Bermuda, servicing Pago Pago, Bora Bora, Guadalcanal, Guam, New Caledonia, Eniwetok, the Philippines, Formosa, Manus, Palawan and Los Negros. Jerry's diary was an example of the distances traveled by thousands of U.S. battleships, aircraft carriers, destroyers, destroyer escorts and cruisers, their crews enduring boredom, constantly following zigzag paths through the ocean to discourage successful torpedo attacks and constantly alert for attacks from the air. One navy man Centerville people learned about from the pages of their *Reader's Digest.* He was Richard Bumgarner, aboard the U.S.S. *Hayter.* Richard helped pull sixty-five unconscious and semiconscious survivors of the torpedoed *F.C. Davis* out of the Pacific, personally reviving three believed dead, working unflaggingly despite the heavy rolling ship deck for three hours, refusing relief so he could maintain resuscitation rhythm.[8]

Illustrating the enormity of Pacific distances was an AP map on the *Centerville Daily Iowegian*'s front page on January 11. The map showed Tokyo, Luzon and Saipan. They formed an isosceles triangle, with each leg of the triangle measuring approximately fifteen hundred miles. The leg from Saipan to Tokyo was being flown by the B-29 Superfortresses bombing Tokyo. An intermediate stop, a halfway house, was needed where damaged aircraft and their fighter escorts could land. Midpoint along that Saipan–Tokyo leg was a tiny, volcanic five-by-four-mile island: Iwo Jima. It was the next military target, and it presented a further reason for attack. The island had three airfields where Japanese interceptors flew to attack the B-29s flying between Saipan and Tokyo. The U.S. Fifth, Fourth and Third Marine Divisions landed on Iwo Jima on February 19. For seventy-two days previously, the island was subjected to naval bombardment and aerial strikes. In that time, some twenty-two thousand Japanese, ordered to defend the island, had hewn vast networks of paved, underground tunnels and fortifications into the island's bedrock of basalt. Some of the tunnels were several floors deep, with hospitals, kitchens and troop barracks. Near the surface were hundreds of concrete and earthen pillboxes and hidden machine-gun emplacements. The surface of the island itself was covered with thick layers of volcanic ash. For the marines landing on Iwo Jima that day in February 1945, it was the worst experience of the Pacific war.[9]

Rathbun's Louis Cortesio passed up a deferment as a coal miner and at twenty-one was one of the initial ten thousand marines in the Fifth Division to land on the southeast Iwo Jima beach code-named "Green." The men immediately sank almost to their knees in volcanic ash that hindered movement forward. Ash filled the air. It filled their mouths and it filled their ears. Louis later credited the ash in his ears with protecting his hearing during the din of battle. The marines were subjected to artillery fire, machine-gun fire and snipers moving suicidally close, having waited until the marines—reduced by the ash to a crawling advance—were one hundred yards inland. The men lying wounded were killed from behind by Japanese soldiers running along their paved subterranean passages. For the marines, there was no harbor. There was no shelter. The volcanic ash shifting and sliding became a death trap for trucks and for tanks. Supplies of water, of food, of ammunition lay on the shoreline in countless immobile piles.[10]

Second Lieutenant Mick Starcevich of Mystic landed with the Third Marine Division. He and his men were directed to fill gaps in the American lines. "When we got there," said Mick, "bodies were lying on the beach like cordwood." Yet despite the enormous casualties, despite the volcanic ash, despite the withering crossfire, by the evening of the first day, the marines had reached the first airstrip and cut off Mount Suribachi. U.S. B-29s were flying from the airstrip before the island was secured.[11]

Five days into fighting, Louis Cortesio, as part of the Twenty-eighth Regiment, witnessed the flag raising on the summit of Mount Suribachi. So did Sergeant Floyd Fisher of Centerville's North Park Avenue. And so did

Sergeant Sam Watson of Stockport in Iowa's Jefferson County. There were two flags raised. Louis witnessed both. The first was smaller than the photographed second. Sergeant Sam Watson wrote home to his parents in Stockport that he was "the fellow planting the staff" and the Japanese flag that was replaced he was sending home to them. The second flag raised, a much bigger one, was placed on top of Mount Suribachi under fire. It was photographed by AP's Joe Rosenthal, who made three exposures with his Speed Graphic, the photograph distributed by the press in a then-rapid seventeen-and-a-half hours later. At the moment the flag was raised by five marines and a navy corpsman, Louis remembered marines on the island yelling, ships blaring their horns, a lump in every American's throat, including Mick Starcevich's. Mick was then fighting for the islands' next two airfields.[12]

Three days later, Louis was wounded in both legs and feet. He waved away those moving to assist him. He crawled to relative safety and was treated and evacuated. Louis's wounds were the result of a mortar shell. For Mick, also wounded, it was a grenade exploding under his leg. He heard his platoon sergeant call for litter bearers, adding, " he won't last the night." It was February 1945 for both men. Mick spent the next two years in hospitals. He could not walk and had an artificial ankle joint inserted, the ankle fused to reduce the pain in 1998.

In Appanoose County, through the Battle of Iwo Jima, the parents of Louis and Mick knew their men were marines and were in the Pacific. Radio reports were broadcasting "a Marine is falling dead or wounded with each second." On February 21, just two days after the landing on Iwo Jima, the *Centerville Daily Iowegian* headline was: "Navy Price for Iwo's Gains! 3,650 Marines Fall in 1st Day on Isle." Three weeks later, the families, still without news, read, "Conquest of Iwo Cost Nation 4,000 Marines."[13]

The actual cost was higher: 6,855 marines were dead and more than 20,000 wounded. For the 22,000 Japanese defending the island, 21,000 were dead, the defenders having died almost to a man. The next Pacific target would be Okinawa, and Iwo Jima was a terrible warning. Iwo Jima was declared secure on March 26. It was spring. In Europe, along the German border and in the mountains of northern Italy, the snow was melting.[14]

Chapter 82

Crossing the River Rhine

Battling at Okinawa

While the people at home waited for reports of th[illegible] Philippines and on Iwo Jima, a sense of confiden[illegible] about the war in Europe. In a letter home to his parents [illegible] Glenn Cridlebaugh, serving with Patton's Third Army, wro[illegible] the edge of the Fatherland ...and we've had some guns on t[illegible] Maginot line forts. We have good warm clothes and plenty of [illegible] helps." Glenn had just tasted his first venison and continued[illegible] war isn't going on in the USA and feel plenty sorry for these [illegible] You know what it would be at home without food or fuel."[1]

Glenn, in Patton's Third Army, was part of eight white-clad [illegible] along the western German border, crossing into Germany and [illegible] River Rhine. From north to south, they were: the Canadians; th[illegible] Airborne; the British; the U.S. Ninth, First, Third and Seventh [illegible] the French First. On the opposite side of Germany, on its east[illegible] as *Centerville Daily Iowegian* headlines were reporting, the Russian [illegible] within ninety miles of Berlin on January 27, fifty-eight miles just four da[illegible]. People across the County were reading Swedish AP correspondents in Berlin. "Panic," wrote one, "is sweeping the nation from east to west." Another who'd got out of Berlin to the safety of Stockholm wrote baldly, "Berlin is a city of the doomed." Eyewitnesses were reporting that flashes of Russian guns could be seen from Berlin in the night skies over the eastern battlefront. German army deserters were flooding into the city. People were barricaded, bewildered and bomb-dulled, each left to his own initiative, his own resources.[2]

For the Americans, the British, the Canadians and the French Armies, the River Rhine was their last remaining major barrier. In Appanoose County, their progress was followed. Radio news bulletins broke into regular broadcasting. Customers listened in stores and in restaurants. Families listened over kitchen tables. Children listened and followed along on world maps pinned to classroom walls. In a futile attempt to delay the Allied advance, German engineers were blowing up the Rhine's bridges. They failed at one. They only damaged the old Ludendorff railroad bridge at Remagen. On March 7 it was serendipitously discovered by a small armored patrol of the U.S. First Army. The first man to cross its twelve-hundred-foot width was thirty-four-year-old Sergeant Alexander Drabnik of Holland, Ohio. Despite constant aerial bombardment, ack-ack fire and artillery shells, infantry and tank divisions of the U.S. First Army—Mystic's Joe Coates and Centerville's Bob Nevins among them—crossed the swaying bridge. So did three signal corpsmen, keeping telephone lines intact, grabbing the wire and running, said one, "like hell across" while machine-gun bullets splattered at their heels. So did unarmed medics, seizing German bicycles to transport medical supplies and then carrying the wounded on their backs. By the time the bridge collapsed, U.S. engineers, including the 254th with Centerville's Bob McGuire, were building a replacement pontoon bridge, completing the job in sixteen hours flat, so ensuring the uninterrupted flow of men and materials across the river.[3]

On March 23, people at home were reading of more Rhine crossings. Patton's Third Army was crossing at Oppenheim, seventy-five miles south of Remagen. With Patton were Rathbun's "Sol" Kauzlarich, Moravia's Marvin Gardner, Udell's Glenn Cridlebaugh and Herbert Burr. Herbert single-handedly drove a tank over a German eighty-eight-millimeter antitank gun at point blank range, deliberately sideswiped and overturned a German truck and then, through a hail of gunfire, aided wounded companions. It would earn him a Congressional Medal of Honor and the pride of his sister, Blanche, who lived on East Van Buren Street and whose husband, Troy Smith, ran the DX station across from the Majestic.[4]

The next day, the talk of Centerville was that the British, Canadians and the U.S. Ninth were crossing the Lower Rhine and meeting up with Allied paratroopers dropped across the Rhine, the four groups in the process trapping thousands of German soldiers. At the same time, south of Patton, the U.S. Seventh Army was crossing at Worms. Private First Class Max Exline, whose sister lived south of Moulton, was noting the date and the time: March 28, six thirty in the evening, while Centerville surveyor Technical Sergeant Keith Gregory was studying maps of the territory ahead. One army remained, the furthest south, the French. They crossed at Speyer on the last day of March. All eight armies were now on the Rhine's eastern shore, connecting with each other and forming joint phalanxes.[5]

The U.S. First Army traveled north from Remagen at breakneck speed, Joe Coates admiring the German autobahn. So fast did the First move that its spearheads lost contact with headquarters. It met with the U.S. Ninth Army moving south from the Lower Rhine. The two armies together formed a steel ring, a giant pincers around the German industrial Ruhr. The German armies, thus enclosed and trapped, pounded on all sides and hammered relentlessly day and night by RAF and USAAF heavy bombers, eventually collapsed. The numbers of prisoners totaled 325,000. Among them, Germany's former chancellor Franz Von Papen was captured by Lieutenant Thomas McKinley, a close friend of Centerville's jockey family, the Garners, well-known in the town from his frequent visits.[6]

On the other side of the world, the battle scene was moving nine hundred miles west of Iwo Jima, nine hundred miles ever closer to Japan. On the last day of March, an *Iowegian* AP article reported that a combined U.S. and British Pacific fleet were, for eight days, bombing and shelling the island of Okinawa. This eighty-mile-long island with five airfields was one of a chain of islands south of Japan. The island lies 325 miles south of the Japanese mainland. It was to be the staging ground for the invasion of Japan.[7]

The invasion of Okinawa itself began on the same day all the Allied armies had crossed the Rhine: Easter Sunday April 1, 1945. Around Okinawa, an armada of thirteen hundred ships moved into position; so did ten U.S. Navy local men. In place at the radar screen of the U.S.S. *Patterson* was Mystic's John Golden. The signal officer on board the aircraft carrier the *Bunker Hill* was Centerville's John Talbot, the hero pilot of the Battle of Midway. On the same ship were two Seymour men, fighter pilot Loren Leach and aviation machinist's mate Edwin O. Wilty. Another machinist's mate, Lloyd Sherer of East State Street, and Corporal Paul Jurchich of South Twenty-second Street were serving on the U.S.S. *West Virginia.* Petty Officer Howard Hobart, whose brother Carl had been killed in an aerial mission over Italy and whose father worked at the *Iowegian*, was on board the U.S.S. *Thatcher.* And there were two more Centerville men: Sergeant First Class Robert Clark of South Main Street was on U.S.S. *Logan Victory*, and a third machinist's mate, Robert Woods of South Eighteenth Street, was on the destroyer *Pringle.*[8]

Lieutenant Joe Wilson, who as a seventeen-year-old was, on the day Pearl Harbor was attacked, delivering copies of the Sunday *Des Moines Register* out on Appanoose County's Soap Creek and who'd survived a kamikaze attack on the U.S.S. *Kitkin Bay*, was the tenth local man in the invasion. Taking off from the aircraft carrier the U.S.S. *Savo Island*, he flew his Grumman F4F Wildcat fighter aircraft in the first wave over Okinawa. The timing was crucial. He, in the first wave, was followed by the second wave, approaching within seconds laterally below him. As Joe banked and turned, he saw in the predawn light a sight much like that which John Koestner witnessed flying back to England after dropping the first paratroopers into Normandy. Joe saw thousands of landing craft, full of marines and infantry, approaching the shore.[9]

Among the marines aboard those landing craft was Centerville's J.B. Kelley. J.B. had been one of the first onto the deadly beaches of Saipan. On Okinawa he faced worse. The Japanese fought with desperate resistance, attempting to hold back the impending invasion of their homeland. On some days, the U.S. advance was less than one hundred yards. Worse again was the southern part of the island. It was honeycombed with caves and tunnels, all natural bunkers, where 120,000 Japanese fought to their deaths. J.B. was able to use a Tommy gun found beside a fallen comrade. This weapon, the

Joe Wilson. *Courtesy of Joe Wilson.*

twenty-seven-year-old invention of a Centerville man, Oscar V. Payne, was the weapon of choice of thousands of soldiers. One marine was quoted he'd "give his left testicle to own one."[10]

The gun was, however, ineffective for what was happening off Okinawa's shores. Beginning five days after the invasion, in successive dense waves lasting for weeks, nine hundred Japanese aircraft, three hundred of them on kamikaze suicide missions, attacked ships as targets. Men aboard the U.S.S. *Patterson* watched, seeing "one plane after the other his nose into the air, twisted onto his back ...dive straight into his target." At the *Patterson*'s radar screen, Mystic's John Golden identified one of the first attacks. He picked up a group of enemy planes closing at thirty-seven miles. The officer on watch at first didn't accept John Golden's identification. John persisted now, identifying the group as six to eight planes at twenty-five miles. At this point his observation was accepted, reported and confirmed over the radio's warning network. But it was too late. The planes were already diving.[11]

The kamikazes attacked battleships, they attacked destroyers and they attacked aircraft carriers. Near the U.S.S. *Patterson* that day was the U.S.S. *Logan Victory*, one of the first targets. On board, Centerville's Sergeant First Class Robert Clark survived. He remained steadfastly firing his guns until ordered to abandon ship. But aboard the U.S.S. *Pringle*, Machinist's Mate First Class Robert Woods, whose parents lived on South Eighteenth Street, was killed. The aircraft carrier the U.S.S. *Bunker Hill* was hit by two suicide bombers, one low and one in a vertical dive. Centerville's John Talbot, the hero pilot of Midway, the ship's signal officer, survived—but barely. The first plane hit thirty feet from where John was standing—on the exact spot where he had been minutes before. On the same boat, Seymour's Loren Leach survived. Seymour's Edwin O. Wilty did not. Edwin was among 396 dead on the *Bunker Hill*.[12]

Throughout April, the war on its three fronts was, for the people at home, all consuming. They searched among the news stories for what was happening to their men: those in the Pacific, those in Germany and those still fighting the forgotten war in Italy. High in the Apennine Mountains of northern Italy, where many of their men were fighting, the snows were melting. Violets could be seen along the ridges, buttercups among the gun emplacements and dugouts. The U.S. Fifth Army was infused with replacements, with reinforcements. Diverse units arrived. They were African Americans, Americans of Japanese descent, British East Indians, Brazilians, South Africans, Italians fighting the Germans and the Tenth Mountain Division of the Eighty-eighth Infantry—the famous Blue Devils, the all-draftee citizen army. Mountains peaks were captured—peaks bearing the names Pratolungo, Grande, Monterumici and

Mount Capello, where Captain Charles Radosevich of Centerville's Dewey Road, transferred to the Tenth Mountain from the 168th Infantry at Cassino, armed fifteen Blue Devils with six grenades apiece, and they pitched their way to the top.

As the armies descended the last foothills, waves of bombers of the Fifteenth USAAF came over the mountains from the south to prepare their path ahead. The soldiers could see the prize, the River Po Valley, tantalizingly near. They could see the clusters of neat houses, the fruit trees, the vineyards, the green pastures interlocked by white roads, villages—and the city of Bologna.[13]

Five hundred miles to the northwest, the Allies were moving rapidly east, taking major German cities—Hannover, Kassel and the Pied Piper town of Hamelyn. Patton's Third Army was racing to Bavaria and Czechoslovakia. The British were moving toward the North Sea so fast, Field Marshal Montgomery was imposing a security blackout to confuse ninety thousand Germans he hoped to trap in Holland. The Canadians were reaching Arnhem and the Zuider Zee.[14]

"V-E Day Soon?" asked the *Centerville Daily Iowegian* on April 12. At the Chamber of Commerce rooms on Thirteenth Street, Centerville businessmen met again to go over the original V-E Day program of celebration. But don't let down yet, they urged. The war in Europe is not over yet, and final victory will not be achieved until both the European and Pacific wars are won. Shocks, they knew, still lay ahead. One of the biggest came the next day. It was then that they read the *Centerville Daily Iowegian*'s headline. The date: Friday, the thirteenth.[15]

Chapter 83

Death of FDR, Concentration Camps, Germany Surrenders

The headline was large: "World Mourns Roosevelt!" Beneath it: "Harry S. Truman Leads Nation." The president had died suddenly and unexpectedly of a "massive" cerebral hemorrhage at 3:35 p.m. the previous day while staying at his Pine Mountain cottage in Warm Springs, Georgia.[1]

The news reached Appanoose County via radio in the early hours of the morning. C.A. Farrington, head of the Appanoose County Telephone Company, reported that for one-and-a-half hours, the local telephone office, with a double complement of operators, could not cope with the tremendous numbers of calls that were coming in. The news broke as the shifts changed. Because of the emergency, both shifts were held for duty. An operator was at each position on the board, another back of her to pick up connections as calls came in. The electricity required to operate the board jumped from a normal ten ampere of electricity to twenty-two.[2]

Centerville mayor Clarence Hood proclaimed a period of respect, mourning and prayer for the following day, Saturday, April 14, between three and five in the afternoon, when the president's funeral service would be nationally broadcast from the East Room of the White House. All Centerville business houses would close at the same time, reported attorney C.W. Howell, president of the Association of Commerce. Robert Baker, the manager of the Majestic and Ritz Theatres, canceled Saturday matinee movies. He arranged with NBC for the funeral to be broadcast in both theaters. Ministers of St. Mary's Catholic Church, the Central Church of Christ and the Methodist church said they would be present to lead prayers. Due to the Jewish custom of not holding services for the dead on Saturdays, Centerville's Jewish businesses closed on Friday almost as soon as the news broke. Local Jews gathered for services at their synagogue on Terry and Fifteenth Streets. All flags in town and in outlying villages were lowered to half-mast.[3]

In London, the president's son boarded an aircraft for Washington, D.C. So did the Earl of Athlone to represent the British royal family. The king of England was in shock and grief. Prime Minister Winston Churchill, fighting emotion, described the president as "the greatest American friend we have ever known." The Irish Parliament closed for the day. Black-edged red flags of Russia were hoisted over the Kremlin. Tributes came from China, Jerusalem, Yugoslavia, Portugal, Poland and Venezuela. General Eisenhower decreed a thirty-day mourning for American troops in Europe. American soldiers and sailors stationed in Britain were seen filing into churches. In a small Bavarian town, Captain K.E. Wilcox of Sioux City, Iowa, had just finished digging shrapnel from an American soldier's arm. The president, he said, will "go down in history as one of the three greatest Presidents: Washington, Lincoln, and Roosevelt..."[4]

Twelve days later, three special trains went through Centerville. They were headed for the San Francisco Peace Conference, where the United Nations was to be inaugurated. They carried delegates, some of the fifty representing the United States, many more representing organizations, some representing the fifty nations attending. As the train passed through town, people were aware of an empty seat: President Roosevelt's. He had planned on giving the inauguration address.[5]

What was now clear: the end of Hitler's Germany was at hand. Allied armies were penetrating into Germany in a fast-moving drama. A letter from Sergeant Jack Barnthouse in the Ninth Army described to the *Centerville Daily Iowegian* readers their speed. In "...16 days the battalion rolled an average of better than 600 miles." AP reporter Hal Boyle, who'd been embedded with the troops since Normandy, watched the American advance. "Worn out by three days and nights of continuous advance, doughboys nod and fall asleep on iron beds—the backs of the tanks they are riding into battle ...German prisoners streaming back guardless with upraised hands are dirty, haggard, and hungry."[6]

As the Allies penetrated further into Germany, Poland and Austria, they discovered one torture camp after another. They found underground Nazi factories crowded with slave laborers, huddled like cattle, starving and waiting in desperation for the Allies to come. They found prisoner-of-war camps where American, British, Russian, Canadian and other Allied nationals had been fed a daily diet of seven hundred calories, resulting in weight loss and malnutrition. Prisoners captured at the Battle of the Bulge three-and-a-half months previously had lost twenty-five to forty pounds. When Staff Sergeant John Koestner in his C-47 flew some of them to American evacuation hospitals near the Rhine or to hospitals in England, ice cream given at their request was quickly vomited. Max Exline with the Seventh Infantry, who'd noted the day and the time he crossed the Rhine in a letter to his sister south of Moulton, wrote again. He'd seen political prisoners and prisoners of war; he told her, "The reports don't make it strong enough. I saw men fight for crackers that we throw away out of our rations. A cigarette would burn their fingers and they couldn't feel it ...They acted as though they could, and some did, try to kiss us."[7]

If the prison camps affected the liberating soldiers, what they found in the concentration camps sickened them. At Buchenwald, Dachau, Belsen, Auschwitz and others, they witnessed the effect of state-organized genocide. The camps were run by people, even physicians, who had absorbed a Nazi contempt for humanity. Gypsies, Germans who had opposed the Nazis, homosexuals and Poles—but, above all, Jews—were killed in the hope of exterminating the entire race, and it was done by scientific experiments, disease, starvation and maltreatment. Private First Class Glen Morrow wrote to his mother in Centerville in such graphic terms about what he'd seen at a place he identified as Orkneuf, much of his letter was deleted. A letter from Centerville's Edson Kratzer told of being at Otting, where he watched his American officers force the camp's SS guards to dig up a mass grave of victims, build coffins for each one and then dig individual graves in the town's best cemetery. Three coffins were put on display. All villagers were forced to file by them and pay tribute by sprinkling each with holy water. At Dachau, Centerville's Major Charles Gragg in Patton's Third Army found thirty-eight flatcars standing on tracks filled with dead prisoners who had been starved to death. He described the SS troopers as "blood thirsty morons." Harold Chapman wrote to family in Centerville that he, too, had seen the flatcars. "When I entered the camp the prisoners appeared to be in a stupor ...Then someone started to sing and it was if the prisoners came to life." They sang the Polish national anthem, the inmates apologizing to the soldiers for not knowing the words of "The Star-Spangled Banner," but they'd made a makeshift American flag and raised it over Dachau.[8]

But of all the concentration camps, Buchenwald was the most disturbing. For Bob McGuire, it was unimaginable that human beings could be so treated. Lawrence "Sam" Mahoney, the engineer who'd been at the rebuilding of Cherbourg, was affected by its images for the rest of his life: the body piles, the mounds of ash, prisoners so starved they couldn't move, lying in bunks "like big grocery store shelves." But the worst image, he said, was the prisoners' eyes. They followed him wherever he moved. Their eyes haunted Sam forever. Another soldier haunted by what he saw was Centerville's Cliff Herndon. After the initial shock, Cliff, a photographer, went back to camp to get his camera. He took pictures of Buchenwald: of prisoners holding up their arms to show their tattooed identification numbers; of men lying in their bunks; of the cremation ovens; of the bodies, "just skin and bones," lying in piles. Cliff sent his photographs to the *Centerville Daily Iowegian* newspaper. "Print them," he said, "...for one day people will refuse to believe what was done to human beings here." Jesse Beck at the *Centerville Daily Iowegian* printed only two, "as others were too horrible to show."[9]

By late April, the Western Allies were rolling, almost unopposed, east to the River Elbe. The Russians were ringing Berlin. Spearheads of the U.S. Ninth and the U.S. First met the Russians at Torgau. An American infantry officer and Russian private squirmed across a girder on a blown bridge over the river, pounded each other on the back and, amid smiles and a "Put it there," shook hands. Germany was severed. Russians greeted Americans, among them Joe Coates, Bob McGuire and Bob Nevins. At the same time, Patton's Third, with "Sol" Kauzlarich, Marvin Gardner and other soldiers, including Elvin Jay, were advancing through southern Germany—to Berchtesgaden, Hitler's retreat, and on into Czechoslovakia.[10]

Hundreds of miles to the south, in northern Italy, the U.S. Fifth, with combat engineers, and the Thirty-fourth "Red Bull" Division, full of Midwestern men, were fighting down from the Apennines out into the River Po Valley. The "Red Bull" Division was the first to enter Bologna, to a rapturous welcome from the civilians and from the Partisans—that solid core of Italian patriotic fighters that had been such an aid to the U.S. Fifth and the British Eighth. The Partisans caught Mussolini as he was fleeing north into Switzerland. Mussolini was shot, his body displayed for public exhibition in Milan. At the same time, German soldiers were flocking into the prisoner-of-war cages. More were trying to escape north into Austria, their route cut off by the Thirty-fourth Division.[11]

In Centerville, for days rumors that Germany had surrendered were rife. Mrs. Harry Longanecker, proprietress of the Samson Electric Store, on April 30 turned on the window lights, which has been turned off under federal order. People called the *Centerville Daily Iowegian.* Phones rang across town. Talk circled the Square. But the rumor was premature.[12]

On Tuesday, May 1, the *Centerville Daily Iowegian*'s banner headline, superimposed by a red E-X-T-R-A, reported "Hitler Killed in Berlin." The following day it read, "Nazis Quit in Italy." Two days later, on Friday the fourth, the Nazis had surrendered Denmark, Holland and northern Germany to British general Montgomery at Lüneberg Heath. People everywhere waited for the next, the full and the total surrender.[13]

At Eisenhower's headquarters, the little red schoolhouse in Reims, northern France, WAC Sergeant Angela Cerato of Numa was one of four WACs working night and day in the general staff section. American, Russian and Nazi generals walked the rooms, negotiating. For hours Angela served tea to the Russians, whiskey and coffee to General Gustav Jodl and his fellow Nazis, coffee to the Americans, hamburgers and sandwiches to them all. Nobody, she said, was drinking much. At one in the morning on Monday, May 7, U.S. Lieutenant General Walter Bedell Smith advised the girls to go home and sleep, for agreement was unlikely that night. Angela's phone rang at two, an hour later. She was told to report back to the schoolhouse. "Can you type?" asked Colonel P.C. Lash. Angela then typed the official cable announcing the Nazi surrender to the world. It was Monday, May 7, at 2:41 a.m. French time, 7:41 Sunday evening Central War Time in Centerville.[14]

Angela Cerato, who typed the press release to announce victory in Europe. *Courtesy of Monica Simms Forbes.*

Early Monday morning, President Truman made the news known via radio to the nation. People across the nation, across Appanoose County listened. Shopkeepers listened. The workers at Hercules Manufacturing listened. Sirens in town blew—first the fire siren on top of City Hall, then the big steam siren on top of the ISU power plant. Businesses closed for half an hour. The liquor store closed. There were special school assemblies, followed by a town parade. It started up Main Street shortly before ten in the morning. It was led by color bearers and a guard of honor: a discharged wounded veteran, an active veteran, members of the American Legion and VFW posts. A column of hundreds of citizens and schoolchildren followed. They carried flags, marched around the Square to the bandstand in the Square's center and sang the national anthem. There were no speakers. The crowd dispersed.[15]

Appanoose County's fighting men heard the news. J.B. Kelley heard it on Okinawa. They heard it in Europe; radio gunner O.R. Parks heard it with his air crew flying over the Pacific. Technical Sergeant (T4) Raymond Ferren working in the signal corps in the Lafayette warehouse on Montparnasse, Paris, heard it, and all the wild celebrations conducted by the Parisians. Centerville's reaction to V-E Day was subdued. There were church services and private words spoken inside homes. Perhaps the town's tone was best exemplified by an advertisement that V-E Day from the Presbyterian church on Main and Maple. It read, "One War Down. One War to Go."[16]

Chapter 84

The Bomb, the Manhattan Project: Local Connections

Six days after the death of President Roosevelt, there was another death. This death was a personal loss to everyone who read his columns—a much larger emotional loss to the GIs he loved. Ernie Pyle was killed on the ten-square-mile island of Ie Shima, west of Okinawa. He died when shot by a Japanese sniper on April 18, 1945. On his body was the rough draft of his next column, in which he anticipated victory in Europe. He wrote that his heart was still in Europe, but he was now with American boys in "the other war not yet ended."[1]

That war "not yet ended" had reached its next logical step: the invasion of Japan. On June 22, the island of Okinawa was declared secure. It had cost Americans more than 12,500 sailors, soldiers and aviators; 50,000 more wounded. It was the bloodiest campaign and an awful warning of what lay ahead. One estimate was that a million Americans would die in an invasion of the Japanese homeland. Centerville's J.B. Kelley, a marine who'd been at the invasions of Saipan, Tinian and Okinawa, knew he'd be one of the first in any invasion.[2]

In Centerville, people read the *Centerville Daily Iowegian* headlines with anxiety. On July 17 they read, "American Task Force Lies Close to Shores of Japan"; days later AP war editor Leonard Milliman wrote, "Tokyo said today Japan would choose 'utter destruction' under admittedly superior Allied might rather than yield to the ...unconditional surrender ultimatum that had been sent by President Truman." That Japanese refusal set the course of history. Truman's reference to "utter destruction" was the result of four years of experiments and developments in atomic fission. Physicists, including Albert Einstein, Enrico Fermi and Leo Szilard, and men escaping Nazi Europe had warned Roosevelt of the German work on uranium fusion. The president in response created the U.S. Office of Scientific Research and Development. Its most secret work was known popularly as the "Manhattan Project." When the scientific goal of fission was achieved, engineers built the community of Oak Ridge, Tennessee, a laboratory at Los Alamos, New Mexico, and other key facilities around the country.[3]

Unknown until the end of the war was the number of Centerville people involved in the project. Guy Evans at the local U.S. Employment Office recruited workers employed on the making of the atom bomb without ever knowing that it was anything other than "a vitally important patriotic" project. The people he hired amounted to 220 people: 125 from Appanoose County, the others from surrounding counties of Wayne, Davis and Putnam. They were hired as waitresses, custodians, craftsmen, plumbers, carpenters, messenger boys and cement finishers. They were paid exceptionally good wages that included room and board. They were sent to Pasco, Washington, to support a community of technicians involved in the bomb.[4]

Centerville's Opal Adamson went in a different direction. She went south to Oak Ridge, Tennessee, in 1943 when it was "a huge mud puddle." It was the Appanoose pioneer blood in her veins, she later said, that caused her to stay there. All the workers were told to seal their lips, and many were astonished to learn later they'd help make the bomb. Another Centerville product, Bob Evans, was the business manager at the Iowa State College plant at Ames, where much research and manufacturing was done. He had charge, he said, of payrolls, inventory and "etc. etc.," referring to items not releasable at the time he spoke. Working at the University of Chicago was Amelia Simmons, of the Simmons family of Darbyville, north of Centerville, whose two brothers-in-law served as medics in the war—Royal on Bougainville and Ray on the first day at Omaha Beach. Amelia was an office clerk, working closely with the scientists, often processing their papers, particularly those of Dr. Arthur Dempster, the discoverer of uranium 235.[5]

There were two bombs. The first, a uranium bomb nicknamed "Little Boy," was dropped on the city of Hiroshima in Japan at nine fifteen in the morning on the sixth of August, 1945. It killed 60,175 people. Around noon on the ninth of August, a second bomb, a plutonium bomb, was dropped on Nagasaki, killing 36,000 more. Even these events had strong connections to Centerville. The first bomb on Hiroshima was dropped from a B-29 aircraft. The aircraft was one of fifteen "Silverplate" Boeing B-29 Superfortresses modified for atomic-bombing missions. The fifteen were built at the Glenn L. Martin Aircraft Company at Bellevue, Nebraska, just south of Omaha, and on the site of the present Offutt Air Base. Selected from the assembly line then making B-26s at the plant was Centerville's Zeph Earhart, one of the engineer-mechanics chosen to work on the fifteen B-29s for the excellence and reliability of his work. Colonel Paul Tibbets from Des Moines selected a B-29, flew it to Tinian in the Mariana Islands and named it "Enola Gay" after his mother.[6]

The Enola Gay, loaded with the atomic bomb, was one of seven planes taking off that day for Hiroshima. They flew in two groups: the first were three weather planes; the second group comprised five planes, the Enola Gay among them. Aboard one of the first three weather planes was Moulton's Sergeant Richard Anselme, responsible for observing and analyzing the weather conditions and reporting them to Tibbets and the crew of the five following aircraft. Exactly the nature of the bomb that they dropped that day none of them knew. They learned it from a shortwave radio report broadcast from the United States.[7]

For the second bomb, the plutonium bomb dropped on Nagasaki, Centerville's Robert "Bob" Buss was significantly involved. A brilliant student through Centerville High School, he won scholarships to California Technical College— "CalTech." He graduated in chemical engineering and then received a master's degree in business from Harvard. Carefully remembered for his scientific ability by his CalTech professors, he joined them in Pasadena on the Manhattan Project. Exploding the plutonium bomb was highly complicated. The detonation had to be precisely and exactly symmetrical. Bob's contribution was in solving and designing the fuse necessary for this accuracy.[8]

On Tuesday, the fourteenth of August, after the unparalleled devastation of these two bombs, the Japanese agreed to the terms of unconditional surrender.[9]

The news reached Centerville at 6:04 p.m. The fire siren on City Hall began to sound, alerting those in the town who might not have heard the news. It sounded for twenty minutes. Wild excitement broke out. The beer taverns and the movie theaters closed. So did the pool halls and the billiard halls. People ran to the Courthouse Square from every direction. They waved flags. Girls screamed. Boys whistled. Horns sounded and dogs barked. People alternated between laughing and crying. War wives, mothers and sweethearts, their men overseas, hugged each other. The courthouse clock struck seven. The high school band began marching. The march was led by the Legionnaires, carrying their own large American flag. High school majorettes and twirlers followed. Behind came a spontaneous procession of cars, trucks, bicycles and wagons. An 1870 car managed to honk its way around the Square. Boys

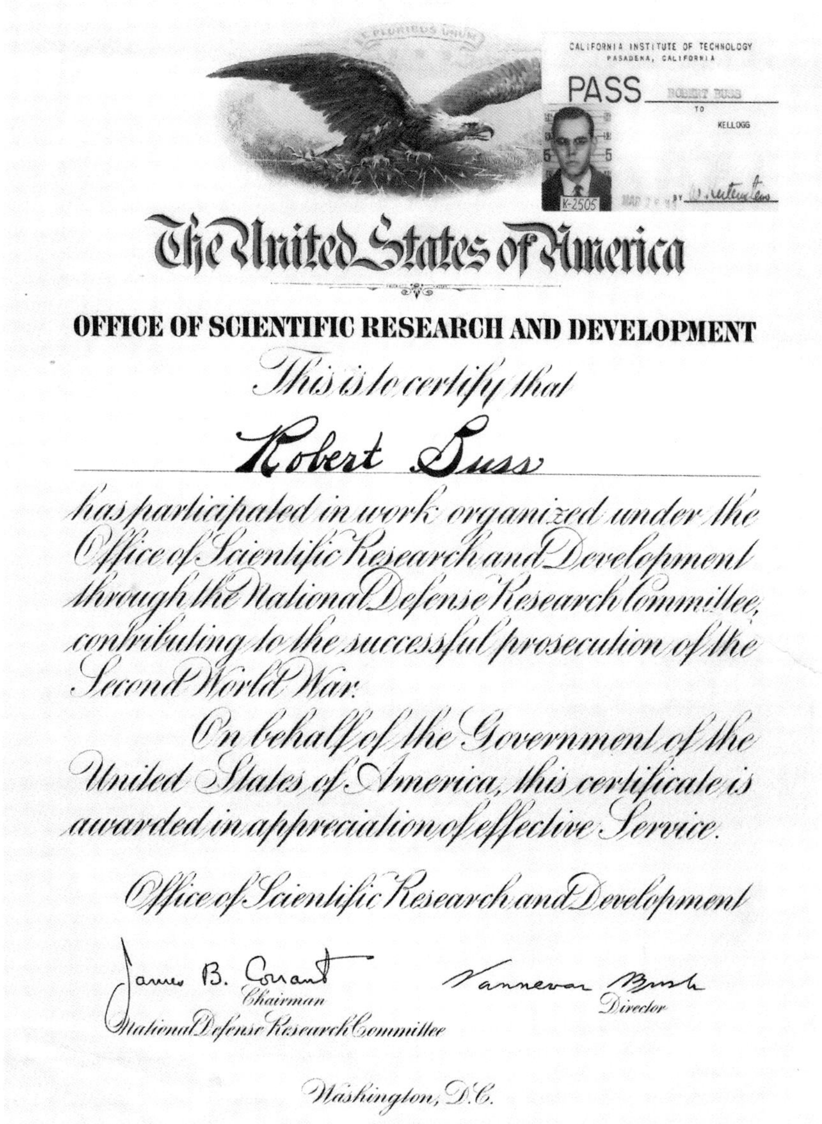

CALIFORNIA INSTITUTE OF TECHNOLOGY
PASADENA, CALIFORNIA

PASS ROBERT BUSS
TO
KELLOGG

K-2505

The United States of America

OFFICE OF SCIENTIFIC RESEARCH AND DEVELOPMENT

This is to certify that

Robert Buss

has participated in work organized under the Office of Scientific Research and Development through the National Defense Research Committee, contributing to the successful prosecution of the Second World War.

On behalf of the Government of the United States of America, this certificate is awarded in appreciation of effective Service.

Office of Scientific Research and Development

James B. Conant
Chairman
National Defense Research Committee

Vannevar Bush
Director

Washington, D.C.

Bob Buss credentials for his work on the Manhattan Project. *Courtesy of William Buss.*

frantically pushed a car, its battery flat. Shrieking girls leaned out of ice trucks. Township John Deere trucks bulged with flags. Trucks seen with "no riders" signs were loaded over capacity, one carrying twenty people. People danced on sidewalks. Confetti flew. Gushes of smoke issued from courthouse screens. At the bandstand, the high school band played "God Bless America" and "The

Star-Spangled Banner." The noise subsided. People sang, their right hands over their hearts. The clock struck eight. Bells rang out across the town. Churches opened, and the crowds dispersed.[10]

In the days that followed, the mood of the town altered. Euphoria gave way to reflection, for some to grief. Across the world's oceans, pockets of violence remained. Somber reminders lay in newspapers. Telegrams were still being delivered to families reporting the dreaded news. There were twenty-four. These were the cruelest telegrams: the County's men cut down only weeks, sometimes just days, before peace had been agreed to in Germany and in Japan.

Two went to Moravia, reporting the deaths of Private First Class Eugene Main on Okinawa, leaving a wife and two children under three, a third child dying as an infant, and the death of Staff Sergeant Paul Stafford, a platoon leader with the Thirty-fourth "Red Bull" Division, fighting in northern Italy. Two went to Exline: Private First Class Francis Hutchison, killed near Limbach, Germany, and Kenneth Hollenbeck, killed in the Philippines. Three were delivered to nearby Cincinnati. Two told of the deaths of two brothers killed a week apart in Germany—Sergeant Gilbert Ayers on March 17, his brother Robert Ayers on March 29, news that prostrated their parents. The third Cincinnati death was Archie Euwer, killed on a destroyer in the Pacific. Three telegrams arrived in Moulton: to the Forsyth family, with the death of Bernard, their son, in Germany; to the Brinegar family, reporting the death of their only son, Junior, aged nineteen; and to the Burgher family, south near Coatsville, news of the death of Staff Sergeant John Burgher, in northern Italy. One telegram was received in Mystic: Staff Sergeant Addison Hunt, killed on Corregidor in the Philippines. One telegram went to Numa—Ensign Wayne Seath, killed by a mortar shell in the invasion of Palau Island. Wayne attended the University of Iowa for three years. In Numa, he left a wife and a baby daughter, Suzanne, he'd never met.[11]

For George and Tina Kauzlarich, a telegram arrived at their Rathbun home to tell of the death of Private John Kauzlarich, lost at sea in the Pacific.[12]

Ten of the telegrams came to Centerville. One went to Mrs. Dorothy Potter of South Sixteenth Street, reporting the death of her husband, Paul, dying of wounds after he'd been torpedoed in the Pacific. Another was to the Malin family, reporting the death of their son, Wayne Junior, on Mindinao in the Philippines. On East Elm Street the news reached the John Marchi family of the death of Guido, shot on a high piece of land overlooking the Old Spanish Trail on Luzon, part of the Philippines. Guido was twenty-two and a star football player in Centerville High School, a member of the third all-state high school team in 1942. On South Main Street, Mrs. Ruby Hanrahan learned of the death of her son, Royal Jim Hanrahan, lost at sea near Iwo Jima, his body never recovered.[13]

Another shock went to Mrs. Elton Hendershot. Her brother, Karl "Hap" Holliday, who lived in Promise City but was known all over Centerville, was dead in Germany. Karl, a graduate of Drake University, a captain with the 561st Field Artillery Battalion, who'd landed on Utah Beach, was killed April 13, 1945. He was traveling in a jeep near the town of Klotz when his convoy was ambushed by German infantry. Karl, his first sergeant, his radio operator and his battery clerk jumped from the jeep. Fighting back with their Thompson submachine guns, they managed to keep the Germans down long enough to permit those in the rear to escape. But all four lost their lives. Karl left a wife and a one-and-a-half-year-old son, Robert.[14]

For Glenn Fry of North Tenth Street, a telegram arrived telling him of the death of his son, Private Alfred Fry, two days after Glenn had received two German Mauser rifles that his son had sent as souvenirs. The Earl Longleys of North Seventeenth learned of the death of their nineteen-year-old son, Private Eugene Longley, killed in Germany serving with Patton's Third Army. A second soldier was Private First Class Mike Countis, the son of Mr. and Mrs. James Countis of South Eighteenth Street. And news came of the death of a third soldier serving under Patton in Germany. It went to Mrs. Rose Cossolotto of South Sixteenth Street, telling her of the death of her son, Nino.[15]

One Centerville telegram was a confirmation of a man missing since January 8, 1944. Technical Sergeant William Whitacre, a crew member of a B-24 Liberator bomber, had departed from northern Australia on January 8 on a bombardment mission to southeastern Celebes in the Pacific and thought to have crashed. After two years of silence, confirmation of his death arrived on February 6, 1946.[16]

And yet another late confirmation of a death was that of ace pilot George H. Brewer. He was shot down over Aachen in Germany in 1944, leaving his parents, his wife and two small sons on West Maple Street hoping for over a year he was alive.[17]

Two years later, there was another death, perhaps the most poignant, but it occurred in Centerville and at home. Curtis Wayne Parson suffered wounds, tropical illness and malaria on Luzon in the Philippines. After hospital stays in San Francisco, in Springfield, Missouri, in Battle Creek, Michigan, and in Hines, Illinois, he came home to his parents at South Main Street. He died on November 8, 1947.[18]

Chapter 85

Celebration on Centerville Square

The *Centerville Daily Iowegian* headline on the morning of Wednesday, August 15, was enormous. Its letters, "War Ends!" measured almost five inches in height. For the people of Appanoose County, as for everyone across the nation, there was one unified goal: to bring their men home. The *Centerville Daily Iowegian* listed the dates, the military units and the arrival times of ships carrying troops into U.S. ports. When the *Queen Mary* slid out of the fog into New York harbor, her sides were hung with so many banners she looked like a huge floating billboard. There were yells, whistles and shouts from the nearly fifteen thousand veterans aboard. The men hung from lanterns and thrust their heads through portholes. One sign read, "Hello America—35th Division" another "Dear Mom—Your Boy has returned." They came down the gangplanks, moving in rhythm to harborside jazz bands.[1]

Seymour's Maurice Stamps aboard the *Lew Wallace* passed under the Golden Gate Bridge in San Francisco Harbor, greeted by flights of carrier planes circling overhead, ships in the harbor blowing whistles and foghorns and crews on navy ships at attention on the rails with their signal flags waving. Centerville's Howard Criswell, entering the same harbor later, remembered a band playing "Sentimental Journey." For Moulton's Clifford Cosby, arriving at the same port, a jazz band played "The St. Louis Blues." Cliff had gone to college in Missouri and thought it the best welcome home he could have ever received. As the men traveled by train across the country to Kansas City, Maurice Stamps, wearing his suntan uniform with six gold bars—one for each of his six months overseas—was assigned a compartment on a

Pullman car with a porter to make up his berth. When he and other veterans went to the dining car, their tabs were paid by civilian travelers before they themselves could pay.[2]

In Centerville when World War I ended, the men came home together and could be welcomed as a group on the Centerville Square. But World War II veterans came home in twos and threes and sometimes on their own. Welcome receptions were with family, with neighbors and with friends.

For some, the war wasn't over. There were thirty-five Purple Hearts in the County, many with injuries that would affect the rest of their lives. Many men were traumatized by what they'd witnessed. Most of them were changed. Lieutenant Colonel Frank Wilder, a former pastor of Centerville's Methodist church, who served on front lines in the Pacific with the men for four years, warned his Centerville audience of this in February, three months before V-E Day, six months before V-J Day. Seven hundred people packed the hall to hear him. "They will be different," he said. "They will be changed ...They'll be practical ...They have lived with death ...They'll have a new conception of missions."[3]

The war was not over for young men still being drafted. They left town to serve in occupational forces in Japan and in Germany. Centerville's Roger Perry was sent to Tokyo Bay to serve with the Forty-third Engineer Construction Battalion. Private First Class Richard Smith entered Japan at Yokohama to instruct maintenance crews. And Centerville's J.B. Kelley, the marine who'd fought at Saipan, Tinian and Okinawa, was sent to Nagasaki on military police duty. "The whole place was devastated," he said. "Of course, no one knew much about radiation in those days ...they issued us to go into Nagasaki ...lead overshoes and a lead jock-strap."[4]

Centerville men were leaving town to serve with the occupational forces in Europe. John Cridlebaugh left to serve at Hamburg, Germany, and passed his returning brother, Glenn, somewhere on the Atlantic. Centerville's Lieutenant Jack Heimes served with the Ninth U.S. Tactical Air Force, flew seventy-eight combat missions over Germany and became a member of the occupational forces, only to be killed in an aircraft accident in Germany four months after V-E Day. Captain David Whitamore, born and raised on Haynes Avenue, appeared on the pages of *Life* magazine. The German war criminals—Goering and von Ribbentrop among them—were being transported to places of confinement, and to ultimate trial at Nuremberg, by Captain Whitamore and the C-47 he commanded.[5]

All returning men had their stories and their memories, which some shared. Captain Max Ellis had worked with the U.S. Eighth Army Air Force in England. He'd planned the combat missions, he'd trained personnel and he'd maintained the Pathfinders—the aircraft that flew first across the English Channel on D-Day, including John Koestner's. Max also was involved in secret radar work at Bletchley Park north of London, a subject he wouldn't talk about. Some twenty-seven Appanoose County men served with the U.S. Army Eighth Air Force, which flew exclusively out of southeastern England bases to bomb Germany. Twenty-eight thousand of them were killed, more than all the marines in World War II. At least eight of these were from Appanoose County, the first being Eugene Wilcox of Moravia. Another death, one that would earn a Congressional Medal of Honor, was that of Darrell Lindsey. Darrell was born in Jefferson but spent much of his high school years in Centerville. On August 9, 1944, on his forty-sixth mission over northern France, the plane he was commanding was hit on the right engine and a wing. Darrell ordered all nine crew members to parachute out. Immediately afterwards, the plane exploded. Darrell's body was never recovered.[6]

Exline's L. Jay Johnson, who opened a funeral home on his return to Centerville, survived the U.S. Eighth Air Force. He won a "Lucky Bastard" award on completion of twenty-five dangerous missions. Steve Zaputil also survived. He told his story to his family and grandchildren. He described to them his missions and how in good, clear weather, he'd see the English coast, passing directly over the White Cliffs of Dover and once almost directly over the Eiffel Tower. He told them he once met a Dutch woman who told him as a child she'd run out of doors to watch the bombers stream over her home. She said at times it took an hour for all to cross, and it was a welcome and awesome sight to see.[7]

For all the men who served, vital support systems were provided by Appanoose men who helped make victory possible. There were armed guards for merchant ships—Ralph Belles, a naval lieutenant in the south Atlantic; Sherman Elgin, a navy signalman on ships carrying oil and gas to refuel aircraft flying across the Atlantic from Trinidad and Brazil; Seymour's Ralph Alshouse, flying aircraft to U.S. bases. In the Pacific, Mystic's Bill McDanel served submarines from the Midway Islands. He worked sixteen hours a day in rotations of two hours sleep, two hours standing watch, two hours sleep, two hours standing watch and sixteen hours work. Exline's Duane Hurley worked as an electrician on submarines at Fremantle, Australia, transferring to submarine patrol runs searching for Japanese ships. Dale Jones was a chief naval radio technician, moving between islands, including New Guinea and Borneo. Lieutenant S.G. Lodwick of Mystic maintained radio communication lines over almost impassable jungle terrain, at the same times supplying rapid artillery in support of infantry, which earned him a Legion of Merit award.[8]

Conducting aerial vigilance of the vitally strategic Panama Canal and serving as a medic on Baltra, one of the Galapagos Islands, was Centerville's Leo Craver. At San Diego, rehabilitating injured returning soldiers, was George Starcevich, and on Leyte Island in the Philippines, working with injured U.S. and Filippino soldiers and children weakened and damaged by war and imprisonment, was Howard Criswell. In the air over the Pacific, help for crewmen O.R. Parks, Bob Seddon and George Russo came from a surprising source: Charles Lindbergh. He advised that by "raising the manifold pressure and lowering revolutions per minute, the engines would consume less gasoline." That knowledge helped pilots fly considerably greater distances.[9]

These were the men that came home to Appanoose County. They came home to a community that had survived pestilence and crime, depression, the KKK and wars. These men came home with energy and discipline, patriotism and focus. They were about to take part in making America into a giant of economic and political power, unprecedented in the pages of history. And for many of them, there was a path in front of them: Public Law 346, the GI Bill of Rights, signed by President Roosevelt on June 22, 1944, when these men were in the thick of fighting in France, Italy and the islands of the Pacific. Jesse Beck reported 23,478 veterans had entered the nation's colleges by June 16, 1945, weeks after being at front-line fighting. At Cedar Falls, enrollment at the Iowa State Teachers College on September 16, 1945, was 2,500, of whom 1,000 were veterans. Centerville Junior College, which had closed a year previously with low enrollment, reopened on October 17, 1945, with thirty-six students, announced the dean of the college, T.C. Ruggles. When a Centerville all-school assembly was held on September 3, 1946, superintendent Fannon asked all GIs to stand—there were forty. The GI Bill offered paths into higher education, into agricultural programs, into aviation and into trades. John Cortesio Sr., who ran the Midwest Modern Shoe Training Service on West Van Buren Street, was one of a handful of individuals selected nationwide under the GI Bill to train returning veterans in shoe repair. John trained 150 students. They set up businesses from Utah to Hawaii. And a map of Iowa, in the back room of his Centerville Shoe Hospital, was peppered with pins showing who started shops in Iowa. Across Centerville Square in the *Iowegian* office on North Main Street, the editor who, for forty-two years, had so superbly informed his community and led it with sound moral leadership was quietly retiring. And, just as quietly, without fanfare and without fuss, his son Robert (Bob) Beck, home from serving in the U.S. Navy, entered the *Iowegian* office, picked up his father's pen and became the newspaper's new editor.[10]

The year 1946 was a Centennial Year. It was the centennial of the State of Iowa and the centennial for Appanoose County. The State of Iowa's celebration culminated on December 28 at the old capitol, the first Statehouse of Iowa in Iowa City.[11]

Centerville's celebration came earlier, in September. There was the inevitable parade that circled the Square and the town's main streets. There was a giant historical pageant at the high school stadium, with contributions and artifacts from the County's small communities. There were recreations of leading historical events and figures. There was a Centennial Flying Farmers event at the airport, with aircraft from all parts of Iowa and northern Missouri. Centennial dances with round dancing, square dancing and jitterbugging competitions occurred, and the Ottumwa Navy Base Band played to crowds at the bandstand on Centerville's Courthouse Square.[12]

Perhaps that day on Centerville's Courthouse Square, someone near the town's Civil War monument made an observation, and perhaps it was a World War veteran. The number of deaths in World War II in Appanoose County was officially 108. At the time, the population size was 24,245. In World War I, with a larger population of 30,600, the number killed was 55. In the Civil War, with a County population of 11,931—less than half that of 1940—the number dead was more than 300.[13]

And if, on that day when the town celebrated, someone had been able to elevate himself into the air over the County courthouse, and then rotate 360 degrees, viewing the ground, he would have seen a sight that would have made Jonathan Stratton smile. For on a late fall day in 1846, Jonathan Stratton walked through the blue-stemmed prairie grass and platted the town. He did it with a vision borne out on this day, one hundred years later. He designed twelve streets entering the Square. He designed them to draw people into the Courthouse Square, into the village, into the heart of social life, into human contact with each other.

Epilogue

In the chaos of the first hours on Omaha Beach on June 6, 1944, the first wounded soldier brought to Ray Simmons for medical attention was so badly wounded, Ray moved to the next victim. Later, when Ray checked on the first soldier, to his surprise he found he was alive. Ray administered plasma and then realized the soldier was a German.

Twenty years passed. Ray was walking in St. Louis, Missouri. A man approached him on the street: "I know who you are. I'll never forget your face. You saved my life on Omaha Beach even though I was a German. I have moved to the United States. I am now an American citizen."

Acknowledgements

In 1996, Lottie Wilson, one of the administrators at Indian Hills Community College, asked me to lead an historic walk of the City of Centerville. That was the beginning. As a European coming from my Welsh hometown of Cowbridge, with a history that predates the Romans by two thousand years, I thought learning the history of an American town that started in 1846 would be swift. I was wrong. Centerville is an almost perfect lens through which to view the growth and turmoil of mid-America. This book is the result. It is also the birth of my dream for the creation of an American museum of mid-America—its location, Centerville, Iowa.

Along the way, my gratitude to the people of Appanoose County has known no bounds. They listened. They shared. They explained, and nothing was too much trouble. This is particularly true of the County's World War II veterans. They had survived thc unimaginable and were prepared to relive it for my benefit.

I am also so grateful to local historian, Gary Craver, for digging out details of people, families and events sometimes at a moment's notice; and to former students, in particular Dr. Jason Roberts, who teaches history at Quincy College, Massachusetts, and who directed me to prime academic sources to uncover the necessary historical and political background. The staff of two libraries—Drake Free Public Library in Centerville and LeCompte Memorial Library in Corydon—were faultless and endlessly cheerful in tracking sources down from sometimes obscure locations. In Corydon, I am also grateful to the staff at the Prairie Trails Museum of Wayne County and to Dennise Andrews at Corydon's Copy Plus.

In translating my versions onto the computer, my great thanks goes to Lisa Eddy, the curator of Appanoose County Historical and Coal Mining Museum. She took over at midpoint, understood my handwriting without complaint and placed it all on computer with her hallmark characteristics of professionalism and artistry. My thanks to Misty Rosenberg and Ann Finch, who assisted Lisa as deadlines approached.

Then there are those who listened to my chapters, offering insights and adjustments. They are Jeanne Harrington Fowler, Phyllis Morrow Cosby, Gary Craver and one long-distance listener who paid for all the phone calls. He is professional history writer Bill Smallwood, who is so thoroughly versed in the twin demands of historical accuracy and clear writing style. Bill has been invaluable.

All these four went further, and in this I include my family and friends on both sides of the Atlantic: they offered me unflagging encouragement and emotional support on the days I felt the whole project was impossible!

To them all, my thanks.

Notes

Chapter 1

1. "'Died' Jonathan Stratton," *Centerville Journal*, August 13, 1884; Mark Hoffman, executive director, Appanoose County Conservation Board, interview with the author, October 25, 2007; Brant Schmell, prairie reconstructionist, interview with the author, May 20, 2007; Obituary of Jonathan Stratton, *Centerville Journal*, August 13, 1884; "Indians Left Appanoose 100 Years Ago," *Centerville Daily Iowegian*, April 30, 1943; "Little Storiees [*sic*] of Early Iowa," *Semi-Weekly Iowegian*, January 18, 1917; Undated papers about the Perjue family, private collection of Kristopher Hoffman, Centerville, Iowa; "Origin of the Dragoon Trail," *Centerville Daily Iowegian*, February 26, 1929; L.L. Taylor, ed., *Past and Present of Appanoose County, Iowa*, vol. 1 (Chicago: The S.J. Clarke Publishing Company, 1913).
2. *History of Appanoose County 1878* (Centerville, Iowa: Appanoose County Genealogy Society, reprint, 1989); Patrick Toscano, "The Arts of Surveying in Seventeenth Century Colonial America," *Professional Surveyor* 21 (2001); Bob Buss, professional land surveyor, interview with the author, September 10, 2001; Bill Buss of Hall Engineering, Centerville, Iowa, interview with the author, October 9, 2005; Surveying equipment from the time of Jonathan Stratton, on display at Prairie Trails Museum of Wayne County, Corydon, Iowa.
3. "How the Appanoose County Seat of Justice Was Located," *Centerville Journal*, June 1, 1922; Taylor, *Past and Present of Appanoose County, Iowa;* "A.J. Perjue Was First Sheriff," *Centerville Daily Iowegian*, April 28, 1928; Obituary of Jonathan Stratton, *Centerville Journal*, August 13, 1884; Jonathan L. Marwil, *A History of Ann Arbor* (Ann

Arbor, Mich.: The Ann Arbor Observer Company, 1987); United States Public Land Survey Corner Certificate, surveyed by Robert Buss, September 10, 1993.

4. "Map of Iowa," U.S. Department of Agriculture, 1936; "Chief Appanoose, Man for Whom County Was Named Was Indian of Fine Qualities," *Centerville Daily Iowegian*, Progress Anniversary Edition, January 1934. On the Sac and Fox Indians: Royce Delbert Kurtz, "Economic and Political History of the Sauk and Meskwaki 1780s–1845," (Ph.D. thesis, University of Iowa, December 1986); William T. Hagan, *The Sac and Fox Indians* (Norman and London: University of Oklahoma Press, 1958); Dan Ehl, "Digging Up the Past: Archaeological Survey Looking for Historic Artifacts and Sites," *Ad Express and Daily Iowegian*, August 3, 2001; *History of Appanoose County 1878*.
5. Leland L. Sage, *A History of Iowa* (Ames: Iowa State University Press, 1974); A.P. Nasatir, ed., *Before Lewis and Clark: Documents Illustrating the History of the Missouri, 1785–1804*, 2 vols. (St. Louis: St. Louis Historical Documents, 1952); M.M. Quaife, ed., extracts from McKay's and Evans's journals, "Historical Introduction," Separate 171, Publications of the State Historical Society of Wisconsin, vol. 22 (State Historical Society of Wisconsin, n.d.); Taylor, *Past and Present of Appanoose County, Iowa*; John M. Faragher, *Daniel Boone: The Life and Legend of an American Pioneer* (New York: Henry Holt Company Owl Book, 1993); Elizabeth A. Moize, "Daniel Boone: First Hero of the Frontier," *National Geographic* 841 (December 1985); J.C. Harvey, "Daniel Boone Is Again Discussed," *Centerville Daily Iowegian*, October 13, 1930; *History of Appanoose County 1878*; J.C. Harvey, "Daniel Boone," *Centerville Daily Iowegian and Citizen*, March 16, 1931; "Harvey Charges Some History Is Erroneous," *Centerville Daily Iowegian*, June 13, 1931; James Coates, *In Mormon Circles* (Reading, Mass.: Addison-Wesley, 1991); John W. Reps, *Cities of the American West: A History of Frontier Urban Planning* (Princeton, N.J.: Princeton University Press, 1979); Willis M. Heusinkveld, ed., "Journal of Andrew Jensen," *Mormon Trails across Appanoose County, Iowa* (Centerville, Iowa: Appanoose County Mormon Trail Association, 1995), 25; "Mormons Crossed Appanoose" *Centerville Daily Iowegian*, Centennial Edition, November 29, 1946; *Mormon Journal*, March 27, 1846.
6. Obituary of Jonathan Stratton, *Centerville Journal*, August 13, 1884; Appanoose County Map, Iowa Department of Transportation with United States Department of Transportation, January 1, 1999; "Map of the Town of Chaldea," Appanoose County Records, J.F. Stratton, county surveyor, County Recorder's Office; Edward T. Price, "The Central Courthouse Square in the American County Seat," *Geographical Review* 58 (1968).
7. Obituary of Jonathan Stratton, *Centerville Journal*, August 13, 1884; Taylor, *Past and Present of Appanoose County, Iowa.*
8. "Spencer Wadlington First Merchant in Centerville," *Centerville Daily Iowegian*, Centennial Edition, November 29, 1946.

9. "Squire Wadlington Sleeps in the Farmyard He Loved in County," *Centerville Daily Iowegian*, November 12, 1959; T.J. Fitzpatrick, "Spencer Wadlington First Merchant in Centerville," *Centerville Daily Iowegian*, Centennial Edition, November 29, 1946; "Doctor and Preacher," *Centerville Daily Iowegian*, Centennial Edition, November 29, 1946; *Centerville Daily Iowegian*, December 27, 1894; *History of Appanoose County 1878*.
10. "Has Wagon Used Almost 90 Years; Still Runs Well," *Centerville Daily Iowegian*, Progress Anniversary Edition, January 10, 1934; *Early Pioneer Stories*, collection of reprints from *Centerville Daily Iowegian*, Progress Anniversary Edition, January 10, 1934 (Centerville, Iowa: Appanoose County Genealogy Society); Taylor, *Past and Present of Appanoose County, Iowa*; *History of Appanoose County 1878*.
11. Appanoose County Courthouse Records, Range 2, Lots 1–2; "Lamp as Old as Centerville," *Centerville Daily Iowegian*, July 23, 1927; Taylor, *Past and Present of Appanoose County, Iowa*; Letter to Lavinia T. Ward, April 19, 1850, Howell family papers, private collection of Patricia Gleason, Centerville, Iowa.
12. *History of Appanoose County 1878*; "First Court House Stood at South East Corner of the Present Square," *Centerville Daily Iowegian*, Iowa Centennial Edition, August 23, 1938.
13. "Wild Hogs Were Cause of People Climbing Trees," *Centerville Daily Iowegian*, Progress Anniversary Edition, January 10, 1934; "A Centerville Man of 1856 Has Some Words of Greeting for One of the Newer Ones Who Has Gained Some Distinction," *Centerville Daily Iowegian*, September 8, 1930.
14. "Sixty Years of Married Life Passed," *Semi-Weekly Iowegian*, December 28, 1915.
15. *History of Appanoose County 1878* (this contains an error; Senter was *not* a governor); "William Tandy Senter, 1801–1848," in *Biographical Directory of the United States Congress, 1774–Present*, http://bioguide.congress.gov/scripts.
16. Frank J. Stork and Cynthia Clingan, *Iowa General Assembly: Our Legislative Heritage 1846–1980* (Des Moines: State of Iowa General Assembly, 1980); Clinton L. Scott, *The Universalist Church of America: A Short History* (Boston, Mass.: Universalist Historical Society, 1957); "Death of Reuben Riggs," *Centerville Citizen*, February 8, 1873; T.J. Fitzpatrick, "Spencer Wadlington First Merchant in Centerville," *Centerville Daily Iowegian*, Centennial Edition, November 29, 1946.
17. "How First Sheriff Got His Man after Cross State Chase," *Centerville Daily Iowegian*, Progress Anniversary Edition, January 10, 1934.
18. Benjamin F. Gue, *History of Iowa from the Earliest Times to the Beginning of the Twentieth Century*, vol. 3 (New York: The Century History Company, 1903), 425 (Wayne), 339 (Decatur), 405–6 (Ringgold), 415–16 (Taylor), 395–96 (Page), 348–49 (Fremont); "Map of the Town of Corydon—Seat of Justice of Wayne County," surveyed October 1851 by J.F. Stratton, county surveyor of Appanoose County, Iowa, and deputy surveyor for Wayne County, Wayne County Engineer's Office, Corydon, Iowa.

19. Erik McKinley Eriksson, "The Honey War," in *The Palimpsest*, vol. 5 (Iowa City: The State Historical Society of Iowa, 1924): 340; Gue, *History of Iowa from the Earliest Times to the Beginning of the Twentieth Century*, vol. 1, 145, 146, 193; Description of the Sullivan Survey, "Our Iowa, Its Beginning and Growth," IAGenWeb Project, http://iagenweb.org/history/history/oibg/Politics.htm.
20. Eriksson, "The Honey War," 340 and 341; *History of Appanoose County 1878*, 331.
21. *History of Appanoose County 1878*, 329 and 330; Taylor, *Past and Present of Appanoose County, Iowa*, 159.
22. Gue, *History of Iowa from the Earliest Times to the Beginning of the Twentieth Century*, vol. 1, 194.
23. Eriksson, "The Honey War," 343–48.
24. Eriksson, "The Honey War," 350; Taylor, *Past and Present of Appanoose County, Iowa*, 242; Bill Heusinkveld, "The Boundary Question," *Daily Iowegian*, April 10, 2003.
25. Taylor, *Past and Present of Appanoose County, Iowa*, 317.

Chapter 2

1. "Two Yoke of Oxen Brought the Davis Family to Iowa," *Centerville Daily Iowegian*, Progress Anniversary Edition, January 10, 1934; "Seeking a Prairie Home," *Centerville Daily Iowegian*, August 21, 1924; "Filled with Interesting Events Pioneers Enjoyed Rugged Life," *Centerville Daily Iowegian*, February 20, 1924; "Took Part in Two Big Movements," *Centerville Daily Iowegian*, March 21, 1924; "Longs Residents of County over Eighty-four Years," *Centerville Daily Iowegian*, special edition supplement, February 17, 1934; "Mr. and Mrs. R.E. Cummins of Moravia Observe 54th Anniversary," *Centerville Daily Iowegian*, April 15, 1938; "Carried Gold in False Bottom of Their Tool Chest," *Centerville Daily Iowegian*, Progress Anniversary Edition, January 10, 1934.
2. U.S. Bureau of the Census, "*1860 Federal Census of Appanoose County*"; "Traces History of Porter Family," *Centerville Daily Iowegian*, Progress Anniversary Edition, January 10, 1934; "Here Is Graphic Story of How the Pioneers Came by Covered Wagon and Established Their Home in the West," *Centerville Daily Iowegian*, Progress Anniversary Edition, January 10, 1934.
3. "Girl of Five Came to County Back in 1849," *Centerville Daily Iowegian*, Progress Anniversary Edition, January 10, 1934; "Traveled Mormon Trail," *Semi-Weekly Iowegian*, July 25, 1911; "Pioneer Tells of Early Iowa Days," *Centerville Daily Iowegian*, January 6, 1931; "Here Is Graphic Story of How the Pioneers Came by Covered Wagon and Established Their Home in the West," *Centerville Daily Iowegian*, Progress Anniversary Edition, January 10, 1934.

4. H.W. Lathrop, *Life and Times of Samuel J. Kirkwood, Iowa's War Governor* (Chicago, Ill.: Press of Regan Publishing House, 1893); John C. Brindley, *History of Road Legislation in Iowa* (Iowa City: State Historical Society of Iowa, 1912), 1, 2.
5. "Here Is Graphic Story of How the Pioneers Came by Covered Wagon and Established Their Home in the West," *Centerville Daily Iowegian*, Progress Anniversary Edition, January 10, 1934; "Longs Residents of County over Eighty-four Years," *Centerville Daily Iowegian*, Progress Anniversary Edition, January 10, 1934.
6. "Appanoose County Land Given as 1812 War Grants to Soldier Widows," *Centerville Daily Iowegian*, Progress Anniversary Edition, January 10, 1934; *History of Appanoose County 1878*, 364; "Old Couple Early in County Lived to Celebrate Their 65th Wedding Day," *Centerville Daily Iowegian*, Progress Anniversary Edition, January 10, 1934.
7. "Came to Iowa in Spring of 1851," *Centerville Daily Iowegian*, February 10, 1934; "Pioneer Homes Quite Simple," *Centerville Daily Iowegian*, April 21, 1927; "County Pioneer Tells of Hard Days Years Ago," *Centerville Daily Iowegian*, September 2, 1925; "Elderly Appanoose Lady is Ninety Two," *Centerville Daily Iowegian*, Progress Anniversary Edition, January 10, 1934; Taylor, *Past and Present of Appanoose County, Iowa*, 229–30 (see chap. 1, n. 1); "Old Settlers Meditation," *Centerville Daily Iowegian*, May 6, 1895; Taylor, *Past and Present of Appanoose County, Iowa*, 230–31 (see chap. 1, n. 1); "Came to Iowa in Spring of 1851," *Centerville Daily Iowegian*, Progress Anniversary Edition, January 10, 1934; "Has Lived Here Longer Than Anyone," *Daily Iowegian*, March 2, 1951; "91st Birthday Is Celebrated by Mrs. Wilson," *Centerville Daily Iowegian*, July 27, 1936.
8. "Some Interesting Early Day History of Points in Davis County, Iowa," *Centerville Daily Iowegian*, July 21, 1924; "Early Day Threshing Outfits Recalled by J.C. Harvey and Changes in Type Are Noted," *Centerville Daily Iowegian*, September 22, 1944; Taylor, *Past and Present of Appanoose County, Iowa*, 233–34 (see chap. 1, n. 1); "Main Interest Getting Along in These Days," *Centerville Daily Iowegian*, Progress Anniversary Edition, January 10, 1934; "Report Bear Was Killed Here in an Early Day," *Centerville Daily Iowegian*, Progress Anniversary Edition, January 10, 1934; Taylor, *Past and Present of Appanoose County, Iowa*, 231–32 and 234–35 (see chap. 1, n. 1); "Circuit Riders of Old Days Had Strenuous Life," *Centerville Daily Iowegian*, Progress Anniversary Edition, January 10, 1934; "Woman of 86 Has Memory of Real Time of Hardship," *Centerville Daily Iowegian*, Progress Anniversary Edition, January 10, 1934; "The Pioneer Doctors Had Many Hardships," *Centerville Daily Iowegian*, Progress Anniversary Edition, January 10 1934; "Born in Iowa in 1843—Lives in Appanoose," *Centerville Daily Iowegian*, Progress Anniversary Edition, January 10, 1934.
9. "Elizabeth Bishop Arrived as Indians Left and Lived Long to Tell the Story of Events in Earliest County History," *Centerville Daily Iowegian*, Progress Anniversary Edition, January 10, 1934; Stanley B. Kimball, "The Mormon Trail Network in Iowa 1838–1863: A New Look," *Brigham Young University Studies* 21, no. 4 (fall 1981): 417–

30; "More on Mormon Trail," *Semi-Weekly Iowegian*, June 2, 1911; "Gets More Data on Mormon Trek across County," *Centerville Daily Iowegian*, April 19, 1927; "Some Appanoose People Interested in Huge Estate of Californian; Counted in Hundreds of Millions," *Centerville Daily Iowegian*, August 3, 1929; "Park Plantings Came from Farm with a History," *Centerville Daily Iowegian*, May 3, 1940; Helen C. Wetmore, *Last of the Great Scouts* (Harrisburg, Penn.: The National Historical Society, 1899; reprint, 1994), 4–8; "Drummer Boy of Waterloo Buried Near Lineville, IA," *Centerville Daily Iowegian*, March 19, 1937; Taylor, *Past and Present of Appanoose County, Iowa*, 243–46 (see chap. 1, n. 1); "Local Angle Is Noted in River City Festival," *Centerville Daily Iowegian*, June 23, 1933; "Story Sent of Ox-Team Train That Left Cincy Century Ago," *Centerville Daily Iowegian*, July 3, 1953.

10. "Elder Wooden Stopped Here before the War," *Centerville Daily Iowegian*, Progress Anniversary Edition, January 10, 1934; "J.R. Wooden Has Been in Business in Centerville for 56 Years," *Semi-Weekly Iowegian*, May 10, 1912.
11. Taylor, *Past and Present of Appanoose County, Iowa*, 317 (see chap. 1, n. 1).
12. Fitzpatrick, "Spencer Wadlington First Merchant in Centerville," *Centerville Daily Iowegian*, Centennial Edition, November 29, 1946.
13. "Old Trails Took Easiest Way, Then Came Auto Highway," *Centerville Daily Iowegian*, Progress Anniversary Edition, January 10, 1934; Bill Heusinkveld, "Early Roads in Appanoose County," *Daily Iowegian*, July 21, 2005; "Johns Township Story," *Centerville Daily Iowegian*, Progress Anniversary Edition, January 10, 1934; "Reports Death of Three 'Old-Timers'; Were Well Known," *Centerville Daily Iowegian*, January 29, 1937.
14. Taylor, *Past and Present of Appanoose County, Iowa*, 315–16 (see chap. 1, n. 1); "Old Stage Driver Died in Past Year," *Centerville Daily Iowegian*, Progress Anniversary Edition, January 10, 1934; "William Strickler of Centerville, Last of Iowa's Stage Coach Pilots Recounts Days When He Was 'Kid Driver' of 1860," *Centerville Daily Iowegian*, September 27, 1930.
15. "Old Stage Driver Died in Past Year," *Centerville Daily Iowegian*, Progress Anniversary Edition, January 10, 1934.
16. "J.R. Wooden Has Been in Business in Centerville for 56 Years," *Semi-Weekly Iowegian*, May 10, 1912.
17. Taylor, *Past and Present of Appanoose County, Iowa*, 315 (see chap. 1, n. 1); "Wm. Bradley Dead," *Centerville Weekly Citizen*, May 20, 1896.
18. Taylor, *Past and Present of Appanoose County, Iowa*, 315 (see chap. 1, n. 1); Mrs. George (Ella Williams) Randle, "Walks around the Square as It Was in Her Girlhood," *Centerville Daily Iowegian*, Progress Anniversary Edition, January 10, 1934; "Fifty Cents a Day Fifty Years Ago," *Semi-Weekly Iowegian*, March 20, 1908.
19. "J.R. Wooden Has Been in Business in Centerville for 56 Years," *Semi-Weekly Iowegian*, May 10, 1912; "Elder Wooden Stopped Here Before the War," *Centerville*

Daily Iowegian, Progress Anniversary Edition, January 10, 1934; Mrs. George (Ella Williams) Randle, "Walks around the Square as It Was in Her Girlhood," *Centerville Daily Iowegian*, Progress Anniversary Edition, January 10, 1934.

20. "Methodist Church Had Beginning in 1846 Built 1852," *Centerville Daily Iowegian*, Progress Anniversary Edition, January 10, 1934; Taylor, *Past and Present of Appanoose County, Iowa*, 345–46, 347 (see chap. 1, n. 1); Fitzpatrick, "Spencer Wadlington First Merchant in Centerville," *Centerville Daily Iowegian*, Centennial Edition, November 29, 1946.

21. "Uncovering Old Well Revives Memories," *Daily Iowegian*, June 17, 1946; "Lamplighting Days Meant Early Rising," *Centerville Daily Iowegian*, Progress Anniversary Edition, January 10, 1934; H.B. Williams, "Early Centerville, Its Business Men, and Incidents That One in Business Here Many Years Recalls," *Centerville Daily Iowegian*, Progress Anniversary Edition, January 10, 1934; Taylor, *Past and Present of Appanoose County, Iowa*, 321 (see chap. 1, n. 1).

22. "Centerville Schools Student Iowegian," *Centerville Daily Iowegian*, January 9, 1946.

23. "Paints a Picture of Old Turkey Pen School as Traditions Have Been Handed Down by Those Who Were Children There," *Centerville Daily Iowegian*, Progress Anniversary Edition, January 10, 1934; "One Who Knew the Pioneer Log School Describes It and Tells of the Class Work and the Diversions of the Time," *Centerville Daily Iowegian*, Progress Anniversary Edition, January 10, 1934; "Centerville as Remembered by One Born Here in 1856 and Knew the People Well," *Centerville Daily Iowegian*, June 13, 1931.

24. Taylor, *Past and Present of Appanoose County, Iowa*, 312–15 (see chap. 1, n. 1); *Centerville Daily Iowegian*, Centennial Edition, November 29, 1946.

25. H.B. Williams, "Early Centerville, Its Business Men, and Incidents That One in Business Here Many Years Recalls," *Centerville Daily Iowegian*, Progress Anniversary Edition, January 10, 1934; "In Memoriam: Mrs. Cora Whitsell," *Centerville Daily Iowegian*, Progress Anniversary Edition, January 10, 1934.

26. "Took Interest Singing School around Udell," *Centerville Daily Iowegian*, Progress Anniversary Edition, January 10, 1934; "Old Fashioned Dance Portrayed in Vivid Style," *Centerville Daily Iowegian*, Progress Anniversary Edition, January 10, 1934; "Old Time Fight in Centerville Drew Big Crowd," *Centerville Daily Iowegian*, Progress Anniversary Edition, January 10, 1934; *History of Appanoose County 1878*, 367–68.

27. Taylor, *Past and Present of Appanoose County, Iowa*, 274 (see chap. 1, n. 1); "Trial of H.W.S. Hinkle," *Ward's Own*, reprinted from *The Appanoose Chieftain*, May 13, 1858; "Describes Spot Where Hinkle Was Hanged in 1858," *Centerville Daily Iowegian*, Progress Anniversary Edition, January 10, 1934; C.E. McGrew, "Locates the Place of Hinkle Hanging West of Orleans," *Centerville Daily Iowegian*, November 26, 1941; "Records on Famous Hinkle Hanging Near Orleans Where He Was

Executed," *Centerville Daily Iowegian*, August 13, 1858; T.J. Fitzpatrick, "Sam Brown, a Rank Fundamentalist an Interesting Early Day Citizen," *Centerville Daily Iowegian*, Centennial Edition, November 29, 1946; "Had Ice Water at Early Hanging," *Centerville Daily Iowegian*, September 2, 1925; "Hinkle Hanging Arouses Memories," *Centerville Daily Journal*, September 27, 1922; "Was Present at Hinkle Hanging," *Centerville Daily Iowegian*, April 25, 1928.

28. Taylor, *Past and Present of Appanoose County, Iowa*, 265, 274 (see chap. 1, n. 1); "Died in Chicago," *Burlington (Iowa) Gazette*, December 14, 1908.

Chapter 3

1. "John Lankford Dead," *Centerville Journal*, February 24, 1916; "John Lankford Died This Morning," *Centerville Daily Citizen*, February 23, 1916; "John Lankford Died at Age Eighty-eight," *Semi-Weekly Iowegian*, February 24, 1916; "Picturesque Old Undertaker Wore Straw Hat All Yr.," *Centerville Daily Iowegian*, Progress Anniversary Edition, January 10, 1934.
2. Robert Dykstra, front flap, *Bright Radical Star: Black Freedom and White Supremacy on the Hawkeye Frontier* (Cambridge, Mass.: Harvard University Press, 1993).
3. Paul Johnson, *A History of the American People* (New York: Harper Collins, 1997), 399–400; "1850 U.S. Federal Census of Appanoose County."
4. Charles Blockson, *The Underground Railroad: First-Person Narratives of Escapes to Freedom in the North* (New York: Prentice Hall Press, 1987); Gue, *History of Iowa from the Earliest Times to the Beginning of the Twentieth Century*, vol. 1, 373–74 (see chap. 1, n. 19); Elliott (no other name given), son of George, letter to Professor Wilbur H. Siebert, November 18, 1895, and Seth Stanton, letter to Hon. W.H. Siebert. (c. 1896), in "The Underground Railroad in Iowa," letters and materials collected by Wilbur H. Siebert, Ohio State University, Columbus, Ohio, with index by John Loveless, Drake University, Des Moines, Iowa, collection held by Ohio Historical Society Collections.
5. Land records in Appanoose County, Iowa, Recorder's Office; "Picture of Mystery Farm Brings Old Time Memories," *Centerville Daily Iowegian*, September 18, 1957.
6. "First House Built Where Cincinnati Now Stands in 1850; Wolves and Deer Were Abundant Those Days," *Centerville Daily Iowegian*, February 13, 1924.
7. Luther R. Holbrook, letter to readers, *The True Wesleyan*, June 29, 1850, Yale Divinity Library, New Haven, Conn.
8. J.H.B. Armstrong, letter to Wilbur H. Siebert, December 12, 1895, in collection held by Ohio Historical Society Collections.
9. Dykstra, *Bright Radical Star*, 29.
10. Ibid., 30.

11. Ibid., 90; J.H.B. Armstrong, letter to W.H. Siebert, December 10, 1895, in collection held by Ohio Historical Society Collections.
12. "J.H.B. Armstrong Dead," *Centerville Daily Citizen*, May 25, 1900; "One of the First Settlers of County," J.H.B. Armstrong obituary, *Cincinnati Review*, May 25, 1900.
13. Taylor, *Past and Present of Appanoose County, Iowa*, 366, 378 (see chap. 1, n. 1); "One of the First Settlers of County," J.H.B. Armstrong obituary, *Cincinnati Review*, May 25, 1900.
14. Land records, Appanoose County, Iowa, Recorder's Office.
15. "J.H.B. Armstrong," *Centerville Weekly Citizen*, March 16, 1872; Louis Pelzer, "The Origin and Organization of the Republican Party in Iowa," *Iowa Journal of History and Politics* 4 (1906): 523–24; David S. Sparks, "The Birth of the Republican Party in Iowa 1854–1856," *Iowa Journal of History* 1 (January 1956).
16. Dykstra, *Bright Radical Star*, 126–32 and 136–37.
17. Pelzer, "The Origin and Organization of the Republican Party in Iowa," 525; Dykstra, *Bright Radical Star*, 134; "Origin of the Republican Party in Iowa," *Weekly Citizen*, July 15, 1871.
18. Dykstra, *Bright Radical Star*, 144–45.
19. Deed Record Book E, 689, Appanoose County, Iowa, Recorder's Office.
20. Biographical and Historical Record of Wayne and Appanoose Counties, Iowa (Chicago: Interstate Publishing Co., 1886); Biographical and Genealogical History of Appanoose and Monroe Counties, Iowa (Chicago and New York: The Thompson Lewis Publishing Company, 1903); individual obituaries.
21. "Reuben Riggs," Taylor, *Past and Present of Appanoose County*, vol. 1, 267 (see chap. 1, n. 1); "Thaddeus H. Stanton: New Paymaster—General of the Army," *Centerville Daily Citizen*, April 22, 1895.
22. "Special Correspondent—Moulton," *Centerville Daily Citizen*, December 10, 1907; "John G. Bridal," *Biographical and Genealogical History of Appanoose and Monroe Counties*; "Grandfather of C.E. Bridal, Late of This City, Was One of Brown's Men," including quotes from a letter from Dr. Mott R. Sawyers, *Centerville Daily Iowegian*, February 14, 1950.
23. Dykstra, *Bright Radical Star*, 156, 158–9; Benjamin F. Shambaugh, *The Constitutions of Iowa* (Iowa City, Iowa: State Historical Society, 1934), 246; Erik Eriksson, "The Framers of the Constitution of 1857," *Iowa Journal of History and Politics* 22 (January 1924): 52–88.

Chapter 4

1. Lathrop, *Life and Times of Samuel J. Kirkwood*, 113–15 (see chap. 2, n. 4).
2. Ibid.

3. Ibid.
4. "Iowa and Civil War," editorial column, reprinted from the *Oskaloosa (Iowa) Herald*, *Centerville Daily Iowegian*, March 18, 1950.
5. "The Vote of Iowa in 1860 …," *Weekly Citizen*, November 5, 1870 (Note: the ellipsis points in this article citation, and all other articles including ellipsis points that are cited hereafter in these notes, indicate articles that were published without headlines; these articles are hereafter identified by the opening words of the first sentence of the article and marked as untitled); "County Not for Lincoln," editorial, *Centerville Daily Iowegian*, May 31, 1950; Taylor, *Past and Present of Appanoose County, Iowa*, 169–75 (see chap. 1, n. 1); "Items Gathered from Old Papers," *Centerville Daily Iowegian*, Progress Anniversary Edition, January 10, 1934.
6. "Recollections and Reminescences [*sic*] of Kos Harris, Wichita, Kansas, on Early Centerville School Days," *Centerville Daily Iowegian*, November 15, 1925; Taylor, *Past and Present of Appanoose County, Iowa*, 177 (see chap. 1, n. 1); *History of Appanoose County 1878*, 407 (see chap. 1, n. 2).
7. "John W. Fuller," *Centerville Daily Iowegian*, Progress Anniversary Edition, January 10, 1934; A.R.S., "Triumps [*sic*] and Achievements of By-Gone Days in Walnut Township and Appanoose County," *Mystic Telegram*, August 21, 1924.
8. L.D. Ingersoll, *Iowa and the Rebellion* (Philadelphia: J.B. Lippincott and Company, 1866); Gue, *History of Iowa from the Earliest Times to the Beginning of the Twentieth Century*, 57 (see chap. 1, n. 18).
9. Stephen N. Kallestad, David L. Snook and Michael J. Musel, "Spirit Lake Massacre," Iowa National Guard, http://www.iowanationalguard.com/Museum/IA_History/SpiritLakeMassacre.htm.
10. "Francis Marion Martin 95 Has 'Been to Doctor' Three Times," *Centerville Daily Iowegian*, January 6, 1950; Lathrop, *Life and Times of Samuel J. Kirkwood, Iowa's War Governor*, 165–67 (see chap. 2, n. 4); Hubert H. Wubben, *Civil War Iowa and the Copperhead Movement* (Ames, Iowa: Iowa State University Press, 1980), 65.
11. A.R.S., "Triumps [*sic*] and Achievements of By-Gone Days in Walnut Township and Appanoose County," *Mystic Telegram*, August 21, 1924.
12. "Recall Stirring Times When War Seemed Near Home," *Centerville Daily Iowegian*, May 29, 1925; "Benjamin Wells" and "Dexter Spooner," *Biographical and Historical Record of Wayne and Appanoose Counties, Iowa*, 619, 602–3 (see chap. 3, n. 20); Ingersoll, *Iowa and the Rebellion*, 711; Lathrop, *Life and Times of Samuel J. Kirkwood, Iowa's War Governor*, 165 (see chap. 2, n. 4).
13. Ingersoll, *Iowa and the Rebellion*, 113.
14. "Departure of the Volunteers," *Appanoose Chieftain*, July 11, 1861; "Recall Old Times," *Daily Iowegian*, February 25, 1921; "Recalls Incidents of Civil War Time," *Centerville Daily Iowegian*, May 23, 1935.

15. Ingersoll, *Iowa and the Rebellion*, 113.
16. James M. McPherson, *Battle Cry of Freedom* (New York: Oxford University Press, 1988).
17. "The Civil War in Iowa," *Centerville Daily Iowegian*, June 26, 1961; Henry H. Wright, *A History of the Sixth Iowa Infantry* (Iowa City, Iowa: State Historical Society of Iowa, 1923), 16–19.
18. "Dedicate Monument to 'Battle of Athens,'" *Centerville Daily Iowegian*, May 24, 1950; "The Civil War in Iowa," *Centerville Daily Iowegian*, June 26, 1961.
19. Wright, A History of the Sixth Iowa Infantry, 21–22.
20. A. Stanton, "Company 'I,' Third Iowa Cavalry," *The Citizen*, July 27, 1887.
21. Ingersoll, *Iowa and the Rebellion*, 396, 397; Stanton, "Company 'I,' Third Iowa Cavalry," *The Citizen*, July 27, 1887; Chas B. DePuy, "Civil War Letters Are Handclasp across Time," *Centerville Daily Iowegian*, October 5, 1961.
22. Geoffrey C. Ward, Ric Burns and Ken Burns, *The Civil War: An Illustrated History* (New York: Alfred A. Knopf, 1990), 74–75.
23. C.K. Holbrook, "Letter from a Soldier Going to the Front," *Centerville Daily Iowegian*, May 19, 1937.
24. Stanton, "Company 'I,' Third Iowa Cavalry," *The Citizen*, July 27, 1887.

Chapter 5

1. Frank L. Klement, *The Copperheads in the Middle West* (Chicago, Ill.: University of Chicago Press, 1960), 5; Bill Heusinkveld, "The Appanoose County Courthouse Centennial," Appanoose Courthouse Centennial Committee, 5; Tom C. Merritt, Early Days in Appanoose County, *Centerville Daily Iowegian*, October 27, 1941; "Mrs. Martha Hiatt of Moravia is Ninety-Four Today; Recalls Many Things Occurred in Past," *Centerville Daily Iowegian*, April 26, 1939.
2. "How Poor People Lived When the Country Was New," *Centerville Daily Iowegian*, Progress Anniversary Edition, January 10, 1934; Merritt, Early Days in Appanoose County, *Centerville Daily Iowegian*, October 27, 1941.
3. H.B. Williams, "Early Centerville, Its Business Men, and Incidents That One in Business Here Many Years Recalls," *Centerville Daily Iowegian* January 10, 1934; *Biographical and Historical Record of Wayne and Appanoose Counties, Iowa* (see chap. 3, n. 20).
4. "Recollections Written by One Now Gone," *Centerville Daily Iowegian*, Progress Anniversary Edition, January 10, 1934; C.B. DePuy, "Uncle Dick and Aunt Lizzie Mannon Reach Sixty Eight Anniversary in Celebrated Petty Mill Valley Near Omaha, Missouri," *Centerville Daily Iowegian*, December 7, 1935; "Uncle Dick

Mannon Taken at 97," *Centerville Daily Iowegian*, November 20, 1943; "Mrs. Nancy Jane Waite Will Observe 94th Birthday This Week," *Centerville Daily Iowegian*, February 27, 1950.

5. "Early Days in Exline Vicinity," *Centerville Daily Iowegian*, Progress Anniversary Edition, January 10, 1934.
6. "Dr. Worthington Farm Now Owned by E.E. Withrow," *Centerville Daily Iowegian*, December 31, 1946; "First Doctor Carried Bullet Fired at Him," *Centerville Daily Iowegian*, August 23, 1938.
7. "Recalls Fear Children Felt during the War," *Centerville Daily Iowegian*, Progress Anniversary Edition, January 10, 1934; "Mrs. Elizabeth Stuckey, 99, Recalls Days of Civil War," *Centerville Daily Iowegian*, March 4, 1957; H.B. Williams, "Early Centerville, Its Business Men, and Incidents That One in Business Here Many Years Recalls," *Centerville Daily Iowegian*, January 10, 1934.
8. Mrs. George (Ella Williams) Randle, "Walks around the Square as It Was in Her Childhood," *Centerville Daily Iowegian*, Progress Anniversary Edition, January 10, 1934; *History of Appanoose County 1878*, 435 (see chap. 1, n. 2).
9. "R.B. Carson Dies at Moulton, Aged Ninety Three Yrs," *Centerville Daily Iowegian*, September 11, 1935; *History of Appanoose County 1878*, 426 (see chap. 1, n. 2); "Joseph W. Curl, Local Resident, Becomes One of the City's Oldest Residents," *Centerville Daily Iowegian*, December 8, 1932.
10. Ward, Burns and Burns, *The Civil War: An Illustrated History*, 96 (see chap. 4, n. 22).
11. Ingersoll, *Iowa and the Rebellion*, 41–43 (see chap. 4, n. 8).
12. Ward, Burns and Burns, *The Civil War: An Illustrated History*, 98 (see chap. 4, n. 22).
13. Ingersoll, *Iowa and the Rebellion*, 41–43 (see chap. 4, n. 8).
14. Ibid., 44–45; Johnson Brigham, *Iowa: Its History and Its Foremost Citizens*, vol. 1 (Chicago, Ill.: S.J. Clarke Publishing Company, 1918), 321.
15. H.B. Williams, "Early Centerville, Its Business Men, and Incidents That One in Business Here Many Years Recalls," *Centerville Daily Iowegian*, January 10, 1934.
16. History of Appanoose County 1878, 408–10 (see chap. 1, n. 2); Ingersoll, *Iowa and the Rebellion* (see chap. 4, n. 8).
17. Ingersoll, *Iowa and the Rebellion*, 115–16 (see chap. 4, n. 8); Wright, *A History of the Sixth Iowa Infantry*, 96 (see chap. 4, n. 17).
18. Wright, A History of the Sixth Iowa Infantry, 97 (see chap. 4, n. 17).
19. Ibid., 98.
20. McPherson, *Battle Cry of Freedom*, 410 (see chap. 4, n. 16); Ward, Burns and Burns, *The Civil War: An Illustrated History*, 116 (see chap. 4, n. 22); "Civil War Veterans List," n.d., Prairie Trails Museum of Wayne County, Corydon, Iowa; Lorena Blount, interview with the author about James C. Duncan, Allerton, Wayne County, Iowa, February 16, 2006.

21. *History of Appanoose County 1878*, 410–15 (see chap. 1, n. 2); Ingersoll, *Iowa and the Rebellion*, 661 (see chap. 4, n. 8); Chas B. DePuy and Mrs. Harold Sayers, "Civil War Centennial Recalls Graybeards from Appanoose," *Centerville Daily Iowegian*, May 19, 1961.
22. "Benjamin F. Pearson's War Diary," *Annals of Iowa*, vol. 15, no. 2 (October 1925): 85–89; Orr Kelly and Mary Davies Kelly, *Dream's End: Two Iowa Brothers in the Civil War* (New York: Kodansha America, Inc., 1998); Taylor, *Past and Present of Appanoose County, Iowa*, 316 (see chap. 1, n. 1); Sharp and Bird's Studio, advertisement, *Weekly Citizen*, November 19, 1870; Strickler's Sunbeam Gallery, advertisement, *The Loyal Citizen*, July 27, 1864.
23. Advertisement for Drake's store, *Bloomfield Union Guard*, December 19, 1863.
24. History of Appanoose County 1878, 410–15 (see chap. 1, n. 2).

Chapter 6

1. Brigham, *Iowa: Its History and Its Foremost Citizens*, vol. 1, 175 (see chap. 5, n. 14).
2. Taylor, *Past and Present of Appanoose County, Iowa*, 274 (see chap. 1, n. 1).
3. "Second Court House Built in 1861," photograph and caption, *Early Pioneer Stories*, 119 (see chap. 1, n. 10); "Early Courthouse History Related," *Centerville Daily Iowegian*, April 14, 1948; *History of Appanoose County 1878*, 385–86 (see chap. 1, n. 2).
4. "Pioneer Ways Were Quaint But Friendly," *Centerville Daily Iowegian*, Centennial Edition, November 29, 1946.
5. Great Western Stage Company, advertisement, *Appanoose Chieftain*, July 11, 1861.
6. J.W. Williams Tin Shop, advertisement, *Appanoose Chieftain*, July 11, 1861.
7. Merritt, Early Days in Appanoose County, *Centerville Daily Iowegian*, December 18, 1941; "Newspaper Recalls Centerville of 1866," *Centerville Daily Iowegian*, October 16, 1949.
8. "Pioneer Ways Were Quaint But Friendly," *Centerville Daily Iowegian*, Centennial Edition, November 29, 1946.
9. "J.B. Maring Here 50 Years, in Business 34 Years," *Semi-Weekly Iowegian*, February 6, 1914.
10. "City Government Dropped during the Civil War," *Centerville Daily Iowegian*, Centennial Edition, November 29, 1946.
11. "85th Anniversary Marked by First National Today," *Centerville Daily Iowegian*, September 23, 1948; "National Bank Is 100 Years Old," *Centerville Daily Iowegian*, August 26, 1955.
12. Recollections and Reminescences [*sic*], of Kos Harris, Wichita, Kansas, On Early Centerville School Days, *Centerville Daily Iowegian*, November 15, 1925;

Advertisements for Harmonial Store, Wooden Hoosier Store, R.N. Glenn, Bradley Mammoth Store, G. Heygis, Callen and Pierson, S.D. Zern and Howell's, *Appanoose Chieftain*, July 11, 1861.

13. Mrs. George W. (Ella Williams) Randle, "Walks around the Square as It Was in Her Girlhood," *Centerville Daily Iowegian*, Progress Anniversary Edition, January 10, 1934.
14. H.B. Williams, "Centerville as Remembered by One Who Was Born Here in 1856 and Knew People Well," *Semi-Weekly Iowegian*, August 27, 1909.
15. "Old Creamery, a Landmark Here Is Being Torn Down," *Centerville Daily Iowegian*, March 16, 1929.
16. "First Editor Had His Principles As Began Publication," *Centerville Daily Iowegian*, Progress Anniversary Edition, January 10, 1934.
17. "Old Settler Gone," *Centerville Journal*, June 8, 1899.
18."Elder Wooden Stopped Here before the War," *Centerville Daily Iowegian*, Progress Anniversary Edition, January 10, 1934; Gue, *History of Iowa: From the Earliest Times to the Beginning of the Twentieth Century*, vol. 2, 382 (see chap. 1, n. 18).
19. Merritt, Early Days in Appanoose County, *Centerville Daily Iowegian*, November 25, 1941.
20. "Longest Time: Wide Mourning in Passing of Ash Henderson," *Centerville Daily Iowegian*, February 5, 1934.
21. "Walter S. Johnson," *Biographical and Historical Record of Wayne and Appanoose Counties, Iowa*, 578 (see chap. 3, n. 20); Rosalie Mahoney's interview of Mildred Probasco, private letter to the author, Unionville, Missouri, October 10, 2005; Biographical appendix, *History of Adair, Sullivan, Putnam and Schuyler Counties, State of Missouri* (Chicago: The Goodspeed Publishing Company, 1886), 1102.
22. "Walter S. Johnson," Biographical and Historical Record of Wayne and Appanoose Counties, Iowa, 578 (see chap. 3, n. 20).
23. Donald C. Elder III, ed., *Love Amid the Turmoil: The Civil War Letters of William and Mary Vermilion* (Iowa City: University of Iowa Press, 2003), 31; Ingersoll, *Iowa and the Rebellion*, 651–53 (see chap. 4, n. 8); "Keokuk Still Has Hospital Building of Civil War Times," *Centerville Daily Journal*, December 13, 1922.
24. Elder, *Love Amid the Turmoil*, 90, 193, 256, 276, 297–98, 301–6, 311–12, 320, 328, 330.
25. "Had Coldest Days Back in 1863–64," *Centerville Daily Iowegian*, Progress Anniversary Edition, January 10, 1934.
26. "Triumps [*sic*] and Achievements of By-Gone Days in Walnut Township and Appanoose County," *Mystic Telegram*, September 4, 1924.
27. Elder, *Love Amid the Turmoil*, 100.
28. *History of Appanoose County* 1878, 374 (see chap. 1, n. 2).
29. Elder, *Love Amid the Turmoil*, 99.
30. Mott R. Sawyers, "The Bravest Soldier I Ever Knew," *Centerville Daily Iowegian*, June 2, 1934.

31. Gladys M. DePuy, "Hattie Nighswonger, 97 Recalls Civil War Days," *Centerville Daily Iowegian*, February 21, 1957.
32. "Some Interesting Davis County History and Events in War Days," *Centerville Daily Iowegian*, January 31, 1925.
33. *History of Davis County, Iowa* (Des Moines, Iowa: Des Moines State Historical Company, 1882), 555, 556.
34. "Recollections and Reminescences [*sic*] of Kos Harris, Wichita, Kansas, on Early Centerville School Days," *Centerville Daily Iowegian*, November 15, 1925.

Chapter 7

1. "Present Location of Iowa Regiments," *Dubuque Herald*, September 26, 1863.
2. Wright, *A History of the Sixth Iowa Infantry*, 193 (see chap. 4, n. 17).
3. Ward, Burns and Burns, *The Civil War: An Illustrated History*, 212 (see chap. 4, n. 22).
4. Ingersoll, *Iowa and the Rebellion*, 653–54 (see chap. 4, n. 8).
5. Ward, Burns and Burns, *The Civil War: An Illustrated History*, 212, 238–41 (see chap. 4, n. 22).
6. "Benjamin F. Pearson's War Diary," *Annals of Iowa*, vol. 15, no. 3 (January 1926): 194, 197.
7. Annie Wittenmyer, *Under the Guns: A Woman's Reminiscences of the Civil War* (Boston, Mass.: E.B. Stillings and Company, 1895), 5, 13, 33, 49.
8. Wittenmyer, *Under the Guns*, 72.
9. Captain Tom Sillanpa, ed., *Annie Wittenmyer, God's Angel* (Hamilton, Ill.: Hamilton Press, Inc., 1972), 21.
10. Wittenmyer, *Under the Guns*, 106–9; Sillanpa, Annie Wittenmyer, *God's Angel*, 16.
11. Ward, Burns and Burns, *The Civil War: An Illustrated History*, 239 (see chap. 4, n. 22); "Has Old Vicksburg War Time Paper," *Centerville Daily Iowegian*, June 4, 1941.
12. Lathrop, *Life and Times of Samuel J. Kirkwood, Iowa's War Governor*, 328–29 (see chap. 2, n. 4).
13. Wittenmyer, *Under the Guns*, 150–51.
14. *History of Appanoose County 1878*, 436 (see chap. 1, n. 2).
15. Elder, *Love Amid the Turmoil*, 162 (see chap. 6, n. 23).
16. Ibid., 168.
17. Ibid., 216–24.
18. "Third Iowa Cavalry," *Citizen*, October 18, 1899.
19. Lathrop, *Life and Times of Samuel J. Kirkwood, Iowa's War Governor* (see chap. 2, n. 4).
20. Ibid., 241, 246–47; Sage, *A History of Iowa* (see chap. 1, n. 5).
21. Frank C. Arena, *Study of Southern Sympathizers in Iowa during the Civil War Period* (Des Moines, Iowa: Drake University, 1951).

22. Ingersoll, *Iowa and the Rebellion*, 691–93 (see chap. 4, n. 8).
23. W.C. Ransom, late major, Sixth Kansas Volunteer Cavalry, "Appanoose County Volunteers Who Served in the 6th Kansas Cavalry," written address to the annual reunion of Company B, Sixth Kansas Volunteer Cavalry, unpublished, n.d., Drake Free Public Library, Centerville, Iowa.
24. "First Editor Had His Principles as Began Publication," *Centerville Daily Iowegian*, Progress Anniversary Edition, January 10, 1934.
25. "Old Issues of Newspapers Had Much Old Lore," *Centerville Daily Iowegian*, October 30, 1933; Wright, *A History of the Sixth Iowa Infantry*, 217–18, 271 (see chap. 4, n. 17).
26. Ingersoll, *Iowa and the Rebellion*, 408–9, 656–58 (see chap. 4, n. 8).
27. Ibid., 697–98; R.W. Porter, "Andersonville Prison Survivor Tells of Those Harrowing Days Spent in a Confederate Stockade," *Centerville Daily Iowegian* (reprinted from *Geneseo [Kansas] Journal*), June 17, 1935; McPherson, *Battle Cry of Freedom*, 796 (see chap. 4, n. 16).
28. Elder, *Love Amid the Turmoil*, 292–93 (see chap. 6, n. 23); Ward, Burns and Burns, *The Civil War: An Illustrated History*, 243–45 (see chap. 4, n. 22).
29. "Capt. John L. Bashore," *Centerville Daily Iowegian*, Progress Anniversary Edition, January 10, 1934.
30. Ibid.; McPherson, *Battle Cry of Freedom*, 796 (see chap. 4, n. 16).
31. Russell Corder, "The Confederate Invasion of Iowa," unpublished paper presented to the Davis County Historical Society, Bloomfield, Iowa, 1997; Walter Davis, "Bloomfield Man Tells of the Guerilla Raid into Iowa with Trail of Murder and Terrors," *Centerville Daily Iowegian* (reprinted from *Des Moines Sunday Register*), April 1, 1928; *History of Davis County, Iowa.*
32. Elder, *Love Amid the Turmoil*, 297 (see chap. 6, n. 23).

Chapter 8

1. Elder, *Love Amid the Turmoil*, 275–330, 269–70 (see chap. 6, n. 23).
2. Wright, *A History of the Sixth Iowa Infantry*, 335–36 (see chap. 4, n. 17); "Ash Henderson, One of Centerville's Two Living Civil War Veterans Tells Thrilling Days Following Famous '61," *Centerville Daily Iowegian*, September 27, 1933.
3. Wright, *A History of the Sixth Iowa Infantry*, 356, 385–87, 395, 423, 462, 468 (see chap. 4, n. 17).
4. Ibid., 380.
5. Ibid., 387, 462–63.
6. Ward, Burns and Burns, *The Civil War: An Illustrated History*, 340–44 (see chap. 4, n. 22); Wright, *A History of the Sixth Iowa Infantry*, 414–45 (see chap. 4, n. 17).

7. "Letter Found That Tells Last Local Death of '61–'65." *Centerville Daily Iowegian*, May 11, 1929; Ward, Burns and Burns, *The Civil War: An Illustrated History*, 340–44 (see chap. 4, n. 22).
8. Samuel E. Morison, *The Oxford History of the American People: Volume Two, 1789 through Reconstruction*, Mentor edition (New York: Oxford University Press, 1972), 491; Wright, *A History of the Sixth Iowa Infantry*, 447 (see chap. 4, n. 17); Elder, *Love Amid the Turmoil*, 315 (see chap. 6, n. 23).
9. Morison, *The Oxford History of the American People*, vol. 2, 495–96.
10. Wright, *A History of the Sixth Iowa Infantry*, 449–51 (see chap. 4, n. 17); "Local Veteran Recalls Night of April '65," *Centerville Daily Iowegian*, April 14, 1927.
11. Elder, *Love Amid the Turmoil*, 316 (see chap. 6, n. 23).
12. "Benjamin F. Pearson's War Diary," *Annals of Iowa*, vol. 15, no. 7 (January 1927): 529–30.
13. *The (Keokuk, Iowa) Daily Gate City*, April 17, 1865.
14. "…town in mourning," (part of newspaper torn off, headline missing) in "Old Centerville Newspapers," *Centerville Daily Iowegian*, February 2, 1951; "Stamps Family Has Paper with Story of Lincoln Death," *Centerville Daily Iowegian*, April 15, 1937; *The (Keokuk, Iowa) Daily Gate City*, April 17, 1865.
15. *Weekly Citizen*, November 5, 1870; "County Not for Lincoln," *Centerville Daily Iowegian*, May 31, 1950; Elder, *Love Amid the Turmoil*, 295 (see chap. 6, n. 23); Wright, *A History of the Sixth Iowa Infantry*, 352 (see chap. 4, n. 17).

Chapter 9

1. Ward, Burns and Burns, *The Civil War: An Illustrated History*, 386–91 (see chap. 4, n. 22); Wright, *A History of the Sixth Iowa Infantry*, 461–67 (see chap. 4, n. 17).
2. "Benjamin F. Pearson's War Diary," *Annals of Iowa*, vol. 15, no. 7 (January 1927): 533–35.
3. Wright, *A History of the Sixth Iowa Infantry*, 468–70 (see chap. 4, n. 17).
4. Ibid., 471–75; Ward, Burns and Burns, *The Civil War: An Illustrated History*, 393–97 (see chap. 4, n. 22).
5. Wright, *A History of the Sixth Iowa Infantry*, 474 (see chap. 4, n. 17).
6. Ibid., 480–94.
7. Elder, *Love Amid the Turmoil*, 330–31 (see chap. 6, n. 23).
8. "Old Prison Diary Kept by Cap. Gedney," *Centerville Daily Iowegian*, special edition supplement, January 27, 1934.
9. *History of Appanoose County 1878*, 427 (see chap. 1, n. 2).
10. Ibid., 406–27; "154 Civil War Pensioners in Appanoose County in 1883," *Centerville Daily Iowegian*, February 19, 1940.

11. "M'Keehans Had Their Trials in a New Country," *Centerville Daily Iowegian*, Progress Anniversary Edition, January 10, 1934.
12. R.W. Porter, "Andersonville Prison Survivor Tells of Those Harrowing Days Spent in a Confederate Stockade," *Centerville Daily Iowegian*, June 17, 1935; "Ash Henderson, One of Centerville's Two Living Civil War Veterans Tells Thrilling Days Following Famous '61," *Centerville Daily Iowegian*, September 27, 1933.
13. R.W. Porter, "Anderson Prison Survivor Tells of Those Harrowing Days Spent in a Confederate Stockade," *Centerville Daily Iowegian*, June 17, 1935; R.W. Porter, "Anderson Prison Survivor Tells of Confederates' Efforts to Sway Union Men to Cause of the South," *Centerville Daily Iowegian*, June 22, 1935; R.W. Porter, "Anderson Prison Survivor Tells of Convalescence, Trip from East through Centerville to Home in Mo.," *Centerville Daily Iowegian*, July 1, 1935.
14. Kelly and Kelly, *Dream's End: Two Iowa Brothers in the Civil War*, 245 (see chap. 5, n. 22); "E.B. Brayman…," untitled announcement of death, *Weekly Citizen*, November 11, 1871.
15. Letter from L.G. Parker, *Weekly Citizen*, July 22, 1871.
16. *History of Appanoose County 1878*, 407–15, 417, 418 (see chap. 1, n. 2); "Gets Letter from Civil War Comrade," *Centerville Daily Iowegian*, March 27, 1923.
17. "50 Years of Life in Centerville," *Semi-Weekly Iowegian*, December 21, 1906; Letter from Mary "Dollie" Vermilion to her husband: Captain William Vermilion, November 12, 1862," in chapter 1, "Still I Am Pround of My Gallant Soldier Husband" in Elder, *Love Amid the Turmoil*, 15 (see chap. 6, n. 23); Letter from Caroline Masters to her mother, Margaret C. Jacobs, March 31, 1863, in "Jacobs/Cridlebaugh Family Memoir," unpublished manuscript, 51, Drake Free Public Library, Centerville, Iowa.
18. Biographical and Historical Record of Wayne and Appanoose Counties, Iowa, 694 (see chap. 3, n. 20); Dykstra, *Bright Radical Star*, 227–28, 229, 235 (see chap. 3, n. 2); www.iowawomenattorneys.org.
19. "Walter S. Johnson," *Biographical and Historical Record of Wayne and Appanoose Counties, Iowa*, 579, 610 (see chap. 3, n. 20); "Capt. Joseph B. Gedney," *Centerville Daily Iowegian*, Progress Anniversary Edition, January 10, 1934; Taylor, *Past and Present of Appanoose County, Iowa*, 106 (see chap. 1, n. 1); J.M. Beck, "Many Interesting People Have Lived in the Community through the Years," *Centerville Daily Iowegian*, Fiftieth Year Edition, June 26, 1953; "Major C.A. Stanton," *Centerville Daily Iowegian*, Progress Anniversary Edition, January 10, 1934; "Death of Dr. Nathan Udell, of Denver & Former Centerville Citizen," *Semi-Weekly Iowegian*, March 13, 1903; "A Sad Death: Capt. W.F. Vermilion Passes Away," *Centerville Citizen*, January 2, 1895; "Death of Judge T.M. Fee Affects Community at Large," *Semi-Weekly Iowegian*, April 15, 1910; "Capt. G.W. Wyckoff Dies on Home Farm Aged 87," *Centerville Daily Iowegian*, August 28, 1925; "Capt. M.M. Walden," *Centerville Daily Iowegian*, Progress Anniversary Edition, January 10, 1934; "Gen. J.A. Baker at the End of an Eventful Career," *Semi-Weekly*

Iowegian, April 25, 1911; "General F.M. Drake," *Centerville Daily Iowegian*, Progress Anniversary Edition, January 10, 1934; "Death of Judge Tannehill," *Centerville Journal*, February 28, 1901; "Gen. H.H. Wright Died Last Night Ex-Adj-General and Old Soldier," *Semi-Weekly Iowegian*, April 28, 1901; "Judge Caldwell Pays Tribute to Col. C.A. Stanton, Ideal Citizen," *Centerville Citizen*, January 2, 1913; Wright, *A History of the Sixth Iowa Infantry*, vols. 5–10 (see chap. 4, n. 17); "Ash Henderson," *Centerville Daily Iowegian*, Progress Anniversary Edition, January 10, 1934.

20. "Mrs. Mary Holman Pioneer of City Taken by Death," *Centerville Daily Iowegian*, July 26, 1929; "D.A. Sawyers is Unionville, Iowa, Pioneer Resident," *Centerville Daily Iowegian*, August 8, 1925; "John Daniels," *Centerville Daily Iowegian*, Progress Anniversary Edition, January 10, 1934; "W.H.H. Duckworth Taken by Death," *Centerville Daily Iowegian*, July 5, 1924.
21. Eli Buck, "Comments on the Custer Massacre," letter to the editor, *Centerville Daily Iowegian*, June 24, 1926; "Curry Reed Is Called Was War Veteran," *Centerville Daily Iowegian*, June 18, 1938; "Veteran Past 95 Is Visitor Here," *Centerville Daily Iowegian*, March 16, 1937; "A Banquet and Toast Program," *Semi-Weekly Iowegian*, October 14, 1910; "Entertainment for Civil War Vets Is Planned," *Centerville Daily Iowegian*, July 27, 1926; *History of Appanoose County 1878*, 428–31 (see chap. 1, n. 2); "Enough Money for Gettysburg," *Semi-Weekly Iowegian*, June 1913; "Member Grant's Company Visits His Old Home," *Semi-Weekly Iowegian*, July 21, 1914; "Honoring General U.S. Grant Today," *Centerville Journal*, April 27, 1922; "Anniversary of Lee's Surrender Is Celebrated," *Daily Iowegian*, April 9, 1921; *History of Appanoose County 1878*, 428 (see chap. 1, n. 2).
22. Undated photograph from family collection of Nelma Fuller, in "Civil War Veterans of Mystic," collection of eighteen Civil War soldiers' photographs and short biographies, privately held by Eric Davis; *Early Pioneer Stories* 44–54 (see chap. 1, n. 10); "Ed Streepy 97 Years Old Today," *Centerville Daily Iowegian*, October 30, 1941; "William Hondesheldt Dies," *Centerville Daily Iowegian*, January 31, 1936; "Curry Reed Is Called Was War Veteran," *Centerville Daily Iowegian*, June 18, 1938; "Decoration Day at Centerville," *Weekly Citizen*, June 3, 1871.
23. "Memorial Day," *Centerville Citizen*, June 1, 1872; Himie Voxman, interview with the author, recalling Memorial Day marches, October 4, 2002.

Chapter 10

1. U.S. Census records, 1870; U.S. Census records, 1880; "74 Year Old Letter Tells of Early Day Centerville," *Centerville Daily Iowegian*, November 29, 1956; "Map of the Business Portion of Centerville, Iowa, Population 3,500," United States Commercial Map Company, 1883.

2. "Major C.A. Stanton," *Centerville Daily Iowegian*, Progress Anniversary Edition, January 10, 1934; "Stanton's Store," *Semi-Weekly Iowegian*, holiday supplement, December 19, 1899; "…By reference to the advertisement…," untitled, *Weekly Citizen*, January 6, 1872; S. Thompson Lewis, ed., *Biographical and Genealogical History of Appanoose and Monroe Counties, Iowa* (New York: The Lewis Publishing Company, 1903), 15; "C.W. Lane Co.," *Semi-Weekly Iowegian*, holiday supplement, December 19, 1899.
3. "New Year Presents," advertisement for Morret's Blue Front, *Centerville Citizen*, December 28, 1872; "Map of the Business Portion of Centerville, Iowa," United States Commercial Map Company 1883; "Photographs—Thomas Rattan," *Weekly Citizen*, March 25, 1871; "Mr. H.A. Snedeker," *Centerville Citizen*, May 9, 1873; "Not So Easy for 2nd Generation to Get a Start," *Centerville Daily Iowegian*, Progress Anniversary Edition, January 10, 1934.
4. "New Grocery!" advertisement for J.M. Roberts Groceries, *Centerville Citizen*, April 19, 1873; "Gus Shinogle Early Business Man Here Dead," *Centerville Daily Iowegian*, July 20, 1928; "Thos. E. Sargent Dead," *Centerville Journal*, July 27, 1916; "New Grocery," advertisement for Philadelphia Grocery Store, *Centerville Citizen*, October 5, 1872; "Sturgeon and Crossan," *Weekly Citizen*, September 2, 1871; "Letha Morris Has Clipping Concerning Centerville in 1866," listing of thirty-two stores, their locations and goods sold, *Centerville Daily Iowegian*, February 28, 1961; "Map of the Business Portion of Centerville, Iowa," United States Commercial Map Company, 1883; Merritt, Early Days in Appanoose County, *Centerville Daily Iowegian*, November 22, 1941; "Fresh Fish!" advertisement, *Weekly Citizen*, December 3, 1870, and *Weekly Citizen*, June 3, 1871; "This Where the Jensen Store Now Stands," photograph in *Centerville Daily Iowegian*, Fiftieth Year Edition, June 26, 1953; "Handkerchief with Napoleon at Moscow," *Semi-Weekly Iowegian*, July 2, 1917; "The ice harvest…," untitled, *Weekly Citizen*, January 7, 1871.
5. "Centerville's First Restaurant and Bakery," photograph in *Semi-Weekly Iowegian*, Centennial Edition, November 29, 1946; "Newton C. Michael," *Biographical and Historical Record of Wayne and Appanoose Counties, Iowa,* 371 (see chap. 3, n. 20); "Alhambra Bakery and Cracker Factory," advertisement, *Weekly Citizen*, November 5, 1870; "J.A. Pennington had fitted up…," untitled, *Centerville Citizen*, May 25, 1872; Mrs. George (Ella Williams) Randle, "Walks around the Square as It Was in Her Girlhood," *Semi-Weekly Iowegian*, Progress Anniversary Edition, January 10, 1934.
6. "Geo. L. Barnthouse Answers Summons," *Centerville Daily Iowegian*, March 29, 1923.
7. "To Centerville," *Centerville Citizen*, January 25, 1873; "Next Monday J.K. Boyles…," untitled, *Weekly Citizen*, December 16, 1871; "Last Monday Mr. J.K. Boyles…," untitled, *Weekly Citizen*, December 23, 1871.
8. "History Business—Professional Firms Now in Business: Hotels: Continental Hotel," *Centerville Daily Iowegian*, Progress Anniversary Edition, January 10, 1934;

"Jefferson House…," untitled, *Weekly Citizen*, January 28, 1871; "Continental Hotel Has Long History," *Centerville Daily Iowegian*, August 23, 1936; "Mr. McKee…," untitled, *Weekly Citizen*, November 26, 1870.

9. "Joseph Gray Has the Contract …," untitled, *Centerville Citizen*, February 8, 1873; "Uncovering Old Well Revives Memories Here," *Centerville Daily Iowegian*, June 17, 1946; "Lamplighting Days Meant Early Rising," *Centerville Daily Iowegian*, Progress Anniversary Edition, January 10, 1934.
10. "The town council have acted wisely…," untitled, *Weekly Citizen*, December 17, 1870; "Came in High Hope—Couldn't Find Old Scenes or People," *Centerville Daily Iowegian*, August 30, 1948; Mrs. George (Ella Williams) Randle, "Walks around the Square as It Was in Her Girlhood," *Centerville Daily Iowegian*, Progress Anniversary Edition, January 10, 1934.
11. Taylor, *Past and Present of Appanoose County, Iowa*, 329, 14 (see chap. 1, n. 1); Molly Myers Naumann, *An Architectural and Historical Survey of the Centerville Public Square*, prepared for the Centerville Historic Preservation Commission, Certified Local Government Grant 19-94-90055.008.16; "First National Bank Marks Its 90th Anniversary Friday," *Centerville Daily Iowegian*, March 26, 1954.
12. Merritt, Early Days in Appanoose County, *Centerville Daily Iowegian*, November 22, 1941; "Elder Wooden Stopped Here before the War," *Centerville Daily Iowegian*, Progress Anniversary Edition, January 10, 1934.
13. "Away from Centerville 49 Years He Tells of the Change He Noted Last Time Came Back to a New Modern City," *Centerville Daily Iowegian*, Progress Anniversary Edition, January 10, 1934.
14. "Centerville National Bank," photograph in *Centerville Daily Iowegian*, December 24, 1891; "Banks: Centerville National Bank," *Centerville Daily Iowegian*, Progress Anniversary Edition, January 10, 1934; Lewis, *Biographical and Genealogical History of Appanoose and Monroe Counties, Iowa*, 15; "Centerville National Bank Started by Drakes in 1876," *Centerville Daily Iowegian*, August 23, 1938.
15. "Shows Growth and Progress for Community," *Centerville Daily Iowegian*, October 17, 1949; "Second School House," *Centerville Citizen*, August 4, 1902; "Chicago, December 11—Reverend S.A. Holt…," untitled, *Weekly Citizen*, December 17, 1870, reprinted from *Chicago Republican*, December 11, 1870.
16. *Biographical and Historical Record of Wayne and Appanoose Counties*, Iowa, 646 (see chap. 3, n. 20); C.S. Williams, "School Days of Centerville of Long Ago," *Centerville Daily Iowegian*, Progress Anniversary Edition, January 10, 1934; "J.S. Hamilton & Bro.," advertisement, *Centerville Citizen*, August 3, 1872.
17. "J.R. Wooden & Son…," untitled, *Centerville Citizen*, April 19, 1873; "John Deere's New Cultivator, The Advance," advertisement, *Weekly Citizen*, June 8, 1872.

18. "Agricultural Warehouse—Baker & Farley," advertisement, *Weekly Citizen*, April 27, 1872; "They Burned the Spring Wagon as Too Much Finery," *Centerville Daily Iowegian*, Progress Anniversary Edition, January 10, 1934.
19. W.M. Heusinkveld and O.R. Parks, "A Pictorial History of Towns of Appanoose County Past and Present," unpublished, presented to Centerville Historic Preservation Committee, 2003, collection of Appanoose County Museum, Centerville, 28; J.C. Harvey, Walt Stevenson and Sherman Varner, "Old Hibbsville a Pretentious Town Which Competed with Centerville for Trade and Stood over Half a Century," *Centerville Daily Iowegian*, Progress Anniversary Edition, January 10, 1934; People's Column, letter from J.C. Harvey to the editor, *Centerville Daily Iowegian*, February 3, 1948; "Wire Fence Came; Range Disappeared," *Centerville Daily Iowegian*, Progress Anniversary Edition, January 10, 1934; Alistair Cooke, *Alistair Cooke's America* (New York: Alfred A. Knopf, 1974), 237–38.
20. "Appanoose County Livestock," *Centerville Citizen*, December 23, 1885; "Appanoose Agricultural Society," in *History of Appanoose County 1878*, 396–98 (see chap. 1, n. 2); "Captain Joseph B. Gedney," *Biographical and Historical Record of Wayne and Appanoose Counties, Iowa*, 654–55 (see chap. 3, n. 20).
21. "Appanoose Agricultural Society," in *History of Appanoose County 1878*, 396–98 (see chap. 1, n. 2); Sage, *A History of Iowa*, 100–2 (see chap. 1, n. 5); Gue, *History of Iowa from the Earliest Times to the Beginning of the Twentieth Century*, vol. 3, 26–27 (see chap. 1, n. 18).
22. "Patrons of Husbandry," in *History of Appanoose County 1878*, 398–99 (see chap. 1, n. 2); Gue, *History of Iowa from the Earliest Times to the Beginning of the Twentieth Century*, vol. 3, 55–56 (see chap. 1, n. 18).
23. Taylor, *Past and Present of Appanoose County, Iowa*, 147, 150 (see chap. 1, n. 1).
24. "Ash Henderson," *Centerville Daily Iowegian*, Progress Anniversary Edition, January 10, 1934; "The Union Coal Company…," untitled, *Centerville Citizen*, November 23, 1872.
25. Mrs. George (Ella Williams) Randle, "Walks around the Square as It Was in Her Girlhood," *Centerville Daily Iowegian*, Progress Anniversary Edition, January 10, 1934.

Chapter 11

1. "Centerville as Remembered by One Who Was Born Here in 1856 and Knew People Well," *Semi-Weekly Iowegian*, August 9, 1909; "We expect to record the death…," untitled, *Weekly Citizen*, February 17, 1872, and November 5, 1870.
2. H.B. Williams, "Early Centerville, Its Business Men, and Incidents That One in Business Here Many Years Recalls," *Centerville Daily Iowegian*, Progress Anniversary Edition, January 10, 1934; "Old Centerville Newspapers," *The Loyal Citizen*, August 23, 1865, from the collection of Mrs. George W. Randle; Editorial, *Centerville Daily*

Iowegian, December 11, 1951, from the collection of Mrs. George W. Randle; "Soldiers' Bounty Land Bill," *Centerville Citizen*, January 4, 1873; "A Sad Death, Capt. W.F. Vermilion Passes Away," *Centerville Citizen*, January 2, 1895; "Wright, General Henry Harrison," *Biographical and Historical Record of Wayne and Appanoose Counties, Iowa*, 606 (see chap. 3, n. 20); Wright, *A History of the Sixth Iowa Infantry* (see chap. 4, n. 17); "Johnson, Walter S.," *Biographical and Historical Record of Wayne and Appanoose Counties, Iowa*, 579 (see chap. 3, n. 20); J.M. Beck, "Many Interesting People Have Lived in the Community through the Years," *Centerville Daily Iowegian*, Pictorial Edition, March 2, 1951.

3. Bill Heusinkveld, "Appanoose County 1904–2004: A Proud Heritage, a Promising Future," unpublished, presented to the Appanoose Historical Society, August 2004, collection of Appanoose County Museum, Centerville, 5; "Wells, Benjamin," *Biographical and Historical Record of Wayne and Appanoose Counties, Iowa*, 619 (see chap. 3, n. 20); "Saw Trains of Covered Wagons," *Centerville Daily Iowegian*, Progress Anniversary Edition, January 10, 1934; "When Ghost Walked in Court Park," *Centerville Daily Iowegian*, April 28, 1943.
4. "The Fourth of July at Centerville," *Centerville Citizen*, July 9, 1884; H.B. Williams, "Centerville as Remembered by One Who Was Born Here in 1856 and Knew People Well," *Semi-Weekly Iowegian*, August 27, 1909; "Decoration Day at Centerville," *Centerville Citizen*, June 1, 1887; "Wild Pigeons and Other Birds in Disappearing Class," *Centerville Daily Iowegian*, Progress Anniversary Edition, January 10, 1934; "Died: Stratton," *Centerville Citizen*, August 13, 1884; "Living in Iowa," Iowa Public Television, January 21, 2005; "A Few Briefs from History," *Centerville Daily Iowegian*, January 5, 1960.
5. "Strange Phenomenon," *Weekly Citizen*, August 5, 1871; "Total Eclipse of Sun Scared Them," *Centerville Daily Iowegian*, Progress Anniversary Edition, January 10, 1934; "Besse Family One of Those Coming in an Early Day," *Centerville Daily Iowegian*, August 10, 1934; "Unionville: Mrs. A.S. Dukes Correspondent," *Centerville Daily Iowegian*, August 10, 1934; "Man of Ninety Recalls Civil War and Eclipse," *Centerville Daily Iowegian*, September 25, 1947.
6. "Old Poster Tells of Rope Walking," *Centerville Daily Iowegian*, August 11, 1928; "Cole's Colossal Circus and Animal Exhibition," advertisement, *Centerville Citizen*, July 15, 1871; "Older's Museum, Circus and Menagerie," advertisement, *Weekly Citizen*, August 5, 1871; "Major Geo. Ogle Recalls Old Show Grounds & Walks," *Centerville Daily Iowegian*, December 31, 1946; Gue, *History of Iowa from the Earliest Times to the Beginning of the Twentieth Century*, vol. 3, 39 (see chap. 1, n. 18); Roger North, Fort Dodge historian, interview with the author, May 20, 2006.
7. H.B. Williams, "Centerville as Remembered by One Who Was Born Here in 1856 and Knew People Well," *Semi-Weekly Iowegian*, August 27, 1909; "Old Handbills Reveal Centerville Schools Gave Good Programs Over 57 Years Ago at the Courthouse,"

Centerville Daily Iowegian, August 29, 1930; "There Will Be a Christmas Tree," *Centerville Citizen*, December 23, 1871; "The Concerts on Friday and Saturday…," untitled, *Centerville Citizen*, January 11, 1873.

8. "Literary Society, the Centerville Philomathian Society…," untitled, *Weekly Citizen*, November 26, 1870; on Prohibition, "Literary Society," *Weekly Citizen*, November 26, 1870; on phrenology, "The Lyceum," *Loyal Citizen*, April 3, 1867; "Phrenological Lectures," *Centerville Citizen*, May 16, 1873; on female suffrage, "Literary Society," *Weekly Citizen*, December 3, 1870; on capital punishment, "Literary Society" *Weekly Citizen*, December 24, 1870, and January 7, 1871; Gov. Kirkwood, "Grand Rally," *Loyal Citizen*, September 26, 1866.
9. "The Lyceum," *Loyal Citizen*, September 26, 1866.
10. *History of Appanoose County 1878*, 375–81 (see chap. 1, n. 2); Taylor, *Past and Present of Appanoose County, Iowa*, 243–50 (see chap. 1, n. 1); "Wholesale Robbery," *Weekly Citizen*, May 20, 1871; "Another Year," *Centerville Citizen*, January 11, 1873.
11. *History of Appanoose County 1878*, 433 (see chap. 1, n. 2).
12. "Edward Turner…," untitled, *Weekly Citizen*, July 29, 1871.
13. W.C. Ransom, late major, Sixth Kansas Volunteer Cavalry, "Appanoose County Volunteers Who Served in the 6th Kansas Cavalry," written address to the annual reunion of Company B, Sixth Kansas Volunteer Cavalry, unpublished, n.d., Drake Free Public Library, Centerville, Iowa; T.J. Stiles, *Jesse James: Last Rebel of the Civil War* (New York: Knopf, Borzoi Books, Random House, Inc., 2002), 119–27.
14. "The Far West Not Alone in Early Day Stage Coach Holdups for was One Near Centerville Years Ago," *Centerville Daily Iowegian*, May 7, 1928 (different accounts reverse the names of the stagecoach drivers; I followed this account); "Pioneer Days," *Centerville Citizen*, August 22, 1900; "Story of Stage Coach Robbery from Files of Paper in 1865," *Semi-Weekly Iowegian*, October 4, 1917.
15. "Bold Robbery at Corydon," *Weekly Citizen*, June 10, 1871.
16. "J.W. Swinford Says Saw James Boys in Centerville," *Centerville Daily Iowegian*, February 25, 1939.
17. "James Boys Spent Night at Former Lepper Farm Home," *Centerville Daily Iowegian*, March 2, 1939; "Regarding the 'Old Stone House'…," Around the Town, *Centerville Daily Iowegian*, May 26, 1945; "Bart Lepper Died in Famed 'Stone House,'" *Centerville Daily Iowegian*, May 15, 1945.
18. "More Johns Twp. Old Timers and the James Boys," *Centerville Daily Iowegian Pioneer Editor*, January 10, 1934.
19. "J.W. Swinford Says Saw James Boys in Centerville," *Centerville Daily Iowegian*, February 25, 1939.
20. "The Corydon Bank Robbers," *Weekly Citizen*, June 24, 1871, reprinted from the *(Lineville) Index*; Stiles, *Jesse James: Last Rebel of the Civil War*, 213–14, 217–18.

21. "J.W. Swinford Says Saw James Boys in Centerville," *Centerville Daily Iowegian*, February 25, 1939; Florence Crowder, retired Continental Hotel employee, interview with the author, May 2, 2001.
22. "Promise City," *Centerville Daily Iowegian*, October 14, 1954; "Farm Where Jesse James Stayed May Become Church Retreat," *Centerville Daily Iowegian*, October 21, 1959.
23. "Corydon Resident Saw Jessie [*sic*] James on Day of Robbery There," *Centerville Daily Iowegian*, November 25, 1949.
24. "Bold Robbery at Corydon," *Weekly Citizen*, June 10, 1871.
25. "Farm Where Jesse James Stayed May Become Church Retreat," *Centerville Daily Iowegian*, October 21, 1959.
26. Phyllis Cosby, "Jesse James Saga Surfaces in Moulton," *Daily Iowegian*, February 5, 2004.
27. Cerula M. Michaels, "Daughter Tells of Her Famous Doctor Father," *Centerville Daily Iowegian*, December 31, 1946.

Chapter 12

1. "Chicago & Southwestern Railroad," *Moulton Independent*, March 10, 1870.
2. "Raised $125,000 to Get Railroad within a Mile," *Centerville Daily Iowegian*, Progress Anniversary Edition, January 10, 1934; "Almost Had a Railroad Far Back as 1863," *Centerville Daily Iowegian*, Progress Anniversary Edition, January 10, 1934; *History of Appanoose County 1878*, 393–94 (see chap. 1, n. 2).
3. "About Our City," *Appanoose Iowegian*, December 27, 1894; "Cameron Railroad," *Moulton Independent*, December 3, 1869.
4. H.B. Williams, "News Items Gleaned from Old Files Back in the Seventies Pertaining to Centerville and Williams Family," *Centerville Daily Iowegian*, August 1, 1932; "Chicago & Southwestern Railroad," *Moulton Independent*, October 1, 1869.
5. "We received a call…," untitled, *Moulton Independent*, April 28, 1870; "The Chicago and Southwestern R.R.," *Weekly Citizen*, November 5, 1870; "Rail spikes and joints…," untitled, *Weekly Citizen*, December 3, 1870; "Do You Remember," *Centerville Daily Iowegian*, July 14, 1930.
6. "A breeze…," untitled, *Centerville Daily Iowegian*, January 14, 1871; "E.C. Haynes," advertisement for sale of land, *Weekly Citizen*, December 3, 1870; Mrs. George (Ella Williams) Randle, "Walks around the Square as It Was in Her Childhood," *Centerville Daily Iowegian*, Progress Anniversary Edition, January 10, 1934.
7. "Lively…," untitled, *Weekly Citizen*, December 3, 1870.
8. "Trestle bridge…," untitled, *Weekly Citizen*, January 14, 1871; "Came in 1852 to Unionville Settlement," *Centerville Daily Iowegian*, Progress Anniversary Edition,

January 10, 1934; "By Mr. Dean…," untitled, *Weekly Citizen*, January 7, 1871; "Chicago and Southwestern…," untitled, *Weekly Citizen*, December 17, 1870; "The telegraph wire…," untitled, *Weekly Citizen*, March 25, 1871; "Courthouse Cupola," *Weekly Citizen*, January 14, 1871.

9. "A breeze…," untitled, *Centerville Daily Iowegian*, January 14, 1871.

10. "The Railroad Has Come," *Weekly Citizen*, February 11, 1871; "Chicago and Southwestern R.R.," *Weekly Citizen*, March 4, 1871; "Born with the Citizen Married with the Iowegian, *Centerville Daily Iowegian*, Progress Anniversary Edition, January 10, 1934.

11. "A Card," *Weekly Citizen*, January 14, 1871; M.L. Childs, "Recollections of Old Pioneer," *Centerville Daily Iowegian*, September 15, 1931; "Gen Drake retires…," untitled, *Weekly Citizen*, January 14, 1871; "Former Engineer Here Is Prisoner," *Centerville Daily Iowegian*, April 5, 1943; "Missouri, Iowa and Nebraska Railroad," *Weekly Citizen*, December 3, 1870; "Capt. John Hays, of Corydon …," untitled, *Weekly Citizen*, December 17, 1870.

12. "Railroad Meetings," *Weekly Citizen*, May 27, 1871; "Every businessman is urgently…," untitled, *Weekly Citizen*, February 10, 1872; "The Railroad," *Weekly Citizen*, March 2, 1872.

13. "Henry Clay Dean speaks…," untitled, *Weekly Citizen*, June 17, 1871; "Henry Clay Dean was announced…," untitled, *Weekly Citizen*, January 20, 1872; Mrs. Ruth Harvey Wilson, "Sidelights on Fame and Eccentricity of Henry Clay Dean Whose Home Was on the Border of Appanoose and Mo.," *Centerville Daily Iowegian*, Progress Anniversary Edition, January 10, 1934; "Found House Half Done But Moved In," *Centerville Daily Iowegian*, Progress Anniversary Edition, January 10, 1934; "Walked to Moulton and Stayed There," *Centerville Daily Iowegian*, Progress Anniversary Edition, January 10, 1934.

14. "Dean at Centerville," *Weekly Citizen*, May 20, 1871; "During Gen. Drake's late visit to New York …," untitled, *Weekly Citizen*, February 3, 1873.

15. "Bold Robbery at Corydon," *Weekly Citizen*, June 10, 1871; "Corydon Bank Robbers," *Centerville Daily Iowegian*, October 12, 1925; William Lee Burton, "Adam Ripper, Corydon Resident for 62 Years, Tells of Town's Thrilling History," *Times Republican*, January 14, 1932; John Clayton, "John Stromsten Will Feature Wayne Old Settlers Runion [*sic*]," *Centerville Daily Iowegian*, July 27, 1962; Stiles, *Jesse James: Last Rebel of the Civil War*, 213–14 (see chap. 11, n. 13).

16. "On the M. I. & N. Road to Centerville," *Centerville Citizen*, January 11, 1873, reprinted from the *Lancaster Excelsior*.

17. "Waiting Rooms' Cafeterias…," untitled, *Weekly Citizen*, May 6, 1871; "Clock at Depot…," untitled, *Weekly Citizen*, May 6, 1871; "Dispatches can not be sent…," untitled, *Weekly Citizen*, May 6, 1871; "Completed—Here is the first dispatch…," untitled, *Centerville Citizen*, February 18, 1873.

Chapter 13

1. H.B. Williams, "Looking Back Sixty Years to My Parents Wedding Day," *Centerville Iowegian*, September 28, 1915; "Now that cars are here…," untitled, *Weekly Citizen*, March 11, 1871.
2. History of Appanoose County 1878, 394 (see chap. 1, n. 2).
3. "The Orphan Train Kids," *Midwest Living*, December 1988, 30–34; Madonna M. Harms, email interview with Patsy Bunnell, March 9, 2001; "The Orphan Train Comes to Clarion," *The Palimpsest* (fall 1988): 144–50; Annette Riley Fry, "The Children's Migration," *American Heritage* (December 1974): 5–10, 79–81.
4. "New York Outcasts," *Centerville Journal*, March 5, 1884.
5. "New York Orphan Dies Here a Respected Man," *Centerville Daily Iowegian*, February 1, 1954.
6. Deanna Allen, descendant of orphan adopted in Centerville, interview with the author, April 3, 2003.
7. James W. and Ruth Ann Allen, descendants of orphan adopted in Centerville, interview with the author, April 3, 2003.
8. B.S. Spooner, editor, "A large excursion train from the east…," untitled, *Appanoose Times*, April 28, 1881.
9. "President Grant at Centerville," *Weekly Citizen*, September 30, 1871; "Our citizens will doubtless remember…," untitled, *Centerville Citizen*, July 20, 1872; "Recollects the Visit of Grant to Centerville," *Centerville Daily Iowegian*, Progress Anniversary Edition, January 10, 1934.
10. "The Fourth at Centerville," *Weekly Citizen*, July 8, 1871.
11. "Excursion to Keokuk," *Centerville Citizen*, May 23, 1873; Merritt, Early Days in Appanoose County, *Centerville Daily Iowegian*, December 8, 1941.
12. *History of Appanoose County 1878*, 395 (see chap. 1, n. 2); "Excursion to St. Louis…," untitled, advertisement, *Weekly Citizen*, June 3, 1871.
13. "Col. Haynes Finds Old Menu and Just to Think He Lived thru Good Old Days!" *Centerville Daily Iowegian*, January 7, 1947.
14. "Lives Over Again Those Fierce, Hectic Days When Life on the Levee Was Just One Thing after Another and Not So Very Far after It Either," *Centerville Daily Iowegian*, Progress Anniversary Edition, January 10, 1934; "David Dinning Recalls Events 47 Years Ago," *Centerville Daily Iowegian*, April 12, 1928.
15. "Much dissatisfaction…," untitled, *Weekly Citizen*, December 24, 1870.
16. "J.W. Spooner Died Result of Recent Stroke," *Centerville Daily Iowegian*, June 20, 1928.
17. "When Saloons Ran in S. Centerville," *Centerville Daily Iowegian*, January 3, 1931; "Centerville," *Iowegian*, December 26, 1889; Beaham & Steele's Lumber Yard advertisement, *Centerville Citizen*, October 5, 1872.

18. "Old Landmark Once the Clinton House and Home of the Fleming Family Later Became Burlington Division Offices, Will Soon Be Only a Memory," *Centerville Daily Iowegian*, June 11, 1937; "Famed Landmark Torn Down in '37," *Centerville Daily Iowegian*, February 27, 1962; "When Saloons Ran in S. Centerville," *Centerville Daily Iowegian*, January 3, 1931.
19. "A. Grinspan Died in Seattle Monday," *Semi-Weekly Iowegian*, July 26, 1910; "A. Grinspan," *Iowegian*, December 27, 1894; "When Saloons Ran in S. Centerville," *Centerville Daily Iowegian*, January 3, 1931; "A man named Froud…," untitled, *Weekly Citizen*, December 30, 1871; "Lives Over Again Those Fierce, Hectic Days When Life on the Levee Was Just One Thing after Another and Not So Very Far after It Either," *Centerville Daily Iowegian*, Progress Anniversary Edition, January 10, 1934.
20. "Tramping beggars…," *Weekly Citizen*, November 4, 1871.
21. "Lives Over Again Those Fierce, Hectic Days When Life on the Levee Was Just One Thing after Another and Not So Very Far after It Either," *Centerville Daily Iowegian*, Progress Anniversary Edition, January 10, 1934.
22. "Death in a Saloon," *Appanoose Times*, October 6, 1881; "Sammy Stewart…," untitled, *Centerville Citizen*, June 9, 1886; "On last Thursday…," untitled, *Appanoose Times*, July 7, 1881; "Marshal Swearngin…," untitled, *Centerville Citizen*, June 30, 1886; "Houser Row No More the Place Once Well Known," *Centerville Daily Iowegian*, April 30, 1931; "On the afternoon…," untitled, *Centerville Citizen*, July 6, 1872; "A Woman's Letter," submitted by a writer identified as "Beatrice," *Centerville Daily Iowegian*, July 4, 1873.
23. "When Saloons Ran in S. Centerville," *Centerville Daily Iowegian*, January 3, 1931; "A man named Froud…," untitled, *Weekly Citizen*, December 30, 1871.
24. "Lives Over Again Those Fierce, Hectic Days When Life on the Levee Was Just One Thing after Another and Not So Very Far after It Either," *Centerville Daily Iowegian*, Progress Anniversary Edition, January 10, 1934.

Chapter 14

1. "Our street lamps around the Square…," untitled, *Appanoose Times*, April 12, 1882; "The county is putting in…," untitled, *Appanoose Times*, March 9, 1882; "Mr. Geo. Bryan has been engaged…," untitled, *Appanoose Times*, April 28, 1881; "Geo. Bryan has bought a large telescope…," untitled, *Appanoose Times*, May 19, 1881.
2. "4200 Miners Once Employed in Field," *Centerville Daily Iowegian*, March 2, 1951.
3. "Dean of Mining Men Here Today Recalls History," *Centerville Daily Iowegian*, October 23, 1940.
4. "Very few persons…," untitled, *Weekly Citizen*, May 20, 1871.

5. "Dean of Mining Men Here Today Recalls History," *Centerville Daily Iowegian*, October 23, 1940.
6. "Fourth of July: Programme," *Appanoose Times*, June 14, 1881; "The Fourth passed off…," untitled, *Appanoose Times*, July 7, 1881.
7. "Last Saturday morning…," untitled, *Appanoose Times*, July 7, 1881.
8. "Fourth of July: Programme," *Appanoose Times*, June 14, 1881.
9. Mrs. George (Ella Williams) Randle, "Walks around the Square as It Was in Her Girlhood," *Centerville Daily Iowegian*, Progress Anniversary Edition, January 10, 1934.
10. "About eight o'clock…," untitled, *Appanoose Times*, July 7, 1881.
11. "Early Centerville, Its Business Men, and Incidents that One in Business Here Many Years Recalls," letter to the editor from H.B. Williams, *Centerville Daily Iowegian*, Progress Anniversary Edition, January 10, 1934.
12. "About eight o'clock…," untitled, *Appanoose Times*, July 7, 1881.
13. "President Garfield Is [*sic*] Condition Steadily Growing Better," *Appanoose Times*, July 21, 1881; "Death of President Garfield," *Appanoose Times*, September 22, 1881; "The Death of President Garfield 1881," EyeWitness to History, 1999, http://www.eyewitnesstohistory.com/gar.htm.
14. "Death of President Garfield," *Appanoose Times*, September 22, 1881; "The President Is Dead," *Appanoose Times*, September 22, 1881.
15. "Memorial Services at Centerville," *Appanoose Times*, September 29, 1881; "Among the decorations…," untitled, *Appanoose Times*, September 29, 1881; "The Cupalo [*sic*] of the Courthouse," *Appanoose Times*, September 1, 1881.
16. "At the time of the Memorial Services…," untitled, *Appanoose Times*, November 10, 1881.
17. "Dean of Mining Men Here Today Recalls History," *Centerville Daily Iowegian*, October 23, 1940.
18. Howes, Culp, Greenberg and VanDorpe, research geologists, "Underground Coal Mines of Centerville, Iowa and Vicinity," open file report 86-2 (Iowa City: Geologic Survey Bureau and Iowa Department of Natural Resources, 1986).
19. Taylor, *Past and Present of Appanoose County, Iowa*, 260–61 (see chap. 1, n. 1).
20. "Coal Production of Appanoose County Almost Million Tons Year," *Semi-Weekly Iowegian*, December 15, 1905.

Chapter 15

1. "Early History of Mystic Reveals Town Was Born When Railroad Finished Line," *Centerville Daily Iowegian*, October 6, 1937; Phyllis Cosby, "Thesis Stirs Memories of Coal Mining Towns," *Daily Iowegian*, May 15, 1997.

2. Dorothy Schwieder, *Black Diamonds: Life and Work in Iowa's Coal Mining Communities, 1895–1925* (Ames: Iowa State University Press, 1983), 86–88; Bill Heusinkveld, "The History of Coal Mining in Appanoose County, Iowa," unpublished manuscript written in 2007, collection of Appanoose County Museum.
3. "From Tuesday's Daily: The sleeping populace…," untitled, *Centerville Citizen*, October 16, 1895; Dan Ehl, managing editor, "Seddon Recalls Coal Mining Days," *Daily Iowegian*, April 17, 2003; Bill Smallwood, interview with the author, May 23, 2006; Milo Murphy, "The Birth and Demise of Brazil," unpublished manuscript, copyrighted 1985, printed by Copy Center of Topeka, Kans., in the collection of Drake Free Public Library, Centerville; Richard Gorden, author of *A Step Back in Time: Plano, Iowa*, interview with the author, May 1, 2005; Patsy Cincotta, "Began Working Mines at 16," *Ad-Express/Iowegian*, Heritage section, February 21, 2003; Julie McClure, "Blozovich, Messa Recall Days in County's Mines," *Ad-Express/Iowegian*, Annual Progress Edition, Heritage section, February 20, 1998.
4. Schweider, *Black Diamonds*, 9, 29–31; "Very few persons…," untitled, *Weekly Citizen*, May 20, 1871; "After Following the Coal Business through Its Commercial Development Recalls the Old Time Coal Operators," *Centerville Daily Iowegian*, Progress Anniversary Edition, January 10, 1934.
5. "Miners Recall '8-Hour-Day' as They Work '7,'" *Centerville Daily Iowegian*, April 2, 1936.
6. Ehl, "Seddon Recalls Coal Mining Days," *Daily Iowegian*, April 17, 2003; Iowa State Mine Inspector's Reports, 1891–1929, collection of Appanoose County Museum, Centerville; Patsy Cincotta, "Coal Mining Played Major Role in C'ville Development: Leon Kauzlarich," *Daily Iowegian*, May 8, 1994; "Strike Is Broken," *Centerville Citizen*, October 16, 1895.
7. Patsy Cincotta, "Coal Mining Played Major Role in C'ville Development," interview with Leon Kauzlarich, explaining the role of company stores, *Ad-Express/Daily Iowegian*, May 9, 1994.
8. Schwieder, *Black Diamonds*, 13, 12.
9. "Proceedings of the Appanoose County Miners' Convention," *Centerville Citizen*, June 7, 1885; "The Reynolds or Cassat bill…," untitled, *Centerville Citizen*, March 24, 1886; "Coal! Coal!," advertisement, *Centerville Citizen*, September 29, 1886.
10. "The miners of the various…," untitled, *Appanoose Times*, February 16, 1882; "The reported riot at Rathbun…," untitled, *Centerville Daily Iowegian*, February 21, 1894; "The miners in the Scandinavian Coal works 'came out' last Saturday…," untitled, *Centerville Citizen*, March 11, 1885.
11. "Go Down to Death," *Centerville Citizen*, August 18, 1897.
12. Schweider, *Black Diamonds*, 20; "Recovering the Bodies of the Dead Miners," *Industrial Iwegian* [*sic*], April 7, 1883; "Miners Shot Down," *Centerville Weekly Citizen*,

September 15, 1897; Paul Johnson, *A History of the American People* (New York: HarperCollins, 1997), 566–67.

13. "Richard Trevellick at Centerville, Iowa, July 7, 1883," *Centerville Citizen*, June 1, 1883; "Richard Trevellick of Detroit…," untitled, *Centerville Citizen*, July 11, 1883; "The Labor Agitator," *Industrial Iwegian* [*sic*], August 10, 1883.
14. "Miners Meeting…," untitled, *Centerville Daily Iowegian*, April 16, 1891.
15. "Talking to Slick Kauzlarich…," untitled, Around the Town, *Centerville Daily Iowegian*, April 16, 1947.
16. "At Cincinnati: Serious Trouble at That Point May Possibly Ensue," *Centerville Citizen*, April 10, 1895.
17. "At Cincinnati: The Situation as Reported by the Citizen Correspondent," *Centerville Citizen*, April 17, 1895.
18. Ibid.
19. "Quiet Day at the Cincinnati Mines," *New York Times*, April 16, 1895, ProQuest Historical Newspapers: The New York Times (1851–2001); "Needy Miners," *Daily Citizen*, December 2, 1895.
20. "The Strike," *Centerville Daily Iowegian*, May 7, 1891; Schwieder, *Black Diamonds*, 130.
21. "They Quit Work," *Centerville Citizen*, January 16, 1895; "A man named Myers…," untitled, *Centerville Citizen*, May 24, 1894; "Miners Gather at the Baker Mine on the St. Paul R.R. to Prevent Work," *Centerville Citizen*, January 30, 1895; "Dynamite a Mine," *Centerville Citizen*, September 15, 1897.
22. "The Diamond Coal Company…," untitled, *Centerville Citizen*, May 26, 1886; "The Negro in Iowa," *Iowa Journal of History and Politics* (January 1848): 41; "The status of the coal miners strike…," untitled, *Iowegian*, May 21, 1891; "The Strike," *Iowegian*, June 4, 1891.
23. "After Following the Coal Business through Its Commercial Development Recalls the Old Time Coal Operators," *Centerville Daily Iowegian*, Progress Anniversary Edition, January 10, 1934.
24. E.D. Lewis, *The Rhondda Valleys* (Cardiff, Wales: University College Press, 1958), 148–79 and appendix B, 279–80.
25. James D. Seddon, interview with the author, May 31, 2006; Dr. Brad McConville, interview with the author, May 31, 2006. Both Seddon and McConville are direct descendants of coal owners.
26. Harry H. Ashton, "Was in Charge of Light Brigade," *Semi-Weekly Iowegian*, March 13, 1908; Cecil Woodham Smith, *The Reason Why* (New York: Penguin Putnam, Inc., 1958), 253.
27. "City Gardens Same Age as the Iowegian," *Centerville Daily Iowegian*, Progress Anniversary Edition, January 10, 1934; *Daily Iowegian*, June 6, 1923.
28. "The Negro in Iowa," *Iowa Journal of History and Politics* (January 1848): 41.

29. "Recall Big Coal Booster Caravan in 1896," *Centerville Daily Iowegian*, October 23, 1940.
30. Schwieder, *Black Diamonds*, 132–33.
31. "Mine Workers Will Celebrate," *Iowegian*, March 28, 1899; "City News in Brief: The Mine Workers Celebrate," *Iowegian*, April 4, 1899.

Chapter 16

1. "Tells of First Bicycle Used Here," *Centerville Daily Iowegian*, February 6, 1929.
2. "Ulrich Bros…," untitled, *Appanoose Times*, February 10, 1881.
3. Samuel Eliot Morison, *Oxford History of the American People: Volume Three, 1869–1963*, Mentor edition (New York: Oxford University Press, 1965), 99; "Centerville Wheelmen Perfect the Permanent Organization of a Bicycle Club," *Centerville Daily Citizen*, April 2, 1895; "Bicycle Riding Was Once Favorite Sport with Centerville Young Folks," *Centerville Daily Iowegian*, February 5, 1929; "The Avery Planter Co.'s," advertisement, *Centerville Daily Citizen*, May 13, 1895; "Light, Strong, Beautiful!" advertisement, *Centerville Daily Citizen*, March 26, 1895.
4. "Here Is Centerville of 80's–90's," *Centerville Daily Iowegian*, November 22, 1950; "Centerville Wheelmen Perfect the Permanent Organization of a Bicycle Club," *Centerville Daily Citizen*, April 2, 1895; Donald L. McMurry, "Kelly's Army," *The Palimpsest*, vol. 4, no. 10 (October 1923); "Gen. Kelly and his army…," untitled, *Centerville Citizen*, May 16, 1894; "Kelly's Army," *Centerville Daily Iowegian*, December 20, 1923.
5. "Bicycle Races and Sports Plentiful," *Centerville Daily Iowegian*, August 23, 1938; "Has Picture of Bicycle Racer," *Centerville Daily Iowegian*, February 8, 1929; "Tells of First Bicycle Used Here," *Centerville Daily Iowegian*, February 6, 1929; "The Bicycle Run," *Centerville Citizen*, June 12, 1895.
6. *The Citizen*, June 29, 1892.
7. "Harvey Tells of Old Time Ball Club," *Centerville Daily Iowegian*, August 15, 1933; J.C. Harvey, "There Was a Merchant's Ball Club in Centerville Back in 1901 and It Made All Contenders Sit Up an' Take Notice," *Centerville Daily Iowegian*, August 27, 1932; "Baseball," *Centerville Citizen*, June 10, 1885; J.C. Harvey, "Harvey Recalls Early Colored Baseball Team," *Centerville Daily Iowegian*, August 16, 1933.
8. "There Was a Merchant's Ball Club…," untitled, *Centerville Daily Iowegian*, August 27, 1932; *Des Moines Register*, Sunday morning edition, August 25, 1918.
9. Carl Whiteley, "A Baseball Tour," unpublished, 1893, collection of Prairie Trails Museum, Wayne County; Carl Whiteley, letter to Rilla Whiteley, August 12, 1893, transcripted by Prairie Trails Museum of Wayne County, September 1, 1951; J.C.

Harvey, "Harvey Tells of Old Time Ball Club," *Centerville Daily Iowegian*, August 15, 1933.

10. "The Great Shane Hill Baseball Team," in *Wayne County: Heritage Highlights; A Sesquicentennial History*, Joyce Dicks, ed. (Wayne County Historical Society, 1966), 14, 15; "Comments on Three Pioneers," featuring Henry Whiteley and J. C. Harvey, *Centerville Daily Iowegian*, December 26, 1929; *Des Moines Register*, August 25, 1918.
11. Jerry Marks, "Courthouse Custodian on Night Shift Recalls Gay 90's When He Pitched for New York Giants," newspaper article in the collection of Prairie Trails Museum, Corydon, Iowa.
12. "Harvey Recalls Early Colored Baseball Team," *Centerville Daily Iowegian*, August 16, 1933.
13. "Livery Stable and Race Horse Days Remembered," *Centerville Daily Iowegian*, Progress Anniversary Edition, January 10, 1934.
14. Ibid.
15. Obituary of Sarah Rebecca Neuse Scott, *Centerville Daily Iowegian*, May 18, 1935; "Tells of First Bicycle Used Here," *Centerville Daily Iowegian*, February 6, 1929; "Uncle Ike Manson Attains Three Quarters of Century and 17 Miles of Sidewalk," *Centerville Daily Iowegian*, June 19, 1936.
16. Obituary of Leander Henry Jackson, *Iowegian*, November 15, 1936; "Centerville Driving Club," *Centerville Citizen*, June 28, 1893; "Centerville Noted for Horses," *Centerville Citizen*, June 30, 1902, reprinted from *Marshalltown Times-Republican*; Around the Town, *Centerville Daily Iowegian*, June 17, 1944; "Tells of First Bicycle Used Here," *Centerville Daily Iowegian*, February 6, 1929; "Garner Jockeys Brought Us Fame," *Centerville Daily Iowegian*, Progress Anniversary Edition, January 10, 1934.
17. "Centerville Driving Club," *Centerville Citizen*, June 28, 1893; "The Annual Summer Races of the Centerville Driving Club," *Centerville Citizen*, June 21, 1893, and August 30, 1894.
18. "Tells of First Bicycle Used Here," *Centerville Daily Iowegian*, February 6, 1929.
19. "Strathberry a Winner," *Centerville Citizen*, August 29, 1894.
20. *Iowegian*, October 11, 1894; *Centerville Citizen*, September 11, 1895; "How Strathberry Did It," *Centerville Citizen*, October 9, 1895; "Strathberry Is Home," *Centerville Weekly Citizen*, October 9, 1895.
21. "Dr. W.M. Scott Dies at Age of 82," *Semi-Weekly Iowegian*, February 4, 1918; "Strathberry, Famous Pacer Made New Record," *Centerville Daily Iowegian*, Progress Anniversary Edition, January 10, 1934; Interview with Ken Weingartner, Harness Racing Committee, with official confirmation of Strathberry's record, July 26, 2006; *Centerville Weekly Citizen*, November 13, 1895.
22. "Tells of First Bicycle Used Here," *Centerville Daily Iowegian*, February 6, 1929.

23. "The Drake Robbery," *The Citizen*, November 22, 1893; "Drake Reappears on English Turf," *Centerville Journal*, May 30, 1901; "Centerville Wheelmen Perfect the Permanent Organization of a Bicycle Club," *Centerville Daily Citizen*, April 2, 1895.
24. "Charles Darwin: The Naturalist's Last Days," *Appanoose Times*, May 17, 1882, reprinted from the *London Standard*; "Oscar Wilde, the English Dude…," untitled, *Iowegian*, April 11, 1895; "The Emperor Alexander III of Russia…," untitled, *Appanoose Times*, November 8, 1894; "A Plague-Stricken City," *Centerville Journal*, January 11, 1900; "Explorations in Central American…," untitled, *Centerville Citizen*, October 18, 1894.
25. "Why can we not…," untitled, June 9, 1886; "The down town telegraph office…," untitled, *Centerville Citizen*, May 9, 1895; "The Seymour Enterprise gets off the following: Centerville has got it and got it bad…," untitled, *Appanoose Times*, January 5, 1882.
26. "At last the long talked of telephone line…," untitled, *Appanoose Times*, November 24, 1881; "Our new telephone line…," untitled, *Appanoose Times*, December 15, 1881; "Our telephone line is now complete…," untitled, *Appanoose Times*, December 22, 1881; "Our telephone line is now in fine working order…," untitled, *Appanoose Times*, January 5, 1882; "The material is now on the ground…," untitled, *Centerville Citizen*, September 5, 1883; "The telephone poles are being set…," untitled, *Centerville Citizen*, October 3, 1883.
27. "The vacant room over Miss Oppenheimer's millinery store…," untitled, *Daily Citizen*, November 7, 1895; "The Reading Room is now open to the general public…," untitled, *Iowegian*, November 21, 1895; "The Reading Room," *Centerville Citizen*, December 4, 1895; "Formation of Library Association in Centerville Is Recounted Today by H.B. Williams in Old Time News," *Centerville Daily Iowegian*, December 17, 1932; "Circulating Library," *Centerville Citizen*, December 10, 1884; "Our Reading Room," *Daily Citizen*, November 15, 1895; "New Year's Day: Reading Room Reception," *Centerville Weekly Citizen*, January 8, 1896; "The Reading Room Benefit," *Centerville Citizen*, December 11, 1895; "For the Library," *Centerville Weekly Citizen*, July 15, 1896; "The liberality of C.A. Stanton and A. Grinspan…," untitled, *Centerville Citizen*, February 24, 1897; "A public opening and sociable…," untitled, *Daily Citizen*, November 11, 1895; "The ladies of the Library…," untitled, *Daily Citizen*, June 21, 1900; "Drake Library Was Proposed in 1901 by Past Governor," *Centerville Daily Iowegian*, July 13, 1946.
28. "Our Reading Room," *Daily Citizen*, November 15, 1895; "Formation of Library Association in Centerville Is Recounted Today by H.B. Williams in Old Time News," *Centerville Daily Iowegian*, December 17, 1932.
29. Gue, *History of Iowa from the Earliest Times to the Beginning of the Twentieth Century*, 180–81 (see chap. 1, n. 18).

30. "The Murphy Meeting," *Centerville Citizen*, October 2, 1895; "Did Not Fall by Accident," *Centerville Daily Citizen*, September 29, 1897; Merritt, Early Days in Appanoose County, *Centerville Daily Iowegian*, February 10, 1942.
31. "Some History of Centerville's First 'Wet' Experiment Gleaned from Newspaper Files," *Centerville Daily Iowegian*, April 19, 1933; "Sheriff Silknitter…," untitled, *Centerville Daily Citizen*, February 3, 1897; "Post Office Robbed," *Citizen*, December 6, 1893; "Two drunks appeared…," untitled, *Daily Citizen*, January 20, 1897.
32. "Saturday Evening's Matinee," *Centerville Citizen*, June 26, 1895.
33. "Doings of the Day: Rum Runs Riot at Rathbun," *Centerville Citizen*, January 1, 1896.
34. "A Fatal Shooting," The City in Brief, *Iowegian*, January 20, 1899; "Did Not Fall by Accident," *Centerville Daily Citizen*, September 29, 1897; "When Saloons Operated in S. Centerville," *Centerville Daily Iowegian*, July 6, 1932; "Rum Runs Riot! Our Public Square the Scene of Drunken Disorder," *Centerville Citizen*, January 2, 1895; "A Horrible Deed," *Appanoose Times*, January 6, 1881.
35. Double Murder and Suicide," *Centerville Weekly Citizen*, February 19, 1893.
36. "Lives over Again Those Fierce Hectic Days When Life on the Levee Was Just One Thing after Another and Not So Very Far after It Either," *Centerville Daily Iowegian*, Progress Anniversary Edition, January 10, 1934; "Dr. Peak got off on another tantrum…," untitled, *Centerville Citizen*, January 26, 1895; "Bits of Local News: Dr. Peak Is in the Toils," *Centerville Daily Citizen*, December 18, 1895.
37. "Cemetery Hill Hazel Brush and Road Was Rutted," *Centerville Daily Iowegian*, Progress Anniversary Edition, January 10, 1934; "Death in a Saloon," *Appanoose Times*, October 6, 1881; "Bobby Stewart Killed," *Centerville Citizen*, April 6, 1892; "All this talk about the sheriff…," untitled, *Centerville Citizen*, April 13, 1892; "Old Sammy Stewart is once more in jail…," untitled, *Centerville Citizen*, May 18, 1892.
38. Mrs. T.M. Fee, "An Address," *Centerville Citizen*, December 13, 1893.
39. Margaret C. Needels, "Woman Editor of the Citizen Took up Duties of Well Known Predecessors and Showed That She Could Carry On," *Centerville Daily Iowegian*, Progress Anniversary Edition, January 10, 1934.
40. Major Geo. Landers, letter to the editor, "Major Geo. Landers and Band Career," *Centerville Daily Iowegian*, Progress Anniversary Edition, January 10, 1934; "Our Female Cornet Band…," untitled, *Centerville Citizen*, August 29, 1883; "We noticed several ladies playing billiards…," untitled, *Centerville Citizen*, September 22, 1886.
41. "Mary Gibbs Spooner Is Picked by New York Paper as 'Distinguished'; She Tells 'Home Folks' All about It," *Centerville Daily Iowegian*, July 22, 1932.
42. "Miss Baker's New Book," *Centerville Citizen*, July 15, 1902; "Iowa Girl Takes Chair at Oxford," *Centerville Journal*, January 12, 1905.
43. "No Saloons as Yet," *Centerville Weekly Citizen*, May 6, 1896.

44. "Women after Rum," *Centerville Weekly Citizen*, February 1, 1897.
45. *Centerville Daily Citizen*, February 3, 1897.
46. "Mrs. Carrie Nation came back...," untitled, *Centerville Journal*, January 24, 1900; "Honor Great Man," *Centerville Journal*, February 7, 1901; "Mrs. Nation's Work," *Centerville Citizen*, January 24, 1901; "Smash an Oxford Saloon," *Centerville Journal*, March 14, 1901.
47. "Carrie Nations Raids in 1901," *Centerville Daily Iowegian*, November 29, 1946.

Chapter 17

1. "Tells Some Old Fire History," *Centerville Daily Iowegian*, Anniversary Edition, August 23, 1938; "Another Fire," *Centerville Daily Iowegian*, November 26, 1891; "Monday Morning's Fire," *Centerville Citizen*, December 13, 1893; "A Sunday Blaze," *Centerville Daily Iowegian*, January 3, 1894; A Seven-Thousand Blaze," *Centerville Citizen*, July 11, 1894; "The Keystone in Ashes," *Centerville Citizen*, September 26, 1894; "Mid-Day Alarm," *Centerville Citizen*, December 4, 1895; "A Northside Blaze," The City in Brief, *Centerville Daily Iowegian*, December 20, 1898; "Late City News," The City in Brief, *Centerville Daily Iowegian*, December 23, 1898; "Entire Stock Lost," The City in Brief, *Centerville Daily Iowegian*, January 9, 1899.
2. "In some unexplainable manner Jake Hatzenbeeler's bell...," untitled, *Centerville Citizen*, April 20, 1887; "Passing Centerville Landmark," *Centerville Daily Iowegian*, October 15, 1937.
3. "Ed Swafford Dies: Old Days Fire Recalled," *Centerville Daily Iowegian*, December 31, 1945.
4. "Old Days of Fire Fighters Are Recalled," *Centerville Daily Iowegian*, January 8, 1925; "'Jinks' Ramsey Assistant Chief Resigns from Fire Department; Recalls Some of Its History," *Centerville Daily Iowegian*, February 18, 1943.
5. "Fought Fires with Hand Pumps and Water from Wells," *Centerville Daily Iowegian*, Anniversary Edition, August 23, 1938; "A new hose cart...," untitled, *Centerville Citizen*, August 11, 1886; "Old Fire Fighter Served 32 Years," *Centerville Daily Iowegian*, Progress Anniversary Edition, January 10, 1934.
6. "West Side Square Fire Told," *Centerville Daily Iowegian*, Anniversary Edition, August 23, 1938; "Fought Fires with Hand Pumps and Water from Wells," *Centerville Daily Iowegian*, Anniversary Edition, August 23, 1938.
7. "Another Fire," *Centerville Daily Iowegian*, November 26, 1891.
8. "Fought Fires with Hand Pumps and Water from Wells," *Centerville Daily Iowegian*, Anniversary Edition, August 23, 1938.
9. "Monday Morning's Fire," *Centerville Citizen*, December 13, 1893.

10. "Continental Fire Recalled," *Centerville Daily Iowegian*, November 9, 1945; "About the most convenient thing…," untitled, *Centerville Citizen*, August 18, 1886.
11. "Big Fire," *Centerville Journal*, February 9, 1893.
12. "Hotel Fire in Last Century," *Centerville Daily Iowegian*, Pictorial Edition, March 2, 1951.
13. "Was in Hotel Fire and Tells about It," *Centerville Daily Iowegian*, Progress Anniversary Edition, January 10, 1934.
14. "Continental Fire Recalled," *Centerville Daily Iowegian*, November 9, 1945.
15. "Hotel Fire in Last Century," *Centerville Daily Iowegian*, Pictorial Edition, March 2, 1951.
16. "Continental Fire Recalled," *Centerville Daily Iowegian*, November 9, 1945.
17. "Continental Had Modest Beginning and Became Great," *Centerville Daily Iowegian*, Progress Anniversary Edition, January 10, 1934; Obituary of Susannah McKee, *Centerville Journal*, February 23, 1893.
18. "'Jinks' Ramsey Assistant Chief Resigns from Fire Department; Recalls Some of Its History," *Centerville Daily Iowegian*, February 18, 1943.
19. "The Past Year," *Centerville Citizen*, January 9, 1895.
20. "In Railroad Circles," *Daily Citizen*, November 2, 1895; "Coal Production of Appanoose County Almost Million Tons Year," *Semi-Weekly Iowegian*, December 15, 1905.
21. "Twenty-two full-blooded Cherokee Indians…," untitled, *Daily Citizen*, July 3, 1900; "Reverend Alex Jefferies," *Daily Citizen*, June 16, 1900.
22. "The Gold Fields," *Centerville Weekly Citizen*, August 4, 1897; "Gold Craze Is On," *Centerville Weekly Citizen*, July 28, 1897; "Get into Training," *Centerville Weekly Citizen*, August 11, 1897.
23. "Columbian Exposition," *Centerville Weekly Citizen*, November 3, 1892; "Tickets on sale everyday at the Rock Island depot for the World's Fair…," untitled, *Centerville Citizen*, May 10, 1893; "Take the K. & W.'s Chicago train…," untitled, *Centerville Citizen*, May 17, 1893; "The Dauphin Park Hotel," advertisement, *Iowegian*, November 24, 1892.
24. "A.E. Wooden and family…," untitled, *Centerville Citizen*, June 21, 1893; "Hon. T.M. Fee and family…," untitled, *Centerville Citizen*, June 28, 1893; "Major C.A. Stanton and family…," untitled, *Centerville Citizen*, July 5, 1893; "Mr. and Mrs. F.E. Drake, Mr. and Mrs. Henry Goss and Miss Mamie Drake…," untitled, *Centerville Citizen*, July 5, 1893; H.B. Williams, letter to the editor, "Readers of the Citizen," *Centerville Citizen*, November 8, 1893; "Columbian Exposition," *Centerville Weekly Citizen*, November 3, 1892; "All the preparations for the dedication of the World's Columbian Exposition Buildings and grounds…," untitled, *Centerville Citizen*, October 5, 1892.

25. "What Iowa Will Have at the Fair," *Centerville Citizen*, October 26, 1892; Gue, *History of Iowa from the Earliest Times to the Beginning of the Twentieth Century*, 167–68 (see chap. 1, n. 18); "Appanoose County coal will be represented…," untitled, *Iowegian*, November 3, 1892; "An Address: Delivered by Mrs. T.M. Fee upon the Delivery of Mrs. McKee's Portrait to the Continental," *Centerville Citizen*, December 13, 1893.
26. "Mass Meeting," *Centerville Citizen*, January 19, 1887; "The Centerville Improvement Association had a rousing meeting…," untitled, *Centerville Citizen*, March 2, 1887; "Elsewhere in this issue…," untitled, *Centerville Citizen*, January 12, 1887; "Rules and Regulations of the Board of Health of the City of Centerville, Iowa," July 19, 1894; "Our Alleys Dirty," *Iowegian*, September 26, 1899; "The work of cleaning up the back alleys…," untitled, *Centerville Citizen*, May 9, 1894; "To Beautify Our City," *Iowegian*, January 10, 1899; "Something should be done…," untitled, *Appanoose Times*, May 12, 1881; M.D. Stephenson, health officer, "A Card," *Centerville Times*, April 19, 1882; Dr. D.C. Morgan, health officer, "Office of Board of Health," *Centerville Citizen*, April 25, 1884; "Spring is now at hand…," untitled, *Centerville Citizen*, March 17, 1886.
27. "Wells Furnished Early City with Its Water Supply," *Centerville Daily Iowegian*, Centennial Edition, November 29, 1946; "The family of Mr. Israel…," untitled, *Iowegian*, September 13, 1894; "Ordinance 207…," untitled, *Centerville Citizen*, February 19, 1895; "About the Waterworks," *Centerville Weekly Citizen*, October 15, 1895.
28. "For the first time in the history of the city…," untitled, *Iowegian*, November 7, 1895; "The city began laying the Mains…," untitled, *Iowegian*, November 7, 1895.
29. "A Great Success," *Centerville Citizen*, January 14, 1896; "This City's Needs," *Centerville Weekly Citizen*, January 20, 1897; "The Water Flows," *Centerville Citizen*, February 12, 1896; "Events of a Day," *Centerville Citizen*, February 12, 1896; "City Own the Works," *Centerville Citizen*, February 26, 1896.
30. "Sunday afternoon about 3½ o'clock…," untitled, *Centerville Journal*, June 11, 1884; "The old Alhambra restaurant…," untitled, *Centerville Citizen*, December 26, 1883; "Tom Wales' building…," untitled, *Centerville Citizen*, March 24, 1886; "Thursday Aug. 19th: Grand Opening," *Centerville Citizen*, August 11, 1886; "A.E. Wooden has torn down…," untitled, *Appanoose Times*, May 5, 1881; "The old buildings on the south side…," untitled, *Appanoose Times*, April 21, 1881; "One by one the old landmarks disappear…," untitled, *Iowegian*, June 13, 1895.
31. Royal Simmons, interview with the author, May 20, 2006; William Heusinkveld, interview with the author, September 20, 2008.
32. "Two Famous Landmarks," *Centerville Citizen*, June 12, 1895; "Looking South Down Main Street from Courthouse as It Appeared in the 80's," *Centerville Daily Iowegian*, April 1916; "This Is Centerville before the Turn of the Century," *Centerville Daily*

Iowegian, Pictorial Edition, March 2, 1951; Molly Myers Naumann, *An Architectural and Historical Survey of the Centerville Public Square*, 18, 19, 20, 25, 29 (see chap. 10, n. 11).

33. "Bradley-Hamilton-White Block," *Centerville Daily Citizen*, September 11, 1895; "J.A. White's New Building to Be Erected on the Southwest Corner," *Centerville Daily Citizen*, March 11, 1896.

Chapter 18

1. "Centerville National Marks 75 Years," *Iowegian*, September 14, 1951.
2. "Old Centerville Newspapers from the Collection of Mrs. G.W. Randle, Pasadena, Calif.," including *Centerville Citizen*, April 16, 1890, 26:49, *Centerville Daily Iowegian*, January 14, 1952.
3. "J. Gould and company…," untitled, *Centerville Citizen*, May 16, 1883; "Railroad Kings," *Industrial Iwegian* [*sic*], April 9, 1883.
4. Katherine Bassett, "County Railroads," chapter in *History of Appanoose County, Iowa* (Centerville: Appanoose County Historical Society, 1986), 37–38; Frank P. Donovan Jr., *Iowa Railroads*, ed. H. Roger Grant (Iowa City: University of Iowa Press, 2000), 237.
5. "South Part of Centerville County Seat of Appanoose Co.," *Plat Book of Appanoose County Iowa* (Northwest Publishing Co., 1896; reprint, Moulton, Iowa: Historical Society, 1981), 27–28; "Colorful Pages of City's History Pass with Sawyers Mansion," *Centerville Daily Iowegian*, September 26, 1957; W.M. Heusinkfeld, *Historic Homes of Centerville Iowa* (self-published, 2004), photograph included, 1–2.
6. "Day Observance of Interest Here," *Centerville Daily Iowegian*, May 8, 1924; "A Million Endowment," *Centerville Citizen*, January 17, 1900; "Makes Another Gift," *Semi-Weekly Iowegian*, November 20, 1903; "Hurrah for Drake," *Centerville Citizen*, June 22, 1892; "News at Drake," *Semi-Weekly Iowegian*, November 24, 1903.
7. "A large company of friends and relations…," untitled, *Appanoose Times*, November 3, 1881; "Married," *Appanoose Times*, January 5, 1882.
8. "Hymeneal Bells," *Industrial Iwegian* [*sic*], June 15, 1883; "Wedding Bells," *Centerville Citizen*, June 13, 1883.
9. Obituary of Harriet Jane Drake, *Centerville Citizen*, December 9, 1885.
10. Heusinkfeld, *Historic Homes of Centerville Iowa*, photograph included, 1–2; "Died—Harriet Jane Drake…," untitled, *Centerville Citizen*, December 9, 1885; "History of His Life Told by an Old and Intimate Friend," *Semi-Weekly Iowegian*, November 24, 1903; "Some Incidents and Tributes from His Friends and Neighbors at Home," *Semi-Weekly Iowegian*, November 24, 1903; "Memorial Sermon Tribute to Character," *Semi-Weekly Iowegian*, November 24, 1903; "Dr. Sylvester H. Sawyers," *Centerville Citizen*, February 10, 1892.

11. "Drake Nominated," *Centerville Citizen*, July 17, 1895.
12. "A Big Reception," *Iowegian*, July 18, 1895.
13. "General Drake was up early this morning…," untitled, *Centerville Citizen*, November 6, 1895.
14. "The Official Count," *Centerville Citizen*, November 13, 1895.
15. "Drake Ratification," *Iowegian*, December 9, 1913.
16. "A Grand Reception," *Centerville Weekly Citizen*, November 13, 1895.
17. "The Inauguration," *Daily Citizen*, January 14, 1896.
18. "Drake's Inauguration," *Daily Citizen*, January 16, 1896.
19. Julia Spiegelman, "Campaign Buttons and Slogans Reflect History of Country," *Centerville Daily Iowegian*, October 11, 1960, reprinted from *Christian Science Monitor*.
20. "Torch Parade to Be Staged Here on Nov. 3," *Centerville Daily Iowegian*, October 29, 1932.
21. "Torchlight Parades," *Centerville Daily Iowegian*, August 24, 1932; "The Democratic Jubilee," *The Journal*, November 19, 1884.
22. "Bryan Is Downed," *Centerville Citizen*, November 4, 1896.
23. "Drake on Result," *Centerville Citizen*, November 10, 1897; "The Election," *Centerville Citizen*, November 12, 1884; "Hosts of Wm. McKinley," *Centerville Weekly Citizen*, October 28, 1896.
24. "Events of a Year: Oct. 1 Governor Drake and others…," untitled, *Centerville Weekly Citizen*, January 13, 1897; "The Des Moines Register says…," untitled, *Centerville Citizen*, March 3, 1897.
25. "On to Washington," *Centerville Citizen*, March 3, 1897; "Governor Drake Injured," *Centerville Citizen*, March 10, 1897; "Not in the Best of Health," *Centerville Citizen*, March 10, 1897.
26. "Governor F.M. Drake was in the city over Sunday…," untitled, *Centerville Citizen*, March 10, 1897; "Governor Drake Is Out," *Centerville Citizen*, July 28, 1897.
27. "Gov. Drake Home," *Centerville Weekly Citizen*, August 4, 1897; "Gov. Drake Is Improving," *Centerville Weekly Citizen*, August 4, 1897.
28. "Governor Is Home," *Centerville Citizen*, September 1, 1897; "Governor Drake Improving," *Centerville Citizen*, September 22, 1897.
29. "Gov. Drake Home," *Centerville Citizen*, November 3, 1897.
30. Gue, *History of Iowa from the Earliest Times to the Beginning of the Twentieth Century*, 184 (see chap. 1, n. 18).
31. Ibid., 185.
32. "'Iowa' Named by Local Girl," *Centerville Journal*, November 17, 1922; "Iowa's First Lady," *Centerville Citizen*, January 29, 1896; "'Iowa' Named by Local Girl," *Centerville Daily Iowegian*, November 16, 1922.
33. "The Cuban Rebellion…," untitled, April 4, 1895; "The Cuban Question," *Centerville Weekly Citizen*, December 11, 1895; "Startling Report," *Centerville Citizen*, September

9, 1896; "Affairs of Cuba," *Centerville Citizen*, March 3, 1897; "A Cuban Message," *Centerville Citizen*, May 19, 1897; "May Lead to War," *Centerville Citizen*, May 26, 1897; "Albia Man in Cuba," *Centerville Citizen*, May 7, 1897; "Tale of Cruelty," *Centerville Citizen*, June 2, 1897; "Spanish Cruelty," *Centerville Weekly Citizen*, November 4, 1896.

34. "Gov. Drake Is Hot," *Centerville Weekly Citizen*, December 24, 1896.
35. "Iowa Soldiers for Cuba," *Centerville Citizen*, December 16, 1896; "Will Fight for Cuba," *Centerville Citizen*, December 24, 1896.
36. "The Maine Horror," *Semi-Weekly Iowegian*, February 18, 1898.
37. Morison, *Oxford History of the American People*, 117 (see chap. 16, n. 3).
38. Taylor, *Past and Present of Appanoose County, Iowa*, 225–27 (see chap. 1, n. 1); "Spanish War Vets Recall Great Event," *Centerville Daily Iowegian*, April 22, 1932; "Incidents in Past Recalled by Ira Perjue," *Centerville Daily Iowegian*, August 23, 1938.
39. "Played as Boy Under Sidewalks," *Centerville Daily Iowegian*, Iowa Centennial Edition, August 23, 1938; "Almost 29 Years Since Spanish War Veterans Left Centerville," *Centerville Daily Iowegian*, March 22, 1927; "Company E Centerville," *Centerville Citizen*, May 13, 1898.
40. "Company E Marched away 23 Years Ago," *Centerville Daily Iowegian*, April 27, 1921; "Are Off to War," *Centerville Citizen*, April 26, 1898.
41. "Followers of Teddy Roosevelt," photograph in *Centerville Daily Iowegian*, Centennial Edition, November 29, 1946; "49 Years Ago …They Marched Away," *Centerville Daily Iowegian*, April 26, 1947.
42. "Spanish War Vets Recall Great Event," *Centerville Daily Iowegian*, April 22, 1932.
43. "Only One Survivor of Spanish-American War in Putnam Co.," *Centerville Daily Iowegian*, July 6, 1960; "Private Otto Larson…," untitled, The City in Brief, *Iowegian*, September 9, 1898.
44. "An Imposing Funeral," *Iowegian*, September 27, 1898; "Died in Camp," *Iowegian*, August 12, 1898; "Death of a Soldier," The City in Brief, *Iowegian*, October 18, 1898.
45. "The raising of the large white and blue flagpole…," untitled, *Iowegian*, May 10, 1898.
46. "Co. E Will Be Home Tomorrow," The City in Brief, *Iowegian*, September 20, 1898; "Return of Company E," *Iowegian*, September 23, 1898; "Welcome Soldiers Home," *Iowegian*, September 23, 1898.
47. "Centerville's Band in Army," *Centerville Citizen*, August 30, 1899.
48. "Iowans Arrive Safely," *Iowegian*, October 25, 1899; "Soldiers Arrive Home," *Centerville Citizen*, October 25, 1899; "Landers Receives Welcome," *Centerville Citizen*, October 25, 1899.
49. "G.W. Landers," *Appanoose Times*, April 28, 1881.
50. "Major Geo. Landers and Band Career," *Centerville Daily Iowegian*, Pioneer Edition, January 10, 1934.

Chapter 19

1. "Carnival Here with Fun and Noise," *Semi-Weekly Iowegian*, June 4, 1907.
2. "Carnival in Full Blast Now Big Opening This Afternoon," *Semi-Weekly Iowegian*, September 19, 1905; "Carnival Here Has Many Shows," *Semi-Weekly Iowegian*, September 20, 1910; "Opera House," *Centerville Citizen*, August 31, 1892; C.B. DePuy, Around the Town, *Centerville Daily Iowegian*, July 24, 1943.
3. "Tony Sebastian, the champion acrobatic roller skater…," untitled, *Centerville Citizen*, February 17, 1886; "Almost a hundred little boys…," untitled, *Centerville Citizen*, June 9, 1886; "Recollections of Gladstone," *Iowegian*, February 28, 1899; "Dr. May's Lecture," *Centerville Citizen*, November 25, 1896.
4. "A socialist lecture…," untitled, *Centerville Citizen*, August 16, 1902; "The maddest man in town…," untitled, *Iowegian*, September 6, 1894; "A populist orator, named Anderson…," untitled, *Iowegian*, September 12, 1895.
5. "Run out of Centerville," *Centerville Journal*, March 21, 1902.
6. "Bosco, the snake eater…," untitled, *Centerville Citizen*, July 31, 1902; "She Eats Snakes," *Centerville Citizen*, August 1, 1902.
7. "Balloon Ascension," *Centerville Citizen*, July 4, 1883; "Weather Was Bad," *Centerville Citizen*, May 19, 1897; "It Was a Big Day," *Centerville Citizen*, June 2, 1897; "Woman Going up in Balloon Each Day of the Races," *Semi-Weekly Iowegian*, September 15, 1903.
8. "Aeronaut Killed," *Centerville Weekly Citizen*, June 9, 1897; Obituary from *Leon (Iowa) Reporter*, "John Walters," June 10 1897, http://iagenweb.org/boards/decatur/obituaries/index.cgi?read=16840; "John Walters, a young man twenty-four years of age…," untitled, *Decatur County (Iowa) Journal* (Leon, Iowa), June 10, 1897.
9. "And Now Centerville Sees It," *Centerville Citizen*, April 14, 1897.
10. "The Airship Again," *Centerville Citizen*, April 14, 1897.
11. "Was a Big Success," *Centerville Citizen*, June 23, 1897.
12. "Secret Society Day," *Centerville Citizen*, October 4, 1899.
13. "Beautiful Windows," *Centerville Daily Citizen*, September 28, 1899; "Magnificent Carnival," *Centerville Citizen*, June 9, 1897.
14. "Centerville Beauty," *Centerville Citizen*, September 27, 1899; "Military Fairs," *Appanoose Times*, January 6, 1881; "Grand Floral Parade," *Centerville Citizen*, September 27, 1899.
15. "Advertising the Show," *Semi-Weekly Iowegian*, July 7, 1907.
16. "Big Circus Arrives in Centerville," *Centerville Citizen*, July 15, 1898; "Sells Brothers circus arrived safely early Friday morning…," untitled, *Appanoose Times*, July 12, 1894; "The Big Robinson Shows All Right," *Semi-Weekly Iowegian*, June 12, 1906; "Greene Home to New Site," *Centerville Daily Iowegian*, October 29, 1962; "City

Gardens Same Age as the Iowegian," *Centerville Daily Iowegian*, Progress Anniversary Edition, January 10, 1934.

17. "Some of Things Old Timers Missed When Circus Came," *Centerville Daily Iowegian*, August 26, 1925; "Hoopla! The Big Circus Is Coming! The Only Show This Season," *Centerville Citizen*, June 28, 1894.
18. "Was a Sure Circus," *Semi-Weekly Iowegian*, August 1, 1899.
19. "Shows in Town Also a Crowd," *Semi-Weekly Iowegian*, July 23, 1907; "Forepaugh—Sells Circus," *Iowegian*, June 30, 1900; "About Circus Parade," *Semi-Weekly Iowegian*, August 13, 1909; "Fine Street Parade," *Semi-Weekly Iowegian*, September 15, 1908; "The Grand Free Street Parade," *Centerville Citizen*, May 10, 1893; "Campbell Bros. Show," *Semi-Weekly Iowegian*, August 8, 1908; "Best Circus Day Business of Year in Centerville," *Centerville Daily Iowegian*, September 5, 1939.
20. "Hercules, the Iron Horse," *Centerville Citizen*, September 7, 1892; "Thousands Await Circus," *Semi-Weekly Iowegian*, July 9, 1907.
21. "The Great Wallace Shows," advertisement, *Centerville Citizen*, July 5, 1902.
22. "Ringlings Have New Parade," *Semi-Weekly Iowegian*, July 9, 1907; "John Robinson's Circus," *Appanoose Times*, May 15, 1883; "John Robinson's 10 Big Shows," advertisement, *Centerville Journal*, May 2, 1883.
23. "W.W. Cole's circus last Saturday…," untitled, *Appanoose Times*, August 4, 1881; "W.W. Cole's Mammoth Menagerie," *Appanoose Times*, July 21, 1881.
24. "Harvey Gathers Some Data about 'Buffalo Bill,'" *Centerville Daily Iowegian*, September 22, 1927; "Buffalo Bill's Wild West," advertisement, *Centerville Citizen*, September 15, 1899.
25. "Buffalo Bill's Wild West," advertisement, *Centerville Citizen*, September 20, 1899; Helen Cody Wetmore, *Last of the Great Scouts* (Chicago: The Duluth Press Publishing Company, 1899), 246–48.
26. "Buffalo Bill's Wild West," *Centerville Citizen*, September 19, 1899; "City and County: It Is to Educate," *Semi-Weekly Iowegian*, September 28, 1899.
27. "Buffalo Bill Is Here," *Centerville Citizen*, September 29, 1899; "City and County: Wild West Show," *Iowegian*, October 3, 1899; Louis S. Warren, *Buffalo Bill's America* (New York: Alfred A. Knopf, 2005), 246–47.
28. "Buffalo Bill Brought Largest Crowd to City," *Centerville Daily Iowegian*, June 14, 1928; "Local Record for Large Gatherings," *Centerville Daily Iowegian*, June 20, 1929.

Chapter 20

1. "Quite Chilly, Thank You," *Centerville Daily Citizen*, January 2, 1900; "The ice harvest began in Centerville…," untitled, *Centerville Daily Citizen*, January 5, 1900; "Other

People's Business: Once upon a time pond ice cut by hand…," untitled, *Centerville Daily Iowegian*, March 31, 1941; "To Thaw Hydrants," *Centerville Daily Citizen*, January 4, 1900.

2. "A Swell 'Holiday Hop,'" *Centerville Daily Citizen*, December 30, 1899; "Danced with the New Year," *Centerville Daily Citizen*, January 2, 1900.
3. "Interesting Programme," *Centerville Daily Citizen*, January 1, 1900; "Shows up the Evil," *Centerville Daily Citizen*, December 11, 1899.
4. "General News of City: How the Last Sunday of the Year Was Observed in Centerville," *Centerville Daily Citizen*, January 1, 1900; "To Sing 'Old Hundred,'" *Centerville Daily Citizen*, December 28, 1899.
5. "In Latter Days," *Centerville Citizen*, June 6, 1902; "The End of the World," *Centerville Citizen*, June 14, 1899; "Are Flying Rollers," *Semi-Weekly Iowegian*, August 5, 1904.
6. "A New Year's Greeting," *Centerville Daily Citizen*, December 31, 1899; "Centerville Needs: Mayor Callen Tells the Men of Centerville What the City Needs Most," *Centerville Citizen*, February 2, 1900.
7. "1903 Was a Turning Point in City and County History," *Centerville Daily Iowegian*, Centennial Edition, November 29, 1946; "The City of Centerville, Iowa," *Semi-Weekly Iowegian*, May 19, 1905; "1903 Year of Great Local Improvement," *Centerville Daily Iowegian*, Fiftieth Year Edition, June 26, 1953; "1904—The Year That Many Improvements Were Started," *Centerville Daily Iowegian*, Fiftieth Year Edition, June 26, 1953; "Was Time for Congratulation and Hope for Future of City," *Semi-Weekly Iowegian*, November 29, 1904.
8. "Architect Wm. Foster…," untitled, *Centerville Citizen*, February 18, 1885; "At a Meeting of the Board of Supervisors…," untitled, *Centerville Citizen*, February 25, 1885; "The Court House is undergoing…," untitled, *Appanoose Times*, July 28, 1881.
9. "Pronounced Unsafe! Dangerous!" *Centerville Citizen*, August 9, 1893; "Our Court House," *Centerville Citizen*, January 9, 1895; "Our Court House is the general butt…," untitled, *Centerville Citizen*, August 7, 1895; "Saturday Summary," *Centerville Daily Citizen*, November 9, 1895; "Owing to the unsafe condition…," untitled, *Centerville Citizen*, August 9, 1893; "New Court House," *Centerville Citizen*, February 3, 1897.
10. "Petition Started for Sewers Property Owners Ask Council," *Semi-Weekly Iowegian*, May 15, 1903; "Dads Talk Sewerage," *Centerville Citizen*, August 7, 1900.
11. "Stop Slaughter," *Semi-Weekly Iowegian*, October 2, 1903; "Stopped Slaughter of Chickens and Discharged Nineteen Men," *Semi-Weekly Iowegian*, October 9, 1903.
12. "Clean up the City," *Centerville Citizen*, March 27, 1902.
13. "Centerville Needs," *Centerville Citizen*, February 2, 1900.
14. "The Smallpox in Iowa," *Centerville Citizen*, April 25, 1900; "Albia's Smallpox," *Centerville Citizen*, January 10, 1900; "Board of Health Metting [*sic*]," *Centerville Journal*, June 20, 1901.

15. "Has Smallpox," *Centerville Citizen*, April 18, 1900; "Reported Smallpox at Mystic," *Centerville Daily Citizen*, December 20, 1900; "The quarantine between Centerville and Mystic…," untitled, *Centerville Journal*, June 27, 1901; "Three young men of Centerville…," untitled, *Centerville Journal*, May 2, 1901, reprinted from the *Albia Union*.
16. "Paving Ordinance Passes and Paving This Year Is Expected," *Semi-Weekly Iowegian*, July 19, 1904.
17. "Meeting of City Council." *Centerville Journal*, April 11, 1901.
18. "The excavation for a new business building block on the South side of the Square…," untitled, *Centerville Journal*, May 16, 1901; Joe Huston, *Centerville Daily Iowegian*, Progress Anniversary Edition, January 10, 1934, quoted in Robert K. Beck, "The Drake Free Public Library," pamphlet (n.p., n.d.).
19. "Locates New Library," *Centerville Citizen*, May 27, 1901; "Notice to Contractors," *Centerville Journal*, June 27, 1901; "The brick work of the Drake Free Public Library…," untitled, *Centerville Citizen*, March 31, 1902; "The Drake Free Public Library…," untitled, *Centerville Citizen*, August 29, 1902; "Dedication of the Drake Free Public Library; Centerville, Iowa, Thursday, January 15, 1903," *Semi-Weekly Iowegian*, January 16, 1903.
20. "The City News Field," *Centerville Citizen*, April 30, 1902; "Centerville Gets $35,000.00 for a Federal Building," *Centerville Citizen*, April 26, 1902; "The New Post Office," *Centerville Citizen*, May 24, 1902; "Great Blow Out," *Centerville Citizen*, April 26, 1902.
21. "The City News Field," *Centerville Daily Citizen*, August 8, 1902; "Federal Building Plans," letter to the editor, *Centerville Citizen*, July 10, 1902.
22. "The committee on site…," untitled, *Centerville Citizen*, August 30, 1902; "J.P. Gribben has a plan…," untitled, *Centerville Citizen*, June 27, 1902; "Locate the New Building," *Centerville Citizen*, August 1, 1902; "Not on the Square," *Centerville Citizen*, July 12, 1902; "Post Office Building Located," *Centerville Citizen*, September 16, 1902.
23. "J.M. Beck, Dr. F.B. Leffert Tell of Hospital's History," *Centerville Daily Iowegian*, February 13, 1953; "Hospital Site Purchased; Association Buys Grinspan Residence for $3,000," *Centerville Citizen*, November 30, 1902.
24. "Dear Mr. DePuy," letter to Charles DePuy's column Around the Town, *Centerville Iowegian*, June 6, 1966; Mrs. Lola Gorman, letter to Charles DePuy, Around the Town, *Centerville Daily Iowegian*, June 2, 1956; Mrs. N.H., letter to Charles DePuy, Around the Town, *Centerville Daily Iowegian*, June 2, 1956; "Picture Proof," two adjacent photographs, *Centerville Daily Iowegian*, June 15, 1956; "What is now known as St. Joseph's Mercy hospital…," untitled, *Centerville Daily Iowegian*, Progress Anniversary Edition, January 10, 1934.
25. "People Greatly Pleased with the Interior of the New Hospital," *Semi-Weekly Iowegian*, November 20, 1903; Nelma Fuller, "St. Joseph's Mercy Hospital Auxiliary: 45th Anniversary," unpublished St. Joseph Auxiliary bulletin, 1998.

26. "M.X.L. Is Centerville's Oldest Social Organization; Its History," *Centerville Daily Iowegian*, February 7, 1931.
27. "J.M. Beck, Dr. F.B. Leffert Tell of Hospital's History," *Centerville Daily Iowegian*, February 13, 1953.
28. "Mrs. Longanecker," *Centerville Daily Iowegian*, Fiftieth Year Edition, June 26, 1953; Keith Sherman, *Iowa Southern Utilities Company: A Century of Service*, ed. Mary C. Harding (Iowa Southern Utilities Company, 1991); "Old Time Courtroom Scene," photograph and article, *Centerville Daily Iowegian*, July 26, 1941; "A Disgrace to Our County," *Centerville Citizen*, September 18, 1895; "The court house in Centerville…," untitled, *Centerville Citizen*, November 27, 1895; "Twenty Years on Courthouse Job," *Centerville Daily Iowegian*, March 3, 1923; "Notice of Sale of Court House," *Centerville Citizen*, December 30, 1902; "The City News Field: Board of Supervisors Lease Rooms in Citizen Block for County Offices," *Centerville Citizen*, December 4, 1902.
29. "Court House Razed," *Semi-Weekly Iowegian*, February 13, 1903.
30. "Old Corner Stone Is Watched with Interest," *Semi-Weekly Iowegian*, February 10, 1903.
31. "City Is Now Well Lighted at a Very Reasonable Expense," *Semi-Weekly Iowegian*, November 27, 1903; "Centerville Light and Traction Comp'y," *Semi-Weekly Iowegian*, January 23, 1906; "Constructing Heating Plant," *Centerville Daily Citizen*, November 21, 1901.
32. "Commence Electric Car Line," *Centerville Citizen*, June 5, 1902; "Electric Street Car Runs," *Centerville Citizen*, November 1, 1902.
33. "Electric Cars on Square: First Electric Street Cars Run on Square This Morning," *Centerville Citizen*, December 18, 1902; "Will Use Electric Cars for Freight," *Semi-Weekly Iowegian*, March 13, 1903; "To Dedicate Drake Library," *Centerville Citizen*, November 19, 1902.
34. "Will Be January 15," *Centerville Citizen*, December 10, 1902; "Special Train to Carry Visitors," *Semi-Weekly Iowegian*, January 13, 1903; "Dedication of the Drake Free Public Library; Centerville, Iowa, Thursday, January 15, 1903," *Semi-Weekly Iowegian*, January 16, 1903; "Governor Cummins Delivered the Dedicatory Address at the Armory," *Semi-Weekly Iowegian*, January 16, 1903.
35. "Governor Drake Injured," *Centerville Citizen*, October 14, 1902; "Ex-Governor Drake…," untitled, *Centerville Citizen*, November 28, 1902; "Ex-Governor Drake Some Better," *Centerville Citizen*, October 15, 1902; "Gen. Drake Still at Home," *Semi-Weekly Iowegian*, October 23, 1903.
36. "Gen. F.M. Drake Has Had a Turn for Worse and Family Is Called," *Semi-Weekly Iowegian*, November 20, 1903; "Taken from Activities of a Useful Life by Hand of Death," *Semi-Weekly Iowegian*, November 21, 1903.

37. "News Brought Sorrow to Centerville People," *Semi-Weekly Iowegian*, November 24, 1903.
38. "Buried in Metalic [*sic*] Casket," *Semi-Weekly Iowegian*, November 24, 1903; "Distinguished Guests at Funeral Elaborate Floral Offerings," *Semi-Weekly Iowegian*, November 24, 1903.
39. "General Drake's Funeral Attended by Prominent," *Semi-Weekly Iowegian*, November 24, 1903; "Prominent Visitors Attended the Funeral," *Semi-Weekly Iowegian*, November 24, 1903.
40. "General Drake's Funeral Attended by Prominent," *Semi-Weekly Iowegian*, November 24, 1903.

Chapter 21

1. "Notice of Sale of Court House," *Centerville Citizen*, December 7, 1902; "Cleaning Up Debris," *Semi-Weekly Iowegian*, March 20, 1903; "Putting in Basement," *Semi-Weekly Iowegian*, April 21, 1903; "Will Use Electric Cars for Freight," *Semi-Weekly Iowegian*, March 13, 1903.
2. "Court House Work," *Semi-Weekly Iowegian*, March 31, 1903; "Notice," *Semi-Weekly Iowegian*, March 13, 1903; "The bids for heating and plumbing…," untitled, *Semi-Weekly Iowegian*, May 5, 1903; "Work Goes Forward," *Semi-Weekly Iowegian*, May 8, 1903; "City Did Not Stop the Street Car Company," *Semi-Weekly Iowegian*, May 12, 1903.
3. "Will Lay Corner Stone of the Court House May Twenty First," *Semi-Weekly Iowegian*, May 8, 1903; "Track Is Laid," *Semi-Weekly Iowegian*, May 15, 1903; "Big Day Thursday," *Semi-Weekly Iowegian*, May 19, 1903; "Contents of Box Placed in Corner Stone," *Semi-Weekly Iowegian*, May 22, 1903.
4. "Laid the Corner Stone of the New Court House …Rain Kept Crowds away but Good Program Was Given," *Semi-Weekly Iowegian*, May 22, 1903; "Pushing Court House," *Semi-Weekly Iowegian*, June 30, 1903.
5. "Work on the Public Buildings Progressing," *Semi-Weekly Iowegian*, August 25, 1903.
6. "Contract for Court House Furnishings," *Semi-Weekly Iowegian*, December 25, 1903; "Board Buys More for the New Court House," *Semi-Weekly Iowegian*, February 5, 1904; "Tower Goes On," *Semi-Weekly Iowegian*, February 19, 1904; "Move into Court House," *Semi-Weekly Iowegian*, September 2, 1904; "Dedication Monday," *Semi-Weekly Iowegian*, September 9, 1904; Jesse Beck, editorial, *Iowegian*, June 1, 1904.
7. "Chief Justice Deemer Made Address at the Dedication," *Semi-Weekly Iowegian*, September 13, 1904.
8. "Address of Chief Justice Deemer at Dedication of Court House," *Semi-Weekly Iowegian*, September 13, 1904.

9. "Clock for Tower," *Semi-Weekly Iowegian*, May 3, 1904; "Pleased with Progressive Spirit of the People," *Semi-Weekly Iowegian*, December 16, 1904; "James R. Wooden, Pioneer, Passed away Monday Morning," *Centerville Journal*, August 10, 1916.
10. "Thanked for Clock," *Semi-Weekly Iowegian*, March 14, 1905; "Putting in New Clock," *Centerville Daily Citizen*, March 6, 1905.
11. "The Court House Clock," *Semi-Weekly Iowegian*, June 2, 1905; "Thanked Mr. Wooden," *Centerville Daily Citizen*, March 14, 1905.
12. "A New Post Office," *Semi-Weekly Iowegian*, June 26, 1903; "Building New Post Office Comes to Home Contractors," *Semi-Weekly Iowegian*, August 11, 1903; "Dedicate Post Office Building This Evening," *Semi-Weekly Iowegian*, August 16, 1904.
13. "Centerville Beat the Whole Bunch," *Semi-Weekly Iowegian*, October 25, 1904; editorial, *Centerville Journal*, February 6, 1902.
14. "Eleven Miles of Sewerage Ordered," *Semi-Weekly Iowegian*, May 13, 1904.
15. "Sewer Contract Let for $55,000; Will Build Thirteen Miles of It," *Semi-Weekly Iowegian*, June 3, 1904; "Several Hundred Feet of the New Sewer Pipe Has Been Laid," *Semi-Weekly Iowegian*, July 10, 1904; "Fourteen Miles of Sewers the Record of Past Year in City," *Semi-Weekly Iowegian*, December 16, 1904.
16. "Thirty Ton Sewer Ditches Used on Work," *Semi-Weekly Iowegian*, December 16, 1904; "Sewer Diggers Strike for Increase in Their Wages," *Semi-Weekly Iowegian*, April 28, 1905; Bill Buss, Hall Engineering Company, interview with the author, November 11, 2007.
17. "Iowa Engineering Company Directing Power Back of All," *Semi-Weekly Iowegian*, Improvement Edition, December 16, 1904.
18. "Heated Controversy Recalled Revolving around Issue in 1904 Whether Streets Should Be Paved with Brick or Asphalt," *Centerville Daily Iowegian*, July 12, 1939; "Farmers Came to Town on Horseback," *Semi-Weekly Iowegian*, March 13, 1903; "Square Paved in Year 1904," *Centerville Daily Iowegian*, Pictorial Edition, March 2, 1951; "Aaron Cohn Remembers This City as It Was 50 Years Ago," *Centerville Daily Iowegian*, November 7, 1958.
19. "Paving Ordinance Passes and Paving This Year Is Expected," *Semi-Weekly Iowegian*, July 19, 1904; "Paving of Square to Be Done at Once," *Semi-Weekly Iowegian*, September 6, 1904.
20. "Moving the Dirt," *Semi-Weekly Iowegian*, September 30, 1904; "The Citizen is pleased to publish…," untitled, *Centerville Citizen*, May 3, 1902.
21. "Paving Job Pleased the People Names of Those Who Pay for It," *Semi-Weekly Iowegian*, Improvement Edition, December 16, 1904.
22. "Laying of Concrete," *Semi-Weekly Iowegian*, October 21, 1904; "Laying Thousand Yards Now Each Day," *Semi-Weekly Iowegian*, October 28, 1904.

23. "Busy Street Scene during Paving," three photographs, *Semi-Weekly Iowegian*, Improvement Edition, December 16, 1904; "Lay Brick Today," *Semi-Weekly Iowegian*, September 8, 1905; "First Brick Laid," *Centerville Daily Citizen*, October 26, 1904; "This Week Ends It," *Semi-Weekly Iowegian*, November 15, 1904.
24. "Was Time for Congratulations and Hope for Future of City," *Semi-Weekly Iowegian*, November 29, 1904.
25. "The Purington paving brick company…," untitled, *Semi-Weekly Iowegian*, December 9, 1904; "Centerville's $150,000 Paved Streets," map, *Centerville Daily Iowegian*, Progress Edition, December 1905; "Angelus Summons Edward J. Hogan," obituary, *Davenport Democrat and Leader*, April 7, 1912; Sarah Wesson, archivist, Davenport Public Library, interview with the author, November 16, 2006; "On the Paving," *Semi-Weekly Iowegian*, December 6, 1904.
26. "Uncle Ike Manson Attains Three Quarters of Century and 17 Miles of Sidewalk," *Centerville Daily Iowegian*, June 19, 1936; "Permanent Walks," *Semi-Weekly Iowegian Improvement Edition*, December 16, 1904; "Man Who Put Hardwalks in Place of Old Board Ones," *Centerville Daily Iowegian*, Progress Anniversary Edition, January 10, 1934; "New Walks All around Square," *Semi-Weekly Iowegian*, May 14, 1907.
27. "Some Concern over Early Day Concerts," *Centerville Daily Iowegian*, Pictorial Edition, March 2, 1951; Jesse M. Beck, editorial, *Semi-Weekly Iowegian*, June 10, 1904; "Squirrels for Courtyard," *Semi-Weekly Iowegian*, April 22, 1904; "Beautify Park," *Semi-Weekly Iowegian*, May 18, 1906; "Will Unveil P.E.O. Drinking Fountain," *Semi-Weekly Iowegian*, March 29, 1907; "Presented to the City by the P.F.O. [*sic*] Sisterhood," photograph, *Semi-Weekly Iowegian*, October 19, 1906; "P.E.O. Fountain Is Dedicated," *Semi-Weekly Iowegian*, April 2, 1907.
28. "Much Achieved in Improvements in Centerville in Year 1905," *Centerville Daily Iowegian*, Progress Anniversary Edition, January 10, 1934; "Will Dedicate the New Baptist Church," *Semi-Weekly Iowegian*, November 21, 1905; "Dedicate Church," *Semi-Weekly Iowegian*, December 8, 1905; "Handsome $40,000 Methodist Church Being Built," *Semi-Weekly Iowegian*, Improvement Edition, December 16, 1904; "Dedicate New Church Sunday," *Semi-Weekly Iowegian*, June 15, 1906; "Jubilee over Dedication of Methodist Episcopal Church," *Semi-Weekly Iowegian*, June 19, 1906; "Funds for Church," *Semi-Weekly Iowegian*, July 30, 1909; "Proceed with Building," *Semi-Weekly Iowegian*, August 20, 1909; "Dedicate the New Church," *Semi-Weekly Iowegian*, November 27, 1906; *Centerville Citizen*, August 6, 1902; *Centerville Citizen*, October 13, 1902; "Believers and Their Beliefs," *Semi-Weekly Iowegian*, January 11, 1907; "Old Methodist Church Bought by Believers," *Semi-Weekly Iowegian*, January 11, 1907; "Gospel Chapel Assembly Holds 55th Conference," *Centerville Daily Iowegian*, August 30, 1957; "This Minister Follows His Calling without Question," *Centerville Daily Iowegian*, November 24, 1952.

29. "Church of the Latter Day Saints," photo caption, *Semi-Weekly Iowegian*, Progress Anniversary Edition, January 10, 1934; "Hallelujah Wedding," *Centerville Citizen*, December 25, 1895; *Centerville Citizen*, August 1, 1894; "Christian Science Church Home Follows Long Career in City," *Centerville Daily Iowegian*, Iowa Centennial Edition, August 23, 1938; "Strange Tongues Were Spoken," *Semi-Weekly Iowegian*, June 11, 1907; "Tongues and Gift of Healing Come," *Semi-Weekly Iowegian*, July 9, 1907; "Strange Tongues Are Plentiful," *Semi-Weekly Iowegian*, January 24, 1908; "Dr. Graham Returns," *Semi-Weekly Iowegian*, March 9, 1906; "G.G. Graham, Osteopathic Physician," advertisement, *Semi-Weekly Iowegian*, February 7, 1908.
30. "Fine Building and Hall Owned by U.M.W.A. Local No. 563," *Semi-Weekly Iowegian*, December 15, 1905.

Chapter 22

1. "How Sad News Came," *Centerville Daily Citizen*, September 7, 1901; "Iowegian & Citizen Carrier Boys," photograph, *Centerville Daily Iowegian*, Progress Anniversary Edition, January 10, 1934; "Joe Huston Who Figured Largely in City as Editor of the Daily Citizen from 1897 to 1909 Recalls Many Events," *Centerville Daily Iowegian*, Progress Anniversary Edition, January 10, 1934.
2. "Czolgosz Confessed," *Centerville Daily Citizen*, September 9, 1901; "Harry Luther, Centerville's Veteran Auto and Accessory Dealer, Now Looks Forward to His Fourth World's Fair," *Centerville Daily Iowegian*, November 4, 1931.
3. "Extra! Extra! McKinley Assasinated [*sic*]," *Centerville Daily Citizen*, September 6, 1901.
4. "How Sad News Came," *Centerville Daily Citizen*, September 7, 1901.
5. "President May Recover," *Centerville Daily Citizen*, September 7, 1901; "Our President Will Live," *Centerville Daily Citizen*, September 9, 1901; "President Improves," *Centerville Daily Citizen*, September 10, 1901; "Steadily Improving," September 11, 1901; "The President Has a Relapse," *Centerville Daily Citizen*, September 13, 1901; "Our President Dead," *Centerville Daily Citizen*, September 14, 1901.
6. "Honor to Martyred President," *Centerville Journal*, September 19, 1901; "Memorial Services," *Centerville Journal*, September 26, 1901.
7. "Trains All Halt," *Centerville Daily Citizen*, September 20, 1901; "Recalls Death and Memorial for McKinley," *Centerville Daily Iowegian*, February 18, 1933.
8. "Oath Administered," *Centerville Daily Citizen*, September 16, 1901.
9. Frederick Lewis Allen, *The Big Change* (New York: Harper and Brothers, 1952), 114–15.
10. "Fast on Typewriter," *Semi-Weekly Iowegian*, June 5, 1903; "The Smith Premier Typewriter," advertisement, *Semi-Weekly Iowegian*, August 14, 1908; Nellie Argo, "This Week's Personality: Harry E. Luther," *Centerville Daily Iowegian*, April 26, 1963.

11. "Wireless Telegraphy," *Centerville Journal*, January 3, 1900; "Signals across the Ocean," *Centerville Daily Citizen*, December 16, 1901; Erik Larson, *Thunderstruck* (New York: Crown Publishers, 2006), 192–93; "Marconi announces…," untitled, *Centerville Citizen*, March 3, 1902; Guglielmo Marconi, "Wireless Telegraphy Versus Cables," *Semi-Weekly Iowegian*, April 3, 1903.
12. "Marconi Is Outdone," *Centerville Journal*, January 18, 1900; "Former Resident Patented Early Radio Devices," *Centerville Daily Iowegian*, January 21, 1925; "Dr. J.L. Sawyers sent a wireless telegraph message…," untitled, *Semi-Weekly Iowegian*, December 11, 1908; "This Is Wonderful," editorial, *Semi-Weekly Iowegian*, February 2, 1909.
13. "How the Picture Shows Came Here," *Centerville Daily Iowegian*, Progress Anniversary Edition, January 10, 1934.
14. "To the People of Centerville," *Centerville Citizen*, October 25, 1900; "Other People's Business," *Centerville Daily Iowegian*, April 21, 1941; "Growth of Theatres in City Is Traced," *Centerville Daily Iowegian*, March 2, 1951; "The Original Oberammergau Passion Play," advertisement, *Centerville Journal*, October 25, 1900; "The famous Edison life motion pictures…," untitled, *Centerville Citizen*, August 15, 1902; "At the Christian Church…," untitled, *Centerville Journal*, August 21, 1902; "The moving picture exhibition…," untitled, *Centerville Citizen*, August 22, 1902; "At the Opera House…," untitled, *Centerville Citizen*, March 25, 1902; "The Brinton Entertainers…," untitled, *Centerville Citizen*, April 4, 1902; "Something New," *Centerville Citizen*, October 21, 1902; "Don't fail to see…," *Centerville Citizen*, October 25, 1902; "Brinton Entertainers…," untitled, *Centerville Citizen*, October 28, 1902.
15. "Fourth of July Was a Hummer with Crowd of Ten Thousand," *Semi-Weekly Iowegian*, July 5, 1907; "Other People's Business," *Centerville Daily Iowegian*, April 21, 1941; "Growth of Theatres in City Is Traced," *Centerville Daily Iowegian*, March 2, 1951; John R. Bittner, *Mass Communication: An Introduction* (Englewood Cliffs, N.J.: Prentice-Hall, Inc., 1977), 186.
16. "John Drake Great Gambler," *Centerville Daily Iowegian*, Fiftieth Year Edition, June 26, 1953; "John A. Drake of Iowa," *Centerville Citizen*, June 28, 1902; "He Will Take Care of Himself with the Best of 'Em," cartoon, *Centerville Daily Iowegian*, September 26, 1905, reprinted from *Chicago Post* (no date given).
17. "Mrs. John A. Drake Found Half Million," *Semi-Weekly Iowegian*, April 10, 1908; "Centerville Noted for Horses," *Centerville Citizen*, June 30, 1902; "Drake Is Questioned," *Centerville Journal*, March 21, 1902; "Derby Owner Examined," *Centerville Citizen*, June 25, 1902; "T.F. Garner left Saturday…," untitled, *Centerville Citizen*, July 14, 1902; "Wyeth the Winner," *Centerville Citizen*, June 23, 1902; "Wins His First Race," *Centerville Citizen*, June 6, 1902; "John A. Drake's horse…," untitled, *Centerville Citizen*, June 6, 1902; "Drake to Have Big Stable," *Semi-Weekly Iowegian*,

February 27, 1905; "Drake Wins the Futurity," *Centerville Citizen*, September 2, 1902; "Drake Leaves Chicago," *Centerville Citizen*, July 22, 1902.

18. "J.A. Drake Buys Vanderbilt Auto," *Chicago American*, April 3, 1902.

19. "Buys White Ghost," *Centerville Citizen*, April 4, 1902; Wm. J. Willett, "Had the First Car in County," letter to the editor, *Centerville Daily Iowegian*, October 19, 1927.

20. "First Car Attracted Large Curious Crowds When Arrived in 1903," *Centerville Daily Iowegian*, Iowa Centennial Edition, August 23, 1938; Robert K. Beck, "Editorial Ramblings," *Centerville Daily Iowegian*, September 6, 1951; Robert K. Beck, "Publisher's Corner," *Centerville Daily Iowegian*, July 21, 1961; "Dr. Heaton Dies," *Centerville Daily Iowegian*, September 5, 1951.

21. "Colorful Chapter in Local Auto History Were Old Time Cars," *Centerville Daily Iowegian*, December 3, 1941.

22. Charles DePuy, Around the Town, *Centerville Daily Iowegian*, Progress Anniversary Edition, January 10, 1934; "Early Car History Featured Some Outstanding Vehicles," *Centerville Daily Iowegian*, August 5, 1953.

23. "Harry Luther, Appanoose County's Oldest Ford Dealer Recalls Days of Centerville's First Flivver," *Centerville Daily Iowegian*, January 23, 1932; "L. C. Main Recalls Was Proud Man 25 Years Ago Today," *Centerville Daily Iowegian*, June 20, 1934; J.C. Harvey, "Recalls Earlier Events," *Centerville Daily Iowegian*, December 9, 1937.

24. "Centerville streets are…," untitled, *Semi-Weekly Iowegian*, June 21, 1907; "Car DeLuxe of 1902 Period Is Seen on Streets," *Centerville Daily Iowegian*, September 21, 1934; "Keep Your Mouth Shut," *Semi-Weekly Iowegian*, August 13, 1912.

25. "Harry Luther, Appanoose County's Oldest Ford Dealer Recalls Days of Centerville's First Flivver," *Centerville Daily Iowegian*, January 23, 1932.

26. "Harry E. Luther," in *Past and Present of Appanoose County, Iowa*, vol. 2, 67–69 (see chap. 1, n. 1); "Local Residents Have Lived in Extremes of Hot and Cold but in Widely Separated Parts of Earth," *Centerville Daily Iowegian*, January 5, 1928.

27. "Many Firsts to Credit Merchant," *Centerville Daily Iowegian*, Progress Anniversary Edition, January 10, 1934; "Harry Luther, Appanoose County's Oldest Ford Dealer Recalls Days of Centerville's First Flivver," *Centerville Daily Iowegian*, January 23, 1932.

28. "Many Firsts to Credit Merchant," *Centerville Daily Iowegian*, Progress Anniversary Edition, January 10, 1934; "Other People's Business," *Centerville Daily Iowegian*, April 7, 1941; "Not a Single Buggy Sold in Centerville in Ten Years— Davison," *Centerville Daily Iowegian and Citizen*, Iowa Centennial Edition, August 23, 1938; "Ford the Universal Car. H.E. Luther, Agt.," advertisement, *Semi-Weekly Iowegian*, April 11, 1913.

29. "Perhaps You Didn't Know," *Centerville Daily Iowegian*, February 12, 1941.

30. "Many Firsts to Credit Merchant," *Centerville Daily Iowegian*, Progress Anniversary Edition, January 10, 1934; "Big Auto Car Is Here," *Semi-Weekly Iowegian*, January 11,

1908; "An Auto Cab," *Semi-Weekly Iowegian*, October 20, 1908; "Taxicab Service!" advertisement, *Semi-Weekly Iowegian*, December 24, 1909.

Chapter 23

1. "Mud Roads Were…," untitled, *Centerville Daily Iowegian*, April 11, 1946; "Width of Highway," *The Homestead*, February 12, 1903.
2. "All Communities, with Good Roads and Good Markets Flourish," advertisement, *The Homestead*, January 1, 1903; John E. Brindley, *History of Road Legislation in Iowa*, Iowa Economic History Series, ed. Benjamin F. Shambaugh (Iowa City, Iowa: The State Historical Society of Iowa, 1912), 229; "The Way to Get Good Roads," *The Homestead*, October 1, 1903.
3. "Twenty-Five Farmers Promised to Begin Using Split Log Drag," *Semi-Weekly Iowegian*, November 3, 1905; "Make Good Roads," *Semi-Weekly Iowegian*, September 1, 1905; "Hard Dirt Road Special Coming Show How Good Roads Are Made," *Semi-Weekly Iowegian*, October 3, 1905.
4. "Twenty-Five Farmers Promised to Begin Using Split Log Drag," *Semi-Weekly Iowegian*, November 3, 1905; "How to Build and Use Split Log Drag," *Semi-Weekly Iowegian*, June 8, 1908.
5. "Prize Offer of Commercial Club for Good Roads Made by the Drag," *Semi-Weekly Iowegian*, November 3, 1905.
6. "Good Roads Made by the Split Log," *Semi-Weekly Iowegian*, Progress Edition, December 12, 1905; "Rural Route People Getting the Split Log Drag Habit," *Semi-Weekly Iowegian*, November 14, 1905.
7. "Drag Day One of Big Events Held in the City," *Centerville Daily Iowegian*, February 26, 1957.
8. "About Drag Day Winners," *Centerville Daily Iowegian*, May 23, 1913.
9. "Drag Roads Flag Day," *Semi-Weekly Iowegian*, June 10, 1913; "Drag Day Was Hummer," *Semi-Weekly Iowegian*, May 20, 1913; "Girl Beat Them All," *Semi-Weekly Iowegian*, May 23, 1913.
10. Mike Kilen, "The First Great American Road Trip," Iowa Life, *The Des Moines Register*, October 6, 2003; "Oskaloosa to Centerville Auto Race behind Schedule," *Centerville Daily Citizen*, March 30, 1908.
11. Julie M. Fenster, *Race of the Century* (New York: Crown Publishers, a division of Random House, 2005), 13–14, 2–9, 350.
12. "A Notable Automobile Race," editorial, *Centerville Daily Iowegian*, December 29, 1952.
13. Drake Hokanson, *The Lincoln Highway* (Iowa City: University of Iowa Press, 1999), 5–7.

14. "Waubonsie Trail Electric Lighted," *Semi-Weekly Iowegian*, March 21, 1911.
15. "Restore and Mark Old Trail," *Semi-Weekly Iowegian*, February 10, 1911; James Fisk, "The Waubonsie Trail across Iowa," *Daily Iowegian*, February 18, 2006.
16. Phyllis Cosby, "From Old Indian Trails to Highways," *Daily Iowegian*, October 17, 2003; "Mark Waubonsie Poles," *Semi-Weekly Iowegian*, May 26, 1911.
17. "Marking Road Distances," *Semi-Weekly Iowegian*, October 31, 1913.
18. Cosby, "From Old Indian Trails to Highways," *Daily Iowegian*, October 17, 2003.
19. "Greatly Improved Train Service," *Centerville Daily Citizen*, December 14, 1904; "Greatly Improved Train Service," *Semi-Weekly Iowegian*, Improvement Edition, December 16, 1904; "Frisco System," advertisement, *Centerville Citizen*, March 24, 1902.
20. "Now Belongs to the Q," *Centerville Daily Citizen*, November 12, 1900; "1903 Was a Turning Point in City and County History," *Centerville Daily Iowegian*, Centennial Edition, November 29, 1946; "County Railroads," *History of Appanoose County, Iowa*, 37 (see chap. 18, n. 4); "Walter Alexander," *Centerville Daily Iowegian*, Pictorial Edition, March 2, 1951; "New Depot Is Now in Use," *Semi-Weekly Iowegian*, February 6, 1912.
21. "California $25.00 via Union Pacific," advertisement, *Semi-Weekly Iowegian*, May 19, 1905; "Homseekers [*sic*] Excursion Canada," *Semi-Weekly Iowegian*, May 11, 1909; "Burlington Route," advertisement, *Centerville Journal*, August 29, 1901; "New Train Service," *Centerville Citizen*, September 27, 1900.
22. "Iowa State Fair," *Centerville Journal*, June 22, 1901; "Excursion," *Semi-Weekly Iowegian*, July 24, 1906; "Mississippi River Dam at Keokuk," advertisement, *Semi-Weekly Iowegian*, August 22, 1913; "What Rudyard Kipling Said about the Grand Canyon…," untitled, advertisement, *Semi-Weekly Iowegian*, April 8, 1913; "Yellowstone Park Is the Nation's Playground," advertisement, *Semi-Weekly Iowegian*, May 27, 1910; "Homseekers [*sic*] Excursion Canada," *Semi-Weekly Iowegian*, May 11, 1909; "Cheap Homeseekers Rates," *Centerville Journal*, January 24, 1901; "T.J. Fuller is home from Comanche county, Oklahoma…," untitled, *Semi-Weekly Iowegian*, November 2, 1906; "Last Big Land Opening in Oklahoma," advertisement, *Semi-Weekly Iowegian*, November 2, 1906; "Opening of Big Pasture Land," *Semi-Weekly Iowegian*, November 2, 1906; "Free Lands," *Semi-Weekly Iowegian*, July 13, 1906; "One of the few remaining opportunities …the Crow Indian Reservation in Montana…," untitled, *Semi-Weekly Iowegian*, July 13, 1906; "The Leading Land Firms," advertisement," *Semi-Weekly Iowegian*, May 14, 1909.
23. "Major Geo. Landers and Band Career," *Semi-Weekly Iowegian*, Progress Anniversary Edition, January 10, 1934; "Plan a Vicksburg Trip," *Centerville Citizen*, September 21, 1900.
24. "Crowd Went to See President," *Semi-Weekly Iowegian*, October 1, 1907; "Co. E to Escort Roosevelt," *Centerville Citizen*, September 15, 1902; "President Theodore Roosevelt: Large Number Went from Appanoose County," *Semi-Weekly Iowegian*,

April 28, 1903; "Iowans Paid Marked Tribute to President Roosevelt in State," *Semi-Weekly Iowegian*, May 1, 1903; "Band and Company Wanted at Keokuk," *Semi-Weekly Iowegian*, September 24, 1907.

25. "A private car which went through…," untitled, *Centerville Citizen*, October 8, 1902; "White Sox Were Here," *Semi-Weekly Iowegian*, March 5, 1917; "Train Load of Gold Went through as Eggs," *Semi-Weekly Iowegian*, February 26, 1917.
26. "J. Pierpont Morgan Comes Our Way," *Semi-Weekly Iowegian*, September 27, 1910.
27. "Opened the Fair," *Semi-Weekly Iowegian*, May 3, 1904; "World's Fair Magnet," *Centerville Daily Citizen*, September 8, 1904; "World's Fair Greatest and Best Ever Produced by Human Skill," *Semi-Weekly Iowegian*, May 27, 1904; "See a Mummy's Face," *Centerville Daily Citizen*, September 10, 1904; "Quite a Crowd of Centerville's young men…," untitled, *Centerville Daily Citizen*, September 20, 1904; "Fast on Typewriter," *Semi-Weekly Iowegian*, June 5, 1903; Michael W. Lemburger and Leigh Michaels, *Meet Me at the Fair* (Ottumwa, Iowa: PBL Limited, 2006), 5, 49, 100, 112, 113.
28. David McCullough, *The Path between the Seas* (New York: Simon and Schuster, 1977), 462; "Neil Stanton Gets Good Promotion," *Semi-Weekly Iowegian*, May 25, 1906; Lowell Perry, "Down in Panama," letter to his parents, published in *Semi-Weekly Iowegian*, April 20, 1906; Lowell Perry, "Things Seen Down in Canal Zone," letter to his parents, published in *Semi-Weekly Iowegian*, May 8, 1906; "Will Close Them Up," *Semi-Weekly Iowegian*, November 7, 1905.
29. "J.M. Biddle and Family…," untitled, *Semi-Weekly Iowegian*, April 24, 1906; "Tourists Return Home," *Centerville Citizen*, April 4, 1900.
30. "Earthquake Topples Buildings and Kindles Fires," *Semi-Weekly Iowegian*, April 20, 1906; "Was in Santa Rosa Time of Earthquake," letter from Mrs. Maggie Belvel to her brother, *Semi-Weekly Iowegian*, May 4, 1906; Josephine Newcomb Perdew, "Pasadena Letter Tells of the Quake," letter to the editor, *Semi-Weekly Iowegian*, May 8, 1906; Aus Ong, "Aus Ong Safe and Sound in Frisco," letter to the editor, *Semi-Weekly Iowegian*, May 8, 1906; "Phase of San Francisco Disaster That Adds to Losses," letter to J.M. Beck from unnamed uncle, *Semi-Weekly Iowegian*, May 1, 1906; "Death and Ruin in a Hurricane," *Centerville Citizen*, September 10, 1900; "Leaving Galveston," *Centerville Daily Citizen*, September 14, 1900; "Killed in Texas Storm," *Centerville Daily Citizen*, September 14, 1900.

Chapter 24

1. H. Roger Grant, "Electric Traction Promotion in the South Iowa Coalfields," *The Palimpsest*, vol. 58 (1977): 18–31; Jesse M. Beck, editorial, *Semi-Weekly Iowegian*, May 5, 1905.

2. Jesse M. Beck, "Opening of Interurban," editorial, *Semi-Weekly Iowegian*, April 22, 1910; Article about Mrs. Longanecker, *Centerville Daily Iowegian*, Fiftieth Year Edition, June 26, 1953; "Electric Street Car Runs," *Centerville Citizen*, November 1, 1902; Norman Carlson, ed., and Robert J. Levis, research coordinator, *Iowa Trolleys*, bulletin 114 of the Central Electric Railfans' Association (Chicago, Ill.: Central Electric Railfans' Association, 1975), 47; "Work on the new electric street car line…," untitled, *Centerville Citizen*, October 2, 1902; "The City News Field: Centerville's Mule Car Street Railway a Thing of the Past," *Centerville Citizen*, August 4, 1902.
3. "Mercantile Houses," *Semi-Weekly Iowegian*, March 31, 1905; "Many Different Types Business Firms in City Listed in 1905," *Centerville Daily Iowegian*, Fiftieth Year Edition, June 26, 1953; "A Widely Experienced Barber," *Centerville Daily Iowegian*, Iowa Centennial Edition, August 23, 1938; "Clyde Shanks," *Centerville Daily Iowegian*, Pictorial Edition, March 2, 1951; "Alpha A. Breese," *Centerville Daily Iowegian*, Fiftieth Year Edition, June 26, 1953; "The Financial Institutions," *Semi-Weekly Iowegian*, March 31, 1905.
4. "Manufacturing Industries," *Semi-Weekly Iowegian*, March 31, 1905.
5. "Steve Martin," *Centerville Daily Iowegian*, Fiftieth Year Edition, June 26, 1953; "Pure Ice for Centerville," *Centerville Daily Iowegian*, June 18, 1901; "The Pure Ice Company," advertisement, *Centerville Daily Iowegian*, Pictorial Edition, March 2, 1951; "Three Business Men Still Active Who Were Operating Here in 1900," *Centerville Daily Iowegian*, Pictorial Edition, March 2, 1951; "Ice! Ice!!" advertisement, *Semi-Weekly Iowegian*, June 4, 1909; "Put the red card in the window…," untitled, *Semi-Weekly Iowegian*, September 23, 1910.
6. "Other People's Business," *Centerville Daily Iowegian*, March 3, 1941; "Barney Fuller, Well Known Manufacturer Taken by Death Sunday," *Centerville Daily Iowegian*, October 25, 1937; "Product Goes around World," *Semi-Weekly Iowegian*, February 14, 1911; "Miles Bateman Taken by Death; Prominent Here," *Centerville Daily Iowegian*, June 2, 1937; "Joseph Goss Foundry and Hercules Mfg. Co. Employes [*sic*]," 1905 photograph, *Centerville Daily Iowegian*, March 28, 1939; "Most Stump Pullers Here," *Semi-Weekly Iowegian*, May 5, 1911; "Stump Pullers on Czar's Farm," *Semi-Weekly Iowegian*, February 14, 1911.
7. Donald L. Koch, state geologist and bureau chief, "Underground Coal Mines of Centerville, Iowa and Vicinity," open file report 86-2, appendix 2, 81–87, and appendix 3, 89–93, Iowa Department of Natural Resources, Iowa City, 1986; "Coal Production of Appanoose County Almost Million Tons Year," *Semi-Weekly Iowegian*, December 15, 1905.
8. "Wholesale Prices," advertisement, *Centerville Journal*, December 6, 1900.
9. "It Will Work Both Ways," cartoon, *Semi-Weekly Iowegian*, April 17, 1903.

10. Paul Johnson, *A History of the American People* (New York: Harper Collins, 1997), 594–95; John S. Potts, "Menace to All," *Semi-Weekly Iowegian*, January 29, 1907.
11. "Patronize Home Merchants," editorial, *Centerville Journal*, February 16, 1905; "Shopping by Mail," *Semi-Weekly Iowegian*, March 28, 1905; Jesse M. Beck, "One Appanoose county town…," untitled, editorial, *Semi-Weekly Iowegian*, May 10, 1907; "Help! Help! Help!" *Semi-Weekly Iowegian*, November 1, 1907; "Marshal [*sic*] Field & Co. of Chicago…," untitled, *Semi-Weekly Iowegian*, October 6, 1902; "Study Human Nature Advice to Salesmen," *Semi-Weekly Iowegian*, March 19, 1909; Jesse M. Beck, "Burning Mail Order Catalogs," *Semi-Weekly Iowegian*, March 22, 1912; "Mister Brown of Shopless Town," *Semi-Weekly Iowegian*, September 24, 1907.
12. Jesse M. Beck, "The Interurban," *Semi-Weekly Iowegian*, February 2, 1909; "Great Promise for City in 1909," *Centerville Daily Iowegian*, February 28, 1956; "Boosters out in Full Force," *Semi-Weekly Iowegian*, February 1, 1910; "Mass Meeting Again Tonight," *Semi-Weekly Iowegian*, April 16, 1909; "Interurban Given Impetus at Mass Meeting of People," *Semi-Weekly Iowegian*, April 16, 1909; "Big Boost Given the Interurban Railway Cause," *Semi-Weekly Iowegian*, February 2, 1909; "Overwhelming Reasons Why Interurban Should Be Built," *Semi-Weekly Iowegian*, July 2, 1909; "Desperate Appeal to People to Save Future of Centerville, in Hour of Need," statement of Interurban Committee, *Semi-Weekly Iowegian*, July 2, 1909; "The Interurban Line Approved," *Centerville Daily Iowegian*, June 19, 1909.
13. "Laying Rails on the Interurban," *Centerville Daily Iowegian*, October 19, 1909; Patsy Cincotta, staff writer, "Old Interurban Played Important Role," *Ad-Express/Iowegian*, Annual Progress Edition, February 20, 1998; Lisa Eddy, Appanoose County Museum curator, interview with the author, conducted during a tour of the Interurban route, August 8, 2008.
14. "Centerville—Mystic Interurban," *Semi-Weekly Iowegian*, April 22, 1910; Bill Heusinkfeld, electrical engineer, interview with the author, August 15, 2008.
15. "Bond Subscribers See Completed Interurban Work," *Semi-Weekly Iowegian*, April 22, 1910; "In April 1910 Centerville and Mystic businessmen gathered for the dedication of the new electric interurban connecting the two communities," photograph in *History of Appanoose County, Iowa*, 36 (see chap. 18, n. 4); "The Subscribers to Bonds When Help Was Needed," *Semi-Weekly Iowegian*, April 22, 1910; John Huffman, interview with the author, August 19, 2008.
16. "Mystic Interurban Started by Payne," *Daily Iowegian*, Centennial Edition, November 29, 1946; Patsy Cincotta, staff writer, "Old Interurban Played Important Role," *Ad-Express/Iowegian*, Annual Progress Edition, February 20, 1998; John Huffman, interview with the author, August 19, 2008; Curt Oden, "When 'Ding-Ding-Ding' Echoed in the Streets of Centerville," *Daily Iowegian*, part 1 of a two-part series, October 21, 2005; Curt Oden, "Power to Lines Cut July 18, 1967 at 11 a.m.," *Daily*

Iowegian, part 2 of a two-part series, October 22, 2005; "Interurban Schedule," *Semi-Weekly Iowegian*, May 13, 1910.

17. "Interurban Depot on East Side," *Semi-Weekly Iowegian*, May 9, 1910; "The Old Waiting Room," photograph, *Centerville Daily Iowegian*, January 29, 1954.
18. "During the Year Now Closing Centerville Forged Ahead," *Semi-Weekly Iowegian*, December 30, 1910; "Interurban Is Doing Well," *Semi-Weekly Iowegian*, April 26, 1910.
19. "Park Is Now a Popular Place," *Semi-Weekly Iowegian*, June 24, 1910.
20. "Many Strollers out Sunday," *Semi-Weekly Iowegian*, May 9, 1911; "Park Glen Hagan Is Busy Place," *Semi-Weekly Iowegian*, March 17, 1911.
21. "Flying Exhibition!! At Glen Hagan Park," advertisement and photograph, *Semi-Weekly Iowegian*, June 21, 1912; "Flying Exhibition!! At Glen Hagan Park Thursday, June 27th," advertisement, *Semi-Weekly Iowegian*, June 25, 1912; "Big Crowd Coming to See Flight," *Semi-Weekly Iowegian*, June 21, 1912; "Fowler Is a Great Air Man," *Semi-Weekly Iowegian*, June 25, 1912; "To Fly Machine at Glen Hagan Park," *Semi-Weekly Iowegian*, June 18, 1912.
22. "Three Fine Flights Made," *Semi-Weekly Iowegian*, June 28, 1912; "How Man Has Achieved Voyaging by Air Route," *Semi-Weekly Iowegian*, August 9, 1910; "On the very last flight of the ocean to ocean journey…," untitled, *Semi-Weekly Iowegian*, November 14, 1911; "Many Aviators Are Eager for Long Flight Prizes," *Semi-Weekly Iowegian*, October 11, 1910; Bob Taylor, interview with the author, Air Power Museum, Blakesburg, Iowa, August 21, 2008.
23. "Three Flying Coast to Coast," *Semi-Weekly Iowegian*, September 19, 1911.
24. "Balloons in Race Pass Here," *Semi-Weekly Iowegian*, July 11, 1911; "Balloons in Storm and Rain," *Semi-Weekly Iowegian*, July 14, 1911; "That Coal City Balloon," *Semi-Weekly Iowegian*, July 21, 1911; "Announce Air Race Results," *Semi-Weekly Iowegian*, July 25, 1911; "Balloons Went around Us," *Semi-Weekly Iowegian*, July 30, 1912; "Some Discussion of First Plane to Alight Here," *Centerville Daily Iowegian*, Special Air Edition, June 14, 1925; "First Gas Kite Lit at Country Club Is Belief," *Centerville Daily Iowegian*, June 20, 1929; "Albert I. Lodwick Works Hard and Effectively for the Good of American Aviation in General," *Centerville Daily Iowegian*, May 13, 1937; "Air Ship Day: Tuesday Aug. 20th, 1912, at Mystic, Ia.," advertisement, *Semi-Weekly Iowegian*, August 16, 1912; "Talk on Aviation," *Semi-Weekly Iowegian*, March 21, 1913; "Aviator Adans [*sic*] Starts from the Country Club," *Semi-Weekly Iowegian*, June 27, 1913; "Airship Moved," *Semi-Weekly Iowegian*, July 1, 1913; "Cincinnati Had Airplane Wreck," *Semi-Weekly Iowegian*, Centennial Edition, November 29, 1946; "Pearl Adams Boy Aviator Has a Fall," *Semi-Weekly Iowegian*, July 4, 1913.
25. "Centerville Doesn't Realize What a Future It Can Have," *Semi-Weekly Iowegian*, January 21, 1910; "Mass Meeting of Boosters to Get Behind Interurban," *Semi-Weekly Iowegian*, January 28, 1910.

26. "Albia and Centerville Line to Be Transferred into Interurban," *Semi-Weekly Iowegian*, January 21, 1910.
27. "S.I.T. Co. to Run Up Town," *Semi-Weekly Iowegian*, June 4, 1912; "Interurban Trade Coming Up Town," *Semi-Weekly Iowegian*, November 15, 1912; "Interurban Running," *Semi-Weekly Iowegian*, June 3, 1913.
28. H. Roger Grant, "Electric Traction Promotion in the South Iowa Coalfields," *The Palimpsest*, vol. 58 (January/February 1977): 29; Mary Harding, *Iowa Southern Utilities Company: A Century of Service*, ed. Keith Sherman (Iowa Southern Utilities Company, 1991), 7, 8, 9; "Rise and Fall of Interurban," *Centerville Daily Iowegian*, March 1, 1955; Carlson and Levis, *Iowa Trolleys*, 48 (see chap. 24, n. 1); "Electric Line to Albia Assured as Soon as It Can Be Equipped," *Semi-Weekly Iowegian*, January 23, 1914.
29. "Straighten Interuban," *Semi-Weekly Iowegian*, March 3, 1914; "New Cars Bought," *Semi-Weekly Iowegian*, February 24, 1914; "Centerville, Albia & Southern Railway Company," advertisement with photograph, *Semi-Weekly Iowegian*, March 12, 1915; "Shipping New Interurban Cars on Saturday," *Semi-Weekly Iowegian*, August 21, 1914; "Interurban Service Starts on Sunday," *Centerville Iowegian*, August 28, 1914.

Chapter 25

1. "There is a systematic persecution of the Jews…," untitled, *Appanoose Times*, February 9, 1882; "The persecution of the Jews in Russia still continues…," untitled, *Appanoose Times*, April 12, 1882; Jesse M. Beck, "The world has 'once more stood aghast' as it heard of atrocities in Russia with the Jews as victims…," untitled, editorial, *Semi-Weekly Iowegian*, May 29, 1903; "A Jewish City," *Semi-Weekly Iowegian*, January 1, 1907; Johnson, *A History of the American People*, 577–79 (see chap. 24, n. 10); "A great many Russian Jews…," untitled, *Semi-Weekly Iowegian*, November 19, 1891.
2. Rabbi Simon Glazer, *The Jews of Iowa* (Des Moines: Koch Brothers, 1904), 186–89.
3. "A. Grinspan," *Semi-Weekly Iowegian*, December 27, 1894; "A. Grinspan: My New Brick Store," advertisement, *Semi-Weekly Iowegian*, December 24, 1891; "A. Grinspan has rented the Howell block…," untitled, *Centerville Weekly Citizen*, January 19, 1898.
4. "Grinspan Frankel Co. Thank You!" *Semi-Weekly Iowegian*, October 15, 1907; "Silver Jubilee for Grinspan-Frankel Co.," *Semi-Weekly Iowegian*, October 11, 1907; "Grinspan-Frankel: Tailored in the Workshop of Worth," advertisement, *Semi-Weekly Iowegian*, October 9, 1908; "A. Grinspan Died in Seattle Monday," *Semi-Weekly Iowegian*, July 26, 1910; "Mrs. A. Grinspan Dies Aged 84," *Centerville Daily Iowegian*, May 28, 1928; J.J. Frankel, "As I Saw Centerville from 1900 to 1938 in Intimate Contact with Its Progress," *Centerville Daily Iowegian*, Iowa Centennial Edition, August 23, 1938.

5. "Opportunity and American Are One—J.J. Frankel," *Centerville Daily Iowegian*, June 29, 1931; "Charles Frankel Dies in Peoria," *Centerville Daily Iowegian*, December 17, 1923; "Brother of J.J. Frankel Dead," *Centerville Daily Iowegian*, February 11, 1926; "J.J. Frankel's Brother Dies," *Centerville Daily Iowegian*, December 7, 1943; "Joseph J. Frankel," in *Past and Present of Appanoose County Iowa*, vol. 2, 36–40 (see chap. 1, n. 1); "The Grand Opening," *Semi-Weekly Iowegian*, May 23, 1905; "Greatly Pleased with the Store," *Semi-Weekly Iowegian*, March 25, 1910.
6. "Lewis Salinger," in *Past and Present of Appanoose County Iowa*, vol. 2, 54–58 (see chap. 1, n. 1); "Ready for Business!" advertisement, *Centerville Daily Citizen*, July 17, 1895; "A Store for the People," advertisement, *Centerville Journal*, January 16, 1902; "Salinger & Goldstein's Department Store: Grand Opening," advertisement, *Semi-Weekly Iowegian*, August 25, 1903; "On the Square," *Semi-Weekly Iowegian*, April 1, 1910; "Abe Goldstein," in *Past and Present of Appanoose County Iowa*, vol. 2, 29–30 (see chap. 1, n. 1); "Handsome Store Delights Everybody," *Semi-Weekly Iowegian*, October 4, 1910; "Remodeling the S. & G. Store," *Semi-Weekly Iowegian*, February 21, 1913.
7. "Geo. W. Strickler Dates Business Career to 70's," *Centerville Daily Iowegian*, Iowa Centennial Edition, August 23, 1938; "Messrs. Israel Brothers…," untitled, *Appanoose Times*, March 24, 1881; "Business Change—Israel Bros…," untitled, *Centerville Citizen*, June 17, 1885; "Sol Rosenbaum," in *Past and Present of Appanoose County Iowa*, vol. 2, 119–20 (see chap. 1, n. 1).
8. "Sol Rosenbaum Old Business Man," *Centerville Daily Iowegian*, Iowa Centennial Edition, August 23, 1938; "Sol Rosenbaum Taken; One of This City's Oldest Merchants," *Centerville Daily Iowegian*, November 19, 1946; "Rosenbaum Plant Closed," *Centerville Daily Iowegian*, Special Edition, February 27, 1962; "J. Rosenbaum Is Called by Death Here Early Today," *Centerville Daily Iowegian*, August 8, 1934; "Levi Rosenbaum Called by Death Well Known Here," *Centerville Daily Iowegian*, November 2, 1942; "Levee Knew Prosperous, and Happy Days Once," *Centerville Daily Iowegian*, Iowa Centennial Edition, August 23, 1938.
9. "Centerville Bottling Works…," untitled, manufacturing industries section, *Centerville Daily Iowegian*, Improvement Edition, December 16, 1904.
10. "James Gavronsky Taken Suddenly by Heart Attack," *Centerville Daily Iowegian*, October 24, 1938; Sarah Gavronsky, interview with the author, October 1, 2003; "Former Centerville Merchant Suffers Paralytic Stroke," *Centerville Daily Iowegian*, April 13, 1936; Gaba and Bromberg advertisement, *City Directory of Centerville Iowa 1903*, compiled and published by Walter L. Neely and Wayne Harris, August 1903, 14; "After 24 Years Joe Goldstein Takes Vacation," *Centerville Daily Iowegian*, January 30, 1930; "Goldstein Is Heart Victim; Loss Mourned," *Centerville Daily Iowegian*, October 24, 1939.

11. "The New Store," Max Futoransky's grocery store, advertisement, *Centerville Journal*, February 14, 1901; "Max Futoransky has leased…," untitled, *Centerville Journal*, January 31, 1901; "A Great Chance to Buy," Friedlander's Clothing Store advertisement, *Centerville Daily Iowegian*, May 29, 1895; "Friedlander's Clothing Store," advertisement, *Semi-Weekly Iowegian*, June 23, 1905; "J.O. Shutzbank," business section, *Centerville Daily Iowegian*, Improvement Edition, December 16, 1904.
12. "The Jewish synagogue is now completed…," untitled, *Semi-Weekly Iowegian*, September 27, 1894; "Jewish Synagogue Built in 1894 Center of Religious Life of People," *Centerville Daily Iowegian*, Progress Anniversary Edition, January 10, 1934; "Hebrew Cemetery Holds Memories," *Daily Iowegian*, May 27, 1988; Krystyna Phillips, director of Iowa Jewish Historical Society, interview with the author, June 10, 2004; David Gradwohl, professor emeritus of anthropology, Iowa State University, interview with the author, August 28, 2008; Maurice Lamm, *The Jewish Way in Death and Mourning* (Middle Village, N.Y.: Jonathan David Publishers, Inc., 2000), 11–12, 19–20, 54; "All the Jewish stories in the city are closed today…," untitled, *Centerville Citizen*, September 23, 1900; "Every faithful Hebrew will go for…," untitled, *Centerville Citizen*, October 10, 1902; "Jewish Yom Kippur," *Semi-Weekly Iowegian*, September 15, 1915; "The Jewish New Year," *Centerville Citizen*, September 6, 1899; "Jewish New Year Being Observed in Centerville," *Semi-Weekly Iowegian*, September 30, 1913; "New Year of Israel," *Semi-Weekly Iowegian*, September 18, 1914; "Three Weeks of Fasting and Sorrow for Jews," *Semi-Weekly Iowegian*, July 25, 1913; Betty McLeod, interview with the author, December 3, 2006.
13. "Hebrews Dedicate School," *Centerville Daily Citizen*, October 3, 1904; Glazer, *The Jews of Iowa*, 312–13.
14. "Buy Back Palestine," *Semi-Weekly Iowegian*, December 15, 1903; "Helping the Jews," *Semi-Weekly Iowegian*, November 14, 1905.
15. Ruby Shkolnick Mihalovich, interview with the author, August 11, 2002; J.W. Shkolnick, "J.W. Shkolnick Plumbing Company Attains 25 Years of Service to Centerville," *Centerville Daily Iowegian*, August 28, 1936.
16. "Joe Shkolnick Taken by Death Well Known Former Resident," *Centerville Daily Iowegian*, January 17, 1957; J.J. Frankel, "As I Saw Centerville from 1900 to 1938 in Intimate Contact with Its Progress," *Centerville Daily Iowegian*, Iowa Centennial Edition, August 23, 1938; "Lewis Salinger," in *Past and Present of Appanoose County Iowa*, vol. 2, 54–58 (see chap. 1, n. 1); "Abe Goldstein," in *Past and Present of Appanoose County Iowa*, vol. 2, 29–30 (see chap. 1, n. 1); "Sol Rosenbaum," in *Past and Present of Appanoose County Iowa*, vol. 2, 119–20 (see chap. 1, n. 1); Himie Voxman, interview with the author, October 4, 2002; Lamm, *The Jewish Way in Death and Mourning*, 11–12, 19–20, 54.

Chapter 26

1. "Booker T. Washington will lecture…," untitled, *Centerville Journal*, January 18, 1900; "Thirty-six people from Corydon…," untitled, *Centerville Citizen*, January 24, 1900; "Booker T. Washington a Centerville Visitor," *Centerville Daily Iowegian*, Centennial Edition, November 29, 1946.
2. "Pleads for His Race," *Centerville Citizen*, January 24, 1900.
3. "Escaped Slaves Went to School in Cincinnati," *Centerville Daily Iowegian*, Progress Anniversary Edition, January 10, 1934; U.S. Bureau of the Census, "1850 Federal Census of Appanoose County, Iowa."
4. "Early Events at Hilltown by Wells Family," *Centerville Daily Iowegian*, Progress Anniversary Edition, January 10, 1934; Frank Wells obituary, *Centerville Daily Iowegian*, January 29, 1923.
5. J.C. Harvey, "Early Day Events Along the Old Trails—Other Comment by Harvey: George Allen," *Centerville Daily Iowegian*, December 28, 1929; "Tells More of the Story of George Allen," *Centerville Daily Iowegian*, Progress Anniversary Edition, January 10, 1934; Alice McMurry, "The Loving Stranger," *Des Moines Register*, January 2, 1998; George Allen photograph, presented to Prairie Trails Museum of Wayne County, Corydon, Iowa, from the effects of Mose Sager of Seymour, April 1997; "George Allen's Biography Is a Story of an Early Pioneer," *Seymour Herald*, December 7, 1933.
6. "J.C. Harvey Reports That Mormons Will Stage Great Trek over Trails thru This County in the Year 1932," *Centerville Daily Iowegian*, December 21, 1931; "I. Trent, colored, received several votes…," *Weekly Citizen*, March 11, 1871; Tom C. Merritt, Early Days in Appanoose County, *Centerville Daily Iowegian*, December 12, 1941.
7. U.S. Bureau of the Census, "1870 Federal Census of Appanoose County, Iowa"; U.S. Bureau of the Census, "1880 Federal Census of Appanoose County, Iowa"; "1885 Iowa Census Appanoose County, Iowa"; "Negroes Coming to Iowa," *Semi-Weekly Iowegian*, January 12, 1904; Willis Gordy, "Selected Demographics," chap. 2 in *Outside In: African American History of Iowa, 1838–2000*, ed. Bill Silag, Susan Koch-Bridgford and Hal Chase (Iowa City: State Historical Society of Iowa, 2001), 40.
8. Morison, *The Oxford History of the American People*, 107–10 (see chap. 16, n. 3); *Iowa Journal of History and Politics* (January 1948), 82–83; Dykstra, *Bright Radical Star*, 239 (see chap. 3, n. 2); Willis Gordy, "You Live What You Learn," chap. 6 in *Outside In: African American History of Iowa, 1838–2000*, 140; "Colored Student to Be M.A.," *Centerville Citizen*, June 6, 1902.
9. "Recalled Many Stories of the Slave Market," *Centerville Daily Iowegian*, October 5, 1915; "Was Born in Slavery," *Semi-Weekly Iowegian*, February 19, 1917; "Woman Born in Slavery Died at an Old Age," *Semi-Weekly Iowegian*, August 21, 1914; "Mrs. George MacDonald," obituary, *Centerville Daily Iowegian*, April 16, 1943; "J.A. Bandy,"

Seymour Press, November 17, 1886; John Crawford Wooden, "Centerville U.S.A.," unpublished memoir, 1970, first booklet of two, 12, privately held by Robert E. Wooden, Winnetka, Ill.; "Stephen James" and "C.S. James, M.D.," in *Biographical and Genealogical History of Appanoose and Monroe Counties, Iowa*, 212–13 (see chap. 10, n. 1); R.K. Beck, "This is the story of our old colored mammy…," untitled, Editorial Ramblings, *Centerville Daily Iowegian*, September 29, 1950; "Daughter of Slaves Dies Here Widely Know and Loved," *Centerville Daily Iowegian*, January 26, 1959; "He's 70, Farms over 700 Acres, and Bowls for 'Exercise,'" *Centerville Daily Iowegian*, September 13, 1961; "'Aunt Mary' Once a Slave Is Called," *Centerville Daily Iowegian*, April 9, 1943; "Aged Negress Is Taken by Death," *Centerville Daily Iowegian*, March 5, 1926; "George Bolden Is Taken at Age 87," *Centerville Daily Iowegian*, May 19, 1948; "Bud Kearney Dead," *Semi-Weekly Iowegian*, April 12, 1912.

10. "Joe E. Heirriford [*sic*], colored, who used to work at the Continental Hotel…," untitled, *Centerville Citizen*, June 16, 1902; "First Colored Youth to Graduate Local High School Returns after Half Century, to Decorate Grave," *Centerville Daily Iowegian*, August 8, 1934; "Commencement," *Centerville Citizen*, May 27, 1885; "Joe Herriford came up from his home…," untitled, *Centerville Citizen*, September 9, 1885.
11. "Emancipation Celebration," *Centerville Journal*, October 1, 1884; "The Ladies Home and Foreign Missionary Circle…," untitled, *Centerville Daily Iowegian*, December 7, 1897; "Colored People Entertain," *Centerville Daily Iowegian*, June 16, 1899; "The colored people…," untitled, *Centerville Citizen*, March 2, 1887; "Second Baptist Church History," *Centerville Daily Iowegian*, Progress Anniversary Edition, January 10, 1934.
12. "The colored voters…," untitled, *Centerville Journal*, November 5, 1884; "A meeting was advertised…," untitled, *Centerville Daily Iowegian*, October 15, 1891; "The 'colored men's revolt' last night…," untitled, *Centerville Daily Iowegian*, July 30, 1891; "Colored Men Organize," *Centerville Daily Iowegian*, September 27, 1898; "Colored Republicans to Meet," *Centerville Citizen*, July 25, 1900; "Plan of Rough Riders," *Centerville Citizen*, July 27, 1900; "Colored Rough Riders," *Centerville Citizen*, July 28, 1900; "J.A. Bandy," *Seymour Press*, November 17, 1886.
13. Morison, *The Oxford History of the American People*, 108 (see chap. 16, n. 3).

Chapter 27

1. Morison, *The Oxford History of the American People*, 173 (see chap. 16, n. 3); Johnson, *A History of the American People*, 661 (see chap. 24, n. 10).
2. "R.N. Hyde Colored of Des Moines Brings Suit Against J.A. Davis of Moulton for Refusing to Feed Him—Davis Brings Fourth [*sic*] Counter Claim and Is Awarded $500," *Centerville Journal*, December 3, 1903.

3. "Wanted," advertisement, *Semi-Weekly Iowegian*, September 9, 1910; "The Roller Rink Opens Monday Night," *Semi-Weekly Iowegian*, July 24, 1908; "William Hampton," *Centerville Citizen*, December 19, 1902; "Stop the Spitting," *Semi-Weekly Iowegian*, April 17, 1906; "Almost a Riot," *Centerville Citizen*, November 6, 1900; "Petition for Dismissal of the Wright Case," *Centerville Journal*, January 17, 1901; " Homer Rutledge Told of Killing Ol Street from Start to Finish," *Semi-Weekly Iowegian*, February 20, 1906; "General News of City: Lis Edwards Works His Bluff and Escapes from Deputy Sheriff," *Centerville Citizen*, August 31, 1900; "Mayor Callen," *Centerville Citizen*, December 26, 1902; "General News of the City," *Centerville Citizen*, August 30, 1900; "Krebs Murder Case Being Tried," *Semi-Weekly Iowegian*, February 13, 1903 (see subsequent articles: *Semi-Weekly Iowegian*, February 17 and 20, 1903, March 17, 1903); "Is Too Much Married: Reverend Zachary Taylor Queen, of Mystic, Arrested for Bigamy Last Night," *Centerville Citizen*, July 25, 1900; "The City News Field: Herman Owens Found Guilty of Keeping House of Ill-Fame," *Centerville Citizen*, December 9, 1902; "Robbery Done in Broad Daylight," *Centerville Citizen*, September 6, 1899; "Robbers Abroad," *Centerville Citizen*, February 17, 1897; "Bold Burglars," *Centerville Citizen*, December 20, 1894; "Five Money Drawers Broken into Last Night in Centerville," *Semi-Weekly Iowegian*, September 27, 1907; "City News," *Centerville Journal*, March 7, 1902; "Dr. E.M. Reynolds," *Centerville Journal*, May 30, 1901; "'Dutch Joe' Burglarized," *Centerville Citizen*, June 11, 1900; "Burglary," *Centerville Journal*, March 22, 1894; "Our Attention Has Been Called," *Centerville Citizen*, September 18, 1900; "Almost a Riot," *Centerville Citizen*, November 6, 1900; "Suppress the Hoodlums." *Centerville Citizen*, August 30, 1900; "Hearing Evidence," *Centerville Citizen*, April 21, 1897.
4. P.C. Selby, *Biographies of Deceased Faculty Members* (Kirksville, Mo.: North East Missouri State Teachers College, 1962), 48–49.
5. Edwin Black, *War Against the Weak* (New York: Four Walls Eight Windows, 2003), 49–51, 395, 88, 68, 188, 189; John Higham, *Strangers in the Land: Patterns of American Nativism, 1860–1925*, tenth printing (New York: Atheneum, 1970), 313–14.
6. Black, *War Against the Weak*, 269–70, 312, 50.
7. Town Talks, *Centerville Citizen*, January 28, 1905; Town Talks, *Centerville Citizen*, January 30, 1905; "Board of Education Meets," *Centerville Journal*, May 26, 1904; "Planning for Big Debate," *Centerville Daily Citizen*, Friday evening, February 24, 1905; *Centerville Daily Citizen*, March 4, 1905; "Our Public Schools," *Centerville Journal*, February 2, 1905; "Centerville Public Schools," *Centerville Journal*, May 11, 1905; "The pupils of the high school…," untitled, *Centerville Journal*, May 19, 1904; "Class Scrap at High School," *Centerville Daily Citizen*, March 3, 1905; "School Notes: Senior Class Enjoys an Outing This Week and Plants Boulder," *Centerville Daily Citizen*, May 6, 1905; "Senior Boulder Buried," *Centerville Daily Citizen*, May 17, 1905; "A

Disinterment," *Centerville Daily Citizen*, May 18, 1905; "Not Well Done," *Centerville Daily Citizen*, May 23, 1905; "Dynamite Used to Blow Up the Class of '05 Boulder Breaks Many Windows in High School," *Centerville Daily Citizen*, May 26, 1905; "Supt. King Asked to Go to Ames," *Semi-Weekly Iowegian*, January 3, 1905.

8. Harry Laughlin Papers, letter to his mother, dated "Tuesday night," postmarked March 15, 1905, Special Collections Department, Pickler Library, Truman State University, Kirksville, Missouri.
9. "New Books at Drake Library," *Semi-Weekly Iowegian*, September 1, 1905; Richard Schickel, *D.W. Griffith: An American Life* (New York: Proscenium Publishers Inc., 1984, First Limelight Edition, 1996), 77.
10. "Tillman Used His Pitchfork," *Semi-Weekly Iowegian*, August 20, 1906.
11. "Weaver and Tillman on Black Race," editorial, *Semi-Weekly Iowegian*, November 23, 1906.
12. "Since the appearance of Tillman…," untitled, editorial, *Semi-Weekly Iowegian*, July 23, 1907.
13. "Smokey Row," story in "The Rippling Waters Review" no. 109 (April 2002), self-printed newspaper by Milly Morris-Amos, Ottumwa, Iowa; "Militia Is to Protect Junkin," *Semi-Weekly Iowegian*, March 16, 1909; "Junkins Case in a Couple Weeks," *Semi-Weekly Iowegian*, April 27, 1909; "Favor Centerville for Junken [*sic*] Trial," *Semi-Weekly Iowegian*, April 2, 1909; "Will Have Junkin Case," *Semi-Weekly Iowegian*, March 5, 1909.
14. "Feeling Intense for Mob Spirit," *Semi-Weekly Iowegian*, February 9, 1909; "Ottumwa Hunts for the Culprit," *Semi-Weekly Iowegian*, February 23, 1909; "Confession of John Junkin in February," *Semi-Weekly Iowegian*, June 1, 1909; "Negro Confesses Murder of Girl," *Semi-Weekly Iowegian*, March 2, 1909; "Adjutant General to Call out Militia," *Semi-Weekly Iowegian*, June 1, 1909.
15. "John Junkin in Jail Here and Ready for Trial Next Tuesday," *Semi-Weekly Iowegian*, May 21, 1909; "Guard for Junkin on the Alert," *Semi-Weekly Iowegian*, May 25, 1909.

Chapter 28

1. "Junkin Faces Stern Law of Land in Court Room Unmolested," *Semi-Weekly Iowegian*, May 25, 1909; "Amusing Things Happen with Serious," *Semi-Weekly Iowegian*, May 25, 1909; "Jury Will Not Balk at Death Penalty if Crime Warrants It," *Semi-Weekly Iowegian*, May 28, 1909.
2. "Some Notes on the Junkin Murder Trial," *Semi-Weekly Iowegian*, May 28, 1909; "Junkin's Brutal Instincts Made Prominent in Trial for Murder," *Semi-Weekly Iowegian*, May 28, 1909; "Junkin Once Bell Boy in Centerville," *Semi-Weekly Iowegian*, May 25,

1909; "Story of Crime and the Trial," *Semi-Weekly Iowegian*, July 29, 1909; "Rinehart Brothers," in *History of Appanoose County*, vol. 2, 401–2 (see chap. 1, n. 2).

3. "Some Notes on the Junkins [*sic*] Murder Trial," *Semi-Weekly Iowegian*, May 28, 1909; "Junkin's Brutal Instincts Made Prominent in Trial for Murder," *Semi-Weekly Iowegian*, May 28, 1909. (Individual evidences of Mrs. Rosen, Mrs. Clutter, Jacob Redman, Patrolman Frank Harris included.)
4. "Keep Blood Off Conscience Was Appeal to the Jury," *Semi-Weekly Iowegian*, June 1, 1909; "Defense Shows Junkins [*sic*] Most Perfect Type of Degenerate Criminal," *Semi-Weekly Iowegian*, June 1, 1909. (Individual evidences of Amy Junkin [*sic*], Dr. Hoeve, John Junkin included.)
5. "Junkin a Degenerate," *Semi-Weekly Iowegian*, October 29, 1909.
6. "Extra! Extra! Hang by Neck till Dead Friday, July 29th, 1910 Is Sentence of Court," *Semi-Weekly Iowegian*, June 1, 1909; "Instructions of the Court," *Semi-Weekly Iowegian*, June 1, 1909; "Closing Scenes of Famous Trial," *Semi-Weekly Iowegian*, June 4, 1909; "Junkins [*sic*] Gone by Special Train," *Semi-Weekly Iowegian Extra Edition*, June 1, 1909.
7. "Forty to See Junkin Hanged," *Semi-Weekly Iowegian*, July 15, 1910; "Junkin Dropped from Gallows at 12:20 p.m.," *Semi-Weekly Iowegian*, July 29, 1910; "Sheriff Clark Did Work Well," *Semi-Weekly Iowegian*, July 29, 1910.
8. "Take Junkin for Baboon," *Semi-Weekly Iowegian*, May 6, 1910; "Lecture on Junkin's Brain," *Semi-Weekly Iowegian*, March 3, 1911; "Junkins [*sic*] Was Much Like an Animal," *Semi-Weekly Iowegian*, March 31, 1911.
9. "An Individual Killed Clara Rosen," editorial, *Semi-Weekly Iowegian*, Extra Edition, June 1, 1909.
10. "Mutterings at the County Jail," *Semi-Weekly Iowegian*, October 29, 1909; "John Hicks for Serious Crime," *Semi-Weekly Iowegian*, December 10, 1909; "Hicks Plead Guilty After Trial Began," *Semi-Weekly Iowegian*, December 14, 1909.
11. "Civil Rights for the Negro," *Semi-Weekly Iowegian*, June 3, 1910.
12. "To Permit No Fight Pictures," *Semi-Weekly Iowegian*, July 8, 1910.
13. "Shows Race Feeling," editorial, *Semi-Weekly Iowegian*, July 8, 1910.

Chapter 29

1. U.S. Bureau of the Census, "1910 Federal Census of Appanoose County."
2. U.S. Bureau of the Census, "1880 Federal Census of Appanoose County," "1890 Federal Census of Appanoose County," "1900 Federal Census of Appanoose County," "1910 Federal Census of Appanoose County."
3. Virginia Padovan, interview with the author, September 15, 2008; "Croatian Heritage: Proud Tradition of History, Food and Song," pamphlet by the Croatian

Festival Committee, St. Mary's Catholic Church, Centerville, for Croatian Fest, July 28, 1990; "To Become Americans," *Semi-Weekly Iowegian*, June 4, 1915; John Cerato, interview with the author, October 24, 2000.

4. Dale Jones, interview with the author, May 20, 1999; John Cerato, interview with the author, October 24, 2000.
5. Mary R. Howes, Matthew A. Culp, Helene Greenberg and Paul E. VanDorpe, "Underground Coal Mines of Centerville, Iowa and Vicinity" (Iowa City, Iowa: Geological Survey Bureau), 2, and plate 1, fold-out map; Schwieder, *Black Diamonds*, 68 (see chap. 15, n. 2); Dale Jones, interview with the author, May 20, 1999.
6. "Life above Ground: The Roles of Italian-American Women," in Schwieder, *Black Diamonds*, 86–111 (see chap. 15, n. 2); "Croatian Heritage" pamphlet (see chap. 29, n. 3).
7. Dale Jones, interview with the author, May 20, 1999.
8. "A Night on the Square," *Centerville Journal*, July 27, 1916; "Baby's Night on the Square," *Centerville Journal*, August 3, 1916; "Regulate Travel on Sidewalks," *Semi-Weekly Iowegian*, August 20, 1917.
9. Dale Jones, interview with the author, May 20, 1999; "Pretty Cottage at the Standard," *Semi-Weekly Iowegian*, April 1, 1913; "These Banks Are Free," Centerville Trust and Savings Bank, Centerville, Iowa, advertisement, *Semi-Weekly Iowegian*, April 17, 1914; "At Sedgley's," advertisement, *Semi-Weekly Iowegian*, December 8, 1908; "Davison's in New Store," *Semi-Weekly Iowegian*, April 16, 1912; "Base Ball Bulletin," *Semi-Weekly Iowegian*, May 17, 1912; "Old Timers of 1901 and '11 Say Not So Hot," *Centerville Daily Iowegian*, July 23, 1934.
10. "Bandfield Store Wagon," Blind Jim advertisement, *Semi-Weekly Iowegian*, September 13, 1910; "Gus Malina [*sic*] now carries…," untitled, *Semi-Weekly Iowegian*, September 25, 1902; "Gus Milani Sells," *Semi-Weekly Iowegian*, September 14, 1915; "The Milani fruit store…," untitled, *Semi-Weekly Iowegian*, November 9, 1915; "T.L. Allen, owner of Delmonicos," *Centerville Daily Iowegian*, Centennial Edition, November 29, 1946; "E.A. Powers Is Honored for 50 Years Service as Druggist," *Centerville Daily Iowegian*, April 30, 1946; "Perjue Recalls 110 Degree Days," *Centerville Daily Iowegian*, June 7, 1933; "Beer's Drug Store Marks Half Century," *Centerville Daily Iowegian*, August 19, 1948; "Since 1898," Red Cross Drug Store advertisement, *Centerville Daily Iowegian*, Pictorial Edition, March 2, 1951; "Jim Shanks," *Semi-Weekly Iowegian*, Progress Anniversary Edition, January 10, 1934; "The Continental drug store has been bought by…," untitled, *Semi-Weekly Iowegian*, May 5, 1908; "Soft Drinks That Are—," Owl Drug Store advertisement, *Semi-Weekly Iowegian*, June 20, 1913; "The City News Field: Week's Red Cross Drug Store Sold to Sigourney Man Today," *Centerville Citizen*, May 7, 1902; "Opens New Drug Store," *Centerville Citizen*, June 10, 1902; "Carl Weeks, Who Created Red Cross Drug, Is Dead," *Centerville Daily Iowegian*, June 6, 1962; "Fewer

Drug Stores Than in Past Days," *Centerville Daily Iowegian*, March 3, 1923; "Town Improvements," *Semi-Weekly Iowegian*, March 4, 1910; R. Kenneth Evans, "M.H. Beer Has Been Identified with the Drug Business in Centerville for Approximately Thirty-Five Years," *Centerville Daily Iowegian*, March 14, 1933.

11. "Special Clubbing Rates," *Semi-Weekly Iowegian*, December 10, 1907; "Two Leading Papers Are Consolidated," *Semi-Weekly Iowegian*, April 18, 1916; "Russians to Defy Czar; Declaration Adopted," *Semi-Weekly Iowegian*, July 27, 1906; "Russian Soldiers Kill Over 2000 Men, Women and Childred [*sic*] Sunday," *Semi-Weekly Iowegian*, January 24, 1905; "Portugal Has Revolution," *Semi-Weekly Iowegian*, October 7, 1910; "Awful Cruelty," *Centerville Citizen*, December 3, 1902; "Millions Have Been Killed in Earthquake Zone of Italy," *Centerville Iowegian*, January 19, 1915; "Earthquake Has 200,000 Victims," *Semi-Weekly Iowegian*, January 1, 1909; "Widespread Panic," *Centerville Journal*, January 23, 1902; Titinac [*sic*] Down with 1200 Lives," *Semi-Weekly Iowegian*, April 16, 1912; "Band Played Nearer My God to Thee as 1601 Went to Their Death on Steamship Titanic," *Semi-Weekly Iowegian*, April 19, 1912; "Mystic Man Loses Wife and Children," *Semi-Weekly Iowegian*, April 19, 1912.
12. Olivier Mendez, ETResearch, "The Lefebvre Family" and memorial to the Lefebvre family in Lievin, France, erected by the Association Francaise du Titanic, *Encyclopedia Titanica*, http://www.encyclopedia-titanica.org/lefebvre.html.
13. "French Children May Be Are His," *Semi-Weekly Iowegian*, April 23, 1912; "Gives Up Hope of Children," *Semi-Weekly Iowegian*, April 30, 1912.
14. "Frenchman Had Too Many Wives," *Semi-Weekly Iowegian*, July 16, 1912; "Lefevres [*sic*] to Be Deported," *Semi-Weekly Iowegian*, July 19, 1912; "Taken East to Be Deported," *Semi-Weekly Iowegian*, July 30, 1912.
15. "Lights Turned On," *Semi-Weekly Iowegian*, March 3, 1911; "Street Lights on March 1," *Semi-Weekly Iowegian*, February 28, 1911; "Electroliers March 1," *Semi-Weekly Iowegian*, February 24, 1911; "Electroliers to Go on Square," *Semi-Weekly Iowegian*, January 24, 1911; "Now Looks Like Electroliers Soon," *Semi-Weekly Iowegian*, November 15, 1910; "Lighted Square Seems Assured," *Semi-Weekly Iowegian*, November 18, 1910; "Electrical Display Will Be Finest Yet," *Semi-Weekly Iowegian*, September 23, 1915.
16. "A Night on the Square," *Centerville Journal*, July 27, 1916; "'Birth of Nation' Gets Court O.K.," *Centerville Daily Citizen*, May 12, 1916; "D.W. Griffith," in Ephraim Katz, *The Film Encyclopedia* (New York: Putnam, 1979, Pedigree Books, 1982), 509–14.
17. Schickel, *D.W. Griffith: An American Life*, 270 (see chap. 27, n. 8).
18. "Cholera Suspects," *Semi-Weekly Iowegian*, August 18, 1911; "Dr. Hickman on Local Health," *Semi-Weekly Iowegian*, March 15, 1912; "City Health Is Looked After," *Semi-Weekly Iowegian*, April 28, 1914; "Saving in Hospitals," *Semi-Weekly Iowegian*, October 8, 1909; "Consumption Is Not Hereditary," *Semi-Weekly Iowegian*, May 11, 1906; "How to Prevent Tuberculosis," editorial, *Semi-Weekly Iowegian*, March 26,

1907; "Measures to Prevent Disease," *Semi-Weekly Iowegian*, March 15, 1912; "Iowa Small-Pox Situation," *Centerville Citizen*, January 2, 1900; "Small Pox Scare Is Thing of Past," *Semi-Weekly Iowegian*, March 15, 1912; "Dreaded Disease Visits County," *Centerville Journal*, September 7, 1916.

19. "Our last small-pox patient…," untitled, *Appanoose Times*, May 10, 1882; "Expert Tests Show Leprosy," *Semi-Weekly Iowegian*, April 26, 1912; "Leper Suspect in Private Car," *Semi-Weekly Iowegian*, April 30, 1912; "Herman Hirschfield Leper Suspect, Taken Back to Bay City, Mich.," *Semi-Weekly Iowegian*, May 21, 1912; "Three Miles of Cement Sidewalk Ordered in '07," *Centerville Daily Iowegian*, Centennial Edition, November 29, 1946; Charlene Lamb, interview with the author, September 13, 2003; "Cholera Suspects," *Semi-Weekly Iowegian*, August 18, 1911.

20. "Free Lecture at Miners Hall…," untitled, *Semi-Weekly Iowegian*, March 9, 1909; "Little Fresh Air Then White Plague," *Semi-Weekly Iowegian*, March 21, 1909; "Saving in Hospitals," *Semi-Weekly Iowegian*, October 8, 1909; "Take Hand in War on Great White Plague," *Semi-Weekly Iowegian*, December 9, 1913; "Continue Fight on Tuberculosis," *Semi-Weekly Iowegian*, December 2, 1913; "Tuberculosis Day," advertisement, *Semi-Weekly Iowegian*, December 5, 1913; "Vaccinate All School Children," *Semi-Weekly Iowegian*, March 8, 1912; "Be Careful Is Advice Given," *Semi-Weekly Iowegian*, November 18, 1910; "Sample Form for Quarantine Card," *Semi-Weekly Iowegian*, February 14, 1908; "Dreaded Disease Visits County," *Centerville Journal*, September 7, 1916; "Old Pest House Was Full of Scares for Passing Youngsters," *Centerville Daily Iowegian*, Iowa Centennial Edition, August 23, 1938.

21. "Kill the Fly Is Slogan," *Semi-Weekly Iowegian*, May 9, 1911; "Dr. Hickman on Local Health," *Semi-Weekly Iowegian*, March 15, 1912; "Doctor Sounds Alarm for All," *Semi-Weekly Iowegian*, April 16, 1915; "Better Disposal of Garbage," *Semi-Weekly Iowegian*, May 1, 1914; "A Timely Warning," *Semi-Weekly Iowegian*, April 16, 1915; "Begin Swatting the Fly Early," *Semi-Weekly Iowegian*, April 16, 1915; "People Urger [*sic*] to Fight Flies and Germs," *Semi-Weekly Iowegian*, June 18, 1909; "Campaign to Exterminate the Pest," *Semi-Weekly Iowegian*, March 9, 1911; "Disease Germs on Cups," *Semi-Weekly Iowegian*, December 15, 1911; "Like a Clean China Dish," advertisement, *Semi-Weekly Iowegian*, April 16, 1915; "Consumption is less deadly…," untitled, advertisement, *Semi-Weekly Iowegian*, June 7, 1907.

22. "Almost Killed the Sheriff," July 29, 1901; "Italians Not Wanted," *Centerville Daily Iowegian*, October 17, 1895.

23. "Riot Started in Miners' Hall," *Semi-Weekly Iowegian*, April 23, 1912; "The Italian who took the lead…," untitled, *Semi-Weekly Iowegian*, April 26, 1912; "Lively Times in Police Court," *Semi-Weekly Iowegian*, September 26, 1911; "Demented Italian Shot Another and Self," *Semi-Weekly Iowegian*, January 30, 1914; "Booze Hunters Were

Targets for Italians," *Semi-Weekly Iowegian*, September 23, 1913; "Pistol Shots Were Plentiful in Rathbun," *Semi-Weekly Iowegian*, May 14, 1907; "Criminal Work Is in Progress," *Semi-Weekly Iowegian*, November 15, 1912.

24. "Started Game as Friends, Both Dead the Result of Fight," *Semi-Weekly Iowegian*, October 7, 1913; "A Rathbun Row," *Centerville Citizen*, March 20, 1895; "Fenians in Centerville," *Centerville Daily Citizen*, December 30, 1899.

25. "Nagging at Syrian Led to More Trouble," *Semi-Weekly Iowegian*, November 11, 1913; "Goldstein Store Was Victim of Night Breakes [*sic*]," *Semi-Weekly Iowegian*, October 19, 1915; "I. Rosenbaum Robbery," *Semi-Weekly Iowegian*, November 17, 1911; "Silk Robbery Frankel Store," *Semi-Weekly Iowegian*, July 5, 1910; "Murderer of Mexican Gone," *Semi-Weekly Iowegian*, April 18, 1911; "John Schrumm Shot at Joda Mosley Home," *Semi-Weekly Iowegian*, November 28, 1913; "John Schrum [*sic*] Funeral," *Semi-Weekly Iowegian*, December 2, 1913; "Austrian Killed," *Centerville Daily Citizen*, December 29, 1905; "Pick Pockets Fleeced People Starting Home," *Semi-Weekly Iowegian*, July 28, 1914; "Smith Preliminary Draws a Big Crowd," *Centerville Daily Citizen*, May 19, 1916; "Mystic Murder Dead of Night," *Semi-Weekly Iowegian*, February 11, 1911; "Gilmores Pleaded Guilty to Court," *Semi-Weekly Iowegian*, March 7, 1911; "Revolver Play on Interurban," *Semi-Weekly Iowegian*, October 31, 1911.

26. "For stealing suitcase…," untitled, *Semi-Weekly Iowegian*, August 7, 1914; J.M. Beck, editor, "Editorial Sidelights," *Centerville Daily Iowegian*, June 23, 1914; "Burglaries Grow More Numerous," *Semi-Weekly Iowegian*, February 14, 1913; "Victim of Stabbing Shows Improvement," *Semi-Weekly Iowegian*, November 11, 1918; "Shondel Stabbed at Galleyville Last Night," *Centerville Daily Citizen*, May 19, 1916.

27. "The ladies of the Baptist Mission Circle…," untitled, *Semi-Weekly Iowegian*, March 13, 1914; "Wednesday Club to Study Many Things in Year," *Semi-Weekly Iowegian*, October 3, 1913; "Night School for Foreigners Opens," *Semi-Weekly Iowegian*, June 25, 1917; "Court House Flags," *Semi-Weekly Iowegian*, April 14, 1911; "Patriotism in Schools to Be Promoted," *Semi-Weekly Iowegian*, November 18, 1913; "It must be admitted that morality…," untitled, *Semi-Weekly Iowegian*, November 21, 1913; "More Flags for Schools," *Semi-Weekly Iowegian*, March 13, 1914.

28. "Full House for Orchestra," *Semi-Weekly Iowegian*, April 26, 1910; "World's Greatest Singers," *Semi-Weekly Iowegian*, December 27, 1910; "Mountain Ash Concert," *Semi-Weekly Iowegian*, October 20, 1911; "Tango Is Fad That Dancers Are Learning," *Semi-Weekly Iowegian*, December 19, 1913.

29. "The U.S. Marine Band, Centerville, Friday, Oct. 29," *Semi-Weekly Iowegian*, October 15, 1915; "Band Comes in Special Train from Oskaloosa," *Semi-Weekly Iowegian*, October 26, 1915; "U.S. Marine Band 11 Leaders 117 Years," *Semi-Weekly Iowegian*, October 22, 1915; "Special Trains for the Band," *Semi-Weekly Iowegian*, October 29, 1915; "Immense Crowd on Band Day," *Semi-Weekly Iowegian*, December 19, 1913.

30. "Was Best Day He Ever Had," *Semi-Weekly Iowegian*, June 30, 1903; "Thousands Heard," *Semi-Weekly Iowegian*, June 30, 1903; "Helen Keller Is a Marvel," *Centerville Journal*, January 10, 1901; "When Bryan Spoke," editorial, *Centerville Daily Iowegian*, August 16, 1955; "W.J. Bryan Cheered by Hundreds During Speech," *Semi-Weekly Iowegian*, October 15, 1912; "Carry [*sic*] Nation at Centerville," *Semi-Weekly Journal*, August 24, 1909; "Debs Made Great Talk on Socialism," *Semi-Weekly Iowegian*, June 25, 1915; "Had Radical Things to Say," *Semi-Weekly Iowegian*, October 2, 1908; "Chautauqua Locally Active," *Semi-Weekly Iowegian*, Pictorial Edition, 1953; "Wonderful Birds and Dogs Perform," *Semi-Weekly Iowegian*, August 21, 1906; "At One Time Receipts Were More Than $5,000 a Year—Great Day When Bryan Came," *Centerville Daily Iowegian*, Iowa Centennial Edition, August 23, 1938; "Fine Program They All Say," *Semi-Weekly Iowegian*, August 25, 1908; "Chautauqua Programs Provide Entertainment for Everyobdy [*sic*]," *Semi-Weekly Iowegian*, August 17, 1909.
31. "Famous Men and Women Here for Home-Coming Program," *Semi-Weekly Iowegian*, August 28, 1908; Mrs. Ella Williams Randle, "Attended School in First Building," letter dated September 30, 1946, *Centerville Daily Iowegian*, Centennial Edition, November 29, 1946; "Theodore P. Shonts," *Semi-Weekly Iowegian*, October 2, 1919, reprinted from *New York Sun*; "Theodore P. Shonts Died Following a Lingering Illness," *Semi-Weekly Iowegian*, September 22, 1919; McCullough, *The Path Between the Seas*, 463 (see chap. 23, n. 27); "Address of T.P. Shonts on Transportation at Chautauqua Home-Coming Day," *Semi-Weekly Iowegian*, September 1, 1908; Dale Jones, interview with the author, September 20, 1999.
32. "How the Picture Shows Came Here," *Centerville Daily Iowegian*, Progress Anniversary Edition, January 10, 1934; "Moving Picture House Is One of the Best," *Semi-Weekly Iowegian*, October 24, 1913; "Who do you think we bumped into this morning…," untitled, Around the Town, *Centerville Daily Iowegian*, February 28, 1942; "Tillies' Punctured Romance," Drake Avenue Theatre advertisement, *Semi-Weekly Iowegian*, February 2, 1915.

Chapter 30

1. "Austrian Heir Is Assassinated," *Semi-Weekly Iowegian*, June 30, 1914; S.L.A. Marshall, *The American Heritage History of World War I* (New York: Dell Publishing Company, 1964), 24; "Austrian and Servian [*sic*] War May Involve Europe," *Semi-Weekly Iowegian*, July 31, 1914; "Germany and Austria Hurl Powerful Armies against Russia and France," *Semi-Weekly Iowegian*, August 4, 1914.
2. U.S. Bureau of the Census, "1910 Federal Census of Appanoose County"; "Story of Numa Man Who Would Occupy Royal Throne of Servia [*sic*]," *Semi-Weekly Iowegian*,

June 26, 1908; "Group Threatened to Invade Servia [*sic*]," quoting Chicago papers in 1946, *Centerville Daily Iowegian*, Centennial Edition, November 29, 1946.

3. "Lerns [*sic*] of Mother's Death 2 Years Ago," *Semi-Weekly Iowegian*, August 4, 1919; "Mother Goes to Belgium after Missing Daughter," *Daily Iowegian*, October 18, 1920; "Three Appanoose Men Seek Families Lost in the War," *Semi-Weekly Iowegian*, August 4, 1919; "Hears from Family in Lithuania after a Long Separation," *Semi-Weekly Iowegian*, October 16, 1919; Former Local Business Man Visits Greece," *Centerville Daily Iowegian*, July 24, 1931; "H.G. Hanson Saw Conditions Made by War," *Semi-Weekly Iowegian*, September 15, 1914; "C.A. Carlson Is Home from Europe," *Semi-Weekly Iowegian*, October 20, 1914; "Tells of Trip Home from the War Scenes," *Semi-Weekly Iowegian*, August 18, 1914; "Rev. Wm. McCoy from War Zone," *Semi-Weekly Iowegian*, September 11, 1914; "E.G. Campbell Returns Home from England," *Semi-Weekly Iowegian*, September 15, 1914.
4. "Austria vs. Belgium in Centerville," *Centerville Daily Citizen*, April 18, 1916; "Put America First," *Semi-Weekly Iowegian*, August 11, 1914; Thomas Phillips, "Opposed to War," letter to the editor, People's Column, *Semi-Weekly Iowegian*, August 11, 1914.
5. "War in Deadly Progress on Land and Sea," *Semi-Weekly Iowegian*, August 7, 1914; "Eleven Years Ago Today," *Semi-Weekly Iowegian*, March 3, 1914.
6. "Belgians Repulse Fierce Attack of Germans," *Semi-Weekly Iowegian*, August 7, 1914; Barbara Tuchman, *Guns of August* (New York: Dell Publishing Co., Inc., 1962), 196, 197.
7. "War Reporter Tells Horror," *Semi-Weekly Iowegian*, August 14, 1914; "The French, English and Belgians to Take Offensive in the War," *Semi-Weekly Iowegian*, August 11, 1914.
8. "Fighting Is Scattered on Long Battle Front," *Semi-Weekly Iowegian*, August 14, 1914; "Germans Keep up Advance onto Paris," *Semi-Weekly Iowegian*, September 1, 1914.
9. "Germans Drop Paris Bombs," *Semi-Weekly Iowegian*, September 1, 1914; "German Air Fleet Makes English Raid," *Semi-Weekly Iowegian*, January 22, 1915; "British Flyers Damage Factory," *Centerville Journal*, November 26, 1915.
10. "Letter from S.A. Carlson after Trip," *Semi-Weekly Iowegian*, January 26, 1915; "Tells of Trip Home from the War Scenes," *Semi-Weekly Iowegian*, August 18, 1914; "Witnessed Air Battle from Decks of Liner," *Semi-Weekly Iowegian*, January 22, 1915.
11. "H.G. Hanson Saw Conditions Made by War," *Semi-Weekly Iowegian*, September 15, 1914; "C.A. Carlson Is Home from Europe," *Semi-Weekly Iowegian*, October 20, 1914; "Tells of Trip Home from the War Scenes," *Semi-Weekly Iowegian*, August 18, 1914; "Rev. Wm. McCoy from War Zone," *Semi-Weekly Iowegian*, September 11, 1914; "E.G. Campbell Returns Home from England," *Semi-Weekly Iowegian*, September 15, 1914; "Trouble Getting out of Austria," *Semi-Weekly Iowegian*, October 6, 1914.
12. "Appeal for Neutrality," *Semi-Weekly Iowegian*, August 21, 1914; "60,000 Americans to Join Canadians," *Semi-Weekly Iowegian*, August 28, 1914; "Who's Who on County

Ticket," *Centerville Daily Iowegian*, October 26, 1926; "This Week's Personality," *Centerville Daily Iowegian*, April 20, 1962.

13. "The Cost of War," *Semi-Weekly Iowegian*, April 23, 1915; "Battlefields Are Places of Death," *Semi-Weekly Iowegian*, May 21, 1915; "Desperate Battle Raging at Ypres," *Semi-Weekly Iowegian*, April 27, 1915; "Bloodiest Battle of All the War Is in Progress," *Semi-Weekly Iowegian*, October 27, 1914; "Canadians Lose Fourth," *Semi-Weekly Iowegian*, May 4, 1915.
14. "Italy Makes Declaration of War on Austria-Hungary," *Semi-Weekly Iowegian*, May 25, 1915; Marshall, *The American Heritage History of World War I*, 157–59; "Italians Are Called Home to Fight for Italy," *Semi-Weekly Iowegian*, June 8, 1915; "Comes for British Subjects," *Semi-Weekly Iowegian*, October 4, 1917; "Getting Recruits among the British," *Semi-Weekly Iowegian*, October 8, 1917; "Pay Way to Enlist for Englishmen," *Semi-Weekly Iowegian*, October 8, 1917; "Englishmen Disappointed," *Semi-Weekly Iowegian*, October 8, 1917; "Streepy Men to Enlist for England," *Semi-Weekly Iowegian*, October 11, 1917.
15. "Deserter Told of Thrilling Escape," *Semi-Weekly Iowegian*, February 5, 1917; "Native Belgian Nurse at Chautauqua Tells Experiences and Hun Atrocities," *Semi-Weekly Iowegian*, August 19, 1918; "Soldier Singers Please Audiences," *Semi-Weekly Iowegian*, August 19, 1918; "Story of Battle of Verdun Will Be Told Here by an Eye Witness," *Semi-Weekly Iowegian*, March 19, 1917; "Battle of Verdun Year Old Has Cost One Million Human Lives," *Semi-Weekly Iowegian*, February 26, 1917; "Saw Heaps of Dead on the Fields," *Semi-Weekly Iowegian*, February 26, 1915; "Free Lecture Tonight on War by One Who Has Been There," *Semi-Weekly Iowegian*, February 26, 1915; Jesse M. Beck, "Big Army Means War," editorial, *Semi-Weekly Iowegian*, March 5, 1915; A. Clermont Mestraud, "The French Side of It," *Semi-Weekly Iowegian*, March 12, 1915.
16. "U.S. and Germany on Verge of Open Hostilities by Sinking," *Semi-Weekly Iowegian*, March 19, 1917; Colin Simpson, *The Lusitania* (Boston: Little, Brown and Company, 1972), 15, 112–16, 91, 92, 154, 156, 176; "Fourteen Hundred Go Down with the Ship," *Semi-Weekly Iowegian*, May 11, 1915; "Lusitania's Sinking Caused More War Talk in U.S. Than Any Incident Since War Began," *Semi-Weekly Iowegian*, May 11, 1915; "Course U.S. to Take Fraught with Danger," *Semi-Weekly Iowegian*, May 11, 1915; "Eight from Here Escaped Wreck," *Semi-Weekly Iowegian*, May 11, 1915.
17. Jesse M. Beck, "The destruction of the Lusitania…," untitled, editorial, *Semi-Weekly Iowegian*, May 11, 1915.
18. "Berlin Blames Ship Owners," *Semi-Weekly Iowegian*, May 14, 1915.
19. "Some Stories of the Survivors," *Semi-Weekly Iowegian*, May 14, 1915; "War May Possibly Come," *Semi-Weekly Iowegian*, May 11, 1915; "U.S. Demands That Germany Stop It," *Semi-Weekly Iowegian*, May 14, 1915; "Unless Germany Backs Down on Submarine Policy US Will Sever Relations or Go to War," *Semi-Weekly Iowegian*, May

14, 1915; Jesse M. Beck, "Saturday noon the orchestra…," untitled, editorial, *Semi-Weekly Iowegian*, May 11, 1915.

20. "The steamship Transylvania, on which the Centerville party of eight sailed…," untitled, *Semi-Weekly Iowegian*, May 18, 1915; "Centerville People Had Another Escape," *Semi-Weekly Iowegian*, May 21, 1915.
21. "In Hands of President," *Semi-Weekly Iowegian*, May 14, 1915; "Can Uncle Sam Preserve Neutrality?" advertisement for *Cartoons* magazine, *Semi-Weekly Iowegian*, May 18, 1915; "Civilization vs. Barbarism," *Semi-Weekly Iowegian*, May 18, 1915, reprinted from *New York Tribune*; "Torpedo Kept Them Away," *Semi-Weekly Iowegian*, May 21, 1915; Jesse M. Beck, "Raising the 'Lusitania,'" editorial, *Semi-Weekly Iowegian*, June 22, 1915; "Germans Torpedo Big Liner," *Semi-Weekly Iowegian*, August 20, 1915; "Buy Lots of Horses and Mules for Army," *Semi-Weekly Iowegian*, August 10, 1915; "Europe Horse Market," *Semi-Weekly Iowegian*, August 24, 1915; "Shipping Mules to Battlefields," *Semi-Weekly Iowegian*, September 33 [*sic*], 1915; "Do Big Business," *Centerville Journal*, July 20, 1916; "Help Fill Christmas Ship to Carry Cheer to War Stricken Children," *Semi-Weekly Iowegian*, October 23, 1914; "Christmas Ship Money and Packages Coming," *Semi-Weekly Iowegian*, October 27, 1914; "Christmas Ship Contributions," *Semi-Weekly Iowegian*, October 20, 1914; "Christmas Ship Information," *Semi-Weekly Iowegian*, October 23, 1914; "The Cry from Belgium," *Centerville Journal*, November 5, 1914; "Appanoose County Is Waking up on the Belgian Relief Fund," *Centerville Journal*, November 26, 1914; "Shall We Let Belgium Starve," public advertisement, *Centerville Journal*, December 3, 1914; "Help the Starving!" public advertisement, *Centerville Journal*, January 27, 1916; "Other War Victims," *Semi-Weekly Iowegian*, January 8, 1915; "Contributions to Jewish Relief," *Centerville Journal*, January 27, 1916; "Turks Massacre Armenians," *Centerville Daily Citizen*, February 11, 1916; "Jewish Speaker on the Zionist Movement," *Semi-Weekly Iowegian*, May 28, 1917; "Sad Plight of the Armenians," *Semi-Weekly Iowegian*, October 1, 1915.
22. "Expecting War in Germany after Break," *Semi-Weekly Iowegian*, February 5, 1917; "American Flag Is Ordered Down in Belgium—Germany Is Driving America Nearer to War," *Semi-Weekly Iowegian*, February 15, 1917; "Much Patriotic Demonstration Here," *Semi-Weekly Iowegian*, February 8, 1917; "South End Is Strong on Flag Display," *Semi-Weekly Iowegian*, April 23, 1917.

Chapter 31

1. "Remember the Little War—On the Banks of the Rio Grande," *Centerville Daily Iowegian*, June 10, 1960; "16 Americans Are Killed by Bandits," *Centerville Daily Citizen*, January 12, 1916; Morison, *The Oxford History of the American People*, 172 (see

chap. 16, n. 3); "Villa Rebels Invade U.S.; Soldiers and Citizens Killed," *Centerville Daily Citizen*, March 10, 1916.

2. "Greetings for the Homecomers," *Semi-Weekly Iowegian*, February 19, 1917; "Company D Enjoys Home Coming Roster of Members of Company," *Semi-Weekly Iowegian*, February 22, 1917; "Big Welcome for Returned Soldiers," *Semi-Weekly Iowegian*, February 22, 1917.
3. "Company D Was Inspected," *Semi-Weekly Iowegian*, April 2, 1917; "Company D Called on to Recruit to One Hundred Men," *Semi-Weekly Iowegian*, April 2, 1917; "Capt. Glenn Haynes Heads Company," *Semi-Weekly Iowegian*, May 21, 1917.
4. "Enlisting Recruits for the War in the Window of the Goldstein Store," *Semi-Weekly Iowegian*, April 24, 1917; "Nine New Men in Company D," *Semi-Weekly Iowegian*, April 9, 1917; "Five More Join Company D Ranks," *Semi-Weekly Iowegian*, April 12, 1917; "Mass Meeting Gets Enlistments," *Semi-Weekly Iowegian*, April 12, 1917; "The H.E. Link Studio," advertisement, *Semi-Weekly Iowegian*, May 14, 1917.
5. "Encourage Surrounding Towns in Enlisting," *Semi-Weekly Iowegian*, April 12, 1917; "Navy Recruiting Here April 13–16," *Semi-Weekly Iowegian*, March 29, 1917; "Military Training Starts in High School," *Semi-Weekly Iowegian*, April 19, 1917.
6. "War Gardens on the Burlington," *Semi-Weekly Iowegian*, April 23, 1917; "Offers Fifteen Acres for Gardening Purposes," *Semi-Weekly Iowegian*, May 7, 1917; "An European War Would Effect [*sic*] Appanoose County," *Centerville Daily Iowegian*, August 29, 1939; "Red Cross Chapter Work Is Started," *Semi-Weekly Iowegian*, May 14, 1917; "Red Cross Meeting Moravia Friday Eve," *Semi-Weekly Iowegian*, June 28, 1917.
7. "Company D Camp on Bradley Land," *Semi-Weekly Iowegian*, June 28, 1917; "Settle Down to Real Camp Life," *Semi-Weekly Iowegian*, July 2, 1917; "Needs Found in Camp of Company D," *Semi-Weekly Iowegian*, July 9, 1917; "Released Three from Co. D. Ranks," *Semi-Weekly Iowegian*, July 9, 1917; "Young Soldier with Company D," *Centerville Daily Iowegian*, August 21, 1917.
8. "Settle Down to Real Camp Life," *Semi-Weekly Iowegian*, July 2, 1917; "Released Three from Co. D. Ranks," *Semi-Weekly Iowegian*, July 9, 1917; "Company Got Various Gifts from Homefolk," *Centerville Daily Iowegian*, May 19, 1919; "Auto Tour Planned for Soldier Boys," *Semi-Weekly Iowegian*, August 2, 1917; "Company Tour Great Success," *Semi-Weekly Iowegian*, August 9, 1917; "County Picnic Great Success," *Semi-Weekly Iowegian*, July 23, 1917; "Make Comfort Bags for Company D Boys," *Semi-Weekly Iowegian*, July 19, 1917.
9. John H. Taber, *The Story of the 168th Infantry*, vol. 1 (Iowa City: State Historical Society of Iowa, 1925), 8–9; Great London Ovation Given," *Semi-Weekly Iowegian*, August 16, 1917; Marshall, *The American Heritage History of World War I*, 264 (see chap. 30, n. 1).
10. "Local Company Proud of Being Rainbows," *Centerville Daily Iowegian*, May 19, 1919.

11. "Company D Is Preparing to Go," *Semi-Weekly Iowegian*, August 16, 1917; "Big Demonstration for the Company D Men off to War," *Semi-Weekly Iowegian*, August 16, 1917; "Great Tribute of Farewell to Soldiers," *Semi-Weekly Iowegian*, May 14, 1917; "Farewell to Company D," *Semi-Weekly Iowegian*, August 20, 1917.
12. "President's Proclamation Sets in Motion Machinery of the Draft," *Semi-Weekly Iowegian*, July 2, 1917.
13. "Seven Points about Registration," *Semi-Weekly Iowegian*, May 24, 1917; "Twenty-Five Carnival Men Are Registered," *Semi-Weekly Iowegian*, May 24, 1917.
14. "Rumors May Resist the Registration," *Semi-Weekly Iowegian*, June 4, 1917; "Forty Four Jailed for Not Registering," *Semi-Weekly Iowegian*, June 7, 1917; "Claim Seditions Meetings Held," *Semi-Weekly Iowegian*, June 11, 1917; "Mothers and Wives Went to See Accused," *Semi-Weekly Iowegian*, June 11, 1917; "Thirty Seven Are All Free Men," *Semi-Weekly Iowegian*, October 29, 1917; "Louis Markeni Seeks Freedom," *Semi-Weekly Iowegian*, December 12, 1918; "Louis Markeni Taken by Federal Officers," *Semi-Weekly Iowegian*, December 19, 1918.
15. "Ready to Pick the New Army," *Semi-Weekly Iowegian*, July 19, 1917; "Lottery System Is Announced," *Semi-Weekly Iowegian*, July 19, 1917; "About 130 Were Rejected by Board," *Semi-Weekly Iowegian*, August 13, 1917; "Exemption Not Easily Secured," *Semi-Weekly Iowegian*, July 26, 1917; "First 128 to Appear Monday," *Semi-Weekly Iowegian*, August 2, 1917; "Buttons for Those Freed from Service," *Semi-Weekly Iowegian*, July 12, 1917.
16. "New Army Starts for Camp When Ten Leave Wednesday A.M.," *Semi-Weekly Iowegian*, September 3, 1917; "Give First Ten Farewell Send-off," *Semi-Weekly Iowegian*, September 3, 1917; "Farewell to Be Wednesday at Train," *Semi-Weekly Iowegian*, September 17, 1917; "Court Dismissed for Soldiers' Farewell," *Semi-Weekly Iowegian*, September 20, 1917; "Soldiers Farewell Was Impressive," *Semi-Weekly Iowegian*, September 20, 1917; "Nineteen Men Are to Leave Friday," *Semi-Weekly Iowegian*, April 1, 1918; "36 Soldiers to Go from Lancaster, Mo.," *Semi-Weekly Iowegian*, October 21, 1918; "Negroes to Go to Camp Dodge," *Semi-Weekly Iowegian*, October 8, 1917; "Chicken Supper for Soldiers," *Semi-Weekly Iowegian*, October 25, 1917; "Tell Soldiers Good-Bye," *Semi-Weekly Iowegian*, October 25, 1917; "Farewell for Colored Men," *Semi-Weekly Iowegian*, October 29, 1917.
17. David M. Kennedy, *Over Here* (New York: Oxford University Press, 1980), 162–63; Taber, *The Story of the 168th Infantry*, 8, 40, 61, 76–79, 85 (see chap. 31, n. 9); "Twenty U.S. Soldiers Killed, Wounded and Captured in Trench by Germans," *Semi-Weekly Iowegian*, November 5, 1917.
18. "3 Appanoose Co. Boys Killed in Action; 6 Wounded," *Semi-Weekly Iowegian*, March 11, 1918; Taber, *The Story of the 168th Infantry*, 91 (see chap. 31, n. 9); "Russell Selix Is Alive in France," *Semi-Weekly Iowegian*, April 1, 1918; "Another Soldier Is Alive,"

Semi-Weekly Iowegian, April 4, 1918; "Company D Pays in More Lives," *Semi-Weekly Iowegian*, March 21, 1918; "Chaplain's Letter Tells of Funeral," *Semi-Weekly Iowegian*, April 11, 1918.

19. "Judge Towner Tells House of Iowa's Fighting Heroes," *Semi-Weekly Iowegian*, Company D special section, May 19, 1919; Taber, *The Story of the 168th Infantry*, 128, 43 (see chap. 31, n. 9); William Manchester, *American Caesar: Douglas MacArthur, 1880–1964* (Boston: Little, Brown and Company, 1978), 85, 86–88.
20. "A Beautiful Rainbow Led Rainbow Div. to Victory," *Semi-Weekly Iowegian*, April 3, 1919.

Chapter 32

1. "Stamping out Pro Germanism in Iowa," *Semi-Weekly Iowegian*, November 12, 1917; "Iowa Mob Attacked German Adherents," *Semi-Weekly Iowegian*, December 27, 1917; "Alleged Pro-German Is Killed in Fight," *Semi-Weekly Iowegian*, September 9, 1918; "Warning Given to German Enemies Here," *Semi-Weekly Iowegian*, April 12, 1917; "Frieda Hempel Will Not Sing in Iowa," *Semi-Weekly Iowegian*, April 15, 1918; "Talk English or Not at All," *Semi-Weekly Iowegian*, May 27, 1918.
2. "Teacher Suspected as Pro-German," *Semi-Weekly Iowegian*, February 7, 1918; "Investigate Rumors of Pro-Germanism," *Semi-Weekly Iowegian*, April 4, 1918; "Mysterious Woman May Have Been Spy," *Semi-Weekly Iowegian*, April 16, 1917; "Court Plaster Was Being Peddled Here," *Semi-Weekly Iowegian*, August 13, 1917; "Remark about Soldiers Caused Speedy Arrest," *Semi-Weekly Iowegian*, April 30, 1917; "Women Arrested Serious Charge," *Semi-Weekly Iowegian*, September 12, 1918; "Women Reprimanded," *Semi-Weekly Iowegian*, September 16, 1918; "Slacker List Is Published," *Semi-Weekly Iowegian*, November 4, 1918.
3. "Plano Has a Mock Hanging," *Semi-Weekly Iowegian*, October 14, 1918; "Five Men Face Serious Charge," *Semi-Weekly Iowegian*, October 28, 1918; "Effigy Hanging Is Explained," *Semi-Weekly Iowegian*, October 31, 1918; "Yellow Paint Was Used on Fronts," *Daily Iowegian*, May 27, 1918.
4. "Organizing for Liberty Loan," *Semi-Weekly Iowegian*, March 7, 1918; "To Put Loan Over," *Centerville Daily Iowegian*, October 26, 1918.
5. "Liberty Posters Help Drive Here," *Centerville Daily Iowegian*, September 25, 1918; "Unique Window Display," *Centerville Daily Iowegian*, September 28, 1918.
6. "French Army Document," *Semi-Weekly Iowegian*, July 4, 1918; "Peach Stones Are Needed for Masks," *Semi-Weekly Iowegian*, October 21, 1918; "Moravia Sending in Many Peach Stones," *Semi-Weekly Iowegian*, October 21, 1918.

7. "Phip Wells," *Centerville Daily Iowegian*, Anniversary Issue, June 26, 1953; "Auctioneer One of Ten 50-Year Certificate Men," *Centerville Daily Iowegian*, December 13, 1952; "Shane Hill Game Gets Attention," *Centerville Daily Iowegian*, August 1, 1918; "Mystic—The Old Mystic Tigers…," untitled, *Centerville Daily Iowegian*, August 1, 1918; "Albia—The Old Shane Hill base ball club…," untitled, *Centerville Daily Iowegian*, August 1, 1918; "Clio—Holly Sowders and Walter Brumer…," untitled, *Centerville Daily Iowegian*, August 1, 1918; "Shane Hills [*sic*] Defeat Old Timers 12 to 4," *Centerville Daily Iowegian*, September 4, 1918.
8. "Vermin Proof Garments to France," *Semi-Weekly Iowegian*, March 4, 1918; "Colored Women Are Doing Their Share," *Centerville Daily Iowegian*, October 4, 1918; "Big Shipment for the Belgians," *Semi-Weekly Iowegian*, March 17, 1918; "Will Feed 1000 Soldiers Here," *Semi-Weekly Iowegian*, September 3, 1917; "Junior Red Cross School Plans Made," *Semi-Weekly Iowegian*, March 17, 1918; "School Hears from Orphan," *Semi-Weekly Iowegian*, April 18, 1918; "Red Cross to Have Old Clothes Drive," *Semi-Weekly Iowegian*, March 10, 1919; "Christmas Fund for Armenia," *Semi-Weekly Iowegian*, November 7, 1918.
9. "Soldiers in France Need More Books," *Semi-Weekly Iowegian*, November 7, 1918; "Making Service Flag for County," *Semi-Weekly Iowegian*, November 7, 1918.
10. "Americans on Marne Front Drive: Americans Advance Half Mile on Two Mile Front and Take Dominating Points," *Semi-Weekly Iowegian*, July 2, 1918; "30,000 Huns Captured: Soissons Falls before the Victorious Allies," *Semi-Weekly Iowegian*, July 19, 1918.
11. "More Interest in the Parade," *Semi-Weekly Iowegian*, July 25, 1918.
12. "Paraders Went to Mystic," *Semi-Weekly Iowegian*, August 29, 1918; "Centerville Patriots as They Paraded the Streets of Mystic," *Semi-Weekly Iowegian*, September 16, 1918.
13. "Centerville Parades Get into the Metropolitan Press," *Semi-Weekly Iowegian*, November 11, 1918; "Patriotic Parade Brought out Crowd," *Semi-Weekly Iowegian*, August 5, 1918; "Participants in Big Parade Are Praised," *Semi-Weekly Iowegian*, August 22, 1918; "Saturday Night Parade Attracted Large Crowd," *Semi-Weekly Iowegian*, August 26, 1918; "Parade Enjoyed by Large Crowd," *Semi-Weekly Iowegian*, September 2, 1918; "Hats off and Everybody Stand at Salute When Flags Pass Tonight," *Semi-Weekly Iowegian*, September 16, 1918; "Pageant Was Most Pleasing," *Semi-Weekly Iowegian*, September 16, 1918; "Sunday Demonstrations and Parades Witnessed by Thousands," *Semi-Weekly Iowegian*, October 7, 1918.
14. "Uncertain Rumors All Day Sunday," *Semi-Weekly Iowegian*, October 7, 1918.
15. "Centerville to Answer Kaiser," *Centerville Daily Iowegian and Citizen*, October 10, 1918; "Many Visitors Here Saturday," *Semi-Weekly Iowegian*, October 14, 1918.
16. "Centerville Parades Get into the Metropolitan Press," *Centerville Daily Iowegian*, November 4, 1918; "Germans Quit," *Semi-Weekly Iowegian*, November 7, 1918.

17. "People Wild with Delight," *Semi-Weekly Iowegian*, November 7, 1918; "End World War," *Semi-Weekly Iowegian*, November 11, 1918; "Hun Delegates Have Agreed to All Conditions—They Surrender by Signing Them," *Semi-Weekly Iowegian*, November 11, 1918; "Celebrations Are Under Way," *Semi-Weekly Iowegian*, November 11, 1918; "Local People Recall Fateful Nov. 11 1918," *Centerville Daily Iowegian*, November 11, 1957.
18. "Plans for Parade at 7:00 O'Clock," *Semi-Weekly Iowegian*, November 14, 1918; "Celebrations Till Late Hour," *Semi-Weekly Iowegian*, November 14, 1918; "Centerville Mayor Dies and Funeral Will Be on Tuesday Afternoon," *Centerville Daily Iowegian*, October 18, 1920.
19. "Memorial Dedication Impressive," *Centerville Daily Iowegian*, October 20 and 22, 1923; Gary Craver, "Oakland Cemetery Arch of Remembrance," *Daily Iowegian*, May 26, 2006.

Chapter 33

1. Gina Kolata, *Flu* (New York: Farrar, Straus and Giroux, 1999), 4, 12, 8–9, 11, 5.
2. "Much Sickness in School," *Centerville Daily Iowegian*, April 8, 1918; "Francis E. Underwood," *Daily Iowegian*, May 10, 1918; "Charles C. Bailey Death," *Daily Iowegian*, May 15, 1918; "Kirk McDonald Funeral," *Daily Iowegian*, May 3, 1918; "Death Comes as a Great Shock," *Daily Iowegian*, May 3, 1918; "Oliver Hiatt Dead Funeral Friday P.M.," *Daily Iowegian*, May 23, 1918.
3. "Used to Flush City Streets," *Centerville Daily Iowegian*, Centennial Edition, November 29, 1946.
4. "Flu Hits Business," *Semi-Weekly Iowegian*, September 12, 1918; "Spanish 'Flu' Spreads Rapidly," *Centerville Daily Iowegian*, September 20, 1918; "Epidemic Controlled at the Great Lakes," *Centerville Daily Iowegian*, September 24, 1918; Kolata, *Flu*, 15, 16; "Spanish Influenza Cases Total 22,992," *Centerville Daily Iowegian*, September 25, 1918.
5. "More Than the Usual Number of Evil Rumors," editorial, *Semi-Weekly Iowegian*, October 21, 1918; "Blame Germans for Influenza," *Centerville Daily Iowegian*, September 21, 1918; "Loafers Thick in Centerville Sun," *Semi-Weekly Iowegian*, October 21, 1918.
6. "Floyd Mincks Dies in Camp," *Centerville Daily Iowegian*, September 26, 1918; "Everett Traxler Death," *Semi-Weekly Iowegian*, October 7, 1918; "Byron Bradley Dies in Service," *Semi-Weekly Iowegian*, October 28, 1918; "Obituary: Guernsey," *Daily Iowegian and Citizen*, October 18, 1918; "Roscoe Guernsey Funeral," *Semi-Weekly Iowegian*, October 7, 1918; "Influenza Is Claiming Victims," *Semi-Weekly Iowegian*, October 14,

1918; "B.F. Thomasson Was Long Time Resident," *Semi-Weekly Iowegian*, October 7, 1918; "Influenza Is Claiming Victims," *Semi-Weekly Iowegian*, October 14, 1918.

7. "No Quarantine for Centerville," October 14, 1918; "Robert A. McKee Passed Away," October 14, 1918; "Robert A. McKee Funeral," *Semi-Weekly Iowegian*, October 14, 1918.
8. "Don't Go into Panic over Flu," *Semi-Weekly Iowegian*, October 17, 1918; "More Quarantines—Utah Is Closed," *Centerville Daily Iowegian*, October 10, 1918; "May Quarantine State to Stop Speed of Flu—Illinois Is Shut Tight," *Centerville Daily Iowegian*, October 15, 1918; "Des Moines to Be Quarantined," *Centerville Daily Iowegian and Citizen*, October 9, 1918; "Influenza Closing More Iowa Cities," *Semi-Weekly Iowegian*, October 10, 1918; "Quarantines Become General Properties," *Centerville Daily Iowegian and Citizen*, October 16, 1918; "Eighty-Four Towns in Iowa Have Influenza," *Semi-Weekly Iowegian*, October 14, 1918; "Governor Flu Bitten," *Centerville Daily Iowegian and Citizen*, October 19, 1918; "Entire State Is under Quarantine—All Speeches Cancelled," *Centerville Daily Iowegian and Citizen*, October 18, 1918; "Dr. Ingersoll Is Dead at Seymour," October 24, 1918.
9. "No Quarantine for Centerville," *Semi-Weekly Iowegian*, October 14, 1918; "Dr. B.F. Sturdivant to Mayo Institute," *Centerville Daily Iowegian and Citizen*, October 18, 1918; "Centerville under Quarantine Effective for Indefinite Period by Order Sec'y of State Board," *Centerville Daily Iowegian and Citizen*, October 18, 1918; "Anti-Spitting Notice," *Centerville Daily Iowegian and Citizen*, October 18, 1918.
10. "Stores Not Closed," *Centerville Daily Iowegian and Citizen*, October 18, 1918; "Doesn't Stop Parades," *Centerville Daily Iowegian and Citizen*, October 18, 1918; "Loafers Thick in Centerville Sun," *Semi-Weekly Iowegian*, October 21, 1918; "Midway News Stand and Lunch Room," advertisement, *Centerville Daily Iowegian and Citizen*, October 21, 1918; "Majestic," advertisement, *Centerville Daily Iowegian and Citizen*, October 18, 1918; "Flu Quarantine Is Practically Over," *Semi-Weekly Iowegian*, October 24, 1918; "Probably Will Lift Quarantine in City," *Semi-Weekly Iowegian*, October 24, 1918.
11. "Centerville Had Delicious Sunday," *Semi-Weekly Iowegian*, October 28, 1918; Appanoose County Death Records, book 4, County Recorder's Office, Appanoose Courthouse, Centerville, Iowa; Himie Voxman, interview with the author, September 5, 2002; Advertisements: for quinine, "As Influenza," *Semi-Weekly Iowegian*, December 25, 1919; for quinine, aspirin, Dover's Powders, "Spanish Influenza—What It Is and How It Should Be Treated," *Semi-Weekly Iowegian*, October 19, 1918; for Bulgarian Blood Tea, "Healing the Sick," *Centerville Daily Iowegian*, March 2, 1921; for Booth's Hyomei, "Relieves Catarrh in One Hour," *Semi-Weekly Iowegian*, September 29, 1912; for Men-Tho-Eze, "Prevent Spanish Influenza by Anointing Nose," *Semi-Weekly Iowegian*, November 26, 1919; for Chamberlain's Cough Remedy, "Few Escape," *Semi-Weekly Iowegian*, December 5, 1918; for Vick's VapoRub, "Druggists!

Please Note Vick's Vaporub Over Sold Due to Present Epidemic," *Semi-Weekly Iowegian*, October 28, 1918; for Begy's Mustarine, "Quick Action When Pneumonia Attacks," *Daily Iowegian*, November 7, 1919; for Foley's Honey and Tar, "Influenza? LaGrippe?" *Centerville Daily Iowegian and Citizen*, October 12, 1918; for United States Public Health Service, Rupert Blue, surgeon general, "'Spanish' Influenza 'The Flu' Three-Day Fever," *Semi-Weekly Iowegian*, October 21, 1918; "U.S. Health Service Issues Warning," *Semi-Weekly Iowegian*, December 2, 1918; "Need Fresh Air to Offset Influenza," *Semi-Weekly Iowegian*, October 10, 1918.

12. "Mayor Is Home from Meeting," *Semi-Weekly Iowegian*, December 12, 1918; "Will Post Flu Cards on Homes," *Semi-Weekly Iowegian*, December 5, 1918.
13. "Flu Decreases over 50 Per Cent… Raging Outside City," *Semi-Weekly Iowegian*, November 18, 1918; "Moulton Is Winner in Flight with Flu," *Semi-Weekly Iowegian*, December 23, 1918; "Much Influenza in Centerville… Physicians Very Busy… Whole Families Afflicted," *Semi-Weekly Iowegian*, December 5, 1918; "Flu Shuts Up Shop," *Semi-Weekly Iowegian*, December 2, 1918; "Donna Maulsby Death," *Semi-Weekly Iowegian*, December 12, 1918; "Tommy M. Quinn Is Pneumonia Victim," *Semi-Weekly Iowegian*, January 13, 1919; "Well-Known Young Man Passes Away," *Semi-Weekly Iowegian*, November 11, 1918; "Former Nurse Is Flu Victim," *Semi-Weekly Iowegian*, December 2, 1918; "Another Sad Death," *Semi-Weekly Iowegian*, October 14, 1918; "John H. Robey Is Pneumonia Victim," *Semi-Weekly Iowegian*, March 17, 1919; "Harry Mack Is Dead," *Semi-Weekly Iowegian*, November 21, 1918; "Popular Young Man Victim of Influenza," *Semi-Weekly Iowegian*, November 29, 1918; "C.C. Overton Has Passed Away," *Semi-Weekly Iowegian*, October 28, 1918.
14. "Four Deaths in Past 24 Hours… Mexican Boy Dies," *Semi-Weekly Iowegian*, November 25, 1918; "Death Comes to Bradley Home," *Semi-Weekly Iowegian*, November 11, 1918; Obituaries: Stella Burkhiser, *Centerville Daily Iowegian*, October 22, 1918; Henry Thornton, *Semi-Weekly Iowegian*, October 28, 1918; Mrs. James Sneddon, *Semi-Weekly Iowegian*, November 7, 1918; Albert McGuire, *Semi-Weekly Iowegian*, November 11, 1918; Mrs. Hjalmar Olson, *Semi-Weekly Iowegian*, November 14, 1918; Dick Stewart, *Semi-Weekly Iowegian*, December 9, 1918; Mrs. Samuel P. Lathum, *Semi-Weekly Iowegian*, December 9, 1918; Laverne E. Smith, *Semi-Weekly Iowegian*, December 9, 1918; Aaron Johnson, *Semi-Weekly Iowegian*, December 12, 1918; John Miliner, *Semi-Weekly Iowegian*, December 19, 1918; Jess Rogers, *Semi-Weekly Iowegian*, December 19, 1918; Kenneth Ray McCracken, *Semi-Weekly Iowegian*, January 9, 1919; Effie Viola Luse, *Semi-Weekly Iowegian*, February 27, 1919; Mrs. L.L. Titus, *Semi-Weekly Iowegian*, April 7, 1919; Nellie June Allen, *Semi-Weekly Iowegian*, March 24, 1919; "Mystic Still in Grip of the Flu," *Semi-Weekly Iowegian*, December 19, 1918; "Death of Carter Infant," *Semi-Weekly Iowegian*, January 16, 1919; "Two Anniversaries Marked by the Fry and Traxler Family," *Centerville Daily Iowegian*,

March 8, 1948; "Death of Wife Follows Husband," *Centerville Daily Iowegian and Citizen*, October 19, 1918; "Will J. Eddy Is Pneumonia Victim," *Semi-Weekly Iowegian*, November 4, 1918; "Daughters Follows Father in Death," *Semi-Weekly Iowegian*, January 6, 1919; "Triple Weeks Funeral Held," *Semi-Weekly Iowegian*, December 16, 1918; "Four Deaths in Past 24 Hours," November 25, 1918; "Five Deaths Reported Since Wednesday Noon," *Semi-Weekly Iowegian*, November 29, 1918; "Unionville Has Nine Funerals in One Day," *Semi-Weekly Iowegian*, November 18, 1918.

15. Appanoose County Death Records, book 4, p. 24–40; "Flu Is Crowding Local Hospitals," *Daily Iowegian*, February 5, 1920; "City Struggles with Epidemic of the Flu," *Daily Iowegian*, February 16, 1920; "Are Some Cases of Influenza in the City," *Daily Iowegian*, January 23, 1920; Kolata, *Flu*, 292; "Sleeping Sickness Makes Appearance in Appanoose County," *Semi-Weekly Iowegian*, March 27, 1919; Mrs. June Rouse (daughter of Mrs. Tissue), telephone interview with the author, April 23, 2007; "Sleeping Sickness in City," *Daily Iowegian*, January 31, 1921.

Chapter 34

1. Taber, *The Story of the 168th Infantry*, 274–77 (see chap. 31, n. 9); "Iowa Rainbow Boys on Their Way Home," *Semi-Weekly Iowegian*, April 21, 1919; "Company D All Tickled to Get Back into U.S.," *Semi-Weekly Iowegian*, April 28, 1919.
2. "The Welcome Home," *Semi-Weekly Iowegian*, May 8, 1919; "Big Reception for Returning Company D," *Semi-Weekly Iowegian*, April 24, 1919; "Give Money for Company D Welcome," *Semi-Weekly Iowegian*, May 1, 1919; "Club Room for Returned Yanks," *Semi-Weekly Iowegian*, January 30, 1919; "Furnishings Coming in for Soldier Club," *Semi-Weekly Iowegian*, February 3, 1919; "Club Room Is Open to Soldiers Here," *Semi-Weekly Iowegian*, February 13, 1919; "More Furnishings for Soldier Club," *Semi-Weekly Iowegian*, February 13, 1919; "More Interest in Soldier Club Room," *Semi-Weekly Iowegian*, February 13, 1919; "Club Room about Complete," *Semi-Weekly Iowegian*, February 20, 1919; "Soldiers' Club Is a Popular Place," *Semi-Weekly Iowegian*, March 17, 1919; "Will Make Rainbow Shields for Stores," *Semi-Weekly Iowegian*, May 1, 1919; "Big Victory Arch to Stay up Until Later Celebration," *Semi-Weekly Iowegian*, May 1, 1919; "Rainbow Buttons Going with Speed," *Semi-Weekly Iowegian*, May 1, 1919; "Welcome Parade Will Be Biggest Ever Held Here," *Semi-Weekly Iowegian*, May 8, 1919.
3. "To Dismiss Company as Soon as Parade Passes Reviewers," *Semi-Weekly Iowegian*, May 12, 1919.
4. Taber, *The Story of the 168th Infantry*, 278, 279, 280 (see chap. 31, n. 9); "How Parade Will Form before March," *Semi-Weekly Iowegian*, May 15, 1919; "Boys of Company D to Have Long Trip," *Semi-Weekly Iowegian*, May 8, 1919.

5. "Iowa's Famous Unit Is Pelted with Flowers as It Marches by in Review," *Semi-Weekly Iowegian*, May 15, 1919; "Special Train to Des Moines Next Saturday," *Semi-Weekly Iowegian*, April 28, 1919; "Expect Many Troops in Welcome Parade for Company D Boys," *Semi-Weekly Iowegian*, May 12, 1919; Taber, *The Story of the 168th Infantry*, 280–81 (see chap. 31, n. 9); "Last of the Long Journey to War and Back," *Semi-Weekly Iowegian*, May 19, 1919.
6. "Immense Crowd Greeted Them on Arrival," *Semi-Weekly Iowegian*, May 19, 1919; "Company D Has Much up Its Sleeve," *Semi-Weekly Iowegian*, January 27, 1919; "Even the Skies Honor Company D," *Semi-Weekly Iowegian*, May 19, 1919; "Professor Explains Saturday's Rainbow," *Semi-Weekly Iowegian*, May 19, 1919.
7. "Decorate as Never before for Soldiers," *Semi-Weekly Iowegian*, August 25, 1919; "Work of Decorating the City Is Begun," *Semi-Weekly Iowegian*, September 8, 1919; "Soldiers in Big Celebration," *Semi-Weekly Iowegian*, September 11, 1919.
8. "Sgt. Bernard Nelson Given French Cross by Col. J.E. McDonald," *Semi-Weekly Iowegian*, September 11, 1919; "Local Soldiers Will Get Victory Buttons," *Semi-Weekly Iowegian*, September 1, 1919; "Major Haynes and Nate Kendall Will Speak Here Sept. 11," *Semi-Weekly Iowegian*, August 28, 1919; "Airplane Will Be Here Victory Day," *Semi-Weekly Iowegian*, August 28, 1919; "Centerville Jammed by Huge Crowd Honoring Service Men," *Daily Iowegian*, September 11, 1919.
9. "Take Decayed Bone from Soldier's Leg," *Semi-Weekly Iowegian*, July 21, 1919; "Charles Forrest Harrison," obituary, *Centerville Daily Iowegian*, May 29, 1925; "Military Rites for Harry Pryde Here Thursday," *Centerville Daily Iowegian*, July 24, 1931; "Hobart," *Daily Iowegian*, April 14, 1955 (reference to George Wailes, dead in 1927 at thirty-three "from wounds"); "Benjamin Gedney A.E.F. Veteran Called by Death," *Centerville Daily Iowegian*, June 30, 1931; "John Stevens Dies, Tuesday," *Centerville Daily Iowegian*, May 30, 1959; "John Stevens," obituary, *Centerville Daily Iowegian*, June 1, 1959; "Many Veterans Still Suffering Effects of War," *Centerville Daily Iowegian*, August 1, 1924; "Omar Strickler Gassed," *Semi-Weekly Iowegian*, October 31, 1918; "Co. D Man Brought Home in a Basket," *Semi-Weekly Iowegian*, February 17, 1919; "Carroll Horn Was Wounded and Gassed," *Semi-Weekly Iowegian*, February 3, 1919; "Soldiers Tell of Experiences in Europe," *Semi-Weekly Iowegian*, June 9, 1919; "Recovers Voice Lost in Action in France," *Semi-Weekly Iowegian*, July 7, 1919; "Young Unionville Man near Death," *Centerville Daily Iowegian*, May 9, 1925; Bill Smallwood, interview with the author, February 23, 2007.
10. "Shock Victims Get Special Treatment," *Semi-Weekly Iowegian*, August 22, 1918; "Mental Unrest Is Cause for Worry," *Daily Iowegian*, September 18, 1919; "Sad Case of Service Man from Moulton," *Centerville Daily Iowegian*, August 27, 1924; "Found Young Man Seriously Ill," *Daily Iowegian*, August 15, 1921; "Harley Hopkins Suffers from Epileptic Attack," *Centerville Journal*, February 23, 1922; "Is No Trace of Chas.

Lee Stewart," *Centerville Daily Iowegian*, November 14, 1924; "Attempt to Escape from Institution May Prove Fatal," *Centerville Daily Iowegian*, November 17, 1923; "Little Hope for Callen's Recovery," *Centerville Daily Iowegian*, November 19, 1923; "Callen to Recover Is Believed Now," *Centerville Daily Iowegian*, November 24, 1923; "Carl Callen Dead Result of Injury," *Centerville Daily Iowegian*, December 3, 1923.

11. "Story against Red Unfounded," *Centerville Daily Journal*, November 14, 1922; "Sawyers Prominent in City and State," *Centerville Daily Iowegian*, March 22, 1922; "War Seen from Side of One in French Service," *Daily Iowegian*, December 17, 1921; "Like Heroes of Old They Return to Their Proud Home," *Semi-Weekly Iowegian*, May 19, 1919; "Harold Nelson at School," *Semi-Weekly Iowegian*, March 17, 1919; "Told of Some Siberian Ways," *Centerville Daily Iowegian*, February 21, 1925; "Howard Anderson Writes from Siberia," *Semi-Weekly Iowegian*, August 7, 1919; "Company D Vets Pay Tribute to General Glenn Haynes," *Centerville Daily Iowegian*, October 31, 1941; "Rainbow Store Opens on Square," *Daily Iowegian*, July 20, 1920; "Rainbow Ice Cream Parlor," advertisement, *Daily Iowegian*, July 20, 1920; "Centerville Boy Goes to New York for English Bride," *Daily Iowegian*, March 16, 1921.

12. "American Legion Post Is Organized," *Semi-Weekly Iowegian*, October 20, 1919; "Believe Will Be Winners of Murphy's Mug," *Centerville Daily Iowegian*, June 28, 1926; "Military Funeral for Pearl Gillis," *Daily Iowegian*, June 7, 1921; "Fred Young Who Died in France to Be Buried Here," *Daily Iowegian*, June 17, 1921; "Funeral for World War Hero Is Sunday," *Daily Iowegian*, July 21, 1921; "World War Hero to Rest in Native Land," *Daily Iowegian*, July 22, 1921; "Legion to Bury Two War Heroes at Exline," *Daily Iowegian*, July 23, 1921; "Bury Seymour World War Veteran Sunday," *Daily Iowegian*, July 23, 1921; "Unionville and Moravia Heroes Buried Sunday," *Daily Iowegian*, August 2, 1921; "Burgess Funeral Sunday Afternoon," *Daily Iowegian*, August 6, 1921; "Moulton Honors World War Hero," *Daily Iowegian*, August 22, 1921; "World War Hero Was Laid to Rest," *Daily Iowegian*, September 26, 1921; "Soldier's Body Home from France," *Daily Iowegian*, October 18, 1920; "Body of Seymour Soldier Arrives," *Daily Iowegian*, October 22, 1921; "Lieut. Larson Body Arrivems [*sic*] Funeral Monday," *Daily Iowegian*, November 13, 1920; "Hero's Body Brought Home," *Centerville Journal*, April 27, 1922; "Body of War Hero is Enroute [*sic*] Home," *Daily Iowegian*, August 18, 1921; "Veterans Plan Annual Banquet," *Centerville Daily Iowegian*, February 13, 1926; "Legion Posts to Help 'Buddies' in Securing Positions," *Daily Iowegian*, October 6, 1921; "Hobart Named as Janitor for Court House," *Centerville Daily Iowegian*, April 12, 1926; "Tables Turned: French Veteran Was Lost Here," *Centerville Daily Iowegian*, February 3, 1931; "Ex-Soldier Found Friends Here When Was in Distress," *Centerville Daily Iowegian*, March 26, 1923; "Takes Its Part in Memorial for the French," *Daily Iowegian*, May 29, 1920; "Start Local Drive for Belleau Funds," *Centerville*

Journal, February 7, 1922; "Belleau Memorial Drive Continues," *Centerville Journal*, February 14, 1922; "LaClede Banks on This City to Help Welcome Pershing," *Semi-Weekly Iowegian*, September 29, 1919; "General Pershing Spending Day in Des Moines," *Daily Iowegian*, January 7, 1920; "Des Moines Welcomes Gen. Pershing," *Centerville Daily Iowegian*, August 16, 1924; "Centerville Woman Was Neighbor to Pershings," *Centerville Daily Iowegian*, August 4, 1960; "Local Woman Has Spanked Pershing," *Semi-Weekly Iowegian*, September 23, 1918; "L.W. Orr of This City Was Schoolmate of General J.J. Pershing When He Was Just 'John' and a Poor Student at That," *Centerville Daily Iowegian*, March 29, 1933; "World War One," section in "Family Ancestors Who Served in the Wars of the United States of America," unpublished account compiled by Mary Joan Tunnell Richardson Seals, collection of Appanoose County Museum, Centerville; Joan Seals, interview with the author, June 27, 2001.

13. "Killed Three Hours before Armistice," *Semi-Weekly Iowegian*, June 23, 1919; "Sees End of the War from Front Trenches," letter from Private M.F. Houk, *Semi-Weekly Iowegian*, December 16, 1918; "Tells How Men Took News of Armistice," *Semi-Weekly Iowegian*, February 3, 1919; "Almost Killed as the War Came to an End," *Semi-Weekly Iowegian*, March 6, 1919; "Dancing Craze Engulfs Paris," *Semi-Weekly Iowegian*, April 17, 1919.
14. "Rainbow Division Made Best Showing of All U.S. Units," *Semi-Weekly Iowegian*, April 10, 1919; "Clemenceau Praises Soldiers of Rainbow," *Semi-Weekly Iowegian*, April 17, 1919; William Manchester, *American Caesar: Douglas MacArthur, 1880–1964* (Boston: Little, Brown and Company, 1978).
15. "Eight Years Ago and Today Differ as to Excitement," *Centerville Daily Iowegian*, November 11, 1926; "Bells Will Toll and Activities Stop One Minute," *Daily Iowegian*, November 8, 1920; "Stores Close Armistice Day," *Daily Iowegian*, November 7, 1921; "Fritz Haynes Raps Delay and Red Tape at Peace Council," *Semi-Weekly Iowegian*, May 8, 1919; "Recalls Early Hun Scheming," *Semi-Weekly Iowegian*, November 18, 1918.
16. William Butler Yeats, "The Second Coming," in *The Norton Anthology of World Masterpieces*, vol. 2 (New York: W.W. Norton and Company, 1999), 1420.

Chapter 35

1. Richard N. Current, T. Harry Williams, and Frank Freidel, *American History: A Survey*, vol. 1, 4th ed. (New York: Alfred A. Knopf, Inc., 1975), 461; "Official Ballot," *Semi-Weekly Iowegian*, October 8, 1917; "Big Jubilee over Closing of Saloons," *Semi-Weekly Iowegian*, December 28, 1915; "Will Celebrate the Closing," *Centerville Journal*,

December 30, 1915; Sage, *A History of Iowa*, 204 (see chap. 1, n. 5); "After Booze Dealers," *Semi-Weekly Iowegian*, April 16, 1915; "Bringing in Bootlegger," *Semi-Weekly Iowegian*, November 19, 1915.

2. Morison, *The Oxford History of the American People*, 237–38 (see chap. 16, n. 3).

3. "Banishment of J. Barleycorn Empties Jails," *Daily Iowegian*, April 26, 1920; "Rev. Mott Sawyers Has Long and Distinguished Church, YMCA Career," *Centerville Daily Iowegian*, August 23, 1938.

4. "Found Liquor but Still Was Elusive," *Daily Iowegian*, January 6, 1920; "Had Valuable Raisins Souring for Liquor," *Daily Iowegian*, January 7, 1920.

5. "Another 'Grappi' Raid," *Daily Iowegian*, May 1, 1920; "Officers Unearth Illitic [*sic*] Still in Mine near Mystic," *Daily Iowegian*, June 16, 1920.

6. "Was Carrying Grappi to a Trenton Joint," *Daily Iowegian*, September 29, 1920.

7. "Grappi Seizure Netted 13 Pints," *Daily Iowegian*, December 27, 1920; "Grappi Suspect Was Raided and Good Capture Made," *Daily Iowegian*, October 4, 1920.

8. "Mr. Webster Never Heard of 'Grappi,'" *Daily Iowegian*, May 10, 1920; "Held to Grand Jury," *Daily Iowegian*, October 6, 1920; Dale Jones, interview with the author, November 20, 2000; "Federal Agents Were Busy Here," *Centerville Daily Iowegian*, April 1, 1924.

9. "Still Found in Raid Made by Sheriff's Office," *Daily Iowegian*, October 9, 1920.

10. "Stills, Liquor and Mash Taken over Weekend," *Centerville Daily Iowegian*, May 26, 1924; "Liquor Raid Nets 300 Gallons Wine," *Daily Iowegian*, April 21, 1921; "Wine Supply of City Depleted by Officers' Raids," *Centerville Daily Iowegian*, January 3, 1924; "Playing Havoc with Home Brew Supplies," *Daily Iowegian*, June 27, 1921; "Officers Stage Big Booze Raid," *Centerville Daily Journal*, August 20, 1922; "Much Grappi Finds Way to Capital by Automobile Route," *Daily Iowegian*, July 14, 1921.

11. "Liquor Found in Search by Federal Agents," *Daily Iowegian*, February 11, 1921.

12. "Tests Show a Heavy Per Cent in Alcohol," *Daily Iowegian*, May 26, 1921; "They Answered the Call of the Grappi," *Daily Iowegian*, May 25, 1920; "Grappi Seizure Netted 13 Pints," *Daily Iowegian*, December 27, 1920; "Grappi Suspect Was Raided and Good Capture Made," *Daily Iowegian*, October 4, 1920; "Grappi and Still Found in Haul Made by Officers," *Daily Iowegian*, June 24, 1921; "Got Another Still," *Daily Iowegian*, July 16, 1921; "Says Grappi Sold in New York City," *Daily Iowegian*, July 18, 1921.

13. "Figures Indicate Some Booze Left," *Centerville Daily Iowegian*, December 28, 1923.

14. Dale Jones, interview with the author, November 20, 2000; "Booze Thieves in Sunday Night Raid Get Much Liquor," *Daily Iowegian*, April 11, 1921; "Destroying Booze Constables Nabbed in Recent Raids," *Daily Iowegian*, September 9, 1921; "Booze Spilling in Justice Court," *Daily Iowegian*, August 20, 1921; "Found Some

Grappi," *Daily Iowegian*, April 16, 1921; "Some Liquor Lost When Keg of Wine Sprung a Leak," *Daily Iowegian*, April 15, 1921; "Stills Turned into Junk Heap," *Centerville Daily Iowegian*, August 28, 1924.

15. "To War on Booze and Intoxicated Auto Drivers," *Centerville Daily Iowegian*, December 29, 1923; "Bootleggers Bottled Bond Was a Forgery," *Centerville Daily Iowegian*, January 31, 1928; "Offender Played Havoc with Wine," *Centerville Daily Iowegian*, March 5, 1924; "A Boozy Creek," *Centerville Journal*, February 9, 1922.
16. "Centerville Is Opium Center," *Centerville Journal*, May 30, 1922.
17. "Arrest Fred Taylor on Serious Charges of Dope Trafficking," *Daily Iowegian*, November 7, 1919.
18. "Office of Doctor Robbed of Opiates by Drug Addict," *Daily Iowegian*, August 16, 1921; "Drug Addicts Are Frequent Visitors Past Few Weeks," *Daily Iowegian*, August 23, 1921; "Dope Leak Here Officers Believe," *Centerville Daily Iowegian*, October 1, 1923; "Rob Office of Doctor: After Dope," *Centerville Daily Iowegian*, February 9, 1924; "Two Cases Stolen in Hunt for Narcotics," *Centerville Daily Iowegian*, February 25, 1924; "Doctor Victim of Narcotic Thieves," *Centerville Daily Iowegian*, April 7, 1924; "Asked to Explain Dope Possession," *Centerville Daily Iowegian*, June 5, 1925; "Dope Addicts Are Causing Doctors Much Annoyance," *Centerville Daily Iowegian*, December 14, 1928; "Drug Addict in Plea for Help to Conquer Habit," *Centerville Daily Iowegian*, February 13, 1924.
19. "Will Refuse Drugs to All Addicts," *Centerville Daily Iowegian*, September 27, 1923; "Find Some Dope Users in the City," *Centerville Daily Iowegian*, October 25, 1923; "Home Was Searched in Hunt for Dope," *Centerville Daily Iowegian*, November 2, 1923; "Drugs Versus Booze," editorial, *Centerville Journal*, March 28, 1922; "Narcotic Agents in City Again," *Centerville Daily Iowegian*, Janury 26, 1925.
20. "Jail for Drunks without Exception Is Mayor's Decree," *Centerville Daily Iowegian*, April 23, 1923; "Arrest Five Men for Intoxication," *Centerville Daily Iowegian*, October 4, 1922; "Week-End Disturbance," *Centerville Daily Iowegian*, September 24, 1923; "Wine and Women Bring Disaster," *Centerville Journal*, June 8, 1922; "Mistook Window for Door, Injured," *Centerville Daily Iowegian*, November 16, 1923; "Arrest Two on Liquor Charge," *Centerville Journal*, August 1, 1922; "Some Brought in for Intoxication," *Centerville Daily Iowegian*, February 2, 1924; "Says Wild Women Stole His Money," *Centerville Journal*, May 30, 1922; "Dooley Was Unruly," *Centerville Journal*, July 19, 1922; "Hold Corder to the Grand Jury," *Centerville Journal*, September 6, 1922; "Stiff Sentence in Liquor Case," *Centerville Daily Iowegian*, December 16, 1925; "Rates for Jail Lodgings High," *Centerville Daily Iowegian*, May 8, 1925.
21. "Bay Rum Is Used Both as Lotion and Intoxicant," *Centerville Daily Iowegian*, May 4, 1929.

22. "Three Tramps Stage Merry Bay Rum Jag," *Centerville Daily Iowegian*, February 21, 1928; "Found Rubbing Alcohol Has an Awful Effect," *Centerville Daily Iowegian*, September 7, 1928; "One Drunk Fined," *Daily Iowegian*, July 16, 1921.
23. "Filed His Way out of Jail Sentence," *Centerville Daily Iowegian*, February 7, 1923; "To Charge Three with Inebriacy," *Centerville Daily Iowegian*, December 10, 1923; "Gathered in Seven," *Daily Iowegian*, October 25, 1920; "Four to Appear in City Court," *Daily Iowegian*, December 5, 1921; "Bootlegging Charge," *Daily Iowegian*, March 28, 1921; "Week's Haul of Booze a Big One," *Centerville Journal*, February 9, 1922; "Drug Addict in Plea for Help to Conquer Habit," *Centerville Daily Iowegian*, February 13, 1924; "John Doe Is an Awful Bootlegger," *Centerville Daily Iowegian*, February 28, 1923.

Chapter 36

1. "Girl Shoots Six Bullets into the Body of Tony Matto," *Centerville Daily Iowegian*, June 16, 1920; "'I Want to See Him Dead, He Has Taken away My Honor' Girl Said According to Witness at Inquest," *Centerville Daily Iowegian*, June 17, 1920; "Scene of Centerville's Recent Tragedy," *Centerville Daily Iowegian*, June 20 (corrected by hand to June 21), 1920; "Scene of Centerville's Recent Tragedy," *Centerville Daily Iowegian*, June 20 (corrected by hand to June 21), 1920.
2. U.S. Bureau of the Census, "1920 Federal Census for Appanoose County"; U.S. Bureau of the Census, "1930 Federal Census of Peoria and Peoria County, Illinois"; Schwieder, *Black Diamonds*, 67–70 (see chap. 15, n. 2).
3. "Ettore Testo," *Centerville Daily Iowegian*, March 23, 1962; "Attilio Poli Taken at L.A.," *Centerville Daily Iowegian*, December 29, 1956; "Italian Day Great Success," *Semi-Weekly Iowegian*, May 27, 1917; Jesse M. Beck, "Italy Day," editorial, *Semi-Weekly Iowegian*, May 27, 1918.
4. Jesse M. Beck, "The Russo Case," editorial, *Centerville Daily Iowegian*, June 22, 1920; "Accused Girl's Father Tells His Story," *Daily Iowegian*, September 24, 1920; "Defendant Tells Her Story," *Centerville Daily Iowegian*, September 27, 1920; "Insanity and the Unwritten Law to Feature the Defense," *Centerville Daily Iowegian*, September 22, 1920.
5. "Negress Slayer Given Freedom," *Centerville Daily Iowegian*, March 10, 1923; Robert K. Beck, "Weekend Special: Publisher's Corner," *Centerville Daily Iowegian*, June 30, 1961; "Robert Kelly Wipes out Entire Family at Drum and Monkey Mine," *Semi-Weekly Iowegian*, September 16, 1919; "Pearl Traxler Murdered," *Centerville Journal*, June 8, 1916.
6. "Verdict in Murder Case," *Centerville Journal*, September 28, 1916.

7. "Black Hand Is Planted Here," *Semi-Weekly Iowegian*, November 4, 1918; "Another Arrest in DeZorzi Case," *Semi-Weekly Iowegian*, November 21, 1918; "Danna and Falzone Are to Be Tried," *Semi-Weekly Iowegian*, December 5, 1918; "Frank Danna Is Under Indictment," *Semi-Weekly Iowegian*, November 25, 1918; "Seeking Authors of 'Blackhand' Notes at Rathbun," *Semi-Weekly Iowegian*, July 7, 1919; "Death Note Fails to Scare Sheriff," *Centerville Daily Iowegian*, July 18, 1924; "Was Ordered to Place Money at Specified Spot," *Daily Iowegian*, October 25, 1920; "Black Hand Cases Coming," *Semi-Weekly Iowegian*, January 20, 1919.
8. "A Card Game Cause of Shooting Fracas," *Centerville Daily Iowegian*, Centennial Edition, November 29, 1946; "Throat Cut and Placed on Track," *Semi-Weekly Iowegian*, February 2, 1915; "Murder Remains Mystery," *Semi-Weekly Iowegian*, February 5, 1915; "Probable Murderers Are Taken," *Semi-Weekly Iowegian*, February 26, 1915; "Italian Shot from Ambush as He Left His Home in Early Morning Light; Died Soon After," *Centerville Daily Iowegian*, February 10, 1920; "Not Much to Work on in the Vinceri Case," *Centerville Daily Iowegian*, February 11, 1920; "Italian Murder Remains Much of a Mystery," *Centerville Daily Iowegian*, February 27, 1920; "State Presents Case against Russo Girl," *Centerville Daily Iowegian*, September 20, 1920.
9. "Conversations and Observations in the Court Room during the Russo Trial," *Centerville Daily Iowegian*, September 29, 1920; "Love Affairs of Carmela Russo Aired," *Centerville Daily Iowegian*, September 23, 1920; "One of Us Must Die Said Tony Matto," *Centerville Daily Iowegian*, September 25, 1920; "Russo Case Evidence Is All In," *Centerville Daily Iowegian*, September 29, 1920; "Will Ask Court to Issue Parole for Russo Girl," *Centerville Daily Iowegian*, October 4, 1920.
10. "Petitions in Store," *Centerville Daily Iowegian*, October 5, 1920.
11. "Carmela Russo Found Guilty by Jury," *Centerville Daily Iowegian*, October 1, 1920; "Petition Heading to Grant Pardon to Camelo [*sic*] Russo," *Centerville Daily Iowegian*, December 10, 1920; "Carmela Russo Marries; Goes to Prison," *Centerville Daily Iowegian*, October 13, 1920.
12. "Met Tragic Death Near Streepy," *Centerville Daily Iowegian*, June 8, 1923; "Death on Railroad Crossing May Be Probed Further," *Centerville Daily Iowegian*, June 16, 1923; "Mystery Surrounds John Swab Death; Dying When Found," *Daily Iowegian*, November 1, 1921; "Farris Killed by R.I. Train," *Centerville Journal*, March 16, 1922; "Mysteby [*sic*] Seen in Coal City Death," *Centerville Journal*, April 18, 1922; "Find Body of Miner Killed during the Night," *Centerville Daily Iowegian*, April 9, 1927; "Coroner's Jury Finds Weston Was Killed by Blow," *Centerville Daily Iowegian*, December 7, 1927.
13. "T. Montegna Kills Mexican in Quarrel," *Centerville Daily Iowegian*, June 2, 1921; "Ten Year Old Negro Girl Victim of Bullet Fired at Father in the Dark," *Centerville Daily Iowegian*, January 28, 1924.

14. "Seek Murderer of Wm. Hamilton," *Centerville Daily Iowegian*, August 22, 1921; "Indict Two for Hamilton Murder," *Centerville Daily Iowegian*, September 26, 1921; "Suspected of Slaying Hamilton," *Centerville Daily Iowegian*, October 5, 1921; "Hamilton Murder Case Is Closed," *Centerville Daily Iowegian*, December 7, 1921.
15. "Cincinnati Recluse Slain with Axe," *Centerville Daily Iowegian*, June 3, 1925; "Brother of Axe Murder Victim Writes Sheriff," *Centerville Daily Iowegian*, August 6, 1925; "Possible Leads to Solution of Murder Failed," *Centerville Daily Iowegian*, June 18, 1926.
16. "Tire Bursts Car Upsets Killing One," *Centerville Daily Iowegian*, August 9, 1920; "Visitor Hurt in Strange Manner Here Last Night," *Centerville Daily Iowegian*, May 19, 1927; "Much Concern Felt for Missing Man," *Centerville Daily Iowegian*, January 5, 1923; "Alleged Swindler Is Sought Here," *Centerville Daily Iowegian*, August 23, 1921; "Search Is on for Tony Sebben Who Lived Here," *Centerville Daily Iowegian*, May 15, 1924; "Three Bullets Lodged in Head and Still Lives," *Centerville Daily Iowegian*, January 11, 1921.
17. "Rough Stuff by the Toughs," *Centerville Daily Iowegian*, December 13, 1921.
18. "Rumors of Shots and Cries in Night," *Centerville Daily Iowegian*, September 22, 1923; "Held as Killer of Foe's Horses," *Centerville Daily Journal*, December 7, 1922; "Pool Hall Fined," *Semi-Weekly Iowegian*, October 16, 1919; "Women Engage in First Fight," *Centerville Journal*, July 30, 1922; "Women Had Bloody Hand to Hand Fight," *Semi-Weekly Iowegian*, July 5, 1917.
19. "Man Attacks Stepdaughter at Mine Thirty," *Centerville Journal*, July 28, 1922; "Kills Charge against Datto," *Centerville Journal*, July 29, 1922; "Seeks Divorce for Fifth Time," *Centerville Daily Journal*, October 4, 1922; "Gun Play Man to Grand Jury," *Centerville Daily Iowegian*, September 27, 1923; "Guilty, Was Verdict in Brodi Case," *Centerville Daily Iowegian*, November 23, 1923; "Prisoner Declares He Prefers 'Cemetair' to Iowa 'Penitent,'" *Centerville Daily Iowegian*, November 24, 1923; "Brodi Tried to Escape by Death," *Centerville Daily Iowegian*, December 19, 1923.
20. "Hold up Men Busy on Roads near the City," *Daily Iowegian*, November 30, 1921; "Held up and Beaten on the Public Highway," *Centerville Daily Iowegian*, January 17, 1923.
21. "Told His Story of a Hold Up," *Centerville Daily Iowegian*, May 24, 1924; "Holdup Near Thirty, Report," *Centerville Daily Iowegian*, March 6, 1926; "Was Attempted Holdup on No. Thirty Road," *Centerville Daily Iowegian*, March 30, 1926; "Women Work Forgery Gag Here Monday," *Daily Iowegian*, October 11, 1921; "More Bad Checks Are Appearing," *Centerville Daily Iowegian*, July 24, 1924; "Bullet Hit Auto but Occupants of Machine Unhrt [*sic*]," *Centerville Daily Iowegian*, August 2, 1924; "Threw Brick into Mike Buban Home," *Centerville Daily Iowegian*, November 17, 1923.
22. "Registered Mail Pouch Stolen at Depot," *Daily Iowegian*, March 21, 1921; "Seize Two in Chicago in $6,000,000 Thefts," *New York Times*, August 2, 1921, cited from

ProQuest Historical Newspapers, *The New York Times* (1851–2001), file 1857–Current.

23. "Hounds Seek Edwards Assailants," *Centerville Daily Iowegian*, October 11, 1921; "Seek Information Concerning Auto Driven by Crooks," *Centerville Daily Iowegian*, October 11, 1921; "After Bandits Who Shot Officer!" *Centerville Daily Iowegian*, November 7, 1921.
24. "Holding Two Men as Accomplices in Shooting of Edwards," *Centerville Daily Iowegian*, November 9, 1921; "Kennedy Fighting Extradition and May Win Battle," *Centerville Daily Iowegian*, November 10, 1921; "Accused Gunman Lost His Fight!" *Centerville Daily Iowegian*, November 19, 1921.
25. "Luke Kennedy Not Indicted," *Centerville Journal*, January 5, 1922; "Edwards List to Close Soon," *Daily Iowegian*, October 31, 1921; Gary Craver, Edwards's nephew, interview with the author, November 5, 2008; "Who's Who in the Egan and Hogan Gangs and How the Feud Between Them Arose," editorial section, *St. Louis Post-Dispatch*, March 30, 1923; "Egan Gang Exhibit for Philadelphia Fair," *St. Louis Post-Dispatch*, May 11, 1926; William J. Helmer and Arthur J. Bilek, *The St. Valentine's Day Massacre* (Nashville: Cumberland House Publishing Inc., 2004), 4, 275.

Chapter 37

1. "Grass Throwing Is New Prank," *Centerville Daily Iowegian*, August 27, 1924; "Young Vandals Trapped by Law," *Centerville Journal*, April 27, 1922; "After Those Who Plug the Fountain," *Centerville Daily Iowegian*, October 8, 1924; "Defacing Business Buildings," *Daily Iowegian*, November 17, 1920.
2. "After Those Who Mar Grave Stones," *Centerville Daily Iowegian*, May 22, 1924; "Youngsters Play Got on Nerve of Many Travelers," *Centerville Daily Iowegian*, September 3, 1921.
3. "Schooling for Beggars Here," *Centerville Daily Journal*, December 8, 1922; "Young People on Streets," *Semi-Weekly Iowegian*, October 11, 1912.
4. "Start Search for Missing Plano Boy," *Centerville Journal*, November 17, 1922; "Boy Back Home after Short Trip," *Centerville Daily Iowegian*, March 20, 1926; "Local Youth Is Reported Absent," *Centerville Daily Iowegian*, March 11, 1926; "Five Children in Sad Plight," *Centerville Daily Iowegian*, February 28, 1924; "Despondent Boy Dies," *Centerville Daily Iowegian*, March 17, 1925; "Child Suicides Increase," *Daily Iowegian*, November 16, 1921; "Children Suicides," *Centerville Daily Journal*, August 11, 1922; "Youths Causing Parents Concern," *Centerville Daily Iowegian*, August 16, 1924; "Daughter Returns Home after Trouble," *Centerville Daily Journal*, December 16, 1922.

5. "Move to Prevent Corner Loafing," *Centerville Daily Iowegian*, January 26, 1924; "Loafing Given a Severe Jolt," *Centerville Daily Iowegian*, February 27, 1924; "Flirtations and 'Pick Up' Dates Are Taboo Now," *Centerville Daily Iowegian*, May 1, 1924; "Traveling Romeos 'Shieking' [*sic*] Costly," *Centerville Daily Iowegian*, June 13, 1924; "Auto Shieks [*sic*] in Bad with Police," *Centerville Daily Iowegian*, June 6, 1924; "Car Romeos Will Get into Trouble," *Centerville Daily Iowegian*, June 6, 1924; "Picking Up Girls Dangerous Practice," *Centerville Daily Iowegian*, June 29, 1923; "Street Romeos Given Set-Back," *Centerville Daily Iowegian*, March 7, 1925; "Wedding Climax to Benedict Affair," *Centerville Daily Iowegian*, May 10, 1921; "Child Charges Local Man with Heinous Crime," *Centerville Daily Iowegian*, May 18, 1920; "Plano Man Held on Serious Charge," *Centerville Journal*, August 16, 1922; "Local Boy Faces Serious Charge," *Centerville Daily Journal*, August 6, 1922; "Charged with Crime against His Daughter," *Centerville Daily Iowegian*, February 2, 1920; "Window Peepekrs [*sic*] Landed in Jail," *Centerville Daily Iowegian*, December 14, 1920; "More Complaints on Window Peeper," *Centerville Daily Iowegian*, January 5, 1923; "Window Peeping Again Reported," *Centerville Daily Iowegian*, January 31, 1923; "Are Three Window Peepers in City Police Informed," *Centerville Daily Iowegian*, March 20, 1923; "Report Activity of Window Peeper," *Centerville Daily Iowegian*, October 26, 1923; "'Peeping Town' [*sic*] Is Reported in Town," *Centerville Daily Journal*, August 12, 1922.
6. "Horrors! Who Ever Thought Centerville Reeked with Crime and Arch Criminal," *Centerville Daily Iowegian*, July 7, 1921; "Why Is Centerville Known for Its Crimes?" *Centerville Journal*, March 21, 1922.
7. "Notice: Children Off Streets," *Centerville Daily Iowegian*, October 25, 1920; "Loafing Given a Severe Jolt," *Centerville Daily Iowegian*, February 27, 1924; "Flirtations and 'Pick Up' Dates Are Taboo Now," *Centerville Daily Iowegian*, May 1, 1924; "Business Men Insist on More Police Protection," *Centerville Daily Iowegian*, November 4, 1921.
8. "Night Police Pointing out Some Difficulties," *Centerville Daily Iowegian*, November 14, 1921; "Another Officer Added to Night Force of City," *Centerville Daily Iowegian*, November 8, 1921; "Much Negligence in Locking Doors," *Centerville Daily Iowegian*, September 17, 1920; "Clothing Store to Have Burglar Alarm," *Centerville Daily Iowegian*, December 28, 1920.
9. "To Keep Record of All Crimianls [*sic*] Captured in County," *Centerville Daily Iowegian*, October 17, 1921; "Finger Printing Outfit Arrives," *Centerville Daily Iowegian*, December 19, 1921; "Young Men Are Committing Crime," *Centerville Daily Iowegian*, November 18, 1921; "Youthful Crime," quoting Justice James C. Cropsey of the New York Supreme Court from article in *Eagle*, *Centerville Daily Iowegian*, August 12, 1924.
10. "Children Go to Orphan's Home," *Centerville Daily Iowegian*, December 15, 1920; "Deserted Children Taken to a Home," *Daily Iowegian*, September 23, 1920; "Youth in Toils of Law Can Tell Pitiful History," *Centerville Daily Iowegian*, December 20,

1921; "Whipping Child Brought a Fine," *Centerville Daily Iowegian*, July 24, 1924; "Exline Cruelty Case Filed in Court Here," *Centerville Journal*, October 27, 1922; "Small Girl in Poor Health Was Kept in Shed," *Centerville Daily Iowegian*, May 20, 1924; "Miners Demanding Ouster of Father of Abused Child," *Centerville Daily Iowegian*, May 22, 1924.

11. "Watching for Country Prowler," *Centerville Daily Iowegian*, August 27, 1925; "Aroused over Attacks of Unknown Man," *Centerville Daily Iowegian*, September 5, 1925; "Prowler Fined $50 by Mayor," *Centerville Daily Iowegian*, February 28, 1924; "Moravia to Watch for Bad Bandits," *Centerville Daily Iowegian*, May 28, 1921; "Moving to Stop Roadside Parties," *Centerville Daily Iowegian*, June 26, 1924; "Raiders Secured Big Booze Haul at Streepyville," *Centerville Daily Iowegian*, December 24, 1923; "Another Raid at Streepyville," *Centerville Daily Iowegian*, December 26, 1923; "Cincinnati Men Pay Third Visit to Streepyville," *Centerville Daily Iowegian*, December 27, 1923.

12. Jesse M. Beck, "Censoring the Movie," editorial, *Centerville Daily Iowegian*, February 9, 1921.

13. "Church Attendance Runs Too Low in Centerville," *Centerville Daily Iowegian*, February 15, 1923; "Commandments in Force in Centerville," *Centerville Daily Iowegian*, November 29, 1920; Himie Voxman, interview with the author, December 13, 2003.

14. "Back to Pre-War Code," *Centerville Journal*, January 12, 1922; "Arbuckle Is Indicted for Girls [*sic*] Death," *Daily Iowegian*, September 14, 1921; "Jack Pickford's Wife Has Mercury Poison," *Centerville Daily Iowegian*, September 9, 1920; "Wallace Reid Was Loser in Fight for Life," *Centerville Daily Iowegian*, January 19, 1923; "Death Is Slowly Sapping away Life of Barbara LaMarr," *Centerville Daily Iowegian*, November 16, 1925; "Taylor Murder Tale Is Probed," *Centerville Journal*, February 23, 1922; "Report Attempt to Slay Movie Star," *Centerville Daily Iowegian*, August 14, 1923; "Film Queens Questioned in Hollywood Shooting," *Centerville Daily Iowegian*, January 4, 1924; "Pola Negri Awaits a Paris Divorce," *Centerville Daily Iowegian*, November 15, 1929; "Pickford Divorce Case Up," *Centerville Daily Iowegian*, November 27, 1920; "Report Chaplin to Mary [*sic*] Again," *Centerville Daily Iowegian*, November 24, 1924.

15. "Norma Talmadge Death Recalls Centerville's Day in the Films," *Centerville Daily Iowegian*, December 27, 1957; "Centerville and Appanoose in the Movies," *Centerville Journal*, May 24, 1921; "Talmadge Company at Work Here," *Centerville Daily Iowegian*, May 23, 1921.

16. "Norma Talmadge Death Recalls Centerville's Day in the Films," *Centerville Daily Iowegian*, December 27, 1957; "A Daughter of Two Worlds," advertisement, *Centerville Daily Iowegian*, August 4, 1920; "She Loves and Lies," advertisement, *Centerville Daily Iowegian*, April 8, 1920; "The Branded Woman," advertisement, *Centerville Daily*

Iowegian, November 11, 1920; "A Lady in Love," advertisement, *Centerville Daily Iowegian*, July 22, 1920.

17. "Norma Talmadge Coming Sunday," *Centerville Daily Iowegian*, May 21, 1921; "Lincoln Harbold Had Far Flung Hog and Farm Operations," *Centerville Daily Iowegian*, February 28, 1969; "Centerville and Appanoose in the Movies," *Centerville Journal*, May 24, 1921; "'On Location' with Norma Talmadge," *Centerville Daily Iowegian*, May 28, 1921, courtesy of *Des Moines Daily Capital*; "Norma Here to Complete Her Picture," *Centerville Daily Iowegian*, May 24, 1921.
18. "Norma Talmadge Death Recalls Centerville's Day in the Films," *Centerville Daily Iowegian*, December 27, 1957.
19. "Calls Her Radiant Despite Rose Fever," *Daily Iowegian*, May 26, 1921; "Allergic Rhinitis," in *The Merck Manual*, 16th ed., ed. Robert Berkow, M.D. (Rahway, N.J.: Merck Research Laboratories, 1992), 326.
20. "Saw Norma Talmadge," *Centerville Daily Iowegian*, September 22, 1921; "Norma Talmadge Is Just Wholehearted Girl; Loves Her Work," *Centerville Daily Iowegian*, May 24, 1921; "Norma Here to Complete Her Picture," *Centerville Daily Iowegian*, May 24, 1921; Theda K. Long, "Reader Shares Picture Taken 52 Years Ago," *Centerville Daily Iowegian*, January 3, 1973; "Plano People Well Pleased with Film Folks," *Centerville Daily Iowegian*, May 26, 1921.
21. "'On Location' with Norma Talmadge," *Centerville Daily Iowegian*, May 28, 1921, courtesy of *Des Moines Daily Capital*; "Norma Talmadge Death Recalls Centerville's Day in the Films," *Centerville Daily Iowegian*, December 27, 1957.
22. "Picture Done Film Artists Return to East," *Centerville Daily Iowegian*, May 25, 1921.
23. "Photoplay Filmed in Appanoose Co. Released Soon," *Centerville Daily Iowegian*, September 13, 1921; "Talmadge Film Ready to Show," *Centerville Daily Iowegian*, October 10, 1921; "Film Produced in Appanoose Co. a Good Picture," *Centerville Daily Iowegian*, October 12, 1921; "Norma Talmadge in 'The Wonderful Thing': The Picture That Was Made at Bradley-Harbold Farm—Centerville—in 6 Reels," *Centerville Daily Iowegian*, October 12, 1921; "Big Crowds Seeing Picture," *Centerville Daily Iowegian*, October 14, 1921; "Clarence Brand of Plano Got into the Real Movies," *Centerville Daily Iowegian*, June 1, 1921.
24. "Saw Home Picture in Heart of China," *Centerville Daily Iowegian*, April 2, 1924.

Chapter 38

1. "The Payton Jazz Band…," untitled, *Centerville Daily Iowegian*, January 2, 1919; "Select Dance," advertisement, *Semi-Weekly Iowegian*, October 9, 1919; "Select Dance," advertisement, *Centerville Daily Iowegian*, October 28, 1919; "Jazz Music," editorial,

Centerville Journal, April 4, 1922; "Jazz Music Will Last a While Longer," *Centerville Daily Iowegian*, March 30, 1920.

2. "In This Land of Jazz," editorial, *Centerville Journal*, March 21, 1922.
3. "The Dance That's Different," advertisement, *Centerville Daily Iowegian*, May 1, 1920; "Schubert's Jazz Band," *Centerville Daily Iowegian*, February 25, 1920; "Ladies and Gentlemen... But Listen! Eddy's Famous 'Lightning Jazzadores' of Chicago, Ill.," advertisement, *Centerville Daily Iowegian*, July 2, 1920; "Hello Jazzbo," advertisement, *Centerville Daily Iowegian*, November 6, 1920; "Appealing Comedy Picture," *Centerville Daily Iowegian*, August 20, 1920; "New York Cabaret Reproduced in Big Film Coming Here," *Centerville Daily Iowegian*, September 7, 1920.
4. "Jazz Music Is Intoxicating," *Southern Iowa American*, September 29, 1925; "Says Jazz Era Responsible for Much Insanity," *Centerville Daily Iowegian*, April 25, 1925; "Sees a Great Menace in Modern Jazz Music," *Centerville Journal*, January 12, 1922; "Jazz Music Blamed," *Centerville Daily Iowegian*, December 31, 1920; "In This Land of Jazz," editorial, *Centerville Journal*, March 21, 1922.
5. "Official Rule Dancing Must Be within the Law," *Centerville Daily Iowegian*, January 11, 1923; "The Dance Problem," *Centerville Daily Iowegian*, January 12, 1923; "Dance Hall Was Ordered Closed," *Centerville Daily Iowegian*, March 31, 1924; "Sunday Night Dances Taboo," *Centerville Daily Iowegian*, October 17, 1921.
6. "Found Nothing Wrong," *Centerville Daily Iowegian*, July 18, 1921; "In This Land of Jazz," editorial, *Centerville Journal*, March 21, 1922; "Jazz Music," editorial, *Centerville Journal*, April 4, 1922.
7. "Charleston Dances the Rage Now Regardless of Censure or Praise," *Centerville Daily Iowegian*, January 23, 1925; "Wallie Whittington with His Charlestonians...," untitled, *Centerville Daily Iowegian*, December 7, 1925; "Black and White Revue," advertisement, *Centerville Daily Iowegian*, December 9, 1925; "Again Crowded Drake Theatre," *Centerville Daily Iowegian*, January 19, 1925; "Schaffners Syncopating Savages," advertisement, *Centerville Daily Iowegian*, January 13, 1926.
8. "Hubby Will Get Even with Wife," *Centerville Daily Iowegian*, March 1, 1924; "No Bobbed-Haired Teachers Wanted," *Centerville Daily Iowegian*, August 26, 1922; "Bobbed Heads a Mistake," *Centerville Daily Iowegian*, January 20, 1927; "Late Paris Modes," *Centerville Daily Iowegian*, December 2, 1920; "Says Clothes of Women 'Scandal,'" *Centerville Daily Iowegian*, March 3, 1924; "Sleeveless Gown Taboo in Local Catholic Church," *Centerville Daily Iowegian*, July 25, 1924; "Real Crusader after Bare Legs," *Centerville Daily Iowegian*, August 17, 1929; "Short Skirts Prompts a Local Statement," *Centerville Daily Iowegian*, Pictorial Edition, March 2, 1951, reprinted from *Centerville Daily Iowegian*, February 25, 1922; "Corsets Aid to Ideal Figure," *Centerville Daily Iowegian*, special spring number, March 21, 1924; "Madam X Reducing Girdle," advertisement, *Centerville Daily Iowegian*, July 8, 1924; "Miss Laura Jane Blaska

Demonstrating Cara Nome Toilet Preparations," advertisement, *Centerville Daily Iowegian*, March 22, 1928; "To the Ladies of Centerville," advertisement, *Centerville Daily Iowegian*, May 5, 1928; "The Elizabeth Arden Method," advertisement, *Centerville Daily Iowegian*, July 1, 1929; "3 Steps to Beauty by Helena Rubinstein," advertisement, *Centerville Daily Iowegian*, July 2, 1929; "Use Electricity and You Can Have a Hoover Sweeper," advertisement, *Semi-Weekly Iowegian*, December 25, 1919.

9. "Mrs. Thos. Goss Was Elected," *Semi Weekly Iowegian*, March 11, 1913; "Mrs. Thos. Goss Pres. School Board Dies," *Semi-Weekly Iowegian*, October 29, 1915; "Suffrage Wins in Appa.," *Centerville Journal*, June 8, 1916; "Women Have Full Rights by Proclamation," *Centerville Daily Iowegian*, August 26, 1920; "Women of Iowa Now Have Equal Rights with Men," *Centerville Daily Iowegian*, August 19, 1920; "Women Knew How to Register and Do It Quickly," *Centerville Daily Iowegian*, September 26, 1920; "Early Voters Were Many of Them Women," *Centerville Daily Iowegian*, November 2, 1920; "Five Women Are Drawn on the January Jury," *Centerville Daily Iowegian*, December 8, 1920; "Mrs. Mary Dershem First Woman to Serve on Jury," *Centerville Daily Iowegian*, January 11, 1921; "Three Women Sit on the Next Case," *Centerville Daily Iowegian*, January 12, 1921.

10. "Three Famous Women Flyers," *Centerville Daily Iowegian*, June 5, 1929; "Women Fliers Surpass the Men with Fortitude," *Centerville Daily Iowegian*, June 30, 1928; "Youngest Woman Attorney Admitted to California Bar," *Centerville Journal*, August 2, 1922; "Women Lawyers Matched in Fight to Convict Man Accused of Murder," *Centerville Daily Iowegian*, May 9, 1925; "She Makes Houses, Maps and Bridges," *Centerville Daily Iowegian*, August 18, 1921; "She Ranks High Among Engineers," *Centerville Daily Iowegian*, August 31, 1921; "An Engineer She'd Be," *Centerville Daily Iowegian*, February 12, 1927; "Women Executive in Attorney General's Office," *Centerville Journal*, September 9, 1922; "One of Uncle Sam's Able Young 'Portias,'" *Centerville Journal*, August 13, 1922; "Swimming the Channel," editorial, *Centerville Daily Iowegian*, August 9, 1926; "Second Woman Swims Channel," *Centerville Daily Iowegian*, August 28, 1926; "Women Fliers Surpass the Men with Fortitude," *Centerville Daily Iowegian*, June 30, 1928; "Girls Break Records in Athletic Meet," *Centerville Journal*, October 11, 1922; "Is Man's Supremacy on the Track Threatened by Feminine Runners?" *Centerville Daily Iowegian*, April 18, 1924; "Viscountess Anticipates Being First White Woman on Upper Nile," *Centerville Journal*, July 22, 1922; "Heads Society of Women Explorers," *Centerville Daily Iowegian*, October 6, 1926; "Aged Woman Wins Seat in Senate," *Centerville Journal*, November 22, 1922; "Women, Risen from Ranks, Have Important Jobs," *Centerville Daily Iowegian*, January 8, 1925; "First Woman Governor Is Inaugurated," *Centerville Daily Iowegian*, January 3, 1925; "Business as Usual, as Woman Bosses Wyoming," *Centerville Daily Iowegian*, January 17, 1925;

"Mary Garden Arrives to Direct Chicago Opera Co.," *Centerville Daily Iowegian*, October 29, 1921; "Amelia Naughton, First Woman Director to Lead Male Orchestra," *Centerville Journal*, August 27, 1922; "Appanoose County Sculptress Ranks with Leaders in Her Chosen Art," *Centerville Daily Iowegian*, April 17, 1925; "Louise Quist Subject of Article in Watch Magazine," *Centerville Daily Iowegian*, November 25, 1957; "Notable Career as Educator," *Centerville Daily Iowegian*, June 26, 1956; Dan Ehl, managing editor, "Centerville's Lee Regaining Respect in Physical Education," *Daily Iowegian*, March 19, 2002; "Goes to Good Chicago Position," *Centerville Daily Iowegian*, January 7, 1925; "Lady Doctor of Lancaster," *Centerville Daily Iowegian*, June 24, 1948; "Dr. Mary J. Bawden," advertisement, *Semi-Weekly Iowegian*, December 30, 1904; "Mrs. Longanecker," *Centerville Daily Iowegian*, Anniversary Issue, June 26, 1953; Dale Jones, interview with the author, August 2, 2002; Robert K. Beck, publisher emeritus. "School Endowment of $100,000 Dedicated to Mother," *Daily Iowegian*, May 14, 2002; "Mrs. Malaney, over 50 Years in the Printing Trade, Taken at 77 Years," *Centerville Daily Iowegian*, July 6, 1953; "Kendall Will Name Women for Office," *Centerville Daily Iowegian*, December 22, 1920.

11. "Divorce Record Is Appalling," *Southern Iowa American*, April 30, 1926; "Divorce Declared a Public Scandal," *Centerville Daily Iowegian*, May 25, 1920; "Birth Control Advocate Heard," *Centerville Daily Iowegian*, January 28, 1925; "Why Divorces So Much More Numerous Now," *Centerville Daily Iowegian*, November 8, 1920.
12. "Took Carbolic Acid," *Centerville Citizen*, March 7, 1900; "Driven to Desperation by Alleged Conduct of His Wife," *Semi-Weekly Iowegian*, January 5, 1904; "Denies Belonging to Suicide Club," *Semi-Weekly Iowegian*, May 21, 1907; "Woman Took Half Box Headache Capsules and Cannot Live Day Out," *Semi-Weekly Iowegian*, July 5, 1907; "Carbolic Acid Route," *Semi-Weekly Iowegian*, August 13, 1907; "Woman Felt Jilted Drank Lye Water," *Semi-Weekly Iowegian*, August 16, 1907; "Attempts Suicide and Will Recover," *Semi-Weekly Iowegian*, August 27, 1907; "Died on Train from Effects Lye Poison," *Centerville Daily Iowegian*, September 3, 1907; "Effects Lye Poison," *Semi-Weekly Iowegian*, September 3, 1907; "Attempt at Suicide Not Successful," *Semi-Weekly Iowegian*, October 8, 1909; "Left Five Children and Husband," *Semi-Weekly Iowegian*, July 16, 1912; "Attempt at Suicide," *Semi-Weekly Iowegian*, July 8, 1913.

Chapter 39

1. "Klu [*sic*] Klux Klan Split the City of Centerville Back in 1920's," *Centerville Daily Iowegian*, Pictorial Edition, March 2, 1951; Robert K. Beck, publisher emeritus, "What a Difference a Century Makes," *Daily Iowegian*, December 31, 1999.

2. "Klan Organizers Find Centerville Is Barren Field," *Centerville Daily Iowegian*, January 16, 1923; "The Three (Dis)Graces," Rushnell cartoon, *Centerville Daily Iowegian*, January 24, 1923.
3. Mott R. Sawyers, "The K.K.K. in Centerville," *Centerville Daily Iowegian*, January 20, 1923; Charles DePuy, "Dr. Mott Calls at the Iowegian Office," *Centerville Daily Iowegian*, November 27, 1962.
4. Mott R. Sawyers, "Let Us Be Americans," *Centerville Daily Iowegian*, February 3, 1923.
5. "Why I Do Not Oppose the Ku Klux Klan," *Centerville Daily Iowegian*, February 2, 1923; "Gave Address on Why I Do Not Oppose the Ku Klux Klan," *Centerville Daily Iowegian*, February 5, 1923.
6. "Ku Kluxers Seek to Organize Here," *Centerville Daily Iowegian*, July 7, 1923.
7. "Klu [*sic*] Klux Klan Split the City of Centerville Back in 1920's," *Centerville Daily Iowegian*, Pictorial Edition, March 2, 1951.
8. "Centerville, Iowa, Needs Klan," *Arkansas Traveller*, October 15, 1923.
9. "Klan Paper Says City Is in Need of Organization," *Centerville Daily Iowegian*, October 20, 1923; "Race Prejudice Is Admitted in Klan Official Speech," *Centerville Daily Iowegian*, October 25, 1923; "Days of the Ku Klux Klan in Iowa," *The Iowan* (summer 1964), 3 and 4; Kay Johnson, "Ku Klux Klan in Iowa" (master's thesis, Graduate College, University of Iowa, June 9, 1967).
10. Higham, *Strangers in the Land*, 308 (see chap. 27, n. 5); "May Have Typhus Outbreaks over Entire Country," *Centerville Daily Iowegian*, February 19, 1921; "Bomb Kills at J.P. Morgan Co. Offices," *Centerville Daily Iowegian*, September 16, 1920; "Are United on a Large Bomb Plot Theory," *Centerville Daily Iowegian*, September 17, 1920.
11. "Find Plans for May Day Demonstration," *Centerville Daily Iowegian*, April 26, 1921; "Militia Stops Rioting of Strikers," *Centerville Daily Iowegian*, November 16, 1921; "Ottumwa Is Quiet with Troops Present," *Centerville Daily Iowegian*, November 17, 1921; "Budding Revolution in U.S. Is Nipped," *Centerville Daily Iowegian*, January 3, 1920.
12. "Dangerous Radical Literature Spreads Poison among People," editorial, *Centerville Daily Iowegian*, June 11, 1923; "Klan and I.W.W. Literature Here," *Centerville Daily Iowegian*, February 14, 1924.
13. "'Red' Literature Flooding Mails," *Centerville Daily Iowegian*, June 9, 1923.
14. "Give Helping Hand to Foreign Born in America," *Centerville Daily Iowegian*, October 28, 1921.
15. Higham, *Strangers in the Land*, 270–77 (see chap. 27, n. 5); Black, *War against the Weak*, 187–90 (see chap. 27, n. 5); Morison, *The Oxford History of the American People*, 234–35 (see chap. 16, n. 3).
16. "Legion Men—Friends of Glenn C. Haynes Try to Put over Belated Denial," *Cincinnati Review*, June 26, 1924.

Chapter 40

1. "Are Indications Klan Organizing," *Centerville Daily Iowegian*, March 20, 1924.
2. "Fiery Crosses at Cincinnati," *Centerville Daily Iowegian*, March 24, 1924.
3. "Klan Paper Is Well Circulated," *Centerville Daily Iowegian*, April 8, 1924; "Klan Used Plane," *Centerville Daily Iowegian*, May 10, 1924; "Distributed Klan Paper," *Centerville Daily Iowegian*, May 12, 1924; "Flaming Crosses Again Appear," *Centerville Daily Iowegian*, April 10, 1924; "Excitement When Crosses Burned," *Centerville Daily Iowegian*, April 11, 1924.
4. "Progressive G.O.P. Runs Convention," *Cincinnati Review*, July 3, 1924; "Jurors Were Asked If Interested in Law Enforcement," *Centerville Daily Iowegian*, April 29, 1924; Glenn Reed, Americanograms, *Southern Iowa American*, September 18, 1924; "Most Colossal Effort…," untitled, *Southern Iowa American*, microfilm 64A, categorized under "Miscellaneous," no date, Drake Free Public Library, Centerville, Iowa; J. Roy Wright, "Says Jurors Should Believe in Law Enforcement Policy," letter to the public, *Centerville Daily Iowegian*, April 30, 1924; "Qualifications of Jurors," *Centerville Daily Iowegian*, April 30, 1924.
5. "Progressive G.O.P. Runs Convention," *Cincinnati Review*, July 3, 1924; "One Reader Tells Convention Story," *Cincinnati Review*, July 3, 1924; Glenn Reed, Americanograms, *Southern Iowa American*, October 4, 1924.
6. "Lest We Forget: The Ku Klux Klan and Sympathizers," pamphlet (n.p., n.d.), *Southern Iowa American*, microfilm 64A, categorized under "Miscellaneous," no date, Drake Free Public Library, Centerville, Iowa; "Rev. Frank E. Peterson, Local Lutheran Pastor, Disowns Lincoln League," *Southern Iowa American*, March 18, 1925; Robert K. Beck, publisher emeritus, "Klan Turmoil Mirrored the Country," *Ad-Express/Iowegian*, February 23, 2001.
7. "Sermon Preached by Rev. Mott Sawyers Last Sunday on the Coming Election," *Centerville Daily Iowegian*, April 3, 1925; Mott R. Sawyers, "I Am an American," *Centerville Daily Iowegian*, May 16, 1925; "Ministers Endorse Citizens Ticket," advertisement, *Southern Iowa American*, March 28, 1925.
8. "Anti-American Lecturer Advises Violence: Would Influence Foreigners against Officers of Law," *Cincinnati Review*, August 14, 1924; "Kluckers Klean Kounty," *Mystic Telegram*, November 6, 1924; masthead, *Southern Iowa American*, September 20, 1924; Robert Beck, publisher emeritus, "The Iowegian Versus the Ku Klux Klan," *Ad-Express/Iowegian*, February 25, 2000; "Centerville Journal Plant Is Purchased—Will Be a Daily," *Cincinnati Review*, August 21, 1924; "Stockholder List," *Southern Iowa American*, October 8, 1924, microfilm 64A, Drake Public Library, Centerville, Iowa; "Centerville's New Daily Greets Readers First Time Today—Platform," *Southern Iowa American*, September 17, 1924.

9. "Brick Was Harder Than This Negro's Head," *Southern Iowa American*, December 13, 1924; "Koonce's Column: Room for But One Flag," *Southern Iowa American*, November 24, 1924; "Another Chink Killed in N.Y. Tong War," *Southern Iowa American*, October 14, 1924; "A Good Program for Americans," *Cincinnati Review*, August 14, 1924; Americanograms, *Southern Iowa American*, December 3, 1924.
10. "Requests a Klan Burial Service," *Mystic Telegram*, October 9, 1924; "Klan Funeral Held at Mystic," *Southern Iowa American*, November 3, 1924; "Klan Funeral Excites Much Local Interest," *Southern Iowa American*, February 10, 1925.
11. "Appanoose Klan Holds Another Out-Door Meet," *Cincinnati Review*, July 3, 1924; "Dr. Geo. P. Rutledge Gives Klan Lecture," *Cincinnati Review*, July 17, 1924; "Klan Meeting," *Centerville Daily Iowegian*, July 29, 1924; letter from KKK executive committee to its members, *Southern Iowa American*, September 1, 1924, microfilm 64A, Drake Free Public Library, Centerville, Iowa; "Ku Klux Klan Meets Near Iconium Church," *Southern Iowa American*, September 17, 1924; "Klan Lecture at Moravia Tonight," *Southern Iowa American*, October 23, 1924; "Moravia Host to Thousands at Klan Meet," *Southern Iowa American*, October 25, 1924; "Jamboree at Moulton Draws Large Crowd," *Southern Iowa American*, October 10, 1924; "Public Lecture," advertisement, *Centerville Daily Iowegian*, October 7, 1924; "Estimated 7,000 Visitors on Thursday Night," *Centerville Daily Iowegian*, October 10, 1924; "Klan Holds Large Meet Near Moulton," *Southern Iowa American*, October 16, 1924.
12. "Appanoose Klan Holds Another Out-Door Meet," *Cincinnati Review*, July 3, 1924.
13. "Klan Burns Crosses in Neighboring Towns," *Southern Iowa American*, December 3, 1924; "Numa," *Centerville Daily Iowegian*, December 4, 1924.
14. "White Robed Men Brought Gift to Family in Need," *Centerville Daily Iowegian*, May 16, 1924.
15. "Ku Klux Klan Gives an Italian Family $100.00," *Southern Iowa American*, October 1, 1924; James Miller, "The Hooded Order in Appanoose County, Iowa" (honors thesis, University of Iowa May 1996), 1; "Klan Makes $100 Donation," *Mystic Telegram*, October 2, 1924; "Ku Klux Klan Gives to Needy," *Southern Iowa American*, November 24, 1924; Americanograms, *Southern Iowa American*, November 29, 1924; "Thanks to the K.K.K," *Southern Iowa American*, November 29, 1924.
16. "Klan Gives Toys to Bring Cheer," *Southern Iowa American*, December 24, 1924; "Klan Makes Donation to Seymour Family," *Southern Iowa American*, January 24, 1925; "Cincinnati," *Southern Iowa American*, December 3, 1924.
17. "Ku Klux Klan Presents Minister with $50 Purse," *Cincinnati Review*, September 12, 1924; "Confidence Church Remembered by Klan," *Southern Iowa American*, October 29, 1924; "Klan Gives Fifty Dollars to M.E. Church," *Southern Iowa American*, November 8, 1924; "Krusaders Make Gift to Church," *Southern Iowa American*, March

2, 1925; "Klan Makes Donation to Rev. W.O. Jones," *Southern Iowa American*, March 10, 1925; "Klan Gives Purse Numa Churches," *Southern Iowa American*, November 3, 1924; Gail Tuttle, letter to the author, June 30, 2006; Gail Tuttle, letter to the author, July 7, 2006; Gail Tuttle, interview with the author, July 20, 2006.

Chapter 41

1. "Anti-Klan Advertisement," *Centerville Daily Iowegian*, August 6, 1924; "Thursday Night Brought Big Crowd," *Centerville Daily Iowegian*, August 8, 1924; "Paid Advertising," *Centerville Daily Iowegian*, August 11, 1924; "Cincinnati," *Centerville Daily Iowegian*, August 14, 1924; "From One Who Was There," *Mystic Telegram*, August 14, 1924; "Anti-Klan Meeting," *Mystic Telegram*, August 14, 1924; "Plano," *Centerville Daily Iowegian*, August 20, 1924; "Notice," advertisement, *Centerville Daily Iowegian*, August 28, 1924; "Anti-Klan Lecture," advertisement, *Centerville Daily Iowegian*, September 10, 1924; "Anti-Klan Meetings," *Centerville Daily Iowegian*, October 17, 1924.
2. "Cincinnati Review Answers Anti-Americans," advertisement paid for by *Cincinnati Review*, in *Centerville Daily Iowegian*, August 7, 1924; "Notice!" Dr. W.B. Miller statement in *Centerville Daily Iowegian*, November 4, 1924; "Predicted Wilkinson Attack Made," *Southern Iowa American*, November 1, 1924; "Sitting Pretty," *Cincinnati Review*, September 5, 1924; "Peter Has Cooled off a Little," *Mystic Telegram*, September 4, 1924; Glenn Reed, Americanograms, *Southern Iowa American*, November 6, 1924; "Agnessen Double-Crosses Self," *Southern Iowa American*, October 14, 1924; "Pete Agnessen May Be Deported," *Mystic Telegram*, August 21, 1924; "Old Soldiers Are Forgers According to Pete Agnessen," *Cincinnati Review*, September 5, 1924; "G.A.R.'s Ask Agnessen's Deportation," *Cincinnati Review*, August 21, 1924; "Right off the Griddle," *Cincinnati Review*, August 14, 1924; "Slimy Serpent Still Spreads Vile Slush," *Southern Iowa American*, January 19, 1925.
3. "J.J. Frankel Fires Negro Who Reported Russo Dress Theft," *Cincinnati Review*, July 10, 1924; Glenn Reed, Americanograms, *Southern Iowa American*, November 3, 1924; "J.J. Frankel Insulted Mystic Girl in His Store by Vile Insinuations," *Cincinnati Review*, August 7, 1924; "J.J. Frankel has been advertising a 'closing out' sale…," untitled, *Southern Iowa American*, November 22, 1924; "They Say," *Mystic Telegram*, December 4, 1924.
4. "Southern Iowa American Will Start Soon," *Cincinnati Review*, September 5, 1924; Taylor McCoy, letter to the editor, *Southern Iowa American*, September 19, 1924, microfilm 64A, Drake Public Library, Centerville, Iowa; Amos Carr, letter to the editor, *Southern Iowa American*, September 12, 1924, microfilm 64A, Drake Free Public Library, Centerville, Iowa; "It will be remembered…," untitled, *Southern*

Iowa American, September 26, 1924, microfilm 64A, Drake Free Public Library, Centerville, Iowa; "The reason that the atmosphere in the courthouse…," untitled, letter without signature or address, *Southern Iowa American*, October 31, 1924, microfilm 64A, Drake Free Public Library, Centerville, Iowa.

5. "Koontz Klean Koal," advertisement, *Southern Iowa American*, September 17, 1924; "Eat at the American (Formerly Northside) Café When in Centerville. Kool Klean Komfortable," advertisement, *Cincinnati Review*, August 7, 1924; "K.K. Kutlery: Shaw's Hardware," advertisement, *Southern Iowa American*, March 5, 1925; "Only 2 Days More Free Pirate Hats…," untitled, E.K. Elledge Co. advertisement, *Cincinnati Review*, August 21, 1924; "Clark's Specials for Wednesday…," untitled, advertisement, *Southern Iowa American*, October 14, 1924; "Clark's Grocery: 100 percent Effecient [*sic*]," *Cincinnati Review*, August 14, 1924.
6. "'100% Filling Station Service.' Collins Filling Station," advertisement, *Southern Iowa American*, January 28, 1925; "The Cincinnati Bakery," H.L. Adams advertisement, *Southern Iowa American*, February 20, 1925.
7. Robert K. Beck, publisher emeritus, "Klan Turmoil Mirrored the Country," *Ad-Express/Iowegian*, February 23, 2001; Dale Jones, interview with the author, December 24, 2000.
8. "Election Today One of the Old Fashioned Type," *Centerville Daily Iowegian*, June 2, 1924; "Clash Occurred Among Political Workers on Street," *Centerville Daily Iowegian*, June 2, 1924; "Quiet Evening of Election Day," *Centerville Daily Iowegian*, June 3, 1924; "Cincinnati Side of Scrap Here," *Centerville Daily Iowegian*, June 3, 1924; "Election Day Affair Is Ended," *Centerville Daily Iowegian*, June 11, 1924; "Attorney Howell Gathers Evidence," *Mystic Telegram*, June 12, 1924; "A Correction," *Mystic Telegram*, June 12, 1924.
9. A.C. Miller, "The fight, at Numa…," untitled, letter to the editor, *Cincinnati Review*, August 7, 1924, found in *Southern Iowa American* collection, microfilm 64A, Drake Free Public Library, Centerville, Iowa; "Men Threatened after Meeting at Moulton Saturday," *Southern Iowa American*, August 21, 1924; "Some Disturbance at Klan Meeting," *Southern Iowa American*, October 3, 1924; "Rumor Says Was a Lively Time," *Centerville Daily Iowegian*, October 6, 1924; "'White Mule' Makes a Complete Jackass of Ceterville [*sic*] Citizen," *Mystic Telegram*, October 9, 1924; "Anti-Klan Invader Is Repulsed," *Southern Iowa American*, October 9, 1924; "Stephen A. Martin," photograph and caption, *Southern Iowa American*, October 10, 1924.
10. "Sunshine Mine Camp Raided Sat. Night," *Southern Iowa American*, December 8, 1924; "Johnny Delmar Makes Statement," *Centerville Daily Iowegian*, December 9, 1924.
11. "One Fined—Other Stands Trial," *Centerville Daily Iowegian*, December 9, 1924; "Johnny Delmar Makes Attack on Publisher," *Southern Iowa American*, December 9, 1924.

12. "More Fighting on Corner Square and Gun Pulled," *Centerville Daily Iowegian*, December 9, 1924; "Near Rioting in Centerville This Afternoon," *Southern Iowa American*, December 9, 1924; "Proceed Carefully in Disturbances," *Centerville Daily Iowegian*, December 10, 1924; Glenn Reed, Americanograms, *Southern Iowa American*, December 10, 1924; "Arrests Being Made in Cases," *Centerville Daily Iowegian*, December 11, 1924; "Witnesses Give Version of Fight," *Centerville Daily Iowegian*, December 18, 1924.
13. Jesse M. Beck, "Street Fighting," editorial, *Centerville Daily Iowegian*, December 19, 1924; "Klu [*sic*] Klux Klan Tore at Vitals of Community," *Centerville Daily Iowegian*, Pictorial Edition, March 2, 1951; Linda Jacobs Green interview with the author, August 14, 2007; Ralph Newcomer, interview with the author, August 14, 2007.
14. "Fire Destroys Purity Bakery," *Southern Iowa American*, February 2, 1925; Glenn Reed, Americanograms, *Southern Iowa American*, February 2, 1925; "Garage Burned This Morning," *Southern Iowa American*, February 4, 1925; "Comment by Others: The Klan Cycle in Williamson; St. Louis Globe-Democrat," *Centerville Daily Iowegian*, April 28, 1925; "Herrin Fearing More Trouble in Recent Arrests," *Centerville Daily Iowegian*, July 7, 1926.
15. "Gun Permits Are Being Withdrawn," *Centerville Daily Iowegian*, December 10, 1924; "Search of All Occupants of Pool Halls for Guns," *Centerville Daily Iowegian*, December 11, 1924; Sam Carpenter Jr., son of Sam Carpenter, Sunshine Coal Company owner, interview with the author, January 11, 2012.

Chapter 42

1. "First Gun Is Fired in City Contest Today," *Southern Iowa American*, February 25, 1925; Glenn Reed, Americanograms, *Southern Iowa American,* February 25, 1925; "Two Tickets Are Placed in Field for City Jobs," *Centerville Daily Iowegian*, February 25, 1925.
2. Glenn Reed, Americanograms, *Southern Iowa American*, January 27, 1925.
3. Glenn Reed, Americanograms, *Southern Iowa American*, March 9, 1925; Glenn Reed, Americanograms, *Southern Iowa American*, March 13, 1925.
4. "Lincoln League Nominated; Resolutions Express Its Purposes," *Centerville Daily Iowegian*, March 14, 1925; "'Lincoln League' Ticket Filed Late Saturday," *Southern Iowa American*, March 16, 1925.
5. Glenn Reed, Americanograms, *Southern Iowa American*, March 16, 1925; "Republican City Ticket Withdrawn from Race—Strong Resolutions," *Southern Iowa American*, March 18, 1925; "Some Revelations about That So Called 'Republican' Ticket," *Centerville Daily Iowegian*, March 18, 1925.

6. J. Roy Wright, "The Ku Klux Klan and the Jew," *Southern Iowa American*, March 18, 1925; J. Roy Wright, "The Ku Klux Klan and the Roman Catholics," *Southern Iowa American*, March 19, 1925; J. Roy Wright, "The Klan and the Colored Race," *Southern Iowa American*, March 17, 1925.
7. "Jim Keller's Record against Law Enforcement," *Southern Iowa American*, March 25, 1925; "Frank Payne's City Council Paving Policy," *Southern Iowa American*, March 24, 1925; Glenn Reed, Americanograms, *Southern Iowa American*, March 24, 1925; Iowa Southern Utilities Company, "Following Are Copies Given Today to Another Newspaper Correcting Statements Made in It Affecting Our Company," *Centerville Daily Iowegian*, March 24, 1925; "William S. Bradley Writes Open Letter to J. Roy Wright Protesting against Misrepresentation and Defaming Character," *Centerville Daily Iowegian*, March 24, 1925; "Manager of the Iowa Southern Utilities Co. Releases Account of Threat Made against Company," *Centerville Daily Iowegian*, March 23, 1925; "The Dark Doings of Frank Payne, and Co.," *Southern Iowa American*, March 23, 1925; "Old Ring Continues Their 'Wringing,'" *Southern Iowa American*, Extra! edition, March 23, 1925; "'Old Ring' Makes Desperate Effort to Force C'ville Merchants to Endorse 'Liquor' League," *Southern Iowa American*, March 24, 1925; "Frank Payne, Beck, and Staley and Special Privileges," *Southern Iowa American*, March 21, 1925; "Why the Staleys Are Promoters of the Liquor League," *Southern Iowa American*, March 20, 1925; "Campaign of Appaling [*sic*] Misrepresentations Personal Attacks and Calumny Comes to Close—Summary of Outstanding Events," *Centerville Daily Iowegian*, March 28, 1925; "Extra: Warrant Issued for Arrest of McConville," *Southern Iowa American*, March 28, 1925; "McConville Case Was Dismissed," *Centerville Daily Iowegian*, April 4, 1925; J.H. Watson, "The McConville Case," *Centerville Daily Iowegian*, April 6, 1925; "Immigration Dept. Says McConville Is U.S. Citizen," *Centerville Daily Iowegian*, March 30, 1925.
8. Bert Davidson, E.C. Ellis, J.W. Powell, Albert Eckman, Mrs. Alice Vinzant, Lincoln Knapp and Albert Weston, Citizens Ticket advertisements, *Southern Iowa American*, March 25, 1925; Jim Keller, Alva Ratliff, Will Bashaw, Geo. B. Ogle; Louis Anderson, J.B. Bruckshaw, E.J. Riepe, Oscar Bergstrom, advertisements for the Citizens Ticket, *Centerville Daily Iowegian*, March 27, 1925; "Lincoln League Ticket, Resolutions," *Centerville Daily Iowegian*, March 18 and 24, 1925; "Stop! Look! Listen!" *Centerville Daily Iowegian*, March 23, 1925; "Lincoln League Ticket Has Men You Know and Whom You Trust," *Centerville Daily Iowegian*, March 24, 1925; "Don't Mark Wrong O on Your Ballot—Mark 'O' as Shown Here," *Centerville Daily Iowegian*, March 27, 1925; "Lincoln Leaguers Hold Negro Political Meeting," *Southern Iowa American*, March 25, 1925; "City Registration Boards Announced Many to Register," *Centerville Daily Iowegian*, March 13, 1925; "Registration Is Reported Heavy," *Centerville Daily Iowegian*, March 20, 1925.

9. "Lincoln League Endorsement," *Centerville Daily Iowegian*, March 26 and 27, 1925; "Lincoln League Endorsements: Too Late for Insertion in the Regular List," *Centerville Daily Iowegian*, March 27, 1925; "Lincoln League Endorsement," second list, *Centerville Daily Iowegian*, March 28, 1925; "More Endorsers: Some That Came Too Late for the Saturday [March 28] Paper," *Centerville Daily Iowegian*, March 28, 1925.
10. "Abraham Lincoln—The Man of the Ages," advertisement, *Centerville Daily Iowegian*, March 18, 1925.
11. "Election Notice," *Centerville Daily Iowegian*, March 25, 1925; Jesse M. Beck, "The Election," editorial, *Centerville Daily Iowegian*, March 30, 1925; "Heaviest Vote in City's History Is Present Indication," *Centerville Daily Iowegian*, March 30, 1925; Glenn Reed, Americanograms, *Southern Iowa American*, March 30, 1925.
12. "Little Betting on Results of City Election," *Centerville Daily Iowegian*, March 27, 1925; "Warning against Election Scraps," *Centerville Daily Iowegian*, March 25, 1925; Glenn Reed, Americanograms, *Southern Iowa American*, April 1, 1925.
13. "Centerville Election '25," election results, *Centerville Daily Iowegian*, March 31, 1925; "Lincoln League Wins in Monster Vote," *Centerville Daily Iowegian*, March 31, 1925; "Lincoln League Victory Brought a Celebration," *Centerville Daily Iowegian*, March 31, 1925; "City Election Results in Election of Keller—4189 Votes Cast," *Southern Iowa American*, March 31, 1925.

Chapter 43

1. "Lincoln League Win Election," *Southern Iowa American*, March 31, 1925; "Lincoln League Wins in Monster Vote," *Centerville Daily Iowegian*, March 31, 1925; "Lincoln League Victory Brought a Celebration," *Centerville Daily Iowegian*, March 31, 1925; Jesse M. Beck, "Election Day Conduct," editorial, *Centerville Daily Iowegian*, April 4, 1925; "City Election Results in Election of Keller—4189 Votes Cast," *Southern Iowa American*, March 31, 1925.
2. Jesse M. Beck, "Charity for All," editorial, *Centerville Daily Iowegian*, April 4, 1925; Glenn Reed, Americanograms, *Southern Iowa American*, April 2, 1925.
3. "A Question," *Centerville Daily Iowegian*, April 1, 1925; "Another Question," *Centerville Daily Iowegian*, April 3, 1925; "Our Announcement," editorial, *Southern Iowa American*, April 27, 1925; "More Mud," *Mystic Telegram*, April 30, 1925; "And He Said: 'Speak unto the People That They Go Forward,'" *Southern Iowa American*, May 2, 1925; "Glenn Reed Has Again Taken Charge of the Cincinnati Review," advertisement, *Centerville Daily Iowegian*, June 9, 1925; Cincinnati Column, *Centerville Daily Iowegian*, June 22, 1925; "J.M. Beck and the Iowegian Held to View," *Hawkeye X-Ray*, November 16, 1925;

"The Hawkeye X-Ray," advertisement, *Hawkeye X-Ray*, November 16, 1925; "Toughs and the Iowegian Condemned," *Hawkeye X-Ray*, August 27, 1925; Cincinnati Column, *Centerville Daily Iowegian*, January 26, 1926; Cincinnati Column, *Centerville Daily Iowegian*, May 25, 1926; Cincinnati Column, *Centerville Daily Iowegian*, May 12, 1926; "Cincinnati Printing Plant Sold to Missouri Man," *Southern Iowa American*, May 11, 1926; Cincinnati Column, *Centerville Daily Iowegian*, May 12, 1926.

4. "McDonald at Sioux City," *Centerville Daily Iowegian*, September 2, 1925; "Rev. J. Roy Wright Died Unexpectedly through Ill Health," *Centerville Daily Iowegian*, August 4, 1928.
5. "Dr. E.J. Shook," KKK advertisement, *Southern Iowa American*, June 10 and 11, 1925; Robert Beck, publisher emeritus, "Klan Turmoil Mirrored the Country… Ku Klux Klan Split the Community," *Ad-Express/Iowegian*, February 23, 2001; Louie Scott, "Dr. Shook Moved," editorial, *Southern Iowa American*, September 15, 1925; "Farewell for Dr. E.J. Shook," *Centerville Daily Iowegian*, September 18, 1925; "Farewell for Beloved Pastor," *Southern Iowa American*, September 18, 1925.
6. "Our Announcement," editorial, *Southern Iowa American*, April 27, 1925; "The Southern Iowa American Has Passed…," untitled, full-page advertisement, *Southern Iowa American*, September 14, 1925; "Peter Hansen Says…," untitled, advertisement, *Southern Iowa American*, January 19, 1925; "345 New Subscriptions for the American Thus Far This Week—3000 Now," *Southern Iowa American*, October 23, 1924; "A Classified Ad Gets Quick Results," *Southern Iowa American*, October 15, 1924; "A Classified Ad will sell…," untitled, advertisement, *Southern Iowa American*, October 14, 1924; "The Southern Iowa American Cooperative Profit Sharing Salesmanship Club," advertisement (two-page spread), *Southern Iowa American*, June 22 and 25, 1926; "American to Give Almost $4,000 in Prizes," *Southern Iowa American*, June 22, 1926; "Salesmanship Campaign Well Under Way," *Southern Iowa American*, June 29, 1926.
7. "Seeks $25,000 in Counter Claim," *Centerville Daily Iowegian*, January 18, 1927; "Continuance in Scott Case," *Centerville Daily Iowegian*, February 5, 1927; "Settlement in Newspaper Case," *Centerville Daily Iowegian*, May 17, 1927.
8. "Notice K.K.K.," meeting advertisement, *Centerville Daily Iowegian*, September 1, 1928; "Notice K.K.K.," meeting advertisement, *Centerville Daily Iowegian*, May 3, 1929; "Dr. E.E. Bamford Made Victim of Sharp Practice," *Centerville Daily Iowegian*, November 13, 1925; "Dr. Bamford Finds Widespread Plot Operating," *Centerville Daily Iowegian*, November 14, 1925; "Affair between Reed and Cowboy Aired in Court," *Centerville Daily Iowegian*, August 18, 1925; "Heacock Pleads Being Guilty of Plain Assault," *Southern Iowa American*, August 19, 1925; "Assault Case on Trial Today," *Southern Iowa American*, August 18, 1925; "Slay Woman Temperance Worker," *Centerville Daily Iowegian*, September 8, 1925; John W. Tobin, *Tobin Tales* (Iowa City: Penfield Books, 1986), 103; "War within Indiana Klan Bared by Girl's Charges against Leader,"

Centerville Daily Iowegian, April 9, 1925; "D.C. Stephenson Trial July 6th," *Centerville Daily Iowegian*, June 27, 1925; "Find Stephenson's Little Black Box," *Centerville Daily Iowegian*, July 23, 1927.

9. "Pulitzer Prize to Paper Which Opposed Klan," *Centerville Daily Iowegian*, May 4, 1926.
10. Jesse M. Beck, "Newspapers in Centerville," editorial, *Centerville Daily Iowegian*, September 7, 1926; Robert K. Beck, "Memoirs," unpublished, 1997, collection of the Beck family; Raymond Rick, interview with the author, August 20, 2002; Name withheld, interview with the author, August 20, 2002; Rick Bowers, *Superman Versus the Ku Klux Klan* (National Geographic Books, 2012), Stetson Kennedy footnote, 74.

Chapter 44

1. "Today Opening of the Winter Radio Season," *Centerville Daily Iowegian*, October 1, 1924; "Radio: Radio Telephony," *Centerville Journal*, April 11, 1922.
2. "Radio: Radio Telephony," *Centerville Journal*, April 11, 1922; "Wireless Stations Hear Grand Opera," *Daily Iowegian*, November 17, 1921; "Wireless Stations Are Springing up in Centerville," *Daily Iowegian*, May 14, 1921.
3. "Journal Will Have Radio 'Colyum'; Amateurs Asked to Report Stations," *Centerville Journal*, April 6, 1922; "Radio: Hints on Aerial Mast Construction," *Centerville Journal*, May 9, 1922; "Farmers Now Get Markets by Radio," *Centerville Journal*, March 7, 1922; "Listened to Band Concert in Milwaukee," *Daily Iowegian*, December 1, 1921; "Gets His Sunday Sermon by Radio," *Centerville Journal*, March 28, 1922; "Journal Had First Radio," *Centerville Journal*, April 6, 1922; "Radio Popularity Hit Here about Year 1922," *Centerville Daily Iowegian*, Pictorial Edition, March 2, 1951; "Majestic Radio Set Installed," *Centerville Journal*, April 11, 1922.
4. "First National Bank Installs Radio Broadcasting Station," *Centerville Journal*, April 13, 1922; "Radio Broadcasting News: 'WDAX' Heard Over Big Area," *Centerville Journal*, July 16, 1922; "First National Is First," *Centerville Journal*, April 20, 1922.
5. "Send out Wireless Concert and News from Journal Office," *Centerville Journal*, April 20, 1922; "Huge Crowds Enjoy Radio Concert from Journal Office," *Centerville Journal*, April 25, 1922; "Majestic Orchestra Plays Accompaniment to Voices by Radio," *Centerville Journal*, April 25, 1922.
6. "Radio Broadcasting News: Kansas Hears WDAX Station," *Centerville Journal*, July 30, 1922; "Radio Broadcasting News: WDAX Breaks Record Four Times in Week," *Centerville Journal*, August 13, 1922; "Will Broadcast Kid Band Program," *Centerville Journal*, September 20, 1922; "WDAX Broadcast Band Concert," *Centerville Journal*, July 21, 1922; "Sharp Hears Radio thru Bed Springs," *Centerville Journal*, September 29, 1922.

7. "Radio Station Is Dead: No License," *Centerville Daily Iowegian*, December 21, 1923.
8. "Primary Returns by Radiophone," *Centerville Journal*, June 6, 1922; "President Heard over the Radio," *Centerville Daily Iowegian*, April 22, 1924; "New Kennedy Model XV: All Night Radio Party," advertisement, *Centerville Daily Iowegian*, November 1, 1924; Jesse M. Beck, "Millions Will Hear It," editorial, *Centerville Daily Iowegian*, February 18, 1925; "Will Broadcast Inauguration," *Centerville Daily Iowegian*, February 27, 1925; "Thousands Hear the [not legible] of the President," *Centerville Daily Iowegian*, March 4, 1925.
9. "Daily Radio Program," *Centerville Daily Iowegian*, September 29, 1924; "Radio Owner in Enviable Record," *Centerville Daily Iowegian*, November 17, 1925; "Heard Station in Mexico City," *Centerville Daily Iowegian*, March 12, 1924; "Local Radio Fans Were Able to Hear Foreign Stations," *Centerville Daily Iowegian*, November 25, 1925.
10. "Local Radio Fan Says Heard England," *Centerville Daily Iowegian*, November 30, 1923; "Local Radio Fans Were Able to Get Stations Abroad," *Centerville Daily Iowegian*, November 26, 1924; "Radio Listners [*sic*] Received London Program Monday," *Centerville Daily Iowegian*, February 5, 1929.
11. "Centerville Was Broadcasting in Spite of Storm," *Centerville Daily Iowegian*, June 8, 1924; "To Take Radio Set into Gypsum Mine for Test," *Centerville Daily Iowegian*, March 3, 1925; "Radio Experiment Staged Tonight," *Centerville Daily Iowegian*, March 4, 1925; "Experimet [*sic*] with Radio Successful," *Centerville Daily Iowegian*, March 5, 1925; Jesse M. Beck, "Great Is Radio," *Centerville Daily Iowegian*, November 9, 1927.
12. "Fine Radio for Iowa University," *Centerville Daily Iowegian*, February 2, 1924; "WOI Program," *Centerville Daily Iowegian*, March 25, 1924; "WOI Radio Program," *Centerville Daily Iowegian*, March 29, 1924; "University to Conduct Laboratory Test April 15," *Centerville Daily Iowegian*, March 17, 1928; "Nerve Impulse Sounds Heard Over Radio," *Centerville Daily Iowegian*, April 16, 1928; "First Act of 'Aida' to Be Broadcasted from KDKA," *Centerville Journal*, November 5, 1922; "Radiophone Theatre Is Latest Innovation," *Centerville Journal*, October 10, 1922; "Fashion Talks, Adventure Stories and Bedtime Stories Told from the Westinghouse—Radio Corporation Stattion [*sic*] WJZ," *Centerville Journal*, August 6, 1922; "Follies Will Be on the Air," *Centerville Daily Iowegian*, September 26, 1927; "Movie Stars to Broadcast," *Centerville Daily Iowegian*, March 23, 1928; "Girl Whistler Who Lived Here Will Broadcast," *Centerville Daily Iowegian*, February 7, 1924; "Several Heard Whistler Girl," *Centerville Daily Iowegian*, February 8, 1924; "Several Iowans Booked to Win at Drake Event," Centerville Daily Iowegian, April 25, 1932; "World's Series," Luther Radio Company advertisement, *Centerville Daily Iowegian*, October 3, 1924; "Radio Operated by Light Current First Time Here," *Centerville Daily Iowegian*, October 7, 1924; "Radio Carries World Series," *Centerville Daily Iowegian*, October 4, 1927; Dale Jones, interview with the author, October 4, 2000; "S. Centerville Enjoying Radio," *Centerville Daily Iowegian*, August 2, 1928; "Are You Going to See

the Big Fight?" Durhams Radio Service advertisement, *Centerville Daily Iowegian*, September 20, 1927; "Broadcasting of Bout Starts 8 Local Time," *Centerville Daily Iowegian*, September 22, 1927; "Radio Dealers Make Provision for Listners [*sic*]," *Centerville Daily Iowegian*, September 22, 1927.

13. "Stone Coffin of Tut Is Revealed," *Centerville Daily Iowegian*, February 6, 1924; "Tombs Raided for the Spring Styles," *Centerville Daily Iowegian*, March 2, 1923; "They're Blaming Old Tut for This," *Centerville Daily Iowegian*, March 12, 1923; "Now Egyptian Print and Bag to Match," *Centerville Daily Iowegian*, May 25, 1923; "King Tut Styles for Women Arrive," *Centerville Daily Iowegian*, March 22, 1923.
14. "Darrow-Bryan Clash at Famous Scopes Trial Is Described by AP Writer Who Covered Trial," *Centerville Daily Iowegian*, March 14, 1938; John R. Bittner, *Mass Communication: An Introduction* (Englewood Cliffs, N.J.: Prentice-Hall, Inc., 1983), 122; Dale Jones, interview with the author, October 4, 2000; Mott R. Sawyers, "Science and Religion," *Centerville Daily Iowegian*, January 22, February 7, 19 and 26, March 12, 1927; Mott R. Sawyers, "Know the Truth," *Centerville Daily Iowegian*, September 18 and October 23, 1926; "Science Sermons at Presbyterian Prove Popular," *Centerville Daily Iowegian*, January 25, 1927.
15. "Parade Monday Afternoon and Meeting Tonight," *Centerville Daily Iowegian*, April 13, 1926; "Parade Monday Vowed Need of Improved Roads," *Centerville Daily Iowegian*, April 13, 1926.
16. "These Slogans Were Winners in Roads Parade," *Centerville Daily Iowegian*, April 14, 1926; "Eloquent Plea for Good Roads," *Southern Iowa American*, April 13, 1926; "Station PAVE Dismantled after Fine Program," *Centerville Daily Iowegian*, April 14, 1926; "Heavy Voting in Centerville on Paving Proposal," *Centerville Daily Iowegian*, April 14, 1926; "When You Hear Dem Whistles Blowin,'" *Southern Iowa American*, April 13, 1926.
17. "County Goes 2 to 1 for Paving," *Centerville Daily Iowegian*, April 15, 1926; "Mud or Pavement? That's for You to Decide When You Cast Your Vote on November 6th," *Centerville Daily Iowegian*, October 27, 1928; "Paving Is Started on West Road," *Centerville Daily Iowegian*, August 20, 1926; "Pavement Laid from Corydon to Appanoose Line," *Centerville Daily Iowegian*, July 30, 1929; "Automobile Traveled at Speed of 93 Miles Per Hour on Paving West of Centerville Friday, Today," *Centerville Daily Iowegian*, March 31, 1928.

Chapter 45

1. "Speed Giant Sets New Record," *Centerville Daily Iowegian*, April 20, 1928; "Mauretania May Be Near Record of New Bremen This Voyage," *Centerville Daily Iowegian*, August 7, 1929; "Three Local People Aboard Steamer in an Atlantic Race," *Centerville Daily Iowegian*, January 11, 1929; "Vegetable Trains on Rock Isalnd [*sic*] Speeding Through

Here to East," *Centerville Daily Iowegian*, December 24, 1928; "Rock Island Crack Trains thru Here at Greater Speed," *Centerville Daily Iowegian*, March 7, 1928; "Star of Screen Passes Through," *Centerville Journal*, November 28, 1922; "Is Rumor of Super Train," *Centerville Daily Iowegian*, December 11, 1925; "Pola Negri in Centerville on Way for Body," *Centerville Daily Iowegian*, August 27, 1926; "Funeral Train of Valentino in Centerville," *Centerville Daily Iowegian*, September 3, 1926; Charles DePuy, Around the Town, August 1, 1951; Emily W. Leider, *Dark Lover* (New York: Farrar, Straus and Giroux, 2003), 386.

2. Jesse M. Beck, "Up in the Air," editorial, *Semi-Weekly Iowegian*, July 27, 1909; "The Year '09 in the World at Large," *Semi-Weekly Iowegian*, December 31, 1909; "Giant Aircraft to Start Home Tues. Morning," *Semi-Weekly Iowegian*, July 7, 1919; "British Blimp R-34 Reaches Home Port," *Semi-Weekly Iowegian*, July 14, 1919; "British Airmen, Believed Lost, Land in Scotland," *Semi-Weekly Iowegian*, May 26, 1919; "Commander Tells How His Seaplane Was Lost in Fog," *Semi-Weekly Iowegian*, May 19, 1919; "British Flyers Make First Non-Stop Atlantic Flight in 16 Hours and 12 Minutes," *Semi-Weekly Iowegian*, June 16, 1919.
3. "Early Airplanes Barnstormed Here," *Centerville Daily Iowegian*, August 23, 1938; "Lots of Places Where One Can Celebrate 4th," *Semi-Weekly Iowegian*, July 3, 1919; "Airplane Carries Many Passengers," *Semi-Weekly Iowegian*, September 8, 1919; "More Take Air Rides," *Semi-Weekly Iowegian*, September 15, 1919; "Wrigley Flying Circus Is Coming Here Thursday, Oct. 23," *Semi-Weekly Iowegian*, October 20, 1919.
4. "Air Plane Stunts," *Centerville Daily Iowegian*, July 5, 1921; "Excursions by Air Plane Will Be Fourth Feature," *Centerville Daily Iowegian*, June 24, 1921; "Flying Circus to Be a Thriller," *Centerville Daily Iowegian*, October 12, 1921; "Flying Circus!" advertisement, *Centerville Daily Iowegian*, October 13, 1921; "Air Plane Coming to Centerville," *Centerville Daily Iowegian*, May 8, 1920; "Air Plane Coming Last of the Week," *Centerville Daily Iowegian*, May 15, 1920; "Changes Airplanes 80 Miles an Hour," *Centerville Daily Iowegian*, August 4, 1920; "Pilot Is Small but He Sure Flies," *Centerville Daily Iowegian*, September 24, 1920; "Airplane Coming!" advertisement, *Centerville Daily Iowegian*, September 24, 1920.
5. "Plane Woke Many in City Tuesday," *Centerville Daily Iowegian*, November 21, 1928; "Aeroplane Was Making Fast Time," *Centerville Daily Iowegian*, November 2, 1921; "Aviator Forced to Land in City," *Centerville Daily Iowegian*, April 30, 1923; "Airplane Over City," *Semi-Weekly Iowegian*, July 7, 1919.
6. "Plane Travel Common South of This City," *Centerville Daily Iowegian*, September 6, 1928; "Air Travel on Marked Increase," *Centerville Daily Iowegian*, October 17, 1930; "Some Things the Pilot Passing over this County Has to Contend with on Trips," *Centerville Daily Iowegian*, July 16, 1926; "Air Mail-Express Lines Cover the

Whole United States," map, *Centerville Daily Iowegian*, November 28, 1927; "Plan to Mark Airways in Middle States," map, *Centerville Daily Iowegian*, December 19, 1925; "President Approves Air Route," *Centerville Daily Iowegian*, August 13, 1926; "Mail Planes Bring Vision of Air Future," *Centerville Daily Iowegian*, April 2, 1928.

7. "Tries Trans-Country Flight in One Day," *Centerville Journal*, August 5, 1922; "When Aviators MacReady and Kelly Made Non-Stop Flight across U.S.," *Centerville Daily Iowegian*, June 29, 1935; "Non-Stop Flight of 2500 Miles," *Centerville Daily Iowegian*, February 4, 1925; "Progress Made in Aviation Has Been 1926 Event," *Centerville Daily Iowegian*, December 31, 1926; "Aviators Start on World Flight," *Centerville Daily Iowegian*, March 17, 1924; "First around the World," photograph in J. Peterman catalog (Lexington, Ky.: The J. Peterman Company, 2004), 17; "U.S. Airmen Reach Paris Bastile [*sic*] Day," *Centerville Daily Iowegian*, July 14, 1924; A. Scott Berg, *Lindbergh* (New York: G.P. Putnam's Sons, 1998), 91.

8. "Route Mapped by Fonck for New York to Paris Flight," map, *Centerville Daily Iowegian*, September 20, 1926; "End of a Great Adventure," photograph, *Centerville Daily Iowegian*, September 25, 1926; "Tragic Start in New York Paris Flight," *Centerville Daily Iowegian*, September 21, 1926; "Keep up Vigil for Aviators Long Missing," *Centerville Daily Iowegian*, May 12, 1927; "Reward Offers Spur for Missing Airmen," *Centerville Daily Iowegian*, May 16, 1927; Berg, *Lindbergh*, 100, 105; "New Record Seen as Flyers Prepare for Ocean Hop," *Centerville Daily Iowegian*, April 19, 1927.

9. "Tells of Lindy's Earlier Career," *Centerville Daily Iowegian*, November 30, 1929; "Paris Flyer Is Daring Pilot," *Centerville Daily Iowegian*, May 18, 1927; "Lindbergh Starts to Paris," *Centerville Daily Iowegian*, May 20, 1927; "How Story of Great Flight Reacdhed [*sic*] Press," *Centerville Daily Iowegian*, May 24, 1927.

10. "Lindbergh Lands in Paris 3:21," extra edition, *Centerville Daily Iowegian*, May 21, 1927.

11. Dale Jones, interview with the author, October 4, 2000; Nelma Fuller, interview with the author, August 8, 2003.

12. "France Goes Wild over Flier," *Centerville Daily Iowegian*, May 21, 1927; Jesse M. Beck, "Lindbergh's Flight," editorial, *Centerville Daily Iowegian*, May 21, 1927; "Streets Lined to See Airman Passing Through," *Centerville Daily Iowegian*, May 25, 1927; "Cheered Here as Rode to the City Hall," *Centerville Daily Iowegian*, May 26, 1927; "Belgians Greet U.S. Flier," *Centerville Daily Iowegian*, May 28, 1927; "English Honor U.S. Airman," *Centerville Daily Iowegian*, May 31, 1927; "Favors Honor for Air Flier," *Centerville Daily Iowegian*, May 25, 1927; "Planning Great Reception When Lindbergh Comes," *Centerville Daily Iowegian*, May 31, 1927; "Spanish Honor Lindbergh Too," *Centerville Daily Iowegian*, June 2, 1927; "Washington Gives Lindbergh Reception with Fervor Never Displayed on Like Occasions," *Centerville Daily Iowegian*, June 11, 1927; "Lindbergh Is Home to Receive Mighty Welcome of the Nation and

to Greet Waiting Mother," *Centerville Daily Iowegian*, June 11, 1927; "New York Greets Lindbergh," *Centerville Daily Iowegian*, June 13, 1927; "Lindbergh Rides up Broadway," photograph, *Centerville Daily Iowegian*, June 17, 1927; "Local Residents Saw Lindbergh at Washington D.C.," *Centerville Daily Iowegian*, June 17, 1927.

13. "Fifty Stations Linked to Give Lindy's Welcome," *Centerville Daily Iowegian*, June 9, 1927; "Hear Coolidge and Lindbergh on Local Radio," *Centerville Daily Iowegian*, June 11, 1927; "St. Louis Will Broadcast When Lindy Returns," *Centerville Daily Iowegian*, June 17, 1927; "'Lindy Ties' Appear Here," *Centerville Daily Iowegian*, June 18, 1927; Dale Jones, interview with the author, October 4, 2000; "Chance to Go See Lindbergh," *Centerville Daily Iowegian*, August 3, 1927; "Col. Charles A. Lindbergh Visits Des Moines with His Airship 'Spirit of St. Louis' That Flew across the Atlantic," advertisement, *Centerville Daily Iowegian*, August 3, 1927; "You Can See Him Free August 29th," Universal Car Company advertisement, *Centerville Daily Iowegian*, August 10, 1927; "Lindbergh Is Feature Today at Des Moines," *Centerville Daily Iowegian*, August 29, 1927; "Seeing Lindy Was Done on Schedule by Local Caravan," *Centerville Daily Iowegian*, August 30, 1927.

14. "Chamberlain Flight Begun," *Centerville Daily Iowegian*, June 4, 1927; "Was Forced down Near Berlin When Supply of Gas Exhausted but Made Longest Flight," *Centerville Daily Iowegian*, June 6, 1927; "Chamberlin's [*sic*] Home Town Has a Celebration," *Centerville Daily Iowegian*, June 6, 1927; "Centerville Now Boasting an Airplane," *Centerville Daily Iowegian*, June 20, 1927; "First Local Plane Arrived June, 1927," *Centerville Daily Iowegian*, August 5, 1953; "Local Flyer Was among the Clouds Friday Evening," *Centerville Daily Iowegian*, July 14, 1928.

15. Jesse M. Beck, "Centerville Should Be There," editorial, *Centerville Daily Iowegian*, November 1, 1927; "Will Fly Here to Talk Airport to Association," *Centerville Daily Iowegian*, January 28, 1928; "Air Experts Tell C'ville to Go Ahead," *Centerville Daily Iowegian*, March 27, 1928; "Forming Local Branch of Nat'l Aeronautic Assn.," *Centerville Daily Iowegian*, April 7, 1928; "Begin Working out Plans for Big Air Event," *Centerville Daily Iowegian*, May 29, 1928; "Join National Aeronautic Assn.," *Centerville Daily Iowegian*, May 31, 1928; "Planes to Fly for a Thousand Dollar Price," *Centerville Daily Iowegian*, June 1, 1928; "Air Contests and Gala Day with Airplanes," *Centerville Daily Iowegian*, June 4, 1928; Jesse M. Beck, "Centerville's Airport," editorial, *Centerville Daily Iowegian*, June 5, 1928; "Army Planes Ordered Here," *Centerville Daily Iowegian*, June 5, 1928; "More Features Announced for Aviation Day," *Centerville Daily Iowegian*, June 6, 1928; "Model Airplane Contest Put on by Boys Air Day," *Centerville Daily Iowegian*, June 8, 1928; "First Plane Coming Here Thursday Morn," *Centerville Daily Iowegian*, June 13, 1928; "Program: Southern Iowa Aviation Day, Jun 18th," advertisement, *Centerville Daily Iowegian*, June 14, 1928; "Mail Service Plane

Coming," *Centerville Daily Iowegian*, June 14, 1928; "Boys Entering Contest with Plane Models," *Centerville Daily Iowegian*, June 14, 1928.

16. "How Centerville Came to Obtain Its New Airport," *Centerville Daily Iowegian*, June 14, 1928; "Contributors Who Made Possible Centerville's New Airport and Aviation Day Program of Events," *Centerville Daily Iowegian*, June 14, 1928; "Air Filled with Planes Here Monday," *Centerville Daily Iowegian*, June 14, 1928; Jesse M. Beck, "Airports" and "Governor Hammill," editorials, *Centerville Daily Iowegian*, June 14, 1928; "Assistant Secretary of War for Aviation Issues Ordered to Seventh Corps Area," *Centerville Daily Iowegian*, June 14, 1928; "Girl Flyer Reaches England," *Centerville Daily Iowegian*, June 18, 1928; "Girl Aviator Gives Credit to Her Pilots," *Centerville Daily Iowegian*, June 19, 1928.

17. Jim Pollock, "Good Times, Good News," *Des Moines Sunday Register*, January 31, 1999; "See Your City from the Air," advertisement, *Centerville Daily Iowegian*, July 19, 1928; "Forward Looking Centerville Provides Airport Where Some Big Events Have Been Staged," *Centerville Daily Iowegian*, August 23, 1938.

18. "Aviation Day Was Success, Large Crowd," *Centerville Daily Iowegian*, June 19, 1928; "Noted Air Ace Recalled Here by Shkolnick," *Centerville Daily Iowegian*, November 12, 1932; "Negro Flyer Not Believer in Hoodoos," *Centerville Daily Iowegian*, June 19, 1928.

19. Berg, *Lindbergh*, 198 (see chap. 45, n. 7); "Lindbergh Has Opened up New Air Mail Line," *Centerville Daily Iowegian*, February 7, 1929; "Lindbergh Carried Centerville Letter," *Centerville Daily Iowegian*, February 18, 1929; "Another Resident in Receipt of a Lindbergh Letter," *Centerville Daily Iowegian*, February 19, 1929.

20. "Eckener Outlines World Flight," *Centerville Daily Iowegian*, August 3, 1929; "An Uneventful Flight across the Atlantic," *Centerville Daily Iowegian*, August 4, 1929; "Zeppelin Makes New Record," *Centerville Daily Iowegian*, August 10, 1929; "Zeppelin Lands on U.S. Soil," *Centerville Daily Iowegian*, August 26, 1929; "Heads Graf Zeppelin on Iowa Course," *Centerville Daily Iowegian*, August 28, 1929; "Hundreds Wanted to See Ship as It Passed Over," *Centerville Daily Iowegian*, August 28, 1929; Charles B. DePuy, "Seeing the Graf and Recording Emotions That One Had as He Viewed This History-Making Accomplishment," *Centerville Daily Iowegian*, September 4, 1929.

21. "Log of Zeppelin Round World Flight," *Centerville Daily Iowegian*, August 29, 1929; "Rail Men Know What Definition of Hard Luck Is," *Centerville Daily Iowegian*, September 6, 1929; "Morning Sun Had Zeppelin View at 1:45 O'Clock," *Centerville Daily Iowegian*, August 28, 1929; "Zeppelin Makes New Record," *Centerville Daily Iowegian*, August 10, 1929.

Chapter 46

1. Sage, *A History of Iowa*, 254, 255–64 (see chap. 1, n. 5); "Says Low Price of Corn Is Not Cause in Trouble," *Centerville Daily Iowegian*, January 5, 1926; "Appanoose Population: Loss on Farms as Well as in Mining Center," *Centerville Daily Iowegian*, May 14, 1930; "Shortage of Farm Help May Hinder Crop Raising: Farmers Offer Tempting Wages but Jazz, Shows and City Lights Hold Hands Away," *Centerville Daily Iowegian*, March 31, 1920.
2. "Union Troubles All Part of Turbulent Coal History," *Centerville Daily Iowegian*, Fifty-Year Edition, June 21, 1952; "Statement Made by the Coal Operators of This Territory," *Centerville Daily Iowegian*, April 14, 1927; J.P. Agnessen, "Our Coal Problem," letter to the editor, People's Column, *Centerville Daily Iowegian*, April 18, 1925; W.E. Dodds, "What's Wrong with Coal?" letter to the editor, People's Column, *Centerville Daily Iowegian*, April 23, 1925; Claus Johnson, "It Is Just Nubbins," letter to the editor, People's Column, *Centerville Daily Iowegian*, April 25, 1925.
3. "Mine Victims Brought to Top," *Centerville Journal*, September 20, 1922; "Mine Death List Is Increasing," *Centerville Daily Iowegian*, November 24, 1922; "Death Toll in Mine Blast 80," *Centerville Journal*, November 8, 1922; "Gas Blamed for Mine Blast Which Took 38," *Centerville Daily Iowegian*, January 31, 1924; "Recover 162 Bodies from Mathes Mine," *Centerville Daily Iowegian*, May 25, 1928; "Tragedy in Colliery Blast," *Centerville Daily Iowegian*, March 1, 1927; "Tony Montegna Gets 500 Dollar Verdict," *Centerville Journal*, December 2, 1922; "Miner Killed When Roof Fell at Rock Valley," *Centerville Daily Iowegian*, December 24, 1927; Roger Williams and David Jones, *The Cruel Inheritance* (Village Publishing, 1990), 80.
4. "Eleven Cinder Burned Victims Are Intense Sufferers," *Centerville Daily Iowegian*, September 19, 1921; "One of Victims of Explosion of Dump Dies," *Centerville Daily Iowegian*, September 22, 1921; "Another Death Resulted from Mine Explosion," *Centerville Daily Iowegian*, September 26, 1921; "Third Victim of Mine Explosion Died Thursday," *Centerville Daily Iowegian*, October 7, 1921; "Young Man and Boy Hurled over High Dirt Dump," *Centerville Daily Iowegian*, May 21, 1923; "Double Tragedy of Fourth Cost Lives of Two in Old Air Shaft at Cincinnati," *Centerville Daily Iowegian*, July 5, 1918; Walter F. Rutkowski, executive director of Carnegie Hero Fund, letter to Linda Polich, September 2, 1998 (included with the letter was a photocopy of the page from the 1921 "Carnegie Report," a photocopy of the Kauzlarich account card and photographs of the Carnegie Hero Medal inscribed with the name of August Kauzlarich and the date of his death, July 4, 1918), privately held by Fred and Linda Polich of Coal Valley, Ill. (the medal itself is privately held by Norma Belloma of Centerville); Patsy Cincotta, "The Father She Never Knew Was 'Carnegie Hero,'" *Centerville Daily Iowegian*, September 2, 2004;

"Young Man and Boy Hurled over High Dirt Dump," *Centerville Daily Iowegian*, May 21, 1923.

5. Ron Roberts and Kent Sandstrom, "The Appanoose County Mine Wars: 1926 to 1931," unpublished paper, University of Northern Iowa Sociology Department, 1.
6. Tom Longden, "Famous Iowans: Lewis, John L.," DesMoinesRegister.com, A Gannett Company, http://www.desmoinesregister.com/article/99999999/FAMOUSIOWANS/40707003/Lewis-John-L-?nclick_check=1; "John P. White Resigns as President," *Semi-Weekly Iowegian*, October 25, 1917; "Recalls John L. Letter from Dr. Mott Sawyers," editorial, *Centerville Daily Iowegian*, July 27, 1946; "John L. Lewis Address Heard by Many Here," *Centerville Daily Iowegian*, September 9, 1931; Roberts and Sandstrom, "The Appanoose County Mine Wars: 1926 to 1931," 1; "Miners Reject Any Reduction in Wage Scale," *Centerville Daily Iowegian*, February 3, 1927.
7. "Miners Meeting at Kirksville Held a Debate," *Centerville Daily Iowegian*, April 18, 1927; James P. Agnessen, "Pete Agnessen's Statement," letter to the editor, People's Column, *Centerville Daily Iowegian*, May 7, 1927; J.P. Agnessen, letter to the editor, People's Column, *Centerville Daily Iowegian*, July 15, 1927; "Articles of Association: United Brotherhood of Miners," *Centerville Daily Iowegian*, August 15, 1927; "Agnessen to Head U. B. of M.," *Centerville Daily Iowegian*, June 1, 1927.
8. "Mines Prepare to Shut Down Completely," *Centerville Daily Iowegian*, March 31, 1927; "Mine Shutdown in This County near Complete," *Centerville Daily Iowegian*, March 31, 1927; "Union Miners Call at Empire on Men at Work," *Centerville Daily Iowegian*, April 21, 1927; "Two Empire Mine Workers Attend Union Gathering," *Centerville Daily Iowegian*, April 23, 1927.
9. "Many Miners Attend Mass Meeting Here," *Centerville Daily Iowegian*, April 27, 1927; "Speakers at Mass Meeting Condemn New Organization," *Centerville Daily Iowegian*, April 27, 1927; "Urged Miners to Stand with Organizations," *Centerville Daily Iowegian*, April 28, 1927; "Miners Mass Meeting in Centerville April 27," photograph, *Centerville Daily Iowegian*, May 2, 1927; "Activities among the Miners and Laboring Men of This Field," *Semi-Weekly Iowegian*, September 24, 1917; Elliott J. Gorn, *Mother Jones* (New York: Hill and Wang, a Division of Farrar, Straus and Giroux, 2001), back cover; "That New Miners Union," *Centerville Daily Iowegian*, April 23, 1927; "At Mystic When Meeting Called," *Centerville Daily Iowegian*, May 10, 1927; "Union Meeting Held at Mystic on Coal Strike," *Centerville Daily Iowegian*, May 17, 1927.
10. "Injunction Case Involving Mine Union on Trial," *Centerville Daily Iowegian*, May 19, 1927; "Mine Trouble at Mystic Growing More Acute Now," *Centerville Daily Iowegian*, August 2, 1927.
11. "Mystic Is Scene of Daily Picket Demonstrations," *Centerville Daily Iowegian*, August 4, 1927.

12. "Crowd Met at Garfield Mine," *Centerville Daily Iowegian*, August 12, 1927.
13. "Mystic Marshal a Suicide," *Centerville Daily Iowegian*, August 15, 1927.
14. "Garfield Men Attacked at Walnut Bridge," *Centerville Daily Iowegian*, August 19, 1927; "Miner Assault Case Is Heard in Court Today," *Centerville Daily Iowegian*, November 25, 1927; "Assault Case Adjourned over the Weekend," *Centerville Daily Iowegian*, November 26, 1927; "Raney on Stand in Mine Trial Resumed Today," *Centerville Daily Iowegian*, November 28, 1927; "Assault Case Defense Busy with an Alibi," *Centerville Daily Iowegian*, December 2, 1927; "Brazil Bridge Assault Case Is Nearing Close," *Centerville Daily Iowegian*, December 15, 1927; "Jury Verdict of Guilty in Assault Case," *Centerville Daily Iowegian*, December 19, 1927.
15. "Sheriff Makes a Proposal to Dismiss Deputies," *Centerville Daily Iowegian*, November 9, 1927; "Much Controversy in Conference with the Governor," *Centerville Daily Iowegian*, August 27, 1927; "Dispersing a Miners Picket," *Centerville Daily Iowegian*, September 24, 1927.
16. Jesse M. Beck, "Abide by the Law," editorial, *Centerville Daily Iowegian*, September 24, 1927; "Judge Walker's Discussion of Evidence in Contempt Case against Joe Morris and Miners' Union Officials," *Centerville Daily Iowegian*, November 15, 1927.
17. George Cox, "The Garfield Incident," letter to the editor, People's Column, *Centerville Daily Iowegian*, September 28, 1927.
18. "Dispersing a Miners Picket," *Centerville Daily Iowegian*, September 24, 1927; "State Will Send Troops Next," *Centerville Daily Iowegian*, September 24, 1927.

Chapter 47

1. "Dynamite Is Used to Blow up Power Line," *Centerville Daily Iowegian*, September 28, 1927.
2. Jesse M. Beck, "Stop the Violence," editorial, *Centerville Daily Iowegian*, September 28, 1927; Jesse M. Beck, "Abide by the Law," editorial, *Centerville Daily Iowegian*, September 24, 1927.
3. John Eddy, N.C. Blackburn, H.E. Ware and Nick Malett, "Those Extra Deputies," People's Column, *Centerville Daily Iowegian*, October 28, 1927; United Brotherhood of Miners, "Discuss Move to Remove the Police Officers," letter to the editor, *Centerville Daily Iowegian*, October 5, 1927; "Mine Situation Was Discussed at Plano Meeting," *Centerville Daily Iowegian*, September 24, 1927.
4. "Are Keeping up Picketing at Winifred Mine," *Centerville Daily Iowegian*, November 16, 1927; "Women Are Still in County Jail," *Centerville Daily Iowegian*, November 9, 1927; "Miners Cause Presented at Exline Meeting," *Centerville Daily Iowegian*,

November 9, 1927; "Union Officials Busy at Jail and Cleaning Quarters," *Centerville Daily Iowegian*, November 18, 1927; Z.T. Millitzer, "Eating Beans," People's Column, *Centerville Daily Iowegian*, November 18, 1927; "Union Men to Be Released under Order," *Centerville Daily Iowegian*, November 19, 1927; "Union Heads Continue to Stay tn Jail," *Centerville Daily Iowegian*, November 15, 1927.

5. Murphy, "The Birth and Demise of Brazil," 153 (see chap. 15, n. 3); Emile Gerard and Frank Powell, "Miners Explain Decision," letter to the editor, People's Column, *Centerville Daily Iowegian*, November 14, 1927; Lige Burcaski (spelling of last name is unclear; may be Bureaski), "Miner with Family," letter to the editor, People's Column, *Centerville Daily Iowegian*, October 22, 1927; S. Boslem, "U.M.W.A. Miners Friend," People's Column, *Centerville Daily Iowegian*, November 8, 1927; Wm. H. Allan, superintendent, Numa Coal Company, People's Column, *Centerville Daily Iowegian*, November 9, 1927.
6. "Head of State Labor Body Here for Inspection," *Centerville Daily Iowegian*, November 9, 1927; "Miners' Relief Work Continued," *Centerville Daily Iowegian*, October 20, 1928; George Cox, "From Union Standpoint," letter to the editor, People's Column, *Centerville Daily Iowegian*, November 8, 1927.
7. "Supplies for Needy Families Are Arriving," *Centerville Daily Iowegian*, November 17, 1927.
8. "Many Mines to Participate in Scale Meeting," *Centerville Daily Iowegian*, February 10, 1928; Charles Hindley, "Brotherhood Gains," People's Column, *Centerville Daily Iowegian*, January 5, 1928; "Center Miners in Brotherhood," *Centerville Daily Iowegian*, January 21, 1928.
9. "Coal Activities in This Field Draw Attention," *Centerville Daily Iowegian*, February 20, 1928; Dale Jones, interview with the author, October 4, 2000.
10. "Charges Lewis Would Destroy Coal Work Here," *Centerville Daily Iowegian*, February 14, 1928; "Some Questions on Saving the Mines in This Field," People's Column, *Centerville Daily Iowegian*, March 3, 1928.
11. "Comment on What Caused Changes in Coal Industry of the Country," *Centerville Daily Iowegian*, March 8, 1929; "Sheriff Called to Brazil Where Trouble Reported," *Centerville Daily Iowegian*, November 28, 1927; "Brazil Miner Was Victim of Attack, Report," *Centerville Daily Iowegian*, February 13, 1928; "Had Toy Guns to Terrorize Mining Camp," *Centerville Daily Iowegian*, May 9, 1928; "Miner Target for Bullets of Unknown Man," *Centerville Daily Iowegian*, January 5, 1928; "Have No Clues to Assailant," *Centerville Daily Iowegian*, January 6, 1928; "Exline Miner Says He Was Hit," *Centerville Daily Iowegian*, November 1, 1927; "Four Facing Serious Charge," *Centerville Daily Iowegian*, January 18, 1928; "Picketing Cause of Trouble Near the Center Mine," *Centerville Daily Iowegian*, January 17, 1928; "Trouble at Mine Brings Sentence," *Centerville Daily Iowegian*, January 23, 1929; "Trouble at Mine May

Develop into Serious Affair," *Centerville Daily Iowegian*, December 20, 1928; "Mine Trouble Is Improved Today," *Centerville Daily Iowegian*, December 21, 1928; "Nail Ambush for Officer in Brazil Road," *Centerville Daily Iowegian*, March 7, 1928.

12. "No Clues Found to 2000 Gallon Gasoline Theft," *Centerville Daily Iowegian*, January 12, 1928; "Tipple, Shaft of Streepy Mine Wreckage Today," *Centerville Daily Iowegian*, October 10, 1928; "What Was Formerly One of Largest Mines in Southern Iowa Badly Damaged," *Centerville Daily Iowegian*, October 10, 1928; "Following Cave-in Efforts Will Be Made to Ascertain If Workings Are Damaged," *Centerville Daily Iowegian*, October 12, 1928; "At 4:30 p.m. yesterday a portion of the shaft of the Empire Mine…," untitled, *Centerville Daily Iowegian*, June 19, 1929; "Mine Blaze Was Prevented by Watchman," *Centerville Daily Iowegian*, January 12, 1928; "Blaze at Empire Ruins Ventilator Repair Is Rushed," *Centerville Daily Iowegian*, January 5, 1931; "Streepy Tipple Burned Tuesday Night," *Centerville Daily Iowegian*, November 7, 1928; "One of Larger Mines Burned During Night," *Centerville Daily Iowegian*, June 8, 1929; "Mystery Blaze at Climie Home Not Solved as Yet," *Centerville Daily Iowegian*, September 17, 1929; "Flames Menaced Office at Mystic," *Centerville Daily Iowegian*, October 25, 1928; "Believe Attempt Made to Destroy Winifred Mine," *Centerville Daily Iowegian*, October 29, 1927; "Fire Destroys Hawkeye Mine; Launch Probe," *Centerville Daily Iowegian*, December 19, 1927; "Fire Destroys Remainder of Hawkeye Mine," *Centerville Daily Iowegian*, May 1, 1928; Murphy, "The Birth and Demise of Brazil" (see chap. 15, n. 3).

13. "Union Refusal Leaves Strike Yet Unsettled," *Centerville Daily Iowegian*, September 29, 1927; "Agnessen Reports New District Has Joined Southwest," *Centerville Daily Iowegian*, October 23, 1929; "Operators and Miners Hopeful with Agreement," *Centerville Daily Iowegian*, January 18, 1929; "Relief Supplies for Mines Still Being Received," *Centerville Daily Iowegian*, September 8, 1929.

14. "Clash between Officials of IA. Miners' Union," *Centerville Daily Iowegian*, October 10, 1928.

15. "Some Trouble at Union Meeting," *Centerville Daily Iowegian*, January 27, 1927; "Lewis Given Salary Boost," *Centerville Daily Iowegian*, January 31, 1927; J.E. Whitehouse, "Too Much Power," People's Column, *Centerville Daily Iowegian*, May 19, 1930; Charles Hindley, "Is a Delusion," People's Column, *Centerville Daily Iowegian*, February 10, 1928; Maurice Bernard, "French Miner Writes," People's Column, *Centerville Daily Iowegian*, February 16, 1928; James P. Agnessen, "Calls U.M.W.A. Detriment," People's Column, *Centerville Daily Iowegian*, January 24, 1928; "Helm Will Speak to Miners Tonight at Court House," *Centerville Daily Iowegian*, February 13, 1928; "Former Head of Miners' Union Attacks Lewis," *Centerville Daily Iowegian*, February 9, 1928; "Lewis Names Pete Agnessen as

Rebel Mine Order Leader," *Centerville Daily Iowegian*, March 20, 1930; "Miners Strike at Communists," *Centerville Daily Iowegian*, January 29, 1927; "Lewis Flays Opposition in Mine Movement," *Centerville Daily Iowegian*, March 10, 1930; "Sub Officials of the U.M.W.A. Are Expelled," *Centerville Daily Iowegian*, March 25, 1930.

16. "Dissention [*sic*] Rife and Charges and Counter Charges Expected to Come to Head Soon," *Centerville Daily Iowegian*, March 3, 1930; "Miners Here Are Divided between Opposing Groups," *Centerville Daily Iowegian*, March 7, 1930; Alfred Pyner, "Rival Miners Organizations," *Centerville Daily Iowegian*, March 22, 1930; "Labor Leaders Engage in Warm Union Debate," *Centerville Daily Iowegian*, March 26, 1930; "Stormy Session with Outsiders at Miners Meet," *Centerville Daily Iowegian*, November 10, 1930.

17. Herbert Stolz, "From Brotherhood Man," People's Column, *Centerville Daily Iowegian*, April 22, 1930; A. Pyner, "Comments on Agnessen Article," People's Column, *Centerville Daily Iowegian*, April 30, 1930; "Some of Former U.M.W.A. Members Back in the Union," *Centerville Daily Iowegian*, April 7, 1930; John Svob, "Notice," advertisement, *Centerville Daily Iowegian*, May 3, 1930; "Southwest Miners Held Important Meeting Monday," *Centerville Daily Iowegian*, April 1, 1930; J.P. Agnessen, "Southwest Miners Dissolved," *Centerville Daily Iowegian*, May 10, 1930; "Former Local Labor Head Is Coal Salesman," *Centerville Daily Iowegian*, July 11, 1930.

18. "Mass Meeting," advertisement, *Centerville Daily Iowegian*, November 7, 1930; "John L. Lewis to Speak Here This Evening," *Centerville Daily Iowegian*, September 8, 1931; Jesse M. Beck, "Our Coal Mining Future," editorial, *Centerville Daily Iowegian*, September 9, 1931; "Owners and Miners Agree!" *Centerville Daily Iowegian*, September 19, 1931; "Situation Is Bad," *Centerville Daily Iowegian*, July 6, 1929; "Mine Trouble Real Problem for Kentucky," *Centerville Daily Iowegian*, May 14, 1931; "Have Orders to Advance," *Centerville Daily Iowegian*, August 17, 1932; "Guard Planes Sent to Mine Strike Areas," *Centerville Daily Iowegian*, August 18, 1932; "Miners Mass in Illinois Protest Wages," *Centerville Daily Iowegian*, August 18, 1932; "Death Attends Miners' War," *Centerville Daily Iowegian*, August 22, 1932; "Miners Charge an Ambush," *Centerville Daily Iowegian*, August 25, 1932; "Oklahoma Is in Midst of Mine Trouble," *Centerville Daily Iowegian*, October 31, 1932.

19. Jesse M. Beck, "Hoover's Coming," editorial, *Centerville Daily Iowegian*, August 21, 1928; "Iowa Voters Keep State in Republican Ranks Result of Tuesday Election Shows," *Centerville Daily Iowegian*, November 7, 1928; Morison, *The Oxford History of the American People*, 290 (see chap. 16, n. 3).

Chapter 48

1. Jesse M. Beck, "Markets Declines [*sic*]," editorial, *Centerville Daily Iowegian*, November 7, 1927; J.A. Bradley, "Investigate! Go Slow," letter to the editor, *Centerville Daily Iowegian*, August 21, 1919; "Government Indictment Hangs over Short Time Resident of City; Charge Fraud Conspiracy," *Centerville Daily Iowegian*, March 1, 1926; "Charges against Bagby Set out in Late Dispatches," *Centerville Daily Iowegian*, March 6, 1926; "Bagby to Give Permanent Bond," *Centerville Daily Iowegian*, March 2, 1926; "Bagby Remains in Centerville," *Centerville Daily Iowegian*, March 11, 1926; "Centerville Banks," *Centerville Daily Iowegian*, December 31, 1926.
2. Jesse M. Beck, "Centerville Banks," editorial, *Centerville Daily Iowegian*, January 4, 1927; "Sees Centerville as Fortunate with Its Substantial Banks," *Centerville Daily Iowegian*, November 23, 1928; "Our Banks," *Centerville Daily Iowegian*, January 5, 1926; "Bank Statements Seflect [*sic*] Sound Conditions Here," *Centerville Daily Iowegian*, January 7 (crossed out to 6), 1927; "Condensed Report of the Condition of First National Bank," *Centerville Daily Iowegian*, October 8, 1928 (this source is one of dozens of similar reports); "Appanoose Co. Enjoys New Era of Prosperity," *Centerville Daily Iowegian*, April 9, 1927.
3. "Business Rooms Are Filling Up," *Centerville Daily Iowegian*, June 1, 1928; "Locations on the Square Seem at a Premium Just Now," *Centerville Daily Iowegian*, August 16, 1928; "Hamburger Shop Is Joining Ranks for Attractive City," *Centerville Daily Iowegian*, May 21, 1929; "Dillon Grocery Quits Business," *Centerville Daily Iowegian*, August 23, 1928; "Opens Delicatessen and Exchange Here," *Centerville Daily Iowegian*, November 21, 1929; "Ritz Café," advertisement, *Centerville Daily Iowegian*, August 28, 1926; "Mrs. Ed. Armour Buys Tea Room," *Centerville Daily Iowegian*, May 13, 1927; "Tumble Inn," advertisement, *Centerville Daily Iowegian*, June 2, 1928; "Bluebird Cafe," 1928 photograph, *Centerville Daily Iowegian*, April 10, 2004; "New Sandwich Shop Goes Up," *Centerville Daily Iowegian*, October 20, 1927; "Bryant Buys Hamburger Shop," *Centerville Daily Iowegian*, July 11, 1928; "'Roadside Inn' West of City Complete Soon," *Centerville Daily Iowegian*, May 18, 1928; "S. Milani Has Made His Shop a Beauty Spot," *Centerville Daily Iowegian*, April 9, 1927; "Milani Shoppe Will Install a Lunch Service," *Centerville Daily Iowegian*, October 29, 1929; "News Shop Sold to John and Bernice Allen, Announced," *Centerville Daily Iowegian*, February 1, 1929; "Geo. Swearngen [*sic*] Opening Store," *Centerville Daily Iowegian*, August 16, 1927; "Katter Is a Good Centerville Store," *Centerville Daily Iowegian*, August 23, 1938; "Oriental Rugs Katter Bros.," advertisement, *Centerville Daily Iowegian*, March 22, 1928; "Special Toasted Sandwiches. The Red Cross Drug Company," advertisement, *Centerville Daily Iowegian*, September 30, 1926; "New Fountain at

Owl Drug Store," *Centerville Daily Iowegian*, March 30, 1925; "Our New Fountain. Owl Drug Store," *Centerville Daily Iowegian*, March 30, 1925.

4. "Some Business Changes Here Being Noted," *Centerville Daily Iowegian*, October 28, 1927; "Improvements over Business District Many," *Centerville Daily Iowegian*, October 12, 1928; "Wooden Savings Bank Increases Present Quarters," *Centerville Daily Iowegian*, August 31, 1928; "Contract for Bank Structure Awarded Today," *Centerville Daily Iowegian*, January 21, 1928; "Bank in New Home Saturday," *Centerville Daily Iowegian*, August 16, 1928; "Magazine Tells of Local Bank," *Centerville Daily Iowegian*, September 12, 1928.
5. "A & P Enlarged Store Opened on Northside," *Centerville Daily Iowegian*, October 13, 1928; "Fine Fur Storage Vault Provided," *Centerville Daily Iowegian*, April 6, 1925; "Dudley Brothers Store Improved," *Centerville Daily Iowegian*, March 3, 1928; "Milady's Shoppe Is Style Leader," *Centerville Daily Iowegian*, August 23, 1938; "Penney Employe [*sic*] 20 Years Ago," *Centerville Daily Iowegian*, August 29, 1928; "Head of Thousand Stores Hunts up Colored Servant," *Centerville Daily Iowegian*, August 30, 1928; "Penney Store Folks Meeting," *Centerville Daily Iowegian*, August 31, 1928; "Millionaire Merchant Tells How He Did It," *Centerville Daily Iowegian*, August 30, 1928; "Remembers Former Servant," *Des Moines Tribune*, September 8, 1928, quoted in Ethel Lira, "J.C. Penney's Visit to Centerville Recalled," *Centerville Daily Iowegian*, September 11, 2003.
6. "Much Building Done Here the Past Summer," *Centerville Daily Iowegian*, September 13, 1928; "New Fronts and Redecorations Improve Square," *Centerville Daily Iowegian*, May 8, 1929; "Throng in City Saturday Night Gave City Air," *Centerville Daily Iowegian*, June 10, 1929; "Streets Were Jammed Last Night," editorial, *Centerville Journal*, August 6, 1922; "Local Band Larger Than Was Last Year," *Centerville Daily Iowegian*, June 13, 1928; "Band Practice Starts Tonight," *Centerville Daily Iowegian*, April 1, 1924; Himie Voxman, interview with the author, October 3, 2003.
7. "See Section of Ocean Cable," *Centerville Daily Iowegian*, March 8, 1928; "Luther Has Unusual Sign," *Centerville Daily Iowegian*, October 4, 1927; "Perfect Model of Locomotive Built by Local Man," *Centerville Daily Iowegian*, February 6, 1929; "Shows Engine All There but Smaller," *Centerville Daily Iowegian*, August 24, 1929; Dale Jones, interview with the author, October 2, 2001; "Thank You: I.L. Durham," advertisement, *Centerville Daily Iowegian*, August 15, 1927; "Durhams Saw Radio Show," *Centerville Daily Iowegian*, September 28, 1928; "Durham Is Local Distributor of Majestic Radio," *Centerville Daily Iowegian*, November 6, 1929.
8. "Capacity Crowds Attend Talkies at Ritz Theatre," *Centerville Daily Iowegian*, May 10, 1929; "City Council Held Session," *Centerville Daily Iowegian*, March 23, 1926; "Why Sunday Movies," *Centerville Daily Iowegian*, April 7, 1927; "Sunday Movies Were Shown at Local Theatres," *Centerville Daily Iowegian*, April 18, 1927; "Fines Paid for

Sunday Movies," *Centerville Daily Iowegian*, April 29, 1927; "This City to Have Talking Pictures Soon," *Centerville Daily Iowegian*, April 30, 1929; "Ritz," advertisement, *Centerville Daily Iowegian*, April 30, 1929; "Talking Pictures Will Make Bow Here Thursday, May 9," *Centerville Daily Iowegian*, May 2, 1929; "Program of 'Talkies' Will Be Featured at Ritz," *Centerville Daily Iowegian*, May 25, 1929; "Second Theatre Here Is to Be Sound Equipped," *Centerville Daily Iowegian*, July 3, 1929.

9. Harding, *Iowa Southern Utilities Company: A Century of Service*, 16 (see chap. 24, n. 28); "Step Taken to Install Motorbusses [*sic*]," *Centerville Daily Iowegian*, February 14, 1925; "Motor Busses [*sic*] Here to Take Place of Cars," *Centerville Daily Iowegian*, April 20, 1925; "New Busses [*sic*] to Strat [*sic*] Sunday," *Centerville Daily Iowegian*, April 25, 1925.
10. "Notice!" advertisement, *Centerville Daily Iowegian*, April 25, 1925; "Packard," advertisement, *Centerville Daily Iowegian*, January 2, 1928; "Reporter Hears Road Report in New Talking Car," *Centerville Daily Iowegian*, March 5, 1930; "Auto Company in Move to Building on N. Main Street," *Centerville Daily Iowegian*, July 23, 1928; "Ford Agency in Formal Opening March 4 and 5," *Centerville Daily Iowegian*, March 1, 1927.
11. "Governor Sees Bright Future for the State," *Centerville Daily Iowegian*, January 15, 1929; "Local Business Men Will Give Views on County's Outlook for 1929 with Series of Articles Starting Monday," *Centerville Daily Iowegian*, January 19, 1929; C.R. Wooden, "1929—? The Answer by Prominent Local Business Men," *Centerville Daily Iowegian*, January 20, 1929; "1929—? The Answer: B.A. Fuller," *Centerville Daily Iowegian*, January 22, 1929; "1929—? C.A. Farrington," *Centerville Daily Iowegian*, January 23, 1929; "1929—? H. L. Tramp," *Centerville Daily Iowegian*, January 25, 1929; "1929—? Wm. S. Bradley," *Centerville Daily Iowegian*, January 26, 1929; "1929—? Iowa Southern Utilities," *Centerville Daily Iowegian*, January 28, 1929; "1929—? S.B. Rosenbaum—Rosenbaum and Sons," *Centerville Daily Iowegian*, January 29, 1929; "1929—? M.M. Stiverson, Swift & Co.," *Centerville Daily Iowegian*, January 30, 1929; "1929—? Harry Schultz—Centrox Dairy Co.," *Centerville Daily Iowegian*, January 31, 1929; "1929—? Jennings-Christopher," *Centerville Daily Iowegian*, February 1, 1929; "1929—? Geo. Duckworth, Secretary Association of Commerce," *Centerville Daily Iowegian*, February 2, 1929; "School Children Present Some Highly Interesting Facts about the County in Which They Live," *Centerville Daily Iowegian*, May 7, 1929; "Centrox Dairy Valuable Asset to Centerville," *Centerville Daily Iowegian*, March 8, 1928; "Brick Plant: Will Increase Capacity and Add Products," *Centerville Daily Iowegian*, May 17, 1928; "Brick Company Completing Big Project Here," *Centerville Daily Iowegian*, September 25, 1928; "Clay Products Plant Found to Be Efficient One," *Centerville Daily Iowegian*, December 11, 1928; "Clay Products Company Adds a Modern Office," *Centerville Daily Iowegian*, March 4, 1930; "Ice Company Has Another Sub Station," *Centerville Daily Iowegian*, July 27, 1928; "Pure Ice Plant Is Busy

Place as Summer Is Near," *Centerville Daily Iowegian*, April 6, 1929; "Russian Order Being Shipped by Hercules," *Centerville Daily Iowegian*, February 1, 1928; "Business at Hercules Now Showing Growth," *Centerville Daily Iowegian*, August 1, 1925; "Stump Pullers Go to Russia," *Centerville Daily Iowegian*, December 30, 1925; "While in Europe in 1912…," untitled, *Centerville Journal*, January 5, 1922; Dale Jones, interview with the author, including map and photographs, March 3, 1999; "Power Plant Is Taking Place as One of Largest," *Centerville Daily Iowegian*, January 12, 1927; Harding, *Iowa Southern Utilities Company: A Century of Service*, 19 (see chap. 24, n. 28).

12. Jesse M. Beck, "Stocks Gone Mad," editorial, *Centerville Daily Iowegian*, March 28, 1928; "Stocks Continue Dizzy Climb," *Centerville Daily Iowegian*, August 31, 1928; "Went Wild on Stock Markets," *Centerville Daily Iowegian*, August 31, 1928; "Wall Street Has Holiday But in Optimistic Mood," *Centerville Daily Iowegian*, February 12, 1929; "Business in Upward Trend," *Centerville Daily Iowegian*, February 14, 1929; Jesse M. Beck, "Bad Day for Stocks," editorial, *Centerville Daily Iowegian*, March 27, 1929; "Extra: Stocks Crash in Today's Trading; Some in Rallies," *Centerville Daily Iowegian*, October 28, 1929; "Stocks Continue Downward Trend on Today's Trade," *Centerville Daily Iowegian*, October 29, 1929; "Socks [*sic*] Crash at the Close of Today's Trading," *Centerville Daily Iowegian*, November 11, 1929; "Stock Market in Another Slide Downward Today," *Centerville Daily Iowegian*, November 12, 1929; Jesse M. Beck, "Stocks Down Again," editorial, *Centerville Daily Iowegian*, February 13, 1929.

Chapter 49

1. Gail Tuttle, letter to her nephew John, loaned to author by Tuttle, April 5, 1996.
2. Kay McConville Cortesio, "Clock Memories: Letters to the Editor," *Daily Iowegian*, March 20, 2003; "Repairing Tower of Courthouse after Has Stood Quarter Century," *Centerville Daily Iowegian*, June 19, 1929; "Court House Tower Repaired and Clock Cleaned, Repainted," *Centerville Daily Iowegian*, July 1, 1929; "Pigeons Blamed for Trouble with Courthouse Clock," *Centerville Daily Iowegian*, October 3, 1930; "Names of Soldier Dead of Civil War Once again to Be Recorded in Stone on War Monument Here," *Centerville Daily Iowegian*, July 19, 1927; "Bronze Tablets Being Placed on Monument Today," *Centerville Daily Iowegian*, November 23, 1927.
3. "Centerville Is Being Garbed in Holiday Attire," *Centerville Daily Iowegian*, December 5, 1929; "Santa Claus to Arrive by Plane Saturday, 14th," *Centerville Daily Iowegian*, December 5, 1929; "Santa Arrived via Airplane This Morning," *Centerville Daily Iowegian*, December 14, 1929.
4. "Filling Station Count Here near 30, More to Come," *Centerville Daily Iowegian*, August 20, 1929; "Gamble Stores to Open Here Jan. 18," *Centerville Daily Iowegian*,

January 15, 1929; "Formal Opening of Gamble Store Saturday 22nd," *Centerville Daily Iowegian*, February 21, 1930; "Spurgeon Store Will Be Located in Centerville," *Centerville Daily Iowegian*, October 12, 1929.

5. "Mail Order Co. May Establish Store in City," *Centerville Daily Iowegian*, May 5, 1928; "Big Store Man Visits the City," *Centerville Daily Iowegian*, November 3, 1928; "Store Here Now Seems Assured," *Centerville Daily Iowegian*, November 7, 1928; "Furniture Firm Announces Will Close Business," *Centerville Daily Iowegian*, October 17, 1929; "Again Reported Montgomery-Ward May Come Here," *Centerville Daily Iowegian*, October 19, 1929; "Montgoery [*sic*] Ward Store Expected to Open Jan. 1," *Centerville Daily Iowegian*, November 29, 1929; "Not Coming Here with Ward Store," *Centerville Daily Iowegian*, December 15, 1929; Dale Jones, interview with the author, October 4, 2000.

6. "Iowegian Installs Telegraph Printer News Service May 10," *Centerville Daily Iowegian*, May 6, 1927; "Fastest Type News Transmission to Be Given Iowegian Readers by High Speed Automatic Printer Telegraph," *Centerville Daily Iowegian*, November 30, 1929; "Hoover Calls Conference of Business Men," *Centerville Daily Iowegian*, November 16, 1929; Jesse M. Beck, "Believe Ponic [*sic*] Is Over," editorial, *Centerville Daily Iowegian*, November 18, 1929; Robert S. McElvaine, *The Great Depression: America, 1929–1941* (New York: Three Rivers Press, Random House, 1993), 73; "Financial World Has Lost All of Recent Pessimism," *Centerville Daily Iowegian*, December 5, 1929; "Outlook Good for Business as Year Opens," *Centerville Daily Iowegian*, January 1, 1930; "Forecast a Prosperous Year," *Centerville Daily Iowegian*, December 30, 1929; "Believe 1930 Good Year for Banks of Iowa," *Centerville Daily Iowegian*, December 27, 1929; "Bankers Are Told Iowa Is Facing a Good Future," *Centerville Daily Iowegian*, January 7, 1930.

7. "Three Smaller Banks Suspend in Territory," *Centerville Daily Iowegian*, January 22, 1930; Jesse M. Beck, "Closed Banks," editorial, *Centerville Daily Iowegian*, January 23, 1930; "Trustee Named for Handling the Bradley Affairs," *Centerville Daily Iowegian*, January 23, 1930; "Mystic Depositors Held a Meeting," *Centerville Daily Iowegian*, February 10, 1930; "Bradley Petition to Federal Court," *Centerville Daily Iowegian*, February 18, 1930; "Bradley Creditors Meeting Saturday," *Centerville Daily Iowegian*, February 27, 1930.

8. Murphy, "Collapse of a Financial Empire," chapter 13 in "The Birth and Demise of Brazil," 159–68 (see chap. 15, n. 3); Robert K. Beck, *100th Anniversary: Iowa Trust and Savings Bank, Centerville, Iowa 1896–1996* (Centerville: Iowa Trust and Savings Bank, 1996), 15–18; "William Bradley Is Visitor Here," *Centerville Daily Iowegian*, November 19, 1940; "Bradley Quits Commodity Job," *Centerville Daily Iowegian*, November 3, 1945.

9. "Community Chest Really Had Its Origin in 1929 as the Social Service League," *Centerville Daily Iowegian*, October 29, 1946; "Calls for Clothing from Homes of Poor," *Centerville Daily Iowegian*, February 26, 1930.

10. "Drake Avenue Theatre Burns, Rosenbaum Clothing Store Is Badly Damaged over Week End," *Centerville Daily Iowegian*, February 3, 1930; Charles B. DePuy, "Place of Memories Where Living Actors Moved Their Audiences Is Reduced to Blackened Pile of Ashes," *Centerville Daily Iowegian*, February 3, 1930; "Drake Library and Fire Dept. Have Fire Loss," *Centerville Daily Iowegian*, February 7, 1930; "Lew Davidson Saved Fire Truck at Theatre Blaze," *Centerville Daily Iowegian*, February 3, 1930.
11. "More Defaults Listed as Court Takes up Cases," *Centerville Daily Iowegian*, April 2, 1930; "Record Entries Made in Several More Court Cases," *Centerville Daily Iowegian*, April 1, 1931; "Court Disposes of Much More Legal Business," *Centerville Daily Iowegian*, August 26, 1931; "Delinquent Taxes," *Centerville Daily Iowegian*, November 17, 1930; "Notice to Our Friends and Customers: M. Rosenbaum," *Centerville Daily Iowegian*, February 8, 1930; "Committee of Tax League in Meeting Here," *Centerville Daily Iowegian*, November 21, 1930; C.B.D. (Charles B. DePuy), At the Courthouse Keyhole, *Centerville Daily Iowegian*, February 13, 1931; C.B.D., At the Courthouse Keyhole, *Centerville Daily Iowegian*, February 12, 1931; C.B.D., At the Courthouse Keyhole, *Centerville Daily Iowegian*, January 10, 1931; "County Must Be Economical If Is to Avoid Debts," *Centerville Daily Iowegian*, January 28, 1931; Mott R. Sawyers, "Get Appanoose County out of Debt," *Centerville Daily Iowegian*, October 18, 1930; "Says County Must Minimize Cost of Government and Spend Its Money in Judicious Way If Gets out of Debt," *Centerville Daily Iowegian*, October 4, 1930; "County Fund Again Exhausted," *Centerville Daily Iowegian*, November 17, 1930.
12. Jesse M. Beck, "Think About This," editorial, *Centerville Daily Iowegian*, May 14, 1930; "Another Change," *Centerville Daily Iowegian*, May 2, 1930.
13. "Sunshine Co. Acquires Two Properties," *Centerville Daily Iowegian*, April 22, 1931; "Appanoose Co. Coal Entering New Markets," *Centerville Daily Iowegian*, October 8, 1930; "Mystic Mines Get Contract for R.R. Coal," *Centerville Daily Iowegian*, October 8, 1930; "Appanoose Co. Coal Concerns Get Contracts," *Centerville Daily Iowegian*, August 23, 1932; "Appanoose Takes Lead in Coal Tonnage," *Centerville Daily Iowegian*, March 21, 1931; "Sunshine Mine Blasts Another Hoist Record," *Centerville Daily Iowegian*, January 12, 1932; "All Time Coal Tonnage Records in Local Field Broken by McConville Co.," *Centerville Daily Iowegian*, January 12, 1932; "Mines Here Get Contracts," *Centerville Daily Iowegian*, August 19, 1931; "Puts Dustless Fuel on Market," *Centerville Daily Iowegian*, November 11, 1931; "Empire-Dustless-Fuel," advertisement, *Centerville Daily Iowegian*, November 11, 1931; "Empire Fuel Company Start Shipping Their Dustless Fuel in Own Box Cars Spreading Fame of Centerville," article plus photograph, *Centerville Daily Iowegian*, March 21, 1932.
14. "Mine Workers Protest Wage Cut Movement," *Centerville Daily Iowegian*, June 13, 1932; "Get Together Meeting for the Coal Industry," *Centerville Daily Iowegian*, March 28, 1933; Jesse M. Beck, "Miners Protest," editorial, *Centerville Daily Iowegian*, August 22,

1932; "25,000 Miners March," *Centerville Daily Iowegian*, August 23, 1932; "Mine Strikers Await New Turn," *Centerville Daily Iowegian*, August 29, 1932; "Miners Vote to Have New Union," *Centerville Daily Iowegian*, September 2, 1932; "Pickets and Mine Workers Come to Blows," *Centerville Daily Iowegian*, November 16, 1932; "Children of Miners Start Strike of Own," *Centerville Daily Iowegian*, October 3, 1932; "Miners Seeking New Wage Scale in This Field," *Centerville Daily Iowegian*, April 7, 1933.

15. "Claude R. Porter, Former Centerville Resident, Says Railroads at Crisis in Current Issues of 'Nation's Business,'" *Centerville Daily Iowegian*, January 8, 1931; "Citizens Meet with R.R. Men," *Centerville Daily Iowegian*, March 26, 1931.
16. "Appanoose Co. Farmers Seek Greater Yield," *Centerville Daily Iowegian*, May 18, 1927; "Plowing Demonstration," advertisement, *Centerville Daily Iowegian*, October 22, 1927; "Tuesday 16th: Farmers Store," advertisement, *Centerville Daily Iowegian*, October 13, 1928; "Bradley Farms at Sedan See First Southeast Iowa Combine Cutting and Threshing Machine," *Centerville Daily Iowegian*, July 18, 1928.
17. "Twenthieth [*sic*] Annual Alfalfa Banquet Recalls History of Initial Event," *Centerville Daily Iowegian*, November 2, 1946.
18. "Alfalfa Banquets Began in 1927; Henry Wallace Spoke in '28," *Centerville Daily Iowegian*, November 13, 1962; Morison, *The Oxford History of the American People*, 300 (see chap. 16, n. 3); Sage, *A History of Iowa*, 294–95 (see chap. 1, n. 5).
19. "Temperature 95 but Jim Builds New Fireplace," *Centerville Daily Iowegian*, July 1, 1931; "Heat Wave Finds Mercury Rising to Higher Level," *Centerville Daily Iowegian*, July 1, 1931; "Night Plowing Universal Here Due to Humidity," *Centerville Daily Iowegian*, July 1, 1931; "Estimate Toll of 1450 Dead in Heat Wave," *Centerville Daily Iowegian*, July 3, 1931; "Heat Here Is near the Record for This Season," *Centerville Daily Iowegian*, July 27, 1931; "Heat Record for Season Broken as Climbs to 101," *Centerville Daily Iowegian*, July 28, 1931; "Appanoose Is Again in Grip of Torrid Wave," *Centerville Daily Iowegian*, July 30, 1931; "Believe Heat May Have Been Cause of Death," *Centerville Daily Iowegian*, July 30, 1931; "It's Below Zero in Centerville," *Centerville Daily Iowegian*, July 31, 1931; "Temperature 92; Fur Coat Sale Is a Big Success," *Centerville Daily Iowegian*, August 5, 1931; "Temperatures for the Past Week," *Centerville Daily Iowegian*, August 8, 1931.
20. "Grasshoppers Prove Menace to Wide Area," *Centerville Daily Iowegian*, July 27, 1931; "Horde Invades Western Part of the State," *Centerville Daily Iowegian*, July 28, 1931; "No Grasshopper Menace in This County to Date," *Centerville Daily Iowegian*, July 28, 1931; "Moves to Halt Invasion from Other States," *Centerville Daily Iowegian*, July 29, 1931.
21. "Grasshoppers May Yet Prove a Menace Here," *Centerville Daily Iowegian*, July 31, 1931; "'Hoppers' Here Are Numerous but No Menace," *Centerville Daily Iowegian*, August 8, 1931; "City Invaded by Grasshoppers in Large Numbers," *Centerville Daily Iowegian*, August 17, 1931.

Chapter 50

1. "Public Sale Notice: Roy Vandike Farm," *Centerville Daily Iowegian*, October 6, 1930; "Public Sale Notice: Prospect Farm," *Centerville Daily Iowegian*, October 8, 1930; "Public Sale Notice: S.H. Porter," *Centerville Daily Iowegian*, October 9, 1930.
2. "Community Public Auction Notice," *Centerville Daily Iowegian*, February 4, 1931; "Public Auction Notice," *Centerville Daily Iowegian*, February 9, 1932; "Community Public Auction Notice," *Centerville Daily Iowegian*, March 4, 1931; "Land Sale Notice," *Centerville Daily Iowegian*, February 23, 1932; "Land at Auction," *Centerville Daily Iowegian*, February 6, 1932; "Closing out Public Sale Notice," *Centerville Daily Iowegian*, November 15, 1930; "Property Bargains: A.P. Speers," *Centerville Daily Iowegian*, August 25, 1931; "Sheriff Sold Half Million in Properties," *Centerville Daily Iowegian*, April 1, 1932.
3. Dr. E.E. Bamford, "Reasons for Commending the Farm Relief Movement Now Proposed by the General Assembly of the State," *Centerville Daily Iowegian*, February 14, 1931; Sage, *A History of Iowa*, 277 (see chap. 1, n. 5); "Notice," ten Iowa banks listed, *Centerville Daily Iowegian*, June 20, 1931; "Announcement: Centerville National Bank," *Centerville Daily Iowegian*, January 14, 1932; "Centerville National and the Commercial State Banks Unite as One Big Consolidated Bank," *Centerville Daily Iowegian*, January 14, 1932; "Checks in Local Banks Cost $261 in Last 10 Days," *Centerville Daily Iowegian*, July 15, 1932; "Mystic Bank Board Decides to Close," *Centerville Daily Iowegian*, January 7, 1931; "Seymour National Bank Has Closed; Deposit Was Small," *Centerville Daily Iowegian*, December 15, 1931; "Moulton Bank Closed Pending Reorganization," *Centerville Daily Iowegian*, December 26, 1931; "Dean Savings Bank Closed Report Today," *Centerville Daily Iowegian*, January 7, 1932; "Moravia Bank Closed Today," *Centerville Daily Iowegian*, August 4, 1932; "Bank Suspends Until Plan Can Be Worked Out," *Centerville Daily Iowegian*, July 16, 1932.
4. Dr. E.E. Bamford, "Reasons for Commending the Farm Relief Movement Now Proposed by the General Assembly of the State," *Centerville Daily Iowegian*, February 14, 1931.
5. "Comment by Others: Scientific View of Cattle Test," *Centerville Daily Iowegian*, November 14, 1931; J.M. Tucker, "Cattle Testing," letter to the editor, *Centerville Daily Iowegian*, March 16, 1931; "Cedar County Farmers Resist the T.B. Law," *Centerville Daily Iowegian*, March 10, 1931; "Capitol of Iowa Is Besieged," *Centerville Daily Iowegian*, March 19, 1931; "T.B. Test Law Attacks Studied by Assembly," *Centerville Daily Iowegian*, March 20, 1931.
6. "Bowdish Present at Bovine T.B. Protest Meeting," *Centerville Daily Iowegian*, March 20, 1931; "Veterinarian Engeged [*sic*] in Cattle T.B. Tests in Eastern Iowa Tells of Work and Value of the Methods as Applied," *Centerville Daily Iowegian*, November 7,

1931; "Cedar County Renews Battle against Test," *Centerville Daily Iowegian*, August 22, 1931; "Veterinarian Attacked When Attempted Test," *Centerville Daily Iowegian*, August 27, 1931; "Chronology of Fight against Cattle Testing," *Centerville Daily Iowegian*, September 24, 1931.

7. "Martial Law in Cedar Co.," *Centerville Daily Iowegian* September 22, 1931; "Troops to Cedar Co. Farms," *Centerville Daily Iowegian*, September 24, 1931; "Veterinary of this City Will Test at Tipton," *Centerville Daily Iowegian*, September 26, 1931; "Local Guardsmen Find It Quiet on the 'Battlefront,'" *Centerville Daily Iowegian*, September 26, 1931; "Test War Again to Courts," *Centerville Daily Iowegian*, September 26, 1931; "Company G Has Returned Home from Cedar Co.," *Centerville Daily Iowegian*, October 3, 1931; "Extra! Local Guard Again Called into Service," *Centerville Daily Iowegian*, October 21, 1931; Sage, *A History of Iowa*, 277–82 (see chap. 1, n. 5); "Co. G. Returns Today with One of Best Ratings," *Centerville Daily Iowegian*, October 31, 1931; "Twelve Guards of Centerville Back—Cow War," *Centerville Daily Iowegian*, November 26, 1931.

8. Sage, *A History of Iowa*, 276 (see chap. 1, n. 5); "Farmers Strike Is on in Iowa but the Hens Go on Laying, the Cows Give Milk and Corn Thrives," *Centerville Daily Iowegian*, August 8, 1932.

9. "Shot Is Fired in Iowa Farm Strike Today," *Centerville Daily Iowegian*, August 15, 1932; "Striking Iowa Farmers Picket State Highway," photographs, *Centerville Daily Iowegian*, August 18, 1932; "'Ag Holiday,' Movement Spreads Renewing Activity of Leaders," *Centerville Daily Iowegian*, August 18, 1932; "Nebraska Farm Men Have Eyes on Iowa Today," *Centerville Daily Iowegian*, August 19, 1932; Henry A. Wallace, "Farm Publisher Sees Farm Strike as a Gesture That Might Be New Boston Tea Party in Its Results," *Centerville Daily Iowegian*, August 19, 1932; "Farmers Halt Trains as Latest Offensive in Agriculture Strike," *Centerville Daily Iowegian*, August 22, 1932; "Freight Car Opened Hogs Back in Pen," *Centerville Daily Iowegian*, August 24, 1932; "Farm Holiday Movement Spreads through Iowa," *Centerville Daily Iowegian*, August 27, 1932; "Much Mystery Bound up in Strike Events," *Centerville Daily Iowegian*, September 2, 1932; "Picket Victim Skull Fractured," *Centerville Daily Iowegian*, September 3, 1932; "Peaceful End to Farm War Sought Today," *Centerville Daily Iowegian*, September 6, 1932; "Farmer Parade in Des Moines Cooled by Wind," *Centerville Daily Iowegian*, October 4, 1932.

10. "Holiday Men Make Change in Objective," *Centerville Daily Iowegian*, October 27, 1932; "Farmers Storm Courthouse to Aid a Neighbor," *Centerville Daily Iowegian*, December 3, 1932; "Angry Farmers Disarm Sheriff at Foreclosure," *Centerville Daily Iowegian*, March 3, 1933; "Angry Farmers Roar Protests at Legislature," *Centerville Daily Iowegian*, March 13, 1933; "Angry Farmers Attack Sheriff and Deputies," *Centerville Daily Iowegian*, April 27, 1933.

11. "Mob Attacks Elderly Judge," *Centerville Daily Iowegian*, April 28, 1933.
12. "Herring Proclaims Martial Law," *Centerville Daily Iowegian*, April 28, 1933; "State Backed by Public in Drastic Move," *Centerville Daily Iowegian*, April 29, 1933; "Tension in Farm War Areas," *Centerville Daily Iowegian*, April 29, 1933; "Rioting Farmers Checked by Troops," photographs, *Centerville Daily Iowegian*, May 1, 1933; "Have Arrested Ring Leaders in Farm Affair," *Centerville Daily Iowegian*, May 2, 1933.
13. "Will Slacken Martial Rule in Few Days," *Centerville Daily Iowegian*, May 5, 1933; "Farm Revolt Trial Is Near," *Centerville Daily Iowegian*, May 9, 1933.
14. "Special Showing," Ritz Theatre advertisement, *Centerville Daily Iowegian*, May 19, 1933.
15. Jesse M. Beck, "President Hoover's Address," editorial, *Centerville Daily Iowegian*, October 3, 1930; "The worst of the depression is over…," untitled, *Centerville Daily Iowegian*, May 7, 1931; Edson R. Waite, "Stop to Think This Over," *Centerville Daily Iowegian*, April 6, 1931; Jesse M. Beck, "The Story of 1931," editorial, *Centerville Daily Iowegian*, December 31, 1931; Johnson, *A History of the American People*, 742 (see chap. 24, n. 10); "In Many Places Workmen Are Being Called Back to Work, While Strife Elsewhere," *Centerville Daily Iowegian*, January 10, 1931; "Oklahoma City Stage a Riot," *Centerville Daily Iowegian*, January 20, 1931; "Chicago Has Serious Riot," *Centerville Daily Iowegian*, August 4, 1931; "Jobless Men Riot in N.Y.," *Centerville Daily Iowegian*, October 27, 1931; "Salt Lake Is Scene of Riots," *Centerville Daily Iowegian*, November 1, 1931; "'Hunger Marchers' Storm Indiana Legislature," *Centerville Daily Iowegian*, July 21, 1932; "Modern Coxey's Army Moves on Ohio Capital," *Centerville Daily Iowegian*, May 4, 1931; "Missouri Has Coxey's Army," *Centerville Daily Iowegian*, October 23, 1931; "Missouri Unemployed March to Demand Relief," photograph, *Centerville Daily Iowegian*, October 27, 1931; "Father Cox of Unemployed Army Sees Uprisings and Armed Revolt, Presents Resolution to the U.S.," *Centerville Daily Iowegian*, January 7, 1932; "Pinchot Makes Hit with Cox's Jobless Army," *Centerville Daily Iowegian*, January 7, 1932; "Cox's Army Has Reached Capital," *Centerville Daily Iowegian*, January 7, 1932; David Burner, Virginia Bernhard and Stanley Kutler, "The Bonus Army of 1932," in *Firsthand America*, 4th ed. (St. James, N.Y.: Brandywine Press, 1996), 805; "Band of Veterans from Seattle to Washington, D.C.," *Centerville Daily Iowegian*, February 16, 1931; "As World War Veterans Paraded in Washington," photograph, *Centerville Daily Iowegian*, June 9, 1932; "Bonus Army History," *Centerville Daily Iowegian*, July 29, 1932.
16. "State Funds Are Near Exhaustion; Not First Time," *Centerville Daily Iowegian*, January 18, 1933; "Iowa Assembly Is Now Facing Problem of Reducing Taxes in the Face of Greatly Diminished Receipts," *Centerville Daily Iowegian*, January 12, 1933; "Reduction of $1,796,032 a year…," untitled, *Centerville Daily Iowegian*, January 12, 1933; C.B.D., At the Courthouse Keyhole, *Centerville Daily Iowegian*, February 14,

1931; W.E. Elgin, county treasurer, "Semi-Annual Report," *Centerville Daily Iowegian*, February 28, 1931; "Two Appanoose Funds Exhausted; Occurs Annually," *Centerville Daily Iowegian*, September 30, 1931; "Original Notice," *Centerville Daily Iowegian*, March 19, 1931; "More Litigation Is Disposed of," *Centerville Daily Iowegian*, February 13, 1931; "Administrator's Sale," notice, *Centerville Daily Iowegian*, December 19, 1932; "Auction!" notice, *Centerville Daily Iowegian*, May 19, 1933; "'Oh Lady, Lady' Says Auctioneer," *Centerville Daily Iowegian*, May 21, 1931; "Seeks to Prevent Receiverships tn Three Farm Cases," *Centerville Daily Iowegian*, January 28, 1933.

17. "Rosenbaum Quitting," sale notice, *Centerville Daily Iowegian*, November 25, 1930; Chas. Katter, "Closing Out Sale," notice, *Centerville Daily Iowegian*, January 5, 1931; "Morris' Big Closing out Sale," *Centerville Daily Iowegian*, January 28, 1931; "Sad News—We Have Lost Our Lease," Nelson Shoe Store sale notice, *Centerville Daily Iowegian*, February 3, 1931; "Tomorrow morning, Stricklers dry goods store in Centerville begins its closing out sale…," untitled, *Centerville Daily Iowegian*, December 2, 1931; "Graham Store to Close out Stock," *Centerville Daily Iowegian*, February 11, 1933; "Sell Everything!" Davison Bros. sale notice, *Centerville Daily Iowegian*, February 16, 1933; "Sale," Chapman sale notice, *Centerville Daily Iowegian*, November 2, 1933; "Auction Sale," Lowrey Grocery sale notice, *Centerville Daily Iowegian*, December 22, 1933; "Bankrupt Auction Sale," Hibbs Store sale notice, *Centerville Daily Iowegian*, November 27, 1934; "Fewer Cars Sold Here during 1930," *Centerville Daily Iowegian*, September 27, 1930; "Some Cars Stored for Year to Avoid License Payment," *Centerville Daily Iowegian*, October 3, 1930; "Bankruptcy Is Filed against Glen A. Norris," *Centerville Daily Iowegian*, July 16, 1932; "Iowa Mine Wage Scale Down," *Centerville Daily Iowegian*, February 7, 1933; "City Salaries Reduced Make Decided Saving," *Centerville Daily Iowegian*, February 7, 1933; "Action Effects a Saving of Practically $5,000 to Taxpayers of District," *Centerville Daily Iowegian*, April 6, 1932; "This County Official Cuts His Own Salary," *Centerville Daily Iowegian*, January 10, 1933; "Justice Peace Quits Because Business Dull," *Centerville Daily Iowegian*, October 5, 1931; Dale Jones, interview with the author, October 4, 2000; "Black Diamond Yearbooks," Centerville High School, 1929–1930; "Class Picture Will Supplant the Annual," *Centerville Daily Iowegian*, April 15, 1933; "Western Union Office Given Bank Orders," *Centerville Daily Iowegian*, March 4, 1933.

18. "Funeral for W.E. Law to Be Held Monday," *Centerville Daily Iowegian*, March 21, 1931.

19. "Counterfeit U.S. Check Is Located Here," *Centerville Daily Iowegian*, July 29, 1932; "Influx of Bogus Coins Reported," *Centerville Daily Iowegian*, July 27, 1932; "Vendors Ruled from Business District Here," *Centerville Daily Iowegian*, September 23, 1930; "Several Items of Business Attended to and Suggestions Made," *Centerville Daily Iowegian*, March 16, 1931; "It's Catalogue Time in Centerville—Or a Word to

the Wise," *Centerville Daily Iowegian*, August 16, 1932; "Bank Rumors Might Lead to Prosecutions," *Centerville Daily Iowegian*, August 12, 1932; "Severe Penalty for Circulating False Rumors," *Centerville Daily Iowegian*, February 6, 1933; Jesse M. Beck, "Time for Wild Rumors," editorial, *Centerville Daily Iowegian*, March 7, 1933; "Business Good Seen Here on Lapel Buttons," *Centerville Daily Iowegian*, February 13, 1931; "Campaign at Casady Store Ends Tonight," *Centerville Daily Iowegian*, May 16, 1931; "Clear the Deck," Centerville merchants sale notice, *Centerville Daily Iowegian*, January 27, 1931; "North Side Square Offers Big Values through This Week," *Centerville Daily Iowegian*, April 5, 1932; "'Centerville Days' Coming Week Will Mean Much to the People of This Trade Area," *Centerville Daily Iowegian*, March 25, 1933.

20. "What the Poor of Appanoose County Need Is to Be Helped out of Their Poverty She Says," *Centerville Daily Iowegian*, March 2, 1929; "Good Fellow Spirit Abounds," *Centerville Daily Iowegian*, December 12, 1930; Jesse M. Beck, "Local Relief Measures," editorial, *Centerville Daily Iowegian*, November 20, 1931.

21. "Clothing Being Sought for the Needy Children," *Centerville Daily Iowegian*, September 4, 1930; "Food, Clothing for Everyone in County Is Plan," *Centerville Daily Iowegian*, December 9, 1930; "Clothing Plea Is Voiced for Poor Children," *Centerville Daily Iowegian*, October 15, 1932; "Open Room to Handle Clothing for the Needy," *Centerville Daily Iowegian*, January 14, 1932; "Welfare Rooms Need Clothing," *Centerville Daily Iowegian*, January 27, 1933; "Social Worker Will Aid Those Who Help Needy," *Centerville Daily Iowegian*, December 11, 1930; "Ask for Offers of Garden Plots," *Centerville Daily Iowegian*, April 6, 1931; "70 Gardens Are Available Now for the Needy," *Centerville Daily Iowegian*, April 21, 1934; "Mothers of Appanoose to Spin Wool," *Centerville Daily Iowegian*, February 17, 1933.

22. "Help the Needy!" School Section editorials, *Centerville Daily Iowegian*, November 18, 1931; "450 Lbs. Spuds Were Donated to Aid Relief," School Section, *Centerville Daily Iowegian*, November18, 1931; "Vegetables and Old Clothes Are C.H.S. Donations," School Section, *Centerville Daily Iowegian*, November 21, 1931; "The School Nurse Has a Busy Office," School Section, *Centerville Daily Iowegian*, October 4, 1930; "Will Provide a 3 Bed Room at Hospital," *Centerville Daily Iowegian*, December 12, 1930; "Milk Fund Plan Is Progressing," *Centerville Daily Iowegian*, March 22, 1933; "Milk Program in Centerville Has Operated over 20 Years," *Centerville Daily Iowegian*, December 9, 1953; "Milk Bottle Fund in Need," *Centerville Daily Iowegian*, April 18, 1933; "New Plan of Milk Pledges," *Centerville Daily Iowegian*, June 14, 1933; "Milk Fund Drive Is on Full Force," *Centerville Daily Iowegian*, August 25, 1933; "Big Carnival Is Coming to Centerville," *Centerville Daily Iowegian*, September 7, 1933; "Milk Fund Gets Aid from Tickets to the Majestic," *Centerville Daily Iowegian*, August 31, 1933.

23. "Children Bring Food and Admits to the Majestic," *Centerville Daily Iowegian*, December 17, 1930; "Good Fellow Spirit Abounds," *Centerville Daily Iowegian*,

December 12, 1930; "Toy Show Was Great Success," *Centerville Daily Iowegian*, December 12, 1931; "Christmas Toys Warm up Steve's Big Ice Truck," *Centerville Daily Iowegian*, December 12, 1931; "'Toy Show' Will Be a Feature at Ritz Saturday," *Centerville Daily Iowegian*, December 10, 1931; "More Than 400 Children See Ritz Toy Show," *Centerville Daily Iowegian*, December 23, 1932.

24. "Out Today for Needy Families," *Centerville Daily Iowegian*, December 24, 1930; "Thankfulness and Happiness Vie with One Another Here as Good Fellows Baskets Go out to Needy," *Centerville Daily Iowegian*, December 24, 1931; "County Has Heart of Gold," *Centerville Daily Iowegian*, December 26, 1931.

25. "Refrigerator at Auction Saturday for Good Fellows," *Centerville Daily Iowegian*, December 17, 1930; "Good Fellows Have $400 in Their Funds," *Centerville Daily Iowegian*, December 15, 1930; "B.P.W. Party for Children Great Success," *Centerville Daily Iowegian*, December 26, 1932; "Good Fellows Fund Will Keep Heartbreaks from Coming to Little Folks and Will Also Aid Others in Distress thru Its Kind Help," *Centerville Daily Iowegian*, December 17, 1931; "There Is a Santa Claus in Centerville—In the Minds and Hearts of Good Fellows; Christmas Fund Swells to More Than $1000," *Centerville Daily Iowegian*, December 12, 1931; "Social Welfare League to Hold Annual Meeting," *Centerville Daily Iowegian*, November 21, 1930; "Exline Begins Drive to Help Needy on Xmas," *Centerville Daily Iowegian*, December 8, 1931; "Good Fellows of Cincinnati Help the Needy," *Centerville Daily Iowegian*, December 27, 1932.

26. Beck, *100th Anniversary: Iowa Trust and Savings Bank*, 20 (see chap. 49, n. 8); Jesse M. Beck, "Want to Talk It Over," *Centerville Daily Iowegian*, April 13, 1933; Jesse M. Beck, "Prompt Action Is Advisable," editorial, *Centerville Daily Iowegian*, February 3, 1933; "Miners—Owners Are Discussing Wage Reduction," *Centerville Daily Iowegian*, January 19, 1933; "Miners out at Two Mines over Wage Matters," *Centerville Daily Iowegian*, March 30, 1933; "Working out Differences at Coal Mines," *Centerville Daily Iowegian*, March 31, 1933; "Union Miners Called out of Working Shaft," *Centerville Daily Iowegian*, June 22, 1933; "Mineworkers Ask for Conference on Relief Here," *Centerville Daily Iowegian*, January 27, 1933; "Situation in Appanoose County Is Considered at Meeting Held by Interested Organizations," *Centerville Daily Iowegian*, February 2, 1933.

Chapter 51

1. "Tramp Colony in Local Yards," *Centerville Journal*, February 2, 1922; "Tramps Few as Winter Comes," *Centerville Daily Iowegian*, December 4, 1926; "Vagrants More Plentiful since Cold Wave Came," *Centerville Daily Iowegian*, January 12, 1929;

"Railroad Officer Talking to Reporter Tells of the Change That Has Come in Ranks of the Transients and at 'Jungle,'" *Centerville Daily Iowegian*, May 2, 1933; "Too Early to Sleep in Park," *Centerville Daily Iowegian*, March 6, 1925; "Unknown Man Is Puzzle; Created Disturbance Here," *Centerville Daily Iowegian*, February 6, 1930; "Stranger Found Almost Frozen," *Centerville Daily Iowegian*, January 25, 1926; "Amnesia Victim Puzzling Police," *Centerville Daily Iowegian*, July 21, 1933; "Two Killed by Freight as Slept," *Centerville Daily Iowegian*, August 10, 1925; "Transient Given Medical Aid as Result Accident," *Centerville Daily Iowegian*, January 8, 1931; "May Identify Fingerprints," *Centerville Daily Iowegian*, November 29, 1932; "Fingerprints Give Identity of Corpse Here," *Centerville Daily Iowegian*, December 1, 1932.

2. "Young Houdini Does His Stuff in Court Park," *Centerville Daily Iowegian*, August 31, 1933; "Gypsies' Visit Cut Short Here," *Centerville Daily Iowegian*, May 21, 1932; "Modern Gypsies," *Centerville Journal*, August 2, 1922; "Catch Gypsies Who Robbed Restaurant," *Centerville Journal*, September 26, 1922; "Gypsy Band Was Asked to Move On," *Centerville Daily Iowegian*, July 31, 1924; "Gypsies or Indians? Either One They Are on Their Way," *Centerville Daily Iowegian*, July 24, 1934; "Phrenologist Gets in Bad with Cops," *Centerville Daily Iowegian*, June 23, 1920.
3. Phyllis Cosby, "A Visit from Hairbreath [*sic*] Harry," *Centerville Daily Iowegian*, October 17, 2002; "Hairbreadth Is Remembered by Folks in City," *Centerville Daily Iowegian*, April 17, 1947; "'Hobo Preacher' Funeral Is Today," *Centerville Daily Iowegian*, September 29, 1947; "'The Tramp Preacher' Subject of Book," *Centerville Daily Iowegian*, October 6, 1952.
4. "Bums and Bo's Trek Northward Stop At 'Jim's,'" *Centerville Daily Iowegian*, March 18, 1929; Phyllis Cosby, "Riding the Rails Seeking Adventure," *Centerville Daily Iowegian*, July 12, 2002; Charles Magee, "Railroad Officer Talking to Reporter Tells of the Change That Has Come in Ranks of the Transients and at 'Jungle,'" *Centerville Daily Iowegian*, May 2, 1933; Jesse M. Beck, "Hobos, Tramps, and Bums," editorial, *Centerville Daily Iowegian*, October 12, 1925; "Vagrants More Plentiful Since Cold Wave Came," *Centerville Daily Iowegian*, January 12, 1929; "Mayor Warns Professional Alms Seekers," *Centerville Daily Iowegian*, January 7, 1933; "Spooner Hotel Caters This Year to Women as Well as Men and Even Small Children Have Slept Upon Its Floor," *Centerville Daily Iowegian*, October 12, 1932; Jeanne Harrington Fowler, interview with the author, August 15, 2009; Bill Smallwood, interview with the author, August 20, 2009.
5. "Vagrants More Plentiful Since Cold Wave Came," *Centerville Daily Iowegian*, January 12, 1929; "Bums and Bo's Trek Northward Stop at 'Jim's,'" *Centerville Daily Iowegian*, March 18, 1929; "Spooner House for Bo's Is Closed; No Longer Will the City Fathers Itch and Twitch as Centerville's Fate Is Shaped," *Centerville Daily Iowegian*, March 4, 1930.

6. "Centerville Is Getting Bad Rep with Transients," *Centerville Daily Iowegian*, March 9, 1931; "Jail Has Become Busy Place after Quite a Lull," *Centerville Daily Iowegian*, February 9, 1931; "City Dads May Provide New Abode for Unfortunate Men; Asked to Consider Airport Improvement Pending a Lease," *Centerville Daily Iowegian*, October 3, 1931; "South Side Business Men Protest Against 'Jobless Hotel'; Recommend New City Jail," *Centerville Daily Iowegian*, November 7, 1931; "City Dads Turn Thumbs Down on Hotel for Bums," *Centerville Daily Iowegian*, December 8, 1931; "Reporter Visits 'The Jungle' and Finds Life of the 'Jolly Old Bum' Isn't Bad as Many People Are Prone to Believe That It Is," *Centerville Daily Iowegian*, January 29, 1932; "Man, 83, without Money, Friends, Home, Relatives, Health, or Even Suitable Clothes Wants to 'Sleep Out' Again," *Centerville Daily Iowegian*, March 9, 1934.
7. "Another 'Case' of Hard Times Is Heard Here," *Centerville Daily Iowegian*, November 8, 1933; "Depression Brings Another Sad True Story from Real Life in This County," *Centerville Daily Iowegian*, November 7, 1933; "Pitiful Plight Seen in Family Marooned Here," *Centerville Daily Iowegian*, August 23, 1932; Cee Bee Dee (Charles B. DePuy), As Told Around the Town, *Centerville Daily Iowegian*, June 28, 1933; W.B. Russell, correspondent, "Numa," *Centerville Daily Iowegian*, June 26, 1933; "Cooper Bridge Was Bed Chamber for Couple Here," *Centerville Daily Iowegian*, November 4, 1933; "Hard Times Are Hard for Hikers in Open Camps," *Centerville Daily Iowegian*, November 16, 1933.
8. "Pitiful Plight Seen in Family Marooned Here," *Centerville Daily Iowegian*, August 23, 1932; "Prairie Schooners Not Things of Past; One Here Last Night Drawn by Horse; Hardships Still Endure," *Centerville Daily Iowegian*, December 5, 1933; Cee Bee Dee, Around the Town, *Centerville Daily Iowegian*, December 6, 1933.
9. Cee Bee Dee, Around the Town, *Centerville Daily Iowegian*, July 29, 1933; "Tourist Park Camper Sleeps with 'The Wolf,'" *Centerville Daily Iowegian*, October 25, 1933.
10. Beck, *100th Anniversary: Iowa Trust and Savings Bank*, 20 (see chap. 49, n. 7); "Full Car Load Red Cross Flour Comes to County," *Centerville Daily Iowegian*, June 10, 1932; "15,000 Pounds of Flour Will Be Distributed," *Centerville Daily Iowegian*, June 27, 1932; "Half of Relief Flour Divided at Noon Today," *Centerville Daily Iowegian*, June 28, 1932.
11. McElvaine, *The Great Depression: America, 1929–1941*, 78–82 (see chap. 49, n. 6); "Relief Action Begins Today, States Apply," *Centerville Daily Iowegian*, July 19, 1932.
12. Bob Beck, "Vote for Hoover," School Section, *Centerville Daily Iowegian*, October 29, 1932; James Bradley, "Vote for Roosevelt," School Section, *Centerville Daily Iowegian*, October 29, 1932.
13. Dale Jones, interview with the author, October 4, 2000; "Little Change in Early Count Here—Is Report," *Centerville Daily Iowegian*, November 8, 1932; "How Election Returns Will Be Broadcast," *Centerville Daily Iowegian*, November 5, 1932;

"Unofficial Returns of General Election Held Tuesday, November 8, 1932," *Centerville Daily Iowegian*, November 9, 1932.

14. Cee Bee Dee (Charles B. DePuy), As Told Around the Town, *Centerville Daily Iowegian*, July 29, 1933; "Many Seek Jobs at Courthouse; No Bonds Filed," *Centerville Daily Iowegian*, January 6, 1933; "Golden Rule Inn Serves 105 Meals to Hungry People," *Centerville Daily Iowegian*, July 29, 1932.

15. "Situation in Appanoose County Is Considered at Meeting Held by Interested Organizations," *Centerville Daily Iowegian*, February 2, 1933; "Second Meeting on Unemployment Named Committees," *Centerville Daily Iowegian*, February 4, 1933; "S.A. (Steve) Martin Taken Today," *Centerville Daily Iowegian*, February 16, 1957; "Appanoose Manufactured Its Own Money Known as Script [*sic*]," *Centerville Daily Iowegian*, August 26, 1955; "Discussing Use of Scrip in County," *Centerville Daily Iowegian*, February 3, 1933; "Relief Com. Is Putting Scrip Plan in Shape," *Centerville Daily Iowegian*, February 7, 1933; Jesse M. Beck, "Will We Use Scrip Plan?" editorial, *Centerville Daily Iowegian*, February 8, 1933; "Merchants and Professional Men to Consider Scrip," *Centerville Daily Iowegian*, February 8, 1933; "Business Folks Consider Scrip Relief Measure," *Centerville Daily Iowegian*, February 10, 1933; "Points Cited in Favor of Scrip by Charles J. Zylstra, Author, of Hawarden," *Centerville Daily Iowegian*, February 10, 1933; "Scrip Depends Upon All Using," *Centerville Daily Iowegian*, February 11, 1933; "Scrip in Use Early in Week in Two Towns," *Centerville Daily Iowegian*, February 18, 1933; "Scrip Permits 23 Men to Earn Livelihood Now," *Centerville Daily Iowegian*, February 20, 1933; "Scrip Plan Has Filled Aid Need in This County," *Centerville Daily Iowegian*, February 22, 1933; Ethel Lira, "Visiting the Past Part of 'Downsizing,'" *Daily Iowegian*, July 22, 2004; Ethel Lira, telephone interview with the author, September 9, 2009; Scott Swenson, president of Corydon State Bank, telephone interview with the author, September 9, 2009; "Ten More Men Get Employment thru Scrip Use," *Centerville Daily Iowegian*, February 23, 1933; "Windows Give One Day's Work under New Scrip Plan," *Centerville Daily Iowegian*, February 24, 1933; "First Scrip Bill Will Be Sold at Auction—Erskine," *Centerville Daily Iowegian*, February 25, 1933; "$300 in Scrip Is in Circulation over Appanoose," *Centerville Daily Iowegian*, February 28, 1933.

16. "Extra! Appanoose Co. to Get $13,400 from the R.F.C.," *Centerville Daily Iowegian*, February 28, 1933; "Scrip Issue Is Halted Today; Relief Starts," *Centerville Daily Iowegian*, March 6, 1933; "Centerville's Scrip Goes to Great Museum," *Centerville Daily Iowegian*, May 15, 1933.

17. "Appanoose Asks for Government Emergency Fund," *Centerville Daily Iowegian*, February 23, 1933; "Men Appointed to Appanoose Relief Group," *Centerville Daily Iowegian*, March 2, 1933; "Miss Goodson Is New Overseer of Poor in County," *Centerville Daily Iowegian*, July 5, 1932; "450 Given Aid thru Relief Act in This County,"

Centerville Daily Iowegian, March 23, 1933; "Discuss Gardens in Interest of Relief Efforts," *Centerville Daily Iowegian*, March 22, 1933; Jesse M. Beck, "Gardens for the Needy," editorial, *Centerville Daily Iowegian*, March 23, 1933; "Throng Gathers at Payne Bldg. for Free Seed," *Centerville Daily Iowegian*, April 12, 1933; "Enough Relief Garden Seed Was Given out Wednesday to Provide Food for 1,125 of Appanoose County's Unfortunate Residents," *Centerville Daily Iowegian*, April 13, 1933; "Drawings for R.F.C. Garden Plots Thursday," *Centerville Daily Iowegian*, April 19, 1933; "Flour—Money Gone; Relief Gets Big Cut," *Centerville Daily Iowegian*, May 22, 1933.

18. "Organization of Unemployed Held Meetings," *Centerville Daily Iowegian*, June 1, 1933; "R.F.C. Funds Are Low Here; No More Cards," *Centerville Daily Iowegian*, April 24, 1933; "Employment by R.F.C. Funds to Come to An End," *Centerville Daily Iowegian*, May 20, 1933; "Flour—Money Gone; Relief Gets Big Cut," *Centerville Daily Iowegian*, May 22, 1933; "Relief Gardens Need Rain Badly," *Centerville Daily Iowegian*, June 27, 1933; "Must Rely on Gardens More as Funds Fall," *Centerville Daily Iowegian*, June 9, 1933.
19. "Mass Meeting for Unemployed," *Centerville Daily Iowegian*, May 29, 1933; "Organization of Unemployed Held Meetings," *Centerville Daily Iowegian*, June 1, 1933; Cee Bee Dee, As Told Around the Town, *Centerville Daily Iowegian*, May 6, 1933; Cee Bee Dee, As Told Around the Town, *Centerville Daily Iowegian*, June 17, 1933; "Organization of Unemployed Held Meetings," *Centerville Daily Iowegian*, June 1, 1933; "Overseer of the Poor at Charles City Abducted by Angry Mob," *Centerville Daily Iowegian*, August 22 1932; "Punishment Planned for Kidnapers [*sic*]," *Centerville Daily Iowegian*, June 23, 1932; "Arrest Officers for Conspiracy in an Abduction," *Centerville Daily Iowegian*, September 2, 1932.
20. "Organization of Unemployed Held Meetings," *Centerville Daily Iowegian*, June 1, 1933; "Unemployed at Court House Ask for More Relief," *Centerville Daily Iowegian*, June 14, 1933; "Information Is Asked Concerning Relief Need Here," *Centerville Daily Iowegian*, June 1, 1933; "Today Brings New Gathering of Unemployed," *Centerville Daily Iowegian*, June 2, 1933; "Believe Unrest Is Allayed for Time at Least," *Centerville Daily Iowegian*, June 3, 1933.
21. "Unemployed Demand Use Local Labor," *Centerville Daily Iowegian*, June 21, 1933; "Unemployed Seek to Halt Shaling Work," *Centerville Daily Iowegian*, June 22, 1933; "Big Crowd Congregates County Jail," *Centerville Daily Iowegian*, June 22, 1933; "Crowd Dispersed after Demands at the County Jail," *Centerville Daily Iowegian*, June 22, 1933; "Men Released from Jail in Legal Manner," *Centerville Daily Iowegian*, June 23, 1933; "Money All Gone All Relief by Local Fund Now," *Centerville Daily Iowegian*, June 20, 1933; "Poor Relief Being Given by the County," *Centerville Daily Iowegian*, June 27, 1933; Dale Jones, interview with the author, October 4, 2000.
22. Jesse M. Beck, "Our Poor Relief Troubles," editorial, *Centerville Daily Iowegian*, June 23, 1933.

Chapter 52

1. "Roosevelt Inaugurated," *Centerville Daily Iowegian*, March 4, 1933; "Acts Swiftly," *Centerville Daily Iowegian*, March 9, 1933; "Bank Proclamation," *Centerville Daily Iowegian*, March 6, 1933; Jesse M. Beck, "President Acts Promptly," editorial, *Centerville Daily Iowegian*, March 6, 1933; "National Banks in Centerville Open as Usual," *Centerville Daily Iowegian*, March 14, 1933; "Banking Business Fast Returning to the Normal Trend," *Centerville Daily Iowegian*, March 15, 1933.
2. McElvaine, *The Great Depression: America, 1929–1941*, 140–41 (see chap. 49, n. 6); "New Currency Flows to U.S. Banks Today," *Centerville Daily Iowegian*, March 11, 1933; "Iowa Showing Confidence in Bank System," *Centerville Daily Iowegian*, March 15, 1933; "Bankers Asked to Report All Gold Drawers," *Centerville Daily Iowegian*, March 14, 1933; "Hidden Gold Is Being Restored to Circulation," *Centerville Daily Iowegian*, March 14, 1933; "New Optimism Is Apparent; Stocks Mount," *Centerville Daily Iowegian*, March 16, 1933; "Put Quarter Million into Local Banks," *Centerville Daily Iowegian*, March 16, 1933; "Much Gold from Centerville to Federal Reserve," *Centerville Daily Iowegian*, March 18, 1933; "Only Four in Iowa Have More Banks Opened," *Centerville Daily Iowegian*, March 20, 1933.
3. "Henry A. Wallace Officially Named Sec'y Agriculture," *Centerville Daily Iowegian*, February 27, 1933; Morison, *The Oxford History of the American People*, 301 (see chap. 16, n. 3).
4. "Amelia Earhart on Flight with Mrs. Roosevelt," *Centerville Daily Iowegian*, April 21, 1933.
5. Dorothy Owen obituary, *Centerville Daily Iowegian*, February 11, 2004; Raymond Clapper, "Roosevelts Are Smashing Washington Precedents in Wholesale Manner Thus Far," *Centerville Daily Iowegian*, March 29, 1933.
6. "Special Message of Roosevelt Proposes 'Direct Attack' upon U.S. Unemployment Problem," *Centerville Daily Iowegian*, March 21, 1933; "Enrolling Vanguard of Huge Army Today That Will Relieve Unemployment in the U.S.," *Centerville Daily Iowegian*, April 6, 1933; "Many of Bonus Marchers Enlist in Forest Army," *Centerville Daily Iowegian*, May 20, 1933.
7. "Preparing for Workmen When Bill Enacted," *Centerville Daily Iowegian*, March 24, 1933; "Roosevelt Approves More Forest Camps," *Centerville Daily Iowegian*, June 1, 1933.
8. "Camps in Iowa Rumored for Some of Forest Army," *Centerville Daily Iowegian*, April 12, 1933; "Start Enrollment Iowa Unemployed," *Centerville Daily Iowegian*, April 26, 1933; "Are Enlisting Iowa Men for Forest Army," *Centerville Daily Iowegian*, April 27, 1933; "Foresters at Albia Will Do Free Farm Work," *Centerville Daily Iowegian*, May 19, 1933; "First of Iowa's Civilian Recruits to Camp Near Albia," *Centerville Daily*

Iowegian, May 25, 1933; "Reforestation Soil Erosion Program Begun," *Centerville Daily Iowegian*, May 25, 1933; "Foresters for Camp Wapello Go thru Here," *Centerville Daily Iowegian*, June 2, 1933; "More of Civilian Workers Go to Camp," *Centerville Daily Iowegian*, June 2, 1933.

9. "Ten Men Given Call to Camp by Social Worker," *Centerville Daily Iowegian*, May 17, 1933; "First Quota of Forest Army Is Called to Camp," *Centerville Daily Iowegian*, May 18, 1933; "North Site Seems Indicated for the Local CCC Camp," *Centerville Daily Iowegian*, April 5, 1934; "'Straw Bosses' Leave for Camp in Albia Park," *Centerville Daily Iowegian*, May 26, 1933.
10. "Reforestation Work Gets OKeh of Local Youths," *Centerville Daily Iowegian*, September 16, 1933.
11. "CCC Officers Here Preparing for Camp Setup," *Centerville Daily Iowegian*, April 26, 1934; "CCC Camp Is Set up Today at End North 7th," *Centerville Daily Iowegian*, May 12, 1934.
12. "Field Workers from CCC Camp Begin Activity," *Centerville Daily Iowegian*, May 15, 1934; "Centerville's New CCC Camp Now Getting Down to Routine, 198 Officers and Men—Erosion Work Started," *Centerville Daily Iowegian*, May 18, 1934.
13. "Visit to Soil Erosion Projects Now Under Way in Appanoose Co. Indicates Nature of Work Done," *Centerville Daily Iowegian*, June 19, 1934; Bill Smallwood, interview with the author, October 4, 2009.
14. "Extensive Work in State Park by CCC Workers," *Centerville Daily Iowegian*, June 25, 1934; "Are Ready to Consider a State Park Site Located in Some Part of Appanoose," *Centerville Daily Iowegian*, February 23, 1925; "Conserve Flowers on the Railroad Right of Ways," *Centerville Daily Iowegian*, September 28, 1926; "Pammell Opposes Cutting Trees on Hill Slopes," *Centerville Daily Iowegian*, October 21, 1926; Jesse M. Beck, "Iowa Parks," editorial, *Centerville Daily Iowegian*, January 10, 1928; "Pammell Here for Addresses and Conducting Survey," *Centerville Daily Iowegian*, January 9, 1929; "Pammell Addresses the Botany Class," *Centerville Daily Iowegian*, January 12, 1929; "State Board of Conservation Inspection Tour," *Centerville Daily Iowegian*, May 14, 1929; "How to Drive to State Park Site on River," *Centerville Daily Iowegian*, May 9, 1930; "Dr. Pammell Says Is Important That We Stress Beauties of Nature and Preserve Plant Life in State Parks," *Centerville Daily Iowegian*, May 16, 1930; "Complete State Park Action," *Centerville Daily Iowegian*, December 11, 1930; "State Park Here Will Be Improved Soon," *Centerville Daily Iowegian*, June 29, 1931.
15. "Dr. L.H. Pammel, Conservationist, Taken by Death," *Centerville Daily Iowegian*, March 24, 1931.
16. "CCC Camp as Business Asset," *Centerville Daily Iowegian*, August 14, 1934.

Chapter 53

1. "States Given Aid on Basis Money Spent," *Centerville Daily Iowegian*, June 1, 1933; McElvaine, *The Great Depression: America, 1929–1941*, 151, 152 (see chap. 49, n. 6); "Mrs. Blank Goes to Albia as New Social Worker," *Centerville Daily Iowegian*, December 1, 1933; "650 Families Drawing Relief in This County," *Centerville Daily Iowegian*, September 15, 1933; "New Relief Committee Has Outlined Its Policy for Aid with Limited Funds," *Centerville Daily Iowegian*, June 15, 1933; "Many Families of Iowa Given Needed Relief," *Centerville Daily Iowegian*, July 5, 1933; "Appanoose Co. Share of Relief Supplies," *Centerville Daily Iowegian*, December 26, 1933.
2. McElvaine, *The Great Depression: America, 1929–1941*, 153 (see chap. 49, n. 6); "Civil Works Projects in Iowa Now Under Way," *Centerville Daily Iowegian*, November 21, 1933; "Unemployment Front Popping in This County," *Centerville Daily Iowegian*, November 23, 1933; "New Re-Employ Office to Open in Centerville," *Centerville Daily Iowegian*, November 29, 1933; "114 Register as Unemployed Here This A.M.," *Centerville Daily Iowegian*, December 4, 1933; "50 Jobs Will Soon Open Here for Needy Women," *Centerville Daily Iowegian*, December 9, 1933; "Need Material for Women to Sew for Poor," *Centerville Daily Iowegian*, December 22, 1933.
3. "Many Employed in County," *Centerville Daily Iowegian*, December 12, 1933; "City Council Given Review Street Work," *Centerville Daily Iowegian*, January 9, 1934; "Improvement at Courthouse Is Getting Notice," *Centerville Daily Iowegian*, February 8, 1934; "Court House Is Undergoing a Re-Decoration," *Centerville Daily Iowegian*, January 9, 1934; "Soon to Demobilize CWA," *Centerville Daily Iowegian*, February 17, 1934; Cee Bee Dee, As Told Around the Town, *Centerville Daily Iowegian*, August 12, 1933; "Report Shows What Was Done in the County," *Centerville Daily Iowegian*, April 6, 1934.
4. McElvaine, *The Great Depression: America, 1929–1941*, 153 (see chap. 49, n. 6); "Uncle Sam Is Saving Farms in Appanoose County," *Centerville Daily Iowegian*, December 29, 1933; "Wallace Body to Arrive at Home City Tonight," *Centerville Daily Iowegian*, October 28, 1924; "Henry Wallace Ag Secretary Belief Today," *Centerville Daily Iowegian*, February 18, 1933; Sage, *A History of Iowa*, 294–300 (see chap. 1, n. 5); Morison, *The Oxford History of the American People*, 306–7 (see chap. 16, n. 3); "Wm. S. Bradley Is Appointed," *Centerville Daily Iowegian*, July 13, 1933.
5. "Office of Farm Bureau Here Now Very Busy Place," *Centerville Daily Iowegian*, December 29, 1933; "Plan for Distribution of Surplus Grain," *Centerville Daily Iowegian*, January 31, 1934; "Appanoose Has New Farm Debt," *Centerville Daily Iowegian*, April 24, 1934; Roy P. Porter, "Plan to Give Farmers Work Instead Grant," *Centerville Daily Iowegian*, June 5, 1934; "Few More Beans Coming for Sale," *Centerville Daily Iowegian*, June 11, 1934; "Three Thousand Bushels of Soy Beans for County,"

Centerville Daily Iowegian, June 11, 1934; "May Hold off Foreclosures in Appanoose," *Centerville Daily Iowegian*, June 11, 1934; "Farmers Apply for 2250 Bushels Relief Soy Beans," *Centerville Daily Iowegian*, June 13, 1934; "Thursday, June 28th Is Rooster Day," *Centerville Daily Iowegian*, June 26, 1934; "Ship Train Load Distressed Cattle out of C'ville," *Centerville Daily Iowegian*, August 21, 1934; *History of Appanoose County, Iowa*, 56 (see chap. 18, n. 4); "90 Farmers of County Seeking Federal Loans," *Centerville Daily Iowegian*, September 28, 1933; "Wm. S. Bradley Named Officer of Farm Group," *Centerville Daily Iowegian*, August 26, 1936.

6. Morison, *The Oxford History of the American People*, 306 (see chap. 16, n. 3); McElvaine, *The Great Depression: America, 1929–1941*, 156–62 (see chap. 49, n. 6); "Congress Has Record of Accomplishment Unsurpassed by Any Peace-Time Session," *Centerville Daily Iowegian*, June 16, 1933; "Retail Code in Operation," *Centerville Daily Iowegian*, August 1, 1933; "Code Now Established for the Retail Dealers of Nation Has Provision for Hours and Wages," *Centerville Daily Iowegian*, August 1, 1933.

7. "Centerville Business Men Reach Code Agreement," *Centerville Daily Iowegian*, August 1, 1933; "O K President Roosevelt," full-page Cincinnati Firms advertisement, *Centerville Daily Iowegian*, August 3, 1933; "Plumbing—Heating Contractors of Centerville," *Centerville Daily Iowegian*, August 6, 1933; "Centerville Monument Works Notice," *Centerville Daily Iowegian*, August 8, 1933; "Betsy Ross Bakery and Schullian's Quality Bakery," advertisement, *Centerville Daily Iowegian*, August 8, 1933; "Notice," advertisement, *Centerville Daily Iowegian*, August 9, 1933; "Important Announcement," *Centerville Daily Iowegian*, August 18, 1933; "Buy Now Is Necessary Part," *Centerville Daily Iowegian*, August 14, 1933; "Bicycle Craze Is Being Seen in Centerville," *Centerville Daily Iowegian*, August 28, 1933; "Miners Meet to Protest Wages in NRA Code," *Centerville Daily Iowegian*, September 9, 1933; "Mass Meeting of Miners in Strike Areas," *Centerville Daily Iowegian*, September 9, 1933; "More Delay in Making a Coal Code This Area," *Centerville Daily Iowegian*, September 16, 1933.

8. "NRA Parade to Be Sept. 7th," *Centerville Daily Iowegian*, August 31, 1933; "Carl Weeks to Speak Here on NRA Parade Day," *Centerville Daily Iowegian*, September 2, 1933; "All in Readiness for NRA Celebration Thursday," *Centerville Daily Iowegian*, September 6, 1933; "NRA Celebration Brings Crowds; A Splendid Parade," *Centerville Daily Iowegian*, September 7, 1933; Dale Jones, interview with the author, October 4, 2000; "CWA Hours Cut Affects County, Wages Are $7.50," *Centerville Daily Iowegian*, January 29, 1934.

9. "All Local CWA Work Is Halted in This County," February 16, 1934; "Frazier-Lemke Law Illegal," *Centerville Daily Iowegian*, May 27, 1935; Jesse M. Beck, "Outlook for Farm Income Minus AAA," *Centerville Daily Iowegian*, January 13, 1936; "New Program of Relief Started in County Now," *Centerville Daily Iowegian*, May 4, 1934; "Employ Office Opens Today in the Court House," *Centerville Daily Iowegian*, April

30, 1934; McElvaine, *The Great Depression: America, 1929–1941*, 152–53 (see chap. 49, n. 6); Paul R. Beck, "Visits Boulder Dam and Gathers Data on Immensity of the Project Which Is to Irrigate Deserts and Provide Power," *Centerville Daily Iowegian*, April 1, 1935.

10. "Appanoose County Emergency Relief Com. Makes Statement Showing Enormous Sum Now Used in Administering Relief Here," *Centerville Daily Iowegian*, July 29, 1936; "Relief Office Setup Due to Shift, Claim," *Centerville Daily Iowegian*, November 7, 1935; "Uncle Sam Will Soon Mark the Passing of Landmarks in Backyards of This City," *Centerville Daily Iowegian*, June 18, 1936; Jesse M. Beck, "The Swimming Pool," editorial, *Centerville Daily Iowegian*, July 3, 1939; "Pool Dedication Attracts Estimated Crowd of 2,500," *Centerville Daily Iowegian*, July 3, 1939; "New Structures Dot Landscape: In the Back Yards," *Centerville Daily Iowegian*, September 30, 1936; "Presents Defense and Eulogy of WPA," *Centerville Daily Iowegian*, October 8, 1936; "Board Moves to Build New County Home," *Centerville Daily Iowegian*, July 14, 1937; "Iowa to Mark Mormon Trail across State," *Centerville Daily Iowegian*, November 8, 1937; "Temporary Markers Indicate Route Taken by Mormons on Trek through Iowa to Shores of Great Salt Lake," *Centerville Daily Iowegian*, December 16, 1937.

11. "Those over 65 Can Get Social Security Number," *Centerville Daily Iowegian*, May 3, 1937; "This County Has Ten over Share," *Centerville Daily Iowegian*, January 16, 1935; Cee Bee Dee, Around the Town, *Centerville Daily Iowegian*, December 18, 1935; "CWA Worker Is Able to Take Care of Child," *Centerville Daily Iowegian*, December 23, 1933; "Names of Local Persons Sought for Big Greeting," *Centerville Daily Iowegian*, January 25, 1935; Dale Jones, interview with the author, October 4, 2000.

12. "Thurston Opposes Profligacy of the Democrat Regime," *Centerville Daily Iowegian*, September 21, 1934; "Sen. Dickinson Strikes Hard at New Deal," *Centerville Daily Iowegian*, April 3, 1936; Letter from Floyd M. Edwards, Letters to the Editor, *Centerville Daily Iowegian*, March 10, 1937; Letter from T.W. Killion, Letters to the Editor, *Centerville Daily Iowegian*, April 12, 1935.

13. Morison, *The Oxford History of the American People*, 304 (see chap. 16, n. 3); Bill Horine, "Iowa's CCC: A Lasting Legacy," *Iowa Natural Heritage* (fall 2006), 8–10.

14. "Landon Train Slow for Towns Enroute [*sic*]," *Centerville Daily Iowegian*, September 29, 1936; "Seymour to Greet Landon," *Centerville Daily Iowegian*, September 28, 1936; "Landon Stops at Seymour Monday," *Centerville Daily Iowegian*, September 25, 1936; "Landon Stop at Seymour Draws Crowd of 1,500," *Centerville Daily Iowegian*, September 29, 1936.

15. "See a Presidential Train Pass at 3:00 A.M. Something of a Thrill Even If You Don't See the President," *Centerville Daily Iowegian*, September 4, 1936.

16. "Hearst Declares Democracy Given New Life by F.R.," *Centerville Daily Iowegian*, November 5, 1936; "Roosevelt Wins 46 States," *Centerville Daily Iowegian*, November 4, 1936; "State Ticket in Appanoose Went Mostly to Demos," *Centerville Daily Iowegian*, November 4, 1936; "G.O.P. Wins in Iowa," *Centerville Daily Iowegian*, November 6, 1940; "County Goes for Roosevelt and John Valentine," *Centerville Daily Iowegian*, November 6, 1940.

Chapter 54

1. "Still Found in Raid Made by Sheriff's Office," *Daily Iowegian*, October 9, 1920; "Stills, Liquor and Mash Taken over Weekend," *Centerville Daily Iowegian*, May 26, 1924; "Liquor Raid Nets 300 Gallons Wine," *Daily Iowegian*, April 21, 1921; "Says Grappi Sold in New York City," *Daily Iowegian*, July 18, 1921; "Much Grappi Finds Way to Capital by Automobile Route," *Daily Iowegian*, July 14, 1921; "Alleged Liquor Dealer at Liberty Under Heavy Bond," *Centerville Daily Iowegian*, November 13, 1923; "More Raids Bring Booze Supply to 'Scarce' Levels," *Centerville Daily Iowegian*, January 4, 1924; "Booze Airplanes Reported Here," *Centerville Daily Iowegian*, June 5, 1925; "Police Business," *Daily Iowegian*, May 2, 1921.
2. Name withheld, interview with the author, October 24, 2009; Name withheld, interview with the author, October 27, 2009; "Mafia Has Adherents in Many Places," *Daily Iowegian*, January 13, 1921; "Rough Stuff by the Toughs," *Daily Iowegian*, December 13, 1921; "Search Is on for Tony Sebben Who Lived Here," *Centerville Daily Iowegian*, May 15, 1924.
3. "Much Concern Felt for Missing Man," *Daily Iowegian*, January 5, 1923; "Rathbun Man Is Reported Missing," *Centerville Daily Iowegian*, April 12, 1924; "Feud Rages in Italian Section over Cora Affair," *Daily Iowegian*, January 11, 1921; "Wanted Marriage Records Changed Many Years Ago," *Centerville Daily Iowegian*, April 22, 1929; "Three Bullets Lodged in Head and Still Lives," *Daily Iowegian*, January 11, 1921; "Head Chopped from Italian in Another City," *Daily Iowegian*, January 12, 1921; "Former Resident Reported Killed in Chicago Feud," *Centerville Daily Iowegian*, October 27, 1927; "Reported Shot by Jealous Lover," *Centerville Daily Iowegian*, June 3, 1927; "Former Resident of This County Buried Alive," *Centerville Daily Iowegian*, May 16, 1927; "Former Resident of This County Shot in Gangster War," *Centerville Daily Iowegian*, October 20, 1926; "Sam Falzone Is Dead in Chicago," *Centerville Daily Iowegian*, December 9, 1924.
4. "Coras Say Is No Explanation for Shooting," *Daily Iowegian*, January 17, 1921; "Tells of Death of Calabroni," *Centerville Daily Iowegian*, November 9, 1926; U.S. Bureau of the Census, "1920 Federal Census of Appanoose County."

5. Family interview conducted by the author with Goldie Dwight, Patricia Ruggles, Sammy Owens, Larry Owens, Francis Owens, Bobby Owens and Bill Owens, November 13, 2009.
6. "Mike Cogo Held to Federal Grand Jury on Liquor Charge Following Raid near Here," *Centerville Journal*, June 27, 1922.
7. "Pleds [*sic*] Guilty to Liquor Nuisance," *Centerville Daily Iowegian*, March 29, 1923; "Liquor Seller Is Fined $300," *Centerville Journal*, August 18, 1922; "Two Fined Total of $900 before Judge W.M. Walker," *Centerville Daily Iowegian*, June 5, 1924; "Wrong Address Causes Suit," *Centerville Daily Iowegian*, August 20, 1925; "Smaniatta [*sic*] Gets Thousand Dollar Fine in Count," *Centerville Daily Iowegian*, May 5, 1924; "Search for Smaniatta [*sic*] Is Being Made," *Centerville Daily Iowegian*, May 6, 1924; "Smaniatta [*sic*] Still Unheard from and May Stay Away," *Centerville Daily Iowegian*, May 7, 1924; "No Bidding at Smaniatta [*sic*] Sale," *Centerville Daily Iowegian*, August 25, 1924; "First Degree Murder Charged in Indictment," *Daily Iowegian*, August 27, 1920.
8. "Carmela Russo Gets Pardon from Acting Governor," *Centerville Daily Iowegian*, August 31, 1923; "Carmella [*sic*] Milone [*sic*] Sues for Divorce," *Southern Iowa American*, February 17, 1925; "Carmella [*sic*] Russo–Malone Divorced," *Centerville Daily Iowegian*, April 1, 1925; "Death Threats from Husband of Carmella [*sic*] Malone," *Centerville Daily Iowegian*, June 3, 1925.
9. "Searching for Missing Girl," *Centerville Daily Iowegian*, September 26, 1925; "Fear Foul Play in Disappearance of Russo Girl," *Centerville Daily Iowegian*, September 28, 1925; "Arrest Made in Disappearance," *Centerville Daily Iowegian*, October 2, 1925; "Still No Clue to Missing Girl," *Centerville Daily Iowegian*, October 2, 1925; "Last Chapter in Russo Case," *Southern Iowa American*, October 5, 1925; "Russo Girl Is Bride of Sister's Former Husband," *Centerville Daily Iowegian*, October 5, 1925; "New Angle to the Russo Case," *Centerville Daily Iowegian*, October 8, 1925; "Russo Case Is Apparently Ended, Father Returns," *Centerville Daily Iowegian*, October 8, 1925; "Is New Angle to the Russo Case," *Centerville Daily Iowegian*, October 6, 1925.
10. "Russo Girl Shot Today, May Recover," *Centerville Daily Iowegian*, November 4, 1925; "No Sympathies for the Daughter," *Centerville Daily Iowegian*, December 30, 1925; "Constanzo [*sic*] Russo Shot by Probation Husband," *Southern Iowa American*, December 31, 1925; Bob Feeny, "Shot for Abandoning Her 'Probation Honeymoon,'" *Des Moines Sunday Register*, magazine section, January 17, 1926; "Father Blames Daughter for Their Plights," *Centerville Daily Iowegian*, January 1, 1926; "'Father Don't Mean That—He Will Cool Off,'" *Southern Iowa American*, January 2, 1926; "Russo Girl Is Back in City," *Centerville Daily Iowegian*, January 26, 1926; "Girl May Enter State School," *Centerville Daily Iowegian*, January 27, 1926; "Russo Girl to Reformatory," *Centerville Daily Iowegian*, January 29, 1926.

11. "Local Lawyer Murdered," *Centerville Daily Iowegian*, February 28, 1929; "Has New Offices," *Daily Iowegian*, July 13, 1920; "Slayer Taken to Ottumwa," *Centerville Daily Iowegian*, March 1, 1929.
12. Jesse M. Beck, "D. Fulton Rice," editorial, *Centerville Daily Iowegian*, March 1, 1929; "Great Outpouring of People for the D.F. Rice Funeral," *Centerville Daily Iowegian*, March 2, 1929; "D. Fulton Rice: In Memoriam," *Centerville Daily Iowegian*, March 6, 1929.
13. "Standing on the Spot Where One Week before He Killed His Victim," photograph, *Centerville Daily Iowegian*, March 11, 1929; "State Witnesses Are Heard; State Rests," *Centerville Daily Iowegian*, April 24, 1929; "Defendant in Murder Trial Long on Stand," *Centerville Daily Iowegian*, April 25, 1929.
14. "Domyancich Now No Defendant in Slander Suit," *Centerville Daily Iowegian*, April 3, 1929; "Infant Rice Dies Soon after Birth," *Centerville Daily Iowegian*, April 4, 1929; "Domyancich Trial Started," *Centerville Daily Iowegian*, April 22, 1929; "Domyancich Pleads Guilty," *Centerville Daily Iowegian*, April 25, 1929; "Domyancich Is in Prison Now," *Centerville Daily Iowegian*, April 26, 1929; "Slayer of Rice a Suicide," *Centerville Daily Iowegian*, September 4, 1929.
15. "Seven Men Murdered in Daring Gangster Raid in Chicago," *Centerville Daily Iowegian*, February 14, 1929; Helmer and Bilek, *The St. Valentine's Day Massacre*, 139–45, photographs on pages 148–49 (see chap. 36, n. 25).
16. "Assassinations for Mastery of Beer Trade Many," *Centerville Daily Iowegian*, February 15, 1929; "Chicago Again in Terrors of Gang Warfare," *Centerville Daily Iowegian*, February 15, 1929; "Demand a Chicago Cleanup," *Centerville Daily Iowegian*, February 16, 1929; "Ministers Turning Their Attention to Chicago Conditions," *Daily Iowegian*, February 23, 1929.
17. "Pastor Warns Is Time to Act Now before Tragedy," *Centerville Daily Iowegian*, February 18, 1929; "Who's Who in the Egan and Hogan Gangs and How the Feud between Them Arose," editorial, *St. Louis Post-Dispatch*, March 30, 1923; "More Concerning Gangsters Visit to Centerville," *Centerville Daily Iowegian*, April 24, 1928.
18. "Three More Men Are Accused Result Chicago Massacre," *Centerville Daily Iowegian*, March 5, 1929.
19. Helmer and Bilek, *The St. Valentine's Day Massacre*, 116, 155, 159–60 (see chap. 36, n. 25); "Developments in Chicago Massadre [*sic*]," *Centerville Daily Iowegian*, March 8, 1929.
20. "Centerville Boy Has Produced Deadly Weapon," *Daily Iowegian*, November 19, 1920; William J. Helmer, *The Gun That Made The Twenties Roar* (Highland Park, N.J.: The Gun Room Press, 1969), 27–28, 35–36; "Oscar V. Payne," Thompson Collectors News Online Editon, vol. 129, July 15, 2001, Thompson Collectors Association, http://www.nfatoys.com/tsmg/tcn/2001/jul/jul01p4.htm.
21. Helmer and Bilek, *The St. Valentine's Day Massacre*, 178–80 (see chap. 36, n. 25).

22. Helmer and Bilek, *The St. Valentine's Day Massacre*, 180–84 (see chap. 36, n. 25); "Police Making Great Effort to Capture Burke," *Centerville Daily Iowegian*, December 18, 1929; J. Evetts Haley, *Robbing Banks Was My Business: The Story of J. Harvey Bailey, America's Most Successful Bank Robber* (Canyon, Tex.: Palo Duro Press, 1973), 91.

Chapter 55

1. J. Evetts Haley, *Robbing Banks Was My Business*, introduction, xi, 34, 84, xii, 91, xiii, xvi (see chap. 54, n. 22); "Mrs. Amanda Bailey Dies at Farm Home," *Green City (Mo.) Press*, March 22, 1934.
2. Gladys Wells Crumpacker, *The Complete History of Sullivan County Missouri: Vol. 2, 1900–1979* (Milan, Mo.: History Publications, Inc., 1980), 206; Lowry Production, *How Burke Was Captured*, film produced and directed by Fred Lowry, photography by R.D. Pasquale, recorded by Motiophone Film Corporation, 1931; Virgil Rodgers, interview with the author, May 22, 2004.
3. Crumpacker, *The Complete History of Sullivan County Missouri*, 208; Virgil Rodgers, interview with the author, May 22, 2004; C.B. DePuy, "Notorious Burke, Long Sought in Many States Married in Centerville Last June," *Centerville Daily Iowegian*, March 26, 1931; "Burke Picture and Reward Hung in Court House," *Centerville Daily Iowegian*, March 30, 1931.
4. "Plenty Weddings in Appanoose Is Report for June," *Centerville Daily Iowegian*, July 3, 1930; Copy of marriage licenses record number 27, Appanoose County, Iowa, marriage license number 13021 June 17, 1930; "White–Porter," *Milan (Sullivan County, Mo.) Standard*, June 26, 1930, vol. 58, no. 25, page 1, column 2; C.B. DePuy, "Notorious Burke, Long Sought in Many States Married in Centerville Last June," *Centerville Daily Iowegian*, March 26, 1931.
5. "Wife of Burke Is Not Convinced He Is Hard Criminal," *Centerville Daily Iowegian*, March 26, 1931; "Stands by Burke," *Centerville Daily Iowegian*, March 30, 1931; Ramah Peek, interview with the author, May 22, 2004; Evelyn (Vance) Daily, "Her Memories Retold," unpublished account as told to her daughter, circa July 2001, collection of Appanoose County Museum, Centerville.
6. "Hunsaker, Burke's Captor, Glad It's All Over," copy of newspaper article, name of publication unknown, date unknown.
7. "Reward Not Spent Yet," *Milan Standard*, March 27, 1931; Ralph Foster, "The Inside Story of the Capture of Fred Burke," in *Startling Detective Adventures*, 42, 43, 44, 45, 85; "Killer Burke's Bloody Career," *Jim Jam Jems* 21, no. 4 (June-July 1931), Graphic Arts Corporation, St. Paul, Minn.; Lowry Production, *How Burke Was Captured*; "Burke Captors Find Many Are After Custody," *Centerville Daily*

Iowegian, March 27, 1931; "Cities of Ten States Want Killer Fred Burke," *Centerville Daily Iowegian*, March 30, 1931; "Michigan Again Home of Burke, Probably Life," *Centerville Daily Iowegian*, March 30, 1931; "Burke Admits Tight Case Is Against Him," *Centerville Daily Iowegian*, March 30, 1931; Jesse M. Beck, "Burke to Prison," editorial, *Centerville Daily Iowegian*, April 28, 1931; "Burke Starts Life Sentence in Michigan," *Centerville Daily Iowegian*, April 28, 1931; "Killer Burke, Wed in Centerville, Dies in Prison," *Centerville Daily Iowegian*, July 11, 1940; "Fred Burke Died at Michigan State Prison of a Heart Attack," *Milan Republican*, July 11, 1940, page 1, col. 5; "'Killer Burke,' Prison Inmate Since '31, Dies," Marquette, Michigan, *The Daily Mining Journal*, July 11, 1940; "'Killer Burke' Married Here Leaves $8,000," *Centerville Daily Iowegian*, August 26, 1940.

8. "Crime Center of Nation Is Shifting Now," *Centerville Daily Iowegian*, July 14, 1933; "Two Notorious Criminals May Be in County," *Centerville Daily Iowegian*, April 27, 1936.
9. "Crime Center of Nation Is Shifting Now," *Centerville Daily Iowegian*, July 14, 1933; "Capone's Gang Was Syndicate," *Centerville Daily Iowegian*, November 11, 1931; "Expert Criminal Chaser Operating," *Centerville Daily Iowegian*, July 9, 1923; "Nab Moulton Robbery Suspects," *Centerville Daily Iowegian*, March 30, 1923; "Ed Winters, Wanted Here, Held in Mo.," *Centerville Daily Iowegian*, June 20, 1923; "Bank Loot Is Estimated at About $4,300," *Centerville Daily Iowegian*, August 14, 1931; "Bandits Rob Moravia Bank," *Centerville Daily Iowegian*, October 17, 1928; "Bank Robber Trail Lost," *Centerville Daily Iowegian*, October 17, 1928; "Bank Loot Is Estimated at About $4,300," *Centerville Daily Iowegian*, August 14, 1931; "State Agents at Moravia to Probe Robbery of Bank," *Centerville Daily Iowegian*, August 13, 1931; "Moravia Bank Loot Is Found South of Exline," *Centerville Daily Iowegian*, November 11, 1931; "Rob Dean Savings Bank," *Centerville Daily Iowegian*, December 6, 1929; "Man Hunt Continues in Rough Country of North Missouri as Dean Robbers Elude Pursuers," *Centerville Daily Iowegian*, December 7, 1929; "State Bank at Cincinnati Robbed—One Bandit Suicide," *Centerville Daily Iowegian*, May 26, 1932; "Cincinnati Bank Is Robbed—Extra," *Centerville Daily Iowegian*, November 24, 1937; "Iowa Trust Robbed $5,000," *Centerville Daily Iowegian*, October 3, 1932; "Extra! Local Young Man Is Arrested as Suspect in Bank Stickup Here," *Centerville Daily Iowegian*, October 3, 1932; "Jack Budiselich 19-Year-Old Bandit Returns Stolen Money and Tells of Criminal Career," *Centerville Daily Iowegian*, October 4, 1932.
10. "Iowa Thoroughfare for Criminals 'When Heat Is On' Says Schmidt; Creates Crime Problem in State," *Centerville Daily Iowegian*, June 18, 1936; "Bandit Car through City," *Centerville Daily Iowegian*, January 30, 1933; "Desperadoes Sought Here!" *Centerville Daily Iowegian*, September 29, 1933; "'Honeymoon Bandits' Taken," *Centerville Daily Iowegian*, February 17, 1938; "Floyd May Wind up the Year as a Free Bandit,"

Centerville Daily Iowegian, December 26, 1933; Haley, *Robbing Banks Was My Business*, 76, 91, 94, 96, 81 (see chap. 54, n. 22); "Prison Break Leader Known to Local Man," *Centerville Daily Iowegian*, June 5, 1933; "Dillinger Has Escaped," *Centerville Daily Iowegian*, March 3, 1934; "Dillinger Aide Is Killed," *Centerville Daily Iowegian*, June 8, 1934; "Still Search for Dillinger; Camps Visited," *Centerville Daily Iowegian*, June 9, 1934; "Just Walkathon Promoters—Not Notorious Bandit," *Centerville Daily Iowegian*, March 15, 1934; "Militia Guns Are Made Useless in Event Theft," *Centerville Daily Iowegian*, May 4, 1934.

11. "Bandit Report Renews Request for Better Arms," *Centerville Daily Iowegian*, October 19, 1934; Reva Ballard, interview with the author, October 27, 2009; "Extra! May Be Bandit Car Abandoned by Floyd Gang," *Centerville Daily Iowegian*, October 13, 1934; "Almost Positive Floyd Car Found Here," *Centerville Daily Iowegian*, October 15, 1934; "Burned Car Here Is Same as That in Bullet Battle," *Centerville Daily Iowegian*, October 16, 1934; "Floyd's Last Car Sold by Deputy Brunson Today," *Centerville Daily Iowegian*, October 31, 1934; "Was Pretty Boy Floyd in This City Shortly Prior His Death in Ohio–? Many Believe That He Visited Here," *Centerville Daily Iowegian*, October 24, 1934; Leo Craver, interview with the author, October 20, 2011.
12. "Extra! Rumor Chase Barrow Gang," *Centerville Daily Iowegian*, July 29, 1933; "Barrow Gang Chased Here? A Possibility," *Centerville Daily Iowegian*, July 31, 1933; "Farmer's Store Plano Scene of a Robbery," *Centerville Daily Iowegian*, July 31, 1933; "Barrow's Gang in Appanoose?" *Centerville Daily Iowegian*, April 9, 1934; "Widow of Slain Barrow Is Given 10 Year Sentence," *Centerville Daily Iowegian*, September 5, 1933; "Barrow and Girl Killed," *Centerville Daily Iowegian*, May 23, 1934.

Chapter 56

1. Majestic advertisement, *Centerville Daily Iowegian*, February 21, 1934; "Manchuria Fall to Japan," *Centerville Daily Iowegian*, December 30, 1931; "Chinese Children and Women Killed Without Mercy," *Centerville Daily Iowegian*, November 25, 1932.
2. "German War Clouds Gather," *Centerville Daily Iowegian*, August 13, 1932; "Charge Reign of Terror Existing in Germany Now," *Centerville Daily Iowegian*, March 23, 1933; "Nazis Dissolve Catholic Veterans Group," *Centerville Daily Iowegian*, July 23, 1935; "Hitler Greeting Sweeps Germany; How Is Started," *Centerville Daily Iowegian*, September 19, 1933; "Hitler Controls Super System of Secret Police," *Centerville Daily Iowegian*, April 28, 1933; "Jewish Boycott to Be Severe as Rules Announce," *Centerville Daily Iowegian*, March 31, 1933; "Boycott Works as Nazis Push Their Program," *Centerville Daily Iowegian*, April 1, 1933; "Czechs Aided Fleeing Jews from Germany," *Centerville Daily Iowegian*, October 20, 1933; "Hitler Drives Jews into

Spanish Retreat," *Centerville Daily Iowegian*, October 26, 1933; "Man of the Umbrella and Violin Case Pessimistic over the Lay Public," *Centerville Daily Iowegian*, December 10, 1932; "Einstein Comes Here to Study a New Theory," *Centerville Daily Iowegian*, December 30, 1931; "Einstein Again in California; The Third Visit," *Centerville Daily Iowegian*, January 9, 1933; "Assumes New Post," *Centerville Daily Iowegian*, October 23, 1933; "Take Passports," *Centerville Daily Iowegian*, March 30, 1933; "Jews Lose All Political Rights in Nazi Decree," *Centerville Daily Iowegian*, November 15, 1935; Jesse M. Beck, "Another Reign of Terror," editorial, *Centerville Daily Iowegian*, July 2, 1934; "Nazis Bar Jewish War Dead Honors," *Centerville Daily Iowegian*, October 23, 1935.

3. Robert Fell, Strictly Confidential, *Centerville Daily Iowegian*, February 3, 1933; "Report Italians in Ethiopia," *Centerville Daily Iowegian*, October 2, 1935; "Italian, Ethiopian Troops Fight for Critical Area," *Centerville Daily Iowegian*, December 19, 1935; "Official Reports Italian Army Desertions," *Centerville Daily Iowegian*, October 8, 1935; "League Votes Gas Protest," *Centerville Daily Iowegian*, April 9, 1936; "Radical Victory Forces Spanish Gov't to Resign," *Centerville Daily Iowegian*, February 19, 1936; "Italy, Nazis to Recognize Rebels," *Centerville Daily Iowegian*, October 21, 1936; "Rebel Drive Snaps Bilbao Defense Line," *Centerville Daily Iowegian*, April 27, 1937.
4. "See Nazi Victory in Saar Election," *Centerville Daily Iowegian*, January 14, 1935; "Saarites Welcome Hitler with Cheers," *Centerville Daily Iowegian*, March 1, 1935; "Saarlanders Bid Goodby [*sic*] to Homeland and Flee," photograph, *Centerville Daily Iowegian*, February 2, 1935; "Churchill Sees Nazis as Threat," *Centerville Daily Iowegian*, September 26, 1935; "Warns England Endangered by Air Attack," *Centerville Daily Iowegian*, November 17, 1934; Richard Overy, *The Penguin Historical Atlas of the Third Reich* (Harmondsworth, Middlesex, England: Penguin Books, Ltd., 1996), 47, 50.
5. "Churchill Sees Nazis as Threat," *Centerville Daily Iowegian*, September 26, 1935; "England Plans for Increased Air Force," *Centerville Daily Iowegian*, June 13, 1934; "England Begins Recruiting for Royal Air Force," *Centerville Daily Iowegian*, May 23, 1935; "British Vote Rearmament," *Centerville Daily Iowegian*, November 15, 1935; "France Votes Millions More for Defense," *Centerville Daily Iowegian*, November 24, 1934; "France Reinforces Rhine!" *Centerville Daily Iowegian*, March 23, 1935; "Air Forces of France to Begin Maneuvers," *Centerville Daily Iowegian*, October 1, 1935; "Remilitarization of the Rhineland… Hidden Fortification," caption and photograph, *Centerville Daily Iowegian*, March 16, 1936.
6. "Witness of War in Spain Calls Relative Here," *Centerville Daily Iowegian*, February 4, 1937; "Nephew of Mrs. D. Rosenbaum Gives First Hand Account of Bitter Civil War in Spain," *Centerville Daily Iowegian*, February 16, 1937; Obituary of Lester Ziffren, *Washington Post*, November 20, 2007; "Hears Fighting and Helps Take Away Refugees," *Centerville Daily Iowegian*, August 18, 1936; "Another County Resident Writes of Spanish War," *Centerville Daily Iowegian*, August 19, 1936; "Former

Seymour Resident Caught in Spanish War," *Centerville Daily Iowegian*, August 11, 1936; "Capture of Irun by Spanish Rebels Is Told in Letter to Seymour Man," *Centerville Daily Iowegian*, October 7, 1936; "Former Seymour Resident Welcomes Mail from Home; Tells of Civil War," *Centerville Daily Iowegian*, October 23, 1936.

7. "Says Conditions in Russia Worse Than Are Reported," *Centerville Daily Iowegian*, April 3, 1930; "Told of Russia in Earlier Days," *Centerville Daily Iowegian*, March 9, 1933; "Tells of New Rule in Italy," *Centerville Daily Iowegian*, May 31, 1929; Gordon Gammack, "In Dark Clouds of Depression, Girls' Cage Success, Numa's Silver Lining," *Centerville Daily Iowegian*, January 5, 2010, reprinted from *Des Moines Register*, date unknown (early 1940s); Mary Buttel, interview by Gary Craver, March 22, 1991, transcript privately held by Gary Craver; "Death Threatens Local Pastor's Mission Friend," *Centerville Daily Iowegian*, March 27, 1927; "The Japanese Have Gone 'Hog Mad,' Writes L.D. Gholson, Relative of Publisher, from Shanghai, China," *Centerville Daily Iowegian*, February 27, 1932; "Joe Shkolnick Is Elected to Office in Zionist Group," *Centerville Daily Iowegian*, January 31, 1938; Charles DePuy, Around the Town, *Centerville Daily Iowegian*, March 14, 1938; "J.J. Frankel in Drive to Aid Jews of Austria–Germany," *Centerville Daily Iowegian*, June 4, 1938.
8. William Carlson Smith, *Americans in the Making: The National History of the Assimilation of Immigrants* (New York: D. Appleton-Century Company, 1939), 369–86; "History of the Junior College in Centerville," *Centerville Daily Iowegian*, August 25, 1930; "Junior College Will Open Here with Fall Term," *Centerville Daily Iowegian*, April 9, 1930; "Latest Census Bulletin," *Centerville Daily Iowegian*, September 17, 1930; "First Ever School Reunion for Rathbun," *Centerville Daily Iowegian*, June 14, 2002; Sol Kauzlarich, interview by Gary Craver, September 23, 2006, transcript in collection of Appanoose County Museum, Centerville; Gordon Gammack, "In Dark Clouds of Depression, Girls' Cage Success, Numa's Silver Lining," *Centerville Daily Iowegian*, January 5, 2010, reprinted from *Des Moines Register*, date unknown (early 1940s); "Opening of Centerville High School Today Recalls Dedication of Former High School by Famous Chase Osborn," *Centerville Daily Iowegian*, January 8, 1940; Himie Voxman, interview with the author, June 9, 2003.
9. Robert Fell, Strictly Confidential, *Centerville Daily Iowegian*, July 27, 1934.

Chapter 57

1. "Worst Dust Storm in Long Period Sweeps County and Housecleaning Is in Order Today in Many Homes," *Centerville Daily Iowegian*, November 13, 1933; "Dust Storm Is One of the Worst, Over All Iowa," *Centerville Daily Iowegian*, April 23, 1934; "Navy Man Here Says Dust Blow Was 'The Worst,'" *Centerville Daily*

Iowegian, May 3, 1933; "Iowa Corn Husking Almost Completed," *Centerville Daily Iowegian*, November 22, 1933; Jesse M. Beck, "Dust Storms General," editorial, *Centerville Daily Iowegian*, May 16, 1934; "How Dust Storms Turn Day into Night in Kansas," *Centerville Daily Iowegian*, April 6, 1933; "Dust Drifts Like Snow in Drouth-Stricken Area of Middle West," *Centerville Daily Iowegian*, June 7, 1934; "Bad Storm Strikes—Mud Underfoot—Dust in the Air," *Centerville Daily Iowegian*, March 20, 1935; "Dust Storm Strikes Kansas City," *Centerville Daily Iowegian*, March 22, 1935; "Oklahoma Crops Ruined by Severe Dust Storms," *Centerville Daily Iowegian*, March 30, 1935; "Sand Storms Bring Desolation to Western Farms," *Centerville Daily Iowegian*, April 6, 1935; "Worst of Series of Dust Storms Hits Southwest," *Centerville Daily Iowegian*, April 11, 1935; "Masks Used in Dust Storm," *Centerville Daily Iowegian*, April 15, 1935; "Dust Storm from Southwest Swirls over Iowa Today," *Centerville Daily Iowegian*, March 24, 1936; C.B. DePuy, Around the Town, *Centerville Daily Iowegian*, March 31, 1937; "Texas Blinded by Heavy Dust Storm," *Centerville Daily Iowegian*, March 27, 1935; "Children Lost Going Home in Big Dust Storm," *Centerville Daily Iowegian*, April 12, 1935; "Dust Storm Area Black as Night in the Daytime," *Centerville Daily Iowegian*, April 13, 1935; "Wrote of Dust Storm in Kansas," *Centerville Daily Iowegian*, April 8, 1935.

2. "Winter of 35–36 Far Below Zero; Summer in 100's," *Centerville Daily Iowegian*, August 23, 1938; "Storm and Cold Lashes County—Once Again," *Centerville Daily Iowegian*, February 8, 1936; "Weather Slows Court Work in Present Term," *Centerville Daily Iowegian*, February 6, 1936; Dale Jones, interview with the author, October 4, 2000; "Home from the Extreme Cold Is Arranged Here," *Centerville Daily Iowegian*, February 13, 1936; "Shortage of Coal Becomes More Serious," *Centerville Daily Iowegian*, February 15, 1936; "Zero Blasts Block Water Service Here," *Centerville Daily Iowegian*, February 4, 1936; "Cold Breaks Twelve Year Record Here," *Centerville Daily Iowegian*, February 5, 1936; "Snow Blocks Entrance to State Mines," *Centerville Daily Iowegian*, February 8, 1936; "Lack of Water Is New Menace to Local Homes," *Centerville Daily Iowegian*, February 8, 1936; "Customers Buy out Town's One Grocery Store," *Centerville Daily Iowegian*, February 8, 1936; "Coal Problem in Iowa Still Serious Today," *Centerville Daily Iowegian*, February 10, 1936; "Local Schools to Open Again Tues. Morning," *Centerville Daily Iowegian*, February 10, 1936; "Bitter Cold and Blizzard Brings Crisis," *Centerville Daily Iowegian*, February 10, 1936; "Mayor Moves to Aid Refugees of Cold Wave Here," *Centerville Daily Iowegian*, February 10, 1936; "'Cold as Usual'—Report Today; Nine Below Zero," *Centerville Daily Iowegian*, February 11, 1936; "Highway Maintenance Men Here Work 96 Hours with No Sleep, to Open Roadways," *Centerville Daily Iowegian*, February 20, 1936.
3. "Briefs Tell Story of Cold in State," *Centerville Daily Iowegian*, February 10, 1936; "Plea for Aid to Birds in County Is Voiced Here," *Centerville Daily Iowegian*, January

29, 1936; "Frozen Dog Standing by Roadside," *Centerville Daily Iowegian*, August 23, 1938; "Mystic Raise Fund for Birds," *Centerville Daily Iowegian*, February 8, 1936; "CCC Camp Needs Help in Battle for Wildlife," *Centerville Daily Iowegian*, February 4, 1936; C.B. DePuy, Around the Town, *Centerville Daily Iowegian*, February 8, 1936; "Cold Claims 2 More Lives," *Centerville Daily Iowegian*, February 5, 1936; "Jerome Woman Found Frozen at Davenport," *Centerville Daily Iowegian*, February 10, 1936; "Jerome," *Centerville Daily Iowegian*, February 11, 1936; "Evans Vicinity," *Centerville Daily Iowegian*, February 12, 1936; W.B. Russell, correspondent, "Numa," *Centerville Daily Iowegian*, February 12, 1936; "Garretson Funeral Services Postponed," *Centerville Daily Iowegian*, February 8, 1936; "So Much Snow It Was Difficult to Hold Funerals," *Centerville Daily Iowegian*, August 23, 1938; "Dr. Charles A. Manahan of Vinton…," untitled, *Centerville Daily Iowegian*, February 15, 1936; "Doctor Travels on Snow Shoes to Visit Sick," *Centerville Daily Iowegian*, February 12, 1936; "Dr. Leffert Is Second in Race with Stork Sun…," untitled, *Centerville Daily Iowegian*, February 10, 1936.

4. "Remember Winter–Summer 35–36?" *Centerville Daily Iowegian*, January 29, 1958; "Sun Fries Egg near Post Office at Intersection," *Centerville Daily Iowegian*, July 16, 1936; "Bad Egg Yields Good Turkey at Seymour," *Centerville Daily Iowegian*, July 15, 1936; "Corn Near Point of Failure Due to Extreme Heat," *Centerville Daily Iowegian*, July 16, 1936; "Iowa Crop Loss Ten Million Bu. Per Day—Report," *Centerville Daily Iowegian*, July 17, 1936; "Grass Fire Cause of Heavy Loss in Moulton Vicinity," *Centerville Daily Iowegian*, August 20, 1936; "Call Firemen to Fight Grass Fires," *Centerville Daily Iowegian*, July 21, 1936; "Pasture Blaze near Unionville Threatens Town," *Centerville Daily Iowegian*, July 17, 1936; "Field Fire Was Carnival Threat This Morning," *Centerville Daily Iowegian*, July 16, 1936; "30 Acres Swept by Flame on Far West of This City," *Centerville Daily Iowegian*, July 15, 1936; "Fire at Wooden Bank Yesterday," *Centerville Daily Iowegian*, July 15, 1936; "Two Stricken Due to Extreme Heat," *Centerville Daily Iowegian*, July 17, 1936; Himie Voxman, interview with the author, June 9, 2003; Obituary of Wm. M. Henderson, *Centerville Daily Iowegian*, July 17, 1936; "Miller Home Has Announced Three Funerals," *Centerville Daily Iowegian*, July 15, 1936; "Wm. Henderson Victim of Heat at County Home," *Centerville Daily Iowegian*, July 14, 1936; "Death Rides Heat Wave in Centerville," *Centerville Daily Iowegian*, July 14, 1936; "Mrs. S.E. Fannon Succumbs to Heat and Ill Health," *Centerville Daily Iowegian*, July 15, 1936; "Iowa Heat Wave Death Toll Mounts to 397," *Centerville Daily Iowegian*, July 17, 1936; "Local Heat Wave Officially Lasted for Sixteen Days," *Centerville Daily Iowegian*, July 20, 1936; "Snow Shoyels [*sic*] Used to Clean Away Hail," *Centerville Daily Iowegian*, July 20, 1936; "Mercury Climbs above 100 Mark," *Centerville Daily Iowegian*, August 13, 1936; "Break in Heat Sends Mercury to 55 Degrees," *Centerville Daily Iowegian*, August 29, 1936.

5. "Chicago World's Fair, Go Rock Island," advertisement, *Centerville Daily Iowegian*, June 20, 1934; "Jimmy Toussaint," advertisement, *Centerville Daily Iowegian*, June 20, 1934; "Dance Featuring Louis Welk," advertisment, *Centerville Daily Iowegian*, April 5, 1935; Bob Seddon, interview with the author, March 16, 2010; "Dancing!" advertisement, *Centerville Daily Iowegian*, May 2, 1935; "To Play for Last Legion Dance," *Centerville Daily Iowegian*, April 11, 1935; "Easter Ball," advertisement, *Centerville Daily Iowegian*, April 10, 1935; "Noted Choir Is Heard Here in Sunday Concert," *Centerville Daily Iowegian*, April 1, 1935; "Messiah: Great Audience," *Centerville Daily Iowegian*, December 15, 1934; "Majestic: Shirley Temple in *Dimples*," advertisement, *Centerville Daily Iowegian*, November 14, 1936; "Majestic: Charlie Chaplin in *Modern Times*," advertisement, *Centerville Daily Iowegian*, June 9, 1936; "Majestic: Ginger Rogers and Fred Astaire in *Top Hat*," advertisement, *Centerville Daily Iowegian*, January 4, 1935; "Majestic: Clark Gable, Claudette Colbert in *It Happened One Night*," advertisement, *Centerville Daily Iowegian*, April 27, 1935; "Cavalcade Wins Kentucky Derby; Garner the Rider," *Centerville Daily Iowegian*, May 7, 1934; "'Git Along, Horse!' Pleaded Garner; Cavalcade Responded to Win Derby, Giving Jockey Year's Biggest Thrill," *Centerville Daily Iowegian*, January 5, 1935; C.B. DePuy, Around the Town, *Centerville Daily Iowegian*, May 8, 1934; advertisement, "Majestic: Fox News Showing Complete 'The Kentucky Derby' with Mack Garner of Centerville Riding Cavalcade to Win," *Centerville Daily Iowegian*, May 21, 1934.
6. "Age Old Attraction of Circus Draws Crowds to Show Grounds as Russell Bros. Circus Opens," *Centerville Daily Iowegian*, July 7, 1936; "Russell Bros. Circus Proved Unusual Treat," *Centerville Daily Iowegian*, July 8, 1936; "Sunset Carnival Is Scheduled Here," *Centerville Daily Iowegian*, July 10, 1936; "Flying Circus Will Show Here September 17," *Centerville Daily Iowegian*, September 13, 1933; "Huge Crowd at Carnival Here," *Centerville Daily Iowegian*, August 21, 1935; "Live Penguins with Whale Exhibit," *Centerville Daily Iowegian*, September 25, 1935; "Huge Octopus on Exhibition Here with Sea Giant," *Centerville Daily Iowegian*, September 23, 1935; "Flea Circus with Whale Exhibit," *Centerville Daily Iowegian*, September 24, 1935; "A Real Whale Is Coming to Town," *Centerville Daily Iowegian*, September 24, 1935; "Human Fly Will Climb Bank Building," *Centerville Daily Iowegian*, May 31, 1935; "Human Fly Chair Balancing Act," *Centerville Daily Iowegian*, June 1, 1935.
7. "C.H. Students First in Iowa in Literature Tests," *Centerville Daily Iowegian*, May 17, 1929; Jesse M. Beck, "Halt School Taxes," editorial, *Centerville Daily Iowegian*, November 15, 1930; "More of Report Concerning the Splendid School System in Which Centerville Can Take Just Pride," *Centerville Daily Iowegian*, July 31, 1931; "Lee Alexander Honored Again," *Centerville Daily Iowegian*, May 31, 1932; "Harold Swanson Now Author of 'Bermuda Moon,'" *Centerville Daily Iowegian*, August 11, 1932; "Local Theatre Will Show Picture Based on Story Written by Harold

Swanson, Former Centerville Boy," *Centerville Daily Iowegian*, November 1, 1932; "Roy Houser in 'Nation's News,'" *Centerville Daily Iowegian*, May 24, 1937; "Musical Courses Offered in Centerville High School Are Among Best in State," *Centerville Daily Iowegian*, August 23, 1937; "Centerville Native Voxman Honored," *Centerville Daily Iowegian*, July 21, 2000; for other prominent graduates of Appanoose County, see "Appanoose County's Extraordinary Individuals" exhibit, Appanoose County Historical Society, Centerville, Iowa; "CHS Band Winner at Annual State Contest," *Centerville Daily Iowegian*, May 10, 1937; "National Winner," *Centerville Daily Iowegian*, May 19, 1937; "Gower Accepts New Position," *Centerville Daily Iowegian*, February 4, 1939; Jim Senior, interview with the author, March 1, 2010; E.W. Fannon, "Golden Age of Athletics at High School Is Recalled," *Centerville Daily Iowegian*, August 18, 1961; "Unbeaten Centerville Team Ends Season," *Centerville Daily Iowegian*, November 8, 1935; "Agnesson Named on I.D.P.A. All State 3rd Team," *Centerville Daily Iowegian*, December 2, 1935; "Centerville Girls Rack Up First State Cage Championship," *Centerville Daily Iowegian*, March 18, 1935; E.W. Fannon, "State Championship Redettes Return for Reunion This Weekend," *Centerville Daily Iowegian*, October 16, 1961; Jesse M. Beck, "The Centerville Girls," editorial, *Centerville Daily Iowegian*, March 23, 1936.

8. Dan Ehl, managing editor, "Mystic Once Dominated H.S. Girls' Basketball," *Daily Iowegian*, January 10, 2002; Ethel Lira, "'Iowa Boy' Comes to Town," *Ad-Express/Iowegian*, January 17, 2002; "Numa Wins State Title, Seymour Tied," *Centerville Daily Iowegian*, March 17, 1941; "400 Attend Numa Celebration for Champions," *Centerville Daily Iowegian*, March 31, 1941; Gordon Gammack, staff writer for *Des Moines Register*, "In Dark Clouds of Depression, Girls Cage Success, Numa's Silver Lining," *Daily Iowegian*, January 5, 2010, reprint from *Des Moines Register*, date unknown (early 1940s); Molly Banks, Seymour School Board secretary, interview with the author, March 30, 2010; Maurice Stamps, former instructor and coach, interview with the author, March 30, 2010; "Seymour Beats Numa to Take Girls' Cage Championship," *Mason City Globe Gazette*, March 10, 1947.

Chapter 58

1. "U.S. Official Order Citizens from Shanghai," *Centerville Daily Iowegia*, August 16, 1937; "Fear Increased Foreign Casualties," *Centerville Daily Iowegian*, August 17, 1937; "300 Chinese Refugees Slain," *Centerville Daily Iowegian*, September 8, 1937; "Japanese Bombard NanKing," *Centerville Daily Iowegian*, September 20, 1937; "2,000 Slain in Air Raids by Japanese," *Centerville Daily Iowegian*, September 23, 1937; "Japanese Plan Major Drive," *Centerville Daily Iowegian*, August 2, 1937; "Ghastly Film of War

Arrives This Afternoon," *Centerville Daily Iowegian*, September 23, 1937; C.B. DePuy, Around the Town, *Centerville Daily Iowegian*, December 29, 1937.

2. "Hitler Breaks Locarno Pact," *Centerville Daily Iowegian*, March 7, 1936; "German Troops March Again into Rhineland," *Centerville Daily Iowegian*, March 10 1936; "France Reports Extent of Nazi Force on Border," *Centerville Daily Iowegian*, May 13, 1936.
3. "Hitler Returns to Austria," *Centerville Daily Iowegian*, March 12, 1938; "Nazis in Complete Control of Austria," *Centerville Daily Iowegian*, March 12, 1938; "No Force on Earth Can Shake Us Hitler Declares in Speech," *Centerville Daily Iowegian*, March 14, 1938; "Nazi Pageantry Dazzles Austria as Voting Nears," *Centerville Daily Iowegian*, March 19, 1938.
4. "Jewish Lawyers under Nazi Ban," *Centerville Daily Iowegian*, March 14, 1938; "Nations United Hitler Says," *Centerville Daily Iowegian*, March 14, 1938; "Bows to Nazis," *Centerville Daily Iowegian*, March 19, 1938; "Freud Seriously Ill after Visit by Nazi Police," *Centerville Daily Iowegian*, March 22, 1938; "Exiled Freud," *Centerville Daily Iowegian*, June 17, 1938; "Jews Are Driven to Suicide by New German Persecution," *Centerville Daily Iowegian*, November 10, 1938; "Jews Observe Pogrom," *Centerville Daily Iowegian*, November 10, 1951; "Jews Scrub Vienna Streets in Nazi 'Purge,'" photograph, *Centerville Daily Iowegian*, August 16, 1938; "Jews Report Vienna Death Rate Increase," *Centerville Daily Iowegian*, March 22, 1938; "Smugglers Aid 1,000 Jews in Secret Flight," *Centerville Daily Iowegian*, August 20, 1938; Jesse Beck, "The Door Closed," editorial, *Centerville Daily Iowegian*, April 11, 1939.
5. "Germany Concentrates Jews for Deporation [*sic*]," *Centerville Daily Iowegian*, October 29, 1938; "Stable Home of Thousand Expelled Jews," photograph, *Centerville Daily Iowegian*, November 14, 1938; "Germany Is Still Punishing Jews," *Centerville Daily Iowegian*, November 30, 1938; "'Main Streets' Banned to Jews," *Centerville Daily Iowegian*, December 3, 1938; "Germans Order Polish Jews to Leave Country," *Centerville Daily Iowegian*, October 28, 1938; "Jewish Suffering Grows," *Centerville Daily Iowegian*, November 12, 1938; "Germans Levy 20 Per Cent Tax on Jew Residents," *Centerville Daily Iowegian*, November 23, 1938.
6. "World Seeks Homes for Jewish Refugess [*sic*]; Abuse Abates," *Centerville Daily Iowegian*, November 21, 1938; "Boatload of Jews to South America" *Centerville Daily Iowegian*, January 10, 1939; "Fear Suicides among Jews Who Are under Ban," *Centerville Daily Iowegian*, June 1, 1939; "Fear Nazi Refugee Suicide Wave," photograph, *Centerville Daily Iowegian*, June 3, 1939; "Watch Their Kin Sail Back to Germany," photograph, *Centerville Daily Iowegian*, June 5, 1939; "900 Jewish Refugees Fail, Ship Sails to Germany," *Centerville Daily Iowegian*, June 6, 1939; "Refugees Proceeding to Europe Under Full Steam; 907 Aboard," *Centerville Daily Iowegian*, June 14, 1939; "Jewish Refugees Had to Form an Anti-Suicide Pact," *Centerville Daily Iowegian*, June 17,

1939; "Another Boatload of Jewish Refugees Are Seeking Some Haven," *Centerville Daily Iowegian*, June 20, 1939; "500 Jews Seek Refuge in Turkey," *Centerville Daily Iowegian*, August 9, 1939; "Homeless Jews Seek a Refuge at Constanza," *Centerville Daily Iowegian*, August 11, 1939; "Jews Ousted from Poland Territory," *Centerville Daily Iowegian*, November 24, 1939.

7. Jesse M. Beck, "Four in One Telegraph," *Centerville Daily Iowegian*, January 11, 1938; "Milo M. Thompson AP Executive for Europe Coordinating Coverage," map of Europe, *Centerville Daily Iowegian*, October 16, 1939; "Associated Press News Wire System," map, *Centerville Daily Iowegian*, March 23, 1938; "Millions Acclaim New Air Hero, Howard Hughes, in New York," photograph, *Centerville Daily Iowegian*, July 15, 1938; Jesse Beck, "Count on Appanoose," editorial, *Centerville Daily Iowegian*, July 11, 1938.

8. C.B. DePuy, Around the Town, *Centerville Daily Iowegian*, May 12, 1937; "Broadcast of Coronation on Air Early Wed.," *Centerville Daily Iowegian*, May 11, 1937.

9. Bob Edwards, *Edward R. Murrow and the Birth of Radio Journalism* (Hoboken, N.J.: John Wiley and Sons, Inc., 2004) 3, 5; Charles A. Grumish, "War Drama Brings Radio Censorships Demands," *Centerville Daily Iowegian*, October 31, 1938; "Scares Country," *Centerville Daily Iowegian*, November 2, 1938; C.B. DePuy, Around the Town, *Centerville Daily Iowegian*, September 23, 1936; "Iowa's Own 'Dutch' Reagan at Majestic," *Centerville Daily Iowegian*, February 25, 1938.

10. Stanley Cloud and Lynne Olson, *The Murrow Boys: Pioneers on the Front Lines of Broadcast Journalism* (Boston: Houghton Mifflin Company, 1996), 33–34, 32.

11. Ibid., 42, 38; Bill Smallwood, interview with the author, April 22, 2010; Phyllis Morrow Cosby, interview with the author, April 20, 2010; Jeanne Harrington Fowler, interview with the author, April 20, 2010; "Jack Shelley to Share His WWII Correspondent Experiences Wed.," *Ogden Reporter*, June 16, 2004.

12. "Hitler Triumphantly Enters Sudetenland," *Centerville Daily Iowegian*, October 3, 1938; "Hitler's Army in Prague," *Centerville Daily Iowegian*, March 15, 1939; "England Meekly Rebukes Germany," *Centerville Daily Iowegian*, March 15, 1939; "Hitler May Try to Get More Territory," *Centerville Daily Iowegian*, March 16, 1939; "England–France Stand by While Hitler Walks In," *Centerville Daily Iowegian*, March 14, 1939; "British Will Back Poland," *Centerville Daily Iowegian*, July 10, 1939; "Britain–Poland Sign Pact," *Centerville Daily Iowegian*, August 25, 1939.

13. "Nations Urge Nationals to Seek Safety," *Centerville Daily Iowegian*, September 24, 1938; "Americans Find German Frontier Traffic Stopped," *Centerville Daily Iowegian*, September 26, 1938; "Belgian Troops Are Mobilized," *Centerville Daily Iowegian*, September 24, 1938; "Belgium Calls Reserve Army," *Centerville Daily Iowegian*, September 27, 1938; "No War,—Well Just in Case—," *Centerville Daily Iowegian*, August 28, 1939; "Sweden Decides to Call Reserve Class," *Centerville Daily Iowegian*,

April 19, 1939; "Embassy to Be Bombproofed," *Centerville Daily Iowegian*, September 17, 1938; "France Orders Troops Prepare for Emergency," *Centerville Daily Iowegian*, September 23, 1938; "France Sends War Force to Maginot Line," *Centerville Daily Iowegian*, September 6, 1938; "France Moves Reserves toward German Border," *Centerville Daily Iowegian*, September 10, 1938; Cloud and Olson, *The Murrow Boys*, 54; "Blackout Tonight of French Coast Cities Ordered," *Centerville Daily Iowegian*, August 28, 1939; "France Orders Evacuation of Paris at Once," *Centerville Daily Iowegian*, September 26, 1938; "American Hospital Ready for Attack," *Centerville Daily Iowegian*, September 17, 1938.

14. Norman Moss, *19 Weeks: America, Britain, and the Fateful Summer of 1940* (New York: Houghton Mifflin, 2003), 50; "Britain Boosts Income Tax," *Centerville Daily Iowegian*, April 26, 1938; "England Sees War, Defense Work Starts," *Centerville Daily Iowegian*, September 27, 1938; "Britain Calls Out Reserves for Defenses," *Centerville Daily Iowegian*, September 26, 1938; "English Factories Speed Production of War Materials," *Centerville Daily Iowegian*, February 19, 1937; "England Hides Throne," *Centerville Daily Iowegian*, August 25, 1939; "King and Queen of England Are Ready for Raid," *Centerville Daily Iowegian*, April 12, 1939; "London: Guys Hospital," photograph, *Centerville Daily Iowegian*, August 31, 1939; "Cover Signposts," photograph, *Centerville Daily Iowegian*, August 31, 1939; "Conscription in England Is Latest Move," *Centerville Daily Iowegian*, April 26, 1939; "London Zoo Ready for War to Start," *Centerville Daily Iowegian*, September 29, 1938; "To Share in England's Preparedness Campaign," *Centerville Daily Iowegian*, July 26, 1938; "Special Announcement: Evacuation of London," *Centerville Daily Iowegian*, September 6, 1939; "Evacuation Rehearsal Is Fun for Tots," *Centerville Daily Iowegian*, August 28, 1939; "It's Just a Lark to Children," photograph, *Centerville Daily Iowegian*, September 1, 1939; "British Children—Not on Way to School!" photograph, *Centerville Daily Iowegian*, September 11, 1939; author's personal recollections; Suzanne Powell Hudson, interview with the author, April 24, 2010.

15. "U.S. Ship Moves to Thames River," *Centerville Daily Iowegian*, September 14, 1938; "U.S. Cruisers in British Port," *Centerville Daily Iowegian*, September 21, 1938; "U.S. Warships Speed to Europe," *Centerville Daily Iowegian*, September 27, 1938; "U.S. Ministers Leaving Prague," *Centerville Daily Iowegian*, March 21, 1939; "Second Embassy Head Recalled," *Centerville Daily Iowegian*, November 17, 1938; "American Travelers in Berlin Urged to Depart," *Centerville Daily Iowegian*, September 14, 1938; "Nations Urge Nationals to Seek Safety," *Centerville Daily Iowegian*, September 24, 1938; "Americans Find German Frontier Traffic Stopped," *Centerville Daily Iowegian*, September 26, 1938; "Americans Urged to Leave Britain," *Centerville Daily Iowegian*, September 27, 1938; "U.S. Embassy Asks Americans Leave France," *Centerville Daily Iowegian*, September 26, 1938; "The Story in Berlin," *Centerville Daily Iowegian*, August

26, 1939; "Americans Are Rushing Home—," *Centerville Daily Iowegian*, August 25, 1939; "Hurry Amreicans [*sic*] Home from France," *Centerville Daily Iowegian*, August 28, 1939; "Americans Flee War-Tense Europe by Hundreds," *Centerville Daily Iowegian*, August 31, 1939; "1,000 Refugees Left Stranded in Paris Today," *Centerville Daily Iowegian*, September 2, 1939.

16. "Churchill Sees War Imminent," *Centerville Daily Iowegian*, June 28, 1939; "Centerville Looks at Europe and Voices Its Opinions," *Centerville Daily Iowegian*, August 24, 1939; Jesse M. Beck, "War Clouds Hang Over Europe," editorial, *Centerville Daily Iowegian*, August 26, 1939.
17. Charles DePuy, Around the Town, *Centerville Daily Iowegian*, August 30, 1939; "Troops Cross Border Trying for Fast Drive," *Centerville Daily Iowegian*, September 1, 1939; "War: Poland–Germany Locked in Battle," *Centerville Daily Iowegian*, September 1, 1939.
18. "Hitler Responsible for Crisis in Europe Local Residents Say," *Centerville Daily Iowegian*, September 13, 1939.

Chapter 59

1. "U.S. Preparing for War?" *Centerville Daily Iowegian*, November 28, 1938; "$552,000,000 for Defense Is Roosevelt Plea Today," *Centerville Daily Iowegian*, January 12, 1939.
2. "Local Guard Preparing," *Centerville Daily Iowegian*, April 1, 1939; "Company G Has New Equipment," *Centerville Daily Iowegian*, May 2, 1940; "Navy Recruiter to Work Here Saturday," *Centerville Daily Iowegian*, December 10, 1936; "Marine Corps to Send Recruiting Officer to City," *Centerville Daily Iowegian*, February 9, 1939.
3. "Co G Ordered into Emergency War Drill," *Centerville Daily Iowegian*, August 7, 1939; "Officers at War," *Centerville Daily Iowegian*, August 11, 1939; "Co G 'Comes and Gets It,'" photograph, *Centerville Daily Iowegian*, August 11, 1939.
4. "Nazi Patrols Cross Border," *Centerville Daily Iowegian*, August 31, 1939; "Poland Declares State of War Today," *Centerville Daily Iowegian*, September 2, 1939; Philip B. Kunhardt Jr., ed., *Life: World War II* (Boston: Little, Brown and Company, 1990), 25; "Nazis Take Polish Cities," *Centerville Daily Iowegian*, September 5, 1939; "Warsaw Falls," *Centerville Daily Iowegian*, September 8, 1939; Morison, "The Emergent Giants," in *The Oxford History of the American People*, 348 (see chap. 16, n. 3); "Fight to the Finish," *Centerville Daily Iowegian*, September 7, 1939.
5. "Joe Goldstein Builds New Home," *Centerville Daily Iowegian*, July 21, 1938; "Notes of Polonaise Rally Polish Morale," *Centerville Daily Iowegian*, September 12, 1939; John Keegan, *The Second World War* (New York: Penguin Books, 1990), 288–89; "Nazi Patrols Cross Border," *Centerville Daily Iowegian*, August 31, 1939; Frank K. Kappler,

Life: World War II, ed. Philip B. Kunhardt Jr. (Boston: Little, Brown and Company, 1990), 27.

6. "Centerville to Have Chance to Aid German Jews," *Centerville Daily Iowegian*, November 19, 1938; "Author to Talk at Church Next Monday Evening," *Centerville Daily Iowegian*, August 12, 1939; "J.J. Frankel to Jewry Meeting," *Centerville Daily Iowegian*, January 14, 1939; "J.J. Frankel Enlightened Wednesday Club Group on Jewish Affairs, Problems," *Centerville Daily Iowegian*, March 30, 1939; "Humanity Speaks in Behalf of Oppressed Jews," *Centerville Daily Iowegian*, May 20, 1939; "Jewish People Renew an Oath," *Centerville Daily Iowegian*, May 24, 1939; "Noted Lecturer in City Tonight," *Centerville Daily Iowegian*, August 14, 1939.
7. Morison, "The Emergent Giants," in *The Oxford History of the American People*, 348 (see chap. 16, n. 3); "Warsaw's Radio Voice Is Stilled Today," *Centerville Daily Iowegian*, September 28, 1939.
8. "Goldstein Is Heart Victim; Loss Mourned," *Centerville Daily Iowegian*, October 24, 1939.
9. "Canada Acts Quickly in Backing England," *Centerville Daily Iowegian*, September 11, 1939; "Canadian Soldiers Take up Posts," photograph, *Centerville Daily Iowegian*, September 11, 1939; "Released to Britain by Embargo Repeal," photograph, *Centerville Daily Iowegian*, November 5, 1939.
10. Burner, Bernhard and Kutler, *Firsthand America*, 847 (see chap. 50, n. 15); "Submarine Warfare Strikes Blow to British Commerce," *Centerville Daily Iowegian*, September 13, 1939; "Athenia," *Centerville Daily Iowegian*, September 13, 1939; "Miss Bonnett Describes Athenia Sinking," *Centerville Daily Iowegian*, October 13, 1939; "Neighbors Drop in to Welcome Martha Bonnett's Return," *Centerville Daily Iowegian*, October 6, 1939; "Told of Sinking of Athenia and Night of Distress," *Centerville Daily Iowegian*, December 7, 1939; "Reveal That Nazis Sank the Athenia Not the British," *Centerville Daily Iowegian*, January 15, 1946.
11. "Stunned by the Attack, But… Life Goes on as Usual in Denmark," *Centerville Daily Iowegian*, April 10, 1940; "Nazi Troops Advance in Norway," *Centerville Daily Iowegian*, April 10, 1940; "Nazis Bomb Some Norwegian Towns," *Centerville Daily Iowegian*, April 10, 1940; "Extra: Total War at Hand; Germany's War Machine Rolls into Holland, Belgium and Luxembourg; Allies Rush Full Aid; Cities Bombed," *Centerville Daily Iowegian*, May 10, 1940; Max Harrelson, "Nazi Airforce Spans Strong Defenses and Land Troops in Key Centers; Rotterdam Partly in Enemy Hands; Dutch Fight On," *Centerville Daily Iowegian*, May 10, 1940; "Most Gigantic Battle of All Time Is Ahead," *Centerville Daily Iowegian*, May 10, 1940; "Greatest Battle 'Of All Time' Is in First Stages," *Centerville Daily Iowegian*, May 14, 1940; "Allied Outlook Is Very Dark as They Retreat on All Fronts in Total War," *Centerville Daily Iowegian*, May 17, 1940; Dewitt McKenzie, "Biggest Battle of All Time Is Now Taking Form," *Centerville Daily Iowegian*,

May 13, 1940; John Keegan, ed., *Collins Atlas of World War II* (London: HarperCollins Publishers, 2006), 30–31; "May Wipe out Army in Week Germans Warn," *Centerville Daily Iowegian*, May 25, 1940; "Allied Troops Hope to Escape," *Centerville Daily Iowegian*, May 29, 1940; "War Terrors," *Centerville Daily Iowegian*, May 31, 1940; "Flanders Rescue Complete," *Centerville Daily Iowegian*, June 1, 1940; Keegan, *The Second World War*, 78–82 (see chap. 59, n. 5); Nigel Farndale, "Hell and High Water: Dunkirk at 70," *UK Sunday Telegraph*, supplement, 7; Morison, "The Emergent Giants," in *The Oxford History of the American People*, 349 (see chap. 16, n. 3); "As Four German Spearheads Converged on Paris," map, *Centerville Daily Iowegian*, June 11, 1940; "French Fear That Huge Maginot Line May Finally Fall," *Centerville Daily Iowegian*, June 14, 1940; "Nazis Take Paris," *Centerville Daily Iowegian*, June 14, 1940.

12. Around the Town, *Centerville Daily Iowegian*, July 10, 1940; "Letter from Norway Tells of Falling Fears and Rising Hopes as the War Progressed," *Centerville Daily Iowegian*, September 26, 1945; Jesse M. Beck, "Right Type of Foreigner," editorial, *Centerville Daily Iowegian*, May 11, 1940; "Local News," *Centerville Daily Iowegian*, May 14, 1940.
13. "Impromptu Song Feature of the Successful Music Contest," *Centerville Daily Iowegian*, May 13, 1940; "Big Crowd Greets Local Musicians," *Centerville Daily Iowegian*, May 13, 1940.

Chapter 60

1. Robert Fell, Strictly Confidential, *Centerville Daily Iowegian*, May 14, 1940; Dale Jones, interview with the author, October 4, 2000; William L. Shirer, *Berlin Diary* (Boston: Little, Brown and Company, 1941), 389.
2. Rex Ingraham, "United States Is Prepared to Aim," *Centerville Daily Iowegian*, May 15, 1940; "Fight Forward," *Centerville Daily Iowegian*, May 15, 1940; Jesse Beck, "Will We Keep Out?" editorial, *Centerville Daily Iowegian*, May 13, 1940; Robert Fell, Strictly Confidential, *Centerville Daily Iowegian*, May 13, 1940.
3. Morison, "The Emergent Giants," in *The Oxford History of the American People*, 349, 350 (see chap. 16, n. 3); "Churchill Named New British Head," *Centerville Daily Iowegian*, May 10, 1940; "New World to Rescue Empire Premier Says," *Centerville Daily Iowegian*, June 4, 1940; Moss, *19 Weeks*, 157 (see chap. 58, n. 14).
4. "Uncle Sam Looks for Soldiers in This City Today," *Centerville Daily Iowegian*, June 14, 1940; "Government Putting Air School Here," *Centerville Daily Iowegian*, June 10, 1940; "Learn to Fly Free! Attention Student Pilots," *Centerville Daily Iowegian*, June 12, 1940; "Flying School Started Today at College Here," *Centerville Daily Iowegian*, June 20, 1940.

5. "Order Local National Guard Strength Increase," *Centerville Daily Iowegian*, June 19, 1940; "Training for Local Guard Is Underway," *Centerville Daily Iowegian*, July 20, 1940; "Company G at Training Camp," *Centerville Daily Iowegian*, August 12, 1940; "Company G Playing Vital Part in War Games Now in Progress at Big Encampment at Ripley, Minnesota," *Centerville Daily Iowegian*, August 26, 1940.
6. "F.R. Signs Conscription Bill," *Centerville Daily Iowegian*, September 16, 1940; "Young Men Sign up for Service," *Centerville Daily Iowegian* October 16, 1940; "3,500 Appanoose Young Men Register for Army Service," *Centerville Daily Iowegian*, October 16, 1940.
7. "Men Who Registered Being Assigned Serial Numbers," *Centerville Daily Iowegian*, October 19, 1940; C.B. DePuy, Around the Town, *Centerville Daily Iowegian*, October 21, 1940; "Draft Lottery at Washington D.C.," *Centerville Daily Iowegian*, October 29, 1940; "Number 1 Man in County Is Rarin' to Go," *Centerville Daily Iowegian*, October 29, 1940.
8. Moss, *19 Weeks*, 216–23 (see chap. 58, n. 14).
9. "Churchill to Talk Sunday," *Centerville Daily Iowegian*, July 13, 1940; "Local News: Mr. & Mrs. Roy Houser…," untitled, *Centerville Daily Iowegian*, June 25, 1941; C.B. DePuy, Around the Town, *Centerville Daily Iowegian*, June 1, 1940; Edwards, *Edward R. Murrow and the Birth of Radio Journalism*, 1–3, 51–55 (see chap. 58, n. 9); Cloud and Olson, *The Murrow Boys*, 90–92 (see chap. 58, n. 9); John Talbot, interview with the author, October 10, 2002; Bob Seddon, interview with the author, April 15, 2010; "'March of Time' Shows How News of War Gathered," *Centerville Daily Iowegian*, September 25, 1940; Moss, *19 Weeks*, 338–39 (see chap. 58, n. 14).
10. "Back to 1914: Col. Charles Sweeny," *Centerville Daily Iowegian*, August 29, 1939; Moss, *19 Weeks*, 197 (see chap. 58, n. 14); Al Cleveland, interview with the author, April 25, 1999; Pierre Burton, *Marching as to War: Canada's Turbulent Years 1899–1953* (Canada [no city listed]: Doubleday Canada, 2001), 433; "Stimson Denounces Tribune War Story," *Centerville Daily Iowegian*, December 5, 1941; Jesse Beck, "A Roosevelt Enlists," *Centerville Daily Iowegian*, November 22, 1939; "No Risk of U.S. Citizenship If You Fight Nazis," *Centerville Daily Iowegian*, July 17, 1940; "London Needs U.S. Airplane Pilots," *Centerville Daily Iowegian*, July 17, 1940; "500 American Pilots Fighting with British," *Centerville Daily Iowegian*, March 12, 1941; "10,000 Americans with Allied Army," *Centerville Daily Iowegian*, May 8, 1941; DeWitt MacKenszie, "United States Moves toward War in Europe," *Centerville Daily Iowegian*, December 10, 1940; C.B. DePuy, Around the Town, *Centerville Daily Iowegian*, April 17, 1940; C.B. DePuy, Around the Town, *Centerville Daily Iowegian*, June 5, 1940.
11. C.B. DePuy, Around the Town, *Centerville Daily Iowegian*, June 15, 1940; C.B. DePuy, Around the Town, *Centerville Daily Iowegian*, February 15, 1941; "War's Children May Come Here," *Centerville Daily Iowegian*, August 1, 1940; "Local Resident Would Take

Care of Child Refugee," *Centerville Daily Iowegian*, August 2, 1940; "Centerville to Offer Homes to War's Orphans," *Centerville Daily Iowegian*, August 13, 1940; "Three English Children to Be in Centerville," *Centerville Daily Iowegian*, November 22, 1940; "Central Shoe to Aid War Relief Drive for Shoes," *Centerville Daily Iowegian*, October 8, 1940; "Barrels of Shoes to War Refugees," advertisement, *Centerville Daily Iowegian*, October 9, 1940; "Helping the British People," photograph with caption, *Centerville Daily Iowegian*, November 8, 1940; "Centerville Women Knit for War Victims," *Centerville Daily Iowegian*, August 2, 1940; "Wanted: Air Raid Shelter Cots—for Them!" photograph and "Bundles for Britain" caption, *Centerville Daily Iowegian*, January 11, 1941; "33,201 Knitted Articles Sent to England Already by Bundles for Britain," *Centerville Daily Iowegian*, September 9, 1940; "Colonel H.C. Haynes Receives Note of Acknowledgement from British for Splendid Work Done by Local Women," *Centerville Daily Iowegian*, October 4, 1941; Bill Smallwood, interview with the author, June 17, 2010.

12. "Contribute to Finnish Aid," *Centerville Daily Iowegian*, December 28, 939; "This City Will Send Aid to Stricken Finland; The Iowegian Responds to Hoover's Appeal," *Centerville Daily Iowegian*, December 8, 1939; "Greek War Relief Movement in Iowa," *Centerville Daily Iowegian*, November 22, 1940; "Harry Stamos to Direct Drive for Greek Funds Here," *Centerville Daily Iowegian*, December 4, 1940; "Harry Stamos Reports $100 Greek Relief," *Centerville Daily Iowegian*, December 16, 1940; "Mr. Stamos Asks Further Aid for the Greek Cause," *Centerville Daily Iowegian*, December 24, 1940; "Red Cross Seeks $1,000 in County for War Relief," *Centerville Daily Iowegian*, May 11, 1940; "Flight of Europe War Refugees Is 'River of Misery' Writers Say," *Centerville Daily Iowegian*, June 10, 1940; "Garments for War Relief Planned in County Red Cross," *Centerville Daily Iowegian*, May 11, 1940; "Red Cross War Drive Started," *Centerville Daily Iowegian*, August 1, 1940; "Blitzkrieg of Mercy Flight," *Centerville Daily Iowegian*, August 7, 1940; "Bombing Planes to Carry 'Blitzkrieg of Mercy' to Towns in Appanoose Soon," *Centerville Daily Iowegian*, July 11, 1940; "Representative of Red Cross in City Asks Action," *Centerville Daily Iowegian*, May 22, 1940; C.B. DePuy, Around the Town, *Centerville Daily Iowegian*, January 4, 1941; "Women to Volunteer for Red Cross Service," *Centerville Daily Iowegian*, October 4, 1940; "Red Cross Sock Knitters Make Fine Progress," *Centerville Daily Iowegian*, September 24, 1941; "Local Appeal Is Made for More Women to Knit for British and American Soldiers This Winter," *Centerville Daily Iowegian*, October 4, 1941; "Want Knitters for Young Men in Army, Navy," *Centerville Daily Iowegian*, August 29, 1941; "Over $500,000 Raised by Ambulance Corps Since Drive Opening," *Centerville Daily Iowegian*, December 2, 1940.

13. C.B. DePuy, Around the Town, *Centerville Daily Iowegian*, September 4, 1940; "No Fifth Column Danger Noted in This Great State," *Centerville Daily Iowegian*, June 12,

1940; "Eleven Persons Gain Citizenship in Court Today," *Centerville Daily Iowegian*, September 25, 1940; "Citizenship School Here Every Thurs.," *Centerville Daily Iowegian*, February 16, 1940; "Large Group Aliens Nationalized Today," *Centerville Daily Iowegian*, February 16, 1940; "Aliens Must Register," *Centerville Daily Iowegian*, August 19, 1940; "County Aliens Registered," photograph, *Centerville Daily Iowegian*, September 5, 1940; "300 Appanoose Aliens Sign Up," *Centerville Daily Iowegian*, December 27, 1940.

14. "Morrow and Bandy Leave Thanksgiving," *Centerville Daily Iowegian*, November 23, 1940; "Enlisted Draft Enrollees Are Given Sendoff," *Centerville Daily Iowegian*, November 29, 1940; "First Two Appanoose Boys Serving in the Army Now," *Centerville Daily Iowegian*, December 6, 1940; "Pictures of the Year," photograph and caption, *Centerville Daily Iowegian*, December 23, 1940; "Call Two More Men to Service," *Centerville Daily Iowegian*, January 2, 1941; "Two More Men Join the Army," *Centerville Daily Iowegian*, January 9, 1941; "First Seymour Boy Called into Army for U.S. Training," *Centerville Daily Iowegian*, January 10, 1941; "Rosenbaum Will Do Special War Duty This June," *Centerville Daily Iowegian*, June 5, 1940; Jesse Beck, "The War Drums Beat," editorial, *Centerville Daily Iowegian*, March 4, 1941.

15. "Democracy Defended by F.R.," inaugural event, *Centerville Daily Iowegian*, January 20, 1941; "Co. G Received Mobilization Orders," *Centerville Daily Iowegian*, January 21, 1941; "Local Guard Ready to Mobilize," *Centerville Daily Iowegian*, February 8, 1941; "We Are Proud of You," full-page advertisement, *Centerville Daily Iowegian*, February 28, 1941; "City Bids Co. G a Fervent Farewell," *Centerville Daily Iowegian*, March 3, 1941; "Pictures of the Year—Co. G Waves Goodbye," *Centerville Daily Iowegian*, December 19, 1941.

16. "Army Trucks Pass through City in 2 Large Convoys," *Centerville Daily Iowegian*, April 5, 1941; Bill Smallwood, interview with the author, June 17, 2010; "Convoy of 200 Army Trucks thru This City Today," *Centerville Daily Iowegian*, April 21, 1941; "Army Convoy to Pass thru City Tomorrow A.M.," *Centerville Daily Iowegian*, May 5, 1941; "Army Convoy Drives Spring Peace from Countryside," *Centerville Daily Iowegian*, May 6, 1941; "Big Army Convoy Passes through This City Today," *Centerville Daily Iowegian*, May 14, 1941; "New U-Boat Fighter Displayed Here by Des Moines Inventor May Perform in World War No. 2 If Plans Succeed," *Centerville Daily Iowegian*, Marcy 7, 1941; "'Jeeps' Will Be Displayed Here at County Fair," *Centerville Daily Iowegian*, July 19, 1941; "Want $2.50? It's Yours for Small Amount of Blood," *Centerville Daily Iowegian*, January 31, 1941; "38 Donate Blood Here in Cause of Convalescence," *Centerville Daily Iowegian*, February 4, 1941; "Draws 3 Gallons of Blood," *Centerville Daily Iowegian*, March 14, 1941; "10,000 in U.S. Defense Bonds Sold Here Today," *Centerville Daily Iowegian*, May 1, 1941; "History Repeats Itself…," photograph, *Centerville Daily Iowegian*, May 4, 1962; "Centerville Gears to Defense

Work," *Centerville Daily Iowegian*, March 21, 1941; "Speed Training for Defense in Centerville Now," *Centerville Daily Iowegian*, June 6, 1941; "Men Wanted at Once to Work in Aircraft Plants," *Centerville Daily Iowegian*, February 29, 1941; "Opportunity Is About to Knock for Local Men," *Centerville Daily Iowegian*, August 9, 1941; "Employment Chances Are Booming Here," *Centerville Daily Iowegian*, August 25, 1941; "Appanoose Sends 10… 28 Men to Lockheed," *Centerville Daily Iowegian*, September 9, 1941; "Aircraft Workers Wanted," advertisement, *Centerville Daily Iowegian*, February 27, 1941; "Aircraft Workers Wanted," advertisement, *Centerville Daily Iowegian*, August 14, 1941; "Local Young Men Seek Careers in Aviation, Report," *Centerville Daily Iowegian*, August 14, 1941; "Munitions Plant Has Created Real Problem at Burlington," *Centerville Daily Iowegian*, August 6, 1941.

17. Jesse Beck, "A Decision to Make," editorial, *Centerville Daily Iowegian*, April 25, 1941.

Chapter 61

1. "President Roosevelt Declares Unlimited National Emergency; Tells Nazis U.S. Will Resist Any Move into West," *Centerville Daily Iowegian*, May 28, 1941; "Axis Sees War Bid in F.R. Talk," *Centerville Daily Iowegian*, May 28, 1941; Jesse M. Beck, "The President Speaks," editorial, *Centerville Daily Iowegian*, May 28, 1941.
2. "Change Plans to Register Men in Appanoose County," *Centerville Daily Iowegian*, June 17, 1941; "Appanoose Draftees Get Rough Idea of Departure," *Centerville Daily Iowegian*, July 18, 1941; "Lottery Tonight for Second Group of Registrants," *Centerville Daily Iowegian*, July 17, 1941.
3. "Young Men in This Area Are Sought by Navy," *Centerville Daily Iowegian*, July 16, 1941; "U.S. Marine in City Recruiting," *Centerville Daily Iowegian*, July 25, 1941; "Expect National Guard to Serve for Indefinite Time," *Centerville Daily Iowegian*, May 29, 1941; "Service Groups Here Called to Join Campaign," *Centerville Daily Iowegian*, May 23, 1941; Jesse M. Beck, "A Responsibility Faces Us," editorial, *Centerville Daily Iowegian*, May 27, 1941; Jesse M. Beck, "Do It for the Boys," editorial, *Centerville Daily Iowegian*, May 29, 1941; "Home Folks to Show Backing for Soldiers," *Centerville Daily Iowegian*, May 27, 1941; "John Dillon to Head USO in Appanoose," *Centerville Daily Iowegian*, June 1, 1941; "Appanoose U.S.O. Perfects Organization," *Centerville Daily Iowegian*, June 4, 1941; "What U.S.O. Will Do," *Centerville Daily Iowegian*, June 20, 1941.
4. "Company G Boys Tell about Army Life at Camp Claiborne; Routine Is O.K. Except for the Weather, Rain," *Centerville Daily Iowegian*, June 11, 1941; "Hectic Week Is Reported by Boys at Claiborne, LA.," *Centerville Daily Iowegian*, July 10, 1941; "23 Members of Co. G Are on Furlough Here," *Centerville Daily Iowegian*, June 30, 1941.

5. C.B. DePuy, Around the Town, *Centerville Daily Iowegian*, June 21, 1941; "Red Cross Helping Soldiers in the Various Army Camps," *Centerville Daily Iowegian*, June 26, 1941; "Putting Baskets out to Collect Army Magazines," *Centerville Daily Iowegian*, October 15, 1941.
6. "Red Cross Will Help Men Called into U.S. Army," *Centerville Daily Iowegian*, November 6, 1940; "Plan Red Cross Nursing School in Centerville," *Centerville Daily Iowegian*, June 10, 1941; "Red Cross Gives Children Place in U.S. Defense," *Centerville Daily Iowegian*, October 16, 1941.
7. "Britain Calls for U.S. Radio Army," *Centerville Daily Iowegian*, June 18, 1941; Moss, *19 Weeks*, 214–16 (see chap. 58, n. 14); Keegan, *Collins Atlas of World War II*, 38 (see chap. 59, n. 11); Jesse M. Beck, "Training English Flyers," editorial, *Centerville Daily Iowegian*, June 5, 1941; "Albert Lodwick Gives Radio to Iowa Wesleyan," *Centerville Daily Iowegian*, August 28, 1941.
8. "Soviet Border Bulwarks Crumble," *Centerville Daily Iowegian*, June 28, 1941; "Nazi Blitz Drives Deep into Russia," *Centerville Daily Iowegian*, June 24, 1941; "Claim Finland at War with Russia," *Centerville Daily Iowegian*, June 25, 1941; "Red Army Checkmate Nazi Drive," *Centerville Daily Iowegian*, June 26, 1941; "Nazis Advance on Eastern Front," *Centerville Daily Iowegian*, June 27, 1941; "Russia–Nazis Both Claim Gains," *Centerville Daily Iowegian*, June 28, 1941; "Nazi Attack Half-Way to Moscow," *Centerville Daily Iowegian*, June 30, 1941; "Nazis Claim Continued Advance," *Centerville Daily Iowegian*, July 1, 1941; "Nazis Smash Russian Army in East," *Centerville Daily Iowegian*, July 2, 1941; "Entire Russian Army in Disorderly Retreat Nazis Claim," *Centerville Daily Iowegian*, July 3, 1941; "German Army Reports New Gains," *Centerville Daily Iowegian*, July 3, 1941; "Soviet Sets Nazi Losses at Million," *Centerville Daily Iowegian*, July 7, 1941; "Russians Hold Nazi Forces at Bay," *Centerville Daily Iowegian*, July 8, 1941; "See Little Chance for the Reds; U.S. to Speed Help," *Centerville Daily Iowegian*, June 23, 1941; "Condemns Germany Attack against Russia," *Centerville Daily Iowegian*, June 23, 1941; "Stalin Calls for Scorched Earth Policy to Resist Nazis," *Centerville Daily Iowegian*, July 3, 1941; Kappler, "1941 Rape of Russia," in *Life: World War II*, 110–25 (see chap. 59, n. 5); "Nazi Blitz Drives Deep into Russia," *Centerville Daily Iowegian*, June 24, 1941; "Red Troops Stem Nazi Advances on All Fronts—Report," *Centerville Daily Iowegian*, July 7, 1941; "Counter Attack Annihilates Two Nazi Regiments," *Centerville Daily Iowegian*, July 8, 1941; "Russia Reports Smashing Victory over Nazis," *Centerville Daily Iowegian*, July 9, 1941; "3 Million Nazis Killed in Fight on Russian Front," *Centerville Daily Iowegian*, September 9, 1941; "Russian Resistance to Nazis Magnificent President Says," *Centerville Daily Iowegian*, August 1, 1941.
9. Jesse M. Beck, "Hitler and Peace," editorial, *Centerville Daily Iowegian*, August 21, 1941; "Text of Message on Iceland Occupation," *Centerville Daily Iowegian*, July 7, 1941; "300 American Officials Plan Return to U.S.," *Centerville Daily Iowegian*,

July 21, 1941; "Greenland Will Be Used to Give Aid to England," *Centerville Daily Iowegian*, April 15, 1941; "U.S. Enters War in Iceland Move Japan Declares," *Centerville Daily Iowegian*, July 8, 1941; "Explanation of Occupation of Iceland by U.S. Forces," *Centerville Daily Iowegian*, July 12, 1941; "Americans at Work in Ireland Paid by British Govt. Reports," *Centerville Daily Iowegian*, July 11, 1941; "U.S. Technicians Arrive in London for Special Work," *Centerville Daily Iowegian*, July 31, 1941; "U.S. Naval Force Arrives in Iceland," *Centerville Daily Iowegian*, July 7, 1941; "More Americans in Ulster Today," *Centerville Daily Iowegian*, September 2, 1941; Jesse M. Beck, "Roosevelt and Churchill Meeting," editorial, *Centerville Daily Iowegian*, August 14, 1941; "British Newsman at Meet but Not U.S.," *Centerville Daily Iowegian*, August 15, 1941; "Local Youth at Famous Meet," *Centerville Daily Iowegian*, October 1, 1941.

10. "Plan City Aluminum Drive," *Centerville Daily Iowegian*, July 19, 1941; "Aluminum Drive Workers Named in Big Precinct," *Centerville Daily Iowegian*, July 22, 1941; "Aluminum Drive Thursday," *Centerville Daily Iowegian*, July 22, 1941; Bill Smallwood, interview with the author, July 15, 2010.
11. C.B. DePuy, Around the Town, *Centerville Daily Iowegian*, July 26, 1941; "Start Aluminum from Here Friday," *Centerville Daily Iowegian*, July 31, 1941; "320 Pounds of Aluminum Given at Seymour, IA.," *Centerville Daily Iowegian*, August 1, 1941; "3,630 Pounds of Aluminum Gathered in Appanoose County," *Centerville Daily Iowegian*, August 1, 1941; "And Then—Appanoose Rolled In," *Centerville Daily Iowegian*, August 2, 1941.
12. Jesse M. Beck, "Patriotism Still Evident," editorial, *Centerville Daily Iowegian*, July 25, 1941.

Chapter 62

1. "Letters from France Tell of Hunger and Misery There," *Centerville Daily Iowegian*, February 21, 1941; "'It Is Terrible' Writes Wife of Wounded French Soldier; Was Formerly Appanoose Co. Girl," *Centerville Daily Iowegian*, June 5, 1941; "Scotch Mother Sends Letters Telling of War," *Centerville Daily Iowegian*, June 30, 1941; Around the Town, *Centerville Daily Iowegian*, September 24, 1941; Inez Faber, "Out Here on Soap Creek," *Centerville Daily Iowegian*, May 21, 1940.
2. C.B. DePuy, Around the Town, *Centerville Daily Iowegian*, May 31, 1941.
3. Jesse M. Beck, "America Must Not Go to War," editorial, *Centerville Daily Iowegian*, August 20, 1941.
4. "Lindbergh Says Entry into Fight Would End Democracy," *Centerville Daily Iowegian*, May 24, 1941; Berg, *Lindbergh*, 419–22 (see chap. 45, n. 7); "House Votes Down Attempt to Beat Bill," *Centerville Daily Iowegian*, February 6, 1941.

5. Berg, *Lindbergh*, 377–80 (see chap. 45, n. 7); "Ickes Said Lindy Should Turn Back German Decoration; Flier Protests," *Centerville Daily Iowegian*, July 17, 1941.
6. "Lindbergh Works Overtime on Talk at Capital Tonight," *Centerville Daily Iowegian*, September 11, 1941; "Cloudy and Cool Is Lindbergh's Local Forecast," *Centerville Daily Iowegian*, September 11, 1941; "Noisy Meeting: Hecklers Greet Lindy," *Centerville Daily Iowegian*, September 12, 1941; "Lindbergh Blames War Threat on Roosevelt, Jews, and the British," *Centerville Daily Iowegian*, September 12, 1941; Charles DePuy, Around the Town, *Centerville Daily Iowegian*, September 13, 1941; "Lindbergh Plans Another Speech," *Centerville Daily Iowegian*, October 3, 1941; "Lindbergh Fearful of F.R.'s Motives," *Centerville Daily Iowegian*, June 10, 1941.
7. "Report American Ship Torpedoed," *Centerville Daily Iowegian*, June 10, 1941; Jesse M. Beck, "When Does the Shooting Start," editorial, *Centerville Daily Iowegian*, July 10, 1941; "'Shoot Rattle Snake Raiders,'—Is Roosevelt's Command," *Centerville Daily Iowegian*, September 12, 1941; "Hull Denounces Latest Sinking," *Centerville Daily Iowegian*, October 4, 1941; "U.S. Freighter Lehigh Sunk," photograph and caption, *Centerville Daily Iowegian*, October 23, 1941; Jesse M. Beck, "War Spirit," editorial, *Centerville Daily Iowegian*, October 23, 1941; "U.S. Destroyer Sunk," *Centerville Daily Iowegian*, November 1, 1941; "Loss of Life Is Heavy on Sunken U.S. Ship Germany Is Sarcastic," *Centerville Daily Iowegian*, November 2, 1941; "Legion Moves to Lift Bans," *Centerville Daily Iowegian*, September 17, 1941; "Hickenlooper Delivers Fiery Address at Defense Dinner Tuesday Night," *Centerville Daily Iowegian*, November 19, 1941.
8. Jesse M. Beck, "War with Japan," editorial, *Centerville Daily Iowegian*, February 25, 1941; "As fast as they can be shipped and flown…," caption with photograph, *Centerville Daily Iowegian*, February 25, 1941; Keegan, *The Second World War*, map, 246–47 (see chap. 59, n. 5); Morison, *The Oxford History of the American People*, 344, 351 (see chap. 16, n. 3); Burner, Bernhard and Kutler, *Firsthand America*, 852 (see chap. 50, n. 15); "Warns U.S.–Britain," photograph and caption, *Centerville Daily Iowegian*, February 27, 1941.
9. "Nineteen Japanese Boats Are Seized by U.S. in Hawaii," *Centerville Daily Iowegian*, July 30, 1941; "Seattle Blacked out in U.S. Test," *Centerville Daily Iowegian*, March 8, 1941.
10. "Japan Reaffirms Union with Axis," *Centerville Daily Iowegian*, June 14, 1941; Burner, Bernhard and Kutler, *Firsthand America*, 852 (see chap. 50, n. 15); Morison, *The Oxford History of the American People*, 356 (see chap. 16, n. 3).
11. "New Jap Premier?" photograph and caption, *Centerville Daily Iowegian*, October 20, 1941; "Japanese Premier Calls for Unity Among His People," *Centerville Daily Iowegian*, October 20, 1941; Dale Jones, interview with the author, October 4, 2000; "Most Centerville People Shocked and Surprised by War," *Centerville Daily Iowegian*, December 8, 1941; Bob Seddon, interview with the author, March 16, 2010; "U.S. Liners Are Passing up All Japanese Ports," *Centerville Daily Iowegian*, October 23, 1941;

"Americans in Japanese Area Told to Leave," *Centerville Daily Iowegian*, November 26, 1941; "America to Take Rapid Action If Japanese Attack," *Centerville Daily Iowegian*, November 29, 1941; "Far Eastern Situation Very Critical," *Centerville Daily Iowegian*, November 29, 1941; "All Troop Leaves Cancelled in Orient," *Centerville Daily Iowegian*, November 29, 1941; "U.S. Philippine Forces Are Ready for an Emergency," *Centerville Daily Iowegian*, December 1, 1941; "Americans Again Advised to Leave City of Shanghai," *Centerville Daily Iowegian*, December 1, 1941; "Japs Are Massing Strong Land, Sea and Air Patrols," *Centerville Daily Iowegian*, December 3, 1941; "Japan Sizzling over Alleged Encirclement," *Centerville Daily Iowegian*, December 5, 1941; "Prepare for Showdown in the Far East; New Troops Arrive," *Centerville Daily Iowegian*, December 6, 1941.

12. "Christmas Trees All Sizes," advertisement, *Centerville Daily Iowegian*, December 6, 1941; "Plan Elaborate Yule Opening," *Centerville Daily Iowegian*, November 29, 1941; "Many Decorations Noted around City as Christmas Nears," *Centerville Daily Iowegian*, December 4, 1941; "Bob Elgin Store," advertisement, *Centerville Daily Iowegian*, December 9, 1941; "Stevens Walgreen," advertisement, *Centerville Daily Iowegian*, December 2, 1941; "City Book Store," advertisement, *Centerville Daily Iowegian*, December 9, 1941; "Brodys," advertisement, *Centerville Daily Iowegian*, December 4, 1941; "Gambles Store Toyland Opens," *Centerville Daily Iowegian*, November 20, 1941; "Spurgeons," advertisement, *Centerville Daily Iowegian*, November 21, 1941.
13. "Thousands in City for the Yule Opening," *Centerville Daily Iowegian*, December 6, 1941; "Free Candy and Show Assures an Outstanding Day," *Centerville Daily Iowegian*, December 4, 1941; "Kiddies Greet Santa," *Centerville Daily Iowegian*, December 6, 1941.
14. "Tolerance Rally Planned for Sunday," *Centerville Daily Iowegian*, December 1, 1941.
15. Keegan, *Collins Atlas of World War II*, 52 (see chap. 59, n. 11); Morison, *The Oxford History of the American People*, 357 (see chap. 16, n. 3).

Chapter 63

1. Keegan, *The Second World War*, 255 (see chap. 59, n. 5); Morison, *The Oxford History of the American People*, 359 (see chap. 16, n. 3); Keegan, *Collins Atlas of World War II*, 52, 55 (see chap. 59, n. 11).
2. "Clear, Crisp and Mild Iowa Weather," *Centerville Daily Iowegian*, December 6, 1941; "Coming Sunday," Majestic advertisement, *Centerville Daily Iowegian*, December 6, 1941; "Hotel Continental Coffee Shop," advertisement, *Centerville Daily Iowegian*, December 6, 1941.
3. Helen Carlson, interview with the author, March 2, 2010; Betty (Morris) Bear, interview with the author, March 10, 2010; "Catholic, Jew, and Protestant Talk It

Over," *Centerville Daily Iowegian*, December 8, 1941; Robert K. Beck, "Pearl Harbor Remembered," editorial, *Centerville Daily Iowegian*, December 7, 1959; Bob Seddon, interview with the author, March 3, 2010; Dan Ehl, "It Was a Very Long War for Hudson," *Ad-Express/Iowegian*, May 28, 2010; Joe Wilson, interview with the author, April 23, 2010; Maurice Stamps, "Snafus and Love Letters: Memories of an Old G.I.," self-published, May 2008, 5, collection of Appanoose County Museum, Centerville; Virginia Koestner, interview with the author, October 10, 2011.

4. Phyllis (Morrow) Cosby, interview with the author, August 8, 2010; Keegan, *The Second World War*, 255–57 (see chap. 59, n. 5); Morison, *The Oxford History of the American People*, 359–60 (see chap. 16, n. 3); Keegan, *Collins Atlas of World War II*, 52, 55 (see chap. 59, n. 11).
5. "Many Centerville Boys in the Far East Waging War," *Centerville Daily Iowegian*, December 8, 1941; "Over 30 Local Men in U.S. Far East Forces," *Centerville Daily Iowegian*, December 9, 1941; "James K. Lewis Is Retired after 20 Years in Navy," photograph and caption, *Centerville Daily Iowegian*, April 25, 1961; "Receive Both Good and Bad News Locally," *Centerville Daily Iowegian*, December 23, 1941; "Centerville Youth Tells about Dodging Submarines," *Centerville Daily Iowegian*, December 10, 1941; "Shoots at Japs," photograph and caption, *Centerville Daily Iowegian*, March 6, 1942; "Locally Known Boy Is Killed," *Centerville Daily Iowegian*, December 13, 1941; "Another Local Youth Reported as Being 'O.K.,'" *Centerville Daily Iowegian*, December 23, 1941; "Army Officer at Numa for Visit Over Week-End," *Centerville Daily Iowegian*, December 11, 1941; "Passenger on S.S. Lurline in Letter Here," *Centerville Daily Iowegian*, December 16, 1941; "List of Local Men at Combat Scene Growing," *Centerville Daily Iowegian*, December 11, 1941; "Grandson in Cryptic Note from Hawaii," *Centerville Daily Iowegian*, December 31, 1941; "Former Local Boy Reported Missing by U.S. Admiral," *Centerville Daily Iowegian*, December 31, 1941.
6. "Special Request from FBI Comes in Midnight Call," *Centerville Daily Iowegian*, December 8, 1941; "War Declaration Has Its Immediate Local Effects," *Centerville Daily Iowegian*, December 9, 1941.
7. "$13,601 Defense Order Received by Local Plant," *Centerville Daily Iowegian*, September 12, 1941; "War Declaration Has Its Immediate Local Effects," *Centerville Daily Iowegian*, December 9, 1941.
8. Phyllis (Morrow) Cosby, interview with the author, August 8, 2010.

Chapter 64

1. "Most Centerville People Shocked and Surprised by War," *Centerville Daily Iowegian*, December 8, 1941.

2. Bill Smallwood, interview with the author, March 14, 2010; Bob Seddon, interview with the author, March 16, 2010; Phyllis (Morrow) Cosby, interview with the author, August 10, 2010; "Most Centerville People Shocked and Surprised by War," *Centerville Daily Iowegian*, December 8, 1941.
3. "Full Text of the President's Message to U.S. Congress," *Centerville Daily Iowegian*, December 8, 1941.
4. "How Iowegian Received All Its War News," *Centerville Daily Iowegian*, January 5, 1942; Jesse Beck, "Iowegian Gets Full Wire Service," editorial, *Centerville Daily Iowegian*, July 26, 1941; Dan Ehl, interview with the author, August 16, 2010.
5. "Most Centerville People Shocked and Surprised by War," *Centerville Daily Iowegian*, December 8, 1941.
6. "How Iowegian Received All Its War News," *Centerville Daily Iowegian*, January 5, 1942; "War Declared," banner headline, *Centerville Daily Iowegian*, December 8, 1941; Bill Smallwood, interview with the author, March 14, 2010.
7. "Congress Rushes War Vote after President Talks," *Centerville Daily Iowegian*, December 8, 1941; "Britain Will Fight to End against Japs," *Centerville Daily Iowegian*, December 8, 1941.
8. "Air Raids Alarm U.S.," *Centerville Daily Iowegian*, December 9, 1941; "War Briefs!!" *Centerville Daily Iowegian*, December 9, 1941.
9. "San Francisco Experienced 3 Night Scares," *Centerville Daily Iowegian*, December 9, 1941; Paul Beck, "First Hand Story of Blackouts and Western Reaction," *Centerville Daily Iowegian*, December 15, 1941; Clifford Smith, "Letter Written from West Tells of War Activity," *Centerville Daily Iowegian*, December 16, 1941.
10. "F.B.I. Agents Detain These Japanese at San Pedro," photograph and caption, *Centerville Daily Iowegian*, December 9, 1941; "Japs Taken into Custody," photograph and caption, *Centerville Daily Iowegian*, December 9, 1941; "Exline Boy Has Experience in San Francisco," *Centerville Daily Iowegian*, December 15, 1941.
11. Bill Smallwood, interview with the author, March 14, 2010; "Alarmed Nation Awaits Address from President Roosevelt," *Centerville Daily Iowegian*, December 9, 1941; "The President's Address," advertisement for Majestic and Ritz Theatres, *Centerville Daily Iowegian*, December 9, 1941; "Hear President at the Banquet," box announcement, *Centerville Daily Iowegian*, December 9, 1941; "President Roosevelt Claims Surpremacy for United States in the Pacific Ocean," *Centerville Daily Iowegian*, December 10, 1941; "Biggest Annual Alfalfa Banquet in History Held Thursday Night," *Centerville Daily Iowegian*, December 10, 1941.
12. "U.S. and Axis at War; Mussolini and Hitler Plunge into Conflict," *Centerville Daily Iowegian*, December 11, 1941; "U.S. and Axis at War; Congress Votes Unanimously to Fight to Finish," *Centerville Daily Iowegian*, December 11, 1941.

Chapter 65

1. Archie Satterfield, *The Home Front: An Oral History of the War Years in America; 1941–45* (Chicago: Playboy Press/A Division of PEI Books, Inc., 1981), 40–41; "Selective Service Officials Receive Many New Inquiries," *Centerville Daily Iowegian*, January 21, 1942; "Iowa Reacts to War Quickly And in Many Respects," *Centerville Daily Iowegian*, December 11, 1941; "Army Deserters Return Voluntarily to Do Duty," *Centerville Daily Iowegian*, January 8, 1942; "Older Iowans Are Trying to Enlist," *Centerville Daily Iowegian*, December 11, 1941.
2. "Father and Son Enlist in Army, Were Former Centerville Residents," *Centerville Daily Iowegian*, December 15, 1941; E.W. Fannon, "This Week's Personality," *Centerville Daily Iowegian*, April 20, 1962; "Kept His Promise: Mystic Father Joins Son in Army Air Corps," *Centerville Daily Iowegian*, January 26, 1942; "Father of Two Local Soldiers Signs in Draft," *Centerville Daily Iowegian*, February 19, 1942; "Vets of Foreign Wars in Formal Warfare Pledge," *Centerville Daily Iowegian*, December 16, 1941.
3. "Lot of Brothers, with Three Families of Four," *Centerville Daily Iowegian*, October 9, 1942; "Two More Families with Four in Service," *Centerville Daily Iowegian*, October 9, 1942; "Two Members of Iowegian Staff Leave for Duty," *Centerville Daily Iowegian*, March 13, 1942; "Families of 3 in the Service," *Centerville Daily Iowegian*, October 9, 1942; "Brothers Who Are Fighting for Country," *Centerville Daily Iowegian*, October 9, 1942; "Ward Family Serves," *Centerville Daily Iowegian*, April 12, 1945; "Adams Family, Formerly of Exline, Is Definitely All Out for Uncle Sam," *Centerville Daily Iowegian*, October 28, 1943; "4 Brothers Serving under Uncle Sam," *Centerville Daily Iowegian*, October 9, 1942; "Third Mericle Brother Joins Army and Is Honored at Party in His Home Friday Eve," *Centerville Daily Iowegian*, October 20, 1942; "King Family of Udell Has Six Service Sons," *Centerville Daily Iowegian*, October 29, 1943; "Another Five Star Mother Is Announced Today," *Centerville Daily Iowegian*, July 5, 1944; "Five Brothers Join the Navy Together," *Centerville Daily Iowegian*, December 26, 1941; "Anniversary of Death of Five Sullivans," *Centerville Daily Iowegian*, November 14, 1962.
4. "Let American Flags Fly Urges A.C. Secretary," *Centerville Daily Iowegian*, December 11, 1941; "Found Legion Post Here Fall of 1919," *Centerville Daily Iowegian*, October 9, 1942; Charles DePuy, Around the Town, *Centerville Daily Iowegian*, December 17, 1941; "Huge V Shows Student Spirit at CHS Today," *Centerville Daily Iowegian*, December 19, 1941; "V for Victory Sign to Be Erected Soon to Show Patriotism," Student Iowegian Section, *Centerville Daily Iowegian*, December 20, 1941; "War Needs Mooey [*sic*]," *Centerville Daily Iowegian*, December 12, 1941; "Big Demand for Defense Bonds Noted," *Centerville Daily Iowegian*, December 16, 1941.
5. "Centerville to Have New Iowa Guard Unit," *Centerville Daily Iowegian*, December 19, 1941; "Armory Humming with Activity as in Days Past," *Centerville Daily Iowegian*,

January 3, 1942; "Local Defense Movement Is on in Earnest Now," *Centerville Daily Iowegian*, December 11, 1941; "Local Plants Arrange Defense Measures," *Centerville Daily Iowegian*, December 19, 1941; "11 Point Plan Outlined Here Home Defense," *Centerville Daily Iowegian*, December 24, 1941; "Medical Plans Compete for Emergency Service," *Centerville Daily Iowegian*, May 4, 1942; "Scouts Are to Participate in Defense Effort," *Centerville Daily Iowegian*, January 13, 1942; "Expect Six to Join Air Patrol from This City," *Centerville Daily Iowegian*, January 26, 1942; "Don Pullman Is Named Air Squardron [*sic*] Adjutant," *Centerville Daily Iowegian*, January 22, 1942; "Local Women to Form a Rifle Organization," *Centerville Daily Iowegian*, January 21, 1942.

6. "Troop News Is Taboo When It Tells Too Much," *Centerville Daily Iowegian*, December 17, 1941; "Cannot Release Any Weather Information," *Centerville Daily Iowegian*, January 13, 1942; "Civilians Asked to Keep Rumors and Not to Talk," *Centerville Daily Iowegian*, December 29, 1941.
7. "Red Cross Memberships Are Up in This County," *Centerville Daily Iowegian*, January 7, 1942; "Women Busy Preparing Red Cross Material for Shipment," *Centerville Daily Iowegian*, January 9, 1942; "Local Red Cross Chapter Has Grown," *Centerville Daily Iowegian*, January 22, 1942; "American Bundles Organization Now in Appanoose County," *Centerville Daily Iowegian*, May 25, 1942; "American Bundles Secures Location West Side Square," *Centerville Daily Iowegian*, June 9, 1942; "'Bundles for America' Is Being Organized in Centerville," *Centerville Daily Iowegian*, June 19, 1942.
8. "Nothing Turned Over to Officers by County Aliens," *Centerville Daily Iowegian*, January 7, 1942; "Second Warning Issued to Alien Oversight Here," *Centerville Daily Iowegian*, January 9, 1942; "New Orders Are Given to Aliens," *Centerville Daily Iowegian*, February 6, 1942; "Fifty Enemy Aliens Have Been Listed," *Centerville Daily Iowegian*, February 17, 1942.
9. "FBI Investigation Rumors Here Make Good Conversation," *Centerville Daily Iowegian*, Febraury 24, 1942; Charles DePuy, Around the Town, *Centerville Daily Iowegian*, January 3, 1942; "Man Found Dead in Mine," *Centerville Daily Iowegian*, May 11, 1942.
10. "Seek Recruits for Maritime Service Here," *Centerville Daily Iowegian*, December 16, 1941; "Information on Opening in Military Service," *Centerville Daily Iowegian*, January 14, 1942; "Young Men Urged to Join Marines," *Centerville Daily Iowegian*, January 27, 1942; Charles DePuy, Around the Town, *Centerville Daily Iowegian*, January 7, 1942.
11. "Local Organization for Tire Rationing," *Centerville Daily Iowegian*, December 23, 1941; "Tire Rationing Will Be Far More Severe Than Many Had Anticipated," *Centerville Daily Iowegian*, December 27, 1941; "Tire Rationing/Quota Received," *Centerville Daily Iowegian*, January 1, 1942; "Announce New Bus Schedule," *Centerville Daily Iowegian*, July 15, 1942; "Notice: Thrift Store," advertisement, *Centerville Daily Iowegian*, January 3, 1942; Charles DePuy, Around the Town, *Centerville Daily Iowegian*,

March 21, 1942; Charles DePuy, Around the Town, *Centerville Daily Iowegian*, March 21, 1942; Bill Smallwood, interview with the author, October 19, 2010; "Announce Tire Life Extension Plan for Public," *Centerville Daily Iowegian*, January 22, 1942.

12. Jeanne Fowler, interview with the author, October 21, 2010; "Iowa News Flashes of the Week Shown at the Majestic," *Centerville Daily Iowegian*, December 17, 1941; "History Repeats Itself," *Centerville Daily Iowegian*, January 21, 1942; "Library Books in Good Demand," *Centerville Daily Iowegian*, December 6, 1941; "High School Students Well Informed on Current Events," *Centerville Daily Iowegian*, December 10, 1941.
13. Charles DePuy, Around the Town, *Centerville Daily Iowegian*, January 3, 1942; "Convoys of Planes over City Early Today Is Report," *Centerville Daily Iowegian*, February 20, 1942; Charles DePuy, Around the Town, *Centerville Daily Iowegian*, January 24, 1942; "Appanoose County Soldier Held Prisoner by Japanese," *Centerville Daily Iowegian*, February 19, 1942; "First U.S. Army to Reach the British Isles Since Start of War," *Centerville Daily Iowegian*, January 26, 1942; Jesse M. Beck, "Are Our Boys There?" editorial, *Centerville Daily Iowegian*, January 27, 1942.

Chapter 66

1. Rice Yahner, "British Greet A.E.F.," *Centerville Daily Iowegian*, January 27, 1942; Rice Yahner, "Many Iowa Boys among A.E.F.," *Centerville Daily Iowegian*, January 27, 1942.
2. "First U.S. Soldier Ashore in Ireland," photograph, *Centerville Daily Iowegian*, January 31, 1942; "Yanks March in Ireland," photograph, *Centerville Daily Iowegian*, January 28, 1942.
3. "Nurses with New A.E.F.," photograph, *Centerville Daily Iowegian*, January 31, 1942; "How Iowegian Gets Pictures within Hours," *Centerville Daily Iowegian*, January 12, 1942.
4. "Company G Still Stationed East at Fort Dix," *Centerville Daily Iowegian*, February 26, 1942; "John Koziol Is First Appanoose Boy to Arrive in Northern Ireland," *Centerville Daily Iowegian*, February 27, 1942; "First in Ireland," photograph of John Koziol, *Centerville Daily Iowegian*, March 6, 1942; "Second Contingent of U.S. Troops Arrive in Northern Ireland," *Centerville Daily Iowegian*, March 4, 1942; "James [*sic*] Pancrazio Is First Centerville Boy in Ireland," *Centerville Daily Iowegian*, March 4, 1942; "'Many Centerville, Appanoose Boys in Ireland'—Major Bear," *Centerville Daily Iowegian*, March 10, 1942.
5. "Believe Company G Lands in Ireland," *Centerville Daily Iowegian*, May 19, 1942; "Tens of Thousands of Yanks Arrive in Northern Ireland," *Centerville Daily Iowegian*, May 19, 1942; "'Arrived Safely'—Cablegram from Maj. Bear," *Centerville Daily Iowegian*,

May 21, 1942; "Proof That Co. G Is in Britain Is Received Today," *Centerville Daily Iowegian*, May 22, 1942.

6. "Bataan Peninsula Defenses Fall; Over 36,000 Gallant Soldiers Face Death or Capture," *Centerville Daily Iowegian*, April 9, 1942; "The Surrenders That Haunted America" and "March of Death for Bataan's Defenders," in *Life: World War II*, ed. Philip B. Kunhardt Jr. (Boston: Little, Brown and Company, 1990), 166–69; Barbara Vorhees, niece of prisoner Nick Burrell, interview with the author, November 1, 2010; "Corregidor Fort Still Fights," *Centerville Daily Iowegian*, April 10, 1942; "Corregidor Fortress Has Fallen!" *Centerville Daily Iowegian*, May 6, 1942; "Java Defenses Falling to Japs," *Centerville Daily Iowegian*, March 7, 1942; "Japs Claim Mastery of Indies," *Centerville Daily Iowegian*, March 9, 1942; Morison, *The Oxford History of the American People*, 361 (see n. 375); "India Bombed by Japanese Planes," *Centerville Daily Iowegian*, April 6, 1942; Keegan, *The Second World War*, 270 (see chap. 59, n. 5); "Bombers in Raid on the Darwin Port," *Centerville Daily Iowegian*, March 16, 1942; "Curtin Reports on Darwin Raid," *Centerville Daily Iowegian*, March 30, 1942; "Jap Sub Shells California Coast," *Centerville Daily Iowegian*, February 24, 1942; "Los Angeles Gun into Action; Unidentified Object Is Cause of Five Hour Air Raid Alarm and Heavy Firing," *Centerville Daily Iowegian*, February 25, 1942; "Shinogle Writes Back Reactions to U.S. Air Raid," *Centerville Daily Iowegian*, March 14, 1942.

7. Morison, *The Oxford History of the American People*, 369 (see chap. 16, n. 3); Keegan, *The Second World War*, 270–71 (see chap. 59, n. 5); Craig Nelson, *The First Heroes: The Extraordinary Story of the Doolittle Raid, America's First World War II Victory*, (New York: Penguin, 2002), xv–xviii and 131–60; "Say Vital Targets Hit in Tokyo Raid," *Centerville Daily Iowegian*, May 19, 1942.

8. John Talbot, interview with the author, May 25, 2002; "War Hero Honored," *Daily Iowegian*, May 17, 2005; "American Hero Passes Away," *Ad-Express*, June 9, 2010.

9. Dan Ehl, "Remembering the Battle of Midway," *Daily Iowegian*, November 9, 2004; John Talbot, interview with the author, April 16, 2010; "John Talbot in Hospital in Hawaii," *Centerville Daily Iowegian*, June 12, 1942; Charles DePuy, "John Talbot Writes Saga of Sea at Midway," *Centerville Daily Iowegian*, June 18, 1942; Charles DePuy, Around the Town, *Centerville Daily Iowegian*, October 15, 1942; *The Battle of Midway* advertisement for Majestic Theatre, *Centerville Daily Iowegian*, October 15, 1942; Lois Swasick, interview with the author, May 31, 2010; "War Is Serious Says Fighter Pilot Talbot," *Centerville Daily Iowegian*, August 5, 1942.

10. "Largest Group of Selectees Leave This City," *Centerville Daily Iowegian*, January 30, 1942; "37 Men Local to Des Moines for Final Physical," *Centerville Daily Iowegian*, February 18, 1942; "43 County Men off to Army," *Centerville Daily Iowegian*, May 25, 1942; "90 County Men Leave for Induction Center," *Centerville Daily Iowegian*, October 5, 1942; "Farewell Is Planned for Drafted Men,"

Centerville Daily Iowegian, July 6, 1942; "Another Group Goes to War," *Centerville Daily Iowegian*, March 13, 1942.

11. "Iowa Will Have Officer School for Women Army," *Centerville Daily Iowegian*, May 15, 1942; "Women Busy Enrolling for Possible Service," *Centerville Daily Iowegian*, May 27, 1942; "WAAC Already Big Job for Army," *Centerville Daily Iowegian*, May 29, 1942; George S. Mills, "Ft. Des Moines Now Has Sounds Shrill, Feminine," *Centerville Daily Iowegian*, July 20, 1942; "Appanoose Co. Women Going into Service," *Centerville Daily Iowegian*, January 28, 1943; "Many Local Young Women Interested in WAVES, SPARS," *Centerville Daily Iowegian*, January 29, 1943; "Getting Women for the Waves," *Centerville Daily Iowegian*, October 12, 1942; Charles DePuy, Columns Write, *Centerville Daily Iowegian*, February 16, 1943; "Mary L. Padovan," obituary, *Centerville Daily Iowegian*, February 4, 2003; "Colored Draftees Honored at Party Tuesday Evening," *Centerville Daily Iowegian*, July 15, 1942; "Colored Boys Are Given a Farewell at Local Station," *Centerville Daily Iowegian*, July 16, 1942; "Naval Service Is Open to Negroes," *Centerville Daily Iowegian*, April 7, 1942; "Casey Bolden First Colored Navy Recruit," *Centerville Daily Iowegian*, June 25, 1942.
12. "Women in War Work a Solution," *Centerville Daily Iowegian*, April 13, 1942; "All-Girl Cast at Local Theaters," photograph and caption, *Centerville Daily Iowegian*, September 10, 1942; "Local Women Learning Air Raid Warden Duties," *Centerville Daily Iowegian*, July 24, 1942; Obituary of Ruth M. Fuller, *Daily Iowegian*, January 8, 2008; Helen Carlson, interview with the author, November 11, 2010; "Local N.Y.A. Shop 'All-Out' in War Effort," *Centerville Daily Iowegian*, May 14, 1942; "More Girls to Aviation Plants from This City," *Centerville Daily Iowegian*, December 14, 1942; "Women—Men; 500 Needed Now! For Aircraft Work in Kansas City," advertisement, *Centerville Daily Iowegian*, September 18, 1942; "500 Girls Wanted," advertisement for work in airplane factory, *Centerville Daily Iowegian*, August 31, 1942.
13. "Navy Is Dictating How Women Workers Should Be Dressed," *Centerville Daily Iowegian*, March 25, 1942; "Slacks in Step with the Times," Spurgeons advertisement, *Centerville Daily Iowegian*, May 13, 1942; "Slack Suits," Milady's Shoppe advertisement, *Centerville Daily Iowegian*, May 13, 1942; "Long Life Ahead for Slacks," *Centerville Daily Iowegian*, May 21, 1942; "Slack Suits," Jensen's advertisement, *Centerville Daily Iowegian*, May 21, 1942.
14. Barbara Clarke Craver, interview with the author, March 16, 2010; Jean Harrison Seddon, interview with the author, March 15, 2010; Obituary of Doris Hazel Kennedy, *Daily Iowegian*, May 18, 2006; Charlene VanNoy Lamb, interview with the author, November 8, 2010; Leila Riggs Niday, interview with the author, November 14, 2010; Mary A. Large, letter quoted in "More Local Youth in Defense Work from NYA Center," *Centerville Daily Iowegian*, December 23, 1942.

Chapter 67

1. "Local Civilians Will Be Asked to Cooperate," *Centerville Daily Iowegian*, December 27, 1941; Morison, *The Oxford History of the American People*, 368 (see chap. 16, n. 3); "Women Will Aid in Salvage Work in Special Way," *Centerville Daily Iowegian*, November 24, 1942; "Old Phonograph Records," advertisement, *Centerville Daily Iowegian*, July 22, 1942; "Books by Millions for the Soldiers," *Centerville Daily Iowegian*, January 10, 1942; "Plan to Gather Milkweed Over Appanoose Co.," *Centerville Daily Iowegian*, August 22, 1944; "Bomb Shell for Hitler," *Centerville Daily Iowegian*, January 16, 1943; "Stop! Don't Throw Away Ammunition," advertisement, *Centerville Daily Iowegian*, March 6, 1942.
2. "Local Civilians Will Be Asked to Cooperate," *Centerville Daily Iowegian*, December 27, 1941; "Boy Scouts Will Call for Books," *Centerville Daily Iowegian*, January 15, 1942; "Miss Ware Tells about Plans for Big Book Drive," *Centerville Daily Iowegian*, January 14, 1942; "Books by Millions for the Soldiers," *Centerville Daily Iowegian*, January 10, 1942; "Remember Pearl Harbor Scrap Iron Makes Guns!" *Centerville Daily Iowegian*, January 23, 1942; "Co. D Salvage Drive Soon," *Centerville Daily Iowegian*, August 6, 1942; "City Salvage Drive Will Last Ten Days," *Centerville Daily Iowegian*, August 6, 1942.
3. "Life for Johnny Jones Comes Wrapped in Paper," advertisement, *Centerville Daily Iowegian*, January 19, 1944; "Give Rubber to War Chest or Sell as Choose," *Centerville Daily Iowegian*, June 16, 1942; Leo Craver, interview with the author, March 16, 2010; "How to Turn Your Scrap In," advertisement, *Centerville Daily Iowegian*, August 10, 1942; "Scrap Handling Explained Here thru Institute," *Centerville Daily Iowegian*, March 4, 1942; "Want More Fats and Salvage Is Local Plea Today," *Centerville Daily Iowegian*, February 25, 1943; "A Boy on a Bike," *Centerville Daily Iowegian*, June 17, 1942; "Salvage Army Completes Drive for Old Hosiery," *Centerville Daily Iowegian*, January 6, 1943; "Notice: What to Do With Your Waste Paper," *Centerville Daily Iowegian*, January 21, 1944; "We'll beat Hitler…," *Centerville Daily Iowegian*, July 30, 1942.
4. "School Youths Make Citywide Drive Thursday," *Centerville Daily Iowegian*, October 7, 1942; Betty Bear, interview with the author, June 1, 2010; "172,000 Lbs of Rubber Is County Figure," *Centerville Daily Iowegian*, June 29, 1942; "School Children in Local Scrap Drive," *Centerville Daily Iowegian*, October 8, 1942; "Paper Drive to Be Staged on Saturday," *Centerville Daily Iowegian*, February 14, 1944; "Drive for Old Records Going over the Top," *Centerville Daily Iowegian*, July 31, 1942; "Walden Post in This City Leads State of Iowa," *Centerville Daily Iowegian*, August 7, 1942; Mary Josephine Moffitt, interview with her daughter, Mary Sue Zaputil, April 25, 2011; "Women's Salvage Army Will Hold Meeting Monday," *Centerville Daily Iowegian*, November 28, 1942; "170 Pounds of Nylon and Silk

Stockings Sent," *Centerville Daily Iowegian*, March 8, 1943; "PT Troopers Ask for Waste Paper," Student Section, *Centerville Daily Iowegian*, October 17, 1944; "Paper Drive Nets over Eleven Ton," *Centerville Daily Iowegian*, November 7, 1944; "Plan to Gather Milkweed over Appanoose Co.," *Centerville Daily Iowegian*, August 22, 1944; Patsy Cincotta, "May Belle Brain: She Kept Home Fires Burning," *Ad-Express/Daily Iowegian*, February 22, 2002; "Scrap Paper Drive Last Saturday Very Satisfactory," *Centerville Daily Iowegian*, August 26, 1943; "Waste Paper Day for Centerville Friday, Aug 4th," *Centerville Daily Iowegian*, July 31, 1944; "What to Do to Get Ready for Waste Paper Day," *Centerville Daily Iowegian*, August 1, 1944; "Paper Drive Adds 18 Tons of Waste," *Centerville Daily Iowegian*, Augut 16, 1944.

5. "105 Tons of Scrap Metal Collected from County Farms," *Centerville Daily Iowegian*, June 9, 1942; "Salvage Drive Gets Started in Appanoose," *Centerville Daily Iowegian*, August 11, 1942; "'Scrip for Scrap' Planned by Association of Commerce," *Centerville Daily Iowegian*, January 28, 1942; "Lest You Forget: Scrap for Scrip Starts Monday," *Centerville Daily Iowegian*, January 30, 1942; "'Scrip for Scrap' Plan Is Progressing," *Centerville Daily Iowegian*, February 5, 1942; "How to Turn Your Scrap In," advertisement, *Centerville Daily Iowegian*, August 10, 1942; "Five Pounds of Scrap Admits to Show," *Centerville Daily Iowegian*, October 8, 1942; "Trade in Your Scrap Metal for Swift's Baby Chicks," advertisement, *Centerville Daily Iowegian*, October 8, 1942; "School Children in Local Scrap Drive," *Centerville Daily Iowegian*, October 8, 1942.
6. "Local Show Manager in New Rubber Drive," *Centerville Daily Iowegian*, July 10, 1942; Charles DePuy, Around the Town, *Centerville Daily Iowegian*, June 27, 1942; "Mike's Mat Moves Away," *Centerville Daily Iowegian*, July 2, 1942; "Two More Rubber Floor Mats Taken," *Centerville Daily Iowegian*, July 3, 1942; "A Boy on a Bike," *Centerville Daily Iowegian*, June 17, 1942; "172,000 Lbs. of Rubber Is County Figure," *Centerville Daily Iowegian*, June 29, 1942; "Rubber Drive Nets 8 Pounds for Each Person," *Centerville Daily Iowegian*, July 2, 1942.
7. "Trade Your Old Guns for New in Drive from Scrap," *Centerville Daily Iowegian*, September 4, 1942; Dale Jones, interview with the author, October 4, 2000; "Machete from Philippines in Salvage Drive," *Centerville Daily Iowegian*, August 13, 1942; "'Adam and Eve' Lose Their Eden All Over Again," *Centerville Daily Iowegian*, August 15, 1942; "Courthouse Park Cannon Goes Back to War Soon," *Centerville Daily Iowegian*, August 21, 1942; "Legion Cannon in Courthouse Park Is Junked," *Centerville Daily Iowegian*, September 30, 1942; Charles DePuy, Around the Town, *Centerville Daily Iowegian*, September 30, 1942; "Will Tear Up Car Tracks for Scrap Tomorrow," *Centerville Daily Iowegian*, September 3, 1942; "Digging Up Memories," *Centerville Daily Iowegian*, September 23, 1942; Charles DePuy, Around the Town, *Centerville Daily Iowegian*, April 4, 1942.

8. "Key Kampaign Is on Kollect Keys for War Effort," *Centerville Daily Iowegian*, September 30, 1942; "Things Being Done to Get the Scrap," *Centerville Daily Iowegian*, October 1, 1942; "School Children in Local Scrap Drive," *Centerville Daily Iowegian*, October 7, 1942; School Children in Local Scrap Drive," *Centerville Daily Iowegian*, October 8, 1942; "Scrap Drive Adds Another 180,000 Pounds," *Centerville Daily Iowegian*, October 13, 1942; "Junior High Student Iowegian: Scrap Metal Drive," *Centerville Daily Iowegian*, October 10, 1942; "Over 4 Tons of Tin Cans Are Gathered," *Centerville Daily Iowegian*, January 30, 1943; "Boy Scouts to Collect Tin Cans Saturday," *Centerville Daily Iowegian*, May 13, 1943; "Why Important to Collect Tin," *Centerville Daily Iowegian*, August 30, 1944; George Freeborn, interview with the author, July 25, 2005; Jesse M. Beck, "School Children in Local Scrap Drive," *Centerville Daily Iowegian*, October 8, 1942.
9. "Appanoose Exceeds Scrap Iron Quota," *Centerville Daily Iowegian*, September 14, 1942; "Gather 331 Tons Scrap in September," *Centerville Daily Iowegian*, October 5, 1942.
10. "Scrap Roundup Holiday in County Oct. 22," *Centerville Daily Iowegian*, October 14, 1942; "Proclamation," *Centerville Daily Iowegian*, October 15, 1942; "Ready Response Assumes a Big Scrap Holiday," *Centerville Daily Iowegian*, October 15, 1942; "All Joining in Scrap Holiday Program Here," *Centerville Daily Iowegian*, October 16, 1942; "Iowegian Works Wednesday Night Closes Thurs. P.M.," *Centerville Daily Iowegian*, October 16, 1942.
11. "Final Touches to Scrap Holiday Plans Tues. Night," *Centerville Daily Iowegian*, October 19, 1942; "Iowa Counties Make Holidays to Get Scrap," *Centerville Daily Iowegian*, October 15, 1942.
12. Charles DePuy, "Scrap Trucks Start at Zero Hour" *Centerville Daily Iowegian*, October 22, 1942.
13. Charles DePuy, Columns Write, *Centerville Daily Iowegian*, October 23, 1942; "Hope to Reach 500 Ton Total Officials Say," *Centerville Daily Iowegian*, October 22, 1942.
14. Three photographs and captions, *Centerville Daily Iowegian*, October 22, 1942; "Co. Reported as Fifteenth in the State," *Centerville Daily Iowegian*, October 23, 1942; Charles DePuy, "Scrap Trucks Start at Zero Hour," *Centerville Daily Iowegian*, October 22, 1942.

Chapter 68

1. Lisa L. Ossian, *The Homefronts of Iowa, 1939–1945* (Columbia: University of Missouri Press, 2009), 93; "Radio Program Launches Drive Tonight 8 to 9," *Centerville Daily Iowegian*, January 17, 1944; "Bing and Voice Are Together at the Majestic," *Centerville Daily Iowegian*, June 12, 1944; "Help the Invasion—Buy More Bonds," *Centerville Daily Iowegian*, June 12, 1944.

2. Clarence Hood, "Urge Appanoose People to Back War Effort by Pledging Money," *Centerville Daily Iowegian*, March 9, 1942; "Victory Stamp and Bond Drive Parade Success," *Centerville Daily Iowegian*, July 1, 1942; "Largest Sale Is Report of Committee," *Centerville Daily Iowegian*, September 17, 1943; "Two Fire Alarms as Paul Revere Canvass Is Made," *Centerville Daily Iowegian*, September 25, 1942; "Naval Band Is to Be Feature of Bond Rally," *Centerville Daily Iowegian*, January 21, 1944; "War Heroes Are Coming to Aid Victory Drive," *Centerville Daily Iowegian*, September 13, 1943; "Famous Band to Play Here for 'B-Day,'" *Centerville Daily Iowegian*, May 5, 1945; "Bond Battle Is Raging Now," *Centerville Daily Iowegian*, January 25, 1944; "Movie Star Paul Kelly Coming Here," *Centerville Daily Iowegian*, January 15, 1944; "Cavalcade of Hollywood Stars," advertisement, *Centerville Daily Iowegian*, January 21, 1944; "American Heroes Will Highlight Bond Drive Program Here Thursday," *Centerville Daily Iowegian*, September 14, 1943; "Iowegian Take a Bow Because of Compliment," *Centerville Daily Iowegian*, April 4, 1942; "For Victory…," untitled, *Centerville Daily Iowegian*, April 6, 1942; "Early Bond Drive Reports Encouraging," *Centerville Daily Iowegian*, July 3, 1942; "Goal Reached Early After Noon Today," *Centerville Daily Iowegian*, April 29, 1943; "$28,000 Is Total Sold by 3 O'Clock," *Centerville Daily Iowegian*, July 17, 1942; "Pearl Harbor Bond Drive Is over the Top," *Centerville Daily Iowegian*, December 7, 1944; "Oscar Jones to Bomb Tokyo Here in Bond Drive," *Centerville Daily Iowegian*, December 7, 1944; "Pearl Harbor Bond Drive Is Big Success," *Centerville Daily Iowegian*, December 8, 1944.
3. "Want to Honor Boys in Armed Forces Friday," *Centerville Daily Iowegian*, July 14, 1942; Charles DePuy, Around the Town, *Centerville Daily Iowegian*, July 15, 1942; Charles DePuy, Columns Write, *Centerville Daily Iowegian*, July 17, 1942; "Picture Display of Home Soldiers," *Centerville Daily Iowegian*, July 17, 1942; "Disney Cartoon Insignias Seen at Elgin's Here," *Centerville Daily Iowegian*, March 13, 1942; "House to House Canvass Starts Here Next Week," *Centerville Daily Iowegian*, September 3, 1942; "September Bond Drive Gets off to Rousing Start," *Centerville Daily Iowegian*, September 2, 1942; "Girl Scouts in Rapid Fire Sale," *Centerville Daily Iowegian*, September 24, 1942; "True Blue Girls Sell War Bonds To-day on Square," *Centerville Daily Iowegian*, June 10, 1944; "Corsage Days to Boost the Sale of Bonds," *Centerville Daily Iowegian*, July 6, 1942; "Stamp Corsages Will Be Sold on through Sat.," *Centerville Daily Iowegian*, July 10, 1942; "Stamp Corsage Sale a Complete Sell Out," *Centerville Daily Iowegian*, July 11, 1942; "Stamp Corsage Making Contest," *Centerville Daily Iowegian*, September 24, 1942; "City Merchants 'All Out' in National Stamp Drive," *Centerville Daily Iowegian*, June 29, 1942; "Miss Victory Takes to Irish Carriage Here," *Centerville Daily Iowegian*, June 30, 1942; Dorothy Haines, "WWII Patriotism on the Home Front," *Daily Iowegian*, July 21, 2005; "Army Jeep at Fair Wednesday," *Centerville Daily Iowegian*, August 20, 1943; "Car Blasted by Japs to Be Seen Here Tomorrow," *Centerville Daily Iowegian*, August 27, 1942; "The Car from Pearl Harbor," E.A. Hull

Insurance Agency advertisement, *Centerville Daily Iowegian*, August 27, 1942; Charles DePuy, "After seeing 'The Car from Pearl Harbor,'" Around the Town, *Centerville Daily Iowegian*, August 29, 1942.

4. "B-Day after V-E Day," *Centerville Daily Iowegian*, May 8, 1945; "Centerville Banks," advertisement, *Centerville Daily Iowegian*, January 19, 1944; "Wanted Feed Sacks-for-Defense Stamps," Waggoner's advertisement, *Centerville Daily Iowegian*, February 23, 1942; "Bacon and Cigarettes," *Centerville Daily Iowegian*, May 16, 1945; "Centerville Swim Pool to Give U.S. Stamps on Fourth," *Centerville Daily Iowegian*, July 3, 1942; "Two Day Tourney Will Help Boom Stamp Campaign," *Centerville Daily Iowegian*, July 1, 1942; Charles DePuy, Around the Town, *Centerville Daily Iowegian*, April 11, 1942.
5. "Veteran Buys Bonds—Still Is Fighting for U.S.," *Centerville Daily Iowegian*, September 24, 1942; "Tiniest Patriot," *Centerville Daily Iowegian*, April 8, 1942; "Takes First Money Ever Made to Buy Defense Stamps," *Centerville Daily Iowegian*, March 25, 1942; "Junior's a Super Bond Salesman," *Centerville Daily Iowegian*, August 10, 1942; "Junior Roush Sells $908.70 of Bonds," *Centerville Daily Iowegian*, August 20, 1942; "Junior Roush Has New Shoes," *Centerville Daily Iowegian*, September 2, 1942; "Junior's Sales Area Leads to Kansas City," *Centerville Daily Iowegian*, June 3, 1943; "'Minute Man' Banner Now at Swift Co. Plant," *Centerville Daily Iowegian*, April 29, 1943; "Women Take Big Part in Sixth War Loan Drive," *Centerville Daily Iowegian*, October 31, 1944; "Youngest Bond Buyer Has His Say," *Centerville Daily Iowegian*, January 19, 1944; "Young Navy Man at Hospital Has Education Money," *Centerville Daily Iowegian*, February 3, 1944; "Buying Stamps Is Not Spending— But Investing," Student Iowegian Section, *Centerville Daily Iowegian*, April 4, 1942; Carolyn Bauman, interview with the author, March 20, 2010; "Band Salutes Flag at Last Night's Game," *Centerville Daily Iowegian*, November 7, 1942.
6. "Rationing: I Share My Car to Conserve Gas. Tires. Auto," exhibit poster in "World War II Rationing on the Home Front," http://www.ameshistoricalsociety.org/exhibits/events/rationing3.htm; "Finish Assn. of Commerce Budget and Aid Defense," *Centerville Daily Iowegian*, January 6, 1942; "Car Dealer Future Dismal," *Centerville Daily Iowegian*, January 23, 1942; "Only 24 Cars Can Be Sold in Appanoose This Year," *Centerville Daily Iowegian*, March 6, 1942; Charles DePuy, Around the Town, *Centerville Daily Iowegian*, May 2, 1942; Charles DePuy, Around the Town, *Centerville Daily Iowegian*, April 8, 1942; Myrtle Felkner, interview with the author, March 20, 2011; "Increase in Rail Travel Shown Here," *Centerville Daily Iowegian*, April 7, 1942; "Discontinue Bus in Rationing of Travel Service," *Centerville Daily Iowegian*, October 2, 1942; "Local Office for Car Ride Changes Now Established," *Centerville Daily Iowegian*, September 2, 1942; Bill Smallwood, interview with the author, January 3, 2011.

7. "Sugar Sales Being Limited by States," *Centerville Daily Iowegian*, January 24, 1942; "Sugar Is Short in Centerville This Weekend," *Centerville Daily Iowegian*, February 2, 1942; "Will Store War Ration Books in the Courthouse," *Centerville Daily Iowegian*, February 16, 1942; "People Must Register for Sugar Ration," *Centerville Daily Iowegian*, April 30, 1942; "Sugar Ration Zones Explained by Supt. Fannon," *Centerville Daily Iowegian*, May 1, 1942; "How to Get Your Sugar," *Centerville Daily Iowegian*, May 1, 1942; "Local Sugar Rationing in a Slow Start," *Centerville Daily Iowegian*, May 4, 1942; "Victory Sundae," Pure Ice Company advertisement, *Centerville Daily Iowegian*, July 2, 1942; "World War II Rationing—Page 2," in exhibit pages for "World War II Rationing on the Home Front," http://www.ameshistoricalsociety.org/exhibits/events/rationing2.htm; "Numbered and Lettered Coupons in New Ration Book," photograph and caption, *Centerville Daily Iowegian*, October 28, 1942; "Shoe Rationing Will Not Be Serious Hardship in Centerville," *Centerville Daily Iowegian*, February 8, 1943; "Must Declare Certain Canned-Bottled Goods," *Centerville Daily Iowegian*, February 10, 1943; "Zero Hour for Food Rationing Is Drawing Near," *Centerville Daily Iowegian*, February 18, 1943; "The Most Popular Canned Foods: Form Consumer Fills out When She Applies for Ration Book Number 2," *Centerville Daily Iowegian*, February 23, 1943; "2,047 Sign for Ration Book in Centerville," *Centerville Daily Iowegian*, February 23, 1943.
8. "Start Wartime Speed Limit of 35 Miles Per Hour," *Centerville Daily Iowegian*, October 1, 1942; "Drive Too Fast and Face Loss of Driver License," *Centerville Daily Iowegian*, December 1, 1942; "Local Car Owners Get Orders to Have Tires Inspected—Or Face Loss of Gas Ration Cards," *Centerville Daily Iowegian*, December 23, 1942; "Gas Rationing Time in Appanoose—and Elsewhere—Is Near At Hand," *Centerville Daily Iowegian*, November 6, 1942; "City Gas Stations Feel 50 Per Cent Decrease in Sales," *Centerville Daily Iowegian*, December 8, 1942; "World War II Rationing on the U.S. Homefront," http://www.ameshistoricalsociety.org/exhibits/events/rationing.htm; Myrtle Felkner, interview with the author, March 20, 2011.

Chapter 69

1. Jesse M. Beck, "Young Men Are Leaving," *Centerville Daily Iowegian*, February 18, 1943; "46 Appanoose Boys Listed by Recruiter Here," *Centerville Daily Iowegian*, August 28, 1942; "Local Service Men Ordered to Return to Duty," *Centerville Daily Iowegian*, January 28, 1942; "February 16 Is Set for New Registration Day," *Centerville Daily Iowegian*, January 5, 1942; "18-Year-Olds Registering Here Today," *Centerville Daily Iowegian*, December 11, 1942; "42 Leave City for Army Camp Monday Evening," *Centerville Daily Iowegian*, August 24, 1942; "73 County Men Depart for Service,"

Centerville Daily Iowegian, October 19, 1942; "Eighty-Three Answer Call for Service," *Centerville Daily Iowegian*, December 3, 1942; "Colored Boys Are Given Farewell at Local Station," *Centerville Daily Iowegian*, July 16, 1942; "Large Draftee List Entrains During Night," *Centerville Daily Iowegian*, September 21, 1942; "Fine Farewell for County Draftees," *Centerville Daily Iowegian*, July 9, 1942; "Another Large Contingent of Co. Men Leave," *Centerville Daily Iowegian*, September 22, 1942.

2. "42 Leave City for Army Camp Monday Evening," *Centerville Daily Iowegian*, August 24, 1942; "Local Guardsmen Die in Wreck," *Centerville Daily Iowegian*, April 10, 1942; "Extra! Chase Fannon Killed in Air Plane Crash," *Centerville Daily Iowegian*, June 17, 1942; "City Mourns Chase Fannon's Death," *Centerville Daily Iowegian*, June 18, 1942; "Fannon Was Great Amateur Golfer," *Centerville Daily Iowegian*, June 18, 1942; "Javonovich Is Listed Dead in Casualty Report," *Centerville Daily Iowegian*, August 20, 1942; "Dan Lutrell First Mystic War Casualty," *Centerville Daily Iowegian*, August 27, 1942; "Midway Island—Where Death Followed Bullets," photograph and caption, *Centerville Daily Iowegian*, September 9, 1942; "U.S. Loses Lexington, One Destroyer in the Smashing Sea Victory," *Centerville Daily Iowegian*, June 12, 1942; Columns Write, *Centerville Daily Iowegian*, September 22, 1942; "United States Loses a Destroyer," *Centerville Daily Iowegian*, September 24, 1942; "Marines 'Hold Own' on Solomons," *Centerville Daily Iowegian*, August 11, 1942; "Marines in Hand-to-Hand Fight," *Centerville Daily Iowegian*, August 12, 1942; "Local Sailor Tells How Japs Fight Until the End Although Their Efforts May Be Futile," *Centerville Daily Iowegian*, December 26, 1942; "U.S. Forces Are on Solomons," *Centerville Daily Iowegian*, August 10, 1942.
3. Private Maurice Hudson, letter in Columns Write, *Centerville Daily Iowegian*, September 30, 1942; Phyllis Morrow Cosby, interview with the author, September 22, 2008.
4. C.B.D., "This Is 'Hello!'" Columns Write, *Centerville Daily Iowegian*, April 24, 1942; C.B.D., Columns Write, *Centerville Daily Iowegian*, July 24, 1942; Phyllis Cosby, Moulton correspondent, "Letters from 'the Boys' Treasures to Folks Back Home," *Ad-Express/Daily Iowegian*, November 23, 2001; Bill Smallwood, "Walking Down Memory Lane," *Daily Iowegian*, May 25, 2004; Bill Smallwood, correspondence with author, February 1, 2010.
5. C.B.D., on Charles Pancrazio, Columns Write, *Centerville Daily Iowegian*, May 8, 1942; C.B.D., on Tony A. Cortesio, Columns Write, *Centerville Daily Iowegian*, July 3, 1942; C.B.D., on Jack Harman, Columns Write, *Centerville Daily Iowegian*, May 22, 1942; C.B.D., Columns Write, *Centerville Daily Iowegian*, December 10, 1943; "John Buscemi Is Recognized Due Camera Art," *Centerville Daily Iowegian*, March 20, 1943; "Centerville Boy Has Pictures in Noted Magazine," *Centerville Daily Iowegian*, March 13, 1942; "John Buscemi on Yank Staff in the Pacific," *Centerville Daily Iowegian*, June 23, 1943; "John Buscemi Is Featured in Edition of Yank," *Centerville Daily Iowegian*, June 29, 1943.

6. "Newly-Arrived American Troops Down to Business," *Centerville Daily Iowegian*, March 5, 1942; "Yanks 'Over the Top' in Ireland," photograph and caption, *Centerville Daily Iowegian*, May 23, 1942; Members of 34th Infantry Division, *The Story of the 34th Division: Louisiana to Pisa* (Information and Education Section, MTOUSA, no date), 3; "The 34th Infantry (Red Bull): About the Insignia," *Des Moines Sunday Register*, State edition, July 25, 2010; "Co. G Holds First Regular Annual Reunion Here Friday," *Centerville Daily Iowegian*, February 11, 1956.
7. "British Score Victory in Egypt," *Centerville Daily Iowegian*, November 5, 1942; "British Take Tobruk as Allied Pincers Close in on Axis Armies," *Centerville Daily Iowegian*, November 13, 1942; "R.A.F. Bombers in Successful Sweep Over France," *Centerville Daily Iowegian*, May 4, 1942; "Flying Fortresses Given More Praise," *Centerville Daily Iowegian*, September 8, 1942; "Sub Base of Jap's [*sic*] Bombed in Aleutians," *Centerville Daily Iowegian*, October 27, 1942; "United States Loses Destroyer," *Centerville Daily Iowegian*, September 24, 1942; "Stalingrad at Any Price—Hitler," *Centerville Daily Iowegian*, September 11, 1942; "Russians Still Hold Stalingrad," *Centerville Daily Iowegian*, December 12, 1942; "Stalingrad Streets Are Bloody," *Centerville Daily Iowegian*, September 19, 1942; "President Roosevelt Tells of Conference," *Centerville Daily Iowegian*, February 2, 1943.
8. "U.S. to Hit Axis through Tunisia," *Centerville Daily Iowegian*, November 9, 1942; "U.S. Second Front Forces Land in Vichy North Africa," map and caption, *Centerville Daily Iowegian*, November 11, 1942; "Where U.S. Forces Push Second Front," map and caption, *Centerville Daily Iowegian*, November 11, 1942; Tracey Corder, interviews with the author, February 21, 2000, October 10, 2006, and January 21, 2011; Justin F. Gleichauf, "Navy Armed Guard: Unsung Heroes," *American Legion Magazine* 120, no. 4 (April 1986): 24, 25, 51; C.A. Lloyd, chairman of U.S. Navy Armed Guard World War II Veterans, "U.S. Navy Armed Guard WWI and WWII," pamphlet, Raleigh, N.C., undated; Morison, *The Oxford History of the American People*, 377 (see chap. 16, n. 3); "Hero Award to Man Who Planted Flag in Africa," *Centerville Daily Iowegian*, January 21, 1943; "Knecht Tells of Experiences," *Centerville Daily Iowegian*, December 8, 1942.
9. Wes Gallagher, "Algerian Port Falls Few Hours After the Allied Attack Start," *Centerville Daily Iowegian*, November 10, 1942.
10. Maurice (Reese) Hudson, interviews with the author, March 1, 2000, November 11, 2004, and November 13, 2010; Dan Ehl, "It Was a Very Long War for Hudson," *Daily Iowegian*, May 25, 2002; Members of 34th Infantry Division, *The Story of the 34th Division: Louisiana to Pisa*, 3–5 (see chap. 69, n. 6), "Bear Promoted to Lieut.-Col. in U.S. Army," *Centerville Daily Iowegian*, July 29, 1942; C.B.D., Around the Town, *Centerville Daily Iowegian*, April 27, 1946.
11. Jesse M. Beck, "Are Our Boys There?" editorial, *Centerville Daily Iowegian*, November 12, 1942; "Noah Davis Is Killed in Africa," *Centerville Daily Iowegian*, December 11, 1942;

"Chaplain Tells of Noah Davis' Death in Africa," *Centerville Daily Iowegian*, January 9, 1943; "Effects Arrive That Belonged to Sgt. Davis," *Centerville Daily Iowegian*, June 17, 1943; C.B.D., "Letter to Noah Davis' Wife Describing his Death by Joe Hurt," Around the Town, *Centerville Daily Iowegian*, June 29, 1943; "Confirm Death Report in Regard to Noah J. Davis," *Centerville Daily Iowegian*, December 18, 1942; "The Story of Colonel Bear's Actions in Tunis," *Centerville Daily Iowegian*, December 31, 1942; C.B.D., Columns Write," *Centerville Daily Iowegian*, December 15, 1942.

12. "War Brings an Extra Worry to Many People Here," *Centerville Daily Iowegian*, January 21, 1943.
13. "Window Stars in Service Men Homes," *Centerville Daily Iowegian*, March 20, 1942; Bill Smallwood, interview with the author, October 10, 2005; Ethel Lira, "We Remember Those Who Served," *Centerville Daily Iowegian*, November 12, 2002; Richard Gorden and Willis Gorden, *A Step Back in Time: Plano, Iowa* (Plano: Self-published, August 1998), photograph, 162; Phyllis Morrow Cosby, interview with the author, January 20, 2011; "Erect Bill Board for Service Men in Unionville, Mo.," *Centerville Daily Iowegian*, October 12, 1942; "Honor Roll Is Going Forward at This Time," *Centerville Daily Iowegian*, April 1, 1943; C.B.D., Columns Write, *Centerville Daily Iowegian*, March 30, 1943; "Seek Names of All Who Serve from Appanoose," *Centerville Daily Iowegian*, May 3, 1943.
14. Bob Seddon, interview with the author, March 16, 2010; Jean Folkerts and Dwight L. Teeter, *Voices of a Nation* (New York: Macmillan, 1989), 447–48; Cloud and Olson, *The Murrow Boys*, 57–162, 163, 375 (see chap. 58, n. 10); C.B.D., Columns Write, *Centerville Daily Iowegian*, December 8, 1942.
15. "U.S. Troops Landing in Aleutians to Fight on Kiska," photograph and caption, *Centerville Daily Iowegian*, October 7, 1942; "Heads Bowed for Fallen Men on Guadalcanal," photograph and caption, *Centerville Daily Iowegian*, February 4, 1943; "Even the Spuds Prophesy 'V' for Victory," photograph and caption, *Centerville Daily Iowegian*, February 4, 1943; C.B.D., Around the Town, *Centerville Daily Iowegian*, February 26, 1944; C.B.D, Columns Write, *Centerville Daily Iowegian*, October 30, 1942; "Sign of Victory in Sky," *Centerville Daily Iowegian*, April 21, 1942.

Chapter 70

1. C.B.D., Columns Write, *Centerville Daily Iowegian*, January 15, 1943; "Bitter Cold Grips County; Mercury Sinks to 19 Below," *Centerville Daily Iowegian*, January 19, 1943; C.B.D., Columns Write, *Centerville Daily Iowegian*, March 9, 1943.
2. "Juneau—Another Saga of the Sea in World War 2—Suffering and Death," *Centerville Daily Iowegian*, December 13, 1945; "Jap Planes Swarm upon the Hornet,"

Associated Press photo from U.S. Navy, *Centerville Daily Iowegian*, January 13, 1943; "Bud Van Doren on U.S. Hornet When It Sank," *Centerville Daily Iowegian*, January 14, 1943; "Delmar Rak, Exline Youth, Is Missing in Action," *Centerville Daily Iowegian*, December 4, 1942; Obituary of Staff Sergeant Delmar Rak, *Centerville Daily Iowegian*, January 21, 1943; C.B.D., Columns Write, *Centerville Daily Iowegian*, April 16, 1943.

3. "British Army Nearing Tripoli," *Centerville Daily Iowegian*, January 19, 1943; "British 8th Army Enters Axis City," *Centerville Daily Iowegian*, January 22, 1943; "Preparing Final Blow at Rommel," *Centerville Daily Iowegian*, February 10, 1943; "First Days in Tunisia—Skirmishing," chapter 3 in *The Story of the 34th Infantry Division: Louisiana to Pisa*, 3 (see chap. 69, n. 6); Lieutenant General G.S. Patton, Jr., commanding letter to Headquarters 11 Corps, Office of the Corps Engineer, APO 3O2, March 20, 1943; "19th Combat Engineer Regt. Has Put in 550 Days at Front," *Stars and Stripes*, January 16, 1945; Reese Hudson, interview with the author, November 2, 2002.
4. "Nazis at Stalingrad Wiped Out," *Centerville Daily Iowegian*, February 1, 1943; Keegan, *Collins Atlas of World War II*, 85 (see chap. 59, n. 11); "Japs Withdraw from Guadalcanal," *Centerville Daily Iowegian*, February 9, 1943; Around the Town, *Centerville Daily Iowegian*, December 6, 1961; Gary Craver, interview with the author, March 5, 2011; Maurice Stamps, interview with the author, March 22, 2011; "John Ross of Cincinnati Is Victim," *Centerville Daily Iowegian*, April 15, 1943; C.B.D., Columns Write, April 16, 1943; "Local Marine Ignores Wound, Goes to Hospital When Hit by Appendicitis; More about A. Scott," *Centerville Daily Iowegian*, March 15, 1943; "Guadalcanal Diary Is Told Here Today by Red-Haired Veteran of 24, Who Has Jap Teeth in His Pocket as a Memento," *Centerville Daily Iowegian*, April 30, 1943; C.B.D., Columns Write, *Centerville Daily Iowegian*, May 7, 1943; "Chas Davis Is Back from Guadalcanal," *Centerville Daily Iowegian*, September 18, 1943; C.B.D., Columns Write, *Centerville Daily Iowegian*, September 21, 1943.
5. Keegan, *Collins Atlas of World War II*, 96 (see chap. 59, n. 11); *The Story of the 34th Infantry Division: Louisiana to Pisa*, 7, 8 (see chap. 69, n. 6); "U.S. Makes New Retreat in Battle," *Centerville Daily Iowegian*, February 18, 1943; Robert Dvorchak, "GIs Get a Bloody Baptism Courtesy of Afrika Korps," Associated Press, no source, no date, in private papers of Maurice Hudson.
6. "Jap Convoy Sunk in Air Attack," *Centerville Daily Iowegian*, March 4, 1943; "Allied Air Power Hits Jap Bases," *Centerville Daily Iowegian*, March 8, 1943; "Unionville, Missouri Youth Feared by the Japanese," *Centerville Daily Iowegian*, Centennial Edition, November 29, 1946; Robert D. Gibson, www.homeofheroes.com; Robert Probasco, interview with the author, March 15, 2011; John Cortesio, interview with the author, April 2, 2011; Biography of Sandy Cortesio, unpublished manuscript, no date, from family papers in possession of John Cortesio.

7. Keegan, *Collins Atlas of World War II*, 102–3 (see chap. 59, n. 11) ; Keegan, *The Second World War*, 296 (see chap. 59, n. 5); "Yanks Land on Jap Base of Attu," *Centerville Daily Iowegian*, May 14, 1943; "Reveals Bloody Memorial Day for Yanks on Attu," *Centerville Daily Iowegian*, June 10, 1943; "Letter Comes after Boy Is Reported Dead," *Centerville Daily Iowegian*, June 26, 1943; C.B.D., Columns Write, *Centerville Daily Iowegian*, September 21, 1943.
8. "War Department List Four in Messages Sent to Their Families Here This Weekend," *Centerville Daily Iowegian*, March 8, 1943; "Local Youth Dies Due to War Wounds," *Centerville Daily Iowegian*, March 19, 1943; "Ray D. Seals Is Victim of War," *Centerville Daily Iowegian*, May 25, 1943; "John Benac Jr. War Casualty," *Centerville Daily Iowegian*, May 22, 1943; "Two More Local Men Wounded on African Front," *Centerville Daily Iowegian*, May 27, 1943; "Family Here Awaits Word from McCoy," *Centerville Daily Iowegian*, April 14, 1943; "Lt. Pravdica, Paul Tweedy Are Missing," *Centerville Daily Iowegian*, March 9, 1943; "Eight Appanoose Boys Now Listed as Missing on the Africa Front Since Feb 17," *Centerville Daily Iowegian*, March 10, 1943; "Missing in Action," *Centerville Daily Iowegian*, March 11, 1943; "Added to List of Missing Soldiers," *Centerville Daily Iowegian*, March 12, 1943; "Official List Includes Men from Appanoose," *Centerville Daily Iowegian*, March 30, 1943; "Charles Burkhiser Reported Prisoner," *Centerville Daily Iowegian*, April 1, 1943; "Paul Slavin Is Heard Via Nazi Radio," *Centerville Daily Iowegian*, April 15, 1943; "Confirm News Corp. Johnston Nazi Prisoner," *Centerville Daily Iowegian*, August 10, 1943; "Hope Felt by Parents of Missing Soldiers," *Centerville Daily Iowegian*, April 15, 1943; C.B.D., Columns Write, *Centerville Daily Iowegian*, December 15, 1943; C.B.D., Columns Write, *Centerville Daily Iowegian*, August 20, 1943; "Many of Iowans Listed as 'Missing' Are Now Prisoners of the Enemy," *Centerville Daily Iowegian*, May 6, 1943; "Letters from Nazi Prison Camps Arrive," *Centerville Daily Iowegian*, April 27, 1943.
9. "Allied Forces Retake Pass from Rommel," *Centerville Daily Iowegian*, February 26, 1943; "U.S. Forces Regain Kasserine Pass," map, *Centerville Daily Iowegian*, March 1, 1943; "Additional Facts about Appanoose Men in Tunisian Battle Received in Letter from PFC W. Leffler," *Centerville Daily Iowegian*, April 5, 1943; Charles DePuy, "Exline Soldier Lost Month of Life in Africa," *Centerville Daily Iowegian*, August 12, 1943; Obituary of Verl Kenneth Farnsworth, Schmidt Family Funeral Homes, *Centerville Daily Iowegian*, August 19, 2005; Jesse M. Beck, "Our Boys Are Fighting," editorial, *Centerville Daily Iowegian*, May 5, 1943; Richard Wilson, *The Gallant Fight of the 34th Division in the North African Campaign*, articles by Wilson reprinted in booklet form by Des Moines Register and Tribune, September 1, 1943, chapter 7; "Sicily Invaded" *Centerville Daily Iowegian*, July 10, 1943.

Chapter 71

1. Daniel De Luce, "Sicily Invaded; Allied Armies Open 2nd Front," *Centerville Daily Iowegian*, July 10, 1943; *General Marshall's Victory Report on the Winning of World War II in Europe and the Pacific* (War Department of the United States of America, no place, no date), 14–15; Keegan, *The Second World War,* 348 (see chap. 59, n. 5); Keegan, *Collins Atlas of World War II*, 112 (see chap. 59, n. 11).
2. *The Story of the 34th Infantry Division: Louisiana to Pisa*, 26–27 (see chap. 69, n. 6); Tracey Corder, interviews with the author, February 21, 2000, January 21, 2011; Richard Harrington, interview with the author, August 31, 2010; "Allies Blast Axis Supply Lines," map and caption, *Centerville Daily Iowegian*, April 20, 1943; "Allied Bombs Rip Naples, Sicily," *Centerville Daily Iowegian*, June 18, 1943; "Allies Hit Military Objectives in City," *Centerville Daily Iowegian*, July 19, 1943; "Rome Bombed," map and caption, *Centerville Daily Iowegian*, July 20, 1943; "U.S. Planes over Naples," *Centerville Daily Iowegian*, March 19, 1943; "Prelude to Invasion?" map and caption, *Centerville Daily Iowegian*, April 7, 1943; Don Whitehead, "'Came to Bury You Fellows Not to See You Surrender,' Story of Yankee Chaplain," *Centerville Daily Iowegian*, November 15, 1943.
3. Keegan, *Collins Atlas of World War II*, 28 (see chap. 59, n. 11); Stamps, "Snafus and Love Letters: Memories of an Old G.I.," 78–79 (see chap. 63, n. 3).
4. Reese Hudson, interview with the author, November 12, 2010; Lieutenant General O.N. Bradley, letter to Benjamin B. Maxwell, captain, Nineteenth Engineers, Adjutant Headquarters Nineteenth Engineers Regiment, APO 302, U.S. Army, September 24, 1943; C.B.D., Columns Write, *Centerville Daily Iowegian*, August 20, 1943; Ernie Pyle, Ernie Pyle's War Dispatches, "Somewhere in Sicily" with the engineers, *Des Moines Register* and *Sunday Des Moines Register,* September 3, 5, 6, 7, 8, 9, 10 and 12; C.B.D., Columns Write, *Centerville Daily Iowegian*, September 17, 1943; C.B.D., Columns Write, *Centerville Daily Iowegian*, October 5, 1943.
5. "Hints Arrest of Mussolini in Attempt to Flee Country," *Centerville Daily Iowegian*, July 26, 1943; "Mussolini under Arrest Is Rumor," *Centerville Daily Iowegian*, July 26, 1943; "Says Vatican Is Scene of Negotiations," *Centerville Daily Iowegian*, July 27, 1943; "Peace Riots Are Breaking out in Italy," *Centerville Daily Iowegian*, July 28, 1943; *General Marshall's Victory Report on the Winning of World War II in Europe and the Pacific*, 16–18; Keegan, *Collins Atlas of World War II*, 112–13 (see chap. 59, n. 11).
6. Lieutenant General Mark Clark, *Road to Rome* (no place, no date), introduction, 1; *General Marshall's Victory Report on the Winning of World War II in Europe and the Pacific*, 350; Edward Kennedy, "Powerful American and British Forces Landed Near Naples," *Centerville Daily Iowegian*, September 9, 1943; *The Story of the 34th Infantry Division: Louisiana to Pisa*, 28 (see chap. 69, n. 6).

7. John E. Bommarito, *We Kept 'Em Flying* (No place: Author House, April 2004), 168; Jeanne Harrington Fowler, interview with the author, March 1, 2010; "American Girl, Hero," *Centerville Daily Iowegian*, October 7, 1943; "Former Appanoose Woman with 5th," *Centerville Daily Iowegian*, November 25, 1944.
8. Keegan, *The Second World War*, 352–53 (see chap. 59, n. 5); Clark, *Road to Rome*, 3–5, including photo and caption; *The Story of the 34th Infantry Division: Louisiana to Pisa*, 30 (see chap. 69, n. 6); "Allies Throw Back Nazi Forces," *Centerville Daily Iowegian*, September 16, 1943; "Allies Move Forward 11 Miles," *Centerville Daily Iowegian*, September 18, 1943; "Fifth Army Approaching Naples," *Centerville Daily Iowegian*, September 22, 1943; "Naples Evacuated by German Troops," *Centerville Daily Iowegian*, September 30, 1943.
9. Keegan, *The Second World War*, 352, 353–5 (see chap. 59, n. 5); John Sisul, private family videotape of interview with Sisul, December 2, 2000, privately held by Mike Sisul.
10. *The Story of the 34th Infantry Division: Louisiana to Pisa*, 31–42 (see chap. 69, n. 6); Ernie Pyle, "Our Secret Weapon," *Centerville Daily Iowegian*, December 22, 1943.
11. Bommarito, *We Kept 'Em Flying*, 181; "Air Reserve," Staff Sergeant George Cortesio, article and papers in possession of John Cortesio, Des Moines, Iowa, source unknown; Obituary of Giancinto Cortesio, George Cortesio's father, *Centerville Daily Iowegian*, January 25, 1940; C.B.D., Columns Write, *Centerville Daily Iowegian*, November 26, 1943.
12. "Wm. Beers Is Victim of Italy Battle," *Centerville Daily Iowegian*, November 30, 1943; C.B.D., Columns Write, *Centerville Daily Iowegian*, November 30, 1943; "Exline Youth Killed in War on October 13," *Centerville Daily Iowegian*, November 15, 1943; "Exline Boy Was Hero of Italy Drive," *Centerville Daily Iowegian*, January 27, 1944; "Fight over Roads to Rome over for Corporal Wakefield," *Centerville Daily Iowegian*, November 17, 1943; "2 Centerville Boys Wounded," *Centerville Daily Iowegian*, December 3, 1943; "Sgt. Roy Long in Hospital in Italy Is Report," *Centerville Daily Iowegian*, December 18, 1943; "Col. Sparks Is Now in States," *Centerville Daily Iowegian*, March 8, 1944.
13. Keegan, *Collins Atlas of World War II*, 122–23, 120–21 (see chap. 59, n. 11); C.B.D., Columns Write, *Centerville Daily Iowegian*, December 10, 1943; Royal Simmons, interview with the author, March 24, 2011.
14. "'We Will Win in '44' Declares Eisenhower," *Centerville Daily Iowegian*, December 27, 1943; Keegan, *The Second World War*, 359 (see chap. 59, n. 5).

Chapter 72

1. C.B.D., Columns Write, *Centerville Daily Iowegian*, July 2, 1943; George Larry Freeborn, interview with the author, May 26 2008; "January Draft Calls Group to Capital

Today," *Centerville Daily Iowegian*, January 18, 1944; "35 Men Leave for Induction Center Exams," *Centerville Daily Iowegian*, January 18, 1944; "74 Men Leave This City for U.S. Exams," *Centerville Daily Iowegian*, February 23, 1944; "49 Men Leave in Latest Call from This City," *Centerville Daily Iowegian*, June 9, 1944; C.B.D., Around the Town, *Centerville Daily Iowegian*, August 5, 1942; "Big Bomber Plane Went over at Noon," *Centerville Daily Iowegian*, July 25, 1942; "Lt. Logan Flies Home from Kansas Training Center," *Centerville Daily Iowegian*, August 12, 1943; C.B.D., Columns Write, *Centerville Daily Iowegian*, May 1, 1942; "War Birds Roar over Centerville," *Centerville Daily Iowegian*, September 3, 1943; "World's Fastest Medium Bomber Lands at Municipal Port Here," *Centerville Daily Iowegian*, September 17, 1943; "Ottumwa Naval Air Station Ends Training," *Centerville Daily Iowegian*, September 24, 1945; Bill Smallwood, interview with the author, March 1, 2011; C.B.D., Around the Town, *Centerville Daily Iowegian*, December 5, 1942; Richard L. Wakefield, *Good Run Almost Done More to Come?* (Self-published, 2010), 25, collection of Appanoose County Museum, Centerville.

2. "Vital Aircraft Carrier Production Shipyard," advertisement, *Centerville Daily Iowegian*, October 26, 1943; "NYA Students 'Report Back' to Local Shop," *Centerville Daily Iowegian*, March 29, 1943; "Needed Immediately Men and Women to Build Super Bombers," advertisement, *Centerville Daily Iowegian*, January 19, 1944; "Navy Sends Man to Centerville to Seek Clerks," *Centerville Daily Iowegian*, November 23, 1943; "War Jobs in Alaska!" *Centerville Daily Iowegian*, March 15, 1944; "First Step Is Taken in Plan for Peace Era," *Centerville Daily Iowegian*, May 9, 1944; "Essential War Work Pacific Northwest," advertisement, *Centerville Daily Iowegian*, February 3, 1944; "Workers Needed Northwest United States," advertisement, *Centerville Daily Iowegian*, March 20, 1944; "Workers Needed Now," advertisement, *Centerville Daily Iowegian*, March 20, 1944; "Boeing Aircraft Co.," advertisement, *Centerville Daily Iowegian*, October 12, 1944; "Civil Service Seeks Workers in Centerville," *Centerville Daily Iowegian*, April 10, 1944; "FBI on the Hunt for Personnel," *Centerville Daily Iowegian*, March 26, 1943; "NYA Is Seeking Local Women for War Production," *Centerville Daily Iowegian*, April 23, 1943; "Men and Women Urgently Needed—for Work On—Canadian-Alaskan Project," advertisement, *Centerville Daily Iowegian*, July 8, 1943; "Art Charles Makes Good as a Ship Builder," *Centerville Daily Iowegian*, January 29, 1943; "50 Youths out of Centerville NYA Shops to Vital War Tasks; Plan Open House Here March 12," *Centerville Daily Iowegian*, March 3, 1943; "Four NYA Youths Leave for West Coast This P.M.," *Centerville Daily Iowegian*, March 8, 1943; "Open House at NYA Shop Friday; Four More Youths Leave to Take Ship Building Jobs at Seattle," *Centerville Daily Iowegian*, March 11, 1943; "Local People Helped with Atomic Bomb," *Centerville Daily Iowegian*, August 8, 1945.

3. "War Will Affect Centerville in Many, Many Ways," *Centerville Daily Iowegian*, April 1, 1942; "Determined Effort Is Being Made to Furnish Badly Needed Employees

for Centerville Business at This Time," *Centerville Daily Iowegian*, April 29, 1943; "Local Business in Dire Need of More Employees," *Centerville Daily Iowegian*, May 19, 1943; "Woman Wanted," Gamble's advertisement, *Centerville Daily Iowegian*, December 7, 1944; "Go to Work in a War Plant—Hercules Manufacturing Co.," advertisement, *Centerville Daily Iowegian*, October 7, 1943; "Help the War Effort and Earn More Money—John Morrell & Co.," advertisement, *Centerville Daily Iowegian*, March 18, 1944; "Mexican Labor to Bolster Need for Iowa Farm Labor," *Centerville Daily Iowegian*, February 5, 1942; "Wanted! Farm Hands for Iowa Farms Married and Single," *Centerville Daily Iowegian*, March 13, 1943; "Farm Crew to Front Lines," *Centerville Daily Iowegian*, July 16, 1943; "Don't Shoot the Piano Player…," advertisement, *Centerville Daily Iowegian*, September 17, 1943.

4. "British Raid Berlin for Fifth Time," *Centerville Daily Iowegian*, December 3, 1943; "Red Army Regaining Initiative in the War," *Centerville Daily Iowegian*, December 13, 1943; "U.S. Marines and Soldiers Landing on Makin and Tarawa Islands in the Japan Held Gilbert Group," *Centerville Daily Iowegian*, November 23, 1943; "Officers Inspect Battered Tarawa Defenses," AP photograph, *Centerville Daily Iowegian*, December 3, 1943; "Tarawa Observer," AP Wire photo, *Centerville Daily Iowegian*, December 1, 1943; "Marines Charge Jap Pillbox," "Jap Dead on Tarawa's Sand," "Jap Position on Tarawa," 3 AP Wire photos, *Centerville Daily Iowegian*, December 4, 1943; "Japs Who Died Before American Guns," AP Wire photo, *Centerville Daily Iowegian*, December 6, 1943; "Axis Being Hit Hard on Anniversary of Pearl Harbor," *Centerville Daily Iowegian*, December 7, 1943; Keegan, *The Second World War*, 302 (see chap. 59, n. 5); Johnson, *A History of the American People*, 780–81 (see chap. 24, n. 28); David Burner, David, Virginia Bernhard and Stanley Kutler, "Mobilizing the Economy" and "The Citizen Army" in *A History of the United States*, 4th ed. (St. James, N.Y.: Brandywine Press, 1996), 855–56, 857; "Pour a Weld, Sew a Seam," *Centerville Daily Iowegian*, April 20, 1944; "Mary Large Is Pioneer at Seattle," *Centerville Daily Iowegian*, January 29, 1943.
5. Keegan, *The Second World War*, 302 (see chap. 59, n. 5); Ray E. Boomhower, *One Shot: The World War II Photography of John A. Bushemi* (Indianapolis: Indiana Historical Society Press, 2004), 58 (the Buscemi family name was alternately spelled Bushemi); C.B.D., Columns Write, *Centerville Daily Iowegian*, January 4, 1944.
6. Keegan, *The Second World War*, 302–3 (see chap. 59, n. 5); C.B.D., Columns Write, *Centerville Daily Iowegian*, January 11, 1944.
7. Boomhower, *One Shot: The World War II Photography of John A. Bushemi*, 60–65.
8. Bob Traxler, interview with the author, July 8, 2011.
9. C.B.D., Columns Write, *Centerville Daily Iowegian*, May 11, 1944; C.B.D., Columns Write, *Centerville Daily Iowegian*, May 12, 1944; C.B.D., Columns Write, *Centerville Daily Iowegian*, December 15, 1943.

Chapter 73

1. *The Story of the 34th Infantry Division: Louisiana to Pisa*, 62, 68 (see chap. 69, n. 6); David Nichols, ed., *Ernie's War* (New York: Simon and Schuster, 1986), 172, 189–96; Gordon Gammack, "Appanoose Co. Boys Heroes at Cassino," *Centerville Daily Iowegian*, February 12, 1944.
2. *The Story of the 34th Infantry Division: Louisiana to Pisa*, 51–52, 56–57 (see chap. 69, n. 6); Keegan, *The Second World War*, 358 (see chap. 59, n. 5); Reese Hudson, interview with the author, July 27, 2010; "Bombs Hammer Monastery on Mt. Cassino," *Centerville Daily Iowegian*, February 15, 1944; "Lt. Colonel Floyd Sparks Nearing Home Is Interviewed in Iowa," *Centerville Daily Iowegian*, March 25, 1944; "Lt. Col. Floyd Sparks Speaks to the Lions Club Monday Night," *Centerville Daily Iowegian*, June 13, 1944; "'War is Hell,' Says a Soldier of the 34th Division in Italy," *Centerville Daily Iowegian*, June 3, 1944; "Fifth Probes German Lines Near Cassino," *Centerville Daily Iowegian*, January 18, 1944; "Fifth Army Lays Siege to Cassino, Reds in New Push," *Centerville Daily Iowegian*, January 17, 1944; "Cassino Menaced from Third Side by French Units," *Centerville Daily Iowegian*, January 13, 1944; "Yanks Take Mountain," map, *Centerville Daily Iowegian*, January 19, 1944; "Nazi Stronghold Falls to Allies in Cassino Fighting," *Centerville Daily Iowegian*, March 20, 1944; "Fifth Army Flings Back Nazi Attacks on Cassino Sector," *Centerville Daily Iowegian*, March 23, 1944; *The Story of the 34th Infantry Division: Louisiana to Pisa*, 62–63 (see chap. 69, n. 6); Jesse M. Beck, "Air Devastation," editorial, *Centerville Daily Iowegian*, March 16, 1944.
3. Keegan, *Collins Atlas of World War II*, 114, 357–58 (see chap. 59, n. 11); *The Story of the 34th Infantry Division: Louisiana to Pisa*, 65–66 (see chap. 69, n. 6); Clark, *Road to Rome*, 29–30 (see chap. 71, n. 6); *General Marshall's Victory Report on the Winning of World War II in Europe and the Pacific*, 22 (see n. 1434); Nichols, *Ernie's War*, 236–37, 244–45 (see chap. 72, n. 9); "Don't Ever Question Courage of Army Nurses," *Centerville Daily Iowegian*, February 9, 1944; "German Shells Hit U.S. Field Hospital," *Centerville Daily Iowegian*, February 12, 1944; C.B.D., Columns Write, *Centerville Daily Iowegian*, May 12, 1944.
4. J.C. Kilbourn, interview with the author, June 4, 1996; Nichols, *Ernie's War*, 247 (see chap. 72, n. 9); "Don't Ever Question Courage of Army Nurses," *Centerville Daily Iowegian*, February 9, 1944; Jesse M. Beck, "Desperate Fighting," editorial, *Centerville Daily Iowegian*, February 28, 1944; "'Anzio Ann' Is Back Overseas," *Centerville Daily Iowegian*, January 10, 1951; Frank Miles, "Iowa's Share in Present Conflict Told by F. Miles," *Centerville Daily Iowegian*, November 13, 1944; C.B.D., Columns Write, December 8, 1944.
5. "Purple Heart to Relatives of Pfc. Lewis; Award Comes Following the Death of Wilbur M. Lewis in Tank Battle at Cassino," *Centerville Daily Iowegian*, October 17,

1944; "Body of Elder Returned Here," *Centerville Daily Iowegian*, August 7, 1948; "Local Sailor Is Missing in China Sea; Brother Wounded," *Centerville Daily Iowegian*, March 5, 1945; C.B.D., Columns Write, *Centerville Daily Iowegian*, March 7, 1944.

6. "Corporal Harold V. Willits, Former Numa High School Faculty Member Is Killed in Action on Italian Front," *Centerville Daily Iowegian*, March 9, 1944; "Alfred Ostino Is Recovering from Wounds," *Centerville Daily Iowegian*, March 21, 1944; Virginia Padovan, interview with the author, July 26, 2011.

7. "Three Appanoose Boys Die in Armed Services," *Centerville Daily Iowegian*, July 22, 1944; C.B.D., Columns Write, *Centerville Daily Iowegian*, December 29, 1942; "Wounded Again," *Centerville Daily Iowegian*, January 28, 1944.

8. "War Victim," *Centerville Daily Iowegian*, April 19, 1944; "Condolences Are Received by Mrs. Sales," *Centerville Daily Iowegian*, April 15, 1944; "Loren Ross of Cincinnati Is Among Missing," *Centerville Daily Iowegian*, June 22, 1944.

9. "Reports Jack Brown Killed," *Centerville Daily Iowegian*, March 16, 1944; "Word Received Lester Brinegar Killed in Action," *Centerville Daily Iowegian*, July 19, 1944; "Victim of War," *Centerville Daily Iowegian*, July 11, 1944; "Mrs. Johnson Gets News of Soldier's Death," *Centerville Daily Iowegian*, July 8, 1944; "Last Letters Follow News of Soldier's Death," *Centerville Daily Iowegian*, July 10, 1944; "Delmar Kennedy Is Wounded in European War" *Centerville Daily Iowegian*, June 19, 1944; "Amos McGhghy Is Missing in Action—Report," *Centerville Daily Iowegian*, June 26, 1944.

10. Keegan, *Collins Atlas of World War II*, 122–23 (see chap. 59, n. 11); Boomhower, *One Shot: The World War II Photography of John A. Bushemi*, 64–66, 69–73 (see chap. 72, n. 5).

11. "John Buscemi Is Killed in Pacific Area," *Centerville Daily Iowegian*, March 1, 1944; "Centerville Boy Killed," photograph and caption, March 4, 1944; "Gary Post Carries Full Story of Centerville Photographer's Death on Eniwetok Atoll in the Pacific," *Centerville Daily Iowegian*, March 6, 1944; Dale Jones, interview with the author, October 4, 2000.

12. Keegan, *The Second World War,* 306 (see chap. 59, n. 5); Maurice Stamps, interview with the author, April 11, 2011; Larry Alexander, *Shadows in the Jungle* (New York: NAL Caliber–Penguin Group, 2009), 4–5, 11.

13. Trenton Mericle, interview with the author, June 4, 2011; "Bullet Parts Appanoose Co. Soldier's Hair," *Centerville Daily Iowegian*, December 23, 1942.

14. "Cecil Gerdon Is Pacific Victim," *Centerville Daily Iowegian*, December 30, 1943; "Body of Rathbun Soldier Returned," *Centerville Daily Iowegian*, February 10, 1949; "Former Local Young Man Is War Casualty," *Centerville Daily Iowegian*, February 4, 1943; "What Is the Cost?" *Centerville Daily Iowegian*, September 12, 1944; "Millionaire Makes Happiness Gift and Mr. & Mrs. Ed Inman Are to Visit Their Heroic, Wounded Son," *Centerville Daily Iowegian*, November 3, 1944; "Appanoose Soldier,

Who Is Blind, Leads Men, Who Can See to Find Their Way Back in Postwar World," *Centerville Daily Iowegian*, November 21, 1944; "For Some the War *Is* Over," *Centerville Daily Iowegian*, April 6, 1960; C.B.D., Columns Write, *Centerville Daily Iowegian*, November 17, 1944.

15. Keegan, *The Second World War*, 306 (see chap. 59, n. 5).

Chapter 74

1. "Eisenhower Arrives in Britain," photograph and caption, *Centerville Daily Iowegian*, January 19, 1944; "Eisenhower Predicts Victory," photograph and caption, *Centerville Daily Iowegian*, December 30, 1943; David Irving, *The War Between the Generals* (New York: Congdon and Weed, Inc., 1981), 36–37; Charles DePuy, Columns Write, *Centerville Daily Iowegian*, January 4, 1944; "Peace? When?" *Centerville Daily Iowegian*, December 30, 1943.
2. Irving, *The War Between the Generals*, 51; Juliet Gardiner, *"Over Here"—The GI's in Wartime Britain* (London: Collins and Brown, 1992), 6; "U.S. Army Buildup in the United Kingdom, January 1942 to May 1944," Tables 7.1 and 7.2, in Richard M. Leighton and Robert W. Coakley, *Global Logistics and Strategy*, quoted in David Reynolds, *Rich Relations: The American Occupation of Britain 1942–1945* (London: Harper Collins, 1995) 99, 103; "Britain Calls for U.S. Radio Army," *Centerville Daily Iowegian*, June 18, 1941; "Americans at Work in Ireland Paid by British Govt. Reports," *Centerville Daily Iowegian*, July 11, 1941; "U.S. Technicians Arrive in Ulster Today," *Centerville Daily Iowegian*, July 7, 1941; "More Americans in Ulster Today," *Centerville Daily Iowegian*, July 7, 1941; "Coming Sunday: Majestic," advertisement, *Centerville Daily Iowegian*, December 6, 1941; Charles D. Taylor, *Iowans of the Mighty Eighth* (Paducah, Ky.: Turner Publishing Company, 2005), 6, 40, 41, 42, 80; "Actual Bombing Put in Pictures," *Centerville Daily Iowegian*, May 5, 1944; "The Story of 25th Mission of the 'Memphis Belle,'" advertisement, May 5, 1944; Gardiner, "Over Here," 162.
3. "Lieut. Eugene Wilcox Is Shot Down, Survives Two Days, Night on Water," *Moravia Union*, August 19, 1943; "Lieut. Wilcox, in England, Wins Promotion and Air Medal," *Moravia Union*, July 15, 1943; "Air War Saga Depicts Action," *Centerville Daily Iowegian*, November 29, 1946; "Lieut. Wilcox Writes of Raid on Germany," *Moravia Union*, November 25, 1943; "Moravia Boy, Bomber Pilot Reported Lost," *Centerville Daily Iowegian*, October 7, 1943; "Lt. Gene Wilcox Died in Action," *Centerville Daily Iowegian*, August 17, 1945; "Death of Movie Producer Recalls Moravia Airman," *Centerville Daily Iowegian*, January 30, 1963.
4. Morison, *The Oxford History of the American People*, 389 (see chap. 16, n. 3).

5. Manuel Bromberg, interview with the author, April 22, 2011.
6. "Lt. Sumpter Is Missing over Europe," *Centerville Daily Iowegian*, February 19, 1944; "Cincinnati Boy Is Killed in Air Battle," *Centerville Daily Iowegian*, May 18, 1944.
7. "Tuskegee Airmen," *American Profile*, November 7–13, 2010; Phil Brunow, interview with the author, May 1, 2011.
8. "Mystic Boy Killed over Nazi Europe," *Centerville Daily Iowegian*, April 27, 1944; "Moravia Man Hears of Death of Nephew in North Europe," *Centerville Daily Iowegian*, January 7, 1943; "Lt. C.W. Swank Is 'Missing' at English Base," *Centerville Daily Iowegian*, March 8, 1944; "Search for Local Five Star Mothers Reveals Report That Six Star Family Has Been Notified One Son is Missing," *Centerville Daily Iowegian*, May 17, 1944; "Lt. Swank Is Prisoner of War—Report," *Centerville Daily Iowegian*, April 6, 1944; "Two Local Men Are Reported to Be Casualties," *Centerville Daily Iowegian*, December 27, 1943; "Nine Men Killed; Two Live in Riddled Bomber; Local Sergeant Survives Tragedy," *Centerville Daily Iowegian*, July 25 1944.
9. "Clip This! Morning Programs—Afternoon Programs—Evening Programs," *Centerville Daily Iowegian*, October 17, 1944; Morgan Beatty, "Leaders Think People Willing to Sacrifice," *Centerville Daily Iowegian*, January 27, 1943; Jesse Beck, editorial, *Centerville Daily Iowegian*, November 10, 1943; "Comment by Others: Quentin Reynolds," *Centerville Daily Iowegian*, March 31 1944.
10. "Pattern for Invasion," map, *Centerville Daily Iowegian*, May 10, 1943; "Where Invasion Blows May Fall," map, *Centerville Daily Iowegian*, August 21, 1943; "Map of Europe as All Signs Point toward Germany," *Centerville Daily Iowegian*, May 9, 1944; "Invasion Date Has Been Set by Allies," *Centerville Daily Iowegian*, April 6, 1944; "Phoney Invasion Confused Nazis," *Centerville Daily Iowegian*, November 29, 1945.
11. Alexander Swanston and Malcolm Swanston, *The Historical Atlas of World War II* (New York: Chartwell Books, 2008), 268–69; Keegan, *Collins Atlas of World War II*, 134–35 (see chap. 59, n. 11); Morison, *The Oxford History of the American People*, 392 (see chap. 16, n. 3).
12. "Exline Boy Represents Iowa at Ball," *Centerville Daily Iowegian*, May 10, 1944; "Yanks Stage Giant Parade in London," photo and caption, *Centerville Daily Iowegian*, March 31, 1944; "Biggest Yank Parade in London," photo and caption, *Centerville Daily Iowegian*, April 1, 1944; "Centerville Boy Weds English Girl," *Centerville Daily Iowegian*, June 7, 1944; "Fate Joins Callen Boys in England," *Centerville Daily Iowegian*, May 13, 1944; Lowell Marshall, letter in Columns Write, *Centerville Daily Iowegian*, June 9, 1944.
13. "Destination: D-Day," photo and caption, *Centerville Daily Iowegian*, May 10, 1944; "Yanks Being Toughened for Second Front Thrust," photo and caption, *Centerville Daily Iowegian*, April 27, 1944; "Exercise Tiger," http://en.wikipedia.org/wikiExercise_Tiger.

14. Manuel Bromberg, interview with the author, April 22, 2011; Joe Coates, interview with the author, April 20, 2011; Operational Archives, Naval History and Heritage Command, "Exercise Tiger," Department of the Navy, http://www.history.navy.mil/faqs/faq20-1.htm; "Operation Tiger," http://www.combindops.com/Op_Tiger.htm.
15. Dewitt MacKenzie, "The War Today," *Centerville Daily Iowegian*, April 29, 1944; "Raid Pounds Nazi Rocket-Bomb Sites," *Centerville Daily Iowegian*, January 8, 1944; "Yank Bombers Pound Coast of Continent," *Centerville Daily Iowegian*, March 21, 1944; Dewitt MacKenzie, "The War Today," *Centerville Daily Iowegian*, March 25, 1944; "Invasion Coast of France Hit by Liberators," *Centerville Daily Iowegian*, April 5, 1944; "Actual Bombing Put in Pictures," *Centerville Daily Iowegian*, May 5, 1944; "The Story of 25th Mission of the 'Memphis Belle,'" advertisement, May 5, 1944.
16. "New Invasion Jitters Felt in Britain," *Centerville Daily Iowegian*, May 23, 1944; Rhinwedd Lewis et al., interviews with the author, August 5, 1990; DeWitt MacKenzie, "The War Today," *Centerville Daily Iowegian*, March 13, 1944; "Restrict British–Irish Travel," map and caption, *Centerville Daily Iowegian*, March 13, 1944; "Plans to Isolate Southern Ireland 'from the World,'" *Centerville Daily Iowegian*, March 14, 1944; Stephen E. Ambrose, *D-Day: June 6, 1944; The Climactic Battle of World War II* (New York: Simon and Schuster, 1994), 151; Hubert Thomas et al., interviews with the author, August 10, 1993; C.B.D., Columns Write, *Centerville Daily Iowegian*, July 24, 1945; "Centerville Sailor in Epic Sea Battle Aboard U.S. Coast Guard Cutter Campbell in Northern Sea," *Centerville Daily Iowegian*, March 20, 1943; "Lt. Commander Kerschner Home from Caribbean," *Centerville Daily Iowegian*, August 19, 1943; "Calvin Sharp Was War Hero, Says Commanding Officer in Letter to His Parents, Mr. and Mrs. W. Sharp," *Centerville Daily Iowegian*, July 29, 1944.
17. Dan Ehl, "A Front Seat to History: Koestner Remembers Operation Overlord," *Daily Iowegian*, March 28, 2002; Virginia Koestner, interview with the author, March 21, 2011.
18. Ambrose, *D-Day*, 181–88, 196–98.

Chapter 75

1. Keegan, *The Second World War*, 360 (see chap. 59, n. 5); Morison, *Oxford History of the American People*, 383 (see chap. 16, n. 3); Keegan, *Collins Atlas of World War II*, 115 (see chap. 59, n. 11).
2. *The Story of the 34th Infantry Division: Louisiana to Pisa*, 70–71 (see chap. 69, n. 6).
3. *The Story of the 34th Infantry Division: Louisiana to Pisa*, 72–73 (see chap. 69, n. 6); Phil Brunow, interview with the author, March 1, 2010.
4. C.B.D., Columns Write, *Centerville Daily Iowegian*, July 11, 1944.

5. *The Story of the 34th Infantry Division: Louisiana to Pisa*, 74–75 (see chap. 69, n. 6); "Americans Plunge Ahead in Italy," *Centerville Daily Iowegian*, May 26, 1944.
6. Reese Hudson, interview with the author, July 9, 2009; J.C. Kilbourn, interview with the author, October 24, 2001.
7. "Allies Push Nearing Rome," *Centerville Daily Iowegian*, May 29, 1944; "Allies within 18 Miles of Rome," *Centerville Daily Iowegian*, May 31, 1944; "Allies within 14 Miles of Rome," *Centerville Daily Iowegian*, June 3, 1944; "Fifth Army Drives across River," *Centerville Daily Iowegian*, June 5, 1944.
8. Keegan, *The Second World War*, 381 (see chap. 59, n. 5); Brian Jewell, "We'll Go," in *Conquest and Overlord: The Story of the Bayeux Tapestry and the Overlord Embroidery* (London: East-West Publications, 1981), 63.
9. Keegan, *The Second World War*, 382 (see chap. 59, n. 5); Dan Ehl, "Koestner Remembers Operation Overlord," *Daily Iowegian*, March 28, 2002; Joe Coates, interview with the author, March 18, 2006; Robert McGuire, interview with the author, October 20, 2010; Carrie Jean Soper, interview with the author, February 21, 2010; "Veteran Dad of Mystic Is Proud of Son," *Centerville Daily Iowegian*, September 8, 1944.
10. "Invasion Holds," *Centerville Daily Iowegian*, June 6, 1944; "Troops Advancing Inland!" *Centerville Daily Iowegian*, June 7, 1944; "Successful in First Phase of Invasion," *Centerville Daily Iowegian*, June 8, 1944; "Allies Nearing Cherbourg–Berlin," *Centerville Daily Iowegian*, June 9, 1944; "How Roosevelt Received Word of the Invasion," *Centerville Daily Iowegian*, June 6, 1944.

Dewitt Ma
"Within Fou
Cherbourg I
in U.S. Hand

Chapter 76

1. Morison, *The Oxford History of the American People*, 392 (see chap. 16, n. 3).
2. Keegan, *The Second World War*, 381–82, 386, map 384–85 (see chap. 59, n. 5); Patsy Cincotta, "A Lot of History," *Centerville Daily Iowegian*, May 1, 2007.
3. Joe Coates, interview with the author, March 18, 2006; Richard Southern, interview with the author, January 10, 2012; Keegan, *The Second World War*, 386–87 (see chap. 59, n. 5); Ambrose, *D-Day*, 320–21 (see chap. 74, n. 16).
4. Richard Southern, interview with the author, January 10, 2010; Joe Coates, interview with the author, March 18, 2006; Carrie Jean Soper, interview with the author, February 21, 2010; Robert McGuire, interview with the author, October 20, 2011.
5. "How Roosevelt Received Word of the Invasion," *Centerville Daily Iowegian*, June 6, 1944; C.B.D., "Do You Know What Hundreds of People in Your Old Home Country Were Doing Last Night?" Columns Write, *Centerville Daily Iowegian*, March 6, 1944; "Radio to Have Ringside Seat in the Invasion," *Centerville Daily Iowegian*,

March 28, 1944; Wes Gallagher, "Invasion Holds," *Centerville Daily Iowegian*, June 6 1944; "The Smoke Shop East Side Square Will Remain Closed," notice, *Centerville Daily Iowegian*, June 6, 1944.

6. "Troops Advancing Inland," *Centerville Daily Iowegian*, June 7, 1944; "Successful in First Phase of Invasion," *Centerville Daily Iowegian*, June 8, 1944; "Allies Nearing Cherbourg–Berlin," *Centerville Daily Iowegian*, June 9, 1944; "Allies Drive Eighteen Miles into Cherbourg," *Centerville Daily Iowegian*, June 12, 1944.
7. "U.S Prays at Altars Today for Victory," *Centerville Daily Iowegian*, June 7, 1944; "WACS Hear News Some Pray and Others Listen," *Centerville Daily Iowegian*, June 6, 1944.
8. Bill Smallwood, interview with the author, March 1, 2011.

Chapter 77

1. Joe Coates, interview with the author, March 18, 2006; Arnie A. Hove, "Normandy: An American Soldier and Warrior Still Weep," *Ottumwa Courier*, June 6, 2001; Richard Southern, interview with the author, January 10, 2010; Bob McGuire, interview with the author, October 20, 2010.
2. Elvin Jay, interview with the author, January 10, 2010; Nichols, *Ernie's War*, 277–78 (see chap. 72, n. 9); "Reads Boyle Dispatches in Daily Iowegian," *Centerville Daily Iowegian*, June 5, 1944; Hal Boyle, "How It Feels to Face Zero Hour," *Centerville Daily Iowegian*, June 19, 1944; "Eisenhower Calls for Full Victory," photograph and caption, *Centerville Daily Iowegian*, June 8, 1944; "Invasion Casualty Lifted to Troopship," photograph and caption, *Centerville Daily Iowegian*, June 10, 1944; "Walking Wounded Return to England," photograph and caption, *Centerville Daily Iowegian*, June 10, 1944; "American Dead in France," photograph and caption, *Centerville Daily Iowegian*, June 10, 1944; "The Cost of French Invasion," photograph and caption, *Centerville Daily Iowegian*, June 14, 1944; "You've Read: Ernie Pyle's Stories! You've Heard Geo. Hicks on the Radio! Now See the Actual Invasion," Majestic advertisement, *Centerville Daily Iowegian*, June 23, 1944; Ambrose, *D-Day*, 504 (see chap. 74, n. 16).
3. C.B.D., Columns Write, *Centerville Daily Iowegian*, June 9, 1944; "Troops Advancing Inland," *Centerville Daily Iowegian*, June 7, 1944; Richard Harrington, interview with the author, October 24, 2010; "Linda Brown, Ship that Carried War Brass Has FD Reunion," *The Messenger*, Fort Dodge, Iowa, June 9, 1991.
4. Manuel Bromberg, letter to the author, January 14, 2010; Manuel Bromberg, interview with the author, April 22, 2011; "They Drew Fire: Combat Artists of World War II; Manuel Bromberg," Public Broadcasting Service, http://www.pbs.org/theydrewfire/artists/bromberg.html; *They Drew Fire*, movie directed by Brian Lanker, an Actual Films Production, Combat Artists of WW2, Lanker Inc., 1999;

Robert Holliday, interview with the author, April 20, 2010; Donald L. Cross, e-mail forwarded to the author from Jeanne Harrington Fowler, November 25, 2003.

5. Nichols, *Ernie's War*, 289 (see chap. 72, n. 9); C.B.D., Columns Write, *Centerville Daily Iowegian*, July 28, 1944; "Kamerad," photograph and caption, *Centerville Daily Iowegian*, June 13, 1944; Keegan, *The Second World War*, 389–90 (see chap. 59, n. 5); "Weather a Curse in Normandy…," untitled, *Centerville Daily Iowegian*, July 15, 1944.
6. *The Story of the 34th Infantry Division: Louisiana to Pisa*, 74–78 (see chap. 69, n. 6); C.B.D., Columns Write, *Centerville Daily Iowegian*, June 9, 1944.
7. "Bombs Hit Japan," *Centerville Daily Iowegian*, June 15th, 1944; "Local Boy Helps Direct Bombing of Japan," *Centerville Daily Iowegian*, July 14, 1944; "Noted Flyer," *Centerville Daily Iowegian*, July 22, 1944.
8. "Reports Landing Attempts on Two Jap-Held Islands," *Centerville Daily Iowegian*, June 15, 1944; Stamps, "Snafus and Love Letters: Memories of an Old G.I.," 99–100 (see chap. 63, n. 3); Keegan, *Collins Atlas of World War II*, 124–25 (see chap. 59, n. 11); Keegan, *The Second World War*, 307 (see chap. 59, n. 5); "'Old Nameless' Is Still Writing Illustrious History; Four Local Men Share in Her Great History," *[illegible]enterville Daily Iowegian*, April 16, 1945; Patsy Cincotta, "Over There," *Daily Iowegian*, [illegible]ember 7, 2007; J.B. Kelley, interview with the author, March 29, 2011.

[illegible]s B. DePuy, "Iowegian Staff Puts in Word about Its Leader," *Centerville Daily [illegible]*, Centennial Edition, November 29, 1946; John Golden, interview with the [illegible] [illegible]ugust 4, 2011.

[illegible]acKenzie, "The War Today," *Centerville Daily Iowegian*, June 13, 1944; [illegible]cKenzie, "The War Today," *Centerville Daily Iowegian*, June 12, 1944; [illegible]ur Miles of Cherbourg," *Centerville Daily Iowegian*, June 20, 1944; "Fall of [illegible]Expected," *Centerville Daily Iowegian*, June 21, 1944; "Part of Cherbourg [illegible]ds," *Centerville Daily Iowegian*, June 26, 1944; "German Officers Captured [illegible]g," photograph and caption, *Centerville Daily Iowegian*, June 29, 1944; [illegible]rbourg," *Centerville Daily Iowegian*, August 8, 1944; Rosalie Mahoney, [illegible] author, with photograph of four members of the 333rd Engineers, [illegible] 2005, collection of Appanoose County Museum.

11. [illegible]eld, "On Saturday, NBC in Bonds Program," *Centerville Daily Iowegian*, [illegible]; War Department film *The Liberation of Rome*, Majestic advertisement, *[illegible]ly Iowegian*, August 16, 1944; "'Eve of Battle' Coming to Majestic [illegible]Mon," *Centerville Daily Iowegian*, June 15, 1944; "Picture Shows War [illegible]," *[illegible]nterville Daily Iowegian*, July 1, 1944; "Attack—the War Department's [illegible]l of the Battle for New Britain," Majestic advertisement, *Centerville [illegible]*, July 3, 1944; C.B.D., Columns Write, *Centerville Daily Iowegian*, July 18, [illegible] Smith White, "Despite German Rule, French Celebrate Fourth of [illegible] *Daily Iowegian*, August 29, 1944.

12. E.D. Ball, "Quiet, Determined—That Is Patton Directing War," *Centerville Daily Iowegian*, August 16, 1944; Richard Southern, interview with the author, January 10, 2010; C.B.D., Columns Write, *Centerville Daily Iowegian*, March 9, 1945; C.B.D., Columns Write, *Centerville Daily Iowegian*, August 1, 1944; C.B.D., Columns Write, *Centerville Daily Iowegian*, August 23, 1944; "Drive on Paris Begins…," untitled, *Centerville Daily Iowegian*, August 8, 1944; "Gateway to Paris Falls to Yanks," *Centerville Daily Iowegian*, August 9, 1944; "Battle for Paris Begins—Nazis," *Centerville Daily Iowegian*, August 10, 1944; "Falaise Trap Nets These Prisoners," *Centerville Daily Iowegian*, August 25, 1944; Keegan, *The Second World War*, 361–62 (see chap. 59, n. 5).

Chapter 78

1. Arnie A. Hove, "An American Soldier and Warrior Still Weep," *Ottumwa Courier*, June 6, 2001; "Pvt. Harrington Killed in War Report Today," *Centerville Daily Iowegian*, January 5, 1945; "Harrington War Victim, Many Mourn," *Centerville Daily Iowegian*, January 8, 1945.
2. "S-Sgt Richard Patterson Is Reported Missing in Action," *Centerville Daily Iowegian*, July 29, 1944; "Mrs. Patterson Gets Word about Her Missing Son," *Centerville Daily Iowegian*, October 16, 1944; "Find the Body of Moravia Soldier on Battlefield," *Centerville Daily Iowegian*, April 26, 1946; "Pvt. Glasgow Is Casualty of Invasion," *Centerville Daily Iowegian*, August 31, 1944; C.B.D., Columns Write, *Centerville Daily Iowegian*, July 6, 1944; "Former Exline Boy Killed in War in France," *Centerville Daily Iowegian*, September 14, 1944.
3. "Chas. Ward Is Killed in French Drive," *Centerville Daily Iowegian*, August 10, 1944; "G.E. Kennedy Dies in France Victim of War," *Centerville Daily Iowegian*, September 5, 1944; "Warrant Officer Howard Chriss Killed," *Centerville Daily Iowegian*, August 19, 1944; "Young Wife Here Loses Hero Husband," *Centerville Daily Iowegian*, August 23, 1944; "Lt. Theodore Rosenbaum Killed," *Centerville Daily Iowegian*, August 23, 1944; Robert Beck, "Looking for Lt. Rosenbaum," *AdExpress/Iowegian*, May 17, 2002; Sam Carpenter, interview with the author, February 23, 2012; Nan Krapfel, interview with the author, February 23, 2012; "Roy Davis Is Reported Dead by War Dept," *Centerville Daily Iowegian*, November 23, 1944.
4. "Body of Hobart Is Enroute [*sic*] Here," *Centerville Daily Iowegian*, June 22, 1944; "Parents of Local Aerial Engineer to Accept Award," *Centerville Daily Iowegian*, January 12, 1945; "Former Local Boy Killed in Ploesti Raid," *Centerville Daily Iowegian*, August 26, 1944; "Two Boys Lost to Parents in Iconium Area," *Centerville Daily Iowegian*, August 26, 1944.

5. C.B.D., "A U.S. Troop Carrier Base, European Theatre of Operations," Columns Write, *Centerville Daily Iowegian*, December 8, 1944; Tracey Corder, interview with the author, May 12, 2009; Bommarito, "Goodbye Italy, Hello France," in *We Kept' Em Flying*, 221 (see chap. 71, n. 6); "Frank Miles Goes to War Fronts to Write for Iowegian," *Centerville Daily Iowegian*, August 9, 1944; "Frank Miles Letters From Battle Fronts," *Centerville Daily Iowegian*, August 29, 1944; C.B.D., Columns Write, *Centerville Daily Iowegian*, August 29, 1944.
6. "Paris Falls to French," *Centerville Daily Iowegian*, August 23, 1944; "A Jeep…," photograph, *Centerville Daily Iowegian*, August 28, 1944; "Parisiens Celebrate," *Centerville Daily Iowegian*, August 28, 1944; "Thousands Jam Paris Square," photograph and caption, *Centerville Daily Iowegian*, August 31, 1944; "Notre Dame Cathedral Undamaged," photograph and caption, *Centerville Daily Iowegian*, September 1, 1944; "Yanks March in Paris," photograph and caption, *Centerville Daily Iowegian*, September 2, 1944.
7. Nichols, *Ernie's War*, 351–56 (see chap. 72, n. 9).
8. Keegan, *The Second World War*, 410–14 (see chap. 59, n. 5).
9. "Local Girl in Life Magazine Proves Generous," *Centerville Daily Iowegian*, September 25, 1944.
10. Richard Southern, interview with the author, October 2, 2010; "Yanks Visit World War 1 Cemetery," photograph and caption, *Centerville Daily Iowegian*, September 6, 1944.
11. Keegan, *The Second World War*, 439–47 (see chap. 59, n. 5); "Russ Daniels Was Captive; A Short Time," *Centerville Daily Iowegian*, September 12, 1944; "Bridge Builder," *Centerville Daily Iowegian*, May 23, 1945.
12. *General Marshall's Victory Report on the Winning of World War II in Europe and the Pacific*, 23–24 (see chap. 71, n. 1); Jesse Beck, editorial, *Centerville Daily Iowegian*, September 7, 1944; "When War Ends in Europe Will Celebrate Here," *Centerville Daily Iowegian*, September 7, 1944; C.B.D., Columns Write, *Centerville Daily Iowegian*, September 19, 1944.
13. "Give All Once for All These…," War Chest Fund advertisement, *Centerville Daily Iowegian*, October 14, 1944; "Plans for V Day Are Now Finished," *Centerville Daily Iowegian*, Student Iowegian Section, November 7, 1944; "Yule Party for Disabled Vets Is Aided Here," *Centerville Daily Iowegian*, December 4, 1944; "Pre-Induction Schools Here," *Centerville Daily Iowegian*, April 1, 1944; "Pre-Induction School Is Held at Courthouse," *Centerville Daily Iowegian*, June 8, 1944; "Air Patrol of This City Host to Notable Men," *Centerville Daily Iowegian*, May 2, 1944.

Chapter 79

1. "Guy Keaton Is Killed in Nazi Drive," *Centerville Daily Iowegian*, October 13, 1944; "Sammy Frank Killed Says War Telegram," *Centerville Daily Iowegian*, October 30, 1944;

"Jim Sleeth Is Victim of War in France," *Centerville Daily Iowegian*, November 14, 1944; "Killed in Action," *Centerville Daily Iowegian*, December 16, 1944; "Killed in Action," *Centerville Daily Iowegian*, December 16, 1944; "Sgt. Sebben Is Killed in Europe Area," *Centerville Daily Iowegian*, December 12, 1944; "Santos Reyes Dies in Action on German Front," *Centerville Daily Iowegian*, November 21, 1944.

2. "Eugene Clark Killed in War Was Known Here," *Centerville Daily Iowegian*, January 4, 1945; "Lt. Swank Is Victim of War Father Writes," *Centerville Daily Iowegian*, November 21, 1944; "Sgt. Caster Exline Killed Says Telegram," *Centerville Daily Iowegian*, June 7, 1945; "Pvt. W.R. Robbins of Cincinnati Was Killed in Holland," *Centerville Daily Iowegian*, June 22, 1945; "Numa Soldier War Victim on December 11," *Centerville Daily Iowegian*, December 26, 1944; "Sergeant Oral Purvis Killed in Action during Fighting in France, Says War Department," *Centerville Daily Iowegian*, October 24, 1944; "Pvt. Bills of Mystic Killed in French Area," *Centerville Daily Iowegian*, December 22, 1944; "Sgt. Caraccio Dies in France with U.S. Army," *Centerville Daily Iowegian*, December 11, 1944.
3. "Return Body of Edwin M. Mathes," *Centerville Daily Iowegian*, November 9, 1948; "Deaths of Two in the Service Mourned Here," *Centerville Daily Iowegian*, December 8, 1944; "Moulton Boy Is War Victim Report Today," *Centerville Daily Iowegian*, November 6, 1944; "Robert Baker Is Killed in Italy Battle," *Centerville Daily Iowegian*, November 11, 1944; "Body of McGhghy Arrives in U.S.," *Centerville Daily Iowegian*, July 8, 1948.
4. "It Happened," *Centerville Daily Iowegian*, April 10, 1945.
5. John Golden, interview with the author, August 20, 2011; C.B.D., Columns Write, *Centerville Daily Iowegian*, October 21, 1944; C.B.D., Columns Write, *Centerville Daily Iowegian*, October 21, 1944; Dan Ehl, "Veteran Recalls Fighting in the South Pacific," *Daily Iowegian*, November 13, 2000.
6. "Philippine Islands Invaded—Tokyo," *Centerville Daily Iowegian*, October 19, 1944; "I Have Returned—MacArthur," *Centerville Daily Iowegian*, October 20, 1944; "General MacArthur Returns to Philippines," photograph and caption, *Centerville Daily Iowegian*, October 30, 1944.
7. Keegan, *Collins Atlas of World War II*, 148–49 (see chap. 59, n. 11); "Kenneth C. Henke, Soundman Aboard Ill-Fated Destroyer Abner Read…," untitled, *Centerville Daily Iowegian*, December 9, 1944; "Mystic Navy Man Killed in Action," *Centerville Daily Iowegian*, November 10, 1944.
8. "Bob Bandy Among Battle Injured," *Centerville Daily Iowegian*, November 28, 1944; "Bob Bandy, O, S, 2-C Back Home after Harrowing Experience…," untitled, *Centerville Daily Iowegian*, December 22, 1944.
9. "Dr. George Gallup Checks Washington Township," *Centerville Daily Iowegian*, September 23, 1944.
10. "Roosevelt Elected!" *Centerville Daily Iowegian*, November 8, 1944.

Chapter 80

1. "Christmas to Come to the GI at Front," *Centerville Daily Iowegian*, December 23, 1944; Richard Southern, interview with the author, March 3, 2012; Joel Baker, D.O., interview with the author, March 3, 2012; Elvin Jay, interview with the author, May, 10 2011; C.B.D.,Columns Write, *Centerville Daily Iowegian*, July 31, 1945; Louis "Sol" Kauzlarich, interview with the author, March 20, 2011; "Letter Received by the Parents of S. Montegna," *Centerville Daily Iowegian*, November 22, 1944; Dan Ehl, "Montegna Has Permanent Reminder of His Service," *Ad-Express/Iowegian*, November 10, 1999.
2. "Germans 14 Miles from the Fortress of Liege," *Centerville Daily Iowegian,* December 20, 1944; "Northern Luxembourg Crossed by Germans," *Centerville Daily Iowegian*, December 18, 1944; "Jack Shelley, Radio Commentator and War Correspondent…," untitled, *Centerville Daily Iowegian*, June 1, 1945; "Americans Recapture Nazi Town," *Centerville Daily Iowegian*, December 19, 1944.
3. DeWitt MacKenzie, "The War Today," *Centerville Daily Iowegian*, December 22, 1944; "Germans Keep on Moving in Great Assault," *Centerville Daily Iowegian*, December 26, 1944; DeWitt MacKenzie, "The War Today," *Centerville Daily Iowegian*, December 27, 1944; "In Christmas Day Battle, Yanks Throw Back Germans," *Centerville Daily Iowegian*, December 27, 1944; "Nazi Bulge Sliced Down to 13 Miles," *Centerville Daily Iowegian*, December 30, 1944; "Patton Praises His Men in War," *Centerville Daily Iowegian*, January 3, 1945; "Belgium Salient Is Narrowed," *Centerville Daily Iowegian*, January 8, 1945; "Advance over Snow toward Bastogne," photograph and caption, *Centerville Daily Iowegian*, January 8, 1945; "Dick Stockwell, Former CJC Student and Resident of Moulton…," untitled, *Centerville Daily Iowegian*, January 18, 1945; "Schoolmaster Hero," *Centerville Daily Iowegian*, March 10, 1945; "Army Paper Calls Murray Ruby of Seymour a Bullet Proof Vet," *Centerville Daily Iowegian*, December 19, 1944; "Sgt. Golick Was Awarded Bronze Star Recently," *Centerville Daily Iowegian*, July 30, 1945; "Citation Tells of Stirring Act by Livonia Boy," *Centerville Daily Iowegian*, April 6, 1945; "Silver Star to Robert Dudley Is Report Here," *Centerville Daily Iowegian*, February 21, 1945; "Loyd Parcel Given the Silver Star," *Centerville Daily Iowegian*, February 27, 1945.
4. "Meaning of 'Nuts' Clear to Germans," *Centerville Daily Iowegian*, January 4, 1945; Dan Brooks, interview with the author, January 16, 2012; Patsy Cincotta, "From Farm to War," *Daily Iowegian*, April 1, 2006; "Vivid War Picture by Men Who Have Seen It First Hand," *Centerville Daily Iowegian*, April 25, 1945; C.B.D., Columns Write, *Centerville Daily Iowegian*, October 24, 1944; C.B.D., Columns Write, *Centerville Daily Iowegian*, July 31, 1945.
5. "Jess Wyldes Is Missing in Europe Area" *Centerville Daily Iowegian*, December 30, 1944; "Sgt Allan Is Missing in Germany," *Centerville Daily Iowegian*, March 1, 1945.

6. "James Samson Is Killed in Invasion War," *Centerville Daily Iowegian*, January 2, 1945; "Pvt. Seath War Victim in Belgium," *Centerville Daily Iowegian*, January 8, 1945; "Further Word Received about Pvt. W.R. Seath," *Centerville Daily Iowegian*, March 1, 1945; "Robert Bennett Is Killed in Europe Area," *Centerville Daily Iowegian*, February 24, 1945.
7. "Sgt. Bever War Victim in Germany," *Centerville Daily Iowegian*, March 5, 1945.
8. "Pvt. Brundage of This City War Victim," *Centerville Daily Iowegian*, February 28, 1945; "Lt. Collins Dies Results of Wounds," *Centerville Daily Iowegian*, March 13, 1945.
9. "War Victim," *Centerville Daily Iowegian*, February 15, 1945; "Baby Leaves the Hospital Dad Missing," *Centerville Daily Iowegian*, March 19, 1945; "Confirmation of Death of Bruce McKern Received," *Centerville Daily Iowegian*, March 1, 1946.
10. "Two More Men Are Missing in War Area," *Centerville Daily Iowegian*, January 23, 1945; "Letter Tells of Sgt. Harrington Death in Battle," *Centerville Daily Iowegian*, April 7, 1945; "Pvt. Kerby of Sedan Killed in Nazi Area," *Centerville Daily Iowegian*, April 4, 1945; "Killed in Action," *Centerville Daily Iowegian*, March 13, 1945; "Moulton Boy Missing, Now Listed Dead," *Centerville Daily Iowegian*, April 28, 1945.

Chapter 81

1. "Yanks Drive toward Manila," *Centerville Daily Iowegian*, January 10, 1945; John Golden, interview with the author, October 10, 2011; Leroy W. Bergstrom, coordinating author, "The USS *Patterson* DD392 Shipmates and Memories," typed collection of contributions from members of the U.S.S. *Patterson*, privately held by John Golden, 591–92.
2. C.B.D., Columns Write, *Centerville Daily Iowegian*, February 13, 1945.
3. "Ezra Temple's Daughter Is a Victim of the Japs," *Centerville Daily Iowegian*, August 24, 1945.
4. Fred Hampson, "Rescued Yanks Relate Terrors of Prison Camp," *Centerville Daily Iowegian*, February 2, 1945; "Jap Prisoner Three Years Coming Here," *Centerville Daily Iowegian*, March 9, 1945; "Some War News Is Good; Take These Stories!" *Centerville Daily Iowegian*, February 22, 1945.
5. Russell Brines, "Horrors of a Jap Prison Camp Told," *Centerville Daily Iowegian*, January 24, 1945; "Less Than Ten Per Cent of Prisoners Taken by Japs in Philippines," *Centerville Daily Iowegian*, June 16, 1945; "Japs Massacre 2,000 Natives," *Centerville Daily Iowegian*, July 17, 1945.
6. "Home Town Recalls Luzon Jap Fighter," *Centerville Daily Iowegian*, January 17, 1945.
7. Nichols, *Ernie's War*, 384 (see chap. 72, n. 9).

8. Jerry Kirkpatrick, personal diary, kept 1944–45; Ethel Lira, "A Local Hero Richard Bumgarner," Heritage Section, *Centerville Daily Iowegian*, February 22, 2002.
9. "Pacific," map, *Centerville Daily Iowegian*, January 11, 1945; Charles (?) Lindsley, "Taking Iwo Beachhead Was a Bloody Business," *Centerville Daily Iowegian*, March 6, 1945; Keegan, *The Second World War*, 566 (see chap. 59, n. 5).
10. Michael A. Cortesio Sr., "Centerville Marine Took Part in 'Bloodiest Battle,'" *Daily Iowegian*, March 11, 2005.
11. Patsy Cincotta, "WWII Vet Tells How It Was 'Over There,'" *Daily Iowegian*, April 30, 2001; Patsy Cincotta, "Battle for Iwo Jima One of the Bloodiest," *Daily Iowegian*, May 1, 2001.
12. Jesse Beck, "An Iowa Boy Was There," editorial, *Centerville Daily Iowegian*, April 3, 1945; "Proud of It!" *Centerville Daily Iowegian*, May 17, 1945; Marianne Fulton, *Eyes of Time* (New York: Graphic Society, Little, Brown, 1988), 160–61.
13. Al Dopking, "Navy Price for Iwo's Gains! 3,650 Marines Fall in 1st Day on Isle," *Centerville Daily Iowegian*, February 21, 1945.
14. Morison, *The Oxford History of the American People*, 405 (see chap. 16, n. 3).

Chapter 82

1. C.B.D., Columns Write, *Centerville Daily Iowegian*, February 6, 1945.
2. Keegan, *The Second World War*, 518–19 (see chap. 59, n. 5); "Russian Columns Nearer Berlin," *Centerville Daily Iowegian*, January 27, 1945; "Reds 58 Miles from Berlin," *Centerville Daily Iowegian*, January 31, 1945; "Panic Sweeps the Third Reich Swedes Report," *Centerville Daily Iowegian*, January 29, 1945; "Berlin—A City of the Doomed," *Centerville Daily Iowegian*, February 22, 1945.
3. "Rhine Crossed by First," *Centerville Daily Iowegian*, March 8, 1945; "Remagen Bridgehead Expanded," *Centerville Daily Iowegian*, March 12, 1945; A. Drabnik, photo and caption, *Centerville Daily Iowegian*, March 13, 1945; Joe Coates, interview with the author, March 30, 2012; Bob McGuire, interview with the author, April 2, 2012.
4. Jeanne Harrington Fowler, interview with the author, January 8, 2006; "Winner of Highest Honor Is Brother Mrs. Troy Smith," *Centerville Daily Iowegian*, September 8, 1945.
5. C.B.D., Columns Write, *Centerville Daily Iowegian*, April 3, 1945; C.B.D., Columns Write, *Centerville Daily Iowegian*, April 3, 1945.
6. Joe Coates, interview with the author, March 30, 2012; "Von Papen's Captor Well Known Here," *Centerville Daily Iowegian*, April 18, 1945.
7. Keegan, *The Second World War*, 566–73 (see chap. 59, n. 5).

8. Bergstrom, "The USS *Patterson*," 514–16 (see chap. 81, n. 1); Maurice Stamps, "Shoal Creek Legends IV: A Small World; But Far from Home," *Seymour Herald*, March 25, 2010; "Two Centerville Boys on Fighter West Virginia," *Centerville Daily Iowegian*, August 6, 2010; "Howard Hobart in City after Being in Okinawa Fight," *Centerville Daily Iowegian*, July 12, 1945; "Robt. Woods Lost His Life on April 16," *Centerville Daily Iowegian*, June 6, 1945.
9. Joe Wilson, interview with the author, April 23, 2010.
10. J.B. Kelley, interview with the author, September 20, 2011.
11. John Golden, Written Report, January 10, 2011, Copy at Appanoose County Museum, Centerville, Iowa.
12. "Although War Is History Now…," untitled, *Centerville Daily Iowegian*, November 7, 1946; "Lt. John Talbot Had Close Call…," untitled, *Centerville Daily Iowegian*, July 7, 1945.
13. "Italian Government Honors Major Charles Radosevich," *Centerville Daily Iowegian*, April 4, 1947; "Centerville Major Featured in National Magazine Story," *Centerville Daily Iowegian*, August 31, 1946; Sid Feder, "The Blue Devils Stumped the Experts," *Saturday Evening Post*, September 7, 1946; Stan Swinton, "Po Valley—The Promised Land," *Stars and Stripes*, April 1945.
14. Keegan, *Collins Atlas of World War II*, 164–65 (see chap. 59, n. 11).
15. "V-E Day Soon?" *Centerville Daily Iowegian*, April 12, 1945.

Chapter 83

1. "World Mourns Roosevelt!" *Centerville Daily Iowegian*, April 13, 1945.
2. "Telephone Co. Swamped Due Tragic News," April 13, 1945; "City Shocked by FDR Death," *Centerville Daily Iowegian*, February 27, 1962.
3. "Mayor's Proclamation in Solemn Respect," *Centerville Daily Iowegian*, April 13, 1945; "Stores Close at 3 O'Clock Tomorrow," *Centerville Daily Iowegian*, April 13, 1945; "Memorial Held by Jews of City for Roosevelt," *Centerville Daily Iowegian*, April 13, 1945; Jean Harrington Fowler, interview with the author, September 20, 2006.
4. "Death of Roosevelt Mourned by People," *Centerville Daily Iowegian*, April 13, 1945; "Athlone to Attend the FR Funeral," *Centerville Daily Iowegian*, April 14, 1945; "Russia Mourns Loss of FDR," *Centerville Daily Iowegian*, April 14, 1945; "Tribute Paid to Roosevelt," *Centerville Daily Iowegian*, April 14, 1945; "Eisenhower Decrees Period of Mourning," *Centerville Daily Iowegian*, April 14, 1945; "Russians Mourn Roosevelt Death, 'A Real Gentleman,'" *Centerville Daily Iowegian*, April 14, 1945.
5. C.B.D., Around the Town, *Centerville Daily Iowegian*, April 25, 1945.

6. C.B.D., Columns Write, *Centerville Daily Iowegian*, August 17, 1945; Hal Boyle, "Yank Writes of Scenes along Road to Berlin!" *Centerville Daily Iowegian*, March 28, 1945.
7. "Underground Nazi Factory Captured," *Centerville Daily Iowegian*, March 23, 1945; "1277 Americans Liberated from a German Camp," *Centerville Daily Iowegian*, April 2, 1945; "Germans Didn't Like Their American Prisoners Much," *Centerville Daily Iowegian*, March 29, 1945; Virginia Koestner, interview with the author, April 15, 2011; C.B.D., Columns Write, *Centerville Daily Iowegian*, March 28, 1944 [*sic*]; "Brutal Treatment of Prisoners Told by Two American Soldiers," *Centerville Daily Iowegian*, April 7, 1945; "Rudy Buyan Tells about Prison Camp," *Centerville Daily Iowegian*, June 11, 1945; "RAF Legless Airman Freed by Americans," *Centerville Daily Iowegian*, April 18, 1945.
8. C.B.D., Columns Write, *Centerville Daily Iowegian*, May 8, 1945; C.B.D., Edson Kratzer, letter, Columns Write, *Centerville Daily Iowegian*, July 27, 1945; "Centerville Major Reveals Nazi Horror," *Centerville Daily Iowegian*, June 30, 1945; "Saw Horrible Sights at Dachau," *Centerville Daily Iowegian*, June 21, 1945.
9. Bob McGuire, interview with the author, March 22, 2012; "Buchenwald," *Unionville Republican*, May 10, 1995; Katherine Chappell, "Herndon Brings History Back to Iowa," *Southern Iowa Marketing Groups Forever Young*, June 2004; Cliff Herndon, interview with the author, February 25, 2004; "Herndon Pictures of Buchenwald," *Centerville Daily Iowegian*, September 5, 1945.
10. "Historic Meeting on Elbe Came as Surprise," *Centerville Daily Iowegian*, April 27, 1945; Bob McGuire, interviews with the author, March 18, 2011, and March 22, 2012; Louis "Sol" Kauzlarich, interview with the author, August 12, 2011; Elvin Jay, interview with the author, June 7, 2011; Joe Coates, interview with the author, March 25, 2012.
11. "Fifth in a Race to Po River," *Centerville Daily Iowegian*, April 23, 1945; "Fifth Army Along Banks of Po River," *Centerville Daily Iowegian*, April 24, 1945; Stan Swinton, "Po Valley—The Promised Land," *Stars and Stripes*, April 1945; "Allies in Swift Pursuit of Foe in Northern Italy," *Centerville Daily Iowegian*, April 25, 1945; "Reports North Italy Falling to Anti-Nazis," *Centerville Daily Iowegian*, April 26, 1945; "An Unheroic End for the Il Duce," *Centerville Daily Iowegian*, April 30, 1945; C.B.D., Columns Write, *Centerville Daily Iowegian*, March 13, 1945; *The Story of the 34th Infantry Division: Louisiana to Pisa*, 15–19 (see chap. 69, n. 6).
12. "Lights Went On," *Centerville Daily Iowegian*, April 30, 1945.
13. "Hitler Killed in Berlin," *Centerville Daily Iowegian*, May 1, 1945; "Nazis Quit in Italy!" *Centerville Daily Iowegian*, May 2, 1945; "Nazis Surrender Denmark!" *Centerville Daily Iowegian*, May 4, 1945.
14. "Sgt. Cerato Was There," *Centerville Daily Iowegian*, May 29, 1945; Angela Cerato Sims, interview with the author, May 20, 2005; "Surrender Took Place at 2 a.m.," *Centerville Daily Iowegian*, May 7, 1945.

15. "Centerville Celebrates Surrender," *Centerville Daily Iowegian*, May 8, 1945.
16. J.B. Kelley, interview with the author, May 10, 2011; O.R. Parks, interview with the author, April 20, 2011; Raymond Ferren, interview with the author, March 10, 2011; "One War Down One War to Go," *Centerville Daily Iowegian*, May 8, 1945; "V-E Day Calmly Received Here," *Centerville Daily Iowegian*, Centennial Edition, November 29, 1946.

Chapter 84

1. Nichols, *Ernie's War*, 32–33, 418–19 (see chap. 72, n. 9).
2. Keegan, *Collins Atlas of World War II*, 152 (see chap. 59, n. 11); Morison, *The Oxford History of the American People*, 406 (see chap. 16, n. 3); Keegan, *The Second World War*, 574 (see chap. 59, n. 5); J.B. Kelley, interview with the author, May 10, 2011.
3. "American Task Force Lies Close to Shores of Japan," *Centerville Daily Iowegian*, July 17, 1945; "Tokyo Says No Surrender," *Centerville Daily Iowegian*, July 27, 1945; Morison, *The Oxford History of the American People*, 407 (see chap. 16, n. 3).
4. "Local People Helped with Atomic Bomb," *Centerville Daily Iowegian*, August 8, 1945.
5. "Helped on Atomic Bomb at Oak Ridge," *Centerville Daily Iowegian*, August 18, 1945; "Oak Ridge Secret a Well Kept One," *Centerville Daily Iowegian*, August 20, 1945; "Bob Evans Had Hand in Atomic Bomb," *Centerville Daily Iowegian*, August 21, 1945; "In Close Touch with Atomic Bomb," *Centerville Daily Iowegian*, August 8, 1945; "Research on Atomic Bomb Done at Ames," *Centerville Daily Iowegian*, August 8, 1945.
6. "Loose Atomic Bomb on Japs," *Centerville Daily Iowegian*, August 6, 1945; "New Bomb Power at Work Almost Inconceivable," *Centerville Daily Iowegian*, August 6, 1945; "Use Atomic Bomb for Second Time, City of Nagasaki Hit," *Centerville Daily Iowegian*, August 9, 1945; "Iowan Was First to Drop Atomic Bomb," *Centerville Daily Iowegian*, August 8, 1945; Morison, *The Oxford History of the American People*, 408 (see chap. 16, n. 3); Zeph Earhart, interview with the author, May 23, 2011; Zeph Earhart, letter to the author, May 26, 2011.
7. Joe Stuteville, "Saga of the Enola Gay," *American Legion Magazine*, August 1988; "Moulton Paper Has Account of Atom Bomb," *Centerville Daily Iowegian*, December 8, 1945.
8. "Robert Buss Doing War Research Work," *Centerville Daily Iowegian*, April 3, 1942; Bill Buss, interview with the author, February 17, 2012.
9. "Surrender Offered by Japan!" *Centerville Daily Iowegian*, August 10, 1945.
10. "War Ends!" *Centerville Daily Iowegian*, August 15, 1945; "Centerville Scene as World War 2 Comes to an End," *Centerville Daily Iowegian*, August 15, 1945; "Local Victory Celebration Was Noisy But Sane," *Centerville Daily Iowegian*, August 16, 1945; "Taverns Close for Celebration," *Centerville Daily Iowegian*, August 15, 1945.

11. "Peace Talk Is Too Late for Another Veteran of War II from Appanoose," *Centerville Daily Iowegian*, August 13, 1945; "Fourth Gold Star Added to Moravia Flag," *Centerville Daily Iowegian*, April 24, 1945; "Pfc. Hutchinson, Former Exline Resident Killed," *Centerville Daily Iowegian*, June 9, 1945; "Exline Boy Is Killed during Luzon Battle," *Centerville Daily Iowegian*, April 26, 1945; "Soldier's Widow Receives Added Sad War News," *Centerville Daily Iowegian*, April 23, 1945; "Brothers Killed," *Centerville Daily Iowegian*, April 27, 1945; "Archie Euwer Is Killed in Pacific Action," *Centerville Daily Iowegian*, April 30, 1945; "Moulton Boy Dies in War in Germany," *Centerville Daily Iowegian*, April 25, 1945; "Moulton Boy Missing, Now Listed as Dead," *Centerville Daily Iowegian*, April 28, 1945; "Mrs. Burgher Hears of Death of Her Hero," *Centerville Daily Iowegian*, April 5, 1945; "Pacific Death," *Centerville Daily Iowegian*, May 25, 1945; "Pacific Victim," *Centerville Daily Iowegian*, May 17, 1945.
12. "John Kauzlarich," *Centerville Daily Iowegian*, August 17, 1945.
13. "Two Service Men Taken," *Centerville Daily Iowegian*, May 12, 1945; "Pfc. Wayne Malin Killed in Action in Philippines," *Centerville Daily Iowegian*, May 26, 1945; "Guido Marchi War Victim on Isle of Luzon," *Centerville Daily Iowegian*, July 2, 1945; "Local Sailor Is Missing in China Sea," *Centerville Daily Iowegian*, March 5, 1945.
14. "Promise City Mourns Death Capt. Holiday," *Centerville Daily Iowegian*, April 28, 1945; Robert Holiday, interview with the author, April 18, 2012; Robert Holliday, letter to the author, April 22, 2011.
15. "Alfred Fry is Killed on German Front," *Centerville Daily Iowegian*, April 26, 1945; "Pvt. Longley War Victim in Germany," *Centerville Daily Iowegian*, April 24, 1945; "Mike Countis Is Killed in Nazi Battle," *Centerville Daily Iowegian*, April 30, 1945; "Cossolotto War Victim Report Now," *Centerville Daily Iowegian*, March 23, 1945.
16. "Acknowledge Deaths of Two Local Airmen," *Centerville Daily Iowegian*, February 6, 1946.
17. "Lt. Brewer Is Reported As Being Dead," *Centerville Daily Iowegian*, September 18, 1945.
18. "World War 2 Ended for Wayne Parson Here Today," *Centerville Daily Iowegian*, November 8, 1947.

Chapter 85

1. "War Ends!" *Centerville Daily Iowegian*, August 15, 1945; "Summary of Soldiers on the Way Home," *Centerville Daily Iowegian*, July 20, 1945; "Increasing No. of Service Men Coming Home," *Centerville Daily Iowegian*, July 14, 1945; "44th Infantry Division Back in U.S. Today," *Centerville Daily Iowegian*, July 20, 1945; "Queen Mary Looks Like Circus Ship, Brings Boys Home," *Centerville Daily Iowegian*, September 10, 1945; "Queen Mary Arrives with 14,000 Yanks," *Centerville Daily Iowegian*, June 22, 1945.

2. Stamps, "Snafus and Love Letters: Memories of an Old G.I.," 207–9 (see chap. 63, n. 3); Howard Criswell, interview with the author, October 30, 2011; Phyllis Cosby, interview with the author, April 19, 2012.
3. "Lt. Col. Frank Wilder in Fine Address; Audience Packs Church," *Centerville Daily Iowegian*, February 12, 1945; "35 Purple Heart Veterans in Appanoose," *Centerville Daily Iowegian*, April 13, 1946.
4. Roger Perry, interview with the author, August 19, 2011; Richard Smith, interview with the author, May 10, 2009; Patsy Cincotta, "Over There," *Daily Iowegian*, December 7, 2007.
5. Gary Cridlebaugh, interview with the author, September 18, 2011; "Lt. Jack Heimes Killed in Airplane Crash," *Centerville Daily Iowegian*, September 6, 1945; "Centerville Boy Now Escorts War Lords of Germany," *Centerville Daily Iowegian*, September 14, 1945.
6. "Max Ellis Back from Radar Work in European Area," *Centerville Daily Iowegian*, July 3, 1945; Guidebook, Imperial War Museum Duxford, Cambridgeshire, England (London: Imperial War Museum, 2010), 45; Captain Darrell R. Lindsey Memorial Rededication Ceremony, June 12, 1993, Courthouse Square, Jefferson, Iowa.
7. "L. Jay Johnson Dies at 83," *Daily Iowegian*, March 19, 2007; Byron Johnson, interview with the author, April 20, 2011; Steve Zaputil, "World War II Experiences Chronicled for Grandchildren," four installments, *Ad-Express/Iowegian*, April 22, April 29, May 3 and May 9, 2002.
8. "Vivid Rescue Story Told by Lieut. Belles," *Centerville Daily Iowegian*, September 25, 1942; Sherman Elgin, interview with the author, August 12, 2011; Bill McDanel, interview with the author, August 12, 2011; Patsy Cincotta, "To the Bottom of the Deep Blue Sea," *Daily Iowegian*, June 25, 2011; Duane Hurley, interview with the author, March 2, 2004; Dale Jones, interview with the author, October 4, 2004; "Legion of Merit Medal Awarded Lt. S.G. Lodwick," *Centerville Daily Iowegian*, May 6, 1944; Ralph Alhouse, interview with the author, June 20, 2010.
9. Leo Craver, interview with the author, October 20, 2011; Joe Starcevich, interview with the author, November 17, 2011; Howard Criswell, interview with the author, October 20, 2011; Berg, *Lindbergh*, 451 (see chap. 45, n. 7).
10. Edwin Kiester Jr., "The G.I. Bill May Be the Best Deal Ever Made by Uncle Sam," *Smithsonian*, November 1994; Jesse Beck, "Service Men to College," editorial, *Centerville Daily Iowegian*, July 16, 1945; "Record Year Seen for Enrollments in Iowa Colleges," *Centerville Daily Iowegian*, September 16, 1946; "Junior College Re-Opens with 36 Students," Student Iowegian Section, *Centerville Daily Iowegian*, October 17, 1945; "40 Ex-Service Students at '46–'47 School Assembly," *Centerville Daily Iowegian*, September 3, 1946; John Cortesio Jr., interviews with the author, April

2, 2011, and April 22, 2012; Theda K. Long, "Two Total Over 100 Years in Shoe Repair Business," *Centerville Daily Iowegian*, February 21, 1978.

11. "Centennial to End Dec. 28 at Old Capitol," *Centerville Daily Iowegian*, December 12, 1946.

12. "This Week Marks Centennial Observance for Centerville," *Centerville Daily Iowegian*, September 23, 1946; "Centerville Schools Will Present Centennial Pageant in Stadium Friday Night, September 27, at 7," *Centerville Daily Iowegian*, September 25, 1946; "Centennial Flying Farmers Event Attracted 49 Planes," *Centerville Daily Iowegian*, September 30, 1946; "Methodist Church Pageant Carried Centennial Theme, Enjoyed by Large Audience," *Centerville Daily Iowegian*, December 2, 1946; "Navy Band Will Be Here Thursday," *Centerville Daily Iowegian*, September 25, 1946.

13. *Centerville Daily Iowegian*, Centennial Edition, November 29, 1946; U.S. Bureau of the Census, "1860 Federal Census of Appanoose County," showing County population—compared with County's Civil War dead listed on Memorial to War Dead at Centerville Courthouse Square; U.S. Bureau of the Census, "1920 Federal Census of Appanoose County," showing County population—compared with County's WWI dead as numbered in *Semi-Weekly Iowegian*, Company D special section, May 19, 1919; U.S. Bureau of the Census, "1940 Federal Census of Appanoose County," showing County population—compared with County's WWII dead as numbered in "108 War Dead of Appanoose County Listed Chronologically," *Centerville Daily Iowegian*, February 27, 1962.

Index

C

D

H

I

J

Q

R

S

T

Y

Z

About the Author

Author of *Hearst's Other Castle,* Enfys McMurry taught English, Aesthetics and Civilization, World Literature and related subjects at Indian Hills Community College. She is a longtime member of the Appanoose County Historical Society, Wayne County Historical Society and the National Trust for Historic Preservation.